Get started with your **Connected Casebook**

Redeem your code below to access the **e-book** with search, highlighting, and note-taking capabilities; a **study center** complete with practice questions, explanations, and videos; **case briefing** and **outlining** tools to support efficient learning; and more.

1. Go to www.casebookconnect.com
2. Enter your access code in the box and click **Register**
3. Follow the steps to complete your registration and verify your email address

If you have already registered at CasebookConnect.com, simply log into your account and redeem additional access codes from your Dashboard.

ACCESS CODE: STXT56871882017
Scratch off with care.

Is this a used casebook? Access code already redeemed? Purchase a digital version at **CasebookConnect.com/catalog**.

If you purchased a digital bundle with additional components, your additional access codes will appear below.

"I liked being able to search quickly while in class."

"Being able to highlight and easily create case briefs was a fantastic resource and time saver for me!"

"I loved the practice exercises and study questions; they really helped me learn the material!"

For technical support, please visit http://support.wklegaledu.com.

COMMENTARIES AND CASES ON THE LAW OF BUSINESS ORGANIZATION

ASPEN CASEBOOK SERIES

COMMENTARIES AND CASES ON THE LAW OF BUSINESS ORGANIZATION

SIXTH EDITION

William T. Allen
Late Jack Nusbaum Professor of Law and Business
New York University

Reinier Kraakman
Ezra Ripley Thayer Professor of Law
Harvard Law School

Vikramaditya S. Khanna
William W. Cook Professor of Law
The University of Michigan Law School

 Wolters Kluwer

Published by Wolters Kluwer in New York.

Wolters Kluwer Legal & Regulatory U.S. serves customers worldwide with CCH, Aspen Publishers, and Kluwer Law International products. (www.WKLegaledu.com)

To contact Customer Service, e-mail customer.service@wolterskluwer.com, call 1-800-234-1660, fax 1-800-901-9075, or mail correspondence to:

Wolters Kluwer
Attn: Order Department
PO Box 990
Frederick, MD 21705

Printed in the United States of America.

1 2 3 4 5 6 7 8 9 0

ISBN 978-1-5438-1573-3

Library of Congress Cataloging-in-Publication Data

Names: Allen, William T., author. | Kraakman, Reinier H., author. | Khanna,
  Vikramaditya, author.
Title: Commentaries and cases on the law of business organization / William
  T. Allen (Late Jack Nusbaum Professor of Law and Business, New York
  University), Reinier Kraakman (Ezra Ripley Thayer Professor of Law,
  Harvard Law School), Vikramaditya S. Khanna (William W. Cook
  Professor of Law, The University of Michigan Law School).
Description: Sixth edition. | New York : Wolters Kluwer, [2021] | Series:
  Aspen casebook series | Includes bibliographical references and index. |
  Summary: "Law school book on the basic principles of law that undergird
  U.S. legal structures. Covers the fundamentals of organizational law in
  a business setting and addresses the legal regulation of a variety of
  actions, decisions, and transactions that involve or concern the modern
  public corporation"— Provided by publisher.
Identifiers: LCCN 2020055707 (print) | LCCN 2020055708 (ebook) | ISBN
  9781543815733 (hardcover) | ISBN 9781543831016 (epub)
Subjects: LCSH: Corporation law—United States. | Business enterprises—Law
  and legislation—United States. | LCGFT: Casebooks (Law)
Classification: LCC KF1414 .A735 2021 (print) | LCC KF1414 (ebook) | DDC
  346.73/065—dc23
LC record available at https://lccn.loc.gov/2020055707
LC ebook record available at https://lccn.loc.gov/2020055708

About Wolters Kluwer Legal & Regulatory U.S.

Wolters Kluwer Legal & Regulatory U.S. delivers expert content and solutions in the areas of law, corporate compliance, health compliance, reimbursement, and legal education. Its practical solutions help customers successfully navigate the demands of a changing environment to drive their daily activities, enhance decision quality and inspire confident outcomes.

Serving customers worldwide, its legal and regulatory portfolio includes products under the Aspen Publishers, CCH Incorporated, Kluwer Law International, ftwilliam.com and MediRegs names. They are regarded as exceptional and trusted resources for general legal and practice-specific knowledge, compliance and risk management, dynamic workflow solutions, and expert commentary.

Dedication

Chancellor William T. Allen, 1944–2019

We dedicate this edition of *Commentaries and Cases* to our late co-author, Chancellor William T. Allen. Bill Allen needs no introduction in the legal community. He is one of the great judges of the Delaware Court of Chancery. His restless intelligence informs many of the landmark judicial decisions of the past generation. His scholarship, practice, and teaching have left a lasting impression on American corporate law. And no one who knew him can forget his cocked eyebrow and soft smile when he encountered implausible or disingenuous arguments, whether in a brief or in an academic paper.

Bill contributed to the evolution of corporate law on many levels: through judicial opinions, law review articles, professional conferences, academic workshops, and of course as a beloved professor at the NYU School of Law and the Stern School of Business. As compared to his achievements as a jurist, scholar, and teacher, his co-authorship of five editions of *Commentaries and Cases* might seem to be a secondary part of his brilliant career. But describing it this way diminishes its role as a vehicle for integrating Bill's disparate insights from practice, history, and contemporary legal scholarship.

The first edition of this book was authored in large part because Bill wished to have teaching materials that supported his vision of teaching corporate law. He chose the title of the book accordingly, *Commentaries and Cases on the Law of Business Organization*. It is noteworthy here that "commentaries" precedes "cases," which suggests a reading of cases as part of a broader conceptual and historical narrative rather than a focus on explaining them in their full factual and procedural complexity. A second point is that our book's title features "business organization," not "corporations" or even "business associations." As a sophisticated business lawyer, Bill understood that corporate legal problems have analogues in other business entities, and that promoters of business enterprises can select from a menu of statutory legal forms.

Bill's untimely death in October 2019, occurred just after he first indicated an interest in co-authoring a 6th edition of *Commentaries and Cases*. We suspect he would have enthusiastically participated in preparing a new edition. As matters stand, however, we can only hope that he would have approved of the revisions and updates that we have undertaken. But at least we have certain knowledge that he would have approved of most of our new edition, since we have retained almost all of the commentary that he developed in earlier editions of *Commentaries and Cases*.

Reinier Kraakman
Vic Khanna

To those who taught me: the late S. Samuel Arsht and Andrew B. Kirkpatrick of the Delaware bar; Martin Lipton of the New York bar; Hon. Walter K. Stapleton of the Third Circuit Court of Appeals; and especially to those I teach daily, Joshua, Benjamin and William W. Allen who came late in my life, but in time! Bless you all.

— William T. Allen

To those who have made this casebook possible. To Victor Brudney, whose generous mentoring saved me during my first year of teaching corporations; to William T. Allen, whose contributions inform every page of this book; to Guhan Subramanian, who took the laboring oar in three prior editions; to Vic Khanna, whose fresh energy and insight have made this edition possible; to my students and colleagues; and to my wife, Anya, whose patience and affection grace all that I do. I am very fortunate.

— Reinier Kraakman

To those who taught me and made this book possible: particularly, Reinier Kraakman who taught me corporate law when I was a student and whose wisdom, advice, and generosity have been consistently invaluable; my current and former students who continue to enhance my understanding of business organization and enliven my thinking; and to my family and friends, especially my mother, Dr. Santosh Khanna, whose inspiration and constant support are immeasurable and my five year old son, Viraj, who patiently waited for me while I was working on this book – thank you and now let's play!

— Vikramaditya S. Khanna

SUMMARY OF CONTENTS

CONTENTS

2

Contents

4

THE PROTECTION OF CREDITORS

7

NORMAL GOVERNANCE: THE DUTY OF CARE   259

8

THE DUTY OF LOYALTY: CONFLICT TRANSACTIONS   309

9

EXECUTIVE COMPENSATION   **375**

10

SHAREHOLDER LAWSUITS   **407**

13

PUBLIC CONTESTS FOR CORPORATE CONTROL 579

14

TRADING IN THE CORPORATION'S SECURITIES   671

Contents   **xxiii**

PREFACE TO THE SIXTH EDITION

This book represents our effort to assist students and non-specialist lawyers to achieve an understanding of the basic principles of law that undergird the legal structures within which business is conducted in the United States. Our approach in this effort is premised upon a functional perspective of law. Thus, we attempt to ask how these legal structures function to produce desired benefits to parties who enter into agreements and relationships, or how legal structures (or rules) add costs and can impede sensible business organization. In this second aspect, the analytical or critical perspective, our point of view is informed through our understanding of basic principles of economics. The book, however, requires of its readers no formal training or understanding of economics. The concepts are for the most part quite intuitive and easily grasped.

We have organized the book into two segments. The first (and shorter) of these segments — the Introduction and Chapters 1-3 — deals with the fundamentals of organizational law in a business setting. Chapter 1 focuses on agency law, which is no less a predicate for modern enterprises functioning in a market economy than contract or property law. Chapter 2 addresses the partnership form and its modern variants: the limited partnership, limited liability company (LLC), and limited liability partnership. Chapter 3 introduces the corporate form, explicitly contrasted against the partnership and its variants, such as the LLC.

The larger segment of the book, Chapters 4-14, addresses the legal regulation of a variety of actions, decisions, and transactions that involve or concern the modern public corporation. Chapter 4 explores relationships among shareholders, corporations, and corporate creditors. Chapters 5 provides a basic primer on applicable finance concepts useful in understanding issues respecting estimating costs of funding a business and estimating asset values. Chapters 6 and 7 explore what we term "normal governance" — that is, the legal framework that regulates the vast majority of the corporation's ordinary business activities. Chapter 6 addresses the routine functioning of the voting system, including the proxy rules and some current issues in corporate governance. Chapter 7 explores the duty of care, together with the multiple legal devices that insulate corporate officers and directors from shareholder liability, including, most notably, the business judgment rule.

Chapters 8 to 13 are devoted to particular classes of corporate actions and related shareholder transactions that are subject to more specialized regulation by corporate law. Chapter 8 addresses self-dealing and other potential duty of loyalty issues arising from the conduct of corporate officers, directors, and controlling shareholders. Chapter 9 focuses on the particular challenges of executive compensation. Chapter 10 reviews the law and practice of shareholder derivative suits. Chapter 11 examines transactions in corporate control, including sales of control blocks of shares and tender offers. Chapter 12 addresses the specialized legal treatment of so-called fundamental corporate actions, with special attention to merger and acquisition transactions. Chapter 13 turns to the dramatic topic of contests for corporate control, including hostile tender offers and proxy contests. And finally, Chapter 14 examines the regulation of transactions in shares on the public markets, including such topics as insider trading and fraud on the market.

Throughout, the sixth edition contains substantial updating from the fifth edition, especially respecting the topics of alternative business entities (e.g., the new contractual entities such as LLCs), corporate finance, shareholder voting, corporate governance, fiduciary duties of care and loyalty, shareholder litigation, mergers & acquisitions, fair value in appraisals, corporate control contests, and securities regulations. The basic structure and insights of the book remain unchanged, however. These materials continue to be structured in a way that conforms to the simple insight that much of corporate law can be divided into general governance, on the one hand, and discrete areas of specialized governance on the other. We expect some teachers will present the materials in a different sequence. We have taken care to facilitate alternative approaches by recapping in later chapters points more exhaustively made in earlier ones and by supplying cross-references for further review.

The book contains a number of notes that are perhaps a bit longer and more openly explanatory than other authors prefer. In this we have been motivated by our experience as teachers to want to provide a rather full textual basis for a general understanding of each subject. Our aim is to provide for those happy occasions when class gets deeply involved in an interesting discussion. In this event we are comforted by the knowledge that we can move on to the next class knowing that all of the basic information and insights have been made available to the class in the reading assignment.

In the end, what makes this branch of law so interesting (and frustrating) to students, practitioners, and scholars alike is the vital role played in it by the open-textured concept of fiduciary duty. From the early study of agency, to its conclusion with corporate mergers and acquisitions, the field and these materials offer myriad puzzles arising from the admixture of morality and efficiency that is often encountered when courts are required to fill in the specifics of a fiduciary's obligations. In approaching this subject, the book places primary emphasis on the Delaware statute and decisions, as that law grows in its dominant importance for publicly financed corporations in the United States. Opinions by the Delaware Court of Chancery and the Delaware Supreme Court tend to outnumber cases from other jurisdictions.

We must offer very real thanks and appreciation to colleagues and friends who have taught from these materials for some years and who have been generous in their comments, contributions, and suggestions. First among these is Guhan Subramanian, our talented coauthor on several prior editions of this Book. Needless to say, we are grateful for his numerous contributions in the past and, like loyal continuing partners, we are fully prepared to hold him intellectually harmless for the novel content of the 6th Edition. Next among those to whom we owe deep gratitude are Victor Brudney, whose teaching materials provided the starting point for this book, and Henry Hansmann, who has commented so richly and so long that it would be difficult to exaggerate our gratitude. Other colleagues have made useful comments and supplied detailed guidance. Among these are Jennifer Arlen, Ryan Bubb, Lucian Bebchuk, Bernard Black, John Coates, Rob Daines, Jill Fisch, Jesse Fried, Jon Hanson, Hon. Jack B. Jacobs, Marcel Kahan, Ehud Kamar, Stephen J. Lubben, Mark Roe, and Hon. Leo Strine. We acknowledge gladly our debt to them. In addition, numerous anonymous reviewers made very helpful comments, and we hope that they will find the book improved because of their efforts. Finally, we each owe a debt of gratitude to student researchers and secretarial associates. Among students, some especially stand out for their glad assistance: Alison Gooley, NYU, 1999, of the Bar of New South Wales; Ronnie Deutch, NYU, 2002, of the New York bar; Melissa Anderson, HLS, 2009; Jeffrey Young, HLS, 2010; Maria Parra-Orlandoni, HLS, 2015; Divya Suwasin, NYU 2016; Katherine Boothroyd, UMLS, 2022; John C. Friess, UMLS, 2022; Jennifer Grecco, UMLS, 2022; Nam Jun Park, UMLS, 2022; Neal Patel, UMLS, 2022; and Thomas Toman, UMLS, 2022. Susannah Atkins, Carol Bateson, Cara R. Conlin, Linell Hanover, Annie Hard, Barbara Karasinski, Kimberly Peterson, and Paula Prather offered cheerful and highly competent assistance. Our gratitude extends to them all.

William T. Allen
Reinier Kraakman
Vikramaditya S. Khanna

February 2021

ACKNOWLEDGMENTS

We thank the authors and copyright holders of the following works for permitting their inclusion in this book:

Bebchuk and Fried, Pay Without Performance: Overview of the Issues, 30 J. Corp. L. 647(2005).

Cain, Fisch, Solomon and Thomas, [Graph] Fig. 1, Filings by Deal Completion Year, Mootness Fees, 72 Vanderbilt Law Review 1777, 1787 (2019). Reprinted with permission of authors.

Cornerstone Research, [Graph], Fig. 1, Appraisal Petitions and Merger Cases Filed in the Delaware Court of Chancery 2006-2018, Appraisal Litigation in Delaware Trends in Petitions and Opinions 2006-2018, p.4. Reprinted with permission.

Easterbrook and Fischel, Close Corporations and Agency Costs, 38 Stan. L. Rev. 271 (1986). Stanford Law Review by School of Law, Stanford University, Copyright 1986. Reproduced with permission of Stanford Law Review via Copyright Clearance Center.

Easterbrook and Fischel, Corporate Control Transactions, 91 Yale L. J. 698, 715-719 (1982). The Yale Law Journal by Yale Law School, Copyright © 1982. Reproduced with permission of Yale Law Journal Company, Inc. via Copyright Clearance Center.

Easterbrook and Fischel, Limited Liability and the Corporation, 52 U. Chi. L. Rev. 89, 94-97 (1985).

Easterbrook and Fischel, Voting in Corporate Law, 26 J.L. & Econ. 395, 409-411 (1983). Alex Edmans

Edmans, Gabaix and Jenter, Executive Compensation: A Survey of Theory and Evidence, The Handbook of the Economics of Corporate Governance (Benjamin E. Hermalin & Michael S. Weisback, eds) Vol. 1, 383 (2017). Reprinted with permission of Elsevier via CCC and the authors.

Edmans, Gabaix, and Jenter, (2017), Figure 6, Panel A: CEOs in the S & P 500 From 1992 to 2014, [Graph], Executive Compensation: A Survey of Theory and Evidence, The Handbook of the Economics of Corporate Governance (Benjamin E. Hermalin & Michael S. Weisback, eds.) Vol 1. Reprinted with permission of Elsevier via CCC and the authors.

Eisenberg, Self-Interested Transactions in Corporate Law, 13 J. Corp. L. 997, 997-1008 (1988). The Journal of Corporation Law, published by University of Iowa, College of Law, Copyright © 1988. Reproduced with permission of The Journal of Corporation Law via Copyright Clearance Center.

Eisinger, Long & Short: Icahu Cries Foul at Perry's No-Risk Play in Takeover Fight, Wall Street Journal, Eastern Edition, Dec. 15, 2004. Copyright © 2004 by Dow Jones & Company, Inc. Reproduced with permission of Dow Jones & Company, Inc. via Copyright Clearance Center.

Fink, Laurence, A Fundamental Reshaping of Finance (Letter to CEOs), Jan. 2018.

Holmstrom, Bengt, Pay Without Performance and the Managerial Power Hypothesis: A Comment, 30 J. Corp. L. 503 (2005).

Kahan and Rock, Hedge Funds in Corporate Governance and Corporate Control, 155 U. Pa. L. Rev. 1021 (2007). University of Pennsylvania Law Review by University of Pennsylvania Law School.

Markon, Jerry, and Robert Frank, Five Adelphia Officials Arrested on Fraud Charges, Wall Street Journal, Eastern Edition, Jul.25, 2002.

Roe, Mark J., Corporate Strategic Reaction to Mass Tort, 72 Va. L. Rev. 1, 32 (1986). Virginia Law Review Association by Virginia Law Review.

Stanford Law School Securities Class Action Clearinghouse [Graph], Federal Securities Class Action Litigation 1996-YTD.

Thompson and Thomas, The New Look of Shareholder Litigation: Acquisition-Oriented Class Actions, 57 Vand. L. Rev. 133, 166-69 (2004).

COMMENTARIES AND CASES ON THE LAW OF BUSINESS ORGANIZATION

INTRODUCTION

Like much of civil law, the law of business enterprises is concerned with facilitating voluntary economic relationships. Property law and contract law are the legal bedrock of market economies, but other bodies of law are also important. Among these are the laws of security interests, money and credit, bankruptcy, intellectual property, agency, and enterprise organization. This book deals primarily with the last, but hardly the least, of these fields: the law of enterprise organization. In particular, we address the laws of agency, partnership (and related limited liability entities), and corporations.

Because cooperative economic relationships frequently raise the same recurring problems, the law provides a useful menu of standard forms to address these problems. Thus, the laws of agency, partnership, noncorporate limited liability entities, and corporations can be seen as offering parties a set of standard legal forms from which to choose the one most suited to their needs. The choice of a standard form is implicitly a contractual choice. Moreover, these forms themselves are more or less contractual insofar as they may be customized or fine-tuned by the parties by express agreement — and, of course, with the assistance of expert lawyering. But as we shall also see, the laws of agency, partnership, and corporations are not entirely malleable. They are subject to fiduciary duties grounded in equity — a principal focus of this course — that limit the opportunistic use of contractual and even statutory rights. Finally, agency law as well as the law of all business entities have a "property" dimension in addition to a contractual dimension, insofar as they may alter the legal rights of third parties as well as the rights of the parties who enter into these enterprise relationships.

We begin by examining the law of agency. The agency relationship frames the simplest form of business organization. Alternatively, it might be seen as the cohesive force that sets the boundaries of a legal enterprise: Which persons have the power to bind the entity contractually and in tort or criminal law, and which persons act outside the entity? Agency law also prefigures many of the most basic and difficult problems of corporation law, most particularly those arising from the so-called fiduciary duty of loyalty. From agency, we move to the general partnership — which we may think of as the simplest form of a jointly owned business firm. (For our purposes, a "firm" is a form of business relation that has a temporal dimension, a social identity, and a separate pool of dedicated business assets.) And from partnership and other noncorporate forms, we move to our principal subject — the corporate

1

form — which is the most stable, complex, and socially important form in the menu of business forms that the law provides.

Before beginning, we will address here two very general themes that run throughout this book. The first is a policy theme: How does one evaluate and critique enterprise law, and what are the goals of enterprise law? The second theme concerns the role that the morally charged language of enterprise law (it is law, after all) plays in its legitimation and enforcement.

We begin with the policy theme. It goes without saying that the fundamental objective of enterprise law — indeed of all law — is to increase social welfare. Yet, this abstract formulation tells us little about how enterprise law should contribute to social welfare or how it might be tweaked to do a better job. Like many other modern commentators on enterprise law, we sometimes assert that good law is "efficient" law, meaning that it maximizes the size of the economic pie (even if the pie's pieces are allocated quite differently according to whether one is, say, an investor or an employee).[1]

At other times we assert that the goal of the business corporation is to maximize long-term shareholder wealth. Needless to say, there is a gap of some distance between innocuously stating that enterprise law should increase social welfare and asserting that this means furthering the interests of shareholders or other investors of risk capital.

Some commentators argue that large enterprises such as public corporations should not privilege shareholder interests over those of other constituencies such as creditors, employees, suppliers, customers, or even the interests of society as a whole. We explore these alternative goals in Chapter 4 (The Protection of Creditors), Chapter 8 (Conflict Transactions: The Duty of Loyalty), and Chapter 13 (Public Contests for Corporate Control). Elsewhere, we take the primacy of shareholder interests for granted. This is not because we take shareholder welfare to be an axiom of corporate law. Rather it is because we take it to be a rough proxy for social welfare in most cases and the working assumption of American corporate law. The primacy of shareholder interests runs so deeply in American law that it is rarely even stated except when its conflicts with the interests of other constituencies are too sharp to ignore.

We note, as we draft the Sixth Edition of this Book, that there are many who would dispute the proposition that shareholder primacy, or the creation of long-term shareholder value, is central to corporate law, either as a

---

1. Those familiar with the literature addressing various definitions of efficiency will recognize that by "efficiency" we mean "Kaldor-Hicks efficiency." This form of efficiency looks to increasing the size of the pie. In principal, a larger pie is divisible in a way that makes all participants in an enterprise better off. Yet efficient law increases Kaldor-Hicks efficiency by increasing the size of the pie, regardless of how the increased pie is divided. Kaldor-Hicks efficiency is to be contrasted with "Pareto efficiency," under which a change is efficient only if the pie increases and every constituent's piece of pie is also increased. The latter criterion is too demanding to serve as a useful norm in enterprise law.

descriptive matter or as a normative concern. No less an authority than the Business Roundtable, whose members include the CEOs of most of America's largest corporations, has recently asserted that the corporation has a broad social purpose to enhance the welfare of all of its stakeholders.[2] Many of America's largest institutional investors and asset managers assert much the same thing, with perhaps a particular emphasis on the social obligation of corporations to address climate change.[3] In addition, the last five years have seen a striking increase in the size and numbers of "ESG" investment funds that selectively prefer to invest in companies with strong environmental, social, and governance policies. Undoubtedly, then, short-term shareholder profits are not all that matters. Nevertheless, we believe the role of law in serving shareholder interests is the most useful vantage point from which to view corporate law. Those who take a broader vision of corporate purpose as their starting point rarely assert that this conflicts with the creation of long-term shareholder value. Indeed, most argue that companies that pursue a larger vision of stakeholder welfare and societal well-being also maximize long-term shareholder value. And a more immediate reason to take long-term shareholder welfare as a starting point is that most issues that corporate law addresses turn on conflicts among — and between — managers and shareholders. Until relatively recently, larger issues of corporate purpose seldom surfaced in the day-to-day affairs and conflicts attending business associations.

Once shareholder/investor welfare is identified as the principal objective of enterprise law, it follows easily that economic efficiency is the logical criterion for evaluating enterprise law. Shareholders/investors are the "equity holders" or "residual claimants" of business entities — a fancy way of saying that they don't get paid until everyone else is paid first, including business creditors, employees, and suppliers. Any factor that increases residual value of the enterprise to its shareholders (or other equity investors) is "efficient" by this criterion — at least if it does not impose uncompensated costs on third parties such as tort victims. And any factor that reduces the costs of capital, labor, supplies, and the like adds to the residual value of the enterprise. Put differently, efficient law adds to the value of the firm just as any other factor might do, by reducing the costs of the firm's inputs and increasing the value of its outputs.

There are at least three specific ways in which enterprise law can enhance the efficiency of enterprises. The first is by providing standard platforms for business entities as well as agency contracts and creditor protections. Where negotiating parties are involved, these platforms are often an integrated set of default terms open to contractual modification. Where third-party rights are at stake, the analogous standard terms are often mandatory. In both cases, however, standard platforms save time and effort by allowing parties to do business in shorthand, without reinventing the legal wheel. Second, enterprise law adds value by permitting business actors to modify third-party

---

2. See *Statement on the Purpose of a Corporation*, Business Roundtable, August 19, 2019.

3. See, e.g., *Larry Fink's 2018 Letter to CEOs*, BlackRock (January 17, 2018); *State Street Tells Companies ESG Moves No Longer Optional*, Investment News, January 29, 2020.

property rights in circumstances when contract alone cannot do the job. We address this function in Chapters 2 and 3, where we demonstrate how legal entities permit investors to divide their assets among different buckets that serve as collateral for different groups of creditors. This power to assign specific assets to support business creditors is enormously useful and yet, as we will argue, cannot be achieved by contract alone.

Finally, enterprise law provides a variety of rules and standards—collectively termed "fiduciary duties"—that are intended to either prevent or remedy self-interested opportunism by parties within enterprises. The simplest example is that of an agent who agrees to advance his principal's interests, but who exploits his position to pursue his own economic interests in one of many ways, ranging from colluding with third parties in negotiating contracts on the principal's behalf to expropriating the principal's property or private information for his own benefit. This genre of opportunism is a chronic problem in every sort of enterprise, from simple agency relationships to publicly traded corporations. In the academic literature, it is referred to generically as the "agency problem" and the costs that inevitably arise from the fact that agents rather than owners themselves are at work in the enterprise are referred to as "agency costs." This problem and the costs that it produces are not specific to the law of agency at all. Indeed, these are not legal terms of art. But addressing them lies at the core of the understanding and critical analysis of much of enterprise law.

As the problem of mitigating agency costs implies, evaluating the efficiency of a particular legal rule or a particular reform in enterprise law requires a good deal of knowledge about institutional context and enforcement. Research in the social sciences can be helpful here. But at the very least, clarity is essential about one's empirical assumptions about the institutional context as well as the weights assigned to particular costs and benefits. In the end, and over time, the balance of costs and benefits generally determines the survivability of legal doctrine here, as in so many other areas of the law.

However, policy-oriented analysis is certainly not the only aim of the study of organization law by lawyers. If it were, enterprise law would be nothing but a pastiche of applied social sciences—mostly economics and finance perhaps, but with a dash of psychology and organization theory tossed in. The meaning of this imaginary law would be wholly captured in phrases such as "efficiency," "transaction costs," "collective action problems," and the "prisoner's dilemma." Its rules and standards would be understood as more or less well-supported hypotheses. Individual plaintiffs and defendants would occupy roughly the same status as laboratory animals behaving in accordance with the vector of their self-interest and the law's calibration of incentives. Judges would be the investigators-in-chief.

Needless to say, this Orwellian account of enterprise law is not the real thing by a long shot, even if traces of applied social science occur in the case law and large deposits of it may be found in the academic literature. The principal statutes of enterprise law, including the statute that will play the most important role in this book—the Delaware General Corporation Law (DGCL)—read like an integrated set of self-contained rules that erect a legal entity, and describe its governance mechanisms. In the aggregate, they seem to rest on social science no more than the blueprints for large buildings do. Similarly, if one reads an opinion handed down by the Delaware Court of Chancery or the Delaware Supreme Court concerning an issue in corporate law, the number of references to "efficiency" or "transaction costs" is vanishingly small in comparison to that of legal terms of art such as "entire fairness" and the "business judgment rule." Moreover, the language of these opinions is often morally charged and didactic. The authorities cited are statutory provisions and prior case law. This is, in short, law as we know it. The attention to policy concerns is often here, but it resides in the melody rather than in the words. The only remotely "scientific" piece of the typical opinion is the careful attention paid to the facts and institutional context at the outset of the decision. And this resembles anthropology or history more than economics.

Phrased more directly, judges and lawyers occupy a different role than social scientists do. Judges and lawyers are understood to be believers in the language of law. Indeed, they are the high priests and the deacons of the faith. For them, the articulated reason for some judicial act is not simply a concurrence with good policy, but a legally derived cause in itself. In this faith, law is all about the meaning of legal doctrines: statutes, court rules, administrative procedures, judicial precedents, and the rich body of professional learning that allows experienced lawyers to perform their professional functions. These meanings may be unclear at times, but the internal processes of law — canons of construction, rules of authority and judicial processes of discovery, trial and appeal, and even much scholarship — are about clarifying legal meanings as well as their application. This is the "interior" perspective on law.

How, then, can faith and science freely coexist in the study of enterprise law — and perhaps even in its creation?[4] Our long answer to this question lies in the discussion of the materials in this book. The short answer comes in several pieces.

The most obvious piece is that the interior perspective on enterprise law comes first in time. The law's basic entity forms, its morally charged categories, and even the forerunners of today's business statutes long predate the normative claims made by modern economics. Indeed, some fundamental concepts in organizational economics were inspired by enterprise law. Examples include entire subfields of microeconomics such as "the principal-agent problem," the idea of "transaction costs," and the distinction between production by a principal's agents within a legal entity as distinct from acquiring goods or services from independent contractors in the market.

A second aspect of the coexistence of "faith-based" legal analysis and economically oriented policy derives from the policy-making role of the judiciary. Even a judge who is a strict constructionist finds that policy-making choices are inescapably thrust upon her. Linguistic ambiguity alone often requires a judge to make choices. To be sure, in such situations — and they arise frequently in the law of enterprise organization — courts avoid using concepts like "efficiency" to justify their choices, even if these concepts are

---

4. We ask the reader to excuse this phrasing, which borrows from another, more venerable discussion.

central to evaluating the wisdom of the outcome reached. However, this may change over the years as more lawyers trained in economic analysis enter the profession. Even today, one should not underestimate how many lawyers and judges — especially those who are frequently involved in business-related cases — are, if not fully bilingual, able to discourse in the language of economics as well as that of traditional enterprise law. In business law, the lawyer who fails to understand the economics of a problem usually fails to find a satisfactory solution to the problem.

Finally, we hasten to add our prediction that today's coexistence will never result in policy analysis supplanting enterprise law as we know it. There are two reasons. The first is that the vice of microeconomic theory cannot completely close on the complex institutional structures and transactions encountered in enterprise law. Markets and contracts are incomplete, and information is noisy in the real world. Judgments based on the situational insights of sophisticated lawyers and judges, as expressed in the language of the law, will ordinarily dominate judgments mechanically derived from an abstract policy framework. Second and even more important, business actors are not two-dimensional puppets entirely controlled by economic concerns. They are moral individuals (albeit more or less imperfect ones) whose actions often reflect ethical notions as well. In many cases, the soft prodding of conscience or reputation may elicit more legal compliance than will the threat of monetary sanctions. The morally charged language of business law takes aim directly at conscience and reputation. For most of us, it is one thing to be scolded by a court for acting inefficiently and quite another to be charged with acting disloyally or in bad faith. Arguably, in fact, some obligations imposed by enterprise law are enforced exclusively by these soft sanctions. And arguably, this is the way it should be.

ACTING THROUGH OTHERS: THE LAW OF AGENCY

1.1 INTRODUCTION TO AGENCY

The simplest form of joint economic undertaking occurs when one person extends the range of her own activity by engaging another to act — or transact — on her behalf. This is the paradigm of the principal-agent relationship. Think of the successful sole proprietor hiring her first employee. Such a relationship is called an agency.

After property, contract, and tort, agency law is a fundamental building block of market economies. Agency law governs the legal relationships among principals, their agents, and the third parties with whom the agents interact. Because agency law enables an agent to create rights and obligations between a principal and a third party, its own rules must be established by legal fiat rather than by contract. While organizational economists often think about the corporate form as a "nexus of contracts," agency law demonstrates why the law of business organizations must be much more than a subfield of contract law.

The law of agency prefigures some of the basic problems in corporate law. Indeed, these problems are heightened in the context of a widely held public corporation because the putative "principal" — often dispersed shareholders in large U.S. corporations — may be incapable of monitoring its "agent" — the corporation's management. Even though principals in the simpler context of common law agency seldom lose the capacity to select and monitor their agents entirely, many of the core problems of corporation law resemble the problems of principals who must act through agents who are motivated by interests in addition to those of the principals themselves.

Law schools once treated agency as a course on par with contracts, torts, and corporations. Giants of the profession — Professor Warren Seavey at Harvard Law School and Professor Philip Mechem of the University of Pennsylvania School of Law, for example — dedicated much of their lives to explicating its interstices. In today's law schools, agency usually plays the modest role of a pit stop on the fast track to corporation law and big money. Happily, however, the Restatement of the Law of Agency (Third), finalized in 2006, is a fine summary that can assist any student or practitioner in learning about the field.

Here we focus on the aspects of agency law most relevant to corporate law. In particular, we address three problems out of a much wider universe of issues that arise from agency relations. The first is the problem of formation and termination of an agency relationship and the related question of the scope of an agent's power to affect the legal relations of the principal. The second is the problem of the principal's relationship to third parties: What is the principal's responsibility for the agent's authorized and unauthorized contracts and for his unauthorized torts? And, third, what are the duties that the agent owes to the principal, given the agent's capacity to alter the principal's obligations to third parties? Our discussion follows this three-part structure. References are made to the Restatement (Third) Agency for further reading and discussion. Please read the relevant provisions in the Restatement in conjunction with this Chapter.

1.2   AGENCY FORMATION, AGENCY TERMINATION, AND PRINCIPAL'S LIABILITY

1.2.1   Formation

The Restatement (Third) Agency offers this definition: "Agency is the fiduciary relationship that arises when one person (a 'principal') manifests assent to another person (an 'agent') that the agent shall act on the principal's behalf and subject to the principal's control, and the agent manifests assent or otherwise consents so to act." Restatement (Third) Agency §1.01.

An agency is a consensual relationship between the principal, who grants authority to another to bind her in certain respects, and the agent, who accepts this responsibility. Thus, an agent holds a power to affect the principal's legal relations within the scope of the agent's agreed-on appointment (or "employment") and beyond this scope in some circumstances. Agents may be *special agents* (i.e., the agency is limited to a single act or transaction), or they may be *general agents* (i.e., the agency contemplates a series of acts or transactions). Principals may be *disclosed* (i.e., when third parties understand that an agent acts on behalf of a particular principal) or *undisclosed* (i.e., when third parties believe an agent to be the principal), or *partially disclosed* (i.e., when third parties deal with an agent without knowing the identity of their principal).

The principal's right to select and control the agent is an essential aspect of an agency. But this right may vary substantially under the agreement, and its practical effect varies substantially in practice. When a principal secures from her agent the right to control in detail how the agent performs his task — for example, the time he devotes to his tasks or the precautions that he uses — the agent is called an *employee* or, more quaintly in the language of the common law, a *servant*. When the principal's control rights are limited and the agent exercises considerable discretion — for example, when the agent is a professional who is bound to provide independent judgment or when the agent is an established business in its own right, such as a building contractor — the agent is described as an *independent contractor*.

1.2.2   Termination

Either the principal or the agent can terminate an agency at any time. If the contract between them fixes a set term of agency, then the principal's decision to *revoke* or the agent's decision to *renounce* gives rise to a claim for damages for breach of contract. In no event will an agency continue over the objection of one of the parties. The rule that either party may freely terminate is the equivalent to limiting the remedy for breach of an agency contract to monetary damages rather than specific performance. This rule seems unexceptional, since many agencies are employment contracts, and courts will not specifically enforce employment contracts against the wishes of either employees or employers. Doubtless, you have addressed these policies before in your study of contract law. Nevertheless, it is worth asking whether excluding the specific performance remedy in agency might not also preclude contracts that would make both parties better off.

QUESTIONS

Should the law preclude a principal from contracting for an irrevocable agency? Why should this restriction be mandatory as opposed to a default option? Can monetary damages always substitute for specific performance? Note that if a principal grants authority for a stated term, it expires automatically at the end of the term. If no term is stated, authority terminates at the end of a reasonable term. A special agency terminates when the specific act contemplated is performed or after a "reasonable" time has elapsed.

1.2.3   Parties' Conception Does Not Control

Agency relations may be implied even when the parties have not *explicitly* agreed to an agency relationship. An important context in which agency relationships are implied is when a party such as a bank assumes "too much" control under a contract that ostensibly makes for a debtor-creditor relationship. Ask yourself: Why might a court be particularly concerned about a debtor-creditor contract? Consider the following case.

JENSON FARMS CO. v. CARGILL, INC.
309 N.W.2d 285 (Minn. 1981)

Plaintiffs, 86 individuals, partnerships or corporate farmers, brought this action against defendant Cargill, Inc. (Cargill) and defendant Warren Grain & Seed Co. (Warren) to recover losses sustained when Warren defaulted on the contracts made with plaintiffs for the sale of grain. After a trial by jury, judgment was entered in favor of plaintiffs, and Cargill brought this appeal. We affirm.

This case arose out of the financial collapse of defendant Warren Seed & Grain Co.... Warren operated a grain elevator and as a result was involved in the purchase of ... grain from local farmers. The cash grain would be resold through the Minneapolis Grain Exchange or to the terminal grain companies directly. Warren also stored grain for farmers and sold chemicals, fertilizer and steel storage bins....

[I]n 1964 [Warren applied] for financing from Cargill. Cargill's officials from the Moorhead regional office investigated Warren's operations and recommended that Cargill finance Warren.

Warren and Cargill thereafter entered into a security agreement which provided that Cargill would loan money for working capital to Warren on "open account" financing up to a stated limit, which was originally set as $175,000.[2] Under this contract, Warren would receive funds and pay its expenses by issuing drafts drawn on Cargill through Minneapolis banks. The drafts were imprinted with both Warren's and Cargill's names. Proceeds from Warren's sales would be deposited with Cargill and credited to its account. In return for this financing, Warren appointed Cargill as its grain agent for transaction with the Commodity Credit Corporation. Cargill was also given a right of first refusal to purchase market grain sold by Warren to the terminal market.

A new contract was negotiated in 1967, extending Warren's credit line to $300,000 and incorporating the provisions of the original contract. It was also stated in the contract that Warren would provide Cargill with annual financial statements and that either Cargill would keep the books for Warren or an audit would be conducted by an independent firm. Cargill was given the right of access to Warren's books for inspection.

In addition, the agreement provided that Warren was not to make capital improvements or repairs in excess of $5,000 without Cargill's prior consent. Further, it was not to become liable as guarantor on another's indebtedness, or encumber its assets except with Cargill's permission. Consent by Cargill was required before Warren would be allowed to declare a dividend or sell and purchase stock.

Officials from Cargill's regional office made a brief visit to Warren shortly after the agreement was executed. They examined the annual statement and the accounts receivable, expenses, inventory, seed, machinery and other financial matters. Warren was informed that it would be reminded periodically to make the improvements recommended by Cargill. At approximately this time, a memo was given to the Cargill official in charge of the Warren account, Erhart Becker, which stated in part: "This organization (Warren) needs *very strong* paternal guidance."

In 1970, Cargill contracted with Warren and other elevators to act as its agent to seek growers for a new type of wheat called Bounty 208. Warren, as Cargill's agent for this project, entered into contracts for the growing of the wheat seed, with Cargill named as the contracting party. Farmers were paid directly by Cargill for the seed and all contracts were performed in full. In

2. Loans were secured by a second mortgage on Warren's real estate and a first chattel mortgage on its inventories of grain and merchandise in the sum of $175,000 with 7 percent interest....

1971, pursuant to an agency contract, Warren contracted on Cargill's behalf with various farmers for the growing of sunflower seeds for Cargill....

During this period, Cargill continued to review Warren's operations and expenses and recommend that certain actions should be taken.[4] Warren purchased from Cargill various business forms printed by Cargill and received sample forms from Cargill which Warren used to develop its own business forms.

Cargill wrote to its regional office in 1970 expressing its concern that the pattern of increased use of funds allowed to develop at Warren was similar to that involved in two other cases in which Cargill experienced severe losses. Cargill did not refuse to honor drafts or call the loan, however. A new security agreement which increased the credit line to $750,000 was executed in 1972, and a subsequent agreement which raised the limit to $1,250,000 was entered into in 1976.

Warren was at that time shipping Cargill 90% of its cash grain. When Cargill's facilities were full, Warren shipped its grain to other companies. Approximately 25% of Warren's total sales were seed grain, which was sold directly by Warren to its customers.

As Warren's indebtedness continued to be in excess of its credit line, Cargill began to contact Warren daily regarding its financial affairs. Cargill headquarters informed its regional office in 1973 that, since Cargill money was being used, Warren should realize that Cargill had the right to make some critical decisions regarding the use of the funds. Cargill headquarters also told Warren that a regional manager would be working with Warren on a day-to-day basis as well as in monthly planning meetings. In 1975, Cargill's regional office began to keep a daily debit position on Warren. A bank account was opened in Warren's name on which Warren could draw checks in 1976. The account was to be funded by drafts drawn on Cargill by the local bank.

In early 1977, it became evident that Warren had serious financial problems.... In April 1977, an audit of Warren revealed that Warren was $4 million in debt. After Cargill was informed that Warren's financial statements had been deliberately falsified, Warren's request for additional financing was refused....

After Warren ceased operations, it was found to be indebted to Cargill in the amount of $3.6 million. Warren was also determined to be indebted to plaintiffs in the amount of $2 million, and plaintiffs brought this action in 1977 to seek recovery of that sum. Plaintiffs alleged that Cargill was jointly liable for Warren's indebtedness as it had acted as principal for the grain elevator....

The major issue in this case is whether Cargill, by its course of dealing with Warren, became liable as a principal on contracts made by Warren with plaintiffs. Cargill contends that no agency relationship was established with Warren....

---

4. Between 1967 and 1973, Cargill suggested that Warren take a number of steps, including: (1) a reduction of seed grain and cash grain inventories; (2) improved collection of accounts receivable; (3) reduction or elimination of its wholesale seed business and its specialty grain operation; (4) marketing fertilizer and steel bins on consignment; (5) a reduction in withdrawals made by officers; (6) a suggestion that Warren's bookkeeper not issue her own salary checks; and (7) cooperation with Cargill in implementing the recommendations. These ideas were apparently never implemented, however.

Agency is the fiduciary relationship that results from the manifestation of consent by one person to another that the other shall act on his behalf and subject to his control, and consent by the other so to act....

In order to create an agency there must be an agreement, but not necessarily a contract between the parties.... An agreement may result in the creation of an agency relationship although the parties did not call it an agency and did not intend the legal consequences of the relation to follow. The existence of the agency may be proved by circumstantial evidence which shows a course of dealing between the two parties....

... We hold that all three elements of agency could be found in the particular circumstances of this case. By directing Warren to implement its recommendations, Cargill manifested its consent that Warren would be its agent. Warren acted on Cargill's behalf in procuring grain for Cargill as the part of its normal operations which were totally financed by Cargill.[7] ...

A number of factors indicate Cargill's control over Warren, including the following:

(1) Cargill's constant recommendations to Warren by telephone;
(2) Cargill's right of first refusal on grain;
(3) Warren's inability to enter into mortgages, to purchase stock or to pay dividends without Cargill's approval;
(4) Cargill's right of entry onto Warren's premises to carry on periodic checks and audits;
(5) Cargill's correspondence and criticism regarding Warren's finances, officers' salaries and inventory;
(6) Cargill's determination that Warren needed "strong paternal guidance";
(7) Provision of drafts and forms to Warren upon which Cargill's name was imprinted;
(8) Financing of all Warren's purchases of grain and operating expenses; and
(9) Cargill's power to discontinue the financing of Warren's operations.

We recognize that some of these elements, as Cargill contends, are found in an ordinary debtor-creditor relationship. However, these factors cannot be considered in isolation, but, rather, they must be viewed in light of all the circumstances surrounding Cargill's aggressive financing of Warren....

The amici curiae assert that, if the jury verdict is upheld, firms and banks which have provided business loans to county elevators will decline to make further loans. The decision in this case should give no cause for such concern. We deal here with a business enterprise markedly different from an ordinary bank financing, since Cargill was an active participant in Warren's operations rather than simply a financier. Cargill's course of dealing with Warren was, by its own admission, a paternalistic relationship in which Cargill made the key economic decisions and kept Warren in existence.

---

7. Although the contracts with the farmers were executed by Warren, Warren paid for the grain with drafts drawn on Cargill. While this is not in itself significant ... it is one factor to be taken into account in analyzing the relationship between Warren and Cargill.

Although considerable interest was paid by Warren on the loan, the reason for Cargill's financing of Warren was not to make money as a lender but, rather, to establish a source of market grain for its business. As one Cargill manager noted, "We were staying in there because we wanted the grain." . . .

On the whole, there was a unique fabric in the relationship between Cargill and Warren. . . . We conclude that, on the facts of this case, there was sufficient evidence from which the jury could find that Cargill was the principal of Warren within the definitions of agency set forth in Restatement (Second) of Agency §§1 and 140.

QUESTION ON JENSON FARMS CO. v. CARGILL, INC.

If Cargill exercised control over Warren to protect its loan, why should it matter that Cargill made the loan to preserve access to a supply of grain? If Cargill was principally interested in preserving its supply of grain rather than earning interest on its loan, can't it also be said that the farmers' principal interest was selling their grain? Should it matter whether the farmers knew of Warren's precarious financial state? Should it matter whether there were competitive buyers for the farmers' grain nearby?

1.2.4 Liability in Contract

1.2.4.1 *Actual and Apparent Authority*

An agency is an arrangement that confers legal power on the agent and gives rise to duties by both the principal (P) and the agent (A). Both parties must manifest their intention to enter an agency relationship. This manifestation need not necessarily be in writing, nor is it essential that it even be verbal. What is necessary is for the agent to *reasonably understand from the action or speech of the principal that she has been authorized to act on the principal's behalf.*

Thus, the scope of the *actual authority* conferred on the agent is that which a reasonable person in the position of A would infer from the conduct of P. Actual authority includes (unless specifically withheld) *incidental authority* — that is, the authority to do those implementary steps that are ordinarily done in connection with facilitating the authorized act. In addition to actual authority, there is another source of authority. *Apparent authority* is authority that a reasonable third party would infer from the actions or statements of P. Thus, apparent authority is in the nature of an equitable remedy designed to prevent fraud or unfairness to third parties who reasonably rely on P's actions or statements in dealing with A. This will be true even if, unbeknownst to the third party, P had quite explicitly limited the authority of A in a way that precluded A from engaging in that action. See generally Restatement (Third) Agency §2.03.

WHITE v. THOMAS
1991 LEXIS 109 (Ark. App. 1991)

CRACRAFT, Chief Judge.

Appellants Bradford White, Sr., and Northwest National Bank appeal from an order of the Washington County Chancery Court requiring White to specifically perform a contract to convey real estate to Stanley Thomas and Mary Thomas, and directing the bank to release the property from the lien of the mortgage it held. As we find sufficient merit in the argument that appellant White was not bound under the contract, we reverse the chancellor's decree.

The facts are not seriously in dispute. Appellant Bradford White had employed Betty Simpson on a part-time basis for nearly two years. During her employment, Ms. Simpson answered appellant's telephone, watched his house when he was out of town, did some typing, and "fixed up" two houses. She had once signed, on appellant's behalf and under a power of attorney, the closing papers on a piece of property appellant was purchasing.* She also had brought appellant information about other properties for sale, but had never negotiated sales or purchases of land for appellant and had never before gone to an auction to buy property.

In December 1988, appellant White instructed Simpson to attend a land auction and bid, in his behalf, up to $250,000.00 on an entire 220-acre farm, except for the three acres on which a house sat. He signed a blank check for her to use in depositing the required ten percent of the bid. Simpson was given no other instructions, and White left for a trip to Europe before the sale was held.

Appellees attended the auction and were the successful bidders on the three-acre tract on which the residence was located. They also unsuccessfully bid on acreage adjoining the homesite. The 217-acre balance of the land, including that additional acreage in which appellees had shown an interest, was struck off and sold to Ms. Simpson for $327,500.00. When Ms. Simpson realized that her bid had exceeded the amount authorized by appellant, she approached appellees about purchasing from her some of the lands surrounding their house. She signed the agreement with the auctioneer to purchase the 217-acre tract. She then entered into an offer and acceptance with appellees in which she agreed to sell to appellees approximately forty-five acres of the land that she had just purchased for appellant White. The contract was signed by appellees and by "Betty Simpson, POA, Power of Attorney for Brad White."

Appellant White returned from Europe on Friday, December 9. The following Monday, Ms. Simpson told him that she had paid $327,500.00 for the property and he "almost had a heart attack. I was upset but I still went through with the closing." Ms. Simpson later told appellant White that appellees wanted to buy part of the property. This was the first information he

---

* A Power of Attorney (POA) is a written instrument executed by the principal (or "grantor") designating the agent to perform specified acts on the principal's behalf. It is intended to provide written evidence of an agency relationship. — EDS.

had concerning it. He immediately repudiated Ms. Simpson's action in sign-ing the offer and acceptance and so informed appellees. The following day, appellant White's purchase of the 217-acre tract was consummated in part with the proceeds of a purchase-money loan, secured by a lien on the real estate, from the appellant bank.

Appellees then began this action seeking specific performance of the contract and release of the land embraced in the contract from the mort-gage. Appellant White and Simpson both denied that Simpson was expressly authorized to enter into a contract of sale on White's behalf, and appellees do not contend otherwise. The only relevant factual dispute centered around Simpson's representations as to her authority. Appellee Stanley Thomas tes-tified that "[a]t one point in time, before the offer and acceptance, I asked Ms. Simpson whether she had the authority or something, and she said was the power of attorney [sic]. At some point in time, the question crossed my mind as to whether or not Ms. Simpson could convey the property, but I was satisfied with her statement that she had a power of attorney." Ms. Simpson, on the other hand, testified that the auctioneer asked her if she had a power of attorney and "I said, 'No.' Then he asked me if I would send one. There was no more conversation about it." It is undisputed that no such power of attorney actually existed.

At the conclusion of the evidence, the court found that Ms. Simpson had in fact informed appellees that she had a power of attorney granting her the authority she had exercised and that appellees had relied on Ms. Simpson's representations as to her authority. The court concluded that the offer and acceptance was a valid and binding contract, complete in its terms, that the reliance by appellees on the representations of Ms. Simpson was reasonable, and that appellant White was estopped from denying the authority of Ms. Simpson and was legally bound to the terms of the contract as her principal and employer. The court also concluded that it would be inequitable to allow appellant White to ratify Ms. Simpson's act of purchasing the farm, despite her having exceeded his express instructions, but allow him to disaffirm her action in entering into the offer and acceptance with appellees. Finally, the court found that the appellant bank had actual and constructive notice of appellees' claim, and ordered it to release its mortgage lien as to that portion of the lands ordered to be conveyed to appellees....

Although we review chancery cases de novo, we will not reverse a chan-cellor's findings unless they are clearly erroneous....

Here, it is undisputed that Ms. Simpson was not expressly authorized to sell appellant White's property; she was expressly authorized only to pur-chase a 217-acre tract of land for her principal if she could do so for no more than $250,000.00. Nor did she have the implied authority to contract to sell to appellees a portion of the property that she had purchased, as that act was not necessary to accomplish her assigned task of purchasing the entire tract. Therefore, in order for appellant White to be liable for Simpson's actions in entering into the offer and acceptance with appellees, her actions must have fallen within the scope of her apparent authority....

Here, it is undisputed that appellees knew that Simpson's actions at the auction were purportedly being taken on behalf of appellant White. While

Simpson's possession of a blank check signed by White may have indicated some limited authority on her part to make a purchase for him, there is no evidence that White knowingly permitted Simpson to enter into a contract to sell or that he ever held her out as having such authority. Nor can we conclude that the two types of transactions, purchasing and selling, are so closely related that a third person could reasonably believe that authority to do the one carried with it authority to do the other. Indeed, appellees were sufficiently concerned about Simpson's authority to contract to sell White's property that they specifically asked her whether she was so authorized. Appellees made no attempt to contact White concerning Simpson's authority and did not even demand to see the alleged written power of attorney under which Simpson claimed to be acting. Instead, they chose to rely solely upon an admitted agent's own declarations as to her authority.

While the declarations of an alleged agent may be used to corroborate other evidence of the scope of agency, neither agency nor the extent of the agent's authority can be shown solely by his own declarations or actions in the absence of the party to be affected. From our review of the record, we cannot conclude that there is any evidence in this case to support Simpson's statements as to her authority to sell White's property. Therefore, we must conclude that the chancellor's conclusion that appellant White was bound under the contract due to Simpson's apparent authority to enter into it is clearly erroneous. There could be no basis for finding White estopped to deny Simpson's authority either, for, as noted above, there is no evidence that he knew or should have known of her action or declarations.

Nor do we find merit in the argument that because appellant White ratified Simpson's contract to purchase the 217-acre tract, it would be inequitable to allow him to deny the burdens of her action in agreeing to sell forty-five acres of it. . . . Simpson entered into two separate contracts involving different parties.

In view of our conclusion that appellant was not bound by the agreement to sell to appellees, we reverse the order of specific performance and the order that the appellant bank release the property from its mortgage lien. . . .

Reversed and dismissed.

1.2.4.2   Inherent Authority

In addition to actual authority, express or implied, and apparent authority, some courts have identified circumstances in which they find that individuals possess *inherent authority* to bind principals to contracts. Such power might better be described as *inherent power* in order to emphasize that it is not conferred on agents by principals but represents consequences imposed on principals by the law. See Restatement (Second) Agency §§8A, 161, 194. The 2006 Restatement (Third) of Agency no longer conceptualizes the field in this way. According to the reporter: "Other doctrines stated in this Restatement encompass the justifications underpinning [inherent authority] including the importance of interpretation by the agent in the agent's relationship with the principal, as well as the doctrines of apparent authority, estoppel, and restitution." See Restatement (Third) Agency §2.01 comment b.

Inherent authority is perhaps easiest to understand in the context of an undisclosed principal transaction. Imagine, for example, that a principal allows an agent to manage property and hold herself out as its owner but that the principal privately restricts the agent's actual authority to deal with the property in some particular—say, she is not authorized to contract for improvements in excess of $3,000. If the agent makes a contract to clear some of the land for a price of $7,000, is the principal bound by the contract obligation to pay? The third party cannot invoke the doctrine of apparent authority, since she did not even know of the existence of the principal. Nevertheless, it seems plain that, since the principal can force the third party to complete the contract, the principal should not be able to walk away from her obligations. But how is this result obtained?

Under the traditional approach, the doctrine of inherent power gives a general agent the power to bind a principal, whether disclosed or undisclosed, to an unauthorized contract as long as a general agent would ordinarily have the power to enter such a contract and the third party does not know that matters stand differently in this case. See Restatement (Second) Agency §§161, 194. The Restatement (Third) seems to provide the same result for the particular case of an undisclosed principal. See Restatement (Third) Agency §2.06. More generally, the Restatement (Third) provides agency by estoppel and ratification. See Restatement (Third) Agency §§2.05, 2.07. Please review these provisions in your statutory supplement. Is the reporter of the Restatement (Third) correct in stating that these new provisions do the same work as previously done by Restatement (Second) §8A? Which approach do you prefer?

The following case addresses the nature of inherent authority.

GALLANT INS. CO. v. ISAAC
732 N.E.2d 1262 (Ind. App. 2000)

RILEY, Judge.

Plaintiff-Appellant, Gallant Insurance Company (Gallant), appeals from the trial court's grant of summary judgment in favor of Defendants-Appellees, Christina Isaac (Isaac) and Loretta Davis (Davis) (hereinafter referred to collectively as "Insured"), on its complaint for declaratory judgment regarding its insurance coverage of Isaac's accident.

Thompson-Harris is an independent insurance agent. Its authority includes the power to bind Gallant on new insurance policies, as well as interim policy endorsement such as adding a new driver, or changing and adding a vehicle insured under a policy. Although no written agreement describes the relation between Gallant and Thompson-Harris, the Record indicates Gallant became bound to provide insurance coverage at the time and date on which Thompson-Harris faxed or called the required information to Gallant's producing agent, and premiums were paid to Thompson-Harris.

On June 2, 1994, Gallant issued automobile insurance coverage on Isaac's 1986 Pontiac Fiero through its independent agent, Thompson-Harris.... The printed application form, which had been filled out by the agent, showed that

Isaac's coverage was bound as of 2:06 p.m. on June 2, 1994 until December 2, 1994.... With regard to "CHANGES" made to its conditions, the policy states that an agent shall not waive or change any part of the policy, except by endorsement issued to form a part of the policy, which is signed by a duly authorized representative of the company. The policy also stated that the written policy embodied all agreements existing between the insured, the company and all agents relating to the insurance.

On the last day of her insurance coverage, Isaac traded her 1986 Pontiac Fiero for a 1988 Pontiac Grand Prix. To obtain the newly purchased car, the financing bank required Isaac to obtain full coverage on it. That same day, Isaac contacted Thompson-Harris to notify it that she was purchasing the new car, and to discuss enhancing the existing insurance policy to meet bank requirements. Isaac told a Thompson-Harris employee that she must obtain "full insurance coverage" as a condition to receiving a loan. She also told the employee at Thompson-Harris that her current coverage expires on December 3, 1994, the next day.

In response, the Thompson-Harris employee informed Isaac that because their agency was about to close for the weekend, she would immediately "bind" coverage on the 1988 Grand Prix. They decided that Isaac would come in to Thompson-Harris on Monday, December 5, 1994, to complete the paperwork and pay the down payment on the premium. The employee also informed Isaac that the new coverage on her Pontiac Grand Prix would include the same coverage existing from her Pontiac Fiero, along with additional coverage to comply with conditions set by the bank.

The next day, on December 3, 1994, a different employee completed the "Personal Policy Change Request." This form deleted the 1987 Pontiac Fiero from Isaac's Policy and replaced it with the 1988 Pontiac Grand Prix. It also added additional coverage to the policy as well as additional loss payee/lienholder. The Personal Policy Change Request listed the "Agency" and "Producer" as Thompson-Harris, and stated that the "effective date of change" was December 3, 1994. Towards the bottom of the form, the Thompson-Harris employee typed "[s]he will be in at 9:00 a.m. Monday, 12/5/94, to [sic] down [sic] on renewal. What is [sic] new rate? Thanks." This form, which requested the listed changes, was faxed to Insurance Brokers of Indiana, Inc., on December 3, 1994.

On December 4, 1994, while driving her Pontiac Grand Prix, Isaac collided with another car in which Davis was a passenger. The next day, as planned, Isaac went to Thompson-Harris and paid a $133.00 down payment on the new insurance policy. She also reported the accident. Thompson-Harris completed an "Indiana Operator's Vehicle Crash Report," which notified the State Police that Isaac had insurance coverage at the time of the accident, on December, 4, 1994. Thompson-Harris completed that form on behalf of Gallant. Later, on or about December 22, 1994, Gallant renewed Isaac's insurance policy, with an effective period of December 6, 1994 to June 6, 1995.

Soon afterwards, Gallant brought its complaint for declaratory judgment regarding its insurance coverage of Isaac's accident. It sought a judgment that stated Gallant was not liable for any losses incurred because the policy was not in force....

Gallant contends that Isaac's insurance coverage had lapsed at the time Isaac's accident occurred because the policy renewal premium was not paid as dictated in the policy. It is undisputed that Thompson-Harris is Gallant's independent insurance agent. However, Gallant insists that Thompson-Harris had no authority to renew the insurance policy or orally contract in a manner contrary to what the policy states without the approval of Gallant's producing agent, Insurance Brokers of Indiana, Inc. We disagree....

Gallant argues that Thompson-Harris had no actual or apparent authority to renew the insurance policy or orally contract to do so. Specifically, Gallant contends that it, as a principal, did not manifest any act toward Thompson-Harris or Isaac, whether directly or indirectly, that may have granted such authority. However, because we find that neither an actual nor apparent authority theory applies to the particular facts of this case, we instead address *sua sponte* Thompson-Harris's authority to act as Gallant's agent under an inherent authority theory.

Inherent agency power indicates the power of an agent that is derived not from authority, apparent or estoppel, but from the agency relation itself. This inherent authority theory exists for the protection of persons harmed by or dealing with a principal's servant or agent....

In the case at bar, Thompson-Harris's renewal of Isaac's insurance policy constitutes an act which usually accompanies or is incidental to insurance transactions that it is authorized to conduct. Examining Gallant and Thompson-Harris's agency relationship reveals that, as an agent, Thompson-Harris *was authorized to bind Gallant* on new insurance policies, as well as interim policy endorsements, such as changing and adding new drivers, or changing or adding the vehicle insured. For example, Thompson-Harris "had authority to write an application." That application "had to be either called to [Insurance Brokers of Indiana, Inc.] or faxed to them to bind coverage." In general, the power to bind its principal came into being once Thompson-Harris faxed the necessary paperwork to Gallant's producing agent and payment was made.

Thompson-Harris also had a common practice of telling its insured that they were "bound" despite not receiving payment until later, violating instructions by Gallant and provisions found in the policy. For example, the Record indicates that Thompson-Harris would "orally tell the insured that the new schedule vehicle was bound for coverage." Thompson-Harris would then relay that communication on to Gallant, which would then issue the endorsement. We conclude that this common practice of binding coverage verbally, in violation of Gallant's orders, is similar to Thompson-Harris's authorized conduct, given expressly by Gallant, to bind coverage by fax or phone. Therefore, we find that Thompson-Harris acted within the usual and ordinary scope of its authority.

Next ... a court looks to the *agent's* direct and indirect manifestations and determines whether the third party could have reasonably believed that the agent had authority to conduct the act in question.... Here, Isaac could have reasonably believed that Thompson-Harris had authority to orally bind coverage. Isaac's past dealings were all through Thompson-Harris, whether involving payment of premiums, changing or including a driver, or requesting a new estimate. Direct communication between Gallant and Isaac never occurred. Thus, it was reasonable for Isaac to take at face value Thompson-Harris's communication that coverage was bound, and that she could come in at the end of the weekend to pay for the policy renewal. The reasonableness of Isaac's belief is bolstered by the fact that Thompson-Harris completed all the paperwork necessary and faxed the "Personal Policy Change Request," requesting at the bottom of the page an estimate and noting that Isaac will be in on December 5th, after the weekend, to pay.

... Isaac had no reason to second guess a direct communication by Thompson-Harris stating coverage was bound, particularly since that was a common practice of Thompson-Harris.... As such, we find that Thompson-Harris's direct and indirect manifestation over time, and its direct verbal communication to Isaac that coverage was bound, lead Isaac to reasonably believe that Thompson-Harris had the authority to renew the insurance policy.

Isaac lacked notice that Thompson-Harris did not have authority to verbally bind coverage.... [T]he Record fails to indicate whether Isaac was aware that Thompson-Harris had limited authority. It does not mention whether Isaac knew of expressed limitations about the authority of Thompson-Harris to bind insurance coverage without actual payment.... Isaac had no reason to know that when Thompson-Harris bound coverage Gallant must still endorse that verbal binding. Therefore, we find Isaac did not have notice that Thompson-Harris was not authorized to verbally bind coverage, without payment....

If Gallant or its producing agent *informed* insured individuals or potential clients that Thompson-Harris could not verbally bind coverage, or if Thompson-Harris was required to give such notice, Gallant would have satisfied the notice requirement. Instead, however, Thompson-Harris was left unsupervised to establish common practice in violation of Gallant's granted authority.

[W]e conclude that the Record supports the trial court's findings that Isaac's insurance policy was in full force and effect on December 3, 1994, because Thompson-Harris had the inherent authority to bind coverage by Gallant verbally.

Affirmed.

NOTE ON GALLANT

The subsequent history of the *Gallant* opinion perhaps implicitly endorses the Restatement (Third) of Agency's abandonment of the "inherent power" concept. On appeal, the Supreme Court of Indiana affirmed the judgment below, but specifically repudiated the use of the concept of inherent power to do so. Instead, it held that Thompson-Harris's employee had apparent authority in the circumstances sufficient to make the contract binding, even though it was in violation of the express requirements of Gallant that it empowered Thompson-Harris to bind it only upon receipt of a premium payment. In doing so, the court also expressed the standard doctrine that an agent's statements alone will not create authority where the principal has not done so. How did the court square these two aspects of its holding when Gallant had not communicated with Isaac directly concerning the new insurance policy?

It stated:

> Apparent authority is the authority that a third person reasonably believes an agent to possess because of some manifestation from his principal. [citing cases]
> It is essential that there be some form of communication, direct or indirect, by

the principal, which instills a reasonable belief in the mind of the third party.... Statements or manifestations made by the agent are not sufficient to create an apparent agency relationship.

Applying these principles to the case at hand, it seems to us that the key is determining whether Gallant made the "necessary manifestation" to "instill a reasonable belief in the mind of" Isaac that Thompson-Harris had authority to transfer the coverage from her Fiero to her Grand Prix and renew the policy....

First, it is clear that the "manifestations" ... need not be in the form of direct communications, "but rather the placing of the agent in a position to perform acts or make representations which appear reasonable to a third person is a sufficient manifestation to endow the agent with apparent authority." ... "[S]uch a manifestation by the principal may be found ... where the principal clothes or allows a special agent to act with the appearance of possessing more authority than is actually conferred."

In *Old Line Auto. Insurors v. Kuebl*, an insured had for some time prior to the issuance of the auto insurance policy at issue in the case dealt with the insurer through one Donald R. Crabb. He purchased a policy on a Studebaker through Crabb. Crabb subsequently arranged the transfer of the coverage of that policy from the Studebaker to a Dodge. When the insurer sent the insured the policy, it did not tell the insured that it would not be responsible for payments made to its agent Crabb. The insured in fact paid his premiums to Crabb who, at some point in time, failed to forward them to the insurer. When this occurred, the insurer did not notify the insured that the policy was cancelled. The insured subsequently presented a claim, which the insurer denied on the basis that the policy had been cancelled. The Court of Appeals held that "[u]nder these circumstances we believe [the insured] was justified in believing that Crabb, as the agent of [the insurer], had the authority to collect the premiums due on the policy in question here." 127 Ind. App. 445, 455, 141 N.E.2d 858, 862 (1957).

* * *

... [T]he evidence appears to us without dispute that Thompson-Harris had apparent authority to bind Gallant, e.g., Gallant's dealings with Isaac just recited contained the manifestations required under applicable case law to cause Isaac reasonably to believe that Thompson-Harris had authority to bind Gallant.

751 NE2d 672, 678 (Ind. 2001)

QUESTIONS ON GALLANT *AND* WHITE

1. While in fact what is behind the two opinions in *Gallant* is very much the same thing, do you have a preference as to the conceptual basis for the liability? Why?

2. How significant was it in *Gallant* that defendant is an automobile insurance company, that plaintiff had paid premiums for insurance to Gallant both before and immediately after the accident, and that Isaac had acted reasonably in relying on the agent who did not follow instructions perfectly?

3. If we evaluate these cases from an ex ante perspective (meaning that we ask whether they articulate the right rule for governing the actions of similarly situated people in the future), what considerations should bear on our answer?

4. Inherent agency power has been criticized as an unwarranted shift in the traditional (and, it is argued, economically efficient) balance of monitoring costs between principals and third parties. See Steven A. Fishman, *Inherent Agency Power — Should Enterprise Liability Apply to Agents' Unauthorized Contracts?*, 19 Rutgers. L.J. 1 (1987). Do you agree?

5. Consider the apparent and inherent authority doctrines as implicit terms (rules of the road) in contracting between principals and third parties. Why should principals *ever* escape liability for contracts negotiated in their names by bona fide general agents? From an economic perspective, are principals always or usually the least costly monitors of their own agents?

1.2.4.3   *Agency by Estoppel or Ratification*

Finally, even where an agent's act is not authorized by the principal, or is not within any inherent agency power of the agent, the principal may still be bound by the agent's acts by *estoppel* or by *ratification* (Restatement (Third) Agency §2.05). The elements of estoppel are the customary ones: failure to act when knowledge and an opportunity to act arise plus reasonable change in position on the part of the third person (Restatement (Third) Agency §2.05). Alternatively, accepting benefits under an unauthorized contract will constitute acceptance (affirmance, in the language of the section) of its obligations as well as its benefits (Restatement (Third) Agency §§4.01, 4.07). For an exposition on the doctrine of implied ratification, see Elliot Axelrod, *The Doctrine of Implied Ratification — Application and Limitations*, 36 Okla. L. Rev. 849-862 (1983).

1.2.5   Liability in Tort

In most circumstances, principals are liable for torts committed by a class of agents known as "employees," as distinguished from another class of agents (and nonagents) known as "independent contractors." Put differently, only a particular kind of agency relationship, the employer-employee relationship, ordinarily triggers vicarious liability for all torts committed within the agent's scope of employment. Please read Restatement (Third) Agency §§2.04 and 7.07 in your statutory supplement.

HUMBLE OIL & REFINING CO. v. MARTIN
148 Tex. 175, 222 S.W.2d 995 (1949)

Garwood, J.:

Petitioners Humble Oil & Refining Company and Mrs. A.C. Love and husband complain here of the judgments of the trial court and the Court of

Civil Appeals in which they were held liable in damages for personal injuries following a special issue verdict at the suit of respondent George F. Martin acting for himself and his two minor daughters. The injuries were inflicted on the three Martins ... by an unoccupied automobile belonging to the petitioners Love, which, just prior to the accident, had been left by Mrs. Love at a filling station owned by petitioner Humble for servicing and thereafter, before any station employee had touched it, rolled by gravity off the premises into and obliquely across the abutting street, striking Mr. Martin and his children from behind as they were walking into the yard of their home, a short distance downhill from the station.

The trial court rendered judgment against petitioners Humble and Mrs. Love jointly and severally and gave the latter judgment over against Humble for whatever she might pay the respondents. The Court of Civil Appeals affirmed the judgment after reforming it to eliminate the judgment over in favor of Mrs. Love.... The petitioners here respectively complain of the judgment in favor of the Martins, and each seeks full indemnity (as distinguished from contribution) from the other.

The apparently principal contention of petitioner, Humble, is that it is liable neither to respondent Martin nor to petitioner Mrs. Love, since the station was in effect operated by an independent contractor, W.T. Schneider, and Humble is accordingly not responsible for his negligence nor that of W.V. Manis, who was the only station employee or representative present when the Love car was left and rolled away. In this connection, the jury convicted petitioner Humble of the following acts of negligence proximately causing the injuries in question: (a) failure to inspect the Love car to see that the emergency brake was set or the gears engaged; (b) failure to set the emergency brake on the Love car; (c) leaving the Love car unattended on the driveway. The verdict also included findings that Mrs. Love "had delivered her car to the custody of the defendant Humble Oil & Refining Company, before her car started rolling from the position in which she had parked it"; that the accident was not unavoidable; and that no negligent act of either of petitioners was the sole proximate cause of the injuries in question. We think the Court of Civil Appeals properly held Humble responsible for the operation of the station, which admittedly it owned, as it did also the principal products there sold by Schneider under the so-called "Commission Agency Agreement" between him and Humble which was in evidence. The facts that neither Humble, Schneider nor the station employees considered Humble as an employer or master; that the employees were paid and directed by Schneider individually as their "boss," and that a provision of the agreement expressly repudiates any authority of Humble over the employees, are not conclusive against the master-servant relationship, since there is other evidence bearing on the right or power of Humble to control the details of the station work as regards Schneider himself and therefore as to employees which it was expressly contemplated that he would hire.... Even if the contract between Humble and Schneider were the only evidence on the question, the instrument as a whole indicates a master-servant relationship quite as much as, if not more than, it suggests an arrangement between independent contractors. For example, paragraph 1 includes a provision requiring Schneider "to make reports *and perform other duties in connection with the operation of said station that may be required of him from time to time by Company.*" (Emphasis supplied). And while paragraph 2 purports to require Schneider to pay all operational expenses, the schedule of commissions forming part of the agreement does just the opposite in its paragraph (F), which gives Schneider a 75% "commission" on "the net public utility bills paid" by him and thus requires Humble to pay three-fourths of one of the most important operational expense items. Obviously the main object of the enterprise was the retail marketing of Humble's products with title remaining in Humble until delivery to the consumer. This was done under a strict system of financial control and supervision by Humble, with little or no business discretion reposed in Schneider except as to hiring, discharge, payment and supervision of a few station employees of a more or less laborer status. Humble furnished the all-important station location and equipment, the advertising media, the products and a substantial part of the current operating costs. The hours of operation were controlled by Humble. The "Commission Agency Agreement," which evidently was Schneider's only title to occupancy of the premise, was terminable at the will of Humble. The so-called "rentals" were, at least in part, based on the amount of Humble's products sold, being, therefore, involved with the matter of Schneider's remuneration and not rentals in the usual sense. And, as above shown, the agreement required Schneider in effect to do anything Humble might tell him to do. All in all, aside from the stipulation regarding Schneider's assistants, there is essentially little difference between his situation and that of a mere store clerk who happens to be paid a commission instead of a salary. The business was Humble's business, just as the store clerk's business would be that of the store owner. Schneider was Humble's servant, and so accordingly were Schneider's assistants who were contemplated by the contract....

The evidence above discussed serves to distinguish the instant case from *The Texas Company v. Wheat*, 140 Texas 468, 168 S.W.(2d) 632, upon which petitioner Humble principally relies. In that case the evidence ... clearly showed a "dealer" type of relationship in which the lessee in charge of the filling station purchased from his landlord, The Texas Company, and sold as his own, and was free to sell at his own price and on his own credit terms, the company products purchased, as well as the products of other oil companies. The contracts contained no provision requiring the lessee to perform any duty The Texas Company might see fit to impose on him, nor did the company pay any part of the lessee's operating expenses, nor control the working hours of the station....

HOOVER v. SUN OIL CO.
212 A.2d 214 (Del. 1965)

CHRISTIE, J.:

This case is concerned with injuries received as the result of a fire on August 16, 1962 at the service station operated by James F. Barone. The fire started at the rear of plaintiff's car where it was being filled with gasoline and was allegedly caused by the negligence of John Smilyk an employee of

Barone. Plaintiffs brought suit against Smilyk, Barone and Sun Oil Company (Sun) which owned the service station.

Sun has moved for summary judgment as to it on the basis that Barone was an independent contractor and therefore the alleged negligence of his employee could not result in liability as to Sun. The plaintiffs contend instead that Barone was acting as Sun's agent and that Sun may therefore be responsible for plaintiff's injuries.

Barone began operating this business in October of 1960 pursuant to a lease dated October 17, 1960. The station and all of its equipment, with the exception of a tire-stand and rack, certain advertising displays and miscellaneous hand tools, were owned by Sun. The lease was subject to termination by either party upon thirty days' written notice after the first six months and at the anniversary date thereafter. The rental was partially determined by the volume of gasoline purchased but there was also a minimum and a maximum monthly rental.

At the same time, Sun and Barone also entered into a dealer's agreement under which Barone was to purchase petroleum products from Sun and Sun was to loan necessary equipment and advertising materials. Barone was required to maintain this equipment and to use it solely for Sun products. Barone was permitted under the agreement to sell competitive products but chose to do so only in a few minor areas. As to Sun products, Barone was prohibited from selling them except under the Sunoco label and from blending them with products not supplied by Sun.

Barone's station had the usual large signs indicating that Sunoco products were sold there. His advertising in the classified section of the telephone book was under a Sunoco heading, and his employees wore uniforms with the Sun emblem, the uniforms being owned by Barone or rented from an independent company.

Barone, upon the urging of Robert B. Peterson, Sun's area sales representative, attended a Sun school for service station operators in 1961. The school's curriculum was designed to familiarize the station operator with bookkeeping and merchandising, the appearance and proper maintenance of a Sun station, and the Sun Oil products. The course concluded with the operator working at Sun's model station in order to gain work experience in the use of the policy and techniques taught at the school.

Other facts typifying the company-service station relationship were the weekly visits of Sun's sales representative, Peterson, who would take orders for Sun products, inspect the restrooms, communicate customer complaints, make various suggestions to improve sales and discuss any problems that Barone might be having. Besides the weekly visits, Peterson was in contact with Barone on other occasions in order to implement Sun's "competitive allowance system" which enabled Barone to meet local price competition by giving him a rebate on the gasoline in his inventory roughly equivalent to the price decline and a similarly reduced price on his next order of gasoline.

While Peterson did offer advice to Barone on all phases of his operation, it was usually done on request and Barone was under no obligation to follow the advice. Barone's contacts and dealings with Sun were many and their relationship intricate, but he made no written reports to Sun and he alone assumed the overall risk of profit or loss in his business operation. Barone independently determined his own hours of operation and the identity, pay scale and working conditions of his employees, and it was his name that was posted as proprietor.

Plaintiffs contend in effect that the aforegoing facts indicate that Sun controlled the day-to-day operation of the station and consequently Sun is responsible for the negligent acts of Barone's employee. Specifically, plaintiffs contend that there is an issue of fact for the jury to determine as to whether or not there was an agency relationship.

The legal relationships arising from the distribution systems of major oil-producing companies are in certain respects unique.... As stated in an annotation collecting many of the cases dealing with this relationship:

In some situations traditional definitions of principal and agent and of employer and independent contractor may be difficult to apply to service station operations. But the undisputed facts of the case at bar make it clear that Barone was an independent contractor.

Barone's service station, unlike retail outlets for many products, is basically a one-company outlet and represents to the public, through Sunoco's national and local advertising, that it sells not only Sun's quality products but Sun's quality service. Many people undoubtedly come to the service station because of that latter representation.

However, the lease contract and dealer's agreement fail to establish any relationship other than landlord-tenant, and independent contractor. Nor is there anything in the conduct of the individuals which is inconsistent with that relationship so as to indicate that the contracts were mere subterfuge or sham. The areas of close contact between Sun and Barone stem from the fact that both have a mutual interest in the sale of Sun products and in the success of Barone's business....

The facts of this case differ markedly from those in which the oil company was held liable for the tortious conduct of its service station operator or his employees. Sun had no control over the details of Barone's day-to-day operation. Therefore, no liability can be imputed to Sun from the allegedly negligent acts of Smilyk. Sun's motion for summary judgment is granted.

It is so ordered....

QUESTIONS ON HUMBLE OIL AND SUN OIL

1. Both *Humble Oil* and *Sun Oil* involve distributorship relationships between gas station proprietors and oil companies. Why might oil companies prefer to establish such networks of semi-independent distributors instead of staffing stations with their own employees or selling through affiliated retail outlets?

2. Without doubt, Humble Oil reserved more contractual control over Schneider's station than Sun Oil retained over Barone's station. How important were these differences? Did they affect the ability of these two oil companies to prevent accidents?

3. Is Schneider in a better position than Humble Oil to supervise station attendants? If so, what are the consequences of shifting liability from Schneider to Humble Oil? Does it matter whether Schneider is wealthy? Judgment proof?

4. As you might expect after reading the gasoline cases above, franchisor-franchisee situations are a well-established genre in agency law. The core question is often whether the franchisor sufficiently controls the franchisee to establish an agency relationship. If so, the franchisor is vicariously liable for claims against franchisees acting within the scope of their employment. Modern courts have come out differently on similar facts in applying this control test. Compare *Hoffnagle v. McDonald's Corp.*, 522 N.W.2d 808 (Iowa 1994) (applying control test to find that McDonald's was not liable for injuries suffered by a franchisee's employee from an assault by a third party) with *Miller v. McDonald's Corp.*, 945 P.2d 1107 (Or. Ct. App. 1997) (applying control test to find that McDonald's could be liable for injuries to a customer of a franchisee who bit into a Big Mac sandwich with a stone in it). As a policy matter, would it be preferable to hold McDonald's strictly liable for torts of its franchisees? How might McDonald's respond to such a change in legal rules?

1.2.6   Liability in Tort Under the Apparent Authority Doctrine

The doctrine of *respondeat superior* illustrated in the preceding "gasoline station" cases is not the only basis for imposing vicarious liability in tort on an agent's principal. Apparent authority — yes, the same apparent authority that figures prominently in the agency law of contract — is also a basis for imposing vicarious liability in tort without regard to the temporal, spatial, or incentive constraints that arise under the definition of "scope of employment." In particular, a principal is liable for a class of intentional "communicative torts" when her agent speaks on her behalf with apparent authority to do so. See Restatement (Third) Agency §7.08 and §7.08 comments a & b. A paradigmatic example for purposes of this book is a fraudulent misstatement made by the CEO of a public corporation that is intended to inflate the market price of her corporation's shares. A CEO ordinarily possesses authority to speak to the market about the performance of her corporation. Of course, she is ordinarily not authorized to make knowingly false statements. But the issue of actual authority is a fine point. The real question is whether corporate principals might be vicariously liable for all harmful statements that their agents make while appearing to have the requisite authority to make these decisions. The short answer is that principals are liable under the apparent authority doctrine. One important implication is that an investor may sue a corporation for the loss he incurs by purchasing the stock of a corporation in reliance on false statements made by an agent with apparent authority to speak for the company — the company's CEO being the most conspicuous candidate. Indeed, the company is vicariously liable on these facts *even* if its dishonest CEO deceived investors solely for personal gain, as might happen if she could increase her own compensation by manipulating share price.

1.3   THE GOVERNANCE OF AGENCY (THE AGENT'S DUTIES)

1.3.1   The Nature of the Agent's Fiduciary Relationship

In common law, an agent is a fiduciary of her principal. When we say that a legal relationship is fiduciary in character, we generally mean that legal power over property (including information) held by the fiduciary is held for the sole purpose of advancing the aim of a relationship pursuant to which she came to control that property. In testamentary trusts, the purpose is to carry out the will of the deceased. In agencies, it is to advance the purposes of the principal. In corporations, it is for the directors to advance the purposes of the corporation. In each case, the fiduciary is bound to exercise her good-faith judgment in an effort to pursue, under future circumstances, the purposes established at the time of creation of the relationship.

While fiduciaries can have numerous specific duties in particular contexts, generally their duties can be said to fall into three categories. First is the *duty of obedience* to the documents creating the relationship (e.g., Restatement (Third) Agency §8.09). This is the duty to obey the principal's commands while the agency relationship continues. Of course, if optimal use of the assets requires flexibility that cannot be perfectly defined at the time of the creation of the relationship, then the duty of obedience will be insufficient to fully inform the principal-agent relationship. The law of agency therefore incorporates two open-ended duties owed by the agent, the *duty of loyalty* and the *duty of care*. The agent's duty of loyalty is the pervasive obligation to exercise her legal power over the subject of the agency in good faith and in what she believes to be in the best interest of her principal as these have been communicated to her — and not, it goes without saying — in her own personal interest. The duty of care is the duty to act as a reasonable person would act, in similar circumstances, in becoming informed and exercising the power conferred by the principal.

The materials that follow illustrate the duty of loyalty in the contexts of the principal-agent relationship and the beneficiary-trustee relationship. We will return to fiduciary duties in the partnership and corporate contexts in due course. The point here is to ask the broad questions: Why do these duties assume the open-ended form that they do? What remedy should follow if they are breached? And how should they differ according to the particular nature of the fiduciary relationship at issue?

1.3.2   The Agent's Duty of Loyalty to the Principal

QUESTIONS ON RESTATEMENT (THIRD) AGENCY
§§8.01-8.03 AND 8.06

1. Please read these Restatement Agency (Third) sections. If your client learns after the fact that his real estate agent purchased his house on her own account — purportedly after making full disclosure — at 50 percent below the

price of a similar house sold through another agent the next week, how confident are you that you will be able to void the deal?

2. More generally, why should self-dealing transactions that are not disclosed be voidable automatically under §8.03? Why not simply place the burden of proof on the agent to establish that the terms of such an undisclosed transaction were "fair" to the principal?

TARNOWSKI v. RESOP
51 N.W.2d 801 (Minn. 1952)

KNUTSON, J.:

Plaintiff desired to make a business investment. He engaged defendant as his agent to investigate and negotiate for the purchase of a route of coin-operated music machines. On June 2, 1947, relying upon the advice of defendant and the investigation he had made, plaintiff purchased such a business from Phillip Loechler and Lyle Mayer of Rochester, Minnesota, who will be referred to hereinafter as the sellers.... Plaintiff alleges that defendant represented to him that he had made a thorough investigation of the route; that it had 75 locations in operation; that one or more machines were at each location; that the equipment at each location was not more than six months old; and that the gross income from all locations amounted to more than $3,000 per month. As a matter of fact, defendant had made only a superficial investigation and had investigated only five of the locations. Other than that, he had adopted false representations of the sellers as to the other locations and had passed them on to plaintiff as his own. Plaintiff was to pay $30,620 for the business. He paid $11,000 down. About six weeks after the purchase, plaintiff discovered that the representations made to him by defendant were false, in that there were not more than 47 locations; that at some of the locations there were no machines and at others there were machines more than six months old, some of them being seven years old; and that the gross income was far less than $3,000 per month. Upon discovering the falsity of defendant's representations and those of the sellers, plaintiff rescinded the sale. He offered to return what he had received, and he demanded the return of his money. The sellers refused to comply, and he brought suit against them in the district court of Olmsted county. The action was tried, resulting in a verdict of $10,000 for plaintiff. Thereafter, the sellers paid plaintiff $9,500, after which the action was dismissed with prejudice pursuant to a stipulation of the parties.

In this action, brought in Hennepin county, plaintiff alleges that defendant, while acting as agent for him, collected a secret commission from the sellers for consummating the sale, which plaintiff seeks to recover under his first cause of action. In his second cause of action, he seeks to recover damages for (1) losses suffered in operating the route prior to rescission; (2) loss of time devoted to operation; (3) expenses in connection with rescission of the sale and his investigation in connection therewith; (4) nontaxable expenses in connection with prosecution of the suit against the sellers; and (5) attorneys' fees in connection with the suit. The case was tried to a jury, and plaintiff recovered a verdict of $5,200. This appeal is from the judgment entered pursuant thereto....

1. With respect to plaintiff's first cause of action, the principle that all profits made by an agent in the course of an agency belong to the principal, whether they are the fruits of performance or the violation of an agent's duty, is firmly established and universally recognized.

It matters not that the principal has suffered no damage or even that the transaction has been profitable to him....

The right to recover profits made by the agent in the course of the agency is not affected by the fact that the principal, upon discovering a fraud, has rescinded the contract and recovered that with which he parted. Restatement, Agency, §407(2)....

It follows that, insofar as the secret commission of $2,000 received by the agent is concerned, plaintiff had an absolute right thereto, irrespective of any recovery resulting from the action against the sellers for rescission.

... Our inquiry is limited to a consideration of the question whether a principal may recover of an agent who has breached his trust the items of damage mentioned after a successful prosecution of an action for rescission against the third parties with whom the agent dealt for his principal.

The general rule is stated in Restatement, Agency, §407(1), as follows:

> If an agent has received a benefit as a result of violating his duty of loyalty, the principal is entitled to recover from him what he has so received, its value, or its proceeds, and also the amount of damage thereby caused, except that if the violation consists of the wrongful disposal of the principal's property, the principal cannot recover its value and also what the agent received in exchange therefor.

In Comment a on Subsection (1) we find the following:

> ... In either event, whether or not the principal elects to get back the thing improperly dealt with or to recover from the agent its value or the amount of benefit which the agent has improperly received, he is, in addition, entitled to be indemnified by the agent for any loss which has been caused to his interests by the improper transaction....

So far as the right to recover attorneys' fees is concerned, the same may be said in this case. Plaintiff sought to return what had been received and demanded a return of his down payment. The sellers refused. He thereupon sued to accomplish this purpose, as he had a right to do, and was successful. His attorneys' fees and expenses of suit were directly traceable to the harm caused by defendant's wrongful act. As such, they are recoverable....

QUESTIONS ON TARNOWSKI v. RESOP

Is the plaintiff overcompensated in this case? Why should he receive both damages and the agent's secret commission from the sellers? Has he not already recovered almost all of his down payment in a separate action against the sellers?

1.3.3 The Trustee's Duty to Trust Beneficiaries

The private trust is a legal device that allows a "trustee" to hold legal title to trust property, which the trustee is under a fiduciary duty to manage for the benefit of another person, the *trust beneficiary*. The trust resembles the agency relationship insofar as the trustee has obvious power to affect the interests of the beneficiary. The trust differs from agency, of course, insofar as the trustee is subject to the terms of the trust, as these have been fixed by the trust's *settlor* (or creator); the trustee is not ordinarily subject to the control of the beneficiary. Before considering the following case, please read Restatement (Second) of Trusts §§203, 205, and 206.

IN RE GLEESON
124 N.E.2d 624 (Ill. App. 1954)

CARROLL, J.:

Mary Gleeson, who died testate on February 14, 1952, owned among other properties, 160 acres of farm land in Christian County, Illinois. By her will admitted to Probate March 29, 1952, she nominated Con Colbrook, petitioner-appellee (who will be referred to herein as petitioner) executor thereof. Petitioner was also appointed as trustee under the will and the residuary estate, including the aforesaid 160 acres of land, was devised to him in trust for the benefit of decedent's 3 children, Helen Black, Bernadine Gleeson, and Thomas Gleeson, an incompetent, who are respondents herein.

On March 1, 1950, the testatrix leased the 160 acres for the year ending March 1, 1951 to petitioner and William Curtin, a partnership. On March 1, 1951, she again leased the premises to said partnership for the year ending March 1, 1952. Upon the expiration of this latter lease the partnership held over as tenants under the provisions thereof and farmed the land until March 1, 1953, at which time petitioner leased the land to another tenant. While there is no written lease in evidence, the record indicates the terms thereof provided for payment to the lessor of $10 per acre cash rent and a share in the crops of 1/2 of the corn and 2/5 of the small grain.

The petitioner's appointment as trustee was confirmed by the Circuit Court of Christian County on April 29, 1953. On July 22, 1953, he filed his first semi-annual report. This report was not approved and petitioner was ordered to recast the same in accordance with certain directions of the Court. The recast report was filed December 5, 1953. To this report respondents filed certain objections. We are concerned here with only one of the said objections, which is as follows:

> 1. Report shows trustee was co-tenant of trust real estate but fails to account for share of profits received by trustee as co-tenant which by law should be repaid by him to trust estate....

The Courts of this state have consistently followed a general principle of equity that a trustee cannot deal in his individual capacity with the trust property....

Petitioner recognizes the existence of this general rule, but argues that because of the existence of the peculiar circumstances under which the petitioner proceeded, the instant case must be taken to constitute one of the rare exceptions to such rule. The circumstances alluded to as peculiar are pointed out as being the facts that the death of Mrs. Gleeson occurred on February 14, 1952, only 15 days prior to the beginning of the 1952 farm year; that satisfactory farm tenants are not always available, especially on short notice; that the petitioner had in the preceding fall of 1951 sown part of the 160 acres in wheat to be harvested in 1952; that the holding over by the trustee and his partner was in the best interests of the trust; that the same was done in an open manner; that the petitioner was honest with the trust; and that it suffered no loss as a result of the transaction.

Petitioner contends that since only 15 days intervened between the death of Mrs. Gleeson and the beginning of the farm year, and that good tenant farmers might not be available at such a time, it was in the interests of the trust that the petitioner continue to hold over for the year of 1952. No showing is made that petitioner tried to obtain a satisfactory tenant to replace Colbrook and Curtin on March 1, 1952. The record discloses that subsequent to the death of testatrix, petitioner discussed continuance of the farming operation with two of the beneficiaries under the trust and voluntarily raised the cash rent from $6 to $10 per acre. This evidence tending to show that petitioner was interested in continuing a tenancy under which he was leasing trust property to himself would seem to refute any contention that an effort to lease the property to anyone other than the partnership was made. The fact that the partners had sown wheat on the land in the fall of 1951 cannot be said to be a peculiar circumstance. It is not suggested that the trust would have suffered a loss if someone other than the petitioner had farmed the land in 1952 and harvested the wheat. It would appear that a satisfactory adjustment covering the matter of the wheat could have been made between the trust and the partnership without great difficulty.

The good faith and honesty of the petitioner or the fact that the trust sustained no loss on account of his dealings therewith are all matters which can avail petitioner nothing so far as a justification of the course he chose to take in dealing with trust property is concerned. . . .

[T]he petitioner herein, upon the death of the testatrix, instead of conferring with her beneficiaries concerning continuance of his tenancy of the trust property, should have then decided whether he chose to continue as a tenant or to act as trustee. His election was to act as trustee and as such he could not deal with himself.

This Court, therefore, reaches the conclusion that the Circuit Court erred . . . and that petitioner should have been required to recast his first semi-annual report and to account therein for all monies received by him personally as a profit by virtue of his being a co-tenant of trust property during the 1952 crop year, and to pay the amount of any such profit to the trust.

The judgment of the Circuit Court of Christian County is reversed. . . .

QUESTIONS AND NOTE ON IN RE GLEESON

1. If new tenants are hard to find on short notice, why expect Colbrook to look for one?

2. If the trustee relationship is analogized to the agency relationship, whom should we view as the principal in this case? The trust beneficiaries? Mary Gleeson?

3. Does the rule illustrated by this trust law case differ from the parallel agency rule? Is there a functional explanation for why it should differ?

4. Who do you suppose first pressed for an action to challenge the trustee's report?

5. The agency in *Tarnowski* and the trust in *Gleeson* are some of the more common forms of fiduciary relationships, but the one that will likely become most familiar to you all is the lawyer-client fiduciary relationship. It too shares some of the key hallmarks of the agency relationships examined thus far, but it raises a host of its own issues. What features of the lawyer-client relationship might lead you to approach it differently than the fiduciary relationships studied thus far? Do you consider the degree of vulnerability a client has with his lawyer to be closer to that between a business principal and an agent, or between a settlor of a trust and the trustee?

JOINTLY-OWNED FIRMS: THE LAW OF PARTNERSHIP AND OTHER CONTRACTUAL ENTITIES

This Chapter explores the general partnership and other contractual entity forms. The partnership is the earliest jointly-owned business form in the common law tradition. For most of the past two centuries, it was the natural form for small businesses. Like agency, partnership is built on consent. The terms of the partnership are usually memorialized in a partnership agreement. But as in agency law, consent may be inferred from the actions of putative partners. And if a partnership exists, important consequences follow. General partners owe one another the same fiduciary duties as general agents and incur the same liability that principals incur for contracts entered into by co-partners on behalf of the business.

But a partnership is much more than a matrix of interlocking principal-agent relationships. Its foundational agreement provides a plan for a working business by delimiting its scope, structuring its governance principles, and fixing terms on which partners leave the business individually or their entitlements if the entire partnership dissolves and its assets and liabilities are wound up. Where a partnership agreement fails to address questions bearing on the internal relations among partners, the law often provides default answers. Much of the text of partnership statutes is devoted to the standard terms that govern inter-partner relations that are not addressed by a partnership agreement.

Of course, traditional partnership law did not permit partners to shape every legal feature of their firms. In particular, partners remained personally liable on partnership contracts as well as for torts committed within the scope of their firms' activities. In addition, partners could not modify their reciprocal fiduciary duties of care and loyalty. And finally, although partners collectively owned their businesses, they had no individual claim on particular assets committed to the business. But here is the punch line — a half century of novel legislation has worked major changes in these areas of law. These statutes authorize new forms of "contractual entities" that resemble traditional partnerships, insofar as they depend heavily on contract to construct their features, but allow their founders to move away from some of their standard attributes. For example, although the traditional general partnership still survives, the new entity forms can duplicate its features *and* provide owners with limited liability. In effect, personal liability for business obligations has become optional and, it might be added, unusual. The second major change is also one that nominally arises outside of partnership law but is in reality close to its core. Most of the new contractual entities allow their members to contract out of fiduciary duties that partnership law imposes. Here too co-owners of enterprise can construct "partnership-like" entities with bespoke fiduciary duties among members or perhaps none at all.

The general partnership was once ubiquitous but no longer is. It has been displaced largely by other contractual entities, which in one respect — limited liability — more closely resemble the corporate form. The second half of this Chapter reviews three of these entities: the limited partnership (LP), the limited liability partnership (LLP), and the limited liability company (LLC). In conceptual terms, these forms seem to lead naturally to the corporation, but it is important to understand that two of them — the LLC and LLP — were introduced well over a century *after* the introduction of general corporation statutes in the U.S.

There are, however, some ways in which the new contractual forms are not so new after all. Indeed, one might argue that the LLP is not novel at all because it doesn't even have its own authorizing statute. It is typically organized under an addendum to the general partnership statute that permits partners to select limited personal liability by filing with the state and paying their franchise fees. Further, given that one-shareholder corporations provided limited liability since at least 1900, providing this same option to general partners hardly seems revolutionary. Similarly, dedicated LP statutes once extended personal liability to partners active in the business while they shielded limited partners who merely shared in the LP's profits. However, today's LP statutes also accord limited liability to the parties who manage them. Finally, LLC statutes are concededly more innovative than other new statutory entity forms. But, as we argue below, their novelty today seems to reside in enhanced flexibility. They distinguish between "members" and "managers," which roughly coincides with the division between limited and general partners. And because LLC law generally allows actors in the firm to assume one or both of these roles, they combine the virtues of both forms with less creative drafting than might be necessary otherwise.

A more immediate note concerns this Chapter's materials. For the most part, they are traditional partnership cases that reference the Uniform Partnership Act of 1914 (1914 "UPA"), the dominant partnership statute of the twentieth century. We supplement the 1914 UPA with provisions from Delaware's Revised Uniform Partnership Act ("RUPA"), as updated through 2020. And, as previously noted, we devote the last part of this Chapter to more contemporary contractual entities including LLPs, modern LPs, and member- and manager-managed LLCs.

Why do we devote so much of this Chapter to the general partnership? The short answer is that we do it for the sake of clarity, simplicity, and historical perspective. Partnership case law graphically illustrates the fundamental challenges of constructing legal entities for jointly-owned businesses. These are: first, the issue of coordinating property rights when there are multiple claimants on commonly-owned assets; second, the problem of allocating authority and decision-making rights; and finally, the resolution of the rights of entity members and third parties when legal entities dissolve. These questions are central to all contractual entities, but they are most intuitive in the general partnership form where we initially develop them. This approach generalizes easily to statutory entities such as the LLC and modern LP.

A more significant divide between the old and the new lies in the freedom that modern statutes allow the members of entities to regulate their own third-party liability and fiduciary duties. The legal power to "opt in" to limited liability to all business creditors is simultaneously the power to "opt in" to personal liability to selected creditors by offering them personal guarantees. Here the increased contractual flexibility that modern statutes allow the members or partners of these entities is obvious. By contrast, the latitude that statutes allow to members, managers, and general partners to opt out of their duties to one another is constrained by the general norm in contract law of "good faith and fair dealing." The concluding cases in this Chapter address the contested reach of this norm in a modern LP and LLC, respectively. We look to Delaware statutes and case law here, as we do throughout most of this Book, because of their dominant position in U.S. business law. Note too that the growing importance of contractual entities hardly detracts from the continued importance of the corporate form, to which we turn in the next Chapter.[1]

For all the flexibility present in the contractual entities, the corporation will remain for the foreseeable future the dominant form for large businesses seeking "equity" financing on the capital markets. But what is equity financing? Before turning to entity forms, we pause briefly to consider the meaning of capital, economic ownership, and joint ownership of a business in the case of the general partnership.

2.1   INTRODUCTION TO PARTNERSHIP: WHY JOINT OWNERSHIP?

A single entrepreneur starts a business by raising capital to fund the inputs she requires to produce her product. If the business is successful, the revenue from selling her product covers her costs and leaves a surplus to reinvest or consume. That surplus is her profit, the firm's residual earnings. Moreover, our entrepreneur is the sole owner of her business because she receives all of its net returns. But she may not have financed her start-up exclusively with her own capital. One narrative might go like this: she contributed a portion of the initial capital from her savings and borrowed the rest from a rich relative or a bank. So far, she is a sole owner. She keeps her company's profits after paying

---

1. Two insightful essays on the kinship among forms for small businesses are Robert B. Thompson, *Allocating the Roles for Contracts and Judges in Closely Held Firms*, 35 W. New Eng. L. Rev. 369 (2011), and Larry E. Ribstein, *Close Corporation Remedies and the Evolution of the Closely Held Firm*, 35 W. New Eng. L. Rev. 531 (2011).

her suppliers and lenders. But suppose that despite encouraging sales, her creditors are reluctant to lend more capital to sustain her business. She cannot afford the price of new debt, which might include higher interest rates, scaling back her business plans, or pledging what remains of her personal assets. How can she avoid paying this price? The textbook answer is by offering new investors a share in the profits of the business. Or, put differently, our entrepreneur exchanges co-ownership for capital. As a first approximation, capital acquired in the form of co-ownership rights is termed "equity."

We hasten to add that the stock story of the entrepreneur who sells co-ownership rights to finance her fledgling start-up might be more appropriate to Silicon Valley today than to co-ownership in other places and times. Others might embrace co-ownership to reinforce family ties, incentivize co-workers, share economies arising from the division of labor or market power, and motivate cooperation within functioning teams.

2.1.1 Partnership Agreements and Partnership Law

Let us now assume that co-ownership is functional as a means of raising capital, securing other inputs for a common enterprise, or both. What are the terms on which co-owners will contribute to the common venture? One can imagine a spectrum stretching between two extremes. At one of these, participants might contribute to the joint venture as equals on similar terms and assume active roles in managing the new enterprise. At the other extreme, they might contribute passively on the assurance that they will receive a negotiated share of the firm's profits commensurate with their contribution. Roughly speaking, these two extremes correspond to two forms of co-ownership considered here: the general partnership and the limited partnership. Both forms have a long history, stretching back to the middle ages if not before.

One can see these two forms through the lens of agency law reviewed in Chapter 1. If individual partners are co-owners and active proprietors of a business, they are principals who participate in control. But if they participate in the enterprise and act on its behalf, they are also general agents of their fellow co-owners. From this perspective, the general partnership appears as an overlapping grid of principal-agent relationships, with each partner owing fiduciary duties to her co-partners and acting with apparent authority to bind her co-partners when transacting with third parties within the ordinary scope of business. Several legal consequences seem to — and in fact do — follow from this "aggregate" model of the general partnership. First, a general partner has personal liability for the contracts and torts of her business, just as a sole proprietor would have for the contracts and torts of her employees acting within the scope of her business. Second, a general partner acting as a principal or an agent must retain the formal power to terminate the principal-agent relationship at any point. And third, an outsider transacting with an affiliate of a partnership will wish to know whether he is dealing with a general partner, limited partner, or mere agent of his counterparty. That this representative of the counterparty shares in its profits may not be decisive. A limited partner shares in profits but enjoys limited liability because she typically does not participate actively in the enterprise as an agent or manager.[2] The common law and subsequent partnership statutes carry a strong presumption that anyone participating in the profit of a firm is a general partner. To forestall dispute, limited partnerships must register as such with state authorities and identify their general partners. So it is that limited partnerships must give public notice, but general partnerships may be formed without public notice and sometimes even contrary to the intent of their putative partners.

We pause here to address the case law and statutory framework that we are about to present. The law of general partnerships was largely common law until it was first codified in the UPA, promulgated in 1914 and widely adopted thereafter. The UPA was the law of the land until the 1990s. Today, 40 states have adopted variations on the Revised Uniform Partnership Act (RUPA), which was first promulgated in 1997 and has been revised multiple times since then.[3] Nevertheless, the cases we excerpt to develop partnership law mostly predate RUPA and rely on the original UPA. We reproduce these cases not out of perverse antiquarianism, but because they reflect fundamental aspects of the partnership entity form. And although the UPA (1914) is conspicuously out of date, RUPA follows the gross outline of UPA (1914). To be sure, times have changed and some fundamental issues have been resolved. Most importantly, the general partnership is now accorded full-fledged entity status, an issue that sharply divided the drafters of the UPA in 1914. We supplement references to the UPA (1914) in our first few cases with parallel citations to RUPA, as it appears in the Delaware Revised Uniform Partnership Act (2019).[4]

2. The Uniform Limited Partnership Act 1916 said that limited partners would retain limited liability as long as they were passive investors in the entity. This has changed over time. The 2001 Revised Uniform Limited Partnership Act (RULPA) §303(a) grants limited partners limited liability even if they exercise control. Delaware, however, has adopted the 1976 RULPA, or DRULPA (not the 2001 version), which means its §303(a) does not grant such broad limited liability protection, but rather says that a limited partner who participates in the control of the business is liable "only to persons who transact business with the limited partnership reasonably believing, based on the limited partner's conduct, that the limited partner is a general partner." This appears to provide less protection than 2001 RULPA. Delaware still manages to get limited partners limited liability via the recent creation of limited liability limited partnerships (LLLPs), which allow partners to keep limited liability if they meet the requirements for setting up and maintaining LLLPs. See 2019 DRULPA §214(d), which incorporates limited liability for LLLPs by relying on 2019 Delaware Revised Uniform Partnership Act (DRUPA) §306(c).

3. The states that have not adopted some version of the RUPA are: Georgia, Indiana, Louisiana, Massachusetts, Michigan, Missouri, New Hampshire, New York, North Carolina, and Rhode Island. See National Conference of Commissioners for Uniform State Laws (NCCUSL), https://www.uniformlaws.org/committees/community-home?communitykey=52456941-7883-47a5-91b6-d2f086d0bb44&tab=groupdetails.

4. Both UPA and RUPA were promulgated by the NCCUSL, which refers to them, respectively, as UPA (1914) and UPA (1997). We maintain the more common tags here, "UPA" and "RUPA." We will reference Delaware statutes throughout as they are the most used sources of entity law in the U.S. Delaware most recently enacted the 2013 amendments to RUPA.

Our first partnership case illustrates the centrality of participation in profits as a defining feature of partnership and vice versa — how partnership can be inferred from profit sharing on a sufficiently compelling set of facts.

2.2   PARTNERSHIP FORMATION

VOHLAND v. SWEET
433 N.E.2d 860 (Ind. App. 1982)

NEAL, J.:

Plaintiff-appellee Norman E. Sweet (Sweet) brought an action for dissolution of an alleged partnership and for an accounting in the Ripley Circuit Court against defendant-appellant Paul Eugene Vohland (Vohland). From a judgment in favor of Sweet in the amount of $58,733, Vohland appeals . . . . The undisputed facts reveal that Sweet, as a youngster, commenced working in 1956 for Charles Vohland, father of Paul Eugene Vohland, as an hourly employee in a nursery operated by Charles Vohland and known as Clarksburg Dahlia Gardens. Upon the completion of his military service, which was performed from 1958 to 1960, he resumed his former employment. In approximately 1963 Charles Vohland retired, and Vohland commenced what became known as Vohland's Nursery, the business of which was landscape gardening. At that time Sweet's status changed. He was to receive a 20 percent share of the net profit of the enterprise after all of the expenses were paid. . . .

No partnership income tax returns were filed. Vohland and his wife, Gwenalda, filed a joint return in which the business of Vohland's Nursery was reported in Vohland's name on Schedule C. Money paid Sweet was listed as a business expense under "Commissions." Also listed on Schedule C were all of the expenses of the nursery, including investment credit and depreciation on trucks, tractors, and machinery. Sweet's tax returns declared that he was a self-employed salesman at Vohland's Nursery. He filed a self-employment Schedule C and listed as income the income received from the nursery; as expenses he listed travel, advertising, phone, conventions, automobile, and trade journals. He further filed a Schedule C-3 for self-employment Social Security for the receipts from the nursery.

Vohland handled all of the finances and books and did most of the sales. He borrowed money from the bank solely in his own name for business purposes, including the purchase of the interests of his brothers and sisters in his father's business, operating expenses, bid bonds, motor vehicles, taxes, and purchases of real estate. Sweet was not involved in those loans. Sweet managed the physical aspects of the nursery and supervised the care of the nursery stock and the performance of the contracts for customers. Vohland was quoted by one customer as saying Sweet was running things and the customer would have to see Sweet about some problem.

Evidence was contradictory in certain respects. The Vohland Nursery was located on approximately 13 acres of land owned by Charles Vohland. Sweet testified that at the commencement of the arrangement with Vohland in 1963, Charles Vohland grew the stock and maintained the inventory, for which he received 25 percent of the gross sales. In the late 1960's, because of age, Charles Vohland could no longer perform. The nursery stock became depleted to nearly nothing, and new arrangements were made. An extensive program was initiated by Sweet and Vohland to replenish and enlarge the inventory of nursery stock; this program continued until February, 1979. The cost of planting and maintaining the nursery stock was assigned to expenses before Sweet received his 20 percent. The nursery stock generally took up to ten years to mature for market. Sweet testified that at the termination of the arrangement there existed $293,665 in inventory which had been purchased with the earnings of the business. Of that amount $284,860 was growing nursery stock. Vohland, on the other hand, testified that the inventory of 1963 was as large as that of 1979, but the inventory became depleted in 1969. Vohland claimed that as part of his agreement with Charles Vohland he was required to replenish the nursery stock as it was sold, and in addition pay Charles Vohland 25 percent of the net profit from the operation. He contends that the inventory of nursery stock balanced out. However, Vohland conceded on cross-examination that the acquisition and enlargement of the existing inventory of nursery stock was paid for with earnings and, therefore, was financed partly with Sweet's money. He further stated that the consequences of this financial arrangement never entered his mind at the time.

Sweet's testimony, denied by Vohland, disclosed that, in a conversation in the early 1970's regarding the purchase of inventory out of earnings, Vohland promised to take care of Sweet. Vohland acknowledged that Sweet refused to permit his 20 percent to be charged with the cost of a truck unless his name was on the title. Sweet testified that at the outset of the arrangement Vohland told him, "he was going to take . . . me in and that . . . I wouldn't have to punch a time clock anymore, that I would be on a commission basis and that I would be, have more of an interest in the business if I had 'an interest in the business.' . . . He referred to it as a piece of the action." Sweet testified that he intended to enter into a partnership. Vohland asserts that no partnership was intended and that Sweet was merely an employee, working on a commission. There was no contention that Sweet made any contribution to capital, nor did he claim any interest in the real estate, machinery, or motor vehicles. The parties had never discussed losses. . . .

The principal point of disagreement between Sweet and Vohland is whether the arrangement between them created a partnership, or a contract of employment of Sweet by Vohland as a salesman on commission. It therefore becomes necessary to review briefly the principles governing the establishment of partnerships.

It has been said that an accurate and comprehensive definition of a partnership has not been stated; that the lines of demarcation which distinguish a partnership from other joint interests on one hand and from agency on the other, are so fine as to render approximate rather than exhaustive any attempt to define the relationship. *Bacon v. Christian*, (1916) 184 Ind. 517, 111 N.E. 628. . . .

Under U.P.A. §7(4) receipt by a person of a share of the profits is prima facie evidence that he is a partner in the business. . . . Lack of daily involvement for one partner is not per se indicative of absence of a partner-ship. A partnership may be formed by the furnishing of skill and labor by others. The contribution of labor and skill by one of the partners may be as great a contribution to the common enterprise as property or money. . . . It is an established common law principle that a partnership can commence only by the voluntary contract of the parties. . . . In *Bond* it was said, "[t]o be a partner, one must have an interest with another in the profits of a business, as profits. There must be a voluntary contract to carry on a business with intention of the parties to share the profits as common owners thereof." . . . In *Bacon*, supra, in reviewing the law relative to the creation of partnerships, the court said:

> . . . [I]t is apparent to establish the partnership relation, as between the par-ties, there must be (1) a voluntary contract of association for the purpose of sharing the profits and losses, as such, which may arise from the use of capi-tal, labor or skill in a common enterprise; and (2) an intention on the part of the principals to form a partnership for that purpose. But it must be borne in mind, however, that the intent, the existence of which is deemed essen-tial, is an intent to do those things which constitute a partnership. Hence, if such an intent exists, the parties will be partners notwithstanding that they proposed to avoid the liability attaching to partners or [have] even expressly stipulated in their agreement that they were not to become partners. (Citation omitted.) . . .

In the analysis of the facts, we are first constrained to observe that should an accrual method of accounting have been employed here, the enhancement of the inventory of nursery stock would have been reflected as profit, a point which Vohland, in effect, concedes. We further note that both parties referred to the 20 percent as "commissions." To us the term "commission," unless defined, does not mean the same thing as a share of the net profits. However, this term, when used by landscape gardeners and not lawyers, should not be restricted to its technical definition. "Commission" was used to refer to Sweet's share of the profits, and the receipt of a share of the profits is prima facie evidence of a partnership. Though evidence is conflicting, there is evidence that the payments were not wages, but a share of the profit of a partnership. As in *Watson*, supra, it can readily be inferred from the evidence most favorable to support the judgment that the parties intended a community of interest in any increment in the value of the capital and in the profit. As shown in *Watson*, absence of contribution to capital is not controlling, and contribution of labor and skill will suffice. There is evidence from which it can be inferred that the parties intended to do the things which amount to the formation of a partnership, regardless of how they may later characterize the relationship. *Bacon*, supra. From the evi-dence the court could find that part of the operating profits of the business, of which Sweet was entitled to 20 percent, were put back into it in the form of inventory of nursery stock. In the authorities cited above it seems the central factor in determining the existence of a partnership is a division of profits.

From all the circumstances we cannot say that the court erred in finding the existence of a partnership. . . .

Affirmed.

QUESTION AND NOTE ON VOHLAND v. SWEET

1. Why should the receipt of a share of the profits create a presumption of partnership under §7(4) of the UPA, while under §7(3), the sharing of gross returns does not?

2. Assessing profits depends in part on how things are recorded. Smaller businesses often rely on the "cash" method of accounting wherein items are counted as revenues or expenses once they have been received or paid out in cash. An alternative is the "accruals" method where items are recorded as revenues or expenses once they are accrued rather than when cash moves hands. This difference matters where — as is often the case — the time when an obligation occurs and when it is fulfilled are different (e.g., the obligation to pay for a doctor's visit accrues when you go to the doctor, but you may pay later). The Court in *Vohland* refers to "the accrual method of accounting" in the second to last full paragraph of the case and notes that it would have resolved the case. Why?

3. *Vohland v. Sweet* is to partnership much like the agency formation case, *Jenson Farms* in Chapter 1, is to agency law. Both cases are sports in the sense that analogous litigation in which the parties were both sophisticated might not have been decided in the same way.

4. The usual case in which partnership is inferred by the courts despite the absence of an explicit partnership agreement involves a third-party action against an alleged partner to recover damages for breach of contract or tortious harm. This takes us to the topic of creditor rights.

2.3   PERSONAL LIABILITY AND THE NATURE OF PARTNERSHIP PROPERTY

As we observed above, general partners are personally liable for the business debts of their partnership. Personal liability traditionally leads to difficult practical and conceptual problems. First, who is a general partner for purposes of establishing personal liability to business creditors. This issue is explored in Brudney's UPA problems immediately below. It includes a host of ancillary issues such as the continuing liability of former or retired partners for business debts after they leave their partnerships and no longer share control over business decisions taken by their former co-partners. Second, there is a question of property rights among creditors. How should the law reconcile the claims of business creditors and personal creditors on two pools of assets, personal assets and those that belong to the partnership's business? This issue leads to the complex topic of partnership property.

PROFESSOR BRUDNEY'S UPA PROBLEMS[5]

1. Ars, Gratia, and Artis form and operate a business to distribute sporting goods and equipment at wholesale. The enterprise — whose letterhead, billheads, and bank account are in the name Argrar — has built a warehouse for $200,000 (on land supplied by Gratia), which it depreciates to the tax advantage of the individual participants because it reports to the IRS as a partnership. Ars, who has no assets, has furnished his talents as an administrator and manages the internal operations of the business. Gratia contributed the use of his land, which he could have sold for $40,000, and has handled the firm's sales, and Artis contributed $30,000 in cash and has done the purchasing. The three men have agreed that Ars is, in all events, to receive the greater of $5,000 annually, or one-third of the profits. During the first years of the business, the three men divided the annual profits equally among themselves. With the knowledge of the other two, Artis obtained half the cash from Mayer, to whom (unbeknownst to them) Artis has promised half his profits.

    (a) If a customer is injured by equipment that Artis knew was defective, is Ars liable? Is Mayer?

    (b) If a customer loses foreseeable resales because Gratia fails to request timely delivery to the customer, is Artis liable? Ars? Mayer?

Consider §§6, 7, 12-16, and 18 of the UPA. Compare these to §§101(13), 202(a), 202(b), 102(f), 305, 306, 308, and 401 of the Delaware RUPA (2019) ("DRUPA").

2. In a later year, Low, who is Ars's uncle and an investment banker, loaned the business $50,000 for ten years. Since the warehouse was mortgaged to the hilt, he could not get any security for his loan, and he insisted on interest in an amount equal to 25 percent of the profits as well as a right to veto firm expenditures in excess of $10,000. The loan is repayable on demand but is not prepayable without Low's consent. Low also indicated that he would be available to give the others advice about how to finance transactions from time to time.

The parties plan to obtain further necessary financing by a bank loan, which will be senior to Low's loan, and by extracting as much credit as possible from their suppliers.

If Gratia tells the bank that Low has an interest in the business, and the bank makes a loan to the firm and passes the word to suppliers that Low is interested in the business, is Low liable to the bank or any supplier who extends credit? Suppose Low receives a bill from a supplier and forwards it to Ars with instructions to pay it and explain his status, and Ars pays but fails to explain.

---

5. Note that these and subsequent Brudney Problems are designed to spark discussion; the "right" answers will sometimes depend on additional facts not provided in the questions themselves. The task is less to be right than to see the interplay of legal considerations at play.

2.3.1   Partnership Creditors' Claims Against Departing Partners

Dissolution of a partnership does not itself affect a partner's individual liability on partnership debts. When a partner withdraws from a partnership but other partners continue the business, this continuing liability for existing obligations leaves the withdrawing partner in an uncomfortable situation. She is liable for partnership obligations incurred prior to her departure, but she no longer exercises control over the capacity of the continuing business to satisfy those obligations.

Sections 36(2) and 36(3) of the UPA are designed to make life easier for the departing partner. Section 36(2) releases the departing partner of partnership debts if the court can infer an agreement between the continuing partners and the creditor to release the withdrawing partner. Section 36(3) is usually applied to release the departing partner from personal liability when a creditor renegotiates his debt with the continuing partners after receiving notice of the departing partner's exit. See, e.g., *Munn v. Scalera*, 181 Conn. 527, 436 A.2d 18 (1990). These provisions seem to balance competing concerns. On one hand, if departing partners could easily escape their partnership debts, one might expect wealthy partners to jump ship as soon as trouble appeared on the horizon. This would degrade the value of personal liability as creditor protection. On the other hand, it seems unjust to expose former partners to continuing business risk that is now exclusively controlled by the remaining partners. What if, for example, the active partners gamble everything in the hope of saving a failing business? What if they negotiated with partnership creditors to extend the terms and double the interest rates on bank debts that were incurred before the departing partner left the firm? Do you see why a departed partner is at continuing risk for the debts of the partnership even if he is not personally liable for debts incurred after his departure? Partnership law walks the line between protecting the relying creditor and the helpless former partner. See UPA §§36(2) and 36(3), and the parallel DRUPA §703.

2.3.2   Third-Party Claims Against Partnership Property

Partnership's most important contribution to the historical evolution of business entities is its treatment of partnership property. Property held by the UPA partnership is titled in a special form: "tenancy in partnership." Under the UPA, this type of estate allowed the partnership qua firm, rather than its individual partners, to exercise true ownership rights over partnership property. This includes the ability to commit its assets to business creditors should the partnership and some of its individual partners subsequently enter bankruptcy. Favoring business creditors in this way was a fundamental step toward creating a freestanding legal entity with a "personality" distinct from the partners who financed and managed it. Or put differently, a firm that owned its own assets could be a more trustworthy counterparty for third-party suppliers, customers, and employees. The common-law slight-of-hand that initially gave partnership creditors a first claim on partnership assets in 1683[6] was an abrogation of the property rights of individual creditors by legal fiat. It meant, for example, that personal creditors of a partner could no longer seize his partnership contributions if he were to default on his personal debts. And, in the event that the partnership entered bankruptcy, these assets would be lost forever to personal creditors. Today RUPA reaches the same result by recognizing the partnership as an independent legal entity that owns its contributed or accumulated assets in its own right. If partners lack any claim on partnership assets, individual creditors who stand in the shoes of partners defaulting on personal debts do as well. See DRUPA §§501, 502, and 504.

Delimiting a pool of partnership assets is a partitioning between business and personal assets.[7] It does not strip a partner or her personal creditors of all personal property interests in the business. Under common law, and later under UPA and RUPA, a partner retains a transferable interest in her partnership share of *the profits arising from the use of partnership property* and the right to receive partnership distributions. (It is these rights to cash flow that a creditor can attach, or that an heir may succeed to.) Thus, a functional two-level ownership structure characterizes the general partnership as well as most business entities: the contributors of equity capital do not "own" the assets themselves but rather own the rights to the net financial returns that these assets generate. In a general partnership, partners also possess certain governance or management rights but these are personal and non-transferable. See UPA §§26, 27; RUPA §§502, 503. As RUPA §503 makes clear, only a partner's financial interest can be transferred or foreclosed on in most circumstances. RUPA §504 and UPA §28 permit individual creditors of partners (e.g., the bank that has made the partner a personal loan) to obtain a "charging order," which is a lien on the partner's transferable interest that is subject to foreclosure unless it is redeemed by repayment of the debt.

But if personal and partnership assets are partitioned in one direction to reserve business assets for partnership creditors, they are not partitioned in the reverse direction. Of course, a key feature of the general partnership is the personal liability of partners for business debts. In practice, partnership creditors find it difficult to seize the personal assets of partners before exhausting available business assets.[8] Assuming that partnership assets are exhausted, however, business creditors—or more likely, a partnership's trustee in bankruptcy—can proceed against the personal assets of all remaining solvent partners. As long as solvent partners remain, claiming against their net personal assets does not lead to direct conflict with their personal creditors. It follows that there is no partitioning of a partner's personal assets from the claims of business creditors. One of us has previously described partnership

6. See *Craven v. Knight* (1683) 21 Eng. Rep. 664 (Ch.).
7. See Henry Hansmann & Reinier Kraakman, *The Essential Role of Organizational Law*, 110 Yale L.J. 387 (2000).
8. See DRUPA §307(d) and comment which states "this subsection prevents a partner's assets from being the first recourse for a judgment creditor of the partnership, even if the partner is liable for the judgment debt under Section 306."

assets as "weakly partitioned" because all personal assets are theoretically available to satisfy claims of partnership creditors, just as all net personal assets are available to the business creditors of a sole entrepreneur.

Yet there is one more twist. Individual partners and their partnerships often enter bankruptcy simultaneously. One can imagine that partners of a firm in financial distress walk a tightrope between saving their businesses on one hand and their personal finances on the other. The insolvency or bankruptcy of their partnership is likely to occur after they have depleted their individual assets as well. Under these circumstances, the claims of business and personal creditors on personal assets directly conflict. English and American common law evolved a solution during the early nineteenth century informally termed the "jingle rule" — perhaps because it was recited as, "partnership creditors first in partnership assets, separate creditors first in separate assets." Which begs the question, "Is that a jingle?"[9] The jingle rule entered both The Bankruptcy Act of 1898 and the UPA.

By contrast, The Bankruptcy Act of 1978 retained only one half — the most important half — of the jingle rule. Today, §723 of the Bankruptcy Code (11 U.S.C. §723) contemplates a trustee in bankruptcy first administering the estate of the partnership (i.e., its partnership property) and then turning to the assets of general partners to the extent of any deficiency. Pending determination of any deficiency, the court may require a partner to provide indemnity for any deficiency or may "order any such partner . . . not to dispose of property," §723(b). When there is a deficiency in the partnership assets, §723(c) provides that the trustee's claim against the assets of any general partner is on parity with individual creditors of the partner. Thus, partnership creditors still have first priority in the assets of a partnership (as under the jingle rule). But under §723(c), partnership creditors (acting through the trustee in bankruptcy) are placed on parity with individual creditors in allocating the assets of an individual partner when the partnership is bankrupt under Chapter 7.

What happens when the partnership is not being liquidated under Chapter 7, but the estate of an individual partner is itself being administered in bankruptcy? If the partnership business is sound, there will typically not be a problem. Partnership creditors may be content to look to the partnership assets (and the credit of the other general partners) to protect their rights to payment. Nevertheless, any partnership creditor who has a mature claim could assert that claim in the partner's bankruptcy case. In that event, the question again arises of priority between individual creditors and partnership creditors. Here, bankruptcy law creates no special rule; rather, it distributes assets according to the applicable state law that determines the allocation of the partner's assets.

---

9. The jingle rule evolved in the English equity courts at the end of the seventeenth and beginning of the eighteenth centuries. See, e.g., *Craven v. Knight* (1683) 21 Eng. Rep. 664 (Ch.) (giving business creditors priority in business assets); *Ex Parte Crowder* (1715) 23 Eng. Rep. 1064 (Ch.) (giving personal creditors of partners priority in personal assets). In fact, the first part of the jingle rule, giving business creditors first priority in business assets, dates back to the city states in medieval Italy. See generally Henry Hansmann, Reinier Kraakman & Richard Squire, *Law and the Rise of the Firm*, 119 Harv. L. Rev. 1333, 1381 (2006).

The UPA and RUPA diverge on the question of how an insolvent partner's assets should be distributed. The UPA follows the jingle rule, giving the partner's creditors priority over partnership creditors, while RUPA follows the parity treatment rule codified in §723 of the Bankruptcy Code. Thus, the bankruptcy assets of a partner whose partnership is not in Chapter 7 will be distributed according to the jingle rule if the UPA applies and according to the parity rule if the RUPA applies. (Note that regardless of priority rules, if the estate of an insolvent partner were to be required to satisfy a partnership obligation, the estate would have an action for subrogation against the solvent partnership or contribution against its partners in the event of its insolvency.)

State partnership law also applies in cases where the assets of an insolvent partner or of an insolvent partnership are distributed outside of bankruptcy (e.g., in a state insolvency proceeding). Thus, when the assets belong to an insolvent partner, the distribution will depend on whether the UPA or RUPA applies. When the assets belong to the partnership (not the partner), both the UPA and the RUPA give partnership creditors first priority in the assets.

So, in all cases, partnership creditors possess first priority in partnership assets. As to claims against the individual assets of partners, however, partnership creditors are subordinated to the claims of a partner's creditors in the allocation of the partner's assets (as under the jingle rule) if (1) the UPA is controlling state law *and* (2) §723 does not apply (that is, the partnership is not in Chapter 7 or the individual partner is not in bankruptcy). But partnership creditors receive parity treatment if *either* (1) the RUPA is controlling state law *or* (2) §723 applies (the partnership is in Chapter 7 or the individual partner is in bankruptcy). If this sounds complicated, you now see one of the benefits of the corporate form, which we will come to in the next chapter.[10]

QUESTIONS ON PARTNERSHIP PROPERTY AND ASSET PARTITIONING

1. Why repeal the second half of the old jingle rule and make partnership creditors more secure at the expense of personal creditors? Note that the legislative history accompanying §723(c) of the 1978 Bankruptcy Act merely observed that the change would align bankruptcy with partnership law outside of bankruptcy.

2. Why doesn't RUPA provide for a "partnership sole," in which a sole proprietor might designate business assets that, in the event of his insolvency or bankruptcy, would be used first to satisfy the claims of his business creditors, and remaining personal assets to be divided pro rata between unsatisfied business claims and those of his personal creditors?

3. Limiting the liability of partners for partnership debts to their partnership interests would result in "strong" asset partitioning by giving personal

---

10. We are grateful to Professor Jesse Fried for his revisions of earlier versions of this subsection.

and partnership creditors exclusive rights in separate asset pools and would greatly simplify sorting out claims in the wake of simultaneous bankruptcies. Why hasn't the law of general partnerships taken this obvious next step?

4. Alternatively, if partners wanted limited liability, why couldn't they contract with their creditors for it? For example, they might attach a standard disclaimer to every contract made with a third party announcing that by contracting with the so-and-so partnership a counterparty waived all claims on the personal assets of its partners.

2.4 PARTNERSHIP GOVERNANCE AND ISSUES OF AUTHORITY

As noted earlier, general partners are general agents for their partnerships. In the absence of indications that would lead reasonable third parties to think otherwise, general partners have the *apparent* authority to bind their firms to the terms of any contract within the ordinary scope of partnership business. See UPA §9(1) and RUPA §301(1). But do they also have *actual* authority? This depends on the partnership agreement or, alternatively, on the statutory default provisions of partnership law. For example, UPA §18(h) and RUPA §401(j) provide that absent agreement to the contrary, a simple majority of partners can decide contested matters within the scope of partnership business. Of course, this majoritarian rule applies only when the partnership agreement does not specify a bespoke rule of its own that reflects the negotiated preference of particular groups of partners. For example, wealthy partners might successfully negotiate for a power to veto any partnership decision or senior partners might demand two votes while their junior colleagues receive only one. Such contractual flexibility allowed large general partnerships in the past to operate under the leadership of a managing partner or committee of partners. The general partnership form is not necessarily limited to small firms.

There are also instances in which a governance issue is addressed neither in the partnership agreement nor in the statute, in which case courts must fall back on common law precedent. Our next case would be a perfect example if only the amount of money at stake were a bit more dignified.

NATIONAL BISCUIT CO. v. STROUD
249 N.C. 467 (1959)

PARKER, J.:

C.N. Stroud and Earl Freeman entered into a general partnership to sell groceries under the firm name of Stroud's Food Center. There is nothing in the agreed statement of facts to indicate or suggest that Freeman's power and authority as a general partner were in any way restricted or limited by the articles of partnership in respect to the ordinary and legitimate business of the partnership. Certainly, the purchase and sale of bread were ordinary and legitimate business of Stroud's Food Center during its continuance as a going concern.

Several months prior to February 1956 Stroud advised plaintiff that he personally would not be responsible for any additional bread sold by plaintiff to Stroud's Food Center. After such notice to plaintiff, from 6 February 1956 to 25 February 1956, at the request of Freeman, [National Biscuit] sold and delivered bread in the amount of $171.04 to Stroud's Food Center.

In *Johnson v. Bernheim*, 76 N.C. 139, this Court said: "A and B are general partners to do some given business; the partnership is, by operation of law, a power to each to bind the partnership in any manner legitimate to the business. If one partner go to a third person to buy an article on time for the partnership, the other partner cannot prevent it by writing to the third person not to sell to him on time; or, if one party attempt to buy for cash, the other has no right to require that it shall be on time. And what is true in regard to buying is true in regard to selling. What either partner does with a third person is binding on the partnership. It is otherwise where the partnership is not general, but is upon special terms, as that purchases and sales must be with and for cash. There the power to each is special, in regard to all dealings with third persons at least who have notice of the terms." There is contrary authority. 68 C.J.S., Partnership, pp. 578-579. However, this text of C.J.S. does not mention the effect of the provisions of the Uniform Partnership Act.

* * *

Freeman as a general partner with Stroud, with no restrictions on his authority to act within the scope of the partnership business so far as the agreed statement of facts shows, had under the Uniform Partnership Act "equal rights in the management and conduct of the partnership business." Under [UPA §18(h)] Stroud, his co-partner, could not restrict the power and authority of Freeman to buy bread for the partnership as a going concern, for such a purchase was an "ordinary matter connected with the partnership business," for the purpose of its business and within its scope, because in the very nature of things Stroud was not, and could not be, a majority of the partners. Therefore, Freeman's purchases of bread from plaintiff for Stroud's Food Center as a going concern bound the partnership and his co-partner Stroud. . . .

In Crane on Partnership, 2d Ed., p. 277, it is said: "In cases of an even division of the partners as to whether or not an act within the scope of the business should be done, of which disagreement a third person has knowledge, it seems that logically no restriction can be placed upon the power to act. The partnership being a going concern, activities within the scope of the business should not be limited, save by the expressed will of the majority deciding a disputed question; half of the members are not a majority." . . .

At the close of business on 25 February 1956 Stroud and Freeman by agreement dissolved the partnership. By their dissolution agreement all of the partnership assets, including cash on hand, bank deposits and all accounts receivable, with a few exceptions, were assigned to Stroud, who bound himself by such written dissolution agreement to liquidate the firm's assets and discharge its liabilities. It would seem a fair inference from the agreed statement of facts that the partnership got the benefit of the bread sold and delivered by plaintiff to Stroud's Food Center, at Freeman's request, from 6 February 1956 to 25 February 1956. But whether it did or not, Freeman's acts, as stated above, bound the partnership and Stroud.

The judgment of the court below is Affirmed.

QUESTIONS ON NABISCO

1. *Nabisco* illustrates the majority rule that half of a two-person partnership is not a "majority" for purposes of making firm decisions within the ordinary course of business. But why not the reverse rule? If Stroud notifies Nabisco that he will not be bound by Freeman's purchases, why hold Stroud liable on the partnership transaction? More generally, why hold any partner liable who explicitly opts out of a transaction with a third party? How else could Stroud have attempted to halt Freeman's contracting?

2. Return to Professor Brudney's Argrar hypothetical, described above. After the firm (assume it is a partnership) has been in business for several years, the flow of unexpected business requires Ars, Artis, and Gratia to decide whether to make alterations in the building. The partners are in disagreement about how extensive the alterations should be. Gratia signs a contract with a construction company for the erection of a retail storefront addition to the building at a cost of $50,000.

    (a) Are the firm and its individual partners bound?
    (b) Even if Artis tells the construction company to stop before it begins actual work?
    (c) What are the construction company's obligations to inquire before entering into the transaction — whom should it ask for what?

Consider §§9, 12-16, and 18 of the Uniform Partnership Act. Compare RUPA §§301, 102(f), 305, 306, 308, and 401.

2.4.1   Partnership Accounting

An evaluation of the financial status of a partnership begins with an inspection of its balance sheet — a simple statement of the assets that it holds, the liabilities that it owes, and the difference between the two, which is the partners' equity in the firm. Inspecting a balance sheet is just the first step in evaluating its financial status, but it is an important step.

Since a balance sheet is always reported as of a particular date, the first step in undertaking a current evaluation of a partnership is bringing it up to date. Next, one must appreciate that in almost all cases, figures on a balance sheet representing the assets are stated at historical cost (minus a regular periodic charge or reduction for "depreciation," but more on that later). In some

businesses (where there is a fast turnover of inventory, for example), the difference between historical costs and current values may not be great. In all events,
with an ongoing business even the historical figures, if kept in a consistent way
from one period to the next, supply information that is somewhat illuminating.
Here is a hypothetical Partnership Balance Sheet:

Washington Square Pharmacia
Balance Sheet
December 31, 2019

Assets		*Liabilities*	
Cash	$ 5,400	Accounts Payable	$ 74,000
Accounts Receivable	76,000	Notes Payable	136,000
Inventory	189,000	Mortgage Note	350,000
		Total Debt Liabilities	$560,000
Real Estate	463,553	Partners' Capital	$173,953
Total Assets	**$733,953**	**Total Liabilities & Capital**	**$733,953**

After the balance sheet, the second fundamental accounting statement
is one that reflects the results of transactions in which the firm has engaged
over a set period, often a year. This Income Statement is sometimes referred
to as a Statement of Profit and Loss (or, more accurately, profit *or* loss).
For our illustrative purposes, we assume that this partnership keeps its
books on a *cash basis.* Another and probably better technique is *accrual
basis accounting.* In accrual, amounts paid are treated as expenses in the
period to which they relate. So, for example, if Washington Square paid
out $35,000 in November of 2019 to cover radio advertising for the next
ten months, its 12/31/19 Income Statement would report only two-tenths
of that cash outlay as an expense. The rest would not be reported on the
Income Statement at all, but would be reported on the balance sheet as
a prepaid expense. (We did not put it into our sample balance sheet, so
don't look.)

Washington Square Pharmacia
Income Statement
December 31, 2019

Gross Sales	$632,550
Cost of Goods Sold	311,000
GROSS PROFIT	321,550
General Administration Expenses:	
Advertising	48,000
Mortgage (rent)	38,000
Salaries	168,000
Total Expenses	$254,000
NET PROFIT	$ 67,550
(Allocated to Partners' Accounts)	

Accounting for Partners' Capital

Finally, the third category of basic financial statements is the capital account, which will have a report that records the effects on the partners' capital of the operations of the business over the year. For our imagined business on Washington Square, it might look like this:

Washington Square Pharmacia
Capital Accounts
December 31, 2019

	Opening Balance 1/1/19	Income FY2019	Withdrawals FY2019	Closing Balance 12/31/19
Allen	$140,000	$22,517	$64,666	$97,851
Khanna	140,000	22,517	74,666	87,851
Kraakman	30,000	22,517	64,266	(11,749)

QUESTIONS ON THE SAMPLE BALANCE SHEET AND INCOME STATEMENT

1. If advertising expenses during 2019 had been $58,000 instead of $48,000 — and all else had remained the same — how would this affect the income statement? How would it affect the balance sheet, or can you say?

2. Suppose each of the three partners earned $40,000 in salary for the services they performed for the partnership during 2019. What are their taxable incomes from the partnership for 2019?

2.5   TERMINATION (DISSOLUTION AND DISSOCIATION)

A central aspect of partnership law and planning is exit: the terms on which individual partners exit a continuing business or, alternatively, the circumstances under which a partnership must dissolve and wind up the business and the governing procedure in the final distribution of the firm's assets to creditors and among partners.

The default in partnership law is the "partnership at will," which permits individual partners to leave or force dissolution at any time. The traditional alternative is to contract for a "term partnership" in which partners commit to remain for a fixed time period or until the occurrence of a specific event such as the repayment of a partnership loan. An at-will partner can always recover her legal interest in the partnership, but the value and how quickly it is paid will depend on her partnership agreement, bargaining leverage, and the available statutory defaults. RUPA today provides a far more developed regime of partner exit rights than was previously on offer from UPA, most conspicuously because RUPA attends separately to the rights of individual partners who "dissociate" from continuing firms and those of all partners to initiate a wind-up of partnerships and participate in the proceeds of their liquidation. One key difference is that the payback to a dissociating partner turns on her proportionate share of the "going-concern value" of the continuing business whereas wind-up and liquidation rights are measured in proportion to the price fixed in a judicial auction of partnership assets. Another point is that entitlements vary in real terms according to market interest in judicially-auctioned assets. Incumbent managers of small businesses are likely to know much more about their worth than outside appraisers but they may not tip their hands until the auction is over. Finally, both UPA and RUPA treat withdrawals prior to agreed terms or otherwise in breach of their partnership agreements as "wrongful" and therefore entitled to less favorable recoveries of capital.

The following case featuring an apparent conflict between the statutory terms of dissociation under the UPA and the terms of the partnership agreement is instructive. An ancillary issue raised by the case concerns the ownership of "accounts receivable," i.e., invoices for goods delivered or services performed that have not yet been paid.

ADAMS v. JARVIS
127 N.W.2d 400 (Wis. 1964)

Action for declaratory judgment construing a medical-partnership agreement between three doctors. Plaintiff-respondent withdrew from the partnership seven years after it was formed.

The dispute concerns the extent of the plaintiff's right to share in partnership assets, specifically accounts receivable.[11] The relevant portions of the agreement provide:

12. Book of Account. Proper books of account shall be kept by said partners and entries made therein of all matters, transactions, and things as are usually entered in books of account kept by persons engaged in the same or similar business. Such books and all partnership letters, papers and documents shall be kept at the firm's office and each partner shall at all times have access to examine, copy, and take extracts from the same.

13. Fiscal Year — Share of Profits and Losses. The partnership fiscal year shall coincide with the calendar year. Net profits and losses of the partnership shall be divided among the individual[s] in the same proportion as their capital interest in the partnership, except as hereinafter provided for partners who become incapacitated or have withdrawn from the partnership, or the estates of the deceased partners. . . .

15. Conditions of Termination. Partnership shall not terminate under certain conditions. The incapacity, withdrawal or death of a partner shall not terminate this partnership. Such partner, or the estate or heirs of a deceased partner shall continue to participate in partnership profits and losses, as provided in this agreement, but shall not participate in management, the making of partnership decisions, or any professional matters. On the happening of any of the above events, the books of the partnership shall not be closed until the end of the partnership fiscal year.

---

11. Accounts receivable is a balance sheet item that represents amounts owed to a firm by customers who have purchased goods or services on credit. In this case it would be bills to patients who have been treated but have not yet paid. — EDS.

16. Withdrawal. No withdrawal from the firm shall be effective until at least thirty (30) days have elapsed from the date on which written notice of such intention is given the other partners by registered mail to their last known address. As used herein "withdrawal" shall refer to any situation in which a partner leaves the partnership, at a time when said partnership is not dissolving, pursuant to a written agreement of the parties to do so. The withdrawing partner shall be entitled to receive from the continuing partners the following:

(1) Any balance standing to his credit on the books of the partnership;

(2) That proportion of the partnership profits to which he was entitled by this agreement in the fiscal year of his withdrawal, which the period from the beginning of such year to the effective date of withdrawal shall bear to the whole of the then current fiscal year. Such figure shall be ascertained as soon as practicable after the close of the current fiscal year and shall be payable as soon as the amount thereof is ascertained. All drawings previously made during the then fiscal year shall be first charged against the share in net partnership profits as above computed. If there shall have been losses for such fiscal year, or overdrawings, or losses and the whole of any overdrawings or loans, shall be determined and charged against his capital account, and if in excess thereof, shall be paid by him or his estate promptly after the close of the fiscal year, plus

(3) The amount of his capital account on the effective date of his withdrawal (after deduction of any losses required to be paid in subdivision (2) above).

In the event such withdrawing partner dies prior to receiving any or all of the above payments, his personal representative, heirs or assigns shall receive the same payments at the same time as those to which he would have been entitled by the terms had he lived. Payment of the items set forth in subdivisions (1) and (3) above shall be made according to and evidenced by a promissory note, executed by the remaining partners, payable in twelve (12) equal quarterly installments, the first of which shall be payable at the end of the six (6) months following the effective date of such withdrawal. Acceleration of said note shall be permitted at the sole discretion of the remaining partners. Such note shall bear interest at Two (2) Per Cent, payable with each installment.

It is further agreed that in the event of the withdrawal of any partner or partners, any and all accounts receivable for any current year and any and all years past shall remain the sole possession and property of the remaining member or members of THE TOMAHAWK CLINIC....

18. Dissolution. Should this partnership be dissolved by agreement of the parties, all accounts and notes shall be liquidated and all firm assets sold or divided between the partners at agreed valuations. The books of the partnership shall then be closed and distribution made in proportion to the capital interests of the partners as shown by the partnership books. No drawings should be paid once the partnership has begun to wind up its affairs, although liquidating dividends based on estimates may be paid from time to time. No dissolution shall be effective until the end of the then fiscal year, and until ninety (90) days have elapsed from the date on which written agreement to such dissolution shall have been executed by the parties hereto.

This agreement shall be binding not only upon the parties hereto, but also upon their heirs, executors, administrators, successors, and assigns, and the wives of said partners have signed this agreement as witnesses, after being advised of the terms of this agreement.

The trial court decided that the withdrawal of the plaintiff worked a dissolution of the partnership under [UPA §§29, 30]; that the partnership assets should be liquidated and applied to the payment of partnership interests according to the scheme set forth in [UPA §38] for the reason that paragraphs 15 and 16 of the partnership agreement did not apply in the case of a statutory dissolution; that plaintiff's interest was one third of the net worth, including therein accounts receivable of the partnership as of May 31, 1961; that plaintiff should recover from defendants the value of his partnership interest; and gave judgment accordingly, but retained jurisdiction for supplementary proceedings. Defendants appeal.

BEILFUSS, J:

1. Does a withdrawal of a partner constitute a dissolution of the partnership under [UPA §§29, 30],[12] notwithstanding a partnership agreement to the contrary?

2. Is plaintiff, as withdrawing partner, entitled to a share of the accounts receivable?

The partnership agreement as set forth above (paragraph 15) specifically provides that the partnership shall not terminate by the withdrawal of a partner. We conclude the parties clearly intended that even though a partner withdrew, the partnership and the partnership business would continue for the purposes for which it was organized. Paragraph 18 of the agreement provides for a dissolution upon agreement of the parties in the sense that the partnership would cease to function as such subject to winding up of its affairs.

While the withdrawal of a partner works a dissolution of the partnership under the statute as to the withdrawing partner, it does not follow that the rights and duties of remaining partners are similarly affected. The agreement contemplates a partnership would continue to exist between the remaining partners even though the personnel constituting the partnership was changed.

Persons with professional qualifications commonly associate in business partnerships. The practice of continuing the operation of the partnership business, even though there are some changes in partnership personnel, is also common. The reasons for an agreement that a medical partnership should continue without disruption of the services rendered is self-evident. If the partnership agreement provides for continuation, sets forth a method of paying the withdrawing partner his agreed share, does not jeopardize the rights of creditors, the agreement is enforceable. The statute does not specifically regulate this type of withdrawal with a continuation of the business. The statute should not be construed to invalidate an otherwise enforceable contract entered into for a legitimate purpose.

The provision for withdrawal is in effect a type of winding up of the partnership without the necessity of discontinuing the day-to-day business. [UPA §38][13] contemplates a discontinuance of the day-to-day business but does not forbid other methods of winding up a partnership.

---

12. Under the UPA §29 a partner's withdrawal amounts to a dissolution, but that is not the same as a "winding up". Moreover, UPA §30 notes that a partnership is not terminated upon dissolution, but only with a winding up of partnership affairs. Under RUPA, the concept of "dissociation" is introduced (e.g., a partner leaving — see RUPA §601). RUPA §801 clarifies where partner dissociation causes a winding up of the business and RUPA §701 provides that in other situations, there is a buyout of the partner's interest in the partnership rather than a wind up.

13. UPA §38 outlines the process for giving each their appropriate share upon dissolution, whether the dissolution is wrongful (§38(2)) or otherwise (§38(1)).

The agreement does provide that Dr. Adams shall no longer actively participate and further provides for winding up the affairs insofar as his interests are concerned. In this sense, his withdrawal does constitute a dissolution. We conclude, however, that when the plaintiff, Dr. Adams, withdrew, the partnership was not wholly dissolved so as to require complete winding up of its affairs, but continued to exist under the terms of the agreement. The agreement does not offend the statute and is valid.

ACCOUNTS RECEIVABLE

[The court reviews UPA §38(1).][14] The trial court concluded that the withdrawal constituted a statutory dissolution; that partnership assets shall be liquidated pursuant to the statute and that the plaintiff was entitled to a one-third interest in the accounts receivable.

[UPA §38(1)] applies only "unless otherwise agreed." The distribution should therefore be made pursuant to the agreement.

Paragraphs 15 and 16 of the contract as set forth above provide for the withdrawal of a partner and the share to which he is entitled. Subject to limitations not material here, paragraph 16 provides that a withdrawing partner shall receive (1) any balance to his credit on partnership books, (2) his proportionate share of profits calculated on a fiscal year basis, and (3) his capital account as of the date of his withdrawal. Paragraph 16 further provides that in event of withdrawal, "any and all accounts receivable for any current year and any and all years past shall remain the sole possession and property of the remaining member or members of THE TOMAHAWK CLINIC."

The plaintiff contends that provision of the agreement denying him a share of the accounts receivable works *a forfeiture* and is void as being against public policy.

We conclude the parties to the agreement intended accounts receivable to be restricted to customer or patient accounts receivable.

The provision of the agreement is clear and unambiguous. There is nothing in the record to suggest the plaintiff's bargaining position was so unequal in the negotiations leading up to the agreement that the provision should be declared unenforceable upon the grounds of public policy. Legitimate business and goodwill considerations are consistent with a provision retaining control and ownership of customer accounts receivable in an active functioning professional medical partnership. We hold the provision on accounts receivable enforceable. . . .

Because of our determination that the partnership agreement is valid and enforceable, the judgment of the trial court, insofar as it decrees a dissolution of the partnership and a one-third division of the accounts receivable to

---

14. If the dissolution is not wrongful, then under UPA §38(1) each partner is able to have the partnership property applied to discharge its liabilities, with surplus cash being paid out to the partners. However, if the dissolution is wrongful and the leaving (or expelled) partner is discharged from all partnership liabilities (by payment or via §36(2)), then under §38(2) she will receive in cash the net amount due from the partnership.

the plaintiff, must be reversed and remanded to the trial court with directions to enter judgment in conformity with this opinion.

The trial court properly retained jurisdiction for the purpose of granting supplementary relief to plaintiff to enforce a distribution to the plaintiff. The trial court may conduct such proceedings as are necessary to effectuate a distribution pursuant to the agreement.

The parties have stipulated that the plaintiff ceased to be an active partner as of June 1, 1961. The agreement provides that the partnership fiscal year shall coincide with the calendar year. It further provides that his share of the partnership profits upon withdrawal shall be calculated upon the whole year and in proportion to his participation of the whole fiscal year. He is, therefore, entitled to 5/12th of 1/3d, or 5/36th of the profits for the fiscal year ending December 31, 1961.

Such of the accounts receivable as were collected during the year 1961 do constitute a part of the profits for 1961. The plaintiff had no part of the management of the partnership after June 1, 1961; however, his eventual distributive share of profits is dependent, in some degree, upon the management of the business affairs and performance of the continuing partners for the remainder of the fiscal year. Under these circumstances the continuing partners stand in a fiduciary relationship to the withdrawing partner and are obligated to conduct the business in a good-faith manner including a good-faith effort to liquidate the accounts receivable consistent with good business practices.

Judgment reversed with directions to conduct supplementary proceedings to determine distributive share of plaintiff and then enter judgment in conformity with this opinion.

QUESTIONS ON ADAMS v. JARVIS

1. Paragraph 16 of the partnership agreement defines "withdrawal" as "any situation in which a partner leaves the partnership, at a time when said partnership is not dissolving." Compare UPA §29. What should paragraph 16 say?

2. Why did the plaintiff want the accounts receivable? Was the partnership agreement's provision for withdrawing partners unfair on its face (and if so, why did the plaintiff agree to it)?

3. How would you draft a withdrawal provision for a plaintiff's law firm that litigated large class actions and derivative suits, typically lasting several years, in the hope of earning contingent fees?

2.5.1   Statutory Dissolution of a Partnership at Will

What happens if the agreement among general partners at will fails to address the consequences of dissolution and one or more partners serves notice of a statutory dissolution and wind-up to the remaining partners? The residual value of the partnership, after the payment of creditors and the partners' loans and capital accounts, must be divided among the partners in accordance with the partnership agreement, or equally, if the agreement does not provide otherwise. But how is this division to be accomplished?

There are three possibilities. One is to physically divide the partnership's assets in a way that seems plausibly fair. A second is to conduct a judicial auction of the firm. Here, the partnership's assets can be sold intact as a business to the highest bidder if it is profitable to do so, or these assets can be sold for liquidation value — either piecemeal or as a whole. (Selling for liquidation value implies that the partnership assets will be reconfigured in one or more other businesses or perhaps resold piecemeal after renovation, etc.) Or, finally, the court might accept an appraiser's valuation of what the partnership's assets *would be worth to the highest valuing purchaser* if they were auctioned off, and allocate a proportionate share of this value to the partner(s) who no longer wishes to continue in the firm.

A now discredited minority position in the common law held that a court could, in exercising its equitable discretion, divide the partnership's assets physically if it deemed this to be fair. UPA §38(1) categorically rejects this view, as do modern courts that have considered the issue. See, e.g., *Dreifuerst v. Dreifuerst*, 80 N.W.2d 335 (Wis. 1979) (rejecting trial court's physical division of assets as violating Wisconsin's UPA).

On the other hand, the UPA makes no provision for the third alternative, namely, that the court accept an appraisal of the value of the partnership in the hands of its highest valuing purchaser (usually remaining partners who wish to continue the business as a going concern), at least without authorization in the partnership agreement. All that remains is a judicial auction of the partnership's assets. The purchaser in such an auction is usually one or more partners who wish to continue the business. That is, continuing partners typically repurchase the interests of dissenting partners at a price set by the expected outcome of an (explicit or implicit) bidding contest between partners themselves or between third-party bidders.

QUESTIONS

1. What valuation process does the RUPA mandate if a single partner in an at-will partnership insists on a statutory dissolution of the partnership? Assume that the dissolution and wind-up is without fault. See RUPA §§801, 802, and 804. What is the implication of the distinction that RUPA draws between the "dissolution" of a partnership and the "dissociation" of a partner? See RUPA §§601 and 603.

2. Are there reasons why some partners might prefer to divide partnership assets directly rather than subject them to valuation in a judicial auction (a "market test") or an appraisal (an expert's opinion about the likely outcome of a market test)?

3. A last Brudney question: After the Argrar partnership has continued for several years, Artis wants to resign and move across the continent. The business is worth, as a going concern, $700,000, but if it were liquidated and sold piece by piece, it would bring $400,000; and if it were sold intact to a related business that would not have to alter the warehouse, it would bring $500,000. A new person is needed to replace Artis as a purchasing agent. On what terms should Artis fairly leave and the newcomer enter? Consider UPA §§17, 24-27, 36, 41, and 42 (and RUPA §701).

2.5.2   Opportunistic Dissolution and the Duty of Loyalty

PAGE v. PAGE
359 P.2d 41 (Cal. 1961)

TRAYNOR, J.:

Plaintiff and defendant are partners in a linen supply business in Santa Maria, California. Plaintiff appeals from a judgment declaring the partnership to be for a term rather than at will.

The partners entered into an oral partnership agreement in 1949. Within the first two years each partner contributed approximately $43,000 for the purchase of land, machinery, and linen needed to begin the business. From 1949 to 1957 the enterprise was unprofitable, losing approximately $62,000. The partnership's major creditor is a corporation, wholly-owned by plaintiff, that supplies the linen and machinery necessary for the day-to-day operation of the business. This corporation holds a $47,000 demand note of the partnership. The partnership operations began to improve in 1958. The partnership earned $3,824.41 in that year and $2,282.30 in the first three months of 1959. Despite this improvement plaintiff wishes to terminate the partnership.

The Uniform Partnership Act provides that a partnership may be dissolved "By the express will of any partner when no definite term or particular undertaking is specified." U.P.A. §31(1)(b). The trial court found that the partnership is for a term, namely, "such reasonable time as is necessary to enable said partnership to repay from partnership profits, indebtedness incurred for the purchase of land, buildings, laundry and delivery equipment and linen for the operation of such business. . . ." Plaintiff correctly contends that this finding is without support in the evidence.

Defendant testified that the terms of the partnership were to be similar to former partnerships of plaintiff and defendant, and that the understanding of these partnerships was that "we went into partnership to start the business and let the business operation pay for itself, put in so much money, and let the business pay itself out." There was also testimony that one of the former partnership agreements provided in writing that the profits were to be retained until all obligations were paid.

Upon cross-examination defendant admitted that the former partnership in which the earnings were to be retained until the obligations were repaid was substantially different from the present partnership. The former partnership was a limited partnership and provided for a definite term of five years and a partnership at will thereafter. Defendant insists, however, that the method of operation of the former partnership showed an understanding that all obligations were to be repaid from profits. He nevertheless concedes that there was no understanding as to the term of the present partnership in the event of losses. . . .

Viewing this evidence most favorably for defendant, it proves only that the partners expected to meet current expenses from current income and to recoup their investment if the business were successful.

Defendant contends that such an expectation is sufficient to create a partnership for a term under the rule of *Owen v. Cohen*, 19 Cal. 2d 147, 150,

119 P.2d 713. In that case we held that when a partner advances a sum of money to a partnership with the understanding that the amount contributed was to be a loan to the partnership and was to be repaid as soon as feasible from the prospective profits of the business, the partnership is for the term reasonably required to repay the loan. It is true that *Owen v. Cohen*, supra, and other cases hold that partners may impliedly agree to continue in business until a certain sum of money is earned (*Mervyn Investment Co. v. Biber*, 184 Cal. 637, 641-642, 194 P. 1037), or one or more partners recoup their investments (*Vangel v. Vangel*, 116 Cal. App. 2d 615, 625, 254 P.2d 919), or until certain debts are paid (*Owen v. Cohen*, supra, 19 Cal. 2d at page 150, 119 P.2d at page 714), or until certain property could be disposed of on favorable terms (*Shannon v. Hudson*, 161 Cal. App. 2d 44, 48, 325 P.2d 1022). In each of these cases, however, the implied agreement found support in the evidence. . . .

In the instant case, however, defendant failed to prove any facts from which an agreement to continue the partnership for a term may be implied. The understanding to which defendant testified was no more than a common hope that the partnership earnings would pay for all the necessary expenses. Such a hope does not establish even by implication a "definite term or particular undertaking" as required by U.P.A. §31(1)(b). All partnerships are ordinarily entered into with the hope that they will be profitable, but that alone does not make them all partnerships for a term and obligate the partners to continue in the partnerships until all of the losses over a period of many years have been recovered.

Defendant contends that plaintiff is acting in bad faith and is attempting to use his superior financial position to appropriate the now profitable business of the partnership. Defendant has invested $43,000 in the firm, and owing to the long period of losses his interest in the partnership assets is very small. The fact that plaintiff's wholly-owned corporation holds a $47,000 demand note of the partnership may make it difficult to sell the business as a going concern. Defendant fears that upon dissolution he will receive very little and that plaintiff, who is the managing partner and knows how to conduct the operations of the partnership, will receive a business that has become very profitable because of the establishment of Vandenberg Air Force Base in its vicinity. Defendant charges that plaintiff has been content to share the losses but now that the business has become profitable he wishes to keep all the gains.

There is no showing in the record of bad faith or that the improved profit situation is more than temporary. In any event these contentions are irrelevant to the issue whether the partnership is for a term or at will. Since, however, this action is for a declaratory judgment and will be the basis for future action by the parties, it is appropriate to point out that defendant is amply protected by the fiduciary duties of co-partners.

Even though the Uniform Partnership Act provides that a partnership at will may be dissolved by the express will of any partner (§31(1)(b)), this power, like any other power held by a fiduciary, must be exercised in good faith. . . .

[P]laintiff has the power to dissolve the partnership by express notice to defendant. If, however, it is proved that plaintiff acted in bad faith and violated

his fiduciary duties by attempting to appropriate to his own use the new pros-
perity of the partnership without adequate compensation to his co-partner, the
dissolution would be wrongful and the plaintiff would be liable [for damages
for breach of partnership agreement] as provided by U.P.A. §38(2)(a) (rights of
partners upon wrongful dissolution) for violation of the implied agreement not
to exclude defendant wrongfully from the partnership business opportunity.

The judgment is reversed. . . .

QUESTIONS ON PAGE v. PAGE

1. Like *Meinhard v. Salmon*, below, which it resembles, *Page* has excited considerable commentary. See, e.g., Robert W. Hillman, *The Dissatisfied Participant
in the Solvent Business Venture: A Consideration of the Relative Permanence of
Partnerships and Close Corporations,* 67 Minn. L. Rev. 1, 33 (1982).

2. How should *Page* have been decided? Consider three possibilities: (1) by
ruling that the partnership implied a term, as the trial court did; (2) by holding,
with Justice Traynor, that the power to dissolve the partnership was constrained
by fiduciary duty (what would violate this duty?); or (3) by ruling that the statutory power to wind-up the partnership was unconstrained and absolute.

2.6   AGENCY CONFLICTS AMONG CO-OWNERS: FIDUCIARY DUTIES

The partnership introduces the last of the basic agency problems of organizational law: the conflict between controlling and "minority" co-owners.
A good case for thinking about this conflict — and its relationship to the conflict between principal and agent generally — is the most famous American
case in all of organizational law. The case concerns a joint venture[15] between
two "co-venturers," Salmon and Meinhard. This was, in effect, a circumscribed
partnership dedicated to a single investment project. The issue concerns the
scope of the duty of loyalty owed by the managing co-venturer (Salmon) to
the passive co-venturer (Meinhard).

MEINHARD v. SALMON
164 N.E. 545 (N.Y. 1928)

CARDOZO, C.J.:

On April 10, 1902, Louisa M. Gerry leased to the defendant Walter J.
Salmon the premises known as the Hotel Bristol at the northwest corner of

---

15. For purposes of this case, a joint venture is a partnership with a single investment or
project. In today's more casual usage, "joint venture" may refer to a jointly-owned investment
or project that is held by any jointly-owned business entity, including, for example, a corporation or limited liability company.

Forty-Second street and Fifth avenue in the city of New York. The lease was for a term of 20 years, commencing May 1, 1902, and ending April 30, 1922. The lessee undertook to change the hotel building for use as shops and offices at a cost of $200,000. Alterations and additions were to be accretions to the land.

Salmon, while in course of treaty with the lessor as to the execution of the lease, was in course of treaty with Meinhard, the plaintiff, for the necessary funds. The result was a joint venture with terms embodied in a writing. Meinhard was to pay to Salmon half of the moneys requisite to reconstruct, alter, manage, and operate the property. Salmon was to pay to Meinhard 40 percent of the net profits for the first five years of the lease and 50 percent for the years thereafter. If there were losses, each party was to bear them equally. Salmon, however, was to have sole power to "manage, lease, underlet and operate" the building. There were to be certain preemptive rights for each in the contingency of death.

The two were coadventurers, subject to fiduciary duties akin to those of partners. *King v. Barnes*, 109 N.Y. 267, 16 N.E. 332. As to this we are all agreed. The heavier weight of duty rested, however, upon Salmon. He was a coadventurer with Meinhard, but he was manager as well. During the early years of the enterprise, the building, reconstructed, was operated at a loss. If the relation had then ended, Meinhard as well as Salmon would have carried a heavy burden. Later the profits became large with the result that for each of the investors there came a rich return. For each the venture had its phases of fair weather and of foul. The two were in it jointly, for better or for worse.

When the lease was near its end, Elbridge T. Gerry had become the owner of the reversion. He owned much other property in the neighborhood, one lot adjoining the Bristol building on Fifth avenue and four lots on Forty-Second street. He had a plan to lease the entire tract for a long term to some one who would destroy the buildings then existing and put up another in their place. In the latter part of 1921, he submitted such a project to several capitalists and dealers. He was unable to carry it through with any of them. Then, in January, 1922, with less than four months of the lease to run, he approached the defendant Salmon. The result was a new lease to the Midpoint Realty Company, which is owned and controlled by Salmon, a lease covering the whole tract, and involving a huge outlay. The term is to be 20 years, but successive covenants for renewal will extend it to a maximum of 80 years at the will of either party. The existing buildings may remain unchanged for seven years. They are then to be torn down, and a new building to cost $3,000,000 is to be placed upon the site. The rental, which under the Bristol lease was only $55,000, is to be from $350,000 to $475,000 for the properties so combined. Salmon personally guaranteed the performance by the lessee of the covenants of the new lease until such time as the new building had been completed and fully paid for.

The lease between Gerry and the Midpoint Realty Company was signed and delivered on January 25, 1922. Salmon had not told Meinhard anything about it. Whatever his motive may have been, he had kept the negotiations to himself. Meinhard was not informed even of the bare existence of a project. The first that he knew of it was in February, when the lease was an accomplished fact. He then made demand on the defendants that the lease be held in trust as an asset of the venture, making offer upon the trial to share the personal obligations incidental to the guaranty. The demand was followed by refusal, and later by this suit. A referee gave judgment for the plaintiff, limiting the plaintiff's interest in the lease, however, to 25 percent. The limitation was on the theory that the plaintiff's equity was to be restricted to one-half of so much of the value of the lease as was contributed or represented by the occupation of the Bristol site. Upon cross-appeals to the Appellate Division, the judgment was modified so as to enlarge the equitable interest to one-half of the whole lease. With this enlargement of plaintiff's interest, there went, of course, a corresponding enlargement of his attendant obligations. The case is now here on an appeal by the defendants. . . .

Joint venturers, like copartners, owe to one another, while the enterprise continues, the duty of the finest loyalty. Many forms of conduct permissible in a workaday world for those acting at arm's length, are forbidden to those bound by fiduciary ties. A trustee is held to something stricter than the morals of the market place. Not honesty alone, but the punctilio of an honor the most sensitive, is then the standard of behavior. As to this there has developed a tradition that is unbending and inveterate. Uncompromising rigidity has been the attitude of courts of equity when petitioned to undermine the rule of undivided loyalty by the "disintegrating erosion" of particular exceptions. . . . Only thus has the level of conduct for fiduciaries been kept at a level higher than that trodden by the crowd. It will not consciously be lowered by any judgment of this court.

The owner of the reversion, Mr. Gerry, had vainly striven to find a tenant who would favor his ambitious scheme of demolition and construction. Baffled in the search, he turned to the defendant Salmon in possession of the Bristol, the keystone of the project. He figured to himself beyond a doubt that the man in possession would prove a likely customer. To the eye of an observer, Salmon held the lease as owner in his own right, for himself and no one else. In fact he held it as a fiduciary, for himself and another, sharers in a common venture. If this fact had been proclaimed, if the lease by its terms had run in favor of a partnership, Mr. Gerry, we may fairly assume, would have laid before the partners, and not merely before one of them, his plan of reconstruction. The pre-emptive privilege, or, better, the preemptive opportunity, that was thus an incident of the enterprise, Salmon appropriated to himself in secrecy and silence. He might have warned Meinhard that the plan had been submitted, and that either would be free to compete for the award. If he had done this, we do not need to say whether he would have been under a duty, if successful in the competition, to hold the lease so acquired for the benefit of a venture then about to end, and thus prolong by indirection its responsibilities and duties. The trouble about his conduct is that he excluded his coadventurer from any chance to compete, from any chance to enjoy the opportunity for benefit that had come to him alone by virtue of his agency. This chance, if nothing more, he was under a duty to concede. The price of its denial is an extension of the trust at the option and for the benefit of the one whom he excluded.

No answer is it to say that the chance would have been of little value even if seasonably offered. Such a calculus of probabilities is beyond the science of the chancery. Salmon, the real estate operator, might have been preferred to Meinhard, the woolen merchant. On the other hand, Meinhard might have offered better terms, or reinforced his offer by alliance with the wealth of others. Perhaps he might even have persuaded the lessor to renew the Bristol lease alone, postponing for a time, in return for higher rentals, the improvement of adjoining lots. We know that even under the lease as made the time for the enlargement of the building was delayed for seven years. All these opportunities were cut away from him through another's intervention. . . .

Little profit will come from a dissection of the precedents. None precisely similar is cited in the briefs of counsel. What is similar in many, or so it seems to us, is the animating principle. Authority is, of course, abundant that one partner may not appropriate to his own use a renewal of a lease, though its term is to begin at the expiration of the partnership. *Mitchell v. Read*, 61 N.Y. 123, 19 Am. Rep. 252; Id., 84 N.Y. 556. The lease at hand with its many changes is not strictly a renewal. Even so, the standard of loyalty for those in trust relations is without the fixed divisions of a graduated scale. There is indeed a dictum in one of our decisions that a partner, though he may not renew a lease, may purchase the reversion if he acts openly and fairly. *Anderson v. Lemon*, 8 N.Y. 236. It is a dictum, and no more, for on the ground that he had acted slyly he was charged as a trustee. The holding is thus in favor of the conclusion that a purchase as well as a lease will succumb to the infection of secrecy and silence. Against the dictum in that case, moreover, may be set the opinion of Dwight, C., in *Mitchell v. Read*, where there is a dictum to the contrary. (61 N.Y. 123, at page 143). . . .

We have no thought to hold that Salmon was guilty of a conscious purpose to defraud. Very likely he assumed in all good faith that with the approaching end of the venture he might ignore his coadventurer and take the extension for himself. He had given to the enterprise time and labor as well as money. He had made it a success. Meinhard, who had given money, but neither time nor labor, had already been richly paid. There might seem to be something grasping in his insistence upon more. Such recriminations are not unusual when coadventurers fall out. They are not without their force if conduct is to be judged by the common standards of competitors. That is not to say that they have pertinency here. Salmon had put himself in a position in which thought of self was to be renounced, however hard the abnegation. He was much more than a coadventurer. He was a managing coadventurer. *Clegg v. Edmondson*, 8 D. M. & G. 787, 807. For him and for those like him the rule of undivided loyalty is relentless and supreme. . . .

A question remains as to the form and extent of the equitable interest to be allotted to the plaintiff. The trust as declared has been held to attach to the lease which was in the name of the defendant corporation. We think it ought to attach at the option of the defendant Salmon to the shares of stock which were owned by him or were under his control. The difference may be important if the lessee shall wish to execute an assignment of the lease, as it ought to be free to do with the consent of the lessor. On the other hand, an equal division of the shares might lead to other hardships. It might take away from Salmon the power of control and management which under the plan of the joint venture he was to have from first to last. The number of shares to be allotted to the plaintiff should, therefore, be reduced to such an extent as may be necessary to preserve to the defendant Salmon the expected measure of dominion. To that end an extra share should be added to his half. . . .

ANDREWS, J. (dissenting). . . .

It may be stated generally that a partner may not for his own benefit secretly take a renewal of a firm lease to himself. . . .

Where the trustee, or the partner or the tenant in common, takes no new lease but buys the reversion in good faith a somewhat different question arises. Here is no direct appropriation of the expectancy of renewal. Here is no offshoot of the original lease. We so held in *Anderson v. Lemon*, 8 N.Y. 236, and although Judge Dwight casts some doubt on the rule in *Mitchell v. Reed*, it seems to have the support of authority. W. & T. Leading Cas. in Equity, p. 650; Lindley on Partnership (9th Ed.) p. 396; *Bevan v. Webb*, [1905] 1 Ch. 620. The issue, then, is whether actual fraud, dishonesty, or unfairness is present in the transaction. If so, the purchaser may well be held as a trustee. (*Anderson v. Lemon*, cited above.)

With this view of the law I am of the opinion that the issue here is simple. Was the transaction, in view of all the circumstances surrounding it, unfair and inequitable? I reach this conclusion for two reasons. There was no general partnership, merely a joint venture for a limited object, to end at a fixed time. The new lease, covering additional property, containing many new and unusual terms and conditions, with a possible duration of 80 years, was more nearly the purchase of the reversion than the ordinary renewal with which the authorities are concerned. . . .

QUESTIONS ON MEINHARD

1. Imagine that Judge Cardozo is supplying a standard term in the joint venture agreements between the Salmons and Meinhards of this world. What does the term say? What must an active co-venturer like Salmon share with his co-venturer, and what can he keep to himself?

2. Suppose the joint venture agreement had included a term allowing Salmon to accept any renewal or extension of the Gerry lease unilaterally, without consulting Meinhard and at any point before or after the term of the joint venture had run. Would Cardozo enforce this term or disregard it, perhaps because it purported to give Salmon unbounded discretion to breach his joint venturer's duty of undivided loyalty to Meinhard? Meinhard could not possibly have agreed to the unlimited range of particular circumstances in which Salmon might benefit at Meinhard's expense under this provision. Alternatively, would enforcing this provision imply that partners are free to contract out of the duty of loyalty?

3. What terms would Salmon and Meinhard have reached if they had negotiated over Salmon's duties in the event that he was offered a renewal or

an enlarged second lease before the term of the first lease was up? (Of course, these hypothetical negotiations would have occurred before May 1, 1902.) Would Meinhard have insisted on an option to participate with Salmon on the same terms as their initial joint venture provided? Would he have demanded timely disclosure and an opportunity to compete against Salmon for the lease or to negotiate different terms with Salmon? Or finally, might he have agreed to waive any claim on an uncertain second lease in exchange for a slightly higher percentage of the profits from the first lease?[16]

4. Would *Meinhard* be decided differently under RUPA? See RUPA §§403, 404.

2.7   AFTER PARTNERSHIP: THE NEW AND THE "NEW-OLD" CONTRACTUAL ENTITIES

The general partnership is a durable entity for jointly-owned businesses. Yet, it also has drawbacks from the perspective of a transactional lawyer. The personal liability of general partners complicates the allocation of risk between partners and creditors while the uncertain reach of fiduciary duties injects legal risk into relationships among partners. Liability to creditors could be ameliorated by adopting the corporate form of business enterprise, as we develop in the next Chapter. But there were obstacles here too, most conspicuously that all but a narrow class of corporations faced a disadvantageous "two-tier" taxation regime under which corporations were taxed as entities and their investors—their shareholders—were taxed again when they received dividends or corporate distributions. By choosing the limited partnership form, they could escape two-tier corporate taxation and retain limited liability, but only by relinquishing any active role in management ("active" partners initially had unlimited liability).

Thus, legal planners of the mid-twentieth century might have wished for an entity form that combined limited investor liability, like the limited partnership and the corporation, robust control rights, like the general partnership and the corporation, and pass-through taxation, like the limited and general partnerships. If they hoped for more than this, it might well have been statutory authorization to minimize fiduciary risk by contract. The remainder of this Chapter demonstrates that wishes can sometimes come true with careful drafting and innovative state legislatures.

---

16. It is noteworthy that Salmon—who lost the case—seemed to be its biggest beneficiary in the end. Salmon was a well-known real estate investor and champion horse breeder in New York society circles before the commencement of this litigation. The decision came down a few months before the Stock Market Crash of 1929 and the onset of the Great Depression. The resultant decline in property value and losses on the venture were now shared with Meinhard, thereby partially insulating Salmon from them. Being inadvertently saved from financial ruin reportedly led Salmon to send Judge Cardozo a bouquet of flowers every year on the anniversary of the decision. See Geoffrey Miller, *A Glimpse of Society Via a Case and Cardozo*: Meinhard v. Salmon, *in* The Iconic Cases in Corporate Law 12, 26 (Jonathan R. Macey, ed. Thomson West 2008); Nicholas L. Georgakopoulos, Meinhard v. Salmon *and the Economics of Honor*, 1999 Col. Bus. L. Rev. 137, 144 n.11 (1999).

It may seem that the most dramatic development over the last 40 years is the demise of personal liability for equity investors in contractual entities. But this impression may exaggerate the role played by personal liability and fail to appreciate that it is simply a default rule in the case of contractual creditors. Limited liability business forms, such as the corporation and limited partnership, predated the twentieth century. Equity investors in these limited liability entities routinely offered personal guaranties of business debts to obtain favorable credit terms and general partners often asked business creditors to waive personal liability (at some cost in less favorable credit terms). The critical change in the late twentieth century was that the default rule flipped in contractual entities. Although general partners remained personally liable on business debts, new statutory entities such as the LLC changed the default setting to limit investor losses to their capital contributions while the progressive statutory reform of the LP permitted limited partners to exercise more control while retaining limited liability.

We develop these points throughout the remainder of this Chapter. Here, however, we introduce a parallel development that is at least as important as the evolution of contractual entities into limited liability vehicles. This is the statutory leeway new entities provide to waive or reformulate common law fiduciary duties that play a central role in partnership and corporate law.

2.7.1   Opting Out of Fiduciary Duties by Contract

Clauses that modify or eliminate fiduciary duties are common features of the "new-old" limited partnership and the "new" statutory form, the limited liability company (LLC). The Delaware Limited Liability Act ("DLLC Act") has evolved to allow business planners to mimic the structure of either a general (GP) or limited partnership (LP). The principal actors in an LLC are "members" and "managers." Members hold equity interests (termed "units") and managers manage. But members may be managers and vice versa, in which case a "member-managed" LLC might look very much like a general partnership in which the partners have limited liability. And, as if this isn't confusing enough, there are now limited liability partnerships, an entity form that we will address shortly. But for now, we pause to reflect on the statutory license that business planners enjoy to opt out of fiduciary duties.

We begin with a case that features a Delaware LLC but was eventually decided by the New York Court of Appeals under New York contract law rather than under Delaware's LLC Act. Most states provide substantial latitude in LP and LLC authorizing statutes to contract around all fiduciary duties. For example, Delaware's LLC statute affirms its policy "to give maximum effect to the principle of freedom of contract and to the enforceability of limited liability agreements."[17] But the New York case below, *Pappas et al. v. Tzolis*, arguably goes beyond standard fiduciary duty opt-outs in LLCs to hold that two members of an LLC had not only waived the fiduciary protections but also their rights to rely on the representations of the third member of the LLC — and hence any claim that they were victims of fraudulent misrepresentation.

17. 6 Del. C. 18-1101.

PAPPAS ET AL. v. TZOLIS
20 N.Y.3d 231 (N.Y. Ct. App. 2012)

PIGOTT, J.:

Steve Pappas and Constantine Ifantopoulos along with defendant Steve Tzolis formed and managed a limited liability company (LLC), for the purpose of entering into a long-term lease on a building in Lower Manhattan. Pappas and Tzolis each contributed $50,000 and Ifantopoulos $25,000, in exchange for proportionate shares in the company.[18] Pursuant to a January 2006 Operating Agreement, Tzolis agreed to post and maintain in effect a security deposit of $1,192,500, and was permitted to sublet the property. The Agreement further provided that any of the three members of the LLC could "engage in business ventures and investments of any nature whatsoever, whether or not in competition with the LLC, without obligation of any kind to the LLC or to the other Members."

Numerous business disputes among the parties ensued. In June 2006, Tzolis took sole possession of the property, which was subleased by the LLC to a company he owned, for approximately $20,000 per month in addition to rent payable by the LLC under the lease. According to plaintiffs, they "reluctantly agreed to do this, because they were looking to lease the building and Tzolis was obstructing this from happening." Pappas, who wanted to sublease the building to others, alleges that Tzolis "not only blocked [his] efforts, he also did not cooperate in listing the Property for sale or lease with any New York real estate brokers." Moreover, Pappas claims that Tzolis "had not made, and was not diligently preparing to make, the improvements. . . . required to be made under the Lease. Tzolis was also refusing to cooperate in [Pappas's] efforts to develop the Property." Further, Tzolis's company did not pay the rent due.

On January 18, 2007, Tzolis bought plaintiffs' membership interests in the LLC for $1,000,000 and $500,000, respectively. At closing, in addition to an Agreement of Assignment and Assumption, the parties executed a Certificate in which plaintiffs represented that, as sellers, they had "performed their own due diligence in connection with [the] assignments . . . engaged [their] own legal counsel, and [were] not relying on any representation by Steve Tzolis[,] or any of his agents or representatives, except as set forth in the assignments and other documents delivered to the undersigned Sellers today," and that "Steve Tzolis has no fiduciary duty to the undersigned Sellers in connection with [the] assignments." Tzolis made reciprocal representations as the buyer.

In August 2007, the LLC, now owned entirely by Tzolis, assigned the lease to a subsidiary of Extell Development Company for $17,500,000. In 2009, plaintiffs came to believe that Tzolis had surreptitiously negotiated the sale with the development company before he bought their interests in the LLC.

---

18. According to a memo filed by Tzolis, all decisions of the LLC required unanimous member consent.

Plaintiffs commenced this action against Tzolis in April 2009, claiming that, by failing to disclose the negotiations with Extell, Tzolis breached his fiduciary duty to them. They alleged, in all, 11 causes of action.

Tzolis moved to dismiss plaintiffs' complaint. Supreme Court dismissed the complaint in its entirety, citing the Operating Agreement and Certificate. A divided Appellate Division modified Supreme Court's order, allowing four of plaintiffs' claims to proceed — breach of fiduciary duty, conversion, unjust enrichment, and fraud and misrepresentation [although]... [t]he dissenting Justices would have dismissed all the causes of action, relying on our recent decision in *Centro Empresarial Cempresa S.A. v. América Móvil, S.A.B. de C.V.* (17 N.Y.3d 269 [2011]).

The Appellate Division granted Tzolis leave to appeal, ... [we] reverse.

In their first cause of action, plaintiffs claim that Tzolis was a fiduciary with respect to them and breached his duty of disclosure. Tzolis counters that plaintiffs' claim fails to state a cause of action because, by executing the Certificate, they expressly released him from all claims based on fiduciary duty.

In *Centro Empresarial Cempresa S.A.*, we held that "[a] sophisticated principal is able to release its fiduciary from claims — at least where . . . the fiduciary relationship is no longer one of unquestioning trust — so long as the principal understands that the fiduciary is acting in its own interest and the release is knowingly entered into" ... Where a principal and fiduciary are sophisticated entities and their relationship is not one of trust, the principal cannot reasonably rely on the fiduciary without making additional inquiry. For instance, in *Centro Empresarial Cempresa S.A.,* plaintiffs — seasoned and counseled parties negotiating the termination of their relationship — knew that defendants had not supplied them with the financial information to which they were entitled, triggering "a heightened degree of diligence" ... In this context, "the principal cannot blindly trust the fiduciary's assertions" ... The test, in essence, is whether, given the nature of the parties' relationship at the time of the release, the principal is aware of information about the fiduciary that would make reliance on the fiduciary unreasonable.

Here, plaintiffs were sophisticated businessmen represented by counsel. Moreover, plaintiffs' own allegations make it clear that at the time of the buy-out, the relationship between the parties was not one of trust, and reliance on Tzolis's representations as a fiduciary would not have been reasonable. According to plaintiffs, there had been numerous business disputes, between Tzolis and them, concerning the sublease. Both the complaint and Pappas's affidavit opposing the motion to dismiss portray Tzolis as uncooperative and intransigent in the face of plaintiffs' preferences concerning the sublease. The relationship between plaintiffs and Tzolis had become antagonistic, to the extent that plaintiffs could no longer reasonably regard Tzolis as trust-worthy. Therefore, crediting plaintiffs' allegations, the release contained in the Certificate is valid, and plaintiffs cannot prevail on their cause of action alleging breach of fiduciary duty.

Practically speaking, it is clear that plaintiffs were in a position to make a reasoned judgment about whether to agree to the sale of their interests to Tzolis. The need to use care to reach an independent assessment of the value of the lease should have been obvious to plaintiffs, given that Tzolis offered to buy their interests for 20 times what they had paid for them just a year earlier.

Plaintiffs' cause of action alleging fraud and misrepresentation must be dismissed for similar reasons. Plaintiffs principally allege that Tzolis represented to them that he was aware of no reasonable prospects of selling the lease for an amount in excess of $2,500,000. However, in the Certificate, plaintiffs "in the plainest language announced and stipulated that [they were] not relying on any representations as to the very matter as to which [they] now claim [they were] defrauded" . . . [W]hile it is true that a party that releases a fraud claim may later challenge that release as fraudulently induced if it alleges a fraud separate from any contemplated by the release . . . , plaintiffs do not allege that the release was itself induced by any action separate from the alleged fraud consisting of Tzolis's failure to disclose his negotiations to sell the lease. . . .

Accordingly, the order of the Appellate Division . . . should be reversed.

NOTES AND QUESTIONS

1. Can a member of an LLC waive her right to rely on the express representations of a fellow member under the Delaware statutory provision allowing fiduciary opt-out? The Delaware statute bars a provision in an LLC agreement that purports to opting out of "the duty of good faith and fair dealing." §18-1101(c). Did Tzolis' certificate attempt to do exactly this? Did the Certificate amend the LLC Agreement or override it as a separate agreement?

2. Can it be argued that the Certificate was void from the outset because it was signed when the parties were still members of an LLC?

3. How much should it matter that "Tzolis offered to buy their interests for 20 times what they had paid for them just a year earlier"?

4. Is the Certificate itself sufficient to opt out of fiduciary duties owed by managing members of an LLC? Would the Court consider the opt-out effective if there was not a lack of "unquestioned trust"?

5. As the next Section suggests, there are effective ways to opt out of fiduciary duties in Delaware, too. Nonetheless, when the facts are sufficiently egregious, the courts may find that an attempt to opt out is not effective. Consider the Delaware Court of Chancery's decision in *Auriga Capital Corp. v. Gatz Properties, LLC,* 40 A. 3d 839 (2012), affirmed in relevant part by the Delaware Supreme Court.[19] The Court of Chancery held that two "exculpatory clauses" in an LLC operating agreement did not protect the manager and majority member of the LLC from monetary damages for breach of fiduciary duty. The court found that over several years, the manager discouraged, failed to disclose, refused, or otherwise subverted several lucrative third-party offers for the LLC's sole asset (a golf course), while also making "low ball" offers to buy out minority interests. As the economy declined at the end of the (2010) decade, the manager finally purchased the golf course for a fire-sale price in a sham auction. (The auctioneer and potential bidders knew the manager had the power and motivation to reject alternative bids.) The first "exculpatory clause" in the LLC operating agreement

---

19. See *Gatz Props., Ltd. Liab. Co.* v. *Auriga Capital Corp.*, 59 A.3d 1206 (Del. 2012).

required that "affiliated party transactions" (which the sale of the golf course to the manager was) must not be on "terms and conditions which are less favorable ... [to those] which could be entered into with arms-length third parties ...".[20] The court held the defendant had not proved this condition was met. A second "exculpatory clause" provided broad protection from liability based on fiduciary duty breach, but specifically excluded liability for acts committed in bad faith or with willful misrepresentation or gross negligence. The court held that this too was of no avail, because it did not specify that it was *exclusive*. In other words, the manager's buyout of the LLC's minority members was governed by this provision and all other equitable duties not excluded by this general exculpatory provision. And — here is the punch line — this second provision failed to exclude any equitable duty that would have bound the manager as a matter of statutory default under Delaware law. Thus the manager was also liable for bad faith, willful misrepresentation, and gross negligence. In short, the manager was liable no matter which provision applied.

2.7.2   Judicial Review After Effectively Opting Out of Fiduciary Duties?

Delaware's policy of giving "maximum effect to the principle of freedom of contract"[21] remains subject to the implied covenant of good faith and fair dealing. The meaning of this venerable doctrine sounding in contract is illustrated by the two cases discussed below, one involving a limited partnership and the other an LLC.

2.7.2.1   The New (Old) Limited Partnership and the Implied Covenant

The defining features of a limited partnership are (1) one or more general partners who manage the business and bear unlimited liability; (2) one or more limited partners who share in profits but are passive investors who do not participate in control or management; (3) limited liability that restricts the personal liability of limited partners to their ownership stake in the business; (4) wide-ranging contractual flexibility including customizing or eliminating fiduciary duties (with a default mirroring the general partnership);[22] and (5) registration with individual states — almost always a division of a state's office of the attorney general — as a limited partnership. Public registration

---

20. In this context, the terms "affiliated party transaction" and "related party transaction" refer to transactions between the legal entity and another party who, directly or indirectly, exercises control or influence over the legal entity. In most cases, it refers to a partner, member, or shareholder who controls the firm and also controls a third-party entity that transacts with the firm.

21. 6 Del. C. 18-1101.

22. See Del. LLC Act §18-1104. For discussion, see Mohsen Manesh, *Damning Dictum: The Default Duty Debate in Delaware* 39 J. Corp. L. 35 (2013).

puts creditors on notice that they can only rely on the personal assets of the general partners who participate in the control of the business. We have seen the LP mentioned before in *Page v. Page*. There, the passive younger brother had previously invested with his older brother in an LP arrangement in which the elder Page was the active general partner with sole power to manage the business but was constrained from dissolving their partnership at will by a fixed term in their agreement. The prior agreements between the Page brothers illustrate the LP at the simplest level, while the agreements in *Dieckman* below reflect a far more complex modern use of the LP form. The limited partnerships involved are so-called "master limited partnerships," meaning that their limited partnership "units" traded on a public stock exchange, much as if they were shares of stock. There were tax reasons to hold these energy assets in an LP structure, but they need not concern us here. The case is challenging enough if considered only for its discussion of the duty of good faith and loyalty. And don't give up trying to understand the transaction at issue here. This is a foretaste of the complex corporate transactions discussed in the last Chapters of this book.

DIECKMAN v. REGENCY GP LP
155 A.3d 358 (Del. 2017)

[Eds. The court helpfully simplifies the facts of this case. Although many entities were involved, the number can be reduced to three for purposes of discussion. Two were limited partnerships, Regency LP and Sunoco LP, each of which had different investors and held different assets. The third is the "General Partner," which had virtually complete managerial power over both limited partnerships. Both limited partnerships were formed under the Delaware Revised Uniform Limited Partnership Act ("DRULPA"). It is not unusual for a single sponsor to raise capital for multiple LP funds and to manage these LP funds centrally, as happened in this case. Although not central to the court's discussion, it may be of interest that Regency and Sunoco were so-called master limited partnerships ("MLPs") whose limited partnership interests—termed "units"—were publicly traded on the New York Stock Exchange.

The transaction at the heart of the case was the General Partner's decision to merge Regency into Sunoco, which for present purposes can be considered as equivalent to selling Regency to Sunoco. Regency's unitholders were to receive new units in the combined limited partnership as consideration for the loss of their Regency units. The problem was that the General Partner was on both sides of the transaction and was far more heavily invested in Sunoco than Regency, making this a conflicted transaction. The complainant, Dieckman, was a limited partner/unitholder in Regency who sought to block the transaction as unauthorized under Regency's limited partnership agreement.

We continue here with excerpts from Justice Seitz's opinion.]

Seitz, Justice:

In this appeal, we again wade into the details of a master limited partnership agreement to decide whether the complaint's allegations can overcome the general partner's use of conflict resolution safe harbors to dismiss the case. . . .

Because conflicts of interest often arise in MLP transactions, those who create and market MLPs have devised special ways to try to address them. The general partner in this case sought refuge in two of the safe harbor conflict resolution provisions of the partnership agreement — "Special Approval" of the transaction by an independent Conflicts Committee, and "Unaffiliated Unitholder Approval."

Special Approval typically means that a Conflicts Committee composed of members independent of the sponsor and its affiliates reviewed the transaction and made a recommendation to the partnership board[23] whether to approve the transaction. Unaffiliated Unitholder Approval is typically just that — a majority of unitholders unaffiliated with the general partner and its affiliates approve the transaction. Under the partnership agreement, if either [Conflict Committee Approval or Unaffiliated Unitholder Approval is obtained by the general partner], the transaction is deemed not to be a breach of the agreement. . . .

[T]he Court of Chancery [below correctly held] that the implied covenant of good faith and fair dealing cannot be used to supplant the express disclosure requirements of the partnership agreement. But the court focused too narrowly on [disclosure]. Instead, the center of attention should have been on the conflict resolution provision of the partnership agreement. We find that the plaintiff has pled sufficient facts, which we must accept as true at this stage of the proceedings, that neither safe harbor was available to the [G]eneral [P]artner because it allegedly made false and misleading statements to secure Unaffiliated Unitholder Approval, and allegedly used a conflicted Conflicts Committee to obtain Special Approval. Thus, we reverse the Court of Chancery. . . .

Because of the undisputed conflicts of interest in the proposed merger transaction, the General Partner looked to the conflict resolution provisions of the LP Agreement.

Under §7.9(a) of the LP Agreement [LPA], . . . the General Partner can resort to several safe harbors to immunize conflicted transactions from judicial review:

> [A]ny resolution or course of action by the General Partner or its Affiliates in respect of such conflict of interest shall be permitted and deemed approved by all Partners, and shall not constitute a breach of this Agreement . . . or of any duty stated or implied by law or equity, if the resolution or course of action in respect of such conflict of interest is (i) approved by Special Approval,

---

23. [Eds. Large limited partnerships typically have "boards of directors" comprised of representatives of major limited partners. These boards are not to be confused with the boards of directors of corporations, which are addressed in later Chapters. LP boards have limited powers specified in LP agreements. One of these limited powers is the right to vote on fundamental transactions, such as the merger at issue in this case.]

(ii) approved by the vote of a majority of the Common Units (excluding Common Units owned by the General Partner and its Affiliates), (iii) on terms no less favorable to the Partnership than those generally being provided to or available from unrelated third parties, or (iv) fair and reasonable to the Partnership. . . .

The General Partner sought the protections of the safe harbors by Special Approval under §7.9(a)(i) and Unaffiliated Unitholder Vote under §7.9(a)(ii). Special Approval is defined in the LPA as "approval by a majority of the members of the Conflicts Committee." The Conflicts Committee must be:

[A] committee of the Board of Directors of the General Partner composed entirely of two or more directors who are not (a) security holders, officers or employees of the General Partner, (b) officers, directors or employees of any Affiliate of the General Partner[,] or (c) holders of any ownership interest in the Partnership Group other than Common Units and who also meet [certain requirement not at issue here] . . .

Sunoco and the General Partner are [. . .] "Affiliates," under the LP Agreement. Thus, Sunoco board members were not eligible to serve [on] the General Partner's Conflicts Committee . . .

[Nevertheless, t]he General Partner appointed Brannon and Bryant to the Conflicts Committee. The complaint alleges that before the proposed transaction, Brannon was a Sunoco director. On January 16, 2015, [he was appointed] to the General Partner's board, while still a director of Sunoco. The plaintiff claims that, from January 16-20, while a member of both boards, Brannon consulted informally on the proposed transaction . . . Brannon then temporarily resigned from the Sunoco board on January 20, and on January 22, became an official member of the Conflicts Committee when formal resolutions were passed creating the Committee. Brannon and Bryant then negotiated on behalf of Regency . . . and recommended the merger transaction to the General Partner. On April 30, 2015, the day that the merger closed, Brannon was reappointed to the Sunoco board, and Bryant was also appointed to Sunoco board . . .

The LP Agreement only required minimal disclosure when a merger transaction was considered by the unitholders — a summary of . . . the merger agreement. But the General Partner went beyond the minimal requirements [to] gain Unaffiliated Unitholder Approval and the benefit of the safe harbor, [by filing] a 165-page proxy statement[24] and [disseminating] it . . .

The proxy statement stated that the "Conflicts Committee consists of two independent directors: Richard D. Brannon (Chairman) and James W. Bryant." It also stated that the Conflicts Committee approved the transaction, and such approval "constituted 'Special Approval' as defined in

---

24. [EDS. A proxy statement is a public disclosure document intended to solicit investor votes. As we discuss in Chapter 6, it is often mandatory and heavily regulated in the corporate context before shareholder meetings are convened to vote on directors or approve basic transactions. The MLP agreement in this case required only minimal disclosure of the terms of the transaction that General Partner was submitting to the limited partner/unitholders for approval.]

the Regency partnership agreement." The proxy statement did not inform [Regency's] unitholders about ... Bryant's alleged overlapping and shifting allegiances, including reviewing the proposed transaction while still a member of the Sunoco board, his nearly contemporaneous resignation from the Sunoco board and appointment to the General Partner's board and then the Conflicts Committee, or Brannon's appointment and Bryant's reappointment to the Sunoco board the day the transaction closed. At a special meeting of Regency's unitholders on April 28, 2015, a majority of Regency's unitholders, including a majority of its unaffiliated unitholders, approved the merger ...

We start with the settled principles of law governing Delaware limited partnerships. The Delaware Revised Uniform Limited Partnership Act ("DRULPA") gives "maximum effect to the principle of freedom of contract." [EDS. DRULPA §17-1101(c)] One freedom often exercised in the MLP context is eliminating any fiduciary duties a partner owes to others in the partnership structure. The act allows drafters of Delaware limited partnerships to ... eliminate fiduciary-based principles of governance, and displace them with contractual terms.

With the contractual freedom accorded partnership agreement drafters, ... come corresponding responsibilities on the part of investors to read carefully and understand their investment. Investors must appreciate that "with the benefits of investing in alternative entities often comes the limitation of looking to the contract as the exclusive source of protective rights." In other words, investors can no longer hold the general partner to fiduciary standards of conduct, but instead must rely on the express language of the partnership agreement to sort out the rights and obligations among the general partner, the partnership, and the limited partner investors.

Even though the express terms of the agreement govern the relationship when fiduciary duties are waived, investors are not without some protections.... When investors buy equity in a public entity, they necessarily rely on the text of the public documents and public disclosures about that entity ... And, of course, another protection exists. The DRUPLA provides for the implied covenant of good faith and fair dealing, which cannot be eliminated by contract. [EDS. DRUPLA §17-1101(d)]

The implied covenant is inherent in all contracts and is used to infer contract terms "to handle developments or contractual gaps that the asserting party pleads neither party anticipated." It applies "when the party asserting the implied covenant proves that the other party has acted arbitrarily or unreasonably, thereby frustrating the fruits of the bargain that the asserting party reasonably expected." The reasonable expectations of the contracting parties are assessed at the time of contracting. In a situation like this, involving a publicly traded MLP, the pleading-stage inquiry focuses on whether, ... the express terms of the agreement can be reasonably read to imply certain other conditions, or leave a gap, that would proscribe certain conduct, ... to vindicate the apparent intentions and reasonable expectations of the parties.

The Court of Chancery decided that the implied covenant could not be used to remedy [allegedly] faulty safe harbor approvals because the LP

Agreement waived fiduciary-based standards of conduct and contained an express contractual term addressing what disclosures were required in merger transactions.

Although the terms of the LP Agreement did not compel the General Partner to issue a proxy statement, it chose to undertake the transaction, which the LP Agreement drafters would have known required a pre-unitholder vote proxy statement. Thus, the General Partner voluntarily issued a proxy statement to induce unaffiliated unitholders to vote in favor of the merger transaction. The favorable vote led not only to approval of the transaction, but allowed the General Partner to claim the protections of the safe harbor and immunize the merger transaction from judicial review. Not surprisingly, the express terms of the LP Agreement did not address, one way or another, whether the General Partner could use false or misleading statements to enable it to reach the safe harbors.

We find that implied in the language of the LP Agreement's conflict resolution provision is a requirement that the General Partner not act to undermine the protections afforded unitholders in the safe harbor process. Partnership agreement drafters, . . . do not include obvious and provocative conditions in an agreement like "the General Partner will not mislead unitholders when seeking Unaffiliated Unitholder Approval" or "the General Partner will not subvert the Special Approval process by appointing conflicted members to the Conflicts Committee." But the terms are easily implied because "the parties must have intended them and have only failed to express them because they are too obvious to need expression." . . .

Our use of the implied covenant is based on the words of the contract and not the disclaimed fiduciary duties. Under the LP Agreement, the General Partner did not have the full range of disclosure obligations that a corporate fiduciary would have had. Yet once it went beyond the minimal disclosure requirements of the LP Agreement, and issued a 165-page proxy statement to induce the unaffiliated unitholders not only to approve the merger transaction, but also to secure the Unaffiliated Unitholder Approval safe harbor, [the] language of the LP Agreement's conflict resolution provision [implied] . . . an obligation not to mislead unitholders.

Further, the General Partner was required to form a Conflicts Committee . . . . Implicit in the express terms is that the Special Committee membership be genuinely comprised of qualified [independent] members and that deceptive conduct not be used to create the false appearance of an unaffiliated, independent Special Committee. [In addition, the] plaintiff also alleges that the Conflicts Committee members failed to satisfy the audit committee independence rules of the New York Stock Exchange, as required by the LP Agreement.

The plaintiff has therefore pled facts raising sufficient doubt about the General Partner's ability to use the safe harbors to shield the merger transaction from judicial review. Thus, we reverse the judgment of the Court of Chancery. . . .

QUESTIONS

1. What "gap" does the court fill with the implied covenant.

2. What distinguishes a gap from an issue that an LP agreement simply doesn't address? Does an LP agreement address an issue if it delegates discretion to decide the issue to an internal authority, such as an independent committee?

2.7.2.2   *A New (New) Entity Form: The Limited Liability Company and the Implied Covenant*

The approach in *Dieckman* extends beyond LPs to all of the new contractual entities. The *Miller* case below is an example involving the LLC, which we have already seen on a very small scale in the *Pappas* case. The LLC is the firm of choice for modern small businesses as well as for many large firms, such as professional partnerships and corporate joint ventures. The legal characteristics of an LLC can resemble those of any other business entity. Apart from providing limited liability and partnership (i.e., pass-through) taxation, an LLC may be operated by managers, as designated by the LLC — or "operating" — agreement or it may be managed by its members. When an LLC agreement does not address fiduciary duties or other key issues, courts will often look to partnership or corporate law to supply the missing terms. Moreover, organizers of LLCs must file a copy of their articles of organization with the secretary of state, just as sponsors of limited partnerships must do. But unlike the general partners in LPs, the managers of LLCs enjoy limited liability full stop.

The following case features litigation between different classes of investors in a complex LLC. It also illustrates the fate of a start-up company with dimming prospects that faces increasingly severe terms as it strives to raise new capital. The conflict at the center of it all parallels an issue in a prominent line of Delaware corporate law cases featured in Chapter 13. We can avert to this line of cases now without spoiling the suspense: they collectively define Delaware's *Revlon* doctrine. A point that merits review later in this Book is the contrast that the Delaware Chancery Court notes between the law of contractual entities and corporate law.

MILLER v. HCP & CO.
2018 WL 656378 (Del. Ch. 2018)

[EDS. This case features a classic narrative in the world of start-ups. Trumpet Search, the start-up company here, was a Delaware LLC that offered "clinical services to persons with autism and other developmental disabilities, and [focused on] helping disabled children develop skills and cope with behavioral issues." As an LLC, Trumpet had members who, as in the preceding MLP case, are termed "unitholders." It also had a board of "managers" who ran the company. The controlling agreement in an LLC is frequently termed the "operating agreement" or "OA." The plaintiffs in this case are Trumpet's co-founder Christopher Miller and other early unitholders in the company. The defendants are HCP & Company and its affiliates, an outside investment fund that contributed significant capital to Trumpet in 2014 and 2016. We follow the court's convention in referring to the various affiliated HCP companies as "HCP."

Trumpet had issued different units to different investors. As with many start-ups, earlier investors received Class A, B, and C units, while HCP received Classes D and E units that reflected the enhanced rights accorded to recent contributors of capital. Each class of equity investment carried a different bundle of rights. A key difference among classes here is the order in which unitholders were paid when Trumpet was sold to a third-party buyer. Classes D and E were paid first. If the price paid by the buyer barely covered the claims of Classes D and E, holders of Classes A, B, and C would receive very little, which is precisely what happened. The term of art used by the parties and adopted by the court here is the cash "waterfall." The river of cash paid out to unitholders is captured in reverse alphabetical order. As holders of the most recent classes of units are paid first, the flow of cash reaching earlier units declines, even to the point that it dries up completely.

With this in mind, we shift to excerpts from Vice Chancellor Glasscock's opinion.]

GLASSCOCK, V. C.

Before me is the Defendants' Motion to Dismiss an action seeking relief under the implied covenant of good faith and fair dealing inhering to an LLC operating agreement. Co-plaintiff Christopher Miller was a cofounder of the LLC, Trumpet Search ("Trumpet"). As of May 5, 2016, HCP [was the] largest holder . . . of membership units in Trumpet. As of that date, the members executed the Second Amended and Restated Operating Agreement [OA] . . . Under the OA, Trumpet created new "Class E" membership units, which, upon sale of Trumpet, would be entitled to a "first in line" payment of 200% of the holders' investment in the Class E units. [HCP] purchased approximately 80% of these new units, for a capital investment of just under $2 million. The HCP Entities also held nearly 90% of the existing "Class D" units; according to the OA, upon sale these units were next in line, also to receive 200% of the holders' investment. [HCP] had contributed around $12 million for the Class D units. Upon any sale, in other words, according to the waterfall provision of the OA, the HCP Entities were entitled to the bulk of the first $30 million, before sales proceeds would be available to holders of other classes of membership units.

The HCP Entities held a majority of the membership units in Trumpet, and were entitled to appoint four of the seven managers on the Trumpet Board. [The OA mandated that every member consent to a sale of the company [approved by a majority of the Board].] The OA also gave the Board sole discretion as to the manner of any sale, conditioned only on the sale being to an unaffiliated third party. The members explicitly agreed, under the OA, to waive all fiduciary duties, to one another and from the managers to the members.

According to the Plaintiffs, this created a perverse incentive. If ... Trumpet [were sold], 90% of the first $30 million would go to the HCP Entities. [Thereafter, additional sales proceeds would primarily benefit] other classes of members ... In other words, the HCP-dominated Board [had] an incentive to negotiate any sales price up to about $30 million, but little incentive to negotiate further.

In the Plaintiffs' view, this incentive played out predictably. Less than a year after the OA was adopted, HCP championed a sale to an unaffiliated third party.... MTS Health Partners, L.P. ("MTS"). MTS initially offered $31 million. The HCP-allied majority of managers elected not to run an open sales process for Trumpet. They gave the non-affiliated managers—including Plaintiff Miller—little time to find alternative buyers. [T]his ... put pressure on MTS to increase its offer, which it did, to $41.3 million and ultimately to $43 million. The Trumpet Board approved the sale at $43 million. The Plaintiffs argue that an open auction of Trumpet would have resulted in a substantially higher sales price.

Plaintiffs acknowledge that all members eschewed fiduciary duties via the OA. They nonetheless argue that I should find that the implied covenant provides a term that the parties would have employed had they considered the matter: that any sale of Trumpet required an open-market sale or auction to ensure maximum value for all members. Implying an auction condition to any sale is necessary, according to the Plaintiffs, in light of the incentive created by the OA waterfall provisions, . . [But] the problem ... is that the incentive complained of is obvious on the face of the OA. The members, despite creating this incentive, eschewed fiduciary duties, and gave the Board sole discretion to approve the manner of the sale, subject to a single protection for the minority, that the sale be to an unaffiliated third party. It thus appears that the parties to the OA did consider the conditions under which a contractually permissible sale could take place. They avoided ... a self-dealing transaction but otherwise left to the HCP Entities the ability to structure a deal favorable to their interests. Viewed in this way, there is no gap in the parties' agreement to which the implied covenant may apply....

Of course, if the parties had chosen to employ the corporate form here, with its common-law fiduciary duties, this matter would be subject to entire fairness review. Here, the members forwent the suite of common-law protections available with the corporate form ... They did so ... despite the presence of a controller with an incentive to take a quick sale, and a Board with sole discretion to approve such a sale, with the single safeguard that the sale must not be to an insider.

The Plaintiffs now regret agreeing to these provisions. Presumably, however, the OA was drafted to attract capital investment, by allowing an exit on terms favorable to the investors ...

The HCP Entities acquired a Controlling Interest in Trumpet, and Trumpet Members entered into a New Operating Agreement in late 2014 ... On May 5, 2016, Trumpet's members entered into the Second Amended and Restated Operating Agreement [OA]. Under the OA, Trumpet created a new class of membership interests "primarily for HCP Investments." The OA sets out the following distribution waterfall for determining members' returns on capital investment in the event of "a sale or otherwise":

- First, Class E members would receive distributions in proportion to their capital contributions until they received 200% of their respective contributions.
- Second, Class D members would receive distributions in proportion to their capital contributions until they received 200% of their respective contributions . . . of $1,963,354.33 . . .

Thus, under the distribution waterfall, HCP's Class D units . . . would receive a first-position payout of $3,926,708 if Trumpet were sold. . . . Under Section 3.01(a) [of the OA], HCP entities have the authority to appoint a majority of Trumpet's seven-person Board. They exercised that authority by appointing Signoret, Shafer, Russell, and Maruri to the Board . . . Section 8.06 provides that if the Board approves a sale of all of Trumpet's membership units to an independent third party, every member is obligated to consent to the sale. If any member refuses to consent, the Board will . . . be appointed as that member's attorney-in-fact so that it can sign, on the objecting member's behalf, any documentation necessary to consummate the sale.

According to the Plaintiffs, once the HCP entities gained control of Trumpet, they set out to engineer a sale of the company that would give them, as holders of the vast majority of the Class D and E units, a 200% return on their investment . . . Instead of "engag[ing] in a reasonable open-market process to solicit the best available price for the company," the Defendants pushed through a below-market sale that allowed them to receive their 200% return but left the other members with little to nothing. That, according to the Plaintiffs, constitutes a breach of the implied covenant of good faith and fair dealing . . .

The Delaware [LLC] Act permits parties to an LLC agreement to eliminate fiduciary duties that members or managers would otherwise owe to one another . . . That grant of authority reflects the LLC Act's policy "of giv[ing] the maximum effect to the principle of freedom of contract and to the enforceability of limited liability company agreements." But an LLC agreement "may not eliminate the implied contractual covenant of good faith and fair dealing." [See the Delaware LLC Act, §18-1101(c) — EDS.]

Applying the implied covenant [of good faith and fair dealing] is a "cautious enterprise," and the doctrine is "rarely invoked successfully." [It] applies only when one party "proves that the other party has acted arbitrarily or unreasonably, thereby frustrating the fruits of the bargain that the asserting party reasonably expected." A party's reasonable expectations are measured as of the time of contracting, and any implied terms must address "developments or contractual gaps that the asserting party pleads neither party anticipated." The Court will not rewrite a contract simply because a party now wishes it had gotten a better deal . . . Similarly, "fair dealing" here does not imply equitable behavior. The term "fair" is something of a misnomer here; it simply means actions consonant "with the terms of the parties' agreement and its purpose" . . . .

[T]he first step in evaluating an implied covenant claim is to determine whether the contract in fact contains a gap that must be filled. That is because the implied covenant applies only if the contract is silent as to the subject at issue. If the contract directly addresses the matter at hand, "[e]xisting contract terms control ... If, on the other hand, the express terms of the contract do not address the subject at issue, the Court must then consider whether implied contractual terms fill the gap ... [If the Court concludes] from what was expressly agreed upon that [a] ... negotiated ... provision directly [addresses the contested subject] and [that it has not] been violated, it is quite unlikely that a court will find that [an implicit contractual obliga-tion] ... "has been breached." ... The Court does not [apply] its own notions of justice or fairness. Instead, it asks what the parties themselves would have agreed to "had they considered the issue in their original bargaining positions at the time of contracting." ...

Here, the OA waives any fiduciary duties that Trumpet's members or man-agers would otherwise have owed one another. And the OA does not, by its terms, require the Board, once it has decided to sell Trumpet, to conduct an open-market process designed to achieve the highest value reasonably available for all of Trumpet's members. But, according to the Plaintiffs, that requirement should be read into the OA via the implied covenant of good faith and fair dealing. The first question, then, is whether the OA is "truly silent" as to how Trumpet could be marketed and sold. The Defendants point out that Trumpet's OA explicitly addresses the issue of how the company could be sold ...

I agree with the Defendants that the OA does not contain a gap as to how Trumpet could be marketed and sold. The OA is not silent ... it explicitly vests the Board with sole discretion as to the manner in which a sale is conducted, subject to the limitation that the company is ... sold to an unaffiliated third-party buyer. The Plaintiffs' reading of Section 8.06(a) — that it confers sole discretion only as to the structure or form of the transaction, not as to the sales process itself — is, to my mind, unreasonable. The plain ... meaning of that provision is that the Board can market the company in whatever manner it chooses. ...

[T]his Court has ... held that "if the scope of discretion is specified, there is no gap in the contract as to the scope of the discretion, and there is no reason for the Court to look ... to the implied covenant to determine how discretion should be exercised." ...

An unqualified grant of sole discretion presents an obvious problem: the party entitled to exercise that discretion may abuse it for self-interested rea-sons and thereby deprive the other party of the benefit of its bargain. That explains why some courts have applied the implied covenant to sole-discretion clauses. Here, however, the parties explicitly addressed the potential for self-dealing inherent in such clauses by providing that the Board does not retain sole discretion to sell the company to insiders. ...

Even if the Plaintiffs were correct that the OA contains a gap as to how Trumpet could be sold, their implied covenant claim must fail. That is because the Plaintiffs have offered no reason to believe that their reasonable expecta-tions were frustrated by the Defendants' conduct during the sales process. ... The goal of this inquiry is to infer the parties' reasonable expectations from the express terms of the contract. Yet the Plaintiffs have failed to point to any provision in the OA that suggests the parties would have proscribed the manner in which Trumpet was marketed and sold if the issue had come up at the time of contracting. In fact, the express terms of the contract suggest precisely the opposite — that the parties actually contemplated that Trumpet might be sold through private negotiation rather than an open-market process.…

In short, there is no reason to think that the obligation the Plaintiffs ask me to insert into the OA would advance "the purposes reflected in the express language of the contract."…

[Trumpet's] members agreed to a process that would enable investors to structure and time an exit at a very substantial premium to their investment, in a way that encouraged investment at the cost of fiduciary protections for earlier equity holders. Presumably, circumstances warranted these terms. Adding an auction sale requirement … that the parties themselves failed to bargain for would alter — not enforce — the deal actually struck. Moreover, the Defendants' conduct during the sales process was not arbitrary, unreasonable, or unanticipated in light of the deal just described; thus, there is nothing in the Complaint that might justify the use of the "limited and extraordinary legal remedy" of the implied covenant. It is [noteworthy] … that [t]here are no allegations of fraud or a kickback from the buyer. There is no indication that the Defendants acted from any incentive … other than their own self-interest manifest from the waterfall provision of the OA.… [t]he "perverse" incentive at the heart of this case — namely, the Defendants' interest in seeking a quick payout … regardless of the effect on Trumpet's other members — is clear from the distribution waterfall itself.

[I]t cannot have come as a surprise … that the Defendants would exercise their contractual rights to pursue a sale that benefited them at the expense of Trumpet's other members. That dooms the Plaintiffs' implied covenant claim … Plaintiffs … could easily have drafted language requiring the Board to implement a sales process designed to achieve the highest value reasonably available for all of Trumpet's members.…

For the foregoing reasons, the Defendants' Motion to Dismiss is granted.

NOTES AND QUESTIONS

1. The court refuses to imply a covenant to sell Trumpet to the highest bidder in an open auction. Why wouldn't HCP prefer such an auction since it would ensure it the highest price for its units?

2. The Chancery Court states that "[a]n unqualified grant of sole discretion presents an obvious problem [and] explains why some courts have applied the implied covenant doctrine to sole-discretion clauses. Here, however, the parties explicitly addressed the potential for self-dealing inherent in such clauses by providing that the Board does not retain sole discretion to sell the company to insiders." Why should "sole discretion" matter in applying the implied covenant doctrine?

3. The Delaware Supreme Court upheld the Chancery Court's final decision in *Miller*, but clarified that "the mere vesting of 'sole discretion' did not relieve the Board of its obligation to use that discretion consistently with the

implied covenant of good faith and fair dealing [and the] specific provisions addressed to conflict-of-interest transactions [have] relevance to the application of the implied covenant, but [do] not vitiate its application." This suggests the implied covenant is a live issue in "sole discretion" cases, but within a few months the court moved in the other direction in *Oxbow Carbon & Minerals Holdings, Inc. v. Crestview-Oxbow Acquisition, LLC,* No. 538, 2018, 2019 WL 237360 (Del. Jan. 17, 2019). After reading the short note on *Oxbow* below, do you think the implied covenant is still applicable in "sole discretion" situations?

In *Oxbow*, the plaintiffs (minority members in Oxbow Carbon LLC) sued to enjoin a sale of all Oxbow units. They argued that the sale price was less than they were promised by Oxbow's Operating Agreement, namely, 150 percent of their original investment. Defendants — larger minority members in Oxbow who purchased their units earlier than the plaintiffs — urged that the sale should proceed. They argued that although the OA was silent on the plaintiffs' rights in an exit sale, an implied covenant of good faith and dealing should fill this "gap." This, they pointed out, would accord plaintiffs the same price as all other members in the exit sale, after which they would separately receive a "top-off" payment that would assure them 150 percent of their original investment as the OA required. However, the Delaware Supreme Court held that the OA accorded Oxford's Board discretion over plaintiffs' rights when they acquired their units and such discretion did not create a "gap" to be filled. There was thus no basis for invoking the implied covenant. Indeed, the Board's actions indicated that it regarded the plaintiffs as regular members of Oxbow who were due 150 percent of their purchase price in an exit sale. Since plainiffs' units were indistinguishable from those of other members, a sale could occur only if it accorded *all members* 150 percent of their purchase price. As a practical matter, this undermined the sale because the plaintiffs bought in at a substantially higher price than others and hence paying all members 150 percent of what the plaintiffs paid for their units would result in an unrealistically high price for the LLC as a whole. This holding indicates the Delaware Supreme Court's reluctance to imply a covenant where an OA, negotiated between sophisticated parties, had designated a process or a decision-maker to decide an open issue and a decision had been reached accordingly. As the court states, "the implied covenant should not be used as 'an equitable remedy' for rebalancing economic interests" of sophisticated parties.'"

2.7.3   An Overview of the New Contractual Entities

An exhaustive inventory of the new contractual entities is beyond the scope of this Chapter. Apart from the modern LP and LLC, we mention only one other in passing. This is the limited liability partnership (or "LLP"), which as its name implies is a general partnership whose partners enjoy limited liability. The LLP statutes clearly intend to protect professionals such as lawyers, doctors, and accountants.[25] They limit liability only with respect to

---

25. See Christine Hurt, *The Limited Liability Partnership in Bankruptcy*, 89 Am. Bankr. J. 567 (2015).

partnership liabilities arising from the negligence, malpractice, wrongful act, or misconduct of another partner or an agent of the partnership not under the partners' direct control as well as for contractual debts. See, e.g., DRUPA, §15-306(c), in your statutory supplement.[26] In functional terms, these entities share several common features—allowing contractual flexibility (as noted above), permitting business planners to contract on the issue of limited liability, and granting entities the power to select into particular tax treatments.

QUESTION

Is it clearly a mistake for a law firm to organize as a general partnership when limited liability vehicles are now available? If not, what kinds of law firms might retain their general partnership status—or at least be at the end of the line to adopt an alternative limited liability status?

2.7.3.1   Contractual Flexibility

This Chapter began by observing that a traditional general partnership is largely contractual within the constraints of fiduciary duty and personal liability. The new contractual entities subject even these constraints to contract.[27] Sophisticated business actors evidently believe that detailed legal planning from the start is less risky on balance than relying on open-ended duties administered by courts of equity after disputes among co-owners and/or their managers emerge. No doubt this judgment depends in part on the value at stake, alternative means of deciding disputes, and the cost of sophisticated legal planning relative to the ability of courts to pass on complex business disputes after the fact—and, lest we forget—the costs of sophisticated legal representation in courts. A decision to prefer detailed contracting over equity is not necessarily an embrace of "the path trodden in the marketplace" over personal loyalty, as Cardozo's imagery suggests; it is often a preference for a well-marked path informed by prudence over uncertain trust. Given the detail and cumulative experience that well-lawyered LP, LLC, and LLP operating agreements embody, it should not surprise that they can be hundreds of pages in length and are the proprietary information of the parties involved. They are not filed with certificates of formation, which give limited

---

26. Virtually all states provide this kind of protection now. See Christine Hurt & D. Gordon Smith, Bromberg & Ribstein on LLPs, Revised Uniform Partnership Act, and the Uniform Limited Partnership Act T.3.1. (2d ed. 2018).

27. 6 Del. C. 18-1101. The power to customize fiduciary duties is found in the Delaware Revised Uniform Limited Partnership Act (governing LPs) and the Delaware Limited Liability Company Act (governing LLCs), which in 2004 clarified that partners' or members' fiduciary duties "may be expanded or restricted *or eliminated* by provisions in [the agreement] . . . provided, that [the agreement] may not eliminate the implied contractual covenant of good faith and fair dealing" (emphasis added).

information beyond formal notice of the name and good standing of the registered entity. Indeed, Delaware practitioners point to the confidentiality allowed by the Delaware LLC statute, which, unlike statutes in some other states, does not mandate a list of its initial managers or members to appear in its publicly registered Certificate of Formation.

Statutory authorization to contract on (or around) the fiduciary duties that investors and/or managers owe clearly extends the reach of contract. By contrast, the contractual consequences of replacing personal liability with limited liability is less obvious. All of the new contractual entities — LPs, LLCs, and LLPs — set limited liability as the default term in the relationship between entities and business creditors. On first glance this might seem like a naked transfer of risk from entity owners to creditors. And so it might be if creditors are, for example, tort victims. But in the usual case of business credit, the terms offered presumably reflect the credit risk. It may be that risk-averse entity owners and managers prefer to share this risk with business creditors, or it may be that unsecured business creditors derive little comfort from a right to share in the estates of bankrupt partners in a hypothetical future. Either way, both parties might prefer to limit their claims to fit the assets and expectations of their respective creditors. They are better off if the claims of unsecured business creditors are limited to business assets.

Of course, one can posit counter-examples. The simplest might be an entity with a handful of investors that seeks a large bank loan. Investor guarantees here might make a loan's terms less onerous or even decide whether it is approved at all. But there is a ready solution: LLC members or partners can personally guarantee the loan. That is, they can contract out of limited liability selectively. The reverse is less feasible. If the default were personal liability to business creditors, negotiating limited liability with a large and shifting stream of business creditors and documenting these arrangements to the satisfaction of the bank would be a herculean task.

It follows that a shift in the default from personal to limited liability expands contractual flexibility as much as the shift of fiduciary liability from a mandatory to a default regime. The LP provides an example of how this shift from personal to limited liability developed. LPs are generally governed by the Uniform Limited Partnership Act (ULPA) or the Revised Uniform Limited Partnership Act (RULPA). They were traditionally designed to allow two sets of owners to come together in a registered entity — "limited partners" who were passive investors and had limited liability and "general partners" who were active investors and incurred unlimited personal liability. However, from the mid-1970s, these general partners could themselves be, and typically were, limited liability entities such as corporations or limited liability companies making their unlimited liability an atavistic requirement. Early on, if limited partners exercised "control" in some way, they risked becoming de facto general partners as cases in the 1970s and 1980s occasionally so held. This is no longer the case with the demise of the so-called "control" test.[28] Therefore, in modern times, there are usually no individuals whose assets stand behind the LP's obligations, effectively making limited liability the default norm even

28. Over the past 30 years, RULPA has scuttled the "control" test as a trigger for imposing personal liability on limited partners who behave like general partners. Most recently, §303

for LPs. Although the control test is now an anachronism, most LP agreements vest virtually complete control of the enterprise in the hands of its general partners in order simply to centralize management of the business.

2.7.3.2   *Taxation*

The new contractual entities can now all receive the more favorable "partnership" pass-through tax treatment as long as they are not publicly traded. But this was not how things started out, and tracking the changes is important to understanding why certain entities are used more in some sectors than in others.

Prior to 1997, U.S. federal tax law imposed two tiers of tax on corporations under subchapter C of the Internal Revenue Code (IRC). See IRC §7704(a); Treas. Reg. §301.7701-2(b)(7). That is, the enterprise is taxed on its entity income, and its investors are taxed again at individual rates when that income is distributed. Because this resulted in double taxation, many owners were likely to prefer an alternative used for general partnerships — pass-through tax, where partnership income and losses are deemed to be those of the individual partners resulting in a single tier of tax.

LPs were and are popular with many business planners because they combined the tax treatment of partnerships (pass-through tax) with limited liability, giving them a tax advantage over the standard corporate form and a limited liability advantage over the general partnership. The LLC, on the other hand, faced a more challenging path to the pass-through tax treatment that was critical to its rise.

It began in the 1980s, when all LLC statutes were drafted with an eye toward qualifying for pass-through taxation under IRS regulations (repealed in 1997), which provided that an LLC would be taxed like a corporation if it possessed three or more of the following four corporate characteristics: (1) limited liability for the owners of the business, (2) centralized management, (3) freely transferable ownership interests, and (4) continuity of life. During this era, LLC drafters relied on failing the corporate resemblance test by lacking both free transferability of interests and continuity of life.

Limits on continuity of life took the form of requirements that LLCs involuntarily dissolve upon the happening of specified events. Restrictions on transfer took the form of a requirement that transferees of LLC interests not become members unless all or a specified percentage of remaining members consented, as provided in the LLC articles of organization. Transferees

---

of the 2001 RULPA states that a limited partner cannot be personally liable for partnership liabilities "even if the limited partner participates in the management and control of the enterprise." The Comment to §303 of the 2001 Uniform Act states: "This section provides a full, status-based liability shield for each limited partner. . . . In a world with LLPs, LLCs, and, most importantly, LLLPs, the control rule has become an anachronism. This Act therefore takes the next logical step in the evolution of the limited partner's liability shield and renders the control rule extinct." Although Delaware has not yet adopted the 2001 RULPA, the creation of LLLPs in Delaware grants partners in a limited partnership limited liability, even if they exercise control. See DRULPA §214(d).

not approved by remaining members obtain only the distribution rights of the transferor. See Uniform Limited Liability Company Act (ULLCA) §503; Delaware LLCA §18-702.

With the need to contort the entity to obtain favorable tax treatment, it is hardly surprising that LLCs grew slowly and were not as popular as LPs. However, in 1997, after nearly every state had adopted an LLC statute, the Internal Revenue Service (IRS) adopted new rules (known as "check the box" regulations) that abandoned the game of attempting to define a de facto corporation and scrapped the four-factor test. The new rules allow all unincorporated business entities (e.g., general and limited partnerships, LLCs, and LLPs) to *choose* whether to be taxed as partnerships or corporations. Read about these rules in your statutory supplement. See IRS Reg. §§7701-1 through 7701-3; IRS Notice 95-14, 1995-14 IRB 7 (proposing "check the box" rules). The test for double taxation is whether or not ownership interests of the firm are traded either on an established securities market, such as the New York Stock Exchange, or on a secondary market or equivalent, such as the NASDAQ Stock Market. (The blanket rule of double taxation for entities with publicly traded equity has special exceptions for mutual funds, real estate investment trusts, and other entities that satisfy tests in the tax code. For example, IRC §7704(c).)

LLCs now can combine pass-through treatment for federal income tax purposes with limited liability, participation in control by members (without loss of limited liability), free transferability of interests, and continuity of life. In addition, LLC statutes generally offer more flexibility than corporate statutes in the form of near-complete freedom to "opt out" of default rules. Thus, LLCs and LPs now are much closer in their key features than just 20 years ago, and this has undoubtedly contributed to the growing popularity of LLCs.[29]

2.7.3.3   *Where the New Contractual Entities Are Used*

Now that the new contractual entities are so much closer in their key features, a natural question is where do we see them being used and what explains those choices? Although things are fluid, there are some consistent patterns.

In particular, LPs remain the most popular choice for financial firms such as hedge funds, private equity firms, and venture capital firms. Much of this industry formed before the tax treatment of LLCs was on par with LPs which, of course, resulted in a preference for LPs. Once the industry gelled around the LP, the familiarity with it made it difficult to dislodge as a favorite.

---

29. By contrast, closely held corporations that seek pass-through tax treatment must comply with the ownership limitations of subchapter S of the IRC. LLCs and other unincorporated entities also enjoy federal tax advantages beyond those available even to S corporations, such as the ability to pass entity-level debt through to members for income tax purposes. See IRC §752. Subchapter S which still offers some benefits over LLCs and other unincorporated entities. "S corps" (but not LLCs or other firms taxed as partnerships) may participate in tax-free reorganizations with subchapter C corporations (which include all publicly held corporations). See IRC §1371(a). In addition, if managers of a new entity expect to sell stock to the public in the near future, incorporation may be the best choice, given that the IRC taxes all new publicly held businesses as corporations, and many start-ups encounter minimal taxes prior to going public.

Further, the LLC offers little obvious advantage over the LP given that limited partners — like LLC members — can now exercise control and keep limited liability. Moreover, at least two issues further entrench the LP for these firms.

First, limited partnership units can be distributed and traded on exchanges (although, as noted earlier, the LP might lose pass-through tax status if it does).[30] On the other hand, LLCs must generally be marketed as publicly traded partnerships before they can be publicly traded. Thus, we see that when private equity or investment management firms seek to "go public," they tend to do so as LPs, although the firms formed to conduct their operations tend to be LLCs. See, e.g., *Corwin v. KKR Financial Holdings, LLC* (Del. C.A. 629-1914 (September 15, 2015) (a holder of LLC units challenging on fairness grounds a merger between KKR LP and KKR, LLC, in which the LLC was acquired by the LP).[31]

Second, the LP is a fairly well recognized entity outside the U.S., which enhances its familiarity and acceptability to foreign investors (an important source of capital for these funds), foreign firms (which are popular investment targets), and foreign countries (where operations or marketing may occur). LLCs, however, are not that common outside the U.S., and the lack of global familiarity likely hinders their usage for these funds in part because of concerns over whether other jurisdictions will fully recognize them.

LLPs, on the other hand, appear popular for professional practices — law firms, accounting firms, medical practices — but not much beyond.[32] Of course, these are the sectors for which they were designed and thus this seems unsurprising. In New York, however, over time there has been a decline in LLP formations and a large increase in professional practices set up as Professional LLCs (PLLC — an LLC where all members are licensed professionals in the area of practice) and Professional Corporations (PC — a corporation where all shareholders are licensed professionals in the area of practice).[33] As of May 28, 2020, New York had 52,941 PCs, 31,103 PLLCs, and 4,572 LLPs.[34] Although PLLCs and LLPs are quite similar, it seems filing for a PLLC is easier than filing for an LLP.

The LLC has become more attractive ever since it could easily adopt pass-through taxation in 1997. It is beginning to encroach on the turf of the LP in

---

30. However, contractual entities in the oil & gas, real estate, and finance sectors can still be structured in ways to keep pass-through taxation under IRC §7704 because their operating income can be treated as "qualifying income" and grant them pass-through taxation. See Christine Hurt, *Extra Large Partnerships* (January 21, 2020) *in* Firm Governance: The Anatomy of Fiduciary Obligations in Business (Arthur Laby & Jacob H. Russell eds., Cambridge Univ. Press 2020 Forthcoming); BYU Law Research Paper No. 20-01. Available at SSRN: https://ssrn.com/abstract=3523375.

31. Owners can change the organizational form, but that is not costless, so that usually the initial choice sticks until some significant event leads to a change.

32. See Robert W. Hillman, *Organizational Choices of Professional Services Firms, an Empirical Study*, 58 Bus. L. 1387 (2003); Susan Saab Fortney, *Law as a Profession: Examining the Role of Accountability*, 40 Ford. Urb. L.J. 177 (2012).

33. Since 2017, professionals in New York, as in most states, cannot use the LLC, and instead they rely on PLLCs or other limited liability vehicles (e.g., LLPs). See *Jacoby & Meyers, LLP v. Presiding Justices*, 852 F.3d 178 (2d Cir. 2017). In a PLLC, the members are still personally liable for their own malpractice or the malpractice of those under their direct supervision.

34. New York Department of State, Division of Corporations, State Records and Uniform Commercial Code (as of 5/28/2020), https://data.ny.gov/Economic-Development/Active-Corporations-Beginning-1800/n9v6-gdp6.

areas such as real estate investment companies, active investment companies, construction, and the like.[35] The LLC is also becoming a popular choice for a variety of different sectors (a "jack-of-all-trades") because of the wide flexibility it provides combined with its limited liability, attractive tax treatment, and various management options. Of course, this wide flexibility raises concerns that members in LLCs may get weaker protection than their corporate peers. However, recent studies suggest that, although members usually opt out of fiduciary duties,[36] they typically replace them with contractual and other protections that may be as good (or perhaps better?).[37]

Finally, we note that, although virtually all states now sport statutes authorizing LLCs, Delaware still dominates the market in out-of-state LLC formations, albeit not yet to the extent that it dominates the market in corporate franchises. Quite small businesses tend to organize in the state of their principal's residence. But a 2012 study found that of "firms that have 5,000 or more employees, more than 62 percent are formed outside their home state, and of the latter, more than 95 percent are formed in Delaware."[38] These numbers appear to have increased over recent years.[39] The trend lines follow Delaware's overwhelming domination of the market for corporate charters, which we address in the next chapter. Indeed, Delaware's status as the dominant choice for incorporation of large enterprise in the U.S. — and the factors that support that status — doubtlessly enhances its attraction as a legal domicile for out-of-state LLCs. But why is Delaware so dominant in the market for corporate charters, and why are corporations the most popular choice of organizational form for large publicly traded businesses? We turn to these questions next.

QUESTION

Many venture capital (VC) and private equity funds are organized as limited partnerships with ten-year terms. The limited partners give money to the VC for ten years. The general partners pick the investments. The general partners get 2 percent of the total funds under management each year (sometimes negotiated down a bit), plus about 20 percent of the profits at

---

35. See Suren Gomtsian, *Contractual Mechanisms of Investor Protection in Non-Listed Limited Liability Companies*, 60 Vill. L. Rev. 955, 965 (2016).

36. See Peter Molk, *How Do LLC Owners Contract Around Default Statutory Protections?*, 43 J. Corp. L. 24, 27 (2016).

37. See id.; Suren Gomtsian, *The Governance of Publicly Traded Limited Liability Companies*, 40 Del. J. Corp. L. 207, 212-216 (2015).

38. Jens Dammann & Mattias Schündeln, *Where Are Limited Liability Companies Formed? An Empirical Analysis*, 55 J. L. & Econ. 741 (2012). Another study also found that among closely held LLCs with more than 50 employees and formed outside their home state, 61 percent were in Delaware. See Bruce H. Kobayashi & Larry E. Ribstein, *Delaware for Small Fry: Jurisdictional Competition for Limited Liability Companies*, 2011 U. Ill. L. Rev. 91 (2011).

39. See Gomtsian, *supra* note 37, at 1002-1003.

the end of the ten-year term, or on another agreed upon withdrawal date. These funds can be huge, sometimes reaching $10 billion or more. Given that the limited partners exercise no control, what factors protect them from exploitation by the general partners?

THE CORPORATE FORM

3.1 INTRODUCTION TO THE CORPORATE FORM

The corporation is the form of choice for large privately-owned and state-owned enterprises around the world. Until fairly recently, the corporation could be described as the answer to the contracting problems of a UPA-style general partnership. For the individual partner, these included personal liability, the expectation of active participation, and the inability to transfer control (as opposed to economic rights) to a third party or heir. For the partnership as a business, the parallel problems ranged from vulnerability to dissolution that discouraged large fixed investment to collective management that increased decision-making costs and fostered instability. The legal characteristics that define the corporate form are strong counterpoints to the generic weaknesses of partnership. These attributes are:

1. legal personality with indefinite life
2. limited liability for shareholders
3. free transferability of shares
4. centralized management, typically in the form of a board of directors that is
5. appointed by equity investors[1]

To this short list of corporate features one might also add "capital lock-in," or the inability of minority shareholders to reclaim their invested

---

1. A similar list may be found in Robert Charles Clark, *Corporate Law* 4-24 (1986) and, prior to 1997, in the tax law. See Rev. Rul. 88-76 (1988) (recognizing pass-through taxation for certain LLCs). All commercial jurisdictions have at least one statutory form with these five features as default options. Indeed, legal historians use a similar list of features for the large joint stock trading companies of the seventeenth century. See, e.g., Ron Harris, *Going the Distance: Eurasian Trade and the Rise of the Corporation 1400-1700*, pp. 251-254 (2020). However, recent scholarship argues that, at least in Brazil, even when all of the features are present on paper, there may be forces (e.g., business practice, other laws, enforcement) that may blunt or undermine the applicability of these features. See Mariana Pargendler, *How Universal Is the Corporate Form? Reflections on the Dwindling of Corporate Attributes in Brazil*, 58 Colum. J. Transnat'l L. 1 (2019).

capital by forcing a distribution or a dissolution over the objection of a corporation's board of directors and the limited ability of corporate fiduciaries to opt out of the duty of loyalty (although that is changing — see Chapter 8).

Like most short lists, the hallmark features of the corporation — or the "company" — should not be misunderstood. As Chapter 2 makes clear, all of the functional features of the corporate form can be replicated in a contractual entity form today. As a historical matter, the corporation came into its own as a response to the limitations of the partnership for financing increasingly capital-intensive enterprises. But the flexibility of modern business organizations makes any list of canonical corporate features over-inclusive.[2] Legal planners structured corporation-like contractual entities well before 1800 and used the common law trust to evade restrictions on the use of the corporation at the turn of the twentieth century.[3] Our short list of legal features references the corporation in much the same way that the UPA default terms reference the partnership. And like the features of the partnership, they seem to complement one another and are often found together. Limited liability, for example, makes free transferability more valuable by reducing the costs associated with transfers of interest. (The value of shares is independent of the assets of their owners.) Free transferability permits the development of large capital (equity or stock) markets, which are also advanced by the presence of centralized management. (Again, if I must learn about how to manage a business in order to invest in it, I might not invest at all.) These characteristics interact to make the corporation an efficient legal form for enterprise organization, especially when investment opportunities require substantial capital and complex operations benefit from specialized management.

2. The Tax Cuts and Jobs Act of 2017 provides a remarkable illustration of how easily functional enterprises can shapeshift between statutory entity forms. Before the Act, some enormous publicly traded private equity enterprises were formally structured almost entirely as interconnected limited partnerships. After the 2017 Act made the corporate form more tax efficient, they restructured most of these LPs as corporations without meaningfully altering the economic ownership and control rights among related entities. Typically, they created a new corporation and executed a one-to-one transfer of public investors ownership rights from the LP to the new corporation. Then, the corporation invested directly in the LP in exchange for a managing interest. But the catch is that the new corporation also issued special non-economic voting shares to the original LP owners, allowing these owners to retain control of the business while keeping their financial interest in the underlying LP (which could be converted into public equity). This allowed the original LP owners simultaneously to take advantage of the pass-through taxation benefits of the LP and the liquidity and greater access to capital of the corporation. See KKR group and Carlyle group proxy statements in 2018 and 2019.

3. See John D. Morley, *The Common Law Corporation: The Power of the Trust in Anglo-American Business History*, 116 Colum. L. Rev. 2145 (2016); Timothy W. Guinnane, Ron Harris, Naomi Lamoreaux & Jean-Laurent Rosenthal, *Ownership and Control in the Entrepreneurial Firm: An International History of Private Limited Companies*, Yale University Economic Growth Center Discussion Paper #959, December 2007.

3.1.1   Some Analytical Distinctions

Although most corporations possess the "characteristic" legal features of the corporate form, there are important functional distinctions among corporations. One lies between "public" corporations and "private" corporations (which are often described as "closely held," or "close," corporations). A second distinguishes between corporations that are controlled by a single shareholder or group of affiliated persons ("controlled corporations") and corporations that lack a controlling shareholder(s). In the latter case, practical control over the affairs of the corporation often resides with the company's managers.

3.1.2   Public, Private, and Close Corporations

In the U.S., public corporations are those that must register their shares under the federal securities laws and comply with the numerous disclosure and governance rules promulgated by the Securities Exchange Commission ("SEC"). Virtually all companies with actively traded shares are public, although stock in small or unsuccessful public companies may cease to trade actively in the market. Most of the largest U.S. corporations are public. By contrast, private corporations escape SEC regulation and are only subject to state corporation law. The vast majority of private companies are small, but the converse does not hold. Some of America's largest enterprises are also private corporations with estimated values in the tens of billions of dollars.[4] Finally, the terms "closely held" and "close corporation" are often used as synonyms for "private corporation." These categories differ principally in emphasis. "Closely held" suggests that there are few shareholders and may also hint that these entities are "incorporated partnerships" in which the legal roles of shareholder, director, and officer overlap. Alternatively, the shareholders of close corporations may choose to contract out of key corporate default terms. Their charters (or shareholder agreements) may restrict share transfers, allow individual shareholders to force the sale of the business, or, by means of personal guarantees, commit shareholders to personal liability for corporate debts.

Whether a closely held business is structured as a corporation or an alternative contractual entity depends primarily on tax objectives and secondarily on transaction costs. Organizing a small business as a no-frills corporation has some advantage over forming a partnership or LLC of comparable sophistication insofar as corporate statutes supply more structure and require less drafting. Nevertheless, the market share of LLCs continues to grow among small business at the expense of other forms.

---

4. We have encountered one such corporation in the first case in Chapter 1 of this Book, namely, Cargill, Inc., which is now estimated to be worth well over $100 billion. See *Jensen Farms Co. v. Cargill, Inc., supra,* at p. 9. Today, 23 descendants of William Wallace Cargill, who founded the company in 1865, own 88 percent of the company. See Hillary Hoffower, "The 28 richest billionaire families in America, ranked," *Business Insider,* July 31, 2019.

3.1.3   Controlled Corporations

The second analytical distinction relates to the corporation's ownership structure — how a company's stock is held and who controls its voting rights. In some corporations, a single shareholder or group of affiliated shareholders exercises control through its power to appoint the board (these are termed "controlled corporations"). Where there is no such person or group in an actively traded corporation, control is said to be "in the market." In theory, anyone might buy enough stock in the market to control these companies, but until they do, no one exercises control. Buying control is not simple in fact, a topic addressed in Chapters 11 and 13. Nevertheless, control is in the market for most large public corporations in the United States and a few other countries today.[5] And if control is in the market, one would expect a company's directors and managers to exercise considerable autonomous influence over its strategic direction.[6]

Most major problems in corporation law arise from conflicts between "outside" investors, who lack power, and "insiders," who control the company's assets, whether as controlling shareholders or as autonomous managers. To state the obvious, powerful insiders who are not constrained by law, morality, or incentives often seek to increase their share of an enterprise's net returns. In controlled corporations, tensions between public and controlling shareholders arise most clearly in self-dealing transactions or appropriations of corporate opportunities (both addressed in Chapter 8). Where corporations have no controllers, parallel tensions arise between shareholders as a class and corporate management. They emerge most clearly in the areas of executive compensation, insider trading, and contests for corporate control. (See Chapters 9, 13, and 14.)

3.2   CREATION OF A FICTIONAL LEGAL ENTITY

The corporation is considered a separate person in the eyes of the law. This seemingly mundane legal characteristic is extraordinarily important. Consider, for example, the simple act of acquiring a plot of land. As a buyer, the corporation, acting through its authorized agents, may sign a binding contract, close a sale, and so take title in its own name. Thereafter, it may deal with the acquired property as its board of directors deems expedient. Because its principal investors need not execute the transaction or even agree to it, the information and coordination costs of closing the transaction are minimal.

5. See Rafael La Porta, Florencio Lopez-de-Silanes, Andrei Schleifer & Robert W. Vishny, *Corporate Ownership Around the World*, 54 J. Fin. 471 (1999).

6. In the U.S., at least, ownership concentration at widely-held, publicly-traded firms is increasing due to growing holdings and voting power exercised by institutional investors and asset managers. One might think of this as an intermediate point on the spectrum between diffusely held and controlled corporations. We will return to this in more depth in Chapters 6 and 13.

Consider, too, the way in which a corporation's ability to own assets as a legal entity enables it to enter into contracts, such as bank loans. Creditors need to know what stands behind any borrower's promise to pay interest and principal. Enabling corporations to own assets — including businesses — delimits the pool of assets upon which corporate creditors can rely for repayment. If there were no separate corporate entity, a large creditor would be forced to investigate the asset holdings and creditworthiness of all of the joint venturers — i.e., the company's shareholders — on the loan. Thus, the doctrinal fiction of an artificial entity vastly reduces the costs of contracting for credit.[7]

In addition to economizing on the monitoring costs of creditors, the status of the corporation as a fictive legal entity allows it to have an indefinite "life." This enhances the stability of the corporate form. Even without complex drafting, the death or departure of a "principal" need not disturb the operation of a corporation, as it would that of a partnership. Entity status, although seemingly pedestrian, is vital to business continuity, and it also supports the other corporate characteristics of tradable shares, centralized management, and limited liability.

If a defining legal characteristic of the corporation is legal personality, one may sensibly ask in what ways does its legal personality differ from that of natural persons? Do the constitutional protections that limit the extent of governmental power vis-à-vis natural persons extend to corporations? A landmark 1886 opinion of the United States Supreme Court is generally interpreted as providing the precedential basis for the view that corporations are "citizens" and qualify for protections guaranteed by the Fourteenth Amendment to the United States Constitution. See *Santa Clara County v. Southern Pacific Railroad Co.*, 118 U.S. 394 (1886). So, for example, should the Constitution bar taking corporate property without just compensation? Does this fictional person merit the same constitutional right to unencumbered political speech as a natural person? See *Citizens United v. FEC*, 540 U.S. 93 (2010). Such questions are beyond our scope here. Nevertheless, their inherent importance is such that we encourage readers to explore them further.[8]

---

7. See Henry Hansmann & Reinier Kraakman, *The Essential Role of Organizational Law*, 110 Yale L.J. 387 (2000). Evolution of the tenancy in partnership, which we addressed in Chapter 2, also reduces the costs of contracting with partnerships. Thus, the transactional benefits addressed here arise principally from the status of the corporation as an entity with legal personality. The status of corporations as legal personalities able to own and contract in their own names is basic. The legal entity status of partnerships was hotly contested during the drafting of the UPA (1914). Today, of course, contractual entities are legal entities and enjoy the same property and contract rights as corporations do. Should they also share the limited "personal" protections under the Bill of Rights that corporations enjoy? Should it matter today that partnerships were not persons let alone "citizens" when the Bill of Rights was adopted?

8. Analogous questions arise in the interpretation of statutes with constitutional overtones. *Burwell v. Hobby Lobby Stores, Inc.*, 573 U.S. 682 (2014), is the principal case in point. At issue in *Hobby Lobby* was whether a for-profit corporation could refuse health care insurance coverage for contraceptives as mandated by the Department of Health Resources and Services Administration on freedom of religion grounds, either under the First Amendment or the Religious Freedom Restoration Act ("RFRA"). The Supreme Court held that the corporation was a "person" entitled to RFRA's protections since providing contraceptive coverage would have violated its shareholders' religious convictions. It is noteworthy that the corporation was closely held by a religious family whose beliefs pervasively influenced its business practices. The Court did not reach Hobby Lobby's constitutional argument.

3.2.1   A Note on the History of Corporate Formation

Today, anyone can create a corporation as a matter of right — quickly and inexpensively. This was not always so. U.S. law evolved from a system in which incorporation was a privilege granted by state legislatures to one in which the right to incorporate became freely available and easily customized. Its development helps to put the regulation of the corporate form in perspective.

Before the nineteenth century, creating a corporation was seen as a significant public act to be undertaken only to achieve a special public advantage. Indeed, in the England of the seventeenth and eighteenth centuries, corporations were formed chiefly for political or charitable purposes rather than for business ones. As J. Willard Hurst observes, "[T]he first English treatise on corporations [published in 1794] has little to say, and scant authority to cite, concerning use of the corporation for economic enterprise."[9] Thus, we can safely pass over the law of royally chartered English joint-stock companies and begin with American corporation law, which branched out early in the nineteenth century to reflect a distinctly American mix of social forces and ideologies.

3.2.1.1   *Federal-State Division of Jurisdiction*

In the United States, the creation of corporations has from our earliest days been seen as requiring governmental action. The states were held to have reserved the sovereign power to form corporations when they joined the federal union.[10] While the national government also gained the power to form corporations pursuant to its delegated powers, the internal regulation of business corporations was, in general, a matter governed by state law from the Republic's beginning. Specifically, under the so-called internal

---

9. See James Willard Hurst, *The Legitimacy of the Business Corporation in the Law of the United States, 1780-1970,* at 3 (1970); Edwin M. Dodd, *Dogma and Practice in the Law of Associations,* 42 Harv. L. Rev. 977 (1929). Curiously, all corporation-like entities in Continental Europe with the power to own assets and contract in their own name prior to the seventeenth century appear to have been what we would today term "nonprofit corporations." They include the Roman *collegia* as well as the monasteries, charitable institutions, and religious orders of the Middle Ages.

10. During the constitutional debates, Madison twice proposed that the federal government be given the power to grant corporate charters, but each proposal was defeated. James Madison, *Journal of the Federal Convention,* 549-550 (E. Scott ed., 1893); James Madison, *The Debates in the Federal Convention of 1787,* at 420, 557, 563-564, 570 (Gaillard Hunt & James Scott eds., 1920). The federal power to grant such charters is restricted to those that are necessary and proper to accomplish some expressly granted power, such as the power "to coin money and regulate the value thereof." U.S. Const. art. I, §8. It is a fundamental characteristic of our federalism that the various states have reserved the power to form corporations.

affairs doctrine, the law of the state of incorporation governs the internal affairs of a corporation, including such matters as who votes, on what, and how often.[11]

3.2.1.2   *Special Acts of Incorporation*

In the earliest years of our Republic, state legislatures established corporations by passing individual acts of incorporation ("special acts"), which constituted certain named persons as a corporation, with specific enumerated powers, for a stated term. At first, these corporations were typically formed in order to address public needs, such as transportation or infrastructure.[12]

Demand for incorporation grew with the American economy in the early nineteenth century. Supply, however, was restricted by the system of special acts. The task of enacting special bills for corporations became a heavy burden for state legislatures. More important, rationing the incorporation power by means of special acts became increasingly controversial for two reasons.[13] The first was the suspicion that legislatures were creating artificial entities that would in time come to dominate the social landscape.[14] The second basis of criticism of the special chartering system was the more reasonable claim that it corrupted public life by opening the legislature to the possibility of favoritism. The rich or well-connected could, by one technique or another, get a corporate franchise that might otherwise be denied.

---

11. *CTS Corp. v. Dynamics Corp. of America*, 481 U.S. 69, 94 (1987); *Hart v. General Motors Corp.*, 129 A.D.2d 179, 183-184, 517 N.Y.S.2d 490, 492-493 (1987); *Draper v. Gardner Defined Plan Trust*, 625 A.2d 859, 864-868 (Del. 1993).

12. Professor Hurst reports that, "of the 317 separate-enterprise special charters from 1780 to 1801 in the states, nearly two-thirds were for enterprises concerned with transport (inland navigation, turnpikes, toll bridges); another 20 percent were for banks or insurance companies; 10 percent were for the provision of local public services (mostly water companies); and less than 4 percent were for general business corporations." Hurst, *supra* note 9, at 17.

13. Lawrence M. Friedman, *A History of American Law*, 197 (1985).

14. This possibility was deeply upsetting to the egalitarian sensibility of the Jacksonian Democrats of the early to mid-nineteenth century. One critic in 1833, for example, published the view that, "[a]gainst corporations of every kind, the objection may be brought that whatever power is given to them is so much taken from either the government or the people. . . . [T]he very existence of monied corporations is incompatible with equality of rights. . . ." (William M. Gouge, *Short History of Paper Money and Banking in the United States*, 17 (2d ed. 1835). See also Bray Hammond, *Banks and Politics in America from the Revolution to the Civil War*, 54-63 (1957). This first level of criticism tended to conflate the legislative grant of a monopoly franchise with the legislative grant of a corporate franchise. While these two types of franchise may often have been awarded together — as in the case of banks, railroads, or ferries — with respect to increasingly important mercantile or manufacturing businesses, they were not logically tied to one another. See Hurst, *supra* note 9, at 33-42.

3.2.1.3   General Incorporation Statutes

General laws of incorporation, under which the corporate form would be equally available to all citizens through a uniform administrative process, unburdened the legislative process and removed a source of corruption.[15] Although other states permitted incorporation early on for limited purposes,[16] New York led the way in 1811 with the first broadly available incorporation statute.[17] Connecticut followed in 1837 with a general statute that allowed incorporation for "any lawful purpose." Nevertheless, these early statutes failed to slow the flood of special incorporation acts. It was not until 1845, when Louisiana adopted a constitution that banned special corporations (except for political or municipal purposes), that an effective antidote to special legislative incorporation was found.[18] The movement toward exclusive general laws governing incorporation remained the dominant issue of nineteenth-century American corporation law until the 1880s, by which time general acts of incorporation had become the norm.

3.2.1.4   The Erosion of Regulatory Corporate Law

If the dominant corporate law story of the nineteenth century is the movement toward general acts of incorporation, the dominant story of the twentieth century is the movement from the general statutes with mandatory governance terms to today's statutes, which are largely free of substantive regulation. Corporate managers and controlling shareholders drove this process. The fact that corporate law is state law in the United States, rather than federal, gave those who sought a more "liberal" corporate law an important means to achieve their objective at the beginning of the twentieth century. Chartering states that attracted new incorporations reaped franchise fees (a tax levied on the privilege of forming and maintaining a corporation) and their lawyers earned legal fees and attracted new clients.

Of course, this evolution was not driven exclusively by the special interests of corporate managers and controlling shareholders. Larger forces were also at work. The arrival of a freely accessible corporate form tended to complement (or, if you prefer, was driven by) the same forces in the economy that promoted the development of complex new forms of industrial organization. Especially during the last quarter of the nineteenth century, the United States experienced phenomenal economic growth. Burgeoning populations,

15. See, e.g., Henry N. Butler, *Nineteenth Century Jurisdictional Competition in the Granting of Corporate Privileges*, 14 J. Legal Stud. 129 (1985).
16. North Carolina, in 1795, and Massachusetts, in 1799, enacted such statutes for canal companies or aqueducts. See E. Merrick Dodd, *American Business Corporations Until 1860*, at 228 (1954).
17. Laws N.Y. ch. 47 (1811).
18. *Christopher v. Brusselback*, 302 U.S. 500, 502-503 (1938); *Bernheimer v. Converse*, 206 U.S. 516, 528-529 (1907); *Keehn v. Hodge Drive-It-Yourself, Inc.*, 64 N.E.2d 117, 120 (Ohio 1945).

enormous infrastructural investments (railroads, telegraph lines, etc.), and rapidly evolving technologies created large markets and large economies of scale and scope, and thus opportunities for large-scale enterprise that favored the corporate form. In addition, the evolution of a new class of managers and the rise of liquid markets for stock favored the emergence of large corporate structures that could capture the new financial and technical economies.[19]

New Jersey began the process of liberalizing incorporation statutes and rapidly attracted new incorporations as a result. By 1894, one commentator reported, "New Jersey is a favorite state for incorporation. Her laws seem to be framed with a special view to attracting incorporation fees and business fees . . . and she has largely succeeded."[20] New Jersey's statute contained many innovations, but among the most important was that it authorized corporations to own the stock of other corporations.[21] This permitted the holding company structure, which, in turn, made possible corporate joint ventures and networks of corporations related by ownership, sometimes called corporate groups.

States liberated the corporate form in other ways as well. Corporations could now have perpetual (or, more accurately, indefinite) existence. They could do business anywhere. They could be organized for any lawful purpose (with the general exception of banking). Capital requirements became more flexible: Corporations were not required to have a stated minimum capital or a limit on either their authorized equity capital or the debt they could issue. They could amend their certificates of incorporation, own and vote stock of other corporations, own land without limit, and merge with other corporations. While these changes may seem modest today, they raised howls of protest at the time.

States began to compete in a "race" to deregulate.[22] In 1890, New York abandoned its limitation on maximum authorized capital and, to a limited extent, permitted intercorporation ownership of stock.[23] Nevertheless, these

19. Alfred D. Chandler, *The Visible Hand: The Management Revolution in American Business* (1977); Alfred D. Chandler, *Scale and Scope: The Dynamics of Industrial Capitalism* (1990).

20. Cook on Stock and Stockholders 1604-1605 (1894), quoted in *Liggett Co. v. Lee*, 288 U.S. 517, 558 n.34 (Brandeis, J., dissenting).

21. General Corporation Law of New Jersey, §51 (1896).

22. One of the most long-standing and voluminous debates in corporate law is whether this regulatory competition constitutes a "race to the top" or a "race to the bottom." The first commentators on opposing sides of the debate were former SEC Commissioner William L. Cary and Ralph K. Winter. Compare William T. Cary, *Federalism and Corporate Law: Reflections upon Delaware*, 83 Yale L.J. 663 (1974) (describing "this race for the bottom, with Delaware in the lead") with Ralph K. Winter, Jr., *State Law, Shareholder Protection, and the Theory of the Corporation*, 6 J. Legal Stud. 251 (1977) (arguing for a "race to the top"). For the leading modern commentators, compare Lucian Arye Bebchuk, *Federalism and the Corporation: The Desirable Limits on State Competition in Corporate Law*, 105 Harv. L. Rev. 1435, 1440 (1992) (arguing that "state competition produces a race for the top with respect to some corporate issues but a race for the bottom with respect to others") with Roberta Romano, *The Genius of American Corporate Law* 16 (1993) (stating that "the evidence supports the view that states do compete for the chartering business" and that this "benefits rather than harms shareholders").

23. New York Business Corporation Law, ch. 567 §12 (1890); see also *Liggett*, 288 U.S. at 560-565.

changes failed to stem the flow of incorporation to New Jersey, and in 1892, New York amended its statute further to permit corporate ownership of stock without limitation. Other states soon got into the act. In 1899, Delaware adopted what was, in essence, the New Jersey statute as its general law of incorporation.[24] Although Maine and West Virginia did so as well, it was tiny Delaware that took the lead. When New Jersey Governor and future U.S. President Woodrow Wilson cracked down on New Jersey's permissive corporate code in the 1910s, companies flocked to Delaware. Delaware quickly gained a dominant share and never looked back: By 1965, 35 percent of companies listed on the New York Stock Exchange (NYSE) were incorporated in Delaware; by 2000, approximately half of all NYSE companies were incorporated in Delaware, and by 2019, over half of these firms (and two-thirds of the Fortune 500) were incorporated in Delaware.[25]

As corporation statutes evolved over the twentieth century, most of the remaining mandatory regulation of internal corporate governance gradually fell away. More technical, but equally important, liberalizations include the disappearance of shareholder preemptive rights,[26] the broadening of lawful consideration for stock, the disappearance of par value as a minimum consideration for stock, and the repeated liberalization of merger law. The typical corporation statute of today, such as the Delaware General Corporation Law (DGCL), is a nonregulatory "enabling" statute with few mandatory features. However, complementary evolutionary phenomena should also be mentioned. As corporate management's freedom to act grew under the enabling approach of modern statutes, and as shareholders of public companies also grew more numerous and disaggregated, courts came to give greater weight to the judicially created "fiduciary duty" of corporate directors and officers, and the federal government began to regulate public companies under the aegis of securities law, which has some of the rule-like, mandatory flavor of early corporation law. However, even this equilibrium appears to be changing as the rise of institutional investors reshapes governance. See generally Chapters 6, 13, and 14 for greater discussion.

24. See Note, *Little Delaware Makes Bid for the Organization of Trusts*, 33 Am. L. Rev. 418 (1899).

25. See Adam O. Emerich, William Savitt, Sabastian V. Niles & S. Iliana Ongun, *The Corporate Governance Review: United States* (9th ed.), Law Business Research, London, 2019. Available at SSRN: https://ssrn.com/abstract=3399676. For discussion on the Fortune 500, see https://corp.delaware.gov/aboutagency/.

In addition to the arguments canvassed in the "race to top (or bottom)" literature, there are many other reasons suggested by scholars for Delaware's success in the competition for corporate charters including the indeterminacy of its law (see Ehud Kamar, *A Regulatory Competition Theory of Indeterminacy in Corporate Law*, 98 Col. L. Rev. 1208 (1998)) and how Delaware insulates its corporate law-making from partisanship (see Ofer Eldar & Gabriel Rauterberg, *Is Corporate Law Non-Partisan?* (Draft, 2020).

26. Preemptive rights (conferred on shareholders either by statute or in the documents creating the corporation) allow a shareholder to buy stock in any future corporate offering of new stock, up to such amount as is required to permit a shareholder to maintain his or her proportionate interest in the corporation.

3.2.2   The Process of Incorporating Today

The process of incorporating today is nicely reflected in §§2.01 to 2.04 of the Model Business Corporation Act, Revised 2016 (MBCA). A flesh-and-blood individual (or other entity, since corporations and partnerships may themselves form new corporations) called an "incorporator" signs the requisite documents and pays the necessary fees. While incorporators create corporations initially, they are often clerks or secretaries who act in a purely ministerial capacity.[27] The incorporator drafts (or has prepared) and signs a document called either the articles of incorporation (under the MBCA) or the certificate of incorporation (under the DGCL). In both instances, this foundational document is colloquially termed the corporation's "charter." The articles of incorporation state the purpose and powers of the corporation and define all of its special features, with great flexibility being afforded to the designer of the firm's legal structure. Today, the purposes of the corporation are typically put forth in an extremely broad statement, such as "to engage in any lawful act or activity for which corporations may be organized under this title." DGCL §102(a)(3). The company charter will contain any customized features of the new enterprise, such as a complex capital structure or customized voting rights. More often, however, the charter is a generic document with few special features. After it is duly executed, the charter is filed with a designated public official, usually the secretary of state. This filing also identifies the corporation's principal office within the state or, if there is none, the name of an agent in the state upon whom process may be served.

Upon filing, a fee will be due, naturally. In Delaware, the fee may be calculated in part as a function of how many shares the new corporation is authorized to issue. This technique is a crude form of price discrimination because bigger businesses will tend to issue more shares and thus will be willing and able to pay a higher fee.[28] In Delaware, the corporation's legal life begins when its charter is filed. DGCL §106. After the articles are filed and the fee is paid, the secretary of state issues the corporation's charter, which is a copy of the articles attached to a certificate of good standing, signed by the secretary of state. In other jurisdictions, the corporation's existence begins only when the secretary of state issues a charter.

The first acts of business in a newly formed corporation are electing directors (if initial directors are not named in the charter), adopting bylaws, and appointing officers. These actions take place at an organizational meeting, which is called either by the incorporators, who elect the initial board of directors, or, when the initial board is named in the articles of incorporation, by the board members themselves. See DGCL §108; MBCA §2.05. Sample

---

27. Recognition of the ministerial nature of the incorporator's role is reflected in the fact that, while statutes formerly required three or more such persons, one is sufficient under current statutes.

28. See Marcel Kahan & Ehud Kamar, *The Myth of State Competition in Corporate Law*, 55 Stan. L. Rev. 679 (2002).

bylaws and minutes of an organizational meeting of the board of directors are included in your statutory supplement. See also MBCA §2.06.[29]

3.2.3   The Articles of Incorporation, or "Charter"

The articles of incorporation (or charter) may contain any provision that is not contrary to law. Modern American corporation statutes mandate only a few terms in the charter. The charter must, for example, provide for voting stock, a board of directors, and shareholder voting for certain transactions. Contractual freedom is, however, the overriding concept. Thus, the corporate charter will contain the most important "customized" features of the corporation, should there be any. If the corporation is to have a special or limited purpose, it will be stated here. If it is to have some governance oddity — say, that one class of stock will elect 75 percent of the board and a second class will elect the balance — this condition must be spelled out in the charter.

Additionally, the charter must name the original incorporators, state the corporation's name and (very broadly) its business, and fix its original capital structure. Thus, the charter defines how many shares and classes of shares the corporation will be authorized to issue and what the characteristics of those shares will be: Will all shares vote? On all issues? In one class or separately? Will any have enhanced voting rights? Will they have par value?[30] Be redeemable? Be convertible? Will they be cumulatively voted? Will any shares have a preference on liquidation? Will the board be given the power to issue preferred stock with whatever terms it deems expedient (so-called blank-check preferred)? All of these capital structure questions are appropriately answered in the charter and will be explained as we proceed.

Finally, the charter may establish the size of the board or include other governance terms, such as whether directors shall have concurrent one-year terms or staggered three-year terms,[31] and the procedures for removing directors from office.[32] Beyond such essentials, the charter may, as a legal matter, contain any provisions that are not in contravention of law. For example, it may even assign shareholders liability for corporate debts,[33] although this rarely happens.

---

29. Thirty states and the District of Columbia rely on the MBCA for this point. See https://corporations.uslegal.com/basics-of-corporations/state-corporation-laws/.

30. Par value stock — that is, stock with a stated face value — is now largely of historical interest only in U.S. corporation law. Historically, it represented an amount of capital that creditors could rely on having been originally contributed to the firm in exchange for its stock. Corporations could not, and still cannot, pay dividends from amounts in the capital account attributable to par value. The story of how and why this concept was eroded by U.S. law (while still taken seriously in many nations) is an interesting one. See generally Bayless Manning, *A Concise Textbook on Legal Capital* (1977).

31. See DGCL §141(d).

32. Id. §145(k).

33. Id. §102(b)(6).

3.2.4   The Corporate Bylaws

The bylaws are the least fundamental of the corporation's "constitutional" documents, which means they must conform to both the corporation statute and the corporation's charter.[34] Generally, bylaws fix the operating rules for the governance of the corporation. They establish, for example, the existence and responsibilities of corporate offices. If the certificate of incorporation does not mandate the size of the board of directors (which it rarely does) or the manner in which the size of the board is to be established, the bylaws will do so. The bylaws will also establish an annual meeting date or a formula by which such a meeting date will be fixed. They may empower an officer to call a stockholders' meeting, and they may establish procedures for the functioning of the board, such as the board's committee structure or quorum requirements.

Under some statutes, shareholders have the inalienable right to amend the bylaws.[35] Others limit this power to the board of directors.[36] Where shareholders are able to amend the bylaws, however, several questions remain. First, what voting rules apply to these amendments? Can directors overrule a shareholder amendment where the board possesses power to make bylaws itself, and how far can bylaws themselves limit the power to amend the bylaws? Because directors owe a fiduciary duty of loyalty to the corporation and its shareholders, courts have sometimes reviewed the directors' exercise of the power to modify and invalidate bylaws as an abuse of that power.[37] A problem of this type is most likely to arise where directors are arguably amending bylaws in order to protect their incumbency.

A question of current interest (and one that we will touch on in Chapter 6) is this: What limits, if any, restrict the topics that shareholder-initiated bylaws can legitimately govern? One might ask why anything should limit the shareholders in this way (other than their own agreement to such a limit in the corporate charter). This issue underscores the basic tension between the shareholders' powers and the board's power to manage the firm's business.

3.2.5   Shareholders' Agreements

Formal agreements among shareholders play an important part in the legal governance structures of many close corporations and in some controlled public corporations (although not often in widely-held public companies). Shareholders' agreements typically address such questions as restrictions on the disposition of shares, buy/sell agreements, voting agreements,[38] and agreements with respect to the employment of officers or the payment

---

34. Id. §109(b).
35. See DGCL §109(a).
36. See, e.g., 18 Okla. Stat. §1013 (2001).
37. E.g., *State ex rel. Brumley v. Jessup & Moore Paper Co.*, 77 A. 16 (Del. Ch. 1916).
38. See DGCL §218(c).

of dividends. Generally, the corporation is a party to these contracts. Thus, courts will specifically enforce these agreements where all shareholders are parties as well. But where some shareholders are not parties, specific enforcement — especially against the corporation — may turn on whether the agreement is fair to shareholders who were not signatories.[39]

Where the voting of corporate stock is the subject of a shareholders' agreement, the agreement may take an even more formal form. A voting trust is an arrangement in which shareholders publicly agree to place their shares with a trustee who then legally owns them and is to exercise voting power according to the terms of the agreement. This formal arrangement is subject to special statutory restrictions.[40]

3.3 LIMITED LIABILITY

We now turn to another fundamental characteristic of the corporate form: limited liability. Although the phrase is not quite accurate, long-time usage prevails over fussy correctness. Technically, neither corporations nor shareholders have limited liability. Corporations have unlimited liability, and shareholders, by reason of their shareholder status alone, have no liability for the debts or obligations of the corporation. Limited liability simply means that shareholders cannot lose more than the amount they invest (absent some special circumstances, discussed more fully later), unlike the general partner, who, under traditional principles, is legally a party to all partnership agreements and thus liable under them. Of course, limited liability is nothing more than a default term in the corporate form; a shareholder can undertake by contract to be a corporate guarantor. One empirical study finds that, among a sample of small corporations that filed Chapter 11 petitions in 1998, the owners had personally guaranteed the corporation's debt in 56 percent of the cases.[41]

In some ways, limited liability looks like the mirror image of entity status. After all, if the corporation *is* legally a separate person, why ought another legal person (a shareholder) be liable for its debts? While this notion has some surface appeal, it is not a functional argument and, historically, not

---

39. Recent work on shareholder agreements has two principal findings. First, Delaware courts appear to allow shareholders to do things in agreements that would be difficult to do (or prohibited) in charters and bylaws. In particular, shareholders can directly bargain over director appointments. Second, about 15 percent of firms going public in the study's sample have shareholder agreements (usually related to board composition) and these often aim to bind the corporation as well as shareholders. Other matters that regularly appear in shareholder agreements include veto rights on important decisions, restrictions on share transfer, and mandating arbitration of disputes between shareholders subject to the agreement. See Gabriel V. Rauterberg, *The Separation of Voting and Control: The Role of Contract in Corporate Governance*, Draft (2020), on file with authors.

40. Id. §218(a).

41. See Douglas Baird & Edward R. Morrison, *Serial Entrepreneurs and Small Business Bankruptcies*, 105 Colum. L. Rev. 8 (Table 17) (2005).

always a persuasive one. Separate entity status for corporations coexisted with "unlimited" shareholder liability for a substantial period — until the 1930s in California, for example. But limited liability ultimately became the default rule for corporations (as it is fast becoming for partnership-like business forms; see Chapter 2) for sound economic reasons. First, limited liability vastly simplifies the job of evaluating an equity investment. A corporate investor who would naturally be concerned about his own liability can, under a limited liability regime, ignore low-probability events that may bankrupt the firm and, without limited liability, would visit a large liability on her. Nor need she be concerned with the financial status of co-venturers (as in a partnership), since in no event will she end up being jointly and severally liable with her co-investors. These features encourage capital investment in equity securities. Second, the ability of the corporate form to segregate assets may encourage risk-averse shareholders to invest in risky ventures, such as biotech firms designing new medicines. Finally, limited liability may also increase the incentive for banks or other expert creditors to monitor their corporate debtors more closely.

The development of limited liability took time because it represented a radical break with the common law liability rules of agency and partnership. Shareholders only gradually won the protection of limited liability for private business ventures in the United States during the first half of the nineteenth century.[42] Great Britain established it later, with the Limited Liability Act of 1855.[43] Only gradually did limited liability come to be seen as a device that assisted people in arranging voluntary contractual relations. The change in attitude toward limited liability over the nineteenth century is suggested by the following two views. First, an excerpt from an 1824 editorial from *The Times* of London:

> Nothing can be so unjust as for a few persons abounding in wealth to offer a portion of their excess for the information of a company, to play with that excess for the information of a company — to lend the importance of their whole name and credit to the society [i.e., the company], and then should the funds prove insufficient to answer all demands, to retire into the security of their unhazarded fortune, and leave the bait to be devoured by the poor deceived fish.[44]

By contrast, about a century later, *The Economist* took a deeper view:

> The economic historian of the future may assign to the nameless inventor of the principle of limited liability, as applied to trading corporations, a place of honour with Watt and Stephenson, and other pioneers of the Industrial Revolution.

---

42. E. Merrick Dodd, *The Evolution of Limited Liability in American Industry: Massachusetts*, 61 Harv. L. Rev. 1351 (1948).

43. Recent historical scholarship suggests that although the law may have permitted limited liability by the mid-1800s, the reality was that limited liability, as we commonly understand it, did not become prevalent until the early twentieth century. See Ron Harris, *A New Understanding of the History of Limited Liability: An Invitation for Theoretical Reframing* (March 28, 2020). Available at SSRN: https://ssrn.com/abstract=3441083.

44. As quoted in Paul Halpern, Michael Trebilcock & Stuart Turnbull, *An Economic Analysis of Limited Liability in Corporate Law*, 30 U. Toronto L. Rev. 117 (1980).

The genius of these men produced the means by which man's command of natural resources has multiplied many times over; the limited liability company the means by which huge aggregations of capital required to give effect to their discoveries were collected, organized and efficiently administered.[45]

Setting aside the troubling problem of tort creditors (which we will come to shortly), the chief purpose of limited liability is to encourage investment in equity securities and thus to make capital more available for risky ventures.

Judge Frank Easterbrook and Daniel Fischel elaborate on these points in the following excerpt.

FRANK EASTERBROOK & DANIEL FISCHEL, LIMITED LIABILITY AND THE CORPORATION
52 U. Chi. L. Rev. 89, 94-97 (1985)

THE RATIONALE OF LIMITED LIABILITY

... The separation of investment and management requires firms to create devices by which these participants monitor each other and guarantee their own performance. Neither group will be perfectly trustworthy. Moreover, managers who do not obtain the full benefits of their own performance do not have the best incentives to work efficiently. The costs of the separation of investment and management (agency costs) may be substantial. Nonetheless, we know from the survival of large corporations that the costs generated by agency relations are outweighed by the gains from separation and specialization of function. Limited liability reduces the costs of this separation and specialization.

First, limited liability decreases the need to monitor [managers]. All investors risk losing wealth because of the actions of agents. They could monitor these agents more closely. The more risk they bear, the more they will monitor. But beyond a point more monitoring is not worth the cost.... Limited liability makes diversification and passivity a more rational strategy and so potentially reduces the cost of operating the corporation.

Of course, rational shareholders understand the risk that the managers' acts will cause them loss. They do not meekly accept it. The price they are willing to pay for shares will reflect the risk. Managers therefore find ways to offer assurances to investors without the need for direct monitoring; those who do this best will attract the most capital from investors....

Second, limited liability reduces the costs of monitoring other shareholders. Under a rule exposing equity investors to additional liability, the greater the wealth of other shareholders, the lower the probability that any one shareholder's assets will be needed to pay a judgment. Thus existing shareholders would have incentives to engage in costly monitoring of other shareholders to ensure that they do not transfer assets to others or sell to others with less

---

45. Id. (quoting *Economist*, Dec. 18, 1926).

wealth. Limited liability makes the identity of other shareholders irrelevant and thus avoids these costs.

Third, by promoting free transfer of shares, limited liability gives managers incentives to act efficiently.... So long as shares are tied to votes, poorly run firms will attract new investors who can assemble large blocs at a discount and install new managerial teams. This potential for displacement gives existing managers incentives to operate efficiently in order to keep share prices high.

Although this effect of the takeover mechanism is well known, the relation between takeovers and limited liability is not. Limited liability reduces the costs of purchasing shares. Under a rule of limited liability, the value of shares is determined by the present value of the income stream generated by a firm's assets. The identity and wealth of other investors is irrelevant. Shares are fungible; they trade at one price in liquid markets. Under a rule of unlimited liability, ... shares would not be fungible.... An acquiror who wanted to purchase a control bloc of shares under a rule of unlimited liability might have to negotiate separately with individual shareholders, paying different prices to each. Worse, the acquiror in corporate control transactions typically is much wealthier than the investors from which it acquires the shares. The anticipated cost of additional capital contributions would be higher to the [acquiror] than [to other shareholders]. This may be quite important to a buyer considering the acquisition of a firm in financial trouble, for there would be a decent chance of being required to contribute to satisfy debts if the plan for revitalization of the firm should go awry....

Fourth, limited liability makes it possible for market prices to impound additional information about the value of firms. With unlimited liability, shares would not be homogeneous commodities, so they would no longer have one market price. Investors would therefore be required to expend greater resources analyzing the prospects of the firm in order to know whether "the price is right"....

Fifth, as Henry Manne emphasized, limited liability allows more efficient diversification. Investors can minimize risk by owning a diversified portfolio of assets.... Diversification would increase rather than reduce risk under a rule of unlimited liability. If any one firm went bankrupt, an investor could lose his entire wealth. The rational strategy under unlimited liability, therefore, would be to minimize the number of securities held. As a result, investors would be forced to bear risk that could have been avoided by diversification, and the cost to firms of raising capital would rise.

Sixth, limited liability facilitates optimal investment decisions. When investors hold diversified portfolios, managers maximize investors' welfare by investing in any project with a positive net present value. They can accept [risky] ventures (such as the development of new products) without exposing the investors to ruin. Each investor can hedge against the failure of one project by holding stock in other firms....

Both those who want to raise capital for entrepreneurial ventures, and society as a whole, receive benefits from limited liability.... So long as the rule of liability is known, investors will price shares accordingly. The choice of an inefficient rule [of unlimited shareholder liability], however, will shrink the pool of funds available for investment in projects that would subject investors to risk. The increased availability of funds for projects with positive net values is the real benefit of limited liability.

QUESTION

Does limited liability raise a problem for tort claimants — and, if so, what might the law do to ameliorate this problem? Chapter 4 addresses this issue in more detail.

3.4   TRANSFERABLE SHARES

Corporate law everywhere provides that equity investors in the corporate entity legally own something distinct from any part of the corporation's property: They own a share interest. This share, or stock, is their personal legal property, and generally (i.e., absent special restrictions imposed by charter or contract), such a share may be transferred together with all rights that it confers.[46] Transferability permits the firm to conduct business uninterruptedly as the identities of its owners change, which avoids the complications of dissolution and reformation that can affect partnerships.

As Easterbrook and Fischel argue in the excerpt above, the transferability of shares is intimately tied to limited liability. Absent limited liability, the creditworthiness of the firm as a whole could change, perhaps fundamentally, as the identities of its shareholders changed. Consequently, the value of shares would be difficult for potential purchasers to judge. Perhaps more important, each seller of shares could impose a cost on her fellow shareholders by selling to a buyer with fewer assets. It is not surprising, therefore, that limited liability and transferable shares are complementary features of the corporate form. This is in contrast to the partnership form, which lacks both features.

Equally significant, the ability of investors to freely trade stock encourages the development of an active stock market. An active market, in turn, facilitates investment by providing liquidity and allowing the inexpensive diversification of the risk associated with any equity investment. These factors make investing in corporate stock more attractive to savers and so increase the ability of the firm to raise capital. For these reasons, all of the important jurisdictions provide for free transferability of shares as the default regime for at least one class of corporations (sometimes referred to as "open" corporations).

Free transferability is a default provision. If investors see value in agreeing to restrictions on transfer, all jurisdictions provide mechanisms for

---

46. This is the general effect. It is possible for the certificate of incorporation to create a type of stock that, upon transfer, has altered legal characteristics. However, this is rarely done.

permitting agreements to that effect. Sometimes this is done by means of a separate statute, such as the special European statutes for closely held (or close) corporations; sometimes it is done by providing for restraints on transferability as an option under a single general corporation statute, as in the United States.

Additionally (as Easterbrook and Fischel also point out), the free transferability of stock complements centralized management in the corporate form by serving as a potential constraint on the self-serving behavior of the managers of widely held companies.[47] If the stock market distrusts the current management of a company, its share price will fall, and its managers are more likely to be replaced—either because its existing shareholders will throw out the board of directors, or because an acquirer will find it financially attractive to take over the company. As we discuss in Chapter 13, the threat of a takeover can be an important motivator for incumbent managers. Antitakeover defenses that limit the ability of shareholders to sell their stock to would-be acquirors are controversial among scholars and other corporate governance experts, largely because these defenses restrict the power of the market to discipline managers by transferring control to a new management team.

3.5   CENTRALIZED MANAGEMENT

A great advantage of the corporate form is the creation of the institution of centralized management, which can achieve economies of scale in knowledge of the firm, its technologies, and markets. Under modern corporate law, shareholder designated boards of directors, not investors, are accorded the power to initiate corporate transactions and manage the day-to-day affairs of the corporation. But the powerful innovation of centralized management also gives rise to the principal problem of modern corporate governance for publicly-financed firms. Freed of the need to invest in information about the firm and protected by cheap diversification of risk, investors become rationally apathetic. Thus, among the foundational problems for modern corporate law is the determination of the set of legal rules and remedies most likely to ensure that these managers will strive to advance the financial interests of investors *without* unduly impinging on management's ability to manage the firm productively.

There are at least three aspects of this problem. First, what can the law do to encourage managers to be diligent, given that shareholders—not judges—choose the directors who designate managers? Second, how can the

---

47. Of course, partners in a general partnership have a different kind of protective "transfer" right that shareholders lack: the power to force dissolution and liquidation of the business. While free transferability is characteristic of corporate shares, it is not mandatory. Close corporations often restrict the free transfer of their stock, which U.S. corporate law allows as long as conspicuous notice appears on the face of the certificate evidencing the share of stock. See, e.g., DGCL §202.

law assist shareholders in acting collectively vis-à-vis managers, especially in the case of widely-held companies with many small shareholders? Corporate law cannot eliminate this "collective action problem," as it is termed, but the law can mitigate it by specifying when shareholder votes are required, what information they must be given,[48] and how they can vote in convenient ways that do not require physical attendance at a shareholders' meeting. Third, how can the law encourage companies to make investment decisions that are best for shareholders (and therefore, in most states of the world, beneficial for society as a whole)?

Corporate law attempts to mitigate the agency problem in a number of ways. Its main technique is to require, as a default rule, that management be appointed by a board of directors that is elected by the holders of common stock in the company. This centralized directorate structure is, to be sure, a basic feature not only of corporations, but also of large firms generally. (It is typical of accounting partnerships, for example, and even large law firms.) Nevertheless, the corporate form is unique in two respects: First, it makes the centralization of management power in the board a strong default option for firms organized as corporations; and second, by contrast, it vests more power in the board than even large partnerships commonly do. Consider, for example, the typical statutory formulation set forth in §141 of the DGCL:

> (a) The business and affairs of every corporation organized under this chapter shall be managed by or under the direction of a board of directors, except as may be otherwise provided in this chapter or in its certificate of incorporation.

As we previously stated, the details of the board's structure and decision-making procedure are found in a company's charter or bylaws. Generally, however, the board "acts" by adopting resolutions at duly called meetings that are recorded in the board's minutes. The board appoints a firm's officers and is therefore formally distinct from the operational managers of the company. Legally speaking, the corporate officers are agents of the company; on the other hand, corporate law often treats the board as if it were a quasi-principal of the company (although, of course, the board is often thought of as the *economic* agent of shareholders).

The formal distinction between a corporation's board and its management also permits a distinction between the approval of business decisions and their initiation and execution. As a practical matter, initiation and execution are the province of management, whereas monitoring and approval are the province of the board. This separation serves as a check on the quality of delegated decision making[49] and makes the board a convenient focus for control mechanisms based on the legal duties of directors.

The additional distinction between a corporation's board and its shareholders is, as we have already noted, principally a device for reducing the costs

48. Thus, for example, the Securities and Exchange Act requires that certain financial information be publicly filed periodically by covered firms and that the financial data be audited by an independent auditor.

49. See Eugene F. Fama & Michael C. Jensen, *Agency Problems and Residual Claims*, 26 J.L. & Econ. 327 (1983).

of corporate decision making. Between annual meetings and while in office, the board need not respond to shareholder concerns, which makes sense because, putting aside agency problems, boards in public companies are often much better informed than shareholders about the firm's business affairs. Also, empowering boards to act in opposition to the will of shareholder majorities can provide a check on opportunistic behavior by controlling shareholders vis-à-vis minority shareholders or other constituencies, such as employees or creditors.

Finally, the board is usually elected by the firm's shareholders. A U.S. corporation may issue nonvoting stock or, at the opposite extreme, accord voting rights to its bondholders. Nevertheless, few companies modify the general default rule that all stock votes at a ratio of one vote per share, and bondholders are never accorded voting rights except by contract when there is a default on interest payments. The obvious utility of restricting the franchise to holders of common stock is that it helps to ensure that the board will act in the interests of the company's owners; that is, its residual claimants.

3.5.1 Legal Construction of the Board

3.5.1.1 *The Holder of Primary Management Power*

In the United States, corporate law makes the board the ultimate locus of managerial powers. More specifically, board members are not required by duty to follow the wishes of a majority shareholder; thus, the corporation is a "republic," not a direct democracy. Is this what the shareholders want? Consider the following English case from early in the last century.

AUTOMATIC SELF-CLEANSING FILTER
SYNDICATE CO., LTD. v. CUNINGHAME
2 Ch. 34 (Eng. C.A. 1906)

[Plaintiff McDiarmid, who, together with his friends, held 55 percent of the shares of the Automatic Self-Cleansing Filter Syndicate Co., Ltd., wished to sell the company's assets. The articles of the company provided that "the management of the business and the control of the company shall be vested in the directors, subject nevertheless . . . to such regulations . . . as may from time to time be made by extraordinary resolution" (i.e., vote of three-quarters of the shareholders). At a special shareholders' meeting, a resolution to sell the company's assets failed by a vote of 55 percent in favor to 45 percent opposed. Plaintiff then asked the court to order the board to proceed with a sale of assets on specific terms. This request was denied.]

Collins, M.R.
. . . At a meeting of the company a resolution was passed by a majority—I was going to say a bare majority, but it was a majority [of

shareholders] — in favor of a sale [of the company's assets] to a purchaser, and the directors, honestly believing, ... that it was most undesirable in the interests of the company that that agreement should be carried into effect, refused to affix the seal of the company to it, or to assist in carrying out a resolution which they disapproved of; and the question is whether under the memorandum and articles of association here the directors are bound to accept, in substitution of their own view, the views contained in the resolution of the company....

[I]n the matters referred to in article 97(1.) [of the company law], the view of the directors as to the fitness of the matter is made the standard; and furthermore, by article 96 they are given in express terms the full powers which the company has, except so far as they "are not hereby or by statute expressly directed or required to be exercised or done by the company," so that the directors have absolute power to do all things other than those that are expressly required to be done by the company, and then comes the limitation on their general authority — "subject to such regulations as may from time to time be made by extraordinary resolution." Therefore, if it is desired to alter the powers of the directors that must be done, not by a resolution carried by a majority at an ordinary meeting of the company, but by an extraordinary resolution. In these circumstances it seems to me that it is not competent for the majority of the shareholders at an ordinary meeting to affect or alter the mandate originally given to the directors, by the articles of association. It has been suggested that this is a mere question of principal and agent, and that it would be an absurd thing if a principal in appointing an agent should in effect appoint a dictator who is to manage him instead of his managing the agent.

I think that that analogy does not strictly apply to this case. No doubt for some purposes directors are agents. For whom are they agents? You have, no doubt, in theory and law one entity, the company, which might be a principal, but you have to go behind that when you look to the particular position of directors. It is by the consensus of all the individuals in the company that these directors become agents and hold their rights as agents. It is not fair to say that a majority at a meeting is for the purposes of this case the principal so as to alter the mandate of the agent. The minority also must be taken into account. There are provisions by which the minority may be over-borne, but that can only be done by special machinery in the shape of special resolutions. Short of that the mandate which must be obeyed is not that of the majority — it is that of the whole entity made up of all the shareholders. If the mandate of the directors is to be altered, it can only be under the machinery of the memorandum and articles themselves. I do not think I need say more.

[Judge Collins goes on to observe that there would be no point to requiring a "special resolution" — that is, a 75 percent vote — for removal of directors in the company's charter if the company could be sold by majority vote at a general shareholders' meeting over the objection of the board.]

[In a concurring opinion, Cozens-Hardy, L.J., said:]

I am of the same opinion. It is somewhat remarkable that in the year 1906 this interesting and important question of company law should for the first time arise for decision, and it is perhaps necessary to go back to the root principle which governs these cases under the Companies Act, 1862. It has been decided that the articles of association are a contract between the members of the company *inter se.* That was settled finally by the case of *Browne v. La Trinidad*, 37 Ch. D. 1, if it was not settled before. We must therefore consider what is the relevant contract which these shareholders have entered into, and that contract, of course, is to be found in the memorandum and articles. I will not again read articles 96 and 97, but it seems to me that the shareholders have by their express contract mutually stipulated that their common affairs should be managed by certain directors to be appointed by the shareholders in the manner described by other articles, such directors being liable to be removed only by special resolution. If you once get a stipulation of that kind in a contract made between the parties, what right is there to interfere with the contract, apart, of course, from any misconduct on the part of the directors? There is no such misconduct in the present case.

. . . If you once get clear of the view that the directors are mere agents of the company, I cannot see anything in principle to justify the contention that the directors are bound to comply with the votes or the resolutions of a simple majority at an ordinary meeting of the shareholders. I do not think it is true to say that the directors are agents. I think it is more nearly true to say that they are in the position of managing partners appointed to fill that post by mutual arrangement between all the shareholders. So much for principle. On principle I agree entirely with what the Master of the Rolls has said, agreeing as he does with the conclusions of Warrington, J.

. . . For these reasons I think that the appeal must be dismissed. . . .

QUESTIONS ON AUTOMATIC SELF-CLEANSING FILTER SYNDICATE

1. Are there good reasons why investors might prefer a rule that requires a supermajority vote in order to override a board decision? Do these reasons apply equally well to all types of decisions?

2. Could the majority of shareholders of a Delaware corporation sell the company's assets without the concurrence of the board? See DGCL §271. Note that, if the board thwarts the will of a majority of the shareholders, the shareholders have a variety of avenues open to them, including passage of a resolution to remove directors at a special shareholders' meeting — or, in some jurisdictions, by consent solicitation.

3. Even the right of the shareholders meeting to remove directors is weaker in the U.S. than in many jurisdictions, including the U.K. and most of continental Europe.[50] Under most company law statutes, the general

---

50. The primary exception is Germany, where the codetermination law allocates half of the board seats in large companies to employee representatives rather than shareholders. In the case of an evenly divided board, however, the chair — a shareholder representative — casts a second and decisive vote. See Luca Enriques et al., in The Basic Governance Structure: The Interests of Shareholders, in Kraakman et al., eds., *The Anatomy of Corporate Law: A Comparative and Functional Approach*, 3rd ed. (2017).

shareholder meeting is explicitly recognized as the "highest managerial organ," able to countermand the board on any decision.[51] Might this difference be explained by the tendency of U.S. public companies to be widely held while their European counterparts tend toward concentrated ownership?

———————————

Although the board of directors has the primary power to direct or manage the business and affairs of the corporation (e.g., DGCL §141), it rarely exercises nitty-gritty management power. Instead, it designates managers or, more realistically, a chief executive officer, who, in turn, nominates other officers for board confirmation. But the managerial powers of directors, acting as a board, are extremely broad. Beyond the powers to appoint, compensate, and remove officers, they include the power to delegate authority to subcommittees of the board, to officers, or to others; the power to declare and pay dividends; the power to amend the company's bylaws; the exclusive power to initiate and approve certain extraordinary corporate actions, such as amendments to the articles of incorporation, mergers, sales of all assets, and dissolutions; and more generally, the power to make major business decisions, including deciding the products the company will offer, the prices it will charge, the wages it will pay, the financing agreements it will enter, and the like.

3.5.1.2 *Structure and Function of the Board*

The charter may, but customarily does not, provide much structure for the board. It will often set an upper limit on size and allow bylaws or board resolutions to do most of the rest of the work. In default of any special provisions in the charter, all members of the board are elected annually to one-year terms. The charter may provide that board seats are to be elected by certain classes of stock. For example, Class A common stock may elect one-third of the members of the board, while Class B elects the rest. In such situations, however, all directors still owe their fiduciary duty to the corporation as an entity and to *all* its shareholders: Specially elected directors do not owe a particular duty to the class that elected them. All directors have one vote on matters before the board.

The board has inherent power to establish standing committees for the effective organization of its own work, and it may delegate certain aspects of its task to these committees or to ad hoc committees. Insofar as committees are advisory, they may include nondirectors; should they exercise any part of the board's power, they must be composed entirely of directors. Under general practice (and New York Stock Exchange listing requirements), board committees include special committees on audit, nominations, and

———————————

51. See John Armour et al., What is Corporate Law?, in *The Anatomy, supra.*

compensation. These committees are typically filled largely or entirely by "independent" directors.[52] Matters that by statute require board action cannot be delegated to a committee for final action.

While the statutory default in almost all states is that the entire board is elected annually, corporation statutes generally permit corporate charters to create staggered boards in which directors are divided into classes that stand for election in consecutive years. Under Delaware law, there may be up to three such classes (DGCL §141(d)). Under the New York Business Corporation Law, there may be as many as four classes (§704).[53] Thus, under these provisions, an individual director might have a three- or four-year term of office. Since the early 1990s, institutional shareholders have generally opposed staggered boards because they plainly enhance management's ability to resist hostile takeovers.[54] For this reason, established public corporations now rarely ask shareholders to approve the introduction of staggered boards. Indeed, because of institutional investor resistance, staggered boards have fallen to a relatively small percentage of large (S&P 500) firms.[55] Interestingly, however, staggered boards continue to be the norm among new companies selling their shares in the public market for the first time, even though institutional investors are also large buyers of their initial public offerings of stock.[56]

As far as board function is concerned, the statutes do not specify with any particularity what a board is to do. There is, however, general agreement that an effective board should over the annual cycle of its meetings attend to the

52. The definition of "independence" for this purpose may vary. It means, at a minimum, that the director is not an employee or officer of the corporation or a family member of an employee or officer. For one fairly strict definition, see Report of Blue Ribbon Committee on Audit Practices, at www.sec.gov. Also see NYSE definition in its listing standards at www.nyse.com.

53. In New York, a staggered board may be established in the charter or by shareholder-enacted bylaw without board concurrence.

54. Empirical evidence confirms this intuition. See Lucian Arye Bebchuk, John C. Coates IV & Guhan Subramanian, *The Powerful Antitakeover Force of Staggered Boards: Theory, Evidence & Policy*, 54 Stan. L. Rev. 887 (2002).

55. A recent Proskauer, Global Capital Markets IPO Study 2019 (which also discussed results from a Conference Board study) finds that only 13 percent of S&P 500 firms had a staggered board and that the incidence of a staggered board in this set of firms is closely tied to firm size. The larger firms were much less likely to have a staggered board compared to smaller firms (e.g., firms with asset values less than $10 billion or revenue less than $1 billion).

56. The Proskauer study in *supra* note 55 finds that 92 percent of issuers in 2018 went public with a staggered board. Also, the majority of firms had restrictions on shareholders calling special meetings and had exclusive forum provisions. During the COVID-19 pandemic, more firms are also adopting anti-takeover devices. Whether staggered boards (or more generally anti-takeover defenses) increase firm value has generated a voluminous literature. For a sampling see Robert Daines & Michael Klausner, *Do IPO Charters Maximize Firm Value? Anti-Takeover Provisions in IPOs*, 17 J.L. & Econ. 83 (2001); Laura Casares Field & Jonathan M. Karpoff, *Takeover Defenses at IPO Firms*, 57 J. Fin. 1857 (2002); Lucian A. Bebchuk, John C. Coates IV and Guhan Subramanian, *The Powerful Antitakeover Force of Staggered Boards: Theory, Evidence, and Policy*, 55 Stan. L. Rev. 887 (2002); K. J. Martijn Cremers, Lubomir P. Litov & Simone M. Sepe, *Staggered Boards and Long-Term Firm Value, Revisited*, 126 J. Fin. Econ. 422 (2017); Alma Cohen & Charles C. Y. Wang, *Reexamining Staggered Boards and Shareholder Value*, 125 J. Fin. Econ. 637 (2017); Yakov Amihud, Markus Schmid & Steven Davidoff Solomon, *Settling the Staggered Boards Debate*, 166 U. Pa. L. Rev. 1475 (2018).

following major responsibilities: selection, monitoring, and compensating the firm's CEO; assure that an appropriate managerial risk and legal compliance program is in place; engage in CEO succession planning; review and approve strategic planning; be prepared to act in a crisis; assure that the firm acts in a socially responsible way; and assure an appropriate and ethical tone at the top of the firm.

3.5.1.3   Formality in Board Operation

As the *Automatic Self-Cleansing Filter Syndicate* case reflects, corporate directors are not legal agents of the corporation.[57] Governance power resides in the board of directors, not in the individual directors who constitute the board. Thus, it matters whether a majority of the directors find themselves discussing business at a company picnic or at a formal board meeting. At the picnic, they are powerless to act with respect to the corporation's affairs; in the boardroom, they have all of the power created by the firm's constitutional documents.

Legally speaking, directors act as a board only at a duly constituted board meeting and by majority vote (unless the corporate charter requires a supermajority vote on an issue) that is formally recorded in the minutes of the meeting. Proper notice of these meetings must be given, and a quorum must be present. The bylaws of the corporation usually specify what constitutes proper notice and what constitutes a quorum. Statutes usually provide minimums. (See, e.g., DGCL §141(b).) Many states now provide that, in lieu of the traditional board action described above, a board may act without a meeting if the members give their unanimous written consent to the corporate action in question (e.g., DGCL §141(f)).[58]

In *Fogel v. U.S. Energy Systems, Inc.*,[59] U.S. Energy had a four-member board of directors, which consisted of the CEO and three outside directors. Just before a scheduled board meeting, the three outside directors convened and decided to fire the CEO. The outside directors then went to the boardroom and announced their decision to the CEO. Two days later, the CEO called a special meeting of shareholders for the purpose of removing the other directors from office and electing replacements. The question before the court was whether the outside directors had held a valid board meeting when they decided to fire the CEO; if not, the CEO was not properly fired and retained the right to call a special shareholders meeting. The Delaware

57. Like other individuals, directors may, in their individual capacities, enter into an agency relationship and may specifically do so with the corporation. Were a director to do so, however, such a contract would have to be fair to the corporation, since directors are fiduciaries for the corporation. The point in the text is that directors are not agents by reason of their being directors.

58. These provisions were enacted principally to accommodate the realities of practice in close corporations (i.e., corporations with very few shareholders and in which management and shareholders typically overlap). In these situations, the added costs of formality may mean that formality is less observed unless allowances are made. Some statutes also permit directors to hold a meeting by telephone conference, but this is an acknowledgment of possibilities created by new technology rather than a repudiation of the notion that directors should act at a meeting.

59. 2007 WL 4438978 (Del. Ch. 2007).

Chancery Court held that the meeting among the outside directors did not constitute a valid meeting of the board. "The mere fact that directors are gathered does not a meeting make. There was no formal call to the meeting, and there was no vote whatsoever." Is this merely legalistic or is there a policy rationale for requiring formality in board action?

3.5.1.4 A Critique of Boards

American corporate law locates the center of energy and power of the corporate enterprise with the board of directors. In fact, most corporation statutes do not even mention the position of chief executive officer (CEO), the most important single organizational role in the large majority of corporations.

Apart from moments of crisis, board meetings for public corporations may be called for a day or two anywhere between four and twelve times a year. The large majority of board members are typically outside directors who have other full-time responsibilities. So, no matter how experienced or talented they may be, they do not have the time to deeply consider the merits of many complex corporate decisions. They must rely on good systems and well-selected officers to provide the information necessary to make sound decisions—or even to ask informed questions. These practical limitations make the role of the "outside," or independent, director in public companies one of the last great amateur roles in American life.

Consider this excerpt from board experts Colin Carter and Harvard Business School professor Jay Lorsch:

> [T]here is a significant gap between what boards are expected to accomplish and the time and knowledge available to directors to do their work. Put simply, the job is difficult if not impossible to carry out in the time most directors can devote to it. Because of that limited time and the rapidity with which business events occur, most directors find it difficult to keep up with their companies. The more complex the company, the more likely a director is to fall behind the curve.[60]

Carter and Lorsch provide guidelines for effective board structure, but then focus most of their attention on the "soft stuff": building and sustaining the right team; building knowledge and using it wisely; and using board time "behind closed doors" as effectively as possible. Well before the corporate scandals of the early 2000s, one of the authors of this book proposed that institutional investors consider funding a clearinghouse for "professional" directors, experts whose *only* job would be to sit on the boards of a half-dozen large companies to safeguard the interests of shareholders.[61]

---

60. Colin B. Carter & Jay W. Lorsch, *Back to the Drawing Board: Designing Corporate Boards for a Complex World*, 19-20 (2004).

61. See Ronald J. Gilson & Reinier Kraakman, *Reinventing the Outside Director: An Agenda for Institutional Investors*, 43 Stan. L. Rev. 863 (1991). For recent discussion on how boards might be staffed see Stephen M. Bainbridge & M. Todd Henderson, *Boards-R-Us: Reconceptualizing Corporate Boards*, 66 Stan. L. Rev. 1051 (2014) and a recent 2019 symposium in Volume 74 of *The Business Lawyer* addressing this and related issues.

3.5.2   Corporate Officers: Agents of the Corporation

Generally, the corporate charter empowers the board to appoint officers and remove them, with or without cause. By and large, the board has the power to delegate authority to corporate officers as it sees fit. The traditional officers are the president, vice presidents, treasurer, and secretary, although nowadays the most senior officer is frequently designated as the CEO. But this matter of names means very little; for legal purposes, a CEO might just as well be termed the company's Imperial Czar or Grand Pooh-Bah. The only important point is that the corporate officers, unlike directors, are unquestionable agents of the corporation and are therefore subject to the fiduciary duty of agents.

JENNINGS v. PITTSBURGH MERCANTILE CO.
202 A.2d 51 (Pa. 1964)

COHEN, J.:

Appellees, Dan R. Jennings, a Pittsburgh real estate broker, ... instituted this action of assumpsit against Pittsburgh Mercantile Company (Mercantile) to recover a real estate brokerage commission for the alleged consummation of a sale and leaseback of all of Mercantile's real property. Mercantile appeals from the lower court's denial of its motion for judgment n.o.v. after jury verdict for appellees.

The principal issue in this appeal is whether there was sufficient evidence upon which the jury could conclude that Mercantile clothed its agent with the apparent authority to accept an offer for the sale and leaseback thereby binding it to the payment of the brokerage commission, the agent having had, admittedly, no actual authority to so do.

Mercantile is a publicly-held corporation with over 400 shareholders. It is managed by a nine-member board of directors. An executive committee, consisting of the three major officers, functions between the board's quarterly meetings.

The facts in issue viewed in a light most favorable to appellees are as follows: In April, 1958, Frederick A. Egmore, Mercantile's vice-president and treasurer-comptroller, and Walter P. Stern, its financial consultant, met with Jennings, explained Mercantile's desire to raise cash for store modernization and provided Jennings with information concerning Mercantile's finances. Jennings was asked to solicit offers for a sale and leaseback.

At this meeting Egmore made the following representations: (1) the executive committee, of which Egmore was a member, controlled Mercantile and (2) would be responsible for determining whether the company would accept any of the offers produced by Jennings; (3) subsequent board of directors' approval of the acceptance would be automatic. Egmore promised the payment of a commission if Jennings succeeded in bringing in an offer on terms as to amount realized, annual rental, and lease duration acceptable to the executive committee. Egmore outlined preliminarily the terms of an acceptable offer.

In July and August, 1958, Jennings brought Egmore three offers.... The third offer came close to [Egmore's] original terms. On November 4, 1958, Jennings was informed by Stern that the executive committee had "agreed to the deal." However, within a week Egmore informed Jennings that the third offer had been rejected. Mercantile refused to pay Jennings' bill for commission of $32,000 and suit was thereafter instituted.

At the outset, we note that for Mercantile this proposed sale and lease-back was not a transaction in the ordinary course of business. Rather, it was unusual and unprecedented. The transaction envisaged Mercantile's relinquishment of ownership of all its real property, worth approximately $1.5 million, for a period of 30 years. Hence, the apparent authority which appellees seek to establish is the apparent authority to accept an offer for an extraordinary transaction.

Apparent authority is defined as that authority which, although not actually granted, the principal (1) knowingly permits the agent to exercise or (2) holds him out as possessing....

Jennings strongly contends that Egmore's representations gave rise to the apparent authority asserted. We do not agree.... An agent cannot, simply by his own words, invest himself with apparent authority. Such authority emanates from the actions of the principal and not the agent....

Jennings further argues that apparent authority arose by virtue of (1) certain prior dealings of Egmore and (2) the corporate offices held by Egmore....

Focusing on the first of these factors, in order for a reasonable inference of the existence of apparent authority to be drawn from prior dealings, these dealings must have (1) a measure of similarity to the act for which the principal is sought to be bound, and, granting this similarity, (2) a degree of repetitiveness.... Although the required degree of repetitiveness might have been present here, the prior acts relied upon consisted solely of Egmore's provision of financial information to Jennings and other brokers with regard to the sale and leaseback, and Egmore's solicitation of offers through them. The dissimilarities between these acts and the act of accepting the offer in issue are self-evident, and apparent authority to do the latter act cannot be inferred from the doing of the former.

As to the second of the above factors, the corporate offices of vice-president and treasurer-comptroller, which Egmore held, do not provide the basis for a reasonable inference that Mercantile held out Egmore as having the apparent authority to accept the offers produced by Jennings.... We hold ... any other conclusion would improperly extend the usual scope of authority which attaches to the holding of various corporate offices, and would greatly undercut the proper role of the board of directors in corporate decision-making by thrusting upon them determinations on critical matters which they have never had the opportunity to consider....

Finally, the extraordinary nature of this transaction placed appellees on notice to inquire as to Egmore's actual authority, particularly since appellees were an experienced real estate broker and investment counselor-attorney team.... Had inquiry been made, appellees would have discovered that the board never considered any of the proposals and obviously did not delegate actual authority to accept offers.

Appellees having failed to produce sufficient evidence upon which the jury could reasonably have found the existence of apparent authority to accept an offer for the sale and leaseback of all of Mercantile's real property, appellant is entitled to judgment n.o.v.

NOTE

For an analogous Delaware case that looks to the corporation statute to limit the apparent/inherent authority of corporate officers, see *Grimes v. Alteon, Inc.*, 804 A.2d 256 (Del. 2002). In *Grimes*, a CEO was held to lack the authority to enter an oral contract to sell 10 percent of any new issue of stock to an existing shareholder who wished to maintain his proportionate shareholdings. The Delaware Supreme Court held that such a contract constituted a "right" in the company's securities and thus required board approval under DGCL §§152 and 157. While this construction might not have been compelling on the face of DGCL §§152 and 157 alone, it was, according to the court, required by the spirit animating a broader set of DGCL provisions as well as the fundamental social policies of protecting the board's power to regulate corporate capital structure and ensuring the certainty of property rights in corporate shares.

QUESTIONS ON JENNINGS

1. Why would extending apparent authority to Egmore, Mercantile's vice president and treasurer, undercut the role of the board?
2. Should the outcome differ if Mercantile's board had made a firm decision to enter a sale and leaseback transaction on the best terms available?

THE PROTECTION OF CREDITORS

Corporate creditors share the same problems as other creditors. Debtors might misrepresent their income or assets before borrowing, or they might divert the income or assets that back their credit afterwards. Debtors can shift value from corporate creditors in many ways. They can shift assets beyond the reach of creditors, dilute the claims of unsecured creditors by taking on senior debt, increase the riskiness of their debt by altering investment policy, or merely operate their businesses badly. In addition, debtors can externalize costs to involuntary creditors such as tort victims by incurring excess debt before the claims of involuntary creditors mature. Corporate creditors enjoy the same protections as other creditors, but corporate law generally provides them additional protections. An obvious question is why? The most plausible explanation is that limited liability gives rise to the potential for special abuse.

Limited liability exacerbates the problems of creditors in two ways. First, it opens opportunities for both express and tacit misrepresentation in transactions with voluntary creditors. Individuals who employ the corporate form in contracting with others may play a game of "bait and switch." They mislead others about corporate assets and simply walk away if the business fails. Indeed, shareholders may contract through companies with no assets whatsoever, while at least implicitly representing otherwise. Second, limited liability makes it quite easy to shift assets out of the contracting corporation after a creditor has extended credit. It is a simple thing for shareholders to distribute assets to themselves, while leaving the debts with their corporation in violation of an implicit representation to continue to operate a solvent business. Or more subtly, shareholders can undertake highly risky (volatile) investments or increase leverage in order to shift uncompensated risk onto the shoulders of both voluntary and involuntary creditors.

All of these opportunistic moves would lose much of their appeal if shareholders or other entity controllers lacked the shield of limited liability to protect their personal assets from contractual default on the part of their entities.

Of course, entity creditors can (and should) minimize the costs of shareholder opportunism by exercising vigilance and negotiating for contractual protections. They can, for example, take security interests in particular corporate assets or negotiate specific covenants that give them early warning of credit problems. Indeed, the most effective creditor protections in the real world are contractual. But such protections are costly to negotiate, perhaps too much so for small debtors and creditors. Moreover, some debtor opportunism is so blatant that no amount of contracting offers protection from it. It follows that special protections for limited-liability creditors seem easy to justify. In this Chapter, we leave aside contractual protections available through negotiation, and focus instead on the law's default provisions that protect corporate creditors.[1]

Corporate law has three generic strategies for protecting creditors. First, it can impose disclosure duties on corporate debtors. Second, it can promulgate (usually de minimis) rules to regulate the amount and disposition of corporate capital. Finally, it can impose duties to safeguard creditors on corporate participants such as directors, creditors, and shareholders. We consider each strategy in turn.

4.1   MANDATORY DISCLOSURE

Mandatory disclosure of financial information is one plausible answer to debtor opportunism that turns on misrepresentation or concealment of information. Federal securities law imposes extensive mandatory disclosure obligations on public corporations, which benefit corporate creditors as well as shareholders. Public issues of debt also require extensive disclosure under the Securities Act of 1933. But state corporation law makes little use of mandatory disclosure to protect creditors of closely held corporations, which are not regulated under federal securities law. No U.S. state requires closely held corporations to prepare audited financial statements or to file financial statements — audited or not — with a commercial register or the attorney general's office.[2] In this respect, U.S. law contrasts with that of European Union (EU) jurisdictions, where large private companies must file audited financial statements annually[3] and even the smallest corporations must often file unaudited statements for creditor inspection.

Are the European requirements for small firm disclosure worth their administrative costs? Maybe so, but arguably credit bureau reports, which are generally available for small businesses as well as individuals in the United

---

1. We assume that creditor protections have similar effects for all limited liability entities, although U.S. corporation statutes have accounting rules that are specific by design to the corporate form. The materials below will suggest how this observation and roughly equal creditor protection can be reconciled across all limited liability entities.

2. A few states, such as Michigan, require all corporations to prepare financial statements annually for distribution to shareholders, but these disclosures are not intended to benefit corporate creditors. See Mich. Bus. Corp. Act §901.

3. Art. 2(1)(f), EU First Company Law Directive. Note that there has been quite some resistance to having smaller EU companies disclose their financial statements (see Case C-191/95, *Commission of the European Communities v. Federal Republic of Germany*, 1998 ECR-I 5485). Thus, in the United Kingdom, corporations with total sales in excess of £6.5 million must present audited financial statements. See Companies Act, 2006, §477.

States, are more useful for evaluating the credit risks of limited liability entities. Annual financial statements quickly grow stale.

4.2 CAPITAL REGULATION

Regulation of the capital committed to the corporation — by, for example, requiring a minimal investor contribution of capital to a new corporation or by restricting the subsequent distribution of its capital — is a very direct legal strategy for protecting corporate creditors. Many rules aim to regulate corporate capital, some much more protective (and restrictive) than others, across jurisdictions and even among state corporation laws. But to discuss these rules as they have evolved, we must first introduce the corporate balance sheet and the arcane concept of legal capital.

4.2.1 Financial Statements

Accounting is a standardized methodology for describing a firm's past financial performance. In the United States, generally accepted accounting principles (GAAP) are set by the Financial Accounting Standards Board (FASB), a self-regulatory body authorized by the Securities Exchange Commission to establish accounting standards.

It is important for novices to appreciate both the significance and the limitations of accounting reports. We start here with the corporate versions of the two principal accounting statements that we introduced for a general partnership in Chapter 2: the balance sheet and the income statement (sometimes called the profit and loss statement). The balance sheet represents the financial picture of a business organization as it stands on a particular day, in contrast to the income statement, which presents the results of business operations over a specified period. A firm customarily presents the balance sheet and income statement for two or more years in order to show how the firm's situation has changed over time.

A principal limitation of the entries on the balance sheet is that they reflect historical costs instead of current economic (market) values. Thus, each asset is listed at its acquisition cost (minus depreciation charges, which are only loosely correlated with deterioration in economic value). Book value (the value found on the balance sheet) may therefore differ quite a bit from an asset's current economic value. A balance sheet might show a value for shareholder equity that is much more than shareholders would realize in a sale of the firm or, more likely in an inflationary period, much less than the firm's market value. Thus liabilities reflect a historical rather than an economic approach to valuation. Moreover, the income statement (not shown) suffers limitations as well — its account of profit or loss does not reflect the actual amount of cash that a business throws off (or makes available to its owners) in the year. The figure that accountants report as net profit may differ from the cash available for distribution for many reasons. For example, depreciation

Washington Square Pharmacia Balance Sheet December, 31, 2019

ASSETS*	2019	2018
Current assets		
Cash	$ 51,000	$ 25,000
Marketable securities — cost (Market value: 2019 $71,400; 2018 $57,800)	$ 68,000	$ 54,400
Accounts receivable (less allowance for doubtful accounts): 2019 $5,100.00; 2018 $4,037.50)	$ 265,200	$ 246,500
Inventories	$ 326,000	$ 315,000
Prepaid expenses	$ 6,800	$ 5,100
Total current assets	$ 717,000	$ 646,000
Fixed assets		
Land	$ 51,000	$ 51,000
Buildings	$ 212,500	$ 201,450
Machinery	$ 365,500	$ 316,370
Office Equipment	$ 35,500	$ 20,400
Total property, plant, and equipment	$ 664,500	$ 589,220
Less accumulated depreciation	$ 212,700	$ 164,900
Net fixed assets	$ 451,800	$ 424,320
Intangible assets	$ 3,400	$ 3,400
TOTAL ASSETS	$ 1,172,200	$ 1,073,720

LIABILITIES	2019	2018
Current liabilities		
Accounts payable	$ 122,400	$ 117,300
Notes payable	$ 86,700	$ 103,700
Accrued expenses payable	$ 51,000	$ 61,200
Federal income taxes payable	$ 28,900	$ 25,500
Total current liabilities	$ 289,000	$ 307,700
Long-term liabilities		
Deferred income tax	$ 17,000	$ 15,300
Debentures 5%, due 2021	$ 231,200	$ 231,200
TOTAL LIABILITIES	$ 537,200	$ 554,200
STOCKHOLDERS' EQUITY		
Preferred stock ($5.83 cumulative, $100 par value, authorized 60,000 shares, outstanding 60,000 shares)	$ 6,000	$ 6,000
Common stock ($5.00 par value, 20,000,000 shares authorized, outstanding 2019 15,000,000 shares, 2018 14,500,000 shares)	$ 75,000	$ 72,500
Capital surplus	$ 27,000	$ 12,750
Accumulated retained earnings	$ 527,000	$ 428,270
Total stockholders' equity	$ 635,000	$ 519,520
TOTAL LIABILITIES & STOCKHOLDERS' EQUITY	$ 1,172,200	$ 1,073,720

* All sums in thousands of dollars

is a noncash charge reflected in the income statement; it reduces net profit, but it does not affect the amount of cash that can be made available that year to owners. On the other hand, some cash expenditures may reduce cash available to the corporation but not reduce net profit, since they are treated in accounting as capital investments. In sum, the income statement does not reflect the cash available to the firm's owners, just as the balance sheet does not reflect current economic value of its assets. Nevertheless, investors and analysts rely on these statements heavily when evaluating a firm's performance or estimating its value.

The balance sheet is particularly important in traditional corporation statutes. As the hypothetical statement above illustrates, a corporate balance sheet is divided into two columns: on the left side are assets while on the right are liabilities, which represent the debts of the business and stockholders' equity (or partners' capital if the business is a partnership). Although we have presented the assets, liabilities, and stockholders' equity side-by-side, some prefer to present this information sequentially (assets first, then liabilities, and then stockholders' equity). But, however they are displayed, the asset and liability portions of the balance sheet must always balance. Every element of a corporation's value (asset column) must be accounted for by an equivalent debt or equity claim in the liability column. The assets column includes all of a business's tangible property, intellectual property, goodwill, and even outstanding legal claims against third parties that have come to judgment but have not yet been collected. The liabilities column lists all of the business' debts that are payable to others. The stockholders' equity category brings the assets and liabilities into balance. It represents the difference between the asset values and the liability values. This is the amount of equity, or the ownership stake, that shareholders have in the business (although, of course, it does not reflect the market value of their equity).

Look first to the asset side of the balance sheet. Current assets include cash, marketable securities, accounts receivable, inventories, and prepaid expenses. These are the "working" assets of the corporation that constantly cycle through the firm's production processes, from raw materials to inventory to receivables to cash. In contrast, fixed assets, which are sometimes termed "property, plant, and equipment" ("PP&E") and sometimes termed "capital assets," represent those assets not intended for sale, which are used for lengthy periods in order to manufacture, display, warehouse, and transport the product. Accordingly, this category includes land, buildings, machinery, equipment, furniture, and vehicles. Note again that under GAAP, the balance sheet fixes asset values at historical cost and adjusts these figures downward to reflect depreciation. The resulting valuations may bear little relationship to market values (or replacement costs), which are often much higher. An open question for the accounting profession is whether this accounting bias toward "objective" historical costs should continue or whether the profession ought to introduce some version of "mark to market" accounting. Since both approaches have difficulties, a market-oriented standard is unlikely to displace historical costs any time soon.

Similarly, the liabilities side of the balance sheet divides into current liabilities (due within the year) and long-term liabilities (due over a longer period). A comparison of current assets with current liabilities gives a sense of the liquidity (or the capacity of noncash assets to be converted into cash) of a company's assets and the likelihood that it can pay its obligations or make new investments in the near future. To facilitate comparison, both current assets and current liabilities are listed in current dollars. Long-term liabilities also tend to be stated in units that approximate real economic dollars. Thus, if our hypothetical company has 5 percent debentures, with a principal value of $231.2 million, due in 2021, the true economic value of this liability may be in the neighborhood of $231.2 million *if* 5 percent is a reasonable risk-adjusted interest rate for the company at this time. If the company is currently significantly riskier (weaker) than when it issued the note, then the economic value of the note (liability) will be less than the principal amount the company is legally obligated to pay. (If you don't see why, ask in class.) In this event, a weak company will be able to buy its notes on the market at a price lower than its legal repayment obligation — that is, if it has the resources to do so.

The third major division of the corporate balance sheet is stockholders' equity. This is the book value of the owners' economic interests. Stockholders' equity is always a "plug figure"; i.e., it is the difference between corporate assets and liabilities. In our example, the 2019 equity accounts equal the difference between total assets ($1,172,200) and total liabilities ($537,200), or $635,000. For both legal and accounting reasons, the stockholders' equity is divided into three accounts: stated (or legal) capital, capital surplus, and accumulated retained earnings (or earned surplus).

Stated capital is also known as capital stock, or the corporation's legal or nominal capital. This item represents all or a portion of the value that shareholders transferred to the corporation at the time of the original sale of the company's stock to its original shareholders. The amount of stated capital, expressed in dollars, is usually the product of the par value[4] of the stock multiplied by the number of issued shares (although the board may fix a higher level). Alternatively, if a corporation chooses to issue "no par stock," which U.S. corporation statutes generally permit, the board of directors must set aside some (discretionary) portion of the sale price as the company's stated capital. See, e.g., DGCL §154. If the stock is sold for more than its par value, the excess is accounted for in a "capital surplus" or "paid-in surplus" account. Suppose, for example, Typical Co. issues 15 million shares of common stock, with a par value of $5 a share, at an average price of $6.066 per share. Typical then receives $91 million for its common stock and allocates $75 million to capital stock or legal capital and $16 million to its capital surplus account.

Finally, consider the third shareholder equity account: accumulated retained earnings, or earned surplus. Retained earnings are merely the amounts that a profitable corporation earns but has not distributed to its shareholders as dividends. (*Note:* When a company first starts in business, it has no accumulated

---

4. The par value of a stock is an arbitrary dollar amount stated in the articles of incorporation and on the stock certificate. It bears no relationship to the stock's economic (market) value.

retained earnings.) Undistributed amounts of net profit accumulate in the earned surplus or accumulated retained earnings account. For example:

Balance of retained earnings (end of Year 1)	$ 50,000
Net profit for Year 2	+ $ 160,000
Total available for dividends	= $ 210,000
Less: All dividends paid Year 2	$ 75,000
Accumulated retained earnings (end of Year 2)	$ 135,000

4.2.2 Distribution Constraints

How might the balance sheet regulate capital and help to protect creditors? One (rather primitive) idea might be to represent a particular fund on the balance sheet as "permanent capital" that could not be paid out to shareholders and upon which creditors could rely in extending credit. Such an account could be (and often is) called the "legal capital" or "stated capital" account. Most distribution restrictions in corporate statutes look to this account on the balance sheet to block distributions of corporate funds to shareholders. But this constraint is feeble.

U.S. corporate law generally permits boards to pay dividends out of a corporation's capital surplus accounts including its retained earnings. But the fine print goes further. Delaware and New York have a "nimble dividend" test that is as flexible as its nickname suggests. DGCL §170(a) permits a corporation (other than a bank) to pay dividends out of surplus but, if there is no surplus, to pay dividends less than its profits in the current and/or preceding fiscal year. The motivation is apparently to permit boards to reward the shareholders of currently "challenged" firms that are on an upward trajectory. As further evidence of the flexibility of the balance sheet, consider that Delaware corporate directors may freely transfer the stated capital associated with no par stock into a surplus account available for distribution to shareholders. A company may even distribute the capital that reflects the par value of stock (generally a nominal figure for common stock), although this requires shareholders to vote to approve a charter amendment to reduce par value. See DGCL §244(a)(4) (and note that shareholders *in extremis* may not be inclined to help creditors). What really matters to both creditors and shareholders is not these bookkeeping accounts but the real economic value of a company's assets.

If a corporation's assets are worth more (in economic value) than the amount at which they are carried on the firm's books, no law prevents the firm from adjusting its books to reflect that higher value. GAAP allows this if the firm's revaluation is fully disclosed and its outside auditor concurs that it has fairly estimated economic values. Indeed, the DGCL expressly permits this, albeit in somewhat opaque language. DGCL §154. If the assets are marked up to market value, the additional value must be recognized by an equal increase on the liabilities side of the balance sheet. Since the write-up involves no increase in the firm's liabilities, the only account available to make this adjustment is some sort of capital surplus account, which we could call "revaluation surplus." Because this is a surplus account, a board of directors can pay dividends from it. See D.A. Drexler, L.S. Black, Jr. & A.G. Sparks, 1 *Delaware Corporation Law and Practice* §20.03 (LEXIS, 2019).

Section 6.40(c) of the MBCA is similar. It is a traditional distribution test but also expressly recognizes the possibility of revaluing a firm's assets for balance sheet purposes. The general rule is the same everywhere: Corporations may not pay dividends if, as a result of doing so, (1) they cannot pay their debts as they come due or (2) their assets are less than their liabilities plus the preferential claims of preferred shareholders. In determining whether assets suffice to make distributions under this test, the MBCA expressly permits boards to rely on either GAAP or "a fair valuation or other method that is reasonable in the circumstances." MBCA §6.40(d). The latter clause invites a shift from accounting conventions to alternative measures of value that more accurately reflect economic reality, such as a Discounted Cash Flow estimate of going concern value (see Chapter 5 for more discussion). See MBCA §6.40 comment 3.

Thus, as a practical matter, under the DGCL or the MBCA, the only real protection that creditors have against aggressive dividend payments (except for contractual restrictions that are often found in loan documents) is the restriction that we discuss below under the fraudulent transfers act.

QUESTIONS

Alpha Inc. has the following balance sheet at the end of 2019 (all numbers in millions of dollars):

Current assets		Liabilities	
Cash	1,000	Current liabilities	9,650
Securities	650	Long-term liabilities	5,000
Accounts receivable	6,000	Total liabilities	14,650
Inventory	5,000		
Property, plant, and equipment	3,000	Shareholders' equity	
		Stated capital	200
Total assets	15,650	Capital surplus	300
		Retained earnings	500
		Total shareholders' equity	1,000

Alpha's net profit was $400 million in 2018 and $120 million in 2019. An investment banking firm has valued Alpha at $30 billion using a DCF methodology discussed in Chapter 5, while Alpha's market capitalization (the aggregate market value of its outstanding stock) is $15 billion.

1. What is the maximum dividend that Alpha can pay under the Delaware statute? The MBCA?

2. How can a capital surplus test protect corporate creditors if there is no minimum level of stated capital to serve as a creditor cushion?

3. Which distribution constraint do you prefer? Why?

4.2.3 Minimum Capital and Capital Maintenance Requirements

An obvious objection to distribution constraints based on accounting categories such as capital surplus is that they are easily avoided through the expedient of placing trivial sums in the "trust fund" of legal capital reserved for creditors. A response to this objection might be to require shareholders to commit a stated amount of capital to the firm: a mandatory minimum capital requirement. But within the United States, statutory minimum capital requirements are either truly minimal ($1,000) or entirely nonexistent. (Neither the DGCL nor the MBCA requires a minimum capital amount as a condition of incorporation.) Internationally, minimum capital requirements have historically been significant but have markedly declined over the past two decades. Japan used to impose relatively high capital requirements on corporations[5] but abolished these requirements in 2006, though a Japanese corporation must still have 3 million yen in assets (~$30,000) before it can distribute profits.[6] The European Union imposes a minimum capital requirement of approximately $25,000+ for "open" or public corporations, but the European Commission has from time to time considered relaxing this requirement.[7] Even in jurisdictions where minimum capital requirements continue to exist, they are fixed at levels that seem to provide a form of de minimis screening rather than a substantial form of creditor protection.[8]

One reason that minimum capital requirements cannot be an effective creditor protection is that this check, where it exists, is fixed at the date of organization of the corporation. But, even if companies cannot dip into minimum capital to pay shareholders, normal business activity can easily dissipate a company's capital, leaving nothing on the books or in the kitty for its creditors. For this reason, jurisdictions within the EU have traditionally adopted not only a minimum capital rule but also so-called capital maintenance rules. The main characteristic of these rules is that they accelerate the point at which failing corporations must file for insolvency: EU company law requires member states to mandate that larger companies call a shareholders' meeting to consider dissolution when a serious loss of legal capital causes the firm to violate capital maintenance standards.[9] In fact, many European jurisdictions go beyond the EU minimum. For example, German and Swiss company laws extend the duty to call a shareholders' meeting to smaller as well as larger companies and, in addition, require that directors

5. See Art. 168-4, Japanese Commercial Code (about $100,000 for AGs, or open joint stock companies); Art. 9, Japanese GmbHG (about $30,000 for GmbHs, or closed corporations).
6. See Law No. 86 of Japan ("Kaisha ho") (promulgated July 26, 2005).
7. See *Modernising Company Law and Enhancing Corporate Governance in the European Union — A Plan to Move Forward*, COM (2003) 284 at 18.
8. See John Armour et al., *Transactions with Creditors*, Ch. 5.2.2.1, in Kraakman et al., ed., *The Anatomy of Corporate Law: A Comparative and Functional Approach* (3rd ed., 2017).
9. Art. 17, EU Second Company Law Directive, applicable to société anonyme; Aktiengesellschaft; società per azioni; public company limited by shares. Many EU jurisdictions now have virtually no minimum capital requirements for private companies.

immediately file for bankruptcy when legal capital is totally lost.[10] There are no such requirements in the United States.

QUESTION

What are the costs and benefits of tough minimum capital and capital maintenance requirements? Which do you prefer, regulating shareholder capital from the start or a deregulatory approach that provides for the possible review of the conduct of corporate actors after insolvency?

4.3   STANDARD-BASED DUTIES

Corporate law (and debtor-creditor law) often forces certain participants in financially-distressed corporations to mitigate the losses of arms-length corporate creditors in specific circumstances. These participants are directors, fellow creditors, and — last but not least — shareholders. Requiring any one of these classes of corporate participants to share in the losses of good-faith creditors is suspect for good reason. There are multiple, often overlapping legal claims that might follow corporate bankruptcies or insolvencies. They can arise from state law or federal bankruptcy law and frequently implicate both, as when a trustee in bankruptcy pursues claims arising under state law on behalf of the corporate estate. We focus here on the classes of corporate participants against whom claims might be brought rather than the full spectrum of legal theories that might support these claims. Nevertheless, we hope to cover the most relevant theories for corporate (and entity) law.

4.3.1   Director Liability

Directors are obvious targets for lawsuits by the creditors of bankrupt corporations. Under Delaware law, a director is liable for the full amount of illegal dividends paid to shareholders, including the amount of dividends paid out in excess of the capital represented by outstanding shares. See DGCL §§170 & 174(a). Our preceding discussion suggests that accounting figures in the balance sheet alone are unlikely to block a corporate board that is determined to gamble on the assets that stand behind corporate promises to unsecured creditors. Nevertheless, the implicit policy behind these provisions of the DGCL — and of parallel provisions in other state corporation

---

10. See for Germany: AktG §92(2) and GmbHG §64; for Switzerland: OR Art. 725 and Art. 817.

statutes — seem to invite judicial intervention when boards of corporations on the brink of insolvency decide to wager remaining corporate assets on propositions that can only benefit shareholders.

In a couple of interesting opinions, the Delaware Chancery Court has suggested that when a firm is insolvent (but no one has yet invoked the federal bankruptcy protections), its directors owe a duty to consider the interests of corporate creditors. In one particularly interesting case, the Court of Chancery opined that, when a corporation is "in the vicinity of insolvency," its board may consider not just the immediate interest of shareholders but also the welfare of the community of interests that constitute the corporation. The court stated:

> The possibility of insolvency can do curious things to incentives, exposing creditors to risks of opportunistic behavior and creating complexities for directors. Consider, for example, a solvent corporation having a single asset, a judgment for $51 million against a solvent debtor. The judgment is on appeal and thus subject to modification or reversal. Assume that the only liabilities of the company are to bondholders in the amount of $12 million. Assume that the array of probable outcomes of the appeal is as follows:

> *Expected Value*

> | | | |
> |---|---|---|
> | 25% chance of affirmance | ($51m) | $12.75 |
> | 70% chance of modification | ($ 4m) | 2.80 |
> | 5% chance of reversal | ($ 0m) | 0.00 |
> | Expected Value of Judgment on Appeal | | $15.55 |

Thus, the best evaluation is that the current value of the equity is $3.55 million. ($15.55 million expected value of judgment on appeal — $12 million liability to bondholders). Now assume an offer to settle at $12.5 million (also consider one at $17.5 million). By what standard do the directors of the company evaluate the fairness of these offers? The creditors of this solvent company would be in favor of accepting either a $12.5 million offer or a $17.5 million offer. In either event they will avoid the 75 percent risk of insolvency and default. The stockholders, however, will plainly be opposed to acceptance of a $12.5 million settlement (under which they get practically nothing). More importantly, they very well may be opposed to acceptance of the $17.5 million offer under which the residual value of the corporation would increase from $3.5 to $5.5 million. This is so because the litigation alternative, with its 25 percent probability of a $39 million outcome to them ($51 million − $12 million = $39 million) has an expected value to the residual risk bearer of $9.75 million ($39 million × 25 percent chance of affirmance), substantially greater than the $5.5 million available to them in the settlement. While in fact the stockholders' preference would reflect their appetite for risk, it is possible (and with diversified shareholders likely) that shareholders would prefer rejection of both settlement offers.

But if we consider the community of interests that the corporation represents it seems apparent that one should in this hypothetical accept the best settlement offer available providing it is greater than $15.55 million, and one below that amount should be rejected. But that result will not be reached by a director who thinks he owes duties directly to shareholders only. It will be reached by directors who are capable of conceiving of the corporation as a legal and economic entity. Such directors will recognize that in managing the business affairs of a solvent corporation in the vicinity of insolvency, circumstances may arise when the right (both the efficient and the fair) course to follow for the corporation may diverge from the choice that the stockholders (or the creditors, or the employees, or any single group interested in the corporation) would make if given the opportunity to act.[11]

If we look elsewhere, we note that, as with minimum capital and capital maintenance requirements, the duties of directors to protect the interests of creditors are more developed in EU jurisdictions than in the United States.[12] In particular, directors are responsible in many of these jurisdictions for ensuring that insolvent corporations enter bankruptcy rather than continuing to do business and accumulating further debt. In the United States, where management retains control when the company enters reorganization proceedings under Chapter 11, such duties are usually unnecessary because management often has an incentive to enter bankruptcy voluntarily in the hopes of engineering a successful recapitalization.

QUESTIONS

1. Consider the preceding hypothetical. Isn't it plain that, as a matter of policy, the directors ought to be legally compelled to reject the $12.5 million offer? Should the law also make it their duty to accept the $17.5 million offer even if the equity holders would prefer not to do so? How would you articulate their duty?

2. One interpretation of *Credit Lyonnais Bank Nederland* is not that the court recognized a right of any kind in creditors but rather that it recognized a board of directors' privilege to subordinate loyalty to shareholders to an overriding interest in maximizing joint (debt and equity) wealth. Most commentators overlook this possibility. Would it make sense as the legal rule?

3. In its 2007 decision, *North American Catholic Educational Programming Foundation, Inc. v. Gheewalla*,[13] the Delaware Supreme Court held that creditors of an insolvent corporation could not assert a direct claim against directors (alleging injury to their own interests as creditors) but did

---

11. *Credit Lyonnais Bank Nederland v. Pathe Communications Corp.*, 1991 Del. Ch. LEXIS 215, at *109 n.55 (Del Ch. Dec. 30, 1991).

12. See for France: Ordonnance no. 2000-912: Art. 52, Loi no. 66-537 dated July 24, 1966, now codified in the French *Code de Commerce* under article L. 223-22; Art. 244, Loi no. 66-537 dated July 24, 1966, now codified in the French *Code de Commerce* under article L. 225-251; Art. 180, Loi no. 55-98 dated January 25, 1985. now codified in the French *Code de Commerce* under article L. 651-2.; for Germany: GmbHG §§43, 93 and AktG §116. This approach is a rather recent one, as far as the United Kingdom is concerned: see Insolvency Act of 1986, §214(4); *Dorchester Finance Co. v. Stebbing*, [1989] Butterworths Company Law Cases 498; Christopher A. Riley, *The Company Director's Duty of Care and Skill: The Case for an Onerous but Subjective Standard*, 62 Mod. L. Rev. 697 (1999).

13. 930 A.2d 92 (Del. 2007).

have standing to assert a derivative claim (alleging injury to the corporation). The court stated: "Recognizing that directors of an insolvent corporation owe direct fiduciary duties to creditors would create uncertainty for directors who have a fiduciary duty to exercise their business judgment in the best interest of the insolvent corporation. . . . Directors . . . must retain the freedom to engage in vigorous, good faith negotiations with individual creditors for the benefit of the corporation." In addition, *Gheewalla* bars both direct and derivative actions by creditors against the directors of corporations that are "in the vicinity of insolvency," i.e., maybe not quite there yet. The distinction between direct and derivative corporate lawsuits is further addressed *infra*, in Chapter 10. *Gheewalla* remains Delaware's definitive statement of creditor rights of action under corporate law. Clarifying *Gheewalla*, the Delaware Supreme Court held in *Schoon v. Smith*, 953 A.2d 196, n.46 (Del. 2008) that "*Gheewalla* confers standing upon creditors to bring a derivative action where the corporation is insolvent, but only because the shareholders of an insolvent corporation no longer have an economic interest in the corporate entity — only its creditors have that interest. . . ."[14]

How much should the distinction between "insolvent" (full stop) and "in the vicinity of insolvency" matter to a corporate creditor considering a lawsuit against the firm's directors?

4.3.2   Creditor Protection: Fraudulent Transfers

Fraudulent conveyance law (a general creditor remedy) imposes an effective obligation on parties contracting with an insolvent — or soon to be insolvent — debtor to give fair value for the cash or benefits they receive, or risk being forced to return those benefits to the debtor's estate. Fraudulent conveyance law is among the oldest creditor protections. It is designed to void transfers by a debtor that — speaking loosely — are made under circumstances that are unfair to creditors. More specifically, the statute provides a means to void any transfer made for the purpose of delaying, hindering, or defrauding creditors. The original fraudulent conveyance act was passed in 1571 by the English Parliament. The first uniform statute widely adopted in the U.S. was the Uniform Fraudulent Conveyance Act (UFCA) (1918); modern states divide about evenly between those that rely on the Uniform Fraudulent Transfer Act (UFTA) (1981) and those that have adopted the newer Uniform Voidable Transactions Act (UVTA) (2014), which is in your statutory supplement. Federal bankruptcy law also includes fraudulent transfer provisions.

---

14. The Delaware Chancery Court clarified further in *Quadrant Structured Products Co. v. Vertin*, 2015 WL 2062115 (Del. Ch. May 4, 2015) that dual standing is possible (creditors and shareholders can have standing to bring derivative suits at the same time), but it did not discuss how this would be operationalized. The Delaware Chancery Court refused to extend the *Gheewalla* holding to LLCs because it was barred by statute. See *CML V, LLC* v. *Bax*, 6 A.3d 238, 240–241 (Del. Ch. 2010).

The UVTA and UFTA are substantially similar in their approach. Under either statute, creditors may attack a transfer on two grounds. First, "present or future creditors" may void transfers made with the "*actual intent* to hinder, delay, or defraud any creditor of the debtor." (Emphasis added.) UVTA §4(a)(1) and UFTA §4(a)(1). Second, "creditors" may void transfers made "without receiving a reasonably equivalent value" if the debtor is left with "remaining assets . . . unreasonably small in relation to [its] business," or the debtor "intended . . . believed . . . or reasonably should have believed he would incur debts beyond his ability to pay as they became due," or the debtor is insolvent after the transfer. UVTA §§4(a)(2), 5(a) & (b); UVTA §§4(a)(2), 5(a) & (b). Most fraudulent transfer litigation today takes place under §548 of the U.S. Bankruptcy Code, which takes a virtually identical approach as the UFCA, UFTA, and UVTA or under §544(b) of the Code, which invokes state law doctrine of fraudulent transfer.

Taken as a whole, fraudulent transfer doctrine permits creditors to void transfers by establishing that they were either actual or constructive frauds on creditors. Actual fraud is easy to understand as a basis for voiding a transfer. Constructive fraud under the fraudulent transfer acts is sometimes understood as creating an evidentiary presumption of actual fraud, although it is better understood to describe the reasonable expectations of creditors when negotiating with debtors — that is, as a standard term in creditor-debtor contracts except when the parties explicitly opt out of it. Restated, don't business debtors implicitly represent that their assets, as affected by normal business transactions (e.g., sales for fair value) or diminished by normal wear and tear and legal distributions, will be available to creditors in the event of default?

How easily *future* creditors can void transfers on the grounds that there was no equivalent value and the business was left with unreasonably small capital is unclear. One construction of the references to future creditors in the statute is that they can void transfers only in the event of actual fraud. Compare UVTA §4(b)(9) with §§4(a)(2)(ii) and 4(a)(1). In any event, future creditors who "knew or could easily have found out about" otherwise vulnerable transfers cannot void them. *Kupetz v. Wolf*, 845 F.2d 842, 846 n.16 (9th Cir. 1988).[15]

NOTE AND QUESTION ON LEVERAGED BUYOUTS AND FRAUDULENT TRANSFER DOCTRINE

In a leveraged buyout (LBO), a target firm is usually acquired for cash, which is typically financed in large amounts by high levels of debt secured by the target's assets. This "leveraged" acquisition benefits all concerned if the acquirer can manage or redeploy the target's assets to generate new value. But

---

15. *Kupetz* is cited for this proposition approvingly in *U.S. Bank Nat. Ass'n v. Verizon Communications Inc.*, 479 B.R. 405, 411 (Bankr. N.D. Tex. 2012) and *Lippi v. City Bank*, 955 F.2d 599, 606 (9th Cir. 1992). Professor Robert Clark has argued that fraudulent conveyance law ought to apply to corporate distributions to shareholders *in addition to* the strictures of

of course, such deals sometimes fail to yield the efficiencies that their architects promise, and target companies cannot service the debt they incur and are forced into bankruptcy. In the worst case, a target's pre-LBO unsecured creditors (among other stakeholders), who never stood to gain from the deal, stand to lose badly unless the target's trustee in bankruptcy can recover some of its losses from the parties who initiated the LBO. A bankruptcy trustee may consider several legal theories for this purpose, including fraudulent transfer.

Under fraudulent transfer doctrine, most LBOs appear to be *prima facie* cases of constructive fraud. (Proving actual fraud is very difficult for LBOs.) It is usually straightforward to show that the transaction did not involve reasonably equivalent value because the target firm receives essentially nothing and now carries a large debt burden (recall that it is the target shareholders who receive cash for their shares, not the target firm).[16] The second step — leaving the target with unreasonably small capital or near insolvency — may be met if the target fails because one reason for failure is the inability to pay the large interest costs.[17] In spite of this, it is not common for LBOs to be unwound under fraudulent transfer doctrine. Occasionally, this is because the plaintiff wasn't able to prove the requirements for constructive fraud,[18] but most often because the transaction comes within a statutory safe harbor provided by §546(e) of the Bankruptcy Code which immunizes a transfer from being voided if a "protected entity," such as a financial institution (e.g., bank) or financial intermediary, is involved.[19] Most LBOs can satisfy this requirement through the banks involved in providing debt to the acquirer, although the U.S. Supreme Court has held that the financial institution must have a real role in the transaction and not be simply a "conduit" for the transaction.[20] A later Second Circuit decision, however, has held that this role can include acting as an agent for one of the key parties to the LBO.[21]

4.3.3 Shareholder Liability

Bankruptcy and state courts may, in the right circumstances, deploy two equitable doctrines to render influential creditors and controlling shareholders at least partly responsible for the debts of insolvent corporations. These

---

the more particularistic dividend tests. Robert C. Clark, *Corporate Law*, §2.5, 86-92 (1986). As we note above, dividend limitations function very much like the fraudulent conveyance act. The difference is that under the dividend statute directors are personally liable for illegal dividends while under the UFTA only the transferee (the corporation) is personally liable, although a constructive trust could be impressed upon the dividend.

16. See *MFS/Sun Life Trust-High Yield Series v. Van Dusen Airport Servs. Co.*, 910 F. Supp. 913, 937 (S.D.N.Y. 1995).

17. See *Boyer v. Crown Stock Distribution Inc.*, 587 F.3d 787, 794 (7th Cir. 2009).

18. See, *e.g., Mellon Bank, N.A. v. Metro Communications, Inc.*, 945 F. 2d 635, 647–648 (3rd Cir. 1991), *MFS/Sun Life, supra* note 16.

19. See 11 U.S.C. §546(e).

20. See *Merit Management Group, LP v. FTI Consulting, Inc.*, 138 S.Ct. 883 (2018).

21. See *In re Tribune Co. Fraudulent Conveyance Litigation*, 946 F.3d 66 (2nd Cir. 2019).

are equitable subordination and "piercing the corporate veil." They are markedly different in legal concept but often target the same parties when shareholders are also their companies' creditors.

4.3.3.1   Equitable Subordination

Courts of equity invoke the equitable subordination doctrine when they feel compelled, by considerations of equity, to subordinate the debt owed by a company to its controllers to the debt owed to its arms-length creditors. This remedy is sometimes known as the "Deep Rock doctrine," after the 1939 U.S. Supreme Court case that validated its application under the U.S. Bankruptcy Code.[22] Today it is codified at §510(c)(1) of the U.S. Bankruptcy Code, which permits subordination of a debt claim "under principles of equitable subordination." The doctrine may be (but rarely is) invoked outside of bankruptcy proceedings.

Equitable subordination is a way to protect unaffiliated creditors by giving them rights to corporate assets superior to those of other influential creditors who are almost always significant shareholders of the firm. The critical question is what set of circumstances will lead a court to impose this subordination on a shareholder-creditor. The first requirement is that the creditor be an equity holder and typically an officer of the company. (See UPA §40(b) for the partnership analogy.) In addition, this insider-creditor must have, in some fashion, behaved inequitably toward the corporation and its outside creditors. Consider the following case.

COSTELLO v. FAZIO
256 F.2d 903 (9th Cir. 1958)

Hamley, Cir. J.:

Creditors' claims against the bankrupt estate of Leonard Plumbing and Heating Supply, Inc., were filed by J.A. Fazio and Lawrence C. Ambrose. The trustee in bankruptcy objected to these claims, and moved for an order subordinating them to the claims of general unsecured creditors. The referee in bankruptcy denied the motion, and his action was sustained by the district court. The trustee appeals.

The following facts are not in dispute: A partnership known as "Leonard Plumbing and Heating Supply Co." was organized in October, 1948. The three partners, Fazio, Ambrose, and B.T. Leonard, made initial capital contributions to the business aggregating $44,806.40. The capital contributions of the three partners, as they were recorded on the company books in September 1952, totaled $51,620.78, distributed as follows: Fazio, $43,169.61; Ambrose, $6,451.17; and Leonard, $2,000.

---

22. See *Taylor v. Standard Gas and Electric Company*, 306 U.S. 307 (1939).

In the fall of that year, it was decided to incorporate the business. In contemplation of this step, Fazio and Ambrose, on September 15, 1952, withdrew all but $2,000 apiece of their capital contributions to the business. This was accomplished by the issuance to them, on that date, of partnership promissory notes in the sum of $41,169.61 and $4,451.17, respectively. These were demand notes, no interest being specified. The capital contribution to the partnership business then stood at $6,000 — $2,000 for each partner.

The closing balance sheet of the partnership showed current assets to be $160,791.87, and current liabilities at $162,162.22. There were also fixed assets in the sum of $6,482.90, and other assets in the sum of $887.45. The partnership had cash on hand in the sum of $66.66, and an overdraft at the bank in the amount of $3,422.78.

Of the current assets, $41,357.76, representing "Accounts receivable — Trade," was assigned to American Trust Co., to secure $50,000 of its $59,000 in notes payable. Both before and after the incorporation, the business had a $75,000 line of credit with American Trust Co., secured by accounts receivable and the personal guaranty of the three partners and stockholders, and their marital communities.

The net sales of the partnership during its last year of operations were $389,543.72, as compared to net sales of $665,747.55 in the preceding year. A net loss of $22,521.34 was experienced during this last year, as compared to a net profit of $40,935.12 in the year ending September 30, 1951.

Based on the reduced capitalization of the partnership, the corporation was capitalized for six hundred shares of no par value common stock valued at ten dollars per share. Two hundred shares were issued to each of the three partners in consideration of the transfer to the corporation of their interests in the partnership. Fazio became president, and Ambrose, secretary-treasurer of the new corporation. Both were directors. The corporation assumed all liabilities of the partnership, including the notes to Fazio and Ambrose.

In June 1954, after suffering continued losses, the corporation made an assignment to the San Francisco Board of Trade for the benefit of creditors. On October 8, 1954, it filed a voluntary petition in bankruptcy. At this time, the corporation was not indebted to any creditors whose obligations were incurred by the preexisting partnership, saving the promissory notes issued to Fazio and Ambrose.

Fazio filed a claim against the estate in the sum of $34,147.55, based on the promissory note given to him when the capital of the partnership was reduced. Ambrose filed a similar claim in the sum of $7,871.17. The discrepancy between these amounts and the amounts of the promissory notes is due to certain setoffs and transfers not here in issue.

In asking that these claims be subordinated to the claims of general unsecured creditors, the trustee averred that the amounts in question represent a portion of the capital investment in the partnership. It was alleged that the transfer of this sum from the partnership capital account to an account entitled "Loans from Copartners," effectuated a scheme and plan to place copartners in the same class as unsecured creditors. The trustee further alleged, with respect to each claimant: . . . .

If said claimant is permitted to share in the assets of said bankrupt now in the hands of the trustee, in the same parity with general unsecured creditors, he will receive a portion of the capital invested which should be used to satisfy the claims of creditors before any capital investment can be returned to the owners and stockholders of said bankrupt.

A hearing was held before the referee in bankruptcy. In addition to eliciting the above recounted facts, three expert witnesses called by the trustee, and one expert witness called by the claimants, expressed opinions on various phases of the transaction.

Clifford V. Heimbucher, a certified public accountant and management consultant, called by the trustee, expressed the view that, at the time of incorporation, capitalization was inadequate. He further stated that, in incorporating a business already in existence, where the approximate amount of permanent capital needed has been established by experience, normal procedure called for continuing such capital in the form of common or preferred stock.

Stating that only additional capital needed temporarily is normally set up as loans, Heimbucher testified that ". . . the amount of capital employed in the business was at all times substantially more than the $6,000 employed in the opening of the corporation." He also expressed the opinion that, at the time of incorporation, there was "very little hope (of financial success) in view of the fact that for the year immediately preceding the opening of the corporation, losses were running a little less than $2,000 a month. . . ."

William B. Logan, a business analyst and consultant called by the trustee, expressed the view that $6,000 was inadequate capitalization for this company. John S. Curran, a business analyst, also called by the trustee, expressed the view that the corporation needed at least as much capital as the partnership required prior to the reduction of capital.

Robert H. Laborde, Jr., a certified public accountant, has handled the accounting problems of the partnership and corporation. He was called by the trustee as an adverse witness, pursuant to §21, sub. j of the Bankruptcy Act, 11 U.S.C.A. §44, sub. j. Laborde readily conceded that the transaction whereby Fazio and Ambrose obtained promissory notes from the partnership was for the purpose of transferring a capital account into a loan or debt account. He stated that this was done in contemplation of the formation of the corporation, and with knowledge that the partnership was losing money.

The prime reason for incorporating the business, according to Laborde, was to protect the personal interest of Fazio, who had made the greatest capital contribution to the business. In this connection, it was pointed out that the "liabilities on the business as a partnership were pretty heavy." There was apparently also a tax angle. Laborde testified that it was contemplated that the notes would be paid out of the profits of the business. He agreed that, if promissory notes had not been issued, the profits would have been distributed only as dividends, and that as such they would have been taxable. . . .

Laborde expressed no opinion as to the adequacy of proprietary capital put at the risk of the business. On the other hand, the corporate accounts and the undisputed testimony of three accounting experts demonstrate that stated capital was wholly inadequate.

On the evidence produced at this hearing, as summarized above, the referee found that the paid-in stated capital of the corporation at the time of its incorporation was adequate for the continued operation of the business. He found that while Fazio and Ambrose controlled and dominated the corporation and its affairs they did not mismanage the business. He further found that claimants did not practice any fraud or deception, and did not act for their own personal or private benefit and to the detriment of the corporation or its stockholders and creditors. The referee also found that the transaction which had been described was not a part of any scheme or plan to place the claimants in the same class as unsecured creditors of the partnership.

On the basis of these findings, the referee concluded that, in procuring the promissory notes, the claimants acted in all respects in good faith and took no unfair advantage of the corporation, or of its stockholders or creditors.

Pursuant to §39, sub. c of the Bankruptcy Act, 11 U.S.C.A. §67, sub. c, the trustee filed a petition for review of the referee's order. The district court, after examining the record certified to it by the referee, entered an order affirming the order of the referee.

On this appeal, the trustee advances two grounds for reversal of the district court order. The first of these is that claims of controlling shareholders will be deferred or subordinated to outside creditors where a corporation in bankruptcy has not been adequately or honestly capitalized, or has been managed to the prejudice of creditors, or where to do otherwise would be unfair to creditors.

As a basis for applying this asserted rule in the case before us, the trustee challenges most of the findings of fact noted above.

The district court and this court are required to accept the findings of the referee in bankruptcy, unless such findings are clearly erroneous. . . .

It does not require the confirmatory opinion of experts to determine from this data that the corporation was grossly undercapitalized. In the year immediately preceding incorporation, net sales aggregated $390,000. In order to handle such a turnover, the partners apparently found that capital in excess of $50,000 was necessary. They actually had $51,620.78 in the business at that time. Even then, the business was only "two jumps ahead of the wolf." A net loss of $22,000 was sustained in that year; there was only $66.66 in the bank; and there was an overdraft of $3,422.78.

Yet, despite this precarious financial condition, Fazio and Ambrose withdrew $45,620.78 of the partnership capital — more than eighty-eight percent of the total capital. The $6,000 capital left in the business was only one-sixty-fifth of the last annual net sales. All this is revealed by the books of the company.

But if there is need to confirm this conclusion that the corporation was grossly undercapitalized, such confirmation is provided by three of the four experts who testified. The fourth expert, called by appellees, did not express an opinion to the contrary.

We therefore hold that the factual conclusion of the referee, that the corporation was adequately capitalized at the time of its organization, is clearly erroneous.

The factual conclusion of the trial court, that the claimants, in withdrawing capital from the partnership in contemplation of incorporation, did not act for their own personal or private benefit and to the detriment of the corporation or of its stockholders and creditors, is based upon the same accounting data and expert testimony.

Laborde, testifying for the claimants, made it perfectly clear that the depletion of the capital account in favor of a debt account was for the purpose of equalizing the capital investments of the partners and to reduce tax liability when there were profits to distribute. It is therefore certain, contrary to the finding just noted, that, in withdrawing this capital, Fazio and Ambrose did act for their own personal and private benefit.

It is equally certain, from the undisputed facts, that in so doing they acted to the detriment of the corporation and its creditors. The best evidence of this is what happened to the business after incorporation, and what will happen to its creditors if the reduction in capital is allowed to stand. The likelihood that business failure would result from such under-capitalization should have been apparent to anyone who knew the company's financial and business history and who had access to its balance sheet and profit and loss statements. Three expert witnesses confirmed this view, and none expressed a contrary opinion.

Accordingly, we hold that the factual conclusion, that the claimants, in withdrawing capital, did not act for their own personal or private benefit and to the detriment of the corporation and creditors, is clearly erroneous.

Recasting the facts in the light of what is said above, the question which appellant presents is this:

Where, in connection with the incorporation of a partnership, and for their own personal and private benefit, two partners who are to become officers, directors, and controlling stockholders of the corporation, convert the bulk of their capital contributions into loans, taking promissory notes, thereby leaving the partnership and succeeding corporation grossly undercapitalized, to the detriment of the corporation and its creditors, should their claims against the estate of the subsequently bankrupted corporation be subordinated to the claims of the general unsecured creditors?

The question almost answers itself. In allowing and disallowing claims, courts of bankruptcy apply the rules and principles of equity jurisprudence. . . . Where the claim is found to be inequitable, it may be set aside, or subordinated to the claims of other creditors. . . . [T]he question to be determined when the plan or transaction which gives rise to a claim is challenged as inequitable is "whether, within the bounds of reason and fairness, such a plan can be justified."

Where, as here, the claims are filed by persons standing in a fiduciary relationship to the corporation, another test which equity will apply is "whether or not under all the circumstances the transaction carries the earmarks of an arm's length bargain." *Pepper v. Litton, supra*, 308 U.S. at page 306. . . .

Under either of these tests, the transaction here in question stands condemned.

Appellees argue that more must be shown than mere undercapitalization if the claims are to be subordinated. Much more than mere under-capitalization was shown here. Persons serving in a fiduciary relationship to the corporation actually withdrew capital already committed to the business, in the face of recent adverse financial experience. They stripped the business of eighty-eight percent of its stated capital at a time when it had a minus working capital and had suffered substantial business losses. This was done for personal gain, under circumstances which charge them with knowledge that the corporation and its creditors would be endangered. Taking advantage of their fiduciary position, they thus sought to gain equality of treatment with general creditors.

In . . . other cases, there was fraud and mismanagement present in addition to undercapitalization. Appellees argue from this that fraud and mismanagement must always be present if claims are to be subordinated in a situation involving undercapitalization.

This is not the rule. The test to be applied . . . is whether the transaction can be justified "within the bounds of reason and fairness."

The fact that the withdrawal of capital occurred prior to incorporation is immaterial. This transaction occurred in contemplation of incorporation. The participants then occupied a fiduciary relationship to the partnership; and expected to become controlling stockholders, directors, and officers of the corporation. This plan was effectuated, and they were serving in those fiduciary capacities when the corporation assumed the liabilities of the partnership, including the notes here in question.

Nor is the fact that the business, after being stripped of necessary capital, was able to survive long enough to have a turnover of creditors a mitigating circumstance. The inequitable conduct of appellees consisted not in acting to the detriment of creditors then known, but in acting to the detriment of present or future creditors, whoever they may be. . . .

Reversed and remanded for further proceedings not inconsistent with this opinion.

QUESTIONS ON COSTELLO v. FAZIO

1. Which creditors benefit from equitable subordination: old partnership creditors, new corporate creditors, or all creditors?

2. Suppose there had been no past history of partnership and the business had been started as a corporation with $6,000 in stated capital and $50,000 in loans from its shareholders. Would such a new firm have involved the same inequitable conduct? What result under the doctrine of equitable subordination?

3. What result if the business had limped along for five years on its capital before going under?

4. Would the case have had the same outcome under UVTA §4(a)?

5. In *Gannett Co. v. Larry*,[23] Gannett, a newspaper publishing company, bought all of the shares of Berwin, a paper manufacturing company, in 1951. Gannett promptly reconfigured Berwin's machines to produce newsprint, which Gannett feared would be in short supply in 1952. Gannett also loaned Berwin money for this purpose and to fund its operations. But when the newsprint shortage failed to materialize, Berwin became unprofitable and,

---

23. 221 F.2d 269 (2d Cir. 1955).

without Gannett's assistance, was forced to file for bankruptcy in May 1953. In an ensuing appeal, the Second Circuit ruled that Gannett's loans should be equitably subordinated to those of other Berwin creditors. It distinguished a similar case that had held differently on the grounds that Berwin's losses "were suffered, not in an attempt by Gannett primarily to make [its] subsidiary a financially profitable proposition, but to turn it into a source of newsprint, of no interest to the other creditors." Does this distinction recall the facts of our first case in Chapter 1, *Jenson Farms Co. v. Cargill, Inc., supra* p. 9. Does it make sense to you?

6. Bankruptcy courts sometimes consider the third-party effects of equitable subordination (and other ex post creditor remedies). The infamous Enron bankruptcy provides an illustration. Some of Enron's creditors sold their claims to third parties after it filed for bankruptcy. Enron's trustee in bankruptcy argued that the original creditors were subject to equitable subordination and that, for this reason, the later creditors to whom they sold their claims should be similarly subordinated. But the U.S. District Court disagreed, holding that the subordination of a bona fide purchaser of claims must be assessed on the basis of its own behavior rather than that of the original creditor. This may permit original creditors to evade equitable subordination. Nevertheless, the court held that it was dictated by statute as well as policy concerns. It noted that "in the distressed debt market context, where sellers are often anonymous and purchasers have no way of ascertaining whether the seller (or a transferee up the line) has acted inequitably or received a preference [then] it is unclear how the market would price such unknowable risk." *In Re Enron Corp.*, 379 B.R. 425 (S.D.N.Y. 2007). Should bankruptcy courts consider the external market in corporate debt as relevant in determining priority among the claims of corporate creditors?

4.3.3.2   *Piercing the Corporate Veil*

The most frequently invoked — and radical — form of shareholder liability in the cause of creditor protection is the equitable power of the court to set aside the entity status of the corporation ("piercing the veil") to hold its shareholders liable directly on contract or tort obligations. This, too, is an "equitable" device through which courts declare that they will not permit the attributes of the corporate form to be used to perpetrate a fraud.

As with all doctrines that are "equitable" in character (e.g., the equitable subordination doctrine), the guidelines for veil piercing are vague. One common formulation is the *Lowendahl* test, under which veil piercing requires that plaintiff shows the existence of a shareholder who completely dominates corporate policy and uses her control to commit a fraud or "wrong" that proximately causes plaintiff's injury. The domination required for this test often includes a failure to treat the corporation's formality seriously. Another formulation of the test calls on courts to disregard the corporate form whenever recognition of it would extend the principle of incorporation "beyond its legitimate purposes and [would] produce injustices or inequitable consequences." *Krivo Industrial Supply Co. v. National*

Distillers & Chem. Corp., 483 F.2d 1098, 1106 (5th Cir. 1973). All courts applying traditional veil-piercing standards agree that some abuse of the corporate form is required in order to ignore the separate legal identity of the corporation. All agree that veil piercing should be done sparingly; the question remains how sparingly. A number of factors may play a role in veil-piercing decisions: a disregard of corporate formalities, thin capitalization, and active involvement by shareholders in management are but a few. Consider the basis for applying the veil-piercing doctrine in the two following contract cases.

SEA-LAND SERVICES, INC. v. THE PEPPER SOURCE
941 F.2d 519 (7th Cir. 1991)

BAUER, C.J.:

This spicy case finds its origin in several shipments of Jamaican sweet peppers. Appellee Sea-Land Services, Inc. ("Sea-Land"), an ocean carrier, shipped the peppers on behalf of The Pepper Source ("PS"), one of the appellants here. PS then stiffed Sea-Land on the freight bill, which was rather substantial. Sea-Land filed a federal diversity action for the money it was owed. On December 2, 1987, the district court entered a default judgment in favor of Sea-Land and against PS in the amount of $86,767.70. But PS was nowhere to be found; it had been "dissolved" in mid-1987 for failure to pay the annual state franchise tax. Worse yet for Sea-Land, even had it not been dissolved, PS apparently had no assets. With the well empty, Sea-Land could not recover its judgment against PS. Hence the instant lawsuit.

In June 1988, Sea-Land brought this action against Gerald J. Marchese and five business entities he owns: PS, Caribe Crown, Inc., Jamar Corp., Salescaster Distributors, Inc., and Marchese Fegan Associates. Marchese also was named individually. Sea-Land sought by this suit to pierce PS's corporate veil and render Marchese personally liable for the judgment owed to Sea-Land, and then "reverse pierce" Marchese's other corporations so that they, too, would be on the hook for the $87,000. Thus, Sea-Land alleged in its complaint that all of these corporations "are alter egos of each other and hide behind the veils of alleged separate corporate existence for the purpose of defrauding plaintiff and other creditors." Not only are the corporations alter egos of each other, alleged Sea-Land, but also they are alter egos of Marchese, who should be held individually liable for the judgment because he created and manipulated these corporations and their assets for his own personal uses. (Hot on the heels of the filing of Sea-Land's complaint, PS took the necessary steps to be reinstated as a corporation in Illinois.)

In early 1989, Sea-Land filed an amended complaint adding Tie-Net International, Inc., as a defendant. Unlike the other corporate defendants, Tie-Net is not owned solely by Marchese: he holds half of the stock, and an individual named George Andre owns the other half. Sea-Land alleged that, despite this shared ownership, Tie-Net is but another alter ego of Marchese and the other corporate defendants, and thus it also should be held liable for the judgment against PS.

Through 1989, Sea-Land pursued discovery in this case, including taking a two-day deposition from Marchese. In December 1989, Sea-Land moved for summary judgment. In that motion — which, with the brief in support and the appendices, was about three inches thick — Sea-Land argued that it was "entitled to judgment as a matter of law, since the evidence including deposition testimony and exhibits in the appendix will show that piercing the corporate veil and finding the status of an alter ego is merited in this case." Marchese and the other defendants filed brief responses.

In an order dated June 22, 1990, the court granted Sea-Land's motion. The court discussed and applied the test for corporate veil-piercing explicated in *Van Dorn Co. v. Future Chemical and Oil Corp.*, 753 F.2d 565 (7th Cir. 1985). Analyzing Illinois law, we held in *Van Dorn*:

> [A] corporate entity will be disregarded and the veil of limited liability pierced when two requirements are met: [F]irst, there must be such unity of interest and ownership that the separate personalities of the corporation and the individual [or other corporation] no longer exist; and second, circumstances must be such that adherence to the fiction of separate corporate existence would sanction a fraud or promote injustice.

753 F.2d at 569-70 (quoting *Macaluso v. Jenkins*, 95 Ill. App. 3d 461, 420 N.E.2d 251, 255 (1981)) (other citations omitted). . . . As for determining whether a corporation is so controlled by another to justify disregarding their separate identities, the Illinois cases . . . focus on four factors: "(1) the failure to maintain adequate corporate records or to comply with corporate formalities, (2) the commingling of funds or assets, (3) under-capitalization, and (4) one corporation treating the assets of another corporation as its own." 753 F.2d at 570 (citations omitted). . . .

Following the lead of the parties, the district court in the instant case laid the template of *Van Dorn* over the facts of this case. The court concluded that both halves and all features of the test had been satisfied, and, therefore, entered judgment in favor of Sea-Land and against PS, Caribe Crown, Jamar, Salescaster, Tie-Net, and Marchese individually. These defendants were held jointly liable for Sea-Land's $87,000 judgment, as well as for post-judgment interest under Illinois law. From that judgment Marchese and the other defendants brought a timely appeal.

Because this is an appeal from a grant of summary judgment, our review is de novo. . . .

The first and most striking feature that emerges from our examination of the record is that these corporate defendants are, indeed, little but Marchese's playthings. Marchese is the sole shareholder of PS, Caribe Crown, Jamar, and Salescaster. He is one of the two shareholders of Tie-Net. Except for Tie-Net, none of the corporations ever held a single corporate meeting. (At the handful of Tie-Net meetings held by Marchese and Andre, no minutes were taken.) During his deposition, Marchese did not remember any of these corporations ever passing articles of incorporation, bylaws, or other agreements. As for physical facilities, Marchese runs all of these corporations (including Tie-Net) out of the same, single office, with the same phone line, the same expense accounts, and the like. And how he does "run" the expense accounts! When he fancies to, Marchese "borrows" substantial sums of money from these corporations — interest free, of course. The corporations also "borrow" money from each other when need be, which left at least PS completely out of capital when the Sea-Land bills came due. What's more, Marchese has used the bank accounts of these corporations to pay all kinds of personal expenses, including alimony and child support payments to his ex-wife, education expenses for his children, maintenance of his personal automobiles, health care for his pet — the list goes on and on. Marchese did not even have a personal bank account! (With "corporate" accounts like these, who needs one?)

And Tie-Net is just as much a part of this as the other corporations. On appeal, Marchese makes much of the fact that he shares ownership of Tie-Net, and that Sea-Land has not been able to find an example of funds flowing from PS to Tie-Net to the detriment of Sea-Land and PS's other creditors. So what? The record reveals that, in all material senses, Marchese treated Tie-Net like his other corporations: he "borrowed" over $30,000 from Tie-Net; money and "loans" flowed freely between Tie-Net and the other corporations; and Marchese charged up various personal expenses (including $460 for a picture of himself with President Bush) on Tie-Net's credit card. Marchese was not deterred by the fact that he did not hold all of the stock of Tie-Net; why should his creditors be?

In sum, we agree with the district court that there can be no doubt that the "shared control/unity of interest and ownership" part of the *Van Dorn* test is met in this case: corporate records and formalities have not been maintained; funds and assets have been commingled with abandon; PS, the offending corporation, and perhaps others have been undercapitalized; and corporate assets have been moved and tapped and "borrowed" without regard to their source. Indeed, Marchese basically punted this part of the inquiry before the district court by coming forward with little or no evidence in response to Sea-Land's extensively supported argument on these points. That fact alone was enough to do him in; opponents to summary judgment motions cannot simply rest on their laurels, but must come forward with specific facts showing that there is a genuine issue for trial. . . . Regarding the elements that make up the first half of the *Van Dorn* test, Marchese and the other defendants have not done so. Thus, Sea-Land is entitled to judgment on these points.

The second part of the *Van Dorn* test is more problematic, however. "Unity of interest and ownership" is not enough; Sea-Land also must show that honoring the separate corporate existences of the defendants "would sanction a fraud or promote injustice." *Van Dorn*, 753 F.2d at 570. This last phrase truly is disjunctive:

> Although an intent to defraud creditors would surely play a part if established, the Illinois test does not require proof of such intent. Once the first element of the test is established, *either* the sanctioning of a fraud (intentional wrongdoing) or the promotion of injustice, will satisfy the second element.

Id. (emphasis in original). Seizing on this, Sea-Land has abandoned the language in its two complaints that make repeated references to "fraud" by Marchese, and has chosen not to attempt to prove that PS and Marchese intended to defraud it — which would be quite difficult on summary judgment. Instead,

Sea-Land has argued that honoring the defendants' separate identities would "promote injustice."

But what, exactly, does "promote injustice" mean, and how does one establish it on summary judgment? These are the critical, troublesome questions in this case. To start with, as the above passage from *Van Dorn* makes clear, "promote injustice" means something less than an affirmative showing of fraud — but how much less? In its one-sentence treatment of this point, the district court held that it was enough that "Sea-Land would be denied a judicially-imposed recovery." Sea-Land defends this reasoning on appeal, arguing that "permitting the appellants to hide behind the shield of limited liability would clearly serve as an injustice against appellee" because it would "impermissibly deny appellee satisfaction." Appellee's Brief at 14-15. But that cannot be what is meant by "promote injustice." The prospect of an unsatisfied judgment looms in every veil-piercing action; why else would a plaintiff bring such an action? Thus, if an unsatisfied judgment is enough for the "promote injustice" feature of the test, then every plaintiff will pass on that score, and *Van Dorn* collapses into a one-step "unity of interest and ownership" test.

Because we cannot abide such a result [How is that for candor! — EDS.] we will undertake our own review of Illinois cases to determine how the "promote injustice" feature of the veil-piercing inquiry has been interpreted. In *Pederson* [*v. Paragon Enterprises*, 214 Ill. App. 3d 815, 158 Ill. Dec. 371, 373, 547 N.E.2d 165, 167 (1st Dist. 1991)], . . . the court offered the following summary: "Some element of unfairness, something akin to fraud or deception or the existence of a compelling public interest must be present in order to disregard the corporate fiction." 214 Ill. App. 3d at 821, 158 Ill. Dec. at 375, 574 N.E.2d at 169. (The court ultimately refused to pierce the corporate veil in *Pederson*, at least in part because "[n]othing in these facts provides evidence of scheming on the part of defendant to commit a fraud on potential creditors [of the two defendant corporations]." *Id.* at 823, 158 Ill. Dec. at 376, 574 N.E.2d at 169.)

The light shed on this point by other Illinois cases can be seen only if we examine the cases on their facts. . . .

Generalizing from these cases, we see that the courts that properly have pierced corporate veils to avoid "promoting injustice" have found that, unless it [*sic*] did so, some "wrong" beyond a creditor's inability to collect would result: the common sense rules of adverse possession would be undermined; former partners would be permitted to skirt the legal rules concerning monetary obligations; a party would be unjustly enriched; a parent corporation that caused a sub's liabilities and its inability to pay for them would escape those liabilities; or an intentional scheme to squirrel assets into a liability-free corporation while heaping liabilities upon an asset-free corporation would be successful. Sea-Land, although it alleged in its complaint the kind of intentional asset-and-liability-shifting found in *Van Dorn*, has yet to come forward with evidence akin to the "wrongs" found in these cases. Apparently, it believed as did the district court, that its unsatisfied judgment was enough. That belief was in error, and the entry of summary judgment premature. We, therefore, reverse the judgment and remand the case to the district court.

On remand, the court should require that Sea-Land produce, if it desires summary judgment, evidence and argument that would establish the kind of additional "wrong" present in the above cases. For example, perhaps Sea-Land could establish that Marchese, like Roth in *Van Dorn*, used these corporate facades to avoid its responsibilities to creditors; or that PS, Marchese, or one of the other corporations will be "unjustly enriched" unless liability is shared by all. Of course, Sea-Land is not required fully to prove intent to defraud, which it probably could not do on summary judgment anyway. But it is required to show the kind of injustice to merit the evocation of the court's essentially equitable power to prevent "injustice." It may well be that, after more of such evidence is adduced, no genuine issue of fact exists to prevent Sea-Land from reaching Marchese's other pet corporations for PS's debt. Or it may be that only a finder of fact will be able to determine whether fraud or "injustice" is involved here. In any event, the record as it currently stands is insufficient to uphold the entry of summary judgment.

REVERSED and REMANDED with instructions.

NOTE ON SEA-LAND SERVICES

Sea-Land's substance is more traditional than its prose. This is a fair summary of Illinois law and probably reflects the majority view on when the veil should be pierced. Notably in this case, and in most cases where the piercing remedy is invoked, there is a failure to treat the corporate fiction seriously. Thus, as in *Sea-Land*, courts find it significant when parties fail to observe corporate formalities.

On remand, the district court entered a judgment for Sea-Land and against Marchese for $86,768 plus post-judgment interest of $31,365. To support its legal conclusion that maintaining the corporate veil would "sanction a fraud or promote injustice," the court relied on the fact that Marchese had committed blatant tax fraud and that Marchese had assured a Sea-Land representative that his freight bill would be paid, even though he was planning to manipulate the corporate funds to ensure there would not be funds to pay Sea-Land's bills. The district court's decision to pierce was subsequently affirmed by the Seventh Circuit. *Sea-Land Services, Inc. v. The Pepper Source*, 993 F.2d 1309 (7th Cir. 1993).

QUESTIONS ON SEA-LAND SERVICES

1. What does "reverse piercing" mean in this case? And why isn't Sea-Land content to pierce through to Marchese's assets — won't it acquire the stock (and hence the value) of his other corporations if Marchese is found to be personally liable? Who might legitimately complain that this novel remedy is unfair to them (other than the expected whining of Marchese himself)?

2. Why doesn't a creditor's inability to collect "unjustly enrich" the owners of a defaulting corporation, and hence "promote injustice" under the test?

3. Is there a principle lurking behind the court's various examples of "injustice" that falls short of fraud? Can you generalize (as the court fails to do)?

KINNEY SHOE CORP. v. POLAN
939 F.2d 209 (4th Cir. 1991)

CHAPMAN, SENIOR CIR. J.:

Plaintiff-appellant Kinney Shoe Corporation ("Kinney") brought this action in the United States District Court for the Southern District of West Virginia against Lincoln M. Polan ("Polan") seeking to recover money owed on a sublease between Kinney and Industrial Realty Company ("Industrial"). Polan is the sole shareholder of Industrial. The district court found that Polan was not personally liable on the lease between Kinney and Industrial. Kinney appeals asserting that the corporate veil should be pierced, and we agree. . . .

The district court based its order on facts which were stipulated by the parties. In 1984 Polan formed two corporations, Industrial and Polan Industries, Inc., for the purpose of re-establishing an industrial manufacturing business. The certificate of incorporation for Polan Industries, Inc. was issued by the West Virginia Secretary of State in November 1984. The following month the certificate of incorporation for Industrial was issued. Polan was the owner of both corporations. Although certificates of incorporation were issued, no organizational meetings were held, and no officers were elected.

In November 1984 Polan and Kinney began negotiating the sublease of a building in which Kinney held a leasehold interest. The building was owned by the Cabell County Commission and financed by industrial revenue bonds issued in 1968 to induce Kinney to locate a manufacturing plant in Huntington, West Virginia. Under the terms of the lease, Kinney was legally obligated to make payments on the bonds on a semi-annual basis through January 1, 1993, at which time it had the right to purchase the property. Kinney had ceased using the building as a manufacturing plant in June 1983.

The term of the sublease from Kinney to Industrial commenced in December 1984, even though the written lease was not signed by the parties until April 5, 1985. On April 15, 1985, Industrial subleased part of the building to Polan Industries, for fifty percent of the rental amount due Kinney. Polan signed both subleases on behalf of the respective companies.

Other than the sublease with Kinney, Industrial had no assets, no income and no bank account. Industrial issued no stock certificates because nothing was ever paid in to this corporation. Industrial's only income was from its sublease to Polan Industries, Inc. The first rental payment to Kinney was made out of Polan's personal funds, and no further payments were made by Polan or by Polan Industries, Inc. to either Industrial or to Kinney.

Kinney filed suit against Industrial for unpaid rent and obtained a judgment in the amount of $166,400 on June 19, 1987. A writ of possession was issued, but because Polan Industries, Inc. had filed for bankruptcy, Kinney did not gain possession for six months. Kinney leased the building until it was sold on September 1, 1988. Kinney then filed this action against Polan individually to collect the amount owed by Industrial to Kinney. Since the amount to which Kinney is entitled is undisputed, the only issue is whether Kinney can pierce the corporate veil and hold Polan personally liable.

The district court held that Kinney had assumed the risk of Industrial's undercapitalization and was not entitled to pierce the corporate veil. Kinney appeals, and we reverse. . . .

We have long recognized that a corporation is an entity, separate and distinct from its officers and stockholders, and the individual stockholders are not responsible for the debts of the corporation. . . . This concept, however, is a fiction of the law " 'and it is now well settled, as a general principle, that the fiction should be disregarded when it is urged with an intent not within its reason and purpose, and in such a way that its retention would produce injustices or inequitable consequences.' " *Laya v. Erin Homes, Inc.*, 352 S.E.2d 93, 97-98 (W. Va. 1986). . . . Piercing the corporate veil is an equitable remedy, and the burden rests with the party asserting such claim. A totality of the circumstances test is used in determining whether to pierce the corporate veil, and each case must be decided on its own facts. The district court's findings of facts may be overturned only if clearly erroneous.

Kinney seeks to pierce the corporate veil of Industrial so as to hold Polan personally liable on the sublease debt. The Supreme Court of Appeals of West Virginia has set forth a two-prong test to be used in determining whether to pierce the corporate veil in a breach of contract case. This test raises two issues. First, is the unity of interest and ownership such that the separate personalities of the corporation and the individual shareholder no longer exist; and second, would an inequitable result occur if the acts were treated as those of the corporation alone. *Laya*, 352 S.E.2d at 99. Numerous factors have been identified as relevant in making this determination.

The district court found that the two prong test of *Laya* had been satisfied. The court concluded that Polan's failure to carry out the corporate formalities with respect to Industrial, coupled with Industrial's gross undercapitalization, resulted in damage to Kinney. We agree.

It is undisputed that Industrial was not adequately capitalized. Actually, it had no paid-in capital. Polan had put nothing into this corporation, and it did not observe any corporate formalities. As the West Virginia court stated in *Laya*, "[i]ndividuals who wish to enjoy limited personal liability for business activities under a corporate umbrella should be expected to adhere to the relatively simple formalities of creating and maintaining a corporate entity." *Laya*, 352 S.E.2d at 100, n.6. . . . This, the court stated, is "a relatively small price to pay for limited liability." *Id.* Another important factor is adequate capitalization. "[G]rossly inadequate capitalization combined with disregard of corporate formalities, causing basic unfairness, are sufficient to pierce the corporate veil in order to hold the shareholder(s) actively participating in the operation of the business personally liable for a breach of contract to the party who entered into the contract with the corporation." *Laya*, 352 S.E.2d at 101-02.

In this case, Polan bought no stock, made no capital contribution, kept no minutes, and elected no officers for Industrial. In addition, Polan attempted to protect his assets by placing them in Polan Industries, Inc. and interposing Industrial between Polan Industries, Inc. and Kinney so as to prevent Kinney from going against the corporation with assets. Polan gave no explanation or justification for the existence of Industrial as the intermediary between Polan Industries, Inc. and Kinney. Polan was obviously trying to limit his liability and the liability of Polan Industries, Inc. by setting up a paper curtain constructed of nothing more than Industrial's certificate of incorporation. These facts present the classic scenario for an action to pierce the corporate veil so as to reach the responsible party and produce an equitable result. Accordingly, we hold that the district court correctly found that the two-prong test in *Laya* had been satisfied. In *Laya*, the court also noted that when determining whether to pierce a corporate veil a third prong may apply in certain cases. The Court stated:

> When, under the circumstances, it would be reasonable for that particular type of a party [those contract creditors capable of protecting themselves] entering into a contract with the corporation, for example, a bank or other lending institution, to conduct an investigation of the credit of the corporation prior to entering into the contract, such party will be charged with the knowledge that a reasonable credit investigation would disclose. If such an investigation would disclose that the corporation is grossly undercapitalized, based upon the nature and the magnitude of the corporate undertaking, such party will be deemed to have assumed the risk of the gross undercapitalization and will not be permitted to pierce the corporate veil.

Laya, 352 S.E.2d at 100. The district court applied this third prong and concluded that Kinney "assumed the risk of Industrial's defaulting" and that "the application of the doctrine of 'piercing the corporate veil' ought not and does not [apply]." While we agree that the two-prong test of *Laya* was satisfied, we hold that the district court's conclusion that Kinney had assumed the risk is clearly erroneous.

Without deciding whether the third prong should be extended beyond the context of the financial institution lender mentioned in *Laya*, we hold that, even if it applies to creditors such as Kinney, it does not prevent Kinney from piercing the corporate veil in this case. The third prong is permissive and not mandatory. This is not a factual situation that calls for the third prong, if we are to seek an equitable result. Polan set up Industrial to limit his liability and the liability of Polan Industries, Inc. in their dealings with Kinney. A stockholder's liability is limited to the amount he has invested in the corporation, but Polan invested nothing in Industrial. This corporation was no more than a shell — a transparent shell. When nothing is invested in the corporation, the corporation provides no protection to its owner; nothing in, nothing out, no protection. If Polan wishes the protection of a corporation to limit his liability, he must follow the simple formalities of maintaining the corporation. This he failed to do, and he may not relieve his circumstances by saying Kinney should have known better. . . .

For the foregoing reasons, we hold that Polan is personally liable for the debt of Industrial, and the decision of the district court is reversed and this case is remanded with instructions to enter judgment for the plaintiff.

REVERSED AND REMANDED WITH INSTRUCTIONS.

QUESTIONS ON KINNEY SHOE

1. Should we feel sorry for Kinney Shoe? It had a rent obligation and was apparently desperate to get someone else on the premises. It took a substantial risk with a newly formed business. If there were no misrepresentations by Polan about putting minimum capital in Industrial, why not conclude with the district court that Kinney "assumed the risk of Industrial's defaulting"? Do you imagine that Kinney asked Polan to personally guarantee the lease payments and he refused?

2. Where was Polan's lawyer? Is this sort of deal one that we should try to prevent? If not, then what should Polan do next time to ensure that the veil will not be pierced?

3. Would the Seventh Circuit, applying the Illinois law of *Sea-Land*, reach the same result in *Kinney Shoe*? How would you characterize the difference between the *Sea-Land* test and the three-prong West Virginia test described in *Kinney Shoe*?

A more general question is how courts should evaluate a contract creditor's claim that the court pierce the liability shield. Professor Robert Clark, in his treatise, attempts to organize veil-piercing law under the norms that he perceives as central to fraudulent conveyance law. Commentators in the law and economics tradition, however, tend to see the appropriate norm in simpler terms: Limited liability is merely a standard term in the contract between the real debtor (the shareholder-owners of the corporation) and the creditor. It follows that the term should be enforced unless there is an element of misrepresentation without which the deal would not have been done.

Note, however, that misrepresentation can come in "hard" and "soft" varieties. Hard misrepresentations are explicit lies. Soft misrepresentations include nondisclosure of facts that contradict the legitimate expectations of creditors and actions that thwart these expectations.

One study examined all veil-piercing cases appearing in Westlaw through 1985. The study found that the corporate veil was pierced in 92 percent of the cases in which there was a judicial finding of misrepresentation, in 8 percent of the cases in which there was a finding of no misrepresentation, and in 33 percent of the remaining cases in which misrepresentation was not explicitly addressed by the court. Somewhat surprisingly, the study also found that courts were considerably more likely to pierce on behalf of contract creditors than on behalf of tort creditors—perhaps because the presence of explicit misrepresentation in many of the contract cases made the justification for piercing especially persuasive. See Robert B. Thompson, *Piercing the Corporate Veil: An Empirical Study*, 76 Cornell L. Rev. 1036 (1991).

4.4   VEIL PIERCING ON BEHALF OF INVOLUNTARY CREDITORS

Tort creditors of thinly capitalized corporations differ from contract creditors in at least two key respects. First, they probably do not rely on the creditworthiness of the corporation in placing themselves in a position to suffer a loss. Second, they generally cannot negotiate with a corporate tortfeasor ex ante for contractual protections from risk. Indeed, tort creditors may be unaware of the existence of the tortfeasor and much less able to monitor its capitalization or insurance coverage. These distinctions between tort and contract creditors are well established in the law of agency and partnership, and are generally recognized as important by commentators on corporate law. Nevertheless, until recently they received surprisingly little explicit recognition in veil-piercing doctrine. The leading tort case remains *Walkovszky v. Carlton*, excerpted below. The general rule of veil piercing remains: Thin capitalization alone is insufficient ground for piercing the corporate veil.

WALKOVSZKY v. CARLTON
223 N.E.2d 6 (N.Y. 1966)

Fuld, J.:

This case involves what appears to be a rather common practice in the taxicab industry of vesting the ownership of a taxi fleet in many corporations, each owning only one or two cabs.

The complaint alleges that the plaintiff was severely injured four years ago in New York City when he was run down by a taxicab owned by the defendant Seon Cab Corporation and negligently operated at the time by the defendant Marchese. The individual defendant, Carlton, is claimed to be a stockholder of 10 corporations, including Seon, each of which has but two cabs registered in its name, and it is implied that only the minimum automobile liability insurance required by law (in the amount of $10,000) is carried on any one cab. Although seemingly independent of one another, these corporations are alleged to be "operated . . . as a single entity, unit and enterprise" with regard to financing, supplies, repairs, employees and garaging, and all are named as defendants. The plaintiff asserts that he is also entitled to hold their stockholders personally liable for the damages sought because the multiple corporate structure constitutes an unlawful attempt "to defraud members of the general public" who might be injured by the cabs.

The defendant Carlton has moved . . . to dismiss the complaint on the ground that as to him it "fails to state a cause of action." The court at Special Term granted the motion but the Appellate Division, by a divided vote, reversed, holding that a valid cause of action was sufficiently stated. The defendant Carlton appeals to us, from the nonfinal order, by leave of the Appellate Division on a certified question.

The law permits the incorporation of a business for the very purpose of enabling its proprietors to escape personal liability . . . but, manifestly, the privilege is not without its limits. Broadly speaking, the courts will disregard the corporate form, or, to use accepted terminology, "pierce the corporate veil," whenever necessary "to prevent fraud or to achieve equity." . . . [W]henever anyone uses control of the corporation to further his own rather than the corporation's business, he will be liable for the corporation's acts "upon the principle of respondeat superior applicable even where the agent is a natural person." . . . Such liability, moreover, extends not only to the corporation's commercial dealings . . . but to its negligent acts as well.

In the *Mangan* case (247 App. Div. 853 . . .), the plaintiff was injured as a result of the negligent operation of a cab owned and operated by one of four corporations affiliated with the defendant Terminal. Although the defendant was not a stockholder of any of the operating companies, both the defendant and the operating companies were owned, for the most part, by the same parties. The defendant's name (Terminal) was conspicuously displayed on the sides of all the taxis used in the enterprise and, in point of fact, the defendant actually serviced, inspected, repaired and dispatched them. These facts were deemed to provide sufficient cause for piercing the corporate veil of the operating company — the nominal owner of the cab which injured the plaintiff — and holding the defendant liable. The operating companies were simple instrumentalities for carrying on the business of the defendant without imposing upon it financial and other liabilities incident to the actual ownership and operation of the cabs. . . .

In the case before us, the plaintiff has explicitly alleged that none of the corporations "had a separate existence of their own" and, as indicated above, all are named as defendants. However, it is one thing to assert that a corporation is a fragment of a larger corporate combine which actually conducts the business. (See Berle, "The Theory of Enterprise Entity," 47 Col. L. Rev. 343, 348-350.) It is quite another to claim that the corporation is a "dummy" for its individual stockholders who are in reality carrying on the business in their personal capacities for purely personal rather than corporate ends. . . . Either circumstance would justify treating the corporation as an agent and piercing the corporate veil to reach the principal but a different result would follow in each case. In the first, only a larger corporate entity would be held financially responsible . . . while, in the other, the stockholder would be personally liable. . . .

At this stage in the present litigation, we are concerned only with the pleadings and, since CPLR §3014 permits causes of action to be stated "alternatively or hypothetically," it is possible for the plaintiff to allege both theories as the basis for his demand for judgment. . . . Reading the complaint in this case most favorably and liberally, we do not believe that there can be gathered from its averments the allegations required to spell out a valid cause of action against the defendant Carlton.

The individual defendant is charged with having "organized, managed, dominated and controlled" a fragmented corporate entity but there are no allegations that he was conducting business in his individual capacity. Had the taxicab fleet been owned by a single corporation, it would be readily apparent that the plaintiff would face formidable barriers in attempting to establish personal liability on the part of the corporation's stockholders. The fact that the fleet ownership has been deliberately split up among many corporations does not ease the plaintiff's burden in that respect. The corporate form may not be disregarded merely because the assets of the corporation, together with the mandatory insurance coverage of the vehicle which struck the plaintiff, are insufficient to assure him the recovery sought. If Carlton were to be held individually liable on those facts alone, the decision would apply equally to the thousands of cabs which are owned by their individual drivers who conduct their businesses through corporations organized pursuant to section 401 of the Business Corporation Law, . . . and carry the minimum insurance. . . . These taxi owner-operators are entitled to form such corporations . . . and we agree with the court at Special Term that, if the insurance coverage required by statute "is inadequate for the protection of the public, the remedy lies not with the courts but with the Legislature." It may very well be sound policy to require that certain corporations must take out liability insurance which will afford adequate compensation to their potential tort victims. However, the responsibility for imposing conditions on the privilege of incorporation has been committed by the Constitution to the Legislature. . . .

This is not to say that it is impossible for the plaintiff to state a valid cause of action against the defendant Carlton. However, the simple fact is that the plaintiff has just not done so here. While the complaint alleges that the separate corporations were undercapitalized and that their assets have been intermingled, it is barren of any "sufficiently particular(ized) statements" . . . that the defendant Carlton and his associates are actually doing business in their individual capacities, shuttling their personal funds in and out of the corporations "without regard to formality and to suit their immediate convenience." *Weisser v. Mursam Shoe Corp.*, 127 F.2d 344. . . . Nothing of the sort has in fact been charged, and it cannot reasonably or logically be inferred from the happenstance that the business of Seon Cab Corporation may actually be carried on by a large corporate entity composed of many corporations which, under general principles of agency, would be liable to each other's creditors in contract and in tort.[3]

In point of fact, the principle relied upon in the complaint to sustain the imposition of personal liability is not agency but fraud. Such a cause of action cannot withstand analysis. If it is not fraudulent for the owner-operator of a single cab corporation to take out only the minimum required liability insurance, the enterprise does not become either illicit or fraudulent merely because it consists of many corporations. The plaintiff's injuries are the same regardless of whether the cab which strikes him is owned by a single corporation or part of a fleet with ownership fragmented among many corporations. Whatever rights he may be able to assert against parties other than the registered owner of the vehicle come into being not because he has been defrauded but because, under the principle of respondeat superior, he is entitled to hold the whole enterprise responsible for the acts of its agents.

In sum, then, the complaint falls short of adequately stating a cause of action against the defendant Carlton in his individual capacity.

The order of the Appellate Division should be reversed, with . . . leave to serve an amended complaint.

---

3. In his affidavit in opposition to the motion to dismiss, the plaintiff's counsel claimed that corporate assets had been "milked out" of, and "siphoned off" from the enterprise. Quite apart from the fact that these allegations are far too vague and conclusory, the charge is premature. If the plaintiff succeeds in his action and becomes a judgment creditor of the corporation, he may then sue and attempt to hold the individual defendants accountable for any dividends and property that were wrongfully distributed (Business Corporation Law, §§510, 719, 720).

KEATING, J. (dissenting):

The defendant Carlton, the shareholder here sought to be held for the negligence of the driver of a taxicab, was a principal shareholder and organizer of the defendant corporation which owned the taxicab. The corporation was one of 10 organized by the defendant, each containing two cabs and each cab having the "minimum liability" insurance coverage mandated by section 370 of the Vehicle and Traffic Law. The sole assets of these operating corporations are the vehicles themselves and they are apparently subject to mortgages.*

From their inception these corporations were intentionally undercapitalized for the purpose of avoiding responsibility for acts which were bound to arise as a result of the operation of a large taxi fleet having cars out on the street 24 hours a day and engaged in public transportation. And during the course of the corporations' existence all income was continually drained out of the corporations for the same purpose.

The issue presented by this action is whether the policy of this State, which affords those desiring to engage in a business enterprise the privilege of limited liability through the use of the corporate device, is so strong that it will permit that privilege to continue no matter how much it is abused, no matter how irresponsibly the corporation is operated, no matter what the cost to the public. I do not believe that it is.

Under the circumstances of this case the shareholders should all be held individually liable to this plaintiff for the injuries he suffered. . . . At least, the matter should not be disposed of on the pleadings by a dismissal of the complaint. . . .

The policy of this State has always been to provide and facilitate recovery for those injured through the negligence of others. The automobile, by its very nature, is capable of causing severe and costly injuries when not operated in a proper manner. The great increase in the number of automobile accidents combined with the frequent financial irresponsibility of the individual driving the car led to the adoption of section 388 of the Vehicle and Traffic law which had the effect of imposing upon the owner of the vehicle the responsibility for its negligent operation. It is upon this very statute that the cause of action against both the corporation and the individual defendant is predicated.

In addition the Legislature, still concerned with the financial irresponsibility of those who owned and operated motor vehicles, enacted a statute requiring minimum liability coverage for all owners of automobiles. The important public policy represented by both these statutes is outlined in section 310 of the Vehicle and Traffic Law. That section provides that: "The legislature is concerned over the rising toll of motor vehicle accidents and the suffering and loss thereby afflicted. . . ."

The defendant Carlton claims that, because the minimum amount of insurance required by the statute was obtained, the corporate veil cannot and should not be pierced despite the fact that the assets of the corporation

---

* It appears that the medallions, which are of considerable value, are judgment proof. (Administrative Code of the City of New York, §4362.0.) — EDS.

which owned the cab were "trifling compared with the business to be done and the risks of loss" which were certain to be encountered. I do not agree.

The Legislature is requiring minimum liability insurance of $10,000, no doubt intended to provide at least some small fund for recovery against those individuals and corporations who just did not have and were not able to raise or accumulate assets sufficient to satisfy the claims of those who were injured as a result of their negligence. It certainly could not have intended to shield those individuals who organized corporations, with the specific intent of avoiding responsibility to the public, where the operation of the corporate enterprise yielded profits sufficient to purchase additional insurance. . . .

The defendant contends that a decision holding him personally liable would discourage people from engaging in corporate enterprise.

What I would merely hold is that a participating shareholder of a corporation vested with a public interest, organized with capital insufficient to meet liabilities which are certain to arise in the ordinary course of the corporation's business, may be held personally responsible for such liabilities. Where corporate income is not sufficient to cover the cost of insurance premiums above the statutory minimum or where initially adequate finances dwindle under the pressure of competition, bad times or extraordinary and unexpected liability, obviously the shareholder will not be held liable. . . .

The only type of corporate enterprises that will be discouraged as a result of a decision allowing the individual shareholder to be sued will be those such as the one in question, designed solely to abuse the corporate privilege at the expense of the public interest.

For these reasons I would vote to affirm the order of the Appellate Division.

DESMOND, C.J., and VAN VOORHIS, BURKE and SCILEPPI, JJ.,concur with FULD, J.

KEATING, J., dissents and votes to affirm in an opinion in which BERGAN, J., concurs.

Order reversed, etc.

NOTES AND QUESTIONS ON WALKOVSZKY v. CARLTON

1. Following the decision in *Walkovszky*, the plaintiff amended his complaint. The Appellate Division held that "the amended complaint sufficiently alleges a cause of action against appellant, i.e., that he and the other individual defendants were conducting the business of the taxicab fleet in their individual capacities." *Walkovszky v. Carlton*, 29 A.D.2d 763 (1968). The court of appeals affirmed, noting that the amended complaint "now meets the pleading requirements set forth in [our prior] opinion and states a valid cause of action." 244 N.E.2d 55 (N.Y. 1968).

2. Taxicab medallions, which even after Uber are very valuable, are no longer judgment proof in New York City as they were at the time of the *Walkovszky* case. In addition, a new owner of a medallion in an execution sale must pay off any tort victims of the former owner — in effect, prioritizing tort claims in bankruptcy.

3. What precisely might the plaintiff have alleged in the amended complaint to keep Carlton and his associates in the litigation?

4. *Walkovszky* observes: "The law permits the incorporation of a business for the very purpose of enabling its proprietors to escape personal liability." Does this imply that the corporate veil is legitimately treated as a costless substitute for liability insurance? How sensible would it be, for example, to require every taxi company (which may be a one or two automobile enterprise) to hold e.g., $1 million or more in capital in order to satisfy a large personal injury judgment? Alternatively, what range of annual cost would you expect by requiring a $1 million liability insurance policy? Is mandatory liability insurance a more efficient way than unlimited liability to assure that an appropriate amount of assets is available to satisfy foreseeable damage claims?

NOTE ON STATUTORY SHAREHOLDER LIABILITY

Shareholders may be held liable for third-party losses under particular statutory provisions that, while not explicitly linked to corporate law, feel very much like local extensions of veil piercing in the service of regulatory objectives. Perhaps the best-known example is the liability provision of the Comprehensive Environmental Response, Compensation, and Liability Act of 1980 (CERCLA §107), which allows the Environmental Protection Agency (EPA) to recover environmental cleanup costs from, among others, "any person who at the time of disposal of any hazardous substance owned or operated any facility" where disposal occurred.

The hallmark case is *United States v. Bestfoods, Inc.*, 524 U.S. 51 (1998). Bestfoods, a multi-brand conglomerate, became the 100 percent owner of the much smaller Ott Chemical Co. (Ott), which in turn owned a manufacturing facility that had polluted the soil and groundwater at its site. When the EPA discovered that cleaning up the site would cost tens of millions of dollars, it filed a §107 action in 1989 to recover its reimbursable costs from Bestfoods' corporate forerunner, which we call the parent corporation ("Parent") here to simplify exposition. The key issue faced by the Supreme Court was whether the Parent, Ott's 100 percent owner, had "operated" Ott's facility, as §107(a)(2) of CERCLA required for reimbursement purposes. The Court, per Justice Souter, held that there were two sources of Parent liability under this section. One was indirect (or "derivative"[24]) liability which is determined under the corporate standard for veil piercing. The second is "direct" liability of a parent for "operating" a polluted facility. The Court affirmed the lower court's decisions that Parent liability under the usual criteria for veil piercing was inapplicable given the facts of the case. This left the district court's holding, which had been reversed by the Sixth Circuit, that the Parent was liable for the environmental cleanup directly, as the "operator" of the polluting facility within CERCLA's meaning.

---

24. "Derivative" liability in this context is unrelated to shareholder derivative suits, explored *infra* in Chapter 10.

In deciding this question, the Court took a Goldilocks position between the district court's expansive "actual control" rule that tied "operator" to the parent-subsidiary relationship rather than to the particular facility in question, and the Sixth Circuit's narrow view that Parent could only have "operated" Ott's facility by managing it directly or in a "sort of joint venture." Instead, the Court sanctioned a middle path of holding a parent liable if its agent participated in decision making associated with the polluting facility without a formal appointment in the subsidiary's organization (such as a directorship). The Court noted that a candidate for such a shadowy agent was present in the *Bestfoods'* record and remanded the case back to the district court for further proceedings consistent with its decision. The Court added in a footnote that parent's agent exercising influence over a facility without a formal position was not the only sort of actor that might lead to CERCLA liability. In particular, dual parent and subsidiary officers or directors might also lead to parent liability for polluting facilities, depending on how well these dual actors had observed "the norms of corporate behavior." Finally, the Court took care to stress that its decision should not be read to undermine the legal separation between corporate parents and their subsidiaries.[25] The Note that follows further elaborates.

QUESTIONS ON BEST FOODS

1. Insofar as the trial court in *Bestfoods* weighed Parent's 100 percent ownership and power to appoint management in its "direct control" test of "operator" liability under CERCLA, could it be said to have followed the traditional agency doctrine of *respondeat superior*? What could be wrong with that? See the next note on "enterprise liability."

2. How does the Court's insistence on tying particular parent agents to the management of polluting facilities differ from the Sixth Circuit's view that parental liability for the cleanup of these facilities should turn on their direct parental management?

3. Other national regulatory statutes also extend the liability of controlling shareholders for third-party losses beyond the standard limits of traditional corporate veil-piercing doctrine. An example is the Employee Retirement Income Security Act (ERISA), which may impose liability on the parent companies of underfunded multiemployer pension plans.[26]

---

25. Again, norms of corporate behavior (undisturbed by any CERCLA provision) are crucial reference points.... " '[A]ctivities that involve the facility but which are consistent with the parent's investor status, such as monitoring of the subsidiary's performance, supervision of the subsidiary's finance and capital budget decisions, and articulation of general policies and procedures, should not give rise to direct liability.' . . . The critical question is whether, in degree and detail, actions directed to the facility by a parent's agent are eccentric under accepted norms of parental oversight." 524 U.S. 51, 72 (1998).

26. See *Sun Capital Partners III, LP v. New England Teamsters & Trucking Industry Pension Fund*, No. 16-1376 (1st Cir. 2019); *Laborer's Pension Fund v. Lay-Com, Inc.*, 580 F.3d 602 (7th Cir. 2009); *Board of Trustees v. Valley Cabinet & Mfg. Co.*, 877 F.2d 769 (9th Cir. 1989).

NOTE ON THE "ENTERPRISE" THEORY OF PIERCING THE CORPORATE VEIL

As we note above, the dominant test for piercing the corporate veil requires the plaintiff to prove both a "unity of interests" between the corporation and the defendant — e.g., controlling it, not observing formalities, intermingling funds, etc. — and an element of injustice in use of the corporate form, which is sometimes stated as abuse of the form. It is impossible to catalog the many types of conduct that are later said to be abusive. In contract cases, at least, the classic example is a misrepresentation or deception that later leads a creditor to reasonably believe that the corporation is a legitimate enterprise with substantial assets.

There are, however, other theories that may have utility to plaintiff's counsel, especially in tort cases. The majority opinion in *Walkovszky* discusses an agency theory. Although this theory can be deployed against an individual stockholder, it has greatest traction when a corporate parent controls a subsidiary corporation and plaintiff seeks to hold the parent liable for the obligations (including tort liabilities) of the subsidiary. This is, of course, exactly the fact pattern described in the preceding Note on CERCLA liability. The gist of it is simple: One might well contend that, in some circumstances at least, a wholly owned subsidiary is simply an agent of its parent corporation and, as we know, a principal is liable for its agent's conduct within the course of the agency. On this theory it is urged that a parent corporation that directs and controls the subsidiary cannot avoid the liabilities of the subsidiary. To some extent and in some ways parent corporations typically do control their subsidiaries, at least those that are wholly owned. They approve strategy, performance targets, and the incentive compensation of the CEO, either formally or more likely through the voice of the representatives placed on the subsidiary's board of directors. But haven't we also learned that the control leading to tort liability in agency law is control over the *details* of the agent's performance? Of course, the liability of independent contractors does not pass through to principals. So is the answer to the agency theory that a parent who only exercises normal shareholder voting rights (and does not control the details of its subsidiary's actions) escapes liability? See the preceding Note on *Bestfoods.*

Closely related to agency theory but of greater appeal to some courts is the "single business enterprise theory." This theory originated in a law review article written by Columbia Law School Professor Adolph Berle, *The Theory of Enterprise Entity,* 47 Col. L. Rev. 343 (1947), although it is also a distant cousin of the "real entity" conception of organizational forms that emerged in nineteenth-century European jurisprudence. Berle asserted, indisputably, that modern business had grown into large networks of corporations under the common control of a central holding company and argued that as the holding company or parent ultimately controls and directs the entire network for the benefit of its shareholders, it *should* be liable for the legal obligations of all entities in the network. From a policy point of view, provided that all of the subsidiaries are adequately capitalized and treated with procedural dignity, one's agreement with the "should" here might turn on whether one believes that the efficiency benefits of this network form, coupled with the legislature's ability to impose mandatory insurance obligations, is socially worthwhile. Professor Stephen Presser argues we may be losing sight of the deep importance of limited liability to our economy. See, e.g., Stephen B. Presser, *The Bogalusa Explosion, "Single Business Enterprise," "Alter Ego" and Other Errors,* 100 Nw. L. Rev. 405 (2006). On the other hand, the single business enterprise theory, which would not recognize a corporation's ability to create limited liability entities under its control, has energetic academic backers who urge its acceptance. See, e.g., Phillip I. Blumberg, *The Increasing Recognition of Enterprise Principles in Determining Parent and Subsidiary Corporation Liabilities,* 28 Conn. L. Rev. 295, 297 (1995-1996).

Some lower state courts have adopted this theory and we expect others may do so from time to time, but either the utility of limited liability in our economic order or the weight of the status quo is such that we do not expect to see the highest courts in commercially sophisticated jurisdictions doing so.

NOTE ON SUBSTANTIVE CONSOLIDATION

Substantive consolidation is a controversial equitable remedy in bankruptcy that pools the assets of a parent corporation and its subsidiaries to simplify the allocation of value among creditors. It resembles enterprise liability up to a point in that it allows creditors to go after assets held by all firms in a corporate group upon bankruptcy.[27] For example, amending the fact pattern of *Walkovszky* only slightly, let us suppose that Carlton controlled a holding company — Carlton Industries (CI) — on top of a much larger and more diverse corporate group. Imagine CI has first-level subsidiaries specializing in taxicabs, retail clothing, and building materials; and that these firms have multiple levels of other subsidiaries that, at their bottom rung, control CI's operating companies that hold its many valuable assets. Now also assume that these subsidiaries have different creditors but own stock in one another and cross guarantee one another's debt. Most conspicuously, CI's operating companies at the pyramid's base individually guarantee portions of the bank debt owed by the CI holding company at the pyramid's apex. Finally, suppose that this holding company files for bankruptcy, seeks reorganization under Chapter 11, and drags all of its direct and indirect subsidiaries with it.

Valuing the claims of individual creditors here is difficult and reaching agreement on a plan of reorganization might be harder still. It might seem that the creditors of CI's operating companies are best placed to recover since these firms own real assets, yet if guarantees run in the opposite direction (as noted in our hypothetical) then the picture looks much more complicated.

Our hypothetical is not wholly fanciful. Large U.S. public companies frequently own hundreds of subsidiaries, directly or indirectly. And there

27. See Henry Hansmann & Richard Squire, *External and Internal Asset Partitioning: Corporations and Their Subsidiaries,* The Oxford Handbook of Corporate Law and Governance (Jeffrey N. Gordon & Wolf-Georg Ringe eds., 2018).

are legitimate reasons for doing so ranging from tax considerations to regulatory requirements, just as there are plausible reasons for providing intra-group credit guarantees. But the costs of unwinding intra-group ties have often led courts and major creditors to support substantive consolidation. Adelphia Communications, Enron, Global Crossing, K-Mart, Owens-Corning, and WorldCom are prominent recent examples of substantive consolidation in bankruptcy proceedings. Professor William Widen finds that among 315 large public-company bankruptcies between 2000 and 2005, 57 percent of the cases involved substantive consolidation. Among the 124 largest bankruptcies in this sample, the incidence of substantive consolidation increases to 62 percent.[28] U.S. Circuit Courts typically cite several justifications when they uphold substantive consolidation on appeal. The "blurriness" of boundaries among a group's constituent entities is one, but two other questions are more decisive: (1) Did contract creditors rely on the credit of individual entities or that of the entire group? or (2) Were intra-group relationships so entangled (as they might be in our hypothetical) that consolidation would benefit all creditors?[29]

Substantive consolidation is controversial, even though creditor majorities approve it and bankruptcy courts have granted it for at least five decades. It is not expressly authorized in the Bankruptcy Code, and the wholesale "veil piercing" that it fosters hardly complies with the traditional law of corporate veil piercing. We are troubled by the prevalence of substantive consolidation as reported in Professor Widen's study reviewed above and as implemented in some recent cases.[30] As a threshold matter, substantive consolidation represents yet another area where federal law undermines well-established state corporate law doctrine on veil piercing. However, our concern goes beyond federalism principles. If bankruptcy courts regularly collapse entities in an exercise of their equitable powers, the corporate form may lose utility as a device for "asset partitioning" and risk allocation.[31] Academic discussion of the policy merits of protecting intra-group subsidiary structure through and beyond bankruptcy have champions on both sides.[32] What do you think?

---

28. See William H. Widen, Report to the American Bankruptcy Institute: *Prevalence of Substantive Consolidation in Large Public Company Bankruptcies from 2000 to 2005*: 16 Am. Bankr. Inst. L. Rev. 2008.

29. See Dennis J. Connolly, *Current Approaches to Substantive Consolidation*, 2019 Norton Annual Survey of Bankruptcy Law, Pt. I, 9-10 (2019). Substantive consolidation might well be in the interests of the creditors of all members of a corporate group depending on the amount and distribution of the future costs of delay and extended bargaining over the entitlements of the creditors of separate companies in the group. We also note that Federal Courts of Appeal have not converged on a single standard for reviewing substantive consolidation. They consider the factors we mention but define and weight them differently.

30. See *In re ADPT DFW Holdings, LLC*, 574 B.R. 87 (Bankr. N.D. Tex. 2017) where the Court, while acknowledging that substantive consolidation should be used rarely, said a more liberal standard for "mega-bankruptcy" cases (in this case, it involved 140 debtor entities) was appropriate, especially as here the consolidation did not harm any creditor.

31. See Henry Hansmann & Reinier Kraakman, *The Essential Role of Organizational Law*, 110 Yale L.J. 387 (2000).

32. Compare Hansmann & Squire, *supra* note 27 with David A. Skeel & George Triantis, *Bankruptcy's Uneasy Shift to a Contract Paradigm*, 166 U. Pa. L. Rev. 1777, 1811-1816 (2018).

NOTE ON DISSOLUTION AND SUCCESSOR LIABILITY

The empirical literature suggests that many small firms such as chemical manufacturers undertaking dangerous activities are not only thinly capitalized but also likely to dissolve and liquidate before the full extent of their potential tort liability becomes known. See Al H. Ringleb & Steven N. Wiggins, *Liability and Large-Scale, Long-Term Hazards*, 90 J. Pol. Econ. 574 (1990). For the liability of shareholders after the dissolution of the firm, see Del. §§278 and 282 and MBCA §14.07(c)(3). Is this what you expected?

Although shareholders can eventually escape all liability through the simple act of dissolving the corporation and abandoning its assets, it may be more difficult to escape tort costs by selling the corporation's assets. As Professor Mark Roe wrote in the mid-1980s:

> Several state supreme courts have devised a doctrine of successor corporation liability. Under this doctrine, the buyer of the liquidating firm's product line picks up the tort liability of the seller, at least as that liability relates to the purchased product line. Anticipating the liability, the purchasing firm will reduce the offering price by the amount of the expected liability. Thus, the potential liquidator cannot escape liability through sale of the damage-causing product line and distribution of the proceeds. Only purchaser miscalculation or ignorance would make sale of the defective product line profitable for the liquidating shareholders.
>
> To avoid imposition of successor corporation liability, the purchasing firm must have no operation identifiable as continuous with the selling firm's product line. But when selling the defective product line, the seller usually must shatter some of its own operational going concern value to accomplish this result. The factories that made the offending product might have to be dismantled and sold off piece by piece, machine by machine; the sale force might have to be cut back; and trademarks might have to be destroyed.[33]

Professor Roe was writing at the height of successor liability, in the 1980s. Since then the doctrine has atrophied somewhat, though some commentators argue that there has been a recent resurgence. The Restatement (Third) of Torts: Products Liability states that the majority of jurisdictions maintain a traditionally restrictive approach to successor liability.[34] This is disputed, though, by others who find a growing number of cases adopting broad principles of successor liability.[35] What are the pros and cons of a doctrine of successor liability? We return to this topic in Chapter 12.5.1, in the context of asset acquisitions.

33. Mark J. Roe, *Corporate Strategic Reaction to Mass Tort*, 72 Va. L. Rev. 1, 32 (1986).
34. Restatement (Third) of Torts: Products Liability, §12 comment b (1997).
35. See Richard L. Cupp, Jr., *Redesigning Successor Liability*, 1999 U. Ill. L. Rev. 845 (1999). But see John H. Matheson, *Successor Liability*, 96 Minn. L. Rev. 371, 396, 398-400 n.115 (2011) (noting that there are now multiple approaches to successor liability).

NOTE ON THE LAW AND ECONOMICS OF LIMITED
LIABILITY IN TORT

A deep issue is whether limited liability for corporate torts can be justified at all within a law-and-economics framework. No one doubts that limiting liability for torts carries social costs; the question is whether the transaction costs savings it produces can justify those costs. Certainly, limited liability can lead firms to invest too little in safety, and produce too much product at too low a price (e.g., too many under-serviced taxis charging underpriced fares). Put differently, limited liability effectively subsidizes firms that are unable to pay the full costs of the torts that they may commit. Should lawmakers permit entrepreneurs to "opt out" of tort liability in this fashion?

Some authors argue that ex post shareholder liability for corporate torts may be an answer, at least if shareholders faced pro rata rather than joint-and-several liability for corporate torts. Under this regime, after the firm's assets were exhausted in bankruptcy proceedings, its shareholders would be compelled to pay pro rata for any remaining tort liability.

However, there are a variety of less radical approaches to the externalization problem posed by limited liability. One strategy is direct regulation. If the state has sufficient information to impose optimal safety procedures, tort liability is unnecessary. A second strategy is to impose mandatory insurance requirements, which taps the insurance market to price tort risks and motivate safety precautions. A third strategy is to accord first priority in corporate bankruptcies to tort creditors, which would incentivize corporate lenders to press for robust safety precautions or deep insurance coverage.

Which, if any, of these strategies seem reasonable to you?

DEBT, EQUITY, AND ECONOMIC VALUE[1]

A business corporation needs long-term capital to invest and fund its operations. There are two broad classes of legal claims that it may sell for this purpose. First, it might borrow money, either directly (say, from a bank) or by issuing debt instruments. Second, it can sell claims on its profits by issuing equity, usually in the form of stock. While we previously introduced this distinction between corporate debt and equity through the lens of the balance sheet, this chapter examines it from the perspectives of legal priority and economic value. It emphasizes sources of long-term capital and touches on concepts that properly fall into the domain of corporate finance, such as "capital structure," "discounted present value," and market pricing. As with our mention of accounting in Chapter 4, our treatment of debt, equity, and value in this chapter is brief. We aim to provide intuition about matters that are as critical for understanding corporate law as accounting conventions. And as with accounting, our hope is that a modest investment now will make our later Chapters more accessible and also encourage further inquiry.[2]

5.1 CAPITAL STRUCTURE

Large public corporations employ both debt and equity as sources of long-term capital. They can rely on debt from many potential lenders and in many forms, from bilateral loans negotiated with large individual lenders to issues

---

1. We owe special thanks in this Chapter to Professor Marcel Kahan for most of the exercises that appear here and to Professor Mark Roe for numerous specific revisions.

2. In a more practicable vein, we note that it is difficult to imagine how a practitioner of corporate law can serve business clients and work alongside of tax specialists, commercial and investment bankers, accountants, and regulators without a working knowledge of accounting and the materials introduced in this Chapter. Lucid development of the topics in this Chapter are available in several introductory finance texts, notably including Richard A. Brealey, Stewart C. Myers & Franklin Allen, *Principles of Corporate Finance* (13th ed., 2020) and Stephen A. Ross, Randolph W. Westerfield, Jeffrey Jaffe & Bradford D. Jordan, *Corporate Finance* (11th ed., 2016).

of debt securities that might be actively traded on public markets. Large companies typically rely more heavily on issues of debt securities that can be sold to multiple purchasers (i.e., lenders) for the same price and at the same time. But these securities are not necessarily actively traded. Although the U.S. market for privately-placed debt securities that are issued to small numbers of investors is smaller than that for publicly-traded debt, the market for private placements dominates that for public debt everywhere else.[3] Relatively short-term debt securities that must be repaid within five years are frequently termed "notes" or "debentures," while longer-term, unsecured obligations are termed "bonds." These definitions are malleable, but everyone knows what they mean in context.

Equity, like debt, takes many forms. While it generally appears as "stock" on the balance sheet, there may be multiple classes of stock. Every corporation must have at least one class of common stock outstanding by law that shares in the residual assets of the firm after all other claims on its value are satisfied. But a company may also have preference shares with economic claims superior to those of its common shares, just as it might have two or more classes of common stock that differ in their voting rights. To further complicate matters, companies might issue hybrid securities such as convertible preferred stock, which can be exchanged for common stock when this might be advantageous for its holders.

The mix of long-term debt and equity claims that fund a corporation's activities is its "capital structure." One way to think about capital structure is to look at the order in which claims get paid if the firm is dissolved (usually called "priority"). Secured debt and senior unsecured debt are paid before all others followed by junior unsecured debt then preferred stock and ending with common stock. Finally, hybrid securities (e.g., preferred stock that is convertible into common stock) have the same level of priority as its most senior claim (here the preferred stock).

The one basic point that this picture fails to capture is the crucial legal distinction between all equity claims on one hand and all debt claims on the other. We now develop this distinction.

5.1.1   Legal Character of Debt

Ordinarily, corporate debtholders have the contractual right to receive periodic payments of interest and to be repaid their principal — the money they had originally loaned — at fixed maturity dates. If a corporation fails to make any of these payments, the creditor has legal remedies, which ordinarily include the basic right to sue the company and to have the sheriff seize the debtor's property for the creditor's benefit if the debtor corporation fails

---

3. This difference is less significant than it might seem, however, since the U.S. market in debt is dominated by institutional investors who trade in negotiated "over-the-market" deals rather than on the major exchanges. Such transactions in corporate debt are typically much less frequent than transactions in public stocks on major exchanges.

to pay. The creditor typically also gets a contractual right to "accelerate" payment of the principal amount if the debtor defaults (for long enough) in paying an interest payment. The debtor and creditor usually write this "acceleration clause" into loan agreements. Moreover, the debtor generally must pay the amounts currently due to its creditors before the debtor can distribute funds or other things of value to equity owners. Debt securities are contracts. Typically, these loan agreements are filled with terms and are often heavily negotiated. But even an "I.O.U." is still a contract, just a very simple one. If the debt takes the form of publicly sold bonds, the loan agreement takes the form of an *indenture*, which is a contract between the bonds' issuer and a trustee who represents the interests of the bond buyers. Whatever its form, the debt contract — the loan agreement — has great flexibility in design.

Lawyers who specialize in negotiating and drafting loan agreements might even argue that they are a higher form of art. They can construct whatever terms the parties desire, as long as these terms do not violate positive law in some respect. Thus, when we speak of the legal "characteristics" of debt, we are largely talking about general patterns of contractual terms — of the terms that have become typical or customary (such as the acceleration clause we have just mentioned). For the most part, we are not speaking of definitional categories or mandatory terms that are strictly enforced. One can think of the loan agreement as allocating risks and responsibilities between the debtor and the creditor and, in more complex companies, among each of several classes of creditors. As such, its terms can range from low risk for the creditor (we must be repaid come hell or high water, as one recurring contract phrase might have it) to high risk for the creditor — and, conversely, from lower risk for the equity holder (if there is no need to repay in this or that circumstance) to higher risk.

5.1.1.1 Maturity Date

The single most common characteristic of debt is a maturity date. That is, the issuer of debt will have (almost always) a legal obligation to repay at a stated date in the future. The repayment obligation is often to repay the principal amount of the bond (typically the amount the creditor originally lent) plus any outstanding interest not yet paid by the maturity date. Bonds typically bear interest at a stated rate (or according to a formula), which the debtor must pay periodically, often semiannually. As we said, their terms can vary almost infinitely. Although most bonds pay interest semiannually, one type that became popular in recent decades has no obligation to pay interest. Instead, the debtor must repay at maturity an amount larger (usually much larger) than the amount the creditor originally lent it. (These are called "zero coupon" bonds.)

If any interest or principal is not paid when due (or upon the expiration of any grace period that the documents may create), bonds are said to be in default. The debtor is said to have defaulted on its debt. Ordinarily, a default in an interest payment, under the terms of the bond, allows the creditor to accelerate the payment of the principal from its original maturity date, perhaps deep in the future, to the current date. The creditor can demand, after the debtor's default on paying interest, that the debtor repay the principal amount in full — immediately. And the mechanisms for the creditor to use to sue the debtor are typically specified in the loan agreement.

Corporate investors choose between investing in equity by buying shares or investing in debt (as a creditor) by lending directly or by buying the debtor's bonds. A critical advantage of bonds is that the investor generally faces less risk as a creditor than as an equity holder because creditors have a legal right to periodic payment of a return (interest) and, most importantly, a priority claim over the company's shareholders on corporate assets in the event that the corporation defaults. And if the creditors are not paid on time, they can do more than ask the company to pay them. They can sue on their contract while stockholders unhappy with paltry dividends have no such recourse against their company. Moreover, bond agreements can be constructed to reduce the financial risk of default through devices such as protective covenants (discussed briefly below) or security interests in specific property that further assure repayment.

5.1.1.2   *Tax Treatment*

Tax is another important feature of debt as a source of finance. Interest paid by the borrower is a deductible cost of business when the firm calculates its taxable income. The corporation, like all taxpayers, pays tax only on its taxable income, which is roughly its revenues minus expenses and any deductions. Thus, the net cost to the corporation of capital that it arranges through borrowing is much less than the stated interest rate on the bonds that it sells: If the corporate tax rate is 50 percent, then for each dollar the corporation pays in interest, its taxable income is reduced by a dollar, and it saves $0.50 in taxes. (In fact, the federal income tax rate for corporations has remained at 21 percent since 2017, well below tax rates in previous decades.) By contrast, there is no deduction for dividends or distributions paid to the corporation's stockholders. In this respect, the cost to the corporation of debt is less than that of equity. (Other factors besides the deductibility of interest, however, also bear on the relative cost of debt, including the higher risk of equity investments, the tax rates of investors in debt or equity, and the costs of financial distress, which increase with a company's debt burden.)

5.1.2   Legal Character of Equity

At the risk of sounding repetitive, the most important observation to make about equity claims is that they are not debt. For example, they have no contractual right to periodic payments (e.g., dividends). They receive distributions from the corporation only on the approval of its board of directors.

5.1.2.1 Common Stock

As we have already noted, there are many kinds of equity, but the most important is common stock, even though its holders are the last to get paid from the corporation's assets (i.e., they are the residual claimants). What is particularly notable about common stock is the apparent fragility of its legal protections. Its holders have no right to any periodic payment, nor can they demand the return of their investment from the corporation. Nor, as we shall see in due course, can they typically tell the firm's managers what to do. They merely have a right to vote, as we will later explore. And common stockholders cannot vote directly on the decision to pay dividends.

Of course, the legal character of common stock can also be seen as essentially contractual in nature, but in this instance, the law fixes clear default rules on the contract. The most important of these rules are that owners of stock can vote to elect directors and that stock carries one vote per share, as a default (any deviations from this need to appear in the charter). This then is what equity has: not the right to payment but (usually) the right to vote on certain other important matters. Further, the charter contains the specifics of the firm's equity securities, including whether there are multiple types of stock with different voting rights, preferences upon liquidation (by which some stockholders get more than others if the firm liquidates), or other terms that affect the company's stock.[4]

Common stockholders are often said to "own" their corporations because we associate ownership with rights to control an asset and claim its residual cash flows. Common stock holds both control rights, through its power to elect the board, and the residual claim on the corporation's assets and income.

5.1.2.2 Preferred Stock

Any equity security on which the corporate charter confers a special right, privilege, or limitation is referred to as a "preferred stock." Preferred stocks are just as malleable as bonds. Generally, they carry a stated dividend, but unlike a bond "coupon" or interest rate obligation, this dividend is payable only when it is declared by the board. Payment of these dividends is usually enforced indirectly, by a provision in the terms of the preferred stock

---

4. Important examples of such "other terms" include the company's redemption and call rights and the shareholder's exchange, conversion, and put rights. A redeemable stock is one that the corporation may redeem on terms stated in the charter, either at the election of the board or at some set time. An exchange right is a right to switch one security for another. Closely related is a conversion right, which is the right to convert one security into another at a stated conversion rate. In this context, a put right is the shareholder's right to force the company to buy her security at a fixed price, while a call right is the corporation's option to force shareholders to surrender their stock at a fixed price. The difference between a call right and a redemption right relates to the status of the security after the right is exercised. Stock that is called becomes the company's "Treasury" stock that continues to be issued but is no longer outstanding in the market. Stock that is redeemed is cancelled and may not be reissued.

stipulating that any unpaid dividends accumulate and that all accumulated dividends must be paid to preferred stockholders before any dividend can be paid to common stockholders. Sometimes preferred stockholders also get votes, or designated board seats, if the preferred stock dividend has been skipped for long enough. Preferred stock is ordinarily less risky than common stock in the same corporation because it typically has a preference over common stock in liquidation as well as dividends. This means that, if the corporation fails and plans to dissolve, a designated amount of money must first be paid to the preferred stockholders before the liquidating corporation can distribute any property to holders of common stock.

Ordinarily, preferred stock does not vote so long as its dividend is current. If its dividend is in default, however, the holders of preferred shares can sometimes elect a stated number (or all) of the directors (as provided by the corporation's charter). On certain fundamental matters, such as mergers in which their rights may be affected, holders of preferred stock are accorded a class vote under some statutes, which can mean that they exercise a veto right on the proposed deal. Under the Delaware statute, however, this right must be created specifically in the document creating and defining the preferred stock. See DGCL §242 (b)(2).

5.2   Conceptions of Value

All else being equal, a corporation's founders wish to attract long-term capital at the lowest possible cost while potential investors in the firm's debt and equity wish to receive the best possible value for their up-front commitment of long-term capital. This much is intuitive. But what does the price of capital or the value of investments mean? They might mean the price and value we arrive at when using a set of first principles from finance and economics. Or, they could mean market prices or the price and value arrived at via negotiation between contracting parties. There could be other contenders too, but mercifully these approaches often lead to comparable results. Indeed, they are most likely to diverge when there are economy-wide factors at play, such as the financial crisis of 2008 or the COVID-19 pandemic that is sweeping the world as we write.

We highlight here the traditional approach of corporate finance, which derives value and predicts market price from first principles. As with corporate accounting discussed in Chapter 4, we intend our treatment to be a sketch — a first introduction to the economic concept of value. We invite readers who are already familiar with this approach to skip the next pages. Even for these readers, however, the Phantasia question on page 177 might provide an interesting puzzle.[5]

Thus, we now turn to a common starting point for understanding value in finance that is developed in the introductory curriculum of business school and widely used by corporate lawyers and investment bankers (with

---

5. This question and the "National Hotel" question that precedes it are among the generous contributions of Prof. Marcel Kahan to earlier editions of this book.

adjustments as noted in Section 5.4). The four basic concepts underlying this understanding of value are: (1) the time value of money, (2) risk and return, (3) systematic risk and diversification, and (4) capital market price efficiency.

5.2.1 The Time Value of Money

Intuitively, we understand that one of the reasons money is valuable is because it can be used to earn more money. The simplest example is just a bank savings deposit. If the market requires banks to pay 5 percent to attract savings deposits (as it once did!) then $1,000 you deposit today will be worth $1,050 in one year. There are other ways to invest your thousand dollars for the year but most of them will entail some degree of risk, which for the moment we wish to ignore (we will get back to risk in a moment). Thus, we could say that the *future value* of $1,000 in one year is $1,050.

Expressed algebraically: FV = PV x [1+ r], where FV is future value, PV is present value of the money invested, and r is the rate of expected return.

If our investment will cover several years, this calculation will be done for each year in order to calculate the future value at the end of the investment period.

The economic concept of *present value* is the inverse of future value. Present value is the value today of a future payment. Again, assuming no risk, and the same interest rate environment as the previous example, we can say that the present value of a certain promise to pay $1,050 in one year is $1,000. Thus, in order to calculate the present value of a future payment we must *discount* that payment by a discount rate reflecting the value of that amount during the period. The rate used for this discount will reflect both the current market rate (the market for money) and an increment for the risk that the payment may not be made when required. But for the moment we continue to ignore the element of risk or the risk premium.

Expressed algebraically: PV = FV/ 1 + r, where PV is Present Value, FV is Future Value, and r is the discount rate which is determined from the time value of money in that place and time, again ignoring the important element of riskiness of the investment.

DISCOUNTING EXERCISES

1. What is the present value of $1.10 one year from now if the discount rate is 5 percent?

2. What is the present value of $1 ten years from now if the discount rate for each of the ten years is 10 percent?

3. What is the relationship between present value and discount rate? Will $100 one year from now have a higher present value if the discount rate is 7 percent or 8 percent? Can you tell the answer without calculating the present values?

4. If the present value of $150 one year from now is $120, what is the discount rate?

The concepts introduced above of future value and present value, related to one another by a discount rate, are the basics. There are other concepts that float through finance, many of which are variations of present value and future value.

You may have encountered other kinds of rates. One is the rate of return: the percentage that you would earn if you invested in a particular project. For example, if you invested $1,000 a year ago and receive $1,200 today, your rate of return is 20 percent. This does not mean that the present value of $1,200 one year from now is $1,000. When you made the investment, you might have expected to make more, or less. But the return you actually got is 20 percent. For instance, if the appropriate discount rate was 10 percent, this was a great investment. But if the appropriate discount rate when you made the investment was, say, 25 percent, this investment was a loser when compared to other potential uses of the money.

Projects for which the present value of the amount invested ($1,000) is less than the present value of the amount received in return are called *positive net present value projects*. In more ordinary language, these are good, profitable projects. (Net present value is just the difference between the present value of the amounts invested and the present value of those received in return.) Investing in such projects is a good idea for investors: If they play out as expected, they will pay out more than is needed to compensate for the time value of money. Their rate of return (say, 20 percent) is higher than the market rate of return (say, a 10 percent rate that investors typically demand to finance this kind of project).

"Interest" is the money you are promised when you lend out money or the amount you have to pay if you borrow money. The interest rate is that amount expressed as a percentage of the amount lent. Thus, if you borrow $10,000 for one year and have to return, at the end of that year, the $10,000 borrowed plus $850 in interest, the rate of interest you have to pay is 8.5 percent.

Thus far, we have distinguished interest returns from other returns. But the same concepts used so far apply to stock and to debt. Stock has its return in two possible albeit uncertain forms: dividends and capital appreciation (or increase in the stock market value of the stock). Stockholders individually and stock markets collectively expect some return and discount the future return to present value, which is expressed in the stock's market price. Investors implicitly compare their estimate of discounted future value to the stock's present price on the market. If their estimated discounted future value is higher than the present price they may buy. If lower, they may not or perhaps they will "short" the stock.[6]

---

6. There are many ways to short stock. The old-fashioned way was to borrow the stock today — many parties will lend it at a price — and then to sell it at today's high price in anticipation of bad public news to come that will lower market price of the stock. After the bad news enters the market, the stock can be repurchased at a low price and returned to its original lender. If all goes well, the prescient trader earns the difference between today's high price minus tomorrow's low price plus interest paid for borrowing the stock. But of course, the trader must also invest in detective work to find private information that is not already reflected in today's stock price.

QUESTION ON NET PRESENT VALUE

What is the present value of the $10,850 you have to repay a year from now if the discount rate is 7 percent? If it is 8.5 percent? If it is 10 percent? What is the net present value of $10,000 borrowed at an 8.5 percent interest rate at each of these discount rates?

5.2.2   Risk and Return

So far, we have dealt with a world of certainty. But future returns on most investments are uncertain. Assessing that uncertainty is a big job. In some ways, it may be the stock market's biggest job. So, to evaluate risky investments — which is to say, nearly all investments — the investor has to consider the probability of their success or failure.

To attempt this rationally, an investor would calculate what we now call the *expected return*. If a return a year from now on an investment will be either $2,000 or zero, each with equal likelihood, the expected return on the investment is $1,000. Thus, to calculate the present value of this investment opportunity, the investor will discount $1,000 to present value, neither $2,000 nor zero.[7]

The expected return is a weighted average of the possible future values of the investment. It is the sum of what the returns would be from the investment at the end of some period, multiplied by the probability of those outcomes. Some possible outcomes will be successful, and some will reflect losses if the investment is risky.

For example, consider the following array of potential outcomes of a risky investment of $1 million by XYZ Corporation. These estimates were made by XYZ's senior executives after exhaustive discussion by its management team. The investment is to be liquidated at the end of one year.

Returns During Year	Value at Termination	Total Return	Probability
50,000	300,000	350,000	10%
125,000	800,000	925,000	20%
200,000	1,300,000	1,500,000	30%
200,000	1,400,000	1,600,000	20%
500,000	1,400,000	1,900,000	10%
0	0	0	10%

What is the expected value of this investment opportunity? To calculate it, we must add the two forms of return for each probability, multiply the sum by the corresponding probability, and add the results for all probabilities

---

7. The investor could discount both $2,000 and zero to present value and take the average, which gives the same answer as discounting $1,000 to present value. But to our minds, this approach is not as logical.

together. In this instance, the expected (future) value of the investment
would be $1.18 million.

Total Return	Probability	Expected Return
350,000	10%	35,000
925,000	20%	185,000
1,500,000	30%	450,000
1,600,000	20%	320,000
1,900,000	10%	190,000
0	10%	0
Total expected value:		$1,180,000

Thus the investors can think of this opportunity as the equivalent of a
promise to pay $1,180,000 in one year, although no one actually made that
promise. Of course, another step would be required to calculate the present
expected value of this opportunity.

Now we introduce the concept of financial risk. Compare this array
of expected returns with the hypothetical return on a $1 million one-year
Treasury note issued at par bearing stated interest at 9 percent. Such an
investment has no array of probable outcomes. Its expected (future) value is
simply $1,090,000. Since there is no volatility in its return, we characterize
this investment as riskless. (Finance-types will want to add some risk: maybe
not that the United States of America will default but the risk that inflation will
increase. Ignore the finance/inflation risk here. Think of this as a sure thing.)
However, the XYZ project, as shown in the two tables, may have an actual
return ranging from $0 to $1.9 million, although its expected future return in
$1.18 million. The potential returns for XYZ are risky.

An investor is said to be risk neutral if all she is concerned about is the
expected return of an investment — that is, if she is indifferent to receiving
the $1.18 million in cash one year from now or receiving the returns from the
XYZ investment project. Most investors are not risk neutral but are, instead,
risk averse. This means that volatile payouts are worth less to them — they
might well value the XYZ project and the Treasury note at the same price, or
even prefer the Treasury note to the XYZ project, notwithstanding the fact
that it has a lower future expected value.

Consider an even simpler investment opportunity, the right to purchase
the outcome of a coin flip. Risk-averse investors — i.e., most investors — would
prefer a coin flip that paid them $9,000 for tails and $11,000 for heads over a
flip that paid them $5,000 for tails and $15,000 for heads. Although both flips
have the same $10,000 expected value, the variance in the outcomes of the
second is wider than that of the first. (True, some investors are risk preferring,
but their number is small.) The additional amount that risk-averse investors
demand for accepting higher-risk investments in the capital markets is termed
the risk premium. Like many things, risk has its market price.

The risk premium does not compensate the investor for the possible out-
of-pocket losses associated with the probability that an investment might fail.
Even a risk-neutral investor demands compensation for these losses because

failure lowers the expected return of an investment. In our XYZ investment payout table, there is a 40 percent chance that the company will get back less than it invests, i.e., that the actual outcome of the investment will be a loss. Even risk-neutral investors care about these real losses and reduce the expected return on investments to account for these losses. But again, these reductions in the expected payout of an investment are not part of the risk premium. Instead, the risk premium is compensation for the intrinsic unpleasantness of volatile returns to the risk-averse investors who dominate market prices. Most investors like the $9,000–$11,000 flip more than the $5,000–$15,000 flip. Everyone takes the downside ($5,000 or $9,000) and the upside ($11,000 or $15,000) into account. Risk-averse investors have to be compensated for taking the $5,000–$15,000 flip. Risk-neutral investors do not have to be paid to switch.

Let's tie this discussion of risk and return to the discussion of the time value of money. We noted earlier that future cash flows must be discounted to arrive at their present value. We now assert that most investors are risk averse and demand extra compensation for bearing risk. This means, in effect, that in order to calculate the present value of risky expected future cash flows (remember that we always discount expected cash flows), we need to discount these cash flows at a rate that reflects *both* the time value of money and the market price of the risk involved. We call this combined rate a *risk-adjusted rate*. By contrast, the rate at which we discount future cash flows that are certain is the risk-free rate. The difference between the risk-adjusted rate and the risk-free rate is the risk premium. More risk in expected future cash flows yields a higher risk premium and a higher risk-adjusted rate. That is to say, the more risky an investment is the higher its risk premium is, and thus the higher the rate of return must be to attract investment capital.

QUESTIONS ON RISK AND NET PRESENT VALUE

National Hotel Corporation wants to borrow $10,000,000 from First City Bank for one year. National Hotel Corporation offers to repay to First City Bank $11,300,000, as principal and interest, at the end of the one-year term. First City Bank believes that, if it extends the loan, it has a 95 percent chance of being repaid in full at the year's end and a 5 percent chance of receiving nothing because National Hotel Corporation will be bankrupt and worth nothing at all. The risk-free discount rate is 6.5 percent. But the risk-averse managers of First City Bank require a 2 percent risk premium to extend a loan to a borrower with the characteristics of National Hotel Corporation.

1. What is the nominal interest rate that National Hotel offers to pay for the loan?

2. Assuming National Hotel obtains a loan at the rate it demands, what is First City's expected return on the $10 million that it would lend?

3. What is the net present value of the loan extended on National Hotel's terms if investors are generally risk neutral? What discount rate would these investors use?

4. What is the net present value of the loan if First City's managers correctly assess the risk premium that most investors in the market would charge for the National Hotel loan? What discount rate does First City use in this case? Should it extend the loan on National Hotel's terms?

5.2.3   Diversification and Systematic Risk

There is, finally, one more twist to the basic intuition about a risk premium. And it turns out to be an important one, not just in the world of investors but also in the world of corporate law and corporate takeovers.

Begin with this "riddle": Imagine that all investments are risky. And imagine that all investors are risk averse. Yet financial promoters figure out how to sell some of these investments—conceivably all of them—without having to put up with a risk premium.

How?

Consider a large class of $5,000 or $15,000 coin-flip-type investments. Let's say that, for investment A, the payout is $5,000 if the Democrats win the next election and $15,000 if the Republicans win. But for investment B, the payout if the Republicans win the next election is $5,000, and if the Democrats win, it is $15,000.

Now you see it. If the two investments can be packaged together, they turn into a $20,000 certain investment, or a $20,000 actual return no matter what the outcome of the election. The risk-averse investor who would demand a premium for either investment alone desists from demanding any premium at all for a package of the two investments together.

A somewhat different example of the same point is as follows. Suppose we flip a coin ten times and pay out $1,500 for each head and $500 for each tail. The expected value of a package of these ten coin flips (the "ten-pack") is $10,000, just as it was for the single $15,000/$5,000 coin flip. But a risk-averse investor will demand a much lower premium to invest in the ten-pack than she would to invest in the single big flip. Unlike the two-investment case we considered above, there is still some risk associated with the ten-pack, but this risk is much less than that associated with the single $15,000/$5,000 investment. Think of it this way: While you might end up with $15,000 or $5,000 by investing in the ten-pack, you are much more likely to end up somewhere in between—say, with six heads and four tails or the other way around, which yield payouts of $11,000 and $9,000, respectively.[8]

The packaging of investments to reduce risk is a big business on Wall Street: It is the construction of mutual funds, the construction of a diversified investment portfolio.

---

8. In the two-investment case, investments A and B are said to be perfectly negatively correlated if, whenever one does well, the other fails, and vice versa. In the ten-pack coin-flip investment, each coin flip is uncorrelated with the others. As the examples suggest, investments with negatively correlated outcomes are very efficient in eliminating risk. But uncorrelated investments are not far behind. Ten coin flips really do get rid of 90 percent of the risk associated with flipping coins by some measures. We do not explore how risk is measured here, but the intuition is easy to understand.

Of course, risk-averse investors are averse only to risks that they actually must bear. But if a risky investment is held as part of a portfolio that includes other risky investments, then these risks balance each other out to a lesser or greater extent. Each such risky investment will be worth more when held in such a portfolio than if held alone. In a portfolio, the odds are that even if one or two investments go sour, most of them will succeed. The investor is said to have diversified across a portfolio that has less total risk than its individual components. This is a fancy way of saying that risk-averse investors should not put all their eggs into one basket — unless, as always, they are paid to do so. But notice the implication: Since investors can hold portfolios, in a competitive capital market, risky investments such as stock will tend to be priced to reflect the fact that investors need not bear all the risk associated with holding a single investment.

If investors can hold very large portfolios, why must corporations pay them a risk premium at all in order to induce them to invest in their risky stock? Why doesn't all stock sell at exactly its expected return? The reason is that not every risk is diversifiable — i.e., not every risk disappears if you hold it in a very large portfolio. While an increase in value for some investments correlates with a decline in value for other investments, there is always some level of risk that affects the entire system or market (e.g., the entire economy going up or down). This is called systematic risk and is something even the most diversified investor must bear, and for which this risk-averse investor still demands a premium.

QUESTIONS ON SYSTEMATIC AND UNSYSTEMATIC RISK

Assume that a person living in Phantasia can invest only in the following four investment projects. She can loan money to the Phantasia government at an interest rate of 6 percent (in which case she is sure to be repaid). She can buy stock of either (or both) of Phantasia's two leading baseball teams. If the Phantasia Mets win the annual baseball championship, Mets stock will sell for $100 a share and the stock of the losing Phantasia Yankees will sell for $50 a share a year from now; if the Yankees win, Yankee stock will sell for $100 a share and Mets stock for $50 a share at that time. Assume that each team has a 50 percent chance of winning the championship. Finally, assume that our investor can buy stock of Phantasia Tourism Inc., a local hotel and restaurant operator. If Phantasia completes construction of its airport one year from now, tourists will start flocking in, and Phantasia Tourism stock will be worth $300 a share. However, if the airport is not completed one year from now, Phantasia Tourism stock will be worth only $30. The likelihood that the airport will be completed in time is 20 percent.

1. What is the expected value one year from now of (a) $1,000 of Phantasia government bonds, (b) one share of Mets stock, (c) one share of Yankee stock, and (d) one share of Phantasia Tourism stock?

2. Which of these investments involve risk? Which involve risk that is fully diversifiable? Which involve risk that is partly undiversifiable?

3. In light of your answer to question 2, what price would you expect Mets stock to sell for today? Yankee stock? Phantasia Tourism stock? (If you cannot figure out an exact price, can you estimate a range of reasonable prices?)

4. How would your answers to question 2 change if you learned that Phantasia's airport will definitely be completed by next year if the Mets win the pennant and that it definitely will not be completed if the Yankees win? (Notice that the probabilities of a completed airport and a Mets victory are now both 50 percent.)

In the Phantasia problems above, we encountered risky projects that involved only diversifiable risk and risky projects that involved partly undiversifiable risk. In reality, most projects involve a combination of diversifiable and undiversifiable risk. For instance, the value of General Motors (GM) stock depends both on the quality of the new GM models compared to Ford, Toyota, and BMW models (diversifiable risk, since you could buy Ford, Toyota, and BMW stock) and on whether the world economy is going to enter a period of prolonged recession (undiversifiable risk). The appropriate risk premium and risk-adjusted discount rate, however, depend only on the undiversifiable portion of the risk. Thus, to modify our conclusion above, the greater the undiversifiable risk is, the greater the risk premium and the risk-adjusted discount rate are.

5.3   VALUING ASSETS

5.3.1   The Discounted Cash Flow (DCF) Approach

A basic understanding of capital structure, time value of money, and the connection between risk and return give us all the building blocks we need to be able to estimate the value of tangible and financial assets, such as stocks and bonds. These building blocks all come together in the "discounted cash flow" (DCF) approach to valuing assets. At the highest level of abstraction, DCF valuation requires a prediction of all future cash flows that an asset is expected to produce, and an estimated discount rate to bring those cash flows back to the present to yield a "net present value" (NPV).

Of course, this is easier said than done, and employing DCF valuation to estimate intrinsic value is something of an art. Nevertheless, DCF analysis is sometimes the only rational way to estimate present values based on an uncertain future. We therefore present a basic conceptual approach to the valuation of assets. The goal of this brief overview is not to make you an expert in the valuation of assets — such an objective would take at least a semester and perhaps a lifetime to achieve — but rather to make you an educated "consumer" of valuations presented by others. We then discuss, in Section 5.4, examples of how these valuation concepts and modern finance theory are of use to corporate lawyers when it comes to working with clients, courts, and regulators.

The first step in the DCF valuation process is the estimation of all future cash flows generated by the asset. Of course, as with any predictions about the future, this step is fraught with uncertainty. Adding further complexity is the fact that many assets typically have indefinite life, while estimating future cash flows can only sensibly be done over a finite number of periods. The solution that valuation experts often use is to estimate a "terminal value," which brings all cash flows from a future year (say, Year 5) and going into perpetuity, into that future year (Year 5). In many DCF valuations, this terminal value is a large fraction of the overall cash flows—sometimes 60 to 70 percent, depending on the discount rate used and the number of discrete cash flow periods that are available. As a result, small changes in assumptions about what happens going into perpetuity (for example, the growth rate of the cash flows) can make a big difference in the overall NPV.

Once one has estimated future net cash flows, the second step in a DCF valuation is the calculation of an appropriate discount rate. The simplest, perhaps most well-accepted, approach is to calculate a weighted-average cost of capital (WACC) and use that as the appropriate discount rate. WACC is calculated as the firm's weighted average of the cost of debt and its cost of equity, where the weights are the relative amounts of debt and equity in the capital structure. The debt side of this calculation is often simple (especially if the firm has traded bonds outstanding).

The before-tax cost of debt for a firm is the interest rate that the firm would pay if it were to seek new debt financing today (i.e., not the historical interest rate on its existing debt). Of course, the after-tax cost of debt is usually significantly lower, because companies can deduct interest payments from their taxable income. For simplicity, if a company with a 50 percent marginal tax rate on its earnings has a current 6 percent before-tax cost of debt, its after-tax cost of debt is only 3 percent as a first approximation.

Estimating the cost of equity is more complicated. Although equity does not have mandated payments like debt, equity plainly has a cost in the sense that investors implicitly demand an expected return when they calculate the price they are willing to pay for shares of the firm's equity. This return will have two potential components: expected future dividend payments and expected (estimated) capital appreciation or stock price growth. This expected return to investors then is the cost of the equity to the firm. But how can one estimate this implicit cost of equity?

Perhaps the most well-accepted, conceptually pure method for estimating a cost of equity is the capital asset pricing model (CAPM), developed originally by Professor William Sharpe of Stanford University. This model is built on the insight that well-functioning markets will themselves link risk and return. That is, informed capital markets will require risky ventures to offer a higher return to the suppliers of their capital in order to compensate investors for their risk aversion. But how then can one measure the degree of risk inherent in an equity investment in order to estimate its expected return (or implied cost)? The CAPM does this by linking securities risk to the volatility of the security prices.

In the real world of investments, investors have a price history by which they can estimate how the returns of a particular stock are likely to react to future events. Risk from future events can be said to be of two types: systemwide, or systematic, risk and company-specific, or idiosyncratic (unsystematic) risk. The first kind is a risk that investors cannot get rid of, no matter how they construct their portfolio. The second kind is a risk that investors can get rid of (as by matching a $5,000–$15,000 flip with a $15,000–$5,000 flip).

Finance scholars have developed a measure of the systematic risk associated with any particular security. By looking at the trading history of the stock and how its price moves in relation to the stock market as a whole, these scholars believe that the amount of systemic (or systematic) risk in a stock's returns can be estimated. The finance coefficient for this risk is called the stock's "beta," and the term "beta" has taken on a life of its own in the finance literature. But it means nothing more than the estimated systemic, nondiversifiable risk of the stock measured as a proportion of the systematic risk of a diversified portfolio, such as a weighted portfolio of stocks in S&P 500 companies.

In the world of corporate finance, each traded stock has a calculated "beta." It measures the historical sensitivity (either negative or positive) that the price of that stock has to overall price movements in the market over a given period. So a relatively risky stock will be one that shows greater volatility in its price over that period than does the market as a whole (its beta coefficient will be greater than 1). When the general market goes up it tends to go up even more, and when the market falls, it will tend to fall more. On the other hand, a beta coefficient less than 1 means a stock will tend to go up or fall less than the market as a whole, based upon its historical performance. It is less risky than the market as a whole. The size of the coefficient reflects the degree of this sensitivity to the overall market.

These risk coefficients or betas then can be used to derive the implied cost of a particular company's equity. This would be done as follows. The cost of capital contributed as equity will be the sum of (a) the riskless cost of money (typically proxied by the current 90-day U.S. Treasury Note rate) plus (b) the market equity risk premium[9] times (c) the stock's beta.

The company's WACC then (the discount rate that would be used in the NPV calculation) will be the weighted average of its cost of debt plus its cost of equity.

There is another, down-and-dirty technique for estimating the cost of equity. It is simpler, but, perhaps unsurprisingly, less precise than CAPM.

It is based on historical average equity risk premia data. It requires a calculation of the firm's before-tax cost of debt and recognizes that, historically, equity has been priced at a cost that is approximately 8 percent higher than the before-tax cost of debt on average. Although imprecise, this technique has the advantage of not requiring one to calculate equity betas.

5.3.2   The Relevance of Prices in the Securities Market

Traditional discounting concepts are a sturdy guide to the underlying logic of valuing assets. These concepts yield a theoretically satisfying notion

9. The market equity risk premium is that number (for a stated period) by which the percentage returns of the whole stock market — meaning both the dividends paid and the capital appreciation that occurs over that period) — exceed the U.S. Treasury rate for that period. One might use the S&P 500 Index stocks as a proxy for the whole market. This is an estimate of what the market is telling us is the systematic risk at that point.

of intrinsic value. To be sure, they are difficult to apply. Predicting future cash flow is problematic. Determining an appropriate risk premium for a risky investment is inherently problematic as well. Fortunately, for some assets such as stock and oil, an alternative mode of valuation is available. These assets are bought and sold in a well-functioning market with many traders. Thus, finding a market price for a share of stock or a barrel of Brent crude oil is easy. In the case of stock, we need only pick up the business section of almost any newspaper listing the closing prices of exchange-traded stocks from the preceding day. In the case of oil, we do not have to figure out the future cash flows from owning 100,000 barrels of oil. We can pick up the finance section of the paper and see how much a barrel of oil trades for. This raises an obvious question: How do the market prices of publicly traded stocks relate to possible estimates of stock value based on discounting their expected cash flows?

It would be exceedingly convenient — not to say socially valuable — if the prices of securities reflected well-informed estimates, based on all available information, of the discounted value of the expected future pay-outs of corporate stocks and bonds. That is, it would simplify matters greatly if market prices aggregated the best estimates of the best-informed traders about the underlying present value of corporate assets — net of payments to creditors, taxes, and all the rest.

One of the core working hypotheses of modern financial economics is that the stock market manages to do just this. Much empirical research indicates that stock market prices rapidly reflect all public information bearing on the expected value of individual stocks. This is generally known as the efficient capital market hypothesis (ECMH). As you will see in Chapter 14, the ECMH has had an important influence on developments in securities law at the federal level. It has met with a more skeptical reception in corporate law developments at the state level, especially in Delaware.

In this book, we remain agnostic about the more aggressive claims that have been made on behalf of the ECMH. It is sufficient for us that prices in a large, liquid, informed market for shares should be regarded as prima facie evidence of the true value of traded shares. Whether the market price of a company's shares also reflects, in a straightforward way, the value of the entire company (or all of its equity in aggregate) is a more complicated question that we will touch on in later chapters. We will also remind you periodically that the accuracy of market prices depends entirely on the quality of information that informs trading — which, in turn, depends on the integrity of all major actors in the market, including top corporate management, accounting firms, law firms, investment banks, security analysts, and even the portfolio managers who invest on behalf of institutional investors.

5.4 VALUATION, MODERN FINANCE THEORY, AND TODAY'S CORPORATE LAWYER

We close this Chapter by exploring where and how valuation principles and modern finance theory are likely to interact with corporate law practice. Although there are many nuances, we focus on three key areas to provide a flavor of the interactions and to whet the appetite. The object is simply to underscore the importance of having an intuitive understanding of the materials in this chapter. Any of the popular finance texts used in business schools can take over from here.

5.4.1   Clients

One very good reason for learning about valuation principles and modern finance theory is that business clients rely on the them, particularly in the contexts of investment decisions and dealmaking. Effective lawyers must speak the same language to serve these clients and to speak with their bankers and other financial advisers. Graham and Harvey (2001) found that both DCF and Internal Rate of Return (IRR) were commonly used by Chief Financial Officers (CFOs) of large firms to assess whether to invest in business opportunities.[10] Larger firms used valuation methods that were more information intensive (and hence costly), while smaller firms seemed to economize and relied on simpler methods such as "multiple of invested capital" (MOIC) (e.g., if investing "X," it expects to receive a multiple of "X" when it exits the investment, such as "5X") or the IRR rule (e.g., invest in a project if its rate of return is above the rate that would lead to a net present value of zero (sometimes called the "hurdle" rate)).[11] In a pair of recent papers, Paul Gompers, Steven Kaplan, and co-authors surveyed private equity (PE) and venture capital (VC) funds to ascertain how they make decisions.[12] On valuation, it appears that both PE and VC funds are more likely to rely on IRR and MOIC than DCF (VCs even more than PEs).[13] This appears consistent with economizing on difficult (and costly) to obtain information, especially for early-stage ventures, and, as the authors suggest, with how investors in PE and VC funds assess the funds' performance.[14] In addition, consistent with the greater uncertainty in VC and PE investments, their required IRR typically sets a higher bar for expected returns (before accepting investments) than we might expect

---

10. See John R. Graham & Campbell R. Harvey, *The Theory and Practice of Corporate Finance: Evidence from the Field*, 60 J. Fin. Econ. 187 (2001).

11. See id. PE funds may set a MOIC or IRR threshold (usually over some period of time) that an investment project must meet before it is accepted. Both measures are absolute in the sense that they are determined independently of other performance measures (such as the market rate of return) and essentially create a target that needs to be met before a project is accepted. This also means neither measure explicitly accounts for investment risk, except perhaps implicitly by affecting what MOIC or IRR threshold is desired. For greater discussion of IRR see Brearley, Myers & Allen, *supra* note 2, at 103-115 and Graham & Harvey, *supra* note 10.

12. See Paul Gompers, Steven N. Kaplan & Vladimir Mukharlyamov, *What Do Private Equity Firms Say They Do?*, 121 J. Fin. Econ. 449 (2016) [*hereinafter Private Equity*]; Paul Gompers, Will Gornall, Steven N. Kaplan & Ilya Strebulaev, *How Do Venture Capitalists Make Decisions?*, 135 J. Fin. Econ. 169 (2020) [*hereinafter Venture Capitalists*].

13. See Gompers et al, *Private Equity, supra* and Gompers et al, *Venture Capitalists, supra*, at 179-180.

14. See Gompers et al, *Private Equity, supra* and Gompers et al, *Venture Capitalists, supra*, at 182-183.

under comparable DCF analysis.[15] Of course, as the side bar below notes, not every investment an investor makes is driven by the valuation concerns noted above. Sometimes, they go with their "gut feeling" and at times this works out and at times it ends with a punch in the gut.

SIDE BAR—INVESTING ON A "GUT FEELING"

In 2000, SoftBank's Masayoshi Son decided to invest $20 million in Jack Ma's Chinese e-commerce company, Alibaba, based on a five-minute meeting. That investment in 2020 is worth about $150 billion. Son invested in Alibaba even though "[Ma] had no business plan, and zero revenue, employees maybe 35 or 40, but his eyes were very strong . . . strong eyes . . . shining eyes . . . I could tell by the way he talked, the way he looked at me, that he had charisma, he had leadership. His business model was wrong. It was the way he talked. It was the way he could bring young Chinese people to follow him."[16] Son later said that he had this same feeling with only one other founder—Adam Neumann of WeWork. Son invested about $4 billion in 2016 after less than half an hour with Neumann, but that investment tanked. SoftBank had to bail out the firm and wrote-down its investment by 50 percent. When asked whether his "gut feeling" for Neumann may have affected his investing judgment, Son said, "[w]e added more investment because we over-evaluated Adam ... Anyway, about loving Adam too much, again, I learned a harsh lesson."[17]

5.4.2   Courts

Courts must often rely on valuation principles and modern finance theory when they are called upon to value a firm. For example, as we will learn in Chapter 12, when a majority shareholder attempts to buy out the minority shareholders from a firm, the law will usually allow the minority to petition the court to seek a "fair value" for their shares. The *In re Emerging Communications, Inc. Shareholder Litigation* C.A. No. 16415, 2004 WL 1305745 (Del. Ch. June 4, 2004) case discussed below is an example and highlights some of the issues that arise when assessing fair value.

The Delaware Court of Chancery was required to value the minority's shares where a controlling shareholder had in effect forced the minority

---

15. The mean IRR was 22 percent for PE funds (see Gompers et al, *Private Equity, supra*) and 31 percent for VCs with an MOIC of above 5 (see Gompers et al, *Venture Capitalists, supra*, at 179-180). This is also consistent with their finding that late-stage investors rely on more information-intensive methods relative to early-stage investors. In addition, nearly 30 percent of respondents said they did not use forecasts, which is not that surprising given the large uncertainty and number of possible scenarios for these sorts of firms. See Gompers et al, *Venture Capitalists, supra*, at 180-181. The focus instead was on the management team at early-stage firms—one of the few things more capable of assessment at this early stage (short of relying on clairvoyance). See id., at 177-179. It is interesting that most VC funds (90 percent) thought "unicorns" were overvalued even though 40 percent had invested in them. See id. at 181-182.

16. *The David Rubenstein Show*, Bloomberg, Oct. 11, 2017, available at: https://www .youtube.com/watch?reload=9&v=Sa2_VBu0d7k.

17. Richard Beales, *Nasty Pieces of WeWork*, Reuters BreakingViews, Dec. 17, 2019, available at: https://breakingviewsfeatures-wework.weebly.com/.

shareholders to accept a buy-out offer of $10.25 per share at a time when the shares had been trading at $7 per share. Although many issues arise, we focus on the court's treatment of two of them: the calculation of the cost of equity, and the relevance of the market price of the company's stock for valuation purposes.

The company, Emerging Communications, Inc. (ECM), operated a telephone company on a small Caribbean island. Both sides had hired experts to provide DCF estimates of the fair value of the minority's stake in the firm and the difference in their estimates was largely driven by different cost of equity figures relied on by the experts. Plaintiffs' expert derived a cost of equity of about 10 percent and defendants' expert used a cost of equity of about 14 percent. (Can you see why the defendants would prefer a larger cost of equity?) The difference was due to the defendants' expert including a "small stock premium" of 1.7 percent, a "super small stock premium" of 1 to 1.5 percent, and a "hurricane risk premium" of 0.9 to 1.4 percent.

The court found support in both finance theory and Delaware case law for the "small stock premium" holding that "stocks of smaller companies are riskier than securities of large ones and, therefore, command a higher expected rate of return in the market."[18] The court did not, however, find evidence to support the defendants' other increments to the cost of equity. It first held that defendants' assertion that very small firms, such as ECM, merited a larger increment was not supported by finance theory and ran contrary to the lower risks ECM faced because although:

> ECM [is] small. . . it is also a utility that was unusually protected from the hazards of the market-place. ECM was well established, it had no competition, it was able to borrow at below-market rates, and it was cushioned by regulators from extraordinary hazards (for example, by tax abatements). Implicit in the defendants' position, but nowhere straightforwardly argued, is the assumption that these advantages, however extraordinary, were not enough to offset the added risk created by ECM's "supersmall" size. It is the defendant's burden to support that assumption, and they have not done that.

Finally, on the "hurricane risk premium," the court held that "[t]he absence of theoretical and evidentiary support leaves this Court unpersuaded that the risk of unrecoverable hurricane damage loss is so embedded in ECM's business as to require a structural increase in ECM's cost of equity." The court was also skeptical that this risk was really important to ECM, especially because ECM did not even disclose this as a material risk in its public filings. In the end the court chose to accept only one of the defendants' increments to the cost of equity, which led to a fair value estimate of $38.05 per share — almost four times the deal price of $10.25 per share and more than five times the market price of $7 per share.

Of course, one could argue the court's task would be easier if it had relied on stock market price as its talisman of fair value. Indeed, the court noted that "Delaware law recognizes market price should be considered in an

18. *In re Emerging Communications* at 54.

appraisal, [although] the market price of shares is not always indicative of fair value." Nevertheless, for several reasons, the court did not think market price (however helpful it may be in other cases), was useful here. First, the court did not think ECM traded in an efficient market because it was thinly traded and wasn't really followed by Wall Street analysts. It would thus take time for the market to incorporate information about ECM. Indeed, the defendant controller of ECM (Prosser) seemed to share similar views. Second, the court noted concerns about relying on market price, even in an efficient market. For example:

> [Defendants' expert] admitted that markets occasionally make errors, that the market could have been wrong about ECM, and that it is possible for a stock that trades even in an efficient market to be mispriced, especially in the short run. [Defendants' expert] also conceded that the market may be inefficient if material information is withheld from it. In the case of ECM, while the stock was trading freely . . . the market never had the benefit of any disclosed earnings or projections of future results, including the June Projections . . . For these reasons, the Court rejects the defendants' argument that the market price of ECM stock corroborates the $10.25 price as the fair or intrinsic value of ECM on the date of the merger. In this case, ECM's unaffected stock market price merits little or no weight.[19]

QUESTION ON EMERGING COMMUNICATIONS

If the court is correct that the intrinsic value of the minority shares was $38.05, why did 60 percent of the ECM minority shareholders approve of (by tendering) Prosser's freeze-out offer at $10.25 per share? More generally, how can a market price of $7 be consistent with a "fair value" of $38.05? We return to these questions in Chapter 12.

Courts also rely on valuation principles and modern finance theory in other business law contexts. For example, in determining whether misleading or fraudulent statements about a firm's performance can generate liability under the federal securities laws, courts often rely on modern finance theory through the use of event studies to understand market price responses. There is a large literature exploring the use of event studies in corporate and securities litigation. Although we do not discuss it in any depth here, we note its importance to practice and encourage interested readers to explore it further.[20]

---

19. Some of the court's comments dovetail with those in the "behavioral finance" literature. For interested readers, please see Robert J. Shiller, *Irrational Exuberance*, Princeton University Press (2000).

20. *See, e.g.,* Lucian A. Bebchuk & Allen Ferrell, *Rethinking Basic,* 69 The Business Lawyer 671 (2014); Sanjai Bhagat & Roberta Romano, *Empirical Studies of Corporate Law* in Vol. 2 Handbook of Law and Economics (A. Mitchell Polinsky & Steven Shavell, eds. 2007); Holger Spamann, *On Inference When Using State Corporate Laws for Identification* (December 6, 2019). Harvard Law School John M. Olin Center Discussion Paper No. 1024 (2019); European Corporate Governance Institute — Finance Working Paper No. 644/2019. Available at SSRN: https://ssrn.com/abstract=3499101.

5.4.3   Regulators

A last important reason to stay current with finance theory and valuation concepts is that regulators and policy makers often rely on them. One important example is Federal Securities Laws (and regulations and enforcement thereunder), which are premised upon certain understandings of modern finance theory. Thus, business lawyers must be familiar with them too. We address some of these matters in Chapter 14 when discussing insider trading regulation, but note this their importance spans much beyond this particular topic.

NORMAL GOVERNANCE: THE VOTING SYSTEM

6.1 INTRODUCTION: SHAREHOLDER VOTING IN THE NEW CORPORATE GOVERNANCE

The corporate form derives much of its utility by according broad discretion to a centralized management structure. Of course, there are some limits to the discretion of corporate boards, including those imposed by the fiduciary duties of directors. And corporate charters can tie the hands of directors (and controlling shareholders) in many ways, as in fact they often do in closely held companies. But remarkably few public companies restrict board discretion in their charters. Instead, dispersed shareholders in public corporations largely rely on three powers to counter overreaching by corporate boards. Professor Robert Clark has aptly summarized these powers as the right to vote, the right to sell, and the right to sue. This Chapter focuses on shareholder voting rights in the selection of directors and in the approval of resolutions sponsored by either the board or by shareholders. And, as between these sorts of voting rights, we emphasize the shareholder's right to elect the members of the board of directors. Subsequent Chapters examine the right to vote on fundamental transactions in more detail, as well as the rights to sue and sell.

Understanding the role of shareholder voting in corporate governance requires a review of the legal machinery that constitutes what might be described as part of the "normal governance" of the corporation. This includes shareholder meetings, procedures for electing and removing directors, proxy voting, shareholder information rights, and judicial superintendence of shareholder voting. We also touch on the SEC's proxy rules that govern mandatory disclosure and proxy voting in public companies, with particular attention to a shareholder's right to bring resolutions concerning corporate governance and social responsibility to a vote at annual shareholders meetings. But before addressing these topics, we introduce two considerations that are broadly relevant to the governance of publicly traded companies: the distribution of share ownership and the rise of institutional investing.

6.1.1   Ownership Structure and the Collective Action Problem

All else being equal, the importance of shareholder voting in corporate governance is tied to ownership structure; that is, to how shares are distributed among shareholders. This is easy to see at the two extremes of a continuum of the possible distributions of voting rights — firms with controlling shareholders and those held by widely-dispersed small shareholders. In companies with controlling shareholders, a single shareholder or group of shareholders might control sufficient votes to appoint the entire board of directors unilaterally. In this case the votes of minority shareholders simply do not matter to the composition of the board (although they matter to shareholder votes on other critical matters such as fundamental corporate transactions).[1]

Controlling or dominant shareholders are more common than is generally appreciated, but most large U.S. companies have, to one degree or another, a more dispersed shareholder base. The polar opposite of the controlled company is thus at least as important for understanding the limits of shareholder voting, and it is at this extreme that the shareholders' collective action problem is most severe. A stylized hypothetical makes the point. Assume that a widely held corporation has 100,000 shareholders, each of whom holds $100 of its stock. Suppose also that this corporation has performed badly for a decade and that its directors, whose average tenure is 25 years, show no signs of responding to their company's slow decline. The question is whether the company's many small investors can replace the incumbent board with new directors committed to change, which might mean anything from devising a new business plan to auctioning off the company to the highest bidder. The answer is probably not, at least not without outside intervention and perhaps not even with it.[2]

If the company's many small shareholders are rational, none of them will individually undertake to recruit new board candidates and solicit other shareholders to support them at the next shareholders meeting (triggering what is termed a "proxy contest"). Leading such a campaign against incumbent directors would be far more costly than the pro rata benefit a small shareholder might receive from saving the company. Even a doubling of firm value only benefits an individual shareholder by $100, which is far less than the costs in time and resources of running a proxy campaign.

But might a large outside investor intervene, say, by buying 10 percent of the company's stock before undertaking a proxy contest? Maybe, because

---

1. Majority-of-minority shareholder votes, sometimes termed "MOM" votes, may affect the standard of review that courts employ when passing on fundamental transactions sponsored by controlling shareholders with conflicted interests. More on this in Chapters 8, 11, and 13. Controlling shareholders routinely appoint financially independent directors to the boards of their companies, in part to deflect charges that they favor their private interests over those of minority shareholders.

2. You might respond that shareholders can jump off the train by selling their shares. But consider that if the market is well informed about the company's trajectory, the price at which they can sell their shares will fully reflect their company's dismal prospects.

such an investor has a greater incentive to gather information and act on it, in contrast to the small shareholders who have little incentive to inform themselves beyond occasionally glancing at share prices. And even if a concerted effort left small investors favorably disposed toward the insurgent side in a proxy contest, it might not be enough to attract their votes. They might reasonably believe that their individual votes won't matter to the outcome of the contest and skip the bother of voting at all. The lesson here is that shareholder voting matters most where there is no controlling shareholder *and* where some shareholders hold stakes large enough to initiate a proxy contest if they think their company is struggling. However, even here generating informed shareholder action is not easy.

Throughout much of the twentieth century, share ownership has seemed too dispersed to support collective shareholder governance via voting. The dominant view of public corporations has tracked the analysis developed by Adolf Berle and Gardiner Means in their seminal 1932 study of the American corporation.[3] These authors confirmed what must have already been obvious in their day, that dispersed small shareholders are largely irrelevant to corporate governance. But they took this observation to the next level by examining the inheritors of control after many controlling shareholders left the scene — namely a rising class of expert and seemingly autonomous managers. This class, they argued, was a novel development in the evolution of the business enterprise because it marked a radical "separation of ownership and control."[4] In the decades after Berle and Means' monograph, most commenters came to accept their description of the large American corporation, even though they differed widely over its policy implications. The focus on retail investors affected securities regulation as well. A popular view after the passage of the Securities Exchange Act of 1934 was that the federal agency created to regulate the securities markets, the Securities and Exchange Commission (SEC), should exercise its powers to protect small shareholders from manipulation by large shareholders, even if a casual reading of Berle and Means might have suggested otherwise, namely that incumbent managers — not small shareholders — were the most likely beneficiaries of policies that discouraged collective action among larger shareholders. Indeed, prior to a significant reform of the SEC's proxy rules in 1992, a strong case could be made that SEC regulations worked to diminish the franchise of all shareholders, small and large.[5]

During the 1980s and 1990s, influential commentators offered other views on the collective action problem of disaggregated public shareholders. Two perspectives that emerged in the law-and-economics and finance literatures argued that market developments already compensate for some organizational disabilities inherent in diffuse shareholder ownership. One argued that corporate governance concerns are — or can be — answered in significant part by competitive markets in products, capital, managerial expertise,

---

3. Adolf Berle & Gardiner Means, *The Modern Corporation and Private Property* (1932).
4. *Id.* at 5.
5. See John Pound, *Proxy Voting and the SEC*, 29 J. Fin. Econ. 241 (1991).

and corporate control.[6] A second account points to the growing importance of concentrated private ownership in the form of private equity and venture capital in many sectors of the economy.[7] But the literature most salient for this Chapter addressed the implications of pervasive institutional ownership for the governance of publicly-traded corporations.

6.1.2   Institutional Investors and Shareholder Voting

As of 2019, institutions held about 80 percent of the shares in public companies listed in the Russell 3000, a broad-gauge index of public corporations.[8] Since the 1980s, institutional ownership has been recognized as a potential game-changer for shareholder participation in corporate governance.[9] Expectations grew after large state pension funds successfully lobbied for an overhaul of the SEC's proxy rules. After the 1992 reforms, shareholders could more freely share their views with more than a handful of their peers about pending corporate issues and publicly disclose how they would vote in shareholders meetings. No one in the 1960s or 1970s could have foreseen that institutional investors would pressure boards during the 1990s to fire CEOs at leading firms such as General Motors, IBM, Sears, Westinghouse, and American Express. Nor could they have anticipated the reforms in statutory law and governance practice that followed after the 1990s. Among the open questions today are the limits on institutional engagement in the governance of individual companies, the values that institutions champion and, of course, the costs and benefits of their interventions.

The gross statistics on institutional ownership of U.S. public companies and the sheer size of asset managers such as BlackRock, Vanguard, State Street, and Fidelity suggest a re-concentration of voting power in public corporations. This reduces the shareholders' collective action problem and might, in some measure, reverse the separation of ownership and control identified by Berle and Means. But of course, the world of institutional investing is not so simple. The institutional owners of shares — the mutual funds, pension funds, bank trust departments, insurance companies, and endowments — have different objectives and face different incentives. And many of these owners contract out the management of their assets and voting rights to investment advisors, which introduces yet another layer of agency relationships and costs. For example, asset managers are generally compensated in proportion to the size of the assets under management rather than by increases in the value of the portfolios they manage. There are also other important differences that undercut the alignment of interests between institutional owners

---

6. See, e.g., Frank H. Easterbrook & Daniel R. Fischel, *The Economic Structure of Corporate Law* (1991).

7. See, e.g., Michael C. Jensen, *Eclipse of the Public Corporation*, Harv. Bus. Rev. (Sept.-Oct. 1989).

8. See Charles McGrath, *80% of Equity Market Cap Held by Institutions*, Pensions & Investments, April 25, 2017.

9. See, e.g., Bernard Black, *Agents Watching Agents, The Promise of Institutional Investor Voice*, 39 UCLA L. Rev. 811 (1991).

and fund managers. Thus, how managers will engage in the affairs of portfolio companies by voting or otherwise is by no means clear.

We touch on the world of institutional investing again in Section 6.8. But it may be helpful to keep this world and the collective action problem in mind while reviewing the legal structure of shareholder voting rights.

6.2   ELECTING AND REMOVING DIRECTORS

6.2.1   Electing Directors

Corporate law requires that every corporation have at least one class of voting stock to elect its board of directors. Moreover, every corporation must have a board of directors, even if this "board" has only a single member. DGCL §141(a). Unless the corporate charter provides otherwise, the statutory default is that each share of stock has one vote — no more, no less. DGCL §212(a). However, since the charter can provide otherwise, the legal mandate that there be *some* voting stock is by itself a trivial constraint on governance design. Public corporations usually stick to the plain vanilla default of issuing a single class of voting common stock, although an important exception — that we will address shortly — is companies that issue a class of low-vote common stock but whose founders or other insiders retain a lock on control by holding second or third classes of common stock with multiple voting rights.

So-called "dual-class" common stock is the exception that proves the rule. But it also raises another question: Why Is voting stock mostly common stock rather than preferred stock or a hybrid security that mimics the features of corporate debt? (Warning: There are also important exceptions to this rule of thumb.[10]) One explanation is that common shareholders value voting rights more than other investors. Common shares have no maturity date and no legal right to periodic payments. By contrast, bondholders are protected by a hard, contractual right to interest payments and to the return of their principal, usually on a stated maturity date and sometimes secured with property of the debtor. Likewise, preferred shareholders enjoy contractual protections such as liquidation preferences and prior claims on corporate dividends. Put differently, the right to appoint corporate directors is the only protection that common stockholders have. Even if these stockholders are too dispersed to influence the boards they elect, they have the comfort of knowing that control of the board will not fall into the hands of other classes of investors and stakeholders whose interests are inimical to their own.[11] But if, more optimistically, common stock can command the allegiance of the board, there may be yet another reason to award it exclusive voting rights.

---

10. Among these exceptions is venture capital ("VC") financing, where VC funds conventionally take convertible preferred stock with voting rights while entrepreneurs retain voting common stock.

11. For a classic analysis of the apportionment of control rights among different enterprise constituencies, see Henry Hansmann, *The Ownership of Enterprise* (1996).

As residual claimants, common stockholders have stronger incentives than other constituencies to increase the value of the corporate enterprise as a whole. Of course, this observation rests on other assumptions as well — that common shareholders agree on maximizing long-term firm value as their common objective, and they also agree on the policies or managers that can best advance this objective.

Another mandatory feature of the voting system is the *annual* election of directors.[12] Each year, holders of voting stock elect either the whole board when there is a single class of directors, or some fraction of the board. For example, shareholders elect one-third of the board annually when the charter provides for a "staggered" or "classified" board made up of three "classes" of directors, each serving three-year terms. See DGCL §141(d). At the annual shareholders meeting, elected directors must meet the affirmative vote requirements provided in their company's bylaws or charter or, if these are not provided, elected directors need only receive a plurality of votes at the shareholders meeting as long as Delaware's easy quorum requirements are satisfied. DGCL §216. Thus, Delaware's statutory default sets a low threshold for election. Under the plurality default, 5 percent of the shares present at the meeting can elect a director, even if 95 percent of the shares present withhold their votes. Should such embarrassing discrepancies arise, however, one form of redress available to Delaware shareholders is to amend their company's bylaws to require that a nominee's election requires an affirmative vote of a majority of the votes of the shareholders present. The Delaware statute bars boards of directors from amending or repealing a stockholder-adopted bylaw that fixes vote requirements. Thus, a shareholder resolution suffices to implement a majority vote requirement. This may be one reason why the boards of most large public companies have implemented a majority-of-votes-cast election rule on their own initiative.[13] Another reason might be the uncomfortable optics of opposing majority elections.

Corporate law facilitates the election of directors by creating a flexible framework for holding the annual meeting of shareholders. Generally, state statutes fix a minimum and maximum notice period (e.g., 10-60 days, DGCL §222(b)) and a quorum requirement for the general meeting (e.g., DGCL §216). The statutes also establish a minimum and maximum period for the board to fix a so-called record date. Shareholders who are registered as shareholders as of the record date are legal shareholders entitled to vote at the meeting (e.g., DGCL §211(c)). Within the range of alternatives permitted by statute, a corporation's actual notice period, quorum requirement, and record

---

12. See DGCL §211. In non-U.S. jurisdictions, directors' terms are frequently longer; for example, four years in Germany and six years in France. Closely held private corporations in the United Kingdom occasionally elect directors *for life*. In all of these cases, however, shareholders retain a mandatory right to remove directors.

13. In a contested election, usually the nominee with the highest vote prevails. Where a majority vote is required for election and no candidate gets a majority of the vote cast, the incumbent will hold over in office. However, most firms have a policy, insisted on by institutional investors, that the holdover submit his resignation to the board promptly.

date will be established in the charter or in a bylaw or, in the case of record date and notice, by the board in the manner authorized by those documents.

CUMULATIVE VOTING

The default voting regime provides that each shareholder gets one vote for each share of voting stock owned and may cast it for each directorship (or board position) that is to be filled at the election. Thus, if there are seven places on the board to be filled each year, an owner of one share casts one vote for a candidate for each office. This allows the holder of a 51 percent voting block to designate the complete membership of the board of directors, while the holder of a sizable minority block of stock (say, 49 percent) can be left without representation on the board. To some, this seems undesirable.

An alternative technique for voting first sprang up late in the nineteenth century. This technique, called *cumulative voting*, is designed to increase the possibility for minority shareholder representation on the board of directors. In a cumulative voting regime, each shareholder may cast a total number of votes equal to the number of directors for whom she is entitled to vote, multiplied by the number of voting shares that she owns, with the top overall vote-getters being seated on the board.

To see how cumulative voting works, consider a simple example. Family Corp. has 300 shares outstanding. Shareholder A owns 199 shares and Shareholder B owns 101 shares. Family Corp. has a three-person board elected to annual terms. Assume that shareholders A and B support different candidates for the board. Under "straight" voting, A would win each seat 199 to 101. Under cumulative voting, B could cast 303 votes (= 101 shares × 3 seats up for election) all for a single candidate. Thus B would be guaranteed to get one seat on the board, because A's 597 votes (= 199 shares × 3 seats) cannot be divided three ways so that all three of A's candidates receive more than 303 votes. This example illustrates how cumulative voting can allow significant minority shareholders to get board representation roughly in proportion to their shareholdings.

While cumulative voting was popular among state legislatures and certain shareholders a century ago, it was never popular with managers who preferred collegial boards able to reach unanimous decisions without deadlock or untoward dissent. Boards with divided shareholder allegiances were said to be too adversarial. Thus, few companies have adopted cumulative voting during the last fifty years.[14] Where a corporate charter does mandate cumulative voting, however, it affects the exercise of the shareholders' rights to remove directors (since it makes little sense to permit a straight majority vote to remove a director without cause when he or she was elected by a cumulative vote).

6.2.2 Removing Directors

State corporate law provides for the right to remove directors, which is no less important than the right to elect them. Under the DGCL,

---

14. See Jeffrey N. Gordon, *Institutions as Relational Investors: A New Look at Cumulative Voting*, 94 Colum. L. Rev. 124 (1994).

shareholders may remove directors from office at any time and for any reason, except in the case of "staggered boards," in which case they may do so only "for cause," unless the charter provides otherwise. DGCL 141(k). Removal may be accomplished at a shareholders meeting or by written consent, as explained below.

When a board is staggered (DGCL §141(d)), removal is difficult. The leading case, *Campbell v. Loew's Inc.*,[15] establishes that a director is entitled to certain due process rights before he or she can be removed for cause. Just what these rights are remains unclear, as does the meaning of "good cause." Certainly, fraud or unfair self-dealing give cause to remove a director, but what about abysmal business judgment? If one views the directorship as a sort of property right, which seems to be the predicate of the "cause" requirement, then poor business judgment alone would not be cause for removal. See DGCL §141(k), which confers broad removal power on shareholders.

Most corporate statutes, including the DGCL, bar directors from removing fellow directors, for cause or otherwise, without express shareholder authorization. This means, for example, that a board typically cannot adopt a bylaw that purports to authorize it to exercise a removal power. Some statutes, however, permit shareholders to grant the board power to remove individual directors for cause. See, e.g., NYBCL §706. In all events, a board uncovering cause for removal can petition a court of competent jurisdiction to remove the director in question from office. It is generally conceded that any court of equity supervising the performance of any fiduciary has an inherent power to remove for cause.[16]

PROBLEM: THE UNFIREABLE CEO

Village, Inc., is a Delaware corporation that provides online fashion advice and individualized consulting services to law students and young lawyers. The firm had its initial public offering (IPO) two years ago, but after a meteoric rise, its stock has fallen steadily for the past 18 months. Wildman West, who is Village's CEO, owns 25 percent of its single class of common stock. The balance of its stock is widely held. Since West is the only large blockholder of Village shares, he has appointed all of its directors since its IPO. Over the past year, however, the word on the street has been that Village's sagging share price could make it a possible target for a takeover attempt. West and his directors responded to these alarming rumors by amending Village's bylaws to mandate a nine-member board divided into three classes, of which only one class is subject to a shareholder vote annually (a classified or staggered board). In addition, West's board solicited and received shareholder approval to amend the Company's charter to (1) vest exclusive power

---

15. 134 A.2d 852 (Del. Ch. 1957).

16. Ordinarily, only the courts of a corporation's home state can remove one of its directors because the law of a company's legal domicile governs its internal affairs. However, federal courts may exercise this authority as well when a corporation is publicly traded, and therefore registered under the Securities Exchange Act of 1934.

to amend its bylaws in the board, and (2) require the election of directors by cumulative voting.

Six months after these events, the infamous takeover artist, Barracuda Manning, silently acquired 51 percent of Village's outstanding shares from its many small shareholders who lost faith in West after the decline in the Company's share price accelerated. Now Barracuda wants to take operational control of Village's affairs ASAP. However, Barracuda's former counsel advised him that he may have to wait three years before securing majority control of the seats on the Company's board.

Why did Barracuda's former counsel advise that it might take three years to control Village's board? Is there a way around the legal obstacles that seem to impede taking control immediately or at least within a much shorter time-span? Consider what might be done by amending the certificate of incorporation, amending the bylaws, increasing the size of the board, and/or removing incumbent directors. Key DGCL provisions to review include DGCL §109(a), §141(k), §223, and §242(b)(1). Do you need to make additional assumptions before deciding on a legal strategy and, if so, what are they? Finally, would your advice change if West had persuaded Village's shareholders to approve a classified board in the Company's charter in addition to the bylaw and cumulative voting charter amendments?

NOTE ON STAGGERED BOARDS

As the preceding problem illustrates, a staggered board makes it more difficult for a shareholder — even a shareholder who holds 51 percent of the stock — to gain control of the board of directors immediately. Under a "unitary" board, in which all directors are elected annually, a majority shareholder has a clean shot at electing a full board once a year. But when the board is staggered, a shareholder may need to win two elections, which can be as long as 13 to 15 months apart, in order to gain majority control of the board.

Of course, majority shareholders may be able to "disassemble" a staggered board to avoid the two-election problem, depending on whether it is located in a company's charter or in its bylaws. If the staggered board is established in a bylaw, shareholders may be able to eliminate it through a bylaw amendment. If it is established in the charter, shareholders may be able to evade it by amending the bylaws to enlarge the board (restrictions on the size of the board are usually placed in the bylaws but can be located in the charter). Increasing board size opens up vacant board seats, which a majority shareholder can fill if the charter happens to authorize shareholders to fill open board seats. See DGCL §226. But if a staggered board is "effective" (non-evadable) — as is usually the case — then a new majority shareholder who wishes to control the board may have to wait at least one year after acquiring a majority of shares and possibly as long as two years, depending on the time between the acquisition of shares and the next annual shareholders meeting.

The difference between unitary and staggered boards is particularly salient in the context of hostile takeover bids. As we shall see in Chapter 13, the invention of the "poison pill" in the mid-1980s made control of the board a prerequisite for acquiring a large block of a company's shares without the incumbent board's cooperation. A staggered board makes acquiring board control more difficult. Sure enough, empirical work shows that targets of hostile takeover bids are more likely to remain independent when they have a staggered board than when they have a unitary board.[17] The data further shows that targets that remain independent do not, on average, achieve the same returns for their shareholders as they would have received by accepting the hostile takeover bid.[18] Putting these facts together suggests that staggered boards, on average, "entrench" boards and managers in ways that deter value-increasing hostile takeover bids.

The claim of those who support staggered boards rests not on their effect on takeovers, but on claimed benefits to firm operations over time. They assert that such structures permit boards to plan and execute long-term strategy more effectively. Can empirical studies resolve this dispute? Not perfectly. The studies that show unitary boards having higher returns are "cross-sectional" studies — they measure firm performance at a moment in time.[19] Such studies cannot definitively determine whether underperforming firms choose staggered board structures (perhaps because they are particularly at risk of takeover) or whether the board structure itself causes the underperformance. Longitudinal studies — which measure firms over time in comparison to their industry or other metric — require more effort and there are far fewer of them. But some of these studies report that over a longer term, firms with staggered boards tend to outperform firms with unitary board structures, all else held constant.[20] However, the studies are not sufficiently definitive to resolve this problem with certainty.

More importantly, many institutional shareholders and their allies believe that staggered boards are undesirable and have lobbied boards to dismantle them. Their efforts have had remarkable success among very large public companies. In 2002, more than 60 percent of S&P 500 firms had staggered boards, but by 2018 that number had declined to about 10 percent. This trend continues among very large firms. Interestingly, however, staggered boards are the dominant board structure at the IPO stage (greater than 90 percent of IPOs have this structure).[21] Institutional investors continue to invest in firms with this structure at that stage.

17. See Lucian Arye Bebchuk, John C. Coates IV & Guhan Subramanian, *The Powerful Antitakeover Force of Staggered Boards: Theory, Evidence & Policy*, 54 Stan. L. Rev. 887 (2002); Lucian Arye Bebchuk, John C. Coates IV & Guhan Subramanian, *The Powerful Antitakeover Force of Staggered Boards: Further Findings and a Reply to Symposium Participants*, 55 Stan. L. Rev. 885 (2002).

18. See Bebchuk, Coates & Subramanian, *Further Findings, supra* note 17.

19. See, e.g., Lucian A. Bebchuk & Alma Cohen, *The Cost of Entrenched Boards*, 78 J. Fin. Econ. 409 (2005).

20. See K.J. Martin Cremers, Lubomir Litov & Simone Sepe, *Staggered Boards and Long-Term Firm Value, Revisited*, 126 J. Fin. Econ. 422 (2017).

21. See Proskauer's Global Capital Markets IPO Study 2019; David F. Larcker & Brian Tayan, *Loosey-Goosey Governance: Four Misunderstood Terms in Corporate Governance* (October 7, 2019).

QUESTION

What alternative explanations might you suggest to explain why established firms consent to drop their staggered boards while young firms issuing shares in the public market for the first time prefer to install staggered board provisions in their charters? We can think of at least two, but there may be others.

6.3 SHAREHOLDER MEETINGS AND ALTERNATIVES

In addition to the election of the board at the annual meeting, shareholders may consider other business. Thus, shareholders may also vote to adopt, amend, and repeal bylaws; to remove directors; and to adopt shareholder resolutions that may ratify board actions or request the board to take certain actions. Should the board fail to convene an annual meeting within 13 months of the last meeting, courts will entertain a shareholder's petition and promptly require that a meeting be held in a summary action. See, e.g., DGCL §211.

6.3.1 Special Meetings

Special meetings of shareholders are those other than the annual meeting called for special purposes. Often, they are called to permit shareholders to vote on fundamental transactions such as mergers. Additionally, in most jurisdictions, a special meeting is the only way that shareholders can initiate action (such as the amendment of the charter or the removal from office of directors) between annual meetings. Therefore, *who* may call a special meeting and *how* a special meeting is called are matters of considerable importance.

If you were designing an ideal corporate governance structure, when would you permit shareholders to call a special meeting over the objection of the board? Presumably, the more that investors monitor corporate management, *ceteris paribus*, the lower the level of wasteful agency costs and other deviations from shared shareholder preferences will be, and to that extent, the lower the firm's cost of capital will be.[22] This factor weighs in favor of permitting shareholders to call special meetings easily, where, for example, they might act to remove directors. Yet shareholder meetings are costly, especially for public companies. Their potential costs include not only funding to support special shareholder meetings and the distractions they pose for senior managers, but also, and perhaps more seriously, the risk of magnifying the decision-making costs that arise when shareholders are sharply divided over

---

22. But is this presumption necessarily true? If a major source of the utility of the corporate form is the deep knowledge and expertise of centralized management, is it not logically possible that increasing shareholder control of the board — while reducing agency costs — might at some point also reduce effectiveness of management and possibly lower efficiency, thus raising the company's cost of capital?

their company's business plan and sufficiently committed to the composition of the board. In all events, as with many issues of corporate law, we
can easily state a general principle such as "maximize the value of the firm,"
but find that it is difficult to apply it without controversy. Either encouraging special meetings (and accepting the costs) or discouraging them
(and allowing directors freer rein) may increase or decrease the value of
a firm.

Putting the matter of meetings in the corporate charter allows corporate
planners to decide for themselves in particular cases. The Model Business
Corporation Act (MBCA, 2016 Revision) offers a typical solution. Under
§7.02, a corporation must hold a special meeting of shareholders if (1) such
a meeting is called by the board of directors or a person authorized in the
charter or bylaws to do so, or (2) the holders of at least 10 percent of all votes
entitled to be cast demand such a meeting in writing. Delaware law has no
such mandated minimum; it provides that special meetings may be called by
the board or by such persons as are designated in the charter or bylaws. See
DGCL §211(d).

6.3.2   Shareholder Consent Solicitations

Shareholders often have an alternative to special meetings in the form
of a statutory provision permitting them to act in lieu of a meeting by filing
written consents. Delaware was an innovator in establishing this alternative
technique for shareholder action, although at the time it was adopted, it was
thought to be little more than a cost-reducing measure for small corporations.
As we will see later, however, this mechanism can also assist in hostile takeovers where acquirers wish to displace the boards of public companies.

The stockholder consent statute in Delaware provides that *any action*
that may be taken at a meeting of shareholders (e.g., amendment of bylaws
or removal of directors from office) may also be taken by the written concurrence of the holders of the number of voting shares required to approve that
action at a meeting attended by all shareholders. See DGCL §228. Other states
are less "liberal." The MBCA, for example, requires unanimous shareholder
consent. See MBCA §7.04(a).

6.4   Proxy Voting and Its Costs

Shareholder meetings require a quorum to act. Dispersed share ownership
ensures that most shareholders of public companies will not physically attend
shareholder meetings. To meet quorum requirements and provide a sem-
blance of collective decision making, the boards and officers of these companies collect proxies — essentially agency agreements — that authorize agents
at these meetings to vote in accordance with the shareholder's instructions.
It is important to note, however, that the standard proxies distributed to the
shareholders of public corporations today differ from the conventional ballots

that voters receive in political elections in one key respect. Modern proxies allow shareholders to vote in favor of the board nominees proposed by the party distributing its proxy cards or to withhold their vote from some or all of this party's nominees, but they do not allow shareholders to vote another party's candidates on the same proxy card. The "political" convention allows voters to mix and match candidates from contesting parties on a single ballot. Such ballots are not unknown in the corporate context where they are termed "universal proxies," but they are exceedingly rare for both legal and institutional reasons. One must also consider that the vast majority of corporate elections are uncontested and the board's proxy card is the only one that shareholders receive. In these "normal" shareholder meetings, there is no difference between a conventional proxy and a universal proxy.

State law does not prescribe a particular form for corporate proxies any more than it regulates agency agreements in other contexts. Under state law, all that is required for a valid proxy is that a shareholder designate the proxy holder and authenticate the grant of the proxy. The proxy holder, in turn, is bound to exercise the proxy as directed. Proxies usually include a list of the specific nominees and specific issues on which the proxy holder proposes to vote. But proxy holders are generally free to exercise independent judgment on issues arising at the shareholder meeting for which they have not received specific instruction. Although the traditional form of a corporate proxy was and still is a signed "proxy card," modern statutes recognize that electronic communications may also be used to designate a proxy, so long as sufficient evidence of authenticity is supplied. See DGCL §212(c)(2).[23]

But if state law is relaxed about the form that corporate proxies may take and the ways in which they may be solicited, federal securities law regulates a great deal about the solicitation and use of proxies in publicly traded firms. As we mentioned above, federal regulation centers on Section 14(a) of the Securities Exchange Act of 1934, which vests the SEC with the authority to promulgate its highly prescriptive Proxy Rules and supports an extensive body of case law in the federal courts that addresses all aspects of proxy regulation, but most particularly the regime of mandatory disclosure under Section 14(a) and the broad scope of its antifraud provision. We return to these topics in Section 6.9 below.

A significant consideration bearing on shareholder voting is the expense of mounting a proxy contest in a publicly traded company. This is yet another example of the familiar collective action problem. One measure of independent shareholder participation in corporate governance might be the ease

---

23. See also the "Eproxy rules," SEC Rule 14a-16, requiring all public companies to post their proxy materials on a publicly available website and requiring a mail "Notice of Internet Availability of Proxy Materials." The rule adopted in 2007 has not yet revolutionized practice. See Rachel Geoffroy, *Electronic Proxy Statement Dissemination and Shareholder Monitoring* (November 30, 2018). Available at SSRN: https://ssrn.com/abstract=3264846.

When shareholders grant two conflicting proxies, the more recent one automatically revokes its predecessor unless the first proxy was given to protect an important interest of the recipient rather than merely to instruct an agent about a shareholder's voting preferences. See DGCL §212(e); *Haft v. Haft*, 671 A.2d 413 (Del. Ch. 1995) (proxy held by CEO was irrevocable because of proxy holder's interest as officer of the corporation).

with which proxy voting allows them to challenge incumbent directors at shareholder meetings. And here the obvious constraint on shareholder choice is that they cannot displace incumbent directors unless they can vote for a credible slate of competing nominees. This means, in turn, that disaggregated shareholders can directly influence the composition of corporate boards only if some person or organization undertakes the considerable expense of running a campaign. This entails recruiting insurgent board candidates, soliciting the support of influential shareholders, making the insurgent case to other shareholders and the press, and retaining a team of professionals — lawyers, proxy solicitors, and PR consultants — whose services are essential for success. Of course, no one initiates a proxy contest solely because it would benefit shareholders as a class. The insurgents who launch a proxy campaign must expect a private benefit commensurate with the costs they incur. Little wonder, then, that contested corporate elections are uncommon and that shareholders can express dissatisfaction with their board only in more oblique ways, such as refusing to vote for some or all of management's nominees (so called "withholding" their votes).

But is the absence of effective shareholder choice in 99 percent of corporate elections a bug or a feature? From the management's perspective, too many proxy contests might seem to be a nightmare. They would threaten to destabilize firm leadership, disrupt long-term business planning, and open the boardroom to the candidates of poorly informed shareholder factions and conflicting agendas. Corporate law must address these concerns as well. In "normal" or uncontested corporate elections, the corporate treasury pays the bills for soliciting proxies on behalf of the board's nominees. It could hardly be otherwise. Each year, public corporations prepare proxy statements that disclose their financial statements, management's discussion of the state of the business, and much more including the board's candidates for election at the annual shareholders meeting. A proxy statement on file with the SEC allows a company to solicit shareholder proxies to ensure that it will have a quorum at the shareholders meeting and acceptable shareholder support for its incoming board.[24] Financing the proxy statement and soliciting shareholder approval is a normal business expense that the company pays for as a matter of course. But should the same rules apply if the company incurs extraordinary expenses to defend the incumbent board in a proxy fight? Expensive proxy contests in S&P 500 companies can cost north of $50 million, while the typical contest in smaller public companies seems and lie between $750,000 and $2 million.[25]

Champions of shareholder rights might point out that the standard practice of funding management's side in proxy contests handicaps insurgents and

---

24. DGCL §216 provides a quorum requirement of "a majority of shares entitled to vote, present in person or represented by proxy." Note that if the meeting has only non-routine matters on which to vote (e.g., a merger), then a broker cannot vote the shares of the beneficial owner without instructions from the owner (NYSE Rule 452). These broker non-votes are not counted toward quorum. See Douglas K. Schnell & Angela Chen, *Counting Shareholder Votes*, 33 Insights 3 (May 2019), available at: https://www.wsgr.com/publications/PDFSearch/insights-2019-05-31.pdf.

25. See Investment Company Institute, *Analysis of Fund Proxy Campaigns: 2012-2019* (Dec. 2019), available at: https://www.sec.gov/comments/4-725/4725-6580709-201124.pdf; Mike Coronato, *2017 Proxy Fights: High Cost, Low Volume*, FactSet (Nov. 6, 2017), https://insight.factset.com/2017-proxy-fights-high-cost-low-volume).

favors incumbent control. If these critics are right, there are too few proxy contests rather than too many. Still, what can be done to mitigate incumbent bias? Any proposal to scale back corporate support for incumbent boards seems like a non-starter. No one expects directors to pay personally to defend policies that they believe to be in the corporation's best interests. Perhaps an alternative, then, is to require corporations to reimburse insurgents partially for their reasonable expenses. From one perspective, this might seem absurd. Why should corporations defend incumbent boards to the end, and also fund their opponents, thereby increasing the costs of defending the board? But from an institutional perspective, reimbursing insurgents might seem plausible if proxy contests are thought to benefit all shareholders by challenging poorly performing managers. Chapter 10 addresses an analogous paradox that arises in the context of shareholder lawsuits. To demonstrate that this is a live question in the context of proxy voting, we need only cite DGCL §113, which authorizes shareholders or boards to enact a bylaw providing for the partial reimbursement of the costs of a losing insurgent campaign in certain circumstances. We do not know how many companies actually have a §113 bylaw provision.

The problem below and the leading case that follows it explore the majority common law position on the reimbursement of proxy solicitation expenses. We suggest reading the problem first and the case next, and then returning to the problem and the commentary that follows the case.

PROBLEM: ONLY INCUMBENTS AND WINNERS GET FREE PROXIES

A group of dissident shareholders controls 20 percent of the voting shares of Incumbent Air, a poorly run airline catering to corporate executives. Suppose that the dissidents believe they stand a 50 percent chance of winning a proxy fight and that they will spend $2 million in mobilizing shareholder support, as will the incumbent managers. Assume that management can use the corporate purse to pay its solicitation costs.

If the dissidents have to pay their own legal and other proxy expenses out of pocket, under what circumstances will they actually go through with the proxy fight (assuming they are risk-neutral, rational profit-maximizers)? What is the total gross gain in corporate value that the dissidents must expect before they will initiate a proxy contest? What effect would there be if the dissidents were reimbursed for their proxy expenses regardless of the outcome?

ROSENFELD v. FAIRCHILD ENGINE & AIRPLANE CORP.
128 N.E. 2d 291 (N.Y. 1955)

Froessel, J.:

In a stockholder's derivative action brought by plaintiff, an attorney, who owns 25 out of the company's over 2,300,000 shares, he seeks to compel the return of $261,522, paid out of the corporate treasury to reimburse both sides in a proxy contest for their expenses. The Appellate Division has unanimously affirmed a judgment of an Official Referee dismissing plaintiff's complaint on the merits, and we agree. Exhaustive opinions were written by both courts below, and it will serve no useful purpose to review the facts again.

Of the amount in controversy $106,000 were spent out of corporate funds by the old board of directors while still in office in defense of their position in said contest; $28,000 were paid to the old board by the new board after the change of management following the proxy contest, to compensate the former directors for such of the remaining expenses of their unsuccessful defense as the new board found was fair and reasonable; payment of $127,000, representing reimbursement of expenses to members of the prevailing group, was expressly ratified by a 16 to 1 majority vote of the stockholders.

Other jurisdictions and our own lower courts have held that management may look to the corporate treasury for the reasonable expenses of soliciting proxies to defend its position in a bona fide policy contest. . . .

If directors of a corporation may not in good faith incur reasonable and proper expenses in soliciting proxies in these days of giant corporations with vast numbers of stockholders, the corporate business might be seriously interfered with because of stockholder indifference and the difficulty of procuring a quorum, where there is no contest. In the event of a proxy contest, if the directors may not freely answer the challenges of outside groups and in good faith defend their actions with respect to corporate policy for the information of the stockholders, they and the corporation may be at the mercy of persons seeking to wrest control for their own purposes, so long as such persons have ample funds to conduct a proxy contest. The test is clear. When the directors act in good faith in a contest over policy, they have the right to incur reasonable and proper expenses for solicitation of proxies and in defense of their corporate policies, and are not obliged to sit idly by. The courts are entirely competent to pass upon their bona fides in any given case, as well as the nature of their expenditures when duly challenged.

It is also our view that the members of the so-called new group could be reimbursed by the corporation for their expenditures in this contest by affirmative vote of the stockholders. With regard to these ultimately successful contestants, as the Appellate Division below has noted, there was, of course, "no duty . . . to set forth the facts, with corresponding obligation of the corporation to pay for such expense." However, where a majority of the stockholders chose — in this case by a vote of 16 to 1 — to reimburse the successful contestants for achieving the very end sought and voted for by them as owners of the corporation, we see no reason to deny the effect of their ratification nor to hold the corporate body powerless to determine how its own moneys shall be spent.

The rule then which we adopt is simply this: In a contest over policy, as compared to a purely personal power contest, corporate directors have the right to make reasonable and proper expenditures, subject to the scrutiny of the courts when duly challenged, from the corporate treasury for the purpose of persuading the stockholders of the correctness of their position and soliciting their support for policies which the directors believe, in all good faith, are in the best interests of the corporation. The stockholders, moreover, have the right to reimburse successful contestants for the reasonable and bona fide expenses incurred by them in any such policy contest, subject to like court scrutiny. That is not to say, however, that corporate directors can, under any circumstances, disport themselves in a proxy contest with the corporation's moneys to an unlimited extent. Where it is established that such moneys have been spent for personal power, individual gain or private advantage, and not in the belief that such expenditures are in the best interests of the stockholders and the corporation, or where the fairness and reasonableness of the amounts allegedly expended are duly and successfully challenged, the courts will not hesitate to disallow them.

The judgment of the Appellate Division should be affirmed, without costs. . . .

Despite a vigorous dissent, Judge Froessel's opinion for the court has carried the day. The doctrine is that, win or lose, incumbent managers are reimbursed for expenses that are reasonable in amount and can be attributed to deciding issues of principle or policy. As a practical matter, any disagreement (including "I am a better manager than you are") tends to satisfy the difference in policy requirement for reimbursement. Insurgents, on the other hand, stand a good chance of being reimbursed only if they win. See, e.g., *Steinberg v. Adams*, 90 F. Supp. 604 (S.D.N.Y. 1950). The rationale is that, when dissidents triumph, shareholders have decided that their expenses were made in a good-faith effort to advance a corporate interest. Without shareholder ratification, however, reimbursements to successful dissidents might be attacked as self-dealing. See *Heineman v. Datapoint Corp.*, 611 A.2d 950 (Del. 1992).

But does the Froessel rule fix the right incentives for proxy contests? If not, should the courts perhaps instead adopt a "super-Froessel" rule: Reimburse both sides for expenses, regardless of whether they win or lose? Or perhaps a pro rata rule in which each side is reimbursed in proportion to the votes they receive? What are the incentive effects of these options? Alternatively, is the Froessel rule the best second-best rule after all? For an analysis of incentives to mount proxy contests, see Lucian A. Bebchuk & Marcel Kahan, *A Framework for Analyzing Legal Policy Toward Proxy Contests*, 78 Calif. L. Rev. 1073 (1990).

NOTE ON PROXY SOLICITORS

Proxy solicitors, such as Okapi Partners, are the specialists who corral votes. They search through records to identify the actual parties entitled to vote on an issue and follow through to encourage them to vote. These may seem like pedestrian concerns, but they are central concerns in a voting contest (see Section 6.8). Proxy solicitors understand the dynamics and "plumbing" of the voting process and are indispensable players in our modern system — for which they usually receive handsome fees.

6.5   CLASS VOTING

Voting regimes always present the risk that majority blocks will advance their private interests. In the political sphere, the problem of majority coalitions is mitigated by the fact that voters typically have a range of cross-cutting identifications — geographic, economic, ethnic or racial, professional, religious, etc. — and a variety of shifting and sometimes inconsistent interests. In the corporate sphere, however, economic interests usually prevail. Thus, to the extent the interests of classes of shareholders diverge, as they may, for example, between preferred and common stock, the minority needs structural protection against exploitation by the majority. This protection is offered by the class voting requirement. A transaction that is subject to class voting simply means that a majority (or such higher proportion as may be fixed) of the votes in every class that is entitled to a separate class vote must approve the transaction for its authorization. Class votes sometimes occur in the normal governance context: when the charter creates rights of special classes to elect designated seats on the board. For example, the charter may provide that the Class A common stock will elect five directors and the Class B common stock will elect two. Of course, regardless of such differences, all corporate directors owe fiduciary loyalty to the corporation and to all of its shareholders equally, even when they are elected by a separate class of stock.

The more interesting class voting problems arise not in normal governance but in voting on fundamental transactions such as mergers and charter amendments. Here it may be necessary to protect the interests of separate classes of shares to ensure that the transaction is fair not only to shareholders in the aggregate but also to those subgroups. But notice that conferring class votes also gives each class a veto right and such rights themselves can be used opportunistically.

Again, Delaware and the MBCA approach this topic a bit differently. The DGCL provides that the charter may define such rights but provides very limited class voting rights in default of contracting for them in the charter. See DGCL §241 (b)(2). The Model Act and many state statutes provide more fully for statutory class voting rights on mergers or amendments to the charter. See MBCA §§10.04, 11.04(f).

PROBLEM: WHEN THE PREFERRED STOCK PREFERS NOT

Avonex Corp. has two classes of stock: 5 million shares of no par common stock and 500,000 shares of 6 percent cumulative preferred with a par value of $10 million. Business has not been good recently. Last year the firm had a net after-tax income of only $745,000. No dividend was paid on the common stock, but the preferred dividend was paid. Avonex has an interesting, if somewhat risky, new project. The company's lines of credit with banks are exhausted, and the banks will not lend more unless the firm raises additional equity. Management proposes that Avonex amend its charter to permit it to issue a new class of stock: an 11 percent senior cumulative preferred stock. In particular, it proposes that Avonex sell $5 million worth of this new security to institutional investors and several very wealthy individuals. The money raised by the new issue will permit the company to invest in the new project, which, if it succeeds, will begin to throw off cash in about two years. Projections indicate that, in five years, the new project will generate more than $1 million per year of net cash flow.

Of course, the charter must be amended before the new issue can proceed. You are the lawyer to whom holders of the preferred stock come for advice. They do not like the proposal — why not, do you suppose? If the projections are reliable, are the stockholders wise to want to oppose the proposal?

Assume Avonex is a New York corporation. Can the preferred stock vote to prevent the transaction? See NYBCL §804.

What if, instead, Avonex proposed to issue 1 million additional shares of the 6 percent cumulative preferred at a large discount and all that management's proposal required was a vote to increase the number of shares authorized in the existing charter? Would the preferred stock have a class vote?

Now assume Avonex is a Delaware corporation. Would this yield the same result? See DGCL §242(b)(2).

6.6 SHAREHOLDER INFORMATION RIGHTS

Shareholders must be informed in order to vote intelligently. State corporate law in the United States leaves the function of informing shareholders largely to the market. State law mandates neither an annual report nor any other financial statement. By contrast, federal securities law and the rules promulgated by the Securities and Exchange Commission mandate extensive disclosure for publicly traded securities. We discuss those requirements in later chapters. Now we focus on the limited state corporation law rights to information.

At common law, shareholders were recognized to have a right to inspect the company's books and records for a proper purpose. This right is codified in modern statutes. See, e.g., DGCL §220; MBCA §§16.02-16.03; NYBCL §624. Each statutory scheme differs, but the elements are similar. The Delaware statute provides, in part, as follows:

> (b) Any stockholder . . . shall upon written demand under oath stating the purpose thereof, have the right during the usual hours of business to inspect for any proper purpose, the corporation's stock ledger, a list of its stockholders and its other books and records, and to make copies and extracts there from. A proper purpose shall mean a purpose reasonably related to such person's interests as a stockholder.[26]

In administering this statutory right of access to information for a proper purpose, the Delaware courts recognize two fundamentally different types of requests: a request for a "stock list" and a request for inspection of "books and records" of the corporation. These two applications for judicial assistance

26. DGCL §220.

have different consequences for the corporation and are treated differently by the courts, even though both hinge on demonstrating a "proper purpose."

6.6.1 The Stock List

A corporate stock list discloses the identity, ownership interest, and address of each registered owner of company stock. Since the stock list does not contain proprietary information and is easy to produce, the law makes this list readily available to registered owners of the corporation's stock. "Proper purpose" for acquiring the stock list is broadly construed, and once it is shown, the court will not consider whether the shareholder has additional, "improper" purposes.[27] As a practical matter, Delaware courts permit only very limited discovery in litigation in which the stock list is sought. These cases are brought quickly to trial (in a matter of weeks) and ordinarily settle prior to trial, since, if the plaintiff is in fact a shareholder, she will ordinarily prevail.

In today's practice, a stock list is unlikely to be a mere piece of paper listing the names and addresses of the corporation's shareholders. First, it will be digitally stored and delivered. Second, a corporation that is required to produce a stock list will also be required to produce related, identifying information. Thus, an order to produce the stock list will carry with it an obligation to update this list, to produce a second list of stock brokerage firms whose stock is registered in the name of the Depository Trust Co., and to furnish daily trading information. Of importance is the fact that the order will often require the company to also furnish a "non-objecting beneficial owners" (NOBO) list, if the company has such a list.[28] The NOBO list is important to those who want to communicate directly with the real owners (and voters) of the stock.

6.6.2 Inspection of Books and Records

After requests for the shareholder list, the second kind of informational petition a court entertains is a request to examine a company's books and records. Here a plaintiff may allege the need for very broad access to the company's records in order to uncover suspected wrongdoing, mismanagement, unequal treatment of shareholders, and so forth. Such a request, however, can trench on legitimate corporate interests. Producing books and records is far more expensive than furnishing a stock list. In addition, it may jeopardize proprietary or competitively sensitive information. It follows that these requests

---

27. See *Bureau Reports, Inc. v. Credit Bureau of St. Paul, Inc.*, 290 A.2d 691 (Del. 1972) (requiring a corporation to disclose the stockholder list even though it was sought to solicit proxies to force management to deal more favorably with suppliers, one of whom was the plaintiff stockholder); and *Food and Allied Service Trades Dept., AFL-CIO v. Wal-Mart Stores, Inc.*, 1992 Del. Ch. LEXIS 108 (stock list requested to inform shareholders that imported goods were made with prison labor was a proper purpose). But see *State ex rel. Pillsbury v. Honeywell, Inc.*, 191 N.W.2d 406 (Minn. 1971) (purpose to communicate to shareholders concerning company's production of war material was not proper under Delaware law).

28. See *Shamrock Associates v. Texas American Energy Corp.*, 517 A.2d 658 (Del. Ch. 1986).

are reviewed with care. Under Delaware law, this is reflected formally by requiring plaintiffs to carry the burden of showing a proper purpose and, informally, by carefully screening plaintiff's motives and the likely consequences of granting her request. Consider, for example, the different matters bearing upon the granting or denial of relief in *Thomas & Betts Corp. v. Leviton Manufacturing Co., Inc.*, 685 A.2d 702 (Del. Ch. 1995) (scope of inspection right carefully delineated by the court in a books and records case).[29] It is noteworthy that Delaware courts have rejected books and records requests when the sole purpose is a fishing expedition to run a proxy contest. See *High River Limited Partnership v. Occidental Petroleum Corporation*, 2019 WL 6040285 (Del. Ch. Nov. 14, 2019). Do you agree that seeking books and records in order to determine whether to bring a proxy contest (or how to run one) is not a proper purpose in itself? On the other hand, recently Delaware courts have been more open to books and records requests when used as "quasi-discovery" devices prior to bringing *shareholder suits*. See, e.g., *AmerisourceBergen Corp. v. Lebanon Cty. Employees' Ret. Fund.* No. 60, 2020, 2020 WL 7266362 (Del. Dec. 10, 2020).[30]

6.7   TECHNIQUES FOR SEPARATING CONTROL FROM CASH FLOW RIGHTS

As noted earlier, one sensible reason to attach voting rights to common stock is that its holders comprise the corporate constituency with the strongest interest in maximizing corporate value. Nevertheless, the law's policy of aligning control with residual returns is not monolithic. For example, corporate law permits capital structures with dual-class voting, which clearly misaligns control rights and return rights. But corporate law also proscribes other devices that serve to misalign incentives — most notably a statutory prohibition against a corporation voting shares in itself that it owns or controls. See DGCL §160(c). Another context in which the law is sensitive to voting incentives is in its treatment of vote buying. "Circular voting," vote buying, and dual-class stock (and other controlling minority structures) are addressed in the three sections that follow.

6.7.1   Circular Control Structures

Imagine, for a moment, a moderately bad person (MBP) who gains control of a corporation as its CEO. MBP isn't likely to engage in murder or mayhem,

---

29. New York law adopts a different approach and grants shareholders a statutory right to inspect the firm's key financial statements and access to stock lists and meeting minutes unless the company can show that the shareholder lacks a proper purpose. Beyond this, the New York statute simply provides that courts retain the common law power to compel inspection in a proper case.

30. Books and records requests were important and favorably received in both the *Rales* case (discussed in Chapter 10) and *Corwin* (examined in Chapter 13). If this trend continues, it may partially offset new restrictions on shareholder discovery imposed by other lines of case law. See, e.g., our discussion in Section 10.5.2. Delaware has also permitted books and records requests when the requester alleged wrongdoing or mismanagement but held a short position in the firm. See *Deephaven Risk Arb Trading Ltd. v. UnitedGlobalCom, Inc.*, No. Civ.A. 379-N, 2005 WL 1713067 (Del. Ch. July 13, 2005).

but he is lazy, greedy, and conspiratorial. If the corporation is large, MBP can live very well, so long as he has control of the corporate treasury. Naturally, MBP wants to keep this control. (At least he is not aimless!) One way to do so would be to use the corporate treasury to buy the corporation's stock and control its voting rights. This plan is too direct, however. The law prohibits management from voting stock owned by the corporation. As a result, MBP must come up with something a bit more complicated — a subsidiary or a joint venture — in which his company owns only a minority interest.

PROBLEM: ROUND AND ROUND THE VOTES GO

MBP is CEO of ExploitCorp, a Delaware corporation that manufactures law textbooks. ExploitCorp's shares are owned by the general public (45 percent), Follow Inc. (45 percent), and MBP himself (10 percent). Recently, a group of dissatisfied shareholders met to discuss MBP's wasteful management style, including the yearly renovations of MBP's office, the use of corporate jets to fly MBP's children to law school, and the purchase of luxury cars for senior executives. A representative of the dissatisfied shareholders, who collectively hold 35 percent of ExploitCorp's shares, met with MBP and threatened to launch a proxy fight for control of the company, should MBP continue his lavish spending. Angered by the challenge to his authority, MBP responded, "Don't even think about a proxy fight. To succeed, you'll need Follow Inc.'s votes, and you'll never get them." Soon after, the shareholder representative discovered that ExploitCorp owns 30 percent of Follow Inc. and MBP is a Follow Inc. director.

Could MBP rely on Follow Inc.'s 45 percent stake in ExploitCorp, together with his own 10 percent, in a proxy fight? Would your answer change if ExploitCorp controlled 51 percent of Follow Inc.? See DGCL §160(c).

SPEISER v. BAKER
525 A.2d 1001 (Del. Ch. 1987)

ALLEN, C.:

The present action is brought under Section 211(c) of our corporation law and seeks an order requiring the convening of an annual meeting of shareholders of Health Med Corporation, a Delaware corporation. The Answer admits that no annual meeting of stockholders of that corporation has been held for several years, but attempts to allege affirmative defenses to the relief sought. In addition, that pleading asserts an affirmative right to a declaratory judgment unrelated, in my opinion, to the annual meeting.

Pending is a motion by plaintiff seeking (1) judgment on the pleadings and (2) dismissal of defendant's affirmative claim for relief. That motion raises two distinct legal issues. The first relates to plaintiff's Section 211 claim: it is whether defendant, having admitted facts that constitute a *prima facie* case for such relief, has pleaded facts which, if true, would constitute an equitable defense to the claim.

The second issue is raised by plaintiff's motion to dismiss claims asserted by defendant as cross-claims and counterclaims. It is whether the circular ownership of stock among the companies involved in this litigation violates Section 160(c) of our general corporation law. Stated generally, Section 160(c) prohibits the voting of stock that belongs to the issuer and prohibits the voting of the issuer's stock when owned by another corporation if the issuer holds, directly or indirectly, a majority of the shares entitled to vote at an election of the directors of that second corporation.

Plaintiff is Marvin Speiser, the owner of 50% of Health Med's common stock. Mr. Speiser is also president of Health Med and one of its two directors. Named as defendants are the company itself and Leon Baker, who owns the remaining 50% of Health Med's common stock and is Health Med's other director. Because of the particular quorum requirements set forth in Health Med's certificate, Baker, as the owner of the other 50% of Health Med's common stock, is able to frustrate the convening of an annual meeting by simply not attending. Thus, the need for the Section 211 action.

Despite the admission of facts constituting a *prima facie* case under Section 211, Baker asserts that a meeting should not be ordered. He contends, in a [counterclaim] . . . that the meeting sought is intended to be used as a key step in a plan by Mr. Speiser to cement control of Health Med in derogation of his fiduciary duty to Health Med's other shareholders. . . [T]o thwart [this] allegedly wrongful scheme Baker seeks a declaratory judgment [that Section 160(c) prohibits Health Chem (hereafter "Chem") from voting its own shares that are held by] . . . another Delaware corporation — Health Med. . . I conclude that Mr. Speiser is now entitled to judgment on his claim seeking to compel the holding of an annual meeting by Health Med, but that plaintiff's motion to dismiss the counterclaim must be denied. . .

I

The facts of the corporate relationships involved here are complex even when simplified to their essentials.

There is involved in this case a single operating business — Chem, a publicly traded company (American Stock Exchange). On its stock ledger, Chem's stockholders fall into four classes: the public (40%), Mr. Speiser (10%), Mr. Baker (8%) and Health Med (42%). In fact, however, Health Med is itself wholly owned indirectly by Chem and Messrs. Speiser and Baker. Thus, the parties interested in this matter (as owners of Chem's equity) are Speiser, Baker and Chem's public shareholders.

How the circular ownership here involved came about is not critical . . . What is relevant is that Chem (through a wholly owned subsidiary called Medallion Corp.) owns 95% of the equity of Health Med.[1] However,

---

1. Health Med's stock interest in Chem is treated as treasury stock on Chem's books.

Chem's 95% equity ownership in Health Med is not represented by owner-ship of 95% of the current voting power of Health Med. This is because what Chem owns is an issue of Health Med convertible preferred stock which, while bearing an unqualified right to be converted immediately into com-mon stock of Health Med representing 95% of Health Med's voting power, in its present unconverted state, carries the right to only approximately 9% of Health Med's vote. In its unconverted state the preferred commands in toto the same dividend rights (i.e., 95% of all dividends declared and paid) as it would if converted to common stock.

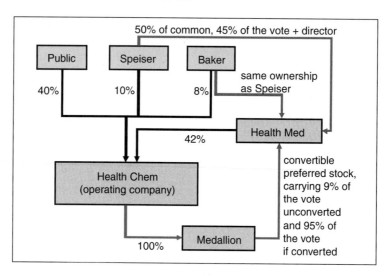

Speiser and Baker own the balance of Health Med's voting power. Each presently votes 50% of Health Med's only other issue of stock, its common stock. [See illustration above. — Eds.] This circular structure was carefully constructed as a means to permit Messrs. Speiser and Baker to control Chem while together owning less than 35% of its equity. It has functioned in that way successfully for some years. Speiser has served as president of all three corporations. When Speiser and Baker's mutual plan required shareholder votes, Speiser apparently directed the vote of Health Med's holdings of Chem stock (its only substantial asset) in a way that together with the vote of Speiser and Baker's personal Chem holdings, assured that their view would prevail.

The conversion of Chem's (Medallion's) preferred stock in Health Med would result in the destruction of the Baker-Speiser control mechanism. Under Section 160(c) of the Delaware corporation law (quoted and discussed below), in that circumstance, Health Med would certainly be unable to vote its 42% stock interest in Chem. As a result, the other shareholders of Chem (i.e., the owners of the real equity interest in Chem) would have their voting power increased . . . from 40% to 65.6%.

For reasons that are not important for the moment, Speiser and Baker have now fallen out. Control of Health Med and the vote of its Chem stock thus has now become critical to them. Mr. Speiser, by virtue of his office as President of Medallion and of Health Med, is apparently currently in a position to control Health Med and its vote. Baker asserts, not implausibly, that Speiser now seeks a Health Med stockholders meeting for the purpose of removing

Baker as one of Health Med's two directors in order to remove his independent judgment from the scene.

None of Chem's public shareholders have heretofore complained that the failure to convert Chem's (Medallion's) preferred stock in Health Med to common constituted a wrong. Several shareholders have, however, now moved to intervene in this action and asked to be aligned with Mr. Baker. This application is resisted by Mr. Speiser — who asserts some estoppel arguments personal to Mr. Baker as a ground for dismissing Baker's counterclaim.

II

Despite defendant Baker's pleading, which intermingles aspects of his affirmative defense to the Section 211(c) claim with elements of his affirmative claim for declaratory relief, I believe the two issues raised by this motion can most appropriately be analyzed independently. The allegedly wrongful control of Chem that is at the center of the [Baker's] claim for affirmative relief is not a matter that will be voted upon at (nor be significantly affected by) a Health Med stockholder meeting. The Section 160 claim is not that Chem (Medallion) ought not to be permitted to vote its stock at a Health Med meeting, but that Health Med is precluded from exercising rights as a Chem shareholder. Thus, while the two claims are factually related, they are, in my opinion, essentially independent claims legally. I therefore analyze them separately and turn first to Speiser's motion for judgment on the pleadings with respect to his Section 211(c) claim.

Section 211(b) of our corporation law contains a mandatory requirement that every Delaware corporation "shall" hold an "annual meeting of stockholders . . . for the election of directors." . . .

The facts alleged [here] . . . do state a claim, as I hold below, for relief, but what seems clear is that they allege no wrong to Health Med or its shareholders that will occur by reason of the holding of Health Med's annual meeting statutorily required by subsection (b) of Section 211. All that is really alleged with respect to Health Med is that Baker will likely be voted out of office as a Health Med director and the company will fall under the complete domination of Speiser. The answer to that, of course, is if the votes entitled to be cast at the meeting are cast so as to obtain that result, so be it.

III

I turn now to Speiser's motion to dismiss the counterclaim seeking a declaratory judgment that Health Med may not vote its 42% stock interest in Chem. The prohibition contained in Section 160 of our corporation law is asserted as the principal basis for such relief.

The pertinent language of the statute is as follows:

> Shares of its own capital stock belonging to the corporation or to another corporation, if a majority of the shares entitled to vote in the election of directors of such other corporation is held directly or indirectly, by the corporation, shall neither be entitled to vote nor counted for quorum purposes.

The statutory language of Section 160(c) which Baker relies upon, when read literally does not, in my opinion, proscribe the voting of Health Med's stock in Chem. That is, I cannot conclude that Chem (or its Medallion subsidiary) presently "holds," even indirectly, a majority of the stock "entitled to vote" in Health Med's election of directors. The stock entitled to vote in such an election, and the extent of its voting power, is technically defined in Health Med's certificate of incorporation. In its unconverted state, Medallion's holding of preferred simply does not represent a majority of the voting power of Health Med.

However, acceptance of Speiser's argument does not end the matter. The clause the parties argue over, even when read as Speiser reads it, does not purport to confer a right to vote stock not falling within its literal terms; it is simply a restriction. More importantly, other statutory words may be read to extend Section 160(c) prohibition to the voting of Health Med's Chem holdings. Specifically, the principal prohibition of the statute is directed to [a corporation voting] its own capital stock "belonging to the corporation." This phrase is not a technically precise term whose literal meaning is clear; it requires interpretation. I turn then to the analysis of these statutory words that leads me to conclude that they do reach the facts pleaded in the counterclaim. . . .

[We] then begin our inquiry into what the legislature meant and intended by the words "belonging to," as used in Section 160(c). . . .

Almost from the earliest stirrings of a distinctive body of law dealing with corporations, courts have been alert to the dangers posed by structures that permit directors of a corporation, by reason of their office, to control the votes . . . of [a] company's stock owned by the corporation itself or a nominee or agent of the corporation.

[The common law that corporations may not vote their own shares] . . . arose as a judicial gloss on the statutory right to vote shares. The reason for the rule is not mysterious. Such structures deprive the true owners of the corporate enterprise of a portion of their voice in choosing who shall serve as directors in charge of the management of the corporate venture. . . .

The predecessor of our present general corporation law statute, first adopted in 1899, contained an expression of the rule typical for that period:

> Section 24. Shares of stock of the corporation belonging to the corporation shall not be voted upon directly or indirectly.

21 Del. Laws 453 (1899).

[However, the mischief that this rule dealt with reemerged in corporate subsidiary structures. The first case in which the courts addressed subsidiary share ownership was] *Italo Petroleum Corp. v. Producers Oil Corporation*, Del. Ch., 174 A. 276[, which] construed a version of the statutory prohibition not materially different from the section of the 1899 Act quoted above. Chancellor Wolcott there rejected the argument that stock belonging to a 99% owned subsidiary was not stock "belonging to the [parent] corporation" because it was owned legally by the subsidiary. Thus, he construed the statutory prohibition against voting (directly or indirectly) stock belonging to the corporation as a prohibition against voting stock belonging (directly or indirectly) to the corporation. In so holding, this court was motivated by the same concerns that underlay the pre-statute cases and the statutory codification itself:

> It seems to me to be carrying the doctrine of distinct corporate entity to an unreasonable extreme to say that, in a contest over control of a corporation those in charge of it should be allowed to have votes counted in their favor which are cast by a subsidiary stockholder wholly owned, controlled, dominated and therefore dictated to by themselves as the spokesmen of the parent. . . .

The statutory language construed in *Italo* remained substantially unchanged until 1967 when a version similar to . . . Section 160(c) was enacted.[6] . . . One knowledgeable commentator has referred to the 1967 amendment as codifying the result of *Italo Petroleum. . . .* Actually, it did that and something more; it specified instances in which stock owned by a subsidiary would be conclusively presumed to be stock "belonging to" its parent. The critical question is, however, did the 1967 amendment . . . intend to create a conclusive statutory presumption that, in no event would stock owned by another corporation that did not satisfy the new test (a majority of shares entitled to vote, etc.) be deemed to be stock "belonging to the corporation?"

There is no hint [that the legislature intended] . . . such a result. [If that had been its intention] . . . the policy of the statute would require a clear expression of such an intention before it could be found. Moreover, there seems slight reason . . . for the legislature to have intended to create a safe harbor for entrenchment schemes implemented through the use of corporate subsidiaries while leaving all other agencies through which such plans could be executed governed by the general language "belonging to."

Accordingly, attempting to read these words in a sensible way consistent with the underlying purpose of the enactment, I conclude that stock held by a corporate "subsidiary" may, in some circumstances, "belong to" the issuer and thus be prohibited from voting, even if the issuer does not hold a majority of shares entitled to vote at the election of directors of the subsidiary.

Assuming the truth of the facts alleged in the counterclaim, I am of the view that this is such a case. Here the substantial ownership of Chem in Health Med is not simply large, it is — at 95% — practically complete. . . .

The facts alleged exemplify the very problem Section 160(c) was intended to resolve. That is, here the capital of one corporation (Chem) has been invested in another corporation (Health Med) and that investment, in turn, is used solely to control votes of the first corporation. The principal (indeed the sole) effect of this arrangement is to muffle the voice of the public shareholders of Chem in the governance of Chem as contemplated by the certificate of incorporation of that corporation and our corporation law. In purpose and effect the scheme here put in place is not materially different

---

6. The 1967 version did not include the "directly or indirectly" language, which was restored in 1970. See 57 Del. Laws, Ch. 649 (1970).

from the schemes repeatedly struck down for more than one hundred fifty years by American courts. . . .

For the foregoing reason, the motion to dismiss the counterclaim will be denied.

QUESTIONS ON SPEISER v. BAKER

1. Is anyone hurt by Speiser's and Baker's control scheme?
2. Can Baker still thwart a quorum at the court-ordered annual share-holders meeting by not showing up? And if so, does it matter whether Health Med's shares of Health Chem are votable or not? See DGCL §211(c).

6.7.2   Vote Buying

It is often said that a shareholder may not sell her votes other than as part of a transfer of the underlying shares.[31] But why limit the separation of control rights (the vote) over cash flow rights (the dividends)? Isn't a stock investment just an economic decision with a single, profit-maximizing pur-pose? If so, why shouldn't investors be permitted to split up share rights in any way that they deem profitable? What supports this apparent preference for keeping votes and cash flow rights together?

Consider the following account of the common law prohibition of vote buying.

FRANK EASTERBROOK & DANIEL FISCHEL,
VOTING IN CORPORATE LAW
26 J.L. & Econ. 395, 409-411 (1983)

It is not [legally] possible to separate the voting right from the equity inter-est. Someone who wants to buy a vote must buy the stock too. The restriction on irrevocable proxies . . . also ensures that votes go with the equity interest. These rules are, at first glance, curious limits on the ability of investors to make their own arrangements. Yet they are understandable . . . Attaching the vote firmly to the residual equity interest ensures that an unnecessary agency cost will not come into being. Separation of shares from votes introduces a disproportion between expenditure and reward.

---

31. E.g., *Hall v. Isaacs*, 146 A.2d 602 (Del. Ch. 1958). A court of equity will be inclined to require a transferor, who sells stock after a record date (the date determining if a share-holder is entitled to vote on an issue), to give his transferee a proxy to vote the stock — unless the transferor specifically retained the voting right to protect a legal interest in the stock or the corporation substantial enough to support the grant of an irrevocable proxy. See, e.g., *Commonwealth Assocs. v. Providence Health Care*, 641 A.2d 155 (Del. Ch. 1993); *In re Giant Portland Cement Co.*, 21 A.2d 697 (Del. Ch. 1941).

For example, if the owner of 20 percent of the residual claims acquires all of the votes, his incentive to take steps to improve the firm (or just to make discretionary decisions) is only one-fifth of the value of those decisions. The holder of the votes will invest too little. And he will also have an incentive to consume excessive leisure and perquisites and to engage in other non-profit-maximizing behavior because much of the cost would be borne by the other residual claimants. The risk of such shirking would reduce the value of investments in general, and the risk can be eliminated by tying votes to shares.

One possible response is that the agency costs created would be eliminated if the owner of 20 percent of the residual claims could obtain returns disproportionate to his equity interest. So long as there is a market in votes that parallels the market in shares, competition among vote-buyers could be sufficient to compensate equity investors for the value of the dilution of their interests.

This is intriguing but, we think, unsatisfactory. Transactions in votes would present difficult problems of valuation and create other costs without conferring any apparent benefit over transactions in votes tied to shares. Moreover, the collective choice problem would exert a strong influence over the market price of votes. Because no voter expects to influence the outcome of the election, he would sell the vote . . . for less than the expected dilution of his equity interest. He would reason that if he did not sell, others would; he would then lose on the equity side but get nothing for the vote. Thus any nonzero price would persuade him to sell.

Competition among those bidding for votes might drive the price up, but not ordinarily all the way to the value of the expected equity dilution. Each person bidding for votes would be concerned that he would end up with less than a majority, and unless he obtained a majority he would have nothing at all. Thus he would offer less than the prospective value of the equity dilution. One cannot exclude the possibility that competition among buyers of votes would fully compensate the sellers. In that event, however, the bidders would see no difference between buying votes and buying shares, which, after the votes had been cast, could be held or resold to their former owners. The only time buying the votes without the shares is advantageous is when the buyer is planning to dilute the interests of the other equity owners. As we have argued elsewhere, investors would agree to prohibit such dilutions in order to ensure that all control changes are value increasing. Thus the legal rules tying votes to shares increase the efficiency of corporate organization.

QUESTION

Exactly what is the difference between selling a vote and entering a sale-and-repurchase agreement that allows the purchaser to hold a share just long enough to vote it, i.e., to hold it on the record date before the shareholders meeting?

SCHREIBER v. CARNEY
447 A.2d 17 (Del. Ch. 1982)

[Plaintiff, a shareholder in Texas International Airlines, Inc., challenged the propriety of the company's loan to defendant Jet Capital Corporation ("Jet Capital"), which owned 35 percent of Texas International's common stock. Jet Capital also held warrants in Texas International shares and a small class of its preferred stock. At this point, Texas International was considering a merger with a Delaware holding company, Texas Air. Under the proposed terms of the deal, Texas International would become a wholly owned subsidiary of Texas Air and its shareholders would receive Texas Air shares in exchange for their Texas International shares. The Company's shareholders wanted the deal to succeed since their company was in financial distress. Jet Capital's two principal owners, Carney and Lorenzo, also had good reason to support the merger because it would allow them to control the new Texas Air by virtue of their 65 percent joint ownership of Jet Capital. Notwithstanding all of this, Carney and Lorenzo, acting in their capacity as Jet Capital directors, threatened to veto the merger by exercising the class voting rights of Jet Capital's preferred stock unless Jet Capital received a below-market rate loan to exercise its Texas International warrants, which would otherwise have received unfavorable tax treatment had they been exchanged for Texas Air warrants.

As the court saw it, the below-market rate loan raised the issue of vote buying. Curiously, Lorenzo's name is never mentioned in the opinion, although he and Carney held equal stakes in Jet Capital, he was CEO of Texas International, and he went on to become Texas Air's CEO after the merger was finally consummated.]

FRANK LORENZO

Born into a family of Spanish immigrants, Frank Lorenzo graduated from Columbia University and Harvard Business School. As CEO of Texas International Airlines during the 1970s, he honed his cost-cutting skills through innovations such as the "peanut flight," a low-fare, off-peak flight that offered peanuts instead of a full meal. Not content with the Texas market, in 1980 Lorenzo formed New York Air and launched a hostile takeover bid for Continental Airlines. Continental's employees attempted to purchase majority ownership in the company through an Employee Stock Purchase Plan, in a dramatic but unsuccessful effort to prevent the takeover. Once in control of Continental, Lorenzo realized the employees' worst fears by demanding severe wage cuts and benefit reductions. When the unions refused to comply, Lorenzo filed for Chapter 11 bankruptcy as a strategy to keep labor costs low. In 1986, Lorenzo acquired Eastern Airlines and similarly plunged it into bankruptcy, making him the only person in U.S. history to bankrupt two airlines. During the Eastern bankruptcy proceedings, Lorenzo was declared "unfit" to run the airline. He resigned his position as CEO and sold his ownership.

When Lorenzo again attempted to found an airline in 1993, his petition was refused by the U.S. Department of Transportation. The U.S. Centennial of Flight Commission, known for its celebration of individuals who contributed to air travel, referred to Lorenzo as "one of the most notorious players in the history of commercial aviation in the United States."

HARTNETT, V.C.:

In order to overcome [the impasse in the negotiations between Texas International and Jet Capital, it was suggested that they] explore the possibility of a loan by Texas International to Jet Capital in order to fund an early exercise of the warrants. Because Texas International and Jet Capital had several common directors, the defendants recognized the conflict of interest and endeavored to find a way to remove any taint or appearance of impropriety. It was, therefore, decided that a special independent committee would be formed to consider and resolve the matter. The three Texas International directors who had no interest in or connection with Jet Capital were chosen to head up the committee. After its formation, the committee's first act was to hire independent counsel. Next, the committee examined the proposed merger and, based upon advice rendered by an independent investment banker, the merger was again found to be both a prudent and feasible business decision. The committee then confronted the "Jet Capital obstacle" by considering viable options for both Texas International and Jet Capital and, as a result, the committee determined that a loan was the best solution.

After negotiating at arm's length, both Texas International and Jet Capital agreed that Texas International would loan to Jet Capital $3,335,000 at 5% interest per annum for the period up to the scheduled 1982 expiration date for the warrants. After this period, the interest rate would equal the then prevailing prime interest rate. The 5% interest rate was recommended by an independent investment banker as the rate necessary to reimburse Texas International for any dividends paid out during this period. Given this provision for anticipated dividends and the fact that the advanced money would be immediately paid back to Texas International upon the exercise of the warrants, the loan transaction had virtually no impact on Texas International's cash position. . . .

The directors of Texas International unanimously approved the proposal as recommended by the committee and submitted it to the stockholders for approval — requiring as a condition of approval that a majority of all outstanding shares *and* a majority of the shares voted by the stockholders other than Jet Capital or its officers or directors be voted in favor of the proposal. After receiving a detailed proxy statement, the shareholders voted overwhelmingly in favor of the proposal. . . .

The complaint attacks the loan transaction on two theories. First, it is alleged that the loan transaction constituted vote-buying and was therefore void. Secondly, the complaint asserts that the loan was corporate waste. In essence, plaintiff argues that even if the loan was permissible and even if it was the best available option, it would have been wiser for Texas International to have loaned Jet Capital only $800,000 — the amount of [its] increased tax liability — because this would have minimized Texas International's capital commitment and also would have prevented Jet Capital from increasing its control in Texas International on allegedly discriminatory and wasteful terms. . . .

[Plaintiff contends] that vote-buying existed and, therefore, the entire transaction including the merger was void because Jet Capital, in consideration for being extended an extremely advantageous loan, withdrew its opposition to the proposed merger. . . . The critical inquiry, therefore, is whether the loan in question was in fact vote-buying and, if so, whether vote-buying is illegal, per se.

It is clear that the loan constituted vote-buying. . . Vote-buying, despite its negative connotation, is simply a voting agreement supported by consideration personal to the stockholder, whereby the stockholder divorces his discretionary voting power and votes as directed by the offeror. The record clearly indicates that Texas International purchased or "removed" the obstacle of Jet Capital's opposition. Indeed, this is tacitly conceded by the defendants. However, defendants contend that the analysis of the transaction should not end here because the legality of vote-buying depends on whether its object or purpose is to defraud or in some manner disenfranchise the other stockholders. . . . Whether this is valid depends upon the status of the law.

The Delaware decisions dealing with vote-buying leave the question unanswered. . . . In each [decision], the Court [has] summarily voided the challenged votes as being purchased and thus contrary to public policy and in fraud of the other stockholders. However, the facts in each case indicated that fraud or disenfranchisement was the obvious purpose of the vote-buying. . .

The present case presents a peculiar factual setting in that the proposed vote-buying consideration was conditional upon the approval of a majority of the disinterested stockholders after a full disclosure to them of all pertinent facts and was purportedly for the best interests of all Texas International stockholders. It is therefore necessary to do more than merely consider the fact that Jet Capital saw fit to vote for the transaction after a loan was made to it by Texas International. . . .

There are essentially two principles which appear in these cases. The first is that vote-buying is illegal per se if its object or purpose is to defraud or disenfranchise the other stockholders. A fraudulent purpose is as defined at common law, as a deceit which operates prejudicially upon the property rights of another.

The second principle which appears . . . is that vote-buying is illegal per se as a matter of public policy, the reason being that each stockholder should be entitled to rely upon the independent judgment of his fellow stockholders. Thus, the underlying basis for this latter principle is again fraud but as viewed from a sense of duty owed by all stockholders to one another. The apparent rationale is that by requiring each stockholder to exercise his individual judgment as to all matters presented, "[t]he security of the small stockholders is found in the natural disposition of each stockholder to promote the best interests of all, in order to promote his individual interests." *Cone v. Russell*, 48 N.J. Eq. 208, 21 A. 847, 849 (1891). In essence, while self interest motivates a stockholder's vote, theoretically, it is also advancing the interests of the other stockholders. Thus, any agreement entered into for personal gain, whereby a stockholder separates his voting right from his property right was considered a fraud upon this community of interests.

The often cited case of *Brady v. Bean*, 221 Ill. App. 279 (1921), is particularly enlightening. In that case, the plaintiff—an apparently influential stockholder—voiced his opposition to the corporation's proposed sale of assets. The plaintiff feared that his investment would be wiped out because the consideration for the sale appeared only sufficient enough to satisfy the corporation's creditors. As a result and without the knowledge of the other stockholders, the defendant, also a stockholder as well as a director and substantial creditor of the company, offered to the plaintiff in exchange for the withdrawal of his opposition, a sharing in defendant's claims against the corporation. In an action to enforce this contract against the defendant's estate, the Court refused relief stating:

> Appellant being a stockholder in the company, any contract entered into by him whereby he was to receive a personal consideration in return for either his action or his inaction in a matter such as a sale of all the company's assets, involving, as it did, the interests of all the stockholders, was contrary to public policy and void, it being admitted that such contract was not known by or assented to by the other stockholders. *The purpose and effect of the contract was apparently to influence appellant, in his decision of a question affecting the rights and interests of his associate stockholders, by a consideration which was foreign to those rights and interests and would be likely to induce him to disregard the consideration he owed them and the contract must, therefore, be regarded as a fraud upon them.* Such an agreement will not be enforced, as being against public policy. . . .

In addition to the deceit obviously practiced upon the other stockholders, the Court was clearly concerned with the rights and interests of the other stockholders. Thus, the potential injury or prejudicial impact which might flow to other stockholders as a result of such an agreement forms the heart of the rationale underlying the breach of public policy doctrine.

An automatic application of this rationale to the facts in the present case, however, would be to ignore an essential element of the transaction. The agreement in question was entered into primarily to further the interests of Texas International's other shareholders. Indeed, the shareholders, after reviewing a detailed proxy statement, voted overwhelmingly in favor of the loan agreement. Thus, the underlying rationale for the argument that vote-buying is illegal per se, as a matter of public policy, ceases to exist when measured against the undisputed reason for the transaction.

Moreover, the rationale that vote-buying is, as a matter of public policy, illegal per se is founded upon considerations of policy which are now outmoded as a necessary result of an evolving corporate environment. According to 5 Fletcher Cyclopedia Corporation (Perm. Ed.) §2066:

> The theory that each stockholder is entitled to the personal judgment of each other stockholder expressed in his vote, and that any agreement among stockholders frustrating it was invalid, is obsolete because it is both impracticable and impossible of application to modern corporations with many widely scattered stockholders, and the courts have gradually abandoned it. . . .

Recently, in *Oceanic Exploration Co. v. Grynberg*, Del. Supr., 428 A.2d 1 (1981), the Delaware Supreme Court applied this approach to voting trusts[, where the Court approved a] liberal approach to all contractual arrangements limiting the incidents of stock ownership. Significantly, *Oceanic* involved the giving up of voting rights in exchange for personal gain. There, the stockholder, by way of a voting trust, gave up his right to vote on all corporate matters over a period of years in return for "valuable benefits including indemnity for large liabilities."

Given the holdings in *Ringling* and *Oceanic*, it is clear that Delaware has discarded the presumptions against voting agreements. Thus, under our present law, an agreement involving the transfer of stock voting rights without the transfer of ownership is not necessarily illegal and each arrangement must be examined in light of its object or purpose. To hold otherwise would be to exalt form over substance. . . . [V]oting agreements in whatever form, therefore, should not be considered to be illegal per se unless the object or purpose is to defraud or in some way disenfranchise the other stockholders. This is not to say, however, that vote-buying accomplished for some laudable purpose is automatically free from challenge. Because vote-buying is so easily susceptible of abuse it must be viewed as a voidable transaction subject to a test for intrinsic fairness. . . .

I therefore hold that the agreement, whereby Jet Capital withdrew its opposition to the proposed merger in exchange for a loan to fund the early exercise of its warrants was not void per se because the object and purpose of the agreement was not to defraud or disenfranchise the other stockholders but rather was for the purpose of furthering the interest of all Texas International stockholders. The agreement, however, was a voidable act. Because the loan agreement was voidable it was susceptible to cure by shareholder approval. *Michelson v. Duncan*, Del. Supr., 407 A.2d 211 (1979). Consequently, the subsequent ratification of the transaction by a majority of the independent stockholders, after a full disclosure of all germane facts with complete candor precludes any further judicial inquiry of it. . . .

QUESTIONS AND NOTES ON SCHREIBER v. CARNEY

1. *Schreiber* deals with the birth of Texas Air, a holding company that for a period owned Eastern and Continental, among other airlines. One anticipated result of the proposed merger was that if Texas International became a subsidiary, its corporate parent, Texas Air, would be free to acquire other airlines without the regulatory obstacles to mergers between operating airlines subsidiaries.

Jet Capital was a kind of investment company founded by Carney and Lorenzo that invested in cash-strapped Texas International (TI) prior to the events featured in *Schreiber v. Carney* and had received common stock, preferred stock, and warrants for its infusions of capital. Its warrants — rights to purchase common stock at a fixed price — were valuable in part because their exercise price was lower than the value of TI's stock. But they were valuable to Jet Capital because they, in addition to Jet Capital's convertible preferred stock, shifted voting control to Jet Capital after the TI-Texas merger. Given this account, would Jet Capital have carried through on its threat to block the merger if the *Schreiber* court had found TI's loan to be void per se?

2. Suppose that Jet Capital's only interest in TI was a small investment in its TI's preferred stock that happened to be entitled to a class vote on the TI-Texas merger, and that Jet Capital had demanded a cash payment to vote for the merger that was much larger than the market value of its preferred stock. Would TI's shareholders agree to Jet Capital's demand? If so, should a Delaware court also sanction such naked vote buying?

3. *Schreiber* notes that constraints on vote buying have been eroded by the wide latitude accorded shareholders to enter voting agreements and voting trusts in exchange for personal consideration. See DGCL §218(c). In light of this development, why are there any constraints on vote buying at all? *Schreiber* singles out the venerable case of *Brady v. Bean* to illustrate a fact pattern in which the traditional remedy of voiding a vote-buying agreement may still be apt. What, precisely, is wrong about the *Brady v. Bean* agreement, and how much does this turn on the fact that the agreement was not disclosed to other shareholders? Should it matter if shareholders are paid to vote against the interests of the shareholder class? Or should it make a difference who the purchaser is — another shareholder, management, or a third party? See *Williams v. Ji*, C.A. No. 12729-VCMR (Del. Ch. Jun. 28, 2017).

4. As the sidebar on Mylan illustrates, vote-buying issues have surfaced recently in the derivative markets. Today, derivative contracts are available that allow the legal owner of shares to trade away some or all of the economic risk of her shares while retaining legal title and thus the right to vote her shares. In theory, a person with no economic interest can vote shares, or what is worse, a person with a net short position can vote despite her incentive to encourage share prices to fall. The law has not fully come to terms with the derivative markets,[32] but

---

CARL ICAHN AT MYLAN LABORATORIES

Consider the following excerpt:

Long & Short: Icahn Cries Foul at Perry's No-Risk Play in Takeover Fight
Wall Street Journal (December 15, 2004)

. . . Here's how it works: Perry [a hedge fund] owns 9.9% of Mylan, or 26.6 million shares. But the firm has no economic interest in the stock, having entered into hedging transactions for its entire position. While Perry was buying all that stock, it had a cooperative brokerage firm (or firms) short an equal amount of Mylan stock — selling shares borrowed from shareholders. At the same time, Perry got the right to sell its shares back to the brokerage, while the brokerage received the right to call the stock back from Perry — all at the same price. The result is a wash. That means Perry is indifferent to the price of Mylan, having no economic interest in it. Nevertheless, it retains nearly 10% of Mylan's voting rights, becoming one of its most powerful shareholders.

Why would Perry go through all this trouble? Because the hedge fund owns seven million shares of King and wants Mylan's takeover bid to go through, boosting the value of Perry's stake in King.

Question: To what extent are Perry's maneuverings de facto vote buying? To what extent should corporate law regulate such behavior? (And if so, how might corporate law accomplish this?)

---

32. See, e.g., *CSX Corp. v. The Children's Investment Fund Management (U.K.) LLP*, 2011 WL 2750913 (2d Cir. July 18, 2011) (declining to rule on whether certain derivative contracts should be counted for purposes of §13(d) reporting by a shareholder).

the legal literature seems to be successfully advocating enhanced disclosure requirements.[33] Indeed, in the particular instance of Mylan, the Perry fund was subsequently forced to settle with the SEC over its failure to disclose its derivative positions.

5. In *Portnoy v. Cryo-Cell International, Inc.*,[34] a 6 percent shareholder group led by Andrew Filipowski threatened a proxy contest at the upcoming annual meeting of Cryo-Cell, a Delaware company. To settle the matter, the board agreed to add Filipowski to the management slate in exchange for his votes at the meeting, despite the fact that he did not meet the board's criteria for director nominees. Management's slate, including Filipowski, won by a hair against a slate led by David Portnoy, another dissident shareholder. Portnoy brought suit alleging illegal vote buying. The Delaware Chancery Court concluded that the board's deal with Filipowski constituted vote buying, but declined to apply the intrinsic fairness test: "Subjecting an agreement to add a potential insurgent to a management slate to the *Schreiber* intrinsic fairness test would, in my view, be an inadvisable and counterproductive precedent. . . . [It] could result in creating litigable factual issues about a large number of useful compromises that result in the addition of fresh blood to management slates. . . ." Do you think the court would have reached the same result if, in addition to providing a board seat, the company had paid Filipowski $10 million in cash? How could a different result be rationalized?

6. In *Crown Emak Partners v. Kurz*, 992 A.2d 377 (Del. 2010), the insurgents (represented by Kurz) bought from a former corporate employee (Boutros) the economic interest (future cash flow rights) and the right to vote just enough shares to secure a majority in a heated proxy contest. This transaction did not take the normal form of a sale of stock because Boutros was contractually prohibited from selling the shares until March 2011. Thus bare legal title was left in his hands. The incumbents challenged the transaction as impermissible vote buying. The Delaware Chancery Court upheld the transaction:

> I find no evidence of fraud in the transaction. The record indicates that Boutros was fully informed about the ongoing consent solicitations. . . . Boutros understood what he was selling, the circumstances under which he was selling it, and what he was getting in return.
>
> This brings me to the alignment of interests. Although Kurz did not take title to the 150,000 shares that Boutros owned, and although I assume the Restricted Stock Grant Agreement prohibits Boutros from transferring title to Kurz until March 3, 2011, Boutros nevertheless transferred to Kurz, and Kurz now bears, 100% of the economic risk from the 150,000 shares. If the value of EMAK's shares drops further, then Kurz will suffer. If EMAK goes bankrupt and its shares become worthless, then Kurz will have a paper souvenir. Conversely, if EMAK turns itself around and prospers, then Kurz will benefit. Kurz has already paid Boutros. Kurz's only interest lies in how EMAK performs.
>
> Because Kurz now holds the economic interest in the shares, Delaware law presumes that he should and will exercise the right to vote. The proxy Boutros

33. See, e.g., Henry T.C. Hu & Bernard Black, *The New Vote Buying: Empty Voting and Hidden (Morphable) Ownership*, 79 S. Cal. L. Rev. 811 (2006).
34. 940 A.2d 43 (Del. Ch. 2008).

granted to Kurz under the Purchase Agreement comports with what our law expects.

On appeal, the Delaware Supreme Court affirmed on the vote-buying claim, "because the economic interests and the voting interests of the shares remained aligned since both sets of interests were transferred from Boutros to Kurz by the Purchase Agreement." Nevertheless, the court held that the Boutros shares could not be voted because the transfer violated a contractual agreement between Boutros and the company.

6.7.3 Controlling Minority Structures

Vote buying and circular voting structures are not the only way to separate control rights from cash flow rights. There are three common and widely accepted structures that accomplish the same thing. They are dual-class share structures, stock pyramids, and cross-ownership ties. These patterns of ownership might be termed "controlling minority structures" (CMSs) because they permit a shareholder to control a firm while holding only a minority of its shares.

LUCIAN A. BEBCHUK, REINIER KRAAKMAN & GEORGE G. TRIANTIS, STOCK PYRAMIDS, CROSS-OWNERSHIP, AND DUAL CLASS EQUITY
Concentrated Corporate Ownership 295 (R. Morck ed., 2000)

CMS structures are common outside the U.S., particularly in countries whose economies are dominated by family-controlled conglomerates.[1] Because these structures can radically distort their controllers' incentives, however, they put great pressure on non-electoral mechanisms of corporate governance, ranging from legal protections for minority shareholders to reputational constraints on controlling families. . . .

Each of the three basic CMS forms [EDS. — dual-class voting, pyramidal ownership, and circular ownership] entrench minority control. In each case, the CMS form can be used in principle to separate cash flow rights from control rights, to any desired extent. We denote the degree of separation induced by a CMS structure between control and cashflow rights by [alpha], which represents the fraction of the firm's equity cash flow rights held by the controlling-minority shareholder. . . .

The most straightforward CMS form is a single firm that has issued two or more classes of stock with differential voting rights. . . . Calibrating the separation of cash flow and control rights in a dual-class equity structure is child's

---

1. LaPorta, et al., who conduct a comprehensive survey of ownership structures around the world, demonstrate that controlling minority shareholder structures, and particularly stock pyramids, are widespread. [See R. LaPorta, F. Lopez-de-Silanes & A. Shleifer, *Corporate Ownership Around the World*, 54 J. Fin. 47 (1999). — EDS.]

play. A planner can simply attach all voting rights to the fraction of shares that are assigned to the controller, while attaching no voting rights to the remaining shares that are distributed to the public or other shareholders.[2] . . .

Despite its simplicity, however, dual class equity is not the most common CMS structure worldwide . . . [M]any jurisdictions restrict both the voting ratio between high- and low-vote shares, and the numerical ratio between high- and low-vote shares that a firm is permitted to issue[, which implicitly mandate[s] a lower bound on the size of [alpha]. [The most popular CMS structure worldwide is the pyramid.] In a pyramid of two companies, a controlling minority shareholder holds a controlling stake in a holding company that, in turn, holds a controlling stake in an operating company. In a three-tier pyramid, the primary holding company controls a second-tier holding company that in turn controls the [first-tier holding] company. . . .

For any fraction alpha, however small, there is a pyramid that permits a controller to completely control a company's assets without holding more than alpha of the company's cash flow rights. [To see how rapidly pyramiding separates equity from control, consider a three-tier pyramid in which the controlling minority shareholder holds 50 percent of the shares at each level. Here, the minority investor in the first tier controls the operating company with only 12.5 percent of its cash flow rights. — EDS.]

[C]ross-holding structures differ from pyramids chiefly in that the voting rights used to control the corporate group are distributed over the entire [corporate] group rather than concentrated in the hands of a single company or shareholder. . . . Neither pyramids nor cross-ownership [is] popular in the U.S. . . . One reason . . . in the U.S. is [the] . . . income tax on inter-corporate dividends[, which imposes] a significant tax penalty on moving corporate distributions through two or more levels of corporate structure. A second reason is [that] the Investment Company Act of 1940 . . . imposes stringent regulatory and reporting requirements on [corporate] group structures. . . [T]he only ownership structure suitable for separating cash flow from ownership in the U.S is [multi-class] common stock.

———————

American corporate law does not require all shares to have voting rights, nor does it require all voting shares to have equal voting rights.[35] Thus, most U.S. jurisdictions permit super-voting stock. As Bebchuk, et al., suggest, dual-class voting stock is the most effective (and most obvious) device in the U.S. for separating voting rights from cash flow rights and entrenching a controlling minority shareholder. Dual-class stock in the United States raises several interesting questions. How many of these firms are there? And are these structures really as inefficient as agency theory suggests that they should be?

Some answers are clear, some are not. To begin, dual-class share structures are relatively rare among public companies — about 7 percent of Russell

2. In their sample of U.S. dual class firms, De Angelo and De Angelo (1985) found that insiders held a median of 56.9% of the voting rights but only 24% of the common stock claims to cash flow.

35. See, e.g., DGCL §151(a); NYBCA §613. Note that some non-U.S. jurisdictions, such as Germany, have adopted a mandatory one-share, one-vote rule.

3000 firms. Some commentators suggest a historical explanation for this. For many years, the NYSE would not list common stock that did not possess equal rights.[36] Since access to the NYSE was essential, public companies simply did not adopt dual-class structures. But was this restriction on dual-class listings justified? Some commentators argue that restrictions on dual-class listings are unnecessary at the IPO stage because entrepreneurs bear the costs of offering shares with differential voting rights. Perhaps vesting control rights in the hands of founding entrepreneurs is optimal and could enhance firm value, or even if it can't, these entrepreneurs would never take their companies' shares to the public market unless they could retain control because they value it for its own sake and are happy to accept a discount on the price they receive on their shares to indulge their taste for control.

However, dual-class structures are problematic when they are adopted in "mid-stream," after the firm's shares are already publicly trading. Corporate law permits corporations with a single class of voting stock to transfer voting control to insiders by a charter amendment that itself requires a majority vote. But a majority vote is unlikely to protect the interests of public shareholders who face a collective action problem.[37] Consider an insider-proposed charter amendment that offers public shareholders a minor benefit in exchange for accepting diluted voting power. For example, the corporation might offer to exchange one share of old common stock for either one share of new Class A common stock or one share of new Class B common stock. The Class A common stock will retain all of the rights of the old common stock, plus it will pay out a one-time special dividend of 50 cents a share. The new Class B stock will also receive the rights of the old common stock except that it will have no right to a special dividend but it will have ten votes per share. [38] Most small shareholders will opt for Class A shares and the special dividend because they rationally believe that their vote doesn't matter. However, management and other insiders choose Class B shares and soon consolidate voting control over the company. One suspects that this development might not work to the long-term benefit of the majority of common stockholders who choose to accept Class A shares, in part because the special dividend they receive bears no necessary relationship to the class-wide value of their votes.

There is a storied history behind efforts to bar mid-stream dual-class recapitalizations after the NYSE first amended its Rules in 1986 to permit dual-class voting.[39] The outcome today is that the NYSE, NASDAQ, and the SEC

---

36. New York Stock Exchange Listed Company Manual §313.00.

37. See Jeffrey N. Gordon, *Ties That Bond: Dual Class Common Stock and the Problem of Shareholder Choice*, 76 Calif. L. Rev. 1 (1988); Ronald J. Gilson, *Evaluating Dual Class Common Stock: The Relevance of Substitutes*, 73 Va. L. Rev. 807 (1987).

38. See, e.g., *Lacos Land Company v. Arden Group, Inc.*, 517 A.2d 271 (Del. Ch. 1986) (injunction against shareholder vote on management's effort to amend charter in a similar way; basis was that management wrongfully coerced the vote by threatening breach of duty if approval was not forthcoming). Compare *Blasius Indus., Inc. v. Atlas*, in Chapter 13.

39. In brief, competition with NASDAQ over listings prompted the NYSE to allow dual-class stock listings. Widespread protests by institutional shareholders and many others prompted the SEC to intervene in 1989 under its statutory authority to regulate securities exchanges. This resulted in Rule 19c-4, which prohibited the listing of shares with unequal

bar low-vote shares arising from mid-stream recapitalizations in their listing requirements, but allow new listings of low-vote shares in IPOs, including those from established public companies that do not dilute the voting rights of existing common stock.

QUESTION

Does today's consensus fully answer the concerns posed by the hypothetical mid-stream dual-class recapitalization described above?

NOTE: THE RETURN OF DUAL-CLASS STOCK?

A large number of very successful high-tech firms have gone public with dual-class voting structures over the last decade including Google and Facebook. Some estimate that around 20 percent of recent IPOs have involved firms with dual-class stock.[40] Traditionally, dual-class voting was structured to preserve family control for family-owned companies that required outside equity capital. Family-owned newspapers are a notable example. It is often said that entrenching family control serves not only the family's interest but also the public's interest in independent editorial content bonded by the family's commitment and reputation. Of course, this explanation hardly makes the case for entrenching the founders of today's high-tech firms. Conventional theory suggests that a misalignment of voting rights and economic ownership creates so-called "agency costs" because a company's controllers will manage the firm in their own interests rather than those of all shareholders. Imagine, for example, that the wealthy founders of a high-tech firm acquire a taste for yacht racing and divert their company's R&D budget from e-commerce, which generates most of their company's revenues, to yacht design, which shows little prospect of becoming profitable. For the founders who control the company with high-vote shares but hold only a 10 percent economic stake in it, investing in yacht design may be entirely rational. They capture all of the "returns" as passionate hobbyists but pay only 10 percent of the costs. This hypothetical is of course fanciful, and yet it goes some way to explain the strong distaste that most institutional investors have for dual-class voting.

But what is to be said on the other side? There are several views. One is that the dangers of dual-class IPOs are overrated. Institutional investors

voting rights unless initially offered to the market in that structure. The D.C. Circuit Court of Appeals subsequently struck down Rule 19c-4 as unauthorized regulation of internal corporate governance matters. *Business Roundtable v. SEC*, 905 F.2d 406 (D.C. Cir. 1990). But by this point, institutional opposition had made it nearly impossible to win shareholder approval for mid-stream dual-class charter amendments. Later amendments to the NYSE and NASDAQ listing requirements reflected the facts on the ground more than they changed them.

40. See Wilson, Sonsini, Goodrich & Rosati, *2019 Technology and Life Sciences IPO Report*; Larcker & Tayan, *supra* note 21. Further, there is a resurgence of dual-class stock globally. See Hal S. Scott & John Gulliver, *Reforming U.S. Capital Markets to Promote Economic Growth* (2020). Committee on Capital Markets Regulation, May 2020, (e.g., Sweden).

continue to invest in issues of low-vote shares despite their distaste. Moreover, it is unclear whether they suffer losses from them on average. The risk of future agency costs is clear when dual-class firms go public. Under standard assumptions, these costs should be priced into the stock's offering price. If the founders of successful start-ups willingly accept discounts on the shares they sell to indulge their personal taste for control, why not let them? Otherwise they might not take their companies public at all. Another view is more enthusiastic. It claims that dual-class voting structures at the IPO stage affirmatively increase the value of some companies in the eyes of shareholders. The conjecture is that dual-class voting serves to retain, not entrench, dedicated and visionary entrepreneurs who might otherwise be displaced by activist shareholders intent on short-term gains.[41]

The empirical literature on whether low-vote IPOs diminish or increase shareholder returns is inconclusive. Instead, policy debates over these IPOs address modest reforms. If the principal concern is that even visionary entrepreneurs grow stale over time, then an obvious fix is a sunset provision that converts high-vote shares into ordinary common stock at the end of a fixed period, or even better, puts the continuation of the dual-class structure to an up or down vote by the low-vote shares.[42] Other possible reforms seek to limit the extent to which high-vote shareholders can reduce their economic ownership of the company, transfer their shares to their heirs, or even sell them to third parties. Current dual-class regimes generally provide that high-vote shares lose their special voting rights upon transfer but are less likely to feature sunsetting clauses. As always, the devil is in the details.

QUESTION

What is the functional difference between a firm issuing both a class of "no-vote" shares and a class with 10 votes per share versus a firm issuing a class of one-vote shares and a class with 10 votes per share? Are there reasons to prefer the issuance of no-vote shares in this example?

6.8   VOTING IN TODAY'S CORPORATION

As the introduction to this chapter noted, institutional owners and asset managers now vote most shares in U.S. public corporations. The big asset managers such as BlackRock, Vanguard, Fidelity, and State Street offer their clients

---

41. For a related argument in the context of publicly traded firms, see Zohar Goshen & Assaf Hamdani, *Corporate Control and Idiosyncratic Vision*, 125 Yale L. J. 560 (2016).

42. See Lucian A. Bebchuk & Kobi Kastiel, *The Untenable Case for Perpetual Dual-Class Stock*, 103 Va. L. Rev. 585 (2017); Robert J. Jackson, Jr., *Perpetual Dual Class Stock: The Case Against Corporate Royalty* (Feb. 15, 2018). See also Jill E. Fisch & Steven Davidoff Solomon, *The Problem of Sunsets* 99 B.U. Law Rev. 1057 (2019); Scott & Gulliver, *supra* note 40, at 28–30.

a variety of funds in which to invest that are usefully divided into passive and active. Passive funds track various indices such as the S&P 500, while active funds allow their managers to add and remove portfolio companies in an effort to beat the market. While the managers of both kinds of funds earn fees based on their total assets under management, active funds recruit new investors by increasing the value of their portfolios relative to the market in general. It may be, in fact, that the managers of active funds follow individual companies more closely across the broad range of all service providers. Curiously, however, in the important case of giant fund families, such as BlackRock, the voting of managed shares seems to be coordinated at the family level rather than at the level of individual funds, whether they are active or passive, and presumably reflect the blended interests of all family funds.[43]

In total, a handful of the largest fund families are thought to control over $20 trillion in passive or indexed assets, which represents about 25 percent of the stock in U.S. publicly traded firms by recent estimates.[44] Thus, the voting incentives of these fund families is no small matter, even though they also include a smaller proportion of actively-managed firms. On its face, it would seem that passive fund managers should have no interest in the performance of individual portfolio companies. Were they to spend on monitoring firm governance, their fees would rise, they would lose investors, and perhaps most galling of all, increases in firm value that followed would necessarily be shared with their competitors' funds. Much of the literature reflects this view.[45] Nevertheless, other thoughtful commentators argue that the competitive pressures facing passive funds to attract more investor capital, the potential economies of scale and scope in monitoring arising from their size, their relatively large stakes in investee firms, and public expectations and reputational incentives suffice to motivate managers of passive portfolios to play an active and benevolent role in corporate governance.[46] These factors may also lead passive funds to pursue general good governance initiatives that might increase firm value across many firms in their portfolios rather than in any particular company.

---

43. See, e.g., *Proxy Voting and Shareholder Engagement FAQ*, BlackRock, Inc. (Jan. 2020); Vanguard, "Principles and Policies," https://about.vanguard.com/investment-stewardship/principles-policies/).

44. See Lucian A. Bebchuk & Scott Hirst, *Index Funds and the Future of Corporate Governance: Theory, Evidence, and Policy*, 119 Col. L. Rev. 2029 (2019); John C. Coates, *The Future of Corporate Governance Part I: The Problem of Twelve* (September 20, 2018), Harvard Public Law Working Paper No. 19-07.

45. See Bebchuk & Hirst, *supra* note 44. Further, Morley argues that coordination on activism within big asset managers is unlikely given the internal conflicts in fund families. See John D. Morley, *Too Big to Be Activist*, 92 S. Cal. L. Rev. 1407 (2019). The extent of concerns over benefits to competitor funds from activism is mitigated somewhat by the fact that there are more indices than U.S. stocks, so that a particular index fund may be narrow enough that there are few other funds tracking its exact composition.

46. See Coates, *supra* note 44; Marcel Kahan and Edward B. Rock, *Index Funds and Corporate Governance: Let Shareholders Be Shareholders* (April 4, 2019). NYU Law and Economics Research Paper No. 18-39; Jill Fisch, Assaf Hamdani and Steven Davidoff Solomon, *The New Titans of Wall Street: A Theoretical Framework for Passive Investors*, 168 U. Pa. L. Rev. 17 (2019).

A less widely noted wrinkle in the voting of institutional shares in public companies is the widespread practice of share lending. The institution that owns or manages the shares often "lends" them (for a fee) to another entity for a short period of time.[47] This may be to "short" the stock or for other purposes too. These lending fees become an additional important source of revenue to institutions, especially for index funds which compete on offering wafer-thin fees to their investors. However, when this practice occurs around votes, then there is the very real prospect that the party entitled to vote may only be holding the shares for a very short period of time, or perhaps only for the purpose of voting, raising concerns similar to vote buying. (See side bar on the recent Gamestop Proxy Contest.)

6.8.1 Proxy Advisory Firms

Proxy advisory firms, such as Institutional Shareholder Services (ISS) and Glass Lewis, are key players in modern shareholder voting. They are for-profit entities providing recommendations to institutions on how they should vote on specific issues (e.g., whether to reappoint a director, de-staggering the board). Large institutional investors and asset managers often use their recommendations when developing their own voting policies, while others go further and pre-commit to follow their advice.[48] Proxy advisory firms can thus sway a large section of voting shareholders, which makes understanding their incentives important. Although their compensation doesn't depend on returns or share price movements per se (they usually charge subscription-based fees to receive their recommendations),[49] some worry whether they suffer from conflicts of interest or other considerations affecting their objectivity. This and related concerns led to the SEC's promulgation of a new set of proxy rules in July 2020, which many argue encumber proxy advisory firms in providing voting recommendations. See Section 6.9.1 below.

6.8.2 Institutional Shareholder Activists

Over the last two decades, activist hedge funds have become increasingly significant. Their investment strategies differ, of course, but in general they investigate opportunity, do sophisticated analysis, and acquire a substantial position in only a handful of target companies unlike the typical large passive index fund. Their strategy can be as simple as seeking to dividend

---

47. See Reena Aggarwal, Pedro A.C. Saffi & Jason Sturgess, *The Role of Institutional Investors in Voting: Evidence from the Securities Lending Market*, 70 J. Fin. 2309 (2015).

48. See Sean J. Griffith, *Opt-In Stewardship: Toward an Optimal Delegation of Mutual Fund Voting Authority*, 98 Tex. L. Rev. 983, 992 (2020); David F. Larcker, Allan L. McCall & Gaizka Ormazabal, *Outsourcing Shareholder Voting to Proxy Advisory Firms*, 58 J. L. & Econ. 173 (2015).

49. See Andrey Malenko & Nadya Malenko, *Proxy Advisory Firms: The Economics of Selling Information to Voters*, 74 J. Fin. 2441 (2019).

excess cash on the balance sheet of that company, or as complex as split-off or spin-off transactions or a sale of the company. They rarely, if ever, want to take over control and management of the business. Once they have their investment position the activist will approach the CEO or the board to demand fundamental changes in the company's business plan. In the entirely predictable event that management and the board are not welcoming, their major tool is to threaten a short slate proxy contest (explained in the discussion of proxy contests, Section 6.9.2 below). The following excerpt explains why some commentators see these hedge funds as well positioned to make positive change.

MARCEL KAHAN & EDWARD B. ROCK, HEDGE FUNDS IN CORPORATE GOVERNANCE AND CORPORATE CONTROL
155 U. Pa. L. Rev. 1021 (2007)

Hedge funds are emerging as the most dynamic and most prominent shareholder activists. On the bright side, this generates the possibility that hedge funds will, in the course of making profits for their own investors, help overcome the classic agency problem of publicly held corporations. . . In doing so, the bright side holds, hedge funds would enhance the value of the companies they invest in for the benefit of both their own investors and their fellow shareholders. . . . But the bright-side story of hedge funds. . . has an element of déjà vu. Twenty years ago, similar stories were told about another set of large and sophisticated investors: mutual funds, pension funds, and insurance companies — or "institutional investors" as they became known. While, on the whole, the rise of these traditional institutional investors has probably been beneficial, they have hardly proven to be a silver bullet.

Are there reasons to think that the newly prominent hedge funds will be more effective? . . . The incentives for hedge funds to monitor portfolio companies differ in several important respects from those of traditional institutional investors. First, hedge fund managers are highly incentivized to maximize the returns to fund investors. The standard hedge fund charges a base fee equal to 1-2% of the assets under management and a significant incentive fee, typically 20% of the profits earned. This fee structure gives hedge fund managers a very significant stake in the financial success of the fund's investments. These stakes are even higher when, as is frequently the case, a hedge fund manager has invested a significant portion of her personal wealth in the hedge fund.

Secondly, many hedge funds strive to achieve high absolute returns, rather than returns relative to a benchmark. . .

Thus, unlike mutual funds, hedge funds benefit directly and substantially from achieving high absolute returns. For successful managers, the resulting profits can be extraordinarily high.

The debate on the effects of hedge fund activism, which has parallels to that around hostile takeovers in the 1980s, has generated an outpouring of empirical work focusing on the central question of whether hedge fund activism encourages "short-termism" at the expense of the long term. Although most scholars find a positive immediate stock price response to activism, greater debate accompanies discussions on longer-term effects on firm value and on stakeholders and society. In an influential 2015 article, Bebchuk, Brav, and Jiang argue that there is scant evidence for negative long-term firm value effects of hedge fund activism and rather good evidence for positive long-term effects on firm value.[50] More recent work expresses greater skepticism on the longer-term firm value gains[51] or finds that the longer-term gains are more likely when activism leads to acquisitions or the formation of significant ownership blocks.[52] Research on the effects of activism outside of the target firm is quite recent and is beginning to generate its own unresolved debate.[53] Given the intense interest in these questions, perhaps the wisest thing to say is stay tuned.

SIDE BAR ON GAMESTOP'S 2020 PROXY CONTEST AND SECURITIES LENDING:

Dawn Lim, "How Investing Giants Gave Away Voting Power Ahead of a Shareholder Dispute," *Wall Street Journal*, June 10, 2020

GameStop Corp. shareholders vote this week to resolve a fight over the embattled videogame retailer's board. But the company's largest investors won't cast much of a vote.

The three biggest money managers in GameStop reported that their funds held some 40% of shares in the first quarter. When it was time to commit to voting, they controlled roughly 5% of ballots, according to count estimates reviewed by The Wall Street Journal. . . .

The main reason for the disparity is that BlackRock Inc. Vanguard Group and Fidelity Investments [and others] chose to loan out substantial GameStop shares for the rich stream of fees their investors stood to gain, according to people with knowledge of the matter. . .

While investing giants have raised their voices to prod companies to address society's most pressing problems, they sometimes decide not to control the ballots that drive change. . .

---

50. See Lucian A. Bebchuk, Alon Brav & Wei Jiang, *The Long-Term Effects of Hedge Fund Activism*, 115 Col. L. Rev. 1085 (2015).

51. See Ed deHaan, David Larcker & Charles McClure, *Long-Term Economic Consequences of Hedge Fund Activist Interventions*, 24 Rev. Account. Stud. 536 (2019); John C. Coffee & Darius Palia, *The Wolf at the Door: The Impact of Hedge Fund Activism on Corporate Governance*, 1 Annals of Corporate Governance 1 (2016).

52. See Matthew Denes, Jonathan M. Karpoff & Victoria McWilliams, *Thirty Years of Shareholder Activism: A Survey of Empirical Research*, 44 J. Corp. Fin. 405 (2017); K. J. Martijn Cremers, Erasmo Giambona, Simone M. Sepe & Ye Wang, *Hedge Fund Activism and Long-Term Firm Value* (May 28, 2020) (arguing that the gains are from hedge funds' superior trading skills, not governance changes).

53. One recent study finds positive spillovers on non-targeted firms. See Nickolay Gantchev, Oleg R Gredil & Chotibhak Jotikasthira, *Governance Under the Gun: Spillover Effects of Hedge Fund Activism*, 23 Rev. of Fin. 1031 (2019). Another paper finds negative effects on social performance. See Mark R. DesJardine & Rodolphe Durand, *Disentangling the Effects of Hedge Fund Activism on Firm Financial and Social Performance*, 41 Strategic Mgmt. J. 1054 (2020).

"Securities lending has changed the way ownership is understood," said Richard Grubaugh, senior vice president of D.F. King & Co., a firm that assists companies with shareholder outreach. "Ownership and economic interests are decoupled from voting." . . . Some SEC staffers were worried there wasn't yet full visibility into how securities lending affects voting patterns, said a person familiar with the matter. . .

The extent to which investment firms forgo votes for lending fees isn't known. Meanwhile, public companies rely on proxy solicitors to stitch together estimates . . . and information on voting power tied to different investors is typically kept under wraps . . .

6.9   THE FEDERAL PROXY RULES

Nowhere are one's views on the severity of the collective action problem more salient than in an evaluation of the effects of the federal proxy rules on the operation of the voting system in public companies.

The federal proxy rules originate with the provisions of the Securities Exchange Act of 1934 (the Exchange Act or sometimes the 1934 Act), chiefly §14(a)-(c), which regulate virtually every aspect of proxy voting in public companies. These provisions support an array of rules promulgated and enforced by the Securities and Exchange Commission.

The federal proxy rules consist of four major elements:

1. Disclosure requirements and a mandatory vetting regime that permit the SEC to assure the disclosure of relevant information and to protect shareholders from misleading communications;
2. Substantive regulation of the process of soliciting proxies from shareholders;
3. A specialized "town meeting" provision (Rule 14a-8) that permits shareholders to gain access to the corporation's proxy materials and to thus gain a low-cost way to promote certain kinds of shareholder resolutions; and
4. A general anti-fraud provision (Rule 14a-9) that allows courts to imply a private shareholder remedy for false or misleading proxy materials.

In this section, we present, in plain English, a brief overview of the federal proxy rules adopted by the SEC under §14 of the 1934 Act. We then present two of the rules in greater detail — Rule 14a-8, the town meeting rule, and Rule 14a-9, the antifraud rule.

6.9.1   Rules 14a-1 Through 14a-7: Disclosure and Shareholder Communication

Unlike company law in EU jurisdictions, corporate law in most U.S. states has never imposed an affirmative obligation on corporations to inform shareholders of the state of the company's business or even to distribute a balance sheet and income statement.[54] At most, shareholders could demand stock lists and sometimes gain access to detailed books and records. Presumably, in an earlier age, the power to replace the board was seen in the United States as a sufficient inducement for firms to disclose. Matters changed, however, after the Great Depression when federal legislation adopted the core strategy of mandating public disclosure. While much of this legislation was designed to inform investors in the initial offer and secondary markets, some of it — in particular, §14(a) of the Securities Exchange Act of 1934 — addressed disclosure in connection with the solicitation of proxies.

Section 14(a) made it unlawful for any person, in contravention of any rule that the commission may adopt, to "solicit" any "proxy" to vote any "security" registered under §12 of the Act. The SEC soon gave each of these terms — "solicit," "proxy," and "security" — a very broad interpretation in Regulation 14A. The basic scheme of the Regulation was (and is) to state with great detail the types of information that any person must provide when seeking a proxy to vote a covered security. These rules were drafted to force disclosure by corporations to the shareholders from whom they sought proxies. These rules, however, apply not only to an issuing corporation but also to a third party who might seek to oust incumbent management by a proxy fight. Thus, they had the unintended consequence of discouraging proxy fights. The 1966 case of *Studebaker Corporation v. Gittlin*[55] illustrates the point. In that case, a request to 42 stockholders of a large public company to join in a petition to inspect the shareholders' list (necessary because, under state law, the list was available only on the demand of more than 5 percent of the company's stock) was held to constitute a "solicitation" of a "proxy" requiring the preparation, filing, and distribution of a proxy statement. By 1990, the risks and expense that the proxy rules imposed on governance activities became the subject of widespread criticism. Consider the following excerpt from an op-ed by Professor Mark Roe:

> Today [December 1991], if a dozen shareholders want to talk to one another about the company that they own, they must file a proxy statement with the SEC, informing it of what they want to say, and usually letting SEC staffers edit their statement. Even a simple newspaper ad usually requires clearance from the SEC. If stockholders have doubts about the quality of their management, they must act publicly, in costly, stilted, potentially embarrassing ways. Publicity instills silence. Why stick your neck out and publicly question management if no one else is going to go along? Before testing whether the water is over your head, you must commit to jumping in. . . . It might seem incredible if during a presidential election, voters could not talk to one another, other than through a formal statement filed with a government agency. But this is the situation in corporate elections.[56]

---

54. There are a few exceptions to this generalization. See, e.g., Mich. Bus. Corp. Act §901, which requires corporations to distribute financial statements to shareholders.
55. 360 F.2d 692 (2d Cir. 1966).
56. Mark Roe, *Free Speech for Shareholders?*, Wall St. J. (December 18, 1991).

In 1992, the SEC responded by amending the rules in several important ways. In general, the 1992 amendments to Regulation 14A limited the term "solicitation" in Rule 14(a)-1(l) and created new exemptions under Rule 14(a)-2, which released institutional shareholders, in limited circumstances, from the requirement to file a disclosure form before they could communicate with other shareholders about a corporation. Prior to these amendments, institutional investors who communicated with other investors about a company ran a serious risk of being deemed to have solicited a proxy, which would have required them to file a costly proxy statement.

Rule 14a-3 contains the central regulatory requirement of the proxy rules. No one may be solicited for a proxy unless they are, or have been, furnished with a proxy statement "containing the information specified in Schedule 14A." When the solicitation is made on behalf of the company itself (the "registrant") and relates to an annual meeting for the election of directors, it must include considerable information about the company, including related party transactions (see Schedule 14A, Item 6) and detailed information about the compensation of top managers (see Item D). When the proxy statement is filed by anyone other than management, it requires detailed disclosure of the identity of the soliciting parties, as well as their holdings and the financing of the campaign.

Rule 14a-3 raises the central question of what constitutes a "proxy" and a "solicitation." Rule 14a-1 provides sweeping definitions of these terms — a "proxy," for example, can be any solicitation or consent whatsoever. Rule 14a-2 provides important exemptions from these broad definitions. For instance, Rule 14a-2(b)(2) provides an exemption for solicitations to less than ten shareholders. Rule 14a-2(b)(1), added in 1992, provides an exemption for ordinary shareholders who wish to communicate with other shareholders but do not themselves intend to seek proxies. In addition, Rule 14a-1(l)(2)(iv) provides that announcements by shareholders on how they intend to vote, even if such announcements include the shareholders' reasoning, are not subject to the proxy rules. Of course, the SEC 1992 Release made clear that these changes did not exempt investors from Rule 14a-9 (discussed below), which prohibits false or misleading statements in connection with written or oral solicitations.[57]

Rules 14a-4 and 14a-5 regulate the form of the proxy — in effect, the actual "vote" itself — and the proxy statement, respectively. For example, the proxy must instruct shareholders that they can withhold support for a particular director on the solicitor's slate of candidates by crossing through her name (see Rule 4(b)(2)(ii)). Similarly, subsection (d)(4) deals with circumstances under which a dissident can solicit votes for some but not all of management's candidates for the board (the so-called short-slate rule).

Rule 14a-6 lists formal filing requirements, not only for preliminary and definitive proxy materials but also for solicitation materials and Notices of

---

57. Regulation of Communications Among Shareholders, Release No. 34-31326, 52 S.E.C. Docket 2028, Release No. IC-19031 (1992).

Exempt Solicitations. Rule 14a-12 contains special rules applicable to contested directors — or, more specifically, solicitations opposing anyone else's (usually management's) candidates for the board. In particular, Rule 14a-12(a) permits dissident solicitations prior to the filing of a written proxy statement as long as dissidents disclose their identities and holdings, and do not furnish a proxy card to security holders. Finally, Rule 14a-12(b) deals with the treatment and filing of proxy solicitations made prior to the delivery of a proxy statement.

Rule 14a-7 sets forth the list-or-mail rule under which, upon request by a dissident shareholder, a company must either provide a shareholders list or undertake to mail the dissident's proxy statement and solicitation materials to record holders (i.e., the intermediaries) in quantities sufficient to assure that all beneficial holders can receive copies.

PROBLEM: THE PROXY RULES MEET THE ACTIVE INSTITUTIONAL SHAREHOLDER

You are counsel to Midland Capital Management, a hedge fund whose investment premise is to make large investments in firms that can be improved, promote positive change, and if resisted, get on the board and do so from inside. If necessary Midland will try to acquire control, but its preferred technique is to be exposed through stock purchases and derivatives to no more than 20 percent of a target firm's equity. Midland holds 1 percent of the outstanding shares of HLS, Inc. Since it has long been dissatisfied with HLS's lackluster management, Midland is considering a proxy campaign to elect three reputable business professors to HLS's 9-member board. Before initiating a campaign, however, Midland wishes to test the waters by circulating a memo outlining the prospective campaign to 15 other institutions that hold a total of 15 percent of HLS's outstanding stock. If its sister institutions respond favorably, Midland plans to file a proxy statement, distribute materials in support of its nominees to all HLS shareholders, and seek a public endorsement of its nominees from Institutional Shareholder Services (ISS), a shareholder rights group.

Advise Midland on the difficulties it may expect to confront. Is there a problem with nominating only three candidates? Who must file what, with whom, and when? At what points can the SEC intervene? Can Midland expect to incur any litigation costs? What access does Midland have under Rule 14a-7 to the HLS shareholder list? What access does it have under DGCL §219 or §220? Under which provision would you recommend it proceed?

Consider, in this regard, the proxy rules under Regulation 14A and Schedule 14A, in your statutory supplement. Look closely at the following rules in connection with Midland's query: 14a-1(f) & (l); 14a-2(a)(6), (b)(1), (b)(2) & (b)(3); 14a-3(a); 14a-6(a) to (c) & (g); 14a-7(a) & (e); 14a-9; and 14a-12(a) & (b). Please do *not* explore every clause of the proxy rules in thinking about this question.

Whether the proxy rules or other legal barriers impede collective action by shareholders depends not only on the rules themselves, but also on the identity of the shareholders. Large, passive institutions might well be deterred by the prospect of a lawsuit when scrappy value investors, hedge funds, like Midland or other activist shareholders, are not. For an excellent analysis of the proxy rules from the perspective of the professional insurgent, see Thomas W. Briggs, *Shareholder Activism and Insurgency Under the New Proxy Rules*, 50 Bus. Law 99 (1994).

NOTE ON NEW PROXY VOTING ADVICE RULES

In July 2020, the SEC adopted rules that impose substantial regulatory burdens on proxy advisory firms as well as subjecting them to new liability risks. These rules were conspicuously targeted at ISS and Glass Lewis. They follow the structure of the proxy rules by treating the recommendations of proxy advisors as proxy "solicitations" that are potentially subject to antifraud liability and the full panoply of disclosure rules under Regulation 14A. Rule 14a-1(l).[58] They then exempt proxy advisors from most of the 14A disclosure mandates providing that these advisors comply with an alternative set of requirements. Rules 14a-2(b) and 14a-2(b)(9). These new disclosure mandates include: (1) requiring detailed disclosure of material conflicts of interest in the proxy advice, (2) providing the company to which the advice relates the opportunity to review the proxy advice and provide feedback before, or simultaneously with, its issuance to investors as well as notifying investors that the firm intends to, or has provided, a response, and (3) permitting the firm to have its views made available to readers of the proxy advice via hyperlink.

In addition, the new rules illustrate when failure to disclose material information might be misleading and hence subject to liability. For instance, a failure to disclose information on the proxy advisor's methodology, sources of information, conflicts of interest, and use of standards materially different from those approved by the SEC. Rule 14a-2(b)(9). The accompanying SEC release also notes that advisors may need to disclose "business practices . . . that might reasonably . . . call into question [the advice's] objectivity and independence [for example] selectively consulting with certain clients before issuing [a recommendation]."

Finally, supplemental advice accompanying the rules indicates that investment advisors (e.g., asset managers), who are among the principal consumers of proxy advisor recommendations, have a duty to consider firm responses to these recommendations before voting their shares.[59]

The new proxy advisor rules were sharply contested prior to their adoption.[60] On one hand, proxy recommendations released to the public were not

---

58. See *Final Rule: Exemptions from the Proxy Rules for Proxy Voting Advice*, SEC (July 22, 2020).

59. See *Supplement to Commission Guidance Regarding Proxy Voting Responsibilities of Investment Advisers,* available at: https://www.sec.gov/rules/policy/2020/ia-5547.pdf.

60. See Council of Institutional Investors, Comment Letter, January 30, 2020; Business Roundtable Public Comments to SEC on Amendments to Exemptions from the Proxy Rules for

always well informed, and the business model in which advisors promulgate governance standards while charging clients for advice on corporate governance flags an apparent — albeit a transparent — conflict of interest. On the other hand, without the low-cost recommendations of ISS and Glass Lewis, institutional investors might not have perspective on governance matters other than those of management.

QUESTIONS

1. It's too early to assess the long-term effects of the new proxy advisor rules. But will these effects be positive if the new rules discourage proxy advisors from providing recommendations in contested proxy battles? Are the policy considerations here different from those in other contexts where legal rules can influence the outcome of proxy contests, for example, the regime for reimbursing proxy solicitation costs addressed in the *Rosenfeld* case above?

2. The 1992 amendments to the proxy rules are often described as deregulating the exchange of views and information among shareholders. Could the new proxy advisor rules be described as re-regulating communication among key actors in corporate governance?

6.9.2   Activist Investors and the Short Slate Proxy Contest

Classically, proxy contests involve an effort by an insurgent group to replace the existing board through election. Completely aside from their regulatory costs, proxy contests for control are, however, hard to win. This is largely because existing investors are often suspicious about delivering control of the company to an unknown new group or individual. For this reason tender offers for control — which offer cash instead of promised reforms — rather than proxy contests became the more heavily used technique for hostile attempts to change corporate control. But over the recent past the proxy contest has returned again, thanks to the innovation of the short slate proxy contest, which was made possible by a 1992 change in SEC rules as well as Delaware case law that makes tender offers without board approval very difficult.

One of the most significant developments of the twentieth century in corporate governance has been the emergence of so-called activist hedge fund investors. Today, no company can hope to escape the attention of activists on the basis of size alone. It is reported that there are more than 100 hedge funds that have engaged in activism, with well over an estimated $100

Proxy Voting Advice, February 3, 2020; SEC Commissioner Robert J. Jackson, Jr., *Statement on Proposals to Restrict Shareholder Voting*, U.S. Securities and Exchange Commission, November 5, 2019.

billion of assets under management. But their real power comes not just from their own capital under management but from marshalling the support of the much larger institutional investors and asset managers, among others.

Typically, the activist fund will have prepared a thoughtful whitepaper outlining the basis for the change in policy or practice that it seeks. These sorts of suggestions from outsiders are almost always resisted by incumbent boards. Thus, a major challenge for activist investors is to find levers that will get their proposals serious attention from senior management and the board. The principal way this is done is through the threat or the execution of a short slate proxy contest.

A short slate proxy contest is one in which the insurgent offers nominees for only a minority of board positions; the other positions on the insurgent's proxy card are filled in with some of the company's nominees. This technique is made possible by SEC regulations that permit the short slate proponent to round out its proxy card with nominees from the management slate.[61] The short slate proxy contest offers the great advantage of giving dissatisfied shareholders an opportunity to "shake up" existing management without turning control over to the activists completely. Thus, successful short slate contests are much more frequent than contests for the whole board, which are rare today. Interventions by activists have grown from just 29 in 2000 to nearly 300 in 2018, according to Wachtell Lipton memoranda on the subject. And these efforts meet increasing success. In approximately 50 percent of their efforts activists win board representation, either through a vote or settlement.

6.9.3   Access to the Company's Proxy Statement: Rule 14a-8: Shareholder Proposals

Rule 14a-8 — the town meeting rule — entitles shareholders to include certain proposals in the company's proxy materials. From the perspective of a shareholder, this has the advantage of low costs: she can advance a proposal for vote by her fellow shareholders without filing with the SEC or mailing her own materials out to shareholders.

From the perspective of corporate management, Rule 14a-8 is at best a costly annoyance and at worst an infringement of management's autonomy. Management has a legitimate interest in excluding some materials from the proxy statement. The length of the proxy statement affects its intelligibility. Loyal agents would desire the proxy statement to be as concise as is consistent with effective communication of material matters and compliance with the law. But management may also have other motives for excluding shareholder materials from the proxy statement. Management prefers to control the content of communications made by a corporation to its shareholders. Thus, access to the proxy statement is an important issue that, in the world of events, demands a great deal of attention from corporate counsel.

61. See Securities Exchange Act Rule 14a-4(d)(4).

Regulation 14A provides a number of specific grounds to permit corporations to exclude shareholder-requested matter from the corporation's proxy solicitation materials. The most important is Rule 14a-8(i) which lists 13 grounds that permit firms to exclude proposals from the company's solicitation materials.[62] These grounds include 14a-8(i)(1) — approval of the proposal would be improper under state law — and 8(i)(7) — the proposal relates to a matter of ordinary business. Matters of ordinary business, which you might suppose would be of interest to shareholders, are correctly regarded as the province of the board under the design of the corporate form. Companies that wish to exclude a shareholder proposal generally seek SEC approval to do so. See Rule 14a-8(j). The SEC's approval of such a request is called a "no-action letter," since it takes the form of a letter stating that the SEC's Division of Corporate Finance will not recommend disciplinary action against the company if the proposal is omitted. The shareholder proponent has the opportunity to respond to the request for a no-action letter.

Most Rule 14a-8 shareholder proposals fall into one of two categories: corporate governance proposals or corporate social responsibility (CSR) proposals. Before 1985, Rule 14a-8 proposals were mostly about CSR, which embraced topics ranging from environmental policies to personnel practices. During the 1990s until around the mid-2010s, corporate governance proposals dominated. In the last few years, however, CSR proposals have come to outnumber governance proposals once again, and they have also received more shareholder support than ever, even if usually this support does not rise to the 50 percent level.

6.9.3.1   *Corporate Governance Proposals*

Hedge fund activists, labor unions, and others have been submitting proposals for years on such topics as separation of the board chair and CEO positions, compensation disclosure, redemption of poison pills, de-staggering of boards, election of directors by majority vote in uncontested elections rather than plurality, and access to the company's proxy to nominate directors. For example, Professors Randall Thomas and James Cotter found that 72 percent of Rule 14a-8 proposals submitted between 2002 and 2004 dealt with corporate governance issues.[63] Although these proposals are typically drafted in

---

62. Shareholder proposals must also satisfy certain formal criteria: They must state the identity of the shareholder (Rule 14a-8(b)(1)), the number of proposals (Rule 14a-8(c)), the length of the supporting statement (Rule 14a-8(d)), and the subject matter of the proposal (Rule 14a-8(i)).

63. See James F. Cotter & Randall S. Thomas, *Shareholder Proposals in the New Millennium: Shareholder Support, Board Response, and Market Reaction*, 13 J. Corp. Fin. 368, 373-374 (2007) (Table 1). These proposals addressed issues ranging from executive compensation (27 percent of the Thomas & Cotter sample) to "internal" corporate governance proposals such as the separation of the chairman and CEO roles (19 percent of the sample) to "external" corporate governance proposals such as dismantling poison pill or staggered board takeover defenses (23 percent of the sample).

a precatory form; that is, as recommendations to the board of directors for adoption,[64] they remain a useful governance technique because they place the issue before shareholders at large and register their sentiment. Further, a large affirmative shareholder vote often has a dramatic effect even when a resolution is only precatory. Simply put, astute management may hesitate to offend a shareholder majority, even if its will is not binding. For instance, we noted above the stark decrease in staggered boards in S&P 500 companies (from more than 60 percent of all such firms in 2000 to approximately 10 percent in 2018), which appears to be almost entirely due to investor pressure tied to these proposals. Recent years have, however, witnessed fewer governance proposals because, for many companies, most of these battles have been won by now.

NOTE ON SHAREHOLDER PROXY ACCESS TO NOMINATE DIRECTORS

Few issues in corporate governance have been so warmly contested and for so long as the question of when, if at all, a shareholder should have the right to submit nominations for the board of directors into the company's proxy statement. Being able to put insurgent nominees into the company's own proxy materials would save some printing and mailing costs that were thought to be important. Management, on the other hand, has resisted this effort from the start. They claim that it would make the company's proxy confusing and would not be beneficial because boards function best collegially and when some nominees are proposed by "special interest investors" the quality of board function will be injured. We pass over an evaluation of these positions for the moment.

   The issue of proxy access for shareholder nominations has a federal law aspect and a state corporation law aspect. During the period up to 2011 most of the effort to allow shareholders to gain access to the company's proxy to nominate directors was directed at the SEC to promulgate a mandatory rule to govern all public companies. Since 2012, however, the effort to gain that access has proceeded company-by-company, largely in conjunction with urging accomodating changes in state corporate law. Our treatment of this lengthy and complex issue is necessarily summary.

   It was always possible for a charter or bylaw provision to mandate that a company provide its shareholders with access to its proxy under some conditions.[65] But such access was not generally available because (1) management did not favor it and thus did not suggest it, and (2) SEC regulations

---

64. We note in passing that the SEC has effectively encouraged shareholders to frame corporate governance resolutions in a precatory form. Precatory resolutions sidestep questions concerning the scope of shareholder authority under state law. See the note following Rule 14a-8(i)(1).

65. In Delaware, this was confirmed in 2009 when, perhaps in an effort to preempt the issue, the legislature amended the DGCL to confirm that shareholders could amend the company's bylaws to permit proxy access. See DGCL §112.

barred shareholders from placing an issue on the company's proxy to allow a shareholder vote. Thus, no shareholder in a public company could put such a bylaw up for a shareholder vote without shouldering the cost of printing and distributing her own proxy solicitation materials. The point of the early SEC prohibition on including shareholder nominees in the company proxy was presumably to avoid confusion about who management's nominees really were.

Beginning in 2007, after alternate circuit court decisions and SEC rule changes, the ability of activists to implement proxy access regimes through Rule 14a-8 proposals has largely been left to private ordering. Institutional investors — led by state pension funds and labor union pension funds — have waged a sustained effort to persuade individual companies to adopt proxy access bylaws under state law.

When a shareholder proposes a proxy access bylaw, the substantive issues will be principally four. First, the size of the shareholding that will qualify for access. Second, the length of continuous ownership required to qualify. Third, the number of shareholders that may join together to satisfy the share ownership requirement. And fourth, the maximum number of directors that may be nominated. There are other subsidiary issues, but these four structure the debate. The "market" has for now settled around a 3 percent, three-year qualification for ownership (the SEC's standard in Rule 14a-11). The number of shareholders in the nominating group rarely exceeds 20 and the percentage of the positions open for election rarely exceeds 25 percent of the open seats.

Prior to the 2015 proxy season (typically April to June) there were just 16 firms that had faced a shareholder vote on proxy access, and of these proxy access had won shareholder support in ten. But in 2015, proxy access emerged as a key issue, with the NYC Comptroller's "2015 Boardroom Accountability Project" seeking to install proxy access at 75 U.S. companies of diverse industries and market capitalizations. Several large pension funds supported the project (e.g., CalPERS) and similar efforts (e.g., TIAA-CREF). Multiple companies subsequently announced company-sponsored moves to provide proxy access voluntarily, with 3 percent/three-year thresholds (e.g., GE, Bank of America) or 5 percent/three-year thresholds (e.g., Priceline). Other companies resisted and recommended against a shareholder proposal: some prevailed (e.g., Apple, Coca-Cola), while others did not. By 2019, roughly 70 percent of S&P 500 companies had proxy access provisions in their charters.

6.9.3.2   Corporate Social Responsibility Proposals

There is a long tradition of "pro-social" activism that seeks to change corporate behavior in ways that their proponents believe are socially beneficial. Should shareholders have a federal right to place proposals on the corporation's proxy statement that urge the board to comply with fixed carbon emission standards or to nominate at least five women candidates to the company's board of twelve directors at the next annual shareholders meeting? If so, under what circumstances? Generally, Regulation 14A permits management to exclude matters that fall within the ordinary business of the corporation (Rule 14a-8(i)(7)). Suppose, for example, that the corporation decides to buy from the cheapest available source, a foreign supplier. Assume that this source is suspected of using child labor and that a shareholder group believes this is immoral and bad for business (arguing the corporation will suffer long-term reputational damage). Can these shareholders include a precatory resolution in the company's proxy requesting that the board cease doing business with this suspect foreign source under Regulation 14A?

The SEC has waffled on social responsibility proposals. In 1991, it strayed from its earlier policy, under which the (then current) Rule 14a-8(c)(7) required issuers to include proposals that related to "matters which have significant policy, economic or other implications in them." In its 1991 no-action letter to the Cracker Barrel Old Country Store, Inc., the SEC agreed that Cracker Barrel could omit a shareholder proposal calling on the board to prohibit employment discrimination based on sexual orientation. The SEC asserted that it could not easily determine which employment-related matters fell within the "ordinary business exclusion" and would therefore permit the exclusion of all such proposals.

However, in July 1997, the SEC waffled back, proposing changes to Rule 14a-8, including a reversal of its *Cracker Barrel* policy and a return to its previous interpretation of the "ordinary business" exclusion with respect to a company's personnel policies. Consider the SEC's explanation.

The Interpretation of Rule 14a-8(c)(7): The "Ordinary Business" Exclusion

In a 1992 no-action letter issued to the Cracker Barrel Old Country Stores, Inc., the Division announced that the fact that a shareholder proposal concerning a company's employment policies and practices for the general workforce is tied to a social issue will no longer be viewed as removing the proposal from the realm of ordinary business operations of the registrant. Rather, determinations with respect to any such proposals are properly governed by the employment-based nature of the proposal. . . .

The *Cracker Barrel* interpretation has been controversial since it was announced. While the reasons for adopting the *Cracker Barrel* interpretation continue to have some validity, as well as significant support in the corporate community, we believe that [its] reversal . . . is warranted . . . Reversal will require companies to include proposals in their proxy materials that some shareholders believe are important to companies and fellow shareholders. . . . That is, employment-related proposals focusing on significant social policy issues could not automatically be excluded under the "ordinary business" exclusion.

Under this proposal, the "bright line" approach for employment-related proposals established by the *Cracker Barrel* position would be replaced by the case-by-case analysis that prevailed previously. . . .

Despite return to a case-by-case, analytical approach, some types of proposals raising social policy issues may continue to raise difficult interpretive questions. For instance, reversal of the *Cracker Barrel* position would not automatically result in the inclusion of proposals focusing on wage and other issues for companies' operations in the Maquiladora region of Mexico, or on "workplace practices."

Finally, we believe that it would be useful to summarize the principal considerations in the Division's application of the "ordinary business" exclusion. . . The general underlying policy of this exclusion is consistent with the policy of most state corporate laws: to confine the resolution of ordinary business problems to management and the board of directors since it is impracticable for shareholders to decide how to solve such problems. . . .

The policy underlying the rule includes two central considerations. The first relates to the subject matter of the proposal. Certain tasks are so fundamental to management's ability to run a company on a day-to-day basis that they could not, as a practical matter, be subject to direct shareholder oversight. Examples include the management of the workforce, such as the hiring, promotion and termination of employees, decisions on production quality and quantity, and the retention of suppliers. However, proposals relating to such matters but focusing on significant social policy issues generally would not be considered to be excludable, because such issues typically fall outside the scope of management's prerogative.

The second consideration relates to the degree to which the proposal seeks to "micro manage" the company by probing too deeply into "matters of a complex nature that shareholders, as a group, would not be qualified to make an informed judgment on, due to their lack of business expertise and lack of intimate knowledge of the (company's) business." This consideration may come into play in a number of circumstances, such as where the proposal seeks intricate detail, or seeks to impose specific time-frames or methods for implementing complex policies. . . .

After reading this analysis, are you clear what the SEC's criteria for inclusion on management's proxy were after it withdrew the *Cracker Barrel* no-action letter and returned to a "case-by-case analytic" for determining whether issues relating to employment practices were excludable or of sufficient importance to be an appropriate subject of a Rule 14a-8 resolution?[66] As you might expect, this distinction has continued be murky.

For some years, the SEC had come to emphasize micromanagement as a key issue in its decisions to grant no-action letters. In 2018, the SEC's Division of Corporate Finance doubled down by giving "micromanagement" pride of place in a more general discussion of its exclusion policies.[67] One example it provided noted the inappropriate specificity of an Apple shareholder proposal recommending that the technology giant reach net-zero greenhouse gas emissions by 2030. During the 2019 proxy season, micromanagement was among the reasons the SEC cited for granting 64 of the 105 no-action letter requests it received relating to environmental and social matters (E&S).[68] The SEC also granted such requests when shareholder proposals recommended compliance with parts of the Paris Climate Agreement on the grounds that these proposals sought to tie management's hands with respect to complex matters of business policy and implementation.[69]

---

66. See SEC Release No. 34-40018, Fed. Sec. L. Rep. (CCH) ¶86,018.

67. See SEC Staff Legal Bulletin No. 14J(CF), October 23, 2018. Available at: https://www.sec.gov/corpfin/staff-legal-bulletin-14j-shareholder-proposals.

68. See Richard Alsop & Yoon-Jee Kim, Shearman & Sterling LLP, *Shareholder Proposals 2019 — ESG No-Action Letter Trends and Strategies*, Harvard Law School Forum on Corporate Governance, March 25, 2020.

69. See id. (referring to no-action letter requests by, among others, ExxonMobil Corporation, The Goldman Sachs Group, Inc., and Wells Fargo & Company).

Today, corporate social responsibility (CSR) and E&S are major concerns for large companies and their boards. In the 2020 proxy season, shareholders submitted over 400 E&S proposals, which outnumbered governance-related proposals. Most of these addressed political spending, climate change, gender and race diversity, and workplace environment.[70] The percentage of these proposals that receive majority shareholder support has been increasing.[71] In addition, many other resolutions are withdrawn because their proponents settle with management over changes in company policies. Such settlements have become increasingly common. The broad range of E&S proposals testifies not only to their rising popularity, but also to the emergence of new activist groups that rely on the shareholder proposal system.[72] We discuss broader issues related to E&S proposals in Chapter 8.

However, the shareholder proposal system also faces significant new challenges. The same package of proposed SEC reforms that led to the recent regulation of proxy advisors also targeted Rule 14a-8 shareholder proposals. The SEC adopted these rules on September 23, 2020. Among the changes they make are increasing the share ownership threshold that proponents must satisfy to be eligible to submit Rule 14a-8 proposals,[73] increasing the threshold of prior shareholder support required to resubmit proposals that had previously failed to pass,[74] and allowing companies to exclude resubmitted proposals whose support had declined over their past two submissions. The last two of these rule changes are particularly likely to affect E&S proposals, which often see rising shareholder support over the course of several annual submissions. As one might expect, these new rule changes are almost as warmly contested as the SEC's newly adopted proxy advisory rules.[75]

---

70. See *Proxy Preview 2020*, March 19, 2020; Hannah Orowitz & Brigid Rosati, *An Early Look at the 2020 Proxy Season*, Harvard Law School Forum on Corporate Governance, June 10, 2020.

71. Thus far, in the 2020 cycle, 7 out of 23 E&S proposals have passed (double the percentage that passed in 2019), including one where Chevron shareholders voted to recommend enhanced disclosure of climate lobbying. Even this understates the number because some governance proposals are really tied to E&S issues, such as two proposals recommending splitting the board chair and CEO positions which passed this year. Orowitz & Rosati, *supra* note 70.

72. See Paul Rissman & Andrew Behar, *A Successful Season for SASB-Based Shareholder Resolutions*, Harvard Law School Forum on Corporate Governance, June 12, 2020. Activism is also going "global." See, e.g., Marco Becht et al., *Returns to Hedge Fund Activism: An International Study*, 30 Rev. Fin. Stud. 2933 (2017).

73. A shareholder would need to show a continuous holding of either $2,000 of a company's voting securities for at least three years, or "$15,000 of these securities for two years, or $25,000 for at least one year." *See Procedural Requirements and Resubmission Thresholds under Exchange Act Rule 14a-8: Proposed Rule*, SEC (November 5, 2019). This contrasts with the existing rule requiring a continuous holding of $2,000 of these securities for at least one year.

74. See id, at 51 which changes the thresholds for resubmission from 3 percent (for the first time a proposal is voted on), 6 percent (for the second time), and 10 percent (for the third time) to 5, 15, and 25 percent, respectively.

75. See, e.g., Council of Institutional Investors, Comment Letter, January 30, 2020; Business Roundtable Public Comments to SEC on Procedural Requirements and Resubmission Thresholds under Exchange Act Rule 14a-8, February 3, 2020; Jackson, *supra* note 60.

QUESTIONS ON SHAREHOLDER PROPOSALS

1. Should a firm be able to place a binding provision in its charter or bylaws allowing its shareholders to vote *only* on management's resolutions or those required by law? This so-called "Skadden Scheme" seems to have received the blessing of the SEC's Division of Corporate Finance in the context of business trusts. The argument might be that if the foundational documents of a business trust — its charter and bylaws — do not contemplate investor votes on matters other than those expressly provided for, their investors are not "entitled to vote" and therefore may not submit Rule 14a-8 shareholder proposals even when business trusts are otherwise subject to the SEC's proxy rules. If this were *not* the argument behind the Skadden Scheme, what would be the implications for Rule 14a-8 shareholder proposals? *See* Phillip Goldstein, *Can a Public Company Effectively Opt-Out of Rule 14a-8?*, Harvard Law School Forum on Corporate Governance, March 30, 2020.

2. Unlike other aspects of shareholder voting in the corporate form, the right to submit Rule 14a-8 shareholder proposals is only trivially attached to share ownership requirements — only one shareholder is necessary to bring a Rule 14a-8 proposal, although more would be needed to vote to approve it. Moreover, corporate law has always permitted one shareholder willing to bear the costs to mount a costly proxy solicitation. Nevertheless, does Rule 14a-8 hint at a different vision of the public corporation from that embodied by state corporation law. Does it see the corporation as a kind of civic organization, or should it be read to provide yet another mechanism to protect the interests of small shareholders from the despotism of large shareholders and corporate managers; that is, another mechanism for mitigating the shareholder collective action problem? This latter vision harkens back in some sense to the one-person, one-vote default rule in partnership and in some companies at the dawn of corporate law.

6.9.4 Rule 14a-9: The Antifraud Rule

Mandating disclosure is typically more credible when backed up by sanctions (public or private) for misrepresentations or misleading statements. As we will see in later chapters, private suits by investors alleging injury as a result of a violation of the federal securities laws have, over the last 40 years, emerged as an important device for enforcing these laws. Congress did not create most of the provisions of private rights of action that are important today. Only the SEC is expressly authorized to enforce the securities acts and the rules adopted under them. The federal courts, however, have implied private rights of action under the securities acts, starting modestly in 1946 (see the *Kardon* case, implying a private right of action under Rule 10b-5, discussed in Chapter 14) and accelerating markedly in the 1960s. The U.S. Supreme Court addressed the question of whether a private right of action arose under §14(a) and Rule 14a-9 in the 1964 case of *J.I. Case v. Borak*, 337 U.S. 426. The Court held that such a right of action exists and began the process of delineating all of its elements.

The golden age of implied private rights of action under the federal securities laws ended when the Supreme Court established a more restrictive test for implying such private remedies in *Cort v. Ash*, 422 U.S. 66 (1975). Under this test, an implied right must satisfy three criteria: "First is the plaintiff one of the class for whose *especial* benefit the statute was enacted? . . . Second, is there any indication of legislative intent, explicit or implicit, either to create such a remedy or deny one? . . . And finally, is the cause of action one traditionally relegated to state law, in an area basically the concern of the States, so that it would be inappropriate to infer a cause of action based solely on federal law?" Id. at 78. Since *Cort*, the Supreme Court has been ambivalent toward implied private rights of action. This ambivalence is especially clear in cases construing private remedies under Rule 10b-5, which we address at length in Chapter 14, but it also marks litigation under Rule 14a-9 — the antifraud rule governing proxy solicitations.

Proxy Rule 14a-9 is the SEC's general proscription against false or misleading proxy solicitations. It is one of the half-dozen antifraud rules in federal securities legislation that supports much of the plaintiff's bar and an enormous edifice of federal case law. (We encounter two other such rules later in dealing with tender offers (Chapter 11) and misrepresentation generally (Chapter 14)).

As with any implied right of action, recognizing the right is only a first step. The devil is in the details of working out the elements of the right and limiting its scope without legislative guidance. In the case of Rule 14(a)-9, a series of Supreme Court decisions has established the key elements, roughly following the pattern of common law fraud. These elements include the following:

a. *Materiality.* A misrepresentation or omission in a proxy solicitation can trigger liability only if it is "material," that is, "there is a substantial likelihood that a reasonable shareholder would consider it important in deciding how to vote." *TSC Indus., Inc. v. Northway, Inc.*, 426 U.S. 438, 449 (1976).

b. *Culpability.* The Supreme Court has not yet determined a standard of culpability under Rule 14a-9. The Second and Third Circuits have adopted a negligence standard. See, e.g., *Gerstle v. Gamble-Skogmo, Inc.*, 478 F.2d 1281 (2d Cir. 1973) (Friendly, J.); *Herskowitz v. Nutri/System, Inc.*, 857 F.2d 179 (3d Cir.), *cert. denied*, 489 U.S. 1054 (1988). The Sixth Circuit has required proof of scienter (intentionality or extreme recklessness). See *Adams v. Standard Knitting Mills, Inc.*, 623 F.2d 422 (6th Cir.), *cert. denied sub nom. Adams v. Peat Marwick, Mitchell & Co.*, 449 U.S. 1067 (1980).

c. *Causation and Reliance.* The Supreme Court has ruled that, unlike a traditional case of fraud, a plaintiff need not prove actual reliance on a misrepresentation to complete a Rule 14a-9 cause of action. Instead, causation of injury is presumed if a misrepresentation is material and the proxy solicitation "was an *essential link* in the accomplishment of the transaction." *Mills v. Electric Auto-Lite Co.*, 396 U.S. 375, 385 (1970) (emphasis added).

d. *Remedies.* The *Mills* Court contemplated that courts might award injunctive relief, rescission, or monetary damages. See Robert C. Clark, Corporate Law, §9.4.5, pp. 387-388 (1986).

Two of these elements — materiality and causation — are addressed in the *Virginia Bankshares* decision, which is the Supreme Court's most recent effort to articulate the limits of Rule 14a-9. In reading the opinion consider whether the Court's arguments are sound. Does the holding advance the purposes of Rule 14a-9, or is it undermining its effectiveness?

VIRGINIA BANKSHARES, INC. v. SANDBERG
501 U.S. 1083 (1990)

SOUTER, J.:

In *J.I. Case Co. v. Borak*, 377 U.S. 426 (1964), we first recognized an implied private right of action for the breach of §14(a) as implemented by SEC Rule 14a-9, which prohibits the solicitation of proxies by means of materially false or misleading statements.

The questions before us are whether a statement couched in conclusory or qualitative terms purporting to explain directors' reasons for recommending certain corporate action can be materially misleading within the meaning of Rule 14a-9, and whether causation of damages compensable under §14(a) can be shown by a member of a class of minority shareholders whose votes are not required by law or corporate bylaw to authorize the corporate action subject to the proxy solicitation. We hold that knowingly false statements of reasons may be actionable even though conclusory in form, but that respondents have failed to demonstrate the equitable basis required to extend the §14(a) private action to such shareholders when any indication of congressional intent to do so is lacking.

I

In December 1986, First American Bankshares, Inc., (FABI), a bank holding company, began a "freeze-out" merger, in which the First American Bank of Virginia (Bank) eventually merged into Virginia Bankshares, Inc., (VBI), a wholly owned subsidiary of FABI. VBI owned 85% of the Bank's shares, the remaining 15% being in the hands of some 2,000 minority shareholders. FABI hired the investment banking firm of Keefe, Bruyette & Woods (KBW) to give an opinion on the appropriate price for shares of the minority holders, who would lose their interests in the Bank as a result of the merger. Based on market quotations and unverified information from FABI, KBW gave the Bank's executive committee an opinion that $42 a share would be a fair price for the minority stock. The executive committee approved the merger proposal at that price, and the full board followed suit.

Although Virginia law required only that such a merger proposal be submitted to a vote at a shareholders' meeting, and that the meeting be preceded by circulation of a statement of information to the shareholders, the directors nevertheless solicited proxies for voting on the proposal at the annual meeting set for April 21, 1987. In their solicitation, the directors urged the proposal's adoption and stated they had approved the plan because of its opportunity for the minority shareholders to achieve a "high" value, which they elsewhere described as a "fair" price, for their stock.

Although most minority shareholders gave the proxies requested, respondent Sandberg did not, and after approval of the merger she sought damages in the United States District Court for the Eastern District of Virginia from VBI, FABI, and the directors of the Bank. She pleaded two counts, one for soliciting proxies in violation of §14(a) and Rule 14a-9, and the other for breaching fiduciary duties owed to the minority shareholders under state law. Under the first count, Sandberg alleged, among other things, that the directors had not believed that the price offered was high or that the terms of the merger were fair, but had recommended the merger only because they believed they had no alternative if they wished to remain on the board. . . .

The jury's verdicts were for Sandberg on both counts, after finding violations of Rule 14a-9 by all defendants and a breach of fiduciary duties by the Bank's directors. The jury awarded Sandberg $18 a share, having found that she would have received $60 if her stock had been valued adequately. . . .

On appeal, the United States Court of Appeals for the Fourth Circuit affirmed the judgments. . . .

II

The Court of Appeals affirmed petitioners' liability for two statements found to have been materially misleading in violation of §14(a) of the Act, one of which was that "The Plan of Merger has been approved by the Board of Directors because it provides an opportunity for the Bank's public shareholders to achieve a high value for their shares." App. to Pet. for Cert. 53a. Petitioners argue that statements of opinion or belief incorporating indefinite and unverifiable expressions cannot be actionable as misstatements of material fact within the meaning of Rule 14a-9, and that such a declaration of opinion or belief should never be actionable when placed in a proxy solicitation incorporating statements of fact sufficient to enable readers to draw their own, independent conclusions.

A

We consider first the actionability per se of statements of reasons, opinion or belief. Because such a statement by definition purports to express what is consciously on the speaker's mind, we interpret the jury verdict as finding that the directors' statements of belief and opinion were made with knowledge that the directors did not hold the beliefs or opinions expressed, and we confine our discussion to statements so made.

That such statements may be materially significant raises no serious question. The meaning of the materiality requirement for liability under §14(a) was discussed at some length in *TSC Industries, Inc. v. Northway, Inc.*, 426 U.S. 438 (1976), where we held a fact to be material "if there is a substantial likelihood that a reasonable shareholder would consider it important in deciding how to vote." *Id.*, at 449. We think there is no room to deny that a statement of belief by corporate directors about a recommended course of action, or an explanation of their reasons for recommending it, can take on just that importance. . . .

B

But, assuming materiality, the question remains whether statements of reasons, opinions, or beliefs are statements "with respect to . . . material facts" so as to fall within the strictures of the Rule. . . .

[D]irectors' statements of reasons or belief . . . are factual in two senses: as statements that the directors do act for the reasons given or hold the belief stated and as statements about the subject matter of the reason or belief expressed. In neither sense does the proof or disproof of such statements implicate the concerns expressed in *Blue Chip Stamps*. The root of those concerns was a plaintiff's capacity to manufacture claims of hypothetical action, unconstrained by independent evidence. Reasons for directors' recommendations or statements of belief are, in contrast, characteristically matters of corporate record subject to documentation, to be supported or attacked by evidence of historical fact outside a plaintiff's control.

In this case, whether $42 was "high," and the proposal "fair" to the minority shareholders depended on whether provable facts about the Bank's assets, and about actual and potential levels of operation, substantiated a value that was above, below, or more or less at the $42 figure, when assessed in accordance with recognized methods of valuation.

Respondents adduced evidence for just such facts in proving that the statement was misleading about its subject matter and a false expression of the directors' reasons. Whereas the proxy statement described the $42 price as offering a premium above both book value and market price, the evidence indicated that a calculation of the book figure based on the appreciated value of the Bank's real estate holdings eliminated any such premium. . . . There was, indeed, evidence of a "going concern" value for the Bank in excess of $60 per share of common stock, another fact never disclosed. However conclusory the directors' statement may have been, then, it was open to attack by garden-variety evidence, subject neither to a plaintiff's control nor ready manufacture, and there was no undue risk of open-ended liability or uncontrollable litigation in allowing respondents the opportunity for recovery on the allegation that it was misleading to call $42 "high." . . .

The question arises whether disbelief, or undisclosed belief or motivation, standing alone, should be a sufficient basis to sustain an action under §14(a), absent proof by the sort of objective evidence described above that the statement also expressly or impliedly asserted something false or misleading about its subject matter. We think that proof of mere disbelief or belief undisclosed should not suffice for liability under §14(a), and if nothing more had been required or proven in this case we would reverse for that reason. . . .

III

The second issue before us, left open in *Mills v. Electric Auto-Lite Co.*, 396 U.S., at 385, n.7, is whether causation of damages compensable through the implied private right of action under §14(a) can be demonstrated by a member of a class of minority shareholders whose votes are not required by law or corporate bylaw to authorize the transaction giving rise to the claim. . . .

The *Mills* Court . . . held that causation of damages by a material proxy misstatement could be established by showing that minority proxies necessary and sufficient to authorize the corporate acts had been given in accordance with the tenor of the solicitation, and the Court described such a causal relationship by calling the proxy solicitation an "essential link in the accomplishment of the transaction." . . .

In this case, respondents address *Mills*' open question by proffering two theories that the proxy solicitation addressed to them was an "essential link" under the *Mills* causation test. They argue, first, that a link existed and was essential simply because VBI and FABI would have been unwilling to proceed with the merger without the approval manifested by the minority shareholders' proxies, which would not have been obtained without the solicitation's express misstatements and misleading omissions. On this reasoning, the causal connection would depend on a desire to avoid bad shareholder or public relations, and the essential character of the causal link would stem not from the enforceable terms of the parties' corporate relationship, but from one party's apprehension of the ill will of the other.

In the alternative, respondents argue that the proxy statement was an essential link . . . because it was the means to satisfy a state statutory requirement of minority shareholder approval, as a condition for saving the merger from voidability resulting from a conflict of interest on the part of one of the Bank's directors, Jack Beddow, who voted in favor of the merger while also serving as a director of FABI. . . . On this theory, causation would depend on the use of the proxy statement for the purpose of obtaining votes sufficient to bar a minority shareholder from commencing proceedings to declare the merger void. . . .

A

Blue Chip Stamps set an example worth recalling as a preface to specific policy analysis of the consequences of recognizing respondents' first theory, that a desire to avoid minority shareholders' ill will should suffice to justify recognizing the requisite causality of a proxy statement needed to garner that minority support. It will be recalled that in *Blue Chip Stamps* we raised concerns about the practical consequences of allowing recovery, under §10(b) of the Act and Rule 10b-5, on evidence of what a merely hypothetical buyer or seller might have done on a set of facts that never occurred, and foresaw that any such expanded liability would turn on "hazy" issues inviting self-serving testimony, strike suits, and protracted discovery, with little chance of reasonable resolution by pretrial process. . . . These were good reasons to deny recognition to such claims in the absence of any apparent contrary congressional intent.

The same threats of speculative claims and procedural intractability are inherent in respondents' theory of causation linked through the directors' desire for a cosmetic vote. Causation would turn on inferences about what the corporate directors would have thought and done without the minority shareholder approval unneeded to authorize action. . . .

B

The theory of causal necessity derived from the requirements of Virginia law dealing with postmerger ratification seeks to identify the essential character of the proxy solicitation from its function in obtaining the minority approval that would preclude a minority suit attacking the merger. . . . [T]his theory of causation rests upon the proposition . . . that §14(a) should provide a federal remedy whenever a false or misleading proxy statement results in the loss under state law of a shareholder plaintiff's state remedy for the enforcement of a state right. Respondents agree with the suggestions of counsel for the SEC and FDIC that causation be recognized, for example, when a minority shareholder has been induced by a misleading proxy statement to forfeit a state-law right to an appraisal remedy by voting to approve a transaction. . . .

This case does not, however, require us to decide whether §14(a) provides a cause of action for lost state remedies, since there is no indication . . . that the proxy solicitation resulted in any such loss. The contrary appears to be the case. Assuming the soundness of respondents' characterization of the proxy statement as materially misleading, the very terms of the Virginia statute indicate that a favorable minority vote induced by the solicitation would not suffice to render the merger invulnerable to later attack on the ground of the conflict. The statute bars a shareholder from seeking to avoid a transaction tainted by a director's conflict if, inter alia, the minority shareholders ratified the transaction following disclosure of the material facts of the transaction and the conflict. Va. Code §13.1-691(A)(2) (1989). Assuming that the material facts about the merger and Beddow's interests were not accurately disclosed, the minority votes were inadequate to ratify the merger under state law, and there was no loss of state remedy to connect the proxy solicitation with harm to minority shareholders irredressable under state law. . . .

KENNEDY, J. (concurring in part and dissenting in part). . . .

The severe limits the Court places upon possible proof of nonvoting causation in a §14(a) private action are justified neither by our precedents nor any case in the courts of appeals.

To the extent the Court's analysis considers the purposes underlying §14(a), it does so with the avowed aim to limit the cause of action and with undue emphasis upon fears of "speculative claims and procedural intractability." . . . The result is a sort of guerrilla warfare to restrict a well-established implied right of action. . . .

The Court seems to assume, based upon the footnote in *Mills* reserving the question, that [the respondent] bears a special burden to demonstrate causation because the public shareholders held only 15 percent of the Bank's stock. . . .

The Court's distinction presumes that a majority shareholder will vote in favor of management's proposal even if proxy disclosure suggests that the transaction is unfair to minority shareholders or that the board of directors or majority shareholder are in breach of fiduciary duties to the minority. . . . Of course, when the majority shareholder dominates the voting process, as was the case here, it may prefer to avoid the embarrassment of voting against its own proposal and so may cancel the meeting of shareholders at which the vote was to have been taken. For practical purposes, the result is the same: because of full disclosure the transaction does not go forward and the resulting injury to minority shareholders is avoided. The Court's distinction between voting and nonvoting causation does not create clear legal categories. . . .

There is no authority whatsoever for limiting §14(a) to protecting [only] those minority shareholders whose numerical strength could permit them to vote down a proposal. One of Section 14(a)'s "chief purposes is 'the protection of investors.' " *J.I. Case Co. v. Borak*, 377 U.S., at 432. Those who lack the strength to vote down a proposal have all the more need of disclosure. The voting process involves not only casting ballots but also the formulation and withdrawal of proposals, the minority's right to block a vote through court action or the threat of adverse consequences, or the negotiation of an increase in price. The proxy rules support this deliberative process. These practicalities can result in causation sufficient to support recovery.

The facts in the case before us prove this point. [The respondent] argues that had all the material facts been disclosed, FABI or the Bank likely would have withdrawn or revised the merger proposal. The evidence in the record . . . meets any reasonable requirement of specific and nonspeculative proof.

FABI wanted a "friendly transaction" with a price viewed as "so high that any reasonable shareholder will accept it." App. 99. Management expressed concern that the transaction result in "no loss of support for the bank out in the community, which was important." *Id.*, at 109. . . .

The theory that FABI would not have pursued the transaction if full disclosure had been provided and the shareholders had realized the inadequacy of the price is supported not only by the trial testimony but also by notes of the meeting of the Bank's board which approved the merger. . . .

Directors of the Bank testified they would not have voted to approve the transaction if the price had been demonstrated unfair to the minority. Further, approval by the Bank's board of directors was facilitated by FABI's representation that the transaction also would be approved by the minority shareholders.

These facts alone suffice to support a finding of causation, but here . . . more evidence [was available] to link the nondisclosure with completion of the merger. FABI executive Robert Altman and Bank Chairman Drewer met on the day before the shareholders' meeting when the vote was taken. Notes produced by petitioners suggested that Drewer, who had received some shareholder objections to the $42 price, considered postponing the meeting and obtaining independent advice on valuation. Altman persuaded him to go forward without any of these cautionary measures. . . .

Though I would not require a shareholder to present such evidence of causation, this case itself demonstrates that nonvoting causation theories are quite plausible where the misstatement or omission is material and the damage sustained by minority shareholders is serious. . . .

The majority avoids the question whether a plaintiff may prove causation by demonstrating that the misrepresentation or omission deprived her of a state law remedy. I do not think the question difficult, as the whole point of federal proxy rules is to support state law principles of corporate governance. Nor do I think that the Court can avoid this issue if it orders judgment for petitioners. The majority asserts that respondents show no loss of a state law remedy, because if "the material facts of the transaction and Beddow's interest were not accurately disclosed, then the minority votes were inadequate to ratify the merger under Virginia law." . . . This theory requires us to conclude that the Virginia statute governing director conflicts of interest, Va. Code §13.1-691(A)(2) (1989), incorporates the same definition of materiality as the federal proxy rules. I find no support for that proposition. If the definitions are not the same, then Sandberg may have lost her state law remedy. For all we know, disclosure to the minority shareholders that the price is $42 per share may satisfy Virginia's requirement. If that is the case, then approval by the minority without full disclosure may have deprived Sandberg of the ability to void the merger. . . .

I would affirm the judgment of the Court of Appeals.

6.10   FIDUCIARY SUPERINTENDENCE OF SHAREHOLDER VOTING

In Chapter 8, we expand on the directors' and officers' fiduciary duty of loyalty to the corporation and its shareholders. Here we simply introduce two specific applications of the directors' and officers' fiduciary obligation: the duty not to unfairly manipulate the voting process for their own advantage and the duty to make truthful statements when addressing the shareholders and perhaps when making public statements respecting the firm.

The fundamental nature of shareholder voting in corporate governance, coupled with the wide and flexible power of management in elections to influence voting outcomes have led courts to exercise broad equitable powers in supervising the voting process under a fiduciary standard of good faith. In the classic case of *Schnell v. Chris-Craft Industries, Inc.*, for example, dissident shareholders were negotiating with the incumbent board up to the last minute, in the hopes of avoiding a full-fledged proxy contest for control of the company. The incumbent board (arguably) strung along the dissidents then, with only a couple of months left before the annual meeting, amended the bylaws to advance the annual meeting date by one month to mid-December (and, for good measure, moved the meeting to a small town in upstate New York). The board explained that it wished to avoid the Christmas mail rush in sending out its solicitation materials. But whatever the board's intention and statutory authorization, the practical effect of rescheduling the shareholders' meeting was to leave very little time for the dissidents to organize and solicit proxies for their slate.

The dissidents brought suit, seeking an injunction to postpone the annual meeting. The Chancery Court recognized the incumbents' maneuvering as a hardball tactic, but refused to grant the injunction. On appeal, the Delaware Supreme Court took a different approach.

SCHNELL v. CHRIS-CRAFT INDUSTRIES, INC.
285 A.2d 437 (Del. 1971)

HERRMANN, J.:

This is an appeal from the denial by the Court of Chancery of the petition of dissident stockholders for injunctive relief to prevent management from advancing the date of the annual stockholders' meeting from January 11, 1972, as previously set by the by-laws, to December 8, 1971. . . .

In our view, [the conclusions of the court below] amount to a finding that management has attempted to utilize the corporate machinery and the Delaware Law for the purpose of perpetuating itself in office; and, to that end, for the purpose of obstructing the legitimate efforts of dissident stockholders in the exercise of their rights to undertake a proxy contest against management. These are inequitable purposes, contrary to established principles of corporate democracy. The advancement by directors of the by-law date of a stockholders' meeting, for such purposes, may not be permitted to stand. Compare *Condec Corporation v. Lunkenheimer Company*, Del. Ch., 230 A.2d 769 (1967).

When the by-laws of a corporation designate the date of the annual meeting of stockholders, it is to be expected that those who intend to contest the reelection of incumbent management will gear their campaign to the by-law date. It is not to be expected that management will attempt to advance the date in order to obtain an inequitable advantage in the contest. Management contends that it has complied strictly with the provisions of the new Delaware Corporation Law in changing the by-law date. The answer to that contention, of course, is that inequitable action does not become permissible simply because it is legally possible. . . .

We are unable to agree with the conclusion of the Chancery court that the stockholders' application for injunctive relief here was tardy and came too late. The stockholders learned of the action of management unofficially on Wednesday, October 27, 1971; they filed this action on Monday, November 1, 1971. Until management changed the date of the meeting, the stockholders had no need of judicial assistance in that connection.

There is no indication of any prior warning of management's intent to take such action; indeed, it appears that an attempt was made by management to conceal its action as long as possible. Moreover, stockholders may not be charged with the duty of anticipating inequitable action by management, and of seeking anticipatory injunctive relief to foreclose such action, simply because the new Delaware Corporation Law makes such inequitable action legally possible.

Accordingly, the judgment below must be reversed and the cause remanded. . . .

Wolcott, C.J. (dissenting):

I do not agree with the majority of the Court in its disposition of this appeal. The plaintiff stockholders concerned in this litigation have, for a considerable period of time, sought to obtain control of the defendant corporation. These attempts took various forms.

In view of the length of time leading up to the immediate events which caused the filing of this action, I agree with the Vice Chancellor that the application for injunctive relief came too late.

I would affirm the judgment below on the basis of the Vice Chancellor's opinion. . . .

Schnell v. Chris-Craft Industries expresses a most fundamental rule of fiduciary duty: Legal power held by a fiduciary may not be deployed in a way that is intended to treat a beneficiary of the duty unfairly. The case law reflecting this broad equitable superintendence of fiduciary power predates the classic academic recognition of this practice. See Adolf Berle, *Corporate Powers as Powers in Trust*, 44 Harv. L. Rev. 1049 (1931). Delaware courts have been willing to use this power, as in *Schnell*, to protect the integrity of the shareholder franchise. We return to this topic, and its implications for hostile takeovers, in Chapter 13. Among the aspects of loyalty is, naturally enough, the obligation not to lie to one to whom the duty extends. Until recently, state law did not go beyond this in regulating communications between directors and shareholders (at least where there was no conflicting interest between the corporation and the director). Thus, state law has traditionally done little to regulate proxy solicitation by management. A plaintiff could always charge the common law tort of fraud if she could prove all of its difficult elements — a knowingly false statement of a material fact, relied upon, with the effect of causing injury. But corporate law itself offered no real assistance to shareholders when their own management sought to solicit their proxies.

Now, however, matters stand differently. Corporation law has evolved since the enactment of the Securities Exchange Act in 1934. Throughout the twentieth century, two large themes stand out. The first is the gradual disappearance of substantive regulation: no more par value for stock, no more required shareholder preemption rights, and no more right to continue an equity interest in the corporation or its successor in a merger. These and similar developments have rendered the corporate form more flexible (or, from a different perspective, more empty). The second theme is the growing importance of fiduciary duties. Courts have gradually become more willing to insert themselves ex post into disputes between shareholders and corporate managers. One example of this is a new, duty-based law of corporate disclosure.

In 1976, the Delaware Supreme Court held that a controlling shareholder making a cash tender offer for stock held by minority shareholders had a fiduciary duty to make full disclosure of all germane facts. See *Lynch v. Vickers Energy Corp.*, 383 A.2d 278 (Del. 1977). There followed a long series of cases applying this principle to corporate directors (e.g., *In re Anderson Clayton Shareholders Litigation*, 519 A.2d 680, 688 (Del. Ch. 1986)) as well as controlling shareholders. The principle was applied to proxy solicitations as well as tender offers. See, e.g., *Kahn v. Roberts*, 679 A.2d 460 (Del. 1996) (collecting cases).

Until recently, most of the Delaware cases minimized potential conflict between state corporate law and the massive body of federal law governing corporate disclosure. They did so in two ways. First, they crafted the state law duty of candor to look like the federal law that preceded it. The basic obligation is the same — to make full disclosure of all material facts, with materiality being similarly defined. Of course, this basic similarity does not ensure identical legal duties in all cases. See Lawrence A. Hamermesh, *Calling Off the Lynch Mob: A Corporate Director's Fiduciary Duty to Disclose*, 49 Vand. L. Rev. 1087 (1996).

Second, the Court of Chancery minimized potential conflict with federal law by limiting the fiduciary duty of candor to circumstances in which a corporation (or a controlling shareholder) asked shareholders to take action of some sort. This meant that mere press releases or other public statements by corporate directors or officers, without a concomitant call for shareholder action, did not violate the duty of candor. The rationale for this limitation was that the state law was concerned with the governance of the corporation, not with disclosures to the market. That is the subject of the federal securities laws.

However, in *Malone v. Brincat*, 722 A.2d 5 (Del. 1998), the Delaware Supreme Court abandoned this limitation. *Malone* was pleaded as a case involving a long-term fraud in which the directors made (or permitted the corporation to make) false filings with the SEC and distributed false financial statements to shareholders. These false statements were alleged to have caused the complete ruin of the company. The Court of Chancery dismissed the suit in deference to SEC regulation of fraud in the public markets. The Delaware Supreme Court affirmed the dismissal of the complaint but stated a different view of the merits that permitted the plaintiffs to replead. In its decision, the Supreme Court asserted: "Whenever directors communicate publicly or directly with shareholders about the corporation's affairs, with or without request for shareholder actions directors have a fiduciary duty . . . to exercise care, good faith and loyalty. . . . [T]he sine qua non of director's fiduciary duty is honesty." 722 A.2d 10. Thus, the Court held that a claim could be stated on the *Malone* facts. Plaintiffs were given the right to replead their claim as a derivative claim or an individual claim.

The court was mindful of the potential overlap with federal law that its ruling might entail.

It cited an earlier case in which it declined to recognize a "fraud on the market" theory of recovery for shareholders. More important though, it implied that the cause of action that it recognized in *Malone* was restricted to plaintiffs who still held their shares. Since these shareholders did not sell their shares, the Delaware court stated that they would not be protected by SEC Rule 10b-5 — the principal federal antifraud provision regulating misleading disclosure in the public markets. Thus, the court attempted to minimize conflict between its holding and federal law.

NORMAL GOVERNANCE: THE DUTY OF CARE

7.1 INTRODUCTION TO THE DUTY OF CARE

The shareholders' right to elect directors is not the law's only strategy for corporate governance. Fiduciary standards also play a role in normal governance, just as they do in agency and partnership law.

The duties of a fiduciary are essentially three. The first, and most basic, is sometimes called the "duty of obedience." This duty plays a significant role in agency law but is less prominent in corporate law. The remaining duties are the duties of loyalty and care (or attention). The duty of loyalty (which we address in Chapter 8) requires that corporate fiduciaries exercise their authority in a good-faith attempt to advance corporate purposes. In particular, it bars corporate officers and directors from competing with the corporation (without informed consent); from misappropriating its property, information, or business opportunities; and especially from transacting business with it on unfair terms. These requirements account for much of the mandatory content of U.S. corporate law.

By contrast, the duty of care is more general. In its classic formulation, it requires that officers and directors act with "the care of an ordinarily prudent person in the same or similar circumstances" in all matters concerning their corporate duties. Despite its sweeping scope, however, the duty of care is less litigated than the duty of loyalty, primarily because the law insulates officers and directors from liability based on negligence (as opposed to knowing misconduct or omissions). In this chapter, we address the duty of care and the insulating law that mitigates its effects on directors and officers. First, however, we offer a brief excursus on the evolution of fiduciary duties at common law.

7.2 THE DUTY OF CARE AND THE NEED TO MITIGATE DIRECTOR RISK AVERSION

From the beginnings of Anglo-American corporate law, courts have maintained that a corporate director must do more than pursue the corporation's interests in good faith; a director also has the duty to act as a reasonable person would in overseeing the company's operations.

An English Court of Chancery case decided in 1742 evidences the foundational nature of the duty of care. The report relates that the King chartered the Charitable Company in the early eighteenth century as a stock company, "to assist poor persons with sums of money by way of loans, and to prevent their falling into the hands of pawnbrokers, &c."[1] It appears that the chief administrative officer of the corporation, with two confederates, soon began to defraud the company by "lending [] more money upon old pledges, without calling in the first sum lent." "The loss which ensued from this mismanagement [was] prodigious . . . not less than 350,000 [pounds]." The liability of those actively engaged in the fraud was easily established by the Lord Chancellor. The more subtle question concerned the possible liability of the "committee-men" (directors), who had not participated in the wrongs, but whose inattention had permitted them to occur. As to them, the Lord Chancellor held that "by accepting of a trust of this sort a person is obligated to execute it with fidelity and reasonable diligence; and it is no excuse to say that they had no benefit from it. . . ."[2] Although we do not know if the directors were forced to pay damages, we do know that the Chancellor appointed a master to determine whether they had acted with reasonable diligence. This much establishes that a director's duty of "reasonable diligence" has been a feature of corporate law for a long time.[3]

How does the law currently express this basic obligation? According to the American Law Institute's (ALI's) Principles of Corporate Governance, a corporate director or officer is required to perform his or her functions (1) in good faith, (2) in a manner that he or she reasonably believes to be in the best interests of the corporation, and (3) with the care that is reasonably expected of an ordinarily prudent person in a comparable position and under similar circumstances.[4] The core of this standard is the level of care that we expect to be exercised by an ordinarily prudent person.[5] This formulation appears to make the duty of care into a negligence rule like any other negligence rule in tort law. However, the duty of care is not just another negligence rule. As we discuss below, there is an important policy reason why a business loss cannot be analogized to a traffic accident or a slip on a banana peel. The reason, bluntly stated, is that corporate directors and officers invest other people's

---

1. *The Charitable Company v. Sutton*, 2 Atk. 400, 406 (Ch. 1742), 26 Eng. Rep. 642 (1742).

2. Id., 26 Eng. Reps. at 645.

3. See, e.g., *Godbold v. Branch Bank of Mobile*, 11 Ala. 191 (1847); *Hodges v. New England Screw Co.*, 1 R.I. 312 (1850); *Bates v. Dresser*, 251 U.S. 524 (1920) (Holmes, J.). It is notable that *Sutton* is not a case in which a loss resulted from a board decision; rather, it was a neglect of attention case. The cases of inattention, rather than poor judgment, are the cases in which one would traditionally find directors liable for breach of care.

4. See ALI, Principles of Corporate Governance §4.01 (1994). See also MBCA §8.30.

5. As of 2005, 40 jurisdictions required that a corporate director discharge the duties of that office in good faith and with a stated standard of care, usually phrased in terms of the care that an ordinarily prudent person would exercise under similar circumstances. Thirty-five of these jurisdictions also expressly required that a director perform these duties in a manner that she reasonably believes to be in the best interests of the corporation. See MBCA §8.30 cmt. 1.

money. They bear the full costs of any personal liability, but they receive only a small fraction of the gains from a risky decision. Liability under a negligence standard might therefore discourage officers and directors from undertaking valuable but risky projects on behalf of shareholders.

Consider the following excerpt from a Delaware Court of Chancery opinion.

GAGLIARDI v. TRIFOODS INTERNATIONAL, INC.
683 A.2d 1049 (Del. Ch. 1996)

ALLEN, C.:

Currently before the Court is a motion to dismiss a shareholders action against the directors of TriFoods International, Inc. . . . In broadest terms the motion raises the question, what must a shareholder plead in order to state a derivative claim to recover corporate losses allegedly sustain[ed] by reason of "mismanagement" unaffected by directly conflicting financial interests? . . .

I start with what I take to be an elementary precept of corporation law: in the absence of facts showing self-dealing or improper motive, a corporate officer or director is not legally responsible to the corporation for losses that may be suffered as a result of a decision that an officer made or that directors authorized in good faith. There is a theoretical exception to this general statement that holds that some decisions may be so "egregious" that liability for losses they cause may follow even in the absence of proof of conflict of interest or improper motivation. The exception, however, has resulted in no awards of money judgments against corporate officers or directors in this jurisdiction. . . .

The rule could rationally be no different. Shareholders can diversify the risks of their corporate investments. Thus, it is in their economic interest for the corporation to accept in rank order all positive net present value investment projects available to the corporation, starting with the highest risk adjusted rate of return first. Shareholders don't want (or shouldn't rationally want) directors to be risk averse. . . .

[But] directors of public companies typically have a very small proportionate ownership interest in their corporations and little or no incentive compensation. Thus, they enjoy (as residual owners) only a very small proportion of any "upside" gains earned by the corporation on risky investment projects. If, however, corporate directors were to be found liable for a corporate loss from a risky project on the ground that the investment was too risky (foolishly risky! stupidly risky! egregiously risky! — you supply the adverb), their liability would be joint and several for the whole loss (with I suppose a right of contribution). Given the scale of operation of modern public corporations, . . . only a very small probability of director liability based on "negligence," "inattention," "waste," etc., could induce a board to avoid authorizing risky investment projects to any extent! Obviously, it is in the shareholders' economic interest to offer sufficient protection to directors from liability for negligence, etc., to allow directors to conclude that, as a practical matter, there is no risk that, if they act in good faith and meet minimal proceduralist standards of attention, they can face liability as a result of a business loss.

The law protects shareholder investment interests against the uneconomic consequences that the presence of such second-guessing risk would have on director action and shareholder wealth in a number of ways. It authorizes corporations to pay for director and officer liability insurance and authorizes corporate indemnification in a broad range of cases, for example. But the first protection against a threat of sub-optimal risk acceptance is the so-called business judgment rule. That "rule" in effect provides that where a director is independent and disinterested, there can be no liability for corporate loss, unless the facts are such that no person could possibly authorize such a transaction if he or she were attempting in good faith to meet their duty. . . ."

As *Gagliardi* states, the law protects corporate officers and directors from liability for breach of the duty of care in many ways, some statutory and some judicial. First, the statutory law authorizes corporations to *indemnify the expenses* (including in some cases the judgment costs) incurred by officers or directors who are sued by reason of their corporate activities. See, e.g., DGCL §145. Second, the statutory law authorizes corporations to purchase liability insurance for their directors and officers, which may even cover some risks that are not subject to indemnification. Third, courts have long recognized the protection of the so-called business judgment rule, as we discuss in Section 7.4. And last, when the business judgment rule proved to be less protective than practitioners had expected,[6] legislatures across the country followed Delaware's lead by authorizing companies to waive monetary liability for directorial acts of negligence or gross negligence. We discuss the first of these statutes, DGCL §102(b)(7), below.

7.3   STATUTORY TECHNIQUES FOR LIMITING DIRECTOR AND OFFICER RISK EXPOSURE

The judge-made business judgment rule is the most fundamental protection against liability for simple mistakes of judgment. But the corporation's statutory power to indemnify losses of corporate officers or directors and its authority to purchase insurance provides officers and directors with the most reliable forms of protection.

7.3.1   Indemnification

Consider indemnification first: Most corporate statutes prescribe mandatory indemnification rights for directors and officers and allow an even broader range of elective indemnification rights. Generally, these statutes authorize corporations to commit to reimburse any agent, employee, officer, or director for reasonable expenses for losses of any sort (attorneys' fees,

---

6. The case of *Smith v. Van Gorkom*, discussed below, was the occasion for this realization.

investigation fees, settlement amounts, and in some instances judgments) arising from any actual or threatened judicial proceeding or investigation. The only limits are that the losses must result from actions undertaken on behalf of the corporation in good faith and that they cannot arise from a criminal conviction. See DGCL §145 (a), (b), (c).

WALTUCH v. CONTICOMMODITY SERVICES, INC.
88 F.3d 87 (2d Cir. 1996)

Jacobs, Cir. J.:

Famed silver trader Norton Waltuch spent $2.2 million in unreimbursed legal fees to defend himself against numerous civil lawsuits and an enforcement proceeding brought by the Commodity Futures Trading Commission (CFTC). In this action under Delaware law, Waltuch seeks indemnification of his legal expenses from his former employer. The district court denied any indemnity, and Waltuch appeals.

NORTON WALTUCH

Norton Waltuch graduated from New Jersey's Fairleigh Dickinson University in the mid-1950s. As a young finance clerk, he became fascinated with the growing futures market and, determined to learn every aspect of the business, took an entry-level position with a futures trading firm.[7] He rose through the ranks of the futures industry and by 1970, at the age of 37, was managing the New York office of ContiCommodity Services. In 1979, Waltuch began placing large bets on the silver futures market on behalf of himself and his wealthy Saudi Arabian clients. His animated behavior on the floor of the New York Commodity Exchange (COMEX) brought attention to his dramatic bids. At the same time, billionaire oil heirs Bunker and Herbert Hunt were also making large investments in silver futures. Together, the Hunts and Waltuch pushed the price of silver to dizzying heights. In a few months, the price of silver climbed from under $10 to an astonishing $50 per ounce. As with many commodities markets, silver futures are vulnerable to the possibility of a speculator illegally "cornering" the market by purchasing a large enough quantity of contracts. Authorities began to suspect that the Hunt brothers and Waltuch were colluding in an effort to corner the silver market. In 1980, COMEX instituted strict trading regulations designed to force the Hunt brothers to sell their investments. The market's subsequent collapse culminated in a 50 percent decline in value on March 27, 1980, a date known as "Silver Thursday."

The silver bubble financially ruined many hapless investors and sent tremors through the banking industry. The Hunt brothers declared bankruptcy and Bunker Hunt was convicted of conspiring to manipulate the market. Norton Waltuch, however, survived criminal investigations and congressional hearings relatively unscathed. Always the savvy investor, he had exited the market before the crash with a $20 million profit.

---

7. Paul Sarnoff, *Silver Bulls* (1980).

As vice-president and chief metals trader for Conticommodity Services, Inc., Waltuch traded silver for the firm's clients, as well as for his own account. In late 1979 and early 1980, the silver price spiked upward as the then-billionaire Hunt brothers and several of Waltuch's foreign clients bought huge quantities of silver future contracts. Just as rapidly, the price fell until (on a day remembered in trading circles as "Silver Thursday") the silver market crashed. Between 1981 and 1985, angry silver specula-tors filed numerous lawsuits against Waltuch and Conticommodity, alleging fraud, market manipulation, and antitrust violations. All of the suits even-tually settled and were dismissed with prejudice, pursuant to settlements in which Conticommodity paid over $35 million to the various suitors. Waltuch himself was dismissed from the suits with no settlement contribu-tion. His unreimbursed legal expenses in these actions total approximately $1.2 million.

Waltuch was also the subject of an enforcement proceeding brought by the CFTC, charging him with fraud and market manipulation. The proceed-ing was settled, with Waltuch agreeing to a penalty that included a $100,000 fine and a six-month ban on buying or selling futures contracts from any exchange floor. Waltuch spent $1 million in unreimbursed legal fees in the CFTC proceeding.

Waltuch brought suit in the United States District Court for the Southern District of New York against Conticommodity and its parent company, Continental Grain Co. (together "Conti"), for indemnification of his unreimbursed expenses. Only two of Waltuch's claims reached us on appeal.

Waltuch first claims that Article Ninth of Conticommodity's articles of incorporation requires Conti to indemnify him for his expenses in both the private and CFTC actions. Conti responded that this claim was barred by sub-section (a) of §145 of Delaware's General Corporation Law, which permits indemnification only if the corporate officer acted "in good faith," something that Waltuch had not established. Waltuch countered that subsection (f) of the same statute permits a corporation to grant indemnification rights out-side the limits of subsection (a), and that Conticommodity did so with Article Ninth (which has no stated good-faith limitation). The district court held that, notwithstanding §145(f), Waltuch could recover under Article Ninth only if Waltuch met the "good faith" requirement of §145(a). On the factual issue of whether Waltuch had acted "in good faith," the court denied Conti's sum-mary judgment motion and cleared the way for trial. The parties then stipu-lated that they would forgo trial on the issue of Waltuch's "good faith," agree to an entry of final judgment against Waltuch on his claim under Article Ninth and §145(f), and allow Waltuch to take an immediate appeal of the judgment to this Court. Thus, as to Waltuch's first claim, the only question left was how to interpret §§145(a) and 145(f), assuming Waltuch acted with less than "good faith." . . .

Waltuch's second claim is that subsection (c) of §145 requires Conti to indemnify him because he was "successful on the merits or otherwise" in the private lawsuits. . . .

I

Article Ninth, on which Waltuch bases his first claim, is categorical and contains no requirement of "good faith":

> The Corporation shall indemnify and hold harmless each of its incumbent or former directors, officers, employees and agents . . . against expenses actually and necessarily incurred by him in connection with the defense of any action, suit or proceeding threatened, pending or completed, in which he is made a party, by reason of his serving in or having held such position or capacity, except in relation to matters as to which he shall be adjudged in such action, suit or proceeding to be liable for negligence or misconduct in the performance of duty.

Conti argues that §145(a) of Delaware's General Corporation Law, which does contain a "good faith" requirement, fixes the outer limits of a corporation's power to indemnify; Article Ninth is thus invalid under Delaware law, says Conti, to the extent that it requires indemnification of officers who have acted in bad faith.

. . . Waltuch argues that §145(a) is not an exclusive grant of indemnification power, because §145(f) expressly allows corporations to indemnify officers in a manner broader than that set out in §145(a). Waltuch contends that the "nonexclusivity" language in §145(f) is a separate grant of indemnification power, not limited by the good faith clause that governs the power granted in §145(a). Conti on the other hand contends that §145(f) must be limited to "public policies," one of which is that a corporation may indemnify its officers only if they act in "good faith." . . .

No Delaware court has decided the very issue presented here; but the applicable cases tend to support the proposition that a corporation's grant of indemnification rights cannot be inconsistent with the substantive statutory provisions of §145, notwithstanding §145(f). . . .

The "consistency" rule suggested by [the] Delaware cases is reinforced by our reading of §145 as a whole. Subsections (a) (indemnification for third-party actions) and (b) (similar indemnification for derivative suits) expressly grant a corporation the power to indemnify directors, officers, and others, if they "acted in good faith and in a manner reasonably believed to be in or not opposed to the best interest of the corporation." These provisions thus limit the scope of the power that they confer. They are permissive in the sense that a corporation may exercise less than its full power to grant the indemnification rights set out in these provisions. By the same token, subsection (f) permits the corporation to grant additional rights: the rights provided in the rest of §145 "shall not be deemed exclusive of any other rights to which those seeking indemnification may be entitled." But crucially, subsection (f) merely acknowledges that one seeking indemnification may be entitled to "other rights" (of indemnification or otherwise); it does not speak in terms of corporate power, and therefore cannot be read to free a corporation from the "good faith" limit explicitly imposed in subsections (a) and (b).

An alternative construction of these provisions would effectively force us to ignore certain explicit terms of the statute. §145(a) gives Conti the power to indemnify Waltuch "if he acted in good faith and in a manner reasonably believed to be in or not opposed to the best interest of the corporation." This statutory limit must mean that there is no power to indemnify Waltuch if he did not act in good faith. . . .

When the Legislature intended a subsection of §145 to augment the powers limited in subsection (a), it set out the additional powers expressly. Thus subsection (g) explicitly allows a corporation to circumvent the "good faith" clause of subsection (a) by purchasing a directors' and officers' liability insurance policy. Significantly, that subsection is framed as a grant of corporate power:

> A corporation shall have power to purchase and maintain insurance on behalf of any person who is or was a director, officer, employee or agent of the corporation . . . against any liability asserted against him and incurred by him in any such capacity, or arising out of his status as such, *whether or not the corporation would have the power to indemnify him against such liability under this section.*

The italicized passage reflects the principle that corporations have the power under §145 to indemnify in some situations and not in others. Since §145(f) is neither a grant of corporate power nor a limitation on such power, subsection (g) must be referring to the limitations set out in §145(a) and the other provisions of §145 that describe corporate power. . . .

Waltuch argues . . . that reading §145(a) to bar the indemnification of officers who acted in bad faith would render §145(f) meaningless. This argument misreads §145(f). . . . Delaware commentators have identified various indemnification rights that are "beyond those provided by statute," . . . and that are at the same time consistent with the statute . . . .

We . . . conclude that §145(f) is not rendered meaningless . . . by the conclusion that a Delaware corporation lacks power to indemnify an officer or director "unless [he] 'acted in good faith and in a manner reasonably believed to be in or not opposed to the best interest of the corporation.'" As a result, . . . Conti's Article Ninth, which would require indemnification of Waltuch even if he acted in bad faith, is inconsistent with §145(a) and thus exceeds the scope of a Delaware corporation's power to indemnify. Since Waltuch has agreed to forgo his opportunity to prove . . . good faith, he is not entitled to indemnification under Article Ninth.

II

Unlike §145(a), which grants a discretionary indemnification power, §145(c) affirmatively requires corporations to indemnify its officers and directors for the "successful" defense of certain claims.

Waltuch argues that he was "successful on the merits or otherwise" in the private lawsuits, because they were dismissed with prejudice without any payment or assumption of liability by him. Conti argues that the claims against Waltuch were dismissed only because of Conti's $35 million settlement payments, and that this payment was contributed, in part, "on behalf of Waltuch." . . .

No Delaware court has applied §145(c) in the context of indemnification stemming from the settlement of civil litigation. One lower court, however, has applied that subsection to an analogous case in the criminal context, and has illuminated the link between "vindication" and the statutory phrase, "successful on the merits or otherwise." In *Merritt-Chapman & Scott Corp. v. Wolfson*, 321 A.2d 138 (Del. Super. Ct. 1974), the corporation's agents were charged with several counts of criminal conduct. A jury found them guilty on some counts, but deadlocked on the others. The agents entered into a "settlement" with the prosecutor's office by pleading nolo contendere to one of the counts in exchange for the dropping of the rest. *Id.* at 140. The agents claimed entitlement to mandatory indemnification under §145(c) as to the counts that were dismissed. . . . [The Court agreed.]. . .

Under *Merritt*'s holding, then, vindication, when used as a synonym for "success" under §145(c) does not mean moral exoneration. Escape from an adverse judgment or other detriment, for whatever reason, is determinative. According to *Merritt*, the only question a court may ask is what the result was, not why it was.

Conti's contention that, because of its $35 million settlement payments, Waltuch's settlement without payment should not really count as settlement without payment, is inconsistent with the rule in *Merritt*. Here, Waltuch was sued, and the suit was dismissed without his having paid a settlement. Under the approach taken in *Merritt,* it is not our business to ask why this result was reached. Once Waltuch achieved his settlement gratis, he achieved success "on the merits or otherwise." And as we know from *Merritt,* success is sufficient to constitute vindication (at least for the purposes of §145(c)). Waltuch's settlement thus vindicated him. . . .

This conclusion comports with the reality that civil judgments and settlements are ordinarily expressed in terms of cash rather than moral victory. . . .

For all of these reasons, we agree with Waltuch, that he is entitled to indemnification under §145(c) for his expenses pertaining to private lawsuits. . . .

NOTE AND QUESTIONS

1. As a matter of statutory construction, this result seems a bit of a stretch. DGCL §145(f) is textually quite independent of §145(a) according to its terms. Yet, as a matter of good policy, this certainly seems like the right result. Was there another way to reach this result?

2. Does this decision suggest that Waltuch is entitled to reimbursement for *all* of his legal expenses including those incurred while defending against the CFTC action?

3. *Hermelin v. K-V Pharmaceutical Company,* 54 A. 3d 1093 (2012) further clarified when indemnification is available in Delaware. On the facts there, plaintiff Hermelin (the former CEO) could seek indemnification in two

ways. First, under §145(c), the firm is *required* to indemnify Hermelin if he obtained "success on the merits or otherwise." Whether he had succeeded under this standard turned on the legal result. Hermelin could not claim success in criminal proceedings where he pled guilty to all of the charges the prosecution brought. Nor could he claim "success on the merits or otherwise" when the government sought to exclude him from particular activities for life and instead only obtained an exclusion for 20 years which, given his age, was no different than a lifetime ban. However, his failure to show success did not affect his contractual claim for indemnification under §145(a), providing that his company had an applicable indemnification agreement in place and he had acted in good faith. As his firm offered such an indemnification agreement, the Court ordered a plenary trial to determine whether Hermelin acted in good faith. What sorts of evidence might be relevant in ascertaining good faith?

7.3.2   Directors and Officers Insurance

The second important aspect of legislation designed to insulate officers and directors from liability for carelessness are the provisions authorizing corporations to pay the premia on directors and officers liability insurance. See, e.g., DGCL §145(f); MBCA §8.57. These group policies, financed by the corporation, place the financial muscle of an insurance company behind the company's pledge to make whole those directors who incur liability as a result of decisions taken in good faith on behalf of their corporations.

These provisions pose an interesting question: Why do corporations purchase insurance for directors and officers rather than raising salaries and board fees to allow directors and officers to purchase insurance on their own accounts? We suppose that the answer lies in the transaction costs and in the details of the institutional environment — which is to say that we don't know the answer. However, several possibilities readily come to mind. First, directors and officers (D&O) insurance might be cheaper if the company acts as a central bargaining agent for all of its officers and directors. Second, there may be advantages when the company, its insurer, and its directors and officers mount a coordinated defense. Third, tax law may favor firm-wide insurance coverage, since D&O insurance is a deductible expense for corporations. Finally, directors may under-invest in D&O insurance if left to themselves, because they may not internalize all the benefits that shareholders obtain from it (e.g., directors receive only a fraction of the benefits that shareholders receive from approving risky, yet higher net present value, projects).

In early 2005, directors of WorldCom and Enron made headlines by paying out of their own pockets to settle shareholder lawsuits arising under federal securities laws. At WorldCom, the independent directors agreed to pay $18 million (20 percent of their collective net worth) toward a

$54 million settlement for their role in WorldCom's $11 billion accounting fraud. At Enron, ten directors agreed to pay $13 million toward a $168 million settlement for their role in Enron's fraudulent accounting practices (but had collectively made $250 million (pre-tax) on the sale of their Enron shares). The natural question arises: Where was the D&O insurance? Most academic commentators and practitioners agree that out-of-pocket liability arose in these two cases due to a "perfect storm" set of facts: Both companies were bankrupt and so could not indemnify the directors; both companies had well-documented paper trails of director inattention and inaction; activist pension funds such as the New York State retirement fund were intent on making examples out of these two companies, which were the largest (WorldCom) and second-largest (Enron) bankruptcies in U.S. history; and the enormous potential liabilities in both cases could have easily exceeded the companies' D&O policies. Consistent with this "perfect storm" conclusion, Professors Black, Chefffins, and Klausner report only one other case (*Van Gorkom*) in which outside directors actually paid out-of-pocket for either damages or legal expenses under U.S. securities law or corporate law for duty of care related claims;[8] and even this case is not really an example of out-of-pocket liability, for reasons described below.

7.4 JUDICIAL PROTECTION: THE BUSINESS JUDGMENT RULE

Long before legislatures acted to protect directors and officers from liability arising from breach of the duty of care, courts fashioned their own protection. Over roughly the past 150 years, U.S. courts have evolved the so-called business judgment rule.[9] Because corporate law varies with each state, there is no canonical statement of the "business judgment rule" across all states. The core idea, however, is universal: Courts should not second-guess good-faith decisions made by independent and disinterested directors. Put differently, the business judgment rule means that courts will not decide (or allow a jury to decide) whether the decisions of corporate boards are either substantively reasonable by the "reasonable prudent person" test or sufficiently well informed by the same test. In the following case, the shareholder plaintiffs had a pretty good argument that the board's decision was not "reasonably prudent." Nevertheless, the court refused to inquire whether an ordinarily prudent person would have made this same decision.

8. Bernard S. Black, Brian R. Cheffins & Michael D. Klausner, *Outside Director Liability*, 58 Stan. L. Rev. 1055 (2006).
9. See generally S. Samuel Arsht, *The Business Judgment Rule Revisited*, 8 Hofstra L. Rev. 93 (1979).

KAMIN v. AMERICAN EXPRESS CO.
383 N.Y.S, 2d 807 (1976)

GREENFIELD, J.:

In this stockholders' derivative action, the individual defendants, who are the directors of the American Express Company, move for an order dismissing the complaint for failure to state a cause of action . . . and alternatively, for summary judgment. . . . The complaint is brought derivatively by two minority stockholders of the American Express Company, asking for a declaration that a certain dividend in kind is a waste of corporate assets, directing the defendants not to proceed with the distribution, or, in the alternative, for monetary damages. . . . It is the defendants' contention that, conceding everything in the complaint, no viable cause of action is made out.

[T]he complaint alleges that in 1972 American Express acquired for investment 1,954,418 shares of common stock of Donaldson, Lufken and Jenrette, Inc. (hereafter DLJ), a publicly traded corporation, at a cost of $29.9 million. It is further alleged that the current market value of those shares is approximately $4.0 million. On July 28, 1975, it is alleged, the Board of Directors of American Express declared a special dividend to all stockholders of record pursuant to which the shares of DLJ would be distributed in kind. Plaintiffs contend further that if American Express were to sell the DLJ shares on the market, it would sustain a capital loss of $25 million, which could be offset against taxable capital gains on other investments. Such a sale, they allege, would result in tax savings to the company of approximately $8 million, which would not be available in the case of the distribution of DLJ shares to stockholders. . . .

It is apparent that all the previously-mentioned allegations of the complaint go to the question of the exercise by the Board of Directors of business judgment in deciding how to deal with the DLJ shares. The crucial allegation which must be scrutinized to determine the legal sufficiency of the complaint is paragraph 19, which alleges:

> All of the defendant Directors engaged in or acquiesced in or negligently permitted the declaration and payment of the Dividend in violation of the fiduciary duty owed by them to Amex to care for and preserve Amex's assets in the same manner as a man of average prudence would care for his own property. . . .

[T]here is no claim of fraud or self-dealing, and no contention that there was any bad faith or oppressive conduct. The law is quite clear as to what is necessary to ground a claim for actionable wrongdoing. In actions by stockholders, which assail the acts of their directors or trustees, courts will not interfere unless the powers have been illegally or unconscientiously executed; or unless it be made to appear that the acts were fraudulent or collusive, and destructive of the rights of the stockholders. Mere errors of judgment are not sufficient as grounds for equity interference, for the powers of those entrusted with corporate management are largely discretionary. . . .

More specifically, the question of whether or not a dividend is to be declared or a distribution of some kind should be made is exclusively a matter of business judgment for the Board of Directors.

. . . Courts will not interfere with such discretion unless it be first made to appear that the directors have acted or are about to act in bad faith and for a dishonest purpose. It is for the directors to say . . . when and to what extent dividends shall be declared. . . . The statute confers upon the directors this power, and the minority stockholders are not in a position to question this right, so long as the directors are acting in good faith. . . .

Thus, a complaint must be dismissed if all that is presented is a decision to pay dividends rather than pursuing some other course of conduct. . . . Courts have more than enough to do in adjudicating legal rights and devising remedies for wrongs. The directors' room rather than the courtroom is the appropriate forum for thrashing out purely business questions which will have an impact on profits, market prices, competitive situations, or tax advantages. . . .

It is not enough to allege, as plaintiffs do here, that the directors made an imprudent decision, which did not capitalize on the possibility of using a potential capital loss to offset capital gains. More than imprudence or mistaken judgment must be shown. . . .

Nor does this appear to be a case in which a potentially valid cause of action is inartfully stated. . . . The affidavits of the defendants and the exhibits annexed thereto demonstrate that the objections raised by the plaintiffs to the proposed dividend action were carefully considered and unanimously rejected by the Board at a special meeting called precisely for that purpose at the plaintiffs' request. The minutes of the special meeting indicate that the defendants were fully aware that a sale rather than a distribution of the DLJ shares might result in the realization of a substantial income tax saving. Nevertheless, they concluded that there were countervailing considerations primarily with respect to the adverse effect such a sale, realizing a loss of $25 million, would have on the net income figures in the American Express financial statement. Such a reduction of net income would have a serious effect on the market value of the publicly traded American Express stock. This was not a situation in which the defendant directors totally overlooked facts called to their attention. They gave them consideration, and attempted to view the total picture in arriving at their decision. While plaintiffs contend that according to their accounting consultants the loss on the DLJ stock would still have to be charged against current earnings even if the stock were distributed, the defendants' accounting experts assert that the loss would be a charge against earnings only in the event of a sale, whereas in the event of distribution of the stock as a dividend, the proper accounting treatment would be to charge the loss only against surplus. While the chief accountant for the SEC raised some question as to the appropriate accounting treatment of this transaction, there was no basis for any action to be taken by the SEC with respect to the American Express financial statement.

The only hint of self-interest which is raised . . . is that four of the twenty directors were officers and employees of American Express and members of its Executive Incentive Compensation Plan. Hence, it is suggested, by virtue of the action taken earnings may have been overstated and their compensation affected thereby. Such a claim . . . standing alone can hardly be regarded as sufficient to support an inference of self-dealing. There is no claim or showing that the four company directors dominated and controlled the sixteen outside members of the Board. Certainly, every action taken by the Board has some impact on earnings and may therefore affect the compensation of those whose earnings are keyed to profits. That does not disqualify the inside directors, nor does it put every policy adopted by the Board in question. All directors have an obligation, using sound business judgment, to maximize income for the benefit of all persons having a stake in the welfare of the corporate entity. . . . The directors are entitled to exercise their honest business judgment on the information before them, and to act within their corporate powers. That they may be mistaken, that other courses of action might have differing consequences, or that their action might benefit some shareholders more than others presents no basis for the super-imposition of judicial judgment, so long as it appears that the directors have been acting in good faith. The question of to what extent a dividend shall be declared and the manner in which it shall be paid is ordinarily subject only to the qualification that the dividend be paid out of surplus (Business Corporation Law Section 510, subd. b). The Court will not interfere unless a clear case is made out of fraud, oppression, arbitrary action, or breach of trust.

. . . Accordingly, the motion by the defendants for summary judgment and dismissal of the complaint is granted. . . .

QUESTIONS

1. Assuming the board acted in good faith in *Kamin*, what is the board's view about the efficiency of the capital markets? If the capital markets are very highly efficient in fact, what does the *Kamin* transaction imply about the wealth-creating impact of this action?

2. The empirical literature in finance suggests that alternative accounting characterizations do not affect share price if they are made publicly and are well understood. Corporate directors and managers typically care a great deal about accounting changes that might lower reported earnings or revenues. If the studies are correct and the market sees through accounting treatments, why might businesspeople act in this way?

7.4.1   Understanding the Business Judgment Rule

Upon reflection, the business judgment rule seems more mysterious than it first appears. More precisely, there are three mysteries. The first is: What exactly *is* this rule? Second, is it a "rule" at all or a standard of judicial review that doubles as a kind of informal pleading requirement for plaintiffs who wish to initiate a shareholder action? Third, how does the rule or standard of review interact with the duty of care?

There is, as we have said, no single canonical statement of the business judgment rule. The closest one can come may be the formulation contained in the American Bar Association's *Corporate Director's Guidebook*, where it is said that a *decision* constitutes a valid business judgment (and gives rise to no liability for ensuing loss) when it (1) is made by *disinterested directors* or officers, (2) who have become *informed* before exercising judgment, and (3) who exercise judgment in a *good-faith* effort to advance corporate interests.[10] Seen as a rule, this formula might be understood as a roundabout statement of directorial authority. Disinterested directors are supposed to make informed decisions for the corporation in good faith. However, the law cannot order directors to make correct or profitable decisions by fiat. It follows that disinterested directors who act deliberately and in good faith are discharging their duties and should not be liable for any resulting losses, no matter how stupid their decisions may seem ex post. But if the *Guidebook* formula is viewed instead as framing a standard of judicial review, it is not so much about director conduct as it is about the circumstances in which a court will entertain a challenge to a board decision.

The doctrinal gain from framing business judgment as a standard of judicial review rather than a marker of directorial authority is that it avoids an unseemly clash with the duty of care mandate that directors act with "the care of an ordinarily prudent person in . . . similar circumstances." Courts wielding business judgment as a standard of review can dismiss lawsuits without commenting on the (mis)conduct that they allege. If, on cursory review, plaintiffs cannot submit plausible and specific allegations that board decisions were conflicted, made in bad faith, or manifestly irrational, the complaint is dismissed. End of story.

The "rule" and the "review" versions of the business judgment rule are both common in corporate law jurisprudence. Delaware courts have come to favor the review concept over the last two decades, although the rule concept dominated in prior years as the *Gagliardi* excerpt above suggests. Thus, in terms of the first mystery we have made progress, even if we have not entirely resolved whether the business judgment rule is a rule, a standard of review, or some quantum legal concept somewhere in between.

But the next mystery is why the law needs a business judgment rule at all? If one takes the "rule" notion seriously, a reasonably informed and unconflicted director acting in what she believes to be in the company's best interest fulfills her legal duties. There is no actionable conduct and no need for insulation. If one favors the "review" notion, why not just say that shareholders lack standing to sue without a specific and plausible allegation of a conflicted board decision? Either version of the business judgment rule — or perhaps no mention of it at all — can get the job done. So then why bother to have a business judgment rule?

There are two reasons, we believe. First, the business judgment rule converts what would otherwise be a question of fact — whether the financially disinterested directors who authorized this money-losing transaction exercised the same care as would a reasonable person in similar circumstances — into

---

10. See American Bar Assn., *Corporate Director's Guidebook* (7th ed. 2019); see also American Law Institute, Principles of Corporate Governance: Analysis and Recommendations §4.01(c) (1994); MBCA §8.30.

a question of law for the court to decide. Recall that courts decide questions of law, while juries ordinarily decide questions of fact. So, the business judgment rule insulates disinterested directors from jury trials, which encourages the dismissal of some claims before trial and allows judicial resolution of the remaining case-based claims that go to trial. And, second, it also means that the question, "Was the standard of care breached?," converts to questions of whether the directors' decisions were truly disinterested and independent and not so inexplicable as to raise questions about good faith. In most circumstances, courts are extremely reluctant to infer that directors lack good faith based on the outcome of board decisions.[11]

What, then, underlies residual ambiguity over whether the business judgment rule is a rule or a standard of judicial review? With some hesitation, we offer the conjecture that there are two different policy objectives embedded in the rule (or standard of review). One is the straightforward concern addressed in *Gagliardi* that negligence-based liability inclines corporate officers and directors to favor low-risk, low-payout decisions at a significant cost to shareholders, since members of management would face personal liability if a high-risk, high-return decision went awry. This concern doubtlessly motivates all forms of liability insulation enjoyed by corporate decision-makers, including indemnification, D&O insurance, and charter waivers of liability addressed in Section 7.4.3 below. In fact, the legal technology insulating directors from personal liability has progressed since the mid-1980s. Directors of public corporations no longer need to rely on the business judgment rule as a first line of defense, although business judgment has become, if anything, even more prominent in shareholder litigation. This points to its second function in shareholder litigation, namely, providing courts with an efficient device for screening out dubious suits while allowing small numbers of promising actions to proceed.

We have no reason to believe that the business judgment rule has been intentionally adapted to this screening function. Later chapters address some of the relevant materials. But putting aside speculative conjectures, one might still wonder why, if the business judgment rule is the puppet master, we bother with the duty of care at all? This is the third mystery: Why *announce* a legal duty to behave as a reasonable director would behave but *apply* a rule that *no good-faith decision* gives rise to liability as long as no financial conflict of interest is involved?

The answer must be that there is social value to announcing a standard ("you must act as a reasonable person would act") that is not enforced with a liability rule. But how? We suggest that when corporate lawyers charge directors with their legal duty of care, most board members will decide how to act based on several considerations, not on their risk of personal liability alone. Nonlegal sanctions such as personal reputation may affect some directors, but many more, we suspect, will be motivated by a simple desire to do the right thing whether or not personal liability is at risk. For such people, articulating

---

11. There is an exception in cases involving a change in corporate control, where directors may have an "entrenchment interest."

the standard of care has the pedagogic function of informing them just what "doing the right thing" means under the circumstances.

7.4.2 The Duty of Care in Takeover Cases: A Note on *Smith v. Van Gorkom*

One of the most interesting features of corporation law over the period 1985-2000 has been the evolution of the law of directors' and officers' duties in the context of hostile takeover attempts. This story is told in Chapter 13 but will be prefaced here. It begins with an unusual 3-2 Delaware Supreme Court decision in 1985, *Smith v. Van Gorkom*,[12] which was met with considerable consternation by the corporate bar. Most corporate law casebooks include an edited version of *Van Gorkom* in their materials on the duty of care because it treats the directors' decision to sign a merger agreement as a breach of their duty of care. Thus, the opinion announces itself to be one about the duty of care — and a unique one at that, insofar as it holds financially disinterested directors personally liable for the consequences of their business decision. By contrast, we believe that subsequent developments have shown *Smith v. Van Gorkom* to be the first in a series of cases in which the Delaware courts struggled to work out a new corporate law of takeovers. Thus, *Van Gorkom* has little to teach about the duty of care in ordinary business decisions of the sort addressed by *Kamin* and *Gagliardi*. Nevertheless, because *Van Gorkom* is an important case that employs the vocabulary of the duty of care, we briefly describe it here.

Van Gorkom arose from an agreement between the Trans Union Corporation and a corporation controlled by the Pritzker family of Chicago. Trans Union had among its assets a substantial net operating loss (NOL) that, under the tax law of the day, could be carried forward for only a limited number of years. During that period, however, the loss could be used to reduce current taxable income. Unhappily, Trans Union was not producing enough net income to use up the carryforward, and thus a valuable asset (the NOL) was being wasted. Trans Union was managed by a board comprised of senior business luminaries from the Chicago area and had as a CEO Jerome Van Gorkom, who had headed the firm for a long time and was now looking toward retirement. The stock had been selling at about $35 per share. Van Gorkom, with little outside advice (no investment banker, no outside lawyer) and little advice from senior staff, set about to arrange a merger agreement with Mr. Pritzker's entity. He discussed the matter with Mr. Jay Pritzker, the leader of the family's business, and Pritzker offered Van Gorkom the cash price that Van Gorkom asked for, $55 per share. At a quickly called board meeting, the board approved the transaction and approved certain "deal protection" features in the merger agreement (see Section 12.6.5 below). No director was alleged to have any financial relationship to Mr. Pritzker or his companies.

---

12. 488 A.2d 858 (Del. 1985).

A Trans Union shareholder sued, alleging that the directors had breached their duty of care in approving the Pritzker offer. While the price represented a large premium over the market price of the company's stock, it was alleged that the board had not acted in an informed manner in agreeing to the deal. A year earlier, the Delaware court had addressed the duty-of-care liability standard in a decision involving self-dealing and management compensation and had declared that directors breached their duty of care only if they were "grossly negligent."[13] Extending this holding against all expectations at the time, the *Van Gorkom* court held that the Trans Union directors had been grossly negligent in their decision making and therefore could not claim the protections of the business judgment rule.

The case was remanded to the Chancery Court for a determination of the value of the Trans Union shares at the time of the board's decision, and for an award of damages to the extent that the fair value exceeded $55 per share. The case was settled prior to this determination for an additional $1.87 per share, or $23.5 million in total. The Trans Union D&O policy covered the first $10 million, which was the policy limit, and nearly all of the remaining $13.5 million was paid by the Pritzker family, apparently motivated by the view that Van Gorkom and the Trans Union board had done nothing wrong.

Van Gorkom was the first Delaware case to actually hold directors liable for breach of the duty of care in a case in which the board had made a business decision. The very few previous cases that had imposed liability for breach of the duty of care had done so in cases in which the board had failed to prevent a corporate fraud. *Van Gorkom* was a shocking result at the time and led to immediate revision in statutory law, to which we now turn. A fuller understanding of the case must await our discussion of the law of mergers and acquisitions.

7.4.3 Additional Statutory Protection: Authorization for Charter Provisions Waiving Liability for Due Care Violations

The immediate reaction to the *Van Gorkom* case was, first, a dramatic rise in the level of premia charged by insurance companies for director and officer (D&O) liability policies and, second, the enactment of §102(b)(7) of the Delaware General Corporation Law. Section 102(b)(7) validated charter amendments that provide that a corporate director has no liability for losses caused by transactions in which the director had no conflicting financial interest or otherwise violated the duty of loyalty.

Between 1985 and 1995, approximately 40 other states followed Delaware's lead in authorizing the release of damage claims for breach of a duty of care for directors. In Delaware, well over 90 percent of public corporations

---

13. *Aronson v. Lewis*, 473 A.2d 805, 812 (Del. 1984). The gross negligence standard, by the way, can be understood as one more way in which courts can articulate a duty of "reasonable care" but enforce a more director-protective standard.

in a large sample had, by 1990, passed charter provisions eliminating liability to the full extent permitted by the statute.[14] Professor Roberta Romano provides an astute analysis of the explosion of D&O liability premia in the mid-1980s (occasioned in part by Delaware case law) and the consequent popularity of liability-limiting statutes in state legislatures. Among other interesting points, Romano reports that insurance companies did not lower premia in response to the passage of §102(b)(7) and that the plaintiffs' bar did not oppose the new legislation.[15] Does this suggest that §102(b)(7) is ineffective? If so, it is news to institutional investors, who generally support charter amendments waiving directorial liability, presumably because, as sophisticated investors, they understand that their self-interest lies in encouraging risk taking by directors.

QUESTIONS

1. Does Delaware's director liability statute raise issues different from those raised by the latitude Delaware firms enjoy to purchase personal liability insurance for their directors and officers? See DGCL §145(g). Could DGCL §102(b)(7) be viewed as simply allowing firms to "self-insure" directors against personal liability arising from gross negligence?

2. Is there reason to distrust a charter amendment, duly approved by shareholders, that eliminates director liability for gross negligence? Why might fully informed investors vote for such an amendment if it were not in their own interests? If the fact of informed shareholder approval of such a liability waiver might be consistent either with the advancement of shareholder economic interests or with a collective action disability of some sort, what might be an empirical methodology to estimate which interpretation of such approval is more likely correct?

3. Statutes such as DGCL §102(b)(7) can be viewed as a device for screening out some or all shareholder suits based on duty-of-care allegations. Is there reason to believe that such actions might be systematically less likely to increase shareholder welfare than duty of loyalty (i.e., conflict of interest) suits? Why? What alternatives, besides the approach used in §102(b)(7), might be worth considering for screening out some shareholder suits? Consider §1701.59, Ohio General Corporation Law (2006).

7.5   THE BOARD'S DUTY TO MONITOR: LOSSES "CAUSED" BY BOARD PASSIVITY

So far, we have discussed the possible liability of directors for failing to take reasonable care in making business decisions that lead to financial losses. We

---

14. Roberta Romano, *Corporate Governance in the Aftermath of the Insurance Crisis*, 39 Emory L.J. 1155, 1160-1161 (1990).

15. Id.

now turn to the related question: What is the scope of director liability for losses that arise, not from business decisions, but rather from causes that the board might arguably have deflected but did not? The business judgment rule protects boards' *decisions*. In fact, however, the relatively few cases that actually impose liability on directors for breach of the duty of care are not cases in which a decision proved disastrously wrong, but cases, like the Enron collapse of 2001, in which directors simply failed to do anything under circumstances in which it is later determined that a reasonably alert person would have taken action.[16]

Directors' incentives are far less likely to be distorted by liability imposed for passive violations of the standard of care than for liability imposed for erroneous decisions. We should not be surprised that actual liability is more likely to arise from a failure to supervise or detect fraud than from an erroneous business decision. Nevertheless, given the disjunction between the scale of operations of many public corporations and the scale of the personal wealth of typical individual directors, the risk of liability for inactivity may still deter talented persons from serving on corporate boards. Despite this danger, the astonishingly rapid collapse of the Enron Corporation in 2001 suggested to many observers that boards may generally be too easily manipulated by company officers. As a corrective, some of these observers believe that the sharp prod of potential liability ought to be more in evidence. But liability for losses in these huge enterprises is a crude ex post method to force appropriate attention. Losses in the Enron case were in the many tens of billions of dollars. Liability for the smallest percentage of this loss would financially destroy corporate directors and would make board service to others desperately unappealing. How then are incentives for director attention to be created that do not deter service? We can, at least, say it cannot be done scientifically.

In this section, we review four cases dealing with directors who are charged with breaching their fiduciary duties by not sufficiently monitoring the corporation and thus by not preventing a loss that the corporation incurred. The seminal case in this field is *Caremark*. However, we begin with some precursors to it that laid the foundation, in part, for its development. We then discuss *Caremark* and examine where its progeny are taking the so-called "duty to monitor."

7.5.1   Prologue to *Caremark*

FRANCIS v. UNITED JERSEY BANK
432 A.2d 814 (N.J. 1981)

[Pritchard & Baird, Inc. was a reinsurance broker that arranged contracts between insurance companies that wrote large policies and other companies

---

16. Recall that the earliest case we find is the 1742 decision of *The Charitable Company v. Sutton*, noted above, in which the board was charged with failing to uncover a fraud. See also the often-cited U.S. Supreme Court case of *Briggs v. Spaulding*, 141 U.S. 132 (1891).

in order to share the risks of those policies thereby avoiding the possibility of a catastrophic loss for any one of them. In this industry, the company that sells insurance to the client pays a portion of the premium to the reinsurance broker, who deducts its commission and forwards the balance to the reinsuring company. The broker thus handles large amounts of money as a fiduciary for its clients.

By 1975, the corporation was bankrupt. This action was brought by the trustees in bankruptcy against Mrs. Pritchard and the bank as administrator of her husband's estate. As to Mrs. Pritchard, the principal claim was that she had been negligent in the conduct of her duties as a director of the corporation. She died during the pendency of the proceedings, and her executrix was substituted as defendant.]

THE FALL OF THE HOUSE OF PRITCHARD[17]

In the mid-1940s, Charles Pritchard, Sr., and George Baird founded one of the first domestic brokerages in the nascent American reinsurance industry. Under the leadership of Charles Pritchard, Sr., Pritchard & Baird became one of America's largest and most prestigious reinsurance intermediaries. After Baird retired in 1964, the Pritchards became the firm's sole shareholders, senior officers, and directors. In 1968, the Pritchard sons, Charles, Jr., and William, assumed sole responsibility for the management of the family firm due to the failing health of their father. Though they were well educated and raised in the family business, Charles, Jr., and William were cut from an altogether different cloth than their father. Where he was moderate, they were greedy; where he was conservative, they were risk-takers; and where he appears to have had integrity, they were unscrupulous.

For several years, the younger Pritchards financed their extravagant lifestyles by misappropriating more than $10 million held in trust by their reinsurance company. But eventually the brothers were discovered, forced into personal bankruptcy, and escaped lengthy prison sentences by a hair's breadth. Shortly thereafter, trustees — including Mr. Francis, the plaintiff in the civil case — were appointed to gather and administer the assets of the various estates. In April 1976, the bankruptcy court directed the trustees for Pritchard & Baird to bring suit against members of the Pritchard family to recover the more than $10 million of client funds misappropriated under the guise of "shareholder loans." Claims were initially filed against all three directors of the company, but the Pritchard brothers were dismissed from the case after being adjudicated bankrupt, leaving their mother — Lillian Pritchard, the only solvent director of Pritchard & Baird — as the main defendant in the case.

The trial court held that if Mrs. Pritchard "had paid the slightest attention to the affairs of the corporation, she would have known what was happening." Consequently, Mrs. Pritchard was found negligent, since "[h]ad she performed her duties with due care, she would readily have discovered

---

17. This account comes from Reinier Kraakman & Jay Kesten, *The Story of Francis v. United Jersey Bank: When a Good Story Makes Bad Law*, Corporate Law Stories (2010). Citations to the trial court opinion and other sources are provided there.

the wrongdoing . . . and she could easily have taken effective steps to stop the wrongdoing." The court rejected the argument that Mrs. Pritchard should be absolved of liability because she was "a simple housewife . . . old and grief-stricken at the loss of her husband" (Charles, Sr., had died in 1973) who merely "served as a director as an accommodation to her husband and sons." Indeed, in an interesting rhetorical twist, Judge Stanton opined that accepting this argument would insult the "fundamental dignity and equality of women." Based on these findings, the trial court held Mrs. Pritchard liable for the more than $10 million of "loans" improperly paid to members of the Pritchard family at the direction of Charlie and Bill between 1970 and 1975. The decision was affirmed by a three-judge panel of the Appellate Division, and the New Jersey Supreme Court granted certification on the question of Mrs. Pritchard's liability as a director.

POLLOCK, J.:

The "loans" were reflected on financial statements that were prepared annually as of January 31, the end of the corporate fiscal year. Although an outside certified public accountant prepared the 1970 financial statement, the corporation prepared only internal financial statements from 1971-1975. In all instances, the statements were simple documents, consisting of three or four 8½ × 11 inch sheets. . . .

	Working Capital Deficit	*Shareholders' Loans*	*Net Brokerage Income*
70	$ 389,022	$ 508,941	$ 807,229
71	NOT AVAILABLE	NOT AVAILABLE	NOT AVAILABLE
72	$ 1,684,298	$ 1,825,911	$1,546,263
73	$ 3,506,460	$ 3,700,542	$1,736,349
74	$ 6,939,007	$ 7,080,629	$ 876,182
75	$10,176,419	$10,298,039	$ 551,598

The statements of financial condition from 1970 forward demonstrated: Mrs. Pritchard was not active in the business of Pritchard & Baird and knew virtually nothing of its corporate affairs. She briefly visited the corporate offices in Morristown on only one occasion, and she never read or obtained the annual financial statements. She was unfamiliar with the rudiments of reinsurance and made no effort to assure that the policies and practices of the corporation, particularly pertaining to the withdrawal of funds, complied with industry custom or relevant law. Although her husband had warned her that Charles, Jr. would "take the shirt off my back," Mrs. Pritchard did not pay any attention to her duties as a director or to the affairs of the corporation. . . .

After her husband died in December 1973, Mrs. Pritchard became incapacitated and was bedridden for a six-month period. She became listless at this time and started to drink rather heavily. Her physical condition deteriorated, and in 1978 she died. The trial court rejected testimony seeking to exonerate

her because she "was old, was grief-stricken at the loss of her husband, sometimes consumed too much alcohol and was psychologically overborne by her
sons." . . . That court found that she was competent to act and that the reason
Mrs. Pritchard never knew what her sons "were doing was because she never
made the slightest effort to discharge any of her responsibilities as a director
of Pritchard & Baird." 162 N.J. Super. at 372. . . .

III

Individual liability of a corporate director for acts of the corporation is
a prickly problem. Generally directors are accorded broad immunity and are
not insurers of corporate activities. The problem is particularly nettlesome
when a third party asserts that a director, because of nonfeasance, is liable for
losses caused by acts of insiders, who in this case were officers, directors and
shareholders. Determination of the liability of Mrs. Pritchard requires findings
that she had a duty to the clients of Pritchard & Baird, that she breached that
duty and that her breach was a proximate cause of their losses. . . .

As a general rule, a director should acquire at least a rudimentary understanding of the business of the corporation. Accordingly, a director should
become familiar with the fundamentals of the business in which the corporation is engaged. . . . Because directors are bound to exercise ordinary care,
they cannot set up as a defense lack of the knowledge needed to exercise the
requisite degree of care. If one "feels that he has not had sufficient business
experience to qualify him to perform the duties of a director, he should either
acquire the knowledge by inquiry, or refuse to act." . . .

Directors are under a continuing obligation to keep informed about the
activities of the corporation. . . . Directorial management does not require a
detailed inspection of day-to-day activities, but rather a general monitoring of
corporate affairs and policies. Accordingly, a director is well advised to attend
board meetings regularly. Indeed, a director who is absent from a board meeting is presumed to concur in action taken on a corporate matter, unless he
files a "dissent with the secretary of the corporation within a reasonable time
after learning of such action." N.J.S.A. 14A:6-13 (Supp. 1981-1982). . . .

While directors are not required to audit corporate books, they should
maintain familiarity with the financial status of the corporation by a regular review of financial statements. In some circumstances, directors may be
charged with assuring that bookkeeping methods conform to industry custom and usage. The extent of review, as well as the nature and frequency of
financial statements, depends not only on the customs of the industry, but
also on the nature of the corporation and the business in which it is engaged.
Financial statements of some small corporations may be prepared internally
and only on an annual basis; in a large publicly held corporation, the statements may be produced monthly or at some other regular interval. Adequate
financial review normally would be more informal in a private corporation
than in a publicly held corporation.

Of some relevance in this case is the circumstance that the financial
records disclose the "shareholders' loans." Generally directors are immune

from liability if, in good faith, they rely upon the opinion of counsel for the corporation or upon written reports setting forth financial data concerning the corporation and prepared by an independent public accountant or certified public accountant or firm of such accountants or upon financial statements, books of account or reports of the corporation represented to them to be correct by the president, the officer of the corporation having charge of its books of account, or the person presiding at a meeting of the board.

The review of financial statements, however, may give rise to a duty to inquire further into matters revealed by those statements. . . . Upon discovery of an illegal course of action, a director has a duty to object and, if the corporation does not correct the conduct, to resign. . . .

[In this case, Mrs. Pritchard] should have realized [from those statements] that, as of January 31, 1970, her sons were withdrawing substantial trust funds under the guise of "Shareholders' Loans." The financial statements for each fiscal year commencing with that of January 31, 1970, disclosed that the working capital deficits and the "loans" were escalating in tandem. Detecting a misappropriation of funds would not have required special expertise or extraordinary diligence; a cursory reading of the financial statements would have revealed the pillage. . . .

Nonetheless, the negligence of Mrs. Pritchard does not result in liability unless it is a proximate cause of the loss. . . .

Cases involving nonfeasance present a much more difficult causation question than those in which the director has committed an affirmative act of negligence leading to the loss. Analysis in cases of negligent omissions calls for determination of the reasonable steps a director should have taken and whether that course of action would have averted the loss.

Usually a director can absolve himself from liability by informing the other directors of the impropriety and voting for a proper course of action. . . . Conversely, a director who votes for or concurs in certain actions may be "liable to the corporation for the benefit of its creditors or shareholders, to the extent of any injuries suffered by such persons, respectively, as a result of any such action." N.J.S.A. 14A:6-12 (Supp. 1981-1982). A director who is present at a board meeting is presumed to concur in corporate action taken at the meeting unless his dissent is entered in the minutes of the meeting or filed promptly after adjournment. N.J.S.A. 14:6-13. In many, if not most, instances an objecting director whose dissent is noted in accordance with N.J.S.A. 14:6-13 would be absolved after attempting to persuade fellow directors to follow a different course of action. . . .

In this case, the scope of Mrs. Pritchard's duties was determined by the precarious financial condition of Pritchard & Baird, its fiduciary relationship to its clients and the implied trust in which it held their funds. Thus viewed, the scope of her duties encompassed all reasonable action to stop the continuing conversion. Her duties extended beyond mere objection and resignation to reasonable attempts to prevent the misappropriation of the trust funds. . . .

A leading case discussing causation where the director's liability is predicated upon a negligent failure to act is *Barnes v. Andrews*, 298 F. 614 (S.D.N.Y. 1924). In that case the court exonerated a figurehead director who served for eight months on a board that held one meeting after his election, a meeting he was forced to miss because of the death of his mother. Writing for the court, Judge Learned Hand distinguished a director who fails to prevent general mismanagement from one such as Mrs. Pritchard who failed to stop an illegal "loan":

> When the corporate funds have been illegally lent, it is a fair inference that a protest would have stopped the loan, and that the director's neglect caused the loss. But when a business fails from general mismanagement, business incapacity, or bad judgment, how is it possible to say that a single director could have made the company successful, or how much in dollars he could have saved? (*Id.* at 616-617) . . .

. . . The wrongdoing of her sons, although the immediate cause of [Pritchard & Baird's] loss, should not excuse Mrs. Pritchard from her negligence which also was a substantial factor contributing to the loss. . . . Her sons knew that she, the only other director, was not reviewing their conduct; they spawned their fraud in the backwater of her neglect. Her neglect of duty contributed to the climate of corruption; her failure to act contributed to the continuation of that corruption. . . .

Analysis . . . is especially difficult . . . where the allegation is that nonfeasance of a director is a proximate cause of damage to a third party. . . . Nonetheless, where it is reasonable to conclude that the failure to act would produce a particular result and that result has followed, causation may be inferred. We conclude that even if Mrs. Pritchard's mere objection had not stopped the depredations of her sons, her consultation with an attorney and the threat of suit would have deterred them. That conclusion flows as a matter of common sense and logic from the record. Whether in other situations a director has a duty to do more than protest and resign is best left to case-by-case determinations. In this case, we are satisfied that there was a duty to do more than object and resign. Consequently, we find that Mrs. Pritchard's negligence was a proximate cause of the misappropriations.

To conclude, by virtue of her office, Mrs. Pritchard had the power to prevent the losses sustained by the clients of Pritchard & Baird. With power comes responsibility. She had a duty to deter the depredation of the other insiders, her sons. She breached that duty and caused plaintiffs to sustain damages.

The judgment of the Appellate Division is affirmed.

NOTE

Although an odd case in some respects, *Francis* reflects the majority view that there is a minimum objective standard of care for directors — that directors cannot abandon their office but must make a good-faith attempt to do a proper job. The case law is divided on whether the minimum standard is the same for all directors or whether sophisticated directors (e.g., lawyers and investment bankers) ought to be held to a higher standard. The law is clear that all directors must satisfy the same legal standard of care, but the determination of liability is a director-by-director determination. A court may conclude that a reasonable engineer or investment banker serving on a board should have acted in certain circumstances while a reasonable person without that training and experience may not have done so. See *In Re Emerging Communications Inc. Shareholders Litigation*, C.A. No. 16415, 2004 WL 1305745 (Del. Ch. June 4, 2004) (investment banker held liable for complicity in controller's breach of loyalty in buyout, while other directors with less knowledge found not liable).

QUESTIONS

1. What would have been the result if Mrs. Pritchard had spotted her sons' activities; if they had responded: "Don't worry, Mama. We were stealing, but we'll stop now and establish a segregated fund for our clients' moneys"; and if her sons had continued to steal as before but pacified their mother with a false financial statement?

2. Courts are reluctant to impose a duty on directors who suspect wrongful activity to do more than protest and resign. Should corporate law impose something tough, such as a whistle-blowing duty (i.e., to go to prosecutors or disclose to shareholders)?

In general, boards of public companies have a particular obligation to monitor their firm's financial performance, the integrity of its financial reporting, its compliance with the law, its management compensation, and its succession planning. Because of the large scale of modern public corporations, the board must monitor largely through reports from others, whether outside auditors, other professionals, or corporate officers. The board authorizes only the most significant corporate acts or transactions: mergers, changes in capital structure, fundamental changes in business, etc. The lesser decisions that are made by officers and employees within the interior of the organization can, however, vitally affect the welfare of the corporation. Recent business history has graphically demonstrated that the failure of appropriate controls can result in extraordinary losses to even very large public companies. Even before the Enron and WorldCom scandals, large losses following monitoring failures resulted in the displacement of senior management and much of the board of Salomon, Inc.;[18] the replacement of senior management of Kidder, Peabody;[19] and extensive financial loss and reputational injury to Prudential Insurance arising from misrepresentations in connection with the sale of limited partnership interests.[20] Financial disasters of this sort raise this

18. See, e.g., *Rotten at the Core*, The Economist, Aug. 17, 1991, at 69-70; Mike McNamee et al., *The Judgment of Salomon: An Anticlimax*, Bus. Week, June 1, 1992, at 106.
19. See Terence P. Pare, *Jack Welch's Nightmare on Wall Street*, Fortune, Sept. 5, 1994, at 40-48.
20. Michael Schroeder & Leah N. Spiro, *Is George Ball's Luck Running Out?*, Bus. Week, Nov. 8, 1993, at 74-76.

question: What is the board's responsibility to assure that the corporation functions within the law to achieve its purposes?

GRAHAM v. ALLIS-CHALMERS MANUFACTURING CO.
188 A.2d 125 (Del. 1963)

WOLCOTT, J.:

This is a derivative action on behalf of Allis-Chalmers against its directors and four of its non-director employees. The complaint is based upon indictments of Allis-Chalmers and the four non-director employees named as defendants herein who, with the corporation, entered pleas of guilty to the indictments. The indictments, eight in number, charged violations of the Federal anti-trust laws. The suit seeks to recover damages which Allis-Chalmers is claimed to have suffered by reason of these violations. . . .

[T]he hearing and depositions produced no evidence that any director had any actual knowledge of the anti-trust activity, or had actual knowledge of any facts which should have put them on notice that anti-trust activity was being carried on by some of their company's employees. The plaintiffs, appellants here, thereupon shifted the theory of the case to the proposition that the directors are liable as a matter of law by reason of their failure to take action designed to learn of and prevent anti-trust activity on the part of any employees of Allis-Chalmers.

By this appeal the plaintiffs seek to have us reverse the Vice Chancellor's ruling of non-liability of the defendant directors upon this theory. . . .

Allis-Chalmers is a manufacturer of a variety of electrical equipment. It employs in excess of 31,000 people, has a total of 24 plants, 145 sales offices, 5000 dealers and distributors, and its sales volume is in excess of $500,000,000 annually. The operations of the company are conducted by two groups, each of which is under the direction of a senior vice president. One of these groups is the Industries Group under the direction of Singleton, director defendant. This group is divided into five divisions. One of these, the Power Equipment Division, produced the products, the sale of which involved the anti-trust activities referred to in the indictments. The Power Equipment Division, presided over by McMullen, non-director defendant, contains ten departments, each of which is presided over by a manager or general manager.

The operating policy of Allis-Chalmers is to decentralize by the delegation of authority to the lowest possible management level capable of fulfilling the delegated responsibility. Thus, prices of products are ordinarily set by the particular department manager, except that if the product being priced is large and special, the department manager might confer with the general manager of the division. Products of a standard character involving repetitive manufacturing processes are sold out of a price list which is established by a price leader for the electrical equipment industry as a whole.

Annually, the Board of Directors reviews group and departmental profit goal budgets. On occasion, the Board considers general questions concerning price levels, but because of the complexity of the company's operations the Board does not participate in decisions fixing the prices of specific products.

The Board of Directors of fourteen members, four of whom are officers, meets once a month, October excepted, and considers a previously prepared agenda for the meeting. Supplied to the Directors at the meetings are financial and operating data relating to all phases of the company's activities. The Board meetings are customarily of several hours duration in which all the Directors participate actively. Apparently, the Board considers and decides matters concerning the general business policy of the company. By reason of the extent and complexity of the company's operations, it is not practicable for the Board to consider in detail specific problems of the various divisions.

The indictments to which Allis-Chalmers and the four non-director defendants pled guilty charge that the company and individual non-director defendants, commencing in 1956, conspired with other manufacturers and their employees to fix prices and to rig bids to private electric utilities and governmental agencies in violation of the anti-trust laws of the United States. None of the director defendants in this cause were named as defendants in the indictments. Indeed, the Federal Government acknowledged that it had uncovered no probative evidence which could lead to the conviction of the defendant directors.

The first actual knowledge the directors had of anti-trust violations by some of the company's employees was in the summer of 1959 from newspaper stories that the TVA proposed an investigation of identical bids. Singleton, in charge of the Industries Group of the company, investigated but unearthed nothing. Thereafter, in November of 1959, some of the company's employees were subpoenaed before the Grand Jury. Further investigation by the company's Legal Division gave reason to suspect the illegal activity and all of the subpoenaed employees were instructed to tell the whole truth.

Thereafter, on February 8, 1960, at the direction of the Board, a policy statement relating to anti-trust problems was issued, and the Legal Division commenced a series of meetings with all employees of the company in possible areas of anti-trust activity. The purpose and effect of these steps was to eliminate any possibility of further and future violations of the antitrust laws.

As we have pointed out, there is no evidence in the record that the defendant directors had actual knowledge of the illegal anti-trust actions of the company's employees. Plaintiffs, however, point to two FTC decrees of 1937 as warning to the directors that anti-trust activity by the company's employees had taken place in the past. It is argued that they were thus put on notice of their duty to ferret out such activity and to take active steps to insure that it would not be repeated.

The decrees in question were consent decrees entered in 1937 against Allis-Chalmers and nine others enjoining agreements to fix uniform prices on condensers and turbine generators. The decrees recited that they were consented to for the sole purpose of avoiding the trouble and expense of the proceeding. . . .

The director defendants and now officers of the company either were employed in very subordinate capacities or had no connection with the company in 1937. At the time, copies of the decrees were circulated to the heads of concerned departments and were explained to the Managers Committee.

In 1943, Singleton, officer and director defendant, first learned of the decrees upon becoming Assistant Manager of the Steam Turbine Department, and consulted the company's General Counsel as to them. He investigated his department and learned the decrees were being complied with and, in any event, he concluded that the company had not in the first place been guilty of the practice enjoined.

Stevenson, officer and director defendant, first learned of the decrees in 1951 in a conversation with Singleton about their respective areas of the company's operations. He satisfied himself that the company was not then and in fact had not been guilty of quoting uniform prices. . . .

Scholl, officer and director defendant, learned of the decrees in 1956 in a discussion with Singleton on matters affecting the Industries Group. He was informed that no similar problem was then in existence in the company. . . .

Under the circumstances, we think knowledge by three of the directors that in 1937 the company had consented to the entry of decrees enjoining it from doing something they had satisfied themselves it had never done, did not put the Board on notice of the possibility of future illegal price fixing. . . .

Plaintiffs are thus forced to rely solely upon the legal proposition advanced by them that directors of a corporation, as a matter of law, are liable for losses suffered by their corporations by reason of their gross inattention to the common law duty of actively supervising and managing the corporate affairs. . . .

The precise charge made against these director defendants is that, even though they had no knowledge of any suspicion of wrongdoing on the part of the company's employees, they still should have put into effect a system of watchfulness which would have brought such misconduct to their attention in ample time to have brought it to an end. However, the *Briggs* case expressly rejects such an idea. On the contrary, it appears that directors are entitled to rely on the honesty and integrity of their subordinates until something occurs to put them on suspicion that something is wrong. If such occurs and goes unheeded, then liability of the directors might well follow, but absent cause for suspicion there is no duty upon the directors to install and operate a corporate system of espionage to ferret out wrongdoing which they have no reason to suspect exists.

The duties of the Allis-Chalmers Directors were fixed by the nature of the enterprise which employed in excess of 30,000 persons, and extended over a large geographical area. By force of necessity, the company's Directors could not know personally all the company's employees. The very magnitude of the enterprise required them to confine their control to the broad policy decisions. That they did this is clear from the record. . . .

In the last analysis, the question of whether a corporate director has become liable for losses to the corporation through neglect of duty is determined by the circumstances. If he has recklessly reposed confidence in an obviously untrustworthy employee, has refused or neglected cavalierly to perform his duty as a director, or has ignored either willfully or through inattention obvious danger signs of employee wrongdoing, the law will cast the burden of liability upon him. This is not the case at bar, however, for as soon as it became evident that there were grounds for suspicion, the Board acted promptly to end it and prevent its recurrence.

Plaintiffs say these steps should have been taken long before, even in the absence of suspicion, but we think not, for we know of no rule of law which requires a corporate director to assume, with no justification whatsoever, that all corporate employees are incipient law violators who, but for a tight check-rein, will give free vent to their unlawful propensities.

We therefore affirm the Vice Chancellor's ruling. . . .

QUESTIONS

1. There is evidence that the exceptionally decentralized operating policy of Allis-Chalmers was accompanied by enormous pressure on the company's semiautonomous units to show steadily growing profits. If this was the management style approved by the Allis-Chalmers board, should there be any implications for the board's duty of care?

2. What function would imposing liability for breach of the duty of care serve in *Allis-Chalmers*? When might it be in the narrow economic interests of shareholders, and when might it not be in the interests of shareholders?

3. To the extent that one is tempted to impose liability on the board for purposes of enforcing the antitrust laws, what alternative enforcement strategies might be available? What about increasing penalties against the company itself?

7.5.2   *Caremark* and the Beginning of a New Era?

Delaware jurisprudence on the Board's duty to monitor took its next big step with the watershed *Caremark* decision. Before discussing it, however, some background is useful in understanding the environment in which *Caremark* was decided.

Over many years, the United States has begun to sometimes treat lapses from statutory or administratively mandated standards of business conduct as criminal matters.[21] Federal statutory law has been a powerful engine of this movement. The Comprehensive Environmental Response, Compensation, and Liability Act (CERCLA),[22] for example, opens up potential civil and criminal liabilities for both corporations and "persons in charge," who may be officers or low-level employees.[23] The Resource Conservation and Recovery Act (RCRA) imposes criminal liability on "any person" who knowingly transports hazardous waste to an unpermitted facility or treats, stores, or disposes of any

---

21. E.g., Flom, *U.S. Prosecutors Take a Tough Line*, Fin. Times, Oct. 31, 1991, at 21.

22. 42 U.S.C.A. §§9601 et seq.

23. E.g., *United States v. Mexico Seed & Feed Co.*, 764 F. Supp. 565, *rev'd in part*, 980 F.2d 473 (8th Cir. 1992).

hazardous waste without a permit.[24] Similarly, the Clean Water Act[25] and the Clean Air Act include criminal penalties applicable to any "person" including "any responsible corporate officer"[26] who violates those Acts. Environmental laws are simply one category of substantive federal regulation in which the criminal law is deployed to promote corporate compliance with regulation. The Occupational Safety and Health Act (OSHA);[27] the Food, Drug, and Cosmetics Act;[28] the antitrust acts; the Foreign Corrupt Practices Act (FCPA);[29] and the acts regulating federally chartered or insured depository institutions[30] and securities markets,[31] all authorize substantial civil or criminal fines against corporations and their officers or employees.

In 1991, pursuant to the Sentencing Reform Act of 1984, the United States Sentencing Commission[32] adopted the Organizational Sentencing Guidelines, which set forth a uniform sentencing structure for organizations convicted of federal criminal violations and provided for penalties that generally exceed those previously imposed on corporations.[33] The Guidelines offer powerful incentives for firms to put compliance programs in place, to report violations of law promptly, and to make voluntary remediation efforts. Under the Guidelines, a convicted organization that has satisfied these conditions will receive a much lower fine. For example, the Guidelines will reduce the base fine of a fully compliant firm by up to 95 percent, while they quadruple the base fine of firms with the highest culpability rating.[34] Thus, with a base fine of say $150 million, the culpability score could cause a variation in a fine from $7.5 million to $600 million for the same offense, depending on the circumstances.[35]

The importance of compliance programs grew even more after the 2003 Department of Justice memorandum entitled "Principles of Federal Prosecution of Business Organizations" (a.k.a. the "Thompson Memo," after then-Deputy Attorney General Larry Thompson) directed U.S. Attorneys to consider the depth and quality of a company's compliance program in connection with charging decisions. This and later memoranda were incorporated into the U.S. Attorneys' Manual which further ensconced the role of

---

24. 42 U.S.C. §6928(d), (e).

25. 33 U.S.C. §§1319(c), 1362(5), 1321(b)(5) (specifically including "any responsible corporate officer").

26. 42 U.S.C. §§7602(e), 7413(c)(6).

27. 21 U.S.C. §333.

28. 21 U.S.C.A. §§301 et seq.

29. 15 U.S.C. §§78m et seq.

30. E.g., Financial Institutions Reform, Recovery, and Enforcement Act of 1989, Pub. L. No. 101-429, 104 Stat. 931 (1990).

31. E.g., Securities Enforcement Remedies and Penny Stock Act of 1990, Pub. L. No. 101-429, 104 Stat. 931 (1990).

32. See Sentencing Reform Act of 1984, Pub. L. No. 98-473, tit. II, ch. II, 98 Stat. 1987 (1984) (codified as amended in scattered sections of 18 and 28 U.S.C.).

33. See United States Sentencing Commission, Guidelines Manual, Ch. 8 (2018), available at: https://www.ussc.gov/sites/default/files/pdf/guidelines-manual/2018/GLMFull.pdf.

34. Id. §8C2.4-2.6.

35. The base fine is the higher of (1) an amount from an offense level table (currently capped at $150 million), (2) "the pecuniary gain to the organization," or (3) "the pecuniary loss from the offense caused by the organization to the extent the loss was caused intentionally, knowingly, or recklessly." Id. §8C2.4. Departures from the Guidelines are discussed in §8C4.

compliance programs in influencing the exercise of prosecutorial discretion.[36] Thus appropriate compliance programs might not only lead to lower sanctions, but also lower charges and a lower likelihood of facing prosecution in the first place.[37]

Designing corporate compliance programs has developed into a new, fast-growing, and highly remunerative legal subspecialty. The enormous potential fines at stake today make it less likely than it was in 1963 that a court construing the duties of corporate directors would pass over a board's failure to implement a legal compliance program as blithely as was done in *Allis-Chalmers.*

IN RE CAREMARK INTERNATIONAL INC. DERIVATIVE LITIGATION
698 A.2d 959 (Del. Ch. 1996)

ALLEN, C.:

Pending is a motion pursuant to Chancery Rule 23.1 to approve as fair and reasonable a proposed settlement of a consolidated derivative action on behalf of Caremark International, Inc. ("Caremark"). The suit involves claims that the members of Caremark's board of directors (the "Board") breached their fiduciary duty of care to Caremark in connection with alleged violations by Caremark employees of federal and state laws and regulations applicable to health care providers. As a result of the alleged violations, Caremark was subject to an extensive four year investigation. . . . In 1994 Caremark was charged in an indictment with multiple felonies. It thereafter entered into a number of agreements with the Department of Justice and others. Those agreements included a plea agreement in which Caremark pleaded guilty to a single felony of mail fraud and agreed to pay civil and criminal fines. Subsequently, Caremark agreed to make reimbursements to various private and public parties. In all, the payments that Caremark has been required to make total approximately $250 million.

This suit was filed in 1994, purporting to seek on behalf of the company recovery of these losses from the individual defendants who constitute the

---

36. See §9-28.000, *Principles of Federal Prosecution of Business Organizations*, U.S. Attorneys' Manual, Department of Justice.

37. The U.S. Supreme Court struck down the federal sentencing guidelines for *individuals* as violating a criminal defendant's Sixth Amendment right to a jury trial. See *United States v. Booker*, 543 U.S. 220 (2005). What this does to the legal status of the sentencing guidelines for *organizations* is murkier because the extent to which the Sixth Amendment applies to corporate defendants isn't clear. Nonetheless, the focus on compliance programs in the U.S. Attorneys' Manual and in plea bargains and settlements underscores the continuing and growing importance of compliance programs. See Jennifer Arlen & Marcel Kahan, *Corporate Governance Regulation through Nonprosecution*, 84 U. Chi. L. Rev. 323 (2017); Timothy L. Dickinson & Vikramaditya S. Khanna, *The Corporate Monitor: The New Corporate Czar?*, 105 Mich. L. Rev. 1713 (2007).

Board of Directors of Caremark.[1] The parties now propose that it be settled and, after notice to Caremark shareholders, a hearing on the fairness of the proposal was held on August 16, 1996.

A motion of this type requires the court to assess the strengths and weaknesses of the claims asserted in light of the discovery record and to evaluate the fairness and adequacy of the consideration offered to the corporation in exchange for the release of all claims made or arising from the facts alleged. . . .

Legally, evaluation of the central claim made entails consideration of the legal standard governing a board of directors' obligation to supervise or monitor corporate performance. For the reasons set forth below I conclude, in light of the discovery record, that there is a very low probability that it would be determined that the directors of Caremark breached any duty to appropriately monitor and supervise the enterprise. . . .

I.   BACKGROUND

. . . I regard the following facts . . . as material. Caremark . . . was created in November 1992. . . . The business practices that created the problem predated the spin-off. During the relevant period Caremark was involved in two main health care business segments, providing patient care and managed care services. . . .

A substantial part of the revenues generated by Caremark's businesses is derived from third party payments, insurers, and Medicare and Medicaid reimbursement programs. The latter source of payments is subject to the terms of the Anti-Referral Payments Law ("ARPL") which prohibits health care providers from paying any form of remuneration to induce the referral of Medicare or Medicaid patients. From its inception, Caremark entered into a variety of agreements with hospitals, physicians, and health care providers for advice and services, as well as distribution agreements with drug manufacturers, as had its predecessor prior to 1992. Specifically, Caremark did have a practice of entering into contracts for services (e.g., consultation agreements and research grants) with physicians at least some of whom prescribed or recommended services or products that Caremark provided to Medicare recipients and other patients. Such contracts were not prohibited by the ARPL but they obviously raised a possibility of unlawful "kickbacks."

As early as 1989, Caremark's predecessor issued an internal "Guide to Contractual Relationships" ("Guide") to govern its employees in entering into contracts with physicians and hospitals. . . . Each version of the Guide stated as Caremark's and its predecessor's policy that no payments would be made in exchange for or to induce patient referrals. But what one might deem a prohibited quid pro quo was not always clear. Due to a scarcity of court decisions interpreting the ARPL, however, Caremark repeatedly publicly stated that there was uncertainty concerning Caremark's interpretation of the law. . . .

---

1. Thirteen of the Directors have been members of the Board since November 30, 1992. Nancy Brinker joined the Board in October 1993.

In August 1991, the HHS [Health and Human Services] Office of the Inspector General ("OIG") initiated an investigation of Caremark's predecessor. Caremark's predecessor was served with a subpoena requiring the production of documents, including contracts between Caremark's predecessor and physicians (Quality Service Agreements ("QSAs")). Under the QSAs, Caremark's predecessor appears to have paid physicians' fees for monitoring patients under Caremark's predecessor's care, including Medicare and Medicaid recipients. Sometimes apparently those monitoring patients were referring physicians, which raised ARPL concerns. . . .

The first action taken by management, as a result of the initiation of the OIG investigation, was an announcement that as of October 1, 1991, Caremark's predecessor would no longer pay management fees to physicians for services to Medicare and Medicaid patients. . . .

During this period, Caremark's Board took several additional steps . . . to assure compliance with company policies concerning the ARPL and the contractual forms in the Guide. In April 1992, Caremark published a fourth revised version of its Guide apparently designed to assure that its agreements either complied with the ARPL and regulations or excluded Medicare and Medicaid patients altogether. In addition, in September 1992, Caremark instituted a policy requiring its regional officers, Zone Presidents, to approve each contractual relationship entered into by Caremark with a physician.

Although there is evidence that inside and outside counsel had advised Caremark's directors that their contracts were in accord with the law, Caremark recognized that some uncertainty respecting the correct interpretation of the law existed. . . .

Throughout the period of the government investigations, Caremark had an internal audit plan designed to assure compliance with business and ethics policies. In addition, Caremark employed Price Waterhouse as its outside auditor. On February 8, 1993, the Ethics Committee of Caremark's Board received and reviewed an outside auditors report by Price Waterhouse which concluded that there were no material weaknesses in Caremark's control structure. Despite the positive findings of Price Waterhouse, however, on April 20, 1993, the Audit & Ethics Committee adopted a new internal audit charter requiring a comprehensive review of compliance policies and the compilation of an employee ethics handbook concerning such policies.

The Board appears to have been informed about this project and other efforts to assure compliance with the law. For example, Caremark's management reported to the Board that Caremark's sales force was receiving an ongoing education regarding the ARPL and the proper use of Caremark's form contracts which had been approved by in-house counsel. On July 27, 1993, the new ethics manual, expressly prohibiting payments in exchange for referrals and requiring employees to report all illegal conduct to a toll free confidential ethics hotline, was approved and allegedly disseminated.[5]

---

5. Prior to the distribution of the new ethics manual, on March 12, 1993, Caremark's president had sent a letter to all senior, district, and branch managers restating Caremark's policies that no physician be paid for referrals, that the standard contract forms in the Guide were not to be modified, and that deviation from such policies would result in the immediate termination of employment.

The record suggests that Caremark continued these policies in subsequent years, causing employees to be given revised versions of the ethics manual and requiring them to participate in training sessions concerning compliance with the law. . . .

On August 4, 1994, a federal grand jury in Minnesota issued a 47-page indictment charging Caremark, two of its officers (not the firm's chief officer), an individual who had been a sales employee of Genentech, Inc., and David R. Brown, a physician practicing in Minneapolis, with violating the ARPL over a lengthy period. According to the indictment, over $1.1 million had been paid to Brown to induce him to distribute Protropin, a human growth hormone drug marketed by Caremark. . . .

In reaction to the Minnesota Indictment . . . [m]anagement reiterated the grounds for its view that the contracts were in compliance with law.

Subsequently, five stockholder derivative actions were filed in this court and consolidated into this action. . . .

On September 21, 1994, a federal grand jury in Columbus, Ohio issued another indictment alleging that an Ohio physician had defrauded the Medicare program by requesting and receiving $134,600 in exchange for referrals of patients whose medical costs were in part reimbursed by Medicare in violation of the ARPL. . . . Caremark was the health care provider who allegedly made such payments. . . .

II.   LEGAL PRINCIPLES . . .

The complaint charges the director defendants with breach of their duty of attention or care in connection with the on-going operation of the corporation's business. The claim is that the directors allowed a situation to develop and continue which exposed the corporation to enormous legal liability and that in so doing they violated a duty to be active monitors of corporate performance. The complaint thus does not charge . . . loyalty-type problems. . . .

1. *Potential liability for directorial decisions:* Director liability for a breach of the duty to exercise appropriate attention may, in theory, arise in two distinct contexts. First, such liability may be said to follow from a board decision that results in a loss because that decision was ill advised or "negligent." . . . What should be understood . . . is that compliance with a director's duty of care can never appropriately be judicially determined by reference to the content of the board decision that leads to a corporate loss, apart from consideration of the good faith or rationality of the process employed. . . .

2. *Liability for failure to monitor:* The second class of cases in which director liability for inattention is theoretically possible entail circumstances in which a loss eventuates not from a decision, but from unconsidered inaction. Most of the decisions that a corporation, acting through its human agents, makes are, of course, not the subject of director attention. . . . As the facts of this case graphically demonstrate, ordinary business decisions that are made by officers and employees deeper in the interior of the organization can . . . vitally affect the welfare of the corporation. . . . [They] raise the question, what is the board's responsibility with respect to the organization and monitoring of the enterprise to assure that the corporation functions within the law to achieve its purposes?

Modernly this question has been given special importance by an increasing tendency, especially under federal law, to employ the criminal law to assure corporate compliance with external legal requirements, including environmental, financial, employee and product safety as well as assorted other health and safety regulations. In 1991, pursuant to the Sentencing Reform Act of 1984, the United States Sentencing Commission adopted Organizational Sentencing Guidelines which impact importantly on the prospective effect these criminal sanctions might have on business corporations. The Guidelines set forth a uniform sentencing structure for organizations to be sentenced for violation of federal criminal statutes and provide for penalties that equal or often massively exceed those previously imposed on corporations. The Guidelines offer powerful incentives for corporations today to have in place compliance programs to detect violations of law, promptly to report violations to appropriate public officials when discovered, and to take prompt, voluntary remedial efforts.

In 1963, the Delaware Supreme Court in *Graham v. Allis-Chalmers Mfg. Co.*, addressed the question of potential liability of board members for losses experienced by the corporation as a result of the corporation having violated the anti-trust laws of the United States. There was no claim in that case that the directors knew about the behavior of subordinate employees of the corporation that had resulted in the liability. Rather, as in this case, the claim asserted was that the directors ought to have known of it. . . . The Delaware Supreme Court concluded that, under the facts as they appeared, there was no basis to find that the directors had breached a duty to be informed of the ongoing operations of the firm. . . .

How does one generalize this holding today? Can it be said today, absent some ground giving rise to suspicion of violation of law, that corporate directors have no duty to assure that corporate information gathering and reporting systems exists which represents a good faith attempt to provide senior management and the Board with information respecting . . . compliance with applicable statutes and regulations? I certainly do not believe so. . . .

[I]n recent years the Delaware Supreme Court has made it clear — especially in its jurisprudence concerning takeovers . . . — the seriousness with which the corporation law views the role of the corporate board. Secondly, I note the elementary fact that relevant and timely information is an essential predicate for satisfaction of the board's supervisory and monitoring role under [DGCL] Section 141. . . . Thirdly, I note the potential impact of the federal organizational sentencing guidelines on any business organization. Any rational person attempting in good faith to meet an organizational governance responsibility would be bound to take into account this development and the enhanced penalties and the opportunities for reduced sanctions that it offers.

[I]t would . . . be a mistake to conclude . . . that corporate boards may satisfy their obligation to be reasonably informed concerning the corporation, without assuring themselves that information and reporting systems exist in the organization that are reasonably designed to provide to senior management and to the board itself timely, accurate information sufficient to allow management and the board, each within its scope, to reach informed judgments concerning both the corporation's compliance with law and its business performance.

Obviously the level of detail that is appropriate for such an information system is a question of business judgment. And obviously too, no rationally designed information and reporting system will remove the possibility that the corporation will violate laws or regulations. . . . But it is important that the board exercise a good faith judgment that the corporation's information and reporting system is in concept and design adequate to assure the board that appropriate information will come to its attention in a timely manner as a matter of ordinary operations, so that it may satisfy its responsibility. . . .

III.   ANALYSIS OF THIRD AMENDED COMPLAINT AND SETTLEMENT

A.   THE CLAIMS

On balance, . . . I conclude that this settlement is fair and reasonable. In light of the fact that the Caremark Board already has a functioning committee charged with overseeing corporate compliance, the changes in corporate practice that are presented as consideration for the settlement do not impress one as very significant. Nonetheless, that consideration appears fully adequate to support dismissal of the derivative claims of director fault asserted, because those claims find no substantial evidentiary support in the record and quite likely were susceptible to a motion to dismiss in all events. . . .

2. *Failure to monitor:* Since it does appear that the Board was to some extent unaware of the activities that led to liability, I turn to a consideration of the other potential avenue to director liability that the pleadings take: director inattention or "negligence." Generally where a claim of directorial liability for corporate loss is predicated upon ignorance of liability creating activities within the corporation, . . . only a sustained or systematic failure of the board to exercise oversight . . . will establish the lack of good faith that is a necessary condition to liability. . . .

Here the record supplies essentially no evidence that the director defendants were guilty of a sustained failure to exercise their oversight function. To the contrary, . . . the corporation's information systems appear to have represented a good faith attempt to be informed of relevant facts. If the directors did not know the specifics of the activities that led to the indictments, they cannot be faulted. . . .

NOTES FOLLOWING CAREMARK

Since *Caremark*, there have been significant legislative and judicial developments. For instance, §404 of the Sarbanes-Oxley Act of 2002 ("SOX" or "Sarbox") requires that the CEO and the CFO of firms with securities regulated under the Securities Exchange Act of 1934 periodically certify that they have disclosed to the company's independent auditor all deficiencies in the design or operation, or any material weakness, of the firm's internal controls for financial reporting. This requirement has generated considerable discussion and controversy. Critics have complained that §404 compliance costs have far exceeded predictions, are irrationally high, and have pushed many companies, particularly smaller companies, out of the public markets.[38] Proponents, on the other hand, argue that §404 forces companies to take a hard look at their control systems, which has long-term benefits that they suppose outweigh the costs. Since 2002, among companies with more than $1 billion in market capitalization, 2 percent have disclosed material weaknesses under §404.[39]

In the event that a firm's internal controls fail to prevent a loss and the CEO *did not* identify any weakness in the control system to the auditors, cases such as *Kamin v. American Express Co.* (above) indicate that state law imposes little risk of directorial liability — unless, under *Caremark,* the board's failure to prevent a loss resulted from a systematic failure to attempt to control potential liabilities. Does §404 of Sarbanes-Oxley change that prediction in any way? What are the arguments, pro and con?

Confirming this point, in 2006, the Delaware Supreme Court in *Stone v. Ritter* endorsed and clarified the *Caremark* standard, stating that: "We hold that *Caremark* articulates the necessary conditions predicate for director oversight liability: (a) the directors utterly failed to implement any reporting or information system or controls; *or* (b) having implemented such a system or controls, consciously failed to monitor or oversee its operations thus disabling themselves from being informed of risks or problems requiring their attention. In either case, imposition of liability requires a showing that the directors knew that they were not discharging their fiduciary obligations." 911 A.2d 362 (Del. 2006).

Another subtle but important point about *Stone* is that it treats violations of the two-prong test above as duty-of-loyalty breaches in the form of not acting in good faith. We address the duty of good faith in more detail in the context of executive compensation in Chapter 9, but here note it because framing *Caremark* obligations in these terms means that such claims cannot be blocked by waivers under §102(b)(7). Further, this makes *Caremark* claims somewhat easier to satisfy for directors because it requires just that the board have some system in place and not consciously fail to oversee it.

7.5.3   *Caremark*'s Progeny

The *Caremark* standard, as clarified in *Stone v. Ritter*, was put to the test in the following Delaware Supreme Court case. The particular issue

---

38. See Ehud Kamar, Pinar Karaca-Mandic & Eric L. Talley, *Going-Private Decisions and the Sarbanes-Oxley Act of 2002: A Cross-Country Analysis,* 25 J. L. Econ. & Org'n 107 (2009); Craig Doidge, G. Andrew Karolyi & Rene M. Stulz, *Has New York Become Less Competitive than London in Global Markets? Evaluating Foreign Listing Choices Over Time,* 91 J. Fin. Econ. 253 (2009).

39. Christine Dunn, *Effective Controls, Clean Opinions Rule the Roost,* Compliance Week (June 2, 2006). One study finds that companies disclosing weaknesses under §404 suffer a 2 percent market-adjusted decline in their stock price on average. See Messod Daniel Beneish et al., *Internal Control Weaknesses and Information Uncertainty,* 83 The Acc. Rev. 665 (2008).

before the court was whether demand was excused, a doctrine we examine in Chapter 10. However, the court's determination on this procedural question was guided by its assessment of the viability of the plaintiffs' substantive claims under *Caremark* and *Stone*.

MARCHAND v. BARNHILL
212 A.3d 805 (Del. 2019)

STRINE, C.J.:

Blue Bell Creameries USA, Inc., one of the country's largest ice cream manufacturers, suffered a listeria outbreak in early 2015, causing the company to recall all of its products, shut down production at all of its plants, and lay off over a third of its workforce. . . . Three people died as a result of the listeria outbreak . . .[and] stockholders also suffered losses. . . .

Based on these unfortunate events, a stockholder brought a derivative suit against . . . Paul Kruse, the President and CEO, and Greg Bridges, the Vice President of Operations [that they] . . . breached their duties of care and loyalty by knowingly disregarding contamination risks and failing to oversee the safety of Blue Bell's food-making operations, and that the directors breached their duty of loyalty under *Caremark*.[1]

The defendants moved to dismiss the complaint for failure to plead demand futility. . . .

As to the *Caremark* claim, the Court of Chancery held that the plaintiff did not plead any facts to support "his contention that the [Blue Bell] Board 'utterly' failed to adopt or implement any reporting and compliance systems." Although the plaintiff argued that Blue Bell's board had no supervisory structure in place to oversee "health, safety and sanitation controls and compliance," the Court of Chancery reasoned that "[w]hat Plaintiff really attempts to challenge is not the existence of monitoring and reporting controls, but [their effectiveness] in particular instances," and "[t]his is not a valid theory under . . . *Caremark*."

In this opinion, we reverse . . . [and] hold that the complaint alleges particularized facts that support a reasonable inference that the Blue Bell board failed to implement any system to monitor Blue Bell's food safety performance or compliance. Under *Caremark* and this Court's opinion in *Stone* v. *Ritter*, directors have a duty "to exercise oversight" and to monitor the corporation's operational viability, legal compliance, and financial performance. A board's "utter failure to attempt to assure a reasonable information and reporting system exists" is an act of bad faith in breach of the duty of loyalty.

As a monoline company that makes a single product — ice cream — Blue Bell can only thrive if its consumers enjoyed its products and were confident that its products were safe to eat. That is, one of Blue Bell's central compliance issues is food safety. Despite this fact, the complaint alleges that Blue Bell's board had no committee overseeing food safety, no full board-level

---

1. *In re Caremark Int'l Inc. Derivative Litig.*, 698 A.2d 959 (Del. Ch.1996) (Allen, C.).

process to address food safety issues, and no protocol by which the board was expected to be advised of food safety reports and developments. Consistent with this dearth of any board-level effort at monitoring, the complaint pleads particular facts supporting an inference that during a crucial period when yellow and red flags about food safety were presented to management, there was no equivalent reporting to the board and the board was not presented with any material information about food safety. Thus, the complaint alleges specific facts that create a reasonable inference that the directors consciously failed "to attempt to assure a reasonable information and reporting system exist[ed]."

I.   Background

A.   BLUE BELL'S HISTORY AND OPERATING ENVIRONMENT [AND] HISTORY

Founded in 1907 in Brenham, Texas, Blue Bell Creameries USA, Inc. ("Blue Bell"), a Delaware corporation, produces and distributes ice cream under the Blue Bell banner. . . .

As a U.S. food manufacturer, Blue Bell operates in a heavily regulated industry. . . . Blue Bell is "required to comply with regulations and establish controls to monitor for, avoid and remediate contamination and conditions that expose the Company and its products to the risk of contamination."

Specifically, [Food and Drug Administration (FDA)] regulations require food manufacturers to conduct operations "with adequate sanitation principles" and, in line with that obligation, "must prepare . . . and implement a written food safety plan." As part of a manufacturer's food safety plan, the manufacturer must include processes for conducting a hazard analysis that identifies possible food safety hazards, identifies and implements preventative controls to limit potential food hazards, implements process controls, implements sanitation controls, and monitors these preventative controls. Appropriate corporate officials must monitor these preventative controls.

Not only is Blue Bell subject to federal regulations, but it must also adhere to various state regulations. At the time of the listeria outbreak, Blue Bell operated in three states, and each had issued rules and regulations regarding the proper handling and production of food to ensure food safety. . . .

B.   THE CAREMARK CLAIM

. . . Although *Caremark* claims are difficult to plead and ultimately to prove out, we nonetheless disagree with the Court of Chancery's decision to dismiss the plaintiff's claim against the Blue Bell board.

Under *Caremark* and *Stone* v. *Ritter*, a director must make a good faith effort to oversee the company's operations. Failing to make that good faith effort breaches the duty of loyalty and can expose a director to liability. In other words, for a plaintiff to prevail on *Caremark* claim, the plaintiff must show that a fiduciary acted in bad faith — "the state of mind traditionally used to define the mindset of a disloyal director."

Bad faith is established, under *Caremark*, when "the directors [completely] fail[] to implement any reporting or information system or controls[,] or . . . having implemented such a system or controls, consciously fail[] to monitor or oversee its operations thus disabling themselves from being informed of risks or problems requiring their attention." In short, to satisfy their duty of loyalty, directors must make a good faith effort to implement an oversight system and then monitor it.

As with any other disinterested business judgment, directors have great discretion to design context- and industry-specific approaches tailored to their companies' businesses and resources. But Caremark does have a bottom-line requirement that is important: the board must make a good faith effort — i.e., try — to put in place a reasonable board-level system of monitoring and reporting. . . .

For that reason, our focus here is on the key issue of whether the plaintiff has pled facts from which we can infer that Blue Bell's board made no effort to put in place a board-level compliance system. That is, we are not examining the effectiveness of a board-level compliance and reporting system after the fact. Rather, we are focusing on whether the complaint pleads facts supporting a reasonable inference that the board did not undertake good faith efforts to put a board-level system of monitoring and reporting in place. . . .

Here, . . . the complaint fairly alleges that before the listeria outbreak engulfed the company:

- no board committee that addressed food safety existed;
- no regular process or protocols that required management to keep the board apprised of food safety compliance practices, risks, or reports existed;
- no schedule for the board to consider on a regular basis, such as quarterly or biannually, any key food safety risks existed;
- during a key period leading up to the deaths of three customers, management received reports that contained what could be considered red, or at least yellow, flags, and the board minutes of the relevant period revealed no evidence that these were disclosed to the board; the board was given certain favorable information about food safety by management, but was not given important reports that presented a much different picture; and
- the board meetings are devoid of any suggestion that there was any regular discussion of food safety issues.

And the complaint goes on to allege that after the listeria outbreak, the FDA discovered a number of systematic deficiencies in all of Blue Bell's plants . . . that might have been rectified had any reasonable reporting system that required management to relay food safety information to the board on an ongoing basis been in place.

In sum, the complaint supports an inference that no system of board-level compliance monitoring and reporting existed at Blue Bell. Although

Caremark is a tough standard for plaintiffs to meet, the plaintiff has met it here. When a plaintiff can plead an inference that a board has undertaken no efforts to make sure it is informed of a compliance issue intrinsically critical to the company's business operation, then that supports an inference that the board has not made the good faith effort that *Caremark* requires.

In defending this case, the directors largely point out that by law Blue Bell had to meet FDA and state regulatory requirements for food safety, and that the company had in place certain manuals for employees regarding safety practices and commissioned audits from time to time. In the same vein, the directors emphasize that the government regularly inspected Blue Bell's facilities, and Blue Bell management got the results.

But the fact that Blue Bell nominally complied with FDA regulations does not imply that the board implemented a system to monitor food safety at the board level. . . . At best, Blue Bell's compliance with these requirements shows only that management was following, in a nominal way, certain standard requirements of state and federal law. It does not rationally suggest that the board implemented a reporting system to monitor food safety or Blue Bell's operational performance. . . .

In decisions dismissing *Caremark* claims, the plaintiffs usually lose because they must concede the existence of board-level systems of monitoring and oversight such as a relevant committee, a regular protocol requiring board-level reports about the relevant risks, or the board's use of third-party monitors, auditors, or consultants. . . . Here, the Blue Bell directors just argue that because Blue Bell management, in its discretion, discussed general operations with the board, a *Caremark* claim is not stated. But if that were the case, then *Caremark* would be a chimera. At every board meeting of any company, it is likely that management will touch on some operational issue. Although *Caremark* may not require as much as some commentators wish,[115] it does require that a board make a good faith effort to put in place a reasonable system of monitoring and reporting about the corporation's central compliance risks. In Blue Bell's case, food safety was . . . critical. The complaint pled facts supporting a fair inference that no board-level system of monitoring or reporting on food safety existed.

If *Caremark* means anything, it is that a corporate board must make a good faith effort to exercise its duty of care. A failure to make that effort constitutes a breach of the duty of loyalty. Where, as here, a plaintiff has . . . plead facts supporting a fair inference that no reasonable compliance system and protocols were established as to the obviously most central consumer safety and legal compliance issue facing the company, that the board's lack of efforts resulted in it not receiving official notices of food safety deficiencies for several years, and that, as a failure to take remedial action, the company exposed

---

115. *See, e.g.,* John Armour et al., *Board Compliance,* 104 Minn. L. Rev. (forthcoming 2020) (manuscript at 47); John Armour & Jeffrey N. Gordon, *Systemic Harms and Shareholder Value,* 6 J. Legal Analysis 35, 46 (2014); Hillary A. Sale, *Monitoring* Caremark's *Good Faith,* 32 Del. J. Corp. L. 719, 753 (2007).

consumers to listeria-infected ice cream, resulting in the death and injury of company customers, the plaintiff has met his onerous pleading burden and is entitled to discovery to prove out his claim. . . .

NOTES AND QUESTIONS ON MARCHAND

Marchand heralds an era of greater scrutiny compared to earlier cases where Delaware courts tended to limit the application of *Caremark*. Two recent Chancery Court cases—decided on the heels of *Marchand*—build upon its holdings. *In Re Clovis Oncology, Inc. Derivative Litigation*, C.A. No. 2017-0222-JRS, 2019 WL 4850188 (Del. Ch. Oct. 1, 2019) involved a case where a biotechnology company, Clovis Oncology, lost substantial value when it was revealed that the Food and Drug Administration (FDA) refused to grant approval to the firm's "mission critical" drug due to problems with the firm following well-established protocols related to clinical trials. Shareholders brought suit claiming a *Caremark* violation for failure to follow these protocols among other things. Although the board had oversight systems in place, the Chancery Court held that the plaintiffs had pled with sufficient particularity that the board ignored multiple red flags about management's reporting of clinical trials and "consciously failed to monitor or oversee its operations." The Court cited *Marchand* and noted that the firm must engage in greater oversight "when a monoline company operates in a highly regulated industry."

In *Hughes v. Hu,* 2020 WL 1987029 (Del. Ch. Apr. 27, 2020), Kandi Technologies failed to rectify known problems relating to its financial reporting and internal controls leading to a financial restatement. Shareholders brought suit against the audit committee members and some top executives for *Caremark* violations. V. C. Laster held that the plaintiffs pled with sufficient particularity that the audit committee "met sporadically, devoted inadequate time to its work, had clear notice of irregularities, and consciously turned a blind eye to their continuation." Further, "the board never established its own reasonable system of monitoring and reporting, choosing instead to rely entirely on management." Simply put, the directors failed "to make a good faith effort — *i.e.,* try — to put in place a reasonable board-level system of monitoring and reporting."

1. Does the focus on "red flags" and reliance on management in these cases suggest that *Allis-Chalmers* is no longer good law? When can boards now rely on management representations?

2. In *Marchand* and *In Re Clovis*, the court stresses the highly regulated nature of the industries in which the firms conduct business and that each firm had "mission critical" products subject to that regulation. How does this change judicial analysis? What additional factors matter more in these situations?

3. In the *In Re Clovis* decision, the court noted there is a distinction between monitoring for business risks and legal risks. Earlier case law — *In re Citigroup Inc. Shareholder Derivative Litigation*, 964 A. 2d 106 (Del. Ch. 2009) — also seems to press on this point. There plaintiffs brought a

Caremark claim for the very large losses suffered by Citigroup from the subprime mortgage crisis. The court blocked the claim and noted that:

> While it may be tempting to say that directors have the same duties to monitor and oversee business risk [as legal risk], imposing *Caremark*-type duties on directors to monitor business risk is fundamentally different. Citigroup was in the business of taking on and managing investments and other business risks. To impose oversight liability on directors for failure to monitor "excessive" risk would involve courts in conducting hindsight evaluations of decisions at the heart of the business judgment of directors. Oversight duties under Delaware law are not designed to subject directors, even expert directors, to *personal liability* for failure to predict the future and to properly evaluate business risk.[40]

As a policy matter, does it make sense to draw a distinction between establishing a control system to detect employee misconduct and establishing a control system to evaluate business risk properly? Which category would seem to be more within a board's expertise? And which category would shareolders be more concerned about?

4. These cases were decided after the Department of Justice issued its guidance on evaluating compliance programs (see discussion *infra* Section 7.5.4). Should the Department of Justice's guidance influence Delaware in interpreting *Caremark* (as perhaps federal policy influenced *Caremark* itself)? Do these cases suggest that it already has?

7.5.4   *Caremark* Duties and Federal Enforcement

Although *Caremark* duties appear motivated in part by the development of the federal organizational sentencing guidelines and the important role of compliance programs therein, that does not mean federal enforcement and Delaware corporate law are quite the same. There are some important differences. First, a poor monitoring system under Delaware law enhances the risk of *directorial civil* liability while it enhances *corporate criminal* liability under federal law. Second, it is easier to satisfy Delaware's standard for monitoring than the federal one. Under *Caremark*, even the version seen in *Marchand*, it will usually be quite difficult to impose liability on directors because the presence of any compliance system and some attempt to monitor and oversee it by the board are together likely to absolve directors of liability. This is not the case under federal enforcement. Such protean compliance programs are not generally considered "reasonably effective compliance programs" under the organizational sentencing guidelines. Further, as

---

40. *In re Citigroup Inc.*, at 131. As the court says in footnote 78, "If directors are going to be held liable for losses for failing to accurately predict market events, then why not hold them liable for failing to profit by predicting market events that, in hindsight, the director should have seen because of certain red (or green?) flags? If one expects director prescience in one direction, why not the other?" Id.

noted earlier, such lackluster programs would increase the likelihood of the U.S. Department of Justice pursuing a criminal case against a corporation. Indeed, assessments about the effectiveness of a firm's compliance efforts may influence the details of any resolution — whether a deferred prosecution agreement might be given, would an independent monitor be appointed, and a host of other matters.[41]

In light of its importance, a critical question is what amounts to a "reasonably effective compliance program." That is the $64,000 question, or more accurately the multi-billion-dollar question given the size of the compliance industry. Although countless consultants, law firms, and academics have their views on this question, the Department of Justice remained relatively silent until recently when it issued its first policy statements on evaluating compliance programs. This was then updated in June 2020.[42]

The Department of Justice eschews any rigid formula for evaluating compliance efforts and prefers more individualized assessments that take into account a number of factors such as the firm's size, regulatory landscape, industry, and other relevant matters. The key features of the current approach center around three questions: (a) is the corporation's compliance program well designed, (b) is it adequately resourced and empowered to function effectively, and (c) does it work in practice? Although this may appear quite skeletal, the policy statements provide a bit more flesh to tease out some important elements. In particular, they note that a culture of compliance is critical, and this should manifest itself not just sporadically but in the day-to-day operations of the firm. Prosecutors should examine whether compliance and business are at loggerheads or do they try to work together. Moreover, "cookie cutter" compliance efforts are not as impressive as those more customized to a firm's specific context. Indeed, effective compliance is a process, not an end result — good compliance programs continuously learn from experience and try to improve. This will usually involve ongoing risk assessments and training within the firm as well as attempts to learn from the experiences of other similarly situated firms. The Department of Justice further encourages firms to rely on data and data analytics (and removing impediments to them) in making their decisions about compliance and internal controls and that both top and middle management be actively involved and committed to compliance. This level of seriousness should apply not just to the firm's employees but also to third parties utilized by the firm.[43]

---

41. See Arlen & Kahan, *supra* note 37; Brandon L. Garrett, Structural Reform Prosecution, 93 Va. L. Rev. 853 (2007); Dickinson and & Khanna, *supra* note 37.

42. See Evaluation of Corporate Compliance Programs (updated June 2020), U.S. Department of Justice, Criminal Division, available at: https://www.justice.gov/criminal-fraud/page/file/937501/download.

43. This is particularly important with the rise of supply chain structured businesses. In addition, in an interesting section of the Update, the Department of Justice notes that one part of the overall assessment of a firm's compliance efforts may include whether firms "track access [by its employees] to various policies and procedures to understand what policies are attracting more attention from relevant employees."

7.6   "KNOWING" VIOLATIONS OF LAW

In *Caremark*, the court says that directors have a duty to take reasonable steps to see that the corporation has in place an information and control structure designed to offer reasonable assurance that the corporation is in compliance with the law. But does that mean every aspect of our public policy should be deployed to this end? Specifically, in addition to the incentives provided in the federal Organizational Sentencing Guidelines above, should corporate law also command obedience to positive law? When we ask this question, are we necessarily asking whether shareholders should be able to sue directors to recover any loss the corporation may suffer (as in *Caremark*) by reason of a knowing violation of the law? Are there issues present in such a question in addition to whether we want augmented enforcement?

MILLER v. AT&T
507 F.2d 759 (3d Cir. 1974)

SEITZ, C.J.:

Plaintiffs, stockholders in American Telephone and Telegraph Company ("AT&T"), brought a stockholders' derivative action . . . against AT&T and all but one of its directors. The suit centered upon the failure of AT&T to collect an outstanding debt of some $1.5 million owed to the company by the Democratic National Committee ("DNC") for communications services provided by AT&T during the 1968 Democratic national convention. Federal diversity jurisdiction was invoked under 28 U.S.C. §1332.

Plaintiffs' complaint alleged that "neither the officers or directors of AT&T have taken any action to recover the amount owed" from on or about August 20, 1968, when the debt was incurred, until May 31, 1972, the date plaintiffs' amended complaint was filed. The failure to collect was alleged to have involved a breach of the defendant directors' duty to exercise diligence in handling the affairs of the corporation, to have resulted in affording a preference to the DNC in collection procedures in violation of §202(a) of the Communications Act of 1934, . . . and to have amounted to AT&T's making a "contribution" to the DNC in violation of a federal prohibition on corporate campaign spending, 18 U.S.C. §610 (1970). . . .

The pertinent law on the question of the defendant directors' fiduciary duties in this diversity action is that of New York, the state of AT&T's incorporation. . . . The sound business judgment rule, the basis of the district court's dismissal of plaintiffs' complaint, expresses the unanimous decision of American courts to eschew intervention in corporate decision-making if the judgment of directors and officers is uninfluenced by personal considerations and is exercised in good faith. . . .

Had plaintiffs' complaint alleged only failure to pursue a corporate claim, application of the sound business judgment rule would support the district court's ruling that a shareholder could not attack the directors' decision. . . . Where, however, the decision not to collect a debt owed the corporation is itself alleged to have been an illegal act, different rules apply. When New York law regarding such acts by directors is considered in conjunction with the underlying purposes of the particular statute involved here, we are convinced that the business judgment rule cannot insulate the defendant directors from liability if they did in fact breach 18 U.S.C. §610, as plaintiffs have charged.

Roth v. Robertson, 64 Misc. 343, 118 N.Y.S. 351 (Sup. Ct. 1909), illustrates the proposition that even though committed to benefit the corporation, illegal acts may amount to a breach of fiduciary duty in New York. In *Roth*, the managing director of an amusement park company had allegedly used corporate funds to purchase the silence of persons who threatened to complain about unlawful Sunday operation of the park. Recovery from the defendant director was sustained on the ground that the money was an illegal payment. . . .

The plaintiffs' complaint in the instant case alleges a similar "waste" of $1.5 million through an illegal campaign contribution. . . .

The alleged violation of the federal prohibition against corporate political contributions not only involves the corporation in criminal activity but similarly contravenes a policy of Congress clearly enunciated in 18 U.S.C. §610. That statute and its predecessor reflect congressional efforts: (1) to destroy the influence of corporations over elections through financial contributions and (2) to check the practice of using corporate funds to benefit political parties without the consent of the stockholders. . . .

The fact that shareholders are within the class for whose protection the statute was enacted gives force to the argument that the alleged breach of that statute should give rise to a cause of action in those shareholders to force the return to the corporation of illegally contributed funds. Since political contributions by corporations can be checked and shareholder control over the political use of general corporate funds is effectuated only if directors are restrained from causing the corporation to violate the statute, such a violation seems a particularly appropriate basis for finding breach of the defendant directors' fiduciary duty to the corporation. Under such circumstances, the directors cannot be insulated from liability on the ground that the contribution was made in the exercise of sound business judgment.

Since plaintiffs have alleged actual damage to the corporation from the transaction in the form of the loss of a $1.5 million increment to AT&T's treasury, we conclude that the complaint does state a claim upon which relief can be granted sufficient to withstand a motion to dismiss.

II

We have accepted plaintiffs' allegation of a violation of 18 U.S.C. §610 as a shorthand designation of the elements necessary to establish a breach of that statute. . . . That such a designation is sufficient for pleading purposes does not, however, relieve plaintiffs of their ultimate obligation to prove the elements of the statutory violation as part of their proof of breach of fiduciary duty. At the appropriate time, plaintiffs will be required to produce evidence sufficient to establish three distinct elements comprising a violation of 18 U.S.C. §610: that AT&T (1) made a contribution of money or anything of value to the DNC (2) in connection with a federal election (3) for the purpose of influencing the outcome of that election. . . . The order of the district court will be reversed and the case remanded for further proceedings consistent with this opinion.

PROBLEM

Knowing violations of law are conceptually distinct from the duty-of-care topics that are addressed in the prior sections of this chapter. To see why, consider a board that deliberates with the utmost care to authorize an action that they know to be illegal. As the *Miller* court tells us, the business judgment rule will not immunize their decision from judicial scrutiny.[44] For this reason, the duty to obey the law can be seen as a judge-created positive overlay on the overall fiduciary duty structure. This imposition seems unproblematic in the case of definite violations of the law, but what about the far more common situation where the legal advice is "some likelihood" or "substantial risk" of violating the law? Could it be the case that corporate law prevents directors from taking *any* risk of violating the law? Or is a balance-of-the-probabilities test required, in which the directors have to know only that it is more likely than not lawful? If an action has some probability of being in violation of a binding regulation, but legal opinion is not that it is more likely than not illegal, how should a board decide? To make the question concrete, consider the following problem:

The board of Acme, Inc. is asked to approve the use of Grade II fuel instead of Grade I fuel in operating a large plant. The board is told that using the lower grade of fuel will cause the company to run an 85 percent risk that the plant will exceed Clean Air Act standards at least once a month, and the best estimate is that it will cause this to happen on average 3.5 times per month. If such a violation were detected and prosecuted, a fine could be levied that would be no more than $10,000 for each violation. Using the lower grade fuel would save more than $80,000 per month at current prices. While this decision would not ordinarily require board action, in this case senior management brings the question to the board because it does involve a possible violation of government regulations.

1. Consider that you are the general counsel of the company. What would you tell the board about its fiduciary duty to the corporation, and what would you say about the corporation's obligation to obey the law and the directors' obligation to cause it to do so?

---

44. See also *Metro Communications Corp. BVI v. Advanced Mobilecomm Technologies, Inc.*, 854 A.2d 121, 131 (Del. Ch. 2004) ("Under Delaware law, a fiduciary may not choose to manage an entity in an illegal fashion, even if the fiduciary believes that the illegal activity will result in profits for the entity.").

2. Would it matter if the probability of violation were 10 percent instead of 85 percent, but the sanction for causing a knowing violation of the standard was incarceration for any person in control of the violator (including directors)?
3. You are personal counsel to one of the outside directors. This action is taken, and the corporation is later determined to have violated applicable clean air standards and fined. What sources of potential risks to your client do you see, and what arguments in her favor exist?

For academic perspectives on this sort of problem, compare, e.g., Robert Cooter, *Prices and Sanctions,* 84 Colum. L. Rev. 1523, 1524-1525 (1984) (drawing the distinction between acts *malum in se* and those *malum prohibitum*) and following the law and economics view that regulations enforced by fines may rationally be regarded (and should be by boards) as ticket prices with Cynthia Williams, *Corporate Compliance with Law in the Era of Efficiency,* 76 N.C. L. Rev. 1265, 1325-1327 (1998) (binding regulatory rules should be complied with on moral as well as legal grounds) and Judd Sneirson, *Shareholder Primacy and Corporate Compliance* 26 Fordham Envir. L. Rev. 450 (2015) (providing alternative grounds for disputing soundness of the view that regulatory prohibitions may be analyzed as "ticket prices").

In what way does the agency problem of the board bear on the question of corporate compliance with known positive regulation?

8

THE DUTY OF LOYALTY: CONFLICT TRANSACTIONS

The core of fiduciary doctrine is the duty of loyalty. In Chapters 6 and 7, we examined the relatively mild legal controls on the board's discretion to make ordinary business decisions: the shareholders' right to appoint directors and the duty of care. These controls are "weak" in the sense that they do not typically limit the board's discretion to enter specific transactions—nor could they without sacrificing the efficiencies that arise from the delegation of managerial power to the board. But there are some specific corporate actions over which it may be sensible to limit board discretion. Indeed, the corporate law in every jurisdiction imposes specific controls on two classes of corporate actions: those in which a director or controlling shareholder has a personal financial interest and those that are considered integral to the existence or identity of the company. In this Chapter, we address the first of these: interested corporate actions. This category naturally includes self-dealing transactions between the company and its directors, but it also extends to appropriations of "corporate opportunities," compensation of officers and directors (dealt with in the following Chapter), and even relations between controlling and minority shareholders. In U.S. corporate law, all of these interested transactions are regulated in large measure by the fiduciary duty of loyalty. In Chapter 12, we explore the second class of corporate actions for which the law imposes specific limitations on board discretion: corporate mergers, dissolutions, and sales of substantially all assets.

The duty of loyalty requires a corporate director, officer, or controlling shareholder to exercise her institutional power over corporate processes or property (including information) in a good-faith attempt to advance the interests of the company. Thus, while the ambit of the duty of loyalty can extend beyond transactions in which a corporate fiduciary has a conflicting financial interest, such "related-party" transactions are the classic situation in which claims of breach of loyalty are made. In these transactions, a corporate fiduciary must fully disclose all material facts to the corporation's disinterested representatives and deal with the company on terms that are intrinsically fair. Corporate officers, directors, and controlling shareholders may not deal with the corporation in any way that benefits themselves at its expense.

The importance of this obligation is greater in the corporation than in the simple agency relationship because corporate directors and officers (like trustees) tend to exercise greater discretion than do ordinary agents. In addition, the duty of loyalty is more complex in the corporate context for two reasons. First, although the corporation is a fictional legal entity, real people invest in it. Some invest financial assets by buying the corporation's debt or equity, while others invest human capital over their years of employment. Communities may invest in the corporation with roads, schools, tax abatements, etc. Thus, when we say that directors owe a duty of loyalty, the logical first question is, "Loyalty to whom?" The second reason the duty of loyalty is more complex in the corporate context relates to the question of how it can be enforced — to whomever it is owed. The enforcement problem is especially pressing in large public corporations, where many constituencies tend to be fragmented and unorganized.

8.1   Duty to Whom?

To whom do directors owe loyalty? The short answer is that they owe their duty to the corporation as a legal entity.[1] Yet the meaning of that answer is still disputed today. The "corporation" has multiple constituencies with often conflicting interests, including stockholders, creditors, employees, suppliers, and customers. To say that directors owe loyalty to the corporation masks conflicts among these constituencies. Happily, in many cases, these conflicts can be reconciled in practice. For a solvent firm, if corporate liability rules, reputation, and contract lead firms to take into account the full effects of their activities on all constituencies, then shareholders, as residual claimants, will only get paid after satisfying the firm's obligations to all other constituencies. In this situation, it makes little difference whether managers think of themselves as furthering long-term shareholder interests or furthering multi-constituency long-term interests.

The question of whose interests ultimately count is of practical importance when the corporation faces insolvency (when by definition there may not be enough corporate assets to satisfy all of the corporation's obligations to all constituencies) or when it contemplates a terminal transaction for equity investors, such as a cash merger (when equity investors will no longer have an interest in the future welfare of the corporation or its other constituencies) or where contract, reputation, or corporate liability rules do not effectively induce firms to take into account their effects on other constituencies. Although these examples counsel for reform in their respective areas of law (e.g., insolvency, corporate liability), they are also examples of when the question of "Duty to whom?" may be most acute.

---

1. In some circumstances, directors deal with stockholders directly, as when they disclose information about a transaction that requires shareholder approval. In these cases, directors owe a duty directly to shareholders. See *In re Cencom Cable Income Partners, L.P. Litigation*, 2000 WL 130629 (Del. Ch. Jan. 27, 2000).

8.1.1   The Shareholder Primacy Norm

That director loyalty to the "corporation" is, ultimately, loyalty to equity investors is an important theme of U.S. corporate law. Shareholders, after all, elect the boards of directors in U.S. corporations, as they do in almost all other jurisdictions. But exactly what additional weight the norm of shareholder primacy carries in corporate law is not always clear. Delaware law and that of a minority of other U.S. jurisdictions make the centrality of shareholder interests in defining the duties of corporate directors clear as an abstract proposition.[2] By contrast, 28 states have adopted so-called constituency statutes that suggest that shareholder primacy is itself a matter of board discretion.[3] But these constituency statutes are themselves a legacy of a period between 1985 and 1990, when management feared that greater board discretion was needed to defend against hostile takeovers. With the emergence of stronger legal defenses against takeovers, the dynamic favoring looser constraints on the formal obligations of boards also lost its force, although not before leaving its mark on many state statutes (not including Delaware, of course).

For most of the history of American corporate law, the dominant role of shareholder interests in defining the duties of directors has more closely resembled a deep but implicit norm rather than a legal rule in any conventional sense. In 1919, the Supreme Court of Michigan recognized this value explicitly as a rule in the famous case of *Dodge v. Ford Motor Co.*[4] The Dodge brothers, who held 10 percent of the shares in Ford Motor Company, had sued to force Ford's board to declare a dividend out of a large pool of earnings that had been retained to fund new projects and to "finance" price reductions on Ford products. Henry Ford, Ford's controlling shareholder, explained his decision to eliminate special dividends on the grounds that Ford had an obligation to share its success "with the public" through price reductions. Taking this claim at face value (see sidebar: The Dodge Brothers and Henry Ford), the Dodge brothers alleged that Ford's directors had wrongfully subordinated shareholder interests to those of consumers by holding back dividends. The court agreed and affirmed the primacy of the shareholders' interests:

> [I]t is not within the lawful powers of a board to shape and conduct the affairs of a corporation for the merely incidental benefit of shareholders and for the primary purpose of benefiting others, and no one will contend that, if the avowed purpose of the defendant directors was to sacrifice the interests of shareholders, it would not be the duty of the courts to interfere.[5]

---

2. See, e.g., Leo Strine, *The Dangers of Denial: The Need for a Clear-Eyed Understanding of the Power and Accountability Structure Established by the Delaware General Corporation Law*, 50 Wake Forest L. Rev. 761 (2015).

3. See Edward Rock, *For Whom Is the Corporation Managed in 2020?: The Debate over Corporate Purpose*, (NYU Law School Working Paper 2020).

4. 204 Mich. 459, 170 N.W. 668 (1919).

5. Id. at 507.

THE DODGE BROTHERS AND HENRY FORD

The Dodge brothers, Horace and John, opened a small machine shop in Detroit, Michigan, in 1901. Their first product was a bicycle with an innovative ball bearing machine, but they quickly moved into the growing automobile industry. Ransom Eli Olds, maker of the Oldsmobile, contracted with the Dodge brothers to make transmissions for his Oldsmobile in 1902. And shortly thereafter, the Dodge brothers became intrigued by Henry Ford's prototype for a new car and engine. The Dodge brothers gave Ford automobile parts and cash in return for a 10 percent stake in Ford Motor Company. Dodge manufactured every part of the Ford car except for the wooden seats and the rubber tires. Sales quickly exploded, and the Dodges' 10 percent stake in Ford became one of the most lucrative investments in business history.

Over the years, the Dodge brothers suggested several improvements to the Model T, which Ford refused to implement. In 1913, the Dodge brothers announced that they would stop building cars for Ford, and would design, build, and sell their own car. In 1914, the first Dodge cars rolled off the assembly line. They were quickly judged to be better than the Model T in every way, and only $100 more. Ford was not happy that the dividends he paid to the Dodge brothers were being used to bankroll his competition. In 1916, Ford announced that his company would stop paying dividends, in an attempt to cut off the cash flow that fueled his rivals' business. The move set the stage for the "trial of the century" (up to 1919) in *Dodge v. Ford Motor Co.*

Dodge is in all corporate law casebooks for a reason: there are few other opinions that actually enforce shareholder primacy as a rule of law — that is, to predicate liability on its breach. Moreover, *Dodge* is an old opinion. A board's good-faith decision today to use retained earnings to fund investments, price reductions, or even increased employee wages would easily be justified as a device to increase long-term corporate earnings and, as such, would be seen as legitimate business judgment, immune from shareholder attack. A question of loyalty would arise only in the odd circumstance that the board claimed to advance non-shareholder interests over those of shareholders. Thus, *Dodge v. Ford Motor Co.* is unique precisely because Mr. Ford announced that he was acting in the interests of non-shareholders. Today, when hedge funds like Elliott Management Corp. push multinational corporations like Hyundai Motor Group to double its proposed dividend to "unlock value" for shareholders, their primary tactic is not litigation of the *Dodge v. Ford Motor Co.* type, but organizing shareholder voting power.

The norm of shareholder primacy dominated discussion of the "purpose" of U.S. corporations during the recent past but it never fully eclipsed a competing norm: the view that directors must act to advance the interests of all constituencies in the corporation, not just the shareholders.[6] As we write

---

6. The classic discussion of this subject is the Depression-era debate between Professor E. Merrick Dodd of Harvard and Professor Adolf Berle of Columbia. *See* Adopf A. Berle, *Corporate Powers as Powers in Trust*, 44 Harv. L. Rev. 1049 (1931); E. Merrick Dodd, *For Whom Are Corporate Managers Trustees?*, 45 Harv. L. Rev. 1145 (1932); Adolf A. Berle, *For Whom Corporate Managers Are Trustees: A Note*, 45 Harv. L. Rev. 1365 (1932). The literature on this subject is voluminous. For a recap of the issue in the age of hostile takeovers, see

today, this "stakeholder" conception of corporate purpose that prevailed from roughly 1940–1970 has made a remarkable comeback. From this perspective, the corporation is more than a private contract; the state bestows the status of legal entity, including limited liability, on the corporation in order to advance the public interest by enabling the board to protect all corporate constituencies, not just shareholders. Of course, sophisticated proponents of the shareholder primacy goal agree that the state is entitled to craft the duty of directors in any way it chooses. They argue, however, that framing the board's mission as maximizing shareholder welfare also serves to maximize the welfare of other corporate constituencies and society as a whole. We summarize how corporate law and civil society have responded to this tension in four contexts: charitable corporate giving, legal release as in the case of constituency statutes, current pronouncements by influential interest groups in management and finance, and the rise of new forms of business enterprise, such as the Public Benefit Corporation, which explicitly allow for consideration of the interests of other constituencies (and public benefits) along with shareholders' interests.

8.1.2 Charitable Contributions

Dodge v. Ford Motor Co. is an unusual case. A more common arena of conflict between different conceptions of corporate purpose and director loyalty prior to the 1980s involved corporate charitable giving. Here one might ask: How can directors *ever* justify giving away some of the corporation's profits to worthy causes (which many firms do) if their principal duty is owed to shareholders? Unsurprisingly, when faced with defendant directors who, unlike Henry Ford, justified their actions by reference to long-term corporate benefits, courts have deferred to director action. The following excerpt deals with a small grant to Princeton University by the A.P. Smith Manufacturing Co.

A.P. SMITH MANUFACTURING CO. v. BARLOW
98 A.2d 581 (N.J. 1953)

Jacobs, J.:

The objecting stockholders have not disputed any of the foregoing testimony nor the showing of great need by Princeton and other private institutions of higher learning and the important public service being rendered by them for democratic government and industry alike. Similarly, they have

---

William T. Allen, *Our Schizophrenic Conception of the Business Corporation*, 14 Cardozo L. Rev. 261 (1992). For a law-and-economics defense of the Merrick-Dodd position that directors must reconcile the interests of disparate corporate constituencies, see Margaret M. Blair & Lynn A. Stout, *A Team Production Theory of Corporate Law*, 85 Va. L. Rev. 247 (1999). For a contrasting view that shareholder primacy is likely to dominate the future development of corporate law, see Henry Hansmann & Reinier H. Kraakman, *The End of History for Corporate Law*, 89 Geo. L.J. 439 (2001).

acknowledged that for over two decades there has been state legislation on our books which expresses a strong public policy in favor of corporate contributions such as that being questioned by them. Nevertheless, they have taken the position that (1) the plaintiff's certificate of incorporation does not expressly authorize the contribution and under common-law principles the company does not possess any implied or incidental power to make it, and (2) the New Jersey statutes which expressly authorize the contribution may not constitutionally be applied to the plaintiff, a corporation created long before their enactment. . . .

In his discussion of the early history of business corporations Professor Williston refers to a 1702 publication where the author stated flatly that "The general intent and end of all civil incorporations is for better government." And he points out that the early corporate charters, particularly their recitals, furnish additional support for the notion that the corporate object was the public one of managing and ordering the trade as well as the private one of profit for the members. . . . However, with later economic and social developments and the free availability of the corporate device for all trades, the end of private profit became generally accepted as the controlling one in all businesses other than those classed broadly as public utilities. Cf. E. Merrick Dodd, Jr., *For Whom Are Corporate Managers Trustees?*, 45 Harv. L. Rev. 1145, 1148 (1932). As a concomitant the common-law rule developed that those who managed the corporation could not disburse any corporate funds for philanthropic or other worthy public cause unless the expenditure would benefit the corporation. . . . *Dodge v. Ford Motor Co.*, 204 Mich. 459 (Sup. Ct. 1919). . . . [C]ourts while adhering to the terms of the common-law rule, have applied it very broadly to enable worthy corporate donations with indirect benefits to the corporations. . . . When the wealth of the nation was primarily in the hands of individuals they discharged their responsibilities as citizens by donating freely for charitable purposes. With the transfer of most of the wealth to corporate hands and the imposition of heavy burdens of individual taxation, [these individuals have] . . . turned to corporations to assume the modern obligations of good citizenship in the same manner as humans do. . . .

More and more [corporations] have come to recognize that their salvation rests upon [a] sound economic and social environment which in turn rests . . . upon free and vigorous nongovernmental institutions of learning. It seems to us that just as the conditions prevailing when corporations were originally created required that they serve public as well as private interests, modern conditions require that corporations acknowledge and discharge social as well as private responsibilities as members of the communities within which they operate. Within this broad concept there is no difficulty in sustaining, as incidental to their proper objects and in aid of the public welfare, the power of corporations to contribute corporate funds within reasonable limits in support of academic institutions. But even if we confine ourselves to the terms of the common-law-rule, . . . such expenditures may likewise readily be justified as being for the benefit of the corporation; indeed, if need be the matter may be viewed strictly in terms of actual survival of the corporation in a free enterprise system. . . .

In 1930 a statute was enacted in our State which expressly provided that any corporation could cooperate with other corporations and natural persons in the creation and maintenance of community funds and charitable, philanthropic or benevolent instrumentalities conducive to public welfare, and could for such purposes expend such corporate sums as the directors "deem expedient and as in their judgment will contribute to the protection of the corporate interests." . . . In 1950 . . . the Legislature declared that it shall be the public policy of our State . . . that encouragement be given to the creation and maintenance of institutions engaged in . . . the betterment of social and economic conditions, and it expressly empowered corporations . . . to contribute reasonable sums to such institutions, provided, however, that . . . the contribution shall not exceed 1% of capital and surplus unless . . . authorized by the stockholders. . . . It may [also] be noted that statutes relating to charitable contributions by corporations have now been passed in 29 states. . . .

The appellants contend that the foregoing New Jersey statutes may not be applied to corporations created before their passage. Fifty years before the incorporation of The A.P. Smith Manufacturing Company our Legislature provided that every corporate charter thereafter granted "shall be subject to alteration, suspension and repeal, in the discretion of the legislature." . . . A similar reserved power . . .is found in our present Constitution. . . .

In the light of all of the foregoing we have no hesitancy in sustaining the validity of the donation by the plaintiff. There is no suggestion that it was made indiscriminately or to a pet charity of the corporate directors in furtherance of personal rather than corporate ends. On the contrary, it was made to a preeminent institution of higher learning, was modest in amount and well within the limitations imposed by the statutory enactments, and was voluntarily made in the reasonable belief that it would aid the public welfare and advance the interests of the plaintiff as a private corporation and as part of the community in which it operate. . . .

QUESTIONS ON SMITH v. BARLOW

1. Suppose that the A.P. Smith Manufacturing Co. board had chosen to donate 2 percent of its capital and surplus to Princeton University without seeking shareholder approval. Would the court have invalidated the donation? Why shouldn't the board's business judgment prevail as to the size of the donation necessary to meet the company's "obligations of good citizenship" and advance its interests as a private corporation?

2. How far does *Barlow*'s holding reach? Can the long-term benefit of the corporation support a financial contribution to a controversial political cause (say, a contraception manufacturer wanting to make a donation to a pro-choice organization)? What about to the favorite charity of a corporate customer or a director? Does it matter which?

3. More fundamentally, what, precisely, is the connection between the observation that the corporation should serve the public interest and the claim that directors ought to have the power to contribute to charity? Could the law deny directors this power in the name of public interest, too?

8.1.3 Constituency Statutes

As noted above, the question "To whom do directors owe loyalty?" acquired much more economic importance in the hostile leveraged buyout transactions of the 1980s. In these transactions, buyers would typically offer shareholders a high premium price for their shares and then, when they had control, sell off significant assets, lay off workers, increase debt on the company's balance sheet, and replace senior management. Thus these transactions advantaged shareholders but left employees out of work and creditors to face an increased risk of default and bankruptcy.[7]

In many of these 1980s transactions, senior managers found themselves in the same precarious position as other non-shareholder stakeholders. Naturally, these managers often resisted being taken over, but in justifying their resistance to high-premium cash offers, they could not persuasively resort to a vision of maximizing long-term economic value of shareholders (as managers had long done for making charitable contributions). Thus, managerial advocates turned to the rationale that directors owe loyalty to something apart from the shareholders alone: the corporation, understood as a combination of all its stakeholders — creditors, shareholders, managers, workers, suppliers, and customers. Although, to be fair, the doctrinal logic of treating the corporation as legal person separate from its shareholders might seem to invite such a conclusion.

With remarkable speed, state legislatures rode to the rescue of managers and other non-shareholder constituencies by enacting statutes that provided, in varying terms, that directors have the power (but not the obligation) to balance the interests of non-shareholder constituencies against the interests of shareholders in setting corporate policy.[8] These statutes may or may not break with our venerable legal tradition of shareholder primacy. A conservative reading of them is that they merely reassert the board's traditional freedom to deal with non-shareholder constituencies in whatever manner it believes best advances the long-term interests of the corporation's shareholders. By contrast, the Corporation Law Committee of the American Bar Association refused to include a constituency provision in the Model Business Corporation Act on the grounds that this would break sharply with the tradition of U.S. corporate law and would undermine much of the established case law.[9] We deal with the constituency problem in greater depth in Chapter 13, in the context of hostile corporate takeovers.

---

7. See Andrei Shleifer & Lawrence H. Summers, *Breach of Trust in Hostile Takeovers*, in Corporate Takeovers: Causes and Consequences, pp. 33-56 (Alan J. Auerbach ed., 1988).

8. Delaware has *not* adopted a constituency statute. However, the Delaware Supreme Court has stated that, in creating takeover defenses, the board may consider the interests of corporate constituencies other than shareholders as long as these have some relationship to long-term shareholder value. *Unocal Corp. v. Mesa Petroleum Co.*, 493 A.2d 946 (Del. 1985). For an argument that the Delaware takeover cases implicitly adopt a paternalistic form of the shareholder primacy norm, see Bernard S. Black & Reinier H. Kraakman, *Delaware's Takeover Law: The Uncertain Search for Hidden Value*, 96 Nw. U. L. Rev. 521, 527-528 (2002).

9. Corporation Law Committee of the American Bar Association, *Report: Other Constituencies Statutes*, 45 Bus. Law. 2253 (1990).

QUESTION ON CONSTITUENCY STATUTES

Given that U.S. constituency statutes do not enable constituencies other than shareholders to sue directors for breach of fiduciary duty, what have these other constituencies gained? Who represents their concerns? Does this color your opinion of these statutes? Recent evidence suggests that constituency statutes did not benefit constituencies, but rather shareholders, management, and the board. See Lucian A. Bebchuk, Kobi Kastiel & Roberto Tallarita, *For Whom Corporate Leaders Bargain* (Working Paper, August 19, 2020).

8.1.4   A Broad Vision of Corporate Purpose Gains New Friends in High Places

In the past few years, financial powerhouses such as the major asset managers and managerial associations such as the Business Roundtable — which includes the CEOs of many of America's largest companies — have joined the conversation about "corporate purpose," and by implication about the duties of corporate directors. Consider the following excerpts from a letter to American CEOs authored by Laurence Fink, the CEO of BlackRock, arguably the world's largest asset manager, and the contrast between the Business Roundtable's most recent pronouncement on corporate purpose and the prior statement that it replaces.

LAURENCE FINK, *A FUNDAMENTAL RESHAPING OF FINANCE* (LETTER TO CEOS), JAN. 2020

Dear CEO,

As an asset manager, BlackRock invests on behalf of others, and I am writing to you as an advisor and fiduciary to these clients. . . .

We believe that all investors, along with regulators, insurers, and the public, need a clearer picture of how companies are managing sustainability-related questions. This data should extend beyond climate to questions around how each company serves its full set of stakeholders, such as the diversity of its workforce, the sustainability of its supply chain, or how well it protects its customers' data. Each company's prospects for growth are inextricable from its ability to operate sustainably and serve its full set of stakeholders.

The importance of serving stakeholders and embracing purpose is becoming increasingly central to the way that companies understand their role in society. **As I have written in past letters, a company cannot achieve long-term profits without embracing purpose and considering the needs of a broad range of stakeholders.** A pharmaceutical company that hikes prices ruthlessly, a mining company that shortchanges safety, a bank that fails to respect its clients – these companies may maximize returns in the short term. But, as we have seen again and again, these actions that damage society will catch up with a company and destroy shareholder value. By contrast, a strong sense of purpose and a commitment to stakeholders helps a company connect more deeply to its customers and adjust to the changing demands of society. **Ultimately, purpose is the engine of long-term profitability. . .** [emphasis in the original].

THE BUSINESS ROUNDTABLE, STATEMENT ON THE PURPOSE OF A CORPORATION (AUG. 2019)

Americans deserve an economy that allows each person to succeed through hard work and creativity and to lead a life of meaning and dignity. We believe the free-market system is the best means of generating good jobs, a strong and sustainable economy, innovation, a healthy environment and economic opportunity for all. . . .

While each of our individual companies serves its own corporate purpose, we share a fundamental commitment to all of our stakeholders. We commit to:

- Delivering value to our customers. We will further the tradition of American companies leading the way in meeting or exceeding customer expectations.
- Investing in our employees. This starts with compensating them fairly and providing important benefits. It also includes supporting them through training and education that help develop new skills for a rapidly changing world. We foster diversity and inclusion, dignity and respect.
- Dealing fairly and ethically with our suppliers. We are dedicated to serving as good partners to the other companies, large and small, that help us meet our missions.
- Supporting the communities in which we work. We respect the people in our communities and protect the environment by embracing sustainable practices across our businesses.
- Generating long-term value for shareholders, who provide the capital that allows companies to invest, grow and innovate. We are committed to transparency and effective engagement with shareholders.

Each of our stakeholders is essential. We commit to deliver value to all of them, for the future success of our companies, our communities and our country.

Signed by 181 CEO members

———————————

As Professor Edward Rock has observed:[10]

"To understand why the Business Roundtable [BRT] statement attracted so much attention [in 2019], it must be compared to the Business Roundtable's

———————————

10. See Rock, *supra* note 3, at 2. Professor Rock's paper provides helpful guidance in unpacking the multiple levels on which the debate over corporate purpose occurs.

September 1997 statement in which the BRT stated that 'the principal objective of a business enterprise is to generate economic returns to its owners' and that:

> "In The Business Roundtable's view, the paramount duty of management and of boards of directors is to the corporation's stockholders; the interests of other stakeholders are relevant as a derivative of the duty to stockholders. The notion that the board must somehow balance the interests of stockholders against the interests of other stakeholders fundamentally misconstrues the role of directors. It is, moreover, an unworkable notion because it would leave the board with no criterion for resolving conflicts between interests of stockholders and of other stakeholders or among different groups of stakeholders."

NOTE AND QUESTIONS ON THE CORPORATE PURPOSE DEBATE

The reinvigoration of the corporate purpose debate was presaged in part by the growth of investing that takes environmental, social, and governance (ESG) considerations into account (sometimes called socially responsible investing).[11] Most of the major asset managers offer ESG-oriented funds whose strategies range from excluding portfolio investments in sectors raising ESG concerns (e.g., oil and gas, tobacco) to actively selecting firms for their portfolios that promise to integrate ESG into their underlying business models. ESG-oriented funds represent the fastest growing sector of the asset management business. Recent estimates suggest that these funds represent north of $1 trillion in assets under management with more growth predicted in years to come.[12]

In addition, many firms actively engage in corporate social responsibility (CSR).[13] This can take many forms including philanthropic activities, reducing harmful firm externalities (e.g., pollution), and weaving social responsibility into the firm's strategy and offerings.

Although these developments, and the statements noted earlier, have led to more discussion on the corporation's purpose, whether this will just result in homilies or something more substantial in terms of business practice or the law is anybody's guess. It is noteworthy that former Chief Justice of the Delaware Supreme Court Leo Strine has argued that Delaware law is quite clear that "directors must make stockholder welfare their sole end, and that

---

11. On the growth of ESG-oriented investing, see Max M. Schanzenbach & Robert H. Sitkoff, *Reconciling Fiduciary Duty and Social Conscience: The Law and Economics of ESG Investing by a Trustee*, 72 Stan. L. Rev. 381 (2020).

12. See Siobhan Riding, *ESG Funds Attract Record Inflows During Crisis*, Financial Times, August 10, 2020; *Why Covid-19 Could Prove to Be a Major Turning Point for ESG Investing*, J.P. Morgan (July 1, 2020), https://www.jpmorgan.com/global/research/covid-19-esg-investing. Both passive and active ESG funds have seen substantial increases. See Hazel Bradford, *Passive ESG on the Rise — Report*, Pensions & Investments, July 28, 2020.

13. The CSR literature is vast. *See, e.g.,* Allen Ferrell, Hao Liang & Luc Renneboog, *Socially Responsible Firms*, 122 J. Fin. Econ. 585 (2016); Hao Liang & Luc Renneboog, *On the Foundations of Corporate Social Responsibility*, 72 J. Fin. 853 (2017).

other interests may be taken into consideration only as a means of promoting stockholder welfare."[14] Further, he argues that pretending that Delaware case law and the DGCL are otherwise is likely to distract and obscure from the reforms that would be more productive — tightening the regulation of externalities (e.g., strengthening corporate liability rules) and developing new business entities that explicitly allow directors to take account of non-shareholder interests, such as perhaps the public benefit corporation discussed below.[15]

1. A plausible guess is that half of the U.S. public equity that BlackRock manages are stocks in Delaware corporations. The DGCL does not include a constituency provision authorizing boards to balance the conflicting interests of corporate stakeholders at their discretion. Is the weight that Larry Fink attaches to stakeholder interests consistent with Delaware law?

2. In Mr. Fink's view, combating environmental degradation, and global warming in particular, should receive top priority in any formulation of corporate purposes. But consider an international oil and gas company such as Exxon. Would the directors of such companies violate their fiduciary duties if they announced that in light of the threat that all corporations faced from global warming, they would discontinue ongoing profitable drilling activities and divert their substantial exploratory drilling budgets to acquiring renewable energy companies?

3. Should pension fund trustees be free to entrust the management of their assets to BlackRock funds promising only to invest in portfolio companies with the highest third-party ESG ratings, i.e., ratings for best conduct on environmental, social, and governance metrics?[16]

4. Is the Business Roundtable's 2019 formulation of a shared component of corporate purpose among its members materially different from that advocated by BlackRock? Is it consistent with Delaware corporate law? And, if so, was the Business Roundtable's standing definition of corporate purpose between 1997-2019 also consistent with Delaware law?

5. Should the courts take notice of the views of the CEO membership of the Business Roundtable, as opposed to the firms for which they work, when addressing issues related to the purpose of the corporation or the duties of its directors? See Lucian Bebchuk & Roberto Tallarita, *"Stakeholder" Capitalism Seems Mostly for Show*, Wall St. J., August 6, 2020. Should the courts be concerned that the focus on stakeholders and corporate purpose may be used to justify opposing hedge fund activism (or shareholder activism more broadly) discussed in Chapter 6?

---

14. Leo Strine, *The Dangers of Denial: The Need for a Clear-Eyed Understanding of the Power and Accountability Structure Established by the Delaware General Corporation Law*, 50 Wake Forest L. Rev. 761, 768 (2015).

15. See id. at 38-40.

16. There are many ESG ratings available — see, e.g., Florian Berg, Julian Kölbel & Roberto Rigobon, *Aggregate Confusion: The Divergence of ESG Ratings* (May 17, 2020). Available at SSRN: https://ssrn.com/abstract=3438533. The Department of Labor also influences ESG investing through its regulation of retirement plan investing and it has recently proposed rules that according to some appear to burden ESG investing. See Jeffrey P. Mahoney, *Comment Letter to DOL*, Harv. Law School Forum on Corp. Gov., August 13, 2020.

8.1.5 Defining Corporate Purpose in the Charter: Public Benefit Corporations

In light of the corporate purpose debate, one might ask: What if a group of individuals wanted to form a for-profit corporation with the aim of pursuing some mission-driven business (say, a delivery service with a minimal carbon footprint) — could they do so under standard corporate law statutes? They probably could if they tried hard enough. They might carefully specify a narrow business purpose in the company charter and lock up control in the hands of directors who could be relied upon to support this purpose. This might mean allocating voting control to disinterested trustees. But the drafting challenges involved would be considerable. Of course, there is always the alternative of forming a nonprofit corporation. But suppose our socially minded entrepreneurs wished the managers of their firm to seek profit in the name of efficiency. Combining these objectives with the framework of for-profit corporation statutes is not easy.

Starting in 2010, state legislatures began making this easier by providing a standard form corporation, generally called a Public Benefit Corporation (PB Corp), which in default provides provisions facilitating this sort of commitment.[17] Delaware's statute is memorialized in DGCL §§361-368. Generally, a PB Corp is formed like other corporations and its shareholders elect the directors, who have the customary broad authority. A major difference is that the statutes contemplate the inclusion in the corporation's charter of one or more specific social purposes along with the profit-making purpose. There is in this case, then, a fiduciary obligation of the directors to the corporation and its shareholders to pursue that purpose in addition to shareholder long-term gain.[18] This gives directors and officers of PB Corps explicit legal protection to pursue the stated social mission and to consider additional stakeholders as well as equity investors.

Management enjoys more protection in a PB Corp in other ways too. For example, derivative suits by shareholders may only be initiated by shareholders owning the lesser of 2 percent of the company's shares or $2,000,000 in value of those shares. (We will see in Chapter 10 that there is no such limitation with respect to ordinary business corporations.) PB Corps managers also used to enjoy some protection from hostile takeovers because PB Corps required a supermajority shareholder vote — a two-third's vote rather than the conventional majority vote — to approve a merger or charter amendment. However, in 2020 Delaware removed this restriction and now a simple majority is all that is required (absent a contrary provision in the PB Corp charter).

---

17. A PB Corp is different from a "B Corp" which is a certification used by B Lab discussed below.

18. Section 365(a) of the DGCL provides: "The board of directors shall manage or direct the business and affairs of the public benefit corporation in a manner that balances the pecuniary interests of the stockholders, the best interests of those materially affected by the corporation's conduct, and the specific public benefit or public benefits identified in its certificate of incorporation."

But while the PB Corp may provide some protections, in the end if a sufficient number of the investors want to cash out, this form itself will not stop that.

Moreover, directors of PB Corps face additional but limited reporting requirements. They must make periodic reports to their shareholders about the activities they have undertaken to advance the social commitments named in their charters. Under the DGCL, such disclosures must be made every two years. See DGCL §366. Statutes in some other states mandate an outside audit of such reports. See, e.g., New York's BSC §1708(2). The DGCL does not require an audit. Nonetheless, third-party certifications for ESG-related matters are available. One of the best known is the "B Corporation" certification provided by the nonprofit organization B Lab, which has granted over 3,000 such certifications in over 70 countries.[19]

Increasing public attention led Delaware to amend the PB Corps provisions of the DGCL in 2020. The new amendments allow PB Corps to convert into a regular corporation and vice versa with a simple majority vote (as compared to the two-thirds vote needed in the earlier version law). The amendments also clarify and further limit the potential liability of directors.[20]

NOTES AND QUESTIONS ON PUBLIC BENEFIT CORPORATIONS

1. In light of the broad discretion granted to corporate directors under the business judgment rule (see Chapter 7) and the capacious interpretation of shareholders' interests witnessed in *Barlow*, what additional discretion is being granted to directors in a PB Corp? Is it simply that PB Corp directors do not need to come up with a reason for how investing in the public benefit work or considering stakeholders' interests furthers shareholders' interests? Consider *eBay Holdings, Inc. v. Newmark* 16 A.3d 1 (Del. Ch. 2010), wherein the founders and controllers of Craigslist, Inc. resisted attempts by a large minority shareholder (eBay) to push for profit-maximization. The founders conceived of the firm as a community service, rather than a profit-maximizing entity, but failed to note that in their charter and incorporated as a standard Delaware corporation. They attempted to block any attempts to remake Craigslist, Inc. by adopting takeover defenses that would have left the firm focused on community benefit into the indefinite future. The Court of Chancery refused to go along. It held that since Craigslist was a Delaware corporation, its directors had an obligation to earn profits. Had Craigslist been formed as a PB Corp, the result would have been otherwise. Of course, that raises the question of whether the founders could have come up with a

---

19. See https://bcorporation.net/.

20. For example, absent a conflict of interest, failing to satisfy the "balancing requirement" is not treated as evidence of bad faith or a duty of loyalty breach unless the charter specifically indicates. Thus, disinterested directors can avail themselves of §102(b)(7) waivers or §145 indemnification for such claims. Further, for a balancing decision, a director is not "interested" just because she owns corporation stock (unless such ownership would create a conflict of interest if the corporation were not a PB Corp). When a firm converts it also eliminates appraisal rights. We discuss appraisal in Chapter 12.

plausible explanation for how their model benefited shareholder interests. Can you?

2. In addition to legislative developments, a couple of PB Corps, such as Lemonade, have recently conducted initial public offerings (IPOs). Lemonade is a PB Corp that aims to "harness novel business models, technologies and private-nonprofit partnerships to deliver insurance products where charitable giving is a core feature, for the benefit of communities and their common causes." In its IPO, Lemonade disclosed that its directors "have a fiduciary duty to consider not only the stockholders' interests, but also the company's specific public benefit and the interests of other stakeholders affected by its actions . . . [Further, if there is] a conflict between [these] interests . . . [Lemonade's] directors must only make informed and disinterested decisions that serve a rational purpose; thus, there is no guarantee such a conflict would be resolved in favor of [Lemonade's] stockholders." Lemonade's IPO was initially well received by the market, though it has cooled since then.[21] Does that suggest the market values broad directorial duties? Or alternatively, might it suggest that the markets expect that Lemonade's directors will behave in much the same way regardless of the company's status as a public benefit corporation?

3. Can Delaware public benefit corporations make credible commitments? If the directors are elected by a majority vote and the majority of shareholders wish to discontinue the firm's public benefit work, can the company do otherwise? Further, if a majority of shareholders elect directors who champion a charter amendment to substitute a new public benefit for the one currently specified in the charter, can minority shareholders faithful to the original benefit enjoin the proposed charter amendment?

8.2   SELF-DEALING TRANSACTIONS

We return now to the traditional model of business corporations in which investors are presumed to be seeking, and directors are obliged to seek, only long-term financial gain. Sometimes directors or controlling shareholders purport to advance shareholder interests by themselves engaging in transactions with the corporation. These related-party transactions offer the paradigmatic circumstance in which courts are required to assess compliance with the duty of loyalty. These cases show that, even if the legal primacy of shareholder interests over those of other constituencies remains uncertain in some cases, it is quite clear that directors and corporate officers may not benefit financially at the expense of the corporation in these self-dealing transactions. The danger in such transactions is apparent, but how should the law deal

21. See Wallace Witkowski, *Lemonade Logs Best U.S. IPO Debut of 2020 with More Than 140% Gain*, MarketWatch (July 2, 2020). On its opening day, Lemonade closed at $69.41, but by the end of August 2020, it was trading at around $57 (having reached a peak of $96.51 on July 7, 2020). See David Moadel, *Don't Try to Squeeze Profits Out of Lemonade Shares*, InvestorPlace, September 1, 2020.

with it? It might simply prohibit all (direct or indirect) transactions between directors or officers and the corporation. This would eliminate the opportunity for insider opportunism, but it would do so at the cost of preventing some mutually beneficial transactions, as when directors are more confident about a corporation's prospects than banks or outside investors. A more nuanced, if operationally more difficult, approach would be to permit interested transactions that are "fair" to the corporation but to proscribe those that are not.

In rationally choosing between these possible legal rules one should also consider the costs of administering the rule chosen. Ideally, the legal regime should be simple (like the preclusion alternative) but discriminating (like the screening alternative), and it should operate without requiring (or inviting) litigation in every such transaction. The evolution of fiduciary law of director self-dealing can be seen as an attempt to balance these three interests.

8.2.1   The Disclosure Requirement

The law has tended to adopt some version of the screening alternative. That is, boards of directors may approve transactions between the corporation and one or more directors or officers. But they may only approve such transactions as are fair to the corporation. What then should a court consider if a related-party transaction is challenged as unfair? The first requirement of valid authorization of a conflicted transaction is that the interested director makes full disclosure of all material facts of which she is aware at the time of authorization. But how far does this disclosure obligation reach?

STATE EX REL. HAYES OYSTER CO. v. KEYPOINT OYSTER CO.
391 P.2d 979 (Wash. 1964)

DENNEY, J.:

Verne Hayes was CEO, director, and 23 percent shareholder of Coast Oyster Co., a public company that owned several large oyster beds. Verne's employment contract barred him from taking part in any business that would compete with Coast except for his activities in Hayes Oyster Co., a family corporation in which he owned 25 percent of the shares and his brother, Sam, owned 75 percent. In the spring of 1960, when Coast was badly in need of cash to satisfy creditors, Hayes suggested that Coast sell its Allyn and Poulsbo oyster beds. Hayes then discussed with Engman, a Coast employee, how Hayes Oyster might help Engman finance the purchase.

On August 11, 1960, Coast's board approved Hayes's plan to sell the Allyn and Poulsbo beds to Keypoint Oyster Co., a corporation to be formed by Engman, for $250,000, payable $25,000 per year, with 5 percent interest, thus improving Coast's cash position and relieving it of the expenses of harvesting the oysters in those beds. On September 1, 1960, Hayes and Engman agreed that Keypoint's shares would be owned half by Engman and half by Hayes Oyster. At a Coast shareholders' meeting on October 21, 1960, the shareholders approved the sale to Keypoint—Hayes voting his Coast shares and others for which he held proxies (in total constituting a majority) in favor. At none of these times did any person connected with Coast (other than Hayes and Engman) know of Hayes's or Hayes Oyster's interest in Keypoint.

In 1961 and 1962, Hayes sold his Coast shares and executed a settlement agreement with respect to his Coast employment contract. Shortly thereafter, Coast's new managers brought suit against Verne and Sam Hayes for their Keypoint shares and all profits obtained by Hayes as a result of the transaction. The trial court absolved Hayes of any breach of duty to Coast.

Coast does not seek a rescission of the contract with Keypoint, nor does it question the adequacy of the consideration which Keypoint agreed to pay for the purchase of Allyn and Poulsbo, nor does Coast claim that it suffered any loss in the transaction. It does assert that Hayes, Coast's president, manager and director, acquired a secret profit and personal advantage to himself in the acquisition of the Keypoint stock by Hayes or Hayes Oyster in the side deal with Engman; and that such was in violation of his duty to Coast, and that, therefore, Hayes or Hayes Oyster should disgorge such secret profit to Coast.

Certain basic concepts have long been recognized by courts throughout the land on the status of corporate officers and directors. They occupy a fiduciary relation to a private corporation and the shareholders thereof akin to that of a trustee, and owe undivided loyalty, and a standard of behavior above that of the workaday world. . . .

Directors and other officers of a private corporation cannot directly or indirectly acquire a profit for themselves or acquire any other personal advantage in dealings with others on behalf of the corporation. . . .

Respondent [Hayes] is correct in his contention that this court has abolished the mechanical rule whereby any transaction involving corporate property in which a director has an interest is voidable at the option of the corporation. Such a contract cannot be voided if the director or officer can show that the transaction was fair to the corporation. However, nondisclosure by an interested director or officer is, in itself, unfair. This wholesome rule can be applied automatically without any of the unsatisfactory results which flowed from a rigid bar against any self-dealing. . . .

The trial court found that any negotiations between Hayes and Engman up to . . . September 1, 1960, resulted in no binding agreement that Hayes would have any personal interest for himself or as a stockholder in Hayes Oyster in the sale of Allyn and Poulsbo. The undisputed evidence, however, shows that Hayes knew he might have some interest in the sale. It would have been appropriate for Hayes to have disclosed his possible interest at the informal meeting in Long Beach on August 4, 1960, and particularly at the meeting of Coast's board of directors on August 11, 1960. It is not necessary, however, for us to decide this case on a consideration of Hayes' obligation to Coast under the circumstances obtaining at that time.

Subsequent to the agreement with Engman, Hayes attended the meeting of Coast stockholders on October 21, 1960, recommended the sale, and voted a majority of the stock, including his own, in favor of the sale to Keypoint.

On the same day, . . . he signed the contract which, among other things, required Keypoint to pay 10 monthly payments amounting to $25,000 per year, to pay interest on [a] deferred balance at 5 percent, to make payments on an option agreement which Coast had with one Smith, to plant sufficient seed to produce 45,000 gallons of oysters per year, inform Coast of plantings, furnish annual reports to Coast, operate the oysterlands in good workmanlike manner, keep improvements in repair, pay taxes, refrain directly or indirectly from engaging in growing, processing or marketing dehydrated oysters or oyster stew, give Coast first refusal on purchase of Keypoint oysters of 10,000 gallons per year or one-fourth of Keypoint's production. Title was reserved in Coast until payment in full of the purchase price of $250,000. . . .

At this juncture, Hayes was required to divulge his interest in Keypoint. His obligation to do so [arose] from the possibility, even probability, that some controversy might arise between Coast and Keypoint relative to the numerous provisions of the executory contract. Coast shareholders and directors had the right to know of Hayes' interest in Keypoint in order to intelligently determine the advisability of retaining Hayes as president and manager under the circumstances, and to determine whether or not it was wise to enter into the contract at all, in view of Hayes' conduct. In all fairness, they were entitled to know that their president and director might be placed in a position where he must choose between the interest of Coast and Keypoint in conducting Coast's business with Keypoint.

Furthermore, after receipt of the Keypoint stock, Hayes instructed the treasurer of Coast to make a payment on the Smith lease-option agreement which Keypoint was required to pay under the provisions of the contract. This action by Hayes grew out of a promise which Hayes made to Engman during their negotiations before the sale to reduce the sale price because of mortality of oysters on Allyn and Poulsbo. There was a clear conflict of interest.

The cases relied upon by respondent are not opposed to the rule condemning secrecy when an officer or director of a corporation may profit in the sale of corporate assets. In *Leppaluoto v. Eggleston*, 57 Wash. 2d 393, 357 P.2d 725, Eggleston secretly chartered his own equipment to a corporation in which he had one-half interest, for $25,000, without the knowledge of the owner of the remaining stock. We held that Eggleston was not required to return the $25,000 to the corporation because there was no proof that the charter arrangement was unfair or unreasonable and no proof that Eggleston made any profit on the transaction and that, absent proof of loss to the corporation or profit to Eggleston, no recovery could be had. In the case before us, profit to Hayes or Hayes Oyster in acquiring 50 percent of Keypoint stock is clear and undisputed. . . .

It is true that Hayes hypothecated his stock in Coast to one of Coast's creditors in early August, 1960. Undoubtedly, this aided Coast in placating its creditors at that time and showed absence of an intent to defraud Coast. It is not necessary, however, that an officer or director of a corporation have an intent to defraud or that any injury result to the corporation for an officer or director to violate his fiduciary obligation in secretly acquiring an interest in corporate property. . . .

Actual injury is not the principle upon which the law proceeds in condemning such contracts. Fidelity in the agent is what is aimed at, and as a means of securing it, the law will not permit the agent to place himself in a situation in which he may be tempted by his own private interest to disregard that of his principal. . . .

Respondent asserts that action by Coast shareholders was not necessary to bind Coast to the sale because it had already been approved by Coast's board of directors. Assuming this to be true, Hayes' fiduciary status with Coast did not change. He could not place himself in an adverse position to Coast by acquiring an interest in the executory contract before the terms of said contract had been performed by Keypoint. Coast had the option to affirm the contract or seek rescission. It chose the former and can successfully invoke the principle that whatever a director or officer acquires by virtue of his fiduciary relation, except in open dealings with the company, belongs not to such director or officer, but to the company. . . .

This rule appears to have universal application. . . . The trial court's finding that Hayes acted on behalf of Hayes Oyster in all of his negotiations with Engman subsequent to July, 1960, does not alter the situation. Sam Hayes knew that Verne Hayes was president and manager of Coast and owed complete devotion to the interests of Coast at the time Verne Hayes first approached him on the subject of sharing with Engman in the purchase of Allyn and Poulsbo. Sam Hayes knew and agreed that any interest of Verne Hayes or Hayes Oyster in Keypoint was to be kept secret and revealed to no one, including Coast. Sam Hayes authorized Verne Hayes to proceed with the deal on behalf of Hayes Oyster on this basis. Verne Hayes became the agent of Hayes Oyster in negotiating with Engman.

. . . Every sound consideration of equity affects Hayes Oyster as well as Verne Hayes. Neither can profit by the dereliction of Verne Hayes. . . .

The decree and judgment of the trial court . . . is reversed with direction to order Keypoint Oyster Company to issue a new certificate for 250 shares of its stock to Coast Oyster Company and cancel the certificates heretofore standing in the name of or assigned to Hayes Oyster Company. . . .

QUESTIONS ON STATE EX REL. HAYES OYSTER CO. v. KEYPOINT OYSTER CO.

Why do courts consider nondisclosure per se unfair? Why shouldn't Hayes be granted the opportunity to show that the consideration received for the oyster beds was completely fair? After all, Hayes Oyster is not attempting to rescind the sale.

MELVIN EISENBERG, SELF-INTERESTED TRANSACTIONS IN CORPORATE LAW
13 J. Corp. L. 997, 997-1009 (1988)

[W]hy isn't fairness of price enough without full disclosure? . . .

[A] rule that fairness of price was enough without full disclosure would in effect remove decision making from the corporation's hands and place it in the hands of the court. Many or most self-interested transactions involve differentiated commodities. . . . In the case of commodities that are differentiated, . . . prices are invariably negotiated. The market may set outside limits on the price — at some point, the price the seller demands is so high that the buyer would prefer a market substitute, or the price the buyer insists upon is so low that the seller would prefer to market his commodity to someone else — but within those limits the price will be indeterminable prior to negotiation. Therefore, if by a "fair price" we mean the price that would have been arrived at by a buyer and a seller dealing at arm's length, in the case of a self-interested transaction involving a differentiated commodity, a court attempting to determine whether the price was fair can do no more than to say that the price was or was not within the range at which parties dealing at arm's length would have concluded a deal. . . .

NOTES ON DISCLOSURE OF CONFLICTED TRANSACTIONS

Requiring a corporate fiduciary to disclose his or her interest in a proposed transaction with the corporation is only the first step. The difficult question is just what must be disclosed beyond the simple fact of self-interest. For example, if a director (call him Jones) offers to buy 50 acres of the corporation's land at a price that he regards as fair, must he disclose his intended use of the property? What if Jones's cousin is a developer who has informed him of his plan for a large residential development in the neighborhood, which will make the property more valuable? Should Jones have to disclose his cousin's plans? Does Jones have to disclose the highest price that he is willing to pay? What principle answers these questions?

The fiduciary's role in negotiating a conflicted transaction with his corporation is not an easy one. Recall the singing phrases of Judge Cardozo in *Meinhard v. Salmon*: Some forms of behavior open to traders in the market are not available to fiduciaries. Among these forms is a range of disingenuous actions that fall short of fraud. The Delaware court's legal standard for disclosure by a conflicted fiduciary is that a director or controlling shareholder must disclose *all* material information relevant to the transaction.[22] In our example, a literal application of this language would require Jones to disclose both what he learned from his cousin and the highest price he would pay. But such a requirement, since it would tend to remove the prospects of any benefit to the fiduciary, might radically reduce the number of mutually beneficial transactions offered. See *Weinberger v. UOP, Inc.*, 457 A.2d 701 (Del. 1983) (en banc) later in this chapter.[23] So, courts would most likely not treat a fiduciary's reservation price as a "fact" that must be disclosed.

---

22. See *Rosenblatt v. Getty Oil Co.*, 493 A.2d 929 (Del. 1985); *Lynch v. Vickers Energy Corp.*, 383 A.2d 278 (Del. 1978).

23. See generally Lawrence A. Hamermesh, *Calling Off the Lynch Mob: The Corporate Director's Fiduciary Disclosure Duty*, 49 Vand. L. Rev. 1087 (1996).

Finally, note that federal securities laws may also regulate disclosure of self-dealing transactions in public corporations. Given that Coast Oyster is a public company, would Verne be compelled to disclose his interest in the oyster bed sale under Regulation S-K, Item 404(a) (in your statutory supplement) if he were to undertake the same transaction with Engman today?[24]

8.3   THE EFFECT OF APPROVAL BY A DISINTERESTED PARTY

A student reading thus far might conclude that litigation about conflicted transactions would focus solely on the adequacy of disclosure or, if the insider actions were fully disclosed, on the intrinsic fairness of their terms. That, however, is not usually the case. The procedural aspects of how such transactions are considered and approved also play a central role. Approvals of self-dealing transactions by disinterested directors or shareholders began to play a key role in the defense of these transactions at least by the early twentieth century. This role was codified in the so-called safe harbor statutes, adopted by states from the mid-twentieth century, and was further developed by the courts since. The principal legal questions raised by disinterested review mechanisms concern (1) whether the disinterested approval has sufficient integrity to be accorded some effect by reviewing courts and (2) the standard of judicial review to be employed *after* disinterested review and approval. For example, is it cursory review under the business judgment standard? Or is it more searching review under some sort of "fairness-lite" standard? And should it matter whether directors or shareholders approve the transaction? (A related issue is: What if the transaction is only disclosed *after* the fact but is then ratified by disinterested directors?)

We explore these issues beyond full disclosure below, beginning with the historical background to the safe harbor statutes.

8.3.1   Early Regulation of Fiduciary Self-Dealing

Understanding safe harbor statutes requires understanding a bit of corporate law history. In the late eighteenth and early nineteenth centuries, American and English courts looked to the law of trusts for guidance in adjudicating disputes over the duties of corporate directors.[25] The trust's division of ownership into legal ownership (with control) and beneficial interest (without control) provided an obvious analogue for the division of ownership powers between the board and shareholders in the widely held corporation.

---

24. Note that the disclosure required of the issuer for related-party transactions must be made in the Form 10-K Annual Report (filed with the SEC) and the annual statement that public companies must distribute to shareholders.

25. *Ex parte Holmes*, 5 Cow. 426 (N.Y. Sup. Ct. 1826); Lawrence E. Mitchell, *Fairness in Trust in Corporate Law*, 43 Duke L.J. 425 (1993).

Early trust law flatly prohibited a trustee from dealing either with trust property on his own account or with the trust beneficiary respecting trust property.[26] Such transactions could be set aside at the insistence of any interested party, without regard to how fair they may have seemed. But with time, the law recognized that a trustee could deal with a beneficiary with respect to trust property,[27] *if* the beneficiary was competent, consented after full disclosure, *and* the transaction was fair.[28] If any of these conditions was not met, however, the transaction between a beneficiary and a trustee was voidable. Thus, transactions with trust beneficiaries were not flatly prohibited, as were transactions between the trustee and the trust itself.[29]

Some commentators argue that, by 1880, the trust rule (prohibition or void) as opposed to the trust beneficiary rule (voidable), had become the general rule of corporation law; conflicted director transactions were simply void.[30] Other commentators dispute this claim.[31] All agree, however, that, beginning in the early twentieth century, courts would uphold as valid a contract between a director and the corporation if it was (1) on fair terms (2) had been approved by a board comprised of a majority of disinterested directors after (3) full disclosure. A contract that did not meet *all aspects* of this test was voidable, meaning that it would be set aside on the application of any party with an interest in the contract.

The practical problem in this approach lay in the requirement that transactions be approved by a majority of disinterested directors. Under early twentieth-century law, an interested director's attendance at a board meeting could not be counted toward a quorum on a question in which he was interested.[32] This rule meant that a corporation could not act to authorize a contract in which a majority of the board was personally interested. No quorum could be had.

There was, however, good reason to make some of these contracts binding; knowledgeable directors might sometimes offer the company better terms than anyone else. One solution was for shareholders to put into the corporation's charter a provision allowing an interested director to be counted

---

26. *Ex parte Holmes*, 5 Cow. 426.

27. *Smith v. Lancing*, 22 N.Y. 520 (1860).

28. *U.S. Rolling Stock Co. v. The Atlantic and Great Western Railroad Co.*, 34 Ohio St. 450 (1878).

29. See, e.g., *In re Gleeson*, 124 N.E.2d 624 (Ill. App. 1954).

30. *See* Harold Marsh Jr., *Are Directors Trustees?*, 22 Bus. Law. 35 (1966). Professor Marsh's interpretation has been widely accepted. See, e.g., 2 Model Bus. Corp. Act. Annot. §8.60, at 8-406 (3d ed. 1994). ("[A]s late as the end of the nineteenth century the rule appeared settled that the corporation had the power to avoid all such transactions without regard to the fairness of the transaction or the manner in which it was originally approved by the corporation.")

31. Professor Norwood Brevenridge urges that, at times in the nineteenth century, judges were willing to permit interested director transactions to stand if they found them fair in all respects. See Norwood P. Brevenridge, Jr., *The Corporate Director's Fiduciary Duty of Loyalty: Understanding the Self-Interested Director Transaction*, 41 DePaul L. Rev. 655 (1992) (Professor Marsh was completely wrong; the rule was opposite of that which he asserts: If an interested contract was fair, it was sustained (citing the leading treatise, 1 V. Morowitz, The Law of Public Corporations 214 (2d ed. 1843)).

32. See *Blish v. Thompson Automatic Arms Corp.*, 64 A.2d 602 (Del. 1948).

toward a quorum. In that event, a meeting could be held, and the contract approved. Courts upheld the validity of these provisions, and this innovation thus permitted interested transactions involving a majority of the board to be accomplished.[33] Nevertheless, courts continued to require directors to prove that such transactions were fair — that is, these transactions remained voidable following "interested" approval, but only if they were unfair or inadequately disclosed. This was essentially the nineteenth-century trust beneficiary rule, applied to the corporation.

The next stage in the development of the law of director conflict occurred in the mid-twentieth century, with the movement to enact legislative provisions governing director conflict transactions.[34] These provisions were, in effect, a statutory embodiment of earlier charter provisions that sought to ensure that interested transactions would *not be void per se.* That is, they were a statutory effort to give all corporations of the jurisdiction the benefit of a charter provision that allowed a quorum to exist and to vote to authorize a transaction between the corporation and one or more directors. These "safe harbor" statutes are discussed below.

8.3.2   Judicial Review of Self-Dealing Today: The Limited Role of Safe Harbor Statutes

As we indicated, the safe harbor statutes initially sought to permit boards to authorize transactions in which a majority of directors had an interest. Most U.S. jurisdictions now have such statutes. Almost all of these statutes provide that a director's self-dealing transaction is not voidable simply because it is interested, or in the language of the Delaware version, such a transaction is not voidable "solely" because it is interested, so long as it is adequately disclosed and approved by a majority of disinterested directors or shareholders, or it is fair. See, e.g., DGCL §144; *accord* NYBCL §713; Cal. Corp. Code §310. However, these statutes might also be interpreted to mean that a conflict transaction is *never* voidable if it is fully disclosed and authorized or approved by the board and shareholders in good faith *or* if it is fair to the corporation at the time it is authorized. Courts have traditionally resisted such a broad reading. Consider the following case.

COOKIES FOOD PRODUCTS v. LAKES WAREHOUSE
430 N.W.2d 447 (Iowa 1988)

NEUMAN, Justice.
This is a shareholders' derivative suit brought by the minority shareholders of a closely held Iowa corporation specializing in barbecue sauce, Cookies Food Products, Inc. (Cookies). The target of the lawsuit is the majority

33. E.g., *Sterling v. Mayflower Hotel Corp.*, 93 A.2d 107, 117 (Del. 1952).
34. See, e.g., Cal. Corp. Code §310; DGCL §144; NYBCL §713; MBCA §8.60.

shareholder, Duane "Speed" Herrig and two of his family-owned corporations, Lakes Warehouse Distributing, Inc. (Lakes) and Speed's Automotive Co., Inc. (Speed's). Plaintiffs alleged that Herrig, by acquiring control of Cookies and executing self-dealing contracts, breached his fiduciary duty to the company and fraudulently misappropriated and converted corporate funds. Plaintiffs sought actual and punitive damages. Trial to the court resulted in a verdict for the defendants, the district court finding that Herrig's actions benefited, rather than harmed, Cookies. We affirm. . . .

L. D. Cook of Storm Lake, Iowa, founded Cookies in 1975 to produce and distribute his original barbeque sauce. Searching for a plant site in a community that would provide financial backing, Cook met with business leaders in seventeen Iowa communities, outlining his plans to build a growth-oriented company. He selected Wall Lake, Iowa, persuading thirty-five members of that community, including Herrig and the plaintiffs, to purchase Cookies stock. All of the investors hoped Cookies would improve the local job market and tax base. The record reveals that it has done just that.

Early sales of the product, however, were dismal. After the first year's operation, Cookies was in dire financial straits. At that time, Herrig was one of thirty-five shareholders and held only two hundred shares. He was also the owner of an auto parts business, Speed's Automotive, and Lakes Warehouse Distributing, Inc., a company that distributed auto parts from Speed's. Cookies' board of directors approached Herrig with the idea of distributing the company's products. It authorized Herrig to purchase Cookies' sauce for twenty percent under wholesale price, which he could then resell at full wholesale price. Under this arrangement, Herrig began to market and distribute the sauce to his auto parts customers and to grocery outlets from Lakes' trucks as they traversed the regular delivery route for Speed's Automotive.

In May 1977, Cookies formalized this arrangement by executing an exclusive distribution agreement with Lakes. Pursuant to this agreement, Cookies was responsible only for preparing the product; Lakes, for its part, assumed all costs of warehousing, marketing, sales, delivery, promotion, and advertising. Cookies retained the right to fix the sales price of its products and agreed to pay Lakes thirty percent of its gross sales for these services.

Cookies' sales have soared under the exclusive distributorship contract with Lakes. Gross sales in 1976, the year prior to the agreement, totaled only $20,000, less than half of Cookies' expenses that year. In 1977, however, sales jumped five-fold, then doubled in 1978, and have continued to show phenomenal growth every year thereafter. By 1985, when this suit was commenced, annual sales reached $2,400,000.

As sales increased, Cookies' board of directors amended and extended the original distributorship agreement. In 1979, the board amended the original agreement to give Lakes an additional two percent of gross sales to cover freight costs for the ever expanding market for Cookies' sauce. In 1980, the board extended the amended agreement through 1984 to allow Herrig to make long-term advertising commitments. Recognizing the role that Herrig's personal strengths played in the success of the joint endeavor, the board also amended the agreement that year to allow Cookies to cancel the agreement with Lakes if Herrig died or disposed of the corporation's stock.

In 1981, L. D. Cook, the majority shareholder up to this time, decided to sell his interest in Cookies. He first offered the directors an opportunity to buy his stock, but the board declined to purchase any of his 8100 shares. Herrig then offered Cook and all other shareholders $10 per share for their stock, which was twice the original price. Because of the overwhelming response to these offers, Herrig had purchased enough Cookies stock by January 1982 to become the majority shareholder. His investment of $140,000 represented fifty-three percent of the [outstanding shares]. . . .

Shortly after Herrig acquired majority control he replaced four of the five members of the Cookies' board with members he selected. . . . Subsequent changes made in the corporation under Herrig's leadership formed the basis for this lawsuit.

First, under Herrig's leadership, Cookies' board has extended the term of the exclusive distributorship agreement with Lakes and expanded the scope of services for which it compensates Herrig and his companies. In April 1982, when a sales increase of twenty-five percent over the previous year required Cookies to seek additional short-term storage for the peak summer season, the board accepted Herrig's proposal to compensate Lakes at the "going rate" for use of its nearby storage facilities. . . .

Second, Herrig moved from his role as director and distributor to take on an additional role in product development. This created a dispute over a royalty Herrig began to receive. . . . Herrig developed a recipe [for taco sauce] because he recognized that taco sauce, while requiring many of the same ingredients needed in barbeque sauce, is less expensive to produce. . . . In August 1982, Cookies' board approved a royalty fee to be paid to Herrig for this taco sauce recipe. This royalty plan was similar to royalties the board paid to L.D. Cook for the barbeque sauce recipe. That plan gives Cook three percent of the gross sales of barbeque sauce; Herrig receives a flat rate per case. Although Herrig's rate is equivalent to a sales percentage slightly higher than what Cook receives, it yields greater profit to Cookies because this new product line is cheaper to produce.

Third, since 1982 Cookies' board has twice approved additional compensation for Herrig. In January 1983, the board authorized payment of a $1000 per month "consultant fee" in lieu of salary, because accelerated sales required Herrig to spend extra time managing the company. Averaging eighty-hour work weeks, Herrig devoted approximately fifteen percent of his time to Cookies' and eighty percent to Lakes' business. In August, 1983, the board authorized another increase in Herrig's compensation. Further, at the suggestion of a Cookies director who also served as an accountant for Cookies, Lakes, and Speed's, the Cookies board amended the exclusive distributorship agreement to allow Lakes an additional two percent of gross sales as a promotion allowance to expand the market for Cookies products outside of Iowa. As a direct result of this action, by 1986 Cookies regularly shipped products to several states throughout the country.

As we have previously noted, however, Cookies' growth and success has not pleased all its shareholders. The discontent is motivated by two factors that have effectively precluded shareholders from sharing in Cookies' financial success: the fact that Cookies is a closely held corporation, and the fact that it has not paid dividends. Because Cookies' stock is not publicly traded, shareholders have no ready access to buyers for their stock at current values that reflect the company's success. Without dividends, the shareholders have no ready method of realizing a return on their investment in the company. This is not to say that Cookies has improperly refused to pay dividends. The evidence reveals that Cookies would have violated the terms of its loan with the Small Business Administration had it declared dividends before repaying that debt. That SBA loan was not repaid until the month before the plaintiffs filed this action.

Unsatisfied with the status quo, a group of minority shareholders commenced this equitable action in 1985. Based on the facts we have detailed, the plaintiffs claimed that the sums paid Herrig and his companies have grossly exceeded the value of the services rendered, thereby substantially reducing corporate profits and shareholder equity. Through the exclusive distributorship agreements, taco sauce royalty, warehousing fees, and consultant fee, plaintiffs claimed that Herrig breached his fiduciary duties to the corporation and its shareholders because he allegedly negotiated for these arrangements without fully disclosing the benefit he would gain. The plaintiffs sought recovery for lost profits, an accounting to determine the full extent of the damage, attorneys' fees, punitive damages, appointment of a receiver to manage the company properly, removal of Herrig from control, and sale of the company in order to generate an appropriate return on their investment.

Having heard the evidence. . ., the district court filed a lengthy ruling that reflected careful attention to the testimony of the twenty-two witnesses and myriad of exhibits admitted. The court concluded that Herrig had breached no duties owed to Cookies or to its minority shareholders. . . .

II. FIDUCIARY DUTIES

Herrig, as an officer and director of Cookies, owes a fiduciary duty to the company and its shareholders. . . . Herrig concedes that Iowa law imposed the same fiduciary responsibilities based on his status as majority stockholder. . . . Conversely, before acquiring majority control in February 1982, Herrig owed no fiduciary duty to Cookies or plaintiffs. . . . Therefore, Herrig's conduct is subject to scrutiny only from the time he began to exercise control of Cookies. . . .

[T]he legislature enacted section 496A.34, . . . that establishes three sets of circumstances under which a director may engage in self-dealing without clearly violating the duty of loyalty:

> No contract or other transaction between a corporation and one or more of its directors or any other corporation, firm, association or entity in which one or more of its directors are directors or officers or are financially interested, shall be either void or voidable because of such relationship or interest . . . if any of the following occur:
>
> 1. The fact of such relationship or interest is disclosed or known to the board of directors or committee which authorizes, approves, or ratifies the contract or transaction . . . without counting the votes . . . of such interested director.

2. The fact of such relationship or interest is disclosed or known to the shareholders entitled to vote [on the transaction] and they authorize . . . such contract or transaction by vote or written consent.

3. The contract or transaction is fair and reasonable to the corporation.

Some commentators have supported the view that satisfaction of any *one* of the foregoing statutory alternatives in and of itself, would prove that a director has fully met the duty of loyalty. . . . We are obliged, however, to interpret statutes in conformity with the common law wherever statutory language does not directly negate it. . . . Because the common law and section 496A.34 require directors to show "good faith, honesty, and fairness" in self-dealing, we are persuaded that satisfaction of any one of these three alternatives under the statute would merely preclude us from rendering the transaction void or voidable *outright* solely on the basis "of such [director's] relationship or interest." . . . We thus require directors who engage in self-dealing to establish the additional element that they have acted in good faith, honesty, and fairness. . . .

. . . The crux of appellants' claim is that the [trial] court should have focused on the fair market value of Herrig's services to Cookies rather than on the success Cookies achieved as a result of Herrig's actions.

We agree with appellants' contention that corporate profitability should not be the sole criteria by which to test the fairness and reasonableness of Herrig's fees. . . .

Given an instance of alleged director enrichment at corporate expense . . . the burden to establish fairness resting on the director requires not only a showing of "fair price" but also a showing of the fairness of the bargain to the interests of the corporation. . . . Applying such reasoning to the record before us, however, we cannot agree with appellants' assertion that Herrig's services were either unfairly priced or inconsistent with Cookies corporate interest.

There can be no serious dispute that the four agreements in issue — for exclusive distributorship, taco sauce royalty, warehousing, and consulting fees — have all benefited Cookies, as demonstrated by its financial success. Even if we assume Cookies could have procured similar services from other vendors at lower costs, we are not convinced that Herrig's fees were therefore unreasonable or exorbitant. Like the district court, we are not persuaded by appellants' expert testimony that Cookies' sales and profits would have been the same under agreements with other vendors. As Cookies' board noted prior to Herrig's takeover, he was the driving force in the corporation's success. Even plaintiffs' expert acknowledged that Herrig has done the work of at least five people — production supervisor, advertising specialist, warehouseman, broker, and salesman. While eschewing the lack of internal control, for accounting purposes, that such centralized authority may produce, the expert conceded that Herrig may in fact be underpaid for all he has accomplished. We believe the board properly considered this source of Cookies' success when it entered these transactions, as did the district court when it reviewed them. . . .

[T]he record before us aptly demonstrates that all members of Cookies' board were well aware of Herrig's dual ownership in Lakes and Speed's. We are unaware of any authority supporting plaintiffs' contention that Herrig was obligated to disclose to Cookies' board or shareholders the extent of his profits resulting from these distribution and warehousing agreements; nevertheless, the exclusive distribution agreement with Lakes authorized the board to ascertain that information had it so desired. Appellants cannot reasonably claim that Herrig owed Cookies a duty to render such services at no profit to himself or his companies. Having found that the compensation he received from these agreements was fair and reasonable, we are convinced that Herrig furnished sufficient pertinent information to Cookies' board to enable it to make prudent decisions concerning the contracts. . . .

AFFIRMED.

SCHULTZ, J. (dissenting). . . .

Much of Herrig's evidence concerned the tremendous success of the company. I believe that the trial court and the majority opinion have been so enthralled by the success of the company that they have failed to examine whether these matters of self-dealing were fair to the stockholders. While much credit is due to Herrig for the success of the company, this does not mean that these transactions were fair to the company.

I believe that Herrig failed on his burden of proof by what he did not show. He did not produce evidence of the local going rate for distribution contracts or storage fees outside of a very limited amount of self-serving testimony. He simply did not show the fair market value of his services or expense for freight, advertising and storage cost. He did not show that his taco sauce royalty was fair. This was his burden. He cannot succeed on it by merely showing the success of the company.

The shareholders, on the other hand, . . . have put forth convincing testimony that Herrig has been grossly overcompensated for his services based on their fair market value. . . .

QUESTIONS

1. Should the limited effect of the safe harbor statute be given if the directors who approved the transaction were under the influence or control of a majority shareholder (as presumably was the case in *Cookies*)? Should it matter that the shareholders who authorize or ratify an interested transaction include the votes of the interested shareholder? Further, should Herrig's status as a controlling shareholder matter in this decision?

2. The *Cookies* court does not base its decision solely on Cookies' enhanced profitability under Herrig, but why not? Isn't it enough that Herrig brought Cookies and its minority tremendous financial success (and that Herrig disclosed the self-interested transactions)? Why allow minority shareholders any daylight to seek further money from Herrig? Won't that make controllers in the future reluctant to put forth their full efforts for the firm?

8.3.3   Judicial Review When Transaction Has Been Approved by a Disinterested Majority of the Board

As we noted, under the conventional interpretation of the safe harbor statutes, the approval of an interested transaction by a fully informed board has the effect only of authorizing the transaction, not of foreclosing judicial review for fairness.[35]

That interpretation of the safe harbor statutes leaves open the critical question: What standard of judicial review should courts employ when a related-party transaction approved under the safe harbor statute is nonetheless attacked by shareholders as unfair? Two possibilities come to mind: First, courts may conclude that compliance with the statute means that they should apply the business judgment rule, or alternatively, they might apply some form of fairness evaluation. In the following except, Professor Eisenberg argues that even if the independent director approval process has integrity, courts should continue to review interested transactions for fairness of price or other terms. Section 5.01 of the Principles of Corporate Governance reflects Professor Eisenberg's view.

MELVIN EISENBERG, SELF-INTERESTED TRANSACTIONS IN CORPORATE LAW
13 J. Corp. L. 997, 997-1009 (1988)

The real question is whether a self-interested transaction that has been approved by disinterested directors after full disclosure will still be subject to a test of fairness, or will [be accorded the protection of the business judgment rule].

There are two reasons why such a transaction should be subject to some sort of fairness test. First, directors, by virtue of their collegial relationships, are unlikely to treat one of their number with the degree of wariness with which they would approach a transaction with a third party. Second, it is difficult if not impossible to utilize a legal definition of disinterestedness in corporate law that corresponds with factual disinterestedness. A factually disinterested director would be one who had no significant relationship of any kind with . . . the subject matter of the self-interested transaction. . . .

A review of the fairness of price of a self-interested transaction may be thought of as a surrogate for a review of the fairness of the process by which the transaction was approved. . . . If a self-interested transaction that has been approved by "disinterested" directors is substantively unfair, it can normally be inferred that either the approving directors were not truly disinterested, or that they were not as wary as they should have been because they were dealing with a colleague.

35. See, e.g., *Fliegler v. Lawrence*, 361 A.2d 218 (Del. 1976); *Kahn v. Lynch Communications Systems*, 638 A.2d 1110 (Del. 1994); *Gaillard v. Natomas Co.*, 256 Cal. Rptr. 702, 208 Cal. App. 3d 1250 (Ct. App. 1989); *Cohen v. Ayers*, 596 F.2d 733 (7th Cir. 1979).

NOTES AND QUESTIONS

Professor Eisenberg posits a rough equivalence: ". . . A review of the fairness of price of a self-interested transaction may be thought of as a surrogate for a review of the fairness of process by which the transaction was approved. . . ." But if there is a rough equivalence between an authorization process that has integrity and a price that is fair to the corporation, one might ask which side of the equation is a court most likely to be able to reliably determine? Why privilege price determination as Eisenberg would? Might not courts be even better at reliably detecting the quality of corporate processes and inferring from a good process an acceptably fair result? In fact, as we will see in this Chapter and more clearly in Chapter 12, Delaware courts in many contexts tend to equate fair process with fair price and not the other way around.

Consider the case of a single director (Jones, again) who is personally interested in a transaction that a corporation proposes to enter. Recall that Jones offered to buy 50 acres of land adjacent to the company's main plant. Assume further that Jones fully disclosed his interest to the other directors (as we discussed above) and withdrew from deliberation over the transaction as well as from voting on it. (While withdrawal from discussion is not technically required, it is helpful in persuading a reviewing court that the corporate interest was protected.) Finally, assume that the board, after due deliberation, approved the proposed transaction as being in the corporation's best interests. What effect, if any, should this procedure have on a derivative suit claiming that the transaction constituted a breach of loyalty?

There are several possibilities. First, the derivative suit might be dismissed for failing to state a claim in light of the board's approval, unless the shareholder could plead fraud. This would be a literal application of the statutory safe harbor language, and it is quite close to the approach adopted by the MBCA §§8.61 et seq. Second, a court might apply the business judgment rule to the substance of the transaction — that is, the transaction is not actionable so long as it is not irrational or egregious.[36] Finally, a court could give the approval a more modest effect by following the approach advocated by Professor Eisenberg and the ALI: that is, simply shifting the burden of proving fairness from the defendant to the plaintiff and possibly also stretching the fairness category to include "a reasonable belief in fairness."

Which of these positions seems implied in the following decision? Note, however, that the facts of this case do not present a classic self-dealing transaction, with a fiduciary acting both as a buyer and a seller; rather it is a case in which defendant directors are claimed to have had a collateral personal interest as creditors of the corporation in choosing this particular buyer of the company.

---

36. One of us interprets this language to mean "not a good faith exercise of judgment"; see *In re RJR Nabisco, Inc. Shareholders Litigation,* 1989 WL 7036, at *13 (Del. Ch. Jan. 31, 1989).

COOKE v. OOLIE
2000 WL 710199 (Del. Ch. May 24, 2000)

CHANDLER, C.:

This case involves a dispute between two directors of The Nostalgia Network, Inc. ("TNN" or the "Company"), Sam Oolie and Morton Salkind, [on a four-person board of directors] and TNN's shareholders. . . .

[In an earlier opinion,] I granted shareholder plaintiffs further discovery on the sole issue of whether the two director defendants, Oolie and Salkind, breached their fiduciary duty of loyalty by electing to pursue a particular acquisition proposal that allegedly best protected their personal interests as TNN creditors, rather than pursue other proposals that allegedly offered superior value to TNN's shareholders. . . .

The Court begins with the presumption that the business judgment rule applies to Oolie's and Salkind's decision to pursue the USA acquisition proposal. . . . The plaintiffs bear the burden of rebutting the presumption that the business judgment rule applies to Oolie and Salkind.

To do so, the plaintiffs allege that the defendants failed to act with disinterest and independence and, therefore, do not deserve the protection of the business judgment rule. The USA deal, argue the plaintiffs, provided the greatest benefit to Oolie and Salkind as individuals, but did not necessarily provide the best option for all shareholders in general. . . .

Even assuming that the facts supported the plaintiffs' claim, the two disinterested directors voted to pursue the USA proposal, which removes the alleged taint of disloyalty. Although [DGCL §144] does not explicitly apply,[39] I recognize the policy rationale behind the provision's safe harbor. Under §144(a)(1), this Court will apply the business judgment rule to the actions of an interested director, who is not the majority shareholder, if the interested director fully discloses his interest and a majority of the disinterested directors ratify the interested transaction. The disinterested directors' ratification cleanses the taint of interest because the disinterested directors have no incentive to act disloyally and should be only concerned with advancing the interests of the corporation. The Court will presume, therefore, that the vote of a disinterested director signals that the interested transaction furthers the best interests of the corporation despite the interest of one or more directors.

Although Oolie's and Salkind's actions do not fall explicitly within §144, the rationale behind the Legislature's creation of the safe harbor is on all fours. . . . The disinterested directors' vote to pursue the same proposal that Oolie and Salkind voted to pursue provides strong evidence to the Court

---

39. Section 144 does not apply . . . for two reasons. First, the statute [only] applies to transactions between a corporation and its directors or another corporation in which the directors have a financial interest. Although a potential conflict exists between Oolie and Salkind as directors and Oolie and Salkind as creditors of TNN, they neither sit on both sides of the potential USA transaction nor do they have a financial interest in USA. Second, §144 applies to a "contract or transaction," but, in this case, no transaction has occurred. The plaintiffs merely challenge defendants' decision to pursue a transaction which ultimately never took place.

that Oolie and Salkind acted in good faith and with the interests of TNN and its shareholders in mind.[40] If the USA deal favored Oolie and Salkind to the detriment of the other shareholders, then presumably the independent directors would not have voted to pursue the USA deal. As such, the disinterested directors' votes present the Court with another reason why the business judgment rule remains the appropriate standard with which to review Oolie's and Salkind's actions. . . .

In addition to the arguments discussed above, the plaintiffs [fail] . . . to offer any evidence or argument on the issue of whether Oolie and Salkind attempted to derive an improper personal benefit by voting to pursue the USA proposal. . . . Because the facts do not support the plaintiffs' claim, the disinterested directors voted to pursue the USA deal, and the plaintiffs themselves abandoned this claim at oral argument, I grant summary judgment for the defendants. . . .

8.3.4   Approval by a Minority of Directors: Special Board Committees

The threat to shareholder interests posed by self-dealing transactions is greatest when a majority of the members of the board are personally involved in a transaction with the corporation or, as more commonly occurs, are under the control of a dominating shareholder who is contracting with the corporation. We defer this topic for the moment in order to turn to the effect accorded to shareholder ratification of self-dealing transactions by fiduciaries. We return to the discussion of the effect of board approval, when the board is represented by the action of only a minority of directors of the whole board, after we read the famous *Weinberger* case. See Section 8.5.1 below.

8.3.5   Shareholder Ratification of Conflict Transactions

Theoretically shareholders offer another instrumentality capable of considering (on full information, of course) and acting on behalf of the corporation in a related-party transaction. Thus the question arises: What effects should courts give to ratification by informed shareholders of a related-party or self-dealing transaction? Recall that in agency law, a principal can adopt an agent's unauthorized acts through ratification.[37] In corporate law, shareholders may ratify acts of the board, too, but because shareholders are a collectivity, their ratification involves issues not present in the agency model. In particular, the law must limit the power of an interested majority of shareholders

---

40. Additionally, DLJ, the investment bank advising TNN's board, expressed the view that the board should pursue the USA proposal.

37. Restatement (Third) Agency §§4.01, 4.03-4.04.

to bind a minority that is disinclined to ratify a submitted transaction. See ALI, Principles of Corporate Governance §5.02(a)(2)(D). In addition, the power of shareholders to affirm self-dealing transactions is limited by the corporate "waste" doctrine, which holds that even a majority vote cannot protect wildly unbalanced transactions that, on their face, irrationally dissipate corporate assets. See, e.g., ALI, Principles of Corporate Governance §5.02(a)(2)(D).

The following excerpt from a Delaware Court of Chancery opinion indicates why shareholder ratification is not treated as a full answer to a complaint that the deal is unfair.

LEWIS v. VOGELSTEIN
699 A.2d 327 (Del. Ch. 1997)

ALLEN, C.:

Ratification is a concept deriving from the law of agency which contemplates the ex post conferring upon or confirming of the legal authority of an agent in circumstances in which the agent had no authority or arguably had no authority. *Restatement (Second) of Agency* §82 (1958). To be effective, of course, the agent must fully disclose all relevant circumstances with respect to the transaction to the principal prior to the ratification. . . . Beyond that, since the relationship between a principal and agent is fiduciary in character, the agent in seeking ratification must act not only with candor, but with loyalty. Thus an attempt to coerce the principal's consent improperly will invalidate the effectiveness of the ratification. . . .

Application of these general ratification principles to shareholder ratification is complicated by three other factors. First, most generally, in the case of shareholder ratification there is of course no single individual acting as principal, but rather a class or group of divergent individuals — the class of shareholders. This aggregate quality of the principal means that decisions to affirm or ratify an act will be subject to collective action disabilities (see Robert C. Clark, Corporate Law at 181-182); that some portion of the body doing the ratifying may in fact have conflicting interests in the transaction; and some dissenting members of the class may be able to assert more or less convincingly that the "will" of the principal is wrong, or even corrupt and ought not to be binding on the class. In the case of individual ratification these issues won't arise, assuming that the principal does not suffer from multiple personality disorder. . . . The second, mildly complicating factor present in shareholder ratification is the fact that in corporation law the "ratification" that shareholders provide will often not be directed to lack of legal authority of an agent but will relate to the consistency of some authorized director action with the equitable duty of loyalty. Thus shareholder ratification sometimes acts not to confer legal authority — but as in this case — to affirm that action taken is consistent with shareholder interests. [The third complicating factor arises because] when what is "ratified" is a director conflict transaction, the statutory law — in Delaware Section 144 of the Delaware General Corporation Law — may bear on the effect [of ratification]. . . .

These [complicating factors] lead to a difference in the effect of a valid ratification in the shareholder context. The principal novelty added to ratification law generally by the shareholder context, is . . . that . . . shareholder ratification [may be held to be] . . . ineffectual (1) because a majority of those affirming the transaction had a conflicting interest with respect to it or (2) because the transaction that is ratified constituted a corporate waste. As to the second of these, it has long been held that shareholders may not ratify a waste except by a unanimous vote. *Saxe v. Brady*, Del. Ch., 184 A.2d 602, 605 (1962). The idea behind this rule is apparently that a transaction that satisfies the high standard of waste constitutes a gift of corporate property and no one should be forced against their will to make a gift of their property. In all events, informed, uncoerced, disinterested shareholder ratification of a transaction in which corporate directors have a material conflict of interest has the effect of protecting the transaction from judicial review except on the basis of waste. . . .

The judicial standard for determination of corporate waste is well developed. Roughly, a waste entails an exchange of corporate assets for consideration so disproportionately small as to lie beyond the range at which any reasonable person might be willing to trade. . . . Most often the claim is associated with a transfer of corporate assets that serves no corporate purpose; or for which no consideration at all is received. . . .

NOTE ON SHAREHOLDER RATIFICATION

Does (should) every shareholder vote affirming a transaction, so long as it is on full information and not coerced, have the effect of a ratification even if the vote is statutorily required to effect the transaction, such as in a merger or sale of substantially all assets? In 2009, the Delaware Supreme Court suggested that a vote that was required by statute to authorize a transaction could not itself also act as a shareholder ratification of the transaction. See *Gantler v. Stephens*, 965 A.2d 695 (Del. 2009). But in 2015, the Court affirmed a holding that in a post-closing damages action a favorable vote by a fully informed, uncoerced majority of the disinterested shareholders would invoke the business judgment rule for a merger not involving a conflict. *Corwin v. KKR Financial Holdings LLC*, 125 A.3d 304 (Del. 2015). But what about transactions that do involve conflicts? For simple conflicts, such as a conflict with a single director or a minority of directors, an uncoerced shareholder approval if on full information should have the same effect of triggering business judgment not entire fairness review. For the special case of controlling shareholder transactions, treated below, the current law is the *M&F Worldwide* case, set forth in Chapter 12 below.

8.4   Corporate Directors and the Duty of Good Faith

Some confusion in the area of fiduciary duty was occasioned by the practice of the Delaware courts to use the term "good faith" in describing in summary way the duty of corporate directors. This practice together with the language of §102(b)(7) of the DGCL (which listed the claims for which damages could not be waived as breaches of loyalty and good faith separately), gave rise to the notion that lack of good faith constituted a basis for a claim of breach of duty separate from claims for breach of care or loyalty. The idea was incorrect and the court got a chance to clarify this narrow topic in two cases in 2006.

In June 2006, the Delaware Supreme Court affirmed the Chancellor's post-trial dismissal of a shareholders' action challenging the hiring and then firing without cause of Michael Ovitz, the number two executive of The Walt Disney Company, Inc.[38] Under Ovitz's employment contract he was entitled to the princely sum of more than $140 million as compensation for this discharge. There was no claim of conflict of interest in the hiring of Ovitz. The appeal affirmed the dismissal. The theories of the complaint included negligence, waste, and lack of good faith. The most significant part of the court's affirmance is not the holding, which was doctrinally unremarkable, but rather the guidance that the court provided on the "duty of good faith." Writing for the court, Justice Jack Jacobs provided a spectrum of behavior for identifying "bad faith" conduct. On one end of the spectrum, fiduciary conduct that is "motivated by an actual intent to do harm" constitutes "classic, quintessential bad faith." On the other end of the spectrum, grossly negligent conduct, without any malevolent intent, cannot constitute bad faith. In between lies conduct that involves "intentional dereliction of duty, a conscious disregard for one's responsibilities." The court concluded that "such misconduct is properly treated as a non-exculpable, non-indemnifiable violation of the fiduciary duty to act in good faith." While the court clarified a good deal of ground, in a footnote it left open a question of interest: "[W]e do not reach or otherwise address the issue of whether the fiduciary duty to act in good faith is a duty that, like the duties of care and loyalty, can serve as an independent basis for imposing liability upon corporate officers and directors."[39]

Five months later, in *Stone v. Ritter*,[40] the Delaware Supreme Court answered that question. First, *Stone v. Ritter* affirmed the Delaware Chancery Court's articulation of the *Caremark* standard for assessing directors' oversight of control systems within the company, which we have already discussed in Chapter 7. Second, and more relevant for present purposes, the court clarified that the "duty of good faith" is not an independent duty:

> [B]ecause a showing of bad faith conduct, in the sense described in *Disney* and *Caremark*, is essential to establish director oversight liability, the fiduciary duty violated by that conduct is the duty of loyalty. This view of a failure to act in good faith results in two additional doctrinal consequences. First, although good faith may be described colloquially as part of a "triad" of fiduciary duties that includes the duties of care and loyalty, the obligation to act in good faith does not establish an independent fiduciary duty that stands on the same footing as the duties of care and loyalty. Only the latter two duties, where violated,

---

38. 906 A.2d 27 (Del. 2006).
39. Id. at 67 n.112.
40. 911 A.2d 362 (Del. 2006).

may directly result in liability, whereas a failure to act in good faith may do so, but indirectly. The second doctrinal consequence is that the fiduciary duty of loyalty is not limited to cases involving a financial or other cognizable fiduciary conflict of interest. It also encompasses cases where the fiduciary fails to act in good faith.[41]

In summary, post–*Disney* and *Stone v. Ritter*, Delaware law reflects the following formal structure of director liability for loss when no conflicting interest is present. First, mere director negligence — lacking that degree of attention that a reasonable person in the same or similar situation would be expected to pay to a decision — does not itself give rise to liability. In this circumstance, the business judgment rule forecloses liability and generally permits dismissal at the motion to dismiss phase of the litigation. See *Gagliardi* and *Kamin*, supra. Second, facts that establish gross negligence may (as in *Smith v. Van Gorkom*) be the basis for a breach of duty finding and result in liability for any losses that result. However, under §102(b)(7), such liability for gross negligence alone can be waived (and in most public companies is waived) through a shareholder-approved amendment to the corporate charter. Third, such waivers, however, *may not* waive liability that rests in part upon breach of the duty of loyalty and, under the statutory language, that inability to waive damages is extended to acts (or omissions) not done in "good faith." Therefore, there is conceptually a third level of inattention — we could call it conscious disregard for the welfare of the firm or abandonment of office as some old cases did — in which a director's inattention is so profound that the court concludes that the director lacked good faith. This extreme level of inattention is treated as a breach of loyalty, and neither the business judgment rule nor the waiver authorized by §102(b)(7) will protect the defendant from liability.

8.5   CONTROLLING SHAREHOLDERS AND THE FAIRNESS STANDARD

8.5.1   Different Treatment for Controlling Shareholders?

It is a short step from the fiduciary duties of a shareholder-director to those of a controlling shareholder. In fact, controlling shareholders have more practical power over the corporation in the long run than does any single director. Thus, corporation law has long recognized a fiduciary duty on the part of controlling shareholders to the company and its minority shareholders.[42] Control in this context should be determined by a practical test rather

41. Id. at 370. For implications of this re-articulated duty of good faith in the context of arm's length mergers, see *Lyondell Chemical Co. v. Ryan*, in Chapter 13.
42. *Sterling v. Mayflower Hotel Corp.*, 93 A.2d 107, 109-110 (Del. 1952); *Allied Chemical & Dye Corp. v. Steel & Tube Co.*, 120 A. 486, 491 (Del. Ch. 1923); *Jones v. Missouri-Edison*

than a formalistic one. A shareholder with less than 50 percent of the outstanding voting power of the firm may have a fiduciary obligation by reason of the exercise of corporate control. A shareholder with 50 percent or more of the vote will be deemed to owe such a duty. Despite the judicial consensus in the United States that controlling shareholders owe a duty of fairness to minority shareholders should they undertake *to exercise or command the exercise of corporate powers*, an additional consideration complicates the articulation of the controller's duty. This consideration is that the controller is also a shareholder, after all, and is therefore entitled to pursue her own investment interests in that capacity. Thus, two values collide. The dominant value (at least in Delaware law) is that a controlling shareholder's power over the corporation, and the resulting power to affect other shareholders, gives rise to a duty to consider their interests fairly whenever the corporation enters into a contract with the controller or its affiliate. The subsidiary value is the entitlement of all shareholders — even controlling shareholders — to sell or vote in their own interests.[43]

The first principle clearly governs when a controlling shareholder engages in a conflicted transaction with the corporation. But what about situations in which a controller exercises influence without authorizing a conflicted transaction? For example, what if a controlling shareholder causes the board to launch a risky new product that results in a substantial loss? Directors are protected by the business judgment rule, but might the controlling shareholder be liable for the resulting loss if it was a reckless or negligent choice? What if the controller believes the company is too large and replaces the board at the next annual meeting to reduce its size? Has the controller breached any duty to others? Do minority shareholders have a cognizable injury if the controller influences the board to declare dividends because it wants the money, even if others would prefer new investments? The next case provides a useful structure for thinking about situations in which a controlling shareholder's interest is not a direct conflict-of-interest transaction.

SINCLAIR OIL CORP. v. LEVIEN
280 A.2d 717 (Del. 1971)

Wolcott, C.J.:

This is an appeal by the defendant, Sinclair Oil Corporation (hereafter Sinclair), from an order of the Court of Chancery, 261 A.2d 911, in a derivative action requiring Sinclair to account for damages sustained by its subsidiary, Sinclair Venezuelan Oil Company (hereafter Sinven), organized by Sinclair for the purpose of operating in Venezuela, as a result of dividends

Electrical Co., 144 F. 765, 771 (8th Cir. 1906); *May v. Midwest Refining Co.*, 121 F.2d 431, 439 (1st Cir. 1941).

43. *Tanzer v. International General Industries, Inc.*, 379 A.2d 1121, 1124 (Del. 1977); *Thorpe v. CERBCO, Inc.*, 676 A.2d 436 (Del. 1996) (controller can vote against sale of all assets that public shareholders regard as advantageous without having to justify fairness because this is purely exercising power as shareholder).

paid by Sinven, the denial to Sinven of industrial development, and a breach of contract between Sinclair's wholly-owned subsidiary, Sinclair International Oil Company, and Sinven.

Sinclair, operating primarily as a holding company, is in the business of exploring for oil and of producing and marketing crude oil and oil products. At all times relevant to this litigation, it owned about 97% of Sinven's stock. The plaintiff owns about 3000 of 120,000 publicly held shares of Sinven. Sinven, incorporated in 1922, has been engaged in petroleum operations primarily in Venezuela and since 1959 has operated exclusively in Venezuela.

Sinclair nominates all members of Sinven's board of directors. The Chancellor found as a fact that the directors were not independent of Sinclair. Almost without exception, they were officers, directors, or employees of corporations in the Sinclair complex. By reason of Sinclair's domination, it is clear that Sinclair owed Sinven a fiduciary duty. . . . Sinclair concedes this.

The Chancellor held that because of Sinclair's fiduciary duty and its control over Sinven, its relationship with Sinven must meet the test of intrinsic fairness. The standard of intrinsic fairness involves both a high degree of fairness and a shift in the burden of proof. Under this standard the burden is on Sinclair to prove, subject to careful judicial scrutiny, that its transactions with Sinven were objectively fair. . . .

Sinclair argues that the transactions between it and Sinven should be tested, not by the test of intrinsic fairness with the accompanying shift of the burden of proof, but by the business judgment rule. . . . A board of directors enjoys a presumption of sound business judgment, and its decisions will not be disturbed if they can be attributed to any rational business purpose. A court under such circumstances will not substitute its own notions of what is or is not sound business judgment.

We think, however, that Sinclair's argument in this respect is misconceived. When the situation involves a parent and a subsidiary, with the parent controlling the transaction and fixing the terms, the test of intrinsic fairness, with its resulting shifting of the burden of proof, is applied. . . . The basic situation for the application of the rule is the one in which the parent has received a benefit to the exclusion and at the expense of the subsidiary. . . .

A parent does indeed owe a fiduciary duty to its subsidiary when there are parent-subsidiary dealings. However, this alone will not evoke the intrinsic fairness standard. This standard will be applied only when the fiduciary duty is accompanied by self-dealing — the situation when a parent is on both sides of a transaction with its subsidiary. Self-dealing occurs when the parent, by virtue of its domination of the subsidiary, causes the subsidiary to act in such a way that the parent receives something from the subsidiary to the exclusion of, and detriment to, the minority stockholders of the subsidiary.

We turn now to the facts. The plaintiff argues that, from 1960 through 1966, Sinclair caused Sinven to pay out such excessive dividends that the industrial development of Sinven was effectively prevented, and it became in reality a corporation in dissolution.

From 1960 through 1966, Sinven paid out $108,000,000 in dividends ($38,000,000 in excess of Sinven's earnings during the same period). The

Chancellor held that Sinclair caused these dividends to be paid during a period when it had a need for large amounts of cash. Although the dividends paid exceeded earnings, the plaintiff concedes that the payments were made in compliance with 8 Del. C. §170, authorizing payment of dividends out of surplus or net profits. However, the plaintiff attacks these dividends on the ground that they resulted from an improper motive — Sinclair's need for cash. The Chancellor, applying the intrinsic fairness standard, held that Sinclair did not sustain its burden of proving that these dividends were intrinsically fair to the minority stockholders of Sinven.

Since it is admitted that the dividends were paid in strict compliance with 8 Del. C. §170, the alleged excessiveness of the payments alone would not state a cause of action. Nevertheless, compliance with the applicable statute may not, under all circumstances, justify all dividend payments. If a plaintiff can meet his burden of proving that a dividend cannot be grounded on any reasonable business objective, then the courts can and will interfere with the board's decision to pay the dividend.

Sinclair contends that it is improper to apply the intrinsic fairness standard to dividend payments even when the board which voted for the dividends is completely dominated. In support of this contention, Sinclair relies heavily on *American District Telegraph Co. (ADT) v. Grinnell Corp.*, (N.Y. Sup. Ct. 1969) *aff'd*, 33 A.D.2d 769, 306 N.Y.S.2d 209 (1969). Plaintiffs were minority stockholders of ADT, a subsidiary of Grinnell. The plaintiffs alleged that Grinnell, realizing that it would soon have to sell its ADT stock because of a pending anti-trust action, caused ADT to pay excessive dividends. Because the dividend payments conformed with applicable statutory law, and the plaintiffs could not prove an abuse of discretion, the court ruled that the complaint did not state a cause of action. . . .

We do not accept the argument that the intrinsic fairness test can never be applied to a dividend declaration by a dominated board, although a dividend declaration by a dominated board will not inevitably demand the application of the intrinsic fairness standard. . . .

If such a dividend is in essence self-dealing by the parent, then the intrinsic fairness standard is the proper standard. For example, suppose a parent dominates a subsidiary and its board of directors. The subsidiary has outstanding two classes of stock, X and Y. Class X is owned by the parent and Class Y is owned by minority stockholders of the subsidiary. If the subsidiary, at the direction of the parent, declares a dividend on its Class X stock only, this might well be self-dealing by the parent. It would be receiving something from the subsidiary to the exclusion of and detrimental to its minority stockholders. This self-dealing, coupled with the parent's fiduciary duty, would make intrinsic fairness the proper standard by which to evaluate the dividend payments.

Consequently it must be determined whether the dividend payments by Sinven were, in essence, self-dealing by Sinclair. The dividends resulted in great sums of money being transferred from Sinven to Sinclair. However, a proportionate share of this money was received by the minority shareholders of Sinven. Sinclair received nothing from Sinven to the exclusion of its minority stockholders. As such, these dividends were not self-dealing. We hold therefore that the Chancellor erred in applying the intrinsic fairness test as to these dividend payments. The business judgment standard should have been applied.

We conclude that the facts demonstrate that the dividend payments complied with the business judgment standard and with 8 Del. C. §170. The motives for causing the declaration of dividends are immaterial unless the plaintiff can show that the dividend payments resulted from improper motives and amounted to waste. The plaintiff contends only that the dividend payments drained Sinven of cash to such an extent that it was prevented from expanding.

The plaintiff proved no business opportunities which came to Sinven independently and which Sinclair either took to itself or denied to Sinven. As a matter of fact, with two minor exceptions which resulted in losses, all of Sinven's operations have been conducted in Venezuela, and Sinclair had a policy of exploiting its oil properties located in different countries by subsidiaries located in the particular countries.

From 1960 to 1966 Sinclair purchased or developed oil fields in Alaska, Canada, Paraguay, and other places around the world. The plaintiff contends that these were all opportunities which could have been taken by Sinven. The Chancellor concluded that Sinclair had not proved that its denial of expansion opportunities to Sinven was intrinsically fair. He based this conclusion on the following findings of fact. Sinclair made no real effort to expand Sinven. The excessive dividends paid by Sinven resulted in so great a cash drain as to effectively deny to Sinven any ability to expand. During this same period Sinclair actively pursued a company-wide policy of developing through its subsidiaries new sources of revenue, but Sinven was not permitted to participate and was confined in its activities to Venezuela.

However, the plaintiff could point to no opportunities which came to Sinven. Therefore, Sinclair usurped no business opportunity belonging to Sinven. Since Sinclair received nothing from Sinven to the exclusion of and detriment to Sinven's minority stockholders, there was no self-dealing. Therefore, business judgment is the proper standard by which to evaluate Sinclair's expansion policies.

Since there is no proof of self-dealing on the part of Sinclair, it follows that the expansion policy of Sinclair and the methods used to achieve the desired result must, as far as Sinclair's treatment of Sinven is concerned, be tested by the standards of the business judgment rule. Accordingly, Sinclair's decision, absent fraud or gross overreaching, to achieve expansion through the medium of its subsidiaries, other than Sinven, must be upheld.

Even if Sinclair was wrong in developing these opportunities as it did, the question arises, with which subsidiaries should these opportunities have been shared? No evidence indicates a unique need or ability of Sinven to develop these opportunities. The decision of which subsidiaries would be used to implement Sinclair's expansion policy was one of business judgment with which a court will not interfere absent a showing of gross and palpable overreaching. . . .

QUESTIONS AND NOTES ON SINCLAIR OIL

1. Is plaintiff's complaint in this case really about self-dealing or an alleged misappropriation of corporate opportunity? How can the pro rata payment of dividends be a basis for either complaint?

2. Do you think that Sinclair would have forced Sinven to pay such large dividends if additional drilling opportunities had been available in Venezuela? How would *Sinclair Oil* have been decided under ALI Principles of Corporate Governance §5.12 and §8.70 MBCA (both in your statutory supplement)?

3. In *GAMCO Asset Management Inc. v. iHeartmedia, Inc.*, WL 6892802 (Del. Ch. Nov. 23, 2016), V.C. Slights summarizes Delaware law on when a transaction at a controlled firm triggers entire fairness review while dismissing the plaintiff's suit:

> The first [category of cases] is where the controller stands on both sides of the transaction. . . . The second category . . . involve [cases] in which the controller "competes with the common stockholders for consideration." These cases exist in three subsets:. . . [1] In a "disparate consideration" case, the controller takes more monetary consideration from the third-party transaction than is given to the minority. . . [2] In a "continuing stake" case, the controller receives more consideration from the third-party transaction than the other stockholders in a form other than money — typically by retaining a continuing equity stake in the surviving entity while the minority common stockholders are cashed out. . . [3] In a "unique benefit" case, "the controller receives some sort of special benefit not shared with the other stockholders." [e.g., a transaction occasioned by the controller's liquidity crisis but offers the same nominal consideration to all shareholders. The court acknowledges that these cases involve "extreme" facts. — Eds].[44]

While parent-subsidiary dealings can take a wide range of forms, much of the litigation challenging these transactions arises from cash-out mergers (that is, a merger in which all shareholders other than the controller receive cash in exchange for their shares and the controller is left owning all of the shares of the corporation that survives the merger). The body of law dealing with parent-subsidiary transactions was reenergized in the 1983 cash-out merger case of *Weinberger v. UOP, Inc.*, 457 A.2d 701 (Del. 1983).

WEINBERGER v. UOP, INC.
457 A.2d 701 (Del. 1983)

Moore, J.:

This post-trial appeal was reheard en banc from a decision of the Court of Chancery. It was brought by the class action plaintiff below, a former shareholder of UOP, Inc., who challenged the elimination of UOP's minority shareholders by a cash-out merger between UOP and its majority owner, The Signal Companies, Inc. . . .

---

44. Id at 41–45. The "unique benefit" line of cases involve unusual facts, where narrow circumstances sustain entire fairness review. For example, the liquidity crisis argument "would have to involve a crisis, fire sale where the controller, in order to satisfy an exigent need. . . agreed to a sale of the corporation without any effort to engage in a sales process that would reflect the market value." Id. at 44–45 (quoting then V.C. Strine in *In re Synthes, Inc. S'holder Litig.*, 50 A.3d 1022, 1036 (Del. Ch. 2012)).

Signal is a diversified, technically based company operating through various subsidiaries. Its stock is publicly traded on the New York, Philadelphia and Pacific Stock Exchanges. UOP, formerly known as Universal Oil Products Company, was a diversified industrial company. . . . Its stock was publicly held and listed on the New York Stock Exchange. [In 1974, Signal acquired 50.5 percent of UOP at $21 per share when UOP shares had traded at $14 per share.] . . .

Although UOP's board consisted of thirteen directors, Signal nominated and elected only six. Of these, five were either directors or employees of Signal. The sixth, a partner in the banking firm of Lazard Freres & Co., had been one of Signal's representatives in the negotiations and bargaining with UOP concerning the tender offer and purchase price of the UOP shares.

However, the president and chief executive officer of UOP retired during 1975, and Signal caused him to be replaced by James V. Crawford, a long-time employee and senior executive vice president of one of Signal's wholly-owned subsidiaries. Crawford succeeded his predecessor on UOP's board of directors and also was made a director of Signal.

By the end of 1977 Signal basically was unsuccessful in finding other suitable investment candidates for its excess cash, and by February 1978 considered that it had no other realistic acquisitions available to it on a friendly basis. Once again its attention turned to UOP.

The trial court found that at the instigation of certain Signal management personnel, including William W. Walkup, its board chairman, and Forrest N. Shumway, its president, a feasibility study was made concerning the possible acquisition of the balance of UOP's outstanding shares. This study was performed by two Signal officers, Charles S. Arledge, vice president (director of planning), and Andrew J. Chitiea, senior vice president (chief financial officer). Messrs. Walkup, Shumway, Arledge and Chitiea were all directors of UOP in addition to their membership on the Signal board.

Arledge and Chitiea concluded that it would be a good investment for Signal to acquire the remaining 49.5% of UOP shares at any price up to $24 each. Their report was discussed between Walkup and Shumway who, along with Arledge, Chitiea and Brewster L. Arms, internal counsel for Signal, constituted Signal's senior management. In particular, they talked about the proper price to be paid if the acquisition was pursued, purportedly keeping in mind that as UOP's majority shareholder, Signal owed a fiduciary responsibility to both its own stockholders as well as to UOP's minority. It was ultimately agreed that a meeting of Signal's Executive Committee would be called to propose that Signal acquire the remaining outstanding stock of UOP through a cash-out merger in the range of $20 to $21 per share.

The Executive Committee meeting was set for February 28, 1978. As a courtesy, UOP's president, Crawford, was invited to attend, although he was not a member of Signal's executive committee. On his arrival, and prior to the meeting, Crawford was asked to meet privately with Walkup and Shumway. He was then told of Signal's plan to acquire full ownership of UOP and was asked for his reaction to the proposed price range of $20 to $21 per share. Crawford said he thought such a price would be "generous," and that it was certainly one which should be submitted to UOP's minority shareholders for their ultimate consideration. He stated, however, that Signal's 100% ownership could cause internal problems at UOP. He believed that employees would have to be given some assurance of their future place in a fully-owned Signal subsidiary. Otherwise, he feared the departure of essential personnel. Also, many of UOP's key employees had stock option incentive programs which would be wiped out by a merger. Crawford therefore urged that some adjustment would have to be made, such as providing a comparable incentive in Signal's shares, if after the merger he was to maintain his quality of personnel and efficiency at UOP.

Thus, Crawford voiced no objection to the $20 to $21 price range, nor did he suggest that Signal should consider paying more than $21 per share for the minority interests. . . .

Thus, it was the consensus that a price of $20 to $21 per share would be fair to both Signal and the minority shareholders of UOP. Signal's executive committee authorized its management "to negotiate" with UOP "for a cash acquisition of the minority ownership in UOP, Inc., with the intention of presenting a proposal to [Signal's] board of directors . . . on March 6, 1978." Immediately after this February 28, 1978 meeting, Signal issued a press release stating [that Signal and UOP were negotiating for the cash purchase of the 49.5 percent of UOP that Signal did not presently own, without reference to the price. Nevertheless, the announcement referred to UOP's closing market price of $14.50 per share. — EDS.]

Two days later, on March 2, 1978, Signal issued a second press release stating that its management would recommend a price in the range of $20 to $21 per share for UOP's 49.5% minority interest. This announcement referred to Signal's earlier statement that "negotiations" were being conducted for the acquisition of the minority shares.

Between Tuesday, February 28, 1978 and Monday, March 6, 1978, a total of four business days, Crawford spoke by telephone with all of UOP's non-Signal, i.e., outside, directors. Also during that period, Crawford retained Lehman Brothers to render a fairness opinion as to the price offered the minority for its stock. He gave two reasons for this choice. First, the time schedule between the announcement and the board meetings was short (by then only three business days) and since Lehman Brothers had been acting as UOP's investment banker for many years, Crawford felt that it would be in the best position to respond on such brief notice. Second, James W. Glanville, a long-time director of UOP and a partner in Lehman Brothers, had acted as a financial advisor to UOP for many years. Crawford believed that Glanville's familiarity with UOP, as a member of its board, would also be of assistance in enabling Lehman Brothers to render a fairness opinion within the existing time constraints.

. . . Glanville's immediate personal reaction was that a price of $20 to $21 [for UOP shares] would certainly be fair, since it represented almost a 50% premium over UOP's market price. Glanville sought a $250,000 fee for Lehman Brothers' services, but Crawford thought this too much. After further discussions Glanville finally agreed that Lehman Brothers would render its fairness opinion for $150,000. . . .

[T]he Lehman Brothers team concluded that "the price of either $20 or $21 would be a fair price for the remaining shares of UOP." They telephoned this impression to Glanville, who was spending the weekend in Vermont.

On Monday morning, March 6, 1978, Glanville and the senior member of the Lehman Brothers team flew to Des Plaines to attend the scheduled UOP directors meeting. Glanville looked over the assembled information during the flight. The two had with them the draft of a "fairness opinion letter" in which the price had been left blank. Either during or immediately prior to the directors' meeting, the two-page "fairness opinion letter" was typed in final form and the price of $21 per share was inserted.

On March 6, 1978, both the Signal and UOP boards were convened to consider the proposed merger. Telephone communications were maintained between the two meetings. Walkup, Signal's board chairman, and also a UOP director, attended UOP's meeting with Crawford in order to present Signal's position and answer any questions that UOP's non-Signal directors might have. Arledge and Chitiea, along with Signal's other designees on UOP's board, participated by conference telephone. . . .

First, Signal's board unanimously adopted a resolution authorizing Signal to propose to UOP a cash merger of $21 per share. . . . This proposal required that the merger be approved by a majority of UOP's outstanding minority shares voting at the stockholders' meeting at which the merger would be considered, and that the minority shares voting in favor of the merger, when coupled with Signal's 50.5% interest would have to comprise at least two-thirds of all UOP shares. Otherwise the proposed merger would be deemed disapproved.

UOP's board then considered the proposal. Copies of the agreement were delivered to the directors in attendance. . . . In addition they had Lehman Brothers' hurriedly prepared fairness opinion letter finding the price of $21 to be fair. Glanville, the Lehman Brothers partner, and UOP director, commented on the information that had gone into preparation of the letter.

Signal also suggests that the Arledge-Chitiea feasibility study, indicating that a price of up to $24 per share would be a "good investment" for Signal, was discussed at the UOP directors' meeting. The Chancellor made no such finding, and our independent review of the record, detailed infra, satisfies us by a preponderance of the evidence that there was no discussion of this document at UOP's board meeting. Furthermore, it is clear beyond peradventure that nothing in that report was ever disclosed to UOP's minority shareholders prior to their approval of the merger.

After consideration of Signal's proposal, Walkup and Crawford left the meeting to permit a free and uninhibited exchange between UOP's non-Signal directors. Upon their return a resolution to accept Signal's offer was then proposed and adopted. . . .

On March 7, 1978, UOP sent a letter to its shareholders advising them of the action taken by UOP's board with respect to Signal's offer. . . .

Despite the swift board action of the two companies, the merger was not submitted to UOP's shareholders until their annual meeting on May 26, 1978. In the notice of that meeting and proxy statement sent to shareholders in May, UOP's management and board urged that the merger be approved. The proxy statement also advised:

> The price was determined after *discussions* between James V. Crawford, a director of Signal and Chief Executive Officer of UOP, and officers of Signal which took place during meetings on February 28, 1978, and in the course of several subsequent telephone conversations. (Emphasis added.)

In the original draft of the proxy statement the word "negotiations" had been used rather than "discussions." However, when the Securities and Exchange Commission sought details of the "negotiations" as part of its review of these materials, the term was deleted and the word "discussions" was substituted. . . .

As of the record date for UOP's annual meeting, there were 12,488,302 shares of UOP common stock outstanding, 5,688,302 of which were owned by the minority. At the meeting only 56%, or 3,208,652, of the minority shares were voted. Of these, 2,953,812, or 51.9% of the total minority, voted for the merger, and 254,840 voted against it. When Signal's stock was added to the minority shares voting in favor, a total of 76.2% of UOP's outstanding shares approved the merger while only 2.2% opposed it.

By its terms the merger became effective on May 26, 1978, and each share of UOP's stock held by the minority was automatically converted into a right to receive $21 cash. . . .

A primary issue mandating reversal [of the Court of Chancery's judgment] is the preparation by two UOP directors, Arledge and Chitiea, of their feasibility study for the exclusive use and benefit of Signal. This document was of obvious significance to both Signal and UOP. Using UOP data, it described the advantages to Signal of ousting the minority at a price range of $21-24 per share. Mr. Arledge, one of the authors, outlined the benefits to Signal:

PURPOSE OF THE MERGER

1. Provides an outstanding investment opportunity for Signal — (Better than any recent acquisition we have seen).
2. Increases Signal's earnings.
3. Facilitates the flow of resources between Signal and its subsidiaries — (Big factors — works both ways).
4. Provides cost savings potential for Signal and UOP.
5. Improves the percentage of Signal's "operating earnings" as opposed to "holding company earnings."
6. Simplifies the understanding of Signal.
7. Facilitates technological exchange among Signal's subsidiaries.
8. Eliminates potential conflicts of interest.

Having written those words, solely for the use of Signal, it is clear from the record that neither Arledge nor Chitiea shared this report with their fellow directors of UOP. We are satisfied that no one else did either. This conduct hardly meets the fiduciary standards applicable to such a transaction. . . .

The Arledge-Chitiea report speaks for itself in supporting the Chancellor's finding that a price of up to $24 was a "good investment" for Signal. It shows that a return on the investment at $21 would be 15.7% versus 15.5% at $24 per share. This was a difference of only two-tenths of one percent, while it meant over $17,000,000 to the minority. Under such circumstances, paying UOP's minority shareholders $24 would have had relatively little long-term effect on Signal, and the Chancellor's findings concerning the benefit to Signal, even at a price of $24, were obviously correct. . . .

Certainly, this was a matter of material significance to UOP and its shareholders. Since the study was prepared by two UOP directors, using UOP information for the exclusive benefit of Signal, and nothing whatever was done to disclose it to the outside UOP directors or the minority shareholders, a question of breach of fiduciary duty arises. This problem occurs because there were common Signal-UOP directors participating, at least to some extent, in the UOP board's decision-making processes without full disclosure of the conflicts they faced.[7] . . .

Given the absence of any attempt to structure this transaction on an arm's length basis, Signal cannot escape the effects of the conflicts it faced, particularly when its designees on UOP's board did not totally abstain from participation in the matter. There is no "safe harbor" for such divided loyalties in Delaware. When directors of a Delaware corporation are on both sides of a transaction, they are required to demonstrate their utmost good faith and the most scrupulous inherent fairness of the bargain. . . .

There is no dilution of this obligation where one holds dual or multiple directorships, as in a parent-subsidiary context. . . . The record demonstrates that Signal has not met this obligation.

The concept of fairness has two basic aspects: fair dealing and fair price. The former embraces questions of when the transaction was timed, how it was initiated, structured, negotiated, disclosed to the directors, and how the approvals of the directors and the stockholders were obtained. The latter aspect of fairness relates to the economic and financial considerations of the proposed merger, including all relevant factors: assets, market value, earnings, future prospects, and any other elements that affect the intrinsic or inherent value of a company's stock. However, the test for fairness is not a bifurcated one as between fair dealing and price. All aspects of the issue must be examined as a whole since the question is one of entire fairness. However, in a non-fraudulent transaction we recognize that price may be the preponderant consideration outweighing other features of the merger. Here, we address

7. Although perfection is not possible, or expected, the result here could have been entirely different if UOP had appointed an independent negotiating committee of its outside directors to deal with Signal at arm's length. . . . Since fairness in this context can be equated to conduct by a theoretical, wholly independent, board of directors acting upon the matter before them, it is unfortunate that this course apparently was neither considered nor pursued. . . . Particularly in a parent-subsidiary context, a showing that the action taken was as though each of the contending parties had in fact exerted its bargaining power against the other at arm's length is strong evidence that the transaction meets the test of fairness. . . .

the two basic aspects of fairness separately because we find reversible error as to both.

Part of fair dealing is the obvious duty of candor required by *Lynch I*, supra. Moreover, one possessing superior knowledge may not mislead any stockholder by use of corporate information to which the latter is not privy. . . . With the well-established Delaware law on the subject, . . . it is inevitable that the obvious conflicts posed by Arledge and Chitiea's preparation of their "feasibility study," derived from UOP information, for the sole use and benefit of Signal, cannot pass muster.

The Arledge-Chitiea report is but one aspect of the element of fair dealing. How did this merger evolve? It is clear that it was entirely initiated by Signal. The serious time constraints under which the principals acted were all set by Signal. It had not found a suitable outlet for its excess cash and considered UOP a desirable investment, particularly since it was now in a position to acquire the whole company for itself. For whatever reasons, and they were only Signal's, the entire transaction was presented to and approved by UOP's board within four business days. . . .

. . . So far as negotiations were concerned, it is clear that they were modest at best. Crawford, Signal's man at UOP, never really talked price with Signal, except to accede to its management's statements on the subject, and to convey to Signal the UOP outside directors' view that as between the $20-$21 range under consideration, it would have to be $21. The latter is not a surprising outcome, but hardly arm's length negotiations. Only the protection of benefits for UOP's key employees and the issue of Lehman Brothers' fee approached any concept of bargaining.

As we have noted, the matter of disclosure to the UOP directors was wholly flawed by the conflicts of interest raised by the Arledge-Chitiea report. . . .

This cannot but undermine a conclusion that this merger meets any reasonable test of fairness. The outside UOP directors lacked one material piece of information generated by two of their colleagues, but shared only with Signal. True, the UOP board had the Lehman Brothers' fairness opinion, but that firm has been blamed by the plaintiff for the hurried task it performed, when more properly the responsibility for this lies with Signal. There was no disclosure of the circumstances surrounding the rather cursory preparation of the Lehman Brothers' fairness opinion. Instead, the impression was given UOP's minority that a careful study had been made, when in fact speed was the hallmark, and Mr. Glanville, Lehman's partner in charge of the matter, and also a UOP director, having spent the weekend in Vermont, brought a draft of the "fairness opinion letter" to the UOP directors' meeting on March 6, 1978 with the price left blank. We can only conclude from the record that the rush imposed on Lehman Brothers by Signal's timetable contributed to the difficulties under which this investment banking firm attempted to perform its responsibilities. Yet, none of this was disclosed to UOP's minority.

Finally, the minority stockholders were denied the critical information that Signal considered a price of $24 to be a good investment. Since this would have meant over $17,000,000 more to the minority, we cannot conclude that the shareholder vote was an informed one. Under the circumstances, an approval by a majority of the minority was meaningless. . . .

QUESTIONS ON WEINBERGER

1. What is the significance of the fact that, at $24 per share, UOP stock would have been a good investment for Signal? Must a controlling shareholder inform minority shareholders of the top price it is willing or able to pay? If so, how could the negotiating committee device, endorsed in footnote 7, work in practice? If not, why did the court lay emphasis on the fact that Signal could have rationally paid more? See *Kahn v. Tremont Corp.*, 694 A.2d 422 (Del. 1997).

2. Regarding the negotiating committee idea mentioned in footnote 7, how much protection to the minority would that device offer even if undertaken in good faith? Specifically, what is the source of negotiating leverage that such a committee might have? See *Kahn v. Lynch Communications*, below (i.e., "the power to say no").

3. To what extent does this result represent disapproval by the court of an apparent failure to observe proper and formal corporate governance practices? Did Arledge and Chitiea use confidential data for Signal's purposes? If they had not been UOP directors and had only used public information, would the case have been decided differently? Why the speed to get UOP board approval when no external force drove the schedule?

8.5.2   Approval by a Board Minority of "Independent" Directors: Special Committees

How should courts approach judicial review of a related-party transaction approved by a minority of the board? Following the *Weinberger* case there has evolved a standard template — not a mandatory template but one that is widely employed — for controlled transactions between a subsidiary corporation and its parent or affiliates.[45] Parent companies have a clear obligation to treat their subsidiaries fairly when the subsidiaries have public shareholders and they can expect shareholder lawsuits to trigger judicial scrutiny of large transactions with their subsidiaries. Therefore, techniques that assure the appearance as well as the reality of a fair deal are useful. Formation of a special committee of disinterested independent directors to consider and recommend the transaction is the most common such technique. Two aspects of this technique deserve mention: the operation of the special committee and its effects, if it is well executed.

To be given effect under Delaware law, a special committee must minimally be properly charged by the full board, comprised of independent members, and vested with the resources to accomplish its task. The charge is critical. Committee members must understand that their mission is not only to negotiate a fair deal but also to obtain the best available deal.

---

45. Some jurisdictions, such as Germany, dedicate an entire subfield of corporate law to protecting minority shareholders and creditors from the risk of exploitation in such intragroup transactions.

Therefore, a special committee's conclusion that a deal is merely within a range of fairness will not serve to shift the burden of proof if the deal is attacked.[46] Moreover, a committee must "just say no" when a controlling shareholder refuses to consider advantageous alternatives unless the controller proposes terms that are their financial equivalent. Make no mistake, a committee has real bargaining power in this context because the courts are likely to be skeptical of any deal forced on the minority shareholders without the committee's approval.

Every aspect of the operation of the special committee is important in assuring that its recommendation receives judicial respect. Almost universally, the committee will retain outside investment bankers and lawyers to advise it. The choice of such firms and, in the case of bankers, the method of their compensation may be important. Since the principal reason for appointing a special committee is to assure that honest, independent judgment is brought to bear, it is a mistake to allow any shadow to fall on that process.[47]

The functioning and effect of a committee of independent directors in a parent-sub merger is an important topic that has received a good deal of judicial attention. We will return to it when we consider freeze-out mergers in Chapter 12.

8.6   CORPORATE OPPORTUNITY DOCTRINE

A distinctive form of potential conflict transaction involves the question: When may a fiduciary pursue a business opportunity on her own account if that opportunity might arguably "belong" to the corporation? The corporate opportunity cases tend to focus on the rules of recognition; that is, when is an opportunity "corporate" rather than personal and hence off-limits to the corporation's managers? This is in contrast to the typical self-dealing case, where the usual issue is whether a self-dealing transaction violates the duty of loyalty rather than whether a given transaction is "interested" in the first instance.

Like most duty of loyalty problems, corporate opportunity doctrine is better described with standards than with tightly drawn rules (although many courts still try to formulate business opportunity problems in rule-like language). The chief questions that arise in the corporate opportunity context are three: first, whether an opportunity is a corporate opportunity, second, whether the case presents circumstances in which even if it is so, a fiduciary may nevertheless justify pursuing the opportunity in a personal capacity, and, finally, if he or she has breached her duty of loyalty in taking an opportunity deemed in equity to belong to the corporation, what remedies will be available.

46. See *In re First Boston Shareholders Litigation*, 1990 WL 201388 (Del. Ch. Dec. 13, 1990).
47. See, e.g., *Kahn v. Tremont Corp.*, 694 A.2d 422, 429 (Del. 1997).

8.6.1   Determining Which Opportunities "Belong" to the Corporation

There are three general lines of corporate opportunity doctrine. The first includes those cases that tend to give the narrowest protection to the corporation by applying an "expectancy or interest" test. As applied by the leading case of *Lagarde v. Anniston Lime & Stone Inc.*, 28 So. 199 (Ala. 1900), the expectancy or interest must grow out of an existing legal interest, and the appropriation of the opportunity will in some degree "balk the corporation in effecting the purpose of its creation." Id. at 201. This language dates from an era in which corporations frequently had a single business purpose. Today, corporations are generally formed for all legal business activities. Thus, more recent cases applying the expectancy or interest test look to the firm's practical business expectancy or interest. Yet this test is still relatively narrow.

The second test, known as the "line of business" test, classifies any opportunity falling within a company's line of business as its corporate opportunity. In other words, anything that a corporation could be reasonably expected to do is a corporate opportunity. Factors affecting this determination include (1) how this matter came to the attention of the director, officer, or employee; (2) how far removed from the "core economic activities" of the corporation the opportunity lies; and (3) whether corporate information is used in recognizing or exploiting the opportunity. *Guft v. Loft, Inc.*, 5 A.2d 503, 511 (Del. 1939), is perhaps the most cited case applying the line of business test.

Finally, some courts employ a more diffuse test that relies on multiple factors—a "fairness" test—to identify corporate opportunities. A court employing the fairness test will look into factors such as how a manager learned of the disputed opportunity, whether he or she used corporate assets in exploiting the opportunity, and other fact-specific indicia of good faith and loyalty to the corporation, in addition to a company's line of business.[48]

As noted above, Delaware is associated with the line of business test, but decisions in the last 20 or so years include factors from other approaches hinting at a broadening of what counts as a corporate opportunity. For example, in *Broz v. Cellular Info. Sys.*, 673 A. 2d 148 (Del. 1996), the Delaware Supreme Court noted as relevant whether "the corporation has an interest or expectancy in the opportunity . . . and [will] the corporate fiduciary . . . be placed in a position inimical to his duties to the corporation." Recently, in *Personal Touch Holding Corp. v. Glaubach*, 2019 WL 937180 (Del. Ch. Feb. 25, 2019), the Court of Chancery held that an opportunity outside of the firm's usual line of business could trigger the corporate opportunity doctrine. Plaintiff was in the home healthcare business and wanted to expand its operations by purchasing a nearby building (the alleged opportunity), but the firm's president (and director) secretly purchased the property from underneath the firm. Given that the firm intended to use the property to expand its core business and had an interest (or expectancy) in the property, the court

---

48. For a critical review of the competing common law doctrines, see Victor Brudney & Robert C. Clark, *A New Look at Corporate Opportunities*, 94 Harv. L. Rev. 997 (1981).

considered it unnecessary to interpret "line of business" in a manner limited to home healthcare services.[49]

NOTE AND QUESTION ON WHICH OPPORTUNITIES "BELONG" TO A CORPORATION

When is a business idea concrete enough to rise to the level of being an "opportunity" that may belong to the corporation? This question was addressed by the Court of Chancery in *Outlaw Beverage, Inc. v. Collins*, C.A. No. 2019-0342-AGB (Del. Ch. June 18, 2019). Plaintiff Outlaw Beverage alleged that defendant (its former director) usurped a corporate opportunity when he developed a private-label energy drink for his own business after attending a meeting for Outlaw where a business customer noted that he wanted a private-label energy drink for distribution. The court rejected plaintiff's claim on multiple grounds including that the idea of a private-label energy drink at the meeting was not concrete enough to amount to a "corporate opportunity" and that it "did not concern a tangible product, an actual business, or anything concrete in form. Rather the opportunity that was presented was little more than a general idea or concept."[50] This was insufficient to ground a corporate opportunity claim. What else should be necessary before this "concept" ripens into an opportunity? Related to the notion of "concreteness" is whether a *chance* to do something could be an "opportunity" — an example is when a firm and its director both submit competing bids for something. Delaware has rejected this as being a corporate opportunity because there was "virtually no certainty that the [firm] would win [the bid]." *Triton Construction Company v. Eastern Short Electrical Services, Inc.* 2009 WL 1287115 (Del. Ch. May 18, 2009). Can you think of examples of where the "certainty" objection might be overcome? See *Leased Access Preservation Ass'n v. Thomas*, C.A. No. 2019-0310-KSJM (Del. Ch, Jan. 8, 2020).

8.6.2 When May a Fiduciary Take a Corporate Opportunity?

Some courts have held that a fiduciary may take an opportunity if the corporation is not in a financial position to do so.[51] Incapacity is related to

49. Moreover, the Court was concerned that the defendant's behavior—the secrecy involved and the use of corporate information and employees—placed him in a "position inimical to his duties." Id. at 17.
50. *Outlaw* (TRANSCRIPT) p. 15. The court also found that the private-label energy drink was developed by the defendant in his individual capacity and not as a director of the firm because all the product development, marketing, and so forth was done by the defendant and not utilizing any of Outlaw's resources.
51. See *Miller v. Miller*, 202 N.W.2d 71 (Minn. 1974) (recognizing company's "financial incapacity" to exploit opportunity as a defense).

disinterest and implies that a corporation's board has determined not to accept the opportunity. In either event, it is reasoned, a fiduciary should be free to take the opportunity. What is critical in these cases, as in other instances of fiduciary analysis, is whether the board has evaluated the question of whether to accept the opportunity in good faith. Financial inability may seem an odd reason for a public corporation to reject an opportunity, at least if the opportunity promises a return that implies a positive net present value and exceeds the corporation's implicit costs of capital. Similarly, a board's decision to permit one of its directors to take a profitable opportunity might be regarded as inherently suspicious. Nevertheless, most courts accept a board's good-faith informed decision not to pursue an opportunity as a complete defense to a suit challenging a fiduciary's acceptance of a corporate opportunity on her own account.[52] Of course, this defense is effective only if a court is persuaded that the decision to reject a valuable opportunity on financial grounds is the genuine business judgment of a disinterested and informed decision maker. The fiduciary who takes the opportunity bears the burden of establishing this defense.[53]

What if the director never presented a business opportunity to the board, in the good-faith belief that it was not a corporate opportunity? While presenting the opportunity to the board seems clearly the safer practice for the fiduciary and the better corporate governance practice, it is not required under Delaware law. In *Broz* the court stated: "It is not the law of Delaware that presentation to the board is a necessary prerequisite to a finding that a corporate opportunity has not been usurped." Instead, the court stated that presenting an opportunity to the board "simply provides a kind of 'safe harbor' for the director, which removes the specter of a *post hoc* judicial determination that the director or officer has improperly usurped a corporate opportunity." See id. at 157.

In 2000, the Delaware legislature added §122(17) to the Delaware corporate code, which explicitly authorizes waiver in the charter of the corporate opportunity constraints for officers, directors, or shareholders "as related to specified business opportunities or specified classes or categories of business opportunities that are presented to the corporation or 1 or more of its officers, directors or stockholders." DGCL §122(17). The amendment was motivated, at least in part, by the growing culture of "interlocking" boards at Silicon Valley companies, in which entrepreneurs from closely related businesses would sit on each others' boards. Waiver of corporate opportunity doctrine, it was argued, was needed in order to induce these entrepreneurs to serve as directors.

---

52. In the past, courts sometimes refused to accept the financial incapacity defense. Thus, in *Irving Trust Co. v. Deutsch*, 75 F.2d 121 (2d Cir. 1934), the court framed a rigid rule forbidding directors of solvent corporations from taking over for their own profit a corporate contract on the plea of the corporation's financial inability to perform. This rule would represent a rational choice of guaranteed purity over messy efficiency. That is, this rule would foreclose some transactions that would be socially useful in order to assure no, or fewer, corrupt transactions occur. It represents a rational choice, but not inevitably the best one, and has not tended to prevail in history.

53. See *Klinicki v. Lundgren*, 695 P.2d 906 (Or. 1985).

Of course, this raises the question: When will courts accept a waiver of corporate opportunity? In a series of cases over the last two years, Delaware's judiciary has started to carve out an answer. In *Alarm.com Holdings, Inc. v. ABS Capital Partners, Inc. et al.*, C.A. No. 2017-0583-JTL (Del. Ch. June 15, 2018), the Court of Chancery examined a waiver that permitted ABS to invest in firms competing with plaintiff Alarm.com (in which ABS was also invested), as long as ABS did not rely on confidential information obtained from Alarm.com in making that investment. ABS invested in a competitor — Resolution — but Alarm.com did not allege the use of confidential information. The court dismissed the suit and held in part that the waiver applied because ABS did what was specifically anticipated in the waiver. However, in an important footnote, the court demurred on whether less specific waivers would be upheld. It said "[n]o one has challenged the scope of the waiver, and this decision provides no opportunity to opine on the validity of a broad and general renunciation of corporate opportunities, as contrasted with a more tailored provision addressing a specified business opportunity or a well-defined class or category of business opportunities."[54] This is consistent with the language of §122(17) and suggests that the specificity of a waiver influences its effectiveness and perhaps more directly that carte blanche waivers of corporate opportunity constraints are likely to face greater judicial headwinds.

Following quickly on the heels of *Alarm.com*, the Court of Chancery held in *Outlaw*, noted earlier, that a waiver targeting specific opportunities was enforceable. There the waiver stated that the corporation gave up any interest or expectancy in opportunities coming to non-employee directors "unless such [opportunity], . . . comes into the possession of [this director] expressly and solely [due to her position] as a director of this corporation." On the facts, plaintiff Outlaw did not show that the opportunity came to the director "solely" in his capacity as a director.

Shortly after this decision, the Court of Chancery refused to dismiss a case based on a purported waiver in *Armored Combat League, LLC v. Brooks*, C.A. No. 2019-0463-MTZ (Del. Ch. July 2, 2019). Plaintiff Armored Combat provided a tournament league in which individuals dressed in medieval armor and staged fights with blunted weapons. As feuding between the founding members worsened, one of them blocked other members from accessing the firm's website, re-directed traffic to his own competing website, and posted negative statements about the firm. Defendant argued that language in the unsigned operating agreement for the LLC (a form that, as you may recall, allows for broad contractual opt-outs of fiduciary duty) insulated him from suit. The relevant provision stated that "[any manager or member] may engage in or possess an interest in other profit-seeking or business ventures. . .whether or not such ventures are competitive with the Company and the doctrine of corporate opportunity, or any analogous doctrine, shall not apply." The court held that the waiver was targeted at permitting members to run their own competing businesses, not sabotaging Armored Combat through such methods.[55]

---

54. *Alarm.com*, at 8 n.46.
55. Although we do not discuss it here, courts have held that the process of obtaining the waiver is subject to fiduciary duty analysis. Thus, seeking a waiver by providing insufficient

NOTE AND QUESTIONS ON WAIVERS OF CORPORATE OPPORTUNITY

1. DreamWorks Animation SKG, a collaboration among entertainment moguls Steven Spielberg, Jeffery Katzenberg, and David Geffen has a waiver in its charter saying:

> None of the Founding Stockholders [Spielberg, Katzenberg, and Geffen] or any director, officer, member, partner, stockholder or employee of any Founding Stockholder (each a "Specified Party"), independently or with others, shall have any duty to refrain from engaging directly or indirectly in the same or similar business activities or lines of business as the Corporation and that might be in direct or indirect competition with the Corporation. In the event that any Founding Stockholder or Specified Party acquires knowledge of a potential transaction or matter that may be a corporate opportunity for any Founding Stockholder or Specified Party, as applicable, and the Corporation, none of the Founding Stockholders or Specified Parties shall have any duty to communicate or offer such corporate opportunity to the Corporation, and any Founding Stockholder and Specified Party shall be entitled to pursue or acquire such corporate opportunity for itself or to direct such corporate opportunity to another person or entity and the Corporation shall have no right in or to such corporate opportunity or to any income or proceeds derived therefrom.

Why would DreamWorks put such a clause in its charter? What questions and concerns would arise for potential investors reading this clause? How might they rationally react to such concerns?

2. Recent scholarship argues that publicly traded firms have started using the waivers under §122(17) with gusto. Gabriel Rauterberg and Eric Talley study the adoption of corporate opportunity waivers between 1995 and 2016 and find that they are increasingly common.[56] They find that many hundreds of publicly traded firms have them (along with estimating that thousands more do) and that firms adopting such waivers are usually profitable (with sizeable revenues), fairly large, and carry some indicia of being well governed. They run event studies to examine market reactions to announcements of waivers and find that they are generally positive. Collectively, this runs contrary to the narrative that waiving firms are less scrupulous or more infected with agency costs. Rather, it is more consistent with the view that waivers are being adopted in ways consistent with efficiency (or at least not violently opposed to it) by, for example, making it easier for certain investors to hold overlapping directorships, or perhaps the market views them positively because the waiver removes one way in which corporations might have to bear litigation costs. They also find that the waivers are granted across the

---

information to shareholders voting on the waiver violates fiduciary duty among other things. See *Armored Combat League*, at 18 n.46.

56. *See* Gabriel V. Rauterberg & Eric L. Talley, *Contracting Out of the Fiduciary Duty of Loyalty: An Empirical Analysis of Corporate Opportunity Waivers*, 117 Colum. L. Rev. 1075 (2017).

spectrum of corporate fiduciaries with most benefiting directors, but a sizeable number benefit controlling shareholders and executives. Also, many of them are drafted in fairly broad terms rather than the specificity that appears intended by the statutory language and preferred by courts.

8.7   THE DUTY OF LOYALTY IN CLOSE CORPORATIONS

Virtually all of the legal characteristics of the corporate form, including limited liability, may fail to capture significant features of the "bargain" among the small numbers of equity participants in closely held corporations. European jurisdictions have long recognized the close or private corporation as a distinct form. France has the *société à responsabilité limitée* (S.A.R.L.), Germany has the *Gesellschaft mit beschränkte Haftung* (G.m.b.H.), and England provides customized statutory treatment for private companies.

In the United States, explicit statutory and judicial recognition of the unique features of the private corporation (with overlapping management and ownership) did not emerge until the late 1960s. Today, however, American corporate statutes allow legal planners enormous latitude in customizing the form of the close corporation. Most often, this new flexibility is characterized by a "unified" corporations statute, which explicitly permits planners to contract around statutory provisions through either general opt-out clauses ("unless otherwise provided in the charter") or opt-out provisions restricted to close corporations. *See, e.g.,* MBCA §8.01(b); F. Hodge O'Neal & Robert Thompson, *O'Neal's Close Corp.,* §1.14 (3d ed. 1971). Other states, by contrast, provide specialized close corporation statutes, which companies meeting the statutory criteria of a close corporation can elect to be governed by, in lieu of general corporation law. Here DGCL §§341-356 are an excellent illustration. (DGCL §342 defines eligible close corporations as those that have, inter alia, 30 or fewer shareholders.)

Notwithstanding the great freedom that business planners now have to customize the form of a close corporation, problems arise, since every contingency cannot be anticipated when the corporation is established. As in the case of dissolving partnerships, shareholder disputes in close corporations often raise questions about the proper role of courts in superintending ongoing businesses. The difference, of course, is that equity participants in close corporations have selected the corporate form — with its associated characteristics of permanence, centralized management, etc. — to frame their long-term deal. Consider the approach developed in the following Massachusetts cases.

DONAHUE v. RODD ELECTROTYPE CO.
328 N.E.2d 505 (Mass. 1975)

TAURO, C.J.:

The plaintiff, Euphemia Donahue, a minority stockholder in the Rodd Electrotype Company of New England, Inc. ("Rodd Electrotype"), a Massachusetts corporation, brings this suit against the directors of Rodd Electrotype, Charles H. Rodd, Frederick I. Rodd and Mr. Harold E. Magnuson, against Harry C. Rodd, a former director, officer and controlling stockholder of Rodd Electrotype and against Rodd Electrotype (hereinafter called "defendants"). The plaintiff seeks to rescind Rodd Electrotype's purchase of Harry Rodd's shares in Rodd Electrotype and to compel Harry Rodd "to repay to the corporation the purchase price of said shares, $36,000, together with interest from the date of purchase." The plaintiff alleges that the defendants caused the corporation to purchase the shares in violation of their fiduciary duty to her, a minority stockholder of Rodd Electrotype.[4]

The trial judge, after hearing oral testimony, . . . found that the purchase was without prejudice to the plaintiff and implicitly found that the transaction had been carried out in good faith and with inherent fairness. . . .

[Briefly, the facts were as follows: In the mid-1930s, Harry Rodd and Joseph Donahue were employees of Royal Electrotype, (Rodd Electrotype's predecessor). Donahue had never participated in the management of the business, but Rodd advanced rapidly within the company. By 1955, he was president and Rodd and Donahue became Royal's sole shareholders, owning 80 percent and 20 percent of its stock, respectively. In 1960, the corporation was renamed Rodd Electrotype, and Harry Rodd's two sons, Charles and Frederick, soon became managers. In 1965, Charles succeeded his father as president and general manager.

In 1970, Harry Rodd was 77 years old and not in good health, and he was contemplating retirement. He had already distributed 117 of his 200 shares equally among his two sons and his daughter, and he had returned 2 shares to the corporate treasury. Before retiring, he wished to dispose of the remaining 81 shares. Accordingly, Charles, acting for the company, offered to repurchase 45 of Harry's shares for $800/share — a price that, Charles testified, reflected book and liquidating value. The company's board — then consisting of Charles, Frederick, and a lawyer — authorized the repurchase in July 1970. Subsequently, Harry Rodd sold 2 shares to each of his three children at $800/share and gave each child 10 shares as a gift. Meanwhile, Donahue had died, and his 50 shares had passed to his wife and son. When the Donahues learned of the repurchase of Harry Rodd's shares, they offered to sell their shares to the company on the same terms, but their offer was rejected. Between 1965 and 1969, the company offered to purchase the Donahue shares for amounts between $2,000 and $10,000 ($40 to $200 a share). The Donahues rejected these offers. — EDS.]

The court continued:

In her argument before this court, the plaintiff has characterized the corporate purchase of Harry Rodd's shares as an unlawful distribution of

---

4. In form, the plaintiff's bill of complaint presents, at least in part, a derivative action, brought on behalf of the corporation, and, in the words of the bill, "on behalf of . . . [the] stockholders" of Rodd Electrotype. Yet the plaintiff's bill, in substance, was one seeking redress because of alleged breaches of the fiduciary duty owed to *her*, a minority stockholder, by the controlling stockholders.

We treat that bill of complaint (as have the parties) as presenting a proper cause of suit in the personal right of the plaintiff.

corporate assets to controlling shareholders. She urges that the distribution constitutes a breach of the fiduciary duty owed by the Rodds, as controlling shareholders, to her, a minority stockholder in the enterprise, because the Rodds failed to accord her an equal opportunity to sell her shares to the corporation. . . . For the reasons hereinafter noted, we agree with the plaintiff and reverse the decree of the Superior Court. However, we limit the applicability of our holding to "close corporations," as hereinafter defined. Whether the holding should apply to other corporations is left for decision in another case, on a proper record.

A. Close Corporations.   In previous opinions, we have alluded to the distinctive nature of the close corporation but have never defined precisely what is meant by a close corporation. There is no single, generally accepted definition. Some commentators emphasize an "integration of ownership and management" . . . in which the stockholders occupy most management positions. Others focus on the number of stockholders and the nature of the market for the stock. In this view, close corporations have few stockholders; there is little market for corporate stock. . . . We accept aspects of both definitions. We deem a close corporation to be typified by: (1) a small number of stockholders; (2) no ready market for the corporate stock; and (3) substantial majority stockholder participation in the management, direction and operations of the corporation.

As thus defined, the close corporation bears striking resemblance to a partnership. Just as in a partnership, the relationship among the stockholders must be one of trust, confidence and absolute loyalty if the enterprise is to succeed. . . .

Although the corporate form provides advantages for the stockholders (limited liability, perpetuity, and so forth), it also supplies an opportunity for the majority stockholders to oppress or disadvantage minority stockholders. The minority is vulnerable to a variety of oppressive devices, termed "freezeouts," which the majority may employ. An authoritative study of such "freezeouts" enumerates some of the possibilities: "The squeezers . . . may refuse to declare dividends; they may drain off the corporation's earnings in the form of exorbitant salaries and bonuses to majority shareholder-officers and perhaps to their relatives, or in the form of high rent by the corporation for property leased from majority shareholders; they may deprive minority shareholders of corporation offices and of employment by the company. . . ."

The minority can, of course, initiate suit against the majority and their directors. Self-serving conduct by directors is proscribed by the director's fiduciary obligation to the corporation. However, in practice, the plaintiff will find difficulty in challenging dividend or employment policies. Such policies are considered to be within the judgment of the directors. . . .

[G]enerally, plaintiffs who seek judicial assistance against corporate dividend or employment policies do not prevail. . . .

Thus, when these types of "freezeouts" are attempted by the majority stockholders, the minority shareholders, cut off from all corporation-related revenues, must either suffer their losses or seek a buyer for their shares. Many minority stockholders will be unwilling or unable to wait for an alteration in majority policy. Typically, the minority stockholder in a close corporation has a substantial percentage of his personal assets invested in the corporation. The stockholder may have anticipated that his salary from his position with the corporation would be his livelihood. Thus, he cannot afford to wait passively. He must liquidate his investment in the close corporation in order to reinvest the funds in income-producing enterprises.

At this point, the true plight of the minority stockholder in a close corporation becomes manifest. He cannot easily reclaim his capital. In a large public corporation, the oppressed or dissident minority stockholder could sell his stock in order to extricate some of his invested capital. By definition, this market is not available for shares in the close corporation. In a partnership, a partner who feels abused by his fellow partners may cause dissolution by his "express will . . . at any time" and recover his share of partnership assets and accumulated profits. By contrast, the stockholder in the close corporation or "incorporated partnership" may achieve dissolution and recovery of his share of the enterprise assets only by compliance with the rigorous terms of the applicable chapter of the General Laws.

Thus, in a close corporation, the minority stockholders may be trapped in a disadvantageous situation. No outsider would knowingly assume the position of the disadvantaged minority. The outsider would have the same difficulties. To cut losses, the minority stockholder may be compelled to deal with the majority. This is the capstone of the majority plan. Majority "freezeout" schemes which withhold dividends are designed to compel the minority to relinquish stock at inadequate prices.

Because of the fundamental resemblance of the close corporation to the partnership, the trust and confidence which are essential to this scale and manner of enterprise, and the inherent danger to minority interests in the close corporation, we hold that stockholders[17] in the close corporation owe one another substantially the same fiduciary duty in the operation of the enterprise[18] that partners owe to one another. In our previous decisions, we have defined the standard of duty owed by partners to one another as the "utmost good faith and loyalty." *Cardullo v. Landau*, 329 Mass. 5, 8, 105 N.E.2d 843 (1952). . . . Stockholders in close corporations must discharge their management and stockholder responsibilities in conformity with this strict good faith standard. They may not act out of avarice, expediency or self-interest in derogation of their duty of loyalty to the other stockholders and to the corporation.

We contrast this strict good faith standard with the somewhat less stringent standard of fiduciary duty to which directors and stockholders of all corporations must adhere in the discharge of their corporate responsibilities. . . .

---

17. We do not limit our holding to majority stockholders. In the close corporation, the minority may do equal damage through unscrupulous and improper "sharp dealings" with an unsuspecting majority. . . .

18. We stress that the strict fiduciary duty which we apply to stockholders in a close corporation in this opinion governs *only* their actions relative to the operations of the enterprise and the effects of that operation on the rights and investments of other stockholders. We express no opinion as to the standard of duty applicable to transactions in the shares of the close corporation when the corporation is not a party to the transaction. . . .

The more rigorous duty of partners and participants in a joint adventure, here extended to stockholders in a close corporation, was described by then Chief Judge Cardozo of the New York Court of Appeals in *Meinhard v. Salmon*. . . . "Joint adventurers, like copartners, owe to one another, while the enterprise continues, the duty of the finest loyalty. Many forms of conduct permissible in a workaday world for those acting at arm's length, are forbidden to those bound by fiduciary ties. . . . Not honesty alone, but the punctilio of an honor the most sensitive, is then the standard of behavior." . . . 164 N.E. at 546.

B. Equal Opportunity in a Close Corporation.   Under settled Massachusetts law, a domestic corporation, unless forbidden by statute, has the power to purchase its own shares. An agreement to reacquire stock "[is] enforceable, subject, at least, to the limitations that the purchase must be made in good faith and without prejudice to creditors and stockholders." When the corporation reacquiring its own stock is a close corporation, the purchase is subject to the additional requirement, in the light of our holding in this opinion, that the stockholders, who, as directors or controlling stockholders, caused the corporation to enter into the stock purchase agreement, must have acted with the utmost good faith and loyalty to the other stockholders.

To meet this test, if the stockholder whose shares were purchased was a member of the controlling group, the controlling stockholders must cause the corporation to offer each stockholder an equal opportunity to sell a ratable number of his shares to the corporation at an identical price. Purchase by the corporation confers substantial benefits on the members of the controlling group whose shares were purchased. These benefits are not available to the minority stockholders if the corporation does not also offer them an opportunity to sell their shares. The controlling group may not, consistent with its strict duty to the minority, utilize its control of the corporation to obtain special advantages and disproportionate benefit from its share ownership. . . .

The purchase also distributes corporate assets to the stockholder whose shares were purchased. Unless an equal opportunity is given to all stockholders, the purchase of shares from a member of the controlling group operates as a *preferential* distribution of assets. In exchange for his shares, he receives a percentage of the contributed capital and accumulated profits of the enterprise[, which the other stockholders do not]. Although the purchase price for the controlling stockholder's shares may seem fair to the corporation and other stockholders under the tests established in the prior case law . . . , the controlling stockholder whose stock has been purchased has still received a relative advantage over his fellow stockholders, inconsistent with his strict fiduciary duty — an opportunity to turn corporate funds to personal use.

. . . We hold that, in any case in which the controlling stockholders have exercised their power over the corporation to deny the minority such equal opportunity, the minority shall be entitled to appropriate relief. . . .

C. Application of the Law to This Case.   We turn now to the application of the learning set forth above to the facts of the instant case.

The strict standard of duty is plainly applicable to the stockholders in Rodd Electrotype. Rodd Electrotype is a close corporation [under the test set out above]. . . .

In testing the stock purchase from Harry Rodd against the applicable strict fiduciary standard, we treat the Rodd family as a single controlling group. . . . From the evidence, it is clear that the Rodd family was a close-knit one with strong community of interest. . . .

Moreover, a strong motive of interest requires that the Rodds be considered a controlling group. When Charles Rodd and Frederick Rodd were called on to represent the corporation in its dealings with their father, they must have known that further advancement within the corporation and benefits would follow their father's retirement and the purchase of his stock. . . .

On its face, then, the purchase of Harry Rodd's shares by the corporation is a breach of the duty which the controlling stockholders, the Rodds, owed to the minority stockholders, the plaintiff and her son. The purchase distributed a portion of the corporate assets to Harry Rodd, a member of the controlling group, in exchange for his shares. The plaintiff and her son were not offered an equal opportunity to sell their shares to the corporation. In fact, their efforts to obtain an equal opportunity were rebuffed by the corporate representative.

Because of the foregoing, we hold that the plaintiff is entitled to relief. Two forms of suitable relief are set out hereinafter. The judge below is to enter an appropriate judgment. The judgment may require Harry Rodd to remit $36,000 with interest at a legal rate from July 15, 1970, to Rodd Electrotype in exchange for forty-five shares of Rodd Electrotype treasury stock. This, in substance, is the specific relief requested in the plaintiff's bill of complaint. Interest is manifestly appropriate. . . . In the alternative, the judgment may require Rodd Electrotype to purchase all of the plaintiff's shares for $36,000 without interest. In the circumstances of this case, we view this as the equal opportunity which the plaintiff should have received. Harry Rodd's retention of thirty-six shares, which were to be sold and given to his children within a year of the Rodd Electrotype purchase, cannot disguise the fact that the corporation acquired one hundred percent of that portion of his holdings (forty-five shares) which he did not intend for his children to own. The plaintiff is entitled to have one hundred percent of her forty-five shares similarly purchased. . . .

WILKINS, J. (concurring).

I agree with much of what the Chief Justice says in support of granting relief to the plaintiff. However, I do not join in any implication (see, e.g., footnote 18 and the associated text) that the rule concerning a close corporation's purchase of a controlling stockholder's shares applies to all operations of the corporation as they affect minority stockholders. That broader issue, which is apt to arise in connection with salaries and dividend policy, is not involved in this case. The analogy to partnerships may not be a complete one.

FRANK EASTERBROOK & DANIEL FISCHEL, CLOSE CORPORATIONS AND AGENCY COSTS
38 Stan. L. Rev. 271 (1986)

C.   STRICT STANDARDS OF FIDUCIARY DUTY

Minority shareholders who believe those in control have acted wrongfully may bring an action for breach of fiduciary duty. Because the parties cannot anticipate every contingency, contractual arrangements of any complexity necessarily will be incomplete. Fiduciary duties serve as implicit standard terms in contractual agreements that lower the cost of contracting. Properly interpreted, fiduciary duties should approximate the bargain the parties themselves would have reached had they been able to negotiate at low cost.

The usefulness of fiduciary duties as a guide for conduct is limited, however, because it is often difficult for a court to determine how the parties would have contracted had they anticipated this contingency. Because of this and other problems with liability rules as a means for assuring contractual performance, the parties have incentives to adopt governance mechanisms to resolve problems that cannot be anticipated. . . .

The same rule could be applied in [publicly held and] closely held corporations, but its application would vary because of differences between the two types of firms. For example, the decision to terminate an employee in a publicly held corporation is a classic example of the exercise of business judgment that a court would not second guess. In a closely held corporation, by contrast, termination of an employee can be a way to appropriate a disproportionate share of the firm's earnings. It makes sense, therefore, to have greater judicial review of terminations of managerial (or investing) employees in closely held corporations than would be consistent with the business judgment rule. The same approach could be used with salary, dividend, and employment decisions in closely held corporations where the risks of conflicts of interests are greater. . . .

If a court is unavoidably entwined in a dispute, it must decide what the parties would have bargained for had they written a complete contingent contract. The difficulties that result when a court misses this point are illustrated by the much applauded case of *Donahue v. Rodd Electrotype Co.* . . .

Grave reflections on the plight of minority investors in closely held corporations and stirring proclamations of the fiduciary duty of the majority fill the opinion. Completely overlooked in all of this rhetoric was any consideration of the basic question—which interpretation of fiduciary duties would the parties have selected had they contracted in anticipation of this contingency? Although no one can answer such a question with certainty (precisely because the parties did not), it is most unlikely that they would have selected a rule requiring an equal opportunity for all. Buy-out arrangements on contingencies such as retirement are common in closely held corporations. Such agreements provide some liquidity and ensure that the identity of the managers and the investors remains the same, reducing agency problems. At the same time, [limiting buyout rights to managers or employees] minimizes the costs of requiring cash payouts or disrupting hard-won patterns of investment.

In comparable corporations, a commonly used agreement requires a firm to purchase all shares if it buys any. Firms often undertake to buy the shares of all who retire, and the court might have made something of this. The plaintiff was the widow of a long-time employee whose shares were not purchased when he died. Among the firms that have written explicit contracts concerning the repurchase of shares, some allow selective repurchases from departing employees and some make repurchase mandatory. It would have been difficult to determine into which category a firm such as Rodd best fit. The court did not pursue this line, however, and it did not suggest that anything turned on the employment history of the current owners of the shares.

Several states seem to follow *Donahue* in imposing a fiduciary duty running directly from shareholder to shareholder in close corporations.[57] The Delaware Supreme Court, however, seems to endorse Easterbrook and Fischel's analytical approach to the problem. See *Nixon v. Blackwell*, 626 A.2d 1366 (Del. 1993) (quoting Easterbrook and Fischel in support of reversing a Delaware Chancery Court ruling that had required close corporations to provide similar insurance benefits to all shareholders). Even Massachusetts has cut back on the *Donahue* rule somewhat. One year after *Donahue*, in *Wilkes v. Springside Nursing Home, Inc.*,[58] the Supreme Judicial Court of Massachusetts qualified the duty of "utmost good faith and loyalty" with a balancing test that recognized the controlling shareholder's right of "selfish ownership." Specifically, if the controlling shareholder can demonstrate a "legitimate business purpose" for its actions, then there is no breach of fiduciary duty unless the minority shareholder can demonstrate "that the same legitimate objective could have been achieved through an alternative course of action less harmful to the minority's interest."[59]

A recent case teases out what this qualification means. *Koshy v. Sachdev*, 477 Mass. 759 (2017) involves an all too common tale of friendship deteriorating into enmity over business issues. Koshy and Sachdev set up Indus Systems Inc. in 1987 to provide computer aided design (CAD) services where each had nearly 50 percent of the shares. The firm was successful, but by the mid-2000s both parties had divergent views on the future of the business leading to this suit. Koshy argued, among other things, that Sachdev had violated the duty of utmost good faith and loyalty by refusing to accede to tax and dividend distributions and by making a "low-ball" offer to buy out Koshy's stake. The Supreme Judicial Court of Massachusetts disagreed and held that Sachdev had legitimate concerns with the distributions — issuing dividends when the firm's largest contract was set to expire might cause financial instability as might making tax distributions when Koshy had unilaterally withdrawn a sizeable amount of assets from the firm. Similarly, the "low-ball" offer was not made in bad faith and there is no duty, absent a contrary agreement, that a close corporation shareholder owes to another shareholder in purchasing

57. See Douglas K. Moll, *Shareholder Oppression and "Fair Value": Of Discounts, Dates, and Dastardly Deeds in the Close Corporation*, 54 Duke L.J. 293, 305 (2004).
58. 353 N.E.2d 657 (Mass. 1976).
59. Id. at 663.

their shares. See id. at 773. Although this latter holding might seem contrary to *Donahue,* one must recall that there the defendants violated their duties by getting the *corporation* to purchase only Rodd's shares at a premium. Here the firm — Indus — was not a potential party to the purchase of shares. Any such purchase was directly between the shareholders — Koshy and Sachdev.

SMITH v. ATLANTIC PROPERTIES, INC.
422 N.E.2d 798 (Mass. App. 1981)

CUTTER, J.:

In December 1951, Dr. Louis E. Wolfson agreed to purchase land in Norwood for $350,000, with an initial cash payment of $50,000. . . . Dr. Wolfson offered a quarter interest each in the land to Mr. Paul T. Smith, Mr. Abraham Zimble, and William H. Burke. Each paid to Dr. Wolfson $12,500, one quarter of the initial payment. Mr. Smith, an attorney, organized the defendant corporation (Atlantic) in 1951 to operate the real estate. Each of the four subscribers received twenty-five shares of stock. Mr. Smith included, both in the corporation's articles of organization and in its by-laws, a provision reading, "No election, appointment or resolution by the Stockholders and no election, appointment, resolution, purchase, sale, lease, contract, contribution, compensation, proceeding or act by the Board of Directors or by any officer or officers shall be valid or binding upon the corporation until effected, passed, approved or ratified by an affirmative vote of eighty percent (80%) of the capital stock issued outstanding and entitled to vote." This provision (hereinafter referred to as the 80% provision) was included at Dr. Wolfson's request and had the effect of giving to any one of the four original shareholders a veto in corporate decisions.

Atlantic purchased the Norwood land . . . [and after] the first year [was] profitable and showed a profit every year prior to 1969. . . .

Salaries of about $25,000 were paid only in 1959 and 1960. Dividends in the total amount of $10,000 each were paid in 1964 and 1970. By 1961, Atlantic had about $172,000 in retained earnings, more than half in cash.

For various reasons, which need not be stated in detail, disagreements and ill will soon arose between Dr. Wolfson, on the one hand, and the other stockholders as a group.[3] Dr. Wolfson wished to see Atlantic's earnings devoted to repairs and possibly some improvements in its existing buildings and adjacent facilities. The other stockholders desired the declaration of dividends. Dr. Wolfson fairly steadily refused to vote for any dividends. Although it was pointed out to him that failure to declare dividends might result in the imposition by the Internal Revenue of a penalty under the Internal Revenue Code, I.R.C. §531 et seq. (relating to unreasonable accumulation of corporate earnings and profits), Dr. Wolfson persisted in his refusal to declare dividends. The other shareholders did agree over the years to making at least the most urgent repairs to Atlantic's buildings. . . .

---

3. At least one cause of ill will on Dr. Wolfson's part may have been the refusal of the other shareholders to consent to his transferring his shares in Atlantic to the Louis E. Wolfson Foundation, a charitable foundation created by Dr. Wolfson.

The fears of an Internal Revenue Service assessment of a penalty tax were soon realized. Penalty assessments were made in 1962, 1963, and 1964. These were settled by Dr. Wolfson for $11,767.71 in taxes and interest. Despite this settlement, Dr. Wolfson continued his opposition to declaring dividends. The record does not indicate that he developed any specific and definitive schedule or plan for a series of necessary or desirable repairs and improvements to Atlantic's properties. At least none was proposed which would have had a reasonable chance of satisfying the Internal Revenue Service that expenditures for such repairs and improvements constituted "reasonable needs of the business," I.R.C. §534(c), a term which includes (see I.R.C. §537) "the reasonably anticipated needs of the business." Predictably . . . the Internal Revenue Service assessed further penalty taxes for the years 1965, 1966, 1967, and 1968. [It is] apparent that Atlantic has incurred substantial penalty taxes and legal expense largely because of Dr. Wolfson's refusal to vote for the declaration of sufficient dividends to avoid the penalty, a refusal which was (in the Tax Court and upon appeal) attributed in some measure to a tax avoidance purpose on Dr. Wolfson's part.

On January 23, 1967, the shareholders, other than Dr. Wolfson, initiated this proceeding in the Superior Court, later supplemented to reflect developments after the original complaint. The plaintiffs sought a court determination of the dividends to be paid by Atlantic, the removal of Dr. Wolfson as a director, and an order that Atlantic be reimbursed by him for the penalty taxes assessed against it and related expenses. . . .

The trial judge made findings (but in more detail) of essentially the facts outlined above and concluded that "Dr. Wolfson's obstinate refusal to vote in favor of . . . dividends was . . . caused more by his dislike for other stockholders and his desire to avoid additional tax payments than . . . by any genuine desire to undertake a program for improving . . . [Atlantic] property." She also determined that Dr. Wolfson was liable to Atlantic for taxes and interest amounting to "$11,767.11 plus interest from the commencement of this action, plus $35,646.14 plus interest," . . . She also ordered the directors of Atlantic to declare "a reasonable dividend at the earliest practical date and reasonable dividends annually thereafter consistent with the good business practice." In addition, the trial judge directed that jurisdiction of the case be retained in the Superior Court "for a period of five years to [e]nsure compliance." . . .

The trial judge, in deciding that Dr. Wolfson had committed a breach of his fiduciary duty to other stockholders, relied greatly on broad language in *Donahue v. Rodd Electrotype Co.*, in which the Supreme Judicial Court afforded to a minority stockholder in a close corporation equality of treatment (with members of a controlling group of shareholders) in the matter of the redemption of shares. The court (at 592-593, 328 N.E.2d 505) relied on the resemblance of a close corporation to a partnership and held that [stockholders owe a duty to one another in the operation of the enterprise of] "utmost good faith and loyalty." [They] . . . "may not act out of avarice, expediency or self-interest in derogation of their duty of loyalty to the other stockholders and to the corporation." Similar principles were stated in *Wilkes v. Springside Nursing Home, Inc.*, but with some modifications, . . . of the sweeping language of the *Donahue* case. . . .

In the *Donahue* case, . . . the court recognized that cases may arise in which, in a close corporation, majority stockholders may ask protection from a minority stockholder. Such an instance arises in the present case because Dr. Wolfson has been able to exercise a veto concerning corporation action on dividends by the 80% provision (in Atlantic's articles of organization and by-laws) already quoted. The 80% provision may have substantially the effect of reversing the usual roles of the majority and the minority shareholders. The minority, under the provision, becomes an ad hoc controlling interest.[6]

It does not appear to be argued that this 80% provision is not authorized by G.L. c. 156B [which] . . . was intended to provide desirable flexibility in corporate arrangements. . . . In the present case, Dr. Wolfson testified that he requested the inclusion of the 80% provision "in case the people [the other shareholders] whom I knew, but not very well, ganged up on me." The possibilities of shareholder disagreement on policy made the provision seems a sensible precaution.[8] A question is presented, however, concerning the extent to which such a veto power possessed by a minority shareholder may be exercised as its holder may wish, without a violation of the "fiduciary duty" referred to in the *Donahue* case. . . .

With respect to the past damage to Atlantic caused by Dr. Wolfson's refusal to vote in favor of any dividends, the trial judge was justified in finding that his conduct went beyond what was reasonable. The other stockholders shared to some extent responsibility for what occurred by failing to accept Dr. Wolfson's proposals with much sympathy, but the inaction on dividends seems the principal cause of the tax penalties. Dr. Wolfson had been warned of the dangers of an assessment under the Internal Revenue Code, I.R.C. §531 et seq. He had refused to vote dividends in any amount adequate to minimize that danger and failed to bring forward, within the relevant taxable years, a convincing, definitive program of appropriate improvements which could withstand scrutiny by the Internal Revenue Service. Whatever may have been the reason for Dr. Wolfson's refusal to declare dividends (and even if in any particular year he may have gained slight, if any tax advantage from withholding dividends) we think that he recklessly ran serious and unjustified risks of precisely the penalty taxes eventually assessed, risks which were inconsistent

---

6. The majority shareholders, in the event of a deadlock, at least may seek dissolution of the corporation if forty percent of the voting power can be mustered, whereas a single stockholder with only twenty-five percent of the stock may not do so. See G.L. c. 156B, §99(b), as amended by St. 1969, c. 392, §23.

8. Dr. Wolfson himself had discovered the business opportunity which led to the formation of Atlantic, had made the initial $50,000 payment which made possible the Norwood purchase, and had given the other shareholders an opportunity to share with him in what looked like a probably profitable enterprise. It was reasonably foreseeable that there might be differences of opinion between Dr. Wolfson, a man with substantial income likely to be in a high income tax bracket, and less affluent shareholders on such matters of policy as dividend declarations, salaries, and investment in improvements in the property. The other shareholders, two of whom were attorneys, should have known that it was as open to Dr. Wolfson reasonably to exercise the veto provided to him by the 80% provision in favor of a policy of reinvestment of earnings in Atlantic's properties, which would probably avoid taxes and increase the value of the corporate assets, as it was for them (possessed of the same veto) to use reasonably their voting power in favor of a more generous dividend and salary policy.

with any reasonable interpretation of a duty of "utmost good faith and loyalty." The trial judge (despite the novelty of the situation) was justified in charging Dr. Wolfson with the out-of-pocket expenditure incurred by Atlantic for the penalty taxes and related counsel fees of the tax cases.[10] . . .

QUESTIONS ON SMITH v. ATLANTIC PROPERTIES

1. Does the fact that the minority protection device at issue in *Smith* was clearly bargained for undermine a contractualist rationale for invoking a fiduciary remedy? What about the fact that the majority in *Smith* could have forced a statutory dissolution? See note 6 in *Smith*.

2. Recent decisions continue to address the interactions between contracting and the fiduciary remedy. *Merriam v. Demoulas Super Markets, Inc.*, 464 Mass. 721 (2013) involved a sale of shares that threatened the close corporation's favorable tax status. However, the Supreme Judicial Court of Massachusetts held the sale was conducted according to the "comprehensive and bargained-for procedure for disposing of [shareholder] interests" laid out in the charter and that the suit in this case fell entirely within this procedure. Id. at 727. Because of that they held the defendant's behavior satisfied the duty of utmost good faith and loyalty indicating that the duty can be limited via contracting. Indeed, the court went further and noted that if the parties were concerned about tax status changes upon the sale of stock, they could have negotiated for that in the charter. Given that the predicate for treating an entity as a "close corporation" under *Donahue* seems to presuppose a high level of trust, does it make sense to then expect such parties to engage in this kind of sophisticated negotiating with each other?[60]

---

10. We do not now suggest that the standard of "utmost good faith and loyalty" may require some relaxation when applied to a minority ad hoc controlling interest, created by some device, similar to the 80% provision, designed in part to protect the selfish interests of a minority shareholder. This seems to us a difficult area of the law best developed on a case-by-case basis. . . .

60. The Supreme Judicial Court of Massachusetts has recently stated that if an LLC meets the requirements for being treated as a "close corporation" under *Donahue*, then the duty of utmost good faith and loyalty can be imposed. See *Allison v. Eriksson*, 479 Mass. 626 (2018).

9

EXECUTIVE COMPENSATION

9.1 INTRODUCTION

Viewed from a great height, corporation law can be seen to have two main social goals. The first is to facilitate economic enterprise. This goal is advanced by all of the fundamental features of the corporate form discussed in Chapter 3 but, most conspicuously, by a powerful centralized management able to make and implement business decisions efficiently. The second aim of corporate law is to efficiently control the agency costs that accompany this powerful managerial institution. This is especially true for companies that raise equity through public distribution of their shares. We emphasize the *efficient* control of agency costs because steps taken to reduce managerial discretion might also deter managers from pursuing new business opportunities that are in the best interests of shareholders and the company. In reducing agency costs, it is possible to have "too much of a good thing."

Shareholder actions to enforce the duty of loyalty are conspicuously directed toward reducing agency costs. But enforcing legal duties in court is a costly and highly imperfect way to encourage senior managers to loyally advance shareholder interests. An *ex ante* approach — that is, an approach that creates incentives for managers to work diligently to increase long-term corporate (and shareholder) wealth — would, if feasible, obviously be better. Such incentive systems are in fact widely used and are at the core of modern executive compensation. Designing and approving executive compensation regimes is one of the principal concerns of modern corporate governance.

But nothing is simple. Designing compensation regimes to align managers' personal interests with corporate wealth production is itself a complex task that is bound to have an imperfect outcome. First, it is difficult to identify what the best measures of corporate performance are for this purpose. Among the many possibilities here are earnings per share, stock price, sales or revenue, or more complex departmental or product-oriented metrics. Second, even if measures of production can be identified, attributing that production to individual members of the management team is complicated. Most production in firms is team production. Third, selecting the time-frame over which production is to be measured is problematic. Investors naturally think in terms of quarterly or annual returns. But firms in different industries and with different challenges may plan in shorter or longer cycles and measurement might optimally differ among them. Fourth, whatever metric is chosen over whatever time-frame, those who will be paid in relation to it will have incentives to "game" the system, i.e., managing to maximize the metrics rather than overall corporate performance. Even worse, as recent corporate scandals illustrate, managers might use guile or deception to maximize their compensation metrics.

These challenges are the central focus of this Chapter. We also address the academic debates about how well public-company boards succeed in shaping these incentives (judged by their results) and the regulatory responses to the problems associated with setting compensation. Finally, we sketch the limited role that judicial review can play in monitoring compensation plans both for senior executives and corporate directors.

9.2   THE CHALLENGE OF EXECUTIVE PAY

Incentive compensation is intended in the first instance to induce senior managers to make the extra effort to create corporate value. A second rationale for high-powered incentives is based on a presumed difference between the risk preferences of managers and diversified shareholders. A conventional assumption is that, all else being equal, senior executives would prefer to manage more conservatively than shareholders would like because they cannot diversify the human capital they have invested in their positions. Thus, in addition to rewarding effort, incentive compensation can serve to offset the differences in risk preferences between executives and shareholders. The fundamental challenge of designing stock-based compensation plans (including options, restricted stock and/or phantom stock rights) lies in creating incentives for senior executives to act energetically to advance shareholder interests by assuming risk intelligently—but not to overdo it by taking on excessive risk or to game it by massaging accounting numbers or managing investment to inflate short-term profits at the expense of long-term returns. How well boards manage to "fine tune" compensation incentives is an open question. Executives are people after all, not sports cars; and as between CEOs and the directors on compensation committees, it may not always be clear who is driving whom.

9.2.1   Creating Incentives that Align the Interests of Managers and Investors

In the 1970s and 1980s, CEOs and other top executives were, for the most part, compensated like all other employees of the company, with most of their compensation coming in the form of an annual salary, and then an additional, discretionary bonus paid at the end of the year. The only difference between the CEO and other employees was that the CEO's pay would be set by the board of directors; then the CEO would be responsible, directly or indirectly, for setting the pay for all other employees. During this era, the level of CEO pay was only occasionally controversial; rather, most of the criticism focused on the way in which CEOs were compensated. In 1990, Professors Michael Jensen and Kevin Murphy made the point sharply that CEOs had inadequate financial incentive to maximize value for their shareholders: "[C]orporate America pays its most important leaders like bureaucrats" was their famous claim. If the company did well, the CEO didn't get much more money; and if the company did poorly, she didn't really feel the loss. The correlation between CEO compensation and overall firm performance was low.[1]

One implication of this observation was the conjecture that managerial agency costs were large. If the CEO received a trivially small fraction of any benefits created for the corporation, and suffered only a trivially small fraction of any costs imposed, would he not, for example, be more likely to approve investing in a corporate headquarters palace, rather than a more utilitarian headquarters building? Would he work 24/7 or might he leave the office at 3:00 p.m. some afternoons to play golf? Famous stories, such as RJR Nabisco CEO Ross Johnson flying his dog on the corporate jet at large expense to the corporation, fueled the popular perception during this era that the "private benefits of control" for public-company CEOs were large. Jensen and others argued that the particular compensation system that was commonplace during this era led to increased agency costs and a reduction in overall corporate value.

Business owners had always understood the importance of creating incentives for important employees. Stock options, for example, became an accepted part of executive pay by the early 1950s. Still, Professor Jensen's criticism was that the levels of these incentives were far too small. By the 1990s, the more high-powered performance-based pay began to broadly emerge. Although several metrics could be used to measure performance, such as revenue growth, earnings growth, or subjective assessments, corporate boards gravitated primarily to stock performance as a measure of CEO productivity. Stock-based pay is straightforward: In addition to an annual salary and bonus, the CEO would at the beginning of a pay cycle receive a specified number of shares or options on the shares of the company. If the company did well, the CEO's stock would appreciate in value. Only slightly less intuitive is option-based compensation. A stock option in this context (technically a "call" option) is the right to purchase a share of stock from the company for a fixed price, known as the "strike price" of the option, i.e., the amount that must be paid to the company for a share of its stock. If the strike price is the market price of the stock at the time the grant is made, as is

1. See, e.g., Michael C. Jensen & Kevin J. Murphy, *Performance Pay and Top-Management Incentives*, 98 J. Pol. Econ. 225 (1990) (calculating that CEOs receive, on average, $3.25 for every $1,000 increase in shareholder wealth).

normally the case, the option is an "at the money" option. If the strike price is lower than the current market price, the option is granted "in the money." And if the strike price is higher than the current market price, the option is granted "out of the money."

To take a simplified example, a company might grant its CEO the right to buy 100 shares of XYZ Corporation at the current share price of $100 per share. Typically, the option — often called a "warrant" — would have a ten-year exercise period (much longer than exercise periods for options that trade in the financial markets), which means that if the share price of XYZ Corporation went above $100 (say, to $110), the CEO could exercise his right to buy 100 shares of the company at $100, and then sell those shares into the marketplace at $110. In this example, the CEO would make a profit of $10 per share × 100 shares = $1,000. If, instead, the share price of XYZ Corporation stayed at or below $100 for the full ten-year exercise period, the CEO would have no incentive to exercise the options, and the options would expire unexercised.

There are variants on this basic model. "Restricted stock" plans make grants of actual shares of stock that vest over a certain period, typically three years. The executive obtains title to the stock only after certain conditions have been met, typically continued employment, but occasionally, hitting certain performance targets as well. "Cliff vesting" stock vests all at once — for example, after continued employment for three years. "Pro rata vesting" stock vests over time — for example, one-third of the stock grant vests each year, for three years. The general idea of restricted stock, of course, is to create incentives for managers to act in the long-term best interests of the corporation. For example, a management decision that might create a temporary increase in the company's stock price might be tempting for a manager who holds stock or stock options in the company, unless the stock or options only vest over some longer period of time.[2]

Stock and stock-option compensation (collectively, "performance-based pay") exploded during the 1990s. The following chart documents the growth of CEO pay at S&P 500 firms during this period and the dramatic shift to performance-based pay, going from a modest level in 1992 to approximately 60 percent of total compensation for the median CEO by 2014. By 2018, it was closer to 70 percent according to ISS Analytics. The chart shows that the greatest part of growth in CEO pay was in the value of share-based incentives, the rise of which reflected in part a general increase in stock market prices across the economy as a whole during those years.[3]

---

2. There is also "phantom stock," which provides a cash or stock bonus based on the stock price at some future date. If structured properly, phantom stock creates the same economic incentives for the manager as actual stock.

3. Using stock as a metric for senior officer productivity raises some problems because stock price reflects many things unconnected with senior officers performance, such as the Federal Reserve Board's interest rate policy, to name just one obvious factor.

Panel A: CEOs in the S&P 500

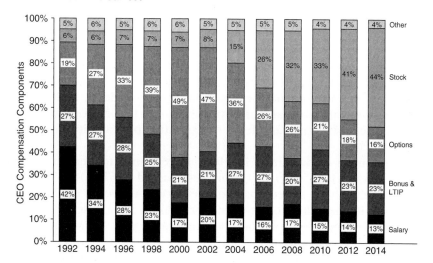

Stock markets don't always rise, of course, and when the stock of any company falls enough, its options lose some of their incentive effect. When this occurred in the 1990s, some firms undertook to "reprice" option strike prices by resetting the strike price to something closer to current market. It was thought that the options would recapture the incentive effect that they were designed to create. Of course, this represented a windfall to executives, because their previously "out of the money" options now became substantially more valuable "at the money" options. Critics of this practice pointed out that if executives expected options to be repriced, then the link between pay and performance had been severed.[4] Similar issues may face executive compensation design during the coronavirus pandemic.

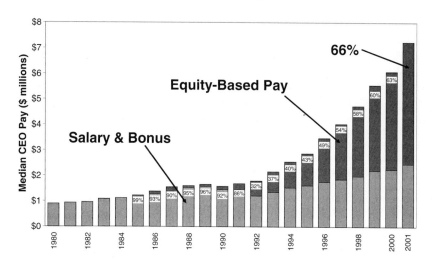

4. Yet another pay practice that diluted the incentive effect of stock-option compensation was option "reloading." With reload options, once an executive had exercised her options,

9.2.2   Political and Regulatory Responses to Executive Pay

Clearly, some of the trend toward stock-based pay was influenced by pay experts, directors, and other observers who sought to establish a tighter link between pay and performance. But other factors also were at work in explaining the shift to performance-based pay. Indeed, action by both political and regulatory organs of government has had important effects on both the modern structure and level of executive pay, albeit not always the intended effects.[5]

Perhaps most importantly, in 1993, in response to perceived general unhappiness with high CEO pay, Congress passed §162(m) of the Internal Revenue Code, which stated that compensation above $1 million for the CEO and any of the other four top officers would not be deductible to the corporation for income tax purposes unless it was "performance-based compensation." Stock and stock-option compensation clearly qualified as performance-based compensation, and therefore avoided the $1 million cap. Corporate boards responded to this change in law by increasing the proportion of stock or option-based compensation in the pay packages of senior officers. Although Congress removed the §162(m) exemption for performance-based compensation in 2017, that hardly slowed the move to performance-based pay because by then over 50 percent of the total long-term compensation for Russell 3000 firms was performance-based — underscoring how important it has become.[6]

Boards liked stock-based compensation for accounting reasons as well. Unless they were "in the money" at the time of the grant (which was rare), stock options *were not an expense* to the company under applicable accounting rules.[7] Therefore they did not reduce closely watched performance metrics such as earnings per share (EPS) and price-earnings ratios. In an efficient market, of course, accounting treatment of options should not matter to stock price because investors should "see through" accounting rules to understand that CEOs were taking value out of the company through stock options. In the real world, however, investors seemed to care about accounting measures, and boards, in turn, seemed to view stock-option compensation as a cheap

---

she would get the same number of new options, struck at the current market price. Of course, reload options created incentives to "ratchet up." Each time the stock price blipped upward, executives might exercise their vested options and then receive new options struck at the new market price. This practice has largely disappeared under institutional investor pressure.

5. The effect, sometimes perverse, of government regulation on the level and structure of executive pay is an understudied aspect of this subject, according to some leading scholars. See, e.g., Kevin Murphy, "Executive Compensation: Where We Are and How We Got There," in Handbook of the Economics of Finance, edited by George Constantinides, Milton Harris & René Stulz (Elsevier Science North Holland 2013).

6. See Matteo Tonello, CEO and Executive Compensation Practices: 2019 Edition, The Conference Board, Inc. (2019).

7. Those rules, Generally Accepted Accounting Principles (GAAP), are promulgated by FASB (Financial Accounting Standards Board), which is the private body charged by the SEC with their development.

tool for compensating the CEO, relative to salary, bonus, or stock — but this changed. In 2004, FASB Statement No. 123 was issued, which required companies to expense the "fair market value" of options at the time of grant.[8] But until then, it is no exaggeration to say that many boards viewed stock options as essentially a "free" way to compensate the CEO.[9]

Ironically, other regulatory measures played a role in rising CEO pay. Also in 1993, the SEC established new rules requiring corporations to make far more detailed public disclosures about the compensation of their top five corporate officers. Three elements were particularly noteworthy. First, companies had to disclose, in a standardized Summary Compensation Table, the annual compensation (salary, bonus, etc.), long-term compensation (restricted stock awards, option awards, etc.), and all other compensation for the top five employees in the company. Second, the 1993 reforms required a narrative description of all employment contracts with top executives, and disclosure of a Compensation Committee report explaining the committee's compensation decisions. Finally, the reforms required a graph showing the company's cumulative shareholder returns for the previous five years, along with a broad-based market index and a peer-group index for the same period.

The net effect of these reforms was increased transparency. Here is the irony: These additional disclosures, rather than dampening CEO compensation, seem to have had the opposite effect. This was due to the particular way in which CEO pay is set. Typically, the compensation committee of the board will hire a compensation consultant, who then identifies a set of comparable companies. Beginning in 1993, the consultant would have excellent visibility of the pay of the top executives at these comparable companies. Using this information, the consultant would prepare a report for the compensation committee. Typically, compensation committees would want to pay their CEO above the 50th percentile among comparable companies (often, for example, at the 75th or 90th percentile),[10] reflecting the fact that their CEO is (of course) above average. But if all boards are aiming to pay their CEO at the 50th percentile or above, then we get a general ratcheting up of CEO pay levels along the lines of what is documented in the chart above. The 1993

---

8. Although Rule 123 does not require a specific method for valuing the options, the vast majority of U.S. companies have used the Black-Scholes option pricing formula. Critics complain that the Black-Scholes formula overstates the value of options on the income statement because, for example, among other reasons, the Black-Scholes formula assumes that the option-holder is perfectly diversified, which is not the case for managers who are over-invested in their own companies. Even if their financial portfolios were perfectly diversified, managers' "human capital" is invested 100 percent in the company, and cannot be diversified.

9. The New York Stock Exchange and NASDAQ listing standards now require listed companies to seek shareholder approval for *all* stock-option plans except those that are offered as an inducement to new employees or in connection with a merger or acquisition. See www.nyse.com/pdfs/finalruletext303A.pdf; nasd.complinet.com/nasd/display/index.html (Rule 4350-5). Formerly, the NYSE and NASDAQ excluded "broadly based" option plans from required shareholder votes.

10. See, e.g., J.M. Bizjak, M. Lemmon & T. Nguyen, *Are All CEOs Above Average? An Empirical Analysis of Compensation Peer Groups and Pay Design*, 100 J. Fin. Econ. 538 (2011); M. Faulkender & J. Yang, *Is Disclosure an Effective Cleansing Mechanism? The Dynamics of Compensation Peer Benchmarking*, 26 Rev. Fin. Stud. 806 (2013).

disclosure requirement fueled this trend by creating greater visibility on the pay of (arguably) comparable CEOs.

The public perception problem grew worse. In July 2001, *Fortune* magazine, led with a cover story entitled "Inside the Great CEO Pay Heist" and added for good measure: "Why the madness won't stop." In October 2003, the cover story in *The Economist* lamented, "Where's the stick? The problem with lavish executive pay." According to their editors: "CEOs are selected for their cleverness and determination, and they have directed these qualities at boosting their own pay. The more the public spotlight is thrown on one aspect of bosses' remuneration, it seems, the more it rises elsewhere."

Given the way CEO pay is structured today, rising stock markets mean rising pay. CEO pay thus grew dramatically with the market. In 2006, the SEC returned to the issue of executive compensation. As in 1993, the focus of the 2006 reforms was increased disclosure of executive compensation. The new SEC rule required a single number that captured all compensation for each of the top executives, as well as improved disclosures on retirement pay-outs, perquisites, directors' pay, and related-party transactions. As we noted above, designing incentive pay is a delicate problem requiring balance. The danger of stimulating too much risk became apparent in the financial crisis of 2008. Some commentators argued that the massive turn to incentive compensation in the banking and finance industries especially — not just at the most senior executive level but throughout the firms — added fuel to the financial crisis by encouraging executives to make excessively risky investments. If these investments paid off, the stock price or other metric of their performance would go up. They might become wealthy, or at least wealthier, overnight. But they personally had no capital at risk in their trades, so if the investments didn't pay off the corporation would lose, the stock price would fall, and while they would make nothing from that trade or for that year, it would be shareholders and (perhaps) creditors who would experience the full downside consequences. In this analysis, the highly leveraged investments that seemed excessively risky in hindsight were the inevitable consequences of sophisticated managers responding rationally to their compensation systems.

The U.S. Congress, of course, does not need to determine root causes in order to respond to a perceived problem of executive pay. After each of the two major stock market meltdowns of the past two decades, Congress enacted significant reforms in the area of executive compensation. In 2002, Congress passed the Sarbanes-Oxley Act, which among other things responded to several instances from the early 2000s in which top executives reaped large performance-based payments, only later to disclose that the accounting statements that the market had responded to were false or misleading. One might think that if the performance had been a mirage, as it turned out, that they should return the money. Section 304 of the Act provides that if a company must restate its financials as a result of executive misconduct, the CEO and CFO must pay back to the company any bonuses, other incentive-based or equity-based pay, and/or trading profits realized in the 12 months after the incorrect financial information was publicly disclosed. In 2010, §954 of the Dodd-Frank Wall Street Reform and Consumer Protection Act added a more stringent clawback requirement. Publicly listed companies that restate their financial statements due to material noncompliance with GAAP reporting requirements must seek repayment from any current or former executive officer of any incentive-based compensation (including stock options) paid during the three-year period prior to the restatement date.

The clawback provisions in Dodd-Frank cover all publicly traded companies. They go beyond the provisions in the Sarbanes-Oxley Act in three important ways. First, the look-back period is extended from 12 months to three years. Second, clawback coverage is extended from the CEO and CFO to any current or former executive. Third, the Act's provision eliminates the requirement of misconduct to trigger clawbacks. Under the new provision, incentive-based compensation can be recovered in the event of accounting restatements due to a company's material noncompliance with financial reporting requirements, regardless of whether the restatements resulted from executive misconduct. In July 2015, about five years after the passage of Dodd-Frank, the SEC finally issued proposed rules implementing these features of the Act's clawback rules. The proposed rules contemplate requiring the stock exchanges to mandate these standards for all listed companies. Although these rules have not yet been finalized by the SEC, many firms are implementing their own privately designed "clawback" provisions as part of their executive compensation packages. These target not only financial restatements, but also other behavior that firms and their investors wish to discourage (e.g., activities contributing to climate risk, acts of moral turpitude, and other misconduct).[11]

The Dodd-Frank Act also initiated a "Say on Pay" shareholder vote. That is, it requires a shareholder advisory vote at least once every three years to approve or reject the compensation of public companies' named executive officers.[12] In addition, the Act requires a non-binding advisory vote to determine whether Say on Pay votes should occur every one, two, or three years. This requirement mirrors the rule that has governed British companies since 2002. Sweden and Australia have also followed the U.K. advisory-vote approach, while the Netherlands, Switzerland, and Norway have gone further on Say on Pay, providing shareholders with a *binding* annual vote on top executive compensation.[13] By the close of the 2019 proxy season, the pattern on these votes had been established. Shareholders generally approve the compensation practices of the firms in which they are invested.[14] Over

11. For a discussion on connecting compensation and compliance efforts see Karl Hofstetter, Reinier H. Kraakman & Eugene F. Soltes, Compliance, Compensation and Corporate Wrongdoing (May 1, 2018). Conclusions from a Roundtable at Harvard Law School of May 18, 2018, available at SSRN: https://ssrn.com/abstract=3373718.

12. Dodd-Frank Wall Street Reform and Consumer Protection Act, Pub. L. No. 111-203, §951, 124 Stat. 1376, 1899 (2010).

13. Steven Davis, Does "Say on Pay" Work? Lessons on Making CEO Compensation Accountable, 1622 PLI/Corp 33, 46 (2007).

14. See Jill Fisch, Darius Palia & Steven Davidoff Solomon, *Is Say on Pay All About Pay?: The Impact of Firm Performance*, 8 Harv. Bus. L. Rev. 101 (2018) (noting that at most firms shareholder support for executive pay packages is very high, but providing some evidence that the instances of low shareholder support are more likely driven by weak firm performance than the structure of the pay package).

the last nine years, around 97 percent of firms per year obtained majority shareholder approval for executive pay packages and average shareholder support at these firms hovered around 90 percent. The vast majority of firms (91 percent) achieved at least 70 percent shareholder support over the last four years. Larger public companies tended to do a bit better than smaller ones on these votes.[15] These votes are taken with extreme seriousness by corporate management. It has been noted that a failed Say on Pay vote makes it statistically ten times more likely that the next equity pay plan put to the shareholders will also fail. Despite the appearance of general acceptance by shareholders of pay practices, these votes changed corporate governance practice and are useful in focusing compensation committees on the fact that their work will be subject to investor scrutiny.

In addition, §951 of the Dodd-Frank Act regulates "golden parachute" compensation through related disclosure and shareholder approval provisions. Any solicitation of shareholder votes to approve an acquisition, merger, consolidation, or proposed sale of all or substantially all of a public company's assets requires the disclosure of any executive compensation arrangements, including the aggregate amount of potential payments, related to the M&A transaction. Moreover, the Act requires a non-binding shareholder advisory vote in connection with the approval of such compensation arrangements.

Finally, §953 of the Dodd-Frank Act directs the SEC to adopt executive compensation disclosure rules that require public companies to include the relationship between executives' compensation and company performance in annual proxy statements. In addition, companies are required to disclose the median employee annual compensation, the CEO's annual compensation, and the ratio of these figures. Only in April 2015 did the SEC propose rules that aim to give investors greater clarity about the link between what corporate executives are paid each year compared to total shareholder return (TSR) — the annual change in stock price plus reinvested dividends. One report finds that from 2014 to 2018 CEO pay growth at the S&P 500 (at 23 percent) trailed TSR at the S&P 500 (at 50 percent).[16] Further, the SEC rules also require companies to disclose top executives' "actual pay," that is, how much its five highest-paid executives received, after excluding certain contingent components of compensation, such as share grants that have yet to vest.

In August 2015, the SEC also adopted new regulations requiring disclosure of the ratio between CEO pay and that of the median worker.[17] This was a directive of Congress. In an editorial on the day after the new regulation was

---

15. There have been some notable close calls in 2019, such as at Disney and Netflix, where the executive pay packages received 53 percent and 49.8 percent support, respectively. See Jill Goldsmith, As Rich 2019 Pay Roll In, Media CEO Salaries Will Be Hard to Justify in A *COVID-19* Economy, Deadline, May 1, 2020.

16. See Joseph Bachelder, *CEO Pay Growth and Total Shareholder Return*, Harv. L. School Forum on Corp. Gov., October 12, 2019.

17. Section 953(b) of the Dodd-Frank Act states that "[a] company will be required to calculate the annual total compensation of its CEO in accordance with Item 402(c)(2)(x) of Regulation S-K."

adopted, the *Wall Street Journal* asked whether any investor sensibly needed this disclosure. Recently, Equilar noted that "[t]he CEO Pay Ratio has yet to garner the impact that many key stakeholders initially thought it would have prior to its implementation. . . . The CEO Pay Ratio presents difficulties as a benchmarking figure. It is difficult to incorporate this measurement when setting CEO compensation because the ratio varies on a number of different factors, including company size or the inclusion of international workers."[18] But query, was the "Pay Ratio" in the Act ever really intended to assist compensation committees in designing CEO pay or shareholders in evaluating CEO pay?

QUESTIONS

1. McDonald's Corporation recently filed suit to recover its former CEO Steve Easterbrook's separation (i.e., severance) pay because he allegedly violated terms of his 2019 separation (and termination) agreement. Under the separation agreement, the CEO kept his severance benefits (worth north of $40 million), but the agreement had a clause that allowed the severance plan administrator to block future payments and clawback payments already made if the administrator found that, at any time, the CEO engaged in behavior that would amount to a basis for "cause" termination while employed at McDonald's. "Cause" included lying, fraud, violating "McDonald's Standard of Business Conduct" ("Standards"), or other acts of "moral turpitude." The allegations in the complaint were that the former CEO lied and concealed evidence relating to a consensual physical relationship with an employee (and an associated grant of restricted stock units to that employee) that would have violated McDonald's Standards and the clause in the separation agreement. Indeed, the complaint states the board would never have approved the 2019 separation agreement had it known about these allegations. See Scott Spector, David Bell & Elizabeth Garland, *McDonald's Clawback Suit Against Former CEO: A Cautionary Tale*, Harv. L. School Forum on Corp. Gov., August 26, 2020. How does this type of private ordering compare to the disclosure-based regulation discussed above?

2. In 2019, the SEC amended its disclosure rules so that Item 407(i) of Regulation S-K now requires firms to detail "any practices or policies it has adopted regarding the ability of its directors, officers and employees to purchase securities or other financial instruments, or otherwise engage in transactions, that hedge or offset, or are designed to hedge or offset, any decrease in the market value of equity securities granted as compensation, or held directly or indirectly by the employee or director." This was targeted at concerns that executives could use trading in derivatives markets or securities markets to unwind the incentive effects of performance-based pay packages. These concerns parallel those in Chapter 6 where large institutional investors

---

18. See Amit Batish & Courtney Yu, *Say on Pay and the Effects of the CEO Pay Ratio: Key Findings from the 2020 Proxy Season*, Harv. L. School Forum on Corp. Gov., June 24, 2020.

can engage in transactions that separate voting rights and economic interest. Does the prospect of unwinding the incentive components of executive pay packages worry you? Is disclosure the best way to police this? Do you think that firms police such behavior themselves via the terms of employment contracts or executive pay packages?

9.3   ARE CEOs PAID TOO MUCH?

Are CEOs paid too much? Reasonable people might have different views, yet the topic evokes far more controversy than whether other people, such as top athletes, movie stars, and hedge fund managers, are paid too much. This is so even though the median CEO of an S&P 500 firm makes less than top earning celebrities and hedge fund managers. Estimates by both ISS Analytics and Pay Governance suggest that the median pay for this group of CEOs in 2018 was around $12.2-$12.4 million.[19] Further, an influential literature argues that among the constellation of factors contributing to a firm's success, no single controllable factor is more important than the skill, energy, and leadership of the firm's CEO.[20] So then why the skeptical attention?

In our view, this attention is not primarily due to the size of executive pay or the intrinsic importance of the CEO's contribution to firm performance. Rather, it is due to the opaque process by which CEO pay is determined — opaque, that is, to outsiders and perhaps even to some insiders, despite the extensive disclosure that SEC rules now require. One might well wonder whether the outsized presence of the CEO on the board might not influence the judgment of the board's compensation committee and its compensation consultant, making negotiations over CEO pay something less than arms-length bargaining.[21] Conversely, one might wonder whether arms-length bargaining between the board and the incumbent CEO is either possible or desirable as long as both parties recognize external norms of compensation that accord with the pay practices of comparable firms.[22] Either way, evaluating the number is nearly impossible without a deep dive into confidential board deliberations and consultant methodologies. Indeed, there is no single number, since compensation arrangements have many parts, ranging from salaries and bonuses to equity compensation to a variety of retirement and contingent severance benefits.[23]

---

19. See also Alex Edmans, Xavier Gabaix & Dirk Jenter, *Executive Compensation: A Survey of Theory and Evidence*, in The Handbook of the Economics of Corporate Governance (Benjamin E. Hermalin & Michael S. Weisbach, eds.) Vol. 1, 383 (2017) (finding that median CEO pay at the S&P 500 during the 2007-2010 financial crises fell from $9.3 million in 2007 to $7.8 million in 2009 and then rose to nearly $9.3 million in 2010 and $10.1 million by 2014 as the stocks rebounded).

20. See, e.g., id.

21. See the Lucian Bebchuk and Jesse Fried insert, *infra* at page 388.

22. See the Bengt Holmstrom excerpt, *infra* at page 391.

23. Public companies must disclose several numbers for the "total direct compensation" of their top managers, which vary by their components and valuation methodologies.

By contrast, the earnings of celebrities are negotiated at arm's length with sophisticated counterparties, and the quality of their performance is not only available but is often a matter of intense public interest. There are performance statistics for athletes and Oscars for actors, not to speak of weekly box office receipts. Thus, a transparent market may aid in legitimating their compensation. It seems to confirm that they earn what the market will bear. No doubt an elite circle of directors, consultants, and analysts also keep track of rising executive talent in particular industries but their assessments are confidential and their metrics are likely to be fuzzy. If superstar CEOs are "priced" in the eyes of the public, it is typically — as in the case of Steve Jobs — in the twilight of their careers.

These and related considerations have sparked significant scholarly debate on CEO pay. On one hand, Professors Lucian Bebchuk and Jesse Fried, leading representatives of the "agency cost" theory of executive pay, argue in their seminal book *Pay Without Performance: The Unfulfilled Promise of Executive Compensation* (2004), that the process of setting executive pay is not arm's length and the power of managers over the pay-setting process can explain many of the practices that do not seem consistent with financial economic theory — in particular, that CEO pay often does not appear to closely track measures of corporate performance, such as shareholder returns.[24] They provide evidence that CEO pay has grown considerably over the last three decades and is only weakly tied to firm performance, underscoring concerns of board capture by powerful managers. This is consistent with a series of other studies as well.[25]

On the other hand, there is academic research examining some other explanations for CEO pay. In a recent paper surveying the academic literature on executive compensation, Professors Alex Edmans, Xavier Gabaix, and Dirk Jenter highlight that in addition to the agency cost explanation, there is the institutional explanation (i.e., that executive pay is driven by legal, regulatory, and tax factors) and the shareholder value explanation (i.e., that CEO contracts are the outcome of shareholder value maximizing firms that compete with each other in an efficient market for managerial talent).[26] They argue that support can be found for all three approaches in the empirical literature, but that models of shareholder value can explain a great deal of observed behavior.[27]

---

24. That is, it is less variable than firm performance (but then all worker compensation is steadier than stock market returns). One reason for this is that owners of capital have available to them methods to cheaply diversify the risks embedded in any specific investment, while labor — whether executives or shop-floor employees — cannot do so easily or inexpensively.

25. See, e.g., Kevin J. Murphy, *Executive Compensation*, in Handbook of Labor Economics [1st pg. of excerpt] (Orley Ashenfelter & David Card eds., 1999) (finding that the ratio of CEO pay to the pay of the average worker rose from 25 in 1970 to over 200 by 1996); Franz Christian Ebert, Raymond Torres & Konstantinos Papadakis, Executive Compensation: Trends and Policy Issues (2008), http://www.ilo.org/public/english/bureau/inst/publications/discussion/dp19008.pdf (finding that CEO pay in the United States over 2003-2007 grew in real terms by 45 percent compared to 15 percent for the average executive, and 2.7 percent for the average American worker). See also Lucian Bebchuk & Yaniv Grinstein, *The Growth of Executive Pay*, 21 Oxford Rev. Econ. Pol'y 283 (2005) (finding significant increases in CEO pay not fully explained by improvements in firm performance).

26. See Edmans et al., *supra* note 19.

27. For example, in an influential paper, Professors Xavier Gabaix and Augustin Landier developed a model of CEO pay that assumed only that there is such a thing as managerial talent,

Yet another, more benign, view is offered by Professor Bengt Holmstrom's extract below. Of course, CEOs are usually talented managers and, while powerful, they don't control all of the features of the business environment; when exerting observed effort in a board-approved strategy, poor performance in any one year may be temporary and due to bad luck, not insufficient talent or diligence, and thus not deserving of punishing discipline. Firms are not exactly like markets; they are places in which relational contracting occurs. Boards and (less so) those outside the firm can never know the counter-factual of what performance would have been achieved with the next best CEO.

Although the debate on CEO pay continues vigorously, it is important to note that reaching scientific judgments about it is complicated, in part, because it is difficult to estimate the market price for unique executive talent. Senior officers are not fungible. Moreover, the recent period of high growth in CEO compensation has also been a time of substantially greater CEO turnover, much of it forced.[28] If CEOs get fired more often today than before (something that is not fully consistent with the managerial power/ agency costs thesis), then economic theory suggests that we would expect CEO compensation to rise in response to reduced job security. Yet many have significant skepticism about the process of setting executive compensation. Moreover, there are some cases of abusive CEO pay and the general level of CEO pay, compared to that of the average worker, is such that even if it might be efficient,[29] it may create political challenges for corporate boards.

So are CEOs paid too much? Before deciding, read over the three excerpts below.

LUCIAN BEBCHUK & JESSE FRIED, PAY WITHOUT PERFORMANCE: OVERVIEW OF THE ISSUES
30 J. Corp. L. 647 (2005)

. . . Financial economists studying executive compensation have typically assumed that pay arrangements are produced by arm's-length contracting,

which is rare, that the market for it is competitive, and, most importantly, that this talent produces value as a function of the value of the assets it has the power to direct. Thus, a talented manager can produce more value if he has $10 billion in assets to manage than if he has $1 billion in assets to manage. This simple model predicted that CEO pay should increase one-to-one with the average market capitalization of large firms in the economy. They then find that the roughly six-fold increase in market capitalization of large U.S. companies between 1980 and 2003 can fully explain the roughly six-fold increase in CEO pay during the same period. So for them there is no general problem of excessive CEO pay — just the market for talent working to distribute the rare resource. See Xavier Gabaix & Augustin Landier, *Why Has CEO Pay Increased So Much?*, 123 Q.J. Econ. 49 (2008).

28. See Steven N. Kaplan & Bernadette A. Minton, *How Has CEO Turnover Changed?*, 12 Int'l Rev. Fin. 57 (March 2012).

29. In an era of increasing global competition and technological innovation, shop floor wages in the United States are depressed by low-cost manufacturing options elsewhere and perhaps more efficient manufacturing technologies. These constraints are arguably less pertinent with respect to the market for top managerial talent, especially at large global firms.

contracting between executives attempting to get the best possible deal for themselves, and boards trying to get the best possible deal for shareholders. This assumption has also been the basis for the corporate law rules governing the subject. We aim to show, however, that the pay-setting process in U.S. public companies has strayed far from the arm's-length model.

Our analysis indicates that managerial power has played a key role in shaping executive pay. The pervasive role of managerial power can explain much of the contemporary landscape of executive compensation, including practices and patterns that have long puzzled financial economists. We also show that managerial influence over the design of pay arrangements has produced considerable distortions in these arrangements, resulting in costs to investors and the economy. This influence has led to compensation schemes that weaken managers' incentives to increase firm value and even create incentives to take actions that reduce long-term firm value. . . .

Many take the view that concerns about executive compensation have been exaggerated. Some maintain that flawed compensation arrangements have been limited to a relatively small number of firms, and that most boards have carried out effectively their role of setting executive pay. Others concede that flaws in compensation arrangements have been widespread, but maintain that these flaws have resulted from honest mistakes and misperceptions on the part of boards seeking to serve shareholders. According to this view, now that the problems have been recognized, corporate boards can be expected to fix them on their own. Still others argue that even though regulatory intervention was necessary, recent reforms that strengthen director independence will fully address past problems; once these reforms are implemented, boards can be expected to adopt shareholder-serving pay policies.

Our work seeks to persuade readers that such complacency is unwarranted. To begin with, flawed compensation arrangements have not been limited to a small number of "bad apples;" they have been widespread, persistent, and systemic. Furthermore, the problems have not resulted from temporary mistakes or lapses of judgment that boards can be expected to correct on their own. Rather they have stemmed from structural defects in the underlying governance structure that enable executives to exert considerable influence over their boards. The absence of effective arm's-length dealing under today's system of corporate governance has been the primary source of problematic compensation arrangements. Finally, while recent reforms that seek to increase board independence will likely improve matters, they will not be sufficient to make boards adequately accountable. Much more needs to be done. . . .

Before proceeding, we want to emphasize that our critique of existing pay arrangements and pay-setting processes does not imply that most directors and executives have acted less ethically than others would have in their place. Our problem is not with the moral caliber of directors and executives, but rather with the system of arrangements and incentives within which directors and executives operate. As currently structured, our corporate governance system unavoidably creates incentives and psychological and social forces that distort pay choices. Such incentives and forces can be expected to lead most people serving as directors to go along with arrangements that favor their firms' executives, as long as these arrangements are consistent with prevailing practices and conventions and thus not difficult to justify to themselves and to others. If we were to maintain the basic structure of the system and merely replace current directors and executives with a different set of individuals, the new directors and executives would be exposed to the very same incentives and forces as their predecessors and, by and large, we would not expect them to act any differently. To address the flaws in the pay-setting process, we need to change the governance arrangements that produce these distortions. . . .

ALEX EDMANS, XAVIER GABAIX & DIRK JENTER, EXECUTIVE COMPENSATION: A SURVEY OF THEORY AND EVIDENCE

The Handbook of the Economics of Corporate Governance (Benjamin E. Hermalin & Michael S. Weisbach, eds.) Vol. 1, 383 (2017)

There is considerable debate among both academics and practitioners on what causes the observed trends in pay. There are three broad perspectives. One is the "shareholder value" view, which argues that compensation contracts are chosen to maximize value for shareholders, taking into account the competitive market for executives and the need to provide adequate incentives. . . . [Another is] the "rent extraction" view, which argues that contracts are set by executives themselves to maximize their own rents. . . . A third perspective . . . is that pay is shaped by institutional forces, such as regulation, tax, and accounting policies.

[W]e make the following broader points:

*   Observed compensation arrangements result from a combination of potentially conflicting forces — shareholders' desire to maximize firm value, executives' desire to maximize their rents, and the influence of legislation, taxation, accounting policies, and social pressures. No one perspective can explain all of the evidence. . . .
*   Recent theoretical contributions make clear that shareholder value models can be consistent with a wide range of observed compensation patterns and practices, including the large increase in executive pay since the 1970s [as noted below — Eds.].
*   Theories of executive pay must take into account the specific features of executives' jobs; models of the general principal-agent problem are not automatically applicable to executives. For example, the skills of executives may be particularly scarce, and CEOs have a much larger impact on firm value than rank-and-file employees, which can fundamentally change the nature of the optimal contract.
*   Attempts to improve CEO pay should focus on the incentives created, and especially on the sensitivity of CEO wealth to long-term performance. The level of pay receives the most criticism, but usually amounts to only

a small fraction of firm value. Badly structured incentives, on the other hand, can easily cause value losses that are orders of magnitudes larger.

[S]hareholder value . . . identifies three mechanisms that might explain the rise in CEO pay since the 1970s. First, the difference between the CEO's contribution to firm value and that of the next best manager may have increased, perhaps because the importance of CEO ability has grown. Second, the CEO's expected earnings in the next best job may have increased, perhaps because CEO skills have become more portable. Third, the CEO's disutility from the optimal contract may have increased, perhaps because risk and effort levels have increased.

BENGT HOLMSTROM, PAY WITHOUT PERFORMANCE AND THE MANAGERIAL POWER HYPOTHESIS: A COMMENT
30 J. Corp. L. 503 (2005)

. . . Let me start with one anecdotal piece of evidence that explains why I think [Bebchuk & Fried's] basic premise that boards should deal with the executives at arm's-length is rather misguided. I have been on the board of my wife's family business for sixteen years. It is a closely held, global company headquartered in Finland with about 3000 employees and one billion dollars in revenue. There is an outside CEO, but the family controls the board and owns over ninety-five percent of the equity. The chairman of the board, my brother-in-law, is the former CEO. I think it is safe to say that the company does not face the sorts of agency problems that Bebchuk and Fried consider crucial. Yet many of the compensation patterns that the book attributes to a toxic combination of CEO power and wimpy boards can also be found in this reasonably successful family firm.

To determine a CEO's compensation, we consider several factors. We call in a compensation consultant. We look at compensation levels in companies of comparable size. We look at the CEO's mix of bonus and salary. We ask the compensation consultants what they think is appropriate. We ask the CEO what he expects to be paid and how. We are concerned about incentive effects, but in the end we closely follow common practice. The CEO has options as well as a bonus plan, with the bonus tied to strategic goals. Currently, we pay him in the top quartile, because we think it is important that he feels appreciated. When all is said and done, it looks pretty much boilerplate.

Why are we this unimaginative? After thirty years of studying compensation and incentives, do I not have better ideas?

My answer comes in three parts. First, and most importantly, we want to avoid arm's-length bargaining. Compensation is a sensitive matter. We benchmark to remove potentially contentious negotiations from the agenda. If we err, we would rather err a bit on the generous side. Second, we have tried to be more creative about structure, including the use of relative performance evaluation. But the executives did not like the use of relative performance evaluation much and in the end we felt that it would cost us more than it was worth to force acceptance. Third, years of experience with incentive design has made me cautious about experimenting too much. The law of unintended consequences never fails to surprise (we have certainly made our share of mistakes), and when it does it can cause a lot of frustration. Following norms and relying on outside expertise is not so bad after all — let the others be guinea pigs.

One data point does not prove a broader thesis, of course, but I would be rather surprised if my experience differed much from the experience of most family boards. I feel fairly confident in saying that CEO pay is very unlikely to be determined by arm's-length bargaining in most companies, whether they are publicly traded or closely held. But that does not mean that a board should go along with whatever the CEO demands. Benchmarking and staying within norms provide a good defense against overly aggressive demands. The biggest pay excesses have occurred in firms that have used unusual structures (the use of mega-grants is illustrative) and that have not benchmarked properly (Oracle, Siebel Systems and Apple are three examples). For this reason, it is surprising that the Conference Board's recent expert panel on executive compensation recommends that boards should avoid benchmarking and use their own judgment in its place. I know of no economic price which individuals can reliably determine by looking at intrinsic value without regard to the price of comparable products or services. Why should executive markets be any different? . . .

QUESTIONS

1. Much of the literature on the rise in CEO pay focuses on the terms of the compensation package and how it is negotiated rather than the process for how CEOs are hired (or fired). Shouldn't that matter? A recent study exploring how CEOs are hired finds "that firms hire from a surprisingly small pool of candidates. More than 80% of new CEOs are insiders. . . . More than 90% of new CEOs are executives firms are already familiar with. . . . Firms raid CEOs of other firms in only 3% of cases. . . . The evidence . . . suggests that firm-specific human capital and personal connections determine CEO hiring." Peter Cziraki & Dirk Jenter, *The Market for CEOs* (July 6, 2020). Available at SSRN: https://ssrn.com/abstract=3644496. How does this influence your thinking on what theory or theories explain the rise in CEO pay?

2. Consider the following description of how CEO pay is set. "[E]very board I have ever sat on or researched benchmarked itself at the 50th, 75th, or 90th percentile, therefore targeting CEO pay at similarly exalted levels. Benchmarking below the 50th percentile says, 'We are a lousy company and don't even aspire to be better.' So in this sense all CEOs are above average: To be benchmarked at or above the 50th percentile, they need not do anything other than report to a board that considers its own company exceptional." Steven Clifford, *How Companies Actually Decide What to Pay CEOs*, The Atlantic, June 14, 2017. Assuming that this is an accurate description, what does it tell us about the factors that might drive CEO pay?

9.4 JUDICIAL REVIEW OF COMPENSATION

9.4.1 The Law of Executive Officer Compensation

Some might think that judicial review would act as an important constraint on executive compensation, perhaps as a backstop when other mechanisms fail — it is not — unless actual corruption in the process of awarding compensation can be shown. Delaware courts, if asked to review executive compensation, will defer to the business judgment of the board of directors by deploying the "waste" standard of judicial review. Although specific definitions vary, perhaps the best articulation in this context was set forth in *Gottlieb v. Hayden Chemical Corporation* in 1952. A wasteful transaction is one "that no person of ordinarily sound business judgment would be expected to entertain the view that the consideration furnished. . . . is a fair exchange."[30]

The Delaware judicial approach reflects both the enormous difficulty in assessing executive pay from outside the boardroom, and the courts' traditional respect for the decisions of non-conflicted corporate directors. The compensation practices at large financial institutions during the financial crisis tested this approach to reviewing compensation decisions. Newspapers were filled with accounts of top professionals getting paid astronomical sums, while taxpayers funded bailouts of their banks. Famed investment banking house Goldman Sachs was a special object of this critical review and plaintiff-shareholders did challenge Goldman's pay practices in Delaware Chancery Court. The opinion, excerpted below, fairly illustrates the unwillingness of the Delaware courts to bend to what may be thought to be the popular sentiment on executive pay.

IN RE THE GOLDMAN SACHS GROUP, INC. SHAREHOLDER LITIGATION
2011 WL 4826104 (Del. Ch. Oct. 12, 2011)

GLASSCOCK, V.C.

C. COMPENSATION

[Opinion on Defendant's Motion to Dismiss the Complaint — EDS.] Goldman employed a "pay for performance" philosophy linking the total compensation of its employees to the company's performance. Goldman has used a Compensation Committee since at least 2006 to oversee the development and implementation of its compensation scheme. The Compensation Committee was responsible for reviewing and approving the Goldman executives' annual compensation. To fulfill their charge, the Compensation

---

30. 90 A.2d 660 (Del. 1952).

Committee consulted with senior management about management's projections of net revenues and the proper ratio of compensation and benefits expenses to net revenues (the "compensation ratio"). [Net revenue is gross revenue minus the cost of goods sold and thus does not include the cost of compensation or taxes. Net *earnings* are net revenue less operating expenses (which includes compensation) and less taxes. Goldman Sachs continues to rely on a similar compensation structure.* — Eds.]

The Plaintiffs allege that from 2007 through 2009, the Director Defendants approved a management-proposed compensation structure that caused management's interests to diverge from those of the stockholders. According to the Plaintiffs, in each year since 2006 the Compensation Committee approved the management-determined compensation ratio, which governed "the total amount of funds available to compensate all employees including senior executives," without any analysis. Although the total compensation paid by Goldman varied significantly each year, total compensation as a percentage of net revenue remained relatively constant. Because management was awarded a relatively constant percentage of total revenue, management could maximize their compensation by increasing Goldman's total net revenue and total stockholder equity. The Plaintiffs contend that this compensation structure led management to pursue a highly risky business strategy that emphasized short term profits in order to increase their yearly bonuses.

D.   Business Risk

The Plaintiffs allege that management achieved Goldman's growth "through extreme leverage and significant uncontrolled exposure to risky loans and credit risks." The trading and principal investment segment is the largest contributor to Goldman's total revenues; it is also the segment to which Goldman commits the largest amount of capital. The Plaintiffs argue that this was a risky use of Goldman's assets, pointing out that Goldman's Value at Risk (VAR) increased between 2007 and 2009, and that in 2007 Goldman had a leverage ratio of 25 to 1, exceeding that of its peers.

The Plaintiffs charge that this business strategy was not in the best interest of the stockholders, in part, because the stockholders did not benefit to the same degree that management did. Stockholders received roughly 2% of the revenue generated in the form of dividends — but if the investment went south, it was the stockholders' equity at risk, not that of the traders.

The Plaintiffs point to Goldman's performance in 2008 as evidence of these alleged diverging interests. In that year, "the Trading and Principal Investment segment produced $9.06 billion in net revenue, but as a result of discretionary bonuses paid to employees lost more than $2.7 billion." This contributed to Goldman's 2008 net income falling by $9.3 billion. The Plaintiffs contend that, but for a cash infusion from Warren Buffett, federal

---

* See The Goldman Sachs Group Inc., Proxy Statement 2019. Available at: https://www.sec.gov/Archives/edgar/data/886982/000119312519082951/d635602ddef14a .htm. See also *Goldman Sachs Cuts Bankers' Bonus Pot by 20% as Profits Fall*, The Guardian, April 15, 2019.

government intervention and Goldman's conversion into a bank holding company, Goldman would have gone into bankruptcy.

The Plaintiffs acknowledge that during this time Goldman had an Audit Committee in charge of overseeing risk. The Audit Committee's purpose was to assist the board in overseeing "the Company's management of market, credit, liquidity, and other financial and operational risks." The Audit Committee was also required to review, along with management, the financial information that was provided to analysts and ratings agencies and to discuss "management's assessment of the Company's market, credit, liquidity and other financial and operational risks, and the guidelines, policies and processes for managing such risks." . . .

III.   ANALYSIS

A.   APPROVAL OF THE COMPENSATION SCHEME

The Plaintiffs challenge the Goldman board's approval of the company's compensation scheme on three grounds. They allege (1) that the majority of the board was interested or lacked independence when it approved the compensation scheme, (2) the board did not otherwise validly exercise its business judgment, and (3) the board's approval of the compensation scheme constituted waste.

B.   OTHERWISE THE PRODUCT OF A VALID EXERCISE OF BUSINESS JUDGMENT

. . . Plaintiffs contend that the entire compensation structure put in place by the Director Defendants was done in bad faith and that the Director Defendants were not properly informed when making compensation awards. I find that the Plaintiffs have not provided particularized factual allegations that raise a reasonable doubt whether the process by which Goldman's compensation scheme allocated profits between the employees and shareholders was implemented in good faith and on an informed basis.

1.   *Good Faith*

. . . The Plaintiffs allege that "[n]o person acting in good faith on behalf of Goldman consistently could approve the payment of between 44% and 48% of net revenues to Goldman's employees year in and year out" and that accordingly the Director Defendants abdicated their duties by engaging in these "practices that overcompensate management." The complaint is entirely silent with respect to any individual salary or bonus; the Plaintiffs' allegation is that the scheme so misaligns incentives that it cannot have been the product of a good faith board decision.

The Plaintiffs' problems with the compensation plan structure can be summarized as follows: Goldman's compensation plan is a positive feedback loop where employees reap the benefits but the stockholders bear the losses. Goldman's plan incentivizes employees to leverage Goldman's assets and engage in risky behavior in order to maximize yearly net revenue and their yearly bonuses. At the end of the year, the remaining revenue that is not paid as compensation, with the exception of small dividend payments to stockholders, is funneled back into the company. This increases the quantity of assets Goldman employees have available to leverage and invest. Goldman employees then start the process over with a greater asset base, increase net revenue again, receive even larger paychecks the next year, and the cycle continues. At the same time, stockholders are only receiving a small percentage of net revenue as dividends; therefore, the majority of the stockholders' assets are simply being cycled back into Goldman for the Goldman employees to use. The stockholders' and Goldman employees' interests diverge most notably, argue the Plaintiffs, when there is a drop in revenue. If net revenues fall, the stockholders lose their equity, but the Goldman employees do not share this loss.[138]

. . . The Plaintiffs acknowledge that the compensation plan authorized by Goldman's board, which links compensation to revenue produced, was intended to align employee interests with those of the stockholders and incentivize the production of wealth. To an extent, it does so: extra effort by employees to raise corporate revenue, if successful, is rewarded. The Plaintiffs' allegations mainly propose that the compensation scheme implemented by the board does not perfectly align these interests; and that, in fact, it may encourage employee behavior incongruent with the stockholders' interest. This may be correct, but it is irrelevant. The fact that the Plaintiffs may desire a different compensation scheme does not indicate that equitable relief is warranted. Such changes may be accomplished through directorial elections, but not, absent a showing unmet here, through this Court.

Allocating compensation as a percentage of net revenues does not make it virtually inevitable that management will work against the interests of the stockholders. Here, management was only taking a percentage of the net revenues. The remainder of the net revenues was funneled back into the company in order to create future revenues; therefore, management and stockholder interests were aligned. Management would increase its compensation by increasing revenues, and stockholders would own a part of a company which has more assets available to create future wealth.**

---

138. In actuality, of course, a drop in revenue does have a direct negative impact on employees, because their income is tied to revenue.

** The 2007 to 2009 Annual Reports for Goldman Sachs reveal the following ($ in millions):

	2009	2008	2007
Net revenue	$45,173	$22,222	$45,987
Compensation ("Comp")	$16,193	$10,934	$20,190
Comp as % of net revenue	35.8%	49.2%	43.9%
Net earnings	$12,192	$2,041	$11,407

The Plaintiffs' focus on percentages ignores the reality that over the past 10 years, in absolute terms, Goldman's net revenue and dividends have substantially increased. Management's compensation is based on net revenues. Management's ability to generate that revenue is a function of the total asset base, which means management has an interest in maintaining that base (owned, of course, by the Plaintiffs and fellow shareholders) in order to create future revenues upon which its future earnings rely.

. . . The Plaintiffs do not allege that the board failed to employ a metric to set compensation levels; rather, they merely argue that a different metric, such as comparing Goldman's compensation to that of hedge fund managers rather than to compensation at other investment banks, would have yielded a better result. But this observance does not make the board's decision self-evidently wrong, and it does not raise a reasonable doubt that the board approved Goldman's compensation structure in good faith.

2.   Adequately Informed

. . . The Plaintiffs allege that the Director Defendants fell short of this reasonableness standard in several ways. . . . They point out that the Director Defendants never "analyzed or assessed the extent to which management performance, as opposed to the ever-growing shareholder equity and assets available for investment, has contributed to the generation of net revenues." The Plaintiffs also argue that because the amount of stockholder equity and assets available for investment was responsible for the total revenue generated, the Director Defendants should have used other metrics, such as compensation levels at shareholder funds and hedge funds, to decide compensation levels at Goldman. The Plaintiffs allege that Goldman's performance, on a risk adjusted basis, lagged behind hedge fund competitors, yet the percentage of net revenue awarded did not substantially vary, and that the Director Defendants never adequately adjusted compensation in anticipation of resolving future claims.

Nonetheless, the Plaintiffs acknowledge that Goldman has a compensation committee that reviews and approves the annual compensation of Goldman's executives. The Plaintiffs also acknowledge that Goldman has adopted a "pay for performance" philosophy, that Goldman represents as a way to align employee and shareholder interests. The Plaintiffs further acknowledge that Goldman's compensation committee receives information from Goldman's management concerning Goldman's net revenues and the ratio of compensation and benefits expenses to net revenues. . . .

	2009	2008	2007
Ratio Comp/Net earnings	1.33	5.36	1.77
Common stock dividends	$588	$642	$639
Preferred stock dividends	$ 1,076	$204	$192
Total dividends	$ 1,664	$846	$831

Rather than suggesting that the Director Defendants acted on an uninformed basis, the Plaintiffs' pleadings indicate that the board adequately informed itself before making a decision on compensation. The Director Defendants considered other investment bank comparables, varied the total percent and the total dollar amount awarded as compensation, and changed the total amount of compensation in response to changing public opinion. None of the Plaintiffs' allegations suggests gross negligence on the part of the Director Defendants, and the conduct described in the Plaintiffs' allegations certainly does not rise to the level of bad faith such that the Director Defendants would lose the protection of an 8 Del. C. §102(b)(7) exculpatory provision.

At most, the Plaintiffs' allegations suggest that there were other metrics not considered by the board that might have produced better results. The business judgment rule, however, only requires the board to reasonably inform itself; it does not require perfection or the consideration of every conceivable alternative. . . .

3.   *Waste*

The Plaintiffs also contend that Goldman's compensation levels were unconscionable and constituted waste. . . . Specifically, to excuse demand on a waste claim, the Plaintiffs must plead particularized allegations that "overcome the general presumption of good faith by showing that the board's decision was so egregious or irrational that it could not have been based on a valid assessment of the corporation's best interests."[152]

"[W]aste entails an exchange of corporate assets for consideration so disproportionately small as to lie beyond the range at which any reasonable person might be willing to trade."[153] Accordingly, if "there is any substantial consideration received by the corporation, and if there is a good faith judgment that in the circumstances the transaction is worthwhile, there should be no finding of waste."[154] The reason being, "[c]ourts are ill-fitted to attempt to weigh the 'adequacy' of consideration under the waste standard or, ex post, to judge appropriate degrees of business risk."[155] Because of this, "[i]t is the essence of business judgment for a board to determine if a particular individual warrant[s] large amounts of money."[156] . . .

The Plaintiffs consciously do not identify a particular individual or person who received excessive compensation, but instead focus on the average compensation received by each of Goldman's 31,000 employees. The Plaintiffs allege that "Goldman consistently allocated and distributed anywhere from two to six times the amounts that its peers distributed to each employee," and

---

152. *Citigroup*, 964 A.2d at 136 (quoting *White v. Panic*, 783 A.2d 543, 554 n.36 (Del. 2001)).

153. *Lewis v. Vogelstein*, 699 A.2d 327, 336 (Del. Ch. 1997).

154. Id.

155. Id.

156. *Brehm*, 746 A.2d at 263 (internal quotations omitted).

the Plaintiffs provide comparisons of Goldman's average pay per employee to firms such as Morgan Stanley, Bear Stearns, Merrill Lynch, Citigroup, and Bank of America. The Plaintiffs note that these firms are investment banks, but do not provide any indication of why these firms are comparable to Goldman or their respective primary areas of business. The Plaintiffs do not compare trading segment to trading segment or any other similar metric. A broad assertion that Goldman's board devoted more resources to compensation than did other firms, standing alone, is not a particularized factual allegation creating a reasonable doubt that Goldman's compensation levels were the product of a valid business judgment.

The Plaintiffs urge that, in light of Goldman's increasing reliance on proprietary trading, Goldman's employees' compensation should be compared against a hedge fund or other shareholder fund. The Plaintiffs allege that Goldman's compensation scheme is equal to 2% of net assets and 45% of the net income produced, but a typical hedge fund is only awarded 2% of net assets and 20% of the net income produced. The Plaintiffs paradoxically assert that "no hedge fund manager may command compensation for managing assets at the annual rate of 2% of net assets and 45% of net revenues," but then immediately acknowledge that in fact there are hedge funds that have such compensation schemes. It is apparent to me from the allegations of the complaint that while the majority of hedge funds may use a "2 and 20" compensation scheme, this is not the exclusive method used to set such compensation. Even if I were to conclude that a hedge fund or shareholder fund would be an appropriate yardstick with which to measure Goldman's compensation package and "even though the amounts paid to defendants exceeded the industry average," I fail to see a "shocking disparity" between the percentages that would render them "legally excessive."

In the end, while the Goldman employees may not have been doing, in the words of the complaint and Defendant Blankfein, "God's Work," the complaint fails to present facts that demonstrate that the work done by Goldman's 31,000 employees was of such limited value to the corporation that no reasonable person in the directors' position would have approved their levels of compensation. Absent such facts, these decisions are the province of the board of directors rather than the courts. . . .

[The court also considered and rejected the plaintiffs' claim that the board had breached its duty to monitor as required under *Caremark*.]

9.5   JUDICIAL REVIEW OF DIRECTOR COMPENSATION

The role of the corporate board in the practical operation of corporate governance of large public companies has been transformed over the past 25 years. Today's board is in general more engaged as an active agent in monitoring and directing the major affairs of the firm than was the case in earlier decades. Concomitantly, service on the board of a public company today takes greater commitment in time and effort. One result of these greater demands is a rise in compensation that is paid to directors of large public companies.

In the past, a shareholder's derivative suit alleging excessive director compensation was unusual. This was principally because in the days when directorial compensation ranged between $75,000 and $200,000, the plaintiffs bar seldom found initiating a derivative suit to be worth the candle. However, more recently directors' pay has been rising. For instance, in tech start-ups stock or option-based compensation for lucky directors can be very large.[31] Large enough, anyway, to merit close scrutiny by corporate boards.

The fundamental difference between compensation of directors as opposed to officers is that director compensation is a self-dealing transaction requiring more careful judicial review. In the case of director compensation, the only available "cleansing" agency is a shareholder ratification vote. Corporations virtually always seek shareholder approval of such grants, typically by asking for shareholder approval of a board-adopted incentive plan covering officers, directors, and sometimes others. Therefore, when director compensation is challenged as a breach of fiduciary duty, the issues inevitably revolve around how specifically the director grants are defined or limited in the plan which shareholders have approved.

IN RE INVESTORS BANCORP, INC. STOCKHOLDER LITIGATION
177 A.3d 1208 (Del. 2017).

[The shareholders of Investor Bancorp in 2015 overwhelmingly approved an "equity incentive plan" (EIP) that allowed directors to grant themselves, executives, employees, and a handful of others restricted stock awards, restricted stock units, and incentive stock options, etc. . . . with the specific details to be determined by directors when exercising their discretion at a future point in time. This was subject to only very general limits. After this approval the compensation committee met several times and awarded over $50 million in equity incentive compensation leading to a derivative suit claiming breach of fiduciary duty based on allegations of unfair and excessive compensation. The Chancery Court dismissed the suit because it held that the shareholder approval resulted in the business judgment standard of review. Plaintiff appealed. We pick up with Justice Seitz's opinion — EDS.]

SEITZ, Justice:
In the absence of stockholder approval, if a stockholder properly challenges equity incentive plan awards the directors grant to themselves, the directors must prove that the awards are entirely fair to the corporation. But, when the stockholders have approved an equity incentive plan, the affirmative defense of stockholder ratification comes into play. Stated generally,

---

31. One publication lists 12 companies that paid stipends between $500,000 and $1,000,000 to each of their directors in 2011, including Amazon and HP, Inc., http://www.oxbusiness.com/business-leaders/2012/06/08/12-companies-with-highest-paid-boards-directors/.

stockholder ratification means a majority of fully informed, uncoerced, and disinterested stockholders approved board action, which, if challenged, typically leads to a deferential business judgment standard of review.

For equity incentive plans in which the award terms are fixed and the directors have no discretion how they allocate the awards, the stockholders know exactly what they are being asked to approve. But, other plans — like the equity incentive plan in this appeal — create a pool of equity awards that the directors can later award to themselves in amounts and on terms they decide. The Court of Chancery has recognized a ratification defense for such discretionary plans as long as the plan has "meaningful limits" on the awards directors can make to themselves. . . .[1]

Stockholder ratification serves an important purpose — directors can take self-interested action secure in the knowledge that the stockholders have expressed their approval. But, when directors make discretionary awards to themselves, that discretion must be exercised consistent with their fiduciary duties. Human nature being what it is,[2] self-interested discretionary acts by directors should in an appropriate case be subject to review by the Court of Chancery.

We balance the competing concerns — utility of the ratification defense and the need for judicial scrutiny of certain self-interested discretionary acts by directors — by focusing on the specificity of the acts submitted to the stockholders for approval. When the directors submit their specific compensation decisions for approval by fully informed, uncoerced, and disinterested stockholders, ratification is properly asserted as a defense in support of a motion to dismiss. The same applies for self-executing plans, meaning plans that make awards over time based on fixed criteria, with the specific amounts and terms approved by the stockholders. But, when stockholders have approved an equity incentive plan that gives the directors discretion to grant themselves awards within general parameters, and a stockholder properly alleges that the directors inequitably exercised that discretion, then the ratification defense is unavailable to dismiss the suit, and the directors will be required to prove the fairness of the awards to the corporation.

Here, the Equity Incentive Plan ("EIP") approved by the stockholders left it to the discretion of the directors to allocate up to 30% of all option or restricted stock shares available as awards to themselves. The plaintiffs have alleged facts leading to a pleading stage reasonable inference that the directors breached their fiduciary duties by awarding excessive equity awards to themselves under the EIP. Thus, a stockholder ratification defense is not available to dismiss the case, and the directors must demonstrate the fairness of the awards to the Company. . .

1. *Seinfeld v. Slager*, C.A. No. 6462-VCG, 2012 WL 2501105, at *11-12 (Del. Ch. June 29, 2012).

2. *Gottlieb v. Heyden Chem. Corp.*, 90 A.2d 660, 663 (1952) ("Human nature being what it is, the law, in its wisdom, does not presume that directors will be competent judges of the fair treatment of their company where fairness must be at their own personal expense. In such a situation the burden is upon the directors to prove not only that the transaction was in good faith, but also that its intrinsic fairness will withstand the most searching and objective analysis.").

I

Investors Bancorp is a holding company for Investors Bank, a New Jersey chartered savings bank with corporate headquarters in Short Hills, New Jersey. The Company operates 143 banking branches in New Jersey and New York. . . .

The board sets director compensation based on recommendations of the Compensation and Benefits Committee ("Committee"), composed of seven of the ten non-employee directors. In 2014, the . . . annual compensation for all non-employee directors ranged from $97,200 to $207,005, with $133,340 as the average amount of compensation per director [composed mainly of cash payments and perquisites and personal benefits].

Just a few months after setting the 2015 board compensation, in March, 2015, the board proposed the 2015 EIP. The EIP was intended to "provide additional incentives for [the Company's] officers, employees and directors to promote [the Company's] growth and performance and to further align their interests with those of [the Company's] stockholders . . . and give [the Company] the flexibility [needed] to continue to attract, motivate and retain highly qualified officers, employees and directors."

The Company reserved 30,881,296 common shares for restricted stock awards, restricted stock units, incentive stock options, and non-qualified stock options for the Company's 1,800 officers, employees, non-employee directors, and service providers. The EIP has limits within each category. Of the total shares, a maximum of 17,646,455 can be issued for stock options or restricted stock awards and 13,234,841 for restricted stock units or performance shares. Those limits are further broken down for employee and non-employee directors. . . .

According to the proxy sent to stockholders, "[t]he number, types and terms of awards to be made pursuant to the [EIP] are subject to the discretion of the Committee and have not been determined at this time, and will not be determined until subsequent to stockholder approval." At the Company's June 9, 2015 annual meeting, 96.25% of the voting shares approved the EIP. . . .

Three days after stockholders approved the EIP, the Committee held the first of four meetings and eventually approved awards of restricted stock and stock options to all board members. According to the complaint, these awards were not part of the final 2015 compensation package nor discussed in any prior meetings. . . .

The board awarded themselves 7.8 million shares . . . The non-employee director awards totaled $21,594,000 and averaged $2,159,400. Peer companies' non-employee awards averaged $175,817. Cummings [the CEO and President] received 1,333,333 stock options and 1,000,000 restricted shares, valued at $16,699,999 and alleged to be 1,759% higher than the peer companies' average compensation for executive directors. Cama [the COO] received 1,066,666 stock options and 600,000 restricted shares, valued at $13,359,998 and alleged to be 2,571% higher than the peer companies' average. According to the complaint, the total fair value of the awards was $51,653,997. . . .

After the Company disclosed the awards, stockholders filed three separate complaints in the Court of Chancery alleging breaches of fiduciary duty by the directors for awarding themselves excessive compensation. . . .

The Court of Chancery . . . dismissed the plaintiffs' complaint. Relying on the court's earlier decisions in *In re 3COM Corp.*[28] and *Calma on Behalf of Citrix Systems, Inc. v. Templeton,*[29] the court dismissed the complaint against the non-employee directors because the EIP contained "meaningful, specific limits on awards to all director beneficiaries." . . .

II

Although authorized to do so by statute, when the board fixes its compensation, it is self-interested in the decision because the directors are deciding how much they should reward themselves for board service. [Usually,] the entire fairness standard of review will apply.

Other factors do sometimes come into play. When a fully informed, uncoerced, and disinterested majority of stockholders approve the board's authorized corporate action, the stockholders are said to have ratified the corporate act. . . . Here, we address the affirmative defense of stockholder ratification of director self-compensation decisions. . . .

A.

Early Supreme Court cases recognized a ratification defense by directors when reviewing their self-compensation decisions. . . .

[In both] *Kerbs* and *Gottlieb*, directors could successfully assert the ratification defense when the stockholders were fully informed and approved stock option plans containing specific director awards. But the award of "specific bargains not yet proposed" could not be ratified by general stockholder approval of the compensation plan.[53]

Our Court has not considered ratification of director self-compensation decisions since *Kerbs* and *Gottlieb*. The Court of Chancery has, however, continued to develop this area of the law.

[T]he Delaware doctrine of ratification does not embrace a "blank check" theory. . . . [T]he mere approval by stockholders of a request by directors for the authority to take action within broad parameters does not insulate all future action by the directors within those parameters from attack. . . . Rather, it is best understood as a decision by the stockholders to give the directors broad legal authority and to rely upon the policing of equity to ensure that that authority would be utilized properly. . . .

28. C.A. No. 16721, 1999 WL 1009210 (Del. Ch. Oct. 25, 1999).
29. 114 A.3d 563 (Del. Ch. 2015).
53. *Gottlieb*, 91 A.2d at 58.

III

A.

As ratification has evolved for stockholder-approved equity incentive plans, the courts have recognized the defense in three situations — when stockholders approved the specific director awards; when the plan was self-executing, meaning the directors had no discretion when making the awards; or when directors exercised discretion and determined the amounts and terms of the awards after stockholder approval. The first two scenarios present no real problems. When stockholders know precisely what they are approving, ratification will generally apply. The rub comes, however, in the third scenario, when directors retain discretion to make awards under the general parameters of equity incentive plans. The defendants rely on *3COM* and *Criden*, where the Court of Chancery recognized a stockholder ratification defense even though the directors' self-compensation awards were not submitted for stockholder approval. [I]n *3COM*, the Court . . . recognized ratification for director-specific compensation plans, where the plans contained specific limits for awards depending on factors set forth in the plan. In *Criden*, the court upheld a ratification defense when the plan authorized the directors to re-price the options after stockholder approval.

The court's decisions in *3COM* and *Criden* opened the door to the difficulties raised in this appeal. After those decisions, the Court of Chancery had to square *3COM* and *Criden* — and their expanded use of ratification for discretionary plans — with existing precedent, which only recognized ratification when stockholders approved the specific awards. The Court of Chancery [in *Seinfeld*] tried to harmonize the decisions by requiring "meaningful limits" on the amounts directors could award to themselves.

We think, however, when it comes to the discretion directors exercise following stockholder approval of an equity incentive plan, ratification cannot be used to foreclose the Court of Chancery from reviewing those further discretionary actions when a breach of fiduciary duty claim has been properly alleged. . . .When stockholders approve the general parameters of an equity compensation plan and allow directors to exercise their "broad legal authority" under the plan, they do so "precisely because they know that that authority must be exercised consistently with equitable principles of fiduciary duty."

. . . Other cases reinforce the same point — when a stockholder properly alleges that the directors breached their fiduciary duties when exercising their discretion after stockholders approve the general parameters of an equity incentive plan, the directors should have to demonstrate that their self-interested actions were entirely fair to the company.

B.

The Investors Bancorp EIP is a discretionary plan as described above. It covers about 1,800 officers, employees, non-employee directors, and service providers. Specific to the directors, the plan reserves 30,881,296 shares of common stock for restricted stock awards, restricted stock units, incentive stock options, and non-qualified stock options for the Company's officers, employees, non-employee directors, and service providers. Of those reserved shares and other equity, the non-employee directors were entitled to up to 30% of all option and restricted stock shares, all of which could be granted in any calendar year. But, "[t]he number, types, and terms of the awards to be made pursuant to the [EIP] are subject to the discretion of the Committee and have not been determined at this time, and will not be determined until subsequent to stockholder approval."

When submitted to the stockholders for approval, the stockholders were told that "[b]y approving the Plan, stockholders will give [the Company] the flexibility [it] need[s] to continue to attract, motivate and retain highly qualified officers, employees and directors. . . ."

After stockholders approved the EIP, the board eventually approved just under half of the stock options available to the directors and nearly thirty percent of the shares available to the directors as restricted stock awards, based predominately on a five-year going forward vesting period. The plaintiffs argue that the directors breached their fiduciary duties by granting themselves these awards because they were unfair and excessive. According to the plaintiffs, the stockholders were told the EIP would reward future performance, but the Board instead used the EIP awards to reward past efforts . . . which the directors had already accounted for in determining their 2015 compensation packages. Also, according to the plaintiffs, the rewards were inordinately higher than peer companies'. As alleged in the complaint, the Board paid each non-employee director more than $2,100,000 in 2015, which "eclips[ed] director pay at every Wall Street firm." This significantly exceeded the Company's non-employee director compensation in 2014, which ranged from $97,200 to $207,005. It also far surpassed the $198,000 median pay at similarly sized companies and the $260,000 median pay at much larger companies. . . .

The plaintiffs have alleged facts leading to a pleading stage reasonable inference that the directors breached their fiduciary duties in making unfair and excessive discretionary awards to themselves after stockholder approval of the EIP. Because the stockholders did not ratify the specific awards the directors made under the EIP, the directors must demonstrate the fairness of the awards to the Company.

[Reversed and remanded.]

NOTES AND QUESTIONS

In *Stein v. Blankfein et al.*, No. 2017-3454-SG, 2019 WL 2323790 (Del. Ch. May 31, 2019), the plaintiffs brought suit claiming that Goldman Sachs' directors received grossly excessive annual compensation averaging over $600,000 per director — nearly double that of its self-identified peers — even though Goldman was less profitable than them in 2016. The defendant directors moved to dismiss arguing that the stock incentive plan (SIP) was approved by shareholders with a provision that said "no member of the Board . . . shall have any liability to any person . . . for any action taken or omitted to be taken or any determination made in good faith with respect to the [SIP] or any Award." They argued this meant that shareholders waived entire fairness review, absent bad faith, with respect to the SIPs and that the directors "exercised their good faith judgment in setting their own compensation, and that even though their compensation is higher than their [peers] . . . they are well worth it. . . because Goldman Sachs' directors are, well, *Goldman Sachs directors.*"

Vice Chancellor Glasscock was "dubious that a majority of stockholders can waive the corporation's right to redress for future and *unknown* unfair self-dealing transactions" given the decision in *Investors Bancorp.* However, he did not need to reach that question because the provision at issue was not specific enough to support a waiver, even if such self-dealing waivers were possible. Generally, for a waiver to be effective, a party must know she has a right, have knowledge of all pertinent facts related to that right, and then voluntarily waive the right. Here the SIPs mostly involved directors approving awards to employees and officers, not to themselves, and thus the SIPs would not have appeared to be self-dealing transactions when the shareholders approved them. In light of that, the shareholder approval cannot satisfy the requirements for an effective waiver of self-dealing director compensation. For that, "[d]efendants would at minimum have to inform stockholders that the SIPs contemplated self-interested transactions subject to entire fairness, and provide that a vote in favor amounted to a waiver of the right to redress for such transactions, even if unfair, absent bad faith."

Would a provision with this specificity meet the requirements of *Investors Bancorp*? If not, then what would be necessary to satisfy *Investors Bancorp*? Finally, if some formulation could satisfy *Investors Bancorp* and result in an effective waiver, then is there much difference in when parties can opt out of fiduciary duties in Delaware corporations and the LLCs and LPs discussed in Chapter 2?

SHAREHOLDER LAWSUITS

We now turn from the content of the fiduciary duties of directors and officers to the lawsuits that enforce them. In considering shareholder suits, we address a uniquely American mode of private enforcement — one that, taken as a whole, is without parallel in other jurisdictions.

There are two principal forms of shareholder suits: *derivative suits* and *direct actions*, the latter of which are customarily brought as *class actions*. A class action merges together many individual claims that share important common features. (See Fed. R. Civ. P. 23.) Such a suit seeks to recover damages suffered by class members directly — in this context, shareholders directly — or to block the injury that these shareholders might otherwise suffer due to imminent corporate actions. The derivative suit, on the other hand, asserts a *corporate claim* against an officer or director (or third party), which charges them with a wrong to the corporation. Such an injury only indirectly (or "derivatively") harms shareholders. Thus, the derivative suit is said to represent two suits in one. The first suit is against a corporation's directors, charging them with *improperly* failing to sue on the existing corporate claim. The second is on the underlying claim of the corporation itself. These suits typically allege that the corporation's directors have failed to vindicate its claims because they themselves are the wrongdoers and therefore fail to bring suit on the corporation's behalf.

Both class suits and derivative suits have their roots in the English Court of Chancery and in the Rules of Equity Practice, which preceded the modern Rules of Federal Civil Procedure. Both of these legal actions are important features of American corporate law. As we will see, academics disagree about the utility of these devices. Suffice it to say, however, that fiduciary duties can deter misconduct only if the shareholders can bring claims of fiduciary breach to court. The virtue of class actions and derivative suits is that they bring claims of fiduciary breach to court on behalf of disaggregated shareholders; the vice of these actions is that they may encourage the plaintiff's bar to bring too many, or the wrong sort of, fiduciary claims to court.

10.1 DISTINGUISHING BETWEEN DIRECT AND DERIVATIVE CLAIMS

Since, technically speaking, directors owe their loyalty principally to the corporation itself, alleged breaches of corporate law obligations by directors and officers are most often brought as derivative suits. However, the numerous suits arising under the federal securities laws are direct actions; the injury alleged is to a personal interest, such as the right to vote shares, rather than to a corporate interest. Often the same behavior that gives rise to a derivative suit will also support a class action alleging securities fraud (e.g., a failure to disclose the fact that the transaction was a self-dealing transaction). Depending on the circumstances, plaintiffs' attorneys may bring one or both kinds of actions.

The distinction between derivative suits and class actions is important for several reasons. On the most basic level, it is important because the derivative suit advances a corporate claim, which implies that any recovery that results *should go directly to the corporation* itself. Occasionally, courts approve direct payment to minority shareholders in derivative litigation,[1] but this offends the formal character of corporate law and, more important, may be unfair to corporate creditors. If, for example, minority shareholders successfully sue a controlling shareholder for looting, the company's creditors will very much prefer to have the resulting recovery go to the corporation, which owes them money, rather than to the minority shareholders, who do not. Procedural law supplies a second reason why characterization of a shareholders' suit as derivative or direct may be important. As we shall shortly see, derivative suits have a number of special procedural hurdles designed to protect the board of directors' role as the primary guardian of corporate interests. A suit that is correctly characterized as a derivative suit may be dismissed if it does not satisfy the provisions of Rule 23.1 of the Federal Rules of Civil Procedure (or similar rules in state court systems).[2]

Although the class action and the derivative suit differ in concept (and to some extent in procedure), they share important commonalities. Both require plaintiffs to give notice to the absent interested parties; both permit other parties to petition to join in the suit; both provide for settlement and release only after notice, opportunity to be heard, and judicial determination of fairness of the settlement; and in both actions, successful plaintiffs are customarily compensated from the fund that their efforts produce. Compare Fed. R. Civ. P. 23 (class actions) and Fed. R. Civ. P. 23.1 (derivative actions).

Professors Matthew Cain, Jill Fisch, Steven Solomon, and Randall Thomas provide the following table of shareholder litigation associated with mergers and acquisitions deals, an area of increasing litigation, between 2003 and 2018.

---

1. See ALI, Principles of Corporate Governance §7.01(d) (1992).
2. Note that Delaware follows the Federal Rules of Civil Procedure with respect to class actions and derivative actions.

Table 1   Filings by Deal Completion Year

	Deals	Deals with Litigation	Delaware*	Other States*	Federal*	Mean # of Suits Filed per Deal
2003	41	34%	7%	100%	7%	1.6
2004	140	33%	43%	78%	0%	2.7
2005	159	37%	39%	66%	7%	2.3
2006	210	39%	21%	82%	12%	2.3
2007	287	42%	28%	86%	13%	3.2
2008	152	43%	23%	92%	21%	2.9
2009	58	76%	34%	98%	20%	3.8
2010	134	90%	49%	88%	26%	4.5
2011	131	92%	50%	88%	40%	5.4
2012	121	90%	56	88%	34%	5.1
2013	120	96%	52%	83%	32%	4.8
2014	117	91%	55%	73%	15%	4.5
2015	147	89%	60%	51%	19%	4.2
2016	172	74%	34%	62%	37%	3.4
2017	174	83%	10%	19%	87%	2.5
2018	157	83%	5%	18%	92%	2.7
Total	2,320	66%	37%	68%	35%	3.7

* Percentages sum to greater than 100% each year due to multi-jurisdictional filings.

Source: Matthew D. Cain, Jill E. Fisch, Steven Davidoff Solomon & Randall S. Thomas, *Mootness Fees*, 72 Vand. L. Rev. 1777, 1787 (2019) (Table 1).

Although the average number of deals hovers around 150 per year in their sample, the likelihood of suit and the jurisdiction in which suits are filed has fluctuated considerably. In the mid-2000s, shareholders challenged about one-third to 40 percent of deals, but after 2010 this percentage has usually exceeded 80 percent and in 2013 reached an astounding 96 percent. Further, the courts in which suits are filed has also changed dramatically. Prior to 2015, between 40 to 50 percent of deals were challenged in the Delaware courts, but this percentage dropped precipitously to five percent in 2018. Federal litigation, however, has gone the other way: between 2003 to 2007 only about 10% of deals in the sample were challenged in federal courts, but by 2018 this percentage had risen to 92%. If you suspect that suits migrate between state and federal courts — and between securities law and fiduciary duty claims — in response to new legislation and evolving case law, you are on to something. We explore this topic in greater depth in Section 10.5.

Although the incidence of deal litigation is fairly high, most of these suits are not derivate suits, but rather direct suits and class actions.[3] But the number of filings alone may not be the best measure of legal significance. In any case, we will pay a good deal of attention to derivative complaints in this chapter, where the procedural requirements are more intricate and the

3. See Sean J. Griffith, *Class Action Nuisance Suits: Evidence from Frequent Filer Shareholder Plaintiffs*, ECGI Working Paper No. 502/2020 at 8 (2020) (Table 1) (finding a low incidence of derivative suits for frequent filer shareholder plaintiffs between 2014 and 2018).

conceptual issues more challenging. The difference between derivative and direct (class action) claims is reasonably clear in theory although it is often problematic in practice. Consider the following problem.

PROBLEM: A FRIEND IN DEED IS A FRIEND IN NEED

The board of directors of Acme Forge Inc. defeated a coalition of insurgents at the annual shareholders' meeting. Shortly before the record date for voting at the meeting, Acme issued a 15 percent block of common stock to the Friendship Investment Company, which is widely believed to invest in companies at bargain prices and subsequently vote for management in hard-fought proxy contests. Acme's board authorized the sale of its common stock at a price that was 10 percent below its share price immediately before the announcement of the deal. The board noted that this transaction would not only supply Acme with much needed equity capital to pay down its debt, but that it would also recruit a long-term "anchor shareholder" who would stand by Acme during future ups and downs of the economy. In addition to these considerations, the board noted, the discount market price that it offered to Friendship was necessary to offset the decrease in Acme's share price that would inevitably follow from injections of a large block of new shares into the market.

After the deal, Acme's share price dropped by well over 10 percent, just as its board had predicted. And shortly thereafter, Acme's share price dropped even more when its board prevailed in a hard-fought proxy contest in which Friendship provided the critical margin of votes to reelect the incumbent directors.

Should a disgruntled public shareholder who learns of these facts after the shareholder meeting bring suit, and if so should she bring a derivative suit or pursue a direct suit and seek class certification? What is the appropriate remedy, assuming there has been a breach of the incumbent directors' duty of loyalty?

NOTE ON TOOLEY

In *Tooley v. Donaldson, Lufkin & Jenrette, Inc.*, 845 A.2d 1031 (Del. 2004), the Delaware Supreme Court attempted to clarify the distinction between direct (class) suits by shareholders and derivative suits brought by shareholders in the name of the corporation. The suit was brought by minority shareholders as a direct (class) action alleging that the board had breached a fiduciary duty to them by agreeing to a 22-day delay in closing a proposed cash merger. The claim was that the extension of time to close deprived them of the time value of the merger proceeds for the period of the delay.

The Delaware Chancery Court dismissed, stating that the only potential claim belonged to the corporation because it was a claim held equally by all shareholders. The court focused on language in earlier cases that emphasized that a shareholder had to suffer some special injury in order to state a direct claim. The Delaware Supreme Court affirmed the dismissal, but in doing so restated the test for determining whether a suit is to be treated as derivative or direct: "We set forth in this Opinion the law to be applied henceforth in determining whether a stockholder's claim is derivative or direct. That issue must turn *solely* on the following questions: (1) who suffered the alleged harm (the corporation or the suing shareholders); and (2) who would receive the benefit of any recovery or other remedy (the corporation or the stockholders individually)?" Thus, the Supreme Court removed from the analysis the question of special injury as being the mark of a direct claim.

In *Tooley*, the Supreme Court dismissed the complaint on the grounds that the shareholder plaintiffs had no individual right to have the merger occur at all. From the corporation's perspective as well, there was no wrong alleged. Nevertheless, if there had been a claim stated, it would have been a direct claim, because a shareholder does have a right to bring a direct action for injuries affecting his or her legal rights as a shareholder.

This case shows the limited utility of the special injury concept. Here, while the claim (such as it was) was shared by all shareholders and thus was not "special," it was nevertheless individual (if a legal right had been asserted at all). The restatement in *Tooley* is clarifying, but does not constitute a change in the law.[4]

10.2   SOLVING A COLLECTIVE ACTION PROBLEM: ATTORNEYS' FEES AND THE INCENTIVE TO SUE

As was observed in Chapter 6, the collective action problem is fundamental in the governance of public companies with dispersed share ownership. Where all investors hold small stakes in the enterprise, no single investor has a strong incentive to invest time and money in monitoring management. Nor are derivative or class suits practical if shareholders lack the time and money necessary to prosecute them. Of course, if minority shareholders own large fractions of company shares, as is common in closely held companies, their stakes alone might induce them to bring suit. But if the shareholder suit is to enforce fiduciary duties in widely held corporations, small shareholders must be motivated to prosecute meritorious claims. Incentives for small shareholders — or at least a proxy for them — evolved from the court of equity's practice of awarding attorneys' fees to plaintiffs whose litigation created a common fund that benefited all shareholders. Consequently, a large majority of shareholder suits against the directors and officers of public companies today are initiated by the plaintiffs' bar. The attorneys who bring these suits seek to earn fees from positive outcomes for the "real parties" of interest, the corporation and

---

4. Recently, the Delaware Supreme Court relied on *Tooley* again in *Citigroup Inc. v. AHW Investment Partnership*, 140 A.3d 1125 (Del. 2016).

its shareholders. Plaintiffs' attorneys are paid — or not — by order of the court or as part of a settlement at the conclusion of the litigation. In form, these attorneys are the economic agents of their shareholder-clients. In substance, they are legal entrepreneurs motivated by the prospect of attorneys' fees.

Whether an attorney for the plaintiff in a shareholder action receives a fee at all turns on whether the suit is dismissed or a judgment is entered in the suit, either through litigation (rare) or settlement (common). The plaintiffs' attorney receives nothing when a derivative suit is dismissed because there is no recovery and no benefit. When a derivative suit succeeds on the merits or settles (the usual outcome), the corporation is said to benefit from any monetary recovery or governance change resulting from the litigation. However, the corporation and its insurer also generally bear the bulk of litigation costs on both sides. The company is likely to have advanced the cost of defense to its managers (e.g., via indemnification agreements), and it must usually pay the plaintiff a sum for "costs" that, in the case of monetary recoveries, range from a couple of percent (where the financial benefit is very large) up to as much as 30 percent in some cases. While the formulas used to calculate attorneys' contingent fees differ by jurisdiction and suit, the percentage of the recovery awarded for legal costs remains surprisingly stable.[5]

FLETCHER v. A.J. INDUSTRIES, INC.
72 Cal. Rptr. 146, 266 Cal. App. 2d 313 (1968)

RATTIGAN, A.J.:

This appeal is from certain orders entered in a stockholders' derivative action against appellant A.J. Industries, Inc. (hereinafter called the "corporation," or "AJ"). . . . The named defendants included the corporation; respondents Ver Halen and Malone . . . [and other members of A.J.'s board of directors].

The complaint alleged generally that . . . Ver Halen had dominated and controlled the board and the management of the corporation . . . and that, in consequence, the corporation had been damaged in the various transactions. . . . The complaint prayed for several forms of relief on behalf of the corporation, including a money judgment against Ver Halen for $134,150 and one against all the individual defendants in the amount of $1,000,000. . . .

During the course of a protracted hearing . . . a settlement of the action was negotiated. . . .

The "executory provisions" of the stipulation included these agreements: Four incumbent directors were to be replaced by persons acceptable to plaintiffs, to Ver Halen, and to the corporation; failing their agreement, the new directors were to be appointed by the trial court. The corporation agreed to employ a new officer who would be in charge of its "operations," and who would be one of the four new directors. In the election of future

---

5. See Roberta Romano, *The Shareholder Suit: Litigation Without Foundation?*, 7 J.L. Econ. & Org. 55 (1991).

directors, Ver Halen's voting powers as a stockholder were to be limited so as to permit him to elect only two of the board's nine members. His employment contract was to be amended to provide that he could be employed as president of the corporation or, at the board's option, as chairman of the board. Malone was to be one of the directors replaced, and he was to resign as the corporation's treasurer.

Several of the specific charges alleged in plaintiffs' complaint related to claimed mismanagement of the corporation due to Ver Halen's "domination" of its affairs; to Malone's allegedly excessive salary; and to Ver Halen's asserted breach of his employment contract. The stipulated agreements summarized above apparently disposed of these matters.

Most of the other charges made in the complaint related to specific transactions in which plaintiffs asserted misconduct on the part of Ver Halen. In other "executory provisions" of the stipulation it was agreed that these would be referred to arbitration. . . .

Whether the corporation was entitled to monetary recovery in any respect was, thus, to be determined in the future. In contrast, the stipulated agreements — providing for the reorganization of the corporation's board of directors and its management, the ouster of Malone, and the amendment of Ver Halen's contract of employment — were to be performed immediately.

The stipulation further provided that the arbitrator could award attorneys' fees, to be paid by the corporation, to any counsel who appeared in the arbitration proceeding, except that plaintiffs' attorneys could be awarded fees only in the event the corporation received a monetary award. The parties acknowledged (1) that plaintiffs' . . . attorneys intended to apply to the trial court — as distinguished from the future arbitrator — for fees and costs to be paid to them by the corporation "in connection with this action," but (2) that the corporation could take "any position in connection with such applications that it may choose." . . .

In its order granting plaintiffs' application for attorneys' fees and costs, the trial court found that they had employed their attorneys to prosecute the derivative action, in good faith, on behalf of themselves and the other stockholders of the corporation, and that the corporation was able to pay the fees and costs incurred. The court also found that by reason of the action, and its settlement, "substantial benefits have been conferred" upon the corporation.[2]

2. [I]n the following particulars, to wit:

a) That by reason of the settlement of said action, and without regard to whether plaintiffs or defendants would have been successful in the ultimate outcome thereof, the defendant A.J. Industries, Inc., a corporation, has been saved substantial expenditures for attorneys' fees, costs, and the loss of valuable time of valued employees by reason of the fact that the settlement and compromise obviates the necessity of a trial of this cause on its merits. Probable expenditures by the corporation, aforesaid, have been estimated by witnesses offered by defendants to be in excess of the sum of $200,000.00.

b) That by reason of said settlement the rights of the defendant corporation, if any, to recover from the defendant C.J. Ver Halen monies . . . has been fully protected and reserved in that a fair and equitable arbitration proceeding is provided for as a part of the terms of said settlement. . . .

Based upon these findings, the court ordered the corporation to pay plaintiffs' attorneys' fees ($64,784) and costs ($2,179.26).

. . . Under the general rule in California and in most American jurisdictions, the party prevailing in an action may not recover attorneys' fees unless a statute expressly permits such recovery. . . .

An exception to the general rule is found, however, in the so-called common-fund doctrine. . . . "It is a well-established doctrine of equity jurisprudence that where a common fund exists to which a number of persons are entitled and in their interest successful litigation is maintained for its preservation and protection, an allowance of counsel fees may properly be made from such fund. By this means *all* of the beneficiaries of the fund pay their share of the expense necessary to make it available to them." . . .

Under the "substantial benefit" rule, a variant of the common-fund doctrine as applied more recently in other jurisdictions, the successful plaintiff in a stockholder's derivative action may be awarded attorneys' fees against the corporation if the latter received "substantial benefits" from the litigation, although the benefits were not "pecuniary" and the action had not produced a fund from which they might be paid. . . .

In the present case, some of the causes of action alleged in plaintiffs' complaint might have produced a "common fund" in the form of a money judgment against appellant corporation. None, however, did: they were referred to an arbitration proceeding which was to be conducted in the future. For the obvious reason that no fund existed, the trial court applied the substantial-benefit rule . . . under which the award of attorneys' fees is charged directly against the corporation. . . .

[W]e conclude, that under the California rule (1) an award of attorneys' fees to a successful plaintiff may properly be measured by, and paid from, a common fund where his derivative action on behalf of a corporation has recovered or protected a fund in fact; but (2) the existence of a fund is not a prerequisite of the award itself. . . .

The stockholder's derivative suit . . . is an effective means of policing corporate management. [It] should not be inhibited by a doctrine which limits the compensation of successful attorneys to cases which produce a monetary recovery: the realization of substantial, if nonpecuniary, benefits by the corporation should [also] be the criterion. . . .

The final question . . . is whether the benefits realized by the corporation were sufficiently "substantial" to warrant the award. To find that they were, . . . [i]t will suffice if the [trial] court finds, upon proper evidence, that the results of the action "maintain the health of the corporation and raise the standards of 'fiduciary relationships and of other economic behavior,'" or "*prevent* an abuse which would be prejudicial to the rights and interests of the corporation or affect the enjoyment or protection of an essential right to the stockholder's interest." [Citation omitted.] . . .

It is not significant that the "benefits" found were achieved by settlement of plaintiffs' action rather than by final judgment. The authorities recognizing the substantial-benefit rule have permitted attorneys' fee awards in settled cases. . . . This is in keeping with the law's general policy favoring settlements . . . and in a stockholder's derivative action the trial court is in a position to scrutinize the fairness of a settlement because the court alone can authorize the action's dismissal. . . .

Some of the "benefits" found by the trial court in the present case related to the comparative economy to be realized by proceeding in arbitration rather than in conventional adversary litigation. Other "benefits," though, were realized in the form of immediate changes in the corporate management. The corporation argues that some of these had been under consideration by its board of directors before plaintiffs sued and settled, and that the real value of others is speculative. But the trial court found that the changes were substantial as benefits to the corporation and, in effect, that plaintiffs' action had brought them about. The finding is supported by ample evidence, and it is decisive on the appeal. We therefore affirm the award of attorneys' fees.

CHRISTIAN, J. (dissenting in part).

. . . The majority opinion refers to certain considerations of policy which appear to indicate that it would be a good thing to allow attorneys' fees against a corporation when one of its shareholders succeeds in a derivative action and substantial benefit to the corporation results. . . . But countervailing policy arguments are not lacking: for example, if the existence of a "common fund" . . . is not prerequisite to the allowance of fees the officers and directors [of the corporation] may well be faced with a liquidation of assets to pay fees, even though resulting harm to the corporation might be disproportionate to the "substantial benefits" derived from the lawsuit. Considerations of this character can better be appraised in the legislative process than by the [courts]. Moreover, it appears likely that the new enlargement of the "common fund" exception to the rule laid down in the statute may greatly outweigh in practical importance the court-created exception on which it is to be grafted. The variety of shareholders' actions in which "substantial benefit" to the corporation may be found is literally boundless. . . .

QUESTIONS ON FLETCHER v. A.J. INDUSTRIES, INC.

1. What was the "substantial benefit" conferred on the corporation by the derivative suit in this litigation?
2. The rationale for shifting from the traditional common fund doctrine to the substantial benefit test for attorneys' fees is obvious. Is there a counterargument as well? What new risk is introduced by the substantial benefit test? How do you imagine courts deal with that risk?
3. Should the avoidance of litigation costs figure among the "benefits" conferred by the settlement of a derivative suit?

NOTE ON AGENCY COSTS IN SHAREHOLDER LITIGATION

The role of lawyer as bounty hunter creates an obvious agency problem in its own right. Legally, the plaintiffs' lawyers are agents of shareholders, just as the defendants are fiduciaries for the corporation and its shareholders. But both sides have important individual interests at stake: lawyers' fees on one side and the potential liability of corporate officers and directors on the other.

Much of the law of derivative suits is an effort to deal with these crosscutting agency problems. One such problem is that plaintiffs' lawyers may initiate so-called strike suits, or suits without merit, simply to extract settlements by exploiting the nuisance value of litigation and the personal fears of liability — even if unfounded — of officers and directors. A second problem is that defendants may be too eager to settle because they bear at least some of the costs of litigation personally (e.g., the pain of depositions and the risk of personal liability), but they do not bear the cost of settling, which is borne by the corporation or its insurer. Strike suits have long been a concern of the corporate bar and are widely discussed in the literature.[6] One controversial article has even argued that the merits of litigation are unrelated to settlement amounts in the related context of securities class actions.[7]

Agency problems also arise when shareholder litigation is meritorious and corporate managers face a serious prospect of liability. In this case, both plaintiffs' attorneys and defendants — if these defendants control their corporations — have an incentive to settle on mutually advantageous terms that allow the defendants to fully escape personal liability for their conduct.

Finally, the legal system itself can generate agency problems by structuring attorneys' fees in dysfunctional ways. For example, awarding plaintiffs' attorneys a percentage of the recovery may encourage premature settlement. The chief alternative fee rule, the so-called lodestar formula sometimes used in federal securities litigation, pays attorneys a base hourly fee for the reasonable time expended on a case, inflated by a multiplier to compensate for unusual difficulty or risk. By decoupling attorneys' fees from the recovery amount, this rule eliminates the incentives of attorneys to settle too soon, but it creates the opposite incentive to spend too much time litigating relative to the likely settlement outcomes.[8] Finally, as a reaction to the evident weaknesses in both techniques for the awarding of attorneys' fees, some courts have experimented with auctioning the rights to represent the corporation (or the class of shareholders) to the law firm that makes the best bid. But even this technique is vulnerable to "gaming" by plaintiffs' attorneys. The

6. See, e.g., Roberta Romano, *The Shareholder Suit: Litigation Without Foundation?*, 7 J.L. Econ. & Org. 55 (1991); John C. Coffee, Jr., *Understanding the Plaintiff's Attorney: The Implications for Private Enforcement of Law Through Class and Derivative Actions*, 86 Colum. L. Rev. 669 (1986).

7. Janet C. Alexander, *Do the Merits Matter? A Study of Settlements in Securities Class Actions*, 43 Stan. L. Rev. 497 (1991). For criticism of this initial study, see, e.g., Leonard B. Simon & William S. Dato, *Legislating on a False Foundation: The Erroneous Academic Underpinnings of the Private Securities Litigation Reform Act of 1995*, 33 San Diego L. Rev. 959, 964 (1996). For more recent empirical work on this question, compare Marilyn F. Johnson, Karen K. Nelson & A.C. Pritchard, *Do the Merits Matter More? The Impact of the Private Securities Litigation Reform Act*, 23 J.L. Econ. & Org. 627 (2007) (finding a "closer relation between factors related to fraud and the filing of securities class actions after the passage of the PSLRA") with Stephen J. Choi, *Do the Merits Matter Less After the Private Securities Litigation Reform Act?*, 23 J.L. Econ. & Org. 598 (2007) (reporting some evidence that meritorious suits were deterred by the PSLRA).

8. See, e.g., John C. Coffee, *The Unfaithful Champion: The Plaintiff as Monitor of Shareholder Litigation*, 48 Law & Contemp. Probs. 5 (1985).

incentives of bidding firms may, for example, lead to low bids that permit a lawyer to control the case in order to negotiate a settlement.[9]

Thus, while paying bounties to plaintiffs' lawyers mitigates the shareholders' collective action problem in widely held corporations, it also gives rise to new risks and challenges for the legal system. Much of what follows in this chapter — specifically the law of pre-suit demand and the law of dismissal by independent board committees — can be understood as judicially created measures intended to fine-tune the power and incentives of plaintiffs' lawyers to pursue shareholder suits.

In addition to these judicial innovations, there have been several statutory responses to the agency problems of fee-driven litigation. Beginning in the 1940s, a number of states adopted "security for expenses" statutes, which permitted corporations to require plaintiffs (or their attorneys) to post a bond to secure coverage of the company's anticipated expenses in the litigation. See, e.g., NYBCL §627; Cal. Corp. Code §800. The purpose of these statutes was to add a stick to the carrot of attorneys' fees — to engineer a fee rule that would discourage strike suits as well as encourage meritorious litigation. But however attractive this approach seems in theory, it appears to have failed in practice. Savvy plaintiffs' attorneys, reluctant defendants, and sympathetic judges together ensure that plaintiffs are rarely forced to post bonds and are virtually never charged with the litigation costs of defendants.[10]

General dissatisfaction with the growth in the number of securities class actions led to enactment of the federal Private Securities Litigation Reform Act (PSLRA) of 1995.[11] That statute embraces a variety of devices to discourage non-meritorious suits, such as particularized pleading requirements, stays in discovery, and changes in substantive law, and to encourage institutional shareholders to assume control of shareholder litigation under the "most adequate plaintiff" rule considered below. The chart below shows the number of securities class actions filed since 1996.

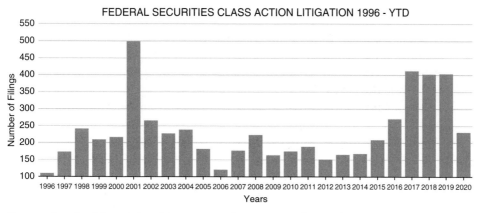

Source: Stanford Law School Securities Class Action Clearinghouse.

9. See Third Circuit Task Force Report on Selection of Class Counsel, 74 Temple L. Rev. 685 (2001).
10. See Robert Clark, Corporate Law §15.5.
11. Pub. L. No. 104-67, 109 Stat. 737 (1995) (codified throughout 15 U.S.C. §§77-78).

Initially, new securities fraud filings decreased after the PSLRA was passed, but only for a year or two. Filings returned to their 1994 (pre-PSLRA) level of approximately 200 new cases per year, then exploded in 2001 with a wave of "IPO Allocation" lawsuits, alleging that underwriters engaged in undisclosed practices in connection with the distribution of IPO (initial public offering) shares. The year 2008 was also a very good year for securities class actions in the wake of the Great Recession against financial institutions. After that, filings stabilized for a few years before increasing dramatically after 2015 to roughly 400 cases annually. These data support the conventional wisdom that the PSLRA was only a minor speed-bump for plaintiffs' lawyers on the way to the courthouse and that the "fundamentals" such as stock market volatility are more important drivers of overall litigation activity.[12] The recent uptick in securities filings during a period of relatively low price volatility reflects a migration of litigation from the Delaware courts to federal courts after an important Chancery Court decision (*In re Trulia*) that we discuss in Section 10.5.2. Visit the Stanford Securities Class Action Clearinghouse on the internet for a trove of data on this topic, including total amount of dollars expended in settlements.

10.3   Standing Requirements

Standing requirements that screen who may bring a derivative suit are established both by statute and by court rule. See, e.g., 10 Del. Code Com. §327; Fed. R. Civ. P. 23.1. They are premised on the assumption that screening for qualified litigants increases the quality of shareholder litigation, that is, that some potential litigants have better incentives to sue than others. (Compare, from this perspective, the various standing requirements for derivative suits in your statutory supplement: Fed. R. Civ. P. 23.1; MBCA §7.41; and ALI, Principles of Corporate Governance §7.02.) Federal Rule 23.1, which Delaware also follows, typifies standing rules for derivative actions. First, the plaintiff must be a shareholder for the duration of the action. (Why? What shapes the incentives of a plaintiff who sues on behalf of a company in which she no longer has any financial interest?) Second, the plaintiff must have been a shareholder at the time of the alleged wrongful act or omission (the "contemporaneous ownership rule"). This requirement reflects the traditional bias of courts against plaintiffs who "buy a lawsuit." In public companies, however, this rule is not very important, since shareholders are easy to find. Third, the plaintiff must be able to "fairly and adequately" represent the interests of shareholders, meaning in practice that there are no obvious conflicts of interest.[13] Finally, the complaint

---

12. See, e.g., Cornerstone Research, Securities Class Action Case Filings: 2005.
13. The requirement that a plaintiff remain a shareholder during the course of litigation, which arises from judicial construction of "fair and adequate" representation under Rule 23.1,

must specify what action the plaintiff has taken to obtain satisfaction from the company's board (a requirement that forms the basis of the "demand requirement") or state with particularity the plaintiff's reason for not doing so.

QUESTIONS ON THE POLICY RATIONALE FOR DERIVATIVE ACTIONS

1. From an incentive standpoint, do you think the contemporaneous ownership requirement makes sense? Current ownership of shares might affect a plaintiff's incentive, but why should past ownership matter?

2. Should the law try to structure attorneys' fees to ensure that every meritorious derivative suit is brought? Why or why not?

3. Evaluate the following proposals for new "standing" rules to govern the right to bring derivative litigation (or class actions):

   a. A rule limiting standing to shareholders holding 2 percent or $500,000 worth of company shares.

   b. A rule assigning the right to control derivative litigation to the largest (nonconflicted) shareholder willing to intervene in the litigation, on the ground that this shareholder is the "most adequate plaintiff." Note that a provision of the Private Securities Litigation Reform Act of 1995 adopts precisely this rule for assigning control over class actions alleging violations of the federal securities laws. See Pub. L. No. 104-67, 109 Stat. 737 (1995).[14]

   c. A rule permitting judges to auction standing to bring derivative actions to the highest bidder — with the proceeds of the auction going to the corporation, a finder's fee to the attorney who filed the initial complaint, and any recovery to the winning bidder who prosecutes the suit.[15]

---

has bite chiefly in the context of corporate mergers and dissolutions, where plaintiffs may cease to be shareholders because the corporations in which they held shares disappear. See, e.g., *Basch v. Talley Industries, Inc.*, 53 F.R.D. 9 (S.D.N.Y. 1971). However, if the plaintiff receives stock in the surviving corporation, the standing requirement is met. See, e.g., *Lambrecht v. O'Neal*, discussed below.

14. For an empirical assessment of this provision, see Stephen J. Choi, Jill E. Fisch & A.C. Pritchard, *Do Institutions Matter? The Impact of the Lead Plaintiff Provision of the Private Securities Litigation Reform Act*, 83 Wash. U. L.Q. 869 (2005) (finding that public pension funds have participated more frequently as lead plaintiff since 1995, but overall institutional participation remains unchanged in four-year samples pre- and post-PSLRA).

15. There is a lively controversy about the policy merits of auctioning shareholder suits. See Jonathan R. Macey & Geoffrey P. Miller, *The Plaintiff's Attorney's Role in Class Action and Derivative Litigation: Economic Analysis and Recommendations for Reform*, 58 U. Chi. L. Rev. 1 (1991). Compare Randall S. Thomas & Robert G. Hansen, *Auctioning Class Action and Derivative Lawsuits: A Critical Analysis*, 87 Nw. U. L. Rev. 423 (1993); Jonathan R. Macey & Geoffrey P. Miller, *Auctioning Class Action and Derivative Suits: A Rejoinder*, 87 Nw. U. L. Rev. 458 (1993).

10.4   BALANCING THE RIGHTS OF BOARDS TO MANAGE THE CORPORATION AND SHAREHOLDERS' RIGHTS TO OBTAIN JUDICIAL REVIEW

An important set of legal doctrines balances the right of boards to manage their companies (including their potential legal claims) against the rights of shareholder-plaintiffs to obtain judicial review of alleged corporate malfeasance. The issue of when a shareholder-plaintiff may pursue a claim on behalf of a corporation without board authorization or despite its opposition arises in several contexts. First, it arises when a company's board considers a shareholder's demand to bring suit, as Rule 23.1 contemplates, but rejects it. Here the court must decide whether or not to defer to the board's business judgment in electing not to prosecute the action. The issue of deference to the board also arises when the shareholder-plaintiff does *not* make demand on the board, on the ground that the board could not exercise disinterested business judgment. Here the court must pass on the validity of the plaintiff's excuse for not making pre-suit demand. In addition, the question of board deference arises when the board seeks to terminate a derivative suit at a later point in the litigation, after the suit has already survived the company's initial motion to dismiss. That is, even if the company's board was disqualified from dismissing the suit as of when the complaint was filed, may be the board subsequently regains competence by delegating authority over the matter to a committee of independent directors who may have been appointed to the board well after litigation began.[16] Finally, the need for courts to balance the rights of management and shareholders in derivative suits also arises in connection with the settlement of shareholder suits. We discuss settlements in Section 10.5.

10.4.1   The Demand Requirement of Rule 23.1

The demand requirement originates in the traditional rule that a derivative complaint must "allege with particularity the efforts, if any, made by the plaintiff to obtain the action he desires from the directors or comparable authority . . . or the grounds for not making the effort." Fed. R. Civ. P. 23.1

---

16. While this may seem like a transparent attempt to defeat and punish derivative plaintiffs, there are circumstances when it is clearly appropriate. Imagine, for example, that a hostile takeover follows the initiation of a derivative suit. Even though the old board may have been implicated in the matter sued on, the new board is not and therefore should be given its rights to manage the company's claim in litigation. The matter becomes far less clear when the company's newfound ability to make a valid business judgment comes, not from a complete turnover of the board, but from the appointment of one or two new directors, who thereafter are appointed to a special committee to review the matter. This is the situation presented in the well-known Delaware case of *Zapata Corp. v. Maldanado*, set forth below.

(Delaware has an identical rule). But under what circumstances may a complaint be dismissed once the plaintiff does — or does not — make a demand on the board? The answer is a matter of common law.

DEMAND EXCUSED: A NOTE ON ARONSON v. LEWIS AND ITS PROGENY

Plaintiffs' attorneys prefer not to make demand on the board for the understandable reason that it is likely to be refused, in which case plaintiffs are treated as having waived any objection to the board's independence. See *Spiegel v. Buntrock*, 571 A.2d 767 (Del. 1990).[17] For Delaware corporations at least, plaintiffs' usual strategy is to plead that demand should be excused because it would be futile — the board is too interested or otherwise muddled to exercise unbiased business judgment. But how should Delaware courts decide "demand-futility" claims? More likely than not, the entire corporate board will be defendants in such cases, making it "interested" in a formal sense. On the other hand, if a court were to require proof that a board was interested in the alleged misconduct prior to any discovery, derivative actions would be almost impossible to bring. The Delaware Supreme Court sought a middle way that implicitly gave the Chancery Court a strong screening function.

The controlling Delaware Supreme Court case is *Aronson v. Lewis*, 433 A.2d 805 (1984). The *Aronson* case involved a favorable deal between a company and its 47 percent shareholder/director. The court, per Justice Moore, rejected plaintiff's demand-futility claim, which had stressed the dominant shareholder's power over board appointments. Instead, the *Aronson* court framed the following test:

> . . . "[I]n determining demand-futility the Court of Chancery in a proper exercise of its discretion must decide whether, under the particularized facts alleged, a reasonable doubt is created that: (1) the directors are disinterested and independent and (2) the challenged transaction was otherwise the product of a valid exercise of business judgment." 473 A2d at 814.

The *Aronson* decision naturally gave rise to later case law parsing the meaning of this test.

Among the more instructive (and amusing) of these cases is *Levine v. Smith*, 591 A.2d 194 (Del. 1991), in which the plaintiffs challenged a transaction between General Motors and its best-known outside director of the time, Ross Perot — an acerbic billionaire and later two-time third-party

---

17. The holding that plaintiffs concede board independence by making demand appears to have been partly qualified by a more recent case, although just how much is difficult to say. See *Scattered Corp. v. Chicago Stock Exchange, Inc.*, 701 A.2d 70 (Del. 1997) ("It is not correct that a demand concedes independence 'conclusively' and in futuro for all purposes relevant to the demand.").

candidate for the U.S. presidency. Perot had sold his company to GM in 1984 and became its largest shareholder and a director, but once on the inside Perot challenged GM's bureaucratic ways and turned to public invective when his suggestions were ignored. One can imagine that GM's management was eager to buy out Perot's stake after its most visible director accused the company of selling "second-rate cars."[18] Whether Perot was simply candid or an astute businessman — or both — we will never know. What is certain is that he received a rich buyout price from GM that almost tripled the value of his holdings in two years. The details of this case are well worth exploring for their own sake, but we restrict ourselves here to *Levine*'s two principal doctrinal contributions.

The first of these was whether the two parts of the *Aronson* test for demand futility were conjunctive or disjunctive. In other words, does establishing demand futility require a reasonable doubt that the board was disinterested *and* that the past transaction at the heart of the complaint was not "the product of a valid exercise of business judgment," or would particularized evidence of either of the propositions suffice? *Levine*'s language indicated that the test was disjunctive, so a reasonable doubt that either today's board is not disinterested *or* that yesterday's challenged transaction was not an exercise of disinterested business judgment might suffice to excuse demand. But how are *Aronson*'s two prongs related? Why should yesterday's board decision affect the ability of today's board to pass on the merits of an action brought by the corporation today? We turn to this second question in the *Rales* case following the note on pre-suit demand.

NOTE ON PRE-SUIT DEMAND

Aronson v. Lewis and *Levine v. Smith* raise many other issues. The most fundamental of these was taken up by the ALI in its Principles of Corporate Governance project: Is the traditional equity rule of pre-suit demand, with its exception for futility, the best way to adjudicate the board's colorable disability to claim sole right to control the adjudication of corporate claims? The drafters of the ALI's Principles concluded that the answer was "no." Instead, the ALI proposed a rule of universal demand, under which a plaintiff would be required to always make a demand, and if, as is likely, she was not satisfied with the board's response to her demand, she could institute suit. If the defendants thereafter sought dismissal of the suit, the court would review the board's exercise of business judgment in making its response. If the court concluded that the board was in a position to exercise a valid business judgment on the question of whether suit should be brought, then it would dismiss the

---

18. This is a tame example. According to a Washington Post article "[n]ot only had [Perot] humiliated Smith [GM's CEO] last fall when he suggested to Business Week that trying to change GM was like "teaching an elephant to tap-dance," he had also slammed the company for coddling executives, producing second-rate cars, and losing the race not only to the Japanese, but to Ford as well." David Remnick, *H. Ross Perot to GM I'll Drive*, The Washington Post, April 19, 1987.

suit. Otherwise, the suit would continue to its merits. See ALI, Principles of Corporate Governance §7.04.

In an odd way, the Delaware Supreme Court has promulgated a rule that is the mirror image of the ALI rule: a rule of "universal non-demand." It has done so through its practice of inferring that, whenever a plaintiff actually does make a pre-suit demand, she automatically concedes that the board is independent and disinterested with respect to the question to be litigated. If independence is conceded by making demand, then the only prong of the *Aronson-Levine* test that the plaintiff is left to contest in the event that the demand is denied (as it usually is) is the test's second prong, which asks whether bad faith or gross negligence may be inferred from the decision itself. Thus, although there is some ex post plausibility in the reasoning of the Delaware courts, the practical effect of this rule is to discourage any pre-suit demand at all. The real policy question then is whether we prefer a universal demand rule or a universal non-demand rule. In either event, the court will ultimately have to pass upon the board's ability to fairly deal with the issue the litigation presents. The ALI approach allows it to do so with more information (but would entail more time and cost by the board).

The *Levine* case itself employs a relaxed modification of the business judgment rule to screen derivative suits: Do the facts alleged "creat[e] a *reasonable doubt* of the 'soundness' of the challenged transaction"? (Emphasis added.) This is presumably because the court is conscious that it is addressing a pleading standard and does not want to prejudge the merits of the claim. Nevertheless, the *Levine* case might be accused of confusing matters because it focuses in part on the identity of the directors at the time of the occurrence of the alleged wrong. What is really relevant, however, is the board's capacity to decide at the time that the suit is brought. That question may, but need not logically, be related to the composition of the board at the time of the wrong. In the following case, the court struggles to overcome this bit of confusion.

RALES v. BLASBAND
634 A.2d 927 (Del. 1993)

Veasey, C.J.:

[Before the court on certification from the United States District Court.] . . .

[Shareholder-plaintiff] Blasband is currently a stockholder of Danaher Corp. Prior to 1990 Blasband owned 1100 shares of Easco Hand Tools, Inc., a Delaware corporation ("Easco"). Easco entered into a [stock-for-stock] merger agreement with Danaher in February 1990 whereby Easco became a wholly-owned subsidiary of Danaher (the "Merger").

Steven M. Rales and Mitchell P. Rales (the "Rales brothers") have been directors, officers, or stockholders of Easco and Danaher at relevant times. Prior to the Merger, the Rales brothers were directors of Easco, and together owned approximately 52 percent of Easco's common stock. They continued to serve as directors of Easco after the Merger.

The Rales brothers also own approximately 44 percent of Danaher's common stock. Prior to the Merger, Mitchell Rales was President and Steven Rales was Chief Executive Officer of Danaher. The Rales brothers resigned their positions as officers of Danaher in early 1990, but continued to serve as members of the [Danaher] Board. The Board consists of eight members. The other six members are Danaher's President and Chief Executive Officer, George Sherman ("Sherman"), Donald E. Ehrlich ("Ehrlich"), Mortimer Caplin ("Caplin"), George D. Kellner ("Kellner"), A. Emmett Stephenson, Jr. ("Stephenson"), and Walter Lohr ("Lohr"). A number of these directors have business relationships with the Rales brothers or with entities controlled by them.

The central focus of the amended complaint is the alleged misuse by the Easco board of the proceeds of a sale of that company's 12.875% Senior Subordinated Notes due 1998 (the "Notes"). On or about September 1, 1988, Easco sold $100 million of the Notes in a public offering (the "Offering"). The prospectus for the Offering stated that the proceeds from the sale of the Notes would be used for (1) repaying outstanding indebtedness, (2) funding corporate expansion, and (3) general corporate purposes. The prospectus further stated that "pending such uses, the Company will invest the balance of the net proceeds from this offering in government and other marketable securities which are expected to yield a lower rate of return than the rate of interest borne by the Notes."

Blasband alleges that the defendants did not invest in "government and other marketable securities," but instead used over $61.9 million of the proceeds to buy highly speculative "junk bonds" offered through Drexel Burnham Lambert Inc. ("Drexel"). Blasband alleges that these junk bonds were bought by Easco because of the Rales brothers' desire to help Drexel at a time when it was under investigation and having trouble selling such bonds. The amended complaint describes the prior business relationship between the Rales brothers and Drexel in the mid-1980s, including Drexel's assistance in the Rales brothers' expansion of Danaher through corporate acquisitions and the role played by Drexel in the Rales brothers' attempt to acquire Interco, Inc. Moreover, Drexel was the underwriter of the Offering of Easco's Notes.

The amended complaint alleges that these investments have declined substantially in value, resulting in a loss to Easco of at least $14 million. Finally, Blasband complains that the Easco and Danaher boards of directors refused to comply with his request for information regarding the investments. . . .

MICHAEL MILKEN

While an MBA student at the University of Pennsylvania's Wharton School, Michael Milken studied the academic literature regarding debt financing and became fascinated with the investment potential of low-grade, high-yield bonds. After graduating in 1970, he traded securities in investment bank Drexel Burnham's low-grade bond department and quickly rose through the ranks to lead the department. He became so adept at promoting and selling "junk bonds," convertible debt issuances with low ratings and high yields, that Drexel Burnham's name became synonymous with the product. Milken was especially skilled at building networks of investors and borrowers for financing deals. Borrowers working with Milken often took a larger loan than necessary and invested the excess in other junk bonds offered by Milken. In the 1980s, Milken financed many of the decade's hostile takeovers with junk bonds, enabling mid-sized companies to make bids for much larger and more established institutions. One of these upstart companies was Danaher, an investment holdings company owned by brothers Steven and Mitchell Rales. The Rales brothers used junk bond financing to fund numerous hostile takeovers, which led to financial success for their company and made them billionaires. Like many of Milken's beneficiaries, they felt a strong sense of loyalty to Michael Milken.

Milken soon became embroiled in controversy as the public became increasingly outraged by the perceived corruption of Wall Street bankers and the greed of corporate raiders. In 1986, U.S. District Attorney Rudolph Giuliani began a two-year investigation of Milken and Drexel Burnham for insider-trading and stock manipulation, which culminated in a ten-year prison sentence for Milken.

The certified question . . . calls upon this Court to decide whether Blasband's amended complaint establishes that demand is excused under the "substantive law of the State of Delaware." It is therefore necessary for this Court to determine what the applicable "substantive law" is before we can decide whether demand on the Board should be excused. . . .

The stockholder derivative suit is an important . . . feature of corporate governance. In such a suit, a stockholder asserts a cause of action belonging to the corporation. . . . In a double derivative suit, such as the present case, a stockholder of a parent corporation seeks recovery for a cause of action belonging to a subsidiary corporation. . . . Because directors are empowered to manage, or direct the management of, the business and affairs of the corporation, 8 Del. C. §141(a), the right of a stockholder to prosecute a derivative suit is limited to situations where the stockholder has demanded that the directors pursue the corporate claim and they have wrongfully refused to do so or where demand is excused because the directors are incapable of making an impartial decision regarding such litigation. *Levine*, 591 A.2d at 200. Fed. R. Civ. P. 23.1, like Chancery Court Rule 23.1, constitutes the procedural embodiment of this substantive principle of corporation law.[7] . . .

Because . . . derivative suits challenge the propriety of decisions made by directors pursuant to their managerial authority, we have repeatedly held that the stockholder plaintiffs must overcome the powerful presumptions of the business judgment rule before they will be permitted to pursue the derivative claim. . . . Our decision in *Aronson* enunciated the test for determining a derivative plaintiff's compliance with this fundamental threshold obligation: "whether, under the particularized facts alleged, a reasonable doubt is created that: (1) the directors are disinterested and independent [or] (2) the

---

7. The United States Supreme Court has recognized that the demand requirements for a derivative suit are determined by the law of the state of incorporation in *Kamen v. Kemper Fin. Servs., Inc.*, 500 U.S. 90, 111 S. Ct. 1711, 114 L. Ed. 2d 152 (1991). . . .

challenged transaction was otherwise the product of a valid exercise of business judgment." 473 A.2d at 814.

Although these standards are well-established, they cannot be applied in a vacuum. Not all derivative suits fall into the paradigm addressed by *Aronson* and its progeny. The essential predicate for the *Aronson* test is the fact that a decision of the board of directors is being challenged in the derivative suit. . . .

Under the unique circumstances of this case, an analysis of the Board's ability to consider a demand requires a departure here from the standards set forth in *Aronson*. The Board did not approve the transaction which is being challenged by Blasband in this action. In fact, the Danaher directors have made no decision relating to the subject of this derivative suit. Where there is no conscious decision by directors to act or refrain from acting, the business judgment rule has no application. *Aronson*, 473 A.2d at 813. The absence of board action, therefore, makes it impossible to perform the essential inquiry contemplated by *Aronson* — whether the directors have acted in conformity with the business judgment rule in approving the challenged transaction.

Consistent with the context and rationale of the *Aronson* decision, a court should not apply the *Aronson* test for demand futility where the board that would be considering the demand did not make a business decision which is being challenged in the derivative suit. This situation would arise in three principal scenarios: (1) where a business decision was made by the board of a company, but a majority of the directors making the decision have been replaced; (2) where the subject of the derivative suit is not a business decision of the board; and (3) where, as here, the decision being challenged was made by the board of a different corporation.

Instead, it is appropriate in these situations to examine whether the board that would be addressing the demand can impartially consider its merits without being influenced by improper considerations. Thus, a court must determine whether or not the particularized factual allegations of a derivative stockholder complaint create a reasonable doubt that, as of the time the complaint is filed, the board of directors could have properly exercised its independent and disinterested business judgment in responding to a demand. If the derivative plaintiff satisfies this burden, then demand will be excused as futile.

In so holding, we reject the defendants' proposal that, for purposes of this derivative suit and future similar suits, we adopt either a universal demand requirement or a requirement that a plaintiff must demonstrate a reasonable probability of success on the merits. The defendants seek to justify these stringent tests on the need to discourage "strike suits" in situations like the present one. This concern is unfounded.

A plaintiff in a double derivative suit is still required to satisfy the *Aronson* test in order to establish that demand on the subsidiary's board is futile. The *Aronson* test was designed, in part, with the objective of preventing strike suits by requiring derivative plaintiffs to make a threshold showing, through the allegation of particularized facts, that their claims have some merit. *Aronson*, 473 A.2d at 811-812. Moreover, defendants' proposal of requiring demand on the parent board in all double derivative cases, even where a board of directors is interested, is not the appropriate protection against strike suits. While defendants' alternative suggestion of requiring a plaintiff to demonstrate a reasonable probability of success is more closely related to the prevention of strike suits, it is an extremely onerous burden to meet at the pleading stage without the benefit of discovery.[10] Because a plaintiff must satisfy the *Aronson* test in order to show that demand is excused on the subsidiary board, there is no need to create an unduly onerous test for determining demand futility on the parent board simply to protect against strike suits.

In order to determine whether the Board could have impartially considered a demand at the time Blasband's original complaint was filed, it is appropriate to examine the nature of the decision confronting it. A stockholder demand letter would, at a minimum, notify the directors of the nature of the alleged wrongdoing and the identities of the alleged wrong-doers. The subject of the demand in this case would be the alleged breaches of fiduciary duty by the Easco board of directors in connection with Easco's investment in Drexel "junk bonds." The allegations of the amended complaint, which must be accepted as true in this procedural context, claim that the investment was made solely for the benefit of the Rales brothers, who were acting in furtherance of their business relationship with Drexel and not with regard to Easco's best interests. Such conduct, if proven, would constitute a breach of the Easco directors' duty of loyalty. . . .

The task of a board of directors in responding to a stockholder demand letter is a two-step process. First, the directors must determine the best method to inform themselves of the facts relating to the alleged wrongdoing and the considerations, both legal and financial, bearing on a response to the demand. If a factual investigation is required,[11] it must be conducted reasonably and in good faith. . . . Second, the board must weigh the alternatives

---

10. Although derivative plaintiffs may believe it is difficult to meet the particularization requirement of *Aronson* because they are not entitled to discovery to assist their compliance with Rule 23.1, see *Levine*, 591 A.2d at 208-10, they have many avenues available to obtain information bearing on the subject of their claims. For example, there are a variety of public sources from which the details of a corporate act may be discovered, including the media and governmental agencies such as the Securities and Exchange Commission. In addition, a stockholder who has met the procedural requirements and has shown a specific proper purpose may use the summary procedure embodied in 8 Del. C. §220 to investigate the possibility of corporate wrongdoing. *Compaq Computer Corp. v. Horton*, Del. Supr., 631 A.2d 1 (1993). Surprisingly little use has been made of §220 as an information-gathering tool in the derivative context. Perhaps the problem arises in some cases out of an unseemly race to the court house, chiefly generated by the "first to file" custom seemingly permitting the winner of the race to be named lead counsel. The result has been a plethora of superficial complaints that could not be sustained. . . . [This became less true after this opinion was issued. More recently, some plaintiffs indeed do file a §220 case to get information prior to filing a derivative claim, although in attacks on mergers of their transactions, the dynamic of the race to the courthouse continues to make the practice rare in those cases — Eds.]

11. In most instances, a factual investigation is appropriate so that the board can be fully informed about the validity, if any, of the claims of wrongdoing contained in the demand letter. Nevertheless, a formal investigation will not always be necessary because the directors may already have sufficient information regarding the subject of the demand to make a decision in response to it. See *Levine*, 591 A.2d at 214. In such a case, the minutes or other writing of the Board may properly reference that information in a summary manner.

available to it, including the advisability of implementing internal corrective action and commencing legal proceedings. . . . In carrying out these tasks, the board must be able to act free of personal financial interest and improper extraneous influences.[12] We now consider whether the members of the Board could have met these standards. . . .

The members of the Board at the time Blasband filed his original complaint were Steven Rales, Mitchell Rales, Sherman, Ehrlich, Caplin, Kellner, Stephenson, and Lohr. The Rales brothers and Caplin were also members of the Easco board of directors at the time of the alleged wrong-doing. Blasband's amended complaint specifically accuses the Rales brothers of being the motivating force behind the investment in Drexel "junk bonds." The Board would be obligated to determine whether these charges of wrongdoing should be investigated and, if substantiated, become the subject of legal action.

A director is considered interested where he or she will receive a personal financial benefit from a transaction that is not equally shared by the stockholders. Directorial interest also exists where a corporate decision will have a materially detrimental impact on a director, but not on the corporation and the stockholders. In such circumstances, a director cannot be expected to exercise his or her independent business judgment without being influenced by the adverse personal consequences resulting from the decision.

We conclude that the Rales brothers and Caplin must be considered interested in a decision of the Board in response to a demand addressing the alleged wrongdoing described in Blasband's amended complaint. Normally, "the mere threat of personal liability for approving a questioned transaction, standing alone, is insufficient to challenge either the independence or disinterestedness of directors. . . ." *Aronson*, 473 A.2d at 815. Nevertheless, the Third Circuit has already concluded that "Blasband has pleaded facts raising at least a reasonable doubt that the [Easco board's] use of proceeds from the Note Offering was a valid exercise of business judgment." *Blasband I*, 971 F.2d at 1052. This determination is part of the law of the case, *Blasband II*, 979 F.2d at 328, and is therefore binding on this Court. Such determination indicates that the potential for liability is not "a mere threat" but instead may rise to "a substantial likelihood."[13]

. . . Common sense dictates that, in light of these consequences, the Rales brothers and Caplin have a disqualifying financial interest that disables them from impartially considering a response to a demand by Blasband.

---

12. Where a demand has actually been made, the stockholder making the demand concedes the independence and disinterestedness of a majority of the board to respond. *Spiegel*, 571 A.2d at 777; *Levine*, 591 A.2d at 212-13. In the present context, however, no demand has been made and the Court must determine whether the Board could have considered a demand without being affected by improper influences. See *Aronson*, 473 A.2d at 816.

13. We emphasize that this assessment of potential liability is based solely on the presumed truthfulness of the allegations of Blasband's amended complaint and the Third Circuit's conclusions thereon, all of which must be accepted by this Court in the present procedural posture. No portion of our decision should be interpreted as a prediction regarding the outcome of this litigation since the Easco defendants have not had the opportunity to rebut Blasband's allegations of wrongdoing.

[W]e must now examine whether the remaining Danaher directors are sufficiently independent to make an impartial decision despite the fact that they are presumptively disinterested. . . . To establish lack of independence, Blasband must show that the directors are "beholden" to the Rales brothers or so under their influence that their discretion would be sterilized. . . . We conclude that the amended complaint alleges particularized facts sufficient to create a reasonable doubt that Sherman and Ehrlich, as members of the Board, are capable of acting independently of the Rales brothers.

Sherman is the President and Chief Executive Officer of Danaher. His salary is approximately $1 million per year. Although Sherman's continued employment and substantial remuneration may not hinge solely on his relationship with the Rales brothers, there is little doubt that Steven Rales' position as Chairman of the Board of Danaher and Mitchell Rales' position as Chairman of its Executive Committee place them in a position to exert considerable influence over Sherman. In light of these circumstances, there is a reasonable doubt that Sherman can be expected to act independently considering his substantial financial stake in maintaining his current offices.

Ehrlich is the President of Wabash National Corp. ("Wabash"). His annual compensation is approximately $300,000 per year. Ehrlich also has two brothers who are vice presidents of Wabash. The Rales brothers are directors of Wabash and own a majority of its stock through an investment partnership they control. As a result, there is a reasonable doubt regarding Ehrlich's ability to act independently since it can be inferred that he is beholden to the Rales brothers in light of his employment.

Therefore, the amended complaint pleads particularized facts raising a reasonable doubt as to the independence of Sherman and Ehrlich. . . .

We conclude that, under the "substantive law" of the State of Delaware, the *Aronson* test does not apply in the context of this double derivative suit because the Board was not involved in the challenged transaction. . . . Instead, the appropriate inquiry is whether Blasband's amended complaint raises a reasonable doubt regarding the ability of a majority of the Board to exercise properly its business judgment in a decision on a demand had one been made at the time this action was filed. Based on the existence of a reasonable doubt that the Rales brothers and Caplin would be free of a financial interest in such a decision, and that Sherman and Ehrlich could act independently in light of their employment with entities affiliated with the Rales brothers, we conclude that the allegations of Blasband's amended complaint establish that DEMAND IS EXCUSED on the Board.

NOTES AND QUESTIONS ON RALES v. BLASBAND

1. The court describes this case as "special" and distinguishes earlier statements indicating that it is the independence and good faith of the board that made the challenged decision (i.e., Easco) that matters for an exemption from pre-suit demand. But is this case special in an important way? Which board's decision should the court review: the decision by the board

to approve a disputed transaction or the decision by a later board to refuse to bring or to dismiss the suit?

The Court of Chancery very recently addressed this question in *United Food & Commercial Workers Union v. Zuckerberg et al.*, C.A. No. 2018-0671-JTL (Del. Ch. Oct. 26, 2020). Facebook's board had first proposed a reclassification of its shares, which it then later withdrew. Plaintiff-shareholder alleged that the board had violated its fiduciary duties when first approving the reclassification and sought to excuse demand by arguing that a narrow majority of the board which would have considered demand had also approved the challenged transaction. Vice Chancellor Laster held that *Aronson*'s analytical framework was "not up to the task" of addressing demand in modern derivative suits and instead relied on *Rales* while injecting some aspects of *Aronson* into it. The court asked for each director "(i) whether the director received a material personal benefit from the alleged misconduct that is the subject of the litigation demand, (ii) whether the director would face a substantial likelihood of liability on any of the claims that are the subject of the litigation demand, and (iii) whether the director lacks independence from someone who received a material personal benefit from the alleged misconduct that is the subject of the litigation demand or who would face a substantial likelihood of liability on any of the claims that are the subject of the litigation demand." *Zuckerberg*, at 42. The court then found that demand was not excused. This decision offers to add greater conceptual clarity by focusing on whether the board considering demand can decide about this litigation impartially and in good faith. Whether the Delaware Supreme Court will adopt this formulation will have to await an appeal.

2. In *Lambrecht v. O'Neal*, 3 A.3d 277 (Del. 2010), the Delaware Supreme Court addressed the question of standing in a double derivative action. The plaintiffs were former Merrill Lynch shareholders, who filed standard derivative actions on behalf of Merrill Lynch, a Delaware corporation, to recover losses Merrill suffered in transactions that occurred before Bank of America acquired Merrill Lynch in a stock-for-stock merger in January 2009. After the merger, the complaints were amended to take the form of double derivative actions, in which the plaintiffs sought the same relief. Applying the conceptualization of double derivative actions articulated by the court in *Rales*, the Delaware Supreme Court held that plaintiffs suing in a double derivative action who were pre-merger shareholders in the acquired company and who are current shareholders, by virtue of a stock-for-stock merger, in the post-merger parent company, are not required to demonstrate that, at the time of the alleged wrongdoing, they owned stock in the acquiring company or that the acquiring company owned stock in the acquired company.

Apart from the relationship between the two prongs of the *Aronson* test, questions remain about what plaintiffs must show to create credible doubt about the business judgment of today's board in responding to a demand request. *Rales v. Blasband* answers these questions in part. Former Chief Justice Strine further clarifies the requirements for demand futility in *Marchand*, the facts and holding of which have already been introduced in Chapter 7.

MARCHAND v. BARNHILL
212 A.3d 805 (Del. 2019)

Strine, C.J.:

The defendants moved to dismiss the complaint for failure to plead demand futility. The Court of Chancery . . . held that [a]lthough the complaint alleged facts sufficient to raise a reasonable doubt as to the impartiality of a number of Blue Bell's directors, the plaintiff ultimately came up one short . . . the plaintiff needed [to raise such doubts about the impartiality of] eight directors but only had seven. . . . [W]e reverse. . . .

We . . . hold that the complaint pleads particularized facts sufficient to create a reasonable doubt that an additional director, W.J. Rankin, could act impartially in deciding to sue Paul Kruse, Blue Bell's CEO, . . . due to Rankin's longstanding business affiliation and personal relationship with the Kruse family. . . . Despite the defendants' contentions that Rankin's relationship with the Kruse family was just an ordinary business relationship from which Rankin would derive no strong feelings of loyalty toward the Kruse family, [the plaintiffs'] allegations are "suggestive of the type of very close personal [or professional] relationship that, like family ties, one would expect to heavily influence a human's ability to exercise impartial judgment."[7] Rankin's . . . ties to the Kruse family raise a reasonable doubt as to whether Rankin could "impartially or objectively assess whether to bring a lawsuit against the sued party."[8] . . .

[T]he Court of Chancery held that the plaintiff "failed to plead particularized facts to raise a reasonable doubt that a majority of the [Blue Bell board] members could have impartially considered a pre-suit demand." Without belaboring the details of the Court of Chancery's thorough analysis, . . . we note that the court essentially ruled that the plaintiff came up one vote short. To survive the Rule 23.1 motion to dismiss, the complaint needed to allege particularized facts raising a reasonable doubt that directors holding eight of the 15 votes could have impartially considered a demand, but the court held that the plaintiff had done so for directors holding only seven votes.

One of the directors who the trial court held could consider demand impartially was Rankin, Blue Bell's recently retired former CFO. Although Rankin worked at Blue Bell for 28 years, the court emphasized that he was no longer employed by Blue Bell, having retired in 2014 [and that other allegations] . . . fell short of Rule 23.1's particularity requirement. Further, the court noted that Rankin voted against rescinding a board initiative to split the CEO and Chairman positions held by Paul Kruse. In the court's view, that act was evidence that Rankin was not beholden to the Kruse family. . . .

A.   RANKIN'S INDEPENDENCE

On appeal, both parties agree that the *Rales* standard applies, and we therefore use it to determine whether . . . a majority of the board was

---

7. *Sandys v. Pincus*, 152 A.3d 124, 130 (Del. 2016).
8. *In re Oracle Corp. Derivative Litig.*, 824 A.2d 917, 942 (Del. Ch. 2003).

independent for pleading stage purposes. "[A] lack of independence turns on 'whether the plaintiffs have pled facts from which the director's ability to act impartially on a matter important to the interested party can be doubted because that director may feel either subject to the interested party's dominion or beholden to that interested party."[86] When it comes to life's more intimate relationships concerning friendship and family, our law cannot "ignore the social nature of humans" or that they are motivated by things other than money, such as "love, friendship, and collegiality. . . ."[87]

From the pled facts, there is reason to doubt Rankin's capacity to impartially decide whether to sue members of the Kruse family. For starters, one can reasonably infer that Rankin's successful career as a businessperson was in large measure due to the opportunities and mentoring given to him by Ed Kruse, Paul Kruse's father, and other members of the Kruse family. The complaint alleges that Rankin started as Ed Kruse's administrative assistant and, over the course of a 28-year career with the company, rose to the high managerial position of CFO. Not only that, but Rankin was added to Blue Bell's board in 2004, which one can reasonably infer was due to the support of the Kruse family. Capping things off, the Kruse family spearheaded charitable efforts that led to a $450,000 donation to a key local college, resulting in Rankin being honored by having Blinn College's new agricultural facility named after him. On a cold complaint, these facts support a reasonable inference that there are very warm and thick personal ties of respect, loyalty, and affection between Rankin and the Kruse family, which creates a reasonable doubt that Rankin could have impartially decided whether to sue Paul Kruse and his subordinate Bridges.

Even though Rankin had ties to the Kruse family that were similar to other directors that the Court of Chancery found were sufficient at the pleading stage to support an inference that they could not act impartially in deciding whether to cause Blue Bell to sue Paul Kruse, the Court of Chancery concluded that because Rankin had voted differently from Paul Kruse on a proposal to separate the CEO and Chairman position, these ties did not matter. In doing so, the Court of Chancery ignored that the decision whether to sue someone is materially different and more important than the decision whether to part company with that person on a vote about corporate governance, and our law's precedent recognizes that the nature of the decision at issue must be considered in determining whether a director is independent.[95]

As important, at the pleading stage, the Court of Chancery was bound to accord the plaintiff the benefit of all reasonable inferences, and the pled facts

---

86. *Sandys v. Pincus*, 152 A.3d 124, 128 (Del. 2016) (quoting *Del. Cty. Emps. Ret. Fund v. Sanchez*, 124 A.3d 1017, 1024 n.25 (Del. 2015)).

87. *In re Oracle Corp. Derivative Litig.*, 824 A.2d 917, 938 (Del. Ch. 2003) ("Delaware law should not be based on a reductionist view of human nature that simplifies human motivations on the lines of the least sophisticated notions of the law and economics movement.") . . .

95. *See Sandys v. Pincus*, 152 A.3d 124, 134 (Del. 2016) ("Causing a lawsuit to be brought against another person is no small matter, and is the sort of thing that might plausibly endanger a relationship."); . . . *In re Oracle Corp. Derivative Litig.*, 824 A.2d 917, 940 (Del. Ch. 2003) (". . . It is, I daresay, easier to say no to a friend, relative, colleague, or boss who seeks assent for an act (e.g., a transaction) that has not yet occurred than it would be to cause a corporation to sue that person [, which may involve finding] . . . that the fellow director has committed serious wrongdoing. . . .")

fairly support the inference that Rankin owes an important debt of gratitude and friendship to the Kruse family for giving him his first job, nurturing his progress from an entry level position to a top manager and director, and honoring him by spearheading a campaign to name a building at an important community institution after him. Although the fact that fellow directors are social acquaintances who occasionally have dinner or go to common events does not, in itself, raise a fair inference of non-independence, our law has recognized that deep and long-standing friendships are meaningful to human beings and that any realistic consideration of the question of independence must give weight to these important relationships and their natural effect on the ability of the parties to act impartially toward each other. As in cases like *Sandys v. Pincus*[97] and *Delaware County Employees Retirement Fund v. Sanchez*,[98] the important personal and business relationship that Rankin and the Kruse family have shared supports a pleading-stage inference that Rankin cannot act independently.

Because the complaint pleads particularized facts that raise a reasonable doubt as to Rankin's independence, we reverse the Court of Chancery's dismissal of the plaintiff's claims against management for failure to adequately plead demand futility.

NOTE AND QUESTIONS ON ABA AND ALI PROPOSALS FOR REFORM

Both the American Bar Association and the American Law Institute have proposed wholesale — and in some respects similar — revisions of the common law screening doctrines developed by the Delaware courts. Read over MBCA §§7.42-7.44, and compare these provisions to ALI, Principles of Corporate Governance §§7.03, 7.08, and 7.10.

1. How would you contrast the common approach of the ALI and the MBCA to the demand requirement with that of the Delaware courts? Which approach do you prefer?

2. How do the approaches of the ALI and the MBCA differ? Which places more faith in the corporate board?

3. Will either reform proposal significantly improve shareholder litigation incentives?

10.4.2 Special Litigation Committees

In contrast to the demand requirement, which is embedded in Rule 23.1 of the Federal Rules of Civil Procedure, there is no basis in positive law for a

---

97. 152 A.3d 124, 130 (Del. 2016) (holding that owning an airplane with the interested party "is suggestive of the type of very close personal relationship that, like family ties, one would expect to heavily influence a human's ability to exercise impartial judgment").

98. 124 A.3d 1017, 1020-22 (Del. 2015) (holding that being "close personal friends for more than five decades" with the interested party gives rise to "a pleading stage inference . . . that it is important to the parties" and suggests that the director is not independent).

procedure under which a court, upon the motion of a special committee of disinterested directors, may dismiss a derivative suit that is already underway. Nevertheless, many state courts adopted such a special litigation procedure under the pressure of growing numbers of shareholder suits in the 1970s and 1980s.[19] The special litigation committee (SLC) is now a standard feature of derivative suit doctrine even though it is not triggered in every case (unlike the demand requirement). Different jurisdictions treated the question differently. The chief divide is between those jurisdictions that follow Delaware's lead in the 1981 case of *Zapata Corp. v. Maldonado* (excerpted below) in giving the court a role in judging the appropriateness of an SLC's decision and those jurisdictions, such as New York, that apply a rule that, if the committee is independent and informed, it is entitled to business judgment deference without any further judicial second-guessing. See *Auerbach v. Bennett*, 393 N.E.2d 994 (N.Y. 1979).

ZAPATA CORP. v. MALDONADO
430 A.2d 779 (Del. 1981)

QUILLEN, J.:

In June, 1975, William Maldonado, a stockholder of Zapata, instituted a derivative action in the Court of Chancery on behalf of Zapata against ten officers and/or directors of Zapata, alleging, essentially, breaches of fiduciary duty. Maldonado did not first demand that the board bring this action, stating instead such demand's futility because all directors were named as defendants and allegedly participated in the acts specified. . . .

By June, 1979, four of the defendant-directors were no longer on the board, and the remaining directors appointed two new outside directors to the board. The board then created an "Independent Investigation Committee" (Committee), composed solely of the two new directors, to investigate Maldonado's actions, as well as a similar derivative action then pending in Texas, and to determine whether the corporation should continue any or all of the litigation. The Committee's determination was stated to be "final . . . not . . . subject to review by the Board of Directors and . . . in all respects . . . binding upon the Corporation."

Following an investigation, the Committee concluded, in September, 1979, that each action should "be dismissed forthwith as their continued maintenance is inimical to the Company's best interests. . . ."* Consequently, Zapata moved for dismissal or summary judgment. . . .

19. See Robert Charles Clark, Corporate Law, at 645-649.
* As reasons for dismissal, the Committee stated: "(1) the asserted claims appeared to be without merit; (2) costs of litigation, exacerbated by likelihood of indemnification; (3) wasted senior management time and talents on pursuing litigation; (4) damage to company from publicity; (5) that no material injury appeared to have been done to company; (6) impairment of current director-defendants' ability to manage; (7) the slight possibility of recurrence of violations; (8) lack of personal benefit to current director-defendants from alleged conduct; (9) that

[W]e turn first to the Court of Chancery's conclusions concerning the right of a plaintiff stockholder in a derivative action. We find that its determination that a stockholder, once demand is made and refused, possesses an independent, individual right to continue a derivative suit for breaches of fiduciary duty over objection by the corporation, . . . is erroneous. . . . *McKee v. Rogers*, Del. Ch., 156 A. 191 (1931), stated "as a general rule" that "a stockholder cannot be permitted . . . to invade the discretionary field committed to the judgment of the directors and sue in the corporation's behalf when the managing body refuses. This rule is a well settled one." 156 A. at 193.

The *McKee* rule, of course, should not be read so broadly that the board's refusal will be determinative in every instance. Board members, owing a well-established fiduciary duty to the corporation, will not be allowed to cause a derivative suit to be dismissed when it would be a breach of their fiduciary duty. Generally disputes pertaining to control of the suit arise in two contexts.

Consistent with the purpose of requiring a demand, a board decision to cause a derivative suit to be dismissed as detrimental to the company, after demand has been made and refused, will be respected unless it was wrongful.[10] . . . A claim of a wrongful decision not to sue is thus the first exception and the first context of dispute. Absent a wrongful refusal, the stockholder in such a situation simply lacks legal managerial power. . . .

But it cannot be implied that, absent a wrongful board refusal, a stockholder can never have an individual right to initiate an action. For, as is stated in *McKee*, a "well settled" exception exists to the general rule. "[A] stockholder may sue in equity in his derivative right to assert a cause of action in behalf of the corporation, *without prior demand* upon the directors to sue, when it is apparent that a demand would be futile, that the officers are under an influence that sterilizes discretion and could not be proper persons to conduct the litigation." . . . A demand, when required and refused (if not wrongful), terminates a stockholder's legal ability to initiate a derivative action. But where demand is properly excused, the stockholder does possess the ability to initiate the action on his corporation's behalf.

These conclusions, however, do not determine the question before us. Rather, they merely bring us to the question to be decided . . . : When, if at all, should an authorized board committee be permitted to cause litigation, properly initiated by a derivative stockholder in his own right, to be dismissed? As noted above, a board has the power to choose not to pursue litigation when demand is made upon it, so long as the decision is not wrongful. If the board

---

certain alleged practices were continuing business practices, intended to be in company's best interests; (10) legal question whether the complaints stated a cause of action; (11) fear of undermining employee morale; (12) adverse effects on the company's relations with employees and suppliers and customers." *Maldonado v. Flynn*, 485 F. Supp. 274, 284 n.35 (S.D.N.Y. 1980). — Eds.

10. In other words, when stockholders, after making demand and having their suit rejected, attack the board's decision as improper, the board's decision falls under the "business judgment" rule and will be respected if the requirements of the rule are met. . . . That situation should be distinguished from the instant case, where demand was not made, and the *power* of the board to seek a dismissal, due to disqualification, presents a threshold issue. . . . We recognize that the two contexts can overlap in practice.

determines that a suit would be detrimental to the company, the board's determination prevails. Even when demand is excusable, circumstances may arise when continuation of the litigation would not be in the corporation's best interests. Our inquiry is whether, under such circumstances, there is a permissible procedure under §141(a) by which a corporation can rid itself of detrimental litigation. If there is not, a single stockholder in an extreme case might control the destiny of the entire corporation. . . .

Section 141(c) allows a board to delegate all of its authority to a committee. Accordingly, a committee with properly delegated authority would have the power to move for dismissal or summary judgment if the entire board did.

Even though demand was not made in this case and the initial decision of whether to litigate was not placed before the board, Zapata's board, it seems to us, retained all of its corporate power concerning litigation decisions. If Maldonado had made demand on the board in this case, it could have refused to bring suit. Maldonado could then have asserted that the decision not to sue was wrongful and, if correct, would have been allowed to maintain the suit. The board, however, never would have lost its statutory managerial authority. . . . Similarly, Rule 23.1, by excusing demand in certain instances, does not strip the board of its corporate power. It merely saves the plaintiff the expense and delay of making a futile demand resulting in a probable tainted exercise of that authority in a refusal by the board or in giving control of litigation to the opposing side. But the board entity remains empowered under §141(a) to make decisions regarding corporate litigation. The problem is one of member disqualification, not the absence of power in the board.

The corporate power inquiry then focuses on whether the board, tainted by the self-interest of a majority of its members, can legally delegate its authority to a committee of two disinterested directors. We find our statute clearly requires an affirmative answer to this question. As has been noted, under an express provision of the statute, §141(c), a committee can exercise all of the authority of the board to the extent provided in the resolution of the board. . . .

We do not think that the interest taint of the board majority is per se a legal bar to the delegation of the board's power to an independent committee composed of disinterested board members. The committee can properly act for the corporation to move to dismiss derivative litigation that is believed to be detrimental to the corporation's best interest.

Our focus now switches to the Court of Chancery which is faced with a stockholder assertion that a derivative suit, properly instituted, should continue for the benefit of the corporation and a corporate assertion, properly made by a board committee acting with board authority, that the same derivative suit should be dismissed as inimical to the best interests of the corporation.

At the risk of stating the obvious, the problem is relatively simple. If, on the one hand, corporations can consistently wrest bona fide derivative actions away from well-meaning derivative plaintiffs through the use of the committee mechanism, the derivative suit will lose much, if not all, of its generally-recognized effectiveness as an intra-corporate means of policing boards of directors. . . . If, on the other hand, corporations are unable to rid themselves of meritless or harmful litigation and strike suits, the derivative action, created to benefit the corporation, will produce the opposite, unintended result. . . . It thus appears desirable to us to find a balancing point where bona fide stockholder power to bring corporate causes of action cannot be unfairly trampled on by the board of directors, but the corporation can rid itself of detrimental litigation.

[T]he question has been treated by other courts as one of the "business judgment" of the board committee. If a "committee, composed of independent and disinterested directors, conducted a proper review of the matters before it, considered a variety of factors and reached, in good faith, a business judgment that [the] action was not in the best interest of [the corporation]," the action must be dismissed. . . . The issues become solely independence, good faith, and reasonable investigation. The ultimate conclusion of the committee, under that view, is not subject to judicial review.[11] . . .

We are not satisfied, however, that acceptance of the "business judgment" rationale at this stage of derivative litigation is a proper balancing point. While we admit an analogy with a normal case respecting board judgment, it seems to us that there is sufficient risk in the realities of a situation like the one presented in this case to justify caution beyond adherence to the theory of business judgment.

The context here is a suit against directors where demand on the board is excused. We think some tribute must be paid to the fact that the lawsuit was properly initiated. It is not a board refusal case. Moreover, this complaint was filed in June of 1975 and, while the parties undoubtedly would take differing views on the degree of litigation activity, we have to be concerned about the creation of an "Independent Investigation Committee" four years later, after the election of two new outside directors. Situations could develop where such motions could be filed after years of vigorous litigation for reasons unconnected with the merits of the lawsuit.

Moreover, notwithstanding our conviction that Delaware law entrusts the corporate power to a properly authorized committee, we must be mindful that directors are passing judgment on fellow directors in the same corporation and fellow directors, in this instance, who designated them to serve both as directors and committee members. The question naturally arises whether a "there but for the grace of God go I" empathy might not play a role. And the further question arises whether inquiry as to independence, good faith and reasonable investigation is sufficient safeguard against abuse, perhaps subconscious abuse.

. . . There is some analogy to a settlement in that there is a request to terminate litigation without a judicial determination of the merits. . . . "In determining whether or not to approve a proposed settlement of a derivative stockholders' action [when directors are on both sides of the transaction], the Court of Chancery is called upon to exercise its own business judgment." *Neponsit Investment Co. v. Abramson*, Del. Supr., 405 A.2d 97, 100 (1979) and cases therein cited. In this case, the litigating stockholder plaintiff facing

---

11. The leading case is *Auerbach v. Bennett*, . . . 393 N.E.2d 994 . . . (1979).

dismissal of a lawsuit properly commenced ought, in our judgment, to have sufficient status for strict Court review. . . .

Whether the Court of Chancery will be persuaded by the exercise of a committee power resulting in a summary motion for dismissal of a derivative action, where a demand has not been initially made, should rest, in our judgment, in the independent discretion of the Court of Chancery. We thus steer a middle course between those cases which yield to the independent business judgment of a board committee and this case as determined below which would yield to unbridled plaintiff stockholder control. In pursuit of the course, we recognize that "[t]he final substantive judgment whether a particular lawsuit should be maintained requires a balance of many factors ethical, commercial, promotional, public relations, employee relations, fiscal as well as legal." *Maldonado v. Flynn, supra*, 485 F. Supp. at 285. But we are content that such factors are not "beyond the judicial reach" of the Court of Chancery which regularly and competently deals with fiduciary relationships, disposition of trust property, approval of settlements and scores of similar problems. We recognize the danger of judicial overreaching but the alternatives seem to us to be outweighed by the fresh view of a judicial outsider. Moreover, if we failed to balance all the interests involved, we would in the name of practicality and judicial economy foreclose a judicial decision on the merits. At this point, we are not convinced that is necessary or desirable.

After an objective and thorough investigation of a derivative suit, an independent committee may cause its corporation to file a pretrial motion to dismiss in the Court of Chancery. The basis of the motion is the best interests of the corporation, as determined by the committee. The motion should include a thorough written record of the investigation and its findings and recommendations. Under appropriate Court supervision, akin to proceedings on summary judgment, each side should have an opportunity to make a record on the motion. As to the limited issues presented by the motion noted below, the moving party should be prepared to meet the normal burden under Rule 56 that there is no genuine issue as to any material fact and that the moving party is entitled to dismiss as a matter of law. The Court should apply a two-step test to the motion.

First, the Court should inquire into the independence and good faith of the committee and the bases supporting its conclusions. Limited discovery may be ordered to facilitate such inquiries. The corporation should have the burden of proving independence, good faith and a reasonable investigation, rather than presuming independence, good faith and reasonableness.[17] If the Court determines either that the committee is not independent or has not shown reasonable bases for its conclusions, or, if the Court is not satisfied for other reasons relating to the process, including but not limited to the good faith of the committee, the Court shall deny the corporation's motion. If, however, the Court is satisfied under . . . [summary judgment] standards that the committee was independent and showed reasonable bases for good faith

---

17. Compare *Auerbach v. Bennett*, 393 N.E.2d 994 (1979). Our approach here is analogous to and consistent with the Delaware approach to "interested director" transactions, where the directors, once the transaction is attacked, have the burden of establishing its "intrinsic fairness" to a court's careful scrutiny. . . .

findings and recommendations, the Court may proceed, in its discretion, to the next step.

The second step provides, we believe, the essential key in striking the balance between legitimate corporate claims as expressed in a derivative stockholder suit and a corporation's best interests as expressed by an independent investigating committee. The Court should determine, applying its own independent business judgment, whether the motion should be granted.[18] This means, of course, that instances could arise where a committee can establish its independence and sound bases for its good faith decisions and still have the corporation's motion denied. The second step is intended to thwart instances where corporate actions meet the criteria of step one, but the result does not appear to satisfy its spirit, or where corporate actions would simply prematurely terminate a stockholder grievance deserving of further consideration in the corporation's interest. The Court of Chancery of course must carefully consider and weigh how compelling the corporate interest in dismissal is when faced with a non-frivolous lawsuit. The Court of Chancery should, when appropriate, give special consideration to matters of law and public policy in addition to the corporation's best interests.

If the Court's independent business judgment is satisfied, the Court may proceed to grant the motion, subject, of course, to any equitable terms or conditions the Court finds necessary or desirable.

. . . [Reversed and remanded.]

NOTES AND QUESTIONS ON ZAPATA v. MALDONADO

1. If, as *Zapata* holds, a court may second-guess the board's evaluation of a derivative action when demand is excused, why shouldn't a court be able to do the same in cases in which demand was required but the board rejected suit? Academic commentary has generally criticized the "demand required/demand excused" distinction,[20] arguing that courts should be able to exercise their own judgment in both classes of cases. As one might expect, corporate counsel have criticized this distinction in the name of *Auerbach v. Bennett* and have urged that the board's business judgment should prevail in both classes of cases.

2. What elements should be included in an appraisal of the corporation's "best interests" in the second step of the *Zapata* test? In particular, what "matters of law and public policy" — if any — should a court consider in addition to the corporation's economic best interests? Would a court's decision to weigh matters other than the company's economic interests be consistent with viewing the derivative suit as an asset "belonging to" the corporation? (One former Delaware Chancery Court judge was heard to confide about

---

18. This step shares some of the same spirit and philosophy of the statement by the Vice Chancellor: "Under our system of law, courts and not litigants should decide the merits of litigation." 413 A.2d at 1263.

20. E.g., Reporters Notes to ALI, Principles of Corporate Governance §7.03 (1994).

the second level of *Zapata* inquiry, "I have no business judgment. If I had I wouldn't be a judge.")

3. In a later case, *Kaplan v. Wyatt*, 499 A.2d 1184 (Del. 1988), the Delaware Supreme Court held that whether to proceed to the second step of the *Zapata* test, and how much discovery to accord derivative plaintiffs, lies entirely within the discretion of the Delaware Chancery Court.

NOTE ON JUDICIAL INQUIRY INTO THE INDEPENDENCE OF A SPECIAL LITIGATION COMMITTEE

As you know from earlier chapters, independence is a key concept in corporate law. Ordinarily, independence means that a person has no *financial* ties to the firm, its executives, directors, and controllers.[21] Sometimes, however, Delaware courts expand the inquiry beyond financial ties to include other considerations for assessing independence, such as social connections. The focus is no longer financial disinterest alone but rather whether the person can act impartially, more generally, as in *Zapata* and the *Marchand* decisions (excerpted above).

Prior to *Marchand*, Chief Justice Strine (when he was Vice Chancellor) had addressed the issue of independence in an earlier SLC case, *In re Oracle Corp. Derivative Litigation*, 824 A. 2d 917 (Del. Ch. 2003). This decision involved allegations that some members of Oracle's top management (including its wealthy founder and controller, Larry Ellison) had engaged in insider trading and that other defendant directors violated *Caremark*. Oracle set up an SLC which, after extensive investigation and consultation, produced a 1,100-plus page tome finding that the suits should be dismissed. Plaintiffs challenged the SLC's recommendation and the independence of two of its members—two well-known and highly regarded professors at Stanford University (one of whom, Professor Joseph Grundfest, was a former SEC Commissioner). The court held that the SLC bore the burden of proving independence and had failed. The court noted that although the SLC members did not have the financial ties that traditionally raised concerns about independence, that did not end the inquiry.

> Delaware law should not be based on a reductionist view of human nature that simplifies human motivations on the lines of the least sophisticated notions of the law and economics movement. . . . To be direct, corporate directors are generally the sort of people deeply enmeshed in social institutions. Such institutions have norms, expectations that, explicitly and implicitly, influence and channel the behavior of those who participate in their operation. . . . Some things are "just not done," or only at a cost, which might not be so severe as a loss of position, but may involve a loss of standing in the institution.

21. See, e.g., *Rales* at 396 noting that "[a] director is considered interested where he or she will receive a personal financial benefit from a transaction that is not equally shared by the stockholders."

The court noted that social and other ties between Stanford, Oracle, and the primary defendants were quite "thick." For example, Oracle, Ellison, and other executives and directors had funded various initiatives at Stanford and were part of the social milieu in the Silicon Valley area. *Oracle* concluded by reiterating that there was no evidence that the two Stanford professors had been biased in favor of their fellow board members, but held that the burden was on Oracle to demonstrate their independence from social as well as economic constraints:

> Nothing in this record leads me to conclude that either of the SLC members acted out of any conscious desire to favor the Trading Defendants or to do anything other than discharge their duties with fidelity. But that is not the purpose of the independence inquiry.
>
> *Zapata* requires independence to ensure that stockholders do not have to rely upon special litigation committee members who must put aside personal considerations that are ordinarily influential in daily behavior in making the already difficult decision to accuse fellow directors of serious wrongdoing.

Following the court's rejection of the SLC's motion for dismissal, the case proceeded a bit further. However, in the end, the plaintiffs dropped their claims against some defendants and the court granted summary judgment in favor of the remaining defendants[22] — reaching the same outcomes that the SLC members had suggested earlier.

NOTES AND QUESTIONS ON IN RE ORACLE

1. The court's rationale for declining to grant the special committee's motion to dismiss is arguably less intrusive than the second step of the inquiry offered by Justice Quillen in *Zapata*. Recall that *Zapata*'s (optional) second step envisions a substantive exercise of judicial business judgment, an exercise without explicit parallels elsewhere in corporate law (although one imagines that, to some degree, courts are always cognizant of the value of shareholder litigation). As a result, *Zapata*'s second step is rarely used by Delaware courts.

2. Initially, the Delaware Supreme Court limited *In re Oracle*'s holding to the SLC context and applied an exclusively financial test of independence for other contexts, such as demand-futility assessments. See *Beam v. Martha Stewart*, 845 A.2d 1040, 1055 (Del. 2004). In the last few years, however, the Delaware Supreme Court has applied *In re Oracle*'s expanded version of independence in demand-futility cases where the firm had a controlling shareholder.[23] Although the cases don't explicitly state so, we speculate that these decisions reflect judicial concerns in assessing independence in a controlled firm rather than a desire to create a uniform independence standard across all contexts. Indeed, one could argue that boards appear more suspect in the

---

22. *In re Oracle Corp. Derivative Litigation*, C.A. No. 18751 (Nov. 24, 2004).

23. See, e.g., *Marchand* excerpted above; *Sandys v. Pincus*, 152 A.3d 124 (Del. 2016); *Del. Cty. Emps. Ret. Fund v. Sanchez*, 124 A.3d 1017 (Del. 2015).

SLC context (because the predicate is that the board appointing the SLC is not independent) and in controlled firms (because the controller appoints the board) than in other contexts, thereby warranting greater judicial scrutiny before dismissing a suit. This appears consistent with *Zapata*'s basic rationale. In light of this, might it make sense to assess independence or disinterestedness differently in different settings?

3. Consider the problem that a board now faces in the aftermath of *In re Oracle*. *Zapata* makes clear that the power to appoint an SLC comes from DGCL §141(c), which means that the SLC must consist entirely of directors. But wouldn't the independence of any current director be questioned given the "'thickness' of the social and institutional connections" between themselves and the defendant directors? And if so, would a board be forced to add new directors whenever it wished to establish an SLC? How would you advise a board that wanted to establish an SLC without changing its size, but also staying within the constraints imposed by *In re Oracle*?

4. At a conceptual level, the broader vision of independence in *In re Oracle* and *Marchand* may be in some tension with the notion of competence. Consider the following: Most people who display the competence and skills necessary to be effective as SLC members or board members are likely to be, as the *Oracle* court notes, "deeply enmeshed in social institutions." If this leads to them not being considered independent, then are we sacrificing competence for the *Oracle* vision of independence? Of course, this tension might not be crippling — for example, if the SLC members came from universities not so closely associated with Oracle — but this suggests that some further guidance may be desirable on what level of social ties are too close.

HOW DOES THE COURT EXERCISE ITS BUSINESS JUDGMENT?

What does it mean to exercise business judgment about whether litigation should go forward? Is litigation "like" an investment in a factory? And does the business judgment of a court resemble the business judgment of a corporate manager, or may the court weigh matters of public interest as well as the private interest of the firm? Consider the following excerpt from a well-known case.

JOY v. NORTH
692 F.2d 880 (2d Cir. 1982)

[In a diversity case, the court predicted that Connecticut would adopt the *Zapata* approach to derivative suits and, exercising its business judgment, rejected a special litigation committee's motion to dismiss.]

WINTER, J.:

[The dissent] is correct in anticipating difficulties in judicial review of the recommendations of special litigation committees. These difficulties are not new, however, but have confronted every court which has scrutinized the fairness of corporate transactions involving a conflict of interest.

Moreover, the difficulties courts face in evaluation of business decisions are considerably less in the case of recommendations of special litigation committees. The relevant decision — whether to continue litigation — is at hand and the danger of deceptive hindsight simply does not exist. Moreover, it can hardly be argued that terminating a lawsuit is an area in which courts have no special aptitude. Citytrust's Special Litigation Committee concluded that there was "no reasonable possibility" that 23 outside defendants would be held liable. A court is not ill-equipped to review the merits of that conclusion. Even when the Committee recommendation arises from the fear of further damage to the corporation, for example, the distraction of key personnel, the cost of complying with discovery, and the possible indemnification of defendants out of the corporate treasury, courts are not on unfamiliar terrain. The rule we predict Connecticut would establish emphasizes matters such as probable liability and extent of recovery. For these reasons we hold that the wide discretion afforded directors under the business judgment rule does not apply when a special litigation committee recommends dismissal of a suit. . . .

In cases such as the present one, the burden is on the moving party, as in motions for summary judgment generally, to demonstrate that the action is more likely than not to be against the interests of the corporation. This showing is to be based on the underlying data developed in the course of discovery and of the committee's investigation and the committee's reasoning, not simply its naked conclusions. The weight to be given certain evidence is to be determined by conventional analysis, such as whether testimony is under oath and subject to cross-examination. Finally, the function of the court's review is to determine the balance of probabilities as to likely future benefit to the corporation, not to render a decision on the merits, fashion the appropriate legal principles or resolve issues of credibility. Where the legal rule is unclear and the likely evidence in conflict, the court need only weigh the uncertainties, not resolve them. The court's function is thus not unlike a lawyer's determining what a case is "worth" for purposes of settlement.

Where the court determines that the likely recoverable damages discounted by the probability of a finding of liability are less than the costs to the corporation in continuing the action, it should dismiss the case. The costs which may properly be taken into account are attorney's fees and other out-of-pocket expenses related to the litigation and time spent by corporate personnel preparing for and participating in the trial. The court should also weigh indemnification which is mandatory under corporate bylaws, private contract or Connecticut law, discounted of course by the probability of liability for such sums. We believe indemnification the corporation may later pay as a matter of discretion should not be taken into account since it is an avoidable cost. The existence or non-existence of insurance should not be considered in the calculation of costs, since premiums have previously been paid. The existence of insurance is relevant to the calculation of potential benefits.

Where, having completed the above analysis, the court finds a likely net return to the corporation which is not substantial in relation to shareholder equity, it may take into account two other items as costs. First, it may consider the impact of distraction of key personnel by continued litigation. Second, it may take into account potential lost profits which may result from the publicity of a trial.

Judicial scrutiny of special litigation committee recommendations should thus be limited to a comparison of the direct costs imposed upon the corporation by the litigation with the potential benefits. We are mindful that other less direct costs may be incurred, such as a negative impact on morale and upon the corporate image. Nevertheless, we believe that such factors, with the two exceptions noted, should not be taken into account.

Quite apart from the elusiveness of attempting to predict such effects, they are quite likely to be directly related to the degree of wrongdoing, a spectacular fraud being generally more newsworthy and damaging to morale than a mistake in judgment as to the strength of consumer demand. . . .

CARDAMONE, Cir. J. dissented in part:

[T]he majority goes beyond [*Zapata*] by requiring that the court *must* proceed to apply its own business judgment, rather than leaving the decision to resort to the second step within the trial court's discretion. . . .

Under [*Zapata*'s] two-step analysis . . . unanswered questions abound. For example, . . . under what circumstances can the trial court conclude that the director's decision [has not satisfied *Zapata*'s criteria]; will evidence be considered by the court that was not before the independent committee; in the exercise of its "business judgment" will the court consider facts not in the record; will the court need to appoint its own experts?

The majority proposes a calculus in an attempt to resolve additional issues engendered by its analysis. This calculus is so complicated, indefinite and subject to judicial caprice as to be unworkable. For example, how is a court to determine the inherently speculative costs of future attorneys' fees and expenses related to litigation, time spent by corporate personnel preparing for trial, and mandatory indemnification "discounted of course by the probability of liability for such sums." How is a court to quantify corporate goodwill, corporate morale and "the distraction of key personnel" in cases in which it "finds a likely net return to the corporation which is not substantial in relation to shareholder equity?" Should a court also take into account the potential adverse impact of continuing litigation upon the corporation's ability to finance its operations? Should future costs be discounted to present value and, if so, at what rate? Must the income tax ramifications of expected future costs be considered and, if so, how? This veritable Pandora's box of unanswered questions raises more problems than it solves.

Even more fundamentally unsound is the majority's underlying premise that judges are equipped to make business judgments. It is a truism that judges really are not equipped either by training or experience to make business judgments. . . . Reasons of practicality and good sense strongly suggest that business decisions be left to businessmen. Whether to pursue litigation is not a judicial decision, rather, it is a business choice.

My colleagues . . . contend that director committees simply cannot be expected to act independently. Where a special litigation committee does not act independently and in good faith, its decision to terminate derivative litigation will not survive judicial scrutiny under *Auerbach*. Thus the contention that director committees will not act independently and in good faith does not support the conclusion that the *Auerbach* standard is inadequate to protect shareholder rights. [In addition, my colleagues argue] that limiting judicial review to the *Auerbach* test would effectively eliminate the fiduciary obligations of directors and officers because the sole method of enforcing these obligations, shareholder derivative suits, could be eliminated upon the recommendation of persons appointed by the officers and directors whose conduct is being challenged. Even if shareholder derivative suits are the only effective method of enforcing the fiduciary obligations of officers and directors, this second objection to *Auerbach* again assumes that director committees reviewing derivative litigation will not act independently and in good faith. Since *Auerbach* will require judicial intervention if the director committees do not so act this second objection to the use of the *Auerbach* standard is similarly without merit. . . .

QUESTIONS ON JOY v. NORTH

1. How does the court's exercise of business judgment in *Joy* compare to the calculus that a 100 percent shareholder (a "sole owner") might use in deciding whether to sue after discovering managerial misconduct? How does the *Joy* rule compare to the calculus of an absolutely loyal and dispassionate director charged with considering whether to sue after discovering managerial misconduct?

2. The *Joy* dissent argues that the decision to pursue a derivative claim is a business decision for the board, just like any other business decision that it might make. Is that right? For a loyal board, is this decision no different than, say, a decision to build a new widget factory?

3. Does the majority in *Joy* disagree that the litigation decision is fundamentally an investment decision?

For board skeptics and reformers, an alternative to the *Zapata* rule might be a more rigorous effort to ensure the independence of the directors who sit on the special litigation committee. Consider Michigan's efforts to codify "independence" in this regard.

MICHIGAN COMPILED LAWS

§450.1107

"Independent director" means a director who meets all of the following requirements:

(a) Is elected by the shareholders.

(b) Is designated as an independent director by the board or the shareholders.

(c) Has at least [five] years of business, legal, or financial experience, or other equivalent experience. . . .

(d) Is not and during the [three] years prior to being designated as an independent director has not been any of the following:

(i) An officer or employee of the corporation or any affiliate of the corporation.

(ii) Engaged in any business transaction for profit or series of transactions for profit, including banking, legal, or consulting services, involving more than $10,000.00 with the corporation or any affiliate of the corporation.

   (iii) An affiliate, executive officer, general partner, or member of the immediate family of any person that had the status or engaged in a transaction described in subparagraph (i) or (ii). . . .

   (f) Does not have an aggregate of more than [three] years of service as a director of the corporation, whether or not as an independent director.

∫495

   (1) The court shall dismiss a derivative proceeding if, on motion by the corporation, the court finds that [one] of the groups specified in subsection (2) has made a determination in good faith after conducting a reasonable investigation . . . that the maintenance of the derivative proceeding is not in the best interests of the corporation. . . . If the determination is made . . . [by a court-appointed panel or by Michigan independent directors], the plaintiff shall have the burden of proving that the determination was not made in good faith or that the investigation was not reasonable.

10.5   DEALING WITH AN ABUNDANCE OF SHAREHOLDER SUITS

Shareholder suits are undoubtedly of use both in deterring and compensating for breaches of duty by controllers and insiders. But there can be too much of a good thing. While the number of derivative suits has vacillated over the last 20 years, a case can be made that they remain too numerous and impose an unjustified tax on M&A transactions. Remarkably, one 2014 study found that nearly 95 percent of recent M&A transactions between public companies valued at $100 million or more were targets of shareholder litigation.[24] The same study reported that the 2014 percentages were almost two and a half times higher than the analogous percentages as recently as 2006. Just as significant, almost half of these suits were brought in multiple jurisdictions by competing teams of lawyers.[25] Here we consider two developments that have sought to contain shareholder litigation in recent years: exclusive forum bylaws and tightened settlement requirements.

   24. Mathew Cain & Steven D. Solomon, *Takeover Litigation in 2014* at 21 (February 20, 2015) (working paper), available at http://papers.ssrn.com/sol13/papers.cfm?abstract_id=2567902.
   25. The mean number of transactions for years 2011 through 2014 subject to suits in more than one jurisdiction as reported by Cain & Solomon is 45 percent.

10.5.1 Exclusive Forum Bylaws

Exclusive forum bylaws emerged as a private ordering device to centralize these multi-jurisdictional claims and thus make adjudication of M&A transactions more efficient.[26] They were first proposed by Wachtell Lipton partner Ted Mirvis in 2007,[27] who argued that any suit brought by a shareholder of the company against its directors or officers to enforce duties created by Delaware law must be brought only in a designated forum. The expectation had been that the Court of Chancery would typically be selected, but as conceived it was possible to designate other jurisdictions as well. The theory is simple: Recall that DGCL §109(b) provides that "[t]he bylaws may contain any provision, not inconsistent with law or with the certificate of incorporation, relating to the business of the corporation, the conduct of its affairs, and its rights or powers *or the rights or powers of its stockholders,* directors, officers or employees" (emphasis added). Thus the exclusive forum bylaw is seen by its proponents as a form of contract among shareholders and the corporation designating a forum for disputes concerning internal affairs that would simplify the costs of such litigation. From the perspective of corporations there seems little downside to such a bylaw and they have been widely and promptly adopted. The only real question has been, are such bylaws valid?

The first Delaware case to deal with the question was *Boilermakers Local 154 Retirement Fund v. Chevron Corp.,* 73 A.3d 934 (Del. Ch. 2013). Then Chancellor Leo Strine stated that he faced two narrow questions: first, whether forum selection bylaws are facially valid under Delaware law and second, whether the unilateral adoption of such a bylaw creates rights and obligations of a contractual nature. On the first subject, the court held that since the bylaw was limited to claims respecting internal affairs and purported only to limit where suit may be brought, not whether a claim exists, it was procedural in nature and a proper subject for a bylaw. On the second issue, the gist of the court's analysis is that since investors buy stock in a Delaware corporation subject to the statutory and governance provisions governing the entity and since they have no "vested right" to freeze governance of the corporation, changes duly authorized are binding upon stockholders just as if they had personally agreed to them. Accordingly, the Chancellor upheld the validity of such bylaws, leaving open the possibility that "as applied" in any particular case, the court may find such a bylaw to constitute an abuse.

After the *Boilermakers* opinion it appears that no court has denied the validity of a forum selection bylaw per se,[28] although one court did refuse to apply such a provision adopted soon after the alleged wrongdoing occurred

---

26. Thanks to Zackary Kravat, NYU Law '15, for research work on this section.

27. *Anywhere But Chancery: Ted Mirvis Sounds an Alarm and Suggests Some Solutions,* M&A J. May 2007 at 17.

28. See Alison Frankel, *Forum Selection Clauses Are Killing Multiforum M&A Litigation,* Reuters Analysis and Opinion (January 24, 2014), available at http://blogs.reuters.com/alison-frankel/2014/06/24.

and in anticipation of the specific suit.[29] In June 2015, the Delaware General Assembly passed a bill validating forum selection bylaws. The bill, however, forbade Delaware corporations from designating courts of another state as the exclusive forum for adjudication of their internal affairs.

It is now clear that corporate bylaws (or charter provisions) that name a Delaware court as the exclusive forum for litigation of matters of internal affairs are valid. Nevertheless, complexities remain. All M&A transactions have the potential for breach of fiduciary duty claims, of course, but they are fertile ground for §§10b-5 and/or 14(a) claims under the Securities Exchange Act of 1934 as well. Whether these claims are matters of internal affairs is a moot question because state courts have no jurisdiction to adjudicate these claims. Corporations can hardly overrule federal venue provisions by enacting a bylaw purporting to do so. Thus, the possibility of something like multi-forum M&A litigation still exists even for firms that adopt exclusive forum bylaws. One suit would be the classic breach of fiduciary duty litigation (in Delaware, for firms adopting an exclusive forum bylaw) and the other would be a federal suit (anywhere federal law would permit) arising from essentially the same facts, but casting the matter as a disclosure or manipulation claim under federal law. But matters stand differently with respect to shareholder suits arising out of §§11 & 12 of the 1933 Act, which accords jurisdiction to both federal and state courts.[30]

In *Salzberg v. Sciabacucchi* (excerpted below) the Delaware Supreme Court examined "federal forum provisions" (FFPs), adopted by three firms in their initial public offerings, which sought to direct all claims under the Securities Act of 1933 to federal courts rather than Delaware state courts. Firms raising capital via IPOs or seasoned public issuances must make tightly regulated disclosures in two key documents — the registration statement and the prospectus — and they and their directors may be held liable for resulting misstatements. See §§11 and 12 of the Act. However, such misstatements may also trigger liability under Delaware corporate law because they may be made to current and potential shareholders. The prospect of facing parallel liability — via private federal class actions and derivative and direct suits in Delaware — raises challenging issues. Corporations typically prefer that such suits occur in federal courts because federal law, unlike Delaware law, stays discovery until motions to dismiss are resolved, requires the imposition of sanctions for frivolous litigation, and limits damages and fees among other things. Unsurprisingly, some corporations prefer to channel such litigation

---

29. *Roberts v. TriQuint SemiConductors, Inc.*, Civ. A. 1402-0244 p. 10 (Or. Cir. Ct. Multnomah Cty. (Aug.14 2014) available at http://www.wlrk.com/docs/triquint_oregon.pdf.

30. Although matters arising under the 1934 Act may not be adjudicated in a state court, they can be validly released — and the whole matter put to rest — in a state court as part of a court-approved settlement of an action that arises from the same facts or transactions as those that gave rise to the federal claim. See *Hyson v. Drummond Coal Co.*, 601 A. 2d 570, 571 (Del. Ch. 1991); *Matsushita Elec. Indus., Ltd. v. Epstein*, 516 U.S. 367 (1996). On the other hand, in a federal 10b-5 action, it remains to be seen if federal courts will conclude that the ordinary pendent jurisdiction that, for reasons of efficiency, they normally have assumed in 10b-5 (and other federal) claims, should be restricted in the case of shareholder internal affairs suits out of deference to the state law of the jurisdiction of incorporation.

to the less plaintiff-friendly federal courts via FFPs. Plaintiff Sciabacucchi brought a facial challenge against the FFPs here; that is, a claim that these provisions cannot operate lawfully or equitably *under any circumstances*. The Chancery Court agreed and held the FFPs were invalid because they attempted to restrict the forum in which *federal* claims would be heard when Delaware law only allows such provisions to choose the forum for "internal" claims (e.g., breach of fiduciary duty claims). The Delaware Supreme Court disagreed. We pick up with Justice Valihura's recent opinion.

SALZBERG v. SCIABACUCCHI
227 A.3d 102 (Del. 2020)

VALIHURA, Justice:

. . . Blue Apron Holdings, Inc., Roku, Inc., and Stitch Fix, Inc. are all Delaware corporations that launched initial public offerings in 2017 [with federal-forum provisions (FFPs) in their charters. An example is]:

> Unless the Company consents in writing to the selection of an alternative forum, the federal district courts of the United States of America shall be the exclusive forum for the resolution of any complaint asserting a cause of action arising under the Securities Act of 1933. . . .

. . . Sciabacucchi ("Appellee") bought shares of each company in its initial public offering or a short time later. He then sought a declaratory judgment . . . that the FFPs are invalid under Delaware law. The Court of Chancery held that the FFPs are invalid because the "constitutive documents of a Delaware corporation cannot bind a plaintiff to a particular forum when the claim does not involve rights or relationships that were established by or under Delaware's corporate law." Because such a provision can survive a facial challenge, we **REVERSE**. . . .

III. ANALYSIS

2. THE FFPS FALL WITHIN THE BROAD, ENABLING TEXT OF SECTION 102(b)(1)

. . . Section 102(b)(1) authorizes two broad types of provisions:
any provision for the management of the business and for the conduct of the affairs of the corporation, and *any* provision creating, defining, limiting and regulating the powers of the corporation, the directors, and the stockholders, or any class of the stockholders, . . . if such provisions are not contrary to the laws of this State.

An FFP could easily fall within either of these broad categories, and thus, is facially valid. FFPs involve a type of securities claim related to the management of litigation arising out of the Board's disclosures to current and prospective stockholders in connection with an IPO or secondary offering. The drafting, reviewing, and filing of registration statements by a corporation and its directors is an important aspect of a corporation's management of its business and affairs and of its relationship with its stockholders. . . . Accordingly, a bylaw that seeks to regulate the forum in which such "intra-corporate" litigation can occur is a provision that addresses the "management of the business" and the "conduct of the affairs of the corporation," and is, thus, facially valid under Section 102(b)(1).

[Further], FFPs can provide a corporation with certain efficiencies in managing the procedural aspects of securities litigation. . . .

When parallel state and federal actions are filed, no procedural mechanism is available to consolidate or coordinate multiple suits in state and federal court. The costs and inefficiencies of multiple cases being litigated simultaneously in both state and federal courts are obvious. The possibility of inconsistent judgments and rulings on other matters, such as stays of discovery, also exists. By directing 1933 Act claims to federal courts when coordination and consolidation are possible, FFPs classically fit the definition of a provision "for the management of the business and for the conduct of the affairs of the corporation." An FFP would also be a provision "defining, limiting and regulating the powers of the corporation, the directors and the stockholders," since FFPs prescribe where current and former stockholders can bring Section 11 claims against the corporation and its directors and officers.

B.   SECTION 102(B)(1) IS NOT LIMITED TO "INTERNAL AFFAIRS" MATTERS

2.   THE TRIAL COURT IMPROPERLY RESTRICTED THE SCOPE OF SECTION 102(B)(1)

The Court of Chancery narrowly interpreted *ATP* by concluding that "intra-corporate litigation" was synonymous with only the state law fiduciary duty claims. . . .

To elaborate, the court below reasoned that, "[t]he *Boilermakers* distinction between internal and external claims answers whether a forum-selection provision can govern claims under the 1933 Act." The [Chancery Court] . . . explained what it meant by an "external" claim:

> Federal law creates the claim, defines the elements of the claim, and specifies who can be a plaintiff or defendant. . . . A claim under the 1933 Act does not turn on the rights, powers, or preferences of the shares, language in the corporation's charter or bylaws, a provision in the DGCL, or the equitable relationships that flow from the internal structure of the corporation. Under *Boilermakers*, a 1933 Act claim is distinct from "internal affairs claims brought by stockholders *qua* stockholders."

[However,] the dicta in *Boilermakers* regarding "external" claims suggests that its definition of "external" claims would exclude "intra-corporate" claims which, as explained above, do fall within Section 102(b)(1)'s broad scope. The two examples of external claims given in *Boilermakers* do not relate to the "affairs" of the corporation or the "powers" of its constituents (a tort claim for personal injury suffered by the plaintiff on the premises of the company or a contract claim involving a commercial contract). As for these types of claims, no Board action is present as it necessarily is in Section 11 claims [under the 1933 Act], and those claims are unrelated to the corporation-stockholder relationship. . . . Thus, FFPs are not "external," and *Boilermakers* does not suggest that they are.

But by creating a binary world of only "internal affairs" claims and "external" claims, the Court of Chancery superimposed the "internal affairs" doctrine onto and narrowed the scope of Section 102(b)(1) — contrary to its plain language. It then concluded that Delaware corporations cannot regulate "external" claims that arise under the laws of other jurisdictions.

[However, t]here is a category of matters that is situated on a continuum between the *Boilermakers* definition of "internal affairs" and its description of purely "external" claims [see Figure 1]. *ATP* suggests that certificate of incorporation provisions governing certain types of "intra-corporate" claims that are not strictly within *Boilermakers*' "internal affairs," can be within the boundaries of the DGCL, and specifically Section 102(b)(1). And because we are dealing here with a facial challenge, it is possible to have a scenario where an FFP could apply to an intra-corporate claim. For example, existing stockholders could assert that a prospectus relating to shares of stock the directors were selling in a registered offering, signed by the directors of a Delaware corporation, contained material misstatements and omissions. That is enough to survive a facial challenge.

Figure 1:

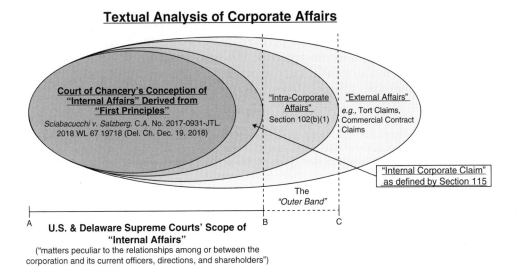

Textual Analysis of Corporate Affairs

. . . It is well-established that matters more traditionally defined as "internal affairs" or "internal corporate claims" are . . . where only one State has the authority to regulate a corporation's internal affairs — the state of incorporation.* There are matters that are not "internal affairs," but are, nevertheless, "internal" or "intra-corporate" and still within the scope of Section 102(b)(1) and the "Outer Band," represented in Figure 1 between points B to C. FFPs are in this Outer Band, and are facially valid under Delaware law because they are within the statutory scope of Section 102(b)(1), as explained above. . . .

[T]his Court recently observed that forum-selection clauses are "presumptively valid." Given that we are addressing a facial challenge, we are not considering hypothetical, contextual situations regarding the adoption or application of FFPs. Such "as applied" challenges are an important safety valve in the enforcement context. As emphasized in *ATP*, whether the specific charter provision is enforceable "depends on the manner in which it was adopted and the circumstances under which it [is] invoked."[152] Charter and bylaw provisions that may otherwise be facially valid will not be enforced if adopted or used for an inequitable purpose. Bremen identifies three bases on which forum-selection provisions might be invalidated on an "as applied" basis: (i) they will not be enforced if doing so would be "unreasonable and unjust"; (ii) they would be invalid for reasons such as fraud or overreaching; or (iii) they could be not enforced if they "contravene[d] a strong public policy of the forum in which suit is brought, whether declared by statute or by judicial decision."[154] In this facial challenge, none of these potential "as applied" challenges are implicated.

QUESTIONS ON SALZBERG

1. The approval of private ordering in the form of forum selection provisions stands in contrast to Delaware's treatment of fee-shifting bylaws. The latter are provisions requiring plaintiffs to pay for the corporation's legal costs in unsuccessful suits. Although approved in principle for non-stock corporations by the Delaware Supreme Court,[31] they were promptly banned by the Delaware legislature. See DGCL §§102(f) and 109(b). Why should they be treated differently than forum selection bylaws? Which do you think is likely to be more effective in enhancing the quality of shareholder litigation? There is, as one might expect, warm debate on this issue.[32]

---

* The figure speaks of internal affairs as covering points A to B, which encompasses the narrow vision of internal affairs the Chancery Court explicated; i.e., claims that do "not involve the rights or relationships that were established under Delaware's corporate law" and instances covered by DGCL §115 which are "claims, including claims in the right of the corporation, (i) that are based upon a violation of a duty by a current or former director or officer or stockholder in such capacity, or (ii) as to which this title confers jurisdiction upon the Court of Chancery."

152. *ATP*, 91 A.3d at 558.

154. *Bremen*, 407 U.S. at 15.

31. *ATP Tour, Inc. v. Deutscher Tennis Bund*, 91 A.3d 554 (Del. 2014).

32. See William B. Chandler III & Anthony A. Rickey, *The Trouble with* Trulia: *Reevaluating the Case for Fee-Shifting Bylaws as a Solution to the Overlitigation of Corporate*

2. Legal niceties aside, doesn't it seem strange that plaintiffs are seeking to enforce a claim based on federal law, but wish to avoid doing so in federal courts?

3. Another move in the shareholder litigation arms race is the attempt to enact bylaws or charter provisions that compel shareholders to arbitrate their disputes rather than bring suit in Delaware or federal courts. The U.S. Supreme Court has approved arbitration provisions in the context of federal employment law claims in *Epic Systems Corp. v. Lewis*, 138 S. Ct. 1612 (2018), but has not yet opined on their validity for shareholder-related disputes (or intra-corporate disputes). Neither, for that matter, have the Delaware legislature or its courts opined on mandatory arbitration bylaws. Might there be reasons, legal or otherwise, to treat arbitration bylaws differently than the bylaws discussed thus far? Which sovereign — Delaware or the United States — do you think is more concerned by such bylaws?

10.5.2   Settlement and Indemnification

The parties are strongly driven to settle in the typical derivative (or class action) suit. From the perspective of plaintiffs' attorneys, litigation becomes increasingly costly as a suit progresses through discovery, and the prospect of a trial imposes the further risk that all suit costs will be lost in the end. Similar considerations motivate defendants to settle. Directors will generally have a right under a company's bylaws to the indemnification of reasonable defense costs, including any amounts paid if the action settles. By contrast, if an action goes to trial, there is a risk of personal liability that can be indemnified only with court approval. Thus, trial imposes an uncompensated risk on defendants as well, and directors and officers (D&O) insurance coverage typically excludes losses arising from "fraud" or self-dealing, while settlements avoiding terms like fraud or self-dealing make available the proceeds of D&O insurance to finance settlement and litigation costs.

DGCL §145(b) accords a corporation broad latitude to indemnify corporate officers, directors, and agents for costs in derivative and shareholder suits. Upon a favorable determination of disinterested board members or outside counsel, a director or officer can be indemnified for any payment made to settle a derivative action as well as for all of her litigation expenses. In the very rare event that the litigation is not settled prior to adjudication, the corporation cannot indemnify officers and directors who are "adjudged to be liable to [it] — except to the extent authorized by the Court of Chancery." However, it can purchase liability insurance for its officers, directors, and agents to cover claims arising out of their status with the corporation, "whether or not the corporation would have the power to indemnify [them] against such liability." DGCL §145(g).

Claims in Can Delaware Be Dethroned?: Evaluating Delaware's Dominance of Corporate Law 145 (Stephen M. Bainbridge, Iman Anabtawi, Sung Hui Kim & James Park, eds., 2018); Matthew D. Cain, Jill E. Fisch, Steven Davidoff Solomon & Randall S. Thomas, *The Shifting Tides of Merger Litigation*, 71 Vand. L. Rev. 603 (2017); Albert Choi, *Fee-Shifting and Shareholder Litigation*, 104 Va. L. Rev. 59 (2018); and Dhruv Aggarwal, Albert H. Choi & Ofer Eldar, *Federal Forum Provisions and the Internal Affairs Doctrine*, 10 Harv. Bus. L. Rev. 383 (2020).

In practice, virtually all public corporations purchase D&O insurance. The standard policy divides into two parts: The first part provides coverage to the corporation for its expenses in defending and indemnifying its officers and directors; the second part provides coverage directly to officers and directors when the corporation does not or cannot indemnify them. In addition, the standard D&O policy excludes criminal penalties and civil recoveries for fraud or fiduciary breach that resulted in a personal gain for officers and directors.[33] A scholarly analysis of several hundred shareholder suits finds (1) that most suits settle and lead to an award of attorneys' fees; (2) that, of the settling suits, about half result in monetary recovery; (3) that D&O insurance pays for most or all of the settlement fund in most cases; and (4) that officers and directors never — in this large sample — face out-of-pocket costs.[34]

Settlement procedures in derivative actions are largely determined by the rules of civil procedure. After the lawyers negotiate a settlement, the court approves the form of the notice of settlement that is conveyed to the shareholders. This notice must describe the claims, the defenses, the settlement consideration, the attorneys' fees sought, and the nature of the release that the settlement gives to the defendants as well as the time and place of a hearing on the fairness of the settlement. While shareholders are thus formally invited to participate in considering the settlement's merits, few ever do in public companies (which is hardly surprising, since shareholder stakes are usually small). Occasionally, however, an institutional shareholder may object to the terms of a settlement or, more likely, to the size of an attorney's fee application.

Incentives to settle are thus strong for most parties, and courts generally favor settlements. However, in the last few years, Delaware courts have demonstrated a willingness to review certain settlements with a skeptical eye.

IN RE TRULIA, INC. STOCKHOLDER LITIGATION
129 A.3d 884 (Del. Ch. 2016)

BOUCHARD, C.

This opinion concerns the proposed settlement of a stockholder class action challenging Zillow, Inc.'s acquisition of Trulia, Inc. in a stock-for-stock merger that closed in February 2015. . . .

The proposed settlement is of the type often referred to as a "disclosure settlement." It has become the most common method for quickly resolving stockholder lawsuits that are filed routinely in response to the announcement of virtually every transaction involving the acquisition of a public corporation. In essence, Trulia agreed to supplement the proxy materials disseminated to

---

33. See generally John F. Olsen & Josiah O. Hatch, Director and Officer Liability: Indemnification and Insurance (1991).

34. See Roberta Romano, *The Shareholder Suit: Litigation Without Foundation?*, 7 J.L. Econ. & Org. 55 (1991).

its stockholders before they voted on the proposed transaction to include some additional information that theoretically would allow the stockholders to be better informed in exercising their franchise rights. In exchange, plaintiffs dropped their motion to preliminarily enjoin the transaction and agreed to provide a release of claims on behalf of a proposed class of Trulia's stockholders. If approved, the settlement will not provide Trulia stockholders with any economic benefits. The only money that would change hands is the payment of a fee to plaintiffs' counsel.

Because a class action impacts the legal rights of absent class members, it is the responsibility of the Court of Chancery to exercise independent judgment to determine whether a proposed class settlement is fair and reasonable to the affected class members. For the reasons explained in this opinion, I conclude that the terms of this proposed settlement are not fair or reasonable. . . . Accordingly, I decline to approve the proposed settlement.

On a broader level, this opinion discusses some of the dynamics that have led to the proliferation of disclosure settlements [and growing concerns with them, as well as] some . . . challenges the Court faces in evaluating disclosure settlements through a non-adversarial [settlement] process.

Based on these considerations . . . to the extent that litigants continue to pursue disclosure settlements, they can expect that the Court will be increasingly vigilant in scrutinizing the "give" and the "get" of such settlements to ensure that they are genuinely fair and reasonable to the absent class members.

I.   BACKGROUND

. . . Because of the posture of the litigation, the recited facts do not represent factual findings, but rather the record as it was presented for the Court to evaluate the proposed settlement.

A.   THE PARTIES

Defendant Trulia, Inc., a Delaware corporation, is an online provider of information on homes for purchase or for rent in the United States. . . .

Defendant Zillow, Inc., a Washington corporation, is a real estate marketplace that helps home buyers, sellers, landlords and others find and share information about homes. Defendant Zebra Holdco, Inc. ("Holdco"), now known as Zillow Group, Inc., is a Washington corporation that was formed to facilitate the merger at issue and is now the parent company of Zillow and Trulia.

Plaintiffs Christopher Shue, Matthew Sciabacucci, Chaile Steinberg, and Robert Collier were Trulia stockholders at all times relevant to this action.

B.   THE ANNOUNCEMENT OF THE MERGER AND THE LITIGATION

On July 28, 2014, Trulia and Zillow announced that they had entered into a definitive merger agreement under which Zillow would acquire Trulia for approximately $3.5 billion in stock. The transaction was structured to include two successive stock-for-stock mergers whereby separate subsidiaries of Holdco would acquire both Trulia and Zillow. After these mergers, Trulia and Zillow would exist as wholly-owned subsidiaries of Holdco, and the former stockholders of Trulia and Zillow would receive, respectively, approximately 33% and 67% of the outstanding shares of Holdco.

After the merger was announced, the four plaintiffs filed class action complaints challenging the Trulia merger and seeking to enjoin it. . . .

On September 11, 2014, Holdco filed a registration statement containing Trulia and Zillow's preliminary joint proxy statement with the United States Securities and Exchange Commission. On September 24, 2014, one of the four plaintiffs filed a motion for expedited proceedings and for a preliminary injunction. . . .

On November 14, 2014, plaintiffs filed a brief in support of their motion for a preliminary injunction [asserting numerous breaches of fiduciary duty and that defendants disseminated] "materially false and misleading disclosures. . . ." The discussion of the merits in that brief, however, focused only on disclosure issues. . . .

C.   THE PARTIES REACH A SETTLEMENT

On November 19, 2014, the parties entered into a Memorandum of Understanding detailing an agreement-in-principle to settle the litigation. . . .

On December 18, 2014, Trulia and Zillow held special meetings of stockholders at which each company's stockholders . . . approved the transaction [with] Trulia's stockholders overwhelmingly support[ing] the transaction. . . .

On June 10, 2015, the parties executed a Stipulation and Agreement of Compromise, Settlement, and Release (the "Stipulation") in support of a proposed settlement reiterating the terms of the Memorandum of Understanding. . . . The Stipulation included an extremely broad release encompassing, among other things, "Unknown Claims" and claims "arising under federal, state, foreign, statutory, regulatory, common law or other law or rule" held by any member of the proposed class relating in any conceivable way to the transaction. The Stipulation further provided that plaintiffs' counsel intended to seek an award of attorneys' fees and expenses not to exceed $375,000, which defendants agreed not to oppose. . . .

II.   LEGAL ANALYSIS

A.   LEGAL STANDARD

Under Court of Chancery Rule 23, the Court must approve the dismissal or settlement of a class action. Although Delaware has long favored the voluntary settlement of litigation,[9] the fiduciary character of a class action requires

---

9. *Rome* v. *Archer*, 197 A.2d 49, 53 (Del. 1964).

the Court to independently examine the fairness of a class action settlement before approving it.[10] "Approval of a class action settlement requires more than a cursory scrutiny by the court of the issues presented."[11] . . . [T]he Court evaluates not only the claim, possible defenses, and obstacles to its successful prosecution,[13] but also "the reasonableness of the 'give' and the 'get,' "[14] or what the class members receive in exchange for ending the litigation.

Before turning to that analysis here, I pause to discuss some of the dynamics that have led to the proliferation of disclosure settlements[15] and the concerns that have been expressed about this phenomenon. . . .

B. CONSIDERATIONS INVOLVING DISCLOSURE CLAIMS IN DEAL LITIGATION

Over two decades ago, Chancellor Allen famously remarked in *Solomon v. Pathe Communications Corporation* that "[i]t is a fact evident to all of those who are familiar with shareholder litigation that surviving a motion to dismiss means, as a practical matter, that economical[ly] rational defendants . . . will settle such claims, often for a peppercorn and a fee."[16] . . .

Today, the public announcement of virtually every transaction involving the acquisition of a public corporation provokes a flurry of class action lawsuits. . . . On occasion, although it is relatively infrequent, such litigation has generated meaningful economic benefits for stockholders. . . . But far too often such litigation serves no useful purpose for stockholders. Instead, it serves only to generate fees for certain lawyers who are regular players in the enterprise of routinely filing hastily drafted complaints on behalf of stockholders . . . and settling quickly on terms that yield no monetary compensation to the stockholders they represent.

In such lawsuits, plaintiffs' leverage is the threat of an injunction to prevent a transaction from closing. Faced with that threat, defendants are incentivized to settle quickly in order to mitigate the . . . expense [and distraction] of litigation . . . , to achieve closing certainty, and to obtain broad releases as a form of "deal insurance." These incentives are so potent that many defendants self-expedite the litigation by volunteering to produce "core documents" to plaintiffs' counsel, obviating the need for plaintiffs to seek the Court's permission to expedite the proceedings . . . thereby avoiding the only gating mechanism . . . the Court has to screen out frivolous cases. . . .

Once the litigation is on an expedited track . . . the most common currency used to procure a settlement is the issuance of supplemental disclosures

10. *Kahn* v. *Sullivan*, 594 A.2d 48, 58 (Del. 1991).

11. *Rome* v. *Archer*, 197 A.2d at 53.

13. See id.

14. *In re Activision Blizzard, Inc. S'holder Litig.*, 124 A.3d 1025, 1043 (Del. Ch. 2015).

15. In this Opinion, I use the term "disclosure settlement" to refer to settlements in which the sole or predominant consideration provided to stockholders in exchange for releasing their claims is the dissemination of [supplementary] disclosures. . . .

16. 1995 WL 250374, at *4 (Del. Ch. Apr. 21, 1995), aff'd, 672 A.2d 35 (Del. 1996).

to the target's stockholders before they are asked to vote on the proposed transaction. . . . Given the Court's historical practice of approving disclosure settlements when the additional information is not material [and of little impact] . . . providing supplemental disclosures is a particularly easy "give" for defendants to make in exchange for a release.

Once an agreement-in-principle is struck to settle for supplemental disclosures, . . . [b]oth sides . . . share the same interest in obtaining the Court's [speedy] approval. . . .

Although the Court commonly evaluates the proposed settlement of stockholder class and derivative actions without the benefit of hearing opposing viewpoints, disclosure settlements present some unique challenges. [There is usually] little or no motion practice . . . and the discovery record is sparse, as is typically the case in an expedited deal litigation leading to an equally expedited resolution. . . . In this case, for example, no motions were decided (not even a motion to expedite), and discovery [and depositions were very limited].

It is beyond doubt in my view that the dynamics described above, . . . have caused deal litigation to explode in the United States beyond the realm of reason. In just the past decade, the percentage of transactions of $100 million or more that have triggered stockholder litigation in this country has more than doubled, from 39.3% in 2005 to a peak of 94.9% in 2014.[26] . . .

Scholars have criticized disclosure settlements, arguing that non-material supplemental disclosures provide no benefit to stockholders and amount to little more than deal "rents" or "taxes," while the liability releases . . . threaten the loss of potentially valuable claims. . . .

Members of this Court also have voiced their concerns [as have j]udges outside of Delaware. . . .

[P]ractitioners should expect that the Court will continue to be increasingly vigilant in applying its independent judgment to its case-by-case assessment of the reasonableness of the "give" and "get" of such settlements in light of the concerns discussed above. To be more specific, practitioners should expect that disclosure settlements are likely to be met with continued disfavor in the future unless the supplemental disclosures address a plainly material misrepresentation or omission, and the subject matter of the proposed release . . . encompass[es] nothing more than disclosure claims and fiduciary duty claims concerning the sale process. . . .

C.   THE SUPPLEMENTAL DISCLOSURES ARE NOT MATERIAL AND PROVIDED NO MEANINGFUL BENEFIT TO STOCKHOLDERS

Under Delaware law, when directors solicit stockholder action, they must "disclose fully and fairly all material information within the board's control."[49] [In Delaware,] [i]nformation is material "if there is a substantial

---

26. Matthew D. Cain & Steven Davidoff Solomon, Takeover Litigation in 2015 2 (Jan. 14, 2016), available at http://ssrn.com/abstract=2715890. . . .

49. *Stroud* v. *Grace*, 606 A.2d 75, 84 (Del. 1992).

likelihood that a reasonable shareholder would consider it important in decid-ing how to vote."[50] In other words, information is material if, from the per-spective of a reasonable stockholder, there is a substantial likelihood that it "significantly alter[s] the 'total mix' of information made available."[51]

Here, the joint Proxy that Trulia and Zillow stockholders received in advance of their respective stockholders' meetings to consider whether to approve the proposed transaction ran 224 pages in length, excluding annexes. It contained extensive discussion [on many relevant issues and in] the case of Trulia, the opinion of J.P. Morgan [its financial advisor] was summarized in ten single-spaced pages.

The Supplemental Disclosures plaintiffs obtained in this case solely con-cern the section of the Proxy summarizing J.P. Morgan's financial analysis, which the Trulia board cited as one of the factors it considered in deciding to recommend approval of the proposed merger. Specifically, these disclosures provided additional details concerning: (1) certain synergy numbers in J.P. Morgan's value creation analysis; (2) selected comparable transaction multi-ples; (3) selected public trading multiples; and (4) implied terminal EBITDA multiples for a relative discounted cash flow analysis. . . .

[N]one of plaintiffs' Supplemental Disclosures were material or even helpful to Trulia's stockholders. The Proxy already provided a more-than-fair summary of J.P. Morgan's financial analysis in each of the four respects crit-icized by the plaintiffs. As such, from the perspective of Trulia's stockhold-ers, the "get" in the form of the Supplemental Disclosures does not provide adequate consideration to warrant the "give" of providing a release of claims to defendants and their affiliates. . . . Accordingly, I find that the proposed settlement is not fair or reasonable. . . .

NOTE AND QUESTIONS ON IN RE TRULIA

In re Trulia had a powerful and immediate effect on deal litigation. Within a year, the number of suits filed in Delaware challenging mergers slowed to a trickle. No doubt plaintiffs were discouraged from pursuing some actions that they might oth-erwise have pursued in the Delaware courts. But the contemporaneous increase in deal litigation elsewhere suggests that many prospective lawsuits may have migrated to other fora with less stringent judicial oversight.[35] If so, however, the attractions of forum shifting proved to be short-lived as both federal courts and some state courts adopted *Trulia*'s skeptical approach to disclosure-only settlements.[36]

---

50. *Rosenblatt* v. *Getty Oil Co.,* 493 A.2d 929, 944 (Del. 1985) (adopting materiality standard of *TSC Indus., Inc.* v. *Northway,* Inc., 426 U.S. 438, 449 (1976)).

51. *Arnold* v. *Soc'y for Sav. Bancorp,* 650 A.2d 1270 at 1277.

35. See Sean J. Griffith, *Class Action Nuisance Suits: Evidence from Frequent Filer Shareholder Plaintiffs,* ECGI Working Paper No. 502/2020 at 7-19 (noting a shift from 82 per-cent of merger claims in his sample being filed in Delaware in 2014 to 87 percent of such claim being filed in federal courts by 2018); Matthew D. Cain, Jill E. Fisch, Steven Davidoff Solomon & Randall S. Thomas, *The Shifting Tides of Merger Litigation,* 71 Vand. L. Rev. 603, 604 (2018).

36. See *In Re: Walgreen Co. Stockholder Litigation,* 832 F.3d 718, 724-725 (7th Cir. 2016) (adopting *Trulia*'s approach); *Griffith v. Quality Distribution Inc.,* Case No. 2D17-3160

Further, the emergence of exclusive forum bylaws (noted earlier) allowed corporations to constrain plaintiffs.

But as in every well-plotted thriller, this was not the end of the game. The ingenuous plaintiffs bar soon found another workaround by agreeing to the voluntary dismissals of their complaints in exchange for so-called "mootness" fees after defendants made a nominal "corrective" in response to the plaintiff's suit, did not seek a liability release, and did not object to payment of plaintiff attorney's fees.[37] This "worked" because for mootness dismissal did not trigger judicial review as settlement might have done and occurred on the eve of a merger vote, thereby leaving other potential plaintiffs little time to intervene. This procedure has the *de facto* effect of a broad release of liability for corporate defendants, and thus mimics the monetary payout of a pre-*Trulia* disclosure-only settlement. Of course, no one can be certain about how long this workaround will last. Indeed, there have been further developments as we write.[38] Suffice it to say that the shareholder litigation arms race is far from over.

1. The role of settlements involving no monetary recovery for the firm has plagued corporate law for some time. Does the approach in *Trulia* differ from that in *Fletcher* (discussed at the beginning of this chapter)?

2. Would a charter provision requiring shareholders to submit their disputes to arbitration be helpful here? Recent commentary is beginning to examine this issue. See, e.g., Ann M. Lipton, *Manufactured Consent: The Problem of Arbitration Clauses in Corporate Charters and Bylaws*, 104 Geo. L.J. 583 (2016).[39]

3. What other steps might Delaware take to curtail frivolous or extortionary shareholder litigation? Given the rise of large institutional investors, might they be prodded to play some kind of supervisory role? Based on your reading of their behavior in voting (see Chapter 6), do you think they would have a better sense about when shareholder suits benefit the firm? There is debate over the effects of a similar provision in the context of federal securities laws.

(Fla. Dist. Ct. App. 2018) (following *Trulia*); *In re Krispy Kreme Doughnuts, Inc., Shareholder Litigation*, 2018 NCBC 58 (favorably citing *Trulia*).

37. See Matthew D. Cain, Jill E. Fisch, Steven Davidoff Solomon & Randall S. Thomas, *Mootness Fees*, 72 Vand. L. Rev. 1777 (2019); Griffith, *supra* note 35.

38. See Pierluigi Matera & Ferruccio M. Sbarbaro, *From* Trulia *to Akorn: A Ride on the Roller Coaster of M&A Litigation*, 44 Del. J. Corp. L. *forthcoming* 2020 (discussing how in *House v. Akorn* 385 F. Supp. 3d 616 (N.D. Ill. 2019) the judge reviewed the mootness fee and disallowed it (the case is on appeal)). Scholarly work continues to explore the effect of *Trulia*, see Giuseppe Dari-Mattiacci & Eric L. Talley, *Being True to* Trulia: *Do Disclosure-Only Settlements in Merger Objection Lawsuits Harm Shareholders?* (March 7, 2019).

39. Recent discussion also examines the proposal put forward at Johnson & Johnson by Hal Scott. For greater discussion see Hal S. Scott & Leslie N. Silverman, *Stockholder Adoption of Mandatory Individual Arbitration for Stockholder Disputes*, 36 Harv. J.L. & Pub. Pol'y 1188 (2013). For additional commentary see Lynn M. LoPucki, *Delaware's Fall: The Arbitration Bylaw Scenario*, in Can Delaware Be Dethroned?: Evaluating Delaware's Dominance of Corporate Law (Stephen M. Bainbridge, Iman Anabtawi, Sung Jui Kim & James Park, eds. 2018); Joseph A. Grundfest, *The Limits of Delaware Corporate Law: Internal Affairs, Federal Forum Provisions, and* Sciabacucchi, 75 Bus. Law. 1319 (2019).

See, e.g., James D. Cox & Randall S. Thomas, *Does the Plaintiff Matter? an Empirical Analysis of Lead Plaintiffs in Securities Class Actions*, 106 Colum. L. Rev. 1587 (2006); Stephen J. Choi, Jill E. Fisch & Adam C. Pritchard, *Do Institutions Matter? The Impact of the Lead Plaintiff Provision of the Private Securities Litigation Reform Act*, 83 Wash. U. L. Q. 869 (2005).

10.6   WHEN ARE DERIVATIVE SUITS IN SHAREHOLDERS' INTERESTS?[40]

The debate over how to address the abundance of shareholder litigation raises the broader question of when is it actually in a shareholder's best interests that a derivative suit be brought against a corporate manager who appears to have violated her fiduciary duty? Presumably, a shareholder (and society as a whole) would prefer a suit to be brought only when it increases corporate value, that is, when its benefits outweigh its costs to the company.

A derivative suit can increase corporate value in two ways. First, the suit may confer something of value on the corporation. For instance, the corporation benefits if it recovers compensation for the past harms inflicted by an errant manager. More subtly, the corporation can benefit in a similar way if a derivative suit forces a governance change that prevents the same manager from inflicting harm on the company in the future (as when, say, the introduction of an independent audit prevents future manipulation of the books). Second, a derivative suit (or, more precisely, the prospect of suit) can add to corporate value by deterring wrongdoing that might otherwise happen in the future. In this second case, unlike the first, the suit adds value only in the contingent sense that it serves to make future would-be wrongdoers *believe* that they will be the target of *another* suit should they also breach their fiduciary duties. Correlatively, any change in circumstances that makes a future suit less likely also reduces the deterrent value of *today's* derivative suit.

As with the benefits of suit, the costs of a derivative suit to the company can be resolved into two categories. First, litigation imposes direct costs on a company. The corporation must pay the price of both defending and (as a practical matter) prosecuting successful derivative suits — in time and energy as well as dollars. As a legal matter, shareholder-plaintiffs (or their attorneys) bear their own costs if they lose, and culpable managers may be charged with defense costs if they lose. See DGCL §145(b). In practice, however, most derivative suits settle, after which the company's liability insurer picks up the costs of both sides in the suit. The insurer, in turn, passes these settlement costs back to the corporation in the form of higher insurance premia.

Second, shareholder suits impose a variety of indirect costs on the corporation and its shareholders. The corporation must pay in advance for at

40. This section borrows from a more extensive discussion in Reiner H. Kraakman, Hyun Park & Steven M. Shavell, *When Are Shareholder Suits in Shareholder Interests?*, 82 Geo. L.J. 1733 (1994).

least some of the prospective costs of managerial liability. In particular, corporate officers and directors must be compensated ex ante for their expected litigation costs or, alternatively, insulated from bearing these costs in the first instance. Again, the legal system facilitates insulation through a variety of mechanisms, the most important of which is the institution of D&O insurance. Derivative suits that are not dismissed generally settle, and settlement costs as well as litigation costs are almost always paid by D&O insurers, who anticipate their own costs in the insurance premia they charge corporations ex ante.

QUESTIONS ON COSTS AND BENEFITS

1. Because D&O insurers generally pay settlement costs, managers are rarely forced to pay out of pocket for alleged breaches of fiduciary duty. So how can the prospect of a derivative suit deter misconduct?

2. Consider the position of a corporation *before* its officers and directors face a derivative suit. Can the company benefit, on an expected value basis, from the certain knowledge that its D&O insurer will make good any losses it suffers if its officers and directors breach their fiduciary duties and are sued as a result? Remember that the company must pay insurance premia, and the insurance corporation is no dummy. Do you have to know how closely underwritten D&O policies are?

3. Consider the following fanciful proposal for reform of the rules for plaintiffs' attorneys: "Attorneys' fees shall be available in settlements of derivative suits only if one of the following criteria is met: (1) The settlement imposes an *uncompensated* financial penalty on alleged wrongdoers; or (2) the settlement results in a monetary recovery in excess of the requested attorneys' fees that is *not* funded, directly or indirectly, by the company or its insurer."

4. Could shareholders validly approve a charter amendment that precludes the institution of derivative suits by shareholders? Are there good policy reasons in favor of or opposed to such an idea?

TRANSACTIONS IN CONTROL

We turn now to transactions in which one shareholder, who has a controlling interest in a corporation's stock, sells that interest to another. Unlike self-dealing transactions initiated by corporate insiders, transactions in shares have traditionally escaped regulation by corporate law. What shareholders do with their own property — their shares — has been seen as their own business and of no concern to the corporation or other shareholders. Over the past 50 years, however, corporate law has come to recognize that share transactions affecting control inevitably have consequences for both the corporation and its minority shareholders.

Unless pressed by urgent necessity, a controller is very unlikely to sell a control block of stock at its current trading price. But why is a buyer willing to pay substantially more than the market price per share for a control block? The academic literature refers to several possible explanations. One popular explanation posits that the premium is a payment for "private benefits of control," by which is meant a range of possible sources of value, from the power to capture salary, perks, and perhaps self-dealing opportunities, to the prestige value of being the company's indisputable boss. Just how controllers extract extra value is important, of course. (For an egregious — and illegal — illustration of how controllers can extract extra value, see the sidebar on the Rigas clan at Adelphia.) But no matter how controllers extract private benefits, these benefits are non–pro rata distributions of value from corporate assets.

Other theorists suggest that control premia are paid not by those seeking to harvest private benefits, but from buyers who have (or believe they have) a superior business plan that will increase the value of the stock in their hands (and coincidentally in the hands of other holders). The acquirer who, for example, will add business A to his existing business B to create an even more valuable business C will be willing to pay a premium if business C will be quite valuable. We might call this "shared" or "public" benefits of control since the remaining shareholders of the company over which the buyer acquires control will participate in the ongoing benefits of the new business.

Other theorists posit that a control premium is simply a function of the nature of capital markets: Anyone attempting to accumulate a control block of stock from many trades quickly will tend to drive up the price of the stock (all else being equal), and thus must pay a premium over the market price. Since control blocks are costly to create, they command a premium on sale.

Each of these theories may explain one transaction better than another. But which one you assume is most frequent may affect what you think of as good corporate law policy with respect to control share transactions.

Other than vigilantly policing conflicted corporate decisions, there is, as a practical matter, little the law can do to regulate controllers' private benefits in the day-to-day operation of the company. But control transactions are more visible and occur less often, so the law could feasibly monitor them more closely if it were thought useful to do so. But any policy position one takes on control premia will inevitably have both costs and benefits. There is no logically superior policy position on the regulation of control transactions.

Consider that investors can acquire control over corporations in two ways, each of which presents different regulatory issues. The first is by purchasing a controlling block of shares from an existing controlling shareholder. In such a sale of control, the incumbent controller will demand a premium over the price of the publicly traded stock for her control block. The acquirer may expect to finance this control premium by putting the assets to a more productive use, by extracting larger private benefits than the incumbent controller already does (in the extreme, by looting the company), or by doing both. Therefore, any regulatory measure that hinders the purchase of control at a premium price will both mitigate the risks of opportunistic transfers of control to "bad" acquirers, but will also hinder the efficient transfer of control to acquirers who will use company assets in more profitable ways. In either case, an incumbent controller who already extracts private gains from a company has no incentive to sell out, except at a premium price that capitalizes his own private benefits.[1]

Five Adelphia Officials Arrested on Fraud Charges
Wall Street Journal (July 25, 2002)

Three members of the Rigas family that founded Adelphia Communications Corp., and two other company executives, were arrested early yesterday morning and charged with looting the nation's sixth-largest cable-television company "on a massive scale." . . . Adelphia also filed suit yesterday seeking more than $1 billion against the entire Rigas family. . . . The suit accuses the family of a violation of the Racketeer Influenced and Corrupt Organizations Act, breaching its fiduciary duties, wasting corporate assets, abusing control, breaching its contracts and other violations.

The Rigases used company jets for private jaunts—including an African safari—borrowed billions of dollars for their closely held companies and used $252 million of company funds to meet margin calls on their private stock, the complaint alleged. After John J. Rigas racked up a personal debt of more than $66 million by early 2001, he was withdrawing so much money from the company for personal use that his son Timothy had to limit him to $1 million a month—which he duly withdrew for 12 months, even as public filings listed his annual compensation at less than $1.9 million, the complaint said. The Rigases also spent $12.8 million of company funds to start construction of a golf course. . . . The company also paid for two apartments in Manhattan—one used rent-free by John's daughter and son-in-law, according to the complaint. (The son-in-law was a member of the board at the time.)

---

1. See Marcel Kahan, *Sales of Corporate Control*, 9 J.L. Econ. & Org. 368 (1993); Lucian Arye Bebchuk, *Efficient and Inefficient Sales of Corporate Control*, 109 Q.J. Econ. 957 (1994).

The second way in which an acquirer might take control of a corporation is by purchasing the shares of numerous smaller shareholders. Here a similar trade-off exists between the law's ambition to protect shareholders from opportunism and its ambition to foster efficient transfers of control. In the absence of ex ante regulation, antitakeover defenses, or ex post derivative litigation, a looter could exploit the collective action problem of disaggregated shareholders by buying 51 percent of a target corporation at a high price and later appropriating a large part of the value of the remaining 49 percent as a private benefit. A variety of regulatory measures directed at acquiring companies — from minimum tender offer periods to mandatory cash-out rights for minority shareholders — mitigate the collective action problem of target shareholders and thereby reduce the risk of inefficient takeovers — but, again, they do so only at the price of also reducing the number of efficient control transfers. Similarly, managers who may use preclusive defensive tactics have a great deal of leverage to bargain on behalf of their shareholders with would-be acquirers, but can also use that power to block efficient transfers for selfish reasons. Managers could abuse such power by, for example, selling the firm to an inefficient acquirer who offers a side deal, or refusing to sell the firm regardless of a potential buyer's price. We consider the latitude of managers to defend the company against a hostile tender offer in Chapter 13.

11.1   SALES OF CONTROL BLOCKS: THE SELLER'S DUTIES

Control blocks in public companies are costly to aggregate and valuable to have. But what rules govern the sale of a control block once it is obtained? We explore three traditional aspects of this issue here: (1) the extent to which the law regulates or should regulate premia from the sale of control (i.e., the difference between the market price of minority shares and the price obtained in the sale of a control block); (2) the law's response to sales of managerial power over the corporation that appear to occur *without* transferring a controlling block of stock (i.e., a "sale of corporate office"); and (3) the duty of the seller of a controlling block of shares to exercise due care to screen out buyers who are potential looters.

11.1.1   The Regulation of Control Premia

While some non–U.S. jurisdictions have statutes that require any acquirer of a control block to offer to acquire all shares at the same price paid in the control transaction, U.S. jurisdictions do not afford to minority shareholders a right to sell their own stock alongside the controlling shareholder, nor a right to sell their stock back to the company, as they might in a corporate merger. The *Zetlin* case, below, illustrates the common law rule, which we call the "market rule" — that is, sale of control is simply a market transaction that creates rights and duties between the parties, but does not confer rights on other shareholders.

A critical tradition of academic commentary, beginning with Professor Adolf A. Berle in the 1950s and extending to Dean Robert Clark's treatise *Corporate Law*, attacks both the fairness and the efficiency of the market rule and proposes in its place a variety of premia-sharing alternatives.[2] Perhaps the best known of these alternatives is the "equal opportunity rule," proposed by Professor William Andrews,[3] under which minority shareholders would be entitled to sell their shares to a buyer of control on the same terms as the seller of control. For a careful review of the literature and case law on sales of control, see Einer R. Elhauge, *The Triggering Function of Sale of Control Doctrine*, 59 U. Chi. L. Rev. 1465 (1992).

Proponents of minority shareholder interests have looked to a handful of cases, including the classic case of *Perlman v. Feldmann*, excerpted below, as legal support for according minority shareholders a claim on control premia. Before examining the interesting facts of *Perlman*, consider the baseline rule, articulated in *Zetlin v. Hanson Holdings*, which continues to represent the law of most jurisdictions.

ZETLIN v. HANSON HOLDINGS, INC.
397 N.E.2d 387 (N.Y. 1979)

MEMORANDUM:

Plaintiff Zetlin owned approximately 2% of the outstanding shares of Gable Industries, Inc., with defendants Hanson Holdings, Inc., and Sylvestri, together with members of the Sylvestri family, owning 44.4% of Gable's shares. The defendants sold their interests to Flintkote Co. for a premium price of $15 per share, at a time when Gable stock was selling on the open market for $7.38 per share. It is undisputed that the 44.4% acquired by Flintkote represented effective control of Gable.

Recognizing that those who invest the capital necessary to acquire a dominant position in the ownership of a corporation have the right of controlling that corporation, it has long been settled law that, absent looting of corporate assets, conversion of a corporate opportunity, fraud or other acts of bad faith, a controlling stockholder is free to sell, and a purchaser is free to buy, that controlling interest at a premium price. . . .

Certainly, minority shareholders are entitled to protection against abuse by controlling shareholders. They are not entitled, however, to inhibit the legitimate interests of the other stockholders. It is for this reason that control shares usually command a premium price. The premium is the added amount an investor is willing to pay for the privilege of directly influencing the corporation's affairs.

In this action plaintiff Zetlin contends that minority stockholders are entitled to an opportunity to share equally in any premium paid for a controlling

2. Adolf A. Berle, Jr., *"Control" in Corporate Law*, 58 Colum. L. Rev. 1212 (1958); Robert Charles Clark, Corporate Law at 491-497 (1986).

3. William D. Andrews, *The Stockholder's Right to Equal Opportunity in the Sale of Shares*, 78 Harv. L. Rev. 505 (1965).

interest in the corporation. This rule would profoundly affect the manner in which controlling stock interests are now transferred. It would require, essentially, that a controlling interest be transferred only by means of an offer to all stockholders, i.e., a tender offer. This would be contrary to existing law and if so radical a change is to be effected it would best be done by the Legislature.

Chief Judge COOKE and Judges JASEN, GABRIELLI, JONES, WACHTLER, FUCHSBERG and MEYER concur in memorandum.

PERLMAN v. FELDMANN

219 F.2d 173 (2d Cir. 1955), cert. denied, 349 U.S. 952 (1955)

CLARK, C.J.:

This is a derivative action brought by minority stockholders of Newport Steel Corporation to compel accounting for, and restitution of, allegedly illegal gains which accrued to defendants as a result of the sale in August, 1950, of their controlling interest in the corporation. The principal defendant, C. Russell Feldmann, who represented and acted for the others, members of his family,[1] was at that time not only the dominant stockholder, but also the chairman of the board of directors and the president of the corporation. Newport, an Indiana corporation, operated mills for the production of steel sheets for sale to manufacturers of steel products, first at Newport, Kentucky, and later also at other places in Kentucky and Ohio. The buyers, a syndicate organized as Wilport Company, a Delaware corporation, consisted of end-users of steel who were interested in securing a source of supply in a market becoming ever tighter in the Korean War.

Plaintiffs contend that the consideration paid for the stock included compensation for the sale of a corporate asset, a power held in trust for the corporation by Feldmann as its fiduciary. This power was the ability to control the allocation of the corporate product in a time of short supply, through control of the board of directors; and it was effectively transferred in this sale by having Feldmann procure the resignation of his own board and the election of Wilport's nominees immediately upon consummation of the sale.

. . . Jurisdiction below was based upon the diverse citizenship of the parties. Plaintiffs argue . . . that in the situation here disclosed the vendors must account to the non-participating minority stockholders for that share of their profit which is attributable to the sale of the corporate power. Judge Hincks denied the validity of the premise, holding that the rights involved in the sale were only those normally incident to the possession of a controlling block of shares, with which a dominant stockholder, in the absence of fraud or foreseeable looting, was entitled to deal according to his own best interests.

---

1. The stock was not held personally by Feldmann in his own name, but was held by the members of his family and by personal corporations. The aggregate of stock thus had amounted to 33% of the outstanding Newport stock and gave working control to the holder. The actual sale included 55,552 additional shares held by friends and associates of Feldmann, so that a total of 37% of the Newport stock was transferred.

Furthermore, he held that plaintiffs had failed to satisfy their burden of proving that the sales price was not a fair price for the stock per se. . . .

The essential facts found by the trial judge are not in dispute. Newport was a relative newcomer in the steel industry with predominantly old installations which were in the process of being supplemented by more modern facilities. Except in times of extreme shortage Newport was not in a position to compete profitably with other steel mills for customers not in its immediate geographical area. Wilport, the purchasing syndicate, consisted of geographically remote end-users of steel who were interested in buying more steel from Newport than they had been able to obtain during recent periods of tight supply. The price of $20 per share was found by Judge Hincks to be a fair one for a control block of stock, although the over-the-counter market price had not exceeded $12 and the book value per share was $17.03. But this finding was limited by Judge Hincks' statement that "[what] value the block would have had if shorn of its appurtenant power to control distribution of the corporate product, the evidence does not show." It was also conditioned by his earlier ruling that the burden was on plaintiffs to prove a lesser value for the stock.

Both as director and as dominant stockholder, Feldmann stood in a fiduciary relationship to the corporation and to the minority stockholders as beneficiaries thereof. . . . Although there is no Indiana case directly in point, the most closely analogous one emphasizes the close scrutiny to which Indiana subjects the conduct of fiduciaries when personal benefit may stand in the way of fulfillment of trust obligations. . . . Directors of a corporation are its agents, and they are governed by the rules of law applicable to other agents, and, as between themselves and their principal, the rules relating to honesty and fair dealing in the management of the affairs of their principal are applicable. They must not, in any degree, allow their official conduct to be swayed by their private interest, which must yield to official duty.

In Indiana, then as elsewhere, the responsibility of the fiduciary is not limited to a proper regard for the tangible balance sheet assets of the corporation, but includes the dedication of his uncorrupted business judgment for the sole benefit of the corporation, in any dealings which may adversely affect it. *Meinhard v. Salmon*, . . . 164 N.E. 545. . . . Although the Indiana case is particularly relevant to Feldmann as a director, the same rule should apply to his fiduciary duties as majority stockholder, for in that capacity he chooses and controls the directors, and thus is held to have assumed their liability. *Pepper v. Litton, supra*, 308 U.S. 295, 60 S. Ct. 238. This, therefore, is the standard to which Feldmann was by law required to conform in his activities here under scrutiny.

It is true . . . that this is not the ordinary case of breach of fiduciary duty. We have here no fraud, no misuse of confidential information, no outright looting of a helpless corporation. But on the other hand, we do not find compliance with that high standard which we have just stated and which we and other courts have come to expect and demand of corporate fiduciaries. In the often-quoted words of Judge Cardozo: "Many forms of conduct permissible in a workaday world for those acting at arm's length, are forbidden to those bound by fiduciary ties. A trustee is held to something stricter than the morals of the market place. Not honesty alone, but the punctilio of an honor the most sensitive, is then the standard of behavior. As to this there has developed a tradition that is unbending and inveterate. Uncompromising rigidity has been the attitude of courts of equity when petitioned to undermine the rule of undivided loyalty by the 'disintegrating erosion' of particular exceptions." *Meinhard v. Salmon, supra,* . . . 164 N.E. 545, 546. . . . The actions of defendants in siphoning off for personal gain corporate advantages to be derived from a favorable market situation do not betoken the necessary undivided loyalty owed by the fiduciary to his principal.

The corporate opportunities of whose misappropriation the minority stockholders complain need not have been an absolute certainty in order to support this action against Feldmann. If there was possibility of corporate gain, they are entitled to recover. . . . [I]n *Irving Trust Co. v. Deutsch, supra,* 2 Cir., 73 F.2d 121, 124, an accounting was required of corporate directors who bought stock for themselves for corporate use, even though there was an affirmative showing that the corporation did not have the finances itself to acquire the stock. . . .

This rationale is equally appropriate to a consideration of the benefits which Newport might have derived from the steel shortage. In the past Newport had used and profited by its market leverage by operation of what the industry had come to call the "Feldmann Plan." This consisted of securing interest-free advances from prospective purchasers of steel in return for firm commitments to them from future production. The funds thus acquired were used to finance improvements in existing plants and to acquire new installations. In the summer of 1950 Newport had been negotiating for cold-rolling facilities which it needed for a more fully integrated operation and a more marketable product, and Feldmann plan funds might well have been used toward this end.

Further, as plaintiffs alternatively suggest, Newport might have used the period of short supply to build up patronage in the geographical area in which it could compete profitably even when steel was more abundant. Either of these opportunities was Newport's, to be used to its advantage only. Only if defendants had been able to negate completely any possibility of gain by Newport could they have prevailed. It is true that a trial court finding states: "Whether or not, in August, 1950, Newport's position was such that it could have entered into 'Feldmann Plan' type transactions to procure funds and financing for the further expansion and integration of its steel facilities and whether such expansion would have been desirable for Newport, the evidence does not show." This, however, cannot avail the defendants, who — contrary to the ruling below — had the burden of proof on this issue, since fiduciaries always have the burden of proof in establishing the fairness of their dealings with trust property. . . .

Defendants seek to categorize the corporate opportunities which might have accrued to Newport as too unethical to warrant further consideration. It is true that reputable steel producers were not participating in the gray market brought about by the Korean War and were refraining from advancing their prices, although to do so would not have been illegal. But Feldmann Plan transactions were not considered within this self-imposed interdiction; the trial court found that around the time of the Feldmann sale Jones & Laughlin Steel Corporation, Republic Steel Company, and Pittsburgh Steel Corporation were all participating in such arrangements. In any event, it ill becomes the defendants to disparage as unethical the market advantages from which they themselves reaped rich benefits.

We do not mean to suggest that a majority stockholder cannot dispose of his controlling block of stock to outsiders without having to account to his corporation for profits or even never do this with impunity when the buyer is an interested customer, actual or potential, for the corporation's product. But when the sale necessarily results in a sacrifice of this element of corporate good will and consequent unusual profit to the fiduciary who has caused the sacrifice, he should account for his gains. So in a time of market shortage, where a call on a corporation's product commands an unusually large premium, in one form or another, we think it sound law that a fiduciary may not appropriate to himself the value of this premium. Such personal gain at the expense of his coventurers seems particularly reprehensible when made by the trusted president and director of his company. In this case the violation of duty seems to be all the clearer because of this triple role in which Feldmann appears, though we are unwilling to say, and are not to be understood as saying, that we should accept a lesser obligation for any one of his roles alone.

Hence to the extent that the price received by Feldmann and his codefendants included such a bonus, he is accountable to the minority stockholders who sue here. . . . And plaintiffs, as they contend, are entitled to a recovery in their own right, instead of in right of the corporation (as in the usual derivative actions), since neither Wilport nor their successors in interest should share in any judgment which may be rendered. . . . Defendants cannot well object to this form of recovery, since the only alternative, recovery for the corporation as a whole, would subject them to a greater total liability.

The case will therefore be remanded to the district court for a determination of the question expressly left open below, namely, the value of defendants' stock without the appurtenant control over the corporation's output of steel. We reiterate that on this issue, as on all others relating to a breach of fiduciary duty, the burden of proof must rest on the defendants. . . .

SWAN, Cir. J. (dissenting).

. . . My brothers' opinion does not specify precisely what fiduciary duty Feldmann is held to have violated or whether it was a duty imposed upon him as the dominant stockholder or as a director of Newport. Without such specification I think that both the legal profession and the business world will find the decision confusing and will be unable to foretell the extent of its impact upon customary practices in the sale of stock.

The power to control the management of a corporation, that is, to elect directors to manage its affairs, is an inseparable incident to the ownership of a majority of its stock, or sometimes, as in the present instance, to the ownership of enough shares, less than a majority, to control an election.

Concededly a majority or dominant shareholder is ordinarily privileged to sell his stock at the best price obtainable from the purchaser. In so doing he acts on his own behalf, not as an agent of the corporation. If he knows or has reason to believe that the purchaser intends to exercise to the detriment of the corporation the power of management acquired by the purchase, such knowledge or reasonable suspicion will terminate the dominant shareholders' privilege to sell and will create a duty not to transfer the power of management to such purchaser. The duty seems to me to resemble the obligation which everyone is under not to assist another to commit a tort rather than the obligation of a fiduciary. But whatever the nature of the duty, a violation of it will subject the violator to liability for damages sustained by the corporation. Judge Hincks found that Feldmann had no reason to think that Wilport would use the power of management it would acquire by the purchase to injure Newport, and that there was no proof that it ever was so used. Feldmann did know, it is true, that the reason Wilport wanted the stock was to put in a board of directors who would be likely to permit Wilport's members to purchase more of Newport's steel than they might otherwise be able to get. But there is nothing illegal in a dominant shareholder purchasing from his own corporation at the same prices it offers to other customers. That is what the members of Wilport did, and there is no proof that Newport suffered any detriment therefrom.

My brothers say that "the consideration paid for the stock included compensation for the sale of a corporate asset," which they describe as "the ability to control the allocation of the corporate product in a time of short supply, through control of the board of directors; and it was effectively transferred in this sale by having Feldmann procure the resignation of his own board and the election of Wilport's nominees immediately upon consummation of the sale." The implications of this are not clear to me. If it means that when market conditions are such as to induce users of a corporation's product to wish to buy a controlling block of stock in order to be able to purchase part of the corporation's output at the same mill list prices as are offered to other customers, the dominant stockholder is under a fiduciary duty not to sell his stock, I cannot agree. For reasons already stated, in my opinion Feldmann was not proved to be under any fiduciary duty as a stockholder not to sell the stock he controlled.

Feldmann was also a director of Newport. Perhaps the quoted statement means that as a director he violated his fiduciary duty in voting to elect Wilport's nominees to fill the vacancies created by the resignations of the former directors of Newport. As a director Feldmann was under a fiduciary duty to use an honest judgment in acting on the corporation's behalf. A director is privileged to resign, but so long as he remains a director he must be faithful to his fiduciary duties and must not make a personal gain from performing them. Consequently, if the price paid for Feldmann's stock included a payment for voting to elect the new directors, he must account to the corporation for such payment, even though he honestly believed that the men he voted to elect were well qualified to serve as directors. He can not take pay for performing his fiduciary duty. There is no suggestion that he did do so, unless the price paid for his stock was more than its value. So it seems to me that decision must turn on whether finding 120 and conclusion 5 of the district judge are supportable on the evidence. They are set out in the margin.[1]

Judge Hincks went into the matter of valuation of the stock with his customary care and thoroughness. He made no error of law in applying the principles relating to valuation of stock. Concededly a controlling block of stock has greater sale value than a small lot. While the spread between $10 per share for small lots and $20 per share for the controlling block seems rather extraordinarily wide, the $20 valuation was supported by the expert testimony of Dr. Badger, whom the district judge said he could not find to be wrong. I see no justification for upsetting the valuation as clearly erroneous. Nor can I agree with my brothers that the $20 valuation "was limited" by the last sentence in finding 120. The controlling block could not by any possibility be shorn of its appurtenant power to elect directors and through them to control distribution of the corporate product. It is this "appurtenant power" which gives a controlling block its value as such block. What evidence could be adduced to show the value of the block "if shorn" of such appurtenant power, I cannot conceive, for it cannot be shorn of it.

The opinion also asserts that the burden of proving a lesser value than $20 per share was not upon the plaintiffs but the burden was upon the defendants to prove that the stock was worth that value. Assuming that this might be true as to the defendants who were directors of Newport, they did show it, unless finding 120 be set aside. Furthermore, not all the defendants were directors; upon what theory the plaintiffs should be relieved from the burden of proof as to defendants who were not directors, the opinion does not explain.

The final conclusion of my brothers is that the plaintiffs are entitled to recover in their own right instead of in the right of the corporation. This appears to be completely inconsistent with the theory advanced at the outset of the opinion, namely, that the price of the stock "included compensation for the sale of a corporate asset." If a corporate asset was sold, surely the corporation should recover the compensation received for it by the defendants. . . .

NOTES AND QUESTIONS ON ZETLIN AND PERLMAN

1. Feldmann sold his control stake for $20/share when the market price was $12/share. Upon remand, the district court determined that the pro rata value of Newport's stock, based on the underlying value of the company's assets, was $14.67/share. This left Feldmann with a premium of $5.33/share, which he was ordered to share pro rata with his fellow shareholders. See

---

1. "120. The 398,927 shares of Newport stock sold to Wilport as of August 31, 1950, had a fair value as a control block of $20 per share. What value the block would have had if shorn of its appurtenant power to control distribution of the corporate product, the evidence does not show.""5. Even if Feldmann's conduct in cooperating to accomplish a transfer of control to Wilport immediately upon the sale constituted a breach of a fiduciary duty to Newport, no part of the moneys received by the defendants in connection with the sale constituted profits for which they were accountable to Newport."

Perlman v. Feldmann, 154 F. Supp. 436 (D. Conn. 1957). Does *Perlman* support a general rule of equal sharing in sales of control blocks, as some have argued, or does its holding turn on the unique circumstances of the case? Put differently, can *Perlman* be reconciled with *Zetlin*?

2. In a parallel case, an earlier panel of the Second Circuit determined that Feldmann had turned down an offer to sell the entire company that would have benefited all of Newport's shareholders and, shortly thereafter, had sold his own shares to the Wilport Group for a slightly higher cash price. Does this fact strengthen the court's holding? Is it conclusive? See *Birnbaum v. Newport Steel Corp.*, 193 F.2d 461, 462 (2d Cir. 1952), *cert. denied*, 343 U.S. 956 (1952).

3. In District Judge Hincks's opinion in *Perlman*, written almost two years after the sale of Feldmann's stock, the court found that the Wilport Group had made substantial improvements in Newport's facilities, that Newport had sold substantial quantities of steel to Wilport at the same prices at which it had sold steel to other customers, and that there was simply no evidence of any sort that Wilport had inflicted economic harm on Newport. See 129 F. Supp. 162, 175-176 (D. Conn. 1952). Does this finding alter your view of the case?

11.1.2 A Defense of the Market Rule in Sales of Control

FRANK H. EASTERBROOK & DANIEL R. FISCHEL, CORPORATE CONTROL TRANSACTIONS
91 Yale L.J. 698, 715-719 (1982)

Investors' welfare is maximized by a legal rule that permits unequal division of gains from corporate control changes, subject to the constraint that no investor be made worse off by the transaction. In essence, this is a straightforward application of the Pareto principle of welfare economics. . . .

A. SALES OF CONTROL BLOCS

Sales of controlling blocks of shares provide a good example of transactions in which the movement of control is beneficial. The sale of control may lead to new offers, new plans, and new working arrangements with other firms that reduce agency costs and create other gains from new business relationships. The premium price received by the seller of the control bloc amounts to an unequal distribution of the gains. . . . [H]owever, this unequal distribution reduces the costs to purchasers of control [because the purchaser need only buy the control bloc and not all shares at the higher price — EDS.], thereby increasing the number of beneficial control transfers, and increasing the incentive for inefficient controllers to relinquish their positions.

Numerous academic commentators, however, argue for some form of sharing requirement. Adolph Berle, for example, has argued that control is a "corporate asset" requiring that premiums paid for control go into the corporate treasury. Another well-known proposal is the "equal opportunity" rule advocated by Professors Jennings and Andrews. This proposal would entitle the minority shareholders to sell their shares on the same terms as the controlling shareholder.

Both of these proposed treatments of the control premium would stifle transfers of control. If the premium must be paid into the corporate treasury, people may not consent to the sale of a controlling bloc; if minority shareholders may sell on the same terms as the controlling shareholder, bidders may have to purchase more shares than necessary, possibly causing the transaction to become unprofitable. Minority shareholders would suffer under either rule, as the likelihood of improvements in the quality of management declined.

[T]he legal treatment of control sales is largely along the lines of wealth maximization. Sales at a premium are lawful, and the controlling shareholder generally has no duty to spread the bounty. The rhetoric of the cases, however, is not uniform. In particular, the famous case of *Perlman v. Feldmann* suggests that the gains may have to be shared in some circumstances.

In *Perlman* the president and chairman (Feldmann) of the board of Newport Steel, a producer of steel sheets, sold his controlling bloc of shares for $20 per share at a time when the market price was less than $12 per share. The purchasers, a syndicate organized as Wilport Company, consisted of end-users of steel from across the country who were interested in a secure source of supply during a period of shortage attributable to the Korean War.

Because of the war, steel producers were prohibited from raising the price of steel. The "Feldmann Plan," adopted by Newport and some other steel producers, effectively raised the price of steel to the market-clearing price. . . .

The Second Circuit held in *Perlman* that the seller of the control bloc had a duty to share the control premium with other shareholders. The court's holding that Feldmann could not accept the premium paid by Wilport without violating his fiduciary duty was based on a belief that the steel shortage allowed Newport to finance needed expansion via the "Plan," and that the premium represented an attempt by Wilport to divert a corporate opportunity — to secure for itself the benefits resulting from the shortage. . . .

There are several problems with this treatment. Foremost is its assumption that the gain resulting from the "Plan" was not reflected in the price of Newport's stock. Newport stock was widely traded, and the existence of the Feldmann Plan was known to investors. The going price of Newport shares prior to the transaction therefore reflected the full value of Newport, including the value of advances under the Feldmann Plan. The Wilport syndicate paid some two-thirds more than the going price and thus could not profit from the deal unless (a) the sale of control resulted in an increase in the value of Newport, or (b) Wilport's control of Newport was the equivalent of looting. To see the implications of the latter possibility, consider the following simplified representation of the transaction. Newport has only 100 shares, and Wilport pays $20 for each of 37 shares. The market price of shares is $12, and hence the premium over the market price is $8 × 37 = $296. Wilport must extract more than $296 from Newport in order to gain from the deal; the extraction comes at the expense of the other 63 shares, which must drop approximately $4.75 each, to $7.25.

Hence the court's proposition that Wilport extracted a corporate opportunity from Newport — the functional equivalent of looting — has testable implications. Unless the price of Newport's outstanding shares plummeted, the Wilport syndicate could not be extracting enough to profit. In fact, however, the value of Newport's shares rose substantially after the transaction. Part of this increase may have been attributable to the rising market for steel companies at the time, but even holding this factor constant, Newport's shares appreciated in price.[43] The sale to the Wilport syndicate took place on August 31, 1950. This pattern of prices certainly does not suggest that the 63% interest excluded from the premium perceived any damage to Newport. The data refute the court's proposition that Wilport appropriated a corporate opportunity of Newport.

It seems, then, that the source of the premium in *Perlman* is the same as the source of the gains for the shares Wilport did not buy: Wilport installed a better group of managers and, in addition, furnished Newport with a more stable market for its products. The gains from these changes must have exceeded any loss from abolition of the Feldmann Plan.

Doubtless not all public shareholders have the same good fortune as those who held Newport Steel. Looting is a profitable transaction under some circumstances. Existing holders of control, no less than prospective purchasers, however, have an incentive to put their hands in the till, and a proposal to ban sales of control at a premium as an antidote to looting is like a proposal to ban investments in common stocks as an antidote to bankruptcy.

If it were feasible to detect looters in advance, it might make sense to put the sellers of control blocs under a duty not to allow shares to pass to the knaves — certainly the sellers of control can detect knavery at a lower cost than the public shareholders who are not parties to the transaction. Indeed, some cases have held that a seller of a control bloc can be liable for failing

---

43. Charles Cope has computed changes in the price of Newport shares using the market model, well developed in the finance literature. . . . Cope found a significant positive [positive abnormal returns] for Newport in the month of the sale to Wilport. . . .

The raw price data are no less telling. The $12 price to which the *Perlman* court referred was the highest price at which shares changed hands before the sale of control. The average monthly bid prices for Newport stock during 1950 were:

July: 6 3/4

August: 8 1/2

September: 10 7/8

October: 12 1/2

November: 12 3/8

December: 12

[Recall that the sale to Wilport took place on August 31. — EDS.]

to investigate adequately a prospective purchaser of control. The wisdom of such holdings is suspect, however, because it is difficult if not impossible to detect looters as they approach. A looter takes the money and runs, and looting is by nature a one-time transaction. . . . Any requirement that owners of control blocs investigate buyers and not sell to suspected looters is equivalent to a program of preventive detention for people who have never robbed banks but have acquisitive personalities.

Although sellers could spend substantial sums investigating buyers . . . and the result of some investigations would be a refusal to sell, almost all of these refusals would be false positives. . . .

We do not suggest that the legal system should disregard looting, but we think it likely that the best remedies are based on deterrence rather than prior scrutiny. Looters, when caught, could be heavily fined or imprisoned, taking into account the frequency with which looting escapes detection. . . . The costs of deterrence are probably much lower than the costs of dealing with looting through a system of prior scrutiny that would scotch many valuable control shifts as a byproduct.

QUESTION ON THE EASTERBROOK AND FISCHEL EXCERPT

Why do Easterbrook and Fischel conclude that the control premium at issue in *Perlman* must have resulted from efficiency gains rather than from Wilport's power to extract for itself the value of the Feldmann plan?

NOTE: BACK TO THE REAL WORLD: HOW MUCH DO THE DELAWARE COURTS REALLY BELIEVE IN THE CONTROLLER'S RIGHT TO A CONTROL PREMIUM?

The market rule is black-letter law in the United States: A controlling shareholder can keep what she gets from the sale of her stock. But how far do modern courts really support this black-letter doctrine? In Delaware, at least, the answer is "not as far as is often thought." Of course, all modern U.S. courts treat the simple sale of a controlling block of stock, unconnected to any corporate activity, as free of any duty to minority shareholders.[4] As noted in *Zetlin v. Hanson Holdings, Inc.*, a control premium is understood to reflect the additional value that accompanies the power to control corporate policy

---

4. There is a minor, and obvious, qualification to this point when the controller has made a contractual commitment to not sell her control block. In *Hollinger Intl. v. Black*, 844 A.2d 1022 (Del. Ch. 2004), the Delaware Chancery Court upheld the Hollinger board's use of a poison pill to prevent Conrad Black from selling his control block in Hollinger to the Barclay brothers because the court found that such a sale would violate a formal contract that Black had made with the Hollinger board. We return to this case in Chapter 12. For present purposes, *Hollinger* would seem to present an exceptional case that does not undermine the controller's fundamental right to sell her stake.

above and beyond the economic value of holding a proportional economic stake in the corporation. However, simple sales of control blocks are rare.

Most recent litigation over control premia has involved a controller's efforts to extract a control premium from a third-party buyer's proposal to purchase an entire company. The narrative in most of these cases is similar: A third-party buyer proposes a transaction that will eventually lead to the acquisition of an entire target company, and the controller uses her influence on the target to ensure that the structure of the transaction provides her with an acquisition premium. This might happen in several ways. For example, the controller might be approached about a purchase of the entire company in her capacity as director and use her ability to veto a deal to encourage the buyer to bid for her control block instead of for the entire company.[5] Alternatively, the seller might threaten to oppose the deal unless an independent committee of the board consents to allow the controller to receive a premium relative to the price received by minority shareholders. The controller's right to a control premium is said to reflect the value of transferring the control of the company with her shares, but the exercise of her power to secure an advantage over minority shareholders in the consideration she receives is suspect.

A classic recent case dealing with a controlling shareholder's right to demand a premium, though arising in a merger in which the controller owned a separate class of shares, also reflects a somewhat skeptical view of the controller's right to receive a premium. The case arose from a proposed arm's length transaction in which TMH, a Japanese corporation, sought to acquire all of the shares of Delphi Financial Group, Inc., a Delaware company in the insurance business. Delphi had been founded by Robert Rosenkranz, who was the CEO and controlled the company by virtue of his Class B share holdings, which, while representing less than 13 percent of the company's capital, carried 49.9 percent of its voting power. Interestingly, the original (1990) IPO charter of Delphi contained a provision that provided that both the A shares and the B shares would receive the same consideration in any merger in which Delphi shares were exchanged for any other consideration. Perhaps critically, the charter did not require that only a supermajority of shares could amend that provision.

IN RE DELPHI FINANCIAL GROUP SHAREHOLDER LITIGATION
2012 WL 729232 (Del. Ch. Mar. 6, 2012)

GLASSCOCK, V.C.:

. . . Delphi is a financial services holding company incorporated in Delaware. Delphi's subsidiaries are insurance and insurance-related businesses

---

5. *In re Digex, Inc. Shareholders Litigation*, 789 A.2d 1176 (Del. Ch. 2000), discussed infra in this chapter, is another example of a controlling shareholder who seeks to sell its controlling shares in a parent company rather than to sell all of the parent's subsidiary shares, which had been the original buyer's proposal. In both cases, the sale of the control block served as a mechanism for capturing a control premium that would otherwise have been shared with the minority shareholders in the parent company.

that provide small to mid-sized businesses with employee benefit services, including group coverage for long term and short term disability, life, travel accident, dental, and health insurance, and workers' compensation. Delphi was founded in 1987 by Defendant Robert Rosenkranz, who is Delphi's current CEO and Chairman.

Delphi's board comprises nine directors, all of whom are Defendants in this action. Seven of the directors are independent and do not hold officer positions within Delphi. . . .

Defendant TMH is a Japanese holding company whose subsidiaries offer products and services in the global property and casualty insurance, reinsurance, and life insurance markets. TMH has no affiliation with Rosenkranz, Delphi, or any of the Director or Executive Defendants.

. . . Following [Delphi's] IPO in 1990, Delphi's ownership was divided between holders of Class A common stock and Class B common stock. Delphi Class A shares are widely held, publicly traded, and entitled . . . to one vote per share. Class B shares are held entirely by Rosenkranz and his affiliates and are entitled to ten votes per share. . . . Although Rosenkranz possesses 49.9% of the Delphi stockholder voting power due to his Class B shares, his stock ownership accounts for roughly 12.9% of Delphi's equity.

. . . [T]he Delphi Charter contains a provision prohibiting disparate consideration between Class A and B stock in the event of a merger. . . . On July 20, 2011, TMH made an unsolicited approach . . . to Delphi to express its interest in acquiring the Company. . . .

At the Delphi Board's August 3rd meeting, Rosenkranz informed the other directors of the Delphi Board of TMH's interest in acquiring Delphi. The Director Defendants authorized preliminary discussions and disclosures with TMH. The directors also discussed the seriousness of TMH's interest, and Rosenkranz suggested 1.5-2.0 times book value as a reference point for an attractive deal, or $45-$60 per share, approximately an 80-140% premium over the Class A stock price at the time.

For most of August, senior management from Delphi and TMH had general discussions regarding a potential merger, with Rosenkranz representing Delphi. . . . Delphi began providing due diligence materials in late August and continued to discuss potential synergies with TMH; however, no discussions of price or other specific terms occurred.

During this time, Rosenkranz considered how he might receive a premium on his Class B shares above what the Class A stockholders would receive in the Merger. Because the Delphi Charter prohibits disparate distributions of merger consideration through a provision that was in place when Delphi went public in 1990, Rosenkranz knew that any premium would require a charter amendment. [Rosenkranz was] [a]pparently undeterred by the fact that . . . Delphi's Charter would likely be viewed by Delphi's public stockholders as expressly prohibiting the differential consideration he sought, and that the Delphi stock price paid by these investors likely reflected a company in which the controlling stockholder, though retaining voting control, had bargained away his right to be compensated disparately for his shares. . . .

On September 7, 2011 . . . [TMH] conveyed [its] interest in acquiring Delphi at a price between $33-$35 per share (a 50-59% premium over Delphi's then-market price of $21.98). After initially responding that TMH's offer was inadequate, Rosenkranz later contacted [TMH] to . . . convey his expectation of an opening offer in the range of 1.5-2.0 times book value, or $45-$60 per share, which was consistent with the price he had suggested to Delphi's Board in early August. Rosenkranz countered with this range despite the fact that he knew at the time that he was unwilling to sell at $45. . . . Several days later . . . [TMH raised] its offer to $45 per share, then a 106% premium over market. Rosenkranz advised [TMH] that he would take the offer to Delphi's Board. . . .

On September 16, 2011, Rosenkranz presented TMH's $45 per share offer to the Board. Rosenkranz acknowledged the offer's substantial premium . . . but he disclosed to the Board that he nonetheless found it inadequate from his perspective as controlling stockholder, and that he would be unlikely to vote his Class B shares in favor of Merger at that price. Because of the conflict of interest Rosenkranz's position created . . . the Board agreed to form a Special Committee, comprising the Board's seven independent directors . . . to evaluate the proposal from TMH, direct further discussions with TMH, and consider alternatives to the TMH proposal. . . .

The Special Committee retained Cravath, Swaine & Moore LLP ("Cravath") as legal advisor and Lazard Frères & Co. LLC ("Lazard") as financial advisor. . . .

. . . [T]he full Delphi Board formally . . . charged the Special Committee with representing the best interests of the Class A stockholders, granted the Special Committee full authority to take any action that would be available to the Board in connection with the transaction, and authorized the Special Committee to pursue and consider alternative transactions to the TMH bid if it deemed such alternatives to be of interest to the Class A stockholders. . . .

The Special Committee then sought advice from its legal and financial advisors on its obligations and the valuation of the Company. Lazard advised the Special Committee that the premium offered by the TMH proposal — more than 100% over Delphi's stock price at the time — was a tremendous deal, and that in light of the significant premium offered, Delphi was unlikely to see a comparable proposal from another buyer. . . . Ultimately, the Special Committee concluded that since TMH was the acquirer most likely to be interested in acquiring . . . shopping Delphi was not worth the impact such a course of action would have on negotiations with TMH or the risk of a potential leak disrupting Delphi's ongoing business. . . .

. . . [S]imultaneously with the negotiations with TMH, [a Sub-Committee of the Special] Committee negotiated with Rosenkranz regarding whether there would be any disparate allocation of the Merger consideration and, if so, what the differential would be. Rosenkranz opened the discussion with a request of $59 per Class B share and $43 per Class A share, asserting to the Special Committee that he did not expect TMH to raise its offer price; that if TMH did raise its price, Rosenkranz expected that increase to be allocated evenly dollar-for-dollar on top of the $59/$43 split; that he was unequivocally not a seller at $45; and that if his demands were not met, he would have no qualms about walking away from the deal. . . . The Sub-Committee reviewed comparable acquisitions of companies with dual-class stock, and, after hearing from its financial and legal advisors that disparate consideration in such cases is unusual and problematic, attempted to persuade Rosenkranz . . . to accept the same price as the Class A stockholders. Nevertheless, Rosenkrantz [refused] to back down on his demand for . . . disparate consideration. . . .

The Sub-Committee engaged in a back-and-forth with Rosenkranz in the days leading up to an October 14, 2011, meeting with TMH representatives . . . neither side wanted to lose momentum in the negotiations with TMH or insult the TMH representatives who were flying in from Japan, and so both sides felt that it was important to keep the October 14th meeting date.

There was also the issue of what role Rosenkranz should have in the upcoming meeting, given his and the Sub-Committee's concurrent sparring over the differential consideration. After consulting with Cravath, the Sub-Committee decided that it was best to allow Rosenkranz to remain the point person, subject to direction and oversight. . . . The Sub-Committee reasoned that Rosenkranz would be an effective negotiator because, as Chairman, CEO, and founder of Delphi, Rosenkranz had intimate knowledge of the business, and that while Rosenkranz's interests were adverse to the Class A stockholders', both Classes' interests were aligned with respect to securing the highest *total* offer from TMH. . . .

[Before] the October 14th meeting, the Special Committee met to decide on Delphi's position with respect to price. After a discussion with Lazard, the Special Committee directed Rosenkranz to request that TMH increase its offer to $48.50 and authorized Rosenkranz to convey to TMH that he would take a price of $47 or higher back to the Special Committee if the circumstances warranted. . . .

Several days later . . . TMH called Rosenkranz to inform him that $45 was TMH's best and final offer. . . . The next day, TMH contacted Rosenkranz to counter with a $1 special dividend; Rosenkranz agreed to take the offer to the Special Committee.

Rosenkranz immediately . . . [informed] the Special Committee . . . that he would not support a transaction based on TMH's revised offer unless the $1 special dividend was split evenly between Class A and Class B shares . . . , and that he would walk away from the transaction if he did not receive $56.50 for each of his Class B shares (with the Class A consideration being $44.50 per share). . . .

With TMH's offer of $46 per share ($45 plus the $1 special dividend) on the table, the Sub-Committee and Rosenkranz continued their negotiations regarding the division of the Merger consideration. . . . Over the course of this back-and-forth, Rosenkranz's gamut of emotions confirmed that the Kübler-Ross Model indeed applies to corporate controllers whose attempts to divert merger consideration to themselves at the expense of the minority stockholders are rebuked by intractable special committees. Rosenkranz began in denial of the fact that he might not receive his original request of $59 per share and was isolated with the formation of the Special Committee, grew angry as the Sub-Committee held firm to its original demand of $45.25 for the Class A shares, began to bargain and revised his proposal to $44.75 for the Class A shares, plunged into depression when the Sub-Committee only reduced its demand to $45 per Class A share, and finally arrived at "acceptance" when Fox, believing the deal to be in jeopardy, proposed $44.875 for Class A and $53.875 for Class B.

. . . [T]he Special Committee . . . approved the differential and agreed to accept TMH's $46 offer and move forward with the remaining terms of the transaction. . . . Rosenkranz relayed the Special Committee's acceptance to TMH and informed TMH for the first time of the differential consideration, toward which TMH reportedly did not express any concern.

In the months following the agreement on price, the Special Committee and TMH negotiated the remaining terms of the Merger. One of the key provisions obtained by the Special Committee was the non-waivable conditioning of the Merger on the affirmative vote of a majority of the disinterested Class A stockholders. . . .

In addition, since Section 7 of Delphi's Charter prohibits the unequal distribution of merger consideration, the parties agreed to condition the Merger on the approval of a charter amendment. . . . The Sub–Committee found such an amendment to be in the best interests of the Class A stockholders as it was . . . the only way to enable the Class A stockholders to obtain a substantial premium on their shares. . . .

II.   THE PLAINTIFFS' CLAIMS

. . . The Plaintiffs allege that the Director Defendants and Rosenkranz breached their fiduciary duties to the Class A stockholders in approving the consideration differential. Additionally, the Plaintiffs assert that Rosenkranz breached his fiduciary and contractual obligations in seeking such a differential in the first instance because the Delphi Charter prohibits the unequal distribution of merger consideration. . . .

III.   ANALYSIS

. . . Although I find that the Plaintiffs have demonstrated a reasonable probability of success on the merits . . . I nonetheless find that injunctive relief here is inappropriate. The threatened harm here is largely, if not completely, remediable by damages. . . .

. . . Plaintiffs' allegations essentially fall under two categories: those attacking the negotiation of the Merger price, and those attacking the differential consideration. . . . Under the latter category, the Plaintiffs challenge Rosenkranz's entitlement to disparate consideration, the effectiveness of the Sub-Committee's negotiations with Rosenkranz. . . .

The Plaintiffs' most persuasive argument . . . is that despite a contrary provision in the Delphi Charter, Rosenkranz, in breach of his contractual and fiduciary duties, sought and obtained a control premium for his shares, an effort that was facilitated by the Executive and Director Defendants. As discussed above, Delphi's Charter contains two classes of stock: Class A, entitled to one vote per share, and Class B, entitled to ten votes per share. Rosenkranz holds all of the Class B shares; thus, even though he only owns 12.9% of Delphi's equity, he controls 49.9% of the stockholders' voting power. As a result, Rosenkranz can effectively block any merger or similar transaction that is not to his liking.

Nevertheless, the Delphi Charter [restricts] . . . Rosenkranz's power. . . . [It] provides that, in a merger, the Class A stockholders and the Class B stockholders must be treated equally. . . .

. . . As Rosenkranz points out, a controlling stockholder is, with limited exceptions, entitled under Delaware law to negotiate a control premium for its shares. Moreover, a controlling stockholder is free to consider its interests alone in weighing the decision to sell its shares or, having made such a decision, evaluating the adequacy of a given price. Rosenkranz contends that as a stockholder he has the right to control and vote his shares in his best interest, which generally includes the right to sell a controlling share for a premium at the expense of the minority stockholders.

The Plaintiffs argue that by including a provision in Delphi's Charter providing that Class B stockholders would accept the same consideration as Class A stockholders in the case of a sale, Rosenkranz gave up his right to a control premium. They argue that by approving a merger conditioned on the Charter Amendment, which restores Rosenkranz's right to obtain disparate consideration for his shares, the Board and Rosenkranz are coercing the stockholders into choosing between approving the Merger at the cost of a substantial premium to Rosenkranz or voting against the Merger and forgoing an otherwise attractive deal (that could nevertheless be more attractive sans the Rosenkranz premium). . . .

The argument of the Director Defendants and Rosenkranz reduces to this syllogism: Rosenkranz, in taking Delphi public in 1990, retained control. Notwithstanding his retention of control, he gave up, through Section 7 of the Delphi Charter, the right to receive a control premium. Consistent with Delaware law, however, the Charter provided for its own amendment by majority vote of the stockholders. Thus, since Rosenkranz is, as a controlling stockholder, generally unconstrained by fiduciary duties when deciding whether to sell his stock, he is permitted to condition his approval of a sale on a restoration of his right to receive a control premium. . . . I find this argument unpersuasive.

. . . [T]he Charter gives the stockholders the right to receive the same consideration, in a merger, as received by Rosenkranz. I assume that the stockholders, in return for the protection against differential merger consideration . . . paid a higher price for their shares. In other words, though Rosenkranz retained voting control, he sold his right to a control premium to the Class A stockholders via the Charter. . . .

Of course, the Charter [also] provided for its own amendment. Presumably, Rosenkranz, clear of any impending sale, could have purchased the right to a control premium back from the stockholders through a negotiated vote in favor of a charter amendment. But to accept Rosenkranz's argument and to allow him to coerce such an amendment here would be to render the Charter rights illusory. . . .

Our Supreme Court has stated that a corporate charter, along with its accompanying bylaws, is a contract between the corporation's stockholders. Inherent in any contractual relationship is the implied covenant of good faith and fair dealing. This implied covenant "embodies the law's expectation that each party to a contract will act with good faith toward the other with respect to the subject matter of the contract." A party breaches the covenant "by taking advantage of [its] position to control implementation of the agreement's terms," such that "[its] conduct frustrates the 'overarching purpose' of the contract." . . .

[Nevertheless] I need not decide at this preliminary stage whether the rights of the stockholder class here sound in breach of contract. . . . Plaintiffs are reasonably likely to be able to demonstrate at trial that in negotiating for disparate consideration and only agreeing to support the merger if he received it, Rosenkranz violated duties to the stockholders. . . .

. . . [T]he price offered by TMH for the Class A shares . . . is 76% above Delphi's stock price on the day before the Merger was announced. No party has suggested that another suitor is in the wings or is likely to be developed at a greater, or even equal, price. . . . In fact, it seems at least as likely that a renegotiated deal may yield a lower price. . . . Having determined that a judicial intervention at this point is unlikely to prove a net benefit to the plaintiff class . . . it is preferable to allow the stockholders to decide whether they wish to go forward with the Merger despite the imperfections of the process leading to its formulation.

[Motion for Preliminary injunction is denied.]

QUESTIONS ON IN RE DELPHI

1. According to the court, "The Plaintiffs' most persuasive argument, based on the preliminary record before me, is that despite a contrary provision in the Delphi Charter, Rosenkranz, . . . sought and obtained a control premium for his shares, an effort that was facilitated by the Executive and Director Defendants." But absent coercion would seeking an agreement to change a charter provision itself constitute a breach of duty?

The core of the court's logic here appears to be that amending the charter to permit disparate merger consideration was invalid because it was "coerced" by a fiduciary. But if Mr. Rosenkranz has the right to vote his shares in his own interest and he has no obligation to sell his shares under any circumstances, unless he freely chooses to do so, and finally, if he truly did not want to sell his shares if the price to him was $45 or so, then is Rosenkranz right in saying (as he apparently did) that he did not coerce agreement, but allowed an option to the public shareholders that would be otherwise unavailable to them?

2. Would it matter to your evaluation of this motion if you believed that Rosenkranz would have been willing to sell at $45 but just wanted to get more per share than other shareholders?

3. How should we define "coercion"? To be analytically useful, is it important to recognize that some coercion is legally permissible and some is wrongful? A parent "grounding" an unruly child may be thought to be trying to coerce correct behavior. What gives rise to the difference between action that we would regard as properly increasing the likelihood of shareholder consent (like raising price) and action that we would regard as wrongfully doing so (e.g., threatening a back-end merger at a lower price)?

4. Was shareholder consent to the charter amendment coerced by Rosenkranz in your opinion?

5. Should a controlling shareholder ever have a right to vote his shares in a way that would be disadvantageous to public shareholders and beneficial to himself?

6. A buyer of control often requires corporate cooperation of some sort to facilitate the sale of a control block. For example, an acquirer might desire a waiver of §203 (discussed in Chapter 13), which might otherwise restrict a buyer's ability to do a merger with the company over which it is acquiring control or the buyer request the board's permission to do due diligence before he buys the control block. These actions require *board* acquiescence and could provide a doctrinal hook for a duty on the part of the board to try to help the minority benefit from the control transaction. Arguably, whenever the corporate board is asked to take action, it should do so only when it believes that it is beneficial to the corporation and all of its shareholders.

In re Digex, Inc. Shareholders Litigation[6] draws a sharp distinction between a controller's "shareholder right" to exercise her voting rights in her private interests but to exercise her de facto controlling power only in the interests of the corporation and all of its shareholders. In *Digex*, an acquirer first approached the board of the controller's partly-held subsidiary with a lucrative offer to purchase the entire company. The controller threatened to exercise its voting power to block the sale of its subsidiary, but then arranged instead to sell *itself* to the acquirer. It thereby retained the control premium paid by the acquirer for its own investors rather than sharing it with the subsidiary's minority shareholders. The Delaware Chancery Court ruled that the controller was entitled to use its voting power to veto the subsidiary's sale, but the court also found that the controller had violated its duty of fairness to minority shareholders by pressing the subsidiary's board to waive the statutory protection that the minority would otherwise have enjoyed under DGCL §203—in essence the the ability to evade a minority freezeout for a period as long as three years after a change in control transaction. (We address §203 more closely in Chapter 13.)

The rationale for *Digex* appears to be that the board may waive the §203 constraint only for the benefit of the corporation and all of its shareholders — not just its controlling shareholder. As a generality, this statement is surely

---

6. 789 A.2d 1176 (Del. Ch. 2000).

correct. But if it is vigorously construed, this norm may seriously weaken a controlling shareholder's entitlement to a control premium in many situations. A controller who wishes to receive premium value for her shares will typically ask the board to waive §203 protections unless the board has already done so. Thus, if such a waiver must be justified on the basis of a corporate benefit, the board must either (1) conclude that the transfer itself is good for the corporation and its minority shareholders or (2) must extract some benefit from the controller to justify the cooperation. Even when §203 is not at issue, boards are commonly asked to cooperate with potential buyers of control in other respects, such as providing access to nonpublic information about the company's operations. Here too, a decision to cooperate with the controlling shareholder arguably requires a benefit for the corporation itself or the minority shareholders.

Recent cases explore when controllers are liable for securing disparate consideration or unique benefits in the context of a sale of the firm.

A more complex recent case is *In re Straight Path Communications Inc. Consol. Stockholder Litig.*[7] Straight Path was spun off from IDT — a telecommunications firm controlled by Howard Jonas — in 2013, with the result that Jonas controlled both firms. As part of the spinoff, IDT agreed to indemnify Straight Path for any liabilities arising before the spinoff. In early 2017, Straight Path entered a consent decree with the Federal Communications Commission (FCC) for alleged violations in the pre-spinoff period that left it with no realistic option but to sell itself and pay 20 percent of the sale proceeds to the FCC as a fine (along with other sanctions). The IDT indemnification agreement required IDT to pay this 20 percent fine, making the agreement very valuable to Straight Path, but potentially very costly to Jonas and his family who owned considerable stock in IDT. Straight Path established an independent committee to run the sales process relying on competitive bids. Initially, the committee wanted to preserve the indemnification claim (given its large value) in a litigation trust, but when Jonas discovered this, he allegedly intervened and told the committee that he would scuttle the sales process if the committee tried to keep the indemnification claim. (He also threw in personal threats against committee members.) He offered to settle the IDT indemnification claim by paying Straight Path $10 million and giving it 22 percent of the sale of some intellectual property assets.[8] The committee accepted because Jonas was the controller and could block any sale. Straight Path was eventually sold to Verizon for over $3 billion, meaning that the FCC 20 percent fine was around $600 million. Thus, an indemnification claim of roughly $600 million was sold for a mere fraction of its worth. The court held that the independent committee's ratification did not change the standard of review because it was coerced by the threats from Jonas and thus the transaction would receive entire fairness review.[9] The court noted that:

7. 2018 WL 3120804, at *16 (Del. Ch. June 25, 2018), *aff'd sub nom. IDT Corp. v. JDS1, LLC*, 206 A.3d 260 (Del. 2019).

8. Jonas also wanted a sale of some of Straight Path's intellectual property assets for $6 million when it appeared to be worth substantially more.

9. *Straight Path* is related to cases where the controller receives a unique benefit. See, e.g., *In re John Q. Hammons Hotels Inc. S'holder Litig.*, C.A. No. 758-CC (Del. Ch. 2011) (examining

Howard Jonas . . . did not "just say no" as was his right as a stockholder. Instead he conditioned his support for the merger on receiving unique, non-ratable benefits at the expense of the company's minority stockholders [who received a lower price for Straight Path]. Worse, he made personal threats against the members of the Special Committee to secure their consent, and he threatened to undercut the sales process if he did not get his way.

11.2 SALE OF CORPORATE OFFICE

How should we analyze the sale of a relatively small block of stock in a widely held firm at a premium price by the CEO or managing directors, who simultaneously promise to resign from the board in favor of the buyer's appointees upon conclusion of the sale? Compare the following cases. In *Carter v. Muscat*, 21 A.D.2d 543, 251 N.Y. 2d 378 (1st Dept. N.Y. 1964), the board of the Republic Corporation appointed a new slate of directors as part of a transaction in which the company's management sold a 9.7 percent block of its stock to a new "controlling" person at a price slightly above market. Despite a shareholder challenge, the court upheld the *re-election* of the new directors at the annual shareholders meeting.

By contrast, in *Brecher v. Gregg*, 392 N.Y.S.2d 776 (1975), Gregg, the CEO of a public company, received a 35 percent control premium on the sale of his 4 percent block of stock, in exchange for his promise to secure the appointment of the buyer's candidate as the company's new CEO and the election of two of the buyer's candidates to the board of directors. Gregg temporarily delivered on his promise, but the company's board soon rebelled and fired the buyer's handpicked CEO. The would-be buyer of control then sued Gregg, unsuccessfully, for a refund of the premium it had paid for his stock. Shortly thereafter, however, a stockholder of the company successfully sued Gregg derivatively and forced him to disgorge his control premium to the company. The New York court observed, inter alia, that paying a premium for control while purchasing only 4 percent of a company's outstanding shares is "contrary to public policy and illegal."

QUESTION

What is the functional argument for requiring sellers of corporate office to disgorge the premia they receive from the sale of their shares to the corporation? Isn't the efficiency argument for allowing the seller to keep her control premium equally strong whether she holds 4 percent of the company's shares or 40 percent? If not, why not?

---

a case where the controller received a suite of unique benefits or disparate consideration — an ownership interest in one of the target's assets, a preferred interest with a liquidating preference, and other contractual rights). The *Straight Path* court also provides an interesting discussion on when direct and derivative suits may be brought in this sort of fact situation.

11.3 LOOTING

Another qualification of the controller's right to take whatever the market will bear for her control stake is the duty that the law imposes to screen against selling control to a looter. Recall what Judge Swan in his dissent in *Perlman v. Feldmann*, above, stated at page 179:

> "If [the controlling shareholder] knows or has reason to believe that the purchaser intends to exercise to the detriment of the corporation the power of management acquired by the purchase, such knowledge or reasonable suspicion will terminate the dominant shareholders' privilege to sell and will create a duty not to transfer the power of management to such purchaser. The duty seems to me to resemble the obligation which everyone is under not to assist another to commit a tort rather than the obligation of a fiduciary. But whatever the nature of the duty, a violation of it will subject the violator to liability for damages sustained by the corporation."

In a similar vein, the Court of Chancery has stated:

> ". . . [I]t does not follow from the proposition that ordinarily a shareholder has a right to sell her stock to whom and on such terms as she deems expedient, that no duty may arise from the particular circumstances to take care in the exercise of that right. It is established American legal doctrine that, unless privileged, each person owes a duty to those who may foreseeably be harmed by her action to take such steps as a reasonably prudent person would take in similar circumstances to avoid such harm to others. While this principle arises from the law of torts and not the law of corporations or of fiduciary duties, that distinction is not, I think, significant unless the law of corporations or of fiduciary duties somehow privileges a selling shareholder by exempting her from the reach of this principle. The principle itself is one of great generality and, if not negated by privilege, would apply to a controlling shareholder who negligently places others foreseeably in the path of injury.
>
> That a shareholder may sell her stock (or that a director may resign his office) is a right that, with respect to the principle involved, is no different, for example, than the right that a licensed driver has to operate a motor vehicle upon a highway. The right exists, but it is not without conditions and limitations, some established by positive regulation, some by common-law. Thus, to continue the parallel, the driver owes a duty of care to her passengers because it is foreseeable that they may be injured if, through inattention or otherwise, the driver involves the car she is operating in a collision. In the typical instance a seller of corporate stock can be expected to have no similar apprehension of risks to others from her own inattention. But, in some circumstances, the seller of a control block of stock may or should reasonably foresee danger to other shareholders; with her sale of stock will also go control over the corporation and with it the opportunity to misuse that power to the injury of such other shareholders. Thus, the reason that a duty of care is recognized in any situation is fully present in this situation. I can find no universal privilege arising from the corporate form that exempts a controlling shareholder who sells corporate control from the wholesome reach of this common-law duty. . . ." *Harris v. Carter*, 582 A.2d 222 (Del. Ch. 1990)

QUESTIONS

1. In the excerpt of their piece on Control Transactions, above, Judge Easterbrook and Professor Fischel argue that placing a burden on a seller of control to investigate whether a buyer is a likely a looter would be an inefficient impediment to control transfers. If you agree, must you disagree with the excerpts above?

2. What standard ought to govern the sale of control to potential looters? Should the same standard apply if the seller merely sells its stock and resigns from the board rather than arranging for his buyer to take the empty board seat[s] he vacates? If looters will have liability for their bad acts, why impose liability on innocent sellers of control?

3. Although *Harris* is cited in looting cases, just how much "due diligence" a seller of control must undertake to protect the minority shareholders whom she leaves in the hands of buyer remains uncertain. In *Abraham v. Emerson Radio Corp.*, 901 A.2d 751, 752 (Del Ch. 2006), the court dismissed a looting claim on the grounds that little evidence was presented to substantiate the claim. However, in dicta, former Chief Justice Strine, then Vice Chancellor, expressed doubt as to whether a controller could be held liable for negligently selling control to someone who later looted the firm:

> I am dubious that our common law of corporations should recognize a duty of care based claim against a controlling stockholder for failing to (in a court's judgment) examine the *bona fides* of a buyer, at least when the corporate charter contains an exculpatory provision authorized by 8 Del. C. § 102(b)(7). After all, the premise for contending that the controlling stockholder owes fiduciary duties in its capacity as a stockholder is that the controller exerts its will over the enterprise in the manner of the board itself. When the board itself is exempt from liability for violations of the duty of care, by what logic does the judiciary extend liability to a controller exercising its ordinarily unfettered right to sell its shares? . . . Lest the point be misunderstood. drawing the line at care would do nothing to immunize a selling stockholder who sells to a known looter or predator, or otherwise proceeds with a sale conscious that the buyer's plans for the corporation are improper. But it would impose upon the suing stockholders the duty to show that the controller acted with scienter and did not simply fail in the due diligence process.

Should controlling shareholders face liability for negligently performing due diligence? Is scienter in *Abraham* more consistent with an exiting controller knowingly endangering the minority shareholders, or with the exiting controller aiding and abetting the new controller's looting?

11.4   TENDER OFFERS: THE BUYER'S DUTIES

In public companies, purchases of control most often occur through a public tender offer, since in the United States, unlike in most of the world, large public companies generally do not have a controlling shareholder. This means that an investor who wishes to purchase a control stake in a widely held company must usually do so by aggregating the shares of many small shareholders, typically through a public tender offer. A tender offer is an offer of cash or securities to the shareholders of a public corporation in exchange for their shares at a premium over market price. Tender offers are always at a premium to the recent market price of the securities subject to the offer. The premium paid by the offeror is often analogized to the control premium paid to a controlling shareholder.

Before the passage of the Williams Act in 1967, cash tender offers were unregulated. Offerors could — and sometimes did — make "Saturday Night Special" offers that left public shareholders only 24 or 48 hours to decide whether to tender their shares, without providing any information about the identity or plans of the offeror. The Williams Act sought to provide shareholders sufficient time and information to make an informed decision about tendering their shares and to warn the market (or the target management) about an impending offer. Arguably, it was also intended to assure shareholders an equal opportunity to participate in offer premia and to discourage hostile tender offers on the margin.

The Williams Act did not define "tender offer," partly because Congress did not wish to be underinclusive and partly because tender offers were an easily recognized market phenomenon, even by 1967. Nevertheless, it is worth asking why, in 1967 and today, efforts to aggregate control usually take the form of public offers for shares rather than long-term gradual efforts to buy shares on the stock market or through negotiated transactions with individual shareholders in "creeping tender offers."

The regulatory structure of the Williams Act, as amplified by the SEC, has four main elements. The first of these elements is an "early warning system" under §13(d), which alerts the public and the company's managers whenever anyone acquires more than 5 percent of the company's voting stock. The SEC rules promulgated under §13(d) include the following.[10]

Rule 13d-1(a) requires investors to file a 13D report within ten days of acquiring 5+ percent beneficial ownership,[11] although Rule13d-1(b) allows certain "qualified institutional investors" to file a shortened 13G report (in lieu of the 13D report) within 45 days of year-end; Rule 13d-1(c) permits passive but nonqualifying investors to file a 13G report (in lieu of the 13D report) within ten days of acquiring their holdings; Rule 13d-2 requires shareholders to amend their 13D and 13G reports annually, or upon acquiring 10+ percent of an issuer's shares; and finally, Rule 13d-5 defines a §13(d) group, subject to §13(d) rules, as multiple shareholders who act together to buy, vote, or sell stock.

---

10. We thank Professor John Coates for contributing this overview of the Williams Act rules.

11. There has been an effort, led by the Wachtell Lipton law firm, to shorten this period from ten days — a period established prior to the internet and digital communications — to a day or two. This is intended as a means to preclude activist hedge funds from using the ten days from the date they acquire a 5 percent interest to rapidly acquire more stock or derivative positions in the stock. The SEC has not seen fit to take up this proposed rule amendment yet.

The second main element of Williams Act regulation is §14(d)(1) (as well as related provisions under §§13 and 14 of the Securities Exchange Act and their associated rules), which mandates disclosure of the identity, financing, and future plans of a tender offeror, including plans for any subsequent going-private transaction. The regulations under these provisions include Rule 14d-3, which requires bidders to file and keep current 14D-1 reports for tender offers; Rule 14e-2, which requires the target's board to comment on the tender offer; Rule 13e-4, which requires companies to make much the same disclosures as third-party offerors when these companies tender for their *own* shares; and Rule 13e-3, which mandates particularly strict disclosure when insiders (including controlling shareholders) plan going-private transactions that would force public shareholders out of the company.

The third element of the Williams Act is §14(e), an anti-fraud provision that prohibits misrepresentations, nondisclosures, and "any fraudulent, deceptive, or misrepresentative" practices in connection with a tender offer. The rules promulgated under this section of the Act include Rule 14e-3, which bars trading on insider information in connection with a tender offer.

Finally, the fourth element of the Williams Act, which builds largely on §§14(d)(4)-(7) and 14(e) of the Act, is a dozen rules that regulate the substantive terms of tender offers, including matters such as how long offers must be left open, when shareholders can withdraw previously tendered shares, and how bidders must treat shareholders who tender. Among the more important of these are Rule 14e-1, which mandates that tender offers be left open for a minimum of 20 business days, and Rule 14d-10, which requires bidders to open their tender offers to *all shareholders* and pay all who tender the same "best" price.

QUESTION ON §13(d) OF THE WILLIAMS ACT

Section 13(d) serves as a disclosure provision and an early warning system for target management. But how does §13(d) (or any parallel disclosure requirement) affect the *proportion* of the value in a premium tender offer that public shareholders are likely to capture? Put differently, if there were no requirement to disclose shareholdings beyond the 5 percent level, and no obstacles to accumulating shares, how would a bidder divide her efforts to accumulate shares between open market purchases and a tender offer? What are the consequences for the total amount she must pay to acquire control?

NOTE: WHAT EXACTLY IS A TENDER OFFER, ANYWAY?

Curiously, the Williams Act does not define "tender offer," the subject of its regulations. One reason may have been that conventional tender offers were unmistakable and self-identifying, even before the Williams Act. A second reason may have been that unconventional "tender offers" are not easy to define.

The absence of a definition in the Act has led to case law on "de facto tender offers." Consider the following case.

BRASCAN LTD. v. EDPER EQUITIES LTD.
477 F. Supp. 773 (S.D.N.Y. 1979)

[Over two days, Edper purchased 24 percent of Brascan, a Canadian company trading in Canada, in the United Kingdom, and on the American Stock Exchange. As a Canadian company, Brascan was not subject to the rules promulgated under §§13(d) and 14(d) of the Williams Act. However, §14(e) of the Act was applicable if Edper's open market purchases on the American Stock Exchange amounted to a de facto tender offer. Edper already held a 5 percent stake in Brascan and had proposed a friendly acquisition, which Brascan had rebuffed. To increase its influence over Brascan, Edper decided to purchase an additional 3 million Brascan shares, and to do so through the American Stock Exchange to avoid Canadian regulations. Edper asked Connacher, president of Gordon Securities Ltd., to advise it. On April 30, 1979, after some initial difficulties in purchasing shares on the American Stock Exchange, Edper informed Connacher that it might purchase up to 3 million shares at a premium price if these were available. Gordon Securities contacted between 30 and 50 institutional investors and 10 to 15 individual investors, who held large blocks of Brascan shares, telling them that Edper might be willing to purchase 3 or 4 million shares at 22¾ (which was several dollars above the trading price).

On April 30, Connacher informed Edper that approximately 1.5 million shares of Brascan might be available at 22¾ per share. Edper authorized its broker to purchase 2.5 million shares at 22¾. Edper's broker on the Exchange floor found very little stock available below 22¾ but when it raised the bid to 22¾, it suddenly acquired 2.4 million shares (2 million of which were offered by Gordon Securities on behalf of the shareholders it had just solicited). By the end of the day, Edper had purchased 3.1 million shares. Edper announced, in response to a demand from Canadian officials, that it had no plans to buy any more shares at that time. Nevertheless, on May 1, without further public announcement, Edper resumed its buying activity, and Gordon Securities again solicited large holders of Brascan. This time Edper managed to purchase 3.2 million shares at 22¾ or slightly higher, almost half of which came from Gordon Securities or its customers.

Brascan sued Edper, seeking to require Edper to divest itself of the shares it had bought, claiming that the failure to announce that it was making further purchases violated §14(e) of the Williams Act and Rule 10b-5 (the general anti-fraud provision under the securities acts). Judge Leval found Edper in violation of Rule 10b-5, but he did not find a violation of §14(e). The judge held that Edper did not make a de facto tender offer within the meaning of the Williams Act.]

LEVAL, J.:

. . . Edper's conduct had very little similarity to what is commonly understood as a tender offer and what was described as a tender offer in the context of the hearings leading to the passage of the Williams Act. Edper did not engage in widespread solicitation of stockholders. Indeed, it scrupulously avoided any solicitation upon the advice of its lawyers. Its purchasing was not contingent on a minimum fixed number of shares being offered, it did not put out an offer at a fixed price and the form of the transaction did not provide for tenders by the selling shareholders to be held for some period of time by the purchaser or a depositary, as is customary in tender offers. What Edper did was to acquire a large amount of stock in open market purchases, bidding cautiously so as to avoid bidding up the price of the stock to excessive levels unless there was large volume available at such prices. This is not a tender offer, even if a large volume of stock is accumulated in such fashion. . . .

Brascan argues that Edper made Connacher its agent so that all of Connacher's and his firm's activity in lining up potential sellers is attributable to Edper in determining whether or not Edper engaged in a tender offer. I do not find this contention supported by the evidence. . . .

Of course Connacher and Edper necessarily had interests in common. A seller's broker always has interests in common with the buyer. If the buyer does not buy, the seller's broker will not earn his commission. Thus, if Connacher as a seller's broker were capable of rounding up a large volume of shares for sale at a price that Edper was willing to pay, Edper's objectives would be satisfied and Connacher would make money. That did not make Connacher Edper's agent for the solicitation of sellers' shares.

Even if Connacher were deemed to have been Edper's agent in the solicitation of shares for sale, still the transaction would not constitute a tender offer within the meaning of the Williams Act. All that Connacher and his firm did was to scout between 30 and 50 large institutional holders of Brascan stock, plus about a dozen large individual investors, to collect a large block for Edper to purchase at a price agreeable to both sides of the transaction. He and his firm did this in the conventional methods of privately negotiated block trades. Such privately negotiated block trading is done on a daily basis in the U.S. securities markets without anyone's ever suspecting that what is being practiced might be a tender offer. . . .

A small number of District Court cases have held that the Williams Act should be deemed applicable to such large scale accumulations. The general thrust of the reasoning is that since the Williams Act was designed to remedy certain problems often found in tender offers, and since similar problems are to be found in other forms of stock accumulation, the Williams Act should be deemed to cover such other forms of stock accumulation even though they are not what is conventionally understood as a tender offer.

There are serious problems with this form of statutory interpretation. First of all the legislative history of the Williams Act shows that it was passed with full awareness of the difference between tender offers and other forms of large scale stock accumulations. . . .

Further the regulatory scheme established by Congress in the Williams Act is incompatible with its application to a program of market purchasing. . . . The consequence of bringing such large scale open market and privately negotiated purchases within the scope of the Williams Act would be to rule, in effect, that no large scale acquisition program may be lawfully accomplished except in the manner of a conventional tender offer. While this may be a sensible legislative provision . . . there is nothing in the legislative history or the text of the Williams Act which suggests that it intended to bring about such consequences.

The Securities Exchange Commission, at this Court's request, submitted a brief amicus curiae. The Commission takes no position as to whether the acts of Edper constituted a tender offer, but lists eight factors which authorities have considered in determining whether acquisitions constitute a tender offer under the Williams Act. The SEC refrains from specifying which of the eight factors or how many must be met or how clearly before an acquisition will be considered a tender offer. I have doubts as to whether this view constitutes either a permissible or a desirable interpretation of the statute. . . .

But more important for purposes of this decision, I find that even if the Commission's eight criteria represented the authorized interpretation of the Williams Act, Edper's actions, even as supplemented by Connacher's, do not sufficiently meet these criteria to come within the definition of a tender offer.

The first criterion calling for "active and widespread solicitation of public shareholders" is clearly not met. The solicitations were directed to only approximately 50 of Brascan's 50,000 shareholders, each of the 50 being either an institution or a sophisticated individual holder of large blocks of Brascan shares.

The third criterion calling for "a premium over the prevailing market price" is met, but only to a slight degree. Edper was unable to purchase large amounts at 21½. Its broker, Balfour, did not encounter sizeable blocks until it went as high as 22⅜ The price at which it accomplished its major volume, 22¾, was only ⅜ of a point above what any purchaser would have had to pay for any significant volume.

Criterion number four that "the terms of the offer are firm rather than negotiable" was not met. Edper, Gordon, and the sellers were feeling their way to find a level at which large volume purchasing could be done. The fact that Gordon spoke to potential sellers during the morning of the likelihood of a price of $26 Cdn. (22¾ U.S.) did not represent a firm bid. I find that it represented Connacher's well educated guess as to where a deal might be put together based on his knowledge of the market and of the buyer's and sellers' desires. He and his traders repeatedly denied to their customers the existence of any firm bid.

The fifth criterion, "whether the offer is contingent on the tender of a fixed minimum number of shares," is met only to a slight degree. It is true that Edper was not interested in bidding up the price too high without acquiring a large number of shares in doing so. And it is true that Connacher advised his customers that he didn't believe a transaction would go through unless sufficient volume were achieved. But these conditions were general, fluid and negotiable. They were not fixed as part of the terms of any offer to purchase shares.

The sixth condition, "whether the offer is open only for a limited period of time," is not met. Since there was no open offer, there was certainly no assurance that any offer would remain open for any period of time. Nor was there any statement to the effect that an offer temporarily available would soon disappear. What was said to the potential sellers by Gordon was that a buyer was interested in accumulating a large volume. Thus the situation did not carry with it the kind of potential pressure which, coupling a high premium with the threat that the offer will disappear as of a certain time, places an offeree under pressure to decide. That is the kind of pressure which the Williams Act was designed to alleviate, by providing information on which to base a decision. That was not present here.

I find that the seventh criterion, "whether the offerees are subjected to pressure to sell their stock," was not met. The offerees were experienced professionals, in most cases institutional portfolio managers. Even assuming that such professional investors can be susceptible to "pressure" in the sense in which the Williams Act is concerned, no such pressures were applied.

Finally, the eighth criterion, "whether public announcements of a purchasing program . . . precede or accompany a rapid accumulation," was not met. Edper had made some public announcements in early April when it was contemplating differently structured programs of acquisition. It announced its application on April 18 to the Ontario Securities Commission for permission to make a conditional circular offering. When permission was refused on April 20, Edper announced the refusal to the public and indicated that it had no specific further plans at that time. No further public statement was made by Edper until the close of business on April 30.

In short, the only one of the SEC's eight criteria which is clearly and solidly met is number two, that "the solicitation is made for a substantial percentage of the issuer's stock." While one might have no disagreement with legislation which imposed pre-acquisition disclosure requirements, comparable to those required by §13(d), whenever a purchaser intended to acquire by any means a large specified percentage of any publicly held stock, that is not what the Williams Act now requires. It is not in my view within the power of a court to so rewrite its provisions.

NOTES AND QUESTIONS ON BRASCAN LTD.

1. In *Wellman v. Dickinson*, which established the eight-factor test that is applied in *Brascan*, a corporate acquirer solicited the sale of stock in a target company from 30 large institutional shareholders and 9 wealthy individuals. The solicitations were made in simultaneous phone calls to the prospective sellers by 30 agents. The offers were made at a fixed price substantially above market price and were left open for only one hour. The solicitees had been told beforehand to expect a phone solicitation but had not been told the offering price. By this method, the acquirer managed to purchase 34 percent of the outstanding stock of its target in a single afternoon. The federal district court, however, ruled that the solicitation campaign was a de facto tender offer subject to the requirements of the Williams Act — each of the eight factors was present except "widespread solicitation." *Wellman v. Dickinson*, 475 F. Supp. 783 (S.D.N.Y. 1979), *aff'd on other grounds*, 682 F.2d 355 (2d Cir. 1982), *cert. denied*, 460 U.S. 1069 (1983).

2. What distinguishes *Wellman* from *Brascan*? Was it important that the *Brascan* purchases were effected over the market rather than as private purchases as in *Wellman*? Should it have been important? Should the fact that none of the selling institutions in *Wellman* complained have weighed against the court's decision? Who was really injured in *Wellman*?

11.5   THE HART-SCOTT-RODINO ACT WAITING PERIOD

Apart from the Williams Act, a second legal constraint on the immediate acquisition of control of large U.S. companies is the Hart-Scott-Rodino Antitrust Improvements Act of 1976 (HSR Act), which was intended to give the Federal Trade Commission (FTC) and the Department of Justice (DOJ) the proactive ability to block deals that violate the antitrust laws. If there are no antitrust issues, the HSR Act affects only the timing of transactions. In most friendly acquisitions, the HSR Act does not even delay a deal because the HSR waiting period is shorter than those imposed by other legal requirements such as the proxy rules and the Williams Act.

Precisely when a filing is required under the HSR Act is a surprisingly complex question. Suffice to say here that a filing is always required for transactions in excess of $94 million in value, and often when they are smaller.[12] Initial filings are relatively short, although the antitrust agencies may later request more information about the deal or the parties.

From the standpoint of corporate law (as opposed to antitrust law), the real significance of the HSR Act lies in the waiting periods it imposes *before* a bidder can close her offer. The effect is something like that of §13(d), only more so, since HSR filings must be disclosed immediately to target companies, and bidders may not close a deal until the relevant waiting period has elapsed. Waiting periods under the HSR Act vary by category of transaction. For cash tender offers, acquirers must wait 15 calendar days after filing before closing; for regulated open market purchases, acquirers must wait 30 days after filing; for mergers, asset deals, and other negotiated acquisitions, both parties must wait 30 days after filing.[13]

---

12. In September 2020, the FTC proposed rule changes under the HSR Act that would require investment funds under common management to aggregate the value of their shares and provide additional details in their filings. The proposed rules also include a new exemption for all acquisitions up to 10 percent of an issuing firm's voting securities (subject to a few exceptions).

13. If a second request is made, further waiting periods apply (10 days from the acquiring person's compliance for tender offers; 20 days from both parties' compliance for open market purchases or negotiated acquisitions). In addition, the antitrust agencies have effective power to extend waiting periods indefinitely if they believe parties have not complied with information requests. In each case, the agencies may grant "early termination" of the applicable waiting period and generally will do so if the deal raises no competitive concerns.

QUESTION ON THE HSR ACT

What would be the effect if the HSR waiting periods had been in place at the time of the *Wellman* transaction? What would have been the effect in the case of the *Brascan* transaction, assuming Brascan and Edper had been U.S. companies?

NOTE ON THE AUCTION DEBATE AND THE SHAREHOLDER COLLECTIVE ACTION PROBLEM

Until the late 1980s, one of the most important effects of the Williams Act was to create a de facto auction period of at least four weeks, which allowed target management to build its defenses and permitted other potential acquirers to jump in. In this way, the Williams Act led directly to broader questions: How should the law structure the purchase of control from disaggregated shareholders? Should it assist shareholders in overcoming their collective action problem by facilitating the highest bid, or should it protect discovery values by facilitating a successful acquisition by the first bidder?

Academic commentators lined up on both sides of this issue. Judge Frank Easterbrook and Professor Daniel Fischel argued strongly that auctioneering is likely to reduce the total number of value-increasing takeovers.[14] Professors Ronald Gilson and Lucian Bebchuk countered that an auction regime enhances the efficiency of individual takeovers, while having relatively little impact on the number of value-enhancing transactions.[15] The empirical evidence on this question is mixed: On one hand, studies showed that returns to U.S. acquirers in tender offers were lower in the 1970s than they were in the 1960s;[16] on the other hand, there is no evidence that acquisition activity declined in the 1970s due to the de facto auction period imposed by the Williams Act.

The legal import of the auction debate reaches well beyond the Williams Act. A related question was how much latitude target managers ought to enjoy under state law to "shop" the company by searching for a higher bidder after a hostile first bid. The auction debate thus feeds into a parallel controversy over the proper role for target management when confronted with a hostile bid. We address this debate in Chapter 13.

14. See, e.g., Frank H. Easterbrook & Daniel R. Fischel, *The Proper Role of a Target's Management in Responding to a Tender Offer*, 94 Harv. L. Rev. 1161 (1981).

15. See Ronald J. Gilson, *Seeking Competitive Bids Versus Pure Passivity in Tender Offer Defense*, 35 Stan. L. Rev. 51 (1982); Lucian Arye Bebchuk, *The Case for Facilitating Competing Tender Offers*, 95 Harv. L. Rev. 1028 (1982); Lucian Arye Bebchuk, *The Case for Facilitating Competing Tender Offers: A Reply and Extension*, 35 Stan. L. Rev. 23 (1982).

16. See, e.g., M. Bradley, A. Desai & E.H. Kim, *Synergistic Gains from Corporate Acquisitions and Their Division Between the Stockholders of Target and Acquiring Firms*, 21 J. Fin. Econ. 3 (1988); (average returns to acquirers declined to 1.3 percent during the 1970s compared to 4.1 percent in the 1960s).

FUNDAMENTAL TRANSACTIONS: MERGERS AND ACQUISITIONS

12.1 INTRODUCTION

Among the most important transactions in corporate law are those that pool the assets of separate companies into either a single entity or a dyad of a parent company and a wholly owned subsidiary (which is practically the same thing, only better). There are three legal forms for such transactions: the merger, the purchase (or sale) of all assets, and — in MBCA jurisdictions — the compulsory share exchange. A merger is a legal event that unites two existing corporations with a public filing of a certificate of merger, usually with shareholder approval. In the classic form, the so-called statutory merger, one of the two companies absorbs the other and is termed the "surviving corporation."[1] This company subsequently owns all of the property and assumes all of the obligations of both parties to the merger. An MBCA share exchange, as we describe below, closely resembles certain kinds of mergers in its legal effects. Finally, "acquisitions" comprise a generic class of "non-merger" techniques for combining companies under one management, which generally involve the purchase of either the assets or the shares of one firm by another. Following an acquisition, the acquiring corporation may or may not assume liability for the obligations of the acquired corporation, as we discuss below.

Mergers and acquisitions by public companies (M&A transactions) are among the most complex of business transactions. They implicate diverse legal questions[2] and profoundly alter the characteristics of shareholder investments. In this Chapter, we first examine economic motives for M&A transactions and then turn to specific protections that the law accords shareholders in these transactions. In particular, M&A transactions provide a useful platform

---

1. A merger in which both parties disappear and are survived by a new third corporation is technically called a consolidation. See, e.g., DGCL §251(a).

2. Even the simplest M&A transaction involving public companies typically raises issues of securities law, tax law, compensation law, and quite possibly competition law, in addition to corporate law, of course. See Martin D. Ginsburg & Jack S. Levin, Mergers, Acquisitions and Buyouts (2006).

for revisiting two fundamental questions of policy in corporate law: the role of shareholders in checking the board's discretion and the role of fiduciary duty in checking the power of controlling shareholders.

12.2   ECONOMIC MOTIVES FOR MERGERS

Like other legal forms of enterprise, the corporate form partitions business assets into discrete pools managed by particular management teams.[3] There is, however, no guarantee that an initial match among assets and managers continues to be the most productive match in a continuously changing economy. The law of M&A transactions provides (relatively) quick and inexpensive ways to reform the partitioning and management of corporate assets. We begin by surveying motives, value-increasing or not, for combining corporate assets.

12.2.1   Integration as a Source of Value

Gains from merging corporate assets arise from what economists term economies of "scale," "scope," and "vertical integration." Economies of scale result when a fixed cost of production — such as the investment in a factory — is spread over a larger output, thereby reducing the average fixed cost per unit of output. Consider two companies, each with a widget factory that operates at half capacity. If these companies merge, the "surviving" company might be able to meet the combined demand for widgets at a much lower cost by closing down one of its two factories and operating the other at full capacity. This source of efficiency often explains so-called "horizontal mergers" between firms in the same industry.

"Economies of scope" provide a similar source of efficiency gains. Here mergers reduce costs not by increasing the scale of production but instead by bundling together a broader range of related business activities. A typical example might be a merger between our widget manufacturer and a major supplier of raw materials that ensures an uninterrupted flow of raw materials of precisely the right quality that minimizes manufacturing costs.[4] Another example might be the widget maker's merger with another company that produces a product often used with widgets and that can be efficiently marketed through the widget maker's sales force. In theory, at least, even a merger

---

3. See our discussion of asset partitioning in Chapter 2.

4. This example illustrates "vertical integration," a special form of economies of scope, which may sometimes arise by merging a company backward, toward its suppliers, or forward, toward its customers. Buying a component on the market has advantages, but so, too, does buying the factory that makes the component. Contracting through the market can be expensive if the component is highly specialized. Moreover, even if a supplier is found, it may behave opportunistically once it determines that its customer has no good substitutes and is therefore dependent on it. Thus, if the component is very important, it may be cheaper in the long term to acquire the supplier through a merger than it would be to buy its product. See

between the widget maker and the manufacturer of a very different product might be said to bring economies of scope if it extends the underutilized talents of the widget maker's management team to a second line of products.[5]

12.2.2   Other Sources of Value in Acquisitions: Tax, Agency Costs, and Diversification

Apart from integration gains, M&A transactions are often said to generate value for at least three other reasons, relating to tax, agency costs, and diversification. Consider tax first. Corporations with tax losses (i.e., deductible expenses greater than income during the tax year) may set those losses off against income in subsequent years for up to 20 years. This ability to carry a net operating loss (NOL) forward is itself a valuable asset — but only if its owner has sufficient taxable income to absorb it. Since an NOL cannot be sold directly, a corporation that lacks sufficient income might prefer to find a wealthy merger partner rather than waste its NOL. In this transaction, the shareholders of the NOL's owner and its merger partner would implicitly share the NOL's present value.[6]

A very different economic motive for M&A transactions is the replacement of an underperforming management team that has depressed the company's stock price. As a company's stock price declines because the market anticipates

---

generally F.M. Scherer & David Ross, Industrial Market Structures and Economic Performance (3d ed. 1990). Professors Brealey and Myers, the finance mavens, offer the following illustration of how integration through ownership can increase efficiency. Suppose that airlines rented their planes on short-term leases but owned their brand names, operated airport gates, advertised, sold tickets, etc. The administrative cost of matching the supply of rented planes with the published schedule of flights would be enormous. Intuitively, any airline that switched to either owning its own planes or leasing them for long periods (which is economically quite similar) could realize huge savings. Thus, we would expect airlines to move to vertical integration — either owning or leasing the vital aircraft input for long periods. Nevertheless, a good thing can be overdone. Professors Brealey and Myers also note that, in the late 1980s, the Polish State Airline owned not only its own planes but also its own hog farms to supply meat to its customers and employees. See Richard A. Brealey & Stewart C. Myers, Principles of Corporate Finance (7th ed. 2003).

5. Thus, a management team with superior "general management" skills could attempt to wring added value from its skills by expanding the asset base over which it exercises its judgment. Something like this idea was a popular rationale for mergers during the "conglomerate merger" movement of the 1960s. Those mergers, however, did not generally prove to be efficient. See, e.g., Ronald W. Melichner & David F. Rush, *The Performance of Conglomerate Firms: Recent Risk and Return Experience*, 28 J. Fin. 381 (1973); David J. Ravenscraft & F.M. Scherer, Mergers, Sell-Offs and Economic Efficiency (1987). Indeed, many commentators believe that the "bust-up" takeover movement of the 1980s was largely about the unwinding of these inefficient mergers of two decades before. See, e.g., Andrei Shleifer & Robert W. Vishny, *The Takeover Wave of the 1980s*, 249 Sci. 745 (Aug. 17, 1990).

6. See Ginsburg & Levin, *supra* note 2, at ch. 12. The Internal Revenue Service not only bars the sale of NOLs but also disallows their deduction if the merger appears to have been structured solely to capture their value. Thus, the surviving company in a tax-driven merger must generally continue to operate the assets acquired from the NOL's owner, at least for a period of time.

that its incumbent managers will mismanage *in the future*, it becomes more likely that an outside buyer can profit by purchasing a controlling block of stock and replacing the incumbent managers.[7] Of course, acquiring a controlling block of stock, by means of a tender offer or otherwise, is usually enough to displace the target company's managers. The point is not merely to depose bad managers, however, but also to realize the maximum economic returns from doing so. Realizing maximum returns will generally require that the target company merge with a subsidiary of the acquiring company.

In the 1980s, most transactions to displace underperforming managers appear to have been hostile. As we discuss in Chapter 13, an acquirer would first bid for a controlling block of stock in a public tender offer and then, when successful, would arrange for a merger to cash out minority shareholders. Once in control, the acquirer would be free to discipline or fire management. Although hostile takeovers have been less common in recent years, the desire to improve management may also motivate friendly acquisitions. Why would poorly performing managers leave if they were not forced to do so? The answer is money, of course. As a matter of fact, poor managers (or good managers) can be bought off as part of the premium that a new investor must pay to acquire the corporation's assets. One device for sharing takeover premia with managers is the "golden parachute" contract, which provides senior managers with a generous payment upon certain triggering events, typically a change in the ownership of a controlling interest in the corporation or a change in the membership of its board. A second compensation technique is a term in a grant of restricted stock or options that allows them to vest immediately upon a change in control when they would otherwise vest over a four- to six-year period.[8]

Yet a third way in which M&A transactions are sometimes said to increase corporate value is by diversifying a company's business projects, thus smoothing corporate earnings over the business cycle. For example, the managers of an air conditioner company might wish to merge with a snow-blower company to ensure stable year-round earnings. Just why this sort of merger should increase the value of corporate assets is unclear, since investors can "smooth" corporate earnings at less cost merely by diversifying their *own* investment portfolios. Nevertheless, such "smoothing" is frequently offered as a rationale for mergers. The reason may be that such mergers simply make life more comfortable for managers,[9] or it may be that they actually can increase company value for some reason as yet undiscovered by financial economists.[10]

7. See Reinier Kraakman, *Taking Discounts Seriously: The Implications of "Discounted" Share Prices as an Acquisition Motive*, 88 Colum. L. Rev. 891 (1981).

8. Single trigger vestings — here, the change in control term — are increasingly viewed with some suspicion. What might be a source of shareholder concern in the example of the control trigger?

9. See Yakov Amihud & Baruch Lev, *Risk Reduces Managerial Motive for Conglomerate Mergers*, 12 Bell J. Econ. 605 (1981).

10. See Ronald J. Gilson & Bernard S. Black, The Law and Finance of Corporate Acquisitions 312-357 (2d ed. 1995). Wholly apart from smoothing earnings, product diversification can add efficiency by combining complementary assets, as when an acquirer can use its

12.2.3 Suspect Motives for Mergers

The discussion thus far has emphasized positive or neutral motives for mergers that increase the value of corporate assets without making anyone else worse off (except the government in tax-driven deals). There are, however, also opportunistic motives to enter mergers that increase shareholder value or management compensation at the expense of another corporate constituency. One example is a squeeze-out merger, in which a controlling shareholder acquires all of a company's assets at a low price, at the expense of its minority shareholders. Another form of opportunistic merger is one that creates market power in a particular product market, and thus allows the post-merger entity to charge monopoly prices for its output. (Of course, the government also attempts to block anticompetitive mergers under the elaborate federal framework of antitrust statutes.[11])

In addition to opportunistic M&A transactions, there is a last class of mergers that destroy value, perhaps even more so than opportunistic mergers. These are "mistaken" mergers that occur because their planners misjudge the difficulties of realizing merger economies. Common errors of judgment include underestimating the costs of overcoming disparate firm cultures; neglecting intangible costs, such as the labor difficulties that might follow wholesale layoffs; and failing to anticipate the added coordination costs that result merely from increasing the size of a business organization.[12] Finally, we note that some mergers are motivated not so much by a vision of making the acquirer more efficient, but to prevent its competitor from achieving some competitive advantage. We see this, for example, in consolidating industries, in which it seems important to each management team to achieve sufficient size to be among the last firms standing. Whether such mergers are efficient

---

distribution channels to sell a target's products. A merger between a snow blower company and an air conditioner company makes good sense if the combined firm can use shared physical facilities or the same trained workers. Economies of scope such as these do increase the real value of the target's assets, and thus the value of the surviving corporation's stock.

11. See Phillip Areeda & Donald F. Turner, Antitrust Law, 5 vols. (1978, 1980); Thomas W. Brunner, Mergers in the New Antitrust Era (1985). The Sherman Antitrust Act, the Clayton Act, and the Federal Trade Commission Act are the three most notable such statutes.

12. While there are often advantages to a larger scale, there is also a special burden that large-scale organizations must bear. That burden is reflected in minor part by the costs of determining transfer prices within large firms and, in a more important way, by the imperfections in these transfer prices. Very large firms may lose market information and discipline by assigning internal costs that differ from true market prices. This problem is small where the input has a comparable market price, in which case internal pricing can be based on an actual price. But as the organization grows large and its inputs become specialized, the costs assigned to them grow unreliable. As a result, the firm comes to lack critical information about the relative efficiency of different aspects of its operations. See Ludwig von Mises, Human Action: A Treatise on Economics (1949) and Ludwig von Mises, Socialism: An Economic and Sociological Analysis (1922) (J. Kahane trans., 1951). In addition, large-scale organizations typically require complex compensation schemes to encourage team cooperation and motivate individual performance. Such plans grow increasingly difficult to design and operate as the scale and complexity of the firm increase. Correlatively, smaller firms are better able to monitor worker productivity and create functional incentives.

or not in any particular case cannot be answered categorically, but it does seem like a risky strategy from the investors' perspective.

12.2.4   Do Mergers Create Value?

There is a vast empirical literature on the wealth effects of mergers. While the magnitude of the result varies widely from study to study, the general weight of the evidence indicates that, measured by immediate stock market price reaction to the merger's announcement, on average, mergers do create value.[13] In one frequently cited study, Professors Gregor Andrade, Mark Mitchell, and Erik Stafford examine 3,688 deals over the period 1973-1998 and find an increase in combined (target and acquirer) wealth of 1.8 percent in the window around the announcement of the deal.[14] This value, however, is not evenly distributed: within the short window the studies use to measure gains, targets generally win, while acquirers break even or lose on average. Andrade and colleagues, for example, report that the targets in their sample experienced positive abnormal returns of 16 percent on average, while the acquirers experienced negative abnormal returns of 0.7 percent.[15] (The combined effect is only modestly positive because acquirers are generally much larger than targets.)

Using a more recent M&A sample, a second study by Moeller and colleagues, reports an acceleration in acquirers' losses from acquisition: Between 1998 and 2001, acquiring firm shareholders lost 12 cents at deal announcement for every dollar spent, as compared to a loss of just 1.6 cents per dollar spent during all of the 1980s.[16] The authors note that their results for the 1998-2001 period are driven by a small number of acquisition announcements with extremely large losses. But a still more recent study by Benjamin Bennett and Robert Dam suggests that most M&A event studies understate the gains from mergers.[17] They estimate that 10 percent of a typical firm's stock price reflects the anticipation of being acquired and receiving a premium, in which case pre-merger stock price understates merger gains because it already reflects the expected value of an acquisition. This cameo summary suffices to show that empirical studies of acquisition gains must be interpreted with caution because we do not have data on the counterfactual — what would have happened to their market values had they opted to remain unattached and avoided acquisition activity?

13. For a comprehensive survey of the empirical evidence, see Robert F. Bruner, Applied Mergers and Acquisitions 47-49 (2004) (summarizing the results from 24 studies and concluding that "M&A does pay the investors in the combined buyer and target firms").

14. Gregor Andrade, Mark Mitchell & Erik Stafford, *New Evidence and Perspectives on Mergers*, 15 J. Econ. Persp. 103, 110 (Table 3) (2001).

15. See id.

16. Sara B. Moeller, Frederick P. Schlingemann & Rene M. Stulz, *Wealth Destruction on a Massive Scale? A Study of Acquiring-Firm Returns in the Recent Merger Wave*, 60 J. Fin. 757 (2005).

17. Benjamin Bennett & Robert A. Dam, *Merger Activity, Stock Prices, and Measuring Gains from M&A* (August 1, 2019). Available at SSRN: https://ssrn.com/abstract=3000574 or http://dx.doi.org/10.2139/ssrn.3000574.

12.3   The Evolution of the U.S. Corporate Law of Mergers

The history of U.S. merger law is one of constantly loosening constraints, driven by dynamic markets and technological change. It begins in a world without any mergers at all and ends in a world in which mergers can force shareholders to divest all of their stock in a company. The fundamental move in this evolution occurred when the law became willing to treat equity investors as a class of interests that could, except where fiduciary duties were triggered, be adequately protected by majority vote and a right to a statutory appraisal of fair value. For convenience, we can divide the history of merger law into two periods.

12.3.1   When Mergers Were Rare

The first period is the era when mergers were rare, which covers the history of U.S. corporate law until roughly 1890. Until about 1840, corporate charters were acts of the sovereign, in theory and in actuality. Legislatures created business corporations by special acts of incorporation, often to facilitate projects with a public purpose: the construction of canals or railroads, the creation of financial intermediaries (banks and insurance firms), or, more rarely, the establishment of manufacturing enterprises. Shareholders naturally lacked the power to amend these legislative charters, and thus, mergers could not occur except by intervention of state legislatures. Beginning around 1840, however, the enactment of general incorporation statutes permitted shareholders to incorporate on their own initiative with a charter of their own design. But until around 1890, state incorporation law uniformly barred shareholders from amending their charters (which a merger would require) without unanimous consent, in order to protect investors who had contributed funds in reliance on the charter. Thus, in this respect, the mid-nineteenth-century corporate form looked rather like the general partnership form.

12.3.2   The Modern Era

Technological change in the last decades of the nineteenth century increased the efficiency scale of many industries. Nevertheless, mergers could not become an economical way to restructure businesses into larger units as long as they required the unanimous consent of shareholders, which created crippling hold-up problems at the hands of minority shareholders. Thus, toward the end of the nineteenth century, corporation statutes were amended to permit mergers and charter amendments that received less than unanimous shareholder approval, providing that they were recommended by the board and approved by a majority (at first a supermajority) of a company's shareholders. Class vote provisions were sometimes added to assure fairness to subgroups of shareholders. Today, Delaware and many other states allow mergers to proceed with the approval of only a bare majority of the outstanding shares of each class of stock that is entitled to vote on them. In addition, a second innovation introduced more than 100 years ago was the establishment of the shareholder's right to dissent from a proposed merger and demand an "appraisal" — or judicial determination of the cash value of her shares — as an alternative to continuing as a shareholder in the new, merged enterprise.

A second important element of merger law in the modern era followed some 50 years later, when states greatly liberalized the permissible forms of merger consideration. Originally, shareholders of a merging company could receive only equity in the surviving company in exchange for their old shares. Under the mid-century statutes, the range of possible forms of consideration moved beyond securities in the surviving corporation to include all forms of property — most notably cash. Thus, from at least mid-century onward, it has been possible under state law to construct a "cash-out" merger, in which shareholders can be forced to exchange their shares for cash as long as the procedural requirements for a valid merger are met.

12.4   THE ALLOCATION OF POWER IN FUNDAMENTAL TRANSACTIONS

Today, the merger is the most prominent among a handful of corporate decisions that require shareholder approval.[18] Of course, those who formulate the corporation's original charter could shape additional shareholder voice in almost any way thought useful. Charters could create shareholder veto power, for example, in the sale of certain assets or in order to leave or enter certain lines of business. But as far as we are aware, no charters of public companies contain such provisions. All rely strictly on the provisions of the statutes to allocate power between the board and shareholders.

So, why does the law usually require shareholder consent for mergers and certain other transactions? Or put differently, how *should* the law draw the line between transactions that are completely delegated to the board and those that also must be approved by shareholders?

To explore this question, consider first the universal requirement that shareholders approve material amendments of the articles of incorporation, the basic "charter" of the corporation. Investors buy shares subject to the terms of the charter, and the board of directors exercises its management powers subject to these same terms. Thus, if it is useful for investors to be able to rely on any constraint in the charter, then the law must preclude unilateral amendment of the charter by the board. In fact, the law in all jurisdictions

---

18. In most U.S. jurisdictions, the other corporate decisions that require shareholder approval include sales of substantially all assets, charter amendments, and voluntary dissolutions. Some states and foreign jurisdictions add other classes of decisions to the short list of fundamental decisions requiring shareholder approval.

does this.[19] Moreover, to protect investors' reasonable expectations, the law must provide a shareholder veto over all transactions that might effectively amend the charter. Thus, shareholders must approve both corporate dissolution, which nullifies the corporate charter, and corporate mergers, in which the surviving corporation's charter may be amended. But the power to change the charter cannot be the only criterion for determining which transactions require a shareholder vote. Other transactions that do not change the charter also require shareholder approval. Specifically, a sale of substantially all of a corporation's assets may not occur unless it has been approved by a vote of the company's shareholders, even though no change in the company's charter occurs.[20] In some non-U.S. jurisdictions, shareholders must approve other transactions as well, such as large share issues and asset purchases.[21] (While in the United States these transactions do not require shareholder approval as a matter of corporation law, the listing rules of the major securities exchanges require shareholder approval if companies issue 20 percent or more of their outstanding stock in a single transaction.[22])

As a general matter, three major considerations ought to determine the allocation of decision-making power within organizations: Who has the best information, who has the most knowledge or skill in regard to this matter, and who has the best incentives? At least in large companies, the answers to these questions are usually not the same. Managers will generally have much better information regarding a company's business and knowledge concerning the specifics of its proposed transactions. But managers may have incentive problems — the most obvious example is the decision to sell the company, which may cost them their job. So the boundary case of complete managerial authority does not seem socially optimal when corporate control transactions are involved. We suggest that, rationally, principals with strong incentives to maximize value will reserve power to veto those matters that are most economically significant and in which they have some capacity to exercise informed judgment. In the corporate context, these criteria suggest that dispersed shareholders will wish to decide at most only very large issues (those that affect their entire investment) and will wish to decide only issues that they can be expected to decide with some competence ("investment-like" decisions rather than "business" decisions).

The general contours of corporate law follow this logic. Bet-the-company operational decisions (take, for example, Microsoft's decision to develop Microsoft Windows; or Boeing's decision to develop the 747 wide-body jet) do not require a shareholder vote. Even though such decisions are of supreme economic importance, shareholders generally lack the ability and information to make them relative to the alternative decision maker, the board and top

19. See, e.g., DGCL §242(b); MBCA §§10.03, 10.04.
20. E.g., DGCL §271; MBCA §12.02. We are focused on charter and bylaw provisions. Shareholders agreements, discussed in Section 3.2.5, may govern shareholder voting in some situations not specifically covered by the charter or bylaws. However, they may not be very common in publicly traded firms.
21. Theodor Baums & Eddy Wymeersch, Shareholder Voting Rights and Practices in Europe and the United States (1999).
22. E.g., NYSE Listed Co. Rule 312.03(c); ASE Co. Guide §712(b).

managers. Likewise, very small acquisitions (sometimes called "whale-minnow" acquisitions) do not require a vote by the whale's shareholders, because they would be rationally apathetic about evaluating the merits of the transaction. Far better to leave both of these kinds of decisions to the board.

What about large-scale M&A? Depending on your intuition about shareholder competence (or information) you might conjecture either that shareholders should vote on *all* large M&A transactions — including mergers, large asset sales and purchases, and share exchanges — or on none of them. The benefits of avoiding errors might seem to be large enough for such transactions that shareholders might plausibly believe that they (or the market) are sufficiently well informed to evaluate these deals.

United States law, however, does not conform to the binary logic of mandating shareholder approval for all or none of these transactions. Mergers require a vote of *both* the target and the acquiring company's shareholders (DGCL § 251(b)) unless the acquiring company is much larger than the target, in which case only the target shareholders vote. Sales of substantially all assets require a vote by the target's shareholders (DGCL §271), but purchases of assets do not require a vote. Thus, even if the seller of substantially all assets is much larger than the buyer, the buyer's shareholders lack a statutory right to approve the deal. What accounts for the different treatment of a very large purchase of assets that transforms the business and a merger that has a similar effect? It cannot be the magnitude of these transactions (and hence the size of potential management error), as both transactions are equally large. Nor can it be the likely quality and cost of shareholder decision making, since similar transactions can take either form. However, there is a third factor bearing on optimal delegation that may have some role here: the potential severity of the agency problem between the principal (the shareholders) and the agent (the board).

By and large, the M&A transactions that require shareholder approval are those that change the board's relationship to its shareholders most dramatically, and thereby reduce the ability of shareholders to displace their managers following the transaction. This is true, for example, in a stock-for-stock merger between equally sized corporations because the shareholders of both corporations will be substantially diluted. It is also true when the board proposes to sell substantially all corporate assets because the company is likely to dissolve after the deal, leaving management to go its own way (perhaps to the purchaser of the assets) with no further ties to the target's shareholders. By contrast, a purchase of assets for cash does not alter the power of shareholders to displace their managers.[23] The purchase of assets for shares is another matter, and it is puzzling why American corporate law does not generally require shareholder votes to authorize large-scale share issues. One (unsatisfying) explanation might be that shareholders have already approved the corporate charter that authorizes such issues. But the major U.S. stock exchanges do require shareholders to authorize large-scale stock issues (20 percent or more).

---

23. This point is developed in Ronald H. Gilson & Bernard Black, The Law of Finance of Corporate Acquisitions 714-722 (1995).

For these reasons, it seems possible that concerns relating to shareholder future control over managers, rather than size or shareholder competence, are the binding functional determinants of when the law requires a shareholder vote. But we can easily see how other jurisdictions might delineate a wider or narrower class of corporate decisions that require shareholder approval.

12.5 OVERVIEW OF TRANSACTIONAL FORM

How is the acquisition of a business to be structured? As we noted above, there are three principal legal forms of acquisitions: (1) The acquirer can buy the target company's assets, (2) the acquirer can buy all of the target corporation's stock, or (3) the acquirer can merge itself or a subsidiary corporation with the target on terms that ensure its control of the surviving entity. In each of these transactional forms, the acquirer can use cash, its own stock, or any other agreed-upon form of consideration. Each form, moreover, has particular implications for the acquisition's transaction costs (including its speed), potential liability costs, and tax consequences. Here we focus on the transaction costs and liability implications of transactional forms. While taxes play an important part in choosing a transaction form, we must leave that large subject to other courses in the curriculum. For those who cannot wait, however, we direct you to the great treatise by Professor Martin Ginsburg and Jack Levin, Esq. cited in note 2, above.

12.5.1 Asset Acquisition

The acquisition of a business through the purchase of its assets has a relatively high transaction cost (but a low liability cost). The purchase of assets — any assets — presents a standard set of contracting problems. One must identify the assets to be acquired, conduct due diligence with respect to these assets (e.g., investigate quality of title and existence of liens or other interests that may exist in the assets by others), establish the representations and warranties that both parties must make respecting the assets or themselves, negotiate covenants to protect the assets prior to closing, fix the price and terms of payment, and establish the conditions of closing. Titled assets, such as land and automobiles, must be transferred formally through documents of title and, frequently, by filing with an appropriate state office. Each of these individual steps is costly, and in the case of purchasing a large firm, aggregate acquisition costs can be quite large.[24]

Finally, as we have just discussed, a sale of substantially all assets is a fundamental transaction for the selling company, which requires shareholder approval under all U.S. corporate law statutes. See, e.g., DGCL §271; MBCA

---

24. See generally American Bar Association, Business Law Section, Negotiated Acquisition Committee, Model Asset Purchase Agreement with Commentary, available at: https://www.americanbar.org/products/inv/book/213895/.

§12.02. But neither the meaning of "all or substantially all" assets nor the policy intent behind these words is always clear.

NOTE ON KATZ v. BREGMAN *AND THE MEANING OF* "SUBSTANTIALLY ALL"

Delaware's approach to "substantially all" assets has changed over time. In the classic *Katz v. Bregman*, 431 A.2d 1274 (Del. Ch. 1981) case, Chancellor Marvel held that when a target sells 51 percent of its assets, producing 45 percent of its sales, that can amount to a sale of "substantially all" assets. In *Katz*, Plant Industries was attempting to sell one of its subsidiaries — Plant National (Quebec) Ltd. (National) — which apparently accounted for roughly 50 percent of Plant Industries' pre-tax profits in 1979 and 1980. There was considerable interest in National with two purchasers vying for it — Vulcan Industrial Packing, Ltd. and Universal Drum Reconditioning Co. National agreed to Vulcan's offer and cut off any further negotiations with Universal because its management reasoned that "a firm undertaking having been entered into with Vulcan, the board of directors of Plant may not legally or ethically negotiate with Universal." Perhaps, unsurprisingly, plaintiff-shareholders brought suit seeking an injunction to block the Vulcan-National merger in order to permit competitive bidding. Chancellor Marvel granted plaintiffs' request for an injunction until a shareholder vote to approve the transaction occurred and held at page 1278 that

> In the case at bar, I am first of all satisfied that historically the principal business of Plant Industries, Inc. has [been] to manufacture steel drums . . . a business which has been profitably performed by National of Quebec. Furthermore, the proposal, after the sale of National, to embark on the manufacture of plastic drums represents a radical departure from Plant's historically successful line of business, namely steel drums. I therefore conclude that the proposed sale of Plant's Canadian operations, which constitute over 51% of Plant's total assets and in which are generated approximately 45% of Plant's 1980 net sales, would, if consummated, constitute a sale of substantially all of Plant's assets. . . .

This outcome might seem surprising. After all, how does 51 percent of the assets reasonably represent "substantially all" of Plant's assets? Others have wondered as well, and no later court has approached this level of liberality in interpreting these words. Moreover, drafters of the Model Business Corporation Act have expressly indicated that "substantially all" is intended to mean much more than 51 percent. See MBCA §12.02(a).

The result in *Katz* can be explained, we think, as an early precursor to the cases decided in 1985 that revolutionized mergers and acquisition law. Specifically, in *Katz* the court is struggling to protect an active bidding contest for control of National. The same task was more aggressively undertaken by the Delaware Supreme Court in its famous *Revlon* case of 1985 (which we take up in Chapter 13). In *Katz*, the court apparently thought either that management had agreed to sell too early (before a higher bidder came along) or that there was something inherently suspect about selecting a lower price over a higher one. Plaintiffs' claim was that management was guilty of a "studied refusal to consider a potentially higher bid. . . ."[25]

Thus, for historians of corporation law (a small set for sure) and for students seeking to uncover the true motivation of courts in reaching decisions (a large set, we believe), *Katz* is an interesting case. We suggest that it represents a court taking up the tools at hand (§271) to reach a result that it thought fairness to shareholders required. For the legal doctrinalist, this case marks the outer boundary of the meaning of the statutes that mandate shareholder votes on sales of assets.

A more recent interpretation of the "substantially all" test under DGCL §271 arises in *Hollinger, Inc. v. Hollinger Intl.*[26] The question presented in that case was whether the sale of the *Telegraph* Group of newspapers (consisting of various newspapers associated with the London-based *Daily Telegraph*) constituted "substantially all" of the assets of Hollinger International ("International"), which owned over 100 other newspapers too. International's controlling shareholder, Conrad Black, claimed that a shareholder vote was required under the substantially all test, which would have allowed him to block the sale.

Examining relative revenue contributions, profitability, and other financial measures, then Vice Chancellor Leo Strine found that the *Telegraph* Group accounted for 56 to 57 percent of International's value, with the *Chicago* Group accounting for the rest. In his characteristically direct (and often entertaining) way, V.C. Strine held that the sale of the *Telegraph* Group did not constitute "substantially all" of International's assets:

> Has the judiciary transmogrified the words "substantially all" in §271 of the [DGCL] into the words "approximately half"? . . . I begin my articulation of the applicable legal principles with the words of the statute itself. There are two key words here: "substantially" and "all." Although neither word is particularly difficult to understand, let's start with the easier one. "All" means "all," or if that is not clear, all, when used before a plural noun such as "assets," means "[t]he entire or unabated amount or quantity of." . . . "Substantially" conveys the same meaning as "considerably" and "essentially." . . . A fair and succinct equivalent to the term "substantially all" would therefore be "essentially everything."[27]

By 2004, then, it would seem that the Delaware courts have moved quite a bit back from *Katz v. Bregman*.

25. *Katz*, at 1275. The court twice cites *Thomas v. Kempner*, which was an unreported 1973 case on preliminary injunction in which Chancellor Marvel, the author of *Katz*, granted an injunction against the closing of a sale of substantially all assets when a higher price emerged after contract signing but before closing. While a contract entered on imperfect information is not rescindable for that reason alone, if the early contract represents an effort to favor one buyer over another for private reasons, it will constitute a breach of duty. The court also cites *Robinson v. Pittsburgh Oil Refining Company*, 126 A. 46 (Del. 1924), an old case that stands for the proposition that a fiduciary must sell for more rather than less cash where price is the only material difference between bidders.

26. 858 A.2d 342 (Del. Ch. 2004).

27. 858 A.2d 342, 377.

NOTE ON ASSET ACQUISITIONS AND POTENTIAL LIABILITY

As we noted above, the chief drawback of asset acquisition as a method of acquiring a company is that it is costly and very time consuming to transfer all of the individual assets of a large business. Offsetting this drawback, it might seem, is that an acquirer accedes only to the assets, and not the liabilities, of the target. In theory, this is true so long as an asset purchase is at arm's length and does not violate the Fraudulent Conveyance Act and its successors (discussed in Chapter 4). However, when the assets at issue constitute an integrated business, courts have identified circumstances in which a purchaser of assets may become responsible for liability associated with those assets. The best-known examples of this doctrine of "successor liability" involve tort claims as a result of defective products manufactured in plants now held by different owners. They also tend to be cases in which the culpable previous owners of the assets — the plants that produced the injury-producing products — have dissolved and paid out a liquidating distribution to their shareholders, leaving no one else to sue but the asset's new owners.[28] Note, however, that courts are less likely to invoke successor liability today than they were in the 1970s and 1980s.

A different legal risk that attends asset acquisition is liability for environmental cleanup expenses that are imposed under various federal statutes on "owners" or "operators" of acquired assets. Thus, the purchase of assets that constitute hazardous environmental conditions may make the new owner jointly liable for cleanup expenses. In response to the risk of successor liability and environmental liability, business planners find it prudent to make acquisitions in the triangular form — that is, through separately incorporated subsidiaries, even when they plan to purchase only the assets of a target firm. When a liability later arises that the acquiring subsidiary cannot pay, courts have not generally "pierced" the corporate existence of this separate legal buyer itself, absent independent grounds to do so (see Section 4 of Chapter 4).[29]

12.5.2 Stock Acquisition

A second transactional form for acquiring an incorporated business is through the purchase of all, or a majority of, the company's stock. As we discussed in Chapter 11, a company that acquires a controlling block of stock in another has, in a practical sense, "acquired" the controlled firm. Thus, tender offers for a controlling block of a company's stock may be thought of as acquisition transactions. In a technical sense, however, the purchase of control by an acquirer is merely a shareholder transaction that does not alter the legal

---

28. See, e.g., *Ray v. Alad Corp.*, 506 P.2d 3 (Cal. 1977). See generally Michael D. Green, *Successor Liability*, 72 Cornell L. Rev. 17 (1986).

29. See *United States v. BestFoods, Inc.*, 524 U.S. 51 (1998) (refusing to pierce the corporate veil to impose CERCLA liability on parent of wholly owned subsidiary).

identity of the corporation. Something more is needed beyond the purchase of control to result in a full-fledged acquisition.

To acquire a corporation in the full sense of obtaining complete dominion over its assets, an acquirer must purchase 100 percent of its target's stock, not merely a control block. As a practical matter, moreover, acquirers typically do not want a small minority of public shares outstanding. There are costs to being a public company, including the costs of complying with SEC regulations and the implicit costs of assuring that all transfers among controlled entities are fair to the public minority. Corporate law recognizes the legitimacy of the desire to eliminate a small public minority by creating the easy-to-execute short-form merger statutes, which allow a 90 percent shareholder to simply cash out a minority unilaterally.[30] Also, some states take the additional step of offering acquirers and targets a statutory device termed a "compulsory share exchange." This permits a direct exchange of target shares for acquirer shares held by the acquirer's subsidiary. The target shareholders become shareholders in the acquirer (or receive cash consideration) while the target becomes a wholly owned subsidiary of the acquirer. The result is a form of acquisition that receives the tax treatment of a tender offer without the attendant holdup problems of a true tender offer or the awkward residue of a minority of public shareholders.[31]

Delaware has no compulsory share exchange statute. Nevertheless, Delaware lawyers can achieve the same result either through a triangular merger, addressed below, or if, for reasons of tax or timing, an initial tender offer is desired, a new Delaware transaction form — the "intermediate-form merger" under DGCL §251(h) — can fit the bill. With the agreement of the target and acquiring corporations' boards, the acquirer first makes a tender offer for the target's shares. If the number of shares tendered would suffice to approve a merger under the voting requirements of the merger statute, then the second-step merger is treated as having been approved (assuming it is at the same price as the first-step tender offer and meets the other requirements of §251(h)). The effect is that the merger can now occur promptly after the tender offer closes.[32]

12.5.3   Mergers

A merger legally collapses one corporation into another. As noted earlier, the corporation that survives with its legal identity intact is, not surprisingly, the "surviving corporation."[33] A management team that wishes to acquire another

---

30. See, e.g., DGCL §253.

31. See MBCA §12.02.

32. The expedited §251(h) process has become an increasingly popular deal structure. See Piotr Korzynski, *"Forcing the Offer": Considerations for Deal Certainty and Support Agreements in Delaware Two-Step Mergers*, Harv. L.S. Forum on Corp. Gov., April 2, 2018. When stock is used as consideration for the target's shares under §251(h)(5), the outcome is identical to a compulsory share exchange.

33. A less common transaction, a "consolidation," collapses two corporations into a new legal entity, the "resulting corporation." In most respects, corporation statutes treat mergers and consolidations identically.

company in a merger typically researches the target and initiates negotiations over the terms of a merger itself—although the target company might also approach a possible acquirer about a possible deal and open its books to facilitate its potential suitor's due diligence. A merger requires the approval of the board, too, of course. But just *when* a CEO raises a proposed merger with the board and *how involved* the board will be are not dictated by law. Courts have, however, plainly signaled that they wish to see boards involved early and deeply in the acquisition or sale process. This means that outside directors should be involved intensively since they constitute most or almost all of the board, excepting only the CEO in the modal case. In all events, the management teams of the two corporations, aided by lawyers and investment bankers, prepare a merger agreement for board approval. (We provide a simple, excerpted example below.) After the board formally authorizes the execution of this agreement, the board will, in most instances, call a shareholders' meeting to obtain shareholder approval of the merger.

In most states, a valid merger requires a majority vote by the outstanding stock of each constituent corporation that is entitled to vote.[34] The default rule is that all classes of stock vote on a merger unless the certificate of incorporation expressly states otherwise.[35] Oddly, the Delaware merger statute, DGCL §251, does not also protect preferred stock with the right to a class vote in most circumstances.[36] Of course, the Delaware statute does give class-voting rights to preferred stock if their rights are adversely affected by a charter amendment. See DGCL §242(b)(2). But this narrow right is triggered only when a charter amendment alters the *formal* rights of the preferred stock, not when it reduces the economic value of the stock.[37] Thus, under Delaware law, the most important source of preferred stock's voting rights either on a merger or on an amendment of the charter is in the corporate charter itself.[38] Competent corporate practitioners working with Delaware incorporated firms do not rely upon statutory defaults but

---

Note that civil law jurisdictions generally have not only a merger transaction but also its statutory inverse, a statutory "separation" transaction, in which a portion of the assets and liabilities of a single large company are *assigned* to a new corporate entity. In the United States, separation is generally accomplished by dropping a portion of a company's assets into a subsidiary and distributing the shares of this subsidiary to the original company's shareholders.

34. See, e.g., DGCL §251(c).

35. E.g., DGCL §212(a). Generally, all common stock votes, although non-voting common is possible. The voting rights of preferred stock are typically more limited. Most commonly, preferred has no right to vote at all except in stated circumstances (e.g., when a preferred dividend has been skipped). But when preferred stock has a right to vote, it is generally the right to a class vote, since preferred votes would otherwise ordinarily be swamped by the votes of common stock if they voted together.

36. Compare MBCA §§11.03, 11.04. Thus, under Delaware law, preferred stockholders are heavily dependent on the terms of their security for their protection and receive scant help from Delaware corporate law. There is an interesting history here for the specialist. See *Federal United Corp. v. Havender*, 11 A.2d 331 (Del. 1940).

37. *Shanik v. White Sewing Machine Corp.*, 19 A.2d 831 (Del. 1941). Compare MBCA §10.04(a)(6) (contra).

38. By contrast, the MBCA creates parallel class-voting tests for charter amendments and mergers. Under these provisions, any special effect on a class of security holders (even

define the voting rights of preferred stock in the document that creates that security, typically called a "Certificate of Preferences, Special Rights and Limitations."

The voting common stock of the "target" or collapsed corporation always has voting rights. The voting stock of the surviving corporation is generally afforded statutory voting rights on a merger *except* when three conditions are met: (1) The surviving corporation's charter is not modified, (2) the security held by the surviving corporation's shareholders will not be exchanged or modified, and (3) the surviving corporation's outstanding common stock will not be increased by more than 20 percent.[39] The rationale for this exemption from the usual requirement that shareholders of both companies approve a merger is that mergers satisfying these conditions have too little impact on the surviving corporation's shareholders to justify the delay and the expense of a shareholder vote.

Of course, higher or special voting requirements for mergers may be established by the corporate charter or by state takeover statutes (e.g., DGCL §203). Moreover, the stock exchanges require a listed corporation to hold a shareholder vote on any transaction or series of related transactions that result in the issuance of common stock (or convertible preferred stock) sufficient to increase outstanding shares by 20 percent. Unlike corporate statutes, the stock exchange rules require approval of 50 percent of shares voting on the matter (a "simple majority"), as opposed to 50 percent of outstanding shares (an "absolute majority"). Thus, if the acquisition contemplates the issuance of more than 20 percent of the acquirer's common stock, shareholders of the acquirer, as well as those of the target, must approve the transaction, regardless of how it is structured.[40]

Following an affirmative shareholder vote, a merger is effectuated by filing a certificate of merger with the appropriate state office. The governance structure of the surviving corporation may be restructured in the merger through the adoption of an amended certificate of incorporation (or articles of incorporation) and bylaws, which will have been approved by the shareholders as part of the merger vote. Shareholders who disapprove of the terms of the merger must dissent from it in order to seek, as an alternative, a judicial appraisal of the fair value of their shares. (Generally, if they have no right to vote on the merger, they will not have appraisal rights for similar reasons.)

---

stock that is made expressly non-voting in the charter) will give that class of security holders a right to vote as a class. See MBCA §§10.04, 11.04(f). Other statutes, including the California and Connecticut codes, give non-voting preferred stock the right to vote on a merger even if the merger does not affect the legal rights of the holders. See also our prior discussion of class voting in Chapter 6.

39. See, e.g., DGCL §251(f); Cal. Corp. Code §1201 (b), (d).

40. It is possible, for example, that the approval of the buyer-parent's shareholders may be required in a reverse triangular stock merger under the NYSE rules even though no vote of parent shareholders would be required under the DGCL. See NYSE Listed Co. Manual ¶B12.03(C), at www.nyse.com. (This situation, in fact, arose in the planned stock acquisition of Warner Communications by Time, Inc. in 1989.) See *Paramount Communications, Inc. v. Time, Inc.*, 1989 WL 79880, Fed. Sec. L. Rep. 94,514, 15 Del. J. Corp. L. 700 (Del. Ch. 1989).

12.5.4   Triangular Mergers

As we have noted, the surviving corporation in a merger assumes the liabilities of both constituent corporations by operation of law. But to expose the acquirer's assets to the (imperfectly known) liabilities of a new acquisition is inevitably a risky step. Thus the acquirer has a strong incentive to preserve the liability shield that the target's separate incorporation confers. This can easily be done by merging the target into a wholly owned subsidiary of the acquirer (or reversing this by merging the subsidiary into the target). And this is precisely what is done. Preserving the liability protection that separate incorporation provides to the acquirer is almost always a highly desirable business goal. Most mergers are accomplished in a way that permits two separate corporate entities to survive the merger.

This maintenance of the liability shield is the premise for the *triangular merger* form. In this structure, the acquirer (A) forms a wholly owned subsidiary (call it NewCo). Imagine that A transfers the merger consideration to NewCo in exchange for all of NewCo's stock. Then Target will merge into NewCo (or NewCo will merge into Target). In either event, at the time of the merger, the merger consideration will be distributed to Target shareholders, and their Target stock will be canceled. The stock of A in Target, if it owned any, will also be canceled. Thus, after the merger, A will own all of the outstanding stock of NewCo, which, in turn, will own all of Target's assets and liabilities. If NewCo is the surviving corporation, the merger is referred to as a "forward triangular merger." If Target is the surviving corporation (its shareholders nevertheless having their shares converted into the merger consideration), the merger is said to be a "reverse triangular merger." Of course, if NewCo is the surviving company, it can immediately change its name to Target, Inc., after the merger and thus preserve the value of Target's brands and goodwill. But no matter which company — NewCo or Target — is the survivor, its charter can be restated (and typically is restated) at the merger to include the governance terms and capital structure that A deems desirable. The merger agreement will be entered into by all three parties — A, Target, and NewCo. In practice, the merger consideration — cash or shares of A typically — will not be transferred first to NewCo, as in our example, but will be distributed at the closing of the transaction directly from A to the holders of Target shares in consideration of the cancellation of those shares.

12.5.5   De Facto Mergers

Should a "merger" be regarded as a functional concept (as implied in Section 12.4), or a formal or technical concept precisely defined by the corporation statute? Might there be functional reasons for treating the concept of a "merger" formally?

Consider, for example, a sale of substantially all assets by one corporation in exchange for stock of the buyer, followed by dissolution of the seller and distribution of buyer's stock to the seller's shareholders. In effect, this resembles a stock-for-stock merger, with the buyer as the surviving entity that owns all of the assets and the investors in both companies owning buyer's stock. Should shareholder sellers be able to seek appraisal of the fair value of their shares from the buyer as they could in a merger? Some U.S. courts have adopted a functionalist approach to questions of this type and have accorded shareholder voting and appraisal rights to all corporate combinations that resemble mergers in effect. These courts have reasoned that when a de facto merger has the same economic effect as a de jure merger, shareholders should have the same protection.[41]

There is, of course, a (functional) counterargument to such a functionalist approach. Corporate law contains a large element of formalism. Corporations exist as entities because certain formal steps are taken. Incorporators sign incorporation documents containing designated information, they hold an organizational meeting at which designated acts are performed, they file a charter in a prescribed form, they make a small payment, and — voila! — a legal person is born.[42] Still other formalities carry the corporation forward in its new life. Boards meet and vote, shareholders elect directors annually (usually), and filings are made. And finally, mergers are consummated by filing with the appropriate state office. All of this is not "mere formality"; it is a source of utility. It permits people to predict accurately the legal consequences of their activities.

Delaware courts, together with most other U.S. courts, take the formalist side of the argument, at least with respect to the range of statutory protections that are available to shareholders in a corporate combination. The provisions of the Delaware statute are said to have "equal dignity" or "independent legal significance." A self-identified sale of assets that results in exactly the same economic consequences as a merger will nonetheless be governed by the (lesser) shareholder protections associated with a sale of assets and not the full panoply of merger protections. A well-known formulation of this position is *Hariton v. Arco Electronics, Inc.*, excerpted below.[43]

HARITON v. ARCO ELECTRONICS, INC.
182 A.2d 22 (Del. Ch. 1962), aff'd, 188 A.2d 123 (Del. 1963)

Short, V.C.:

Plaintiff is a stockholder of defendant Arco Electronics, Inc., a Delaware corporation. The complaint challenges the validity of the purchase by Loral

---

41. Outside of the United States, similar reasoning has been used to extend voting rights to shareholders, especially under German law, where the seminal *Holzmuller* decision extended voting rights in the 1980s to protect an entire class of fundamental transactions. BGHZ, Zivilsenat, II ZR 174/80Y (1980) (German judicial decisions extending shareholder voting rights to apparently fundamental corporate transaction).

42. If corporate organizers get it wrong, courts of equity may resort to a number of devices, such as corporation by estoppel, to try to reach fair outcomes. But if the firm is not formally created, the separate personality does not exist. See Frank William McIntyre, *Note and Comment: De Facto Merger in Texas: Reports of Its Death Have Been Greatly Exaggerated*, 2 Tex. Wesleyan L. Rev. 593 (Spring 1996).

43. A noted American formulation of the opposite position, the de facto merger doctrine, is *Farris v. Glen Alden Corp.*, 393 Pa. 427, 143 A.2d 25 (1958). We do not reproduce the

Electronics Corporation, a New York corporation, of all the assets of Arco. Two causes of action are asserted, namely (1) that the transaction is unfair to Arco stockholders, and (2) that the transaction constituted a de facto merger and is unlawful since the merger provisions of the Delaware law were not complied with. . . .

[At this point,] the only issue before the court, therefore, is whether the transaction was by its nature a de facto merger with a consequent right of appraisal in plaintiff. . . .

In the summer of 1961 Arco commenced negotiations with Loral with a view to the purchase of all of the assets of Arco in exchange for shares of Loral common stock. I think it fair to say that the record establishes that the negotiations which ultimately led to the transaction involved were conducted by the representatives of the two corporations at arm's length. There is no suggestion that any representative of Arco had any interest whatever in Loral, or vice versa. In any event, Arco rejected two offers made by Loral of a purchase price based upon certain ratios of Loral shares for Arco shares. Finally, on October 12, 1961, Loral offered a purchase price based on the ratio of one share of Loral common stock for three shares of Arco common stock. This offer was accepted by the representatives of Arco on October 24, 1961 and an agreement for the purchase was entered into between Loral and Arco on October 27, 1961. This agreement provides, among other things, as follows:

> Arco will convey and transfer to Loral all of its assets and property of every kind, tangible and intangible; and will grant to Loral the use of its name and slogans.
> Loral will assume and pay all of Arco's debts and liabilities. Loral will issue to Arco 283,000 shares of its common stock.
> Upon the closing of the transaction Arco will dissolve and distribute to its shareholders, pro rata, the shares of the common stock of Loral.
> Arco will call a meeting of its stockholders to be held December 21, 1961 to authorize and approve the conveyance and delivery of all the assets of Arco to Loral.
> After the closing date Arco will not engage in any business or activity except as may be required to complete the liquidation and dissolution of Arco.

Pursuant to its undertaking in the agreement for purchase and sale Arco caused a special meeting of its stockholders to be called for December 27, 1961. The notice of such meeting set forth three specific purposes therefor: (1) to vote upon a proposal to ratify the agreement of purchase and sale, a copy of which was attached to the notice; (2) to vote upon a proposal to change the name of the corporation; and (3) if Proposals (1) and (2) should be adopted, to vote upon a proposal to liquidate and dissolve the corporation and to distribute the Loral shares to Arco shareholders. . . .

Plaintiff contends that the transaction, though in form a sale of assets of Arco, is in substance and effect a merger, and that it is unlawful because the

---

Farris decision — partly because its continuing authority is suspect but principally because the underlying issue is identical to that in the *Hariton* case.

merger statute has not been complied with, thereby depriving plaintiff of his right of appraisal.

Defendant contends that since all the formalities of a sale of assets pursuant to 8 Del. C. §271 have been complied with the transaction is in fact a sale of assets and not a merger. In this connection it is to be noted that plaintiffs nowhere allege or claim that defendant has not complied to the letter with the provisions of said section. . . .

The right of appraisal accorded to a dissenting stockholder by the merger statutes is in compensation for the right which he had at common law to prevent a merger. . . . The Legislatures of many states have seen fit to grant the appraisal right to a dissenting stockholder not only under the merger statutes but as well under the sale of assets statutes. Our Legislature has seen fit to expressly grant the appraisal right only under the merger statutes. This difference in treatment of the rights of dissenting stockholders may well have been deliberate, in order "to allow even greater freedom of action to corporate majorities in arranging combinations than is possible under the merger statutes." 72 Harv. L. Rev. 1232, *The Right of Shareholders Dissenting from Corporate Combinations to Demand Cash Payment for Their Shares.*

While plaintiff's contention that the doctrine of de facto merger should be applied in the present circumstances is not without appeal, the subject is one which, in my opinion, is within the legislative domain. Moreover it is difficult to differentiate between a case such as the present and one where the reorganization plan contemplates the ultimate dissolution of the selling corporation but does not formally require such procedure in express terms. . . .

[That] Arco continued in existence as a corporate entity following the exchange of securities . . . only for the purpose of winding up its affairs by the distribution of Loral stock is, in my mind, of little consequence. . . . The right of the corporation to sell all of its assets for stock in another corporation was expressly accorded to Arco by §271 of Title 8, Del. C. The stockholder was, in contemplation of law, aware of this right when he acquired his stock. . . .

I conclude that the transaction complained of was not a de facto merger, either in the sense that there was a failure to comply with one or more of the requirements of §271 of the Delaware Corporation Law, or that the result accomplished was in effect a merger entitling plaintiff to a right of appraisal.

NOTE AND QUESTIONS

1. Which company is the de jure acquirer in this transaction? Which company is likely to have been the functional acquirer? How do you know?

2. The Model Business Corporation Act removes the issue of de facto mergers by giving shareholders a right to dissent and seek appraisal every time a restructuring is authorized. See MBCA §13.02(3).

3. Was *Hariton* rightly decided? Should courts provide identical protections to minority shareholders involved in economically identical transactions? If not, should legislatures do so?

12.6   STRUCTURING THE M&A TRANSACTION

To choose the right structure for an M&A transaction, the lawyer, banker, and client must consider the interaction of many variables. Costs, taxes, speed, liabilities, information known and unknown, accounting treatment, regulatory hurdles, and the possibility of a competing bidder are among the obvious considerations that bear on crafting a deal. In this section, we address a number of these concerns briefly while reserving others, such as deal protections, for the section 12.6.5 and Chapter 13. Thus, M&A agreements contain the customary provisions found in most commercial contracts. In addition to resolving issues of timing, cost, risk, and price that go to the heart of the deal, they typically include terms identifying the property subject to the contract, specifying obligations, fixing the nature and times of performance, and setting forth the representations, warranties, and covenants that the parties undertake.

12.6.1   Timing

Consider first timing. Speed is almost always desirable in acquisition transactions. In dynamic markets, the conditions that make an agreement advantageous may suddenly change. Since each side wants the deal to occur on present information and since neither can predict future market movements, it is rational, once a deal is reached, for businesspeople to be impatient to close it.

An all-cash, multistep acquisition is usually the fastest way to secure control over a target and complete the acquisition of its shares. An all-cash tender offer may be consummated in 20 business days under the Williams Act, as discussed in Chapter 11. By contrast, a merger generally requires a shareholder vote of the target company's shareholders and may require a vote of the acquiring company's shareholders as well. Shareholder votes, in turn, typically take several more months for clearance of the proxy materials and the solicitation of proxies before a shareholder meeting. Of course, the relatively recent adoption of the "intermediate-form merger" introduced by DGCL §251(h), which combines a tender offer and a §251 merger in a single transaction, has done much to mitigate the painful choice between a one-step or two-step transaction in a large class of friendly cash-out deals.[44] However, if lengthy regulatory procedures must be completed before a first-step tender offer can be closed (as is the case in bank acquisitions), a multistep or intermediate-form structure may not offer a timing advantage, in which case a one-step merger may be the best choice.

---

44. For discussion of DGCL §251(h), see *supra* at pp. 510-511.

12.6.2 Regulatory Approvals, Consents, and Title Transfers

As noted above, timing considerations also turn on mechanical aspects of a transaction, such as regulatory approvals, consents, and title transfers. Title transfers are not a matter of concern in a merger, since all assets owned by either corporation vest as a matter of law in the surviving corporation without further action. In a sale of assets, however, title transfers may impose substantial cost and delay. Thus, reverse triangular mergers are the cheapest and easiest methods of transfer because they leave both preexisting operating corporations intact. Stock purchases entail stock transfers and the corresponding costs of documentation (stock certificates, stock powers), but they are nevertheless much simpler to conclude than asset purchases.

Governmental approval and third-party consents vary with the form of transaction. Transaction planners will attempt to choose a structure that minimizes the cost of obtaining regulatory approvals or consents under contracts (e.g., real estate leases, bank loans, service agreements) needed to close the transaction. In addition, planners will wish to make the transfer of corporate assets as cheap as possible.

12.6.3 Planning Around Voting and Appraisal Rights

From the planner's perspective, shareholder votes and appraisal rights are costly and potentially risky. Sometimes planners may voluntarily condition transactions on shareholder approval or provide appraisal rights even when they are not technically required. (Why might they do this?) But ordinarily, they will choose a structure that avoids or minimizes such requirements. Planners are particularly wary of structures that trigger class votes for holders of preferred (or non-voting common) stock, since these votes may enable the holders of such securities to extract a "holdup" payment in exchange for allowing the deal to proceed.[45]

12.6.4 Due Diligence, Representations and Warranties, Covenants, and Indemnification

In any deal, the buyer will wish to acquire reliable information about the target. In many deals involving public companies, acquiring this information is made much easier by public SEC filings and the availability of financial statements audited by an independent public accountant. This is especially true in highly regulated industries such as banking. "Hostile" transactions,

---

45. See, e.g., *Schreiber v. Carney*, 447 A.2d 17 (Del. Ch. 1982); *Warner Communications, Inc. v. Chris Craft Industries, Inc.*, 583 A.2d 962 (Del. Ch. 1989). Chris Craft alleged that it was the sole holder of a class of preferred stock that had a right to a class vote in the merger that created Time-Warner Corp.

of course, are incompatible with due diligence from the target itself. Even if and when such deals turn "friendly," hostile takeovers will rarely provide much opportunity for due diligence. Risk and uncertainty will accordingly be greater.

In negotiated transactions, the representations and warranties contained in a merger agreement will facilitate the due diligence process by requiring the disclosure of accurate information respecting the financial statements of the target, its assets and liabilities, and any other material information that the buyer requires.[46] They establish conditions necessary for closing the transaction as well as allocating between the parties the risks arising from the property subject to the transaction. Target warranties and representations are particularly useful when there is a solvent corporation or individual to stand behind them. When the target is a public corporation, there are generally fewer such provisions because information about these companies is already relatively good, and more importantly, there is no easy way to enforce a breach of warranty against the persons who will have the acquirer's money. It follows that warranties and representations have their greatest use in private deals — that is, where control is acquired through any method from a single entity or small group.[47]

Covenants in merger agreements are another tool for controlling risk. They are designed to offer assurance to the buyer that the company it contracts to acquire should be in roughly the same condition at the time of closing of the transaction. A typical covenant offered by a target in a merger agreement will provide that the business will be operated only in the normal course from the date of the signing of the agreement to the closing and may, for example, require the target to confer with the acquirer before undertaking material transactions. Another typical covenant will require the target to notify the buyer if it learns of any event or condition that constitutes a breach of any representation or warranty. A third standard covenant is a pledge by the target to use its best efforts to cause the merger agreement to close. This often will include a covenant that the board will recommend approval of the merger agreement by the corporation's stockholders (subject usually to a "fiduciary out," discussed in Chapter 13).

46. The most important function of warranties and representations is to force the disclosure of information respecting the target's property and liabilities. To learn about a target's business, an acquirer commonly asks for broad representations and warranties concerning properties owned, potential liabilities, or whatever other information is relevant to value. The acquirer then learns about the business by discussing why such warranties are impractical or what aspect must be excepted from any such warranties. The process is similar with representations. The target must carefully shape each representation on which the acquirer will rely, which teaches the acquirer about the firm.

47. In this context, it is also customary for the acquisition agreement to contain detailed representations concerning the organization of the seller/target; its capital structure; its good standing and the authority to enter into the transaction in question; its financial statements; its tax payments; its licenses, etc., necessary to conduct its businesses; its title to intellectual property and real property; and its insurance and environmental liabilities. While the seller/target will be giving most of the representations and warranties, the buyer/acquirer may be asked to make representations that will go to its ability to close the transaction.

Another fundamental aspect of the agreement will be a statement of the conditions that need to exist before a party can be legally obligated to close the deal. In general, these conditions will include such things as all representations and warranties remain true and correct (except to the extent that all deviations taken together do not constitute a "material adverse change" in the condition or business of the target), any financing condition has been satisfied, and no injunction against closing has been issued. In addition, the parties will customarily indemnify each other for any damages arising from any misrepresentation or breach of warranty. This indemnification has the effect of making every representation a covenant to hold harmless. Thus, the agreement will effectively allocate the burden of undiscovered noncompliance to the party making the representation (ordinarily the seller). Of course, this sort of protection is generally not feasible in a public company acquisition unless it can be negotiated from a large block holder.

12.6.5   Deal Protections and Termination Fees

The period beginning in 1985 witnessed a revolution in the corporate law of mergers and acquisitions. That revolution was initiated by a quartet of surprising Delaware Supreme Court opinions. Those opinions — *Smith v. Van Gorkom*, *Unocal*, *Revlon*, and *Moran v. Household* — and their progeny are examined in Chapter 13, which deals with hostile changes in corporate control. Today, in light of the changes that this revolution wrought, among the most important terms of a friendly merger agreement are those terms that are designed to assure a prospective buyer that its investment in negotiating in good faith with a target will result in a closable transaction. Any discussion of these "deal protection" terms requires an understanding of the doctrine that emerged from the revolutionary cases, and therefore, we take up these provisions in the next chapter.

12.6.6   Accounting Treatment

Under current standards for the accounting for mergers, in a direct merger the surviving corporation will typically record the assets acquired at their fair market value. To the extent the merger consideration exceeds the total of the fair market value of the assets (as it ordinarily will, since the business organization and intangible assets of the target will contribute value to it), the survivor will record this excess as an intangible asset, "goodwill." Under current rules, the value of this goodwill need not be amortized against earnings so long as it continues to represent this economic value. This asset must, however, be periodically evaluated to ensure that the goodwill account continues to be a reasonable approximation of the intangible value embedded in the firm. If it is not, then the goodwill account will be reduced by taking a charge against earnings (a noncash expense) in the amount of its impairment.

12.6.7   A Case Study: Excerpt from Timberjack Agreement and Plan of Merger

AGREEMENT AND PLAN OF MERGER ("Agreement") dated as of this 13th day of April, 1989, by and among RAUMA-REPOLA OY ("Parent"), a corporation organized under the laws of Finland; RAUMA ACQUISITION CORPORATION ("Purchaser"), a Delaware corporation and a direct, wholly-owned subsidiary of Parent; and TIMBERJACK CORPORATION ("Company"), a Delaware corporation.

WITNESSETH

WHEREAS, the respective Boards of Directors of Parent, Purchaser and the Company have approved the acquisition of the Company by Purchaser pursuant to the terms and subject to the conditions set forth in this Agreement;

WHEREAS, as an integral part of such acquisition, Purchaser will make a cash tender offer for all shares of the issued and outstanding common stock, par value $0.01 per share, of the Company (the "Common Stock"), upon the terms and subject to the conditions set forth in this Agreement;

WHEREAS, the Board of Directors of the Company has approved the Offer and has recommended that the stockholders of the Company tender their shares of Common Stock pursuant to the Offer;

WHEREAS, in order to induce Parent and Purchaser to enter into this Agreement, the Company has entered into a Cancellation Fee Agreement with Parent and Purchaser, dated as of an even date herewith (the "Fee Agreement");

NOW, THEREFORE, in consideration of the premises and the representations, warranties, covenants and agreements contained herein and in the Fee Agreement, and intending to be legally bound hereby, Parent, Purchaser and the Company hereby agree as follows:

ARTICLE I
THE OFFER

1.01. *The Offer.* Provided this Agreement has not been terminated pursuant to Section 6.01 hereof, Purchaser shall, as soon as practicable after the date hereof, and in any event within five (5) business days after the date on which Purchaser's intention to make the Offer is first publicly announced, commence a tender offer to acquire any and all issued and outstanding shares of the Common Stock, at a price of $25.00 per share net to the seller in cash (the "Offer"). Subject to the conditions to the Offer set forth in Annex I hereto, including the condition that a minimum amount of at least 70% of the issued and outstanding shares of Common Stock be tendered and available for acquisition (the "Minimum Amount"), Purchaser (a) shall not extend the Offer beyond midnight, New York City time, on the twentieth business day from the date of commencement of the Offer and (b) shall purchase by accepting for payment, and shall pay for, all Common Stock validly tendered and not withdrawn promptly after expiration of the Offer; *provided, however,* that (i) if, as of the then-scheduled expiration of the Offer, in excess of 50%, but less than 90% of the Common Stock have been validly tendered and not withdrawn, Purchaser may, at its sole option, extend the Offer for a period not to extend beyond an additional ten business days in order to qualify for a "short-form merger" in accordance with Section 253 of the Delaware General Corporation Law (the "Delaware Law"), (ii) Purchaser may, at its sole option, extend the Offer with the consent of the Company, (iii) Purchaser may, at its sole option, extend and re-extend the Offer for reasonable periods of time, not to exceed ten business days in any instance, in order to allow a condition to the Offer specified in Annex I to be satisfied that is reasonably likely to be satisfied within the period of such extension and (iv) Purchaser, at its sole option, reserves the right to waive any condition to the Offer set out in Annex I, to purchase fewer than the Minimum Amount and to increase the price per share pursuant to the Offer.

ARTICLE II
THE MERGER

2.01 *The Merger.*

(a) Subject to the terms and conditions hereof, at the Effective Date (as such term is defined in Section 2.01(b)), Purchaser will be merged with and into the Company (the "Merger") in accordance with Delaware Law, the separate existence of Purchaser (except as may be continued by operation of law) shall cease and the Company shall continue as the surviving corporation in the Merger ("the Surviving Corporation").

(b) As soon as practicable after satisfaction or waiver of the conditions set forth in Article V, the parties hereto shall cause the Merger to be consummated by filing with the Secretary of State of Delaware appropriate articles of merger (the "Articles of Merger") in such form as is required by, and executed in accordance with, the relevant provisions of Delaware law, and with this Agreement (the date and time of such filing being referred to herein as the "Effective Date"). . . .

2.02 *Conversion of Shares.* Subject to the terms and conditions of this Agreement, at the Effective Date, by virtue of the Merger and without any action on the part of the Purchaser, the Company or the holder of any of the following securities:

(a) Each share of Common Stock then issued and outstanding, other than (i) shares then held, directly or indirectly, by Parent, Purchaser or any direct or indirect subsidiary of Parent, or (ii) shares held in the Company's treasury, or (iii) Dissenting Shares (as such term is defined in Section 2.03), shall be converted into and represent the right to receive (as provided in Section 2.04) $25.00 net in cash, without any interest thereon (such amount of cash or such higher amount as shall be paid pursuant to the Offer, being referred to herein as the "Merger Consideration"), subject only to reduction for any applicable federal backup withholding or stock transfer taxes which shall be payable by the holder of such Common Stock.

(b) Each share of Common Stock then held, directly or indirectly, by Parent, Purchaser or any direct or indirect subsidiary of Parent shall be canceled and retired without payment of any consideration therefor.

(c) Each share of Common Stock held in the Company's treasury shall be canceled and retired without payment of any consideration therefor.

(d) Each issued and outstanding share of common stock, par value $1.00 per share, of Purchaser shall be converted into and become one validly issued, fully paid and nonassessable share of common stock of the Surviving Corporation. . . .

2.07 *Certificate of Incorporation.* The Restated Articles of Incorporation of the Company in effect immediately prior to the Effective Date (except as such Restated Articles of Incorporation may be amended pursuant to the Articles of Merger) shall be the Articles of Incorporation of the Surviving Corporation until thereafter amended as provided therein and under Delaware Law.

2.08 *By-laws.* The By-laws of the Purchaser, as in effect immediately prior to the Effective Date, shall be the By-laws of the Surviving Corporation until thereafter amended as provided therein and under Delaware Law.

2.09 *Directors.* The directors of Purchaser immediately prior to the Effective Date shall be the initial directors of the Surviving Corporation and will hold office from the Effective Date until their successors are duly elected or appointed and qualified in the manner provided in the Certificate of Incorporation and the By-laws of the Surviving Corporation, or as otherwise provided by law.

2.10 *Officers.* The officers of the Company immediately prior to the Effective Date shall be the initial officers of the Surviving Corporation and will hold office from the Effective Date until their successors are duly elected or appointed and qualified in the manner provided in the Certificate of Incorporation and the By-laws of the Surviving Corporation, or as otherwise provided by law. . . .

ARTICLE III
REPRESENTATIONS AND WARRANTIES

3.02 *Representations and Warranties of the Company.* The Company hereby represents and warrants to Parent and Purchaser that:

(a) *Organization.* The Company and each of its Subsidiaries (as such term is defined in Section 3.02(c)) is a corporation duly organized, validly existing and in good standing (or, with respect to any Subsidiaries organized under the Laws of Canada, subsisting) under the laws of its jurisdiction of incorporation and has all requisite corporate power and authority to own, lease and operate its properties and to carry on its business as now being conducted. The Company and each of its Subsidiaries is duly qualified as a foreign corporation to do business, and is in good standing, in each jurisdiction in which the property owned, leased or operated by it or the nature of the business conducted by it makes such qualification necessary, except where the failure to be so qualified would not have a Material Adverse Effect on the Company and its Subsidiaries. The Company has made available to Purchaser true, correct and complete copies of the Articles of Incorporation and By-laws of the Company and its Subsidiaries, and any amendments thereto. . . .

(d) *Authorization and Validity of Agreements.* The Company has all requisite corporate power and authority to enter into this Agreement and the Documents contemplated to be executed hereunder, including, without limitation, the Fee Agreement, and to perform all of its obligations hereunder and under all documents contemplated to be executed hereunder (subject, in the case of performance of this Agreement, to obtaining the necessary approval of its stockholders if required under Delaware Law). The execution, delivery and performance by the Company of this Agreement and the documents executed hereunder, including, without limitation, the Fee Agreement, and the consummation by it of the transactions contemplated hereby and under all documents executed hereunder, have been duly authorized by the Board of Directors and no other corporate action on the part of the Company is necessary to authorize the execution and delivery by the Company of this Agreement. . . .

(f) *Legal Proceedings.* Except as set forth in the Company Commission Filings (as such term is defined in Section 3.01(g)) or as previously disclosed to Parent or Purchaser in writing, there is no claim, suit, action, proceeding, grievance or investigation pending, or to the Company's best knowledge, threatened against or involving the Company or properties or rights of the Company or its Subsidiaries which, if adversely determined, would have, either individually or in the aggregate, a Material Adverse Effect on the Company and its Subsidiaries. . . .

(h) *Absence of Certain Changes or Events.* Since December 31, 1988, except as disclosed in writing to Parent or Purchaser or in the Company Commission Filings, or as contemplated in this Agreement, the Company and its Subsidiaries have conducted their business only in the ordinary course and in a manner consistent with past practice and have not made any material change in the conduct of the business or operations of the Company and its Subsidiaries taken as a whole, and there has not been (a) any event resulting in any Material Adverse Effect with respect to the Company and its Subsidiaries; (b) any strike, picketing, unfair labor practice, refusal to work, work slowdown or other labor disturbance involving the Company or any of its Subsidiaries; (c) any damage, destruction or loss (whether or not covered by insurance) with respect to any of the assets of the Company or any of its Subsidiaries resulting in any Material Adverse Effect on the Company or any of its Subsidiaries; (d) any redemption or other acquisition of Common Stock by the Company or any of its Subsidiaries or any declaration or payment of any dividend or other distribution in cash, stock or property with respect to Common Stock, other than regularly scheduled cash dividends; (e) any entry into any material commitment or transaction including, without limitation, any material borrowing or material capital expenditure) other than in the ordinary course of business or as contemplated by this Agreement; (f) any transfer of, or any transfer of rights granted under, any material leases, licenses, agreements, patents, trademarks, trade names or copyrights, other than those transferred or granted in the ordinary course of business and consistent with past practice; (g) any mortgage, pledge, security interest or imposition of lien or other encumbrance on any asset of the Company or any of its Subsidiaries that when viewed in the aggregate with all such other encumbrances is material to the business, financial condition or operations of the company and its Subsidiaries taken as a whole; (h) any change in the Certificate of Incorporation or By-laws or equivalent organizational documents of the Company or any Subsidiary; or (i) any change by the Company in accounting principles or methods except insofar as may have been required by a change in generally accepted accounting principles. . . .

(i) *Title to Property.*

(a) The Company and its Subsidiaries have good and marketable title, or valid leasehold rights in the case of leased property, to all real and personal property purported to be owned or leased by them and material to the business and operations of the Company and its Subsidiaries taken as a whole, free and clear of all material liens, security interests, claims, encumbrances and charges, excluding (i) liens securing any revolving term loan with any bank; (ii) liens for fees, taxes, levies, imports, duties or other governmental charges of any kind which are not yet delinquent or are being contested in good faith by appropriate proceedings which suspend the collection thereof; (iii) liens for mechanics, materialmen, laborers, employees, suppliers or similar liens arising by operation of law for sums which are not yet delinquent or are being contested in good faith by appropriate proceedings; (iv) liens created in the ordinary course of business in connection with the leasing or financing of operating assets, including, without limitation, vehicles and office computer and related equipment and supplies and (v) liens, encumbrances or defects in title or leasehold rights that, in the aggregate, do not have a Material Adverse Effect on the Company and its Subsidiaries.

(b) Consummation of the Offer and the Merger will not result in any breach of or constitute a default (or an event which with notice or lapse of time or both would constitute a default) under, or give to others any rights of termination or cancellation of, or require the consent of others under, any material lease under which the Company is a lessee, except for such breaches or defaults which in the aggregate would not have a Material Adverse Effect on the Company and its Subsidiaries. . . .

QUESTIONS ON TIMBERJACK MERGER AGREEMENT

1. What course of events is envisioned by the merger agreement?
2. What happens to the shares of Timberjack upon the merger? Why are all shares not treated in the same way? What will be the charter and the bylaws, and who will be the officers and directors of the surviving corporation?

3. What is the purpose of the provisions in Article III? In what other kind of agreement would you find similar provisions?

12.7   THE APPRAISAL REMEDY

12.7.1   History and Theory

Modern corporation law has abandoned the nineteenth-century idea that shareholders possess "vested rights" in the form of their investment. The introduction of the shareholder non-unanimity rule for authorization of mergers established that shareholder interests are held subject to the exercise of collective shareholder judgment.[48] Today, the shareholder vote (including the right to a class vote created by statute or in charters) is the shareholders' principal protection against unwise or disadvantageous mergers or other fundamental transactions. Through the vote, shareholders can replace an underperforming board or reject a fundamental transaction that requires their authorization. But what if you are a shareholder in a corporation in which the other shareholders have deplorable business judgment? If those shareholders vote to approve a foolish transaction over your objection, should you have a right to require them to buy you out (at a fair price determined by a court) as a condition of their accomplishing their silly deal?

In the United States, corporate law has provided that right — the right to a judicial appraisal of the fair value of one's shares — for more than 100 years. Every U.S. jurisdiction provides an appraisal right to shareholders who dissent from qualifying corporate mergers (more in a minute on which mergers qualify). Most states provide appraisal for shareholders who dissent from a sale of substantially all of the corporation's assets, and in about half of the states, an amendment of a corporate charter gives rise to an appraisal. The Delaware corporate law statute mandates appraisal only in connection with corporate mergers and then only in certain circumstances. See DGCL §262. Charters may, under Delaware law, include a provision granting to shareholders appraisal rights in other fundamental transactions — sale of substantially all assets or charter amendments, for example — but in fact, virtually no corporations include such provisions in their charter at the time of their IPO or later.

This pattern of appraisal statutes raises a basic question: Why do we provide this protection against majority judgments in mergers? Only if we know the purpose of appraisal can we determine whether that statute ought to be interpreted narrowly or broadly, or what the measure of "fair value" for dissenting shareholders should be.

It is often said that the appraisal remedy was granted as a quid pro quo when legislatures first permitted the authorization of mergers to be effectuated with less than unanimous shareholder approval.[49] The stock-for-stock

---

48. See, e.g., *Federal United Corp. v. Havender*, 11 A.2d 331 (Del. 1940).

49. See, e.g., Elliott J. Weiss, *The Law of Take Out Mergers: A Historical Perspective*, 56 N.Y.U. L. Rev. 624 (1981); Hideki Kanda & Saul Levmore, *The Appraisal Remedy and the Goals of Corporate Law*, 32 UCLA L. Rev. 429 (1985).

merger was the only form of merger contemplated at that point, and equity markets were not yet well developed. Thus, a merger at that time might very well have meant that a shareholder would have been forced to accept an illiquid investment in a new company in which she had no desire to invest. A judicial appraisal was a way to provide a liquidity event for such a shareholder, who previously could have prevented the alteration of her investment simply by vetoing a proposed merger.[50] Of course, our equity markets today are very liquid, at least for securities traded on a national securities exchange such as the NYSE or NASDAQ market, which suggests that for public companies the costs of an appraisal procedure are no longer justified by a liquidity rationale. The question then is whether there are other justifications for this remedy that gives it continuing utility for publicly traded firms. We explore that question as we work through the general appraisal materials in the next few subsections. However, we reserve for later discussion in Section 12.8, appraisal in the context of interested mergers where the acquiring firm is owned by the target's controller.

QUESTIONS ON APPRAISAL RIGHTS

1. Many aspects of our lives are subject to the judgments of democratic majorities or institutions subject to majority control. Our land, for example, may be rezoned, but as long as basic procedural norms are observed upon a change in zoning status, we have no right to be paid the fair value of our land. Why should stock in corporations be different?

2. The Delaware statute permits, but does not require, an appraisal remedy when the corporation's charter is amended or when substantially all of its assets are sold. See DGCL §262(c). Yet charters rarely provide an appraisal remedy in these circumstances. If the market for corporate charters responds to investors' economic interests, what inferences do you draw from this observation? Is there a convincing "market failure" story that might account for this fact?

12.7.2   The Market-Out Rule

Section 262 of the Delaware statute is by no means simple to read. After granting the right of judicial appraisal to all qualifying shares of any class in a merger effectuated under the general merger statute (i.e., §251), the Delaware appraisal statute and others (e.g., MBCA §13.02(b)) go on to deny this remedy when shares of target corporations are traded on a national security exchange or held of record by 2,000 registered holders. In addition, an appraisal is denied if the shareholders were not required to vote on the merger — that is,

---

50. The arguments that show the incoherence of the rationales offered for appraisal actions have been masterfully marshalled by Bayless Manning. See Bayless Manning, *The Shareholder's Appraisal Remedy: An Essay for Frank Coker*, 72 Yale L.J. 223 (1962).

they own shares in the acquirer and it is not, for example, issuing 20 percent or more of its own shares in the merger. Then, notwithstanding this, the statute restores the appraisal remedy to target shareholders if they are required to accept in the merger consideration anything *other than* (i) stock in the surviving corporation, (ii) any other shares traded on a national security exchange, (iii) cash in lieu of fractional shares, or (iv) a combination of those items. This is the so-called market out. See DGCL §262(b)(2).[51]

Thus, shareholders in a privately traded firm (with fewer than 2,000 shareholders) will always have appraisal rights in a merger if they are required to vote on it.[52] But consistent with the liquidity rationale of appraisal rights, shareholders in a public company with more than 2,000 shareholders have no appraisal rights in a stock-for-stock merger. The theory, we suppose, is that if one gets traded stock in the merger, then one will not be "forced" to make an investment against one's will. This is a fine theory, but it does not explain why shareholders who receive cash for their shares *do* have appraisal rights. Nor does it acknowledge a role for appraisal as a check on the amount of consideration a shareholder receives (the only plausible rationale for appraisal when the consideration is cash). So how can withholding appraisal in stock-for-stock mergers when shares are publicly traded be reconciled with granting appraisal rights in cash-out mergers?[53] You tell us.

---

51. The 2018 amendments removed a carve-out for intermediate-form mergers (under §251(h)) so that these mergers and long-form mergers are both able to avoid appraisal under the market out. Section 262(e) was also amended so that the surviving firm in an intermediate-form merger only has to disclose the number of shares not tendered or exchanged rather than the shares not voted in favor of the merger (because in an intermediate-form merger there is no shareholder vote). Recent years have witnessed additional amendments. In 2019, amendments allowed shareholders and corporations to rely on electronic communications for certain matters related to appraisals (§§262(d) and (e)) and in 2020, appraisal was removed for conversions into a public benefit corporation status (§363).

52. However, the right to appraisal can, at least in private firms, be waived in some circumstances. *Manti Holdings, LLC v. Authentix Acquisition Co., Inc.,* 2019 WL 3814453 (Del. Ch. Aug. 14, 2019) upheld waivers of (or limitations on) appraisal in private firms through a shareholder agreement where the waiver was clear and the shareholders were sophisticated, informed, and represented by counsel when they signed the agreement. The court found that appraisal rights are merely an available stockholder remedy, not a mandatory one, and thus subject to adjustment via agreement. One wonders how far this ruling might go — could shareholders choose their preferred method of appraisal via contract (e.g., choosing valuation methods, excluding certain synergies)? In any case, the holding of *Manti* has not yet been extended to publicly traded corporations where a shareholder agreement on appraisal is more difficult to achieve. See Jill E. Fisch, *Appraisal Waivers* (August 2, 2020). U of Penn, Inst for Law & Econ Research Paper No. 20-47. Available at SSRN: https://ssrn.com/abstract=3667058.

53. It is noteworthy that Delaware's approach to the "market out" is one of four approaches adopted in the United States. Eleven states deny appraisal rights to shareholders in publicly traded firms even if the merger is with an interested party (e.g., a controller). Thirteen states, including Delaware, make appraisal depend on the type of consideration that is provided. Another 14 states (and the District of Columbia) permit appraisal for shareholders in publicly traded firms when they receive cash or debt, or when the transaction involves an interested party regardless of the type of consideration received. This tracks with the MBCA's approach. Finally, 12 states do not restrict appraisal for shareholders in publicly traded firms — they can seek appraisal regardless of the consideration received or whether an interested party is involved. Here public and private firm shareholders have essentially equivalent access to appraisal. See Gil Matthews, *The "Market Exception" in Appraisal Statutes*, Harv.

QUESTION

Assume a merger agreement provides that minority shareholders may elect to receive *either* cash or shares of the surviving corporation, or a mixture of the two, with no limits on the number of shares or amount of cash that may be elected. Should shareholders who are unhappy about the amount of merger consideration be able to perfect an appraisal under Delaware law? See *Krieger v. Wesco Financial Corp.*, 30 A.3d 54 (Del. Ch. 2011) ("Because Wesco common stockholders were not required to accept consideration other than stock listed on a national securities exchange and cash in lieu of fractional shares, they were not entitled to appraisal rights").

12.7.3   The Nature and Judicial Determination of "Fair Value"

The appraisal right is a put option — an opportunity to sell shares back to the firm at a price equal to their "fair value" immediately prior to the transaction triggering the right. This typically means that dissenting shareholders receive a pro rata portion of the whole firm's value as a going concern less "any element of value arising from the accomplishment or expectation of the merger. In recent years, courts have interpreted "value arising from the accomplishment . . . of the merger" to refer to synergy values. How does one calculate this vision of fair value? Good question.

The meaning of fair value has never been entirely fixed, and the gist of it has shifted several times over the past 50 years. Perhaps wisely, Delaware has left the determination of fair value largely up to the judiciary. Prior to 1983, the Chancery Court settled on the Delaware Block Method, which defied economic intuition by seeming to overweight past company performance in assessing value rather than valuing a company's future prospects. In 1983, *Weinberger* liberated the Chancery Court from the grip of past performance and implicitly recognized that real economic value should rest on future prospects. And from this vantage point, discounted cash flow ("DCF") valuation seemed like the natural way to go, since it promised to value the real cash flows available for distribution to shareholders (see our discussion in Chapter 5). It thus became the de facto standard for over 30 years until 2015 when Delaware's Supreme Court moved to adjusted deal price as the preferred indicator of fair value in arm's length transactions — unless, of course, the negotiations underlying deal price were seriously flawed.

So why the change in 2015? At least two reasons seemed prominent. First, the complexities of DCF models (what discount rate to use, what future cash flows) put judges in an awkward position. The Chancery Court was left to navigate through dozens of key variables guided solely by adversarial

L. Sch. F. Corp. Governance (March 30, 2020), https://corpgov.law.harvard.edu/2020/03/30/the-market-exception-in-appraisal-statues/.

expert reports that might deviate from each other by 100 percent or more in their bottom line valuations. This gave judicial assessments of "fair value" an artificial feel which reliance on deal price in an arm's length bargain avoided.

Second, the courts were alarmed by a rapid increase in so-called "appraisal arbitrage," in which sophisticated hedge funds would buy shares to challenge soft deal prices or alternatively press acquirers to raise deal prices ex ante by threatening to vote against deals. A quirk in the Delaware appraisal statute that specified a generous interest rate made such strategies especially lucrative. Moreover, this occurred at the same time as a general rise in deal litigation (see the Cornerstone Figure below[54]) had begun to trouble courts. And courts responded in the only way they could — by changing their preferred measure of fair value from DCF to adjusted deal price when deal process was not seriously flawed. This meant that deal price became a ceiling on fair value in many appraisals because courts would usually deduct deal synergies from deal price to arrive at a final estimate of fair value.

Of course, deal price had some unattractive features as well. In particular, it risks collapsing fair price into fair process. While relying on arm's length negotiated deal price between sophisticated parties may be a sensible position to adopt — indeed, it has been adopted by courts in many contexts — it seems to ignore the intent of the statute as well as prior case law, both of which imagine that the target has an objective going concern value. If this value is our goal, then we must think that deal price, arrived at via arm's length bargaining, is a better tool for estimating unobservable going concern value than alternative valuation methods, and most particularly, the wide range of estimates that DCF valuation might produce. Since this assumption may not be so self-evident, we should expect that even the formula of "arm's length deal price less synergies" can only proxy for fair value.

In addition, the "deal price less synergies" approach presents other problems that did not arise in DCF valuations. One of these is determining when defects in process — that is, in negotiations between target and acquirer — disqualify deal price as a reasonable basis for estimating fair value. Here, one must remember that there is much that can undercut the credibility of arm's length negotiations between nominally independent acquirers and targets. Possible defects in process on the target's side range from gross negligence in assessing company value to many small conflicts of interest, such as agreements on consulting fees for target managers in the post-deal acquirer or the division of board seats in the post-deal combined company between the former directors of the target and acquirer's boards. A second issue arises if the cumulative effect of process imperfections renders deal value too suspect to support an appraisal estimate. What is the second-best appraisal methodology? Should it be DCF

---

54. See Cornerstone Research, *Appraisal Litigation in Delaware: Trends in Petitions and Opinions 2006-2018* (2019). Available at: https://www.cornerstone.com/publications/reports/appraisal-litigation-delaware-2006-2018.pdf.

Appraisal Petitions and Merger Cases Filed in the Delaware Court of Chancery 2006-2018

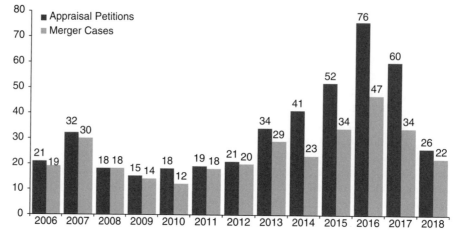

Note: Delaware appraisal rights petitions are identified as those filed in the Chancery Court. Appraisal cases are identified as petitions with a unique respondent name. *Source:* Courthouse News Service

valuation, which recent case law has already rendered suspect, or should it be another valuation methodology contender that has never quite made it to the big time such as the unaffected (i.e., pre-announcement) aggregate market value of target shares? Finally, a third problem concerns the nature of synergy values, which reflect the target's portion of the deal price that arises from the expected surplus of the deal itself. What do courts look at to determine this?

The following two cases illustrate the issues that arise once deal price emerges as the dominant factor in assessing fair value.

VERITION PARTNERS MASTER FUND LTD v. ARUBA NETWORKS, INC.
210 A. 3d 128 (Del. 2019)

PER CURIAM:

In this statutory appraisal case, the Court of Chancery found that the fair value of Aruba Networks, Inc., as defined by 8 Del. C. § 262, was $17.13 per share, which was the thirty-day average market price at which its shares traded before the media reported news of the transaction that gave rise to the appellants' appraisal rights. In its post-trial opinion, the Court of Chancery engaged in a wide-ranging discussion of its view[s]. . . . [T]he key issue before us [is] . . . whether the Court of Chancery abused its discretion . . . in arriving at Aruba's thirty-day average unaffected market price as the fair value of the appellants' shares. Because [its] decision to use Aruba's stock price instead of the deal price minus synergies was rooted in an erroneous factual finding, we . . . reverse [its] judgment. On remand, the Court of Chancery shall enter a final judgment for the petitioners awarding them $19.10 per share, which reflects the deal price minus the portion of synergies left with the seller as estimated by the respondent in this case, Aruba.

I

In August 2014, Hewlett-Packard Company ("HP") . . . approached Aruba . . . about a potential combination. Aruba hired professionals and . . . began to shop the deal. Five other logical strategic bidders were approached, but none of them showed any interest. . . . After several months of negotiations . . . , the Aruba board decided to accept HP's offer of $24.67 per share. News of the deal leaked to the press about two weeks later, causing Aruba's stock price to jump from $18.37 to $22.24. The next day . . . Aruba released its quarterly results, which beat analyst expectations. [Its] stock price rose by [another] 9.7% . . . to close at $24.81 per share, just above the deal price.

Not long after the deal leaked, both companies' boards approved . . . the merger at a price of $24.67 per share. The final merger agreement allowed for another passive market check. However, no superior bid emerged, and the deal closed on May 18, 2015.

On August 28, 2015, the appellants and petitioners below, Verition Partners Master Fund Ltd. and Verition Multi-Strategy Master Fund Ltd. (collectively, "Verition"), filed this appraisal proceeding in the Court of Chancery, asking the court to appraise the "fair value" of their shares under § 262. The respondent was Aruba, albeit an Aruba now 100% controlled by HP . . . Verition maintained that Aruba's fair value was $32.57 per share, [while] Aruba contended that its fair value was either $19.45 per share (before trial) or $19.75 per share (after trial). In its post-trial answering brief, Aruba contended that its "deal price less synergies" value was $19.10 per share. Neither party claimed that Aruba's preannouncement stock price was the best measure of fair value at the time of the merger.

Post-trial argument was scheduled for May 17, 2017, but the Court of Chancery postponed the hearing "once it became clear that the Delaware Supreme Court's forthcoming decision in DFC . . . likely would have a significant effect on the legal landscape." . . . After this Court issued its opinion in DFC, the parties . . . submit[ted] supplemental . . . briefs [to the Court of Chancery]. Both parties continued to argue for their preferred fair value calculation, and neither party advocated for the adoption of the stock price, though Aruba did contend that the stock price was now "informative" of fair value and lent support to its argument that fair value as of the time of the merger was in the $19 to $20 per share range. . . .

On December 14, 2017, this Court issued its opinion in *Dell, Inc.* v. *Magnetar Global Event Driven Master Fund Ltd,*[1] reversing the Court of Chancery's appraisal decision in that case. Six days later, the Vice Chancellor

1. 177 A.3d 1 (Del. 2017).

in this case — who was also the trial judge in *Dell* — [asked . . . the parties for an additional] supplemental briefing on "the market attributes of Aruba's stock" in part because he "learned how many errors [he] made in the *Dell* matter." . . .

[In its] response to the Vice Chancellor's sua sponte request, . . . Aruba argued for the first time that its preannouncement stock price was "the single most important mark of its fair value." Accordingly, Aruba asked the Court of Chancery to award the thirty-day unaffected market price of $17.13 per share. Aruba's brief focused mainly on how the market for its stock was efficient.

On February 15, 2018, the Court of Chancery issued its post-trial opinion finding that the fair value under § 262 was $17.13 per share. [It] considered three different valuation measures: first, the "unaffected market price" of Aruba's stock before news of the merger leaked; second, the deal price minus the portion of synergies left with the seller; and third, flow ("DCF") models.

In weighing the[se] valuation methodologies, the Court . . . gave no weight to the parties' DCF models. [It next] determined that the appropriate deal price minus synergies value was $18.20. In reaching that conclusion, [it] . . . started with an estimate of the total amount of synergies HP expected to realize. [It then] . . . took the midpoint of a study suggesting that "on average, sellers collect 31% of the capitalized value of synergies, with the seller's share varying widely from 6% to 51%." This resulted in a deal price minus synergies value of $18.20 per share, $0.90 lower than Aruba's own estimate of deal price minus synergies. . . . [The Court] failed to explain why [its] estimate of $18.20 per share was more reliable than Aruba's own estimate of $19.10 per share.

However, the Vice Chancellor did not adopt his deal price minus synergies value, in part because he believed that his "deal-price-less-synergies figure continues to incorporate an element of value resulting from the merger" in the form of "reduced agency costs that result from unitary (or controlling) ownership." To remedy this, the Vice Chancellor elected to rely exclusively on the stock price because he thought he would need to estimate and back out these theoretical "reduced agency costs" from the deal price to arrive at a figure that reflected Aruba's value as a going concern. According to the Court, . . . using the "unaffected market price" of Aruba's publicly traded shares "provide[d] a direct estimate" of that endpoint, which led him to find the sole indicator of fair value to be that "unaffected market price" of $17.13 per share. Although § 262 requires the Court of Chancery to assess Aruba's fair value as of "the effective date of the merger," the Court of Chancery arrived at the unaffected market price by averaging the trading price of Aruba's stock during the thirty days before news of the merger leaked, which was three to four months prior to closing.

II

We reverse. . . . Under *Cavalier Oil Corp.* v. *Hartnett*, the Court of Chancery's task in an appraisal case is "to value what has been taken from the shareholder: 'viz. his proportionate interest in a going concern.'" That is, the court must value the company "as an operating entity . . . but without regard to post-merger events or other possible business combinations." *Cavalier Oil* draws this requirement from § 262's command that the court determine fair value "exclusive of any element of value arising from the accomplishment or expectation of the merger or consolidation," which this Court has interpreted as ruling out consideration of not just the gains that the particular merger will produce, but also the gains that might be obtained from any other merger. . . . As a result, fair value "is more properly described as the value of the company to the stockholder as a going concern, rather than its value to a third party as an acquisition." Under this reading of § 262, [a court] must "exclude from any appraisal award the . . . value that the selling company's shareholders would receive because a buyer intends to operate the subject company . . . as a part of a larger enterprise, from which synergistic gains can be extracted."[2] For this reason, in cases where [a trial court] has used the price at which a company is sold [to] a third-party [to estimate going concern value for appraisal purposes], . . . it has excised [any] synergy or other value the buyer expects from changes it plans to make to the company's "going-concern" business plan. . . .

Applying [this] standard, we hold that the Court of Chancery abused its discretion in using Aruba's "unaffected market price" because it did so on the inapt theory that it needed to make an additional deduction [beyond deducting synergy value — EDS.] from the deal price for unspecified reduced agency costs. It [seems] that the Court . . . would have given weight to the deal price minus synergies absent its view that it also had to deduct [these] unspecified agency costs to adhere to . . . [the] going-concern standard. . . . Judging by the law review articles cited by the Court of Chancery, the theory underlying decision [the trial court's decision to deduct agency cost gains as well as synergy values from the deal price — EDS.] appears to be that the acquisition would reduce agency costs essentially because the resulting consolidation of ownership and control would align the interests of Aruba's managers and its public stockholders.[3]

In other words, the theory goes, replacing a dispersed group of owners with a concentrated group of owners can be expected to add value because the new owners are more capable of making sure that management isn't shirking or diverting the company's profits, and that added value must be excluded under § 262 as "arising from the accomplishment or expectation of the merger or consolidation." However, unlike a private equity deal, the merger at issue in this case would not replace Aruba's public stockholders with a concentrated group of owners; rather it would swap one set of public stockholders for another: HP's.

---

2. *Union Ill. 1995 Inv. Ltd. Partnership* v. *Union Fin. Grp., Ltd.,* 874 A.2d at 356; see also *Cavalier Oil,* 564 A.2d at 1144 45; *DFC,* 172 A.3d at 368; *Dell* 177 A.3d at 21; *Global GT LP* v. *Golden Telecom, Inc.,* 993 A.2d 497, 507 (Del. Ch. 2010), aff'd, 11 A.3d 214 (Del. 2010); *Highfields,* 939 A.2d at 42.

3. Cf. Lawrence A. Hamermesh & Michael L. Wachter, *The Short and Puzzling Life of the "Implicit Minority Discount" in Delaware Appraisal Law,* 156 U. Pa. L. Rev. 1, 33-36 (2007).

Indeed, neither party presented any evidence to suggest that any part of the deal price paid by HP, a strategic buyer, involved the potential for agency cost reductions that were not already captured by its synergies estimate. Synergies do not just involve the benefits when, for example, two symbiotic product lines can be sold together. They also classically involve cost reductions that arise because, for example, a strategic buyer believes it can produce the same or greater profits with fewer employees[4] — in English terms, rendering some of the existing employees "redundant." Private equity firms often expect to improve performance and squeeze costs too, including by reducing "agency costs." Here, the Court of Chancery's belief that it had to deduct for agency costs ignores the reality that HP's synergies [in this] case likely already priced any agency cost reductions it may have expected. In short, the record provides no reason to believe that [HP's] estimates omitted any other added value HP thought it could achieve. . . . For this reason, Aruba itself presented a deal price minus synergies value of $19.10 per share as one of its suggested outcomes. . . .

[T]he Court of Chancery's view that some measure of agency costs had to be accounted for finds no basis in the record [or the corporate finance literature].[5] . . . However, instead of [relying on] deal price minus HP's estimate of its expected synergies[, which] was corroborated by the standalone DCF models used by Aruba's and HP's boards in agreeing to the transaction, the Court of Chancery gave exclusive weight to the thirty-day average unaffected market price of $17.13 per share.

In addition . . . the Court of Chancery also seemed to suggest that rote reliance on market prices was compelled based on its reading of *DFC* and *Dell*. Like any human perspective, the trial judge's broader reading of *Dell* and *DFC* is arguable, but [his] sense that those decisions somehow compelled him to make the decision he did was not supported by any reasonable reading of those decisions. . . .

Among other things, the trial judge seemed to find it novel that *DFC* and *Dell* recognized that when a public company . . . is sold at a substantial premium . . . after [competitors have had a fair opportunity to bid against the buyer], the deal price is a strong indicator of fair value, as a matter of economic reality and theory. The apparent novelty the trial judge perceived is surprising, given the long history of giving important weight to market-tested deal prices in the Court of Chancery and this Court. . . .

. . . [W]hen there is an open opportunity for many buyers to buy and only a few bid (or even just one bids), that does not necessarily mean that there is a failure of competition; it may just mean that the target's value is not sufficiently enticing to buyers to engender a bidding war above the winning

---

4. See Robert W. Holthausen & Mark E. Zmijewsji, Corporate Valuation: Theory, Evidence & Practice 681 (2014).

5. Compare Holthausen & Zmijewski, *supra*, at 612–13 (explaining agency cost reductions as a possible motivation for leveraged buyouts), with id. at 677–78, 681–82 (explaining value creation in strategic M&A deals primarily in terms of synergies). See also Michael C. Jensen & William H. Meckling, *Theory of the Firm: Managerial Behavior, Agency Costs and Ownership Structure*, 3 J. Fin. Econ. 305, 308–10, 312–19 (1976).

price.[6] In this case, for instance, Aruba approached other logical strategic buyers prior to signing the deal with HP, and none of those potential buyers were interested. Then, after signing and the announcement of the deal, still no other buyer emerged even though the merger agreement allowed for superior bids. It cannot be that an open chance for buyers to bid signals a market failure simply because buyers do not believe the asset on sale is sufficiently valuable for them to engage in a bidding contest against each other. . . .

In fact, encouraged by *Weinberger* v. *UOP, Inc.,*[7] our courts have for years applied corporate finance principles such as the capital asset pricing model to value companies in appraisal proceedings in ways that depend on market efficiency. The reliable application of valuation methods used in appraisal proceedings, such as DCF and comparable companies analysis, often depends on market data and the efficiency of the markets from which that data is derived. . . .

DFC and *Dell* merely [extended this basic point by recognizing] that a buyer in possession of material nonpublic information about the seller is in a strong position (and is uniquely incentivized) to properly value the seller when agreeing to buy the company at a particular deal price, and that view of value should be given considerable weight by the Court of Chancery absent deficiencies in the deal process.[8]

. . . By asserting that *Dell* and *DFC* "indicate[] that Aruba's unaffected market price is entitled to substantial weight," the Vice Chancellor seemed to suggest that this Court signaled . . . that trading prices should be treated as exclusive indicators of fair value. However, *Dell* and *DFC* did not imply that the market price of a stock was necessarily the best estimate of the stock's so-called fundamental value at any particular time. . . . *Dell*'s references to market efficiency focused on informational efficiency — the idea that markets quickly reflect publicly available information and can be a proxy for fair value — not the idea that an informationally efficient market price invariably reflects the company's fair value in an appraisal or fundamental value in economic terms. Nonetheless, to the extent the Court of Chancery read *DFC* and *Dell* as reaffirming the traditional Delaware view,[10] which is accepted in corporate finance, that the price a stock trades at in an efficient market is an important indicator of its economic value that should be given weight, it was

---

6. See *Dell*, 177 A.3d at 32 (discussing the winner's curse).

7. 457 A.2d 701 (Del. 1983).

8. See *Dell*, 177 A.3d at 35; *DFC Global Corp.* v. *Muirfield Value Partners, L.P.*, 172 A.3d 346, 367 (Del. 2017).

10. See *Dell*, 177 A.3d at 24 ("Further, the Court of Chancery's analysis ignored the efficient market hypothesis long endorsed by this Court. It teaches that the price produced by an efficient market is generally a more reliable assessment of fair value than the view of a single analyst, especially an expert witness who caters her valuation to the litigation imperatives of a well-heeled client."); *DFC Global Corp.*, 172 A.3d at 370 ("Indeed, the relationship between market valuation and fundamental valuation has been strong historically. As one textbook puts it, '[i]n an efficient market you can trust prices, for they impound all available information about the value of each security.' More pithily: 'For many purposes no formal theory of value is needed. We can take the market's word for it.' ") . . .

correct.[11] And to the extent that the Court also read *DFC* and *Dell* as reaffirming the view that when that market price is further informed by the efforts of arm's length buyers of the entire company to learn more through due diligence, involving confidential non-public information, and with the keener incentives of someone considering taking the non-diversifiable risk of buying the entire entity, the [resulting] price . . . is even more likely to be indicative of so-called fundamental value, it was correct.

Here, the price that HP paid could be seen as reflecting a better assessment of Aruba's. . . . For starters, the unaffected market price was a measurement from three to four months prior to the valuation date, a time period during which it is possible for new, material information relevant to a company's future earnings to emerge. Even more important, HP had more incentive to study Aruba closely than ordinary traders in small blocks of Aruba shares, and also had material, nonpublic information that, by definition, could not have been baked into the public trading price. For example, HP knew about Aruba's strong quarterly earnings before the market did, and likely took that information into account when pricing the deal. . . . Based on the record evidence, the Court of Chancery could easily have found that HP and Aruba's back and forth over price, HP's access to nonpublic information, . . . and the currency of the information that they had at the time of striking a bargain had improved the parties' ability to estimate Aruba's going-concern . . . value over that of the market as a whole. In particular, HP had better insight into Aruba's future prospects than the market because it was aware that Aruba expected its quarterly results to exceed analysts' expectations. When those strong quarterly results were finally reported — after the close of the period that the Court of Chancery used to measure the "unaffected market price" — Aruba's stock price jumped 9.7%. Indeed, after the market learned about the strong quarter and the likelihood of a strategic deal with HP, Aruba's stock traded at $24.81, $0.14 away from the actual price HP paid. [Nevertheless,] despite expressing concern . . . that no other bidder emerged to compete with HP at the $24-plus price range, the Court of Chancery [still?] awarded Verition $7.54 per share less than the $24.67 deal price. . . .

Nevertheless, [one can still find a reliable estimate of deal price minus synergies in the record — EDS.] after fixing the double counting problem and hewing to the record . . . [It] is the one that Aruba advanced until the Vice Chancellor himself injected the thirty-day average market price as his own speculative idea. Of course, estimating synergies and allocating a reasonable portion to the seller certainly involves imprecision, but no more than other valuation methods, like a DCF analysis . . . [here] there is no basis to think Aruba was being generous in its evaluation of deal price minus synergies. . . . And,

---

11. See, e.g., Ronald J. Gilson & Reinier Kraakman, *Market Efficiency after the Financial Crisis: It's Still a Matter of Information Costs*, 100 Va. L. Rev. 313, 317 (2014) ("Even if we cannot observe fundamental efficiency, we can with confidence predict that making prices more informationally efficient will move them in the direction of fundamental efficiency."). . . .

as any measure of value should be, Aruba's $19.10 deal price minus synergies value is corroborated by abundant record evidence. . . .

Rather than burden the parties with further proceedings, we order that a final judgment be entered for the petitioners in the amount of $19.10 per share plus any interest to which the petitioners are entitled.

NOTES AND QUESTIONS

The *Aruba* decision followed other Delaware Supreme Court decisions favoring deal price (less synergies) as a measure of fair value provided that it had emerged from arm's length bargaining.[55] But when does a deal's negotiating process reflect an arm's length bargain? The Chancery Court in *In re Appraisal of Columbia Pipeline Group, Inc.,*[56] identified some critical factors: (1) merger negotiations were arm's length with a third party, (2) the board had no conflicts of interest, (3) the buyer conducted extensive due diligence that included obtaining confidential and valuable information about the firm, (4) a pre-signing market check was held and other potential buyers were contacted, (5) multiple price increases were obtained during the negotiations, and (6) post-signing market checks did not lead to any new bidders.[57] The court noted, however, that the sale process need not be perfect to support deal price as a measure of fair value. Rather, the Chancery Court can rely on it if the "facts as a whole" indicate that it is trustworthy.

1. In *Aruba*, the Delaware Supreme Court disapproved the argument that reduced agency costs arising from HP's acquisition of Aruba qualified as synergy gains to be subtracted from deal price when estimating fair value. The court's reasoning was that agency costs netted out in this deal, since Aruba and HP — its acquirer — were both widely held and therefore experienced the same managerial agency costs. Does this suggest that a reduction in agency costs might qualify as "synergies" in transactions where the acquirer is a private equity firm?

2. A related question is how to assess synergies. In *Aruba,* the Court found that Aruba's own estimates of synergies were credible. But what makes a synergy estimate credible?[58] For instance, does this require a court to

---

55. See *Dell, Inc. v. Magnetar Global Event Driven Master Fund Ltd.*, 177 A.3d 1 (Del. 2017); *DFC Global Corp. v. Muirfield Value Partners, L.P.,* 172 A.3d 346 (Del. 2017). For further discussion see Guhan Subramanian, *Appraisal After Dell, in* The Corporate Contract in Changing Times: Is the Law Keeping Up? 222 (Steven Davidoff & Randall Thomas eds., 2019).

56. Cons. C.A. No. 12736-VCL, 2019 WL 3778370 (Del. Ch. Aug. 12, 2019).

57. See *Columbia Pipeline*, at 50–52. For a similar recent case, see *In Re: Appraisal of Stillwater Mining Company*, Consol. C.A. No. 2017-0385-JTL, 2019 WL 3943851 (Del. Ch. Aug. 21, 2019).

58. Recently, the Court of Chancery addressed this in *In re Appraisal of Panera Bread Company*, C.A. No. 2017-0593-MTZ, 2020 WL 506684 (Del. Ch. Jan. 31, 2020). The court held that Panera's fair value was the deal price of $315 less $11.56 in synergies (reflecting cost savings and tax advantages). The court found that a "preponderance of the evidence demonstrate[d] that JAB [the acquirer] formed its bid in anticipation of applying its management playbook" for cost and cash savings. The evidence suggested that JAB had successfully delivered such costs savings over a considerable period of time by implementing similar changes at other firms it had acquired. Indeed, even Panera's expert agreed with these synergies.

determine whether the value expected to be generated by changes in managerial operating procedures are agency costs in the narrow sense that managers consciously impose them for their own personal benefit, or, alternatively, do they result from an ossified culture that traps managers but does not benefit them? More broadly, how specific to a particular acquirer do synergies need to be before they are excluded from fair value? One option might be to count those synergies that *only* this acquirer can obtain. Another is to count those synergies that could be obtained by many acquirers, but that are unlikely to be obtained by the target board as it is currently constituted.[59]

3. The need to deduct synergies from fair value seems to be compelled by the wording of the appraisal statute. But why should synergies be excluded from fair value? For instance, if an individual sells an underutilized asset to a purchaser who can use it more profitably, then typically the sale price will include some of the surplus that the buyer expects to create. Why wouldn't that be true in selling a firm too?

In light of these decisions on fair value, one might suppose that the issue is now resolved. However, the Delaware Supreme Court injected new life into the debate on fair value as we were preparing earlier chapters of this book. The *Jarden* opinion is excerpted below.

FIR TREE VALUE MASTER FUND, LP
v. JARDEN CORP.
236 A.3d 313 (Del. 2020)

[Plaintiffs brought this appraisal action seeking the fair value of their shares in Jarden Corporation, a successful publicly traded firm, which was sold to Newell Brands for $59.21 per share in a blended cash and stock deal. Jarden's Chief Executive Officer and co-founder, Martin Franklin, ran the negotiations for some months without having authorization from Jarden's board or even with its knowledge. Once the board was made aware of this they encouraged Franklin to pursue a sale, which he did. However, he ignored the board's negotiation instructions and dominated the entire sale process. This led the Chancery Court to find that the deal process was flawed and could not support an inference that it reflected the fair value of the firm. The court instead looked at other valuation methods such as discounted cash flow, comparable companies,[60] and unaffected market price. It concluded that on the record at hand, the unaffected market price of $48.31 was the most reliable indicator of Jarden's fair value. Plaintiffs appealed and we pick up with Chief Justice Seitz's opinion — EDS.]

---

59. In *Panera*, the Court rejected petitioner's claim that the synergies were not merger-specific because Panera's management could have made these changes finding that "Panera's management culture and priorities did not support the changes JAB intended to make."

60. Courts may look to comparable deals or comparable firms (even if not involved in deals) assuming these can be identified. It seems the appropriate pool of comparables ought to be comparable deals involving comparable firms — EDS.

Seitz, C.J.:

Martin Franklin co-founded Jarden in the early 2000's. Jarden operated as a decentralized holding company with a large portfolio of consumer product brands in separate operating companies. Franklin served as CEO and board chairman until 2011 when he stepped away from day-to-day operations but remained in charge of capital distribution and M&A activity. . . . Towards the end of 2015, Jarden's market capitalization put it among the top 20% of all publicly traded firms in the United States.

Like Jarden, Newell operated as a large consumer products company with a vast portfolio of products with household names. . . . In 2011, under its new CEO, Michael Polk, Newell implemented . . . Project Renewal [which] sought to streamline Newell's business structure and decrease costs by delayering the business. In 2014, Newell embarked on a strategy of pursuing "transformational M&A." Newell engaged Centerview Partners to generate a list of possible targets [which included Jarden] and to arrange preliminary meetings.

[Roland Phillips of Centerview met with Franklin in July 2015 about other matters and indicated Polk's interest in meeting.] Franklin understood that Polk would likely want to discuss a Newell/Jarden transaction [to which he was amenable so that he could devote more energy to his other businesses, although he was not authorized by Jarden's Board to engage in such discussions and had not even disclosed this to the Board].

Franklin and Polk first met . . . in September 2015 [and Franklin was willing to sell and to engage in greater discussions]. . . . Franklin did not inform the board about his discussions until individual phone calls several days later. [There were further meetings where Franklin reinforced his interest in selling Jarden, suggested a price upwards of $60 per share, entered a mutual confidentiality and standstill agreement, and began to share nonpublic information with Newell all without board approval.]

. . . On October 28, the board held its first formal meeting to discuss a potential Newell transaction. There was no discussion of a pre-signing market check. Instead, the board directed that negotiations continue with Newell. . . .

Newell structured the deal based on $500 million in estimated annual cost synergies, which priced Jarden at $57-$61 per share. . . . Newell offered $57 per share, with $20 in cash plus a fixed exchange ratio of Newell shares. . . . Jarden's board rejected the offer and authorized Franklin to seek a higher offer, but not to make a counteroffer. [H]owever, Franklin made a counteroffer of $63 per share with $21 in cash. Newell balked, . . . and the deal almost died.

Then on November 21, Newell came back with an offer of $21 in cash and target price of $60 per share. The next day, Jarden's board met, decided to accept the offer, and granted Newell exclusivity during the confirmatory due diligence period. . . . [which] disabled any market check. The board thought that Newell was the best and most likely acquirer, and no other companies had the same fit or ability to pay. . . .

Newell wanted Franklin on the board as a sign of confidence to the market. Franklin, Ashken, and Lillie also agreed to a consulting agreement with non-competition covenants in exchange for a $4 million annual fee for three years . . . [and accelerated vesting of their stock incentive plans].

[Both boards approved the deal on December 13 and t]he parties announced the merger on December 14, 2015. . . .

Jarden and Newell stockholders approved the merger on April 15, 2016. As of the closing, the mix of cash and stock valued Jarden at $59.21 per share.

Petitioners sought appraisal. The Court of Chancery held a four-day trial with twenty-five fact witnesses and three expert witnesses. For the petitioners, Dr. Mark Zmijewski . . . relied primarily on his comparable companies analysis to support a fair value of $71.35 per share on the merger date. For Jarden, Dr. Glenn Hubbard . . . concluded that Jarden's fair value on the merger date was $48.01 per share based on his DCF analysis. . . .

After considering the *Aruba* decision and receiving further submissions from the parties, the Court of Chancery found the fair value of each share of Jarden stock on the closing date of the merger at $48.31 using Jarden's unaffected market price. . . .

[T]he court decided not to use the deal price less synergies as a reliable indicator of fair value [because] the Jarden sale process "raise[d] concerns" and "left much to be desired." As the court held, Jarden's CEO acted with "little to no oversight by the Board" and volunteered "a price range the Board would accept to sell the Company before negotiations began in earnest." Also critical, according to the court, was the lack of a pre-signing or post-signing market check and "the difficulty in assessing the extent to which Newell ceded synergies to Jarden in the Merger." . . . After reviewing the evidence, the court decided to "place less weight on this market-based valuation approach in this case because the sales process was not well-conceived or well-executed . . ."

[T]he court rejected the petitioners' comparable companies analysis of $71.35 per share. The court found the credibility of this analysis depended "on the quality of the comparables." The court concluded that "Jarden had no reliable comparables," . . .

[Then], the court refused to adopt either parties' DCF models because of the wildly divergent fair value conclusions. . . . Instead of relying exclusively on either expert's analysis, the court selected its own inputs that led to a DCF fair value of $48.13 per share — a result it ultimately chose not to rely on as a primary source for its fair value award.

[T]he court decided to use Jarden's unaffected stock price — $48.31 per share — as the best evidence of Jarden's fair value. Relying in part on an event study performed by Jarden's expert, the court found that the market for Jarden stock was informationally efficient, meaning the corporation's stock price quickly reflected publicly available information. Further, according to the court, the parties did not have material nonpublic information that would not be reflected in Jarden's unaffected stock price. . . . And the unaffected market price was not stale as of the merger date because the evidence showed that Jarden's financial prospects worsened between the unaffected trading date and closing the merger. . . .

II.

In an appraisal action, the Court of Chancery "shall determine the fair value of the shares exclusive of any element of value arising from the accomplishment or expectation of the merger or consolidation" plus interest. Fair value "is a jurisprudential, rather than purely economic, construct," meaning fair value is a law-created valuation method that excludes elements of value that would normally be captured in economic models.[37] Under the appraisal statute, when "determining such fair value, the Court shall take into account all relevant factors." . . . The court must assess the fair value of each share of stock "on the closing date of the merger" and determine the value of the pre-merger corporation as a going concern. . . . In the end, the trial judge must determine fair value, and "fair value is just that, 'fair.' It does not mean the highest possible price that a company might have sold for."

On appeal, [petitioners] argue that the court erred . . . as a matter of law "because it ignore[d] the long-recognized principle in Delaware law, reinforced in *Aruba*, that stock price does not equal fair value." . . . ; the court should have treated the deal price as a fair value floor; and the court constructed its own flawed DCF model to corroborate its fair value. . . .

Turning to the first ground for error . . . the petitioners argue that our recent *Aruba* decision foreclosed as a matter of law the court's use of unaffected market price to support fair value. The Court of Chancery recognized correctly, however, neither *Aruba* nor our other recent appraisal decisions ruled out using any recognized valuation methods to support fair value.

Our *Aruba* decision followed closely on the heels of two other important Supreme Court appraisal decisions — *DFC Global Corp.* and *Dell*. In *DFC*, . . . [we noted that] "second-guessing the value arrived upon by the collective views of many sophisticated parties with a real stake in the matter is hazardous."[50] [We also] commented on the relevance of a stock's unaffected market price to fair value:

> When, as here, the company had no conflicts related to the transaction, a deep base of public shareholders, and highly active trading, the price at which its shares trade is informative of fair value, as that value reflects the judgments of many stockholders about the company's future prospects, based on public filings, industry information, and research conducted by equity analysts.

In *Dell*, we found that the Court of Chancery erred when it assigned no weight to market value or deal price as part of its valuation analysis. Once again, our Court emphasized that the court must "take into account all relevant factors" and "give fair consideration to 'proof of value by any techniques or methods which are generally considered acceptable in the financial community and otherwise admissible in court.'"[52] Although we cautioned that, in a given case, the market is not always the best indicator of value, . . . we believed that, on the record before the court, ". . . both Dell's stock price and the deal price — have substantial probative value."[53]

And finally, in *Aruba*, we emphasized the "considerable weight" a court should give to the deal price "absent deficiencies in the deal process" . . . We also recognized, however, that "when a market was informationally

37. *DFC*, 172 A.3d at 367.
50. *DFC*, 172 A.3d at 366.
52. *Dell*, 177 A.3d at 21 (quoting *Weinberger*, 457 A.2d at 713).
53. *Id.* at 35.

efficient . . . the market price is likely to be more informative of fundamental value."[55] And how informative of fundamental value an informationally efficient market is depends, at least in part, on the extent of material nonpublic information.[56] . . .

In *DFC*, *Dell*, and *Aruba* we did not, as a matter of law, rule out any recognized financial measurement of fair value. Instead, we remained true to the appraisal statute's command that the court consider "all relevant factors" in its fair value determination. . . . The Vice Chancellor got the "takeaway" exactly right from our recent appraisal decisions: "[w]hat is necessary in any particular [appraisal] case [] is for the Court of Chancery to explain its [fair value calculus] in a manner that is grounded in the record before it."[59] . . .

The Court of Chancery found, and the petitioners agree, that Jarden stock traded in a semi-strong efficient market, meaning the market quickly assimilated all publicly available information into Jarden's stock price.[61] The court considered whether there was sufficient information asymmetry between the market and insiders to render the unaffected market price unreliable. Based on an event study by Dr. Hubbard and [other evidence] the court found it unlikely that there was material nonpublic information not incorporated by the market's estimate of Jarden's value.

[T]he court found it reasonable to rely on Jarden's unaffected market price for fair value. . . .

Experience tells us that sophisticated buyers and sellers typically exchange material confidential information in deal negotiations. . . . Thus, the unaffected market price is not always a better reflection of fair value than the deal price negotiated by those with better [information and] access to the corporation and its advisors.

But in this case, we are satisfied that, on the record before it, the court did not abuse its discretion when it found that the market did not lack material nonpublic information about Jarden's financial prospects. . . .

Based on the record before it, the court could find that the "market was well informed and the Unaffected Market Price reflects all material information." . . .

Having successfully undermined the reliability of the deal price in the Court of Chancery, the petitioners now claim on appeal that the deal price should have at least acted as a floor for the fair value of Jarden stock. . . . Because a better process would have resulted in a higher deal price, and, according to the petitioners, Jarden failed to prove synergies, they contend the deal price is "logically the minimum for any fair value determination."

The petitioners' arguments have some appeal. It makes sense that if a deal negotiation process is flawed, and the seller's negotiator capped the

---

55. *Id.* (quoting *Dell*, 177 A.3d at 7) (alterations in original). . . .

56. *Aruba*, 210 A.3d at 138 n.53 (explaining that when markets reflect all information, rather than just publicly available information, they are "more likely to reflect fundamental value"). . . .

59. *Jarden*, 2019 WL 3244085, at *2 (quoting *DFC*, 172 A.3d at 388) (alterations in original).

61. *Aruba*, 210 A.3d at 138 n.53.

value under what might be achieved in true arm's length negotiations, the deal price might act as a fair value floor in the absence of synergies. But here, synergies cause us to find the Court of Chancery did not err for failing to treat the deal price as a floor for fair value. . . .

As we observed in *Dell*, "the court should exclude 'any synergies or other value expected from the merger giving rise to the appraisal proceeding itself.' "[80] The court here found that "[t]here is no dispute here that synergies were realized in the Merger." . . .

The record supports the court's conclusion. . . . As further evidence of the court's belief that Jarden captured some of those synergies, the court assigned a specific number to deal price less synergies [which] falls between two values Dr. Hubbard identified.[89] Regardless, in the end, the court did not give deal price minus synergies any weight in its final fair value award.

After reviewing the record, however, which contains a mix of valuation ranges supporting either side's valuation position, we find that the court did not abuse its discretion in its review of the conflicting valuations. . . .

QUESTIONS AND NOTES ON JARDEN

1. Although the Chancery Court ultimately relied on unaffected market price to set a fair value of $48.31 per share, its own estimates of deal price less synergies ($46.21) and DCF valuation ($48.13) were very close to unaffected market price. Should the Court have relied on unaffected market price if deal price less synergies and DCF value were not so close?

2. What parts of the deal process seemed most concerning to the Court? Should a Founder CEO's domination of the sale process, by itself, be considered unfair deal process if it led to a price that seemed fair? Are there facts here that might give you pause about the Founder's motives? If so, then why not use deal price as a floor for fair value?

3. The Delaware Supreme Court held that the chosen valuation method must be justified in the record. However, regardless of how one approaches fair value, there are difficult judgment calls. What elements of deal price are "synergies," and how should these be valued? When are acquirers simply good stock pickers, and when do the premia they pay reflect expectations about real operational synergies? How can share prices ever reflect the private information that buyers acquire in friendly deals? If DCF valuation is required, what are the relevant discount rates and how reliable are the projected future cash flows?[61] And finally, how much should we constrain

---

80. 177 A.3d at 21 (quoting *Global GT LP v. Golden Telecom, Inc.*, 993 A.2d 497, 507 (Del. Ch. 2010), *aff'd*, 11 A.3d 214 (Del. 2010)).

89. *Id.* at *50 (assigning $46.21 as "the most reliable estimate of fair value" under the deal price less synergies approach); App. to Opening Br. at A691 (testifying that $41.78 and $47.21 are possible values). Perhaps the court's number, $46.21, is simply a mistyped $47.21.

61. A recent example is *Manichaean Capital, LLC v. SourceHOV Holdings, Inc.*, C.A. No. 2017-0673-JRS (Del. Ch. 2020) which involved an acquisition of a privately held

the discretion of financially savvy judges to make educated decisions about fair value after being fully briefed by the parties? DCF valuations allowed the Delaware Court of Chancery a great deal of discretion but relatively little legal cover. In contrast, a standard that presumptively favors deal price, even when the deal negotiations are "less than perfect," forecloses appraisal as an arena in which to contest sham negotiations and side deals.

4. Concerns over appraisal have generated both judicial responses (as discussed above) and legislative responses. Two recent amendments directly affect the likely success of appraisal actions. The first is §262(g) which requires that shareholders who choose to file appraisal actions must hold at least 1 percent of the firm's outstanding shares or have shares worth more than $1 million in the firm. Although this does not trouble most hedge funds engaging in appraisal arbitrage, it does affect smaller shareholders. A recent study found that nearly one-third of small shareholders who might have in the past brought appraisal actions would not qualify under the new rule.[62] The second is §262(h) which allows firms to pre-pay some or all of the merger consideration to dissenters upon filing of an appraisal action. This appears to reduce the likely interest charges that defendants may face (and appraisal arbitrageurs hope to receive). The effect of this provision is less clear in part because of the uncertainty associated with its application.[63]

5. Over the last 15 years, appraisal actions have witnessed a topsy-turvy run with responses from the judiciary, legislature, and those in practice. What has been the result of all this activity? A recent study by Jiang, Li, and Thomas[64] finds that the returns from appraisal actions declined precipitously in the period 2015-2019 (as legislative and judicial action tightened around appraisal) compared to the 2000-2014 period. Average gross deal returns to appraisal arbitrage declined from 98.2 percent in 2000-2014 to 13.2 percent in 2015-2019. Similarly, the amount over deal price that a judicial valuation provided declined from 50.6 percent in 2000-2014 to −5.3 percent in 2015-2019. The tide had indeed turned, and Jian, Li, and

---

firm — SourceHOV — which did not have an "unaffected market price" (because it did not trade) and its management did not shop the firm around (making deal process more truncated and deal price less reliable). The court did not think there were comparable companies and hence relied on DCF analysis. However, both sides' experts were "solar systems apart" in their DCF estimates, further complicating the court's task. In the end, the court relied on petitioner's expert's analysis, which appeared more reasonable and more grounded in the record.

62. See Wei Jiang, Tao Li, Danqing Mei & Randall Thomas, *Appraisal: Shareholder Remedy or Litigation Arbitrage?*, 59 J. L. & Econ. 697 (2016).

63. See Arthur R. Bookout, Daniel S. Atlas & Andrew D. Kinsey, *Delaware Appraisal Actions: When Does It Make Sense to Prepay?*, Skadden, Arps, Slate, Meagher & Flom, LLP, May 29, 2018, https://www.skadden.com/insights/publications/2018/05/insights-the-delaware-edition/delaware-appraisal-actions.

64. Wei Jiang, Tao Li & Randall S. Thomas, *The Long Rise and Quick Fall of Appraisal Arbitrage* (February 28, 2020). Vanderbilt Law Research Paper No. 20-16, Available at SSRN: https://ssrn.com/abstract=3546281 or http://dx.doi.org/10.2139/ssrn.3546281.

Thomas argue that the primary reasons for this are the trinity of Delaware cases noted above.

12.7.4   Quasi-Appraisal

This is the name given to a remedy that the Delaware courts have announced would be available for valid claims of breach of disclosure obligations in mergers where the merger has closed and a defective disclosure impaired the ability of the plaintiff to elect appraisal in a timely way. Originally arising in short form mergers in which the plaintiff claimed that a defective disclosure impaired his timely election to seek appraisal,[65] the remedy has migrated to arm's length mergers as well.[66] The idea is simple: If material non-disclosures affect the shareholder's election to seek appraisal or not and the merger has already been effectuated, a possible remedy would be to assess the fair value of the shares, as in an appraisal, and award that amount as damages. The theory makes sense. But, while the theory is simple, the "quasi-appraisal" remedy is much different than the statutory appraisal remedy and much more unsettling to those planning corporate transactions.[67]

Why? Recall that in an appraisal preceding the petitioning shareholder must: (1) act affirmatively to vote against the deal and dissent, and (2) forego receipt of merger consideration until the action is concluded. Thus, the appraisal option has costs that tend naturally to limit the size of appraisal classes. But as shaped by the Delaware Supreme Court, the quasi-appraisal remedy is not a costly opt-in action but is an opt-out class action in which no non-dissenting shareholder, having already received the merger consideration, has any incentive to opt-out. Therefore, unlike the appraisal, this form of action has as plaintiffs every public share of target stock. Thus a judgment against the defendants can be orders of magnitude greater, and the existence of this possibility ex ante introduces a new source of risk into transactions.

Vice Chancellor Stephen Lamb attempted to reduce this risk while leaving an effective remedy by making the quasi-appraisal remedy more like the statutory appraisal action by holding that, in order to be included in the quasi-appraisal class, a non-dissenting shareholder would be required affirmatively to opt into the action and, in order to mimic the statutory appraisal action to some extent, would have to tender-back some part of the merger consideration (as fixed by the court).[68] This attempt to make the quasi-appraisal

---

65. *Nebel v. Southwest Bancorp. Inc.*, 1995 WL 405750 (Del. Ch. July 5 1995); *Gilliland v. Motorola, Inc.*, 859 A.2d 80 (Del. Ch. 2004).

66. *Krieger v. Wesco Fin. Corp.*, 2011 WL 4916910 (Del. Ch. 2011). See also *In re Orchard Enterprises, Inc. Stockholder Litigation*, 88 A.3d 1 (Del. Ch. 2014) (noting that the Delaware Supreme Court and the Court of Chancery have permitted quasi-appraisal damages where there is a duty of disclosure breach by a fiduciary in a transaction requiring a stockholder vote).

67. See e.g. W. Savitt, *Dissenters Pose Bigger Risks to Corporate Deals*, Nat. L.J. (February 10, 2014) at 17; R. Schumer, S. Lamb, J. Hamill & J. Christiansen, *Quasi-Appraisal: The New Frontier of Stockholder Litigation?*, 12 The M&A Journal No.2 (2012).

68. *Gilliland v. Motorola Inc.*, 873 A2d at 313-314 (Del Ch. 2004).

remedy function a bit like the statutory appraisal action was rejected by the Delaware Supreme Court in *Berger v. Pubco*.[69] Berger was a short-form merger (8 DGCL §253) in which the disclosure claims were that the parent company had not disclosed how it had fixed the cash-out price and that it had included an out-of-date copy of the appraisal statute. In that setting, the court rejected both aspects of the lower court's effort to fashion balance without any convincing explanation.

Two recent cases, however, may signal more careful scrutiny of suits seeking a quasi-appraisal remedy. In *In re Cyan, Inc. Stockholders Litig.*, No. CV 11027-CB, 2017 WL 1956955 (Del. Ch. May 11, 2017) the Court of Chancery dismissed the plaintiff's suit seeking quasi-appraisal damages for breaches of the duty of disclosure in a stock-for-stock transaction because the firm had in place a §102(b)(7) waiver and the plaintiff had failed to show a non-exculpated breach of the duty of disclosure. In *In re United Capital Corp., Stockholders Litig.*, No. CV 11619-VCMR, 2017 WL 389520 (Del. Ch. Jan. 4, 2017), the Chancery Court held that although quasi-appraisal was a remedy available for breach of the duty of disclosure, "none of the Plaintiff's alleged omissions are material. . . ." The court dismissed the suit and noted that if the plaintiff cannot show fraud, illegality, or a disclosure violation, then the only remedy for dissatisfied minority shareholders is appraisal.

12.7.5   The Appraisal Alternative in Interested Mergers

Prior to the rise of appraisal arbitrage, the appraisal remedy was most often sought in interested mergers. In these circumstances, some judicial remedy to assure fairness seems necessary. A minority shareholder ought not to be at the mercy of a shareholder vote that is either controlled or potentially manipulated by an interested party, as in a parent-subsidiary merger or even a management-sponsored buyout, especially in publicly traded firms.[70]

However, as the discussion of the duties of controlling shareholders in Chapter 8 indicated, the law has provided an equitable remedy in the form of fairness review when minority shareholders challenge a self-interested transaction. Indeed, the development of that remedy provides the grist for our discussion in Section 12.8 below. So, should the law then provide *both* an appraisal action and a fairness action for controlled mergers? And if so, how should these actions relate to each other?

69. 976 A2d 132 (Del. 2009).
70. Where the acquiring company's stock is not publicly traded, an appraisal will provide a liquidity event at a time in which a sudden dramatic change in the firm may make it seem unfair to "force" a dissenting shareholder to continue her investment.

In some aspects, an appraisal action is the easier form of action for shareholders, since the plaintiff need only establish that they properly dissented from the transaction to seek appraisal and need not show that the board or a controlling shareholder breached a fiduciary duty. In most other respects, however, an action alleging breach of entire fairness seems more favorable to plaintiffs. Under the statutory standard, a plaintiff in an appraisal proceeding is entitled to claim only a pro rata share of the fair value of the company *without regard to any gain caused by the merger or its expectation.* By contrast, in a fiduciary "fairness" action against a controlling shareholder, the defendant must prove that a self-dealing transaction was fair in all respects. See *Weinberger v. UOP Inc.*, discussed above in Chapter 8. If the defendant fails in this, the possible remedies are very broad and may include rescission or "rescissory damages." (Rescissory damages are the financial equivalent to what rescission would bring, were it feasible.) Perhaps even more advantageous, at least for plaintiffs' lawyers, fairness claims can be brought as class actions in the name of all minority shareholders — not just those relatively few who will have bothered to dissent. Put differently, the class action procedure gives to plaintiffs and their lawyers the great leverage that results from a large "opt-out" class of shares.

In Section 12.8, we discuss the fascinating development of judicial review of controlled mergers. As you read it over, ask yourself: How do appraisal proceedings and suits for breach of fiduciary duty compare now given recent developments in both areas?

12.8   THE DUTY OF LOYALTY IN CONTROLLED MERGERS

As we discussed in Chapter 8, U.S. corporate law generally provides that controlling shareholders owe to the corporation and its minority shareholders a fiduciary duty of loyalty whenever they exercise any aspect of their control over corporate actions and decisions.[71] All shareholders, however, have the right to vote their shares in their own best interests.[72] Thus, there is some tension between a controlling shareholder's exercise of voting rights, which can arguably reflect her own "selfish" self-interest, and her exercise of "control" over the corporation or its property, which cannot. What precisely is the exercise of control that gives rise to an obligation of fairness? It is best defined as the de facto power to do what other shareholders cannot, such as the controller's power

---

71. *Weinberger v. UOP, Inc.*, 457 A.2d 701 (Del. 1983); *Sinclair Oil Corp. v. Levien*, 280 A.2d 717. (Del. 1971) (*Sinclair Oil* is the source of a particular test for invoking the entire fairness burden: that the corporate transaction under scrutiny treats the controller differently than the other shareholders before the obligation to prove its fairness arises. Of course, this test is typically met in freeze-out mergers).

72. *Tanzer v. International General Industries, Inc.*, 379 A.2d 1221 (Del. 1977).

to access non-public corporate information or influence the board to approve a transaction (e.g., a merger) with another company in which the controller is financially interested.

Controlled mergers, including parent-subsidiary mergers, expose minority shareholders to an acute risk of exploitation. Today, we describe most of these mergers as "cash-out," "freeze-out," or "going-private" mergers. But a merger is not the only technique for accomplishing a cash-out or freeze-out. Asset sales and reverse stock splits can also be freeze-out techniques. For example, a controlling shareholder can cause the company to sell all of its assets to his wholly owned firm, in exchange for cash, which may then be distributed to the company's shareholders in liquidation. Alternatively, a controlling shareholder can cause the company to radically decrease its number of shares and pay off minority shareholders in cash for fractional shares. If the reverse split is dramatic enough, only one shareholder will be left after it is completed.[73]

12.8.1   Cash Mergers or Freeze-Outs

Nineteenth-century corporation lawyers would have been horrified (or maybe delighted) by the cash-out merger. Even after the repudiation of the unanimity rule allowed a qualified majority of shareholders to impose a merger against the will of a disagreeing minority, all shareholders had the right to continue as shareholders of the surviving entity. Indeed, this is still the rule in most non-U.S. jurisdictions that recognize mergers.

Nevertheless, by the 1920s, the idea of cashing out minority shareholders through the merger device no longer shocked the consciences of U.S. corporate lawyers. Florida led the way by amending its statute in 1925 to permit cash consideration in a merger. Other states followed. Delaware

---

73. To better understand a reverse stock split, first consider a normal stock split. In a normal stock split, either the company pays a stock dividend on its outstanding shares, so that each shareholder receives more stock for each share already held, or the company amends its charter to provide that each share is "reclassified" into more than one share. Of course, the company's expected cash flows and earnings are unaffected by simply changing the number of shares outstanding, and the only other certain result of a split is to reduce the company's stock price in proportion (or nearly so) to the split. Typical stock splits are 2-for-1 or 3-for-1 and are used to decrease the per-share price to a "normal" range ($10 to $200). Lower absolute stock prices reduce an investor's threshold investment: Stock is generally traded in round lots of 100 shares, and purchases of smaller ("odd") lots usually involve higher transaction costs. Well-timed splits may thus have the real economic effect of increasing the liquidity of a stock and so may (modestly) increase the total value of outstanding shares.

In a reverse stock split, the opposite effect is achieved. A controlling shareholder amends the corporate charter to provide for the combination of some large number of shares into a single share (e.g., 1-for-10, 1-for-100, etc.). Cash is provided to shareholders holding less than a single share ("fractional share") after the reverse split, pursuant to statute. See DGCL §155. The reverse split ratio is set large enough to ensure that only the controlling shareholder ends up with one or more whole shares of stock; all other shareholders end up with fractional shares (and thus cash).

was customarily cautious; it did not authorize the use of cash in short-form mergers until 1957 and not in long-form mergers until 1967. The MBCA followed in 1968 and 1969, respectively.[74] Cash-out mergers (or freeze-outs) emerged as a controversial topic during the 1960s and 1970s, when a period of low stock market prices followed after a boom in public offerings of stock. The low stock values allowed many controlling shareholders to cash out public shareholders at prices substantially below the prices that these investors had paid for the same shares a short time before. This raised complaints about unfairness. Critics argued, among other things, that such transactions often occurred when the pro rata asset value of these firms greatly exceeded the market price of their publicly traded shares. It was widely thought that, in these circumstances, a "cash-out" even at a premium price allowed controlling shareholders to capture a disproportionate share of the company's value.[75]

At the federal level, the SEC adopted Rule 13e-3 under the Williams Act, which requires a great deal of specified disclosure whenever a controller seeks to tender for the minority shares of its company. See Statutory Supplement. At the state level, courts in Delaware and elsewhere wrestled with the task of protecting minority shareholders without banning freeze-outs altogether. At first, in *Singer v. Magnavox*, 380 A.2d 969 (Del. 1977), the Delaware courts announced that going private transactions would henceforth constitute a breach of duty by a controlling shareholder unless the controller could demonstrate a valid business purpose for the transaction. This rule, however, proved unstable. By 1985, it was replaced by the Delaware Supreme Court's analysis in the *Weinberger* opinion, which we discussed in Chapter 8.

Weinberger thus established the modern articulation of the rule governing controlling-shareholder related-party transactions. Once a plaintiff alleges a freeze out transaction between a controller and a company, the fiduciary controller will be deemed to have the burden of establishing that the transaction is fair in all respects: that is, that the process of the deal and the terms of the deal are entirely fair to the corporation and its minority shareholders.

---

74. See generally Elliott J. Weiss, *The Law of Take Out Mergers: A Historical Perspective*, 56 N.Y.U. L. Rev. 624, 632 (1981); Arthur M. Borden, *Going Private — Old Tort, New Tort or No Tort?*, 49 N.Y.U. L. Rev. 987 (1974).

75. For example, in a much-publicized speech given at the University of Notre Dame in November 1974, SEC Commissioner A.A. Sommer said:

> Daily we read of companies which are offering to buy out all, or substantially all, of their shareholders, thus enhancing the control of the controlling shareholders and freeing the corporation of the "burdens" of being publicly-held. In other instances clever and indeed most imaginative devices are used to afford the small shareholders little, if any, choice in the matter. What is happening is, in my estimation, serious, unfair, and sometimes disgraceful, a perversion of the whole process of public financing, and a course that inevitably is going to make the individual shareholder even more hostile to American corporate mores and the securities markets than he already is.

A.A. Sommer, Jr., Law Advisory Council Lecture, Notre Dame Law School (Nov. 1974) in [1974-1975 Transfer Binder] Fed. Sec. L. Rep. (CCH) 80,010, at 84,695 (Nov. 20, 1974).

The *Weinberger* case left in its wake important undecided issues beyond the central question of just what constituted fair process and fair price in a parent-subsidiary merger. One of these was the hallmarks of "control" that trigger the deployment of the entire fairness standard. Another was the legal effect of interposing an independent negotiating committee between a board and a controlling shareholder. A third was the relationship between a majority-of-the-minority (MOM) shareholder vote of approval and a deal price negotiated by an independent board committee fully empowered to accept or reject a controller's proposed deal.[76] Finally, a last subsidiary issue was whether the entire fairness standard would apply to a two-step freeze-out transaction in which a controller employed a tender offer to obtain 90 percent of outstanding shares and then resorted to DGCL §253 to cash out the remaining minority shareholders. We consider the history of these issues in this section.

Weinberger's forceful suggestion that it might be a good idea in freeze-out transactions to empanel a committee of independent directors to negotiate with the controller at arm's length gave rise to a practice in freeze-out transactions to do just that. In that evolving practice, boards would appoint a committee of independent board members who would, with the help of independent bankers and lawyer advisors, negotiate the deal, presumably saying no to any deal that did not offer both a fair price and the best price available from the controller. The hope of deal planners was that when such transactions were attacked in court as unfair to public shareholders, the courts would accord, some kind of deference to the judgment of the independent committees.

Early on (1988), the Court of Chancery indicated a willingness to review freeze-out mergers under the business judgment rule, if a board committee of independent directors was comprised of truly independent directors and the process otherwise had integrity. (See *In re Trans World Airlines Shareholders Litig.*, CIV. A. No. 9844, 1988 WL 111271 (Del. Ch. Oct. 21, 1988).) but other Chancery opinions of the period held otherwise. This split in authority was not resolved by the Delaware Supreme Court until its 1994 opinion in *Kahn v. Lynch Communication Systems, Inc.*, 638 A.2d 1110 (1994).

KAHN v. LYNCH COMMUNICATION SYSTEMS, INC.
638 A.2d 1110 (Del. 1994)

[Alcatel U.S.A. Corporation (Alcatel), a holding company, is an indirect subsidiary of Compagnie Generale d'Electricite (CGE), a French corporation. In 1981, Alcatel acquired 30.6 percent of the common stock of

---

76. *Weinberger* noted that a majority of the minority shareholder vote in favor of the freeze-out would shift the burden of proof on entire fairness to the plaintiff and soon the courts held a favorable vote by an informed independent committee did too. This of course made the majority of the minority shareholder vote appear superfluous. See Guhan Subramanian, *Fixing Freezeouts*, 115 Yale L.J. 2 (2005).

Lynch Communication Systems, Inc. (Lynch) pursuant to a stock purchase agreement.]

Holland, J.:

By the time of the merger which is contested in this action, Alcatel owned 43.3 percent of Lynch's outstanding stock; designated five of the eleven members of Lynch's board of directors; two of three members of the executive committee; and two of four members of the compensation committee.

In the spring of 1986, Lynch determined that in order to remain competitive in the rapidly changing telecommunications field, it would need to obtain fiber optics technology to complement its existing digital electronic capabilities. Lynch's management identified a target company, Telco Systems, Inc. ("Telco"), which possessed both fiber optics and other valuable technological assets. The record reflects that Telco expressed interest in being acquired by Lynch. Because of the supermajority voting provision, which Alcatel had negotiated when it first purchased its shares, in order to proceed with the Telco combination Lynch needed Alcatel's consent. In June 1986, Ellsworth F. Dertinger ("Dertinger"), Lynch's CEO and chairman of its board of directors, contacted Pierre Suard ("Suard"), the chairman of Alcatel's parent company, CGE, regarding the acquisition of Telco by Lynch. Suard expressed Alcatel's opposition to Lynch's acquisition of Telco. Instead, Alcatel proposed a combination of Lynch and Celwave Systems, Inc. ("Celwave"), an indirect subsidiary of CGE engaged in the manufacture and sale of telephone wire, cable and other related products.

Alcatel's proposed combination with Celwave was presented to the Lynch board at a regular meeting held on August 1, 1986. Although several directors expressed interest in the original combination which had been proposed with Telco, the Alcatel representatives on Lynch's board made it clear that such a combination would not be considered before a Lynch/Celwave combination. According to the minutes of the August 1 meeting, Dertinger expressed his opinion that Celwave would not be of interest to Lynch if Celwave was not owned by Alcatel.

At the conclusion of the meeting, the Lynch board unanimously adopted a resolution establishing an Independent Committee, consisting of Hubert L. Kertz ("Kertz"), Paul B. Wineman ("Wineman"), and Stuart M. Beringer ("Beringer"), to negotiate with Celwave and to make recommendations concerning the appropriate terms and conditions of a combination with Celwave. On October 24, 1986, Alcatel's investment banking firm, Dillon, Read & Co., Inc. ("Dillon Read") made a presentation to the Independent Committee. Dillon Read expressed its views concerning the benefits of a Celwave/Lynch combination and submitted a written proposal of an exchange ratio of 0.95 shares of Celwave per Lynch share in a stock-for-stock merger.

However, the Independent Committee's investment advisors, Thomson McKinnon Securities Inc. ("Thomson McKinnon") and Kidder, Peabody & Co. Inc. ("Kidder Peabody"), reviewed the Dillon Read proposal and concluded that the 0.95 ratio was predicated on Dillon Read's overvaluation of Celwave.

Based upon this advice, the Independent Committee determined that the exchange ratio proposed by Dillon Read was unattractive to Lynch. The Independent Committee expressed its unanimous opposition to the Celwave/ Lynch merger on October 31, 1986.

Alcatel responded to the Independent Committee's action on November 4, 1986, by withdrawing the Celwave proposal. Alcatel made a simultaneous offer to acquire the entire equity interest in Lynch, constituting the approximately 57 percent of Lynch shares not owned by Alcatel. The offering price was $14 cash per share.

On November 7, 1986, the Lynch board of directors revised the mandate of the Independent Committee. It authorized Kertz, Wineman, and Beringer to negotiate the cash merger offer with Alcatel. At a meeting held that same day, the Independent Committee determined that the $14 per share offer was inadequate. The Independent's Committee's own legal counsel, Skadden, Arps, Slate, Meagher & Flom ("Skadden Arps"), suggested that the Independent Committee should review alternatives to a cash-out merger with Alcatel, including a "white knight" third party acquirer, a repurchase of Alcatel's shares, or the adoption of a shareholder rights plan.

On November 12, 1986, Beringer, as chairman of the Independent Committee, contacted Michiel C. McCarty ("McCarty") of Dillon Read, Alcatel's representative in the negotiations, with a counteroffer at a price of $17 per share. McCarty responded on behalf of Alcatel with an offer of $15 per share. When Beringer informed McCarty of the Independent Committee's view that $15 was also insufficient, Alcatel raised its offer to $15.25 per share. The Independent Committee also rejected this offer. Alcatel then made its final offer of $15.50 per share.

At the November 24, 1986 meeting of the Independent Committee, Beringer advised its other two members that Alcatel was "ready to proceed with an unfriendly tender at a lower price" if the $15.50 per share price was not recommended by the Independent Committee and approved by the Lynch board of directors. Beringer also told the other members of the Independent Committee that the alternatives to a cash-out merger had been investigated but were impracticable. After meeting with its financial and legal advisors, the Independent Committee voted unanimously to recommend that the Lynch board of directors approve Alcatel's $15.50 cash per share price for a merger with Alcatel. The Lynch board met later that day. With Alcatel's nominees abstaining, it approved the merger. . . .

Alcatel held a 43.3 percent minority share of stock in Lynch. Therefore, the threshold question to be answered by the Court of Chancery was whether, despite its minority ownership, Alcatel exercised control over Lynch's business affairs. Based upon the testimony and the minutes of the August 1, 1986 Lynch board meeting, the Court of Chancery concluded that Alcatel did exercise control over Lynch's business decisions.

At the August 1 meeting, Alcatel opposed the renewal of compensation contracts for Lynch's top five managers. According to Dertinger, Christian Fayard ("Fayard"), an Alcatel director, told the board members, "you must listen to us. We are 43 percent owner. You have to do what we tell you."

Although Beringer and Kertz, two of the independent directors, favored renewal of the contracts, according to the minutes, the third independent director, Wineman, admonished the board as follows:

> Mr. Wineman pointed out that the vote on the contracts is a "watershed vote" and the motion, due to Alcatel's "strong feelings," might not carry if taken now. Mr. Wineman clarified that "you [management] might win the battle and lose the war." With Alcatel's opinion so clear, Mr. Wineman questioned "if management wants the contracts renewed under these circumstances." He recommended that management "think twice." Mr. Wineman declared: "I want to keep the management. I can't think of a better management." Mr. Kertz agreed, again advising consideration of the "critical" period the company is entering.

The minutes reflect that the management directors left the room after this statement. The remaining board members then voted not to renew the contracts.

At the same meeting, Alcatel vetoed Lynch's acquisition of the target company, which, according to the minutes, Beringer considered "an immediate fit" for Lynch. Dertinger agreed with Beringer, stating that the "target company is extremely important as they have the products that Lynch needs now." Nonetheless, Alcatel prevailed. The minutes reflect that Fayard advised the board: "Alcatel, with its 44% equity position, would not approve such an acquisition as it does not wish to be diluted from being the main shareholder in Lynch." From the foregoing evidence, the Vice Chancellor concluded:

> . . . Alcatel did control the Lynch board, at least with respect to the matters under consideration at its August 1, 1986 board meeting. . . .

The record supports the Court of Chancery's underlying factual finding that "the non-Alcatel [independent] directors deferred to Alcatel because of its position as a significant stockholder and not because they decided in the exercise of their own business judgment that Alcatel's position was correct." The record also supports the subsequent factual finding that, notwithstanding its 43.3 percent minority shareholder interest, Alcatel did exercise actual control over Lynch by dominating its corporate affairs. . . .

A controlling or dominating shareholder standing on both sides of a transaction, as in a parent-subsidiary context, bears the burden of proving its entire fairness. . . .

The logical question raised by this Court's holding in *Weinberger* was what type of evidence would be reliable to demonstrate entire fairness. That question was not only anticipated but also initially addressed in the *Weinberger* opinion. *Id.* at 709-10 n.7. This Court suggested that the result "could have been entirely different if UOP had appointed an independent negotiating committee of its outside directors to deal with Signal at arm's length," because "fairness in this context can be equated to conduct by a theoretical, wholly independent, board of directors." *Id.* Accordingly, this Court stated, "a showing that the action taken was as though each of the contending parties had in fact exerted its bargaining power against the other at arm's length is strong *evidence* that the transaction meets the test of fairness." *Id.* (emphasis added).

. . . In *Weinberger*, this Court recognized that it would be inconsistent with its holding [to abolish the business purpose requirement] to apply the business judgment rule in the context of an interested merger transaction which, by its very nature, did not require a business purpose. Consequently, [an informal vote by a majority of the minority shareholders merely shifts the burden of proof as to proving unfairness. — EDS.] . . .

Even where no coercion is intended, [minority] shareholders voting on a parent subsidiary merger might perceive that their disapproval could risk retaliation of some kind by the controlling stockholder. For example, the controlling stockholder might decide to stop dividend payments or to effect a subsequent cash out merger at a less favorable price, for which the remedy would be time consuming and costly litigation. At the very least, the potential for that perception, and its possible impact upon a shareholder vote, could never be fully eliminated. . . .

Once again, this Court holds that the exclusive standard of judicial review in examining the propriety of an interested cash-out merger transaction by a controlling or dominating shareholder is entire fairness. . . . The initial burden of establishing entire fairness rests upon the party who stands on both sides of the transaction. . . . However, an approval of the transaction by an independent committee of directors or an informed majority of minority shareholders shifts the burden of proof on the issue of fairness from the controlling or dominating shareholder to the challenging shareholder-plaintiff. . . .

[However, t]he mere existence of an independent special committee does not itself shift the burden. At least two factors are required. First, the majority shareholder must not dictate the terms of the merger. . . . Second, the special committee must have real bargaining power that it can exercise with the majority shareholder on an arm's length basis. . . .

[T]he performance of the Independent Committee merits careful judicial scrutiny to determine whether Alcatel's demonstrated pattern of domination was effectively neutralized. . . . The fact that the same independent directors had submitted to Alcatel's demands on August 1, 1986 was part of the basis for the Court of Chancery's finding of Alcatel's domination of Lynch. Therefore, the Independent Committee's ability to bargain at arm's length with Alcatel was suspect from the outset.

The Independent Committee's second assignment was to consider Alcatel's proposal to purchase Lynch. The Independent Committee proceeded on that task with full knowledge of Alcatel's demonstrated pattern of domination. The Independent Committee was also obviously aware of Alcatel's refusal to negotiate with it on the Celwave matter.

The Court of Chancery gave credence to the testimony of Kertz, one of the members of the Independent Committee, to the effect that he did not believe that $15.50 was a fair price but that he voted in favor of the merger because he felt there was no alternative.

The Court of Chancery also found that Kertz understood Alcatel's position to be that it was ready to proceed with an unfriendly tender offer at a lower price if Lynch did not accept the $15.50 offer, and that Kertz perceived this to be a threat by Alcatel. . . .

According to the Court of Chancery, the Independent Committee rejected three lower offers for Lynch from Alcatel and then accepted the $15.50 offer "after being advised that [it] was fair and after considering the absence of alternatives." . . .

Nevertheless, based upon the record before it, the Court of Chancery found that the Independent Committee had "appropriately simulated a third-party transaction, where negotiations are conducted at arm's length and there is no compulsion to reach an agreement." . . .

The Court of Chancery's determination . . . is not supported by the record. . . . [T]he ability of the Committee effectively to negotiate at arm's length was compromised by Alcatel's threats to proceed with a hostile tender offer if the $15.50 price was not approved by the Committee and the Lynch board. The fact that the Independent Committee rejected three initial offers, which were well below the Independent Committee's estimated valuation for Lynch and were not combined with an explicit threat that Alcatel was "ready to proceed" with a hostile bid, cannot alter the conclusion that any semblance of arm's length bargaining ended when the Independent Committee surrendered to the ultimatum that accompanied Alcatel's final offer.

Accordingly, the judgment of the Court of Chancery is reversed. This matter is remanded for further proceedings consistent herewith, including a redetermination of the entire fairness of the cash-out merger to Kahn and the other Lynch minority shareholders with the burden of proof remaining on Alcatel, the dominant and interested shareholder.

QUESTION ON KAHN v. LYNCH COMMUNICATION SYSTEMS

Did the court correctly decide that Alcatel breached its duty of fair dealing with the corporation and its public shareholders? Why can't Alcatel be a tough bargainer? If Alcatel had simply extended a tender offer at the price it was interested in paying, would it have breached its duty?

NOTE ON LIABILITY OF INDEPENDENT DIRECTORS IN CONTROLLER BUYOUT TRANSACTIONS

Weinberger reiterated that a controller owes a duty of entire fairness to minority shareholders when it engineers a cash-out or freeze-out transaction. It also suggested that a controller can enhance the fairness of such a transaction by agreeing to negotiate with a committee of the company's independent directors that is charged with representing the interests of the company and its minority shareholders. The rationale, of course, is that a simulation of arms length bargaining should go part of the way toward providing the protections that one naturally expects in arms length bargaining between a target company and a third-party acquirer. But neither *Weinberger* nor *Kahn v. Lynch* address the question of what liability rules apply to those directors who serve on a committee charged with negotiating with a controlling shareholder.

The members of such an independent committee are in a tough spot if they believe that the controller will stand firm on an unfairly low price. If the controller's proposed deal price offers a premium to minority shareholders relative to the pre-offer market price — but still below the fair value of minority shares — they might agree to the controller's price out of fear that the controller will otherwise pull its offer entirely. Before or after the deal closes, shareholders might allege that the recommendation of the independent committee was "coerced" and that the committee itself was dominated by the controller. The defendants in such an action would include the controller, of course, but they would also include the directors on the independent committee. Since these directors were free of conflicts and presumably recommended the controller's offer in good faith, the only plausible liability theory is a duty of care claim, i.e., gross negligence, recklessness, etc. Since virtually all U.S. public corporations now include an "exculpatory clause" under DGCL §102(b)(7) in their charters, it might seem that claims against independent directors should be dismissed even if the complaint against the controlling shareholder survives a motion to dismiss.

This is, in fact, the law today. But the evolution of doctrine has not always been linear. Two Delaware Supreme Court decisions in 2001 addressed this issue in different contexts. In *Malpiede v. Townson*,[77] the court held that in an acquisition not involving a controlling shareholder a §102(b)(7) waiver would lead to pretrial dismissal of suit against outside directors absent claims of duty of loyalty breaches. On the other hand, the court in *Emerald Partners v. Berlin*,[78] held that in the freeze-out context, where entire fairness is the standard of judicial review, a charter waiver of damages under §102(b)(7) could not be the basis of a pretrial dismissal of suits against outside directors.[79] Given that the typical claim in a freeze-out is that the controller violated the duty of loyalty one might understandably be uncomfortable with dismissing claims against directors appointed by that controller. Nonetheless, this led to the somewhat unsatisfying outcome that pretrial dismissal of suits against outside directors depended on whether the challenged deal was a freeze-out rather than on whether the plaintiff plead a non-exculpable violation. This remained the law until 2015, when another Supreme Court decision,

---

77. 780 A.2d 1075 (Del. 2001).

78. 787 A.2d 85 (Del. 2001).

79. The court stated "when entire fairness is the applicable standard of judicial review, a determination that the director defendants are exculpated from paying monetary damages can be made only after the basis for their liability has been decided [at trial or on summary judgment]." 787 A.2d at 94.

In re Cornerstone Therapeutics Inc Shareholder Litigation,[80] held that even though a controlled going-private transaction was subject to entire fairness review, the company's §102(b)(7) waiver in its charter would require independent directors to remain in the litigation only if plaintiffs could plausibly plead their non-exculpated violation of the duty of loyalty.

12.8.2   The "Proceduralization" of Going-Private Transactions

Until roughly 2000, almost all freeze-out transactions of Delaware corporations took the form of one-step cash-out mergers and faced the prospect of entire fairness judicial review. These were, after all, extreme related-party transactions that eliminated minority shareholder interests entirely. After *Weinberger,* the most that controllers could do to insulate freeze-outs from challenges by minority shareholders was to condition their deals on negotiated outcomes with committees of independent directors or on the outcomes of MOM shareholder votes. However, an influential case in 2001, *In re Siliconix Incorporated Shareholder Litigation*, C.A. No. 18700, 2001 WL 716787 (Del. Ch. June 19, 2001),[81] held that controlling shareholder tender offers to minority shareholders were not subject to entire fairness review (because they are direct offers to shareholders without relying on the board or other corporate organ to approve). Enterprising deal lawyers soon used this holding to fashion a novel transactional model for going-private transactions. A controller might first make a tender offer for minority shares and subsequently cash out the remaining minority shareholders at the tender offer price. This was not novel in a fundamental conceptual way. After all, the Timber Jack transaction described earlier in this chapter shows that two-step acquisitions had already been a common deal practice for decades. Rather, the novelty lay in the way that the two-step templet cabined the risk of unfavorable judicial review. The controller's first-step tender offer did not face entire fairness review. As for the second-step merger, a strong shareholder response to the price offered in the first step tended to suggest that the price was likely to be viewed as fair. Still more important, a controller who held more than 90 percent of her company's shares after a first-step tender offer could execute the second step as a short-form merger under DGCL §253. A contemporaneous Chancery Court decision had held that §253 short-form mergers were not subject to entire fairness review.[82] Thus, the bottom line during this period was that there were two templets for going-private transactions. Under the one-tier, so-called *"Lynch"* templet, entire fairness review was unavoidable, while under the two-tier *"Siliconix"* templet, a cash-out of minority shareholders might proceed with little more than business judgment review.

---

80. 115 A. 3d 1173 (Del. 2015).

81. See also *Solomon v. Pathe Communications Corp.*, 672 A.2d 35 (Del. 1996).

82. *In re Unocal Exploration Corporation*, 793 A.2d 329 (Del. Ch. 2000). Its holding is more accurately described as precluding any remedy other than appraisal in DGCL §253 mergers.

For more than a decade, the disparate treatment of *Lynch* and *Siliconix* freeze-outs was a source of doctrinal tension in Delaware jurisprudence. In 2005, then Vice Chancellor Leo Strine proposed a doctrinal model for bridging the gap between the two templets by increasing the procedural protections of minority shareholders in a two-step freeze-out. In dicta, in a largely unrelated case, Strine proposed substituting a procedural framework — the *Cox* framework[83] — for entire fairness review in two-step freeze-out transactions. The core of this substation was to permit business judgment review for two-step freeze-outs, but only if controllers conditioned their transactions ex ante on both the approval of an independent board committee and an affirmative MOM vote on the transaction — or alternatively, a majority-of-minority tender by minority shareholders in the first-step tender offer.[84]

Case law and scholarly opinion moved gradually in the direction that *Cox*'s dicta had suggested and then Vice Chancellor Laster's opinion, excerpted below, firmly fixed the conditions under which a two-step freeze-out qualified for business judgment review.

IN RE CNX GAS CORPORATION SHAREHOLDERS LITIGATION
C.A. No. 5377-VCL, 2010 WL 2291842 (Del. Ch. May 25, 2010)

LASTER, V.C.:

[CONSOL Energy was a Delaware corporation engaged in the production of coal and methane gas.] In June 2005, CONSOL formed CNX Gas Corp., also a Delaware corporation, to conduct CONSOL's natural gas operations. By April 26, 2010, CONSOL and its affiliates held approximately 83.5 percent of the outstanding shares of CNX. The remaining shares of CNX were held principally by institutional investors. . . . The largest minority stockholder of CNX was T. Rowe Price Associates, Inc., which held 6.3 percent of the CNX outstanding common stock, or 37 percent of the public float. T. Rowe Price also held approximately 6.5 percent of CONSOL's outstanding common stock. . . .

On April 28, 2010, [after negotiating an acceptable price with T. Rowe Price . . .], CONSOL commenced a tender offer to acquire the outstanding public shares of CNX Gas at a price of $38.25 per share in cash (the "Tender Offer"). The price represents a premium of 45.83% over the closing price of CNX Gas's common stock on the day before CONSOL announced the Dominion Transaction and its intent to acquire the shares of CNX Gas that it did not already own ($26.23). The Tender Offer price represents a 24.19% premium over the closing price of CNX Gas's common stock on the day before CONSOL announced the T. Rowe Price agreement ($30.80).

---

83. *In Re Cox Communications, Inc.*, 879 A.2d 604 (Del. Ch. 2005).

84. See generally Guhan Subramanian, *supra* note 76; Guhan Subramanian, *Post-Siliconix Freeze-Outs: Theory & Evidence*, 36 J. Legal Stud. 1 (2007). Note that Strine's dicta in *Cox* drew significantly from Professor Subramanian's research and expert witness testimony. See id., 879 A.2d at 629–631.

CONSOL has committed to effect a short-form merger promptly after the successful consummation of the Tender Offer. In the merger, remaining stockholders will receive the same consideration of $38.25 per share in cash. Consummation of the Tender Offer is subject to a non-waivable condition that a majority of the outstanding minority shares be tendered, . . . The T. Rowe Price shares are included in the majority-of-the-minority calculation. With the T. Rowe Price shares locked up, CONSOL only needs to obtain an additional 3,006,316 shares, or approximately 12% of the outstanding stock, to satisfy the condition.

F.   THE SPECIAL COMMITTEE

After the public announcement of the tender agreement with T. Rowe Price, Lyons, the CFO of CONSOL and CNX Gas, discussed with Pipski, the lone independent director of CNX Gas, the possibility that the CNX Gas board might form a special committee in connection with the CONSOL Tender Offer. . . . [T]he CNX Gas board unanimously approved the formation of a special committee consisting of Pipski (the "Special Committee"). The board did not act on Pipski's request for an additional director. . . .

On May 5, 2010, Pipski and his advisors met in person to determine how to respond to the Tender Offer. Lazard advised Pipski that it would be able to opine that an offer price of $38.25 per share was fair from a financial point of view to holders of CNX Gas common stock other than CONSOL. But Pipski and his advisors believed that CONSOL was not paying the highest price it was prepared to pay.

Even though the Special Committee was technically not authorized to negotiate, Pipski decided to seek a price increase. On May 5, 2010, Skadden advised CONSOL's counsel that Pipski could not recommend the Tender Offer at a price of $38.25 but likely could do so at $41.20. Five days later, on May 10, the day before the Schedule 14D-9 was due, the CNX Gas board retroactively granted the Special Committee authority to negotiate. On the next day, May 11, Pipski and his advisors held a call with CONSOL senior executives and their advisors. CONSOL declined to increase the price.

Later on May 11, the Special Committee issued the Schedule 14D-9. The Special Committee stated in the Schedule 14D-9 that it "determined not to express an opinion on the offer and to remain neutral with respect to the offer." . . .

The Schedule 14D-9 specifically cited the tender agreement with T. Rowe Price as a "potentially negative factor[]" that the Special Committee considered when evaluating the Tender Offer. The Schedule 14D-9 states:

> The Tender Agreement with T. Rowe Price increases the certainty of the offer being successful and, as a result, reduces the likelihood of any increase in the offer price by reducing the negotiation leverage of the "majority of the minority" condition. The Special Committee considered that T. Rowe Price's interests may not be the same as the other minority shareholders due to the fact that T. Rowe Price beneficially owned 6.51% of the outstanding common stock of CONSOL. In addition, the offer price was determined through relatively short

negotiations with T. Rowe Price without the input from any other minority shareholders or the Special Committee . . .

The Tender Offer is scheduled to close tomorrow, May 26, 2010, at 5:00 P.M.

II.   LEGAL ANALYSIS

1.   *The Appropriate Standard of Review for the Tender Offer*

. . . As knowledgeable readers understand all too well, . . . a negotiated merger between a controlling stockholder and its subsidiary is reviewed for entire fairness. But under *In re Siliconix Inc. Shareholders Litigation*, a controller's unilateral tender offer followed by a short-form merger is reviewed under an evolving standard far less onerous. . . .

I question the soundness of the twin cornerstones on which *Siliconix* rests. The first cornerstone is the statutory distinction between mergers and tender offers and the lack of any explicit role in the General Corporation Law for a target board of directors responding to a tender offer. . . .

The second cornerstone has been *Solomon v. Pathe Communications Corp.*, 672 A.2d 35 (Del.1996) [hereinafter, "*Solomon II*"], which has been cited repeatedly for the rule that a tender offeror has no duty to provide a fair price. But *Solomon II* did not involve a freeze-out. . . . *Solomon II* therefore does not hold that controllers never owe fiduciary duties when making tender offers, nor does it eliminate the possibility of entire fairness review for a two-step freeze-out transaction. . . . [T]he question is: What transactional structures result in the controlling stockholder not standing on both sides of a two-step freeze-out? . . .

Under the *Cox Communications* framework, if a freeze-out merger is both (i) negotiated and approved by a special committee of independent directors and (ii) conditioned on an affirmative vote of a majority of the minority stockholders, then the business judgment standard of review presumptively applies. 876 A.2d 606. If the transaction does not incorporate both protective devices, or if a plaintiff can plead particularized facts sufficient to raise a litigable question about the effectiveness of one of the devices, then the transaction is subject to entire fairness review. Id. The viability of a challenge to a controlling stockholder merger in which both protective devices are used thus can be assessed prior to trial, either on the pleadings or via motion for summary judgment. . . .

Likewise, under the *Cox Communications* framework, if a first-step tender offer is both (i) negotiated and recommended by a special committee of independent directors and (ii) conditioned on the affirmative tender of a majority of the minority shares, then the business judgment standard of review presumptively applies to the freeze-out transaction. Id. at 607. As with a merger, if both requirements are not met, then the transaction is reviewed for entire fairness. Id.

2.   *Applying the Unified Standard to this Case*

The Tender Offer does not pass muster under the unified standard. First and most obviously, the Special Committee did not recommend in favor of the transaction. That fact alone is sufficient to end the analysis and impose an obligation on CONSOL to pay a fair price.

Second, the Special Committee was not provided with authority comparable to what a board would possess in a third-party transaction. . . . When Pipski asked for the authority to consider alternatives, the CNX Gas board declined his request. Later, when Pipski requested full board authority to respond to the Tender Offer, the CNX Gas board again declined his request. . . .

Third, the plaintiffs have raised sufficient questions about the role of T. Rowe Price to undercut the effectiveness of the majority-of-the-minority tender condition. Economic incentives matter, particularly for the effectiveness of a legitimizing mechanism like a majority-of-the-minority tender condition or a stockholder vote. . . . T. Rowe Price as a whole owns 6.5% of CONSOL's outstanding common stock versus 6.3% of CNX Gas. T. Rowe Price's roughly equivalent equity interests leave it fully hedged and indifferent to the allocation of value between CONSOL and CNX Gas. To the extent the Tender Offer shortchanges CNX Gas holders, T. Rowe Price gains proportionately through its CONSOL ownership. To the extent CONSOL overpays, T. Rowe Price gains proportionately through its CNX Gas ownership. T. Rowe Price arguably has an incentive to favor CONSOL because of its slightly larger percentage equity ownership and holdings in CONSOL debt. T. Rowe Price's has materially different incentives than a holder of CNX Gas common stock, thereby calling into question the effectiveness of the majority-of-the-minority condition. . . .

It was neither the plaintiffs nor this Court that put the focus on T. Rowe Price and its cross-ownership. It was CONSOL who elected to pre-negotiate the terms of the Tender Offer with T. Rowe Price, a third-party non-fiduciary, rather than negotiating with the Special Committee. It was CONSOL and T. Rowe Price who chose to enter into the tender agreement. T. Rowe Price's incentives are at issue because of decisions that CONSOL and T. Rowe Price chose to make.

. . . T. Rowe Price is the largest minority holder of CNX Gas. It controls 37% of the public float. As the Special Committee itself concluded in the Schedule 14D-9, the tender agreement with T. Rowe Price "increases the certainty of the offer being successful and, as a result, reduces the likelihood of any increase in the offer price by reducing the negotiation leverage of the 'majority of the minority' condition." As the Special Committee also observed, "T. Rowe Price's interests may not be the same as the other minority shareholders due to the fact that T. Rowe Price beneficially owned 6.51 percent of the outstanding common stock of CONSOL." This case is not about "holdings in competitor corporations" or "directional sector bets." It is about a direct economic conflict that at best renders T. Rowe Price indifferent to the allocation of value between CONSOL and CNX Gas and at worst gives T. Rowe Price reason to favor CONSOL. . . .

The absence of Special Committee approval imposes an obligation on the defendants to show that the Tender Offer price is fair. The defendants are free to argue at a later stage of the proceeding and on a fuller record that (i) the negotiations with T. Rowe Price were truly at arms' length and untainted by cross-ownership, and (ii) the majority-of-the-minority condition was effective.

QUESTIONS AND NOTES ON CNX GAS

1. Empirical evidence indicates that minority shareholders received less (measured by shareholder abnormal returns) in tender offer freeze-outs than in merger freeze-outs in the four years following *Siliconix*.[85] One potential response is: So what? Professor Adam Pritchard argues that investors will simply pay less for a minority stake if they know that they will be cashed out at a lower price in a freeze-out down the road.[86] Why, then, is Vice Chancellor Strine concerned about reconciling the doctrinal disconnect between the *Lynch* and *Siliconix* line of cases, beyond simply doctrinal purity? For an efficiency justification for reconciling the competing doctrinal strands, see Subramanian (2005), *supra* note 76.

2. What concerns does the court's treatment of T. Rowe Price raise as a matter of corporate law generally? Is Vice Chancellor Laster's effort to curtail "generalized fishing expeditions into stockholder motives" persuasive?

3. Despite the language excerpted above, Vice Chancellor Laster denied the plaintiffs' motion for a preliminary injunction, holding that the tender offer was not coercive, there were no viable disclosure claims, and any harm to the minority shareholders could be remedied through a post-closing damages action. In July 2010, Vice Chancellor Laster granted the defendant's application to certify this decision to the Delaware Supreme Court for interlocutory appeal, stating:

> The standard of review for a controller's unilateral two-step freeze-out thus presents an issue of first impression for the Delaware Supreme Court. It is an issue with real-world consequences. In his study of post-*Siliconix* freeze-outs, Professor Guhan Subramanian found that stockholders received greater consideration in single-step freeze-outs and negotiated two-step freeze-outs than in unilateral two-step freeze-outs. . . . Professor Subramanian noted that "[i]nterviews as well as informal conversations with New York City and Delaware lawyers indicate that [the finding of lower returns for stockholders in *Siliconix* deals] is consistent with practitioner experience." Id.
>
> Controllers and their advisors take the governing legal regime into account when determining whether and how to proceed with a transaction. Professor Subramanian found that controllers moved decidedly towards unilateral two-step transactions after the blazing of the *Siliconix-Glassman* trail. Id. at 10-11.

---

85. Guhan Subramanian, *Post-*Siliconix *Freeze-Outs: Theory & Evidence*, 36 J. Legal Stud. 1 (2007).

86. Adam Pritchard, *Tender Offers by Controlling Shareholders: The Specter of Coercion and Fair Price*, 1 Berkeley Bus. L.J. 83 (2004).

These data raise policy questions. . . .

Solomon II, Siliconix, and *Pure Resources* rely primarily on market forces, impose few procedural protections, and limit judicial review. All else equal, this approach should lead to more transactions and lower premiums. *Lynch* de-emphasizes market forces, encourages procedural protections, and relies heavily on judicial review. All else equal, this approach should lead to fewer transactions and higher premiums. Prominent commentators have suggested that *Siliconix* and *Pure Resources* may be too lenient towards controllers and under-protective of minority stockholders, while *Lynch* may be too strict and overprotective. They recommend a regime that applies the business judgment rule to a transaction that mimics third party transactional approvals, while allowing controllers the flexibility to employ fewer protections at the cost of some level of fairness review. . . . Only the Supreme Court can determine definitively whether different policies, duties, and standards should govern unilateral two-step freeze-outs.

Because the appropriate standard of review for unilateral two-step freeze-out presents a question of first impression for the Delaware Supreme Court and implicates fundamental issues of Delaware public policy, certification is appropriate.

In re CNX Gas Corp., C.A. No. 5377-VCL, 2010 WL 2705147 at *11-*12 (Del. Ch. July 5, 2010).

The Delaware Supreme Court denied the appeal on the grounds that the issues raised in the case should be addressed after the entry of a final judgment. *In re CNX Gas Corp.,* 30 A. 3d 782 (Del. 2010).

12.8.3   The Other Shoe Drops: One-Step Freeze-Out Mergers

In re CNX Gas Corp. seemed to give a clear roadmap to business judgment review for two-step freeze-out transactions, even though the the Delaware Supreme Court's reluctance to grant an interlocutory appeal on the matter might also be seen to suggest continuing uneasiness about the procedural makeover that *CNX* implied. Another matter to consider was that *CNX* did not resolve the doctrinal incongruity that controllers could obtain business judgment review in a two-step freeze-out but not the one-step freeze-out merger. The then Chancellor, Leo Strine, who earlier had been the first judge to float a proposal to allow business judgment review in freeze-out mergers, was also the first judge to rule that business judgment review was available to controllers in a one-step freeze-out merger. See *In re MFW Shareholders Litig.,* 67 A.3d 496 (Del. Ch. 2013). The Delaware Supreme Court heard this case on appeal shortly after Strine had been appointed to be Chief Justice of the Supreme Court. The opinion below reflects that Court's en banc decision to affirm the Chancery Court's decision below. Our reading of this opinion also reflects a note of hesitation, although there is no doubt that the road to business judgment review that the opinion affirms is now firmly established Delaware law.

KAHN v. M&F WORLDWIDE CORP. ET AL.
88 A.3d 635 (Del. 2014)

HOLLAND, J. for the Court *en banc*:

This is an appeal from a final judgment entered by the Court of Chancery in a proceeding that arises from a 2011 acquisition by MacAndrews & Forbes Holdings, Inc. ("M & F" or "MacAndrews & Forbes") — a 43% stockholder in M & F Worldwide Corp. ("MFW") — of the remaining common stock of MFW (the "Merger") [at a price of $25 per share]. From the outset, M & F's proposal to take MFW private was made contingent upon two stockholder-protective procedural conditions. First, M & F required the Merger to be negotiated and approved by a special committee of independent MFW directors (the "Special Committee"). Second, M & F required that the Merger be approved by a majority of stockholders unaffiliated with M & F. The Merger closed in December 2011, after it was approved by a vote of 65.4% of MFW's minority stockholders.

[After expedited discovery, shareholder-plaintiffs' withdrew a motion for a preliminary injunction and after following further discovery, defendants moved for summary judgment, which was granted.]

COURT OF CHANCERY DECISION

The Court of Chancery found that the case presented a "novel question of law"; specifically, "what standard of review should apply to a going private merger conditioned upfront by the controlling stockholder on approval by both a properly empowered, independent committee and an informed, unco-erced majority-of-the-minority vote." . . .

The Court of Chancery held that, rather than entire fairness, the business judgment standard of review should apply "if, but only if: (i) the control-ler conditions the transaction on the approval of both a Special Committee and a majority of the minority stockholders; (ii) the Special Committee is independent; (iii) the Special Committee is empowered to freely select its own advisors and to say no definitively; (iv) the Special Committee acts with care; (v) the minority vote is informed; and (vi) there is no coercion of the minority."

[It] found that those prerequisites were satisfied and that the Appellants had failed to raise any genuine issue of material fact indicating the contrary. The court then reviewed the Merger under the business judgment standard and granted summary judgment for the Defendants.

APPELLANTS' ARGUMENTS

The Appellants raise two main arguments on this appeal. First, they con-tend that the Court of Chancery erred in concluding that no material dis-puted facts existed regarding the conditions precedent to business judgment review. The Appellants submit that the record contains evidence showing that the Special Committee was not disinterested and independent, was not fully empowered, and was not effective. [Notice that the Court of Chancery did not include "effective" as a prerequisite for application of BJR. — EDS.] . . .

Second, the Appellants submit that the Court of Chancery erred, as a matter of law, in holding that the business judgment standard applies to controller freeze-out mergers where the controller's proposal is conditioned on both Special Committee approval and a favorable majority-of-the-minority vote. Even if both procedural protections are adopted, the Appellants argue, entire fairness should be retained as the applicable standard of review.

. . .

FACTS

MFW is a holding company incorporated in Delaware. Before the Merger . . . MFW was 43.4% owned by MacAndrews & Forbes, which in turn is entirely owned by Ronald O. Perelman. MFW had four business segments. Three were owned through a holding company, Harland Clarke Holding Corporation ("HCHC"). . . .

The MFW board had thirteen members. They were: Ronald Perelman, Barry Schwartz, William Bevins, Bruce Slovin, Charles Dawson, Stephen Taub, John Keane, Theo Folz, Philip Beekman, Martha Byorum, Viet Dinh, Paul Meister, and Carl Webb. Perelman, Schwartz, and Bevins were officers of both MFW and MacAndrews & Forbes. Perelman was the Chairman of MFW and the Chairman and CEO of MacAndrews & Forbes; Schwartz was the President and CEO of MFW and the Vice Chairman and Chief Administrative Officer of MacAndrews & Forbes; and Bevins was a Vice President at MacAndrews & Forbes.

THE TAKING MFW PRIVATE PROPOSAL

In May 2011, Perelman began to explore the possibility of taking MFW private. At that time, MFW's stock price traded in the $20 to $24 per share range. MacAndrews & Forbes engaged a bank, Moelis & Company, to advise it. After preparing valuations based on projections that had been supplied to lenders by MFW in April and May 2011, Moelis valued MFW at between $10 and $32 a share.

On June 10, 2011, MFW's shares closed on the New York Stock Exchange at $16.96. The next business day, June 13, 2011, Schwartz sent a letter proposal ("Proposal") to the MFW board to buy the remaining MFW shares for $24 in cash. The Proposal stated, in relevant part:

> The proposed transaction would be subject to the approval of the Board of Directors of the Company [i.e., MFW] and the negotiation and execution of mutually acceptable definitive transaction documents. It is our expectation that the Board of Directors will appoint a special committee of independent directors to consider our proposal and make a recommendation to the Board of Directors. We will not move forward with the transaction unless it is approved

by such a special committee. In addition, the transaction will be subject to a non-waivable condition requiring the approval of a majority of the shares of the Company not owned by M & F or its affiliates. . . . [Emphasis by Supreme Court.]

   . . . In considering this proposal, you should know that in our capacity as a stockholder of the Company we are interested only in acquiring the shares of the Company not already owned by us and that in such capacity we have no interest in selling any of the shares owned by us in the Company nor would we expect, in our capacity as a stockholder, to vote in favor of any alternative sale, merger or similar transaction involving the Company. If the special committee does not recommend or the public stockholders of the Company do not approve the proposed transaction, such determination would not adversely affect our future relationship with the Company and we would intend to remain as a long-term stockholder. . . .

   In connection with this proposal, we have engaged Moelis & Company as our financial advisor and Skadden, Arps, Slate, Meagher & Flom LLP as our legal advisor, and we encourage the special committee to retain its own legal and financial advisors to assist it in its review.

MacAndrews & Forbes filed this letter with the U.S. Securities and Exchange Commission ("SEC") and issued a press release disclosing substantially the same information.

THE SPECIAL COMMITTEE IS FORMED

   The MFW board met the following day to consider the Proposal . . . Schwartz presented the offer on behalf of MacAndrews & Forbes. Subsequently, Schwartz and Bevins recused themselves from the meeting, as did Dawson, the CEO of HCHC, who had previously expressed support for the proposed offer.

   The independent directors then invited counsel from Willkie Farr & Gallagher—a law firm that had recently represented a Special Committee of MFW's independent directors in a potential acquisition of a subsidiary of MacAndrews & Forbes—to join the meeting. The independent directors decided to form the Special Committee, and resolved further that:

[T]he Special Committee is empowered to: (i) make such investigation of the Proposal as the Special Committee deems appropriate; (ii) evaluate the terms of the Proposal; (iii) negotiate with Holdings [i.e., MacAndrews & Forbes] and its representatives any element of the Proposal; (iv) negotiate the terms of any definitive agreement with respect to the Proposal (it being understood that the execution thereof shall be subject to the approval of the Board); (v) report to the Board its recommendations and conclusions with respect to the Proposal, including a determination and recommendation as to whether the Proposal is fair and in the best interests of the stockholders of the Company other than Holdings and its affiliates and should be approved by the Board; and (vi) determine to elect not to pursue the Proposal. . . . [Emphasis by Court.] [T]he Board shall not approve the Proposal without a prior favorable recommendation of the Special Committee. . . .

. . . [T]he Special Committee [is] empowered to retain and employ legal counsel, a financial advisor, and such other agents as the Special Committee shall deem necessary or desirable in connection with these matters. . . .

The Special Committee consisted of Byorum, Dinh, Meister (the chair), Slovin, and Webb. The following day, Slovin recused himself because, although the MFW board had determined that he qualified as an independent director under the rules of the New York Stock Exchange, he had "some current relationships that could raise questions about his independence for purposes of serving on the Special Committee."

[The special committee retained independent bankers and lawyers to advise it and negotiated a transaction with MacAndrews & Forbes. After trying to get the $24 offer up to $30 and failing, the committee agreed to the $25 price. That deal was then presented to the public shareholders and approved. The suit followed promptly.]

ANALYSIS

WHAT SHOULD BE THE REVIEW STANDARD?

Where a transaction involving self-dealing by a controlling stockholder is challenged, . . . the defendants bear the ultimate burden of proving that the transaction with the controlling stockholder was entirely fair to the minority stockholders. In *Kahn* v. *Lynch Communication Systems, Inc.* however, this Court held that in "entire fairness" cases, the defendants may shift the burden of persuasion to the plaintiff if either (1) they show that the transaction was approved by a well-functioning committee of independent directors; or (2) they show that the transaction was approved by an informed vote of a majority of the minority stockholders.

This appeal presents a question of first impression: What should be the standard of review for a merger between a controlling stockholder and its subsidiary, where the merger is conditioned ab initio upon the approval of both an independent, adequately-empowered Special Committee that fulfills its duty of care, and the uncoerced, informed vote of a majority of the minority stockholders. The question has never been put directly to this Court.

. . . *Lynch* did not involve a merger conditioned by the controlling stockholder on both procedural protections. The Appellants submit, nonetheless, that statements in *Lynch* and its progeny could be (and were) read to suggest that even if both procedural protections were used, the standard of review would remain entire fairness. However, in *Lynch* and the other cases that Appellants cited, *Southern Peru* and *Kahn v. Tremont*, the controller did not give up its voting power by agreeing to a non-waivable majority-of-the-minority condition. That is the vital distinction between those cases and this one. The question is what the legal consequence of that distinction should be in these circumstances.

The Court of Chancery held that the consequence should be that the business judgment standard of review will govern going private mergers with a controlling stockholder that are conditioned ab initio upon (1) the approval of an independent and fully-empowered Special Committee that fulfills its duty of care and (2) the uncoerced, informed vote of the majority of the minority stockholders.

The Court of Chancery [stated]:

> By giving controlling stockholders the opportunity to have a going private trans-action reviewed under the business judgment rule, a strong incentive is created to give minority stockholders much broader access to the transactional struc-ture that is most likely to effectively protect their interests. . . . That structure, it is important to note, is critically different than a structure that uses only one of the procedural protections. The "or" structure does not replicate the pro-tections of a third-party merger under the DGCL approval process, because it only requires that one, and not both, of the statutory requirements of director and stockholder approval be accomplished by impartial decision-makers. The "both" structure, by contrast, replicates the arm's length merger steps of the DGCL by "requir[ing] two independent approvals, which it is fair to say serve independent integrity-enforcing functions."

Before the Court of Chancery, the Appellants acknowledged that "this transactional structure is the optimal one for minority shareholders." Before us, however, they argue that neither procedural protection is adequate to protect minority stockholders, because "possible ineptitude and timidity of directors" may undermine the special committee protection, and because majority-of-the-minority votes may be unduly influenced by arbitrageurs that have an institutional bias to approve virtually any transaction that offers a market premium, however insubstantial it may be. Therefore, the Appellants claim, these protections, even when combined, are not sufficient to justify "abandon[ing]" the entire fairness standard of review.

. . . [T]he Appellants' assertions regarding the MFW directors' inability to discharge their duties are not supported either by the record or by well-established principles of Delaware law. As the Court of Chancery correctly observed:

> Although it is possible that there are independent directors who have little regard for their duties or for being perceived by their company's stockhold-ers (and the larger network of institutional investors) as being effective at pro-tecting public stockholders, the court thinks they are likely to be exceptional, and certainly our Supreme Court's jurisprudence does not embrace such a skeptical view.

Regarding the majority-of-the-minority vote procedural protection, as the Court of Chancery noted, "plaintiffs themselves do not argue that minority stockholders will vote against a going private transaction because of fear of retribution." Instead, as the Court of Chancery summarized, the Appellants' argued as follows:

> [Plaintiffs] just believe that most investors like a premium and will tend to vote for a deal that delivers one and that many long-term investors will sell out when they can obtain most of the premium without waiting for the ultimate vote. But

that argument is not one that suggests that the voting decision is not voluntary, it is simply an editorial about the motives of investors and does not contradict the premise that a majority-of-the-minority condition gives minority investors a free and voluntary opportunity to decide what is fair for themselves.

BUSINESS JUDGMENT REVIEW STANDARD ADOPTED

We hold that business judgment is the standard of review that should govern mergers between a controlling stockholder and its corporate subsidiary, where the merger is conditioned ab initio upon both the approval of an independent, adequately-empowered Special Committee that fulfills its duty of care; and the uncoerced, informed vote of a majority of the minority stockholders. We so conclude for several reasons.

First, entire fairness is the highest standard of review in corporate law. It is applied in the controller merger context as a substitute for the dual statutory protections of disinterested board and stockholder approval, because both protections are potentially undermined by the influence of the controller. However, as this case establishes, that undermining influence does not exist in every controlled merger setting, regardless of the circumstances. The simultaneous deployment of the procedural protections employed here create a countervailing, offsetting influence of equal — if not greater — force. That is, where the controller irrevocably and publicly disables itself from using its control to dictate the outcome of the negotiations and the shareholder vote, the controlled merger then acquires the shareholder-protective characteristics of third-party, arm's length mergers, which are reviewed under the business judgment standard.

Second, the dual procedural protection merger structure optimally protects the minority stockholders in controller buyouts. As the Court of Chancery explained:

> [W]hen these two protections are established up-front, a potent tool to extract good value for the minority is established. From inception, the controlling stockholder knows that it cannot bypass the special committee's ability to say no. And, the controlling stockholder knows it cannot dangle a majority-of-the-minority vote before the special committee late in the process as a deal-closer rather than having to make a price move.

Third, . . . applying the business judgment standard to the dual protection merger structure: . . . is consistent with the central tradition of Delaware law, which defers to the informed decisions of impartial directors, especially when those decisions have been approved by the disinterested stockholders on full information and without coercion. Not only that, the adoption of this rule will be of benefit to minority stockholders because it will provide a strong incentive for controlling stockholders to accord minority investors the transactional structure that respected scholars believe will provide them the best protection, a structure where stockholders get the benefits of independent, empowered negotiating agents to bargain for the best price and say no if the agents believe the deal is not advisable for any proper reason, plus the critical ability to determine for themselves whether to accept any deal that their negotiating agents recommend to them. A transactional structure with both these protections is fundamentally different from one with only one protection. [Emphasis by court.]

Fourth, the underlying purposes of the dual protection merger structure utilized here and the entire fairness standard of review both converge and are fulfilled at the same critical point: price. Following *Weinberger v. UOP, Inc.*, this Court has consistently held that, although entire fairness review comprises the dual components of fair dealing and fair price, in a non-fraudulent transaction "price may be the preponderant consideration outweighing other features of the merger." The dual protection merger structure requires two price-related pretrial determinations: first, that a fair price was achieved by an empowered, independent committee that acted with care;[13] and, second, that a fully-informed, uncoerced majority of the minority stockholders voted in favor of the price that was recommended by the independent committee.

THE NEW STANDARD SUMMARIZED

To summarize our holding, in controller buyouts, the business judgment standard of review will be applied if and only if: (i) the controller conditions the procession of the transaction on the approval of both a Special Committee and a majority of the minority stockholders; (ii) the Special Committee is independent; (iii) the Special Committee is empowered to freely select its own advisors and to say no definitively; (iv) the Special Committee meets its duty of care in negotiating a fair price; (v) the vote of the minority is informed; and (vi) there is no coercion of the minority.[14]

If a plaintiff that can plead a reasonably conceivable set of facts showing that any or all of those enumerated conditions did not exist, that complaint would state a claim for relief that would entitle the plaintiff to proceed and conduct discovery. If, after discovery, triable issues of fact remain about

---

13. In *Americas Mining*, for example, it was not possible to make a pretrial determination that the independent committee had negotiated a fair price. After an entire fairness trial, the Court of Chancery held that the price was not fair. See *Ams. Mining Corp.* v. *Theriault*, 51 A.3d 1213, 1241–44 (Del. 2012).

14. The Verified Consolidated Class Action Complaint would have survived a motion to dismiss under this new standard. First, the complaint alleged that Perelman's offer "value[d] the company at just four times" MFW's profits per share and "five times 2010 pre-tax cash flow," and that these ratios were "well below" those calculated for recent similar transactions. Second, the complaint alleged that the final Merger price was two dollars per share lower than the trading price only about two months earlier. Third, the complaint alleged particularized facts indicating that MFW's share price was depressed at the times of Perelman's offer and the Merger announcement due to short-term factors such as MFW's acquisition of other entities and Standard & Poor's downgrading of the United States' creditworthiness. Fourth, the complaint alleged that commentators viewed both Perelman's initial $24 per share offer and the final $25 per share Merger price as being surprisingly low. These allegations about the sufficiency of the price call into question the adequacy of the Special Committee's negotiations, thereby necessitating discovery on all of the new prerequisites to the application of the business judgment rule.

whether either or both of the dual procedural protections were established, or if established were effective, the case will proceed to a trial in which the court will conduct an entire fairness review.

This approach is consistent with *Weinberger*, *Lynch*, and their progeny. A controller that employs and/or establishes only one of these dual procedural protections would continue to receive burden-shifting within the entire fairness standard of review framework. Stated differently, unless both procedural protections for the minority stockholders are established prior to trial, the ultimate judicial scrutiny of controller buyouts will continue to be the entire fairness standard of review.

Having articulated the circumstances that will enable a controlled merger to be reviewed under the business judgment standard, we next address whether those circumstances have been established as a matter of undisputed fact and law in this case.

[The Court then affirms the Court of Chancery opinion that no issue of material fact had been raised by the plaintiffs on the motion for summary judgment respecting the independence and disinterestedness of the members of the special committee, its due empowerment, or its due care in proceeding to approve the merger. The Supreme Court then affirmed the Chancellor's determination that disclosure was full and fair and that the shareholders were not coerced. . . .

BOTH PROCEDURAL PROTECTIONS ESTABLISHED

Based on a highly extensive record, the Court of Chancery concluded that the procedural protections upon which the Merger was conditioned — approval by an independent and empowered Special Committee and by an uncoerced, informed majority of MFW's minority stockholders — had both been undisputedly established prior to trial. We agree and conclude the Defendants' motion for summary judgment was properly granted on all of those issues.

BUSINESS JUDGMENT REVIEW PROPERLY APPLIED

We have determined that the business judgment rule standard of review applies to this controlling stockholder buyout. Under that standard, the claims against the Defendants must be dismissed unless no rational person could have believed that the merger was favorable to MFW's minority stockholders. In this case, it cannot be credibly argued (let alone concluded) that no rational person would find the Merger favorable to MFW's minority stockholders.

CONCLUSION

For the above-stated reasons, the judgment of the Court of Chancery is affirmed.

NOTES AND QUESTIONS

1. One curiosity of the *MFW* opinion is its emphasis on "fair price." This seems odd in an opinion that approves a process that if properly followed can obviate the need for judicial review of price. More pointedly, the Court states: "Fourth, the underlying purposes of the dual protection merger structure utilized here and the entire fairness standard of review both converge and are fulfilled at the same critical point: price. . . . The dual protection merger structure requires two price-related pretrial determinations: first, that a fair price was achieved by an empowered, independent committee that acted with care . . ." See footnote 13.

But the Court of Chancery did not in this case determine that a "fair price" was achieved but rather that each of the procedural predicates for business judgment rule had been shown on summary judgment record. See also footnote 14 of the case.

2. Another mysterious element in the Court's opinion is its statement that if there is a triable issue respecting any of the pre-conditions for business judgment review the case must be tried under an entire fairness standard of review. But why should a "triable issue" with respect to a predicate for business judgment review require a judicial determination of fair price? If at trial, defendants introduce evidence that shows by a preponderance of the evidence that the "triable issue" must be determined in their favor, why shouldn't logic compel the application of the business judgment rule to determine liability? Or should a court nevertheless go ahead and try to determine fair price under the entire fairness test?

3. Do you expect *MFW* to become the model for all parent sub-freeze-out mergers in the future? A recent study by Fernan Restrepo finds that the incidence of MOM vote conditionality increased dramatically after *MFW* from about 40 percent of subject deals to 80 percent (special committees were already the norm prior to *MFW* due in no small measure to *Weinberger*).[87] Further, target shareholder gains and deal completion rates seemed to remain fairly similar even after the addition of MOM vote conditionality. What do these results suggest about the effectiveness of *MFW*? About MOM votes and shareholder voting more generally?

4. Following *MFW*, the Delaware judiciary emphasized that business judgment review is only available if the *MFW* conditions are put in place prior to any transaction negotiations. This led to litigation over when the beginning stages were and why business judgment review should be conditioned on the *ab initio* acceptance of *MFW* conditions.

In *Flood* v. *Synutra Int'l, Inc.,* 195 A. 3d 754 (Del. 2018), the Delaware Supreme Court provided answers to both questions. Synutra's controlling shareholder, Liang Zhang, sent a letter stating that he intended to take the firm private but did not mention the *MFW* conditions. Two weeks later Zhang sent a second letter conditioning the going-private transaction on

---

87. Fernan Restrepo, *Judicial Deference, Procedural Protections, and Deal Outcomes in Freezeout Transactions: Evidence from the Effect of* MFW (January 19, 2018). Available at SSRN: https://ssrn.com/abstract=3105169.

meeting *MFW*'s requirements. By this time no economic negotiations had taken place and the special committee had not even begun to hire advisors or evaluate Zhang's offer. Plaintiffs' claim hinged on Zhang's first offer not requiring *MFW* conditionality. Affirming the dismissal of the suit, the court held that business judgment review is available if the controller adopts the *MFW* conditions before any substantive economic negotiations begin.[88] The court noted that:

> having *MFW*'s dual requirements in place at the start of economic negotiations — helps replicate a third-party process and . . . incentivizes controllers to precommit to *MFW*'s conditions . . . to take advantage of business judgment review. The essential element of *MFW*, then, is that these requirements cannot be dangled in front of the Special Committee, when negotiations to obtain a better price from the controller have commenced, as a substitution for a bare-knuckled contest over price.
>
> That is, the purpose of the words "*ab initio*," . . . require the controller to self-disable before the start of substantive economic negotiations, and to have both the controller and Special Committee bargain under the pressures exerted on both of them by these protections. . . . In that situation, the Special Committee and the controller know, at all times . . . , that a transaction cannot proceed if the Special Committee says no, and the Special Committee knows that if they agree to a price, their judgment will be subject to stockholder scrutiny and approval.

Within a few months, another case explored the *ab initio* requirement. In *Olenik v. Lodzinski*, 208 A.3d 704 (Del. 2019) — where the *MFW* conditions were put in place about eight months after negotiations had started — the Delaware Supreme Court found that the plaintiffs had pled facts "support[ing] a reasonable inference" that the controlled firm and its controlling stockholder had effectively engaged in "substantive economic negotiations" before the dual protections were in place. The court reversed the Chancery Court's dismissal of the suit.

5. To obtain business judgment review, the controller must not only adopt the *MFW* conditions *ab initio*, but also implement them in the actual negotiations. *In re Dell Technologies Inc. Class V Stockholders Litig.*, C.A. No. 2018-0816-JTL (Del. Ch. June 11, 2020), provides an example of where the court declined to grant business judgment review because the controller did not implement the *MFW* conditions as promised. This suit emanates from Dell's purchase of EMC Corporation for $67 billion in 2016. EMC shareholders received cash and new "Class V" shares in Dell (which tracked the performance of VMware — a publicly traded subsidiary of EMC). The Class V shares could be forcibly converted (by Dell) into Dell Class C shares at a contractually set formula if Dell listed its Class C shares on a national exchange. In January 2018, Dell formed a special committee to negotiate the redemption of Class V shares from former EMC shareholders subject to the *MFW* conditions. However, Dell retained the right to bypass the special committee by engaging in a forced conversion.

---

88. In *Swomley v. Schlecht*, 128 A.3d 992 (Del. 2015), the court held that it can determine whether *MFW* is satisfied at the pleading stage.

During the negotiations, Dell told the committee that if it did not agree to the redemption then Dell would force the conversion of Class V shares into Class C shares (an unattractive option for Class V shareholders). The committee soon recommended a redemption valuing Class V shares at $21.7 billion, which led several large Class V shareholders to object. Dell then ignored the committee and interacted directly with six large Class V shareholders and publicly took steps toward a forced conversion. This led to a redemption value of $23.9 billion, which the committee then approved (in a one-hour meeting) as did a majority of Class V shareholders.

Some former Class V shareholders sued alleging breach of fiduciary duty against Michael Dell (as Dell's controller) and Dell's board. The Chancery Court noted that adopting *MFW* conditions will not result in business judgment review if — as here — the special committee is bypassed in the negotiations, or if its consent (or any resulting favorable shareholder vote) is obtained through coercive acts such as retaining the power to pursue alternatives that are detrimental to the minority (e.g., forcibly converting Class V shares to Class C shares).[89]

In re Dell raises a number of interesting questions. For instance, is retaining the power to pursue alternatives by itself sufficient to torpedo *MFW* cleansing, or must the controller also threaten to (or actually) use that power?

6. As with the appraisal cases, *MFW* places a premium on process considerations. Indeed, *MFW* mirrors the emerging appraisal jurisprudence. When there is fair process (here the *MFW* conditions adopted *ab initio*), then the courts will grant business judgment review and most likely dismiss the suit with no remedy.[90] In appraisal proceedings when the deal price is arrived at in a fair process, then the courts will assess fair value to be deal price less synergies (thereby providing essentially no remedy). That, in turn, raises the question of whether there is much difference between the requirements for *MFW* cleansing and the requirements for fair deal process in the appraisal context.

NOTE ON EXTENDING MFW TO ALL TRANSACTIONS INVOLVING CONTROLLERS

Although *MFW* cleansing developed in the context of freeze-out mergers, a string of recent Chancery Court decisions is starting to extend it beyond that domain. For instance, in *Tornetta v. Musk*, 2019 WL 4566943 (Del. Ch.

---

89. The court notes that other extraneous influences may also undermine *MFW* cleansing. For example, a potential insolvency may provide shareholders with such an unattractive status quo that they may have no other practical choice but to affirm a transaction. In addition, if a transaction is structured in a way that appears coercive (e.g., clubbing a beneficial transaction with a questionable one) then it may not obtain *MFW* cleansing, even if this doesn't necessarily involve any fiduciary duty breaches.

90. Although the courts and commentators tend to describe *MFW* as creating preconditions to obtaining business judgment review, might it also be plausible to describe *MFW* as scripting out the requirements for fair process inquiries under the entire fairness standard? After all, what in addition to *MFW*'s conditions might courts look to in assessing fair process?

September 20, 2019), Vice Chancellor Slights applied *MFW* cleansing to a controller's compensation package. Tesla's board and shareholders overwhelmingly approved Elon Musk's 2018 compensation package, which it preliminarily valued at $2.615 billion (with the potential to grant Musk over $50 billion worth of stock options if the highest milestones are achieved). Plaintiff-shareholders filed direct and derivative claims, and Musk did not contest that he was Tesla's controller. The court held — as a matter of first impression — that a controller's compensation package was subject to entire fairness review rather than business judgment review. It then went further and said that if the compensation decision satisfied the requirements of *MFW*, it would receive business judgment review. Here the Tesla board did not follow *MFW* and thus the court denied defendant's motion to dismiss.

Prior to *Tornetta*, Chancellor Bouchard had already extended *MFW* to a transaction involving a corporate recapitalization in a controlled firm. See *IRA Trust FBO Bobbie Ahmed v. Crane*, 2017 WL 7053964 (Del. Ch. Dec. 11, 2017). Similarly, Vice Chancellor Slights applied *MFW* to cleanse a sale of a controlled firm to an unaffiliated third party, even when there might be side deals with the controlling shareholder. See *In re Martha Stewart Living Omnimedia, Inc. S'holder Litig.*, C.A. No. 11202-VCS (Aug. 18, 2017) (Slights, V.C.). And, of course, *In re Dell* involved the potential application of *MFW* to a redemption of shares rather than a pure freeze-out merger. It appears that satisfying *MFW* conditions may be moving us toward a world where conflicted transactions with controllers may, like conflicted transactions with directors, receive business judgment review.

PUBLIC CONTESTS FOR CORPORATE CONTROL

13.1 INTRODUCTION

Control contests occupy a central place in the theory of U.S. corporate governance. The simplest form of the theory goes something like this: Share prices fall when companies underperform, which in turn attracts the attention of potential acquirers who believe they can do better than incumbent managers and are prepared to offer a premium price for their targets' shares. When incumbent directors agree, they conclude a friendly deal; when they disagree, the stage is set for a hostile contest for corporate control. Thus, successful control contests allow acquiring managers the opportunity to create new value and give target shareholders the opportunity to share in this new value.[1] The flip side is that control contests are profoundly unpleasant for incumbent managers. But many have argued that for this very reason, the threat of a takeover has the salutary effect of encouraging all managers to deliver shareholder value. Thus, control contests can be an important potential constraint on managerial agency costs generally.[2] This chapter reviews the landmark cases in the law of control contests and brings developments in this area up to date.

---

1. Of course, a developed account of the market for corporate control must go well beyond this simple sketch. One also must consider that the evolution of defensive tactics largely excludes the bareknuckle hostile tender offers of the 1980s. Today's best analogy to the hostile takeover contests of that time are activist hedge fund campaigns that were briefly reviewed in Chapter 6.

2. Credit for first articulating the key governance role of control contests goes to Henry Manne. See Henry Manne, *Mergers and the Market for Corporate Control*, 73 J. Pol. Econ. 110 (1965). For subsequent development of the governance role of control contests, see two classic articles from the early 1980s: Frank H. Easterbrook & Daniel R. Fischel, *The Proper Role of a Target's Management in Responding to Hostile Takeovers*, 94 Harv. L. Rev. 1161 (1981); and Ronald J. Gilson, *A Structural Approach to Corporations: The Case Against Defensive Tactics in Tender Offers*, 33 Stan. L. Rev. 819 (1981).

Law is one of the principal determinants of the scope of the takeover market. Traditionally, Anglo-American law opened two avenues for initiating a hostile change in control. The first was the proxy contest — running an insurgent slate of candidates for election to the board. Although the proxy contest is costly and often unsuccessful (at least at first),[3] it was nevertheless the only insurgent technique employed during the infrequent contests for control over widely held companies prior to the 1960s. Moreover, the proxy contest has returned with the rise of activist hedge funds who use proxy fights — or more often, the threat of proxy fights — to press their alternative business plans on corporate boards. But as we discussed in Chapter 6, hedge funds seldom pursue complete control of target companies but rather seek to place a minority of their candidates on target company boards with the aim of promoting change through "constructive engagement" with other board members.

The second technique for obtaining control over a target company is, of course, the tender offer which, as discussed in Chapter 11, is the simple expedient of purchasing enough stock oneself to obtain voting control rather than soliciting the proxies of others. Clearly, a tender offer is even more expensive than a proxy contest if one includes the costs of buying shares. But launching a tender offer also has the great comparative advantage of offering stockholders cash or other consideration up front, rather than seeking to win their votes with promises of future performance. In recent years, moreover, the proxy contest and the tender offer have sometimes merged into a single hybrid form of hostile takeover, as the law's acceptance of potent defensive tactics has sometimes made it difficult to pursue either avenue alone.

The law of corporate control contests has developed in tandem with the steep rise in the number of M&A transactions in the U.S. economy over the past 45 years. At the outset of this period, courts reviewed a board's resistance to a contest for control just as they would review any other corporate action. If the response were self-interested in an immediate financial way, the board would be required to demonstrate that it was intrinsically fair;[4] otherwise, it would be reviewed under the business judgment standard.[5] But this dichotomous approach, which worked well for reviewing self-dealing transactions and disinterested business decisions, seemed less suitable for hostile tender offers and other acquisition-of-control transactions. Management and the board are never truly disinterested in efforts to acquire control over their corporation (and hence over their positions). Nevertheless, responses to takeover offers are not "self-interested" to the same extent as a self-dealing transaction. These offers *are* immensely complicated business propositions that can expose shareholders to serious risks of exploitation by third-party

---

3. Even in those instances in which incumbent managers defeat a proxy fight, history shows that there is a relatively strong probability that incumbent management will be changed within the following year.

4. *Sterling v. Mayflower Hotel Corp.*, 93 A.2d 107 (Del. 1952); *Weinberger v. UOP, Inc.*, 457 A.2d 701 (Del. 1983).

5. *Painter v. Marshall Field & Co.*, 646 F.2d 271, 293-295 (7th Cir.), *cert. denied*, 454 U.S. 1092 (1981); *Johnson v. Trueblood*, 629 F.2d 287, 292-293 (3d Cir. 1980) (Seitz, C.J.); *Treadway Cos. v. Care Corp.*, 638 F.2d 357, 382-383 (2d Cir. 1980).

bidders; boards of directors have a critical role in protecting and advising target shareholders in this context.

The Delaware Supreme Court first began to grapple seriously with the complexities of the board's duties in contests for corporate control in a series of three cases argued during 1985, which together set the framework for the analysis of directors' fiduciary duties in M&A transactions and for defenses against hostile takeovers. Each of these cases involved a different doctrinal question, but all concerned changes in corporate control. The wisdom of hindsight suggests that they were all aspects of a single effort to bring meaningful judicial review to control transactions. The first case was *Smith v. Van Gorkom*,[6] which arose out of a friendly cash-out merger. On its face, *Van Gorkom* appears to be chiefly about the corporate director's duty of care. Nevertheless, *Van Gorkom* held an entire board liable for "gross negligence" under circumstances in which most experts would have said its directors *had* met their standard of care: that is, they had attended all meetings and deliberated about the key corporate decisions at issue. To better understand this surprising case, we suggest looking at it in the context of the law of mergers. Later cases make clear that during this period the Delaware Supreme Court began a project of redefining the role of the corporate board in corporate control transactions.

The second major decision was *Unocal Corp. v. Mesa Petroleum Co.*,[7] which is excerpted below. It dealt with the Unocal board's efforts to defend against a hostile tender offer. *Unocal* articulated for the first time a standard of judicial review between lax business judgment review and tough entire fairness review to address board efforts to defend against a threatened change-in-control transaction.

The third significant case argued in 1985 was *Revlon v. MacAndrews and Forbes Holdings, Inc.*[8] *Revlon* also addressed the efforts of an incumbent board to resist an unwelcome takeover. Revlon's board, however, attempted to resist by pursuing an alternative transaction, which is the focus of the case. Again, the court adopted a form of heightened review short of intrinsic fairness. For want of better terminology, lawyers and judges came to talk of "*Revlon* duties," and more recently, "*Revlon* review" of similar cases in which it was alleged that boards were failing — or had failed — to seek top value for shareholders when their companies were sold. Yet for many years, no one was certain when a board's *Revlon* duties were triggered or exactly what they required.

Although these 1985 cases appeared revolutionary, they had precursors: two earlier cases that sought to introduce flexibility into the business judgment rule/entire fairness dichotomy. The first was *Cheff v. Mathes*,[9] a 1964 Delaware Supreme Court opinion in which shareholders attacked a corporate repurchase at a premium price of all the stock belonging to a dissident shareholder/director. The premium payment was attacked by another

6. 488 A.2d 858 (Del. 1985). See the discussion in Chapter 7.
7. 493 A.2d 946 (Del. 1985).
8. 506 A.2d 173 (Del. 1986).
9. 199 A.2d 548 (Del. 1964).

shareholder as a waste and the whole transaction as simply an effort to entrench the existing board. The court agreed that the repurchase had the effect of securing the directors in control but held that, as long as the board's *primary purpose* was to advance business policies, the buyback did not violate the board's fiduciary duty.[10] The second precursor was *Schnell v. Chris-Craft Industries*[11] which, in contrast to *Cheff*, did find a breach of fiduciary duty when a "disinterested" board advanced the date of the company's annual meeting, as it was permitted to do by statute, solely in order to make a hostile proxy solicitation impossible to mount.[12]

Although *Cheff* and *Schnell* had dealt intelligently with a board's use of corporate power to maintain control, neither case afforded useful doctrinal tools for examining entrenchment measures more generally. However, the extraordinary growth in the number of M&A transactions — and especially hostile tender offers — in the late 1970s and early 1980s made the question of a director's fiduciary duty in the face of a takeover bid inescapable. The courts addressed this question, and so did other institutions. State legislatures passed antitakeover statutes and promulgated standards for evaluating defensive action undertaken by boards. And more important still, private legal innovation, particularly the so-called poison pill, dramatically altered the law governing changes in control of public companies. In fact, this private innovation (together with copious case law that it has stimulated) has made most state takeover legislation, as well as much of the Williams Act (as discussed previously in Chapter 11), very much less significant.

13.2 DEFENDING AGAINST HOSTILE TENDER OFFERS

UNOCAL CORP. v. MESA PETROLEUM CO.
493 A.2d 946 (Del. 1985)

MOORE, J.:

We confront an issue of first impression in Delaware — the validity of a corporation's self-tender for its own shares which excludes from participation a stockholder making a hostile tender offer for the company's stock. . . .

On April 8, 1985, Mesa, the owner of approximately 13% of Unocal's stock, commenced a two-tier "front loaded" cash tender offer for 64 million shares, or approximately 37%, of Unocal's outstanding stock at a price of $54 per share. The "back-end" was designed to eliminate the remaining publicly held shares by an exchange of securities purportedly worth $54 per share.

---

10. The shareholder attacked the corporation marketing strategy, which management defended as a source of real value. The board resolved the disagreement by causing the company to repurchase the dissident's stock at a premium over market price. Plaintiff shareholders claimed that this purchase was wasteful, since the company paid a premium to market price, and that the repurchase was made to entrench the directors in office.

11. 285 A.2d 437 (Del. 1971).

12. See §6.10 above.

However, pursuant to an order entered by the United States District Court for the Central District of California on April 26, 1985, Mesa issued a supplemental proxy statement to Unocal's stockholders disclosing that the securities offered in the second-step merger would be highly subordinated, and that Unocal's capitalization would differ significantly from its present structure. Unocal has rather aptly termed such securities "junk bonds."

Unocal's board consists of eight independent outside directors and six insiders. It met on April 13, 1985, to consider the Mesa tender offer. Thirteen directors were present, and the meeting lasted nine and one-half hours. The directors were given no agenda or written materials prior to the session. However, detailed presentations were made by legal counsel regarding the board's obligations under both Delaware corporate law and the federal securities laws. The board then received a presentation from Peter Sachs on behalf of Goldman Sachs & Co. (Goldman Sachs) and Dillon, Read & Co. (Dillon Read) discussing the bases for their opinions that the Mesa proposal was wholly inadequate. Mr. Sachs opined that the minimum cash value that could be expected from a sale or orderly liquidation for 100% of Unocal's stock was in excess of $60 per share. . . .

Mr. Sachs also presented various defensive strategies available to the board if it concluded that Mesa's two-step tender offer was inadequate and should be opposed. One of the devices outlined was a self-tender by Unocal for its own stock with a reasonable price range of $70 to $75 per share. The cost of such a proposal would cause the company to incur $6.1-6.5 billion of additional debt, and a presentation was made informing the board of Unocal's ability to handle it. The directors were told that the primary effect of this obligation would be to reduce exploratory drilling, but that the company would nonetheless remain a viable entity.

The eight outside directors, comprising a clear majority of the thirteen members present, then met separately with Unocal's financial advisors and attorneys. Thereafter, they unanimously agreed to advise the board that it should reject Mesa's tender offer as inadequate, and that Unocal should pursue a self-tender to provide the stockholders with a fairly priced alternative to the Mesa proposal. . . .

On April 15, the board met again. . . . Unocal's Vice President of Finance and its Assistant General Counsel made a detailed presentation of the proposed terms of the exchange offer. A price range between $70 and $80 per share was considered, and ultimately the directors agreed upon $72. . . . The board's decisions were made in reliance on the advice of its investment bankers. . . . Based upon this advice, . . . the directors unanimously approved the exchange offer. Their resolution provided that if Mesa acquired 64 million shares of Unocal stock through its own offer (the Mesa Purchase Condition), Unocal would buy the remaining 49% outstanding for an exchange of debt securities having an aggregate par value of $72 per share. The board resolution also stated that the offer would be subject to other conditions. . . .

Legal counsel advised that under Delaware law Mesa could only be excluded for what the directors reasonably believed to be a valid corporate purpose. The directors' discussion centered on the objective of adequately compensating shareholders at the "back-end" of Mesa's proposal, which the latter would finance with "junk bonds." To include Mesa would defeat that goal, because under the proration aspect of the exchange offer (49%) every Mesa share accepted by Unocal would displace one held by another stockholder. Further, if Mesa were permitted to tender to Unocal the latter would in effect be financing Mesa's own inadequate proposal. . . .

[Unocal's board subsequently waived the Mesa Purchase Condition as to 50 million shares (roughly 30 percent of outstanding shares), five days after the commencement of its April 17 exchange offer. This waiver — in effect, a self-tender for 30 percent of Unocal — was meant to placate institutional shareholders who correctly anticipated that Unocal's offer would defeat Mesa's bid and feared that it would also lead stock prices to decline to the $30 level, where they had languished prior to Mesa's bid.]

We begin with the basic issue of the power of a board of directors of a Delaware corporation to adopt a defensive measure of this type. . . .

The board has a large reservoir of authority upon which to draw. Its duties and responsibilities proceed from the inherent powers conferred by 8 Del. C. §141(a), respecting management of the corporation's "business and affairs." Additionally, the powers here being exercised derive from 8 Del. C. §160(a), conferring broad authority upon a corporation to deal in its own stock. From this it is now well established that in the acquisition of its shares a Delaware corporation may deal selectively with its stockholders, provided the directors have not acted out of a sole or primary purpose to entrench themselves in office. *Cheff v. Mathes*, Del. Supr., 199 A.2d 548, 554 (1964). . . .

Finally, the board's power to act derives from its fundamental duty and obligation to protect the corporate enterprise, which includes stockholders, from harm reasonably perceived, irrespective of its source. . . .

When a board addresses a pending takeover bid it has an obligation to determine whether the offer is in the best interest of the corporation and its shareholders. In that respect a board's duty is no different from any other responsibility it shoulders, and its decisions should be no less entitled to the respect they otherwise would be accorded in the realm of business judgment. . . . There are, however, certain caveats to a proper exercise of this function. Because of the omnipresent specter that a board may be acting primarily in its own interests, rather than those of the corporation and its shareholders, there is an enhanced duty which calls for judicial examination at the threshold before the protections of the business judgment rule may be conferred. . . .

In the face of this inherent conflict directors must show that they had reasonable grounds for believing that a danger to corporate policy and effectiveness existed because of another person's stock ownership. . . .

[C]orporate directors have a fiduciary duty to act in the best interests of the corporation's stockholders. . . . As we have noted, their duty of care extends to protecting the corporation and its owners from perceived harm whether a threat originates from third parties or other shareholders.[10] But such powers are not absolute. A corporation does not have unbridled discretion to defeat any perceived threat by any Draconian means available.

---

10. It has been suggested that a board's response to a takeover threat should be a passive one. Frank H. Easterbrook & Daniel R. Fischel, *Takeover Bids, Defensive Tactics, and*

The restriction placed upon a selective stock repurchase is that the directors may not have acted solely or primarily out of a desire to perpetuate themselves in office . . . [or take] inequitable action. . . .

A further aspect is the element of balance. If a defensive measure is to come within the ambit of the business judgment rule, it must be reasonable in relation to the threat posed. This entails an analysis by the directors of the nature of the takeover bid and its effect on the corporate enterprise. Examples of such concerns may include: inadequacy of the price offered, nature and timing of the offer, questions of illegality, the impact on "constituencies" other than shareholders (i.e., creditors, customers, employees, and perhaps even the community generally), the risk of non-consummation, and the quality of securities being offered in the exchange. See Lipton and Brownstein, *Takeover Responses and Directors' Responsibilities: An Update*, p. 7, ABA National Institute on the Dynamics of Corporate Control (December 8, 1983). While not a controlling factor, it also seems to us that a board may reasonably consider the basic stockholder interests at stake, including those of short-term speculators, whose actions may have fueled the coercive aspect of the offer at the expense of the long term investor.[11] Here, the threat posed was viewed by the Unocal board as a grossly inadequate two-tier coercive tender offer coupled with the threat of greenmail.

Specifically, the Unocal directors had concluded that the value of Unocal was substantially above the $54 per share offered in cash at the front end. Furthermore, they determined that the subordinated securities to be exchanged in Mesa's announced squeeze out of the remaining shareholders in the "back-end" merger were "junk bonds" worth far less than $54. It is now well recognized that such offers are a classic coercive measure designed to stampede shareholders into tendering at the first tier, even if the price is inadequate, out of fear of what they will receive at the back end of the transaction. Wholly beyond the coercive aspect of an inadequate two-tier tender offer, the threat was posed by a corporate raider with a national reputation as a "greenmailer."[13]

In adopting the selective exchange offer, the board stated that its objective was either to defeat the inadequate Mesa offer or, should the offer still succeed, provide the 49% of its stockholders, who would otherwise be forced

---

Shareholders' Welfare, 36 Business Lawyer (ABA) at 1750 (1981). However, that clearly is not the law of Delaware, and as the proponents of this rule of passivity readily concede, it has not been adopted either by courts or state legislatures. Easterbrook & Fischel, *supra* at note 2, 94 Harv. L. Rev. at 1194 (1981).

11. There has been much debate respecting such stockholder interests. One rather impressive study indicates that the stock of over 50 percent of target companies, who resisted hostile takeovers, later traded at higher market prices than the rejected offer price, or were acquired after the tender offer was defeated by another company at a price higher than the offer price. See Martin Lipton, [*Takeover Bids in the Target's Boardroom*, 35 Bus. Law. 101 (1979)] at 106-109, 132-133. Moreover, an update by Kidder Peabody & Company of this study, involving the stock prices of target companies that have defeated hostile tender offers during the period from 1973 to 1982 demonstrates that in a majority of cases the target's shareholders benefited from the defeat. . . .

13. The term "greenmail" refers to the practice of buying out a takeover bidder's stock at a premium that is not available to other shareholders in order to prevent the takeover. . . .

to accept "junk bonds," with $72 worth of senior debt. We find that both purposes are valid.

However, such efforts would have been thwarted by Mesa's participation in the exchange offer. First, if Mesa could tender its shares, Unocal would effectively be subsidizing the former's continuing effort to buy Unocal stock at $54 per share. Second, Mesa could not, by definition, fit within the class of shareholders being protected from its own coercive and inadequate tender offer.

Thus, we are satisfied that the selective exchange offer is reasonably related to the threats posed. . . . Thus, the board's decision to offer what it determined to be the fair value of the corporation to the 49% of its shareholders, who would otherwise be forced to accept highly subordinated "junk bonds," is reasonable and consistent with the directors' duty to ensure that the minority stockholders receive equal value for their shares.

Mesa contends that it is unlawful, and the trial court agreed, for a corporation to discriminate in this fashion against one shareholder. It argues correctly that no case has ever sanctioned a device that precludes a raider from sharing in a benefit available to all other stockholders. However, as we have noted earlier, the principle of selective stock repurchases by a Delaware corporation is neither unknown nor unauthorized. . . . The only difference is that heretofore the approved transaction was the payment of "greenmail" to a raider or dissident posing a threat to the corporate enterprise. All other stockholders were denied such favored treatment, and given Mesa's past history of greenmail, its claims here are rather ironic.

However, our corporate law is not static. It must grow and develop in response to, indeed in anticipation of, evolving concepts and needs. . . .

[A]s the sophistication of both raiders and targets has developed, a host of other defensive measures to counter such ever mounting threats have evolved and received judicial sanction. These include defensive charter amendments and other devices bearing some rather exotic, but apt, names: Crown Jewel, White Knight, Pac Man, and Golden Parachute. Each has highly selective features, the object of which is to deter or defeat the raider.

Thus, while the exchange offer is a form of selective treatment, given the nature of the threat posed here the response is neither unlawful nor unreasonable. If the board of directors is disinterested, has acted in good faith and with due care, its decision in the absence of an abuse of discretion will be upheld as a proper exercise of business judgment. . . .

In conclusion, there was directorial power to oppose the Mesa tender offer, and to undertake a selective stock exchange made in good faith and upon a reasonable investigation pursuant to a clear duty to protect the corporate enterprise. Further, the selective stock repurchase plan chosen by Unocal is reasonable in relation to the threat that the board rationally and reasonably believed was posed by Mesa's inadequate and coercive two-tier tender offer. Under those circumstances the board's action is entitled to be measured by the standards of the business judgment rule. Thus, unless it is shown by a preponderance of the evidence that the directors' decisions were primarily based on perpetuating themselves in office, or some other breach of fiduciary duty such as fraud, overreaching, lack of good faith, or being uninformed, a Court will not substitute its judgment for that of the board.

. . . If the stockholders are displeased with the action of their elected representatives, the powers of corporate democracy are at their disposal to turn the board out. . . .

QUESTIONS AND NOTES ON UNOCAL

1. What does it mean to characterize the Mesa offer as "coercive"? In what sense can Mesa's two-tier offer be coercive if the pre-bid market price for Unocal shares was, say, $33/share, Pickens's cash price for 37 percent of Unocal was $55/share, and Pickens's back-end cash-out price for the remaining 50 percent of Unocal's shares was around $45/share (the likely market value of junk bonds with a face value of $55/share)? Even the "back end" of the Pickens offer was generally acknowledged to be worth a lot more than Unocal's pre-bid market price.

2. Was the Unocal exchange offer also coercive?

3. What was the logical relevance of Mesa's reputation as a greenmailer to the court's analysis?

4. What are we to make of a discriminatory self-tender? Is it any different from greenmail, which the Delaware Supreme Court had authorized to protect corporate policies since the *Cheff* case? The SEC presumably thought so, since it effectively overruled this aspect of *Unocal* by promulgating Rule 13e-4, which bars discriminatory self-tenders. No SEC rule bars greenmail.

5. Is Justice Moore abandoning shareholder primacy in this opinion? Is the fundamental duty of boards to further the interests of shareholders, to balance the interests of all corporate "constituencies," or to do something else?

6. In footnote 11 of its opinion, the court cites empirical evidence from Martin Lipton and Kidder Peabody indicating that targets remaining independent achieve higher returns for their shareholders than targets that sell to the hostile bidder. The court does not cite Professor Ronald Gilson, who points out several flaws in Lipton's study, including no adjustment for market effects or the time value of money. When these and other factors are considered, Gilson states that "Lipton's data refute his own conclusion."[13] A more recent study, examining targets that remained independent between 1996 and 2002, shows that shareholders received lower returns than they would have received if the company had been sold to the initial bidder or to a white knight[14] — the opposite of what Lipton and Kidder Peabody found 20 years earlier. Whatever the general tendency is, it seems clear, as well, that in individual cases of hostile takeover attempts, shareholders have been made better

---

13. See Gilson, *supra* note 2, at 857-858.

14. Lucian Arye Bebchuk, John C. Coates IV & Guhan Subramanian, *The Powerful Antitakeover Force of Staggered Boards: Further Findings and a Reply to Symposium Participants*, 55 Stan. L. Rev. 885 (2002).

off by management's defeat of a hostile takeover. The *Airgas* case noted later in this Chapter, appears to be such a case.

How should courts utilize empirical evidence in formulating their opinions in individual cases? For one judge's perspective on this "meta-question," see Jack B. Jacobs, *Comments on Contestability*, 54 U. Miami L. Rev. 847 (2000).

7. *Unocal* announces a new standard for reviewing defensive tactics — what the Delaware Supreme Court refers to as "enhanced business judgment review." To earn the protection of the business judgment rule, the board must show that its defensive tactic was "reasonable in relation to the threat posed." How different is this standard from old-fashioned business judgment review? See Ronald J. Gilson & Reinier Kraakman, *Delaware's Intermediate Standard for Defensive Tactics: Is There Substance to Proportionality Review?*, 44 Bus. Law. 247 (1989). Before you answer, take a look at the *Unitrin* case below.

In the 1995 case *Unitrin v. American General Corp.*,[15] the Delaware Supreme Court tried to add some specificity to the *Unocal* test of "reasonable in relation to the threat posed." The case involved a hostile tender offer by American General Corp. (AmGen) for Unitrin at $50^3/_8$ per share, a substantial premium to market price. Unitrin's board was comprised of seven persons, who collectively owned 23 percent of the company's stock.

After concluding that AmGen's offer was inadequate, Unitrin's board sought to defend by implementing a poison pill, an advance-notice bylaw,[16] and a tender offer to repurchase 5 million, or 20 percent, of its outstanding shares. Unitrin's directors announced that they would not participate in this buyback, which, if successful, would increase their proportional share ownership to 28 percent of Unitrin's outstanding stock. Unitrin's charter mandated that any transaction with an entity controlled by or affiliated with a person owning 15 percent of Unitrin's stock required approval by 75 percent of the outstanding stock.

The Chancery Court held that the AmGen offer represented a threat of "substantive coercion."[17] This Orwellian phrase meant that (the board believed) shareholders might be "coerced" because they would not fully understand the value of their stock or the inadequacy of the consideration

---

15. 651 A.2d 1361 (Del. 1995).

16. Advance-notice bylaws generally require any stockholder who intends to nominate an insurgent slate at the next annual shareholders' meeting to give certain information to the corporation concerning the identity of such persons well in advance of the meeting. Sometimes the mandated time is 90 days, but often it is longer (120 days or more). Obviously, as the period increases, so does the constraint on proxy contests. Some such bylaws will be validly subject to a claim that they constitute a manipulation foreclosed by the *Schnell* principle.

17. This phrase was coined in Ronald J. Gilson & Reinier Kraakman, *Delaware's Intermediate Standard for Defensive Tactics: Is There Substance to Proportionality Review?*, 44 Bus. Law. 247, 267 (1989). Although the article advocated "a meaningful proportionality test" when a board alleged substantive coercion, the *Unitrin* court seems to have adopted the term "substantive coercion" without the accompanying hard look at "how — and when — management expects a target's shareholders to do better." Id. at 268. See also *Chesapeake v. Shore*, 771 A.2d 293, 329 (Del. Ch. 2000) (Strine, V.C.) (noting the tension).

offered. Applying *Unocal*, the Court of Chancery held that the pill was a proportional response to this threat but that the repurchase program was not. Increasing the management block from 23 percent to 28 percent of the shares by repurchases would, according to the court, preclude a change in control as a practical matter. The court concluded that this response was "unnecessary" in light of what was only a "mild" threat.

On appeal, the Delaware Supreme Court reversed, holding that "if the board of directors' defensive response is not draconian (preclusive or coercive) and is within a 'range of reasonableness,' a court must not substitute its judgment for the board's." The court found that neither the poison pill nor the repurchase program was coercive or preclusive, because AmGen could run a proxy contest to replace the Unitrin board. The court then remanded the case to the Delaware Chancery Court for a determination as to whether the pill and the repurchase program were within the range of reasonable defenses (with the burden on the Unitrin directors). If the defendant directors *did* establish that the board action was proportionate and within a range of reasonableness, the burden would then shift back to the plaintiffs to prove that the defensive action was nevertheless a breach of the duty; for instance, by being primarily motivated to maintain the board in office.

Unitrin reflects the almost Byzantine complexity of the Delaware corporate law of hostile takeovers. One might think that, if a court concludes that directors have taken an action that is (1) legal, (2) proportionate to a threat, and (3) within a range of reasonable responses, the challenge to the action should be at an end. But under *Unitrin*, such a finding does not justify a dismissal of the complaint — it simply shifts the burden back to the plaintiff. Analogous consequences follow if the defendant directors do *not* establish that a defensive action is proportionate (i.e., if the action *is* deemed either coercive/preclusive or outside the range of reasonableness). Here, too, Delaware law does not simply say that such actions violate a board's fiduciary duty. Rather, according to the cases, it is open to defendants to prove the fairness of the action nevertheless. See, e.g., *Shamrock Holdings, Inc. v. Polaroid Corp.*, 559 A.2d 278 (Del. Ch. 1989).

Unitrin makes clear how limited an "enhancement" to the business judgment rule *Unocal* can be. In this regard, *Unitrin* boils down to three things. First, under *Unocal/Unitrin*, the target's directors, not the plaintiff, bear the burden of going forward with evidence to show that the defensive action was proportionate to a threat. Second, substantively, action that is "preclusive" or "coercive" will fail to satisfy *Unocal*'s test. Third, assuming that a defensive measure passes the preclusive/coercive test (in *Unitrin*'s language, that it is not "draconian"), then it will satisfy *Unocal* so long as it is "within a range of reasonable action." Properly understood, this last aspect of the test is operationally similar to the business judgment rule: An action will be sustained if it is attributable to *any* reasonable judgment. It will not matter if the court would have regarded some other action as more reasonable. Taken together, these three aspects of "enhanced" business judgment in the end may be thought to provide more smoke than warmth. But see *Omnicare v. NCS Healthcare*, at §13.8.2.

13.3   PRIVATE LAW INNOVATION: THE POISON PILL

We turn now to a most remarkable innovation in corporate law, the share-holders' rights plan or "poison pill." This was an audacious invention that has proven to be remarkably effective, although it continues to be controversial. In an arm's length merger, the counter-party must negotiate an agreement with the target board of directors; in a tender offer for corporate control, as of the early 1980s, the board had no formal role. The shareholders' rights plan operates to give a target's board the same bargaining power over a hostile tender offer as DGCL §251 grants the board over merger proposals.

What is now colloquially named the "poison pill" is a private law device, variously said to have been invented by Wachtell Lipton or another prominent law firm. But regardless of who has bragging rights, the pill would not enjoy the prominence it does today without the encouragement of the Delaware courts. The pill was first validated in 1985 by the Delaware Supreme Court in *Moran v. Household International, Inc.*[18] Many academics of the day believed (and still believe) that hostile tender offers are a useful device for dis-ciplining corporate management. But boards and managers believed the suc-cess of hostile bids revealed a profound weakness in corporate governance by leaving disaggregated shareholders vulnerable to abusive tender offer tactics. Moreover, in the late 1970s and early 1980s, the practices of certain takeover entrepreneurs made management's arguments plausible. "Front-end loaded, two-tier" tender offers could unquestionably induce shareholders to sell, even if they believed that the tender offer price was well below what their shares were worth. This much was confirmed by academic research.[19] And to managers and boards, if not necessarily the academic commentators of the day, the implication was clear: Only a loyal bargaining agent — namely, the board — could remedy the bargaining infirmities and collective action prob-lems of dispersed shareholders. The poison pill did just this, it empowered the board to be the shareholders' gatekeeper and bargaining agent.

Shareholders' rights plans take the form of capital instruments: rights to buy a capital asset, such as a bond, common share, or preferred share. Yet, their only real function is to alter the allocation of power between sharehold-ers and boards. The most common form of rights plans today does this rather like the Mesa exclusion in *Unocal.* The rights to buy a company security are "distributed" to all shareholders. (Shareholders do not literally receive a new piece of paper; the rights trade with the stock.) But upon the happening of a triggering event — generally the acquisition by a hostile party of a set percent-age of the company's stock (often 10 or 15 percent) — the rights automati-cally convert into the right to buy the company's stock at a greatly discounted price. Moreover (and this is the key), the person whose stock acquisition triggers the exercise of the rights is itself excluded from buying discounted stock. Thus, its holdings are severely diluted; it retains only a small fraction of its prior voting rights and may lose most of the value of its investment in the

---

18. 500 A.2d 1346 (Del. 1985).
19. See, e.g., Lucian Arye Bebchuk, *Toward Undistorted Choice and Equal Treatment in Corporate Takeovers*, 98 Harv. L. Rev. 1639 (1985).

company stock. The result is that buying a substantial block of stock without the prior consent of the target's board is ruinously expensive and the dilution of voting rights is even more extreme. These consequences give the board an effective veto over a hostile tender offer. However, if the hostile party successfully negotiates a friendly deal with the board before crossing the triggering percentage, the board can waive the pill (called "redeeming" the pill). Thus typical pills always have a so-called "board-out" provision.

Consider this hypothetical example of the pill's operation. T Corp. distributes as a dividend the Shareholders' Rights. Each Right purports to be a right to buy 1/100 of a share of the company's common stock in the future for an extravagant, "out of the money" price: say, $500 (or $5,000 per share) when its common stock is selling for $75 a share. Given its terms, no one really expects this Right ever to be exercised (although the company's lawyers might argue that the Right's high exercise price represents the hidden long-term value of the company's stock). The Rights do not trade separately at this point but are embedded in the common stock on which the dividend is paid. However, should a "triggering event" occur, the Rights detach and are tradable separately. Today, a triggering event might be the acquisition of 10 percent of the company's stock by any single entity or an affiliated group of persons, or the announcement of a tender offer for 10 percent or more of the company's stock.[20]

If a person or group did acquire a 10 percent block, then under a "flip-in" pill, each outstanding Right would "flip-into" a right to acquire some number of shares of the target's common stock at one-half of the market price for that stock. (It could be one-third or some other number, but it usually is one-half.) In other words, the Right's holder would be able to buy stock from the company at half price. Now, if every Right holder bought stock at half price, the aggregate effect is to increase the proportionate holdings of all shareholders *except* the "triggering person," whose Right would be canceled upon the occurrence of the triggering event and who, as a result, would only own a much smaller interest in the company than that for which she initially paid.[21]

---

20. When rights plans were first introduced in the 1980s, triggering events typically involved 30 percent of the company's stock. The size of the triggering threshold has steadily receded, however, and since 1990, triggers have been typically 10 percent. Once the rights are triggered, they are no longer redeemable by the company, and ten days later they are exercisable. For a commentary that examines pill design choices with respect to redeemability, see Guhan Subramanian, *Bargaining in the Shadow of PeopleSoft's (Defective) Poison Pill*, 12 Harv. Neg. L. Rev. 41 (2007).

21. The original rights plans were not "flip-in" plans, but "flip-over" plans which purported to create a right to buy some number of shares *in the corporation whose acquisition of target stock had triggered the right.* In this plan, a triggering event — acquiring a certain percentage of target's shares (when followed by a second triggering event: a merger or sale of more than 50 percent of the target's assets to the triggering shareholder or an affiliate) results in the rights being exercisable. How can the target's board create a right that requires a third party to sell its stock at half price to the target's shareholders? Well, we are not certain that it can be done, since the question of whether a *triggering* shareholder must respect an obligation created by a flip-over plan has never been litigated. The reason these plans are *supposed* to work, however, is that they purport to compel the target's board, as a party to the second triggering event, to put terms in any merger agreement (or asset sale agreement, etc.) with the acquirer that will force the acquirer to recognize flip-over rights.

Rights plans were, and to some extent remain, controversial. One can easily see how they could be beneficial to shareholders, but it is just as easy to see ways in which they might be misused to protect the status quo. When rights plans were first introduced, it was fairly clear that most boards were authorized to issue rights, like those created by rights plans, to raise capital, but whether they could do so solely as a takeover defense was less clear.[22] In *Moran*, the Delaware Supreme Court held that Delaware corporations have the statutory power to issue both shares (DGCL §151) and rights to acquire securities (DGCL §157) even when they are not raising capital; and the accompanying rights do not preclude shareholders from receiving tender offers (although the shareholders may be required to change the board to do so). In approving the power that boards have to adopt rights plans, the Court relied expressly on the fiduciary duty of the board in stating that boards would have a continuing obligation to monitor the rights and to redeem them under the (then) newly adopted *Unocal* test if a tender offer did not represent a threat to the corporation or its shareholders. The use of the pill was thus approved as a takeover defense, but unlike many other takeover defenses, it blocked hostile offers without requiring any real changes to the corporation's business plans, shares, or assets.

Immediately after *Moran* was decided, commentary on Delaware law came to focus on how a target company's board could satisfy its burden to show that, under *Unocal*, an unsolicited tender offer represented a threat to corporate policy or to shareholders that justified leaving a rights plan in place.

QUESTIONS AND NOTES ON STOCK RIGHTS PLANS

1. *Moran* was the first judicial opinion to validate shareholders' rights plans. Other jurisdictions split on their validity at first, but that equivocation ended, state by state. As Professors Emiliano Catan and Marcel Kahan report: "Between 1986 and 1989, court decisions rendered under the laws of Colorado, Georgia, New Jersey, New York, Virginia, and Wisconsin held or strongly suggested that flip-in pills are invalid. The basis for these decisions was that the discriminatory treatment of raiders in flip-in pills violated a statutory requirement that all shares of the same class be treated equally. Court decisions under the laws of Indiana, Maine, Maryland, Michigan, Minnesota, Texas and Wisconsin upheld flip-in pills, reasoning that any discrimination

---

Because of their second trigger, flip-over plans are less effective than flip-in plans. In a flip-over plan, a hostile party may acquire a large block of target stock but propose no transaction which would act as the second trigger activating the rights. It may wait to elect a new board. Indeed, this weakness was demonstrated in one instance and flip-in pills, which did not require the hostile acquirer to take any second step in order to execute the punishing dilution, were designed in response.

22. Firm charters usually had provisions authorizing the board to issue classes of preferred stock (along with deciding on their voting rights, preferences, and so forth) without needing any further stockholder approval. These so-called "blank check" preferred stocks were used by transactional lawyers to set up the pill.

entailed is merely among shareholders, not among shares. But while the reception of flip-in pills by courts was mixed, legislatures embraced them enthusiastically. By 1990, twenty-four states (including all states where courts had invalidated flip-in pills) had adopted statutes validating discriminatory pills. This number now stands at thirty-four."[23]

2. Can we say what effect adoption of poison pills is likely to have on shareholder value? One can easily imagine a narrative either way, depending on whether managers are more likely to deploy the pill to serve as loyal bargaining agents or to deploy it to entrench themselves in the face of buyers who might offer shareholders better value. But testing the effects of pills on corporate value is not easy, in part because every Delaware company might be said to have a pill. That is, companies that do not presently have a pill can adopt one in a matter of days (if not hours) if they are threatened by an impending takeover bid. All that is required is a board meeting, after all, not a shareholder vote. Thus it is difficult to compare measures of value between firms with and without pills. See John C. Coates IV, *Takeover Defenses in the Shadow of the Pill: A Critique of the Scientific Evidence*, 79 Tex. L. Rev. 271 (2000).

3. The Delaware Supreme Court was careful in *Moran* to state that corporate directors continue to exercise power subject to their fiduciary duty after adoption of a stock rights plan. In particular, the court noted that, under *Unocal*, a board might have a duty to redeem rights issued under its rights plan if their effect no longer appears reasonable in relation to the threat posed by an uninvited tender offer. But exactly when must a pill be redeemed? Is the board entitled to keep rights outstanding only long enough to assure that shareholders have a (board-approved) alternative to the unsolicited offer and to complete that alternative, such as a recapitalization, or is the board entitled to "just say no" to a hostile bidder indefinitely, without proposing an alternative to its shareholders?

When faced with boards resisting hostile tender offers, the Delaware courts defer more to boards who just say no (i.e., no to board-disapproved offers and offer no company-approved alternative) than to those boards who do propose an alternative. See, e.g., *TW Services, Inc. v. SWT Acquisition Corp.*, 1989 WL 20290 (Del. Ch. Mar. 2, 1989). The few cases in which the Delaware Court of Chancery did force boards to redeem their pills were ones in which the pills were used to protect company-sponsored alternatives to all-cash tender offers. In *City Capital Associates Ltd. Partnership v. Interco, Inc.*, 551 A.2d 787 (Del. Ch. 1988), the court ordered Interco, Inc., to redeem a stock rights plan that the company used to protect its recapitalization alternative to a hostile all-cash, all-shares tender offer.[24] Similarly, in *Grand Metropolitan Public Ltd. Co. v. Pillsbury Co.*, 558 A.2d 1049 (Del. Ch. 1988), the court required Pillsbury to redeem its rights plan after concluding that

23. Emiliano Catan & Marcel Kahan, *The Law & Finance of Anti-Takeover Statutes*, 68 Stan. L. Rev. 629, 636-637 (2016).

24. After reviewing the company's own restructuring plan, the court concluded that the hostile all-cash, all-shares offer did not constitute a sufficient threat to Interco or its shareholders to justify foreclosing the shareholders indefinitely from choosing to accept the offer.

Pillsbury's own restructuring proposal compared unfavorably in value to a hostile all-cash, all-shares offer from Grand Met. To be sure, these cases were expressly disapproved by the Delaware Supreme Court in dicta in *Paramount Communications, Inc. v. Time, Inc.*, 571 A.2d 1140 (Del. 1989) (*Time-Warner*), excerpted below. The most recent and significant case dealing with this issue, the 2011 *Airgas* opinion, a "just say no" case, is noted below, following a discussion of the Delaware Supreme Court opinion in the *Time-Warner* case.

4. As we have said, many institutional investors have long been skeptical of poison pills. Precatory shareholder resolutions to redeem rights plans have for many years been among the most common subjects of Rule14(a)(8) shareholder proxy access proposals. As a gesture to investor interests, many firms today have allowed their pills to expire. But they have done so knowing that they can put a new pill in place in less than 24 hours should a hostile acquirer approach.

13.4 CHOOSING A MERGER OR BUYOUT PARTNER: *REVLON*, ITS SEQUELS, AND ITS PREQUELS

The board's entrenchment interest can affect not only its takeover defenses but also its choice of a merger or buyout partner. Management can obtain a variety of benefits in "friendly" deals, ranging from such minor things as a place on the surviving corporation's board, to more significant benefits such as consulting contracts, termination payments, and other compensation-related benefits. Traditionally, corporate law treated decisions to initiate merger proposals as business judgments as long as management did not have a conflicting ownership interest. In its third revolutionary takeover opinion of the 1985-1986 season, the Delaware Supreme Court addressed the board's fiduciary duty in arranging for the "sale" of a company. The case was *Revlon, Inc. v. MacAndrews & Forbes Holdings, Inc.*, 506 A.2d 173 (Del. 1986). Even before *Revlon*, however, the Delaware Supreme Court signaled its concern about the possibility that incumbent managers might sell their company at a low price to a favored bidder in the remarkable case of *Smith v. Van Gorkom*, 488 A.2d 858 (Del. 1985). At the time it was issued, the *Van Gorkom* opinion was believed to be an aggressive articulation of the board's general duty of care. (Accordingly, we noted the case in Chapter 7.) In hindsight, however, *Van Gorkom* has come to seem much more like a precursor of the great Delaware takeover cases of the mid-1980s, and especially of *Revlon*. We reproduce portions of this very lengthy opinion below.

SMITH v. VAN GORKOM
488 A.2d 858 (Del. 1985)

HORSEY, J.:

This appeal from the Court of Chancery involves a class action brought by shareholders of the defendant Trans Union Corporation ("Trans Union" or "the Company"), originally seeking rescission of a cash-out merger of Trans Union into . . . a wholly-owned subsidiary of the defendant, Marmon Group, Inc. ("Marmon"). Alternate relief in the form of damages is sought against the defendant members of the Board of Directors of Trans Union. . . .

Trans Union was a publicly-traded, diversified holding company, the principal earnings of which were generated by its railcar leasing business. During the period here involved, the Company had a cash flow of hundreds of millions of dollars annually. However, the Company had difficulty in generating sufficient taxable income to offset increasingly large investment tax credits (ITCs). Accelerated depreciation deductions had decreased available taxable income against which to offset accumulating ITCs. . . .

[At a senior management meeting on September 5, 1980, Trans Union's CFO and COO discussed a leveraged buyout as a solution to the ITC problem.] . . . They did not "come up" with a price for the Company. They merely "ran the numbers" [and t]heir "figures indicated that $50 would be very easy to do but $60 would be very difficult to do under those figures." This work did not purport to establish a fair price for either the Company or 100% of the stock. It was intended to determine the cash flow needed to service the debt that would "probably" be incurred in a leveraged buy-out. . . .

. . . Van Gorkom [Trans Union's CEO for more than 17 years] stated that he would be willing to take $55 per share for his own 75,000 shares. [Nevertheless, h]e vetoed the suggestion of a leveraged buy-out by Management . . . as involving a potential conflict of interest for Management. . . . It is noteworthy in this connection that he was then approaching 65 years of age and mandatory retirement.

For several days following the September 5 meeting, Van Gorkom pondered the idea of a sale. . . .

Van Gorkom [then] decided to meet with Jay A. Pritzker, a well-known corporate takeover specialist and a social acquaintance. However, rather than approaching Pritzker simply to determine his interest in acquiring Trans Union, Van Gorkom assembled a proposed per share price for sale of the Company and a financing structure by which to accomplish the sale. Van Gorkom did so without consulting either his Board or any members of Senior Management except one: Carl Peterson, Trans Union's Controller. Telling Peterson that he wanted no other person on his staff to know what he was doing, but without telling him why, Van Gorkom directed Peterson to calculate the feasibility of a leveraged buy-out at an assumed price per share of $55. Apart from the Company's historic stock market price,[5] and Van Gorkom's long association with Trans Union, the record is devoid of any competent evidence that $55 represented the per share intrinsic value of the Company. . . .

---

5. The common stock of Trans Union was traded on the New York Stock Exchange. Over the five year period from 1975 through 1979, Trans Union's stock had traded within a range of a high of $39½ and a low of $24¼. Its high and low range for 1980 through September 19 (the last trading day before announcement of the merger) was $38¼–$29½.

Van Gorkom arranged a meeting with Pritzker at the latter's home on Saturday, September 13, 1980. Van Gorkom [suggested $55 per share as the price and how to potentially finance it. Pritzker subsequently made a cash offer for Trans Union at $55/share. The offer was to remain open for a period of 90 days, during which Trans Union could accept a higher offer. But this "market test" was defective in the court's view.] . . .

On Friday, September 19 [1980], Van Gorkom called a special meeting of the Trans Union Board for noon the following day. . . .

Ten directors served on the Trans Union Board, five inside . . . and five outside. . . . None was an investment banker or trained financial analyst. All members of the Board were well informed about the Company and its operations as a going concern. . . .

Van Gorkom began the Special Meeting of the Board with a twenty-minute oral presentation. Copies of the proposed Merger Agreement were delivered too late for study before or during the meeting. He reviewed the Company's ITC and depreciation problems and the efforts theretofore made to solve them. He discussed his initial meeting with Pritzker and his motivation in arranging that meeting. Van Gorkom did not disclose to the Board, however, the methodology [for arriving] at the $55 figure, or . . . that he first proposed the $55 price [to] Pritzker.

Van Gorkom outlined the terms of the Pritzker offer as follows . . . for a period of 90 days, Trans Union could receive, but could not actively solicit, competing offers; the offer had to be acted on by the next evening, Sunday, September 21; Trans Union could only furnish to competing bidders published information, and not proprietary information; the offer was subject to Pritzker obtaining the necessary financing by October 10, 1980; if the financing contingency were met or waived by Pritzker, Trans Union was required to sell to Pritzker one million newly-issued shares of Trans Union at $38 per share.

Van Gorkom took the position that putting Trans Union "up for auction" through a 90-day market test would validate a decision by the Board that $55 was a fair price. He framed the decision before the Board not as whether $55 per share was the highest price that could be obtained, but as whether the $55 price was a fair price that the stockholders should be given the opportunity to accept or reject. . . .

On Monday, September 22, the Company issued a press release announcing that Trans Union had entered into a "definitive" Merger Agreement with an affiliate of the Marmon group, Inc., a Pritzker holding company. Within 10 days of the public announcement, dissent among Senior Management over the merger had become widespread. Faced with threatened resignations of key officers, Van Gorkom met with Pritzker who agreed to several modifications of the Agreement. Pritzker was willing to do so provided that Van Gorkom could persuade the dissidents to remain on the Company payroll for at least six months after consummation of the merger. . . .

The next day, October 9, Trans Union issued a press release announcing [the deal, Pritzker satisfying the financing commitment, and] that Trans Union was now permitted to actively seek other offers and had retained Salomon Brothers for that purpose. [Further] if a more favorable offer were not received before February 1, 1981, Trans Union's shareholders would thereafter meet to vote on the Pritzker proposal.

It was not until the following day, October 10, that the actual amendments were delivered to Van Gorkom for execution. [T]he amendments were considerably at variance with Van Gorkom's representations . . . to the Board on October 8; and the amendments placed serious constraints on Trans Union's ability to negotiate a better deal and withdraw from the Pritzker agreement. Nevertheless, Van Gorkom proceeded to execute [them] without conferring further with the Board . . . and apparently without comprehending [their] actual implications. . . .

Salomon Brothers' efforts over a three-month period from October 21 to January 21 produced only one serious suitor for Trans Union — General Electric Credit Corporation ("GE Credit"), a subsidiary of the General Electric Company. However, GE Credit was unwilling to make an offer for Trans Union unless Trans Union first rescinded its Merger Agreement with Pritzker. When Pritzker refused, GE Credit terminated . . . discussions . . . in early January. . . .

On February 10, the stockholders of Trans Union approved the Pritzker merger proposal. . . .

On [this] record . . . , we must conclude that the Board of Directors did not reach an informed business judgment on September 20. . . .

Without any documents before them concerning the proposed transaction, the members of the Board were required to rely entirely upon Van Gorkom's 20-minute oral presentation of the proposal. No written summary of the . . . merger was presented; the directors were given no documentation to support the adequacy of $55 price per share . . . ; and the Board had before it nothing more than Van Gorkom's statement of his understanding of the substance of an agreement which he admittedly had never read. . . .

A substantial premium may provide one reason to recommend a merger, but in the absence of other sound valuation information, the fact of a premium alone does not provide an adequate basis upon which to assess the fairness of an offering price. . . .

Indeed, as of September 20, the Board had no other information [besides its current and historical stock price] on which to base a determination of the intrinsic value of Trans Union as a going concern. As of September 20, the Board had made no evaluation of the Company designed to value the entire enterprise. . . . Thus, the adequacy of a premium is indeterminate unless it is assessed in terms of other competent and sound valuation information that reflects the value of the particular business. . . .

This brings us to the post-September 20 "market test" upon which the defendants . . . rely to confirm the reasonableness of their September 20 decision to accept the Pritzker proposal. . . .

Again, the facts of record do not support the defendants' argument. There is no evidence: (a) that the Merger Agreement was effectively amended [on September 20] to give the Board freedom to put Trans Union up for auction sale to the highest bidder; or (b) that a public auction was in fact permitted to occur. . . .

The October 10 amendments to the Merger Agreement did authorize Trans Union to solicit competing offers, but the amendments had more far-reaching

effects. The most significant change was in the definition of the third-party
"offer" available to Trans Union as a possible basis for withdrawal from its Merger
Agreement with Pritzker. Under the October 10 amendments, a better *offer* was
no longer sufficient to permit Trans Union's withdrawal. Trans Union was now
permitted to . . . abandon the merger only if, prior to February 10, 1981, Trans
Union had either consummated a merger (or sale of assets) with a third party or
had entered into a "definitive" merger agreement more favorable than Pritzker's
and for a greater consideration — subject only to stockholder approval. . . .

Finally, we turn to the Board's meeting of January 26, 1981 . . . [which]
was the first meeting following the filing of the plaintiffs' suit in mid-December
and the last meeting before the previously-noticed shareholder meeting of
February 10. . . .

The defendants characterize the Board's Minutes of the January 26 meeting as a "review" of the "entire sequence of events" from Van Gorkom's initiation of the negotiations on September 13 forward. The defendants . . . argue
that whatever information the Board lacked to make a deliberate and informed
judgment on September 20, or on October 8, was fully divulged to the entire
Board on January 26. Hence, the argument goes, the Board's vote on January
26 to again "approve" the Pritzker merger must be found to [be] an informed
and deliberate judgement. . . .

We must conclude from the foregoing that the Board was mistaken
as a matter of law regarding its available courses of action on January 26,
1981. . . . [T]he Board had but two options: (1) to proceed with the merger
and the stockholder meeting, with the Board's recommendation of approval;
or (2) to rescind its agreement with Pritzker, withdraw its approval of the
merger, and notify its stockholders that the proposed shareholder meeting
was canceled. There is no evidence that the Board gave any consideration to
these, its only legally viable [options].

But the second course of action . . . clearly involved a substantial
risk — that the Board would [face] suit by Pritzker for breach of contract based
on its September 20 agreement as amended October 10. As previously noted,
under the terms of the October 10 amendment, the Board's only ground for
release from its agreement with Pritzker was its entry into a more favorable
definitive agreement to sell the Company to a third party. Thus, in reality, the
Board was not "free to turn down the Pritzker proposal" . . . on January 26
by simply relying on its self-induced failure to [reach] an informed business
judgment at the time of its original agreement. . . .

The defendants ultimately rely on the stockholder vote of February 10
for exoneration. The defendants contend that the stockholders' "overwhelming" vote approving the Pritzker Merger Agreement [cured] any failure of the
Board to reach an informed business judgment. . . .

[W]e find that Trans Union's stockholders were not fully informed of all
facts material to their vote on the Pritzker Merger and that the Trial Court's
ruling to the contrary is clearly erroneous. . . .

We conclude that the Board acted in a grossly negligent manner on
October 8 [in addition to acting in a grossly negligent manner at the initial
meeting on September 20 — Eds.]; and that Van Gorkom's representations on
which the Board based its actions do not constitute "reports" under §141(e)
on which the directors could reasonably have relied. . . .

JAY PRITZKER & JEROME VAN GORKOM

Jay Pritzker was born into a family already prominent in Chicago's business circles. His father, an immigrant from the Ukraine, had arrived in Chicago at the turn of the century with little money and no knowledge of the English language. In time, he went to law school and opened a law office. Gradually he began investing in area businesses and found great success.

At the precocious age of 14, his son, Jay, graduated from high school and began his studies at Northwestern University. After obtaining a law degree from Northwestern and performing military service during World War II, he returned home to join his father at Pritzker & Pritzker and helped manage the family investments. He formed what would become The Marmon Group in 1953 with his brother Robert in order to purchase underperforming industrial companies. Jay Pritzker was known for his ability to swiftly evaluate business deals and his preference for quick and simple transactions. As he told the *Wall Street Journal*, "We've bought a lot of things on just a handshake or a paragraph or two. We're the least legal-minded people you'll ever meet."[25] His investments made him and his family billionaires.

While vacationing at a ski chalet in the Swiss Alps, Jay Pritzker met Jerome Van Gorkom, CEO of Trans Union. Both men were active in the Chicago business community and became friends while working together to rescue the Chicago public school system from severe financial difficulties. Their relationship would lead to a merger of their respective companies and to a groundbreaking legal decision in *Smith v. Van Gorkom.*

NOTE ON SMITH v. VAN GORKOM

As noted above, *Smith v. Van Gorkom* is on its own terms a case about the extent of the directors' duty of care. Yet as argued in Chapter 7, courts generally refuse to examine the reasonableness of decisions made by disinterested directors in the board's regular decision-making process. (Recall the *Kamin* case in particular.) *Smith v. Van Gorkom* was a jolting break with this tradition — so much so that we are persuaded it is something other than the simple application of duty of care doctrine to special facts.[26] In particular, we recommend the interpretation offered by Professors Jonathan Macey and Geoffrey Miller that *Van Gorkom* should be understood *not* as a director negligence case (although the court presented it this way) but rather as the first of several important cases in which the court struggled to construct a new standard of judicial review for "change in control" transactions such as mergers.[27]

---

25. Quoted in William Owen, Autopsy of a Merger (1986).

26. We are unaware of any prior nonbanking case in which directors who have no conflicting interests and who attend meetings and deliberate before authorizing a transaction are held personally liable for breach of a duty of care, let alone a case in which they are held liable for approving a sale of the company at a 50 percent premium to market price.

27. See Jonathan R. Macey & Geoffrey P. Miller, Trans Union *Reconsidered*, 98 Yale L.J. 127, 138 (1988). We stand behind our conviction by locating an excerpt from *Van Gorkom* in this Chapter, rather than Chapter 7, although, of course, we do not object if some of our readers wish to read *Van Gorkom* in conjunction with Chapter 7.

NOTE: INTRODUCING THE REVLON DECISION

The opinion that gave full cry to the courts' desire to modify the business judgment rule in the context of transactions that involved a change in control was the *Revlon* decision, which was handed down the year following *Van Gorkom.* The bidder in *Revlon* was Ronald O. Perelman, a well-known takeover entrepreneur and the chairman of Pantry Pride, Inc. Revlon's management opposed the Perelman/Pantry Pride offer with two defensive tactics. First, it adopted a form of the flip-in rights plan as described above, and second, it repurchased 20 percent of Revlon's stock with unsecured debt (the Notes) at a premium price. This repurchase had two useful effects from the standpoint of Revlon's embattled management. First, these Notes clouded Revlon's balance sheet and thus made it harder for Perelman to find financing to support his buyout. Second, the Notes gave management a vehicle for inserting a covenant that barred Revlon from selling or encumbering its assets without the approval of its independent directors. Again, such a covenant would make it more difficult for Perelman to borrow against Revlon's assets and subsequently pay down his debt by selling assets in typical leveraged buyout fashion.[28]

Perelman proved to be a formidable opponent, however. He countered management's moves by raising his bid price! Soon shareholder pressure on Revlon's board to act became overwhelming. At this point, Revlon's management attempted to reverse course by soliciting a competing bid from a "white knight," or friendly bidder, Forstmann Little & Co., a financial firm in the leveraged buyout business. The board's new strategy aimed at giving shareholders the cash they were demanding by selling Revlon to a friendly buyer (Forstmann and themselves) rather than to Perelman. But for the new strategy to succeed, Revlon had to remove the restrictive covenant contained in the Notes that it had exchanged with its shareholders, since this covenant not only interfered with Perelman's financing but also precluded Forstmann from financing the new alternative transaction. Yet one thing leads to another. Stripping the restrictive covenant from the Notes sharply lowered their value. Within days, lawyers representing Revlon's noteholders (who were erstwhile shareholders) were threatening to sue the board for bad faith and breach of duty.

Forstmann was persuaded to enter the fray and make a bid, but Perelman vowed to beat whatever price Forstmann would offer. Revlon then concluded a final deal with Forstmann: Revlon would assure Forstmann's victory by giving it a "lock-up option" to purchase Revlon's most valuable assets at a bargain price if another bidder (i.e., Perelman) were to acquire more than 40 percent of Revlon's stock. In exchange, Forstmann would increase its offer for Revlon's stock (to $57.25) and support the price of Revlon's Notes (thus satisfying any claims of noteholders).

---

28. A leveraged buyout is a transaction in which a buyer borrows cash that will be used to buy the equity of the target corporation. Repayment of the borrowing comes from the sale of the target's assets (breakup) or is secured by the target's assets.

In response to the new Revlon-Forstmann deal, Pantry Pride increased its offer to $58/share conditional on the lock-up being rescinded or declared invalid. It sought to enjoin Forstmann's lock-up option as well as the agreement not to assist buyers other than Forstmann in the Delaware courts. The Delaware Supreme Court (per Justice Moore) firmly rejected what it considered to be Revlon's attempt to "rig" the bidding, holding that when the sale of the company became "inevitable," "[t]he directors' role changed from defenders of the corporate bastion to auctioneers charged with getting the best price for the stockholders at a sale of the company."

We pick up here with the Delaware Supreme Court opinion after the court approved Revlon's original defensive tactics that were designed to maintain its independence (the poison pill and the exchange offer). Justice Moore now turns to Revlon's decision to sell to Forstmann and the lock-up option.

REVLON, INC. v. MACANDREWS AND FORBES HOLDINGS, INC.
506 A.2d 173 (Del. 1986)

MOORE, J.:

[The Revlon board's focus on its agreement with Forstmann on] shoring up the sagging market value of the Notes in the face of threatened litigation . . . was inconsistent with . . . the directors' responsibilities at this stage of the developments. The impending waiver of the Notes covenants had caused the value of the Notes to fall, and the board was aware of the noteholders' ire as well as their subsequent threats of suit. The directors thus made support of the Notes an integral part of the company's dealings with Forstmann, even though their primary responsibility at this stage was to the equity owners.

The original threat posed by Pantry Pride — the break-up of the company — had become a reality which even the directors embraced. Selective dealing to fend off a hostile but determined bidder was no longer a proper objective. Instead, obtaining the highest price for the benefit of the stockholders should have been the central theme guiding director action. Thus, the Revlon board could not make the requisite showing of good faith by preferring the noteholders and ignoring its duty of loyalty to the shareholders. The rights of the former already were fixed by contract. . . . The noteholders required no further protection, and when the Revlon board entered into an auction-ending lock-up agreement with Forstmann on the basis of impermissible considerations at the expense of the shareholders, the directors breached their primary duty of loyalty.

The Revlon board argued that it acted in good faith in protecting the noteholders because *Unocal* permits consideration of other corporate constituencies. Although such considerations may be permissible, there are fundamental limitations upon that prerogative. A board may have regard for various constituencies in discharging its responsibilities, provided there are rationally related benefits accruing to the stockholders. *Unocal*, 493 A.2d at 955. However, such concern for non-stockholder interests is inappropriate when an auction among active bidders is in progress, and the object no longer is to protect or maintain the corporate enterprise but to sell it to the highest bidder.

Revlon also contended that . . . it had contractual and good faith obligations to consider the noteholders. However, any such duties are limited to the principle that one may not interfere with contractual relationships by improper actions. Here, the rights of the noteholders were fixed by agreement, and there is nothing of substance to suggest that any of those terms were violated. The Notes covenants specifically contemplated a waiver to permit sale of the company at a fair price. The Notes were accepted by the holders on that basis, including the risk of an adverse market effect stemming from a waiver. Thus, nothing remained for Revlon to legitimately protect, and no rationally related benefit thereby accrued to the stockholders. Under such circumstances we must conclude that the merger agreement with Forstmann was unreasonable in relation to the threat posed.

A lock-up is not per se illegal under Delaware law. . . . Current economic conditions in the takeover market are such that a "white knight" like Forstmann might only enter the bidding for the target company if it receives some form of compensation to cover the risks and costs involved. . . . However, while those lock-ups which draw bidders into the battle benefit shareholders, similar measures which end an active auction and foreclose further bidding operate to the shareholders' detriment. . . .

Recently, the United States Court of Appeals for the Second Circuit invalidated a lock-up on fiduciary duty grounds similar to those here. *Hanson Trust PLC, et al. v. ML SCM Acquisition Inc., et al.*, 781 F.2d 264 (2d Cir. 1986). . . .

In *Hanson Trust*, the bidder, Hanson, sought control of SCM by a hostile cash tender offer. SCM management joined with Merrill Lynch to propose a leveraged buy-out of the company at a higher price, and Hanson in turn increased its offer. Then, despite very little improvement in its subsequent bid, the management group sought a lock-up option to purchase SCM's two main assets at a substantial discount. The SCM directors granted the lock-up without adequate information as to the size of the discount or the effect the transaction would have on the company. Their action effectively ended a competitive bidding situation. The *Hanson* Court invalidated the lock-up because the directors failed to fully inform themselves about the value of a transaction in which management had a strong self-interest. . . .

The Forstmann option had a similar destructive effect on the auction process. Forstmann had already been drawn into the contest on a preferred basis, so the result of the lock-up was not to foster bidding, but to destroy it. The board's stated reasons for approving the transaction were: (1) better financing, (2) noteholder protection, and (3) higher price. As the Court of Chancery found, and we agree, any distinctions between the rival bidders' methods of financing the proposal were nominal at best, and such a consideration has little or no significance in a cash offer for any and all shares. The principal object, contrary to the board's duty of care, appears to have been protection of the noteholders over the shareholders' interests.

While Forstmann's $57.25 offer was objectively higher than Pantry Pride's $56.25 bid, the margin of superiority is less when the Forstmann price is adjusted for the time value of money. In reality, the Revlon board ended the auction in return for very little actual improvement in the final bid. The principal benefit went to the directors, who avoided personal liability to a class of creditors to whom the board owed no further duty under the circumstances. Thus, when a board ends an intense bidding contest on an insubstantial basis, and where a significant by-product of that action is to protect the directors against a perceived threat of personal liability for consequences stemming from the adoption of previous defensive measures, the action cannot withstand the enhanced scrutiny which *Unocal* requires of director conduct. See *Unocal*, 493 A.2d at 954-55.

In addition to the lock-up option, the Court of Chancery enjoined the no-shop provision as part of the attempt to foreclose further bidding by Pantry Pride. *MacAndrews & Forbes Holdings, Inc. v. Revlon, Inc.*, 501 A.2d at 1251. The no-shop provision, like the lock-up option, while not per se illegal, is impermissible under the *Unocal* standards when a board's primary duty becomes that of an auctioneer responsible for selling the company to the highest bidder. The agreement to negotiate only with Forstmann ended rather than intensified the board's involvement in the bidding contest.

It is ironic that the parties even considered a no-shop agreement when Revlon had dealt preferentially, and almost exclusively, with Forstmann throughout the contest. After the directors authorized management to negotiate with other parties, Forstmann was given every negotiating advantage that Pantry Pride had been denied: cooperation from management, access to financial data, and the exclusive opportunity to present merger proposals directly to the board of directors. Favoritism for a white knight to the total exclusion of a hostile bidder might be justifiable when the latter's offer adversely affects shareholder interests, but when bidders make relatively similar offers, or dissolution of the company becomes inevitable, the directors cannot fulfill their enhanced *Unocal* duties by playing favorites with the contending factions. Market forces must be allowed to operate freely to bring the target's shareholders the best price available for their equity.[16] Thus, as the trial court ruled, the shareholders' interests necessitated that the board remain free to negotiate in the fulfillment of that duty.

The court below similarly enjoined the payment of the cancellation fee, pending a resolution of the merits, because the fee was part of the overall plan to thwart Pantry Pride's efforts. We find no abuse of discretion in that ruling. . . .

In conclusion, the Revlon board was confronted with a situation not uncommon in the current wave of corporate takeovers. A hostile and determined bidder sought the company at a price the board was convinced was inadequate. The initial defensive tactics worked to the benefit of the shareholders, and thus the board was able to sustain its *Unocal* burdens in justifying those measures. However, in granting an asset option lock-up to Forstmann, we must conclude that under all the circumstances the directors allowed considerations other than the maximization of shareholder profit to affect their judgment, and followed a course that ended the auction for Revlon, absent court intervention, to the ultimate detriment of its shareholders. No such defensive measure can be sustained when it represents a breach of the directors' fundamental duty of

---

16. The directors' role remains an active one, changed only in the respect that they are charged with the duty of selling the company at the highest price attainable for the stockholders' benefit.

care. See *Smith v. Van Gorkom*, Del. Supr., 488 A.2d 858, 874 (1985). In that context the board's action is not entitled to the deference accorded it by the business judgment rule. The measures were properly enjoined. . . .

RONALD PERELMAN & TED FORSTMANN

Born into a wealthy Philadelphia family, Ron Perelman sat in on his father's board meetings as a child and pored over financial statements in his teenage years. After graduating from the University of Pennsylvania's Wharton School, he learned the art of dealmaking while working for his father. In 1978, he moved to Manhattan with no job, but big ambitions. He started by acquiring Hatfield Jewelers and turning it around by selling off many of its underperforming assets. His investment holding company, MacAndrews & Forbes, proceeded to acquire several other companies, including Marvel Comics, First Nationwide Bank, Panavision, and Technicolor. Early on he developed a relationship with "junk bond king" Michael Milken, who financed many of his acquisitions, including Revlon. By installing new management, disposing of assets, and then selling firms at a profit, he became a billionaire. On Wall Street, he was known for his exceptionally aggressive style.

Ted Forstmann graduated from Yale and Columbia Law School, and eventually formed Forstmann Little in 1978. The firm, an innovator in leveraged buyouts, became enormously profitable by buying and selling companies such as Dr. Pepper Co. When junk bonds became popular, however, Forstmann increasingly found himself losing out on deals because he could not raise as much money as junk bond–financed competitors. Forstmann publicly extolled his "old-fashioned" approach to business, which involved avoiding junk bond financing and maintaining good relations with the management of acquired companies. In a column for the *Wall Street Journal* in 1988, he attacked the junk bond industry, writing that "today's financial age has become a period of unbridled excess with accepted risk soaring out of proportion to possible reward."

QUESTIONS AND NOTES ON REVLON

1. What fiduciary duty did Revlon's board violate — a duty of care or a duty of loyalty?

2. According to the court in *Revlon*, what must a board do when it is committed to entering an acquisition transaction with one of two suitors who are locked in a competitive bidding contest? Does your answer imply that Delaware law is ultimately committed to shareholder primacy in board decision making, notwithstanding the dicta in *Unocal* allowing boards to consider nonshareholder interests in evaluating the threat posed by a hostile takeover?

3. In the 1989 case *Barkan v. Amsted Industries, Inc.*,[29] the Delaware Supreme Court clarified the substantive requirements imposed by *Revlon*. The court affirmed the lower court holding that there is no single template

---

29. 567 A.2d 1279 (Del. 1989).

required when selling a company. The classic *Revlon* case occurs when two bidders are engaged in a bidding contest for the target. Here, as in *Revlon* itself, "the directors may not use defensive tactics that destroy the auction process. [F]airness forbids directors from using defensive mechanisms to thwart an auction or to favor one bidder over another."[30] But what if there is only a single bidder at the table? The *Barkan* court stated that the essence of the *Revlon* requirement is that a board be well informed. An auction is a very good way to know what the company is worth, but not the only or the required way. Before becoming bound, the board may engage in a so-called market check to see if a higher bid is available, unless "the directors possess a body of reliable evidence with which to evaluate the fairness of a transaction."[31] Such a check may occur post-signing of the deal provided that the deal does not place serious impediments to the emergence of a higher valuing buyer, such as an unreasonable termination fee (discussed below). We discuss the substance of so-called *Revlon* review in Section 13.6.

4. "*Revlon*" questions haunted Delaware law for years: What *are Revlon* duties specifically; just what do they require, and when are they triggered? It took years of litigation for the confusion to gradually lift. It is now established that *Revlon* created no new duties but dealt with a modified standard of judicial review of the duties of care and loyalty in a particular context.

5. In the 2001 case *In re Pennaco Energy, Inc.* 787 A.2d 691 (Del. Ch. 2001), the board negotiated exclusively with Marathon Oil and reached an agreement at $19 cash per share, with a 3 percent breakup fee and a right for Marathon to match any higher offer that might emerge. Despite the absence of any pre-signing market check of the company, the Court of Chancery found that the target directors had met their *Revlon* duties on the theory that the relatively modest breakup fee and chance for others to come in were they interested in paying more was one reasonable way to sell the business. *Pennaco* shows that while *Revlon* continues to be the brand name opinion, the spirit of *Barkan v. Amsted* captures far better the approach to change of control duties that courts tend to take. See below also for the latest word in the Delaware Supreme Court's 2014 opinion in *C&J Energy Services, Inc. v. City of Miami Employees Union* in Section 13.6.

13.5   PULLING TOGETHER *UNOCAL* AND *REVLON*

During this evolutionary period, whether a hostile takeover succeeded came down to whether the incumbent board eventually gave in under shareholder pressure or the Delaware courts ordered the company's poison pill be redeemed, which happened in the late 1980s, but very rarely. A much-discussed Delaware Supreme Court decision of 1989, *Paramount Communications, Inc. v. Time, Inc.*, addressed both the question of whether the board has a duty to redeem its poison pill and the issue of what triggers

---

30. Id. at 1286-1287.
31. Id. at 1287.

Revlon duties. Discussion of the first issue was dicta, since *Time, Inc.*, the corporate defendant, had not relied on its poison pill to defend against a hostile attack by Paramount Communications, Inc. That characterization, however, detracts little from the force of the court's statements.

PARAMOUNT COMMUNICATIONS, INC. v. TIME, INC.
571 A.2d 1140 (Del. 1989)

[Paramount Communications' unsuccessful bid for Time, Inc. was perhaps the most famous hostile takeover attempt of the 1980s. In brief, Paramount launched its bid after Time had already initiated a friendly merger transaction with Warner Communications. Time succeeded in thwarting Paramount by transforming its original merger deal into a tender offer by Time for Warner, thereby making itself too large (and debt-ridden) to be an attractive target for Paramount. Prior to Time's tender offer, both Paramount and several groups of Time's shareholders sought to enjoin the tender offer in order to give Time's shareholders an opportunity to choose between this offer and Paramount's bid. The Delaware Court of Chancery recognized that Time's shareholders apparently preferred the higher price offered by the Paramount deal but nonetheless refused to enjoin Time's tender offer, on the grounds that, since Time's board was not under a *Revlon* duty to optimize Time's current stock value, the board had acted reasonably in pursuing its long-term plan to create business value.

The facts of the case were as follows. Time's long-term business strategy was to expand from a publishing company into a diversified multimedia and entertainment company. Pursuant to this strategy, Time initiated merger negotiations with Warner Communications. As both companies were in the $10-$12 billion range, the proposed combination was to be a "merger of equals." The negotiations were protracted. The chief sticking points were the management structure of the combined company and the role that Steven Ross, Warner's extraordinarily successful CEO, would play in the new entity.

On March 3, 1989, the parties signed a stock-for-stock merger agreement that cast Time in the role of the surviving corporation but would have transferred 62 percent of Time's common stock to Warner shareholders at an exchange ratio reflecting the current market price of the shares in the two firms (i.e., Warner had a somewhat larger market capitalization). The agreement also provided that the surviving corporation would be renamed Time-Warner Corporation, would have an expanded board to be divided equally between the old Time and Warner directors, and would have shared management with a succession plan. Under the management arrangement, there would be co-CEOs for a period of five years. One would be from the Time organization (Nicholas) and one from the Warner organization (Ross). After the five-year period, Ross would retire and Nicholas would continue as the sole CEO. Ross received a compensation package valued at roughly $200 million. Thus, Time bargained hard to assure the ultimate ascendancy of its managers in the combined firm. A final provision of the agreement gave each party the option to trigger a share exchange in which Time would receive

9.4 percent of Warner's stock and Warner would receive 11.1 percent of Time's stock. The purpose of this option was to deter third-party bids for Time or Warner prior to the merger vote.

On June 7, 1989, Paramount announced a $175 per share cash bid for all of Time's shares, contingent on the termination of the share exchange agreement, the redemption of Time's poison pill, and the resolution of legal difficulties attending the transfer of Time properties to Paramount. Paramount's offer came two weeks before Time's shareholders were scheduled to vote on the Warner merger. Time's shares had traded at a high of $50 prior to the Warner merger agreement and $122 prior to Paramount's offer. After Paramount's offer, they jumped to a high of $188/share.

Time's board rejected Paramount's price as grossly inadequate and concluded that the Warner deal was a better vehicle for Time's strategic goals. On June 16, Wasserstein, Perella, Time's investment banker, informed Time's board that a "control market value" for Time would exceed $250/share, although an earlier Wasserstein valuation conducted in connection with the Time-Warner agreement had valued Time at between $189 and $212 per share. In addition, Wasserstein estimated that Time's stock would trade at between $106 and $188 if the Time-Warner combination succeeded.

Having rejected Paramount's offer, however, Time's management faced a dilemma: It had planned the stock-for-stock merger that required a shareholder vote. But if Time's shareholders were to vote, they would almost certainly reject the proposed merger in the hope of tendering into the higher Paramount offer. Therefore, Time and Warner abandoned their merger agreement and agreed that Time would make a friendly cash tender offer to Warner shareholders and that, following the closing of that offer, a merger between Time and Warner would be effectuated. The governance terms in the new Time-Warner agreement were identical to those in the old agreement. The chief difference was that Time was forced to borrow $10 billion to purchase Warner shares at a 56 percent cash premium over their preagreement market price.

As a result of various delays that were caused by Paramount getting regulatory approval to acquire Time's programming and cable TV franchises, Paramount could not pursue its offer for Time immediately. On June 22, Paramount increased its cash offer to $200/share in the hope of dissuading Time from buying Warner, but to no avail. Paramount then sought to enjoin Time's offer in the Delaware Chancery Court, where it was joined by several groups of Time shareholders also seeking to block Time's maneuver. It was clear that if Time's offer went forward, Paramount would lack the incentive and the resources to bid for the heavily indebted Time-Warner entity that would emerge.

Here we pick up the Delaware Supreme Court's opinion after the statement of facts.]

HORSEY, J.:

The Shareholder Plaintiffs first assert a *Revlon* claim. They contend that the March 4 Time-Warner [Original Stock-for-Stock Merger] agreement effectively put Time up for sale, triggering *Revlon* duties, requiring Time's board to enhance short-term shareholder value and to treat all other interested acquirers on an equal basis. The Shareholder Plaintiffs base this argument on two facts: (i) the ultimate Time-Warner exchange ratio of .465 favoring Warner, resulting in Warner shareholders' receipt of 62% of the combined company; and (ii) the subjective intent of Time's directors as evidenced in their statements that the market might perceive the Time-Warner merger as putting Time up "for sale" and their adoption of various defensive measures.

The Shareholder Plaintiffs further contend that Time's directors, in structuring the original merger transaction to be "takeover-proof," triggered *Revlon* duties by foreclosing their shareholders from any prospect of obtaining a control premium. In short, plaintiffs argue that Time's board's decision to merge with Warner imposed a fiduciary duty to maximize immediate share value and not erect unreasonable barriers to further bids. . . .

Paramount asserts only a *Unocal* claim in which the shareholder plaintiffs join. Paramount contends that the Chancellor, in applying the first part of the *Unocal* test, erred in finding that Time's board had reasonable grounds to believe that Paramount posed both a legally cognizable threat to Time shareholders and a danger to Time's corporate policy and effectiveness. Paramount also contests the court's finding that Time's board made a reasonable and objective investigation of Paramount's offer so as to be informed before rejecting it. Paramount further claims that the court erred in applying *Unocal*'s second part in finding Time's response to be "reasonable." Paramount points primarily to the preclusive effect of the revised agreement which denied Time shareholders the opportunity both to vote on the agreement and to respond to Paramount's tender offer. Paramount argues that the underlying motivation of Time's board in adopting these defensive measures was management's desire to perpetuate itself in office.

The Court of Chancery posed the pivotal question presented by this case to be: Under what circumstances must a board of directors abandon an in-place plan of corporate development in order to provide its shareholders with the option to elect and realize an immediate control premium? . . .

While we affirm the result reached by the Chancellor, we think it unwise to place undue emphasis upon long-term versus short-term corporate strategy. Two key predicates underpin our analysis. First, Delaware law imposes on a board of directors the duty to manage the business and affairs of the corporation. 8 Del. C. §141(a). This broad mandate includes a conferred authority to set a corporate course of action, including time frame, designed to enhance corporate profitability. Thus, the question of "long-term" versus "short-term" values is largely irrelevant because directors, generally, are obliged to charter a course for a corporation which is in its best interest without regard to a fixed investment horizon. Second, absent a limited set of circumstances as defined under *Revlon,* a board of directors, while always required to act in an informed manner, is not under any per se duty to maximize shareholder value in the short term, even in the context of a takeover. In our view, the pivotal question presented by this case is: "Did Time, by entering into the proposed merger with Warner, put itself up for sale?" A resolution of that issue through application of *Revlon* has a significant [b]earing upon the resolution of the derivative *Unocal* issue. . . .

We first take up plaintiffs' principal *Revlon* argument, summarized above. In rejecting this argument, the Chancellor found the original Time-Warner merger agreement not to constitute a "change of control" and concluded that the transaction did not trigger *Revlon* duties. The Chancellor's conclusion is premised on a finding that "[b]efore the merger agreement was signed, control of the corporation existed in a fluid aggregation of unaffiliated shareholders representing a voting majority — in other words, in the market." The Chancellor's findings of fact are supported by the record and his conclusion is correct as a matter of law. However, we premise our rejection of plaintiffs' *Revlon* claim on different grounds, namely, the absence of any substantial evidence to conclude that Time's board, in negotiating with Warner, made the dissolution or breakup of the corporate entity inevitable, as was the case in *Revlon.*

Under Delaware law there are, generally speaking and without excluding other possibilities, two circumstances which may implicate *Revlon* duties. The first, and clearer one, is when a corporation initiates an active bidding process seeking to sell itself or to effect a business reorganization involving a clear break-up of the company. . . . However, *Revlon* duties may also be triggered where, in response to a bidder's offer, a target abandons its long-term strategy and seeks an alternative transaction also involving the breakup of the company. Thus, in *Revlon,* when the board responded to Pantry Pride's offer by contemplating a "bust-up" sale of assets in a leveraged acquisition, we imposed upon the board a duty to maximize immediate shareholder value and an obligation to auction the company fairly. If, however, the board's reaction to a hostile tender offer is found to constitute only a defensive response and not an abandonment of the corporation's continued existence, *Revlon* duties are not triggered, though *Unocal* duties attach. . . .

Finally, we do not find in Time's recasting of its merger agreement with Warner from a share exchange to a share purchase a basis to conclude that Time had either abandoned its strategic plan or made a sale of Time inevitable. The Chancellor found that although the merged Time-Warner company would be large (with a value approaching approximately $30 billion), recent takeover cases have proven that acquisition of the combined company might nonetheless be possible. The legal consequence is that *Unocal* alone applies to determine whether the business judgment rule attaches to the revised agreement. . . .

We turn now to plaintiffs' *Unocal* claim. . . .

. . . Time's decision in 1988 to combine with Warner was made only after what could be fairly characterized as an exhaustive appraisal of Time's future as a corporation. After concluding in 1983-84 that the corporation must expand to survive, and beyond journalism into entertainment, the board combed the field of available entertainment companies. By 1987 Time had focused upon Warner; by late July 1988 Time's board was convinced that Warner would provide the best "fit" for Time to achieve its strategic objectives. The record attests to the zealousness of Time's executives, fully supported by their directors, in seeing to the preservation of Time's "culture," i.e., its perceived editorial integrity in journalism. We find ample evidence in the record to support the Chancellor's conclusion that the Time board's decision to expand the business of the company through its March 3 merger with Warner was entitled to the protection of the business judgment rule. . . .

The Chancellor reached a different conclusion in addressing the Time-Warner transaction as revised three months later. He found that the revised agreement was defense-motivated. . . . Thus, the court . . . analyzed the Time board's June 16 decision under *Unocal.* The court ruled that *Unocal* applied to all director actions taken, following receipt of Paramount's hostile tender offer, that were reasonably determined to be defensive. Clearly that was a correct ruling. . . .

Unocal involved a two-tier, highly coercive tender offer. In such a case, the threat is obvious: shareholders may be compelled to tender to avoid being treated adversely in the second stage of the transaction. . . .

Since Paramount's offer was [not two-tier, but all-shares and] all-cash, the only conceivable "threat," plaintiffs argue, was inadequate value. We disapprove of such a narrow and rigid construction of *Unocal,* for the reasons which follow.

Plaintiffs' position represents a fundamental misconception of our standard of review under *Unocal* principally because it would involve the court in substituting its judgment as to what is a "better" deal for that of a corporation's board of directors. To the extent that the Court of Chancery has recently done so in certain of its opinions, we hereby reject such approach as not in keeping with a proper *Unocal* analysis. See, e.g., *Interco*, 551 A.2d 787, and its progeny. . . .

The usefulness of *Unocal* as an analytical tool is precisely its flexibility in the face of a variety of fact scenarios. *Unocal* is not intended as an abstract standard; neither is it a structured and mechanistic procedure of appraisal. Thus, we have said that directors may consider, when evaluating the threat posed by a takeover bid, the "inadequacy of the price offered, nature and timing of the offer, questions of illegality, the impact on 'constituencies' other than shareholders, the risk of nonconsummation and the quality of securities being offered in the exchange." 493 A.2d at 955. The open-ended analysis mandated by *Unocal* is not intended to lead to a simple mathematical exercise: that is, of comparing the discounted value of Time-Warner's expected trading price at some future date with Paramount's offer and determining which is the higher. Indeed, in our view, precepts underlying the business judgment rule militate against a court's engaging in the process of attempting to appraise and evaluate the relative merits of a long-term versus a short-term investment goal for shareholders. To engage in such an exercise is a distortion of the *Unocal* process and, in particular, the application of the second part of *Unocal*'s test, discussed below.

In this case, the Time board reasonably determined that inadequate value was not the only legally cognizable threat that Paramount's all-cash, all-shares offer could present. Time's board concluded that Paramount's eleventh hour offer posed other threats. One concern was that Time shareholders might elect to tender into Paramount's cash offer in ignorance or a mistaken belief of the strategic benefit which a business combination with Warner might produce. Moreover, Time viewed the conditions attached to Paramount's offer as introducing a degree of uncertainty that skewed a comparative analysis.

Further, the timing of Paramount's offer to follow issuance of Time's proxy notice was viewed as arguably designed to upset, if not confuse, the Time stockholders' vote. Given this record evidence, we cannot conclude that the Time board's decision of June 6 that Paramount's offer posed a threat to corporate policy and effectiveness was lacking in good faith or dominated by motives of either entrenchment or self-interest. . . .

We turn to the second part of the *Unocal* analysis. . . . As applied to the facts of this case, the question is whether the record evidence supports the Court of Chancery's conclusion that the restructuring of the Time-Warner transaction, including the adoption of several preclusive defensive measures, was a reasonable response in relation to a perceived threat.

Paramount argues that, assuming its tender offer posed a threat, Time's response was unreasonable in precluding Time's shareholders from accepting the tender offer or receiving a control premium in the immediately foreseeable future. Once again, the contention stems, we believe, from a fundamental misunderstanding of where the power of corporate governance lies. Delaware law confers the management of the corporate enterprise to the stockholders' duly elected board representatives. The fiduciary duty to manage a corporate enterprise includes the selection of a time frame for achievement of corporate goals. That duty may not be delegated to the stockholders. Directors are not obliged to abandon a deliberately conceived corporate plan for a short-term shareholder profit unless there is clearly no basis to sustain the corporate strategy. See, e.g., *Revlon*, 506 A.2d 173.

Although the Chancellor blurred somewhat the discrete analyses required under *Unocal,* he did conclude that Time's board reasonably perceived Paramount's offer to be a significant threat to the planned Time-Warner merger and that Time's response was not "overly broad." . . .

. . . Time's responsive action to Paramount's tender offer was not aimed at "cramming down" on its shareholders a management-sponsored alternative, but rather had as its goal the carrying forward of a pre-existing transaction in an altered form. Thus, the response was reasonably related to the threat. The Chancellor noted that the revised agreement and its accompanying safety devices did not preclude Paramount from making an offer for the combined Time-Warner company or from changing the conditions of its offer so as not to make the offer dependent upon the nullification of the Time-Warner agreement. Thus, the response was proportionate. We affirm the Chancellor's rulings as clearly supported by the record. . . .

QUESTIONS AND NOTES ON TIME-WARNER

1. Under *Time-Warner*'s restatement of the *Unocal* doctrine, can a hostile bidder ever force management to redeem a poison pill that is said to protect a company's existing business plan? Does it matter whether the business plan appears to constitute a "break-up" of the company as it has existed, such as those in *Interco*? Does it matter whether the plan was in place prior to the offer?

2. *Time-Warner* might be read to imply that a board may maintain a pill defense indefinitely whenever it is pursuing an established business plan, but it fears that shareholders might "mistakenly" conclude that a hostile offer is fairly priced. Can this view be reconciled with *Time-Warner*'s repudiation of *Interco,* in which the Chancery Court had pulled the pill after the company's board had abandoned its prior business plan in order to pursue a leveraged recapitalization (little different from what the hostile bidder proposed).[32]

3. Does a board's fiduciary duty to be informed require it to negotiate with every plausible acquirer that approaches the corporation with a takeover proposal? Since the dominant view among practitioners, managers, and politicians during the 1980s was that there were too many takeovers,[33] it is hardly surprising that the Delaware courts did not construe the duty of care or the duty to be informed in this way. That is, a board that had decided that its company was not for sale could "just say no" without negotiating with would-be acquirers.[34]

4. *Air Products & Chemicals v. Airgas, Inc.,* 16 A.3d 48 (Del. Ch. 2011) is one of latest cases to examine pill redemption. In February 2010, after its friendly overtures were rebuffed, Air Products launched a hostile tender offer for its competitor Airgas, initially at $60 cash per share and eventually reaching $70 as a "best and final" price. The Airgas board rejected these offers, claiming that Airgas was worth at least $78 per share. (Airgas had been trading in the $40s and $50s for most of 2007-2008. Between October 2009 and January 2011, Airgas's stock price ranged from a low of $41.64 to a high of $71.28.) Airgas had a poison pill with a 15 percent trigger and a three-class staggered board comprised of nine members. At the September 2010 Airgas annual meeting, Air Products successfully replaced three Airgas directors with its own nominees. In what was a stunning development, once they joined the board, all three of the new directors, advised by their own bankers and lawyers, agreed with the incumbent directors that the Air Products $70 per share offer was inadequate. The pill stayed in place. Air Products filed a motion in its pending Delaware Chancery Court suit against the Airgas board seeking an injunction against all of the Airgas defenses that impeded its offer from being acted upon by the Airgas shareholders. While expressing personal misgivings about the continued use of a pill against a structurally non-coercive, all-cash offer, Chancellor Chandler upheld Airgas's use of the

---

32. The *Time-Warner* court added at the end of the excerpt reproduced above that "we have found that even in light of a valid threat, management actions that are coercive in nature or force upon shareholders a management-sponsored alternative to a hostile offer may be struck down as unreasonable and non-proportionate responses" (citing *Mills Acquisition Co. v. Macmillan, Inc.*, 559 A.2d 1261 (Del. 1989), and *AC Acquisition Corp.*, 519 A.2d 103 (Del. Ch. 1986)).

33. This was not, of course, the dominant view among financial economists or corporate law professors.

34. That is, boards have the legal power to "just say no" under Delaware case law. As managers in both *Unocal* and *Revlon* learned, however, as a practical matter it may be impossible to say no without offering shareholders an alternative transaction designed to give value comparable to what the acquirer offers.

poison pill: "[T]here seems to be no threat here—the stockholders know what they need to know (about both the offer and the Airgas board's opinion of the offer) to make an informed decision. That being said, however, as I understand binding Delaware precedent, I may not substitute my business judgment for that of the Airgas board. [citing *Unitrin* and *Time-Warner*]."[35] The Chancellor also observed in a footnote: "Our law would be more credible if the Supreme Court acknowledged that its later rulings have modified *Moran* and have allowed a board acting in good faith (and with a reasonable basis for believing that a tender offer is inadequate) to remit the bidder to the election process as its only recourse. The tender offer is in fact precluded and the only bypass of the pill is electing a new board. If that is the law, it would be best to be honest and abandon the pretense that preclusive action is *per se* unreasonable."[36]

Air Products then dropped its offer and over the following year the stock of the target Airgas outperformed the stock of Air Products by a significant margin. In 2015 Airgas agreed to be acquired by a European company for $143 a share.

5. On the *Revlon* side of the *Unocal-Revlon* doctrinal dichotomy, the Delaware Supreme Court in *Time-Warner* appeared to reject the change-in-control test as the trigger for invoking judicial scrutiny. But stay tuned—the moving hand writes, and having written . . ., sometimes writes again. The next chapter in Delaware's law of corporate takeovers, the *QVC* case, which follows, returns to the sale-of-control test for *Revlon* duties.

PARAMOUNT COMMUNICATIONS, INC. v. QVC NETWORK, INC.
637 A.2d 34 (Del. 1994)

[This case features another instance of the Media Industry merger battles which started in the 1980s. This time Paramount is the target firm and the potential acquirers are Viacom (controlled and run by Sumner Redstone) and QVC, whose CEO—Barry Diller—was once CEO of Paramount. Of these three firms only Viacom had a controlling shareholder. The original Paramount-Viacom deal had Viacom making a blended cash and stock offer to acquire Paramount for around $69 per share. The deal had a number of other important terms including (i) a "No-Shop" provision which prohibited Paramount from negotiating or discussing a deal with an alternative bidder unless it was an unsolicited written offer with no financing contingencies and Paramount's Board considered negotiating/discussing necessary to comply with its fiduciary duties; (ii) a termination fee of $100 million if the deal fails for certain specified reasons; and (iii) a Stock Option Plan (SOP), triggered by the same conditions as the termination fee, which grants Viacom the option to purchase 19.9% of Paramount stock at about $69 per share. The SOP was

---

35. *Air Products & Chemicals v. Airgas, Inc.*, 16 A.3d 48 (Del. Ch. 2011).
36. Id. at 122 n.480.

unusual in that it allowed Viacom to either pay for the shares with a note (the "Note Feature") or to have Paramount pay Viacom cash in the amount of the difference between the then-prevailing market price and $69 (the "Put Feature"). The combined effect of these terms was to protect and facilitate the Paramount-Viacom deal and dissuade other suitors.

Yet, QVC was undeterred and offered $80 per share (blended cash and stock) thereby triggering a contest for Paramount. After QVC provided evidence that it would meet the financing contingency, Paramount's board hired Booz-Allen & Hamilton (a management consulting firm) to advise it on the sale. QVC soon thereafter filed suit and publicly announced its $80 per share bid. Paramount then renegotiated a higher offer from Viacom to match QVC's $80, but with no let down in the deal protections. Soon thereafter Viacom amended its offer, seemingly on its own, to $85 per share and QVC responded with a $90 per share offer conditional on removing the SOP. Paramount's board decided to go with Viacom's offer citing too many conditionalities in the QVC bid. The Court of Chancery issued a preliminary injunction blocking some of the deal protections, which was appealed to the Delaware Supreme Court. We pick up with Chief Justice Veasey's discussion of the standard of review.—Eds.]

VEASEY, C.J.:

When a majority of a corporation's voting shares are acquired by a single person or entity, or by a cohesive group acting together, there is a significant diminution in the voting power of those who thereby become minority stockholders. . . .

. . . Absent effective protective provisions, minority stockholders must rely for protection solely on the fiduciary duties owed to them by the directors and the majority stockholder, since the minority stockholders have lost the power to influence corporate direction through the ballot. The acquisition of majority status and the consequent privilege of exerting the powers of majority ownership come at a price. That price is usually a control premium which recognizes not only the value of a control block of shares, but also compensates the minority stockholders for their resulting loss of voting power.

In the case before us, the public stockholders (in the aggregate) currently own a majority of Paramount's voting stock. Control of the corporation is not vested in a single person, entity, or group, but vested in the fluid aggregation of unaffiliated stockholders. In the event the Paramount-Viacom transaction is consummated, the public stockholders will receive cash and a minority equity voting position in the surviving corporation. Following such consummation, there will be a controlling stockholder who will [be able to determine many important aspects of corporate policy]. [Thus, i]rrespective of the present Paramount Board's vision of a long-term strategic alliance with Viacom, the proposed sale of control would provide the new controlling stockholder with the power to alter that vision.

Because of the intended sale of control, the Paramount-Viacom transaction has economic consequences of considerable significance to the Paramount stockholders. . . . Once control has shifted, the current Paramount stockholders will have no leverage in the future to demand another control premium. As a result, the Paramount stockholders are entitled to receive, and should receive, a control premium and/or protective devices of significant value. There being no such protective provisions in the Viacom-Paramount transaction, the Paramount directors had an obligation to take the maximum advantage of the current opportunity to realize for the stockholders the best value reasonably available.

[Because there were no such protective provisions] the directors must focus on one primary objective — to secure the transaction offering the best value reasonably available for the stockholders — and they must exercise their fiduciary duties to further that end. . . . Moreover, the role of outside, independent directors becomes particularly important because of the magnitude of a sale of control transaction and the possibility, in certain cases, that management may not necessarily be impartial. . . .

The *Barkan* [decision] teaches some of the methods by which a board can fulfill its obligation to seek the best value reasonably available to the stockholders. 567 A.2d at 1286-87. . . . They include conducting an auction, canvassing the market, etc. Delaware law recognizes that there is "no single blueprint" that directors must follow. . . .

In determining which alternative provides the best value for the stockholders, a board of directors is not limited to considering only the amount of cash involved. . . . Where stock or other non-cash consideration is involved, the board should try to quantify its value, if feasible, to achieve an objective comparison of the alternatives. . . . While the assessment of these factors may be complex, the board's goal is straightforward: Having informed themselves of all material information reasonably available, the directors must decide which alternative is most likely to offer the best value reasonably available to the stockholders. . . .

Board action in the circumstances presented here is subject to enhanced scrutiny. Such scrutiny is mandated by: (a) the threatened diminution of the current stockholders' voting power; (b) the fact that an asset belonging to public stockholders (a control premium) is being sold and may never be available again[;] and (c) the traditional concern of Delaware courts for actions which impair or impede stockholder voting rights. . . .

The key features of an enhanced scrutiny test are: (a) a judicial determination regarding the adequacy of the decisionmaking process employed by the directors, including the information on which the directors based their decision; and (b) a judicial examination of the reasonableness of the directors' action in light of the circumstances then existing. The directors have the burden of proving that they were adequately informed and acted reasonably.

Although an enhanced scrutiny test involves a review of the reasonableness of the substantive merits of a board's actions,[17] a court should not ignore the complexity of the directors' task in a sale of control. . . . Accordingly, a court applying enhanced judicial scrutiny should be deciding whether the directors made a reasonable decision, not a perfect decision. If a board selected one of

---

17. It is to be remembered that, in cases where the traditional business judgment rule is applicable and the board acted with due care, in good faith, and in the honest belief that they are acting in the best interests of the stockholder (which is not this case), the Court gives great deference to the substance of the directors' decision and will not invalidate the decision. . . .

several reasonable alternatives, a court should not second-guess that choice even though it might have decided otherwise or subsequent events may have cast doubt on the board's determinationThus, courts will not substitute their business judgment for that of the directors, but will determine if the directors' decision was, on balance, within a range of reasonableness. . . .

The Paramount defendants and Viacom assert that the fiduciary obligations and the enhanced judicial scrutiny discussed above are not implicated in this case in the absence of a "break-up" of the corporation. . . .

Although [the earlier] *Macmillan* and *Barkan* [decisions] are clear in holding that a change of control imposes on directors the obligation to obtain the best value reasonably available to the stockholders, the Paramount defendants have interpreted our decision in *Time-Warner* as requiring a corporate break-up in order for that obligation to apply. The facts in *Time-Warner*, however, were quite different from the facts of this case. . . . [However, i]n *Time-Warner*, the Chancellor held that there was no change of control in the original stock-for-stock merger between Time and Warner because Time would be owned by a fluid aggregation of unaffiliated stockholders both before and after the merger. . . .

In our affirmance of the Court of Chancery's well-reasoned decision, this Court held that "The Chancellor's findings of fact are supported by the record and *his conclusion is correct as a matter of law.*" 571 A.2d at 1150 (emphasis added). . . . Nevertheless, the Paramount defendants here have argued that a break-up is a requirement and have focused on the following language in our *Time-Warner* decision:

> Under Delaware law there are, generally speaking and without excluding other possibilities, two circumstances which may implicate *Revlon* duties. The first, and clearer one, is when a corporation initiates an active bidding process seeking to sell itself or to effect a business reorganization involving a clear breakup of the company. However, *Revlon* duties may also be triggered where, in response to a bidder's offer, a target abandons its long-term strategy and seeks an alternative transaction involving the breakup of the company. *Id.* at 1150 (emphasis added) (citation and footnote omitted).

The Paramount defendants have misread the holding of *Time-Warner*. Contrary to their argument, our decision in *Time-Warner* expressly states that the two general scenarios discussed in the above-quoted paragraph are not the only instances where "*Revlon* duties" may be implicated. The Paramount defendants' argument totally ignores the phrase "without excluding other possibilities." Moreover, the instant case is clearly within the first general scenario set forth in *Time-Warner*. The Paramount Board, albeit unintentionally, had "initiated an active bidding process seeking to sell itself" by agreeing to sell control of the corporation to Viacom in circumstances where another potential acquirer (QVC) was equally interested in being a bidder.

The Paramount defendants' position that both a change of control and a break-up are required must be rejected. Such a holding would unduly restrict the application of *Revlon*, is inconsistent with this Court's decisions in *Barkan* and *Macmillan*, and has no basis in policy. There are few events that have a more significant impact on the stockholders than a sale of control or a corporate break-up. Each event represents a fundamental (and perhaps irrevocable) change in the nature of the corporate enterprise from a practical standpoint. It is the significance of each of these events that justifies: (a) focusing on the directors' obligation to seek the best value reasonably available to the stockholders; and (b) requiring a close scrutiny of board action which could be contrary to the stockholders' interests.

Accordingly, when a corporation undertakes a transaction which will cause: (a) a change in corporate control; or (b) a break-up of the corporate entity, the directors' obligation is to seek the best value reasonably available to the stockholders. This obligation arises because the effect of the Viacom-Paramount transaction, if consummated, is to shift control of Paramount from the public stockholders to a controlling stockholder, Viacom. Neither *Time-Warner* nor any other decision of this Court holds that a "break-up" of the company is essential to give rise to this obligation where there is a sale of control. . . .

We now turn to duties of the Paramount Board under the facts of this case and our conclusions as to the breaches of those duties that warrant injunctive relief. . . .

Under the facts of this case, the Paramount directors had the obligation: (a) to be diligent and vigilant in examining critically the Paramount-Viacom transaction and the QVC tender offers; (b) to act in good faith; (c) to obtain, and act with due care on, all material information reasonably available, including information necessary to compare the two offers to determine which of these transactions, or an alternative course of action, would provide the best value reasonably available to the stockholders; and (d) to negotiate actively and in good faith with both Viacom and QVC to that end.

Having decided to sell control of the corporation, the Paramount directors were required to evaluate critically whether or not all material aspects of the Paramount-Viacom transaction (separately and in the aggregate) were reasonable and in the best interests of the Paramount stockholders in light of current circumstances, including: the change of control premium, the Stock Option Agreement, the Termination Fee, the coercive nature of both the Viacom and QVC tender offers,[18] the No-Shop Provision, and . . . [so forth].

These obligations necessarily implicated various issues, including the questions of whether or not those provisions . . . : (a) adversely affected the value provided to the Paramount stockholders; (b) inhibited or encouraged alternative bids; (c) were enforceable contractual obligations in light of the directors' fiduciary duties; and (d) in the end would advance or retard the Paramount directors' obligation to secure for the Paramount stockholders the best value reasonably available under the circumstances.

The Paramount defendants contend that they were precluded by certain contractual provisions including the No-Shop Provision, from negotiating

---

18. Both the Viacom and the QVC tender offers were for 51 percent cash and a "back-end" of various securities, the value of each of which depended on the fluctuating value of Viacom and QVC stock at any given time. Thus, both tender offers were two-tiered, front-end loaded, and coercive. Such coercive offers are inherently problematic and should be expected to receive particularly careful analysis by a target board. See *Unocal*, 493 A.2d at 956.

with QVC or seeking alternatives. Such provisions, whether or not they are presumptively valid in the abstract, may not validly define or limit the directors' fiduciary duties under Delaware law or prevent the Paramount directors from carrying out their fiduciary duties under Delaware law. To the extent such provisions are inconsistent with those duties, they are invalid and unenforceable. . . .

Since the Paramount directors had already decided to sell control, they had an obligation to continue their search for the best value reasonably available to the stockholders. This continuing obligation included the responsibility . . . to evaluate critically both the QVC tender offers and the Paramount-Viacom transaction to determine if . . . the QVC tender offer was, or would continue to be, conditional; [the QVC and Viacom offers could be improved; and other material matters relevant to obtaining the best value reasonably available to stockholders.] . . .

When entering into the Original Merger Agreement, and thereafter, the Paramount Board clearly gave insufficient attention to the potential consequences of the defensive measures demanded by Viacom [that had the effect of making Paramount less attractive to other bidders]. The Stock Option Agreement had a number of unusual and potentially "draconian."[19] The provisions, including the Note Feature and the Put Feature. Furthermore, the Termination Fee, whether or not unreasonable by itself, clearly made Paramount less attractive to other bidders, when coupled with the Stock Option Agreement. Finally, the No-Shop Provision inhibited the Paramount Board's ability to negotiate with other potential bidders, particularly QVC which had already expressed an interest in Paramount . . .

[Moreover, Paramount's board had multiple opportunities to renegotiate the Paramount-Viacom deal to obtain better terms for its shareholders.]

[I]t should have been clear to the Paramount Board that the Stock Option Agreement, coupled with the Termination Fee and the No-Shop Clause, were impeding the realization of the best value reasonably available to the Paramount stockholders. Nevertheless, the Paramount Board made no effort to eliminate or modify these counterproductive devices, and instead continued to cling to its vision of a strategic alliance with Viacom. Moreover, based on advice from the Paramount management, the Paramount directors considered the QVC offer to be "conditional" and asserted that they were precluded by the No-Shop Provision from seeking more information from, or negotiating with, QVC.

. . . [T]he value of the revised QVC offer on its face exceeded that of the Viacom offer by over $1 billion at then current values. This significant disparity of value cannot be justified on the basis of the directors' vision of future strategy, primarily because the change of control would supplant the authority of the current Paramount Board to continue to hold and implement their

19. The Vice Chancellor so characterized the Stock Option Agreement. Court of Chancery Opinion, 635 A.2d at 1272. We express no opinion whether a stock option agreement of essentially this magnitude, but with a reasonable "cap" and without the Note and Put Features, would be valid or invalid under other circumstances. . . .

strategic vision in any meaningful way. Moreover, their uninformed process had deprived their strategic vision of much of its credibility. . . .

When the Paramount directors met on November 15 to consider QVC's increased tender offer, they remained prisoners of their own misconceptions and missed opportunities to eliminate the restrictions they had imposed on themselves. Yet, it was not "too late" to reconsider negotiating with QVC. . . . Nevertheless, the Paramount directors remained paralyzed by their uninformed belief that the QVC offer was "illusory." This final opportunity to negotiate on the stockholders' behalf and to fulfill their obligation to seek the best value reasonably available was thereby squandered. . . .

Viacom argues that it had certain "vested" contract rights with respect to the No-Shop Provision and the Stock Option Agreement. In effect, Viacom's argument is that the Paramount directors could enter into an agreement in violation of their fiduciary duties and then render Paramount, and ultimately its stockholders, liable for failing to carry out an agreement in violation of those duties. Viacom's protestations about vested rights are without merit. This Court has found that those defensive measures were improperly designed to deter potential bidders, and that such measures do not meet the reasonableness test to which they must be subjected. They are consequently invalid and unenforceable under the facts of this case.

The No-Shop Provision could not validly define or limit the fiduciary duties of the Paramount directors. To the extent that a contract, or a provision thereof, purports to require a board to act or not act in such a fashion as to limit the exercise of fiduciary duties, it is invalid and unenforceable. . . .

Viacom, a sophisticated party with experienced legal and financial advisors, knew of (and in fact demanded) the unreasonable features of the Stock Option Agreement. It cannot be now heard to argue that it obtained vested contract rights by negotiating and obtaining contractual provisions from a board acting in violation of its fiduciary duties. . . .

The realization of the best value reasonably available to the stockholders became the Paramount directors' primary obligation under these facts in light of the change of control. That obligation was not satisfied, and the Paramount Board's process was deficient. The directors' initial hope and expectation for a strategic alliance with Viacom was allowed to dominate their decision-making process to the point where the arsenal of defensive measures established at the outset was perpetuated (not modified or eliminated) when the situation was dramatically altered. QVC's unsolicited bid presented the opportunity for significantly greater value for the stockholders and enhanced negotiating leverage for the directors. Rather than seizing those opportunities, the Paramount directors chose to wall themselves off from material information which was reasonably available and to hide behind the defensive measures as a rationalization for refusing to negotiate with QVC or seeking other alternatives. Their view of the strategic alliance likewise became an empty rationalization as the opportunities for higher value for the stockholders continued to develop.

For the reasons set forth herein, the . . . Order of the Court of Chancery has been AFFIRMED, and this matter has been REMANDED for proceedings consistent herewith. . . .

QUESTIONS AND NOTES ON PARAMOUNT v. QVC

1. Suppose Viacom had been widely held, without Sumner Redstone as its controlling shareholder. Would an acquisition agreement between Viacom and Paramount that provided for Viacom to make a cash tender offer for 51 percent of Paramount's shares, followed by a merger in which Paramount's remaining shareholders received Viacom stock, trigger *Revlon* duties on the part of Paramount's board?

2. Is there a policy justification for imposing *Revlon* duties on a target's board when a merger shifts control to a controlling shareholder, as in *Paramount v. QVC*, but not when control remains in a dispersed body of shareholders, as in *Time-Warner*? Suppose, as *QVC* suggests, that minority shareholders are, post-merger, in a vulnerable position when there is a controlling shareholder in the combined company. Can the target ameliorate this problem through contracting? See the 2014 case *C&J Energy Services, Inc.* below (bylaw requiring that the minority must get the same price as others in a future merger, amendable only unanimously).

3. What consequences follow from allowing managers more discretion to defend the corporation's independence under *Unocal* than to choose its acquirer under *Revlon*? Or is this characterization of the case law inaccurate?

4. In *Paramount v. QVC*, the Delaware Supreme Court went back to the Court of Chancery's *Time-Warner* "change-in-corporate-control" trigger to distinguish between *Revlon* and non-*Revlon* deals. That is, it drew the line at the point at which public shareholders are excluded from meaningful participation in governance in the combined company, by a controlling shareholder or otherwise. In applying this principle, courts might look to a de jure or de facto definition of control. In fact, the formation of a 30 percent block of voting stock probably represents the creation of a controlling shareholder in the combined company. Legally, however, control is not certain unless a large shareholder holds more than 50 percent of the company's outstanding stock. Since *QVC*'s analysis rests heavily on policy considerations, we would expect Delaware courts to gravitate toward a practical test for control rather than a formal one. Thus, *Revlon* duties are likely to be triggered when mergers create shareholdings with between 30 and 35 percent of the voting rights in widely held companies.

5. While far from completely clear, the change-in-control test carries a number of specific implications. The most obvious of these is that a stock-for-stock merger between two public companies with no controlling shareholders should not trigger *Revlon* duties. Instead, such a merger ought to be reviewed by courts under some form of the business judgment standard. In the *Time-Warner* merger litigation in 1989, the Court of Chancery held that the merger did not trigger *Revlon* review, but the court then went on to analyze the merger's deal protective aspects under the reasonableness (*Unocal*) version of the business judgment rule. More explicitly, the Delaware Supreme Court affirmed that stock-for-stock mergers do not trigger *Revlon* duties in *In re Santa Fe Pacific Corp. Shareholder Litigation*, 669 A.2d 59 (Del. 1995). There has been a split of opinion among practitioners whether deal protections in such a merger are entitled to "plain vanilla" business judgment review or

"enhanced" business judgment of *Unocal*. One influential Vice Chancellor has let us know his view in an encyclopedic review of Delaware takeover law.[37]

6. A second implication of the change-in-control test is that a cash merger generally triggers *Revlon* duties unless there is *already* a majority shareholder in the target company.[38] In a merger in which all, or a majority, of the public shareholders are cashed out of the enterprise, these public shareholders cannot participate in the long-term strategic value of the combination, no matter how successful it proves to be. Thus, the target's board must have a duty to maximize shareholder value today, not in the future.

7. *Paramount v. QVC* is unclear about how to evaluate board conduct when merger consideration is mixed. For example, suppose a target's board is offered 70 percent of the merger consideration in stock and 30 percent in cash (or the other way around). May the board accept such a deal and "lock it up" (see section on lock-ups) without doing a market check for a higher deal? More basically, what principle distinguishes those cases in which the board should exercise its own business judgment about long-term synergistic benefits of a possible merger and those in which the board must maximize current value? In *In re Smurfit-Stone Container Corp. Shareholder Litigation*,[39] the Delaware Chancery Court held that an approximately 50-50 cash/stock deal, in which the target company's shareholders would hold 45 percent of the combined company, did trigger *Revlon*, but that the target board had satisfied its *Revlon* duties despite no pre-signing canvass of the marketplace, a 3.4 percent termination fee, and a standard no-shop provision with a fiduciary out.[40]

PROBLEM

The stock of T Corp., a producer of audio components, sells for $12 a share on NASDAQ. It has a million shares outstanding and annual sales of $200 million. The stock of Xenor, Inc., a large conglomerate with total sales of $13 billion and sales in its audio division of $500 million, recently traded on the NYSE in the range of $40-$45 per share. Xenor has offered to acquire T in a

---

37. J. Travis Laster, *Revlon Is a Standard of Review: Why Its True and What It Means*, 19 Ford. J. Corp & Fin. L 5 (2013) (all changes in corporate control, if challenged, should be decided under a reasonableness review).

38. A majority shareholder has no obligation to sell her stock. See *Bershad v. Curtis Wright Corp.*, 535 A.2d 840 (Del. 1987). And a controller's desire to accomplish a cash-out of the minority does not obligate it to sell to a third party willing to pay more than it offers. *Mendel v. Carroll*, 651 A.2d 297 (Del. Ch. 1994) (third party must pay a control premium but controller need not do so as it already has control. Thus these bids are not apples to apples comparisons). But cf. *McMullin v. Beran*, 765 A.2d 910 (Del. 2000) (where controller negotiated a merger that paid all shareholders—itself and the small public minority—the same amount, target board's duty was to be informed concerning alternatives for shareholders).

39. 2011 WL 2028076 (Del. Ch. May 20, 2011).

40. See also *In re Santa Fe Pac. Corp. Shareholder Litigation*, 669 A.2d 59, 70-71 (Del. 1995) (transaction involving 33 percent cash did not trigger *Revlon* duties); *In re Lukens Inc. Shareholders Litigation*, 757 A.2d 720, 732 n.25 (Del. Ch. 1999) (suggesting that a deal with 62 percent cash would likely trigger *Revlon*).

merger. For each share of T, Xenor has offered the following consideration with an approximate total value of $14 per T share: 1/10 of a share of Xenor common stock, 1/4 of a share of a new redeemable preferred stock with a 5 percent dividend to be valued at $20 a share at issuance, and $4.50 in cash. Xenor has also offered T's CEO a position in its top management that she finds quite interesting.

Must T's board treat Xenor's proposal as an invitation to a *Revlon* trans-action? Cash represents only 33 percent of the total consideration — but the preferred stock portion of the merger consideration is redeemable and non-voting. On the other hand, Xenor itself is publicly owned, with no controlling shareholder.

Suppose further that T's board decides that *Revlon* does not apply and votes to protect the Xenor merger agreement with a large termination fee payable if it terminates the deal for a better one (under its fiduciary out) or its shareholders vote the deal down. Shortly thereafter a competitor, SoundsaLot, Inc., offers $15 cash per share for T shares, which T's board rejects because it finds the Xenor deal to be a better long-term "fit." The suit will attack the legality of the termination fee and the board's failure to remove it as a violation of its *Revlon* duty. Would you expect the court to hold that the board has an obligation to optimize present value in a shareholder suit seeking an injunction?

AN APPROACH TO THE PROBLEM

Consider the following approach to this problem. In our view, the rules that underlie *Revlon* duties turn on the assumption that, in most circumstances, boards of directors are better able to estimate long-term value of companies than are shareholders — *but* in some circumstances, such as when sharehold-ers will be cashed out of the post-merger enterprise, boards must maximize short-term value, since this is the only value that shareholders are likely to receive.[41] Since courts believe (implicitly) that, in an all-stock deal between two companies of the same size, the board has a substantial advantage over shareholders (and the market) in evaluating the long-term value of the surviv-ing company as well as the long-term value of the merger consideration to be received, courts will defer to the views of boards in these cases (recall that in such cases the shareholders themselves will in any case have to approve the merger by vote). A focus on informational advantage implies that the more the value of merger consideration depends on synergies between the target and the acquiring company (about which the directors have superior infor-mation), the more courts will defer to the judgment of T's directors. In cash deals, courts will not defer; in stock-for-stock mergers of equals, they will defer a great deal.

41. For an elaboration and critique of this account of the judicial theory behind *Revlon* duties, see Bernard S. Black & Reinier H. Kraakman, *Delaware's Takeover Law: The Uncertain Search for Hidden Value*, 96 Nw. U. L. Rev. 521 (2002).

Put differently, judicial deference to a target board's choice is a trade-off. The more opportunity there is for a directorial informational advantage, the more deference is likely. But judges are realists, too. They understand that the agency problem exists. Thus, the greater the "hidden" value that a board must assert to defend its choice of a transaction partner, the more likely a skeptical court is to cite *Revlon* and require the board to seek the highest current value. These two trade-offs create a pragmatic structure for judicial review, not a rule of decision. In the end, the courts must evaluate the bona fides of board judgment.

To return to our problem, when the T board's claim that a Xenor merger would give shareholders better long-term value is evaluated, a court is likely to ask itself how much value can reasonably be attributed to the T directors' informational advantage, given that only 33 percent of the value of the merger consideration is Xenor common stock and that this will be stock in a huge company, most of which will be unaffected by the acquisition of target. In the real world, we suppose that this case would be decided on the basis of whether the context would permit the court to decide that, in choosing a deal apparently worth 7 percent or so less, the board was making a good-faith judgment about achievable future value. Unlike a plain business judgment case, here the board would have to be prepared to explain its decision.

In our view, consideration of the Xenor problem points to the conclusion that the dichotomy between a *Revlon* test and a business judgment test is unstable and has proven unhelpful in deciding many cases. As between two cash bids, a simple injunction to "take more rather than less" decides the winner (if there are no other relevant considerations).[42] But in most cases, the choice is not so clear because the deal consideration is not so easily valued. This ambiguity is not a reason to invoke the traditional business judgment rule, however, because M&A transactions are simply too important to target shareholders for such a rule of wholesale delegation. Ultimately, the test for deciding whether a board's decision to select a merger partner should be respected in the face of an alternative that might seem better in some respects must be whether the board has shown that it decided in an informed manner and made a good-faith effort to advance the interests of the corporation and its shareholders. Of course, whether a board's decision satisfies such a test is not an easy question to answer. When a transaction is very important — a friendly merger in the face of a hostile alternative, for example — a court must examine the board's bona fides very closely, keeping in mind all of the soft conflicts of interest that the deciding incumbents are likely to have in the matter.

For these reasons, we believe that history has shown that the *Revlon*/non-*Revlon* dichotomy is too rigid, both normatively and descriptively. What courts should do — and do in fact — in reviewing authorized corporate action

---

42. This is also an old rule of trust and corporate law; see, e.g., *Robinson v. Pittsburgh Oil Refining Corp.*, 126 A. 46 (Del. Ch. 1924).

is to accord corporate boards degrees of deference along a continuum. Where, as in *Revlon* itself, the merger consideration is cash, courts will not defer to the board's judgment to take less cash. Thus, in such instances, any "deal protection" accorded to the favored merger partner will be closely reviewed to assure it represents a good-faith effort to get the best current price. By contrast, where, as in *Santa Fe*, the consideration is stock of a company of approximately equal size (that is, a situation in which the synergy contribution of the target is greatest and thus directors' inside information is most valuable to target shareholders), deal protections will receive the greatest deference. In the middle range (where the merger represents mixed consideration or the target is vastly smaller than the survivor), courts will inevitably assess deal-protective terms by evaluating the good faith of the corporate directors who approve these terms, which inevitably will be expressed as a reasonableness type of review.

13.6 APPLYING *REVLON*

In the years immediately following *Revlon*, one could have been forgiven for supposing that *Revlon* obligated a corporate board to discharge some ill-defined substantive duties once a decision had been made to sell its company. To be sure, there were early cases that held that "there is no single blueprint that a board must follow to fulfill its duties."[43] But there were also unexpected decisions, such as the *QVC* case discussed earlier in this chapter, which demonstrated that courts might undertake searching review under the auspices of the *Revlon* doctrine. And there were also cross-cutting distinctions that had not yet been fully explored, the most important of which was that between fact patterns in which there was a bidding contest with competing suitors and those in which a company's board had decided to sell the firm, or at least to remain open to a sale should an attractive opportunity present itself.

Two recent opinions, one from 2009 and the other from 2015, by the Delaware Supreme Court give a flavor of the current approach to judicial review of a *friendly* change-in-control transaction. In this context, what does it mean for a target board to be under *Revlon* duties? How active can we expect courts to be in reviewing the actions of disinterested boards?

NOTE ON LYONDELL CHEMICAL CO. v. RYAN, *970 A.2D 235* *(DEL. 2009)*

An abbreviated account of the facts of *Lyondell* goes as follows. Circa 2007, shortly before the financial crisis, specialty chemical companies in the range of $10 billion in market capitalization were anxious to combine with companies in their same circle, so to speak. Lyondell was a member of this exclusive circle, as was a private Luxembourgian company controlled by Blavatnik, a billionaire. At various times, Blavatnik had floated the idea of

---

43. *Barkan v. Amsted Industries, Inc.*, 567 A.2d 1279 (Del. 1989).

a possible merger of his company and Lyondell with Dan Smith, Lyondell's Chairman and CEO. Smith rejected these advances because the price range proposed was well below Smith's expectations. Then in May 2007, Blavatnik disclosed in a Schedule 13D filing with the SEC that his company had acquired the right to purchase an 8.3 percent block of stock from Lyondell's largest shareholder. Lyondell's board, as well as the entire market, understood this filing for what it conventionally meant; namely, a signal that Blavatnik had a strong interest in buying all of Lyondell. In other words, Lyondell was "in play." Reading the market signals, Lyondell's disinterested board of directors immediately met to discuss what it should do. The board's somewhat unusual decision was to do absolutely nothing and adopt a "wait and see" posture. That is, the board did not take defensive measures, nor did it seek to assess Lyondell's value, either internally via a DCF valuation or externally by shopping the company to other third-party buyers.

Over the next two months, Lyondell remained passive, although it received an LBO offer from Blackstone. But passions were fierce within Lyondell's small circle of chemical companies. Without contacting Lyondell, Blavatnik's wandering eye soon shifted to another specialty chemical company, and this time he went so far as to sign a merger agreement with it. But at the last moment, Blavatnik was jilted at the altar when yet a third chemical company made a topping bid for his latest acquisition target. Shortly thereafter, Blavatnik approached Smith with a cash offer to acquire Lyondell. Smith succeeded in pressing Blavatnik to raise his initial offer price from $40/share to $48/share, albeit with a large break-up fee if Lyondell got cold feet. And, after a week of valuations by Lyondell's financial advisors and several (seemingly short) board meetings, Blavatnik and Lyondell's board signed a cash merger agreement which was subsequently approved by a 99 percent majority of Lyondell's shareholders.

Of course, the transaction was challenged by a shareholder class action against Lyondell's disinterested outside directors who had signed off on the deal. On a motion to dismiss at summary judgment, the Delaware Chancery court opined that it could not conclude that Lyondell's independent directors had not failed to discharge their *Revlon* duties without a trial.

The Chancery Court opinion emphasized that these directors had indulged in "two months of slothful indifference despite knowing that the company was 'in play' after Blavatnik filed his Schedule 13D. Moreover, the week between Blavatnik's formal offer and the board's assent left little time for adequate discussion of the offer, and the board had failed "to seriously press" Blavatnik for a higher price (although Smith had done so prior to the board's consideration of the offer).

On interlocutory appeal, the Delaware Supreme Court en banc reversed and granted summary judgment in favor of Lyondell's directors. The paragraphs excerpted below from Justice Berger's opinion for the court capture the gist of the decision:

. . . As the trial court correctly noted, *Revlon* did not create any new fiduciary duties. It simply held that the "board must perform its fiduciary duties in the service of a specific objective: maximizing the sale price of the enterprise." The trial court reviewed the record, and found that Ryan [the shareholder- plaintiff] might be able to prevail at trial on a claim that the Lyondell directors breached their duty of care. But Lyondell's charter includes an exculpatory provision, pursuant to 8 Del. C. §102(b)(7), protecting the directors from personal liability for breaches of the duty of care. Thus, this case turns on whether any arguable short comings on the part of the Lyondell directors also implicate their duty of loyalty, a breach of which is not exculpated. Because the trial court determined that the board was independent and was not motivated by self-interest or ill will, the sole issue is whether the directors are entitled to summary judgment on the claim that they breached their duty of loyalty by failing to act in good faith.

* * *

Directors' decisions [when *Revlon* duties are triggered] must be reasonable, not perfect. "In the transactional context, [an] extreme set of facts [is] required to sustain a disloyalty claim premised on the notion that disinterested directors were intentionally disregarding their duties." The trial court denied summary judgment because the Lyondell directors' "un-explained inaction" prevented the court from determining that they had acted in good faith. But, if the directors failed to do all that they should have under the circumstances, they breached their duty of care. Only if they knowingly and completely failed to undertake their responsibilities would they breach their duty of loyalty. The trial court approached the record from the wrong perspective. Instead of questioning whether disinterested, independent directors did everything that they (arguably) should have done to obtain the best sale price, the inquiry should have been whether those directors utterly failed to attempt to obtain the best sale price.

* * *

. . . [T]his record clearly establishes that the Lyondell directors did not breach their duty of loyalty by failing to act in good faith. In concluding otherwise, the Court of Chancery reversibly erred.

NOTE ON C&J ENERGY SERVICES, INC. v. CITY OF MIAMI GENERAL EMPLOYEES AND SANITATION EMPLOYEES RETIREMENT TRUST, *107 A.3D 1049 (DEL. 2014)*

A very recent statement of the Delaware Supreme Court on the freedom of non-conflicted boards in selling the company to adopt whatever tactic they deem appropriate in the good-faith exercise of their business judgment was contained in the en banc reversal of a preliminary injunction issued by a Vice Chancellor enjoining a deal for 30 days and requiring the board to shop the company more actively. The Vice Chancellor, of course, believed he was ful-filling the mandate of the *Revlon* case.

STRINE, C.J., for the Court en banc:

. . .

The proposed transaction is itself unusual in that C&J, a U.S. corporation, will acquire a subsidiary of Nabors [Inc.], which is domiciled in Bermuda, but Nabors will retain a majority of the equity in the surviving company. To obtain more favorable tax rates, the surviving entity, C&J Energy Services, Ltd. ("New C&J"), will be based in Bermuda, and thus subject to lower corporate tax rates than C&J currently pays.

To temper Nabors majority voting control of the surviving company, C&J negotiated for certain protections, including a bye-law [court notes this is spelling used in Bermuda—EDS.] guaranteeing that all stockholders would share pro rata in any future sale of New C&J, which can only be repealed by a unanimous stockholder vote. [Compare *QVC* and *Delphi Financial* cases above—EDS.] C&J also bargained for a "fiduciary out" if a superior proposal was to emerge during a lengthy passive market check. . . . And during that market check, a potential competing bidder faced only modest deal protec-tion barriers.

Although the Court of Chancery found that the C&J board harbored no conflict of interest and was fully informed about its own company's value, the court determined there was a "plausible" violation of the board's *Revlon* duties because the board did not affirmatively shop the company either before or after signing. On that basis, the Court of Chancery enjoined the stockholder vote for 30 days, despite finding no reason to believe that C&J stockholders — who must vote to approve the transaction — would not have a fair opportunity to evaluate the deal for themselves on its economic merits.

The Court of Chancery's order also required C&J to shop itself in vio-lation of the merger agreement between C&J and Nabors, which prohibited C&J from soliciting other bids. The order dealt with this issue by stating "[t]he solicitation of proposals consistent with this Order and any subsequent nego-tiations of any alternative proposal that emerges will not constitute a breach of the Merger Agreement in any respect."

But the Court of Chancery did not rely on undisputed facts showing a reasonable probability that the board had breached its fiduciary duties when it imposed this mandatory, affirmative injunction. Instead, it is undisputed that a deal with Nabors made strategic business sense and offered substan-tial benefits for C&J's stockholders. Moreover, the order stripped Nabors of its contractual rights even though the Court of Chancery did not make any finding that Nabors was an aider and abettor, . . . finding that there was a rea-sonable probability of a breach by C&J's board that Nabors could have aided and abetted.

We assume for the sake of analysis that *Revlon* was invoked by the pending transaction because Nabors will acquire a majority of New C&J's

voting shares. But we nonetheless conclude that the Court of Chancery's injunction cannot stand. A preliminary injunction must be supported by a finding by the Court of Chancery that the plaintiffs have demonstrated a reasonable probability of success on the merits. The Court of Chancery made no such finding here, and the analysis that it conducted rested on the erroneous proposition that a company selling itself in a change of control transaction is required to shop itself to fulfill its duty to seek the highest immediate value. But *Revlon* and its progeny do not set out a specific route that a board must follow when fulfilling its fiduciary duties, and an independent board is entitled to use its business judgment to decide to enter into a strategic transaction that promises great benefit, even when it creates certain risks. When a board exercises its judgment in good faith, tests the transaction through a viable passive market check, and gives its stockholders a fully informed, uncoerced opportunity to vote to accept the deal, we cannot conclude that the board likely violated its *Revlon* duties. It is too often forgotten that *Revlon*, and later cases like *QVC*, primarily involved board resistance to a competing bid after the board had agreed to a change of control, which threatened to impede the emergence of another higher-priced deal. No hint of such a defensive, entrenching motive emerges from this record. . . .

QUESTIONS AND NOTES

1. There has never been an injunction issued in a *Revlon* case and sustained on appeal where there was not an ongoing bidding contest. Courts are understandably reluctant to enjoin a premium deal for target shareholders because of defects in the target company's sale process when no other premium transaction is at hand. A less than fair premium price is better than no premium at all.

2. Despite the preceding observation, however, *Lyondell* demonstrates why it is difficult to recover damages in a *Revlon* action when board members are independent. Section 102(b)(7) precludes seeking monetary damages from directors unless they act in bad faith, which is extremely difficult to prove.

3. *Lyondell* might lead one to think that we are back to the old-time religion that arm's length mergers are only subject to business judgment review. But this is not entirely the case for transactional lawyers. A lawyer working on negotiating or drafting a friendly acquisition agreement cannot know for certain whether it will meet a shareholder challenge. An alternative deal might come out of the woodworks and challenge the provisions of the agreement that have a defensive effect. Thus, she must draft on the assumption that her work might be closely reviewed.

13.7   REGULATION OF TAKEOVERS IN OTHER LEGAL SYSTEMS

The multiple forces that produced the phenomenon of hostile takeovers in the United States — including changes in technology, financial markets, and the way in which shares are held — were not limited to the United States. In time, other systems too were faced with the question of how best to deal with the phenomenon of large-scale unsolicited takeovers. Everywhere the same questions of managing large-scale change to enhance productivity but limiting the disrupting effects it inevitably causes arose.

NOTE ON THE EUROPEAN UNION TAKEOVER DIRECTIVE

These dynamic forces disrupted the status quo in the European Union in the 1990s. In 2004, the European Union, after 14 years of negotiations, promulgated its Takeover Directive. The Directive was adopted only after the EU member states reached the radical compromise of making its two most important provisions optional — a decision that naturally limits the extent to which the Directive can impose uniformity on takeover policy in the European Union.

The first of these key provisions is Article 9 of the Directive, which prohibits target companies from taking defensive actions to defeat hostile bids without a shareholder vote (sometimes called the "Board Neutrality Rule"). This rule of managerial passivity in the face of a hostile takeover reflects the policy of the British City Code. For firms in member states that do not opt out, it is a mandatory rule of shareholder choice rather than board decision making, which is precisely the reverse of the approach that Delaware law takes, at least as a default rule. France, Spain, and the United Kingdom have opted in to Article 9, while Germany and the Netherlands have opted out, among the larger EU member states.

The second key provision of the Takeover Directive is the so-called breakthrough rule embodied in Article 11. Under the breakthrough rule, a hostile acquirer that obtains more than 75 percent of the voting equity of a target company can remove the board of directors, regardless of any restrictions on the voting rights in the charter (including differential voting rights among multiple classes of stock) and any restrictions on the transfer of securities. All shares vote equally on charter amendments proposed by such an acquirer. In addition, multiple voting class structures and restrictions on shareholder votes are unenforceable under Article 11 against the bidder in a takeover and do not apply to target shareholders who must vote on defensive measures. From a U.S. perspective, this would be very strong medicine. Most EU members (e.g., France, Germany, Italy, the Netherlands, Spain, and the United Kingdom) have opted out of Article 11.

In terms of social welfare maximization, what factors might lead to a preference between Article 9 and Article 11? See John C. Coates IV, *Ownership, Takeovers, and EU Law: How Contestable Should EU Corporations Be?*, in E. Wymeersch & G. Ferrarini eds., Reforming Company and Takeover Law in Europe (2003). It is noteworthy that several large EU member states have enacted restrictions on foreign takeovers in the last few years, limiting the impact of the European Union's harmonization drive in this area. See Jonathan Mukwiri, *The End of History for the Board Neutrality Rule in the EU*, 21 Eur. Bus.

Org. L. Rev. 253 (2020)(discussing restrictions in France, Germany, Italy, and the Netherlands).

*NOTE ON THE JAPANESE GUIDELINES ON
TAKEOVER DEFENSE*

In September 2004, Japan's Ministry of Economy, Trade, and Industry (METI) convened a group of experts and business representatives, chaired by Professor Hideki Kanda of the University of Tokyo, to propose a government response to the hostile takeovers that were beginning to appear on the Japanese corporate landscape. After extensive study and consultation with takeover experts around the world, the Corporate Value Study Group published its report in March 2005. Two months later, METI and the Japanese Ministry of Justice jointly promulgated "guidelines" that adopted the general approach and many of the specific recommendations from the report. On one hand, the Guidelines follow Delaware law by allowing Japanese boards to adopt poison pills without a shareholder vote, and, more generally, requiring that defenses be "necessary and reasonable in relation to the threat posed." (Sound familiar?) On the other hand, the Guidelines indicate that defenses can only be used to maximize shareholder value, not to protect other constituencies as suggested in *Unocal*. In addition, the Guidelines suggest a more stringent form of reasonableness review than the Delaware courts have historically applied. For example, in order to be reasonable, a board-adopted poison pill must provide a mechanism for shareholders to eliminate it, such as through an annual election of all the directors, or a sunset provision.

Taken as a whole, Japan seems to have adopted a middle-ground approach somewhere between Delaware and the EU Takeover Directive. Of course, the Guidelines only provide general principles, and it will take years of judicial interpretation to see how they play out in practice. For an insightful commentary on these developments, see Curtis J. Milhaupt, *In the Shadow of Delaware? The Rise of Hostile Takeovers in Japan*, 105 Colum. L. Rev. 2171 (2005). Indeed, recent scholarship by Professors Koh, Nakahigashi, and Puchniak documents a volte face in Japanese firms' adoptions of the pill after a meteoric rise in the early 2000s.[44] They attribute this to three factors. First, reduced need for the pill as the demand and success of hostile takeovers has petered out in Japan. Second, reduced effectiveness of the pill because Japanese firms typically required shareholder approval before adopting a pill, unlike their American counterparts which only need board action to adopt the pill. Third, reduced institutional support for the pill due in part to recent changes in Japan's corporate law and stewardship

---

44. See Alan K. Koh, Masafumi Nakahigashi, and Dan W. Puchniak, *Land of the Falling "Poison Pill": Understanding Defensive Measures in Japan on Their Own Terms*, 41 U. Pa. J. Int'l L. 687 (2020).

law requiring firms to explain why they have the pill and institutional investors to disclose whether they supported pill renewals.

As the world economy becomes ever more global, other countries are facing takeover-related issues. For a helpful summary of emerging regimes in Asian countries, see Umakanth Varottil and Wai Yee Wan, *Hostile Takeover Regimes in Asia: A Comparative Approach*, 15 Berkeley Bus. L. J. 267 (2019).

13.8 PROTECTING THE DEAL

The deal protection provisions of a merger agreement generally provide the grist for the mill of M&A litigation. Modernly, these provisions typically include covenants against actively shopping the buyer's deal ("no shops" or "no talks"), covenants committing the board to recommend shareholder approval of the deal, and termination fees to be paid in the event that the target exercises its fiduciary out right to terminate the deal, or its shareholders vote the transaction down. Historically, we observed stock lock-ups (as in *Paramount v. QVC*) and "crown jewel lock-ups" (as in *Revlon*), but for reasons we will briefly explain, these have largely disappeared from practice.[45]

Today the termination fee provides the principal deal protection or "lock-up" provision. A lock-up is a colloquial term for a contract provision designed to increase the likelihood that the parties will be able to close the deal. Historically, the two major categories of lock-ups that we find in the cases are asset lock-ups and stock lock-ups.[46] Asset lock-ups create rights to acquire specific corporate assets that become exercisable after a triggering event that signals the deal will not close. Thus, should a third party disrupt the parties' favored transaction, the target corporation will lose, pursuant to the terms of the "lock-up," some of its more attractive assets through the exercise of the lock-up rights. Asset lock-ups have been virtually non-existent since *Revlon*, which, as you will recall, struck down an asset lock-up granted to Forstmann Little.[47]

---

45. In the next section, we discuss "no shops" and "no talks," which are another species of deal protection provisions.

46. An example of a nonfinancial form of lock-up is an agreement providing that, if the target shareholders do not approve the favored merger, the target board will not enter into any other control transaction for a period of, say, 18 months. Such a provision is designed to suppress alternative transactions and pressure shareholders to approve the recommended deal. (Courts in dicta have expressed some skepticism about such provisions.) Note, too, that the term "lock-up" is also used to describe a contract between a large shareholder of a target and the acquirer. See Section 12.6.5. Such a contract may commit the shareholder to sell in a tender offer or give to the acquirer a proxy to vote his shares. Of course, because these lock-ups are given individually, they are fundamentally different from lock-ups that involve corporate, not individual, contracting. Nevertheless, they are extremely important to reducing the risks of failure for a friendly bidder.

47. See John C. Coates IV & Guhan Subramanian, *A Buy-Side Model of M&A Lockups: Theory & Evidence*, 53 Stan. L. Rev. 307, 326-328 (2000).

Stock lock-ups, which were common prior to 2001, are options to buy a block of target company's stock (usually 19.9 percent of the currently outstanding shares) at a stated price. The exercise price of the option was typically the deal price in the "protected transaction." Should a third party disturb the pending transaction, the lock-up provides that the jilted acquirer can acquire the shares and thus participate in the increased value of the target to the extent of its proportionate share in the company's diluted equity (e.g., 19.9 percent). Stock lock-ups were very common, largely because their exercise could force less favorable "purchase" accounting treatment — rather than more favorable "pooling" accounting — on the topping bidder. But following the elimination of pooling of interest accounting treatment for mergers in 2001, stock lock-ups virtually disappeared too. Now the compensation function that was their express rationale can be more directly accomplished through cash termination fees. The Thomson Financial M&A database indicates virtually no stock option lock-ups (<0.1% incidence) since 2002 in U.S. public-company deals larger than $50 million.

Today, then, transactional lawyers are left primarily with "termination fees," or "breakup fees," which are cash payments in the event that the seller elects to terminate the merger or otherwise fails to close. Termination fees are common. They are justified as compensation to a prospective buyer for spending the time, money, and reputation to negotiate a deal with a target when a third party ultimately wins the target. Reasonable payments for this purpose are permitted even when the target is in an auction mode. Lump-sum termination payments no larger than 3 to 4 percent of the deal price are easily accepted by the courts.[48]

Query, however, whether a lock-up that is preclusive, or nearly so — say a 10 percent termination fee — may in some circumstances be permissible to protect a proposed merger transaction?

Imagine, for example, a case in which two bidders are engaged in a lengthy auction-like contest. Target's management finally says: We want your highest and best final cash offer. To ensure that you give us your highest cash offer now, we will give the higher bidder a contract with a 10 percent [or 15 percent!] termination fee. The bidders come up with their last and final bids and target board signs a contract with the higher bidder with a 10 percent termination fee. The losing bidder then makes yet another offer, this one 2 percent higher than the winner's last and final offer. It sues to enjoin the closing of the winning bidder contract and the enforcement of the termination fee, asserting that in a *Revlon* context this termination fee is invalid. Result?

---

48. There have been indications, however, that courts will question the bona fides of amounts beyond a certain range (perhaps 4 to 5 percent of the deal price). See *Phelps Dodge Corp. v. Cyprus Amax Minerals Co.*, 1999 WL 1054255 (Del. 1999) (dicta: "I think 6.3 percent certainly seems to stretch the definition of range of reasonableness and probably stretches the definition beyond its breaking point").

Imagine now a stock-for-stock merger between two high-tech companies. After lengthy negotiations but no market check (as neither wants to merge with anyone else), they agree on terms and include cross-termination fees equal to 7 percent of deal value. They announce that neither company is "for sale" but each seeks the unique benefits that this combination will provide. A private equity fund nevertheless then announces it is prepared to pay 10 percent more than the implied price for one of the two firms on the conditions that (1) its pill is redeemed and (2) the termination fee is invalidated by the court. In a suit to enjoin target company defenses, what is the result?

Doctrinally these two problems are dealt with differently. One is a *Revlon* case and one will be analyzed under *Unocal*'s "enhanced" business judgment. But how much difference will that likely make? Probably not much. In both cases, courts will be looking to the good faith of the board's effort to advance corporate or shareholder interests and evaluating that good faith by the reasonableness of the action taken in the circumstances. Our view is that even a preclusive lock-up will be sustained under the circumstances of the first problem even though that is a *Revlon* transaction. The second case, under the apparently easier *Unocal* standard, is closer probably, but would likely be sustained as well, assuming the court thought the boards had grounds to believe that there were unique benefits to the combination.

A final issue concerns the range of legitimate triggers for termination fees. Buyers' rights under "deal protective" provisions are commonly triggered by (1) a failure of the board to recommend a negotiated deal to shareholders in light of the emergence of a higher offer (thus employing a "fiduciary out," which is discussed in the next section), (2) a rejection of the negotiated deal by a vote of the target's shareholders, or (3) a later sale of assets to another firm. A board decision *not* to recommend a negotiated acquisition is an accepted trigger for a termination payment. Indeed, §146 (formerly §251(c)) of the DGCL was amended in 1998 to validate contracts that require the board to submit a merger proposal to shareholders for a vote even if there is a better offer now on the table — a so-called force-the-vote provision (thus reversing another aspect of *Smith v. Van Gorkom*).[49]

NOTE ON THE UK APPROACH TO TERMINATION FEES

The Takeover Panel in the United Kingdom has taken a different approach to termination fees than the United States. The Takeover Panel had endorsed a bright-line rule that allowed termination fees up to 1 percent of deal value,

---

49. Prior to the amendment, in the event of a later higher-value merger proposal from a third party, target directors could be placed in an untenable position by a contractual provision that requires the corporation to recommend the deal to its shareholders, in light of their fiduciary duty of loyalty (specifically, candor).

substantially lower than the 3-4 percent of deal value allowed under the standards-based approach in the United States. In September 2011, the Takeover Panel went even further, establishing new rules that prohibit any termination fees, as well as any other devices or actions by the target company that might deter competing offers. There is an exception permitting the target of a hostile bid to grant a fee up to 1 percent to one and only one topping bidder.[50]

On one hand, eliminating termination fees maximizes the chance of a third-party overbid after a first bid has been announced. On the other hand, bidders might be deterred from making an initial offer due to the inability to protect the deal from competition or receive compensation in the event of an overbid. Thus, once more, the overall social welfare implications of this change are murky.

13.8.1   "No Shops/No Talks" and "Fiduciary Outs"

Every buyer of an asset wants assurances that her deal will close and she will obtain the asset on the terms agreed. For acquirers in corporate mergers, however, the legal requirement that the target's shareholders vote introduces an irreducible contingency into merger contracts. Something might happen — for example, a second bidder might offer a higher price — before the shareholders vote and the deal closes. Buyers seek protection against this risk in two ways. First, they may seek a large termination fee, as described above. Second, they may seek certain covenants from the seller that will protect their deal. For example, a target board will be asked to covenant (a) not to shop for alternative transactions or supply confidential information to alternative buyers (or more extreme, not to talk at all to others interested in a transaction), (b) to submit the merger agreement (and no other agreement) to the shareholders for approval, and (c) to recommend that shareholders approve this agreement. Such terms are often found in merger agreements, and it is important to recognize that they can serve the interests of target shareholders as well as those of acquirers. Without them, prospective buyers would invest fewer resources in searching for deals and might offer less generous prices.

But what do directors' fiduciary duties require when, despite these covenants, a third party does make a better offer before the shareholders can vote on the original offer? Following the Delaware Supreme Court opinion in *Smith v. Van Gorkom,* corporate lawyers have tended to put in all merger agreements that constitute a change in control (i.e., covered by *Revlon* duties) a provision that allows the target board to terminate the contract in the event that its fiduciary obligation to get the highest available price requires that action. This is the so-called fiduciary out. More specifically, counsel for targets have devised the "fiduciary out" clause, which specifies that, if some triggering event occurs (such as a better offer or an opinion from outside counsel

---

50. The Takeover Panel, Review of Certain Aspects of the Regulation of Takeover Bids (July 21, 2011), *available at* https://www.thetakeoverpanel.org.uk/wp-content/uploads/2008/11/RS201101.pdf.

that the board has a fiduciary duty to abandon the original deal), then the target's board can avoid the contract without breaching it. (The company will, of course, pay a termination fee as provided in the agreement.)

Buyers resist fiduciary outs, since they crave certainty. But where a transaction triggers *Revlon* duties, target counsel typically advise that the legal risk of failing to have a fiduciary out clause is unacceptable. And if a deal is not subject to *Revlon* duties? If there is no legal duty to sell for the highest price, can target directors safely tie their own hands by leaving out a fiduciary out? Even here it would still be imprudent to covenant to make a recommendation to shareholders to vote for a transaction at a future time that left no room for second thoughts when circumstances may have changed by the time the recommendation is to be made.

13.8.2 Shareholder Lock-Ups

If one were to derive general principles from the analysis thus far, it would seem that, whether or not a transaction constitutes a "change in control," if the board's process is deliberate and informed and the board is truly independent, the law must let the board make business decisions without fear of being second-guessed (but see the *Omnicare* case below). When the transaction does constitute a "change in control" that deference will still be accorded unless the board fails to show its actions represent a reasonable attempt to get the best value available. When the transaction is not technically a change in control, the court will be deferential to the board decision of independent directors made in good faith, unless the board cannot show its actions were reasonable in the circumstances. The Delaware corporation law does not appear to mandate specific terms of merger agreements, but requires a process that is informed and honestly pursued in the interests of the corporation and its shareholders. The Delaware Supreme Court's 3–2 decision in *Omnicare v. NCS Healthcare* provides a puzzling exception to this general approach.

OMNICARE, INC. v. NCS HEALTHCARE, INC.
818 A.2d 914 (Del. 2003)

[NCS was a troubled company in the health care industry. In 2001, after defaulting on its debt, the NCS board began exploring a sale of the company. NCS's bankers contacted more than 50 parties, but only received one nonbinding indication of interest, which did not materialize into an offer. In July and August 2001, Omnicare made two proposals to acquire NCS's assets out of bankruptcy, with a small recovery for NCS's noteholders and no recovery for its stockholders. These proposals were rejected by the NCS board, and Omnicare too went away.

In January 2002, Genesis was contacted by representatives of NCS's noteholders about a possible transaction. Genesis had previously lost a bidding contest with Omnicare in a different transaction. According to the Delaware Supreme Court's opinion, reproduced in part below, "This bitter experience for Genesis led to its insistence on exclusivity agreements and lock-ups in any potential transaction with NCS." Genesis and NCS agreed on an exclusive negotiating period that, with extensions, ran through July 31, 2002.

On July 26, 2002, after hearing rumors of a potential Genesis-NCS combination, Omnicare faxed a letter to NCS with an acquisition offer that would pay the NCS debtholders in full and provide $3 cash per share for the NCS shareholders. NCS did not return phone calls from Omnicare to discuss the proposal because of its exclusivity agreement with Genesis, which prevented NCS from "engag[ing] or participat[ing] in any discussions or negotiations with respect to a Competing Transaction or a proposal for one."

Nevertheless, the NCS Independent Committee was able to use the Omnicare proposal to extract better terms from Genesis. On July 27, Genesis agreed to satisfy the NCS debtholders claims in full, increased the offer ratio to one Genesis share for every 10 shares of NCS (worth approximately $1.60 per share on that date), and to reduce the break-up fee in the merger agreement from $10 million to $6 million. In exchange for these financial terms, the Genesis offer required significant "deal protection": most important, a so-called force-the-vote provision under DGCL §251(c) (now codified at DGCL §146), which required the NCS board to submit the deal to the NCS shareholders for their approval even if the NCS board no longer recommended the merger; and voting agreements with Outcalt and Shaw, who were directors and officers of NCS and collectively held a majority of its voting stock. The voting agreements required Outcalt and Shaw, "acting in their capacity as NCS stockholders . . . not in their capacity as NCS directors or officers," to grant to Genesis an irrevocable proxy to vote their shares in favor of the NCS-Genesis merger agreement.

Genesis demanded that the transaction and voting agreements be approved by midnight the next day, July 28, or else Genesis would terminate discussions and withdraw its offer. After receiving reports from the NCS Independent Committee and its legal and financial advisors, the NCS board concluded that "balancing the potential loss of the Genesis deal against the uncertainty of Omnicare's letter, results in the conclusion that the only reasonable alternative for the Board of Directors is to approve the Genesis transaction." In approving the deal, the NCS board understood that it would preclude NCS from engaging in any alternative transaction.

The deal was announced on July 29, 2002. On August 1, Omnicare filed a lawsuit attempting to enjoin the NCS-Genesis merger. On August 8, Omnicare began a tender offer for NCS's shares at a price of $3.50 per share. On October 21, the NCS board withdrew its recommendation that the stockholders vote in favor of the NCS-Genesis merger agreement, and NCS's financial advisors withdrew its fairness opinion of the NCS-Genesis merger agreement as well. Nevertheless, the force-the-vote provision in the merger agreement combined with the shareholder lock-up agreements seemed to make the NCS-Genesis deal a *fait accompli*.

The Delaware Court of Chancery declined to grant an injunction against the NCS-Genesis deal, holding that the NCS directors had not breached their duty of care by entering into the exclusivity and merger agreements with Genesis. Although finding that *Revlon* duties had not been triggered, the court also held that "even applying the more exacting *Revlon* standard, the directors acted in conformity with their fiduciary duties in seeking to achieve the highest and best transaction that was reasonably available to the stockholders." We pick up here with the Delaware Supreme Court's holding on appeal.]

HOLLAND, Justice, for the majority:

In this case, the Court of Chancery correctly held that the NCS directors' decision to adopt defensive devices to completely "lock up" the Genesis merger mandated "special scrutiny" under the two-part test set forth in *Unocal*. . . . The record does not, however, support the Court of Chancery's conclusion that the defensive devices adopted by the NCS board to protect the Genesis merger were reasonable and proportionate to the threat that NCS perceived from the potential loss of the Genesis transaction.

Pursuant to the judicial scrutiny required under *Unocal*'s two-stage analysis, the NCS directors must first demonstrate "that they had reasonable grounds for believing that a danger to corporate policy and effectiveness existed. . . ." To satisfy that burden, the NCS directors are required to show they acted in good faith after conducting a reasonable investigation. The threat identified by the NCS board was the possibility of losing the Genesis offer and being left with no comparable alternative transaction.

The second stage of the *Unocal* test requires the NCS directors to demonstrate that their defensive response was "reasonable in relation to the threat posed." This inquiry involves a two-step analysis. The NCS directors must first establish that the merger deal protection devices adopted in response to the threat were not "coercive" or "preclusive," and then demonstrate that their response was within a "range of reasonable responses" to the threat perceived. A response is "preclusive" if it deprives stockholders of the right to receive all tender offers or precludes a bidder from seeking control by fundamentally restricting proxy contests or otherwise. This aspect of the *Unocal* standard provides for a disjunctive analysis. If defensive measures are either preclusive or coercive they are draconian and impermissible. In this case, the deal protection devices of the NCS board were both preclusive and coercive.

In this case, the Court of Chancery did not expressly address the issue of "coercion" in its *Unocal* analysis. It did find as a fact, however, that NCS's public stockholders (who owned 80% of NCS and overwhelmingly supported Omnicare's offer) will be forced to accept the Genesis merger because of the structural defenses approved by the NCS board.

Consequently, the record reflects that any stockholder vote would have been robbed of its effectiveness by the impermissible coercion that predetermined the outcome of the merger without regard to the merits of the Genesis transaction at the time the vote was scheduled to be taken. Deal protection devices that result in such coercion cannot withstand *Unocal*'s enhanced judicial scrutiny standard of review because they are not within the range of reasonableness.

EFFECTIVE FIDUCIARY OUT REQUIRED

The defensive measures that protected the merger transaction are unenforceable not only because they are preclusive and coercive but, alternatively, they are unenforceable because they are invalid as they operate in this case. Given the specifically enforceable irrevocable voting agreements, the provision in the merger agreement requiring the board to submit the transaction for a stockholder vote and the omission of a fiduciary out clause in the merger agreement completely prevented the board from discharging its fiduciary responsibilities to the minority stockholders when Omnicare presented its superior transaction. "To the extent that a [merger] contract, or a provision thereof, purports to require a board to act or not act in such a fashion as to limit the exercise of fiduciary duties, it is invalid and unenforceable."[74]

Under the circumstances presented in this case, where a cohesive group of stockholders with majority voting power was irrevocably committed to the merger transaction, "[e]ffective representation of the financial interests of the minority shareholders imposed upon the [NCS board] an affirmative responsibility to protect those minority shareholders' interests." The NCS board could not abdicate its fiduciary duties to the minority by leaving it to the stockholders alone to approve or disapprove the merger agreement because two stockholders had already combined to establish a majority of the voting power that made the outcome of the stockholder vote a foregone conclusion.

The Court of Chancery noted that Section 251(c) of the Delaware General Corporation Law now permits boards to agree to submit a merger agreement for a stockholder vote, even if the Board later withdraws its support for that agreement and recommends that the stockholders reject it. The Court of Chancery also noted that stockholder voting agreements are permitted by Delaware law. In refusing to certify this interlocutory appeal, the Court of Chancery stated "it is simply nonsensical to say that a board of directors abdicates its duties to manage the 'business and affairs' of a corporation under Section 141(a) of the DGCL by agreeing to the inclusion in a merger agreement of a term authorized by §251(c) of the same statute."[80]

---

74. [*Paramount Communications Inc. v. QVC Network Inc.*], 637 A.2d 34, 51 (Del.1993) (citation omitted). Restatement (Second) of Contracts §193 explicitly provides that a "promise by a fiduciary to violate his fiduciary duty or a promise that tends to induce such a violation is unenforceable on grounds of public policy." The comments to that Section indicate that "[d]irectors and other officials of a corporation act in a fiduciary capacity and are subject to the rule stated in this Section." Restatement (Second) of Contracts §193 (1981).

80. Section 251(c) was amended in 1998 to allow for the inclusion in a merger agreement of a term requiring that the agreement be put to a vote of stockholders whether or not their directors continue to recommend the transaction. Before this amendment, Section 251 was interpreted as precluding a stockholder vote if the board of directors, after approving the merger agreement but before the stockholder vote, decided no longer to recommend it. See *Smith v. Van Gorkom*, 488 A.2d 858, 887-88 (Del.1985).

Taking action that is otherwise legally possible, however, does not *ipso facto* comport with the fiduciary responsibilities of directors in all circumstances.

Genesis admits that when the NCS board agreed to its merger conditions, the NCS board was seeking to assure that the NCS creditors were paid in full and that the NCS stockholders received the highest value available for their stock. In fact, Genesis defends its "bulletproof" merger agreement on that basis. We hold that the NCS board did not have authority to accede to the Genesis demand for an absolute "lock-up."

The directors of a Delaware corporation have a continuing obligation to discharge their fiduciary responsibilities, as future circumstances develop, after a merger agreement is announced. Genesis anticipated the likelihood of a superior offer after its merger agreement was announced and demanded defensive measures from the NCS board that completely protected its transaction.

Instead of agreeing to the absolute defense of the Genesis merger from a superior offer, however, the NCS board was required to negotiate a fiduciary out clause to protect the NCS stockholders if the Genesis transaction became an inferior offer. By acceding to Genesis' ultimatum for complete protection in futuro, the NCS board disabled itself from exercising its own fiduciary obligations at a time when the board's own judgment is most important, i.e. receipt of a subsequent superior offer.

Any board has authority to give the proponent of a recommended merger agreement reasonable structural and economic defenses, incentives, and fair compensation if the transaction is not completed. To the extent that defensive measures are economic and reasonable, they may become an increased cost to the proponent of any subsequent transaction. Just as defensive measures cannot be draconian, however, they cannot limit or circumscribe the directors' fiduciary duties. Notwithstanding the corporation's insolvent condition, the NCS board had no authority to execute a merger agreement that subsequently prevented it from effectively discharging its ongoing fiduciary responsibilities. . . .

In the context of this preclusive and coercive lock up case, the protection of Genesis' contractual expectations must yield to the supervening responsibility of the directors to discharge their fiduciary duties on a continuing basis. The merger agreement and voting agreements, as they were combined to operate in concert in this case, are inconsistent with the NCS directors' fiduciary duties. To that extent, we hold that they are invalid and unenforceable.

VEASEY, Chief Justice, with whom STEELE, Justice, joins dissenting.
. . . The Majority invalidates the NCS board's action by announcing a new rule that represents an extension of our jurisprudence. That new rule can be narrowly stated as follows: A merger agreement entered into after a market search, before any prospect of a topping bid has emerged, which locks up stockholder approval and does not contain a "fiduciary out" provision, is per se invalid when a later significant topping bid emerges. This bright-line, per se rule would apply regardless of (1) the circumstances leading up to the agreement and (2) the fact that stockholders who control voting power had

irrevocably committed themselves, as stockholders, to vote for the merger. Narrowly stated, this new rule is a judicially created "third rail" that now becomes one of the given "rules of the game," to be taken into account by the negotiators and drafters of merger agreements. In our view, this new rule is an unwise extension of existing precedent.

Although it is debatable whether *Unocal* applies — and we believe that the better rule in this situation is that the business judgment rule should apply[102] — we will, nevertheless, assume arguendo — as the Vice Chancellor did — that *Unocal* applies. Therefore, under *Unocal* the NCS directors had the burden of going forward with the evidence to show that there was a threat to corporate policy and effectiveness and that their actions were reasonable in response to that threat. The Vice Chancellor correctly found that they reasonably perceived the threat that NCS did not have a viable offer from Omnicare — or anyone else — to pay off its creditors, cure its insolvency and provide some payment to stockholders. The NCS board's actions — as the Vice Chancellor correctly held — were reasonable in relation to the threat because the Genesis deal was the "only game in town," the NCS directors got the best deal they could from Genesis and — but for the emergence of Genesis on the scene — there would have been no viable deal.

In our view, the Majority misapplies the *Unitrin* concept of "coercive and preclusive" measures to preempt a proper proportionality balancing. Thus, the Majority asserts that "in applying enhanced judicial scrutiny to defensive devices designed to protect a merger agreement, . . . a court must . . . determine that those measures are not preclusive or coercive. . . ." Here, the deal protection measures were not adopted unilaterally by the board to fend off an existing hostile offer that threatened the corporate policy and effectiveness of NCS. They were adopted because Genesis — the "only game in town"— would not save NCS, its creditors and its stockholders without these provisions.

The Majority — incorrectly, in our view — relies on *Unitrin* to advance its analysis. The discussion of "draconian" measures in *Unitrin* dealt with unilateral board action, a repurchase program, designed to fend off an existing hostile offer by American General. In *Unitrin* we recognized the need to police preclusive and coercive actions initiated by the board to delay or retard an existing hostile bid so as to ensure that the stockholders can benefit from the board's negotiations with the bidder or others and to exercise effectively the franchise as the ultimate check on board action. *Unitrin* polices the effect of board action on existing tender offers and proxy contests to ensure that the board cannot permanently impose its will on the stockholders, leaving the stockholders no recourse to their voting rights.

The very measures the Majority cites as "coercive" were approved by Shaw and Outcalt through the lens of their independent assessment of the

102. The basis for the *Unocal* doctrine is the "omnipresent specter" of the board's self-interest to entrench itself in office. *Unocal Corp. v. Mesa Petroleum Co.*, 493 A.2d 946, 954 (Del.1985). NCS was not plagued with a specter of self-interest. Unlike the Unocal situation, a hostile offer did not arise here until after the market search and the locked-up deal with Genesis.

merits of the transaction. The proper inquiry in this case is whether the NCS board had taken actions that "have the effect of causing the stockholders to vote in favor of the proposed transaction for some reason other than the merits of that transaction."[109]

Outcalt and Shaw were fully informed stockholders. As the NCS controlling stockholders, they made an informed choice to commit their voting power to the merger. The minority stockholders were deemed to know that when controlling stockholders have 65% of the vote they can approve a merger without the need for the minority votes.

Moreover, to the extent a minority stockholder may have felt "coerced" to vote for the merger, which was already a fait accompli, it was a meaningless coercion — or no coercion at all — because the controlling votes, those of Outcalt and Shaw, were already "cast." Although the fact that the controlling votes were committed to the merger "precluded" an overriding vote against the merger by the Class A stockholders, the pejorative "preclusive" label applicable in a *Unitrin* fact situation has no application here.

Therefore, there was no meaningful minority stockholder voting decision to coerce.

In applying *Unocal* scrutiny, we believe the Majority incorrectly preempted the proportionality inquiry. In our view, the proportionality inquiry must account for the reality that the contractual measures protecting this merger agreement were necessary to obtain the Genesis deal. The Majority has not demonstrated that the director action was a disproportionate response to the threat posed. Indeed, it is clear to us that the board action to negotiate the best deal reasonably available with the only viable merger partner (Genesis) who could satisfy the creditors and benefit the stockholders, was reasonable in relation to the threat, by any practical yardstick.

AN ABSOLUTE LOCK-UP IS NOT A PER SE VIOLATION OF FIDUCIARY DUTY

We respectfully disagree with the Majority's conclusion that the NCS board breached its fiduciary duties to the Class A stockholders by failing to negotiate a "fiduciary out" in the Genesis merger agreement. What is the practical import of a "fiduciary out?" It is a contractual provision, articulated in a manner to be negotiated, that would permit the board of the corporation being acquired to exit without breaching the merger agreement in the event of a superior offer.

In this case, Genesis made it abundantly clear early on that it was willing to negotiate a deal with NCS but only on the condition that it would not be a "stalking horse." Thus, it wanted to be certain that a third party could not use its deal with NCS as a floor against which to begin a bidding war.

As a result of this negotiating position, a "fiduciary out" was not acceptable to Genesis. The Majority Opinion holds that such a negotiating position,

---

109. [*Williams v.*] *Geier*, 671 A. 2d [1368] at 1382-83.

if implemented in the agreement, is invalid per se where there is an absolute lock-up. We know of no authority in our jurisprudence supporting this new rule, and we believe it is unwise and unwarranted.

One hopes that the Majority rule announced here — though clearly erroneous in our view — will be interpreted narrowly and will be seen as sui generis. By deterring bidders from engaging in negotiations like those present here and requiring that there must always be a fiduciary out, the universe of potential bidders who could reasonably be expected to benefit stockholders could shrink or disappear.

Nevertheless, if the holding is confined to these unique facts, negotiators may be able to navigate around this new hazard.

Accordingly, we respectfully dissent.

[Justice Steele also filed a separate dissent.]

NOTES AND QUESTIONS ON OMNICARE

1. The court finds that the NCS board went wrong by not negotiating for an effective fiduciary out in the Genesis transaction. What would have happened, do you think, if the NCS board had tried to get a fiduciary out into the Genesis agreement? If Genesis would have walked, was there any business risk that Omnicare would have lowered its bid?

2. In holding that a fiduciary out must be included in the merger agreement's undertaking to call a meeting, the majority quotes the Restatement (Second) of Contracts §193, which provides that a "promise by a fiduciary to violate his fiduciary duty or a promise that tends to induce such a violation is unenforceable on grounds of public policy." The comments to that section indicate that "[d]irectors and other officials of a corporation act in a fiduciary capacity and are subject to the rule stated in this Section." Can you identify a duty that the members of the board violated (or promised to violate) on July 28?

3. Applying a *Unocal/Unitrin* analysis to the execution of the Genesis agreement, what would you identify as the risk that the board sought to protect against? What, in the view of the majority, makes the board's choice "unreasonable"? Does the majority opinion in effect hold that *the law required the board to accept the business risk* that Genesis would walk if it did not get the deal protections it sought? How can you support this result from a policy perspective?

4. In applying *Unocal/Unitrin*, the court states elsewhere in its opinion that: "The latitude a board will have in either maintaining or using the defensive devices it has adopted to protect the merger it approved will vary according to the degree of benefit or detriment to the stockholders' interests that is presented by the value or terms of the subsequent competing transaction." The court seems to be saying that a target board will have less latitude to protect the deal if a higher bid emerges later; that is, the court will assess lock-ups with 20-20 hindsight. In the words of one observer, does the court's holding in *Omnicare* require directors to be omniscient? See *Orman v. Cullman* (described below), 2004 WL 2348395 (Del. Ch. Oct. 20, 2004) at

*8 n.98 ("As formulated, the [*Omnicare*] test would appear to result in judi-cial invalidation of negotiated contractual provisions based on the advantages of hindsight.").

5. Do you think the majority's analysis was affected by the fact that the controlling shareholders did not represent a majority of the equity capital? (The court notes that the public shareholders represented 80 percent of the equity and that, according to the court, they wanted the Omnicare deal.) Is this a legitimate consideration in your opinion?

6. Did Genesis have any obligation *not* to ask for the controller's irrevo-cable proxy, or for the merger term mandating the calling of a shareholder meeting at which the merger would be voted upon (authorized by §146 (formerly §251(c))) or to refrain from giving the seller a 24-hour deadline? If these positions did not violate a duty of any sort, what is the significance to the majority of its taking these positions?

7. *Omnicare* was distinguished in *Orman*. In January 2000, Swedish Match agreed to buy out the minority shareholders of General Cigar for $15.25 in cash per share, with the result that Swedish Match would own 64 percent and the controlling Cullman family would own 36 percent of General Cigar (with the Cullmans retaining control by virtue of their high-vote stock). The merger agreement contained: (1) no break-up fee; (2) a fiduciary out that allowed General Cigar to consider an unsolicited superior proposal; (3) a class vote of the A and B shares separately; and (4) a majority-of-the-minority approval condition from the Class A shareholders. In addition, the Cullman family agreed to vote their controlling interest for the Swedish Match transac-tion, and against any alternative acquisition proposal for 18 months after any termination of the merger. Putting it all together, the minority shareholders could veto the deal, but if they did so they would not be able to see another deal for 18 months. Chancellor Chandler of the Delaware Chancery Court upheld the shareholder lock-up agreement: "In [*Omnicare*], the challenged action was the directors' entering into a contract in their capacity as *directors*. The Cullmans entered into the voting agreement *as shareholders*. . . . [Unlike *Omnicare*,] the public shareholders were free to reject the proposed deal, even though, permissibly, their vote may have been influenced by the exis-tence of the deal protection measures."[51] Do you find the distinction per-suasive? How would you structure a shareholder lock-up in the aftermath of *Omnicare* and *Orman v. Cullman*? It should be noted that other Delaware courts have criticized the majority's opinion in *Omnicare*,[52] and California has explicitly declined to follow its holding.[53]

8. The corporate bar has developed "work-arounds" to the *Omnicare* holding. Two of the more common are (1) controller giving to acquirer a proxy locking-up less than 50 percent of the company's stock (e.g., 35 percent),

---

51. *Orman v. Cullman*, 2004 WL 2348395 at *7 (Del. Ch. Oct. 20, 2004) (emphasis in original).

52. See, e.g., *In re Toys "R" Us, Inc. Shareholder Litigation*, 877 A.2d 975, 1016 n.68 (Del. Ch. 2005) (*Omnicare* "represents . . . an aberrational departure from long accepted principle[s]").

53. *Monty v. Leis*, 193 Cal. App. 4th 1367 (Cal. 2011).

which still offers high assurance, if not certainty, against an interloper, and (2) a provision that the merger will be approved not at a shareholder meeting but by a consent solicitation, which when there is a controller, as in *Omnicare*, may be done the day after board approval of the deal.

13.9 *Corwin* Cleansing

As noted in Chapters 10 and 12, the Delaware courts have been increasingly concerned about deal-related litigation. In the context of freezeout mergers, this has resulted in *MFW* cleansing, and for appraisal proceedings, the increasing reliance on fair deal process in determining fair value. Contests for corporate control have also witnessed increased deal litigation and rising concerns over it. The Delaware Supreme Court entered the fray in 2015 with the *Corwin* decision, excerpted below, and changed the debate over judicial review of corporate control contests.

CORWIN v. KKR FINANCIAL HOLDINGS LLC
125 A.3d 304 (Del. 2015)

Strine, C.J.:

In a well-reasoned opinion, the Court of Chancery held that the business judgment rule is invoked as the appropriate standard of review for a post-closing damages action when a merger that is not subject to the entire fairness standard of review has been approved by a fully informed, uncoerced majority of the disinterested stockholders. For that and other reasons, the Court of Chancery dismissed the plaintiffs' complaint. In this decision, we find that the Chancellor was correct in finding that the voluntary judgment of the disinterested stockholders to approve the merger invoked the business judgment rule standard of review and that the plaintiffs' complaint should be dismissed. For sound policy reasons, Delaware corporate law has long been reluctant to second-guess the judgment of a disinterested stockholder majority that determines that a transaction with a party other than a controlling stockholder is in their best interests. . . .

The plaintiffs filed a challenge in the Court of Chancery to a stock-for-stock merger between KKR & Co. L.P. (KKR) and KKR Financial Holdings LLC (Financial Holdings) in which KKR acquired each share of Financial Holdings's stock for 0.51 of a share of KKR stock, a 35% premium to the unaffected market price. Below, the plaintiffs' primary argument was that the transaction was presumptively subject to the entire fairness standard of review because Financial Holdings's primary business was financing KKR's leveraged buyout activities, and instead of having employees manage the company's day-to-day operations, Financial Holdings was managed by KKR Financial Advisors, an affiliate of KKR, under a contractual management agreement that could only be terminated by Financial Holdings if it paid a termination fee. As a result, the plaintiffs alleged that KKR was a controlling stockholder of Financial Holdings, which was an LLC, not a corporation.[1]

The defendants filed a motion to dismiss, taking issue with that argument. In a thoughtful and thorough decision, the Chancellor found that the defendants were correct that the plaintiffs' complaint did not plead facts supporting an inference that KKR was Financial Holdings's controlling stockholder. Among other things, the Chancellor noted that KKR owned less than 1% of Financial Holdings's stock, had no right to appoint any directors, and had no contractual right to veto any board action. Although the Chancellor acknowledged the unusual existential circumstances the plaintiffs cited, he noted that those were known at all relevant times by investors, and that Financial Holdings had real assets its independent board controlled and had the option of pursuing any path its directors chose.

In addressing whether KKR was a controlling stockholder, the Chancellor was focused on the reality that in cases where a party that did not have majority control of the entity's voting stock was found to be a controlling stockholder, the Court of Chancery, consistent with the instructions of this Court, looked for a combination of potent voting power and management control such that the stockholder could be deemed to have effective control of the board without actually owning a majority of stock. Not finding that combination here, the Chancellor noted:

> According to plaintiffs, [Financial Holdings] serves as little more than a public vehicle for financing KKR-sponsored transactions and the terms of the Management Agreement make [Financial Holdings] unattractive as an acquisition target to anyone other than KKR because of [Financial Holdings]'s operational dependence on KKR and because of the significant cost that would be incurred to terminate the Management Agreement. I assume all that is true. But, every . . . stockholder of [Financial Holdings] knew about the limitations the Management Agreement imposed on [Financial Holdings]'s business [and] also knew that the business and affairs of [Financial Holdings] would be managed by a board . . . subject to annual stockholder elections.
>
>   At bottom, plaintiffs ask the Court to impose fiduciary obligations on a relatively nominal stockholder, not because of any coercive power that stockholder could wield over the board's ability to independently decide whether or not to approve the merger, but because of pre-existing contractual obligations with that stockholder . . . Plaintiffs have cited no legal authority for that novel proposition, and I decline to create such a rule.

After carefully analyzing the pled facts and the relevant precedent, the Chancellor held:

> 1. We wish to make a point. We are keenly aware that this case involves a merger between a limited partnership and a limited liability company, albeit both ones whose ownership interests trade on public exchanges. But, it appears that both before the Chancellor, and now before us on appeal, the parties have acted as if this case was no different from one between two corporations whose internal affairs are governed by the Delaware General Corporation Law and related case law. We have respected the parties' approach to arguing this complex case, but felt obliged to note that we recognize that this case involved alternative entities, and that in cases involving those entities, distinctive arguments often arise due to the greater contractual flexibility given to those entities under our statutory law.

[T]here are no well-pled facts from which it is reasonable to infer that KKR could prevent the [Financial Holdings] board from freely exercising its independent judgment in considering the proposed merger or, put differently, that KKR had the power to exact retribution by removing the [Financial Holdings] directors from their offices if they did not bend to KKR's will in their consideration of the proposed merger.

Although the plaintiffs reiterate their position on appeal, the Chancellor correctly applied the law and we see no reason to repeat his lucid analysis of this question. . . .

On appeal, the plaintiffs further contend that, even if the Chancellor was correct in determining that KKR was not a controlling stockholder, he was wrong to dismiss the complaint because they contend that if the entire fairness standard did not apply, *Revlon*[2] did, and the plaintiffs argue that they pled a *Revlon* claim against the defendant directors.

But, as the defendants point out, the plaintiffs did not fairly argue below that *Revlon* applied and even if they did, they ignore the reality that Financial Holdings had in place an exculpatory charter provision, and that the transaction was approved by an independent board majority and by a fully informed, uncoerced stockholder vote.[3]

Therefore, the defendants argue, the plaintiffs failed to state a non-exculpated claim for breach of fiduciary duty.

But we need not delve into whether the Court of Chancery's determination that *Revlon* did not apply to the merger is correct for a single reason: it does not matter. Because the Chancellor was correct in determining that the entire fairness standard did not apply to the merger, the Chancellor's analysis of the effect of the uncoerced, informed stockholder vote is outcome-determinative, even if *Revlon* applied to the merger.

As to this point, . . . [t]he Chancellor . . . adhered to precedent supporting the proposition that when a transaction not subject to the entire fairness standard is approved by a fully informed, uncoerced vote of the disinterested stockholders, the business judgment rule applies. Although the Chancellor took note of the possible conflict between his ruling and this Court's decision in *Gantler* v. *Stephens*,[4] he reached the conclusion that *Gantler* did not alter the effect of legally required stockholder votes on the appropriate standard of review.

---

2. *Revlon* v. *MacAndrews & Forbes Holdings, Inc.*, 506 A.2d 173 (Del. 1986).

3. The Court of Chancery indicated that the merger was not subject to review under *Revlon* because KKR was a widely held, public company and that Financial Holdings's stockholders would therefore own stock after the merger in a company without a controlling stockholder. On appeal, the plaintiffs argue that that observation was incorrect and that ownership in KKR was not dispersed after the merger because . . . KKR is a limited partnership that is controlled by its managing partner, which is in turn controlled by KKR's founders. The defendants, for their part, stress that the plaintiffs' focus on *Revlon* is a novel one in the course of this case . . . [We do not reach the *Revlon*] issue, . . . [We only] note that . . . the plaintiffs should have fairly raised their *Revlon* argument below . . .

4. 965 A.2d 710 (2010).

Instead, the Chancellor read *Gantler* as a decision solely intended to clarify the meaning of the precise term—ratification. He had two primary reasons for so finding. First, he noted that any statement about the effect a statutorily required vote had on the appropriate standard of review would have been dictum because in *Gantler* the Court held that the disclosures [at issue] . . . —were materially misleading. Second, the Chancellor doubted that the Supreme Court would have . . . overrule[d] extensive Delaware precedent, [that recognizes the ratifying effect of] . . . a statutorily required stockholder vote. . . .

[Eds. At this point, the Chief Justice analyzes the case law to demonstrate that routine statutory voting after major transactions consigns subsequent shareholder complaints to business judgment review. The earlier *Gantler* decision was ambiguous and might have been read to argue that routine shareholder votes on fundamental transactions such as mergers cleanse the transactions at issue but not the procedures that gave rise to it. After this discussion, the court resumes:]

To erase any doubt on the part of practitioners, we embrace the Chancellor's . . . interpretation of *Gantler* as a narrow decision focused on defining a specific legal term, . . . ratification, and not on the question of what standard of review applies if a transaction not subject to the entire fairness standard is approved by an informed, voluntary vote of disinterested stockholders. . . .

Furthermore, although the plaintiffs argue that adhering to the proposition that a fully informed, uncoerced stockholder vote invokes the business judgment rule would impair the operation of *Unocal*[5] and *Revlon*, or expose stockholders to unfair action by directors without protection, the plaintiffs ignore several factors. First, *Unocal* and *Revlon* are primarily designed to give stockholders and the Court of Chancery the tool of injunctive relief to address important M & A decisions in real time, before closing. They were not tools designed with post-closing money damages claims in mind, the standards they articulate do not match the gross negligence standard for director due care liability under *Van Gorkom*,[6] and with the prevalence of exculpatory charter provisions, due care liability is rarely even available.

Second and most important, the doctrine applies only to fully informed, uncoerced stockholder votes, and if troubling facts regarding director behavior were not disclosed that would have been material to a voting stockholder, then the business judgment rule is not invoked. Here, however, all of the objective facts regarding the board's interests, KKR's interests, and the negotiation process, were fully disclosed.

Finally, when a transaction is not subject to the entire fairness standard, the long-standing policy of our law has been to avoid the uncertainties and costs of judicial second-guessing when the disinterested stockholders have had the free and informed chance to decide on the economic merits of a

5. *Unocal Corp.* v. *Mesa Petroleum Co.*, 493 A.2d 946 (Del. 1985).
6. *Smith* v. *Van Gorkom*, 488 A.2d 858 (Del. 1985).

transaction for themselves. There are sound reasons for this policy. When the real parties in interest — the disinterested equity owners — can easily protect themselves at the ballot box by simply voting no, the utility of a litigation-intrusive standard of review promises more costs to stockholders in the form of litigation rents and inhibitions on risk-taking than it promises in terms of benefits to them.[28] The reason for that is tied to the core rationale of the business judgment rule, which is that judges are poorly positioned to evaluate the wisdom of business decisions and there is little utility to having them second-guess the determination of impartial decision-makers with more information (in the case of directors) or an actual economic stake in the outcome (in the case of informed, disinterested stockholders). In circumstances, therefore, where the stockholders have had the voluntary choice to accept or reject a transaction, the business judgment rule standard of review is the presumptively correct one and best facilitates wealth creation through the corporate form.

For these reasons, therefore, we affirm the Court of Chancery's judgment on the basis of its well-reasoned decision.

NOTE AND QUESTIONS ON CORWIN

1. *In re Volcano Corp. Stockholder Litigation*, 143 A.3d 727 (Del. Ch. 2016) held that "acceptance of a first-step tender offer by fully informed, disinterested, uncoerced stockholders representing a majority of a corporation's outstanding shares in a two-step merger under Section 251(h) has the same cleansing effect [as in] *Corwin* . . . [i.e., to grant business judgment review — EDS]." The Court rejected the plaintiff's argument that the board's role in negotiating a first-step tender offer was different than that for a merger because §251(h)'s requirements addressed concerns about potential stockholder coercion in the context of a tender offer. Under §251(h) "(1) the first-step tender offer must be for all of the target company's outstanding stock, (2) the second-step merger must 'be effected as soon as practicable following the consummation of the' first-step tender offer, (3) the consideration paid in the second-step merger must be of 'the same amount and kind' as that paid in the first-step tender offer, and (4) appraisal rights are available in all Section 251(h) mergers." The Delaware Supreme Court affirmed stating "it

---

28. See *Williams*, 671 A.2d at 1381 (where a stockholder vote is statutorily required, such as for a merger or a charter amendment, the stockholders control their own destiny through informed voting, and calling this [the] highest form of corporate democracy") . . . *In re Lear Corp. S'holder Litig.*, 926 A.2d 94, 114-15 (Del. Ch. 2007) (Delaware corporation law gives great weight to informed decisions made by an uncoerced electorate. When disinterested stockholders make a mature decision about their economic self-interest, judicial second-guessing is almost completely circumscribed by the doctrine of ratification.") . . . it is difficult to see the utility of allowing litigation to proceed in which the plaintiffs are permitted discovery and a possible trial. . . . In this day and age in which investors also have access to an abundance of information about corporate transactions from sources other than boards of directors, it seems presumptuous and paternalistic to assume that the court knows better in a particular instance than a fully informed corporate electorate with real money riding on the corporation's performance."

appears to the Court that the judgment of the Court of Chancery should be affirmed for the reasons stated in its decision dated June 30, 2016."

2. Although *Corwin* is famous for its "cleansing effect" holding, it also provides useful guidance on when a shareholder will be considered a controlling shareholder. The court appears to hold that when a shareholder cannot prevent the board from "freely exercising its independent judgment . . . or . . . [did not have] the power to exact retribution by removing . . . [Financial Holdings] directors from their offices if they did not bend to KKR's will . . ." then it is not treated as a controlling shareholder and will not be subject to entire fairness review. This phrasing stresses the independence of the board and the power to remove the board rather than the ability to influence the day-to-day operation of the firm. Is there any daylight between these two versions of control?

3. *Corwin* does not affect *Unocal* or *Revlon* claims prior to closing (because there is unlikely to be the requisite shareholder vote prior to closing), but it can protect directors from liability under *Unocal* or *Revlon* post-closing. How might this work in practice? For instance, *Corwin* cleansing depends on a fully informed and uncoerced vote of disinterested shareholders. If there is a *Unocal* or *Revlon* breach, then that would suggest that a *fully informed* vote at closing would require the board to reveal that there was a *Unocal* or *Revlon* breach (or perhaps at least the underlying material facts triggering such a breach).[54] Also, *Corwin* requires an uncoerced vote — does that mean that a shareholder vote affirming an acquisition after a *Unocal* or *Revlon* violation, which made it impossible (or nearly so) for any acquirer to succeed (except the preferred one), is uncoerced? Do you think a shareholder vote in such circumstances should be treated as an *uncoerced* vote and receive *Corwin* cleansing?

NOTE ON WHEN CORWIN *CLEANSING WILL BE GRANTED*

The Delaware Supreme Court explicitly premised *Corwin* cleansing on a "fully informed, uncoerced vote of the disinterested stockholders." Of course, that led to litigation on what "fully informed" means. The Delaware Supreme Court addressed this issue in *Morrison v. Berry*, 191 A.3d 268 (Del. 2018), *as revised* (July 27, 2018). This case involved the going private transaction of The Fresh Market wherein the plaintiffs alleged multiple fiduciary duty beaches by the board. Defendants argued, following *Volcano*, that when the majority of disinterested shareholders accepted the tender offer part of the going private transaction, that amounted to a fully informed and uncoerced shareholder approval resulting in *Corwin* cleansing. The court disagreed and held that there were material misstatements and omissions

---

54. See *Chester Cty. Employees' Ret. Fund v. KCG Holdings, Inc.*, No. CV 2017-0421-KSJM, 2019 WL 2564093 (Del. Ch. June 21, 2019) where the Chancery Court did not apply *Corwin* to dismiss *Revlon* claims because plaintiffs' allegations, if true, would mean the shareholder vote was uninformed.

in the board's recommendations favoring the going private transaction that vitiated *Corwin* cleansing because there was "a substantial likelihood that a reasonable shareholder would consider [this information] important in deciding how to vote." Id 282-283. The court's finding was based on emails that the plaintiffs provided (relying on a §220 books and records request) which contradicted what was disclosed in the board's recommendation to shareholders. These damning documents sunk the defendants' claims. As the court noted this case "offers a cautionary reminder to directors and the attorneys who help them craft their disclosures: 'partial and elliptical disclosures' cannot facilitate the protection of the business judgment rule under the *Corwin* doctrine."

Soon after *Morrison* the Delaware Supreme Court had another opportunity to provide guidance in *Appel v. Berkman*, 180 A.3d 1055 (Del. 2018). Plaintiffs brought suit arguing that the sale of Diamond Resorts International should not receive business judgment review under *Corwin* because the firm's disclosures to shareholders were materially misleading in that they did not provide the reasons for why the founder, largest shareholder, and Chairman of Diamond Resorts International (Stephen J. Cloobeck) abstained from voting on a sale of the firm. The Chancery Court dismissed the suit, but the Delaware Supreme Court per Chief Justice Strine reversed. The Court held that the "defendants' argument that the reasons for a dissenting or abstaining board member's vote can never be material is incorrect." In particular, here "Cloobeck—a 'key board member' if ever there were one—objected to the timing of the transaction because [he thought] mismanagement had negatively affected the sale price." The Court found it incredulous that the board inadvertently omitted Cloobeck's reasons for abstaining given that his views—as the founder and driving force behind the firm's success—would have been of substantial importance to a reasonable shareholder in deciding what to do (making his views material). In particular, omitting Cloobeck's views made the board's representation that the shareholders would receive a fair price in the merger materially misleading. This meant the requirements for *Corwin* cleansing were not satisfied.

QUESTIONS

1. *Morrison* and *Appel* address whether material misrepresentations and knowing omissions vitiate *Corwin* cleansing. What about unintentional or negligent behavior? For instance, what if the board did not know of some information that made its statements materially misleading (i.e., the board was uninformed)? Would that mean that *Corwin* cleansing would be lost, and the board would be subject to enhanced scrutiny under *Revlon* or *Unocal*? Even if *Corwin* cleansing is lost, that does not mean that the board will be held liable. For example, if a §102(b)(7) waiver of damages for breach of the duty of care by directors is in place, as is usually the case, then the plaintiffs

are unlikely to recover. See *In re USG Corp. S'holder Litig.,* Consol. C.A. No. 2018-0602-SG (Del. Ch. Aug. 31, 2020).

2. Courts carefully scrutinize plaintiffs' claims of materially misleading statements and omissions. In *English v. Narang*, No. CV 2018-0221-AGB, 2019 WL 1300855 (Del. Ch. Mar. 20, 2019), *aff'd*, 222 A.3d 581 (Del. 2019), *and aff'd*, 222 A.3d 581 (Del. 2019), the Court of Chancery rejected plaintiffs' claims that the alleged misstatements were material even though they alleged the misstatements related to financial projections and conflicts of interest attaching to financial advisors. Plaintiffs have had greater success when they have been able to obtain relevant evidence from §220 books and records requests as they did in both *Morrison* and *Appel*.

3. There has been much discussion of *Corwin*. A recent report by Skadden suggests that in the first two years after *Corwin*, the Delaware courts applied it to dismiss a number of plaintiffs' suits, but that trend seemed to reverse by 2018, where most cases did not apply *Corwin*.[55] The report suggests one explanation for this is that plaintiffs started relying more heavily on §220 requests to generate the type of evidence that courts found persuasive in not applying *Corwin* (usually on inadequate disclosure grounds).

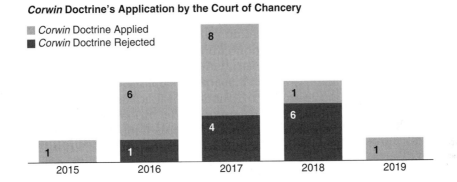

Corwin **Doctrine's Application by the Court of Chancery**

NOTE ON LIABILITY FOR AIDING AND ABETTING BREACHES OF FIDUCIARY DUTY

Given the increasing significance and influence of hedge fund activists, it is perhaps not surprising that plaintiffs have tried to attach liability to them. One recent fascinating case is *In re PLX Technology Inc. Stockholders Litigation* (2018), excerpted below. PLX was a publicly traded Delaware corporation engaged in the business of developing and selling specialized integrated circuits used in connectivity applications. It entered into merger negotiations

---

55. See Edward B. Micheletti, Chad Davis & Mary T. Reale, *Examining* Corwin: *Latest Trends and Results*, Skadden (May 9, 2019), available at https://www.skadden.com/insights/publications/2019/05/insights-the-delaware-edition/examining-corwin-latest-trends-and-results. *Singh v. Attenborough*, 137 A.3d 151 (Del. 2016) was an early case to apply *Corwin* to dismiss a suit.

with IDT (a competitor) in 2011, but those collapsed when the FTC objected on antitrust grounds. As PLX's stock price fell in response an activist hedge fund (Potomac Capital Partners II, L.P.) acquired about 5 percent of its shares and started to agitate for a sale. Eric Singer—Potomac's co-managing member—reasoned that PLX was a bargain at the current price, and there were other firms which could potentially acquire PLX (whose business was improving) at a significant premium. Singer pushed hard for a sale, sent highly critical public letters demanding a sale of the firm, conducted a successful short slate proxy contest with the support of ISS, and got himself appointed to both PLX's board and as Chair of the Special Committee exploring the sale of the firm.

Even before Singer arrived on the board, PLX was working with Deutsche Bank (DB) to explore a sale, and DB had reached out to some bidders (including Avago) who had expressed interest. However, on December 19, 2013, Thomas Krause, the Vice President for Corporate Development at Avago, let DB know that Avago was currently pursuing another entity and when that deal closed it would be open to exploring an acquisition of PLX for around $6.50 a share (a total of about $300 million). DB communicated this to Singer, and thus he knew that Avago was a likely purchaser in a few months and at what approximate price. Neither DB nor Singer communicated Krause's tip to PLX's board, and Singer cooled his jets on pushing for a sale (he thought Avago was likely to be the most interested bidder) until he received another call from DB in May 2014 that Avago was putting things in motion. Within days, he had dinner with Krause where they discussed price and moving with some speed (which again was not disclosed to the board). Within a few weeks Singer shepherded a deal at $6.50 per share (the price suggested in Krause's tip from December 2013). On June 2, 2014, PLX and Avago formally executed an exclusivity agreement lasting 21 days. A number of things happened between these developments and June 22, 2014, when the board met to consider the Avago offer. First, DB reviewed the sale processes over the last two years and noted that there had been several market checks, and that although there were some interested acquirers, they were probably not likely to proceed at this point. Second, DB produced an oral fairness opinion that $6.50 per share was in the fair price range. This was based on projections in June 2014 that the Special Committee had PLX management prepare so that DB could provide its fairness opinion. These were substantially lower than projections prepared just six months earlier. When the PLX board asked for an explanation for the differing projections, they received none except that DB thought the June 2014 projections were the "Base Case" and the earlier projections the "Upside Case."

The board met on June 22 and approved the committee's recommendation to move forward on the Avago deal at $6.50 per share. Avago's deal was a two-step intermediate form merger under §251(h) with the first step tender offer closing on August 11, where about 80 percent of PLX's shares were tendered. There were no competing bids and the merger closed on August 12.

Plaintiff shareholders filed suit against multiple defendants on July 14 and settled with all of them, except Potomac and Singer, on August 17, 2016.

We pick up with Vice Chancellor Laster's opinion addressing the legal analysis for aiding and abetting fiduciary duty breaches. Please note that space constraints require us to drop or compress many of the court's subsection headings, as we have also done in previous cases. We hope our edit leaves most of V.C. Laster's analytical structure intact.

IN RE PLX TECHNOLOGY INC. STOCKHOLDERS LITIGATION
2018 WL 5018535 (Del. Ch. Oct. 16, 2018)

LASTER, V.C.:

II. LEGAL ANALYSIS

The plaintiffs seek damages from Potomac for aiding and abetting breaches of fiduciary duty. This claim has four elements: (i) the existence of a fiduciary relationship, (ii) a breach of the fiduciary's duty, (iii) knowing participation in the breach by a non-fiduciary defendant, and (iv) damages proximately caused by the breach. The plaintiffs established all of the elements except for causally related damages.

A. The Existence of a Fiduciary Relationship

The plaintiffs easily satisfied the first element of their claim. The Company's directors were fiduciaries who owed duties "to the corporation and its shareholders." . . .

B. A Breach of Fiduciary duty

[T]he plaintiffs attack both the sale process and the disclosures . . . To determine what standard of review applies [à la *Corwin*—Eds.] . . . requires an assessment of whether the stockholder decision was fully informed, which in turn requires determining whether the directors breached their duty of disclosure. . . .

1. The Disclosure Claim

[T]he Board owed a "fiduciary duty to disclose fully and fairly all material information within the board's control when it seeks shareholder action." A fact is material "[if there is] a substantial likelihood that the disclosure of the omitted fact would have been viewed by the reasonable investor as having significantly altered the 'total mix' of information made available."

...A stockholder who knew about [Krause's December 2013 tip] could take a very different view of the Board's subsequent efforts to explore alternatives and negotiate with Avago, as well as the role Singer played in the process . . . Rather than appearing like arm's-length negotiations, the quick back-and-forth in May 2014 can be seen as a means of arriving at the $300 million valuation that Krause identified in December 2013. . . . The fact that Deutsche Bank and Singer did not share Krause's tip calls into question their motivations on behalf of PLX. Rather than actors [seeking] the best outcome possible, they look like self-interested agents who were happy with a quick sale that would serve their interests. . . . [These are things a reasonable stockholder would want to know in evaluating the deal.] [Morever,] . . . [i]n light of the circumstances . . . it was misleading for the Recommendation Statement to claim that the June 2014 Projections "were prepared in the ordinary course of business for operating purposes." The June 2014 Projections were prepared after Avago made its bid so that Deutsche Bank could use them in its fairness opinion. . . .

Finally, the plaintiffs argue that the Recommendation Statement was materially misleading because it failed to include a discounted cash flow analysis based on the December 2013 Projections. [which provided] . . . a valuation range of $6.90 to $9.78 per share. . . . The entire range of the analysis exceeded both the directors' counteroffer and the eventual deal price . . . I believe that omitting the May valuation range constituted a misleading partial disclosure. . . .

2.   The Sale Process Claims

In addition to asserting disclosure claims, the plaintiffs contend that the directors breached their fiduciary duties during the sale process . . . by permitting Singer to lead them into a near-term sale when PLX would have been better served by remaining independent, building its business, and potentially pursuing a sale at a later date. . . . The Board approved a sale of PLX to Avago for cash, making enhanced scrutiny the operative standard of review. Under *Corwin*, however, the business judgment rule would apply if the directors had complied with their duty of disclosure. This decision has held that the Recommendation Statement was misleading, so the . . . operative standard of review is therefore enhanced scrutiny. When that standard applies, the defendant fiduciaries bear the burden of proving that they "act[ed] reasonably to seek the transaction offering the best value reasonably available to the stockholders." . . . [A] court applying enhanced judicial scrutiny should be deciding whether the directors made **a reasonable** decision, not **a perfect** decision. If a board selected one of several reasonable alternatives, a court should not second-guess that choice. . . . Thus, courts will not substitute their business judgment for that of the directors, but will determine if the directors' decision was, on balance, within a range of reasonableness. . . .

b. Conflicts of Interest in the Boardroom

The divergent interest that led to a predicate breach of duty in this case was Singer's interest in achieving a near-term sale. As Potomac's agent and co-managing member, Singer faced the dual fiduciary problem identified in *Weinberger v. UOP, Inc.* . . .

Ordinarily, the fact that Potomac held a large block of common stock would be helpful to Singer and undermine any concern about divergent interest.[492] . . . [However,] Delaware law recognizes that in some scenarios, circumstances may cause the interests of investors who hold common stock to diverge. For example, . . . "[a]ctivist hedge funds . . . are impatient shareholders, who look for value and want it realized in the near or intermediate term. . . ."[499] The record in this case convinces me that Singer and Potomac had a divergent interest in achieving quick profits by orchestrating a near-term sale at PLX. During their activist campaign and subsequent proxy contest, Singer and Potomac argued vehemently that PLX should be sold quickly. Singer's thesis for investing in PLX depended entirely on a short-term sale to the other bidder. . . . He lacked any ideas for generating value at PLX other than to sell it. . . . Once on the Board, Singer consistently acted with that intent . . . He only backed off when he learned that Avago could not re-engage for several months. When Avago did re-engage, he got to a deal within days.

In addition to Singer's divergent interest, Deutsche Bank also had significant reasons to favor a near-term sale to Avago. . . . Deutsche Bank's contingent fee arrangement . . . gave Deutsche Bank a powerful financial incentive to favor a sale over having PLX remain independent. The other factor was Deutsche Bank's longstanding and thick [and on-going] relationship with Avago. . . .

c. The Sale Process in this Case

Absent divergent interests, the Board's sale process . . . would fall within a range of reasonableness. The Board combined a narrow, pre-signing canvass with a post-signing market check. This was a reasonable approach. . . .

[However, t]he record in this case indicates that Potomac and Singer succeeded in influencing the directors to favor a sale when they otherwise would have decided to remain independent. . . . [T]he directors agreed to accept less [in the form of Avago's $6.50 per share offer] than what they had rejected when PLX's business was weaker. . . . [T]he directors permitted Singer to take

---

492. This is not a case where a large blockholder owned a security other than common stock with a return profile that created divergent incentives. . . .

499. William W. Bratton & Michael L. Wachter, *The Case Against Shareholder Empowerment*, 158 U. Pa. L. Rev. 653, 682 (2010). . . .

control of the sale process when it mattered most [in May and June 2014]. [Further,] at the time they approved the . . . deal at $6.50, the directors lacked essential information. As in *Rural Metro*, they had not yet received a valuation of the Company on a standalone basis. . . . In contrast to the enhanced scrutiny standard, which requires that directors "seek the transaction offering the best value reasonably available to the stockholders," . . . Singer . . . testified that the Special Committee was focused on [the art of the possible] and maintaining "deal momentum." This testimony provides direct evidence of breach. . . .

. . . Yet in spite of this evidence, I could not conclude that the Board's decisions fell outside the range of reasonableness without one other critical fact: Krause's secret tip to Deutsch Bank in December 2013 about Avago's plans for PLX. . . . [By] withholding this information from the rest of the Board, Singer breached his fiduciary duty and induced the other directors to breach theirs [along with] fatally undermin[ing] the sale process. . . .

C.   KNOWING PARTICIPATION IN THE BREACH

The third element of a claim for aiding and abetting is the third party's knowing participation in the breach. . . . The method of facilitating the breach can include "creating the informational vacuum" in which the board breaches its duty of care. . . . In this case, Singer was a co-managing member of Potomac and its agent, and his knowledge is imputed to Potomac in those capacities . . . Singer directed Potomac's activities and, once elected to the Board, Singer continued to act on Potomac's behalf. By failing to share Krause's tip with the Board, Singer created a critical informational gap that contributed to the Board's breach of duty.

D.   DAMAGES

. . . The plaintiffs sought to prove that the standalone value of the Company was $9.86 per share [relying on] their valuation expert. . . . [However, t]he evidence at trial did not give me sufficient confidence to [agree] . . . [Further, a]lthough this decision has found that the sale process was flawed, largely because of Singer and Deutsche Bank's failure to disclose Avago's tip to the rest of the Board, I believe the sale process was sufficiently reliable to exclude the plaintiffs' damages contention.

. . . The Delaware Supreme Court has . . . commented that a deal price "deserved heavy, if not dispositive weight" when it resulted from a sale process that involved "fair play, low barriers to entry, outreach to all logical buyers, and the chance for any topping bidder to have the support of [the largest stockholder's] votes. . . ." In this case, PLX conducted a quiet outreach campaign during the second half of 2013. By the end of September, Deutsche Bank had contacted fifteen potential bidders, executed nine non-disclosure agreements with companies expressing significant interest, and arranged three meetings. . . . Ultimately, none of the companies made a formal bid, but this process provided the Board with important information about how potential acquirers regarded PLX.

In early 2014, PLX engaged in a quieter market exploration. . . . Although this pre-signing process was not extensive, the contacts provide some support for the reliability of the deal price. . . . More important than the pre-signing process was the post-signing market check. As this decision has explained, the structure of the Merger Agreement satisfied the Delaware Supreme Court's standard for a passive, post-signing market check. No topping bid emerged . . . Another relevant consideration is that the Merger involved a combination between two companies operating in the same industry. As a result, the price likely included synergies. . . .

* * *

Although flawed from a fiduciary standpoint, the details of the sale process that the Board conducted and the nature of the synergistic deal with Avago that it generated means that the plaintiffs received consideration that exceeded the value of the Company on a stand-alone basis. The real-world market evidence from the sale process provides another reason to reject the plaintiffs' damages case. The plaintiffs failed to show causally related damages, and their claim for aiding and abetting therefore fails. . . . Judgment is entered for Potomac.

NOTES AND QUESTIONS ON IN RE PLX

1. The Delaware Supreme Court affirmed the Chancery Court's decision on the issue of damages, but explicitly did not opine on the issue of aiding and abetting a breach of fiduciary duty. It said, "we . . . do not address whether the Court of Chancery was correct in any of its other determinations, including that Potomac was responsible for any breach of fiduciary duty by any PLX director or that any underlying fiduciary duty breach occurred. . . ."[56]

2. The Chancery court highlights the importance of disclosure in determining the standard of review and whether directors have breached their duties (and if someone has aided and abetted those breaches). What level of involvement is required to hold a third party liable for "aiding and abetting" fiduciary breach? Singer dominated the sale process and hid information from the board. Were both necessary?

3. The Court made comments suggesting that the divergent interests of Potomac and Singer from the other shareholders were important. In what way? Does the same argument apply for shareholders who hold different classes of shares?

56. *In re PLX Technology Inc. Stockholders Litigation*, 211 A.3d 137 (2019).

13.10   STATE ANTITAKEOVER STATUTES

13.10.1   First- and Second-Generation Antitakeover Statutes (1968–1987)

Although poison pills were the decisive legal development of the hostile takeover era — and in most respects made state takeover statutes irrelevant, since from the target's perspective the pill was far more effective[57] — states were also active before and after the advent of the pill. State legislation, which came in waves, was generally an attempt by the forces of the status quo to limit the disruption that accompanied hostile takeovers. The first wave of statutes followed the enactment in 1968 of what may be thought of as the first federal antitakeover legislation, the Williams Act.[58] Over the following 13 years, approximately 37 states enacted some version of "first-generation" antitakeover legislation.[59]

The first generation of antitakeover statutes addressed both disclosure and fairness concerns and was generally limited to attempted takeovers of companies with a connection to the enacting state.[60] An example is the Illinois Business Takeover Act of 1979, which required any offer for the shares of qualifying target companies to be registered with the secretary of state, after which the offer entered a 20 day waiting period and then became registered unless, during that period, the secretary called a hearing to adjudicate the substantive fairness of the offer. The secretary exercised discretionary power to call a hearing to protect the shareholders of the target company, but she was required to do so if requested by a majority of the target's outside directors or by Illinois shareholders who owned 10 percent of the class of securities subject to the offer. The secretary was required to deny registration if a tender offer failed to "provide full and fair disclosure to the offerees of all material information concerning the takeover offer" or was "inequitable or would work or tend to work a fraud or deceit upon the offerees." In 1982, the U.S. Supreme Court struck down the Illinois Act[61] as preempted by the federal Williams Act and thus in violation of the Supremacy Clause (and — it seems likely — the Commerce Clause).

---

57. See Catan & Kahan, *supra* note 23, at 634. ("From a lawyer's perspective, finance academics who focus on anti-takeover statutes are barking up the wrong tree. Rather than examine anti-takeover statutes, finance academics should take account of the takeover defense that really matters: the poison pill.").

58. Recall from Chapter 11 that, by creating an auction period and forcing disclosure of takeover plans, the Williams Act raised the costs of takeovers and shifted transaction gains from acquirers to target shareholders. See Easterbrook & Fischel, *supra* at note 2.

59. See Roberta Romano, *Law as a Product: Some Pieces in the Incorporation Puzzle*, 1 J.L. Econ. & Org. 225 (1985).

60. For example, the Illinois Business Takeover Act of 1979 applied to target corporations in which Illinois shareholders held 10 percent or more of the shares subject to the tender offer and to target corporations who satisfied any two of three conditions in an alternative test for local interest: having its principal executive office in Illinois; being organized under the laws of Illinois; or having at least 10 percent of its stated capital and paid-in surplus represented within the state.

61. *Edgar v. MITE Corp.*, 457 U.S. 624 (1982).

After the first generation of antitakeover statutes was invalidated, a second generation of statutes attempted to avoid preemption by the Williams Act by maintaining an appropriate balance between the interests of the offerors and the targets within the overarching policy of investor protection. One example is the "fair price statute," which deters coercive two-tier takeovers by requiring that minority shareholders who are frozen out in the second step of such a takeover receive no less for their shares than the shareholders who tendered in the first step of the takeover. Typically, this result is achieved by requiring a very high supermajority vote to approve a freeze-out merger unless the merger provides shareholders with a statutory "fair price" that equals or exceeds the original tender offer price.[62]

Another example of a second-generation antitakeover statute is the "control share statute," which resists hostile takeovers by requiring a disinterested shareholder vote to approve the purchase of shares by any person crossing certain levels of share ownership in the company that are deemed to constitute "acquisition of control" (usually 20 percent, 33.33 percent, and 50 percent of outstanding shares). Ohio enacted such a statute in 1982 that became the model for other states.[63] Indiana's control share acquisition statute varied the Ohio model by allowing the bidder to cross the relevant ownership thresholds without obtaining shareholder approval but with an automatic loss of voting rights. The offeror could regain voting rights only upon gaining approval from a majority of disinterested shareholders. Indiana's statute was upheld by the U.S. Supreme Court in *CTS Corp. v. Dynamics Corp. of America*, 481 U.S. 69 (1987) against challenges that it violated the Commerce Clause and was preempted by the Williams Act's regulation of tender offers. With respect to the Williams Act preemption claim, the Supreme Court said in part:

> The Indiana Act operates on the assumption, implicit in the Williams Act, that independent shareholders faced with tender offers often are at a disadvantage. By allowing such shareholders to vote as a group, the Act protects them from the coercive aspects of some tender offers . . . [which] furthers the federal policy of investor protection.
>   . . . Unlike the *MITE* statute, the Indiana Act does not give either management or the offeror an advantage in communicating with the shareholders about the impending offer. The Act also does not impose an indefinite delay on tender offers. Nothing in the Act prohibits an offeror from consummating an offer on the 20th business day, the earliest day permitted under applicable federal regulations. . . . Nor does the Act allow the state government to interpose its views of fairness between willing buyers and sellers of shares of the target company. Rather, the Act allows shareholders to evaluate the fairness of the offer collectively. . . .

62. Maryland adopted a fair price statute in 1986. Md. Gen. Corp. L. §§3-601 to 3-603 (1986), and several other states followed suit. See, e.g., Conn. Stock Corp. Act §§33-374a to 33-374c (1986); Ga. Bus. Corp. L. §§232-234 (1985).
    63. Ohio Gen. Corp. L. §1701.32.

The Court of Appeals based its finding of pre-emption on its view that the practical effect of the Indiana Act is to delay consummation of tender offers until 50 days after the commencement of the offer. . . .

[But t]he Act does not impose an absolute 50-day delay on tender offers. . . . If the offeror fears an adverse shareholder vote under the Act, it can make a conditional tender offer, offering to accept shares on the condition that the shares receive voting rights within a certain period of time. The Williams Act permits tender offers to be conditioned on the offeror's subsequently obtaining regulatory approval. . . .

Even assuming that the Indiana Act imposes some additional delay, nothing in *MITE* suggested that any delay imposed by state regulation, however short, would create a conflict with the Williams Act. . . .

Finally, we note that the Williams Act would pre-empt a variety of state corporate laws of hitherto unquestioned validity if it were construed to preempt any state statute that may limit or delay the free exercise of power after a successful tender offer. State corporate laws commonly permit corporations to stagger the terms of their directors. . . . By staggering the terms of directors, and thus having annual elections for only one class of directors each year, corporations may delay the time when a successful offeror gains control of the board of directors. Similarly, state corporation laws commonly provide for cumulative voting. . . .

13.10.2   Third-Generation Antitakeover Statutes

Following the Supreme Court's *CTS* opinion, a third generation of antitakeover statutes were enacted premised on the holding that a state statute would be consistent with both the Williams Act and the Commerce Clause if it allows a bidder to acquire shares, even if it makes such acquisition less attractive in some respects. A prominent example is the so-called business combination statutes. This type of statute prohibits a corporation from engaging in a "business combination" (variously defined) within a set time period after a shareholder acquires more than a threshold level of share ownership. In some statutes, an exception allows a merger to proceed in that time period if a statutory "fair price" is paid in the merger. Such statutes thus act as a ban on immediate liquidation of an acquired entity but not as a bar to takeovers where the acquirer will continue to operate the business of the target. New York adopted the first moratorium statute in 1985, NYBCL §912 (1985), and was followed by other states, including Delaware, DGCL §203 (1988).

NOTE ON DGCL §203

The full text of DGCL §203 is available in your statutory supplement. Like other business combination statutes, DGCL §203 is meant to deter "junk bond"-financed "bust-up" takeovers by preventing acquirers from getting their hands on the assets of target firms. There are two "outs" that may affect the planning of an acquisition. First, the statute's restriction does not apply if the bidder can acquire 85 percent of the outstanding voting stock in a single transaction (on the apparent premise that this level of unity implies a lack of coercion). Second, its restrictions will not be imposed if, after acquiring more than 15 percent, but less than 85 percent, a bidder can secure a two-thirds vote from the remaining shareholders (other than itself) as well as board approval. Obviously, the 85 percent exclusion chills partial bids and low-premium takeovers. The two-thirds vote exception may have a more curious and even paradoxical impact because the more shares a successful bidder gains (short of achieving 85 percent), the greater will be the voting power of any intransigent minority that does not tender. Suppose, for example, that a bidder acquires 80 percent of the voting stock (thus failing to come within the 85 percent exemption in §203(a)(2)). Now, it must secure a two-thirds vote from this remaining 20 percent if it is to escape a three-year moratorium. Thus, if one-third of 20 percent, or 6.6 percent, of the stock is opposed (or wants to hold up the acquirer) or if that percentage simply does not vote (since the statute requires two-thirds of outstanding shareholders to vote affirmatively), the §203(a)(3) exception is not satisfied. Potentially, this could create an incentive to make a partial bid for only 50 percent (if the bidder is uncertain about its ability to acquire 85 percent and it fears falling just short of that level). Alternatively, the bidder could protect itself by specifying an 85 percent minimum tender condition to its obligation to close its tender offer.

Unlike the New York business combination statute, which bars any substantial sale of assets or merger for five years after the threshold is crossed without prior approval, DGCL §203(c)(3) defines the term "business combination" narrowly so as to cover only transactions between the target and the bidder or its affiliates. Thus, a takeover entrepreneur could still seek to acquire control of a company having a liquidation value substantially in excess of its stock market value in order to sell those assets — either piecemeal or in a single sale — to others, and it could then pay out the proceeds of this sale as a pro rata dividend to all remaining shareholders.[64]

QUESTIONS AND NOTES ON DGCL §203

1. If you wished to exploit one of the two loopholes in DGCL §203 in a hostile offer, which would you choose? Could you choose both? What might management do to thwart you?

2. How does DGCL §203 work? Why do acquirers need to get their hands on corporate assets within three years? Isn't it enough to be a controlling shareholder?

3. When DGCL §203 was enacted in 1988, three hostile bidders for Delaware targets challenged its constitutionality on the grounds that the statute was preempted by the Williams Act, among other things. In all three of these cases, the federal district court upheld the constitutionality of DGCL §203, concluding from the evidence presented to the court that the 85 percent "out" in DGCL §203(a)(2) gave bidders a "meaningful opportunity for success," and therefore the statute did not

---

64. It has been estimated that the passage of the Delaware statute by itself extended the protective mantle of a state takeover statute to 80 percent of the business capital in the United States from a prior level of 20 percent. See D. Bandow, *Curbing Raiders Is Bad for Business,* N.Y. Times, Feb. 7, 1988, at F-2.

disrupt the balance between bidders and targets that Congress envisioned. Some scholars assert that all three courts left open the possibility that future evidence could influence, and possibly change, the constitutional conclusion and that subsequent evidence shows that no bidder has subsequently achieved 85 percent on a hostile basis in a tender offer. See Guhan Subramanian, Steven Herscovici & Brian Barbetta, *Is Delaware's Antitakeover Statute Unconstitutional? Evidence from 1988-2008*, 65 Bus. Law. 685 (2010). A second example of the post-*CTS* statutes is the disgorgement statute, which has been adopted by Pennsylvania, 15 Pa. Consol. Stat. Ann. §§2561-2567, and Ohio, Ohio Rev. Code Ann. §1707.043. These statutes mandate the disgorgement of profits made by bidders upon the sale of either stock in the target or assets of the target. Any bidder who acquires a fixed percentage of voting rights, including (in some acts) voting rights acquired by proxy solicitation, is subject to this statute. Thus, under the Pennsylvania statute, any profit realized by a "controlling person" from the sale of any equity security of the target within 18 months of becoming a "controlling person" belongs to the target. A "controlling person" includes any person or group who has acquired, offered to acquire, or publicly disclosed the intent to acquire over 20 percent of the total voting rights. Since the emphasis is on voting rights, a solicitation of proxies triggers the disgorgement provision. The Ohio statute is more circumscribed, providing safe harbors to management proxy solicitations. It also provides safe harbors to insurgent solicitations made in accordance with federal proxy rules where the solicitation of the voting right is limited to the matters described in the proxy statement and constrained by the instructions of the proxy giver. The constitutionality of these statutes remains untested.

"Constituency statutes" comprise the last major class of third-generation statutes.[65] They allow, or in some states require, the board of a target corporation to consider the interests of constituencies other than the shareholders when determining what response to take to a hostile takeover offer. These statutes deter takeovers by releasing directors from some of the fiduciary constraints imposed by case law in the takeover context, thus allowing the board to use a broader range of potential justifications for taking defensive measures.

13.11   PROXY CONTESTS FOR CORPORATE CONTROL

In a world in which corporations are defended by poison pills, those seeing opportunity in a change of management have only two alternatives. The first is to negotiate with the incumbent board. In some cases, board leadership might be convinced that a change-in-control transaction is a good thing. The odds of persuasion are increased by lucrative inducements for CEOs, such as substantial non-vested options that will vest in a change-in-control transaction,

---

65. There are other, more idiosyncratic antitakeover statutes as well. The less common statutes include those that prohibit targets from adopting golden parachutes for their executives or paying greenmail without shareholder approval, Ariz. Rev. Stat. §§1202, 1204; authorize the adoption of discriminatory rights plans without shareholder approval, NYBCL §§501, 505; or require appraisals in management-led buyouts, Cal. Gen. Corp. L. §§181, 1001, 1101.

consultation agreements, or other deal-related compensation. Therefore, one might predict that, as the Delaware Supreme Court will permit boards to leave poison pills in place indefinitely, the number of "friendly deals" will increase.[66]

The second alternative for displacing management is the hostile option of running both a proxy contest and a tender offer simultaneously. In this case, closing the tender offer is conditioned on electing the acquirer's nominees to the board and the board's redemption of the target's poison pill. See, e.g., *Hilton Hotels, Inc. v. ITT Corp.*, 978 F. Supp. 1342 (D. Nev. 1997). Contests of this type leave open a variety of further defensive steps that the target may attempt to take. For example, the target board may attempt to affect the outcome of the proxy fight by issuing stock into friendly hands; it may move the meeting date; it may sell assets that the "raider" presumably treasures — and it may sell them to a friendly party for high-vote stock; it may put covenants in new loan agreements that impede the takeover, and so forth. In other words, a target board may engage in a wide variety of actions that are designed to impede an insurgent from gathering enough support to oust the current board through a shareholder vote. The following cases address the legal test for evaluating board actions that affect proxy contests.

BLASIUS INDUSTRIES, INC. v. ATLAS CORP.
564 A.2d 651 (Del. Ch. 1988)

[Blasius Industries, the owner of about 9 percent of the stock of the Atlas Corporation, proposed a restructuring to Atlas's management that would have resulted in a major sale of Atlas assets, an infusion of new debt financing, and the disbursement of a very large cash dividend to Atlas's shareholders. When management rejected the restructuring proposal, Blasius announced that it would pursue a campaign to obtain shareholder consents to increase Atlas's board from seven to fifteen members, the maximum size allowed by Atlas's charter, and to fill the new board seats with Blasius's nominees. The Atlas board, however, preempted Blasius's campaign by immediately amending the bylaws to add two new board seats and filling these seats with its own candidates. (Remember the "Unfireable CEO" problem in Section 6.2? The Atlas board was classified, needless to say.)]

ALLEN, C.:

. . .

THE MOTIVATION OF THE INCUMBENT BOARD IN EXPANDING THE BOARD AND APPOINTING NEW MEMBERS

In increasing the size of Atlas' board by two and filling the newly created positions, the members of the board realized that they were thereby

---

66. See, e.g., Marcel Kahan & Edward B. Rock, *How I Learned to Stop Worrying and Love the Pill: Adaptive Responses to Takeover Law*, 69 U. Chi. L. Rev. 871 (2002).

precluding the holders of a majority of the Company's shares from placing a majority of new directors on the board through Blasius' consent solicitation, should they want to do so. Indeed the evidence establishes that that was the principal motivation in so acting.

The conclusion that, in creating two new board positions on December 31 and electing Messrs. Devaney and Winters to fill those positions the board was principally motivated to prevent or delay the shareholders from possibly placing a majority of new members on the board, is critical to my analysis of the central issue posed by the first filed of the two pending cases. If the board in fact was not so motivated, but rather had taken action completely independently of the consent solicitation, which merely had an incidental impact upon the possible effectuation of any action authorized by the shareholders, it is very unlikely that such action would be subject to judicial nullification. . . . The board, as a general matter, is under no fiduciary obligation to suspend its active management of the firm while the consent solicitation process goes forward. . . .

I conclude that, while the addition of these qualified men would, under other circumstances, be clearly appropriate as an independent step, such a step was in fact taken in order to impede or preclude a majority of the shareholders from effectively adopting the course proposed by Blasius. . . .

Plaintiff attacks the December 31 board action as a selfishly motivated effort to protect the incumbent board from a perceived threat to its control of Atlas. Their conduct is said to constitute a violation of the principle, applied in such cases as *Schnell v. Chris Craft Industries*, Del. Supr., 285 A.2d 437 (1971), that directors hold legal powers subjected to a supervening duty to exercise such powers in good faith pursuit of what they reasonably believe to be in the corporation's interest. . . .

On balance, I cannot conclude that the board was acting out of a self-interested motive in any important respect on December 31. I conclude rather that the board saw the "threat" of the Blasius recapitalization proposal as posing vital policy differences between itself and Blasius. It acted, I conclude, in a good faith effort to protect its incumbency, not selfishly, but in order to thwart implementation of the recapitalization that it feared, reasonably, would cause great injury to the Company.

The real question the case presents, to my mind, is whether, in these circumstances, the board, even if it is acting with subjective good faith (which will typically, if not always, be a contestable or debatable judicial conclusion), may validly act for the principal purpose of preventing the shareholders from electing a majority of new directors. The question thus posed is not one of intentional wrong (or even negligence), but one of authority as between the fiduciary and the beneficiary (not simply legal authority, i.e., as between the fiduciary and the world at large).

It is established in our law that a board may take certain steps — such as the purchase by the corporation of its own stock — that have the effect of defeating a threatened change in corporate control, when those steps are taken advisedly, in good faith pursuit of a corporate interest, and are reasonable in relation to a threat to legitimate corporate interests posed by the proposed change in control. See *Unocal Corp. v. Mesa Petroleum Co.*, Del. Supr., 493 A.2d 946 (1985). . . . Does this rule — that the reason able exercise of good faith and due care generally validates, in equity, the exercise of legal authority even if the act has an entrenchment effect — apply to action designed for the primary purpose of interfering with the effectiveness of a stockholder vote? Our authorities, as well as sound principles, suggest that the central importance of the franchise to the scheme of corporate governance, requires that, in this setting, that rule not be applied and that closer scrutiny be accorded to such transaction. . . .

The shareholder franchise is the ideological underpinning upon which the legitimacy of directorial power rests. Generally, shareholders have only two protections against perceived inadequate business performance. They may sell their stock (which, if done in sufficient numbers, may so affect security prices as to create an incentive for altered managerial performance), or they may vote to replace incumbent board members.

It has, for a long time, been conventional to dismiss the stockholder vote as a vestige or ritual of little practical importance. It may be that we are now witnessing the emergence of new institutional voices and arrangements that will make the stockholder vote a less predictable affair than it has been. Be that as it may, however, whether the vote is seen functionally as an unimportant formalism, or as an important tool of discipline, it is clear that it is critical to the theory that legitimates the exercise of power by some (directors and officers) over vast aggregations of property that they do not own. Thus, when viewed from a broad, institutional perspective, it can be seen that matters involving the integrity of the shareholder voting process involve consideration not present in any other context in which directors exercise delegated power.

The distinctive nature of the shareholder franchise context also appears when the matter is viewed from a less generalized, doctrinal point of view. From this point of view, as well, it appears that the ordinary considerations to which the business judgment rule originally responded are simply not present in the shareholder-voting context.[2] That is, a decision by the board to act for the primary purpose of preventing the effectiveness of a shareholder vote inevitably involves the question who, as between the principal and the agent,

---

2. Delaware courts have long exercised a most sensitive and protective regard for the free and effective exercise of voting rights. This concern suffuses our law, manifesting itself in various settings. For example, the perceived importance of the franchise explains the cases that hold that a director's fiduciary duty requires disclosure to shareholders asked to authorize a transaction of all material information in the corporation's possession, even if the transaction is not a self-dealing one. See, e.g., *Smith v. Van Gorkom*, Del. Supr., 488 A.2d 858 (1985). . . . A similar concern, for credible corporate democracy, underlies those cases that strike down board action that sets or moves an annual meeting date upon a finding that such action was intended to thwart a shareholder group from effectively mounting an election campaign. See, e.g., *Schnell v. Chris Craft*. . . . The cases invalidating stock issued for the primary purpose of diluting the voting power of a control block also reflect the law's concern that a credible form of corporate democracy be maintained. . . . Similarly, a concern for corporate democracy is reflected (1) in our statutory requirement of annual meetings (8 Del. C. §211), and in the cases that aggressively and summarily enforce that right. . . .

has authority with respect to a matter of internal corporate governance. That, of course, is true in a very specific way in this case which deals with the question who should constitute the board of directors of the corporation, but it will be true in every instance in which an incumbent board seeks to thwart a shareholder majority. A board's decision to act to prevent the shareholders from creating a majority of new board positions and filling them does not involve the exercise of the corporation's power over its property, or with respect to its rights or obligations; rather, it involves allocation, between shareholders as a class and the board, of effective power with respect to governance of the corporation. This need not be the case with respect to other forms of corporate action that may have an entrenchment effect. . . . Action designed principally to interfere with the effectiveness of a vote inevitably involves a conflict between the board and a shareholder majority. Judicial review of such action involves a determination of the legal and equitable obligations of an agent towards his principal. This is not, in my opinion, a question that a court may leave to the agent finally to decide so long as he does so honestly and competently; that is, it may not be left to the agent's business judgment. . . .

QUESTIONS AND NOTES ON BLASIUS

1. Which of the following actions by the board may be prohibited under the *Blasius* rationale? Under what circumstances?

a. During a heated proxy contest for control of the board, the incumbent board purchases stock selectively from a large shareholder who is otherwise likely to vote for the insurgents.

b. Under the same circumstances, the incumbent board issues a large block of additional stock at the market price to shareholders who are likely to support the incumbent board.

c. Under the same circumstances, the incumbent board delays the annual meeting after the meeting date is set when its initial proxy returns suggest that the insurgents may win.

2. In *Blasius* the court went on to reject a per se rule, instead holding that the board bears the "heavy burden of demonstrating a compelling justification" after the plaintiff has established that the board "has acted for the primary purpose of thwarting the exercise of a shareholder vote." Yet it is not easy to fortify the vote with strong fiduciary protections. Since manipulations of the voting process can often be characterized as "defensive," courts may apply *Unocal* which is less demanding than review under *Blasius*. The structure of analysis under either review standard, however, is the same. In both instances, directors have the burden to establish compliance with a standard, and in both instances, the standard is a relative one. In *Unocal*, the action must be reasonable in light of something else (a threat that the act is directed against). Under *Blasius*, the justification for the act must be deemed compelling in light of something else (the threat that the act is directed against). The substantive difference is one of emphasis. *Blasius* requires a very powerful justification to thwart a shareholder franchise for an extended period. But

where a board delays a shareholder vote for a week or two, a less compelling justification may suffice.[67]

There is, however, one critical difference between review under *Unocal* and review under *Blasius.* The Delaware Supreme Court's *Time-Warner* opinion seems to authorize a target board to take defensive action if the company is threatened by what the court terms "substantive coercion." This, in the end, is simply the board's belief that the tender offer is inadequate and that the shareholders do not understand that. Under *Blasius,* however, corporate action to defeat a proxy contest cannot be justified by a parallel belief that the voters simply do not understand the foolishness of voting for the insurgent slate.

Blasius continues to be a significant precedent where board action specifically attempts to impede a shareholder vote. However, *Blasius* is not a radical departure from prior case law, nor is it revolutionary; it is a special case evaluating board conduct under the general principles of fiduciary duty.

3. *Liquid Audio v. MM Companies, Inc.*[68] is a case that lies at the intersection of *Unocal* and *Blasius.* Liquid Audio (LA) was yet another victim of the dot-com bubble, reaching $48 per share at its peak but down to less than $3 per share by 2001. The *Wall Street Journal* reported that LA's business strategy suffered because rivals "offer[ed] similar services free of charge." (How's that for a business problem?) LA rejected a cash offer from MM Companies in favor of a stock-for-stock merger with Alliance Entertainment. MM then forced LA to hold its annual meeting, at which MM planned to: (1) challenge the two incumbent directors who were up for reelection; and (2) propose a bylaw amendment expanding the board from five to nine members. In August 2002, LA added two directors, increasing the board size from five to seven. At the annual meeting one month later, shareholders elected the two MM candidates to replace the LA incumbents, but rejected the MM proposal to add four more board seats. MM brought suit alleging *Blasius* and *Unocal* violations. Vice Chancellor Jack Jacobs upheld LA's defensive tactics under *Unocal,* and declined to apply *Blasius* because LA's actions would not have prevented MM from achieving board control had its board expansion amendment succeeded.[69] The Delaware Supreme Court reversed, holding that *Blasius* applied and invalidated LA's board expansion from five to seven because the "primary purpose" of LA's actions was to reduce the MM directors' ability to influence board decisions.[70]

4. In *Mercier v. Inter-Tel,*[71] the Inter-Tel board delayed a merger vote by 25 days in order to provide more information to shareholders, and because it became clear that shareholders were not going to approve the merger on the original meeting date. Vice Chancellor Strine applied the *Blasius* standard but held that the standard "ought to be consistent with the *Unocal* framework": Directors should bear the burden of proving that their action

---

67. See *Mercier v. Inter-Tel, infra.*
68. 929 A.2d 786 (Del. Ch. 2007).
69. *MM Companies v. Liquid Audio*, 813 A.2d 1118 (Del. 2003).
70. *MM Companies v. Liquid Audio, Inc.*, 813 A.2d 1118, 1132 (Del. 2003).
71. 929 A.2d 786 (Del. Ch. 2007).

(1) serves, and is motivated by, a legitimate corporate objective; and (2) is reasonable in relation to the legitimate objective and not preclusive or coercive. Under this recasting of *Blasius* the Inter-Tel board had met its burden, but the court still noted some room between *Blasius* and *Unocal*: "Lest there be confusion, I do not believe that the use of a test of this kind should signal a tolerance of the concept of 'substantive coercion' in the director election process." A few years later, Strine commented in *Kallick v. Sandridge Energy, Inc.*, 68 A.3d 242, 258-59 (Del. Ch. 2013) that *Blasius'* compelling justification would be invoked when a challenged activity was "taken for the sole or primary purpose of thwarting a shareholder vote." However, he further said "*Blasius'* importance rests more in its emphatic and enduring critical role in underscoring the serious scrutiny that Delaware law gives to director action that threatens to undermine the integrity of the electoral process, than in its articulation of a useful standard of review to decide actual cases."[72]

13.12   DEALS JURISPRUDENCE AND CONTRACTUAL FREEDOM

The current standards for reviewing deals place considerable and often dispositive weight on fair process. Thus, if *MFW*'s conditions are adopted *ab initio* and followed scrupulously, a freeze-out merger is likely to receive business judgment review. Similarly, following *Corwin*'s prescription of an informed uncoerced shareholder vote is likely to ensure business judgment review of all transactions apart from those engineered by a controlling shareholder. And even in appraisal proceedings, a deal price negotiated at arm's length would seem to be a ceiling on a company's fair value — and thus, the major determinant of fair price — unless egregious conflicts of interest or other process failures were to compromise deal price. Of course, the process behind every deal is unique. Nevertheless, the thrust of the new case law is to suggest that appropriate processes are effective substitutes for robust equitable review under most circumstances.

   How should we understand this development? If we focus only on deals, we might infer that if the deal process proxies for arm's length negotiations, deal price is less worrisome than the prospect of wasteful and costly deal litigation. However, a focus on deals may be too narrow. We suggest that a full explanation of the development of the law in the M&A context might also be seen as part of a broader trend across many areas of the law of business organizations to limit equitable review in deference to contractual protections.

---

72. In *Pell v. Kill*, 135 A.3d 764, 785 (Del. Ch. 2016), the Chancery Court said that "the shift from reasonable to compelling requires that directors establish a closer fit between means and ends" and that *Blasius* was not a separate standard of review, but within the enhanced scrutiny standard of review. The court went on to note that it would examine justifications with a "gimlet eye" if the board was aware that the election was likely to be contested. For a critique of cases that appear to narrow *Blasius*, see James D. Cox & Randall S. Thomas, *Delaware's Retreat: Exploring Developing Fissures and Tectonic Shifts in Delaware Corporate Law*, 42 Del. J. of Corp. L. 323, 360-369 (2018).

Think back to Chapter 2, for example, which reviewed how Delaware's legislature and courts allowed a bevy of new contractual entities to slough off traditional fiduciary norms in favor of more clearly articulated contractual protections or no fiduciary protections at all. The simultaneous substitution of limited liability as the default term in the contractual relationship between equity holders and outside creditors had a similar effect insofar as it freed equity holders to contract into personal liability with firm creditors on a case-by-case basis. Corporation law doesn't allow as much latitude to contract out of fiduciary duties as parallel entity forms do. Nonetheless, "contractualization" has made incremental progress here too. Consider statutory authorization to allow shareholders to contract to enter corporate opportunities waivers under §122(17) (discussed in Chapter 8) and to waive monetary damages for directorial breaches of the duty of care under §102(b)(7) (discussed in Chapter 7). The recent deal case law — *MFW, Corwin, Aruba, Dell,* and *DFC* — is a first step in the same direction. Detailing a procedural map around searching judicial review is the functional equivalent of specifying the mandatory terms in a contract that dispenses with traditional fiduciary protections. We do not suggest or expect full convergence between contractual and corporate entities. Standard charter terms in public corporations provide important network advantages that will make lawmakers think twice about further weakening the established legislation and case law that is now an organic part of the corporate contract. Yet it may be that the changes in the trade-off between established expectations and flexibility still has surprises in store for us.

TRADING IN THE CORPORATION'S SECURITIES

We turn now to a large topic: the obligations of directors, officers, and issuing corporations when dealing in the corporation's own securities. For publicly financed corporations, this is primarily an area of federal law. In the public distributions of securities, the Securities Act of 1933 is the principal statute. Thereafter, for shares that continue to trade in the public "secondary" markets (such as the New York Stock Exchange or NASDAQ), the Securities Exchange Act of 1934 is the primary source of regulatory law. The Securities and Exchange Commission has promulgated extensive regulations under both of these statutes, which dominate the legal regulation of disclosure. While state law is not entirely supplanted in this area, the fiduciary doctrines that play such a large role elsewhere in corporate law are decidedly of secondary significance in this field. Even though the law of mandatory disclosure is principally federal, it is helpful to begin with a review of the fraud remedy and the common law of insider trading. In large part, it was the perceived shortcomings of this area of state law that motivated the Depression-era federal securities statutes.

14.1 Common Law of Directors' Duties When Trading in the Corporation's Stock

The nineteenth century was an age of *caveat emptor* — let the buyer beware. Then, as now, fraud was actionable. But prosecuting a claim of common law fraud was not easy, since it required proof of five elements: (1) a *false statement* of (2) *material* fact (3) made with the *intention to deceive* (4) upon which one *reasonably relied* and which (5) *caused injury.* Given these elements, the fraud remedy was generally unavailable when the buyer or seller simply failed to disclose a material fact without overt deception. Equally important, common law fraud was unavailable to redress the losses of persons trading over impersonal markets (such as stock exchanges), since they could not be said to have traded in reliance on statements made by unknown counter-parties.

Moreover, even where parties transacted face-to-face, nondisclosure of a material fact was not usually considered to be a fraud at common law. A buyer who wanted information generally had to bargain for it by demanding a representation or warranty from his seller. There was, however, one area in which the common law imposed a duty of full and fair disclosure on the seller: in contracts between trustees and their beneficiaries. By the late nineteenth century, such contracts were upheld only if there was proof of full disclosure and substantive fairness. (Sound familiar? Look back to Chapters 1 and 8.)

The tough common law requirements of full disclosure and fairness in dealings between trustees and trust beneficiaries raised an obvious question for corporate law at the end of the nineteenth century: Was trading in stock by a corporate officer or director of the issuer sufficiently like trustee self-dealing to merit analysis under the disclosure and fairness rule? Jurisdictions differed on this question.[1] The majority rule was that a director's only duty was to the corporation and, *a fortiori,* he did not owe a duty of disclosure to those with whom he traded shares. Only a handful of jurisdictions imposed a general duty to disclose material information when a director traded opposite shareholders in his company's stock. The U.S. Supreme Court applied an intermediate rule in *Strong v. Repide,* a case in which a shareholder offered to sell his stock to a director who knew that the company would soon obtain a highly favorable contract. The director bought the stock without disclosing the company's good news or counseling delay, at what soon appeared to be a bargain price. The former shareholder sued to rescind the contract for breach of loyalty. The Supreme Court affirmed judgment in favor of the shareholder on the grounds that, where *special facts* exist, a director has an obligation to disclose them to his counter-party in a face-to-face transaction or refrain from trading.

Cases involving transactions on the public markets were more difficult for a shareholder-plaintiff to prosecute successfully. *Goodwin v. Agassiz,* below, discusses what then (1933) seemed to be the weak doctrinal case for imposing a disclosure duty on a corporate director or officer who trades on the basis of material nonpublic information in an anonymous public stock market. *Goodwin* was decided of course shortly before the enactment of the federal securities laws.

GOODWIN v. AGASSIZ
186 N.E. 659 (Mass. 1933)

RUGG, C.J.:

A stockholder in a corporation seeks in this suit relief for losses suffered by him in selling shares of stock in Cliff Mining Company by way of accounting, rescission of sales, or redelivery of shares. . . .

The defendants, in May 1926, purchased . . . on the Boston stock exchange seven hundred shares . . . of the Cliff Mining Company [belonging

---

1. See, e.g., Michael Conant, *Duties of Disclosure of Corporate Insiders Who Purchase Shares,* 46 Cornell L.Q. 53 (1960).

to the plaintiff]. Agassiz was president and director and MacNaughton a director and general manager of the company. They had certain knowledge, material as to the value of the stock, which the plaintiff did not have. The plaintiff contends that such purchase in all the circumstances without disclosure to him of the knowledge was a wrong against him. That knowledge was that an experienced geologist had formulated in writing in March 1926, a theory as to the possible existence of copper deposits under conditions prevailing in the region where the property of the company was located. That region was known as the mineral belt in Northern Michigan, where are located mines of several copper mining companies. Another such company, of which the defendants were officers, had made extensive geological surveys of its lands. In consequence of recommendations resulting from that survey, exploration was started on property of the Cliff Mining Company in 1925. That exploration was ended in May 1926, because completed unsuccessfully, and the equipment was removed. The defendants discussed the geologist's theory shortly after it was formulated. Both felt that the theory had value and should be tested, but they agreed . . . that if the geologist's theory were known to the owners of such other land there might be difficulty in securing options [on adjacent properties], and that that theory should not be communicated to any one unless it became absolutely necessary. . . . The defendants both thought, also that, if there was any merit in the geologist's theory, the price of Cliff Mining Company stock in the market would go up. Its stock was quoted and bought and sold on the Boston Stock Exchange. Pursuant to agreement, they bought many shares of that stock through agents on joint account. The plaintiff first learned of the closing of exploratory operations on property of the Cliff Mining Company from an article in a paper on May 14, 1926, and immediately sold his shares of stock through brokers. It does not appear that the defendants were in any way responsible for the publication of that article. The plaintiff did not know that the purchase was made for the defendants and they did not know that his stock was being bought for them. There was no communication between them touching the subject. The plaintiff would not have sold his stock if he had known of the geologist's theory. The finding is express that the defendants were not guilty of fraud, that they committed no breach of duty owed by them to the Cliff Mining Company, and that that company was not harmed by the nondisclosure of the geologist's theory, or by their purchases of its stock, or by shutting down the exploratory operations.

The contention of the plaintiff is that the purchase of his stock in the company by the defendants without disclosing to him as a stockholder their knowledge of the geologist's theory, their belief that the theory had value, . . . and their plan ultimately to test the value of the theory, constitute actionable wrong for which he as stockholder can recover. . . .

The directors of a commercial corporation stand in a relation of trust to the corporation and are bound to exercise the strictest good faith in respect to its property and business. . . . The contention that directors also occupy the position of trustee toward individual stockholders in the corporation is plainly contrary to repeated decisions of this court and cannot be supported. . . .

A rule holding that directors are trustees for individual stockholders with respect to their stock prevails in comparatively few states; but in view of our own adjudications it is not necessary to review decisions to that effect. . . .

The knowledge naturally in the possession of a director as to the condition of a corporation places upon him a peculiar obligation to observe every requirement of fair dealing when directly buying or selling its stock. Mere silence does not usually amount to a breach of duty, but parties may stand in such relation to each other that an equitable responsibility arises to communicate facts. . . . [Nevertheless,] purchases and sales of stock dealt in on the stock exchange are commonly impersonal affairs. An honest director would be in a difficult situation if he could neither buy nor sell on the stock exchange shares of stock in his corporation without first seeking out the other actual ultimate party to the transaction and disclosing to him everything which a court or jury might later find that he then knew affecting the real or speculative value of such shares. . . . On the other hand, directors cannot rightly be allowed to indulge with impunity in practices which do violence to prevailing standards of upright business men. Therefore, where a director personally seeks a stockholder for the purpose of buying his shares without making disclosure of material facts . . . , the transaction will be closely scrutinized and relief may be granted in appropriate instances. *Strong v. Repide*, 213 U.S. 419. . . .

The precise question to be decided . . . is whether . . . the defendants as directors had a right to buy stock of the plaintiff, a stockholder. . . . The only knowledge possessed by the defendants not open to the plaintiff was the existence of a theory . . . as to the possible existence of copper deposits where certain geological conditions existed. . . . Whether that theory was sound or fallacious, no one knew, and so far as appears has never been demonstrated. The defendants made no representations to anybody about the theory. No facts found placed upon them any obligation to disclose the theory. A few days after the thesis expounding the theory was brought to the attention of the defendants, the annual report by the directors of the Cliff Mining Company for the calendar year 1925, signed by Agassiz for the directors, was issued. It did not cover the time when the theory was formulated. The report described the status of the operations under the exploration which had been begun in 1925. At the annual meeting of the stockholders of the company held early in April 1926, no reference was made to the theory. It was then at most a hope, possibly an expectation. It had not passed the nebulous stage. No disclosure was made of it. The Cliff Mining Company was not harmed by the nondisclosure. There would have been no advantage to it, so far as appears, from a disclosure. The disclosure would have been detrimental to the interests of another mining corporation in which the defendants were directors. In the circumstances there was no duty on the part of the defendants to set forth to the stockholders at the annual meeting their faith, aspirations and plans for the future. . . . Disclosing of the theory, if it ultimately was proved to be erroneous . . . , might involve the defendants in litigation with those who might act on the hypothesis that it was correct. The stock of the Cliff Mining Company was bought and sold on the stock exchange. The identity of buyers and seller of the stock in question in fact was not known to the parties. . . . The defendants caused the shares to be bought through brokers on the stock exchange. They said nothing to anybody as to the reasons actuating them. The plaintiff was no novice. He was a member of the Boston stock exchange and had kept a record of sales of Cliff Mining Company stock. He acted upon his own judgment in selling his stock. He made no inquiries of the defendants or of other officers of the company. The result is that the plaintiff cannot prevail. . . .

QUESTIONS ON GOODWIN v. AGASSIZ

1. Do you disagree with the result? How would today's public investors react to the actions sanctioned by *Goodwin*?

2. Would the court have decided differently if the Agassiz insiders had purchased Goodwin's stock after learning that the geologist was right — the company had struck it rich — but before they could make a public announcement because the company had not yet completed negotiations to secure mining rights from landowners of adjacent properties? Alternatively, what if the insiders had temporarily stopped the company's exploratory drilling deliberately in order to lower share prices while their agents worked the Boston Exchange buying shares?

14.2   THE CORPORATE LAW OF INSIDER TRADING POST-*GOODWIN*

Goodwin was decided in 1933, but little changed in the duties of insiders who traded their companies' shares for the next 30 years. Even the 1934 Securities Exchange Act did not seem to address the issue of insider disclosure to counter-parties in the public markets.

But if state corporate law mostly rejected the view that insiders owed a disclosure duty to their counter-parties when trading in the market, it slowly began to develop another response to insider trading based on a different, and perhaps more natural set of fiduciary duties — namely, the duties that agents and directors owed to the company itself. Basic agency law prohibits agents from employing their principals' confidential information for personal profit.[2] The equitable remedy if this duty is breached is most commonly disgorgement, meaning that the principal can claim the agent's illicit profits. In the corporate context, the company is the principal, and as such it would seem that it should have a strong claim on any profits received by a corporate officer or director after trading on the company's private information. If the corporate board declined to sue the insider, then any shareholder should have standing to sue on the company's behalf. Although the logic seems clear enough, derivative suits to recover insider gains did not emerge until the middle of the twentieth century. The Delaware Chancery Court was the first court to recognize such an action against corporate insiders in *Brophy v. Cities Service Co.*, 70 A.2d 5 (Del. Ch. 1949). Two decades later, the influential New York Court of Appeals built on *Brophy* to articulate the action's rationale in *Diamond v. Oreamuno*, 248 N.E.2d 910 (N.Y. Ct. App. 1969). And

---

2. Restatement (Third) Agency §8.02.

over the next decade, increasing numbers of derivative actions against insider trading succeeded under a *Brophy*-like theory of insider breach of loyalty to their corporations. Today, the Restatement (Third) Agency relies on *Brophy* and *Diamond* in framing the duties of corporate agents. Of course, many courts resisted a "corporate duty" theory of insider liability, most conspicuously when there was no evidence that the corporation had suffered tangible harm from the alleged insider trading. The Delaware Supreme Court definitively rejected actual harm as a precondition for the disgorgement remedy as late as 2011, when it held that the disgorgement remedy required a derivative plaintiff to demonstrate only two propositions: a corporate fiduciary (1) "possessed material, nonpublic company information, and (2) executed trades motivated by the substance of that information." *Kahn v. Kohlberg Kravis Roberts & Co.*, 23 A.3d 831, (Del. 2011).

Why were state courts so slow to adopt the corporate duty theory of insider liability? The case *Freeman v. Decio,* excerpted below, illustrates the arguments made by its sophisticated opponents.[3]

NOTE ON FREEMAN v. DECIO, *584 F.2d 186 (7th Cir. 1978)*

Defendant Decio was the chairman, CEO, and controlling shareholder of a public corporation. A shareholder-plaintiff brought a derivative action alleging that Decio and other insiders had made large profits by buying the company's shares shortly before disclosing record earnings and selling shares before disclosing a sharp drop in company earnings. This was a case of first impression in Indiana, the company's home jurisdiction.[4] More than a decade before it was filed, corporate common law on insider trading had reached an impasse. Rule 10b-5, a broad anti-fraud rule promulgated under the 1934 Securities Exchange Act, had come to dominate insider trading law. We will return to Rule 10b-5 below, but it is enough to say now that a corporate law derivative suit at this time was an odd duck. Judge Wood, Jr., writing for the Seventh Circuit, used the occasion to critique the earlier development of state law on insider trading before concluding that the Indiana courts would reject a derivative action based on an insider's fiduciary duty to the corporation, or a theory of inside information as corporate property. The following excerpt indicates the direction of his argument.

[T]he plaintiff suggests that were the question to be presented to the Indiana courts, they would adopt the holding of the New York Court of

---

3. No doubt other factors are at least as important in explaining the late arrival of actions challenging fiduciary breach of corporate duties in insider trading cases. We suspect that in addition to the doctrinal arguments, evidentiary difficulties and the limited size of recoveries must also have played a role.

4. The second amended complaint contained allegations of violations of §§17(a) and 22(a) of the 1933 Act, §§10(b) and 27 of the 1934 Act, and Rule 10b-5. The appeal did not include claims related to actions under any of these but did include a challenge to the lower court's ruling on §16(b), which the court affirmed. The instant suit was primarily focused on the state law claim the plaintiff advanced when suing the largest shareholder and the directors.

Appeals in *Diamond v. Oreamuno*, 248 N.E.2d 910 (1969): . . . that the officers and directors of a corporation breached their fiduciary duties owed to the corporation by trading in its stock on the basis of material non-public information acquired by virtue of their official positions. . . .

[F]rom a policy point of view it is widely accepted that insider trading should be deterred because it is unfair to other investors who do not enjoy the benefits of access to inside information. The goal is not one of equality of possession of information since some traders will always be better "informed" than others by dint of greater expenditures of time and resources, greater experience, or greater analytical abilities but rather equality of access to information. . . .

Yet, a growing body of commentary suggests that [such] . . . "market egalitarianism" may be costly. In addition to the costs associated with enforcement of the laws prohibiting insider trading, there may be a loss in the efficiency of the securities markets in their capital allocation function. The basic insight of economic analysis here is that securities prices act as signals helping to route capital to its most productive uses and that insider trading helps assure that those prices will reflect the best information available (i.e., inside information) as to where the best opportunities lie. However, even when confronted with the possibility of a trade-off between fairness and economic efficiency, most authorities appear to find that the balance tips in favor of discouraging insider trading. . . .

Absent fraud, the traditional common law approach has been to permit officers and directors of corporations to trade in their corporation's securities free from liability to other traders for failing to disclose inside information. . . .

The *Diamond* court relied heavily on the Delaware case of *Brophy v. Cities Service Co.*, 31 Del. Ch. 241, 70 A.2d 5 (1949), [which was a] . . . significant departure from the traditional common law approach. . . . There, the confidential secretary to a director of a corporation purchased a number of shares of the company's stock after finding out that the corporation was about to enter the market to make purchases of its stock itself, and then sold at a profit after the corporation began its purchases. The Delaware Court of Chancery upheld the complaint in a derivative action on behalf of the corporation to recover those profits. The court stated that the employee occupied a position of trust and confidence toward his employer and that public policy would not permit him to abuse that relation for his own profit, regardless of whether or not the employer suffered a loss . . . . The *Diamond* court also relied on Section 388 of the Restatement (2nd) of Agency. . . .

[However, t]here are a number of difficulties with the *Diamond* court's ruling. Perhaps the thorniest problem . . . is that there is no injury to the corporation which can serve as a basis for recognizing a right of recovery in favor of the latter. . . .

Some might see the *Diamond* court's decision as resting on a broad, strict-trust notion [that] no director is to receive any profit, beyond what he receives from the corporation, solely because of his position. Although . . . this basis for the *Diamond* rule would obviate the need for finding a potential for injury to the corporation, it is not at all clear that current corporation law contemplates such an extensive notion of fiduciary duty. It is customary to view the *Diamond* result as resting on a characterization of inside information as a corporate asset. The lack of necessity for looking for an injury to the corporation is then justified by the traditional "no inquiry" rule with respect to profits made by trustees from assets belonging to the trust *res*. However, to start from the premise that all inside information . . . [is] a corporate asset may presuppose an answer to the inquiry at hand. It might be better to ask whether there is any potential loss to the corporation from the use of such information in insider trading. . . .

Most information involved in insider trading is not [a corporate asset], e.g., knowledge of an impending merger, a decline in earnings, etc. If the corporation were to attempt to exploit such non-public information by dealing in its own securities, it would open itself up to potential liability under federal and state securities laws. . . .

The injury [to the corporation] hypothesized by the *Diamond* court seems little different from the harm to the corporation that might be inferred whenever a responsible corporate official commits an illegal or unethical act using a corporate asset. Absent is the element of loss of opportunity or potential susceptibility to outside influence that generally is present when a corporate fiduciary is required to account to the corporation. . . .

[T]he *Diamond* court's action was motivated in large part by its perception of the inadequacy of existing remedies for insider trading. . . . [O]ver the decade since *Diamond* was decided, the 10b-5 class action has made substantial advances toward becoming the kind of effective remedy for insider trading that the court of appeals hoped that it might become. Most importantly, recovery of damages from insiders has been allowed by, or on the behalf of, market investors even when the insiders dealt only through impersonal stock exchanges. . . . [R]emedies for insider trading under the federal securities laws now constitute a more effective deterrent than they did when *Diamond* was decided.

QUESTION ON FREEMAN v. DECIO

How might insider trading by corporate managers "harm" a corporation? By resulting in the loss of corporate opportunities, by a drop in share prices coincident with its discovery, by raising its cost of equity capital? Conversely, would it be sufficient evidence to show that insider trading has harmed the company if its share price drop sharply after it is disclosed that its officers and directors have engaged in insider trading in the past?

14.3   §16(b) and Rule 16-b Under the 1934 Act

Initially, the only provision of the Depression-era securities statutes to address insider trading was §16 of the Securities Exchange Act. Section 16(a) required so-called "statutory insiders" of publicly traded companies — their directors, officers, and 10 percent shareholders — to file public reports within ten days after transacting in company shares (since reduced to two days). Section 16(b) authorized a shareholder derivative action to recover on the corporation's behalf any so-called "short-swing" gains resulting from the trading activity of statutory insiders. Short-swing gains, in turn, were (and are) defined as gains from buying *and* selling shares- or losses avoided by selling *and* buying shares — within any six-month period.

Several points are worth emphasizing about the §16 enforcement regime. First, it was legislated by Congress, and is therefore independent of fiduciary duties arising under state corporate law. Second, it was intended to be a bright-line, strict liability rule that could reach the most egregious kind of insider trading. The paradigmatic example of the "round-trip trading" targeted by §16 is a scenario (reputed to have been common in the 1920s) in which directors had material information (say, good news that the firm would report favorable earnings), immediately purchased corporate shares, and then resold their shares for a risk-free profit after the good news was publicly disclosed. And third, although the product of legislation, §16 seems to anticipate the development of state case law by relying on private enforcement by derivative suit and adopting the disgorgement remedy. As just discussed, however, state case law did not hold insiders liable to their corporations for trading profits until long after the adoption of §16 in the 1934 Act and, as *Freeman* suggests, some state courts might still disallow a derivative suit to reclaim insider trading profits on behalf of corporations today.

This is not to say that §16 is an adequate response to insider trading. From today's perspective, it is dramatically underinclusive, since only a small fraction of insider trading profits results from short-swing trading. Moreover, §16 is a modest deterrent at most, given that it relies on private enforcement and limits recovery to the disgorgement remedy. And, perhaps more important, to achieve even this much, §16 has imposed challenging interpretative problems despite its apparent simplicity. To begin with: What are short-swing profits when an insider buys and sells at different prices and in multiple transactions, all within a relatively short period? It took no less a figure than Judge Learned Hand to establish the accepted rule in 1951:[5] In calculating the profit realized from a sale (or purchase) of a given class of shares, a statutory insider ("covered person") must first look back six months and match the number of shares sold (or purchased) with the same number of shares purchased (or sold). The same process is repeated looking forward six months. One then deducts the lower total purchase price from the amount realized on the reportable sale to determine the profit, if any, that is payable to the corporation.[6]

Other problems arise in defining "covered persons" and "purchases or sales" under §16. The statute explicitly covers 10 percent shareholders,

---

5. *Gratz v. Claughton* 187 F.2d 46 (2d Cir. 1951).

6. In other words, "if one is seeking an equation of purchase and sale, one may take any sale as the minuend and look back for six months for a purchase at less price to match against it. On the other hand, if one is looking for an equation of sale and purchase, one may take the same sale and look forward for six months for any purchase at a lower price." Id. at 52.

officers, and directors. But who is an "officer" for the purposes of §16? Since titles are often misleading, courts must look behind them to assess the "real" positions of defendants. A "vice-president" who functions as a lowly salesman is not an officer,[7] while a "production manager" with senior responsibilities may be.[8] Regular access to confidential information is key[9] but not always easy to spot. Similar difficulties arise in defining "purchases" and "sales" under §16(b). Is it a §16 sale if a third-party lender sells stock that had served as collateral for an insider's unpaid loan? More complicated still, do corporate officers "buy" stock when they purchase derivative contracts — options and futures — that mimic a stock's financial return; do they sell stock if they use swaps to cash out its economic value while still retaining nominal legal title to it? For guidance on functional equivalents to purchasing or selling stock, see SEC Rule 16b-6.

Finally, corporate mergers raise still more questions. Do target share-holders who receive cash consideration for their stock "sell" their stock? Do they sell it if they receive stock in the surviving company instead?[10] The Supreme Court's decision in *Kern County Land Co. v. Occidental Petroleum Corp.*, 411 U.S. 582 (1973), illustrates the futility of expecting to apply §16(b) mechanically, regardless of context. It held that stock mergers were "unorthodox" transactions, which required case-by-case analysis to determine whether the transfer of stocks involved enabled a defendant to obtain short-swing profits from inside information. More problematically, *Kern County Land Co.* also held that granting a call option was not a "sale" since the option might not be exercised, at least within six months. This holding was to prove troublesome in other contexts. Consult Rule 16b-6 again.

PROBLEM ON §16

On September 15, 2001, Raj pays $5.00 per share for 10,000 shares of common stock in XYZ Corp., which constitutes less than 1 percent of all issued and outstanding XYZ common stock. On October 1, he is appointed treasurer of XYZ Corp. On October 30, Raj buys another 5,000 shares of common stock for $5.50 a share. On December 15, he buys another 3,000 shares of common stock for $5.30 a share. On December 25, Raj sells 2,000 shares of common stock for $5.10 a share. On March 1, 2002, Raj resigns as treasurer of XYZ

---

7. See *Merrill Lynch, Pierce, Fenner & Smith, Inc. v. Livingston*, 566 F.2d 1119 (9th Cir. 1978).

8. See *Colby v. Klune*, 178 F.2d 872 (2d Cir. 1949).

9. See also *Reliance Electric Co. v. Emerson Electric Co.*, 404 U.S. 418 (1972), where the Court found that plaintiffs could not recover profits made in the second of two successive sales of company stock, even though the sale had been split in order to avoid application of §16(b), because at the time of the second sale, the defendant was no longer a covered person under the statute (he owned less than 10 percent of the company's stock).

10. See 17 C.F.R. §240.16b-7 (1998) (stating that mergers and reclassifications of 85-percent-owned subsidiaries are exempt from §16).

Corp. On March 20, Raj sells his remaining 16,000 shares of common stock for $5.70 a share.

1. What statements must Raj file under §16(a)?
2. Is Raj liable for any damages under §16(b)? If so, for how much?

14.4 EXCHANGE ACT §10(b) AND RULE 10b-5

While §16 was the Securities Exchange Act's only explicit attempt to address insider trading, the 1934 Act left open an indirect route for revisiting insider trading. It broadly empowered the SEC to promulgate rules regulating the trading of securities on national stock exchanges or through the means of interstate commerce. One of the Act's most important provisions authorizes SEC rulemaking: Under §10(b) of the Act, it provides in pertinent part that [it shall be unlawful]:

> To use or employ, in connection with the purchase or sale of any security registered on a national securities exchange or any security not so registered, any manipulative or deceptive device or contrivance in contravention of such rules and regulations as the Commission may proscribe as necessary or appropriate in the public interest or for the protection of investors.

14.4.1 Evolution of Private Right of Action Under §10

Rule 10b-5 had a humble birth. No hearings attended its creation, and no deep deliberation led to its choice of language. The facts prompting the adoption of the rule were rather like those of the *Goodwin* case. The SEC had learned that the president of a company in Boston was "going around buying up the stock of the company . . . at $4 a share and he was telling [the shareholders] that the company was doing very badly, whereas in fact the earnings . . . will be $2 a share for this coming year." (If the facts were as reported, the president was engaging in common law fraud.) To enable the SEC's Enforcement Division to seek an injunction against this activity in U.S. district court, Milton Freeman, a young lawyer working for the Commission, rapidly drafted Rule 10b-5 for the members of the Commission to review. The rest is history.

The rule provides in pertinent part that it shall be unlawful:

(a) To employ any device, scheme or artifice to defraud,
(b) To make any untrue statement of a material fact or omit to state a material fact necessary in order to make the statements made, in the light of the circumstances in which they were made, not misleading, or

(c) To engage in any act, practice, or course of business which operates or would operate as a fraud or deceit upon any person, in connection with the purchase or sale of any security.

In drafting a rule to implement §10(b) of the 1934 Act, Mr. Freeman had sought only to empower the SEC's Enforcement Division to ask federal courts to enjoin fraudulent or misleading conduct. Neither he nor the Commission envisioned creating an implied private right of action under Rule 10b-5. Congress had created private rights of action in the securities laws, but had done so sparingly. Although the drafters of the 1934 Act had clearly intended that the SEC use its broad rulemaking authority to implement and enforce the Act's objectives, it was less clear that Congress intended to allow federal courts to amplify SEC anti-fraud rules by creating private rights of action. Law, however, changes, and in this case, the agent of change was William Huntington Kirkpatrick, a brilliant federal district judge from Philadelphia,[11] who first recognized an implied private remedy for violation of Rule 10b-5. The case was *Kardon v. National Gypsum Co.*,[12] and the claim was that defendants had conspired to mislead shareholders into selling their stock at depressed prices. Judge Kirkpatrick concluded that, if true, the allegations would support a federal remedy under Rule 10b-5, even though that rule did not state that a private remedy for damages was intended:

> It is not, and cannot be, questioned that the complaint sets forth conduct on the part of the Slavins directly in violation of the provisions of Sec. 10(b) of the Act and of Rule X-10B-5 which implements it. It is also true that there is no provision in Sec. 10 or elsewhere expressly allowing civil suits by persons injured as a result of violation of Sec. 10 or of the Rule. However, "The violation of a legislative enactment by doing a prohibited act, or by failing to do a required act, makes the actor liable for an invasion of an interest of another if: (a) the intent of the enactment is exclusively or in part to protect an interest of the other as an individual; and (b) the interest invaded is one which the enactment is intended to protect. . . ." Restatement, Torts, Vol. 2, §286. This rule is more than merely a canon of statutory interpretation. The disregard of the command of a statute is a wrongful act and a tort.[13]

14.4.2   Elements of a Rule 10b-5 Claim

Whatever theory one adopts to justify a right of private action under Rule 10b-5, such a right must be grounded in the language of both the statute

---

11. In addition to his opinion in *Kardon*, corporate law scholars know Judge Kirkpatrick's opinion in *Insurance Shares Corp. v. Northern Fiscal Corp.*, 35 F. Supp. 22 (E.D. Pa. 1940) (describing when a controller may be liable to fellow shareholders who are looted by the controller's transferee). Judge Kirkpatrick may be thought of as one of the unsung heroes of American corporate and securities law, whose many opinions, although largely forgotten today, continue to have their effects felt indirectly through case law.
12. 69 F. Supp. 512 (E.D. Pa. 1946).
13. Id. at 513.

and the rule. The statute empowers the SEC to make rules that protect against "manipulative and deceptive" activity "in connection with the purchase or sale of [covered] securities" or the making of untrue statements of material facts or the omission to state material facts in connection with the purchase or sale of a covered security. Thus, the elements of a Rule 10b-5 implied cause of action must resemble those of common law fraud, but they must also reflect the realities of the market-based transactions at which the rule is chiefly directed.

Recall the elements of common law fraud: a (1) false or misleading statement (2) of material fact that is (3) made with intent to deceive another (4) upon which that person reasonably relies, (5) and that reliance causes harm. In addition to these elements, the language of Rule 10b-5 would seem to mandate that the requisite reliance must be by a buyer or seller of stock, the harm must be to a trader in stock, and the misleading statement must be made in connection with a purchase or sale of stock. Ask yourself whether these conditions are met as you consider the Rule 10b-5 action against insider trading.

Our discussion here touches on most of the elements of a private, SEC, or criminal action predicated on Rule 10b-5. We focus, however, on 10b-5 liability in its two most prominent forms. The first, of course, is liability for insider trading. The second is liability in private class actions seeking damages for so-called fraud-on-the-market ("FOM") actions. In contrast to insider trading, FOM class actions seek redress for misrepresentations made to the market rather than for insider trading on undisclosed information. But before exploring class actions, we continue with the evolution of insider trading law under Rule 10b-5.

14.4.3   Early Rule 10b-5 Insider Trading Liability: The Equal Access Theory

A false statement (made with intent to deceive) is the most basic element of common law deceit, and it is likewise a foundation for Rule 10b-5 liability. This is the essence of fraud. By contrast, omissions of material facts are more problematic, as you may recall from our prior discussion of the extremely limited regulation of insider trading under the common law. Liability for failure to disclose under the common law doctrine of fraud required a duty to disclose grounded in a preexisting fiduciary relationship. The 1934 Act did not explicitly reject the common law understanding of fraud. In order to extend Rule 10b-5 liability to insider trading, therefore, the federal courts required a theory on which to predicate a breach of fiduciary duty to disclose. Three different approaches to this problem evolved. As the case below indicates, the SEC and the Second Circuit initially took the aggressive position that any possession of relevant, material, nonpublic information gives rise to a duty to disclose or abstain from trading. The Supreme Court, by contrast, adopted a more limited view of Rule 10b-5 liability for insider trading in the *Chiarella* case, discussed below, but thereafter expanded the doctrinal reach of Rule 10b-5, most conspicuously by adopting the so-called "misappropriation theory" of liability.[14] We begin with the Second Circuit and a fact pattern bearing some resemblance to that featured in our prior common law case, *Goodwin v. Agassiz*.

SEC v. TEXAS GULF SULPHUR CO.
401 F.2d 833 (2d Cir. 1968)

WATERMAN, Cir. J. (en banc):

This action was commenced in the United States District Court by the [SEC] . . . against Texas Gulf Sulphur Company ("TGS") and several of its officers, directors and employees, to enjoin certain conduct by TGS and the individual defendants said to violate Section 10(b) of the Act, and to compel the rescission by the individual defendants of securities transactions assertedly conducted contrary to law. . . .

This action derives from the exploratory activities of TGS begun in 1957 on the Canadian Shield in eastern Canada. In March of 1959, aerial geophysical surveys were conducted over more than 15,000 square miles of this area by a group led by defendant Mollison, a mining engineer and a Vice President of TGS. The group included defendant Holyk, TGS's chief geologist, defendant Clayton, an electrical engineer and geophysicist, and defendant Darke, a geologist. . . .

On October 29 and 30, 1963, Clayton conducted a ground geophysical survey on the northeast portion of the Kidd 55 segment which confirmed the presence of an anomaly and indicated the necessity of diamond core drilling for further evaluation. Drilling of the initial hole, K-55-1, at the strongest part of the anomaly was commenced on November 8. . . . Visual estimates by Holyk of the core of K-55-1 indicated an average copper content of 1.15% and an average zinc content of 8.64% over a length of 599 feet. This visual estimate convinced TGS that it was desirable to acquire the remainder of the Kidd 55 segment, and in order to facilitate this acquisition TGS President Stephens instructed the exploration group to keep the results of K-55-1 confidential and undisclosed even as to other officers, directors, and employees of TGS. The hole was concealed and a barren core was intentionally drilled off the anomaly. Meanwhile, the core of K-55-1 had been shipped to Utah for chemical assay which, when received in early December, revealed an average mineral content of 1.18% copper, 8.26% zinc, and 3.94% ounces of silver per ton over a length of 602 feet. These results were so remarkable that neither Clayton, an experienced geophysicist, nor four other TGS expert witnesses, had ever seen or heard of a comparable initial exploratory drill hole in a base metal deposit. . . .

---

14. See *United States v. O'Hagan, infra.*

During the period, from November 12, 1963 when K-55-1 was completed, to March 31, 1964 when drilling was resumed, certain of the individual defendants . . . purchased TGS stock or calls thereon.* . . .

On February 20, 1964, also during this period, TGS issued stock options to 26 of its officers and employees whose salaries exceeded a specified amount, five of whom were the individual defendants Stephens, Fogarty, Mollison, Holyk, and Kline. Of these, only Kline was unaware of the detailed results of K-55-1, but he, too, knew that a hole containing favorable bodies of copper and zinc ore had been drilled in Timmins. At this time, neither the TGS Stock Option Committee nor its Board of Directors had been informed of the results of K-55-1, presumably because of the pending land acquisition program which required confidentiality. All of the foregoing defendants accepted the options granted them.

[D]rilling was resumed on March 31. . . .

On April 8 TGS began with a second drill rig to drill another hole, K-55-6, 300 feet easterly of K-55-1. . . . On April 10, a third drill rig commenced drilling yet another hole. . . . By the evening of April 10 in this hole, too, substantial copper mineralization had been encountered over the last 42 feet of its 97-foot length.

Meanwhile, rumors that a major ore strike was in the making had been circulating throughout Canada. On the morning of Saturday, April 11, Stephens at his home in Greenwich, Conn. read in the *New York Herald Tribune* and in the *New York Times* unauthorized reports of the TGS drilling which seemed to infer a rich strike from the fact that the drill cores had been flown to the United States for chemical assay. Stephens immediately contacted Fogarty at his home in Rye, N.Y., who in turn telephoned and later that day visited Mollison at Mollison's home in Greenwich to obtain a current report and evaluation of the drilling progress. The following morning, Sunday, Fogarty again telephoned Mollison, inquiring whether Mollison had any further information and told him to return to Timmins with Holyk, the TGS Chief Geologist, as soon as possible "to move things along." With the aid of one Carroll, a public relations consultant, Fogarty drafted a press release designed to quell the rumors, which release, after having been channeled through Stephens and Huntington, a TGS attorney, was issued at 3:00 P.M. on Sunday, April 12, and which appeared in the morning newspapers of general circulation on Monday, April 13. It read in pertinent part as follows: . . .

> During the past few days, the exploration activities of Texas Gulf Sulphur in the area of Timmins, Ontario, have been widely reported in the press, coupled with rumors of a substantial copper discovery there. These reports exaggerate the scale of operations, and mention plans and statistics of size and grade of ore that are without factual basis. . . .
>   The facts are as follows. TGS has been exploring in the Timmins area for six years as part of its overall search in Canada and elsewhere for various

---

* A "call" is a negotiable option contract under which the bearer has the right to buy from the writer of the contract a certain number of shares of a particular stock at a fixed price on or before a certain agreed-upon date. — EDS.

minerals — lead, copper, zinc, etc. During the course of this work, in Timmins as well as in Eastern Canada, TGS has conducted exploration entirely on its own, without the participation by others. Numerous prospects have been investigated by geophysical means and a large number of selected ones have been core-drilled. These cores are sent to the United States for assay and detailed examination as a matter of routine and on advice of expert Canadian legal counsel. No inferences as to grade can be drawn from this procedure.

Most of the areas drilled in Eastern Canada have revealed either barren pyrite or graphite without value; a few have resulted in discoveries of small or marginal [value]. . . .

Recent drilling on one property near Timmins has led to preliminary indications that more drilling would be required for proper evaluation of this prospect. The drilling done to date has not been conclusive, but the statements made by many outside quarters are unreliable and include information and figures that are not available to TGS.

The work done to date has not been sufficient to reach definite conclusions and any statement as to size and grade of ore would be premature and possibly misleading. When we have progressed to the point where reasonable and logical conclusions can be made, TGS will issue a definite statement to its stockholders and to the public in order to clarify the Timmins project. . . .

The release purported to give the Timmins drilling results as of the release date, April 12. . . . Mollison Fogarty had been told of the developments through 7:00 P.M. on April 10, and of the remarkable discoveries made up to that time, detailed supra, which discoveries, according to the calculations of the experts who testified for the SEC at the hearing, demonstrated that TGS had already discovered 6.2 to 8.3 million tons of proven ore having gross assay values from $26 to $29 per ton. TGS experts, on the other hand, denied at the hearing that proven or probable ore could have been calculated on April 11 or 12 because there was then no assurance of continuity in the mineralized zone.

The evidence as to the effect of this release on the investing public was equivocal and less than abundant. On April 13 the *New York Herald Tribune* in an article head-noted "Copper Rumor Deflated" quoted from the TGS release of April 12 and backtracked from its original April 11 report of a major strike but nevertheless inferred from the TGS release that "recent mineral exploratory activity near Timmins, Ontario, has provided preliminary favorable results, sufficient at least to require a step-up in drilling operations." . . . The trial court stated only that "While, in retrospect, the press release may appear gloomy or incomplete, this does not make it misleading or deceptive on the basis of the facts then known." *Id.* at 296. . . .

While drilling activity ensued to completion, TGS officials were taking steps toward ultimate disclosure of the discovery. On April 13, a previously invited reporter for *The Northern Miner*, a Canadian mining industry journal, visited the drill site, interviewed Mollison, Holyk and Darke, and prepared an article which confirmed a 10 million ton ore strike. This report, after having been submitted to Mollison and returned to the reporter unamended on April 15, was published in the April 16 issue. A statement relative to the extent of the discovery, in substantial part drafted by Mollison, was given to the Ontario Minister of Mines for release to the Canadian media. Mollison and

Holyk expected it to be released over the airwaves at 11 P.M. on April 15th, but, for undisclosed reasons, it was not released until 9:40 A.M. on the 16th. An official detailed statement, announcing a strike of at least 25 million tons of ore, based on the drilling data set forth above, was read to representatives of American financial media from 10:00 A.M. to 10:10 or 10:15 A.M. on April 16, and appeared over Merrill Lynch's private wire at 10:29 A.M. and, somewhat later than expected, over the Dow Jones ticker tape at 10:54 A.M.

Between the time the first press release was issued on April 12 and the dissemination of the TGS official announcement on the morning of April 16, the only defendants before us on appeal who engaged in market activity were Clayton and Crawford and TGS director Coates. Clayton ordered 200 shares of TGS stock through his Canadian broker on April 15. . . . Crawford ordered 300 shares at midnight on the 15th and another 300 shares at 8:30 A.M. the next day, and these orders were executed over the Midwest Exchange in Chicago at its opening on April 16. Coates left the TGS press conference and called his broker son-in-law Haemisegger shortly before 10:20 A.M. on the 16th and ordered 2,000 shares of TGS for family trust accounts of which Coates was a trustee but not a beneficiary; Haemisegger executed this order over the New York and Midwest Exchanges, and he and his customers purchased 1,500 additional shares.

During the period of drilling in Timmins, the market price of TGS stock fluctuated but steadily gained overall. On Friday, November 8, when the drilling began, the stock closed at $17\,^3/_8$ . . . . On April 13, the day on which the April 12 release was disseminated, TGS opened at $30\,^1/_8$, rose immediately to a high of 32 and gradually tapered off to close at $30\,^7/_8$. It closed at $30\,^1/_4$ the next day, and at $29\,^3/_8$ on April 15. On April 16, the day of the official announcement of the Timmins discovery, the price climbed to a high of 37 and closed at $36\,^3/_8$. By May 15, TGS stock was selling at $58\,^1/_4$ . . . .

[Rule 10b-5] is based in policy on the justifiable expectation of the securities marketplace that all investors trading on impersonal exchanges have relatively equal access to material information. The essence of the Rule is that anyone who, trading for his own account in the securities of a corporation has "access, directly or indirectly, to information intended to be available only for a corporate purpose and not for the personal benefit of anyone" may not take "advantage of such information knowing it is unavailable to those with whom he is dealing," i.e., the investing public. *Matter of Cady, Roberts & Co.*, 40 SEC 907, 912 (1961). Insiders, as directors or management officers are, of course, by this Rule, precluded from so unfairly dealing. Thus, anyone in possession of material inside information must either disclose it to the investing public, or, if he is disabled from disclosing it in order to protect a corporate confidence, or he chooses not to do so, must abstain from trading in or recommending the securities concerned while such inside information remains undisclosed. So, it is here no justification for insider activity that disclosure was forbidden by the legitimate corporate objective of acquiring options to purchase the land surrounding the exploration site; if the information was, as the SEC contends, material, its possessors should have kept out of the market until disclosure was accomplished. *Cady, Roberts, supra* at 911. . . .

An insider is not, of course, always foreclosed from investing in his own company merely because he may be more familiar with company operations than are outside investors. . . . Nor is an insider obligated to confer upon outside investors the benefit of his superior financial or other expert analysis by disclosing his educated guesses or predictions. The only regulatory objective is that access to material information be enjoyed equally, but this objective requires nothing more than the disclosure of basic facts so that outsiders may draw upon their own evaluative expertise. . . .

[W]hether facts are material within Rule 10b-5 when the facts relate to a particular event . . . will depend . . . upon a balancing of both the indicated probability that the event will occur and the anticipated magnitude of the event in light of the totality of the company activity. Here, knowledge of the possibility, which surely was more than marginal, of the existence of a mine of the vast magnitude indicated by the remarkably rich drill core located rather close to the surface . . . might well have affected the price of TGS stock and would certainly have been an important fact to a reasonable, if speculative, investor in deciding whether he should buy, sell, or hold. . . .

Finally, a major factor in determining whether the K-55-1 mine discovery was a material fact is the importance attached to the drilling results by those who knew about it. In view of other unrelated recent developments favorably affecting TGS, participation by an informed person in a regular stock-purchase program, or even sporadic trading by an informed person, might lend only nominal support to the inference of the materiality of the K-55-1 discovery; nevertheless, the timing by those who knew of it of their stock purchases and their purchases of short-term calls — purchases in some cases by individuals who had never before purchased calls or even TGS stock — virtually compels the inference that the insiders were influenced by the drilling results. . . .

Our decision to expand the limited protection afforded outside investors by the trial court's narrow definition of materiality is not at all shaken by fears that the elimination of insider trading benefits will deplete the ranks of capable corporate managers by taking away an incentive to accept such employment. Such benefits, in essence, are forms of secret corporate compensation . . . derived at the expense of the uninformed investing public and not at the expense of the corporation which receives the sole benefit from insider incentives. Moreover, adequate incentives for corporate officers may be provided by properly administered stock options and employee purchase plans of which there are many in existence.

The core of Rule 10b-5 is the implementation of the Congressional purpose that all investors should have equal access to the rewards of participation in securities transactions. It was the intent of Congress that all members of the investing public should be subject to identical market risks, — which . . . include, of course the risk that one's evaluative capacity or one's capital available to put at risk may exceed another's capacity or capital. The insiders here were not trading on an equal footing with the outside investors. They alone were in a position to evaluate the probability and magnitude of what seemed from the outset to be a major ore strike; they alone could invest safely, secure in the expectation that the price of TGS stock would rise substantially in the event such a major strike should materialize, but would decline little, if at all, in the event of failure, for the public, ignorant at the outset of the favorable probabilities would likewise be unaware of the unproductive exploration, and the additional exploration costs would not significantly affect TGS market prices. Such inequities based upon unequal access to knowledge should not be shrugged off as inevitable in our way of life, or, in view of the congressional concern in the area, remain uncorrected.

We hold, therefore, that all transactions in TGS stock or calls by individuals apprised of the drilling results of K-55-1 were made in violation of Rule 10b-5. . . .

QUESTIONS ON TEXAS GULF SULPHUR

1. The short-term calls at issue in *TGS* are call options, which give holders the right to purchase stock at a fixed price for a fixed period. Why might wayward insiders prefer to buy call options rather than shares? In contrast, a put option is the right to sell stock in the future at a fixed price. How might a wayward insider profit by trading on puts?

2. Who is harmed by insider trading? The shareholders who trade on the opposite side of the insiders? The shareholders who trade on the same side as the insiders? Does it matter whether inside information is good news or bad?

3. Can a public shareholder who would have bought or sold regardless of insider trading activity be harmed by such activity? If so, is the measure of harm the difference between the price the public shareholder received and the price she would have received had the insider refrained from trading? What else could the measure of harm be? Try to illustrate your views on the appropriate measure of harm from the *Texas Gulf Sulphur* case.

4. Are those who know little and seldom trade harmed by insider trading in the few stocks that they do hold? Are savvy (outside) speculators who continuously trade in the same stocks harmed just as much? Might the Wall Street speculators be harmed more than the infrequent traders?

5. Is anyone at all harmed by insider trading if the market correctly anticipates overall levels of insider trading and discounts share prices accordingly? Could we make the same argument about stealing from the corporate treasury — that is, if share prices discount fairly for stealing ex ante, shareholders are not harmed by thieving corporate managers — at least from an ex ante perspective.

NOTE ON THE SUPREME COURT'S EFFORT TO CONSTRAIN RULE 10B-5 LIABILITY IN THE PERIOD FROM 1975 TO 1980

After the influential *Texas Gulf Sulphur* case (and the 1966 liberalization of Federal Rule of Civil Procedure 23, the class action rule), there was an eruption of private litigation under Rule 10b-5 in the lower federal courts. By 1975, the U.S. Supreme Court could be seen as attempting to stem this growth in a series of cases. See, e.g., *Blue Chip Stamps v. Manor Drug*

Stores, 421 U.S. 723 (1975) (claimants must be buyers or sellers of stock; holding stock in reliance on misstatement is not enough); *Ernst & Ernst v. Hochfelder*, 425 U.S. 185 (1976) (scienter required to bring a 10b-5 claim). Most notable among these cases was *Santa Fe v. Green*, which sought to preserve state law as the regulator of internal corporate affairs, including the fiduciary duties that directors and officers owed to the corporation and its shareholders.

SANTA FE INDUSTRIES, INC. v. GREEN
430 U.S. 462 (1977)

WHITE, J.:

The issue in this case involves the reach and coverage of §10(b) of the [1934 Act] and Rule 10b-5 . . . in the context of a Delaware short-form merger transaction used by the majority stockholder of a corporation to eliminate the minority interest. . . .

[EDS. — The transaction at issue here involved a decision by Santa Fe Industries, Inc. (Santa Fe) to freeze out the minority shareholders of its subsidiary, Kirby Lumber, under Delaware's §253 short-form merger provision (which required Santa Fe to have at least 90 percent of Kirby's shares (Santa Fe had 95 percent)). As the Court noted, §253 does not require that minority stockholders consent to a freeze-out merger, but it does permit them to file for appraisal rights if they believe that the freeze-out price is too low . . . However, notice of the merger must be given within ten days after its effective date, and any stockholder who is dissatisfied with the terms of the merger may petition the Delaware Court of Chancery [to order] . . . the surviving corporation to pay him the fair value of his shares. . . . Here we resume with excerpts from Justice White's decision.]

Santa Fe obtained independent appraisals of the physical assets of Kirby — land, timber, buildings, and machinery — and of Kirby's oil, gas, and mineral interests. These appraisals . . . were submitted to Morgan Stanley . . . , an investment banking firm retained to appraise the fair market value of Kirby stock. Kirby's physical assets were appraised at $320 million . . . (amounting to $640 for each of [its] 500,000 shares); Kirby's stock was valued by Morgan Stanley at $125 per share. Under the terms of the merger, minority stockholders were offered $150 per share.

The provisions of the short-form merger statute were fully complied with. The minority stockholders of Kirby were notified the day after the merger became effective and were advised of their right to obtain an appraisal . . . if dissatisfied with the offer of $150 per share. They also received an information statement containing, in addition to the relevant financial data about Kirby, the appraisals of the value of Kirby's assets and the Morgan Stanley appraisal concluding that the fair market value of the stock was $125 per share.

Respondents, minority stockholders of Kirby, objected to the terms of the merger, but did not pursue their [Delaware] appraisal remedy. . . . Instead, they brought this action in federal court . . . seeking to set aside the merger or to recover what they claimed to be the fair value of their shares. The amended complaint asserted that, based on the fair market value of Kirby's physical assets as revealed by [the appraised value of Kirby's assets], Kirby's stock was worth at least $772 per share. The complaint alleged further that the merger took place without prior notice to minority stockholders; that the purpose of the merger was to appropriate the difference between the "conceded pro rata value of the physical assets," . . . and the offer of $150 per share—to "freez[e] out the minority stockholders at a wholly inadequate price;" . . . and that Santa Fe . . . obtained a "fraudulent appraisal" of the stock from Morgan Stanley and offered $25 above that appraisal "in order to lull the minority stockholders into erroneously believing that [Santa Fe was] generous." *Id.*, at 103a. This . . . conduct [allegedly violated] Rule 10b-5 "because defendants employed a 'device, scheme, or artifice to defraud' and engaged in an 'act, practice or course of business which operates or would operate as a fraud or deceit upon any person, in connection with the purchase or sale of any security.'" *Ibid.* Morgan Stanley assertedly participated in the fraud as an accessory by submitting its appraisal of $125 per share. . . .

The language of §10(b) gives no indication that Congress meant to prohibit any conduct not involving manipulation or deception. Nor have we been cited to any evidence in the legislative history that would support a departure from the language of the statute. . . . It is our judgment that the transaction, if carried out as alleged, was neither deceptive nor manipulative and therefore did not violate either §10(b) of the Act or Rule 10b-5. . . .

[M]inority shareholders could either accept the price offered or reject it and seek an appraisal. . . . Their choice was fairly presented, and they were furnished with all relevant information on which to base their decision. . . .

It is also readily apparent that the conduct alleged . . . was not "manipulative" within the meaning of the statute. "Manipulation" is "virtually a term of art when used in connection with securities markets." *Ernst & Ernst*, 425 U.S., at 199. The term refers generally to practices, such as wash sales, matched orders, or rigged prices, that are intended to mislead investors by artificially affecting market activity. . . . Section 10 (b)'s general prohibition of practices deemed by the SEC to be "manipulative"—in this technical sense . . . —is fully consistent with the fundamental purpose of the 1934 Act. . . . No doubt Congress meant to prohibit the full range of ingenious devices that might be used to manipulate securities prices. But we do not think it would have chosen this "term of art" if it had meant to bring within the scope of §10(b) instances of corporate mismanagement such as this, in which the essence [was] that shareholders were treated unfairly by a fiduciary. . . .

The language of the statute is . . . dispositive here, . . . but even if it were not, there are additional considerations that weigh heavily against permitting a cause of action under Rule 10b-5 for the breach of corporate fiduciary duty alleged in this complaint. Congress did not expressly provide a private cause of action for violations of §10(b). . . . [A] private cause of action under the antifraud provisions of the Securities Exchange Act should not be implied where it is "unnecessary to ensure the fulfillment of Congress' purposes" in adopting the Act. *Piper v. Chris-Craft Industries.* . . .

A second factor in determining whether Congress intended to create a federal cause of action in these circumstances is "whether 'the cause of action [is] one traditionally relegated to state law.'" . . . The Delaware Legislature has supplied minority shareholders with a cause of action . . . to recover the fair value of shares allegedly undervalued in a short-form merger. . . .

[In addition,] [t]he reasoning that would bring the alleged fraud in this case under Rule 10b-5 could not be easily contained. It is difficult to imagine how a court could distinguish, for purposes of Rule 10b-5 fraud, between a majority stockholder's use of a short-form merger to eliminate the minority at an unfair price and the use of some other device, such as a long-form merger, tender offer, or liquidation, to achieve the same result; or indeed how a court could distinguish the alleged abuses in these going private transactions from other types of fiduciary self-dealing. . . . The result would be to bring within the Rule a wide variety of corporate conduct traditionally left to state regulation. In addition to posing a "danger of vexatious litigation . . . this extension of the federal securities laws would overlap and quite possibly interfere with state corporate law. . . . Absent a clear indication of congressional intent, we are reluctant to federalize the substantial portion of the law of corporations that deals with transactions in securities, particularly where established state policies of corporate regulation would be overridden.

. . . There may well be a need for uniform federal fiduciary standards to govern mergers such as that challenged in this complaint. But those standards should not be supplied by judicial extension of §10(b) and Rule 10b-5 to "cover the corporate universe."

NOTE AND QUESTION ON SANTA FE AND FAIRNESS IN GOING-PRIVATE MERGERS

1. Compare the policy concerns articulated in *Santa Fe* with those in *Virginia Bankshares*, which was reviewed in Chapter 6. In what ways do the two cases differ?

2. *Santa Fe* deals with a short-form, freeze-out transaction under DGCL §253, which permits a parent that holds 90 percent of the shares in a subsidiary to value the minority interest, merge with the subsidiary, and subsequently pay off the minority shareholders, all without the formality of a shareholder vote. When *Santa Fe* was decided, Delaware law offered minority shareholders little protection in a cash-out merger beyond the appraisal remedy. At the time, few minority shareholders chose to accept the delay and legal cost associated with appraisal litigation. Many contemporaneous commentators condemned the practice, prevalent in the 1970s, of "cashing out" minority shareholders at close to market prices at a time when stock market prices seemed depressed. But with *Santa Fe*, the U.S. Supreme Court placed the ball clearly back in the court of state law. The Delaware Supreme Court seemed to respond to *Santa Fe*'s invitation in *Singer v. Magnavox*,[15] which announced

---

15. 380 A.2d 969 (Del. 1977).

elaborate fiduciary duty protection for minority shareholders in freeze-out transactions. (As we have reviewed in Chapter 12, the Delaware Court's later decision, *Weinberger v. UOP, Inc.* (and its progeny), reaffirmed the controlling shareholder's obligation to pay a "fair price" in such transactions and also modernized the appraisal remedy.)

QUESTIONS ON SANTA FE v. GREEN

1. How do you suppose Morgan Stanley could have valued Kirby's assets at $640/share and its minority stock at $125/share? Could both numbers have referred to real economic values, given the existing legal framework? The pre-merger market price of Kirby stock had ranged between $65 and $92.50.

2. What precisely is the distinction between "deception and manipulation," on the one hand, and an allegation of a breach of fiduciary duty, on the other? Might the Court have decided differently if Santa Fe had given Morgan Stanley inaccurate or insufficient valuation data?

NOTE ON DISCLOSURE OF UNFAIRNESS: GOLDBERG v. MERIDOR

Although *Santa Fe* disapproved extending Rule 10b-5 into the domain of state fiduciary law, lower federal courts did not abandon this effort entirely. For example, it seems clear that if D, a director of Corporation C, persuades C's board, by fraud, to sell him stock, C can sue D under Rule 10b-5 even though it can also sue D for breach of fiduciary duty. Similarly, if C's board does not sue D, a shareholder could sue D under Rule 10b-5 in a derivative action (if she can demonstrate that the board's failure to sue D is not deserving of business judgment deference). What happens then if a controlling shareholder causes a corporation to issue stock to him at an unfair price, not by making false statements but by dominating corporate directors? Is this actionable manipulation in connection with the purchase or sale of a security under Rule 10b-5? The relevant case law in this area has been — and remains — contested since *Goldberg v. Meridor*, 567 F.2d 209 (2d Cir. 1977), *cert. denied*, 434 U.S. 1069 (1978) (holding that a derivative plaintiff could establish a Rule 10b-5 case against the directors of a controlling corporate shareholder that disguised its overpayment in purchasing a subsidiary's assets by failing to disclose material facts to its minority shareholders).

14.4.4   The Equal Access Theory of Rule 10b-5 Liability

We return now to the development of the law of Rule 10b-5 in the wake of *Texas Gulf Sulphur*. Recall that case law has followed three main legal theories of when omissions to disclose may be a predicate for 10b-5 liability.

These are sometimes termed the "equal access," "fiduciary duty," and "misappropriation" theories. The equal access or "duty to the market" theory articulated in *Texas Gulf Sulphur* was the first. In its simplest form, this theory holds that all traders owe a duty to the market to disclose or refrain from trading on material nonpublic corporate information. The basis for this duty is said to be the "inherent unfairness" of exploiting an unerodable informational advantage — that is, confidential information from which other traders are legally excluded.[16] The equal access theory originates in an expansive reading of the best known (and most ambiguous) discussion in the corpus of insider trading case law, which concluded that the application of Rule 10b-5 rested on "two principal elements":

> [F]irst, the existence of a relationship giving access, directly or indirectly, to information intended to be available only for a corporate purpose, and not for the personal benefit of anyone, and second, the inherent unfairness involved where a party takes advantage of such information knowing it is unavailable to those with whom he is dealing.[17]

This sentence originates in *Cady, Roberts & Co.*,[18] the first SEC administrative decision to address insider trading on the open market. Its ambiguity lies in its failure to specify to whom insider trading is inherently unfair, and what fiduciary relationship gives rise to its unfairness. Must all traders relying on confidential information that is legally unavailable to others have a duty to disclose this information or refrain from trading? This was the equal access theory, which, allowing for detours and caveats, the influential Second Circuit seemed to follow for a decade after *Texas Gulf Sulphur* — that is, until it was rejected by the Supreme Court in *Chiarella v. United States*, excerpted below. The equal access theory had the important virtue in that it could reach all insider trading that one might intuitively believe to be unfair. Thus it could reach tippees and financial printers who traded on confidential information, even if they were not company insiders, since the essence of "wrongdoing" on this theory lies in exploiting a protected informational advantage over other traders. Correlatively, the victims of insider trading are easily identified under this theory: They are all the uninformed traders to whom the insider should have disclosed.[19]

In the end, however, the Supreme Court decided that the doctrinal and conceptual weaknesses of the equal access theory were fatal. It is not obvious why the "unfairness" arising from trading on access to superior information defrauds other traders in the absence of misrepresentation or a preexisting

---

16. See Victor Brudney, *Insiders, Outsiders, and Informational Advantages Under the Federal Securities Laws*, 93 Harv. L. Rev. 322, 346 (1979).

17. Id. at 911.

18. 40 S.E.C. 907 (1961).

19. Under Rule 10b-5 jurisprudence, however, only injured purchasers or sellers of securities are allowed a private right of action. See *Blue Chip Stamps v. Manor Drug Stores*, 421 U.S. 723 (1975). The Second Circuit has interpreted Rule 10b-5 to permit a private suit by contemporaneous traders against an insider, with recovery limited to the insider's profit. See *Elkind v. Liggett & Myers, Inc.*, 635 F.2d 156 (2d Cir. 1980).

disclosure duty. These other traders come for their own reasons to the public market seeking to sell (or buy) at the market price. In what sense is information asymmetry alone unfair? Investors continuously exploit differential access to information; indeed, the effort to profit from such disparities is precisely what keeps securities prices informed.[20] Why then should the law seek broadly to impede all trading on nonpublic information?

14.4.5   Elements of Rule 10b-5 Liability: The Fiduciary Duty Theory

Whatever the flaws of the equal access theory, however, a return to the common law of the 1930s was no longer possible in the 1970s and 1980s. Rule 10b-5 liability for insider trading was now well entrenched, both in the case law and social norms more generally. Nor did anyone want to turn the clock back to *Goodwin v. Agassiz*, least of all the Supreme Court. Two U.S. Supreme Court decisions of the early 1980s articulated a more limited theory of liability under Rule 10b-5, which is now termed the "classical" or "fiduciary duty" theory. In the first, the *Chiarella* decision, the Court rejected the equal access theory by overturning the criminal conviction of a financial printer who had traded on confidential foreknowledge of pending takeover bids that he had gained in his employment. More precisely, the Court ruled that the printer did not breach a disclosure duty *to other traders* by trading on nonpublic information. Since the printer had gleaned information from the documents of takeover *bidders*, he lacked a relationship-based duty to shareholders of the *target* companies in whose securities he traded. *Chiarella* is excerpted below. The Supreme Court's second insider trading case, *Dirks v. SEC*, addressed the liability of tippees, i.e., parties who learn confidential information from insiders but do not otherwise have a fiduciary relationship to corporate shareholders.

<u>CHIARELLA v. UNITED STATES</u>
445 U.S. 222 (1980)

POWELL, J.:

The question in this case is whether a person who learns from the confidential documents of one corporation that it is planning an attempt to secure control of a second corporation violates §10(b) of the Securities Exchange Act of 1934 if he fails to disclose the impending takeover before trading in the target company's securities. . . .

Petitioner is a printer by trade. In 1975 and 1976, he worked as a "markup man" in the New York composing room of Pandick Press, a financial printer.

---

20. See generally Ronald J. Gilson & Reinier H. Kraakman, *The Mechanisms of Market Efficiency*, 70 Va. L. Rev. 549 (1984).

Among documents that petitioner handled were five announcements of corporate takeover bids. When these documents were delivered to the printer, the identities of the acquiring and target corporations were concealed by blank spaces or false names. The true names were sent to the printer on the night of the final printing.

The petitioner, however, was able to deduce the names of the target companies before the final printing from other information contained in the documents. Without disclosing his knowledge, petitioner purchased stock in the target companies and sold the shares immediately after the takeover attempts were made public. By this method, petitioner realized a gain of slightly more than $30,000 in the course of 14 months. Subsequently, the [SEC] began an investigation of his trading activities. In May 1977, petitioner entered into a consent decree with the Commission in which he agreed to return his profits to the sellers of the shares. On the same day, he was discharged by Pandick Press.

In January 1978, petitioner was indicted on 17 counts of violating §10(b) of the Securities Exchange Act of 1934 (1934 Act) and SEC Rule 10b-5. After petitioner unsuccessfully moved to dismiss the indictment, he was brought to trial and convicted on all counts.

The Court of Appeals for the Second Circuit affirmed petitioner's conviction. 588 F.2d 1358 (1978). We granted certiorari, 441 U.S. 942 (1979), and we now reverse. . . . This case concerns the legal effect of the petitioner's silence. . . .

[The statute] does not state whether silence may constitute a manipulative or deceptive device. Section 10(b) was designed as a catchall clause to prevent fraudulent practices. . . . But neither the legislative history nor the statute itself affords specific guidance for the resolution of this case. When Rule 10b-5 was promulgated in 1942, the SEC did not discuss the possibility that failure to provide information might run afoul of §10(b).

. . . In *Cady, Roberts & Co.*, 40 S.E.C. 907 (1961), the Commission decided that a corporate insider must abstain from trading in the shares of his corporation unless he has first disclosed all material inside information known to him. The obligation to disclose or abstain derives from:

> [an] affirmative duty to disclose material information[, which] has been traditionally imposed on corporate "insiders," particularly officers, directors, or controlling stockholders. We and the courts have consistently held that insiders must disclose material facts which are known to them by virtue of their position but which are not known to persons with whom they deal and which, if known, would affect their investment judgment. *Id.*, at 911.

The Commission emphasized that the duty arose from (i) the existence of a relationship affording access to inside information intended to be available only for a corporate purpose, and (ii) the unfairness of allowing a corporate insider to take advantage of that information by trading without disclosure. . . .

That the relationship between a corporate insider and the stockholders of his corporation gives rise to a disclosure obligation is not a novel twist of the law. At common law, . . . one who fails to disclose material information prior to the consummation of a transaction commits fraud only when he is under a duty to do so. And the duty to disclose arises when one party has information "that the other [party] is entitled to know because of a fiduciary or other similar relation of trust and confidence between them." In its *Cady, Roberts* decision, the Commission recognized a relationship of trust and confidence between the shareholders of a corporation and those insiders who have obtained confidential information by reason of their position with that corporation. This relationship gives rise to a duty to disclose because of the "necessity of preventing a corporate insider from [taking] unfair advantage of the uninformed minority stockholders." [Citation omitted.]

Thus, administrative and judicial interpretations have established that silence in connection with the purchase or sale of securities may operate as a fraud actionable under §10(b) despite the absence of statutory language or legislative history specifically addressing the legality of nondisclosure. But such liability is premised upon a duty to disclose arising from a relationship of trust and confidence between parties to a transaction. Application of a duty to disclose prior to trading guarantees that corporate insiders, who have an obligation to place the shareholder's welfare before their own, will not benefit personally through fraudulent use of material, nonpublic information.[12] . . .

In this case, the petitioner was convicted of violating §10(b) although he was not a corporate insider and he received no confidential information from the target company. . . . [T]he "market information" upon which he relied . . . only [concerned] the plans of the acquiring company. Petitioner's use of that information was not a fraud under §10(b) unless he was subject to an affirmative duty to disclose it before trading. . . .

The Court of Appeals affirmed the conviction by holding that "[*anyone* —] corporate insider or not — who regularly receives material nonpublic information may not use that information to trade in securities without incurring an affirmative duty to disclose." . . . The Court of Appeals . . . failed to identify a relationship between petitioner and the sellers that could give rise to a duty. Its decision thus rested solely upon its belief that the federal securities laws have "created a system providing equal access to information necessary for reasoned and intelligent investment decisions." . . . The use by anyone of material information not generally available is fraudulent, this theory suggests, because such information gives certain buyers or sellers an unfair advantage over less informed buyers and sellers.

This reasoning suffers from two defects. First, not every instance of financial unfairness constitutes fraudulent activity under §10(b). See *Santa Fe Industries, Inc. v. Green.* . . . Second, the element required to make silence fraudulent — a duty to disclose — is absent in this case. No duty could arise from petitioner's relationship with the sellers of the target company's

---

12. "Tippees" of corporate insiders have been held liable under §10(b) because they have a duty not to profit from the use of inside information that they know is confidential. . . . The tippees' obligation has [thus] been viewed as arising from his role as a participant after the fact in the insider's breach of a fiduciary duty. . . .

securities, for petitioner had no prior dealings with them. He was not their agent, he was not a fiduciary, he was not a person in whom the sellers had placed their trust and confidence. He was, in fact, a complete stranger who dealt with the sellers only through impersonal market transactions.

We cannot affirm petitioner's conviction without recognizing a general duty between all participants in market transactions to forgo actions based on material, nonpublic information. Formulation of such a broad duty, which departs radically from the established doctrine that duty arises from a specific relationship between two parties . . . should not be undertaken absent some explicit evidence of congressional intent.

As we have seen, no such evidence emerges from the language or legislative history of §10(b). Moreover, neither the Congress nor the Commission ever has adopted a parity-of-information rule. Instead the problems caused by misuse of market information have been addressed by detailed and sophisticated regulation that recognizes when use of market information may not harm operation of the securities markets. . . .

Indeed, the theory upon which the petitioner was convicted is at odds with the Commission's view of §10(b) as applied to activity that has the same effect on sellers as the petitioner's purchases. "Warehousing" takes place when a corporation gives advance notice of its intention to launch a tender offer to institutional investors who then are able to purchase stock in the target company before the tender offer is made public and the price of shares rises. In this case, as in warehousing, a buyer of securities purchases stock in a target corporation on the basis of market information which is unknown to the seller. In both of these situations, the seller's behavior presumably would be altered if he had the nonpublic information. Significantly, however, the Commission has acted to bar warehousing under its authority to regulate tender offers [not under §10(b)].

. . . Section 10(b) is aptly described as a catchall provision, but what it catches must be fraud. When an allegation of fraud is based upon nondisclosure, there can be no fraud absent a duty to speak. We hold that a duty to disclose under §10(b) does not arise from the mere possession of nonpublic market information. The contrary result is without support in the legislative history of §10(b) and would be inconsistent with the careful plan that Congress has enacted for regulation of the securities markets. . . .

In its brief to this Court, the United States [also] offers an alternative theory to support petitioner's conviction. It argues that petitioner breached a duty to the acquiring corporation when he acted upon information that he obtained by virtue of his position as an employee of a printer employed by the corporation. The breach of this duty is said to support a conviction under §10(b) for fraud perpetrated upon both the acquiring corporation and the sellers. . . .

The jury instructions demonstrate that petitioner was convicted merely because of his failure to disclose material, non-public information to sellers from whom he bought the stock of target corporations. The jury was not instructed on . . . a duty owed by petitioner to anyone other than the sellers. Because we cannot affirm a criminal conviction on the basis of a theory not presented to the jury, . . . we will not speculate upon whether such a duty exists, whether it has been breached, or whether such a breach constitutes a violation of §10(b).

The judgment of the Court of Appeals is reversed. . . .

BURGER, C.J., dissenting.

I believe that the jury instructions in this case properly charged a violation of §10(b) and Rule 10b-5, and I would affirm the conviction. . . . I would read §10(b) and Rule 10b-5 . . . to mean that a person who has misappropriated nonpublic information has an absolute duty to disclose that information or to refrain from trading.

The language of §10(b) and of Rule 10b-5 plainly supports such a reading. By their terms, these provisions reach *any* person engaged in *any* fraudulent scheme. This broad language negates the suggestion that congressional concern was limited to trading by "corporate insiders" or to deceptive practices related to "corporate information." . . .

. . . The antifraud provisions were designed in large measure "to assure that dealing in securities is fair and without undue preferences or advantages among investors." H.R. Conf. Rep. No. 94-229, p. 91 (1975). These provisions prohibit "those manipulative and deceptive practices which have been demonstrated to fulfill no useful function." S. Rep. No. 792, 73d Cong., 2d Sess., 6 (1934). An investor who purchases securities on the basis of misappropriated nonpublic information possesses just such an "undue" trading advantage; his conduct quite clearly serves no useful function except his own enrichment at the expense of others. . . .

Finally, it bears emphasis that this reading of §10b and Rule 10b-5 would not threaten legitimate business practices. [It] would not impose a duty on a tender offeror to disclose its acquisition plans during the period in which it "tests the water" prior to purchasing a full 5% of the target company's stock. Nor would it proscribe "warehousing." . . . In each of these instances . . . the information has not been unlawfully converted for personal gain. . . .

The Court's opinion, as I read it, leaves open the question whether §10(b) and Rule 10b-5 prohibit trading on misappropriated nonpublic information. . . .

QUESTIONS AND NOTES ON CHIARELLA v. UNITED STATES

1. The fiduciary duty theory articulated in *Chiarella* has at least two important attractions. The first is that it supports an analogy to common law fraud, which eases the assimilation of insider trading liability into the statutory prohibition against securities fraud. Its second, less obvious, attraction is that it allows case-by-case review of the relationship between putative insiders and other traders, and thus enables courts to selectively target insider trading. The drawback of the fiduciary theory of insider-trading liability is that it seems seriously underinclusive to most people, at least if it is not somehow supplemented to reach the many kinds of apparent insider trading that do not involve a breach of a trust relationship between a company's insiders and its

shareholders, e.g., trading by tippees or market outsiders such as Chiarella himself. Of course, the *Chiarella* decision only rejects the equal access theory, but it does not purport to foreclose all other theories of insider trading liability.

2. What is the origin of the "relationship of trust and confidence" between corporate insiders and shareholders? It is from traditional common law, since, as previously discussed, most state courts considered corporate officers and directors to be fiduciaries of the corporation but not necessarily of its shareholders.

3. With whom, exactly, are shareholders in a relationship of trust and confidence after *Chiarella*? An issuer's janitor who discovers material information while cleaning at corporate headquarters? The issuer's investment banker who discovers information in the course of confidential negotiations? The taxi driver who overhears a discussion of merger plans on the way to the airport?

4. Can the corporation itself violate its fiduciary duty of trust and confidence to its shareholders while trading on its own confidential information, i.e., by repurchasing or selling its shares? What if the inside information is bad news and existing shareholders would profit from the sale of treasury shares? See Mark J. Loewenstein & William U.S. Wang, *The Corporation as Insider Trader*, 30 Del. J. Corp. L. 45 (2005).

5. Note that Chief Justice Burger's dissenting discussion of the SEC's misappropriation theory marks the debut of that theory as an independent basis of Rule 10b-5 liability.

6. Scienter is a necessary element of Rule 10b-5 liability, whether for insider trading or fraud. It variously means knowledge or gross recklessness verging on willfulness, depending on the circuit and the nature of the action (civil or criminal). A more subtle requirement for imposing 10b-5 liability in insider trading cases is the condition that a defendant must trade "on the basis of" inside information. What does this mean? One interpretation is that an insider's liability turns on proof that her possession of inside information motivated her decision to trade. Another interpretation is that she incurs liability simply by trading while in possession of information that she knows to be confidential, even if something entirely different motivated her trades (such as her need to pay law school tuition).

The SEC promulgated Rule 10b5-1 in 2000 to assist companies and their executives to decrease their risk of prosecution of insider trading by voluntarily adopting plans that fixed the timing and amount of their sales of company stock *before they acquired inside information*. Although the efficacy of these plans is questionable because they can be terminated at will, they nonetheless provide considerable protection from insider trading liability. As an offset for providing the opportunity to file a 10b5-1 plan, the SEC has adopted the view that anyone who knowingly trades on the basis of inside information consequently incurs liability for insider trading. The SEC position has never been tested in the Supreme Court. Is it correct? Or should insider trading liability require proof than an insider was motivated to trade by inside information rather than by something else, such as a need for liquidity?

14.4.6   The Problem of Tippees after *Chiarella*

DIRKS v. SEC
463 U.S. 646 (1983)

POWELL, J.:

Petitioner Raymond Dirks received material nonpublic information from "insiders" of a corporation with which he had no connection. He disclosed this information to investors who relied on it in trading in the shares of the corporation. The question is whether Dirks violated the antifraud provisions of the federal securities laws by this disclosure. . . .

In 1973, Dirks was an officer of a New York broker-dealer firm who specialized in providing investment analysis of insurance company securities to institutional investors. On March 6, Dirks received information from Ronald Secrist, a former officer of Equity Funding of America. Secrist alleged that the assets of Equity Funding, a diversified corporation primarily engaged in selling life insurance and mutual funds, were vastly overstated as the result of fraudulent corporate practices. Secrist also stated that various regulatory agencies had failed to act on similar charges made by Equity Funding employees. He urged Dirks to verify the fraud and disclose it publicly.

Dirks decided to investigate the allegations. He visited Equity Funding's headquarters in Los Angeles and interviewed several officers and employees of the corporation. The senior management denied any wrongdoing, but certain corporation employees corroborated the charges of fraud. Neither Dirks nor his firm owned or traded any Equity Funding stock, but throughout his investigation he openly discussed the information he had obtained with a number of clients and investors. Some of these persons sold their holdings of Equity Funding securities, including five investment advisers who liquidated holdings of more than $16 million.

While Dirks was in Los Angeles, he was in touch regularly with William Blundell, the *Wall Street Journal*'s Los Angeles bureau chief. Dirks urged Blundell to write a story on the fraud allegations. Blundell did not believe, however, that such a massive fraud could go undetected and declined to write the story. He feared that publishing such damaging hearsay might be libelous.

During the 2-week period in which Dirks pursued his investigation and spread word of Secrist's charges, the price of Equity Funding stock fell from $26 per share to less than $15 per share. This led the New York Stock Exchange to halt trading on March 27. Shortly thereafter California insurance authorities impounded Equity Funding's records and uncovered evidence of the fraud. Only then did the Securities and Exchange Commission (SEC) file a complaint against Equity Funding and only then, on April 2, did the *Wall Street Journal* publish a front-page story based largely on information assembled by Dirks. Equity Funding immediately went into receivership.

The SEC began an investigation into Dirks' role in the exposure of the fraud. After a hearing by an Administrative Law Judge, the SEC found that Dirks had aided and abetted violations of §17(a) of the Securities Act of 1933, . . . §10(b) of the Securities Exchange act of 1934 . . . , and SEC Rule 10b-5 . . . , by repeating the allegations of fraud to members of the investment community who later sold their Equity Funding stock. . . . Recognizing, however, that Dirks "played an important role in bringing [Equity Funding's] massive fraud to light," . . . the SEC only censured him. . . .

In view of the importance to the SEC and to the securities industry of the question presented by this case, we granted a writ of certiorari. . . . We now reverse.

In *Chiarella*, we accepted the two elements set out in *Cady, Roberts* for establishing a Rule 10b-5 violation: "(i) the existence of a relationship affording access to inside information intended to be available only for a corporate purpose, and (ii) the unfairness of allowing a corporate insider to take advantage of that information by trading without disclosure." 445 U.S., at 227. In examining whether Chiarella had an obligation to disclose or abstain, the Court found that there is no general duty to disclose before trading on material nonpublic information, and held that "a duty to disclose under §10(b) does not arise from the mere possession of nonpublic market information." *Id.*, at 235. Such a duty arises rather from the existence of a fiduciary relationship. . . .

We were explicit in *Chiarella* in saying that there can be no duty to disclose where the person who has traded on inside information "was not [the corporation's] agent, was not a fiduciary, [or] was not a person in whom the sellers [of the securities] had placed their trust and confidence." 445 U.S., at 232. . . . This requirement of a specific relationship between the shareholders and the individual trading on inside information has created analytical difficulties for the SEC and courts in policing tippees who trade on inside information. Unlike insiders who have independent fiduciary duties to both the corporation and its shareholders, the typical tippee has no such relationships.[14] In view of this absence, it has been unclear how a tippee acquires the *Cady, Roberts* duty to refrain from trading on inside information.

The SEC's position, as stated in its opinion in this case, is that a tippee "inherits" the *Cady, Roberts* obligation to shareholders whenever he receives inside information from an insider. . . .

In effect, the SEC's theory of tippee liability . . . appears rooted in the idea that the antifraud provisions require equal information among all traders. This conflicts with the principle set forth in *Chiarella* that only some persons, under some circumstances, will be barred from trading while in possession of material nonpublic information. . . .

Imposing a duty to disclose or abstain solely because a person knowingly receives material nonpublic information from an insider and trades on it could have an inhibiting influence on the role of market analysts, which the SEC itself recognizes is necessary to the preservation of a healthy market. It is commonplace for analysts to "ferret out and analyze information," 21 S.E.C.

---

14. Under certain circumstances, such as where corporate information is revealed legitimately to an underwriter, accountant, lawyer, or consultant working for the corporation, these outsiders may become fiduciaries of the shareholders. The basis for recognizing this fiduciary duty is not simply that such persons acquired nonpublic corporate information, but rather that they have entered into a special confidential relationship in the conduct of the business of the enterprise and are given access to information solely for corporate purposes. . . . For such a duty to be imposed, however, the corporation must expect the outsider to keep the disclosed nonpublic information confidential, and the relationship at least must imply such a duty.

Docket, at 1406, and this often is done by meeting with and questioning corporate officers and others who are insiders. And information that the analysts obtain normally may be the basis for judgments as to the market worth of a corporation's securities. The analyst's judgment in this respect is made available in market letters or otherwise to clients of the firm. It is the nature of this type of information, and indeed of the markets themselves, that such information cannot be made simultaneously available to all of the corporation's stockholders or the public generally.

The conclusion that recipients of inside information do not invariably acquire a duty to disclose or abstain does not mean that such tippees always are free to trade on the information. The need for a ban on some tippee trading is clear. Not only are insiders forbidden by their fiduciary relationship from personally using undisclosed corporate information to their advantage, but they also may not give such information to an outsider for the same improper purpose of exploiting the information for their personal gain. . . .

Thus, some tippees must assume an insider's duty to the shareholders not because they receive inside information, but rather because it has been made available to them *improperly.* And for Rule 10b-5 purposes, the insider's disclosure is improper only where it would violate his *Cady, Roberts* duty. Thus, a tippee assumes a fiduciary duty to the shareholders of a corporation not to trade on material nonpublic information only when the insider has breached his fiduciary duty to the shareholders by disclosing the information to the tippee and the tippee knows or should know that there has been a breach. . . . Tipping thus properly is viewed only as a means of indirectly violating the *Cady, Roberts* disclose-or-abstain rule.

In determining whether a tippee is under an obligation to disclose or abstain, it thus is necessary to determine whether the insider's "tip" constituted a breach of the insider's fiduciary duty. All disclosures of confidential corporate information are not inconsistent with the duty insiders owe to shareholders. In contrast to the extraordinary facts of this case, the more typical situation in which there will be a question whether disclosure violates the insider's *Cady, Roberts* duty is when insiders disclose information to analysts. In some situations, the insider will act consistently with his fiduciary duty to shareholders, and yet release of the information may affect the market. For example, it may not be clear — either to the corporate insider or to the recipient analyst — whether the information will be viewed as material nonpublic information. Corporate officials may mistakenly think the information already has been disclosed or that it is not material enough to affect the market. Whether disclosure is a breach of duty therefore depends in large part on the purpose of the disclosure. . . . Thus, the test is whether the insider personally will benefit, directly or indirectly, from his disclosure. Absent some personal gain, there has been no breach of duty to stockholders. And absent a breach by the insider, there is no derivative breach. . . .

In determining whether the insider's purpose in making a particular disclosure is fraudulent, the SEC and the courts are not required to read the parties' minds. Scienter in some cases is relevant in determining whether the tipper has violated his *Cady, Roberts* duty. But to determine whether the disclosure itself "[deceives], [manipulates], or [defrauds]" shareholders, . . . the initial inquiry is whether there has been a breach of duty by the insider. This requires courts to focus on objective criteria, i.e., whether the insider receives a direct or indirect personal benefit from the disclosure, such as a pecuniary gain or a reputational benefit that will translate into future earnings. . . . There are objective facts and circumstances that often justify such an inference. For example, there may be a relationship between the insider and the recipient that suggests a *quid pro quo* from the latter, or an intention to benefit the particular recipient. The elements of fiduciary duty and exploitation of nonpublic information also exist when an insider makes a gift of confidential information to a trading relative or friend. The tip and trade resemble trading by the insider himself followed by a gift of the profits to the recipient.

Determining whether an insider personally benefits from a particular disclosure . . . will not always be easy for courts. But it is essential, we think, to have a guiding principle for those whose daily activities must be limited and instructed by the SEC's inside-trading rules, and we believe that there must be a breach of the insider's fiduciary duty before the tippee inherits the duty to disclose or abstain. . . .

Under the inside-trading and tipping rules set forth above, we find that there was no actionable violation by Dirks. It is undisputed that Dirks himself was a stranger to Equity Funding, with no pre-existing fiduciary duty to its shareholders. He took no action, directly or indirectly, that induced the shareholders or officers of Equity Funding to repose trust or confidence in him. There was no expectation by Dirks' sources that he would keep their information in confidence. Nor did Dirks misappropriate or illegally obtain the information about Equity Funding. Unless the insiders breached their *Cady, Roberts* duty to shareholders in disclosing the nonpublic information to Dirks, he breached no duty when he passed it on to investors as well as to the *Wall Street Journal.*

It is clear that neither Secrist nor the other Equity Funding employees violated their *Cady, Roberts* duty to the corporation's shareholders by providing information to Dirks. The tippers received no monetary or personal benefit for revealing Equity Funding's secrets, nor was their purpose to make a gift of valuable information to Dirks. As the facts of this case clearly indicate, the tippers were motivated by a desire to expose the fraud. . . . In the absence of a breach of duty to shareholders by the insiders, there was no derivative breach by Dirks. . . .

Reversed.

BLACKMUN, J., dissenting. . . .

No one questions that Secrist himself could not trade on his inside information to the disadvantage of uninformed shareholders and purchasers of Equity Funding securities. . . .

The Court also acknowledges that Secrist could not do by proxy what he was prohibited from doing personally. . . . But this is precisely what Secrist did. Secrist used Dirks to disseminate information to Dirks' clients, who in turn dumped stock on unknowing purchasers. Secrist thus intended Dirks to injure the purchasers of Equity Funding securities to whom Secrist had a duty to disclose. Accepting the Court's view of tippee liability, it appears that Dirks' knowledge of this breach makes him liable as a participant in the breach after the fact. . . .

It makes no difference to the shareholder whether the corporate insider gained or intended to gain personally from the transaction; the shareholder still has lost because of the insider's misuse of nonpublic information. The duty is addressed not to the insider's motives, but to his actions and their consequences on the shareholder. Personal gain is not an element of the breach of this duty. . . .

NOTES AND QUESTIONS ON DIRKS v. SEC

1. *Dirks* was intended in part to create a safe harbor for security analysts. Does *Dirks* allow a corporate manager to release material inside information selectively to a prominent securities analyst as a means of assuring "accurate" reporting on the company? Does *Dirks* permit a corporate manager to give away nonpublic information to a favored analyst whom she honestly believes will use the information to publish a favorable report that will raise her company's stock prices to reflect its "real" value?

2. The SEC has successfully established a "benefit" to meet the *Dirks* requirement in most tippee cases. When Paul J. Thayer, a former CEO of LTV, was charged with passing information to a group of eight friends, including a young woman who was a former LTV employee, the SEC successfully argued that Thayer had received a personal benefit in the guise of his "close personal relationship" with the woman. Similarly, in *United States v. Reed*, 601 F. Supp. 686 (S.D.N.Y. 1985), the court refused to dismiss an indictment of a tippee who was the son of the alleged tipper, although there was no evidence apart from the parental relationship that the father had intended to benefit his son by the disclosure of the information at issue.

3. Returning to *Dirks*, why exactly did Secrist *not* breach his duty by telling Dirks about his suspicions of fraud?

4. Consistent with *Dirks*, could a company permit its accountants or lawyers to trade on nonpublic information in exchange for lower fees? Could a company permit its CEO to trade on nonpublic information in exchange for paying a lower salary?

5. On Sept. 23, 2008, just minutes after leaving a Goldman Sachs board meeting, Rajat Gupta, the former head of global management consulting firm McKinsey & Company, called Galleon hedge fund chief, Raj Rajaratnam, to tell him that a $5 billion investment by billionaire Warren Buffett had been approved by the Goldman board. Minutes later, Rajaratnam bought significant amounts of Goldman shares. The next day, with Goldman's shares trading higher on news of Buffett's investment, Rajaratnam sold his position in the bank, making a profit of roughly $840,000. Rajaratnam received a sentence of 14 years for trading on material, nonpublic information. On October 26, 2011, Gupta was criminally charged for tipping Rajaratnam. Although there was no claim that Gupta received direct financial benefits from Rajaratnam for his tips, the prosecution alleged that Gupta and Rajaratnam were close personal friends; Gupta had been an investor in Galleon; and Gupta was being considered for a

Galleon directorship. In June 2012, a Manhattan jury convicted Gupta of conspiracy and leaking confidential information about Goldman to Rajaratnam. Gupta faced a maximum sentence of 25 years in prison.

6. What would the outcome be if Gupta had mentioned Warren Buffett's impending investment to Rajaratnam at a charity event to which both men had been independently invited, and, although Gupta had sold his investment in Galleon a month earlier, the two men remained good friends?

NOTE ON "PERSONAL BENEFITS" UNDER DIRKS

Dirks left the precise elements of tippee liability ambiguous. After *Dirks*, federal prosecutors — most recently Preet Bharara in the Southern District of New York — pressed hard to expand the scope of tippee liability. This led to a series of cases where the contours of the "personal benefits" test came into clearer focus. The first case in this saga is *United States v. Newman*, excerpted below, where the Second Circuit pushed back against the expansion of tippee liability by tightening the scope of "personal benefits" that an alleged tipper must receive before there is a violation of §10(b) and Rule 10b-5 under *Dirks*.

UNITED STATES v. NEWMAN
773 F.3d 438 (2d Cir. 2014)

PARKER, J.

Defendants appellants Todd Newman and Anthony Chiasson appeal from judgments of conviction entered on May 9, 2013, and May 14, 2013, respectively in the United States District Court for the Southern District of New York. . . .

The Government alleged that a cohort of analysts at various hedge funds and investment firms obtained material, nonpublic information from employees of publicly traded technology companies, shared it amongst each other, and subsequently passed this information to the portfolio managers at their respective companies. The Government charged Newman, a portfolio manager at Diamondback Capital Management, LLC ("Diamondback"), and Chiasson, a portfolio manager at Level Global Investors, L.P. ("Level Global"), with willfully participating in this insider trading scheme by trading in securities based on the inside information illicitly obtained by this group of analysts. On appeal, Newman and Chiasson challenge the sufficiency of the evidence as to several elements of the offense, and further argue that the district court erred in failing to instruct the jury that it must find that a tippee knew that the insider disclosed confidential information in exchange for a personal benefit [in order find a violation].

We agree that the jury instruction was erroneous because we conclude that, in order to sustain a conviction for insider trading, the Government must prove beyond a reasonable doubt that the tippee knew that an insider disclosed confidential information and that he did so in exchange for a personal benefit. Moreover, we hold that the evidence was insufficient to sustain a guilty verdict . . . for two reasons. First, the Government's evidence of any personal benefit received by the alleged insiders was insufficient. . . . Second, . . . the Government presented no evidence that Newman and Chiasson knew that they were trading on information obtained from insiders in violation of those insiders' fiduciary duties. Accordingly, we reverse the convictions of Newman and Chiasson on all counts. . . .

BACKGROUND

This case arises from the Government's ongoing investigation into suspected insider trading activity at hedge funds. . . .

At trial, the Government presented evidence that a group of financial analysts exchanged information they obtained from company insiders, both directly and more often indirectly. Specifically, the Government alleged that these analysts received information from insiders at Dell and NVIDIA disclosing those companies' earnings numbers before they were publicly released in Dell's May 2008 and August 2008 earnings announcements and NVIDIA's May 2008 earnings announcement. These analysts then passed the inside information to their portfolio managers, including Newman and Chiasson, who, in turn, executed trades in Dell and NVIDIA stock, earning approximately $4 million and $68 million, respectively, in profits for their respective funds.

Newman and Chiasson were several steps removed from the corporate insiders and there was no evidence that either was aware of the source of the inside information. With respect to the Dell tipping chain, the evidence established that Rob Ray of Dell's investor relations department tipped information regarding Dell's consolidated earnings numbers to Sandy Goyal, an analyst at Neuberger Berman. Goyal in turn gave the information to Diamondback analyst Jesse Tortora. Tortora in turn relayed the information to his manager Newman as well as to other analysts including Level Global analyst . . . Adondakis. Adondakis then passed along the Dell information to Chiasson, making Newman and Chiasson three and four levels removed from the inside tipper, respectively.

With respect to the NVIDIA tipping chain, the evidence established that Chris Choi of NVIDIA's finance unit tipped inside information to Hyung Lim . . . whom Choi knew from church. Lim passed the information to co-defendant Danny Kuo, an analyst at Whittier Trust. Kuo circulated the information to the group of analyst friends, including Tortora and Adondakis, who in turn gave the information to Newman and Chiasson, making Newman and Chiasson four levels removed from the inside tippers. Although Ray and Choi have yet to be charged . . . the Government charged that Newman and Chiasson were criminally liable for insider trading because, as sophisticated traders, they must have known that information was disclosed by insiders in breach of a fiduciary duty, and not for any legitimate corporate purpose.

At the close of evidence, Newman and Chiasson moved for a judgment of acquittal [arguing] that there was no evidence that the corporate insiders provided inside information in exchange for a personal benefit which is required to establish tipper liability under *Dirks v. S.E.C.*, 463 U.S. 646 (1983). . . .

Newman and Chiasson also argued that . . . they were not aware of, or participants in, the tippers' fraudulent breaches of fiduciary duties to Dell or NVIDIA, and could not be convicted of insider trading under *Dirks*. In the alternative, appellants requested that the court instruct the jury that it must find that Newman and Chiasson knew that the corporate insiders had disclosed confidential information for personal benefit in order to find them guilty.

The district court reserved decision on the [acquittal] motions. With respect to the appellants' requested jury charge, [the district court] ultimately found that it was constrained by this Court's decision in *S.E.C. v. Obus*, 693 F.3d 276 (2d Cir. 2012). . . . Accordingly, [it] gave the following instructions on the tippers' intent and the personal benefit requirement:

> Now, if you find that Mr. Ray and/or Mr. Choi had a fiduciary or other relationship of trust and confidence with their employers, then you must next consider whether the [G]overnment has proven beyond a reasonable doubt that they intentionally breached that duty of trust and confidence by disclosing material[,] nonpublic information for their own benefit.

On the issue of the appellants' knowledge, the district court instructed the jury:

> To meet its burden, the [G]overnment must also prove beyond a reasonable doubt that the defendant you are considering knew that the material, nonpublic information had been disclosed by the insider in breach of a duty of trust and confidence. The mere receipt of material, nonpublic information by a defendant, and even trading on that information, is not sufficient; he must have known that it was originally disclosed by the insider in violation of a duty of confidentiality.

[T]he jury returned a verdict of guilty on all counts [against Newman and Chiasson]. . . . This appeal followed. . . .

The classical theory [of insider trading] holds that . . . there is a special "relationship of trust and confidence between the shareholders of a corporation and those insiders who have obtained confidential information by reason of their position within that corporation." Id. at 228. As a result of this relationship, corporate insiders that possess material, nonpublic information have "a duty to disclose [or to abstain from trading] because of the 'necessity of preventing a corporate insider from . . . tak[ing] unfair advantage of . . . uninformed . . . stockholders.'" . . . An alternative, but overlapping, theory of insider trading liability, commonly called the "misappropriation" theory, expands the scope of insider trading liability to certain other "outsiders," who do not have any fiduciary or other relationship to a corporation or its shareholders. [See *United States v. O'Hagan, infra* — Eds.]

The insider trading case law, however, is not confined to insiders or misappropriators. . . . Courts have expanded insider trading liability to reach situations where the insider or misappropriator in possession of material nonpublic information (the "tipper") does not himself trade but discloses the information to an outsider (a "tippee") who then trades on the basis of the information before it is publicly disclosed. See *Dirks*, 463 U.S. at 659. . . .

In *Dirks*, the Supreme Court . . . rejected the SEC's theory that a recipient of confidential information (i.e. the "tippee") must refrain from trading "whenever he receives inside information from an insider." Id. at 655.

Instead, the Court held that "[t]he tippee's duty to disclose or abstain is derivative from that of the insider's duty." Id. at 659. Because the tipper's breach of fiduciary duty requires that he "personally will benefit, directly or indirectly, from his disclosure," id. at 662, a tippee may not be held liable in the absence of such benefit. Moreover, the Supreme Court held that a tippee may be found liable "only when the insider has breached his fiduciary duty . . . and the tippee knows or should know that there has been a breach." Id. at 660 (emphasis added). In *Dirks*, the corporate insider provided the confidential information in order to expose a fraud in the company and not for any personal benefit, and thus, the Court found that the insider had not breached his duty to the company's shareholders and that Dirks could not be held liable as tippee. . . .

[T]he Government . . . contends . . . that it merely needed to prove that the "defendants traded on material, nonpublic information they knew insiders had disclosed in breach of a duty of confidentiality. . . ." Gov't Br. 58.

[It] seeks to revive the absolute bar on tippee trading that the Supreme Court explicitly rejected in *Dirks*.

[T]he Supreme Court was quite clear in *Dirks*. First, the tippee's liability derives only from the tipper's breach of a fiduciary duty, not from trading on material, non-public information. . . . Second, the corporate insider has committed no breach of fiduciary duty unless he receives a personal benefit in exchange for the disclosure. Third, even in the presence of a tipper's breach, a tippee is liable only if he knows or should have known of the breach.

While we have not yet been presented with the question of whether the tippee's knowledge of a tipper's breach requires knowledge of the tipper's personal benefit, the answer follows naturally from *Dirks*. . . . [W]ithout establishing that the tippee knows of the personal benefit received by the insider in exchange for the disclosure, the Government cannot meet its burden of showing that the tippee knew of a breach. . . .

In reaching this conclusion, we join every other district court to our knowledge — apart from Judge Sullivan — that has confronted this question. [Citations omitted.]

. . . Such a requirement is particularly appropriate in insider trading cases where we have acknowledged "it is easy to imagine a . . . trader who receives a tip and is unaware that his conduct was illegal and therefore wrongful." *United States v. Kaiser*, 609 F.3d 556, 569 (2d Cir. 2010). This is also a statutory requirement, because only "willful" violations are subject to criminal provision. . . .

In sum, we hold that to sustain an insider trading conviction against a tippee, the Government must prove each of the following elements beyond a reasonable doubt: that (1) the corporate insider was entrusted with a fiduciary duty; (2) the corporate insider breached his fiduciary duty by (a) disclosing confidential information to a tippee (b) in exchange for a personal benefit; (3) the tippee knew of the tipper's breach, that is, he knew the information was confidential and was divulged for a personal benefit; and (4) the tippee still used that information to trade in a security or tip another individual for personal benefit. See *Jiau*, 734 F.3d at 152-53; *Dirks*, 463 U.S. at 659-64.

[In] reviewing the charge as a whole [we find] that the district court's instruction failed to accurately advise the jury of the law. . . . [T]he Government had to prove beyond a reasonable doubt that Newman and Chiasson knew that the tippers received a personal benefit for their disclosure. . . .

As a general matter, a defendant challenging the sufficiency of the evidence bears a heavy burden, as the standard of review is exceedingly deferential. . . .

[However, t]he circumstantial evidence in this case was simply too thin to warrant the inference that the corporate insiders received any personal benefit in exchange for their tips. As to the Dell tips, the Government established that Goyal and Ray were not "close" friends, but had known each other for years, having both attended business school and worked at Dell together. Further, Ray, who wanted to become a Wall Street analyst like Goyal, sought career advice and assistance from Goyal. The evidence further showed that Goyal advised Ray on a range of topics, from discussing the qualifying examination in order to become a financial analyst to editing Ray's résumé and sending it to a Wall Street recruiter, and that some of this assistance began before Ray began to provide tips about Dell's earnings. The evidence also established that Lim and Choi were "family friends" that had met through church and occasionally socialized together. The Government argues that these facts were sufficient to prove that the tippers derived some benefit from the tip. We disagree.

. . . To the extent *Dirks* suggests that a personal benefit may be inferred from a personal relationship between the tipper and tippee, where the tippee's trades "resemble trading by the insider himself followed by a gift of the profits to the recipient," . . . we hold that such an inference is impermissible in the absence of proof of a meaningfully close personal relationship that generates an exchange that is objective, consequential, and represents at least a potential gain of a pecuniary or similarly valuable nature. . . . [I]n order to form the basis for a fraudulent breach, the personal benefit received in exchange for confidential information must be of some consequence. . . .

Here the "career advice" that Goyal gave Ray, the Dell tipper, was little more than the encouragement one would generally expect of a fellow alumnus or casual acquaintance. . . . Crucially, Goyal testified that he would have given Ray advice without receiving information because he routinely did so for industry colleagues. Although the Government argues that the jury could have reasonably inferred . . . that Ray and Goyal swapped career advice for inside information, Ray himself disavowed that any such quid pro quo existed. Further, . . . Goyal began giving Ray "career advice" over a year before Ray began providing any insider information. . . .

The evidence of personal benefit was even more scant in the NVIDIA chain. Choi and Lim were merely casual acquaintances. The evidence did not establish a history of loans or personal favors between the two. During cross examination, Lim testified that he did not provide anything of value to Choi in exchange for the information. Tr. 3067-68. Lim further testified that Choi did not know that Lim was trading NVIDIA stock (and in fact for the relevant period Lim did not trade stock), thus undermining any inference that Choi intended to make a "gift" of the profits earned on any transaction based on confidential information.

Even assuming that the scant evidence described above was sufficient to permit the inference of a personal benefit, which we conclude it was not, the Government presented absolutely no . . . evidence that Newman and Chiasson knew that they were trading on information obtained from insiders, or that those insiders received any benefit in exchange for such disclosures, or even that Newman and Chiasson consciously avoided learning of these facts. . . .

It is largely uncontroverted that Chiasson and Newman, and even their analysts, who testified as cooperating witnesses . . . , knew next to nothing about the insiders and nothing about what, if any, personal benefit had been provided to them. . . .

[I]t is inconceivable that a jury could conclude, beyond a reasonable doubt, that Newman and Chiasson were aware of a personal benefit, when Adondakis and Tortora, who were more intimately involved in the insider trading scheme as part of the "corrupt" analyst group, disavowed any such knowledge. Alternatively, the Government contends that the specificity, timing, and frequency of the updates provided to Newman and Chiasson about Dell and NVIDIA were so "overwhelmingly suspicious" that they warranted various material inferences that could support a guilty verdict. . . . We disagree.

. . . The evidence established that analysts at hedge funds routinely estimate metrics such as revenue, gross margin, operating margin, and earnings per share through legitimate financial modeling using publicly available information and educated assumptions about industry and company trends. . . . [And witnesses testified] . . . that analysts routinely solicited information from companies in order to check assumptions in their models in advance of earnings announcements. . . .

No reasonable jury could have found beyond a reasonable doubt that Newman and Chiasson knew, or deliberately avoided knowing, that the information originated with corporate insiders. In general, information about a firm's finances could certainly be sufficiently detailed and proprietary to permit [such an] inference. . . . But in this case, where the financial information is of a nature regularly and accurately predicted by analyst modeling, and the tippees are several levels removed from the source, the inference that defendants knew, or should have known, that the information originated with a corporate insider is unwarranted. Moreover, even if detail and specificity could support an inference as to the nature of the source, it cannot, without more, permit an inference as to that source's improper motive for disclosure. That is especially true here, where the evidence showed that corporate insiders at Dell and NVIDIA regularly engaged with analysts and routinely selectively disclosed the same type of information. . . .

In short, the bare facts in support of the Government's theory of the case are as consistent with an inference of innocence as one of guilt. Where the evidence viewed in the light most favorable to the prosecution gives equal . . . support to a theory of innocence as a theory of guilt, that evidence necessarily fails to establish guilt beyond a reasonable doubt. See *United States v. Glenn*, 312 F.3d 58, 70 (2d Cir. 2002).

QUESTIONS ON NEWMAN AND A NOTE ON OTHER GAPS IN THE FIDUCIARY DUTY THEORY

1. Does *Dirks'* theory of tippee liability compel the holding in *Newman*? What was the government's strongest argument in support of the appellants' convictions?

2. Would it be difficult for managers like Newman and Chiasson to inquire where their tippers got their information? Wouldn't it make sense for them to do so — to check the information is reliable — even independent of insider trading concerns?

3. Suppose a single tipper generates multiple tippee chains with five links. The tipper tips five tippees, these tippees each tip five more tippees, and the process repeats through two levels of subsequent tippees. Each tippee (except the original tipper and the fourth tippee in a chain) not only tips but trades; the fourth tippee only trades. Must the government prove that the fourth tippee (in any of the numerous five-link chains) knew about the personal benefits received by the tippees higher up her particular chain: (a) that she herself gave the third tippee in her chain a personal benefit in exchange for her tip; (b) that the original tipper (who never traded) received a personal benefit for breaching his duty of loyalty from the first tippee in her *particular* chain; (c) that the original tipper received a personal benefit from at least one of the five "first-level" tippees regardless of whether this tippee was in her particular tipping chain; or (d) that the original tipper *and* the three tippees that preceded her in her particular chain all received personal benefits?

4. How many people trade on inside information in the preceding hypothetical (assuming there is no overlap among tippees)? Is the information traded by the fourth tippees in these tipping chains still "inside information"? As tipping chains lengthen, does information that was originally material and confidential eventually become public even if it is not announced publicly? Should the number of links in a tipping chain matter to its status as material and confidential informational?

The *Newman* opinion led to much commentary and a flurry of activity with many defendants appealing based on the hope that *Newman*'s reasoning would save them from a conviction. This may have led the Supreme Court to clarify "personal benefits" shortly thereafter in *Salman v. United States*, excerpted below.

SALMAN v. UNITED STATES
137 S. Ct. 420 (2016)

ALITO, J.:

Maher Kara was an investment banker in Citigroup's healthcare investment banking group. He dealt with highly confidential information about mergers and acquisitions involving Citigroup's clients. Maher enjoyed a close relationship with his older brother, Mounir Kara (known as Michael). After Maher started at Citigroup, he began discussing aspects of his job with Michael. . . . Then, while their father was battling cancer, the brothers discussed companies that dealt with innovative cancer treatment and pain management techniques. Michael began to trade on the information Maher shared with him. At first, Maher was unaware of his brother's trading activity, but eventually he began to suspect that it was taking place.

Ultimately, Maher began to assist Michael's trading by sharing inside information with his brother about pending mergers and acquisitions. . . . Without [Maher's] knowledge, Michael fed the information to others—including Salman, Michael's friend and Maher's brother-in-law. By the time the authorities caught on, Salman had made over $1.5 million in profits. . . .

The evidence at trial established that Maher and Michael enjoyed a "very close relationship." . . . Michael was like "a second father to Maher," and Michael was the best man at Maher's wedding to Salman's sister. . . . Maher testified that he shared inside information with his brother to benefit him and with the expectation that his brother would trade on it. While Maher explained that he disclosed the information in large part to appease Michael (who pestered him incessantly for it), he also testified that he tipped his brother to "help him" and to "fulfil[l] whatever needs he had." . . . Maher offered his brother money but Michael asked for information instead. Maher then disclosed an upcoming acquisition. . . .

. . . Michael testified that he became friends with Salman when Maher was courting Salman's sister and later began sharing Maher's tips with Salman. As he explained at trial, "any time a major deal came in, [Salman] was the first on my phone list." Id., at 258. Michael also testified that he told Salman that the information was coming from Maher. . . .

After a jury trial . . . Salman was convicted on all counts . . . [and] appealed to the Ninth Circuit. While his appeal was pending, the Second Circuit issued its opinion in *United States* v. *Newman*, 773 F. 3d 438 (2014), *cert. denied*, 577 U. S. (2015) [discussed above—EDS.]. . . .

Pointing to *Newman*, Salman argued that his conviction should be reversed. While the evidence established that Maher made a gift of trading information to Michael and that Salman knew it, there was no evidence that Maher received anything of "a pecuniary or similarly valuable nature" in exchange—or that Salman knew of any such benefit. The Ninth Circuit . . . affirmed Salman's conviction. . . . The court reasoned that the case was governed by *Dirks*'s holding that a tipper benefits personally by making a gift of confidential information to a trading relative or friend. Indeed, Maher's disclosures to Michael were "precisely the gift of confidential information to a trading relative that *Dirks* envisioned." 792 F. 3d, at 1092 (internal quotation marks omitted). To the extent *Newman* went further and required additional gain to the tipper in cases involving gifts of confidential information to family and friends, the Ninth Circuit "decline[d] to follow it." 792 F. 3d, at 1093.

We granted certiorari to resolve the tension between the Second Circuit's *Newman* decision and the Ninth Circuit's decision in this case.[2] . . .

We adhere to *Dirks*, which easily resolves the narrow issue presented here.

In *Dirks*, we explained that a tippee is exposed to liability for trading on inside information only if the tippee participates in a breach of the tipper's fiduciary duty. Whether the tipper breached that duty depends "in large part on the purpose of the disclosure" to the tippee. 463 U. S., at 662. "[T]he test," we explained, "is whether the insider personally will benefit, directly or indirectly, from his disclosure." Ibid. Thus, the disclosure of confidential information without personal benefit is not enough. In determining whether a tipper derived a personal benefit, we instructed courts to "focus on objective criteria, i.e., whether the insider receives a direct or indirect personal benefit from the disclosure, such as a pecuniary gain or a reputational benefit that will translate into future earnings." Id., at 663. This personal benefit can "often" be inferred "from objective facts and circumstances," we explained, such as "a relationship between the insider and the recipient that suggests a quid pro quo from the latter, or an intention to benefit the particular recipient." Id., at 664. In particular, we held that "[t]he elements of fiduciary duty and exploitation of nonpublic information also exist when an insider makes a gift of confidential information to a trading relative or friend." Ibid. . . . In such cases, "[t]he tip and trade resemble trading by the insider followed by a gift of the profits to the recipient." Ibid. We then applied this gift-giving principle to resolve *Dirks* itself, finding it dispositive that the tippers "received no monetary or personal benefit" from their tips to *Dirks*, "nor was their purpose to make a gift of valuable information to *Dirks*." Id., at 667. . . .

Our discussion of gift giving resolves this case. Maher, the tipper, provided inside information to a close relative, his brother Michael. *Dirks* makes clear that a tipper breaches a fiduciary duty by making a gift of confidential information to "a trading relative," and that rule is sufficient to resolve the case at hand. As Salman's counsel acknowledged, . . . Maher would have breached his duty had he personally traded on the information [at issue] here [and then gifted] the proceeds . . . to his brother. . . . But Maher effectively achieved the same result by disclosing the information to Michael, and allowing him to trade on it. *Dirks* appropriately prohibits that approach, as well. . . . *Dirks* specifies that when a tipper gives inside information to "a trading relative or

---

2. *Dirks* v. *SEC*, 463 U. S. 646 (1983), established the personal-benefit framework in a case brought under the classical theory of insider-trading liability. . . . By contrast, the misappropriation theory holds that a person commits securities fraud "when he misappropriates confidential information for securities trading purposes, in breach of a duty owed to the source of the information". . . . The Court of Appeals observed that this is a misappropriation case, 792 F. 3d, 1087, 1092, n. 4 (CA9 2015), while the Government represents that both theories apply on the facts of this case. . . . We need not resolve the question. . . . The parties do not dispute that *Dirks*'s personal-benefit analysis applies in both classical and misappropriation cases, so we will proceed on the assumption that it does.

friend," the jury can infer that the tipper meant to provide the equivalent of a cash gift. . . . Here, by disclosing confidential information as a gift to his brother with the expectation that he would trade on it, Maher breached his duty of trust and confidence to Citigroup and its clients—a duty Salman acquired, and breached himself, by trading on the information with full knowledge that it had been improperly disclosed.

To the extent the Second Circuit held that the tipper must also receive something of a "pecuniary or similarly valuable nature" in exchange for a gift to family or friends, *Newman*, 773 F. 3d, at 452, we agree with the Ninth Circuit that this requirement is inconsistent with *Dirks*. . . .

. . . Accordingly, the Ninth Circuit's judgment is affirmed.

NOTE AND QUESTIONS ON PERSONAL BENEFITS, NEWMAN *AND* SALMAN

1. There were multiple Second Circuit appeals pending when the Supreme Court announced its decision in *Salman*. Two of those cases—*Martoma* and *Gupta*—appeared to weaken the personal benefits test further. In *United States v. Martoma*, 894 F.3d 64 (2d Cir. 2018), defendant Martoma was convicted under *Dirks* tipping liability because he paid a doctor, who was a consultant on a firm's confidential clinical trials, to feed him information on those trials which he then used to assist his employer in trading. The Court upheld the conviction because Martoma's payments to the doctor satisfied the personal benefits test, but then went further (issuing two opinions) delineating two ways in which the personal benefit test could be met. First, if there was a quid pro quo relationship between the tipper and tippee, or second, if the tipper intended to benefit the tippee. In neither instance did *Newman*'s reasoning seem to matter. Soon thereafter, the Second Circuit decided *Gupta v. United States*, No. 15-2707 (2d Cir.) (2019), which also whittled away at *Newman*. Here Rajat Gupta (noted earlier) appealed his Rule 10b-5 conviction by arguing that he (as the tipper) had not received a personal benefit as this was defined in *Newman*. The Second Circuit upheld his conviction, observing that a personal benefit need not be pecuniary and that a "good relationship with a frequent business partner" could satisfy *Dirks*' personal benefit requirement. The net effect of these decisions makes *Newman* of little ongoing significance.

2. But that still leaves us with the question: What is left of the personal benefits test in *Dirks*? Except in the situations where the tipper reveals information by mistake or with the aim of revealing fraud (as in *Dirks*)—surely not everyday occurrences—how difficult is it for the prosecution to show personal benefit? Pecuniary gain is not necessary, and neither is a "meaningfully close personal relationship" that offers potential future gain. A simple intention to benefit the tippee suffices. Perhaps Justice Blackmun's dissent in *Dirks* ("[p]ersonal gain is not an element of the breach of this duty") prefigures the current state of the law.

3. We now leave the case law on tippee liability. Tippee trading was one aspect of the under-inclusion problem that *Chiarella*'s fiduciary duty theory

of Rule 10b-5 liability left in its wake, but it was not the particular aspect that is most closely tied to *Chiarella*'s fact pattern. That honor belongs to Chiarella himself and the broader class of so-called "market insiders" — or actors who, like Chiarella, receive confidential information about third-party companies in the ordinary course of business. This problem is most acute when market insiders illicitly appropriate such information from their principals. Yet it can also arise when market insiders are freely given information, as when insiders selectively disclose information to favored security analysts with the tacit expectation that this will favorably influence corporate share prices (as is illustrated by the *Newman* fact pattern). We turn first to selective disclosure by corporate agents who, without receiving any personal benefit, tip confidential information to favored analysts because they believe that this best serves the interests of their corporations and their shareholders. Far from obtaining personal benefits, these tippers are only doing their jobs as investor relations officers.

14.4.7   Note on Regulation FD

The SEC addressed the issue of selective insider disclosure to market professionals in 2000. Targeted disclosure by insiders to security analysts, journalists, and other professionals had long been perceived as unfair, and especially so since a majority of professionals were rarely selected. In addition, it was widely argued that selective disclosure threatened to corrupt the integrity of influential security analysts. In response to these concerns, the SEC promulgated Regulation "Fair Disclosure" (or "Reg. FD"), which reads in part:

§243.100 General Rule Regarding Selective Disclosure.

(a) Whenever an issuer, or any person acting on its behalf, discloses any material nonpublic information regarding that issuer or its securities to any person described in paragraph (b)(1) [e.g., brokers, dealers, investment advisors, investment analysts, certain managers, and certain shareholders], the issuer shall make public disclosure of that information . . . (1) Simultaneously, in the case of an intentional disclosure; and (2) Promptly, in the case of a non-intentional disclosure.

§243.101 Definitions.

(a) . . . [D]isclosure . . . is "intentional" when the person making the disclosure either knows, or is reckless in not knowing, that the information he or she is communicating is both material and nonpublic. . . .

§243.102 No Effect on Antifraud Liability.

No failure to make a public disclosure required solely by [this Rule] shall be deemed to be a violation of Rule 10b-5. . . .

QUESTIONS ON REG. FD

1. Consider the following excerpt from the *Wall Street Journal*, published on the day that Reg. FD went into effect:

> Matthew Berler, an analyst at Morgan Stanley Dean Witter & Co., is pouring over spreadsheets covering 887 financial factors affecting his earning expectations for Georgia-Pacific Corp. In the past, he would call executives at the Atlanta forest-products company to quiz them about the more pertinent variables factored into his model. Such one-on-one guidance, he says, was part of a "continuous check on my modeling." . . . [Now] Reg FD has entered the picture, and it means Mr. Berler no longer will have access to all the information he uses in his spreadsheets. The result: He is less certain his earnings estimates will match the profit that Georgia-Pacific reports. . . .[21]

Do you believe that the work of a typical analyst has changed as much as this account suggests in light of the facts reported in the *Newman* case?

2. Several empirical studies have suggested that analyst predictions became less accurate in the years immediately after Reg. FD was adopted.[22] Should we care? Or does *Newman*'s account of pervasive insider tipping imply that Reg. FD no longer matters?

3. Is Reg. FD in tension with *Dirks'* concern that the law protect the institutions that inform prices in the securities markets?

4. Why isn't an intentional violation of Reg. FD also a violation of Rule 10b-5?

A NOTE ON RULE 14E-3

Reg FD addresses insider tipping. But the government's first concern after the *Chiarella* decision was "outsider trading," as illustrated by the facts in *Chiarella* itself. There were two plausible strategies for prosecuting outsider trading as securities fraud. One was to invoke a new source of statutory authority to counter common law intuitions and embrace the SEC's expanded definition of securities fraud, and the other was to offer another theory of liability under Rule 10b-5 — a theory that reached the printer without violating *Chiarella*'s ground rules that excluded market duties and reference to an equal access norm.

We turn first to the SEC's effort to switch statutes and reestablish the equal access norm, albeit just for information about tender offers. This was SEC Rule 14e-3, which prohibits "any person" who "has reason to know"

---

21. Jeff D. Opdyke, *The Big Chill: Street Feels Effect of the New "Fair Disclosure" Rule,* Wall St. J. (Oct. 23, 2000).

22. See, e.g., Anup Agrawal, Sahiba Chadha & Mark A. Chen, *Who Is Afraid of Reg FD? The Behavior and Performance of Sell-Side Analysts Following the SEC's Fair Disclosure Rules,* 79 J. Bus. 2811 (2006).

nonpublic information originating from a bidder or target company from trading, without disclosing, while in possession of this information. Rule 14e-3 easily reaches most actors, agents, and tippees who trade on confidential information about tender offers. (Please consult the text of Rule 14e-3 in your statutory supplement.)

The SEC's authority to promulgate Rule 14e-3 survived an early test in a Second Circuit case decided en banc, *United States v. Chestman*, 947 F.2d 551 (2d Cir. 1991), a decision which also limits insider trading liability under Rule 10b-5.

The facts, roughly summarized, were these. A controlling shareholder planned to sell his publicly traded corporation in a transaction in which he would transfer his control stake directly to the purchaser while minority shareholders in his company would be offered the opportunity to sell out on the same terms in a tender offer. The patriarch informed his wife and trusted children of the impending sale. The information spread through the family, eventually reaching a third-generation in-law, who (inevitably it seems) tipped his broker. The broker (Chestman) bought shares for the in-law, himself, and some of his other clients, all of whom made significant profits. The government convicted the broker on charges of criminal liability for securities fraud under both Rule 10b-5 and Rule 14e-3. On appeal, the Second Circuit dismissed the broker's conviction under Rule 10b-5, after finding that the tipper — the dishonorable in-law — lacked an implied relationship of trust and confidence to his spouse, who was the source of his information. By contrast, the Second Circuit upheld the broker's conviction under Rule 14e-3. It reasoned that the SEC had broader authority to define securities fraud under §14(e) than under §10(b) because §14 was added to the Exchange Act partly in order to increase the Commission's authority to regulate tender offers.

Chestman, then, was a partial victory for the SEC insofar as it upheld the SEC's authority to promulgate and apply Rule 14e-3. However, it was a defeat for the government's theory of liability under Rule 10b-5 insofar as it implied that the broker might have escaped liability if the information had concerned anything other than a tender offer. To fill this gap, the SEC adopted Rule 10b5-2 in late 2000, which clarifies that a duty of trust and confidence arises (1) "whenever a person agrees to maintain information in confidence"; (2) whenever two persons "have a history, pattern, or practice of sharing confidences, such that the recipient of the information . . . reasonably should know that the [speaker] expects that the recipient will maintain its confidentiality"; or (3) "whenever a person receives or obtains material nonpublic information from his or her spouse, parent, child, or sibling" in the absence of contrary evidence that no duty existed.

14.4.8   The Introduction of the Misappropriation Theory

After *Chestman*, most — but not all — federal courts accepted the SEC's authority to promulgate Rule 14e-3. But Rule 14e-3 was limited to trading on confidential information about tender offers. This Rule, had it been promulgated before Chiarella's trades, would have made his criminal prosecution much easier. However, it would not have helped much in prosecuting market insiders who traded on information about matters other than tender offers. Suppose, for example, that Chiarella had traded on confidential merger proposals. To handle this possibility and many more like it, the federal courts were forced to adopt a more far-reaching doctrinal innovation, to wit, a new theory of Rule 10b-5 liability that supplemented, and partially overlapped with, the classical fiduciary duty theory of liability. This was the misappropriation theory, which, like Rule 14e-3, found its home in the Second Circuit well before the Supreme Court finally accepted it in the *O'Hagan* case, excerpted below. In fact, *O'Hagan* was a double victory for the government. It not only accepted the misappropriation theory of liability under Rule 10b-5, but it also validated the SEC's authority to pass Rule 14e-3 under §14(e).

UNITED STATES v. O'HAGAN
521 U.S. 642 (1997)

GINSBURG, J.:

This case concerns the interpretation and enforcement of [SEC] Rule 10b-5 and Rule 14e-3(a). . . . In particular, we address and resolve these issues: (1) Is a person who trades in securities for personal profit, using confidential information misappropriated in breach of a fiduciary duty to the source of the information, guilty of violating §10(b) and Rule 10b-5? (2) Did the Commission exceed its rulemaking authority by adopting Rule 14e-3(a), which proscribes trading on undisclosed information in the tender offer setting, even in the absence of a duty to disclose? . . .

Respondent James Herman O'Hagan was a partner in the law firm of Dorsey & Whitney in Minneapolis, Minnesota. In July 1988, Grand Metropolitan PLC (Grand Met) . . . retained Dorsey & Whitney as local counsel [in] a potential tender offer for the common stock of the Pillsbury Company. . . . Both Grand Met and Dorsey & Whitney took precautions to protect the confidentiality of Grand Met's tender offer plans. O'Hagan did no work on the Grand Met representation. Dorsey & Whitney withdrew from representing Grand Met on September 9, 1988. Less than a month later, on October 4, 1988, Grand Met publicly announced its tender offer for Pillsbury stock.

On August 18, 1988, while Dorsey & Whitney was still representing Grand Met, O'Hagan began purchasing call options for Pillsbury stock. . . . Later . . . O'Hagan made additional purchases of Pillsbury call options. By the end of September, he owned 2,500 unexpired Pillsbury options [each giving the right to purchase 100 shares], apparently more than any other individual investor. . . . O'Hagan also purchased, in September 1988, some 5,000 shares of Pillsbury common stock, at a price just under $39 per share. When Grand Met announced its tender offer in October, the price of Pillsbury stock rose to nearly $60 per share. O'Hagan then sold his Pillsbury call options and common stock, making a profit of more than $4.3 million.

The Securities and Exchange Commission (SEC or Commission) initiated an investigation into O'Hagan's transactions, culminating in a 57-count indictment. The indictment alleged that O'Hagan defrauded his law firm and its client, Grand Met, by using for his own trading purposes material, nonpublic information regarding Grand Met's planned tender offer. . . .

A divided panel of the Court of Appeals for the Eighth Circuit reversed all of O'Hagan's convictions. . . .

. . . We hold, in accord with several other Courts of Appeals, that criminal liability under §10(b) may be predicated on the misappropriation theory. . . .

The "misappropriation theory" holds that a person commits fraud "in connection with" a securities transaction, and thereby violates §10(b) and Rule 10b-5, when he misappropriates confidential information for securities trading purposes, in breach of a duty owed to the source of the information. . . . In lieu of [the classical theory of] premising liability on a fiduciary relationship between company insider and purchaser or seller of the company's stock, the misappropriation theory premises liability on a fiduciary-turned-trader's deception of those who entrusted him with access to confidential information.

The two theories are complementary. . . . The classical theory targets a corporate insider's breach of duty to shareholders with whom the insider transacts; the misappropriation theory outlaws trading on the basis of nonpublic information by a corporate "outsider" in breach of a duty owed not to a trading party, but to the source of the information. . . .

In this case, the indictment alleged that O'Hagan, in breach of a duty of trust and confidence he owed to his law firm, Dorsey & Whitney, and to its client, Grand Met, traded on the basis of nonpublic information regarding Grand Met's planned tender offer for Pillsbury common stock. . . .[5]

We agree with the Government that misappropriation . . . satisfies §10(b)'s requirement that chargeable conduct involve a "deceptive device or contrivance" used "in connection with" the purchase or sale of securities. We observe, first, that misappropriators, as the Government describes them, deal in deception. A fiduciary who "[pretends] loyalty to the principal while secretly converting the principal's information for personal gain," Brief for United States 17, "dupes" or defrauds the principal. . . .

The misappropriation theory advanced by the Government [also] is consistent with *Santa Fe Industries, Inc. v. Green*, 430 U.S. 462. . . . [I]n *Santa Fe Industries*, all pertinent facts were disclosed by the persons charged with violating §10(b) and Rule 10b-5 . . . ; therefore, there was no deception through nondisclosure to which liability under those provisions could

---

5. The Government could not have prosecuted O'Hagan as a Pillsbury insider trader under the classical theory, for O'Hagan was not an insider of Pillsbury, the corporation whose stock he traded. Although an "outsider" with respect to Pillsbury, O'Hagan had an intimate association with, and was found to have traded on confidential information from, Dorsey & Whitney, counsel to tender offeror Grand Met. Under the misappropriation theory, O'Hagan's securities trading does not escape Exchange Act sanction, as it would under the dissent's reasoning, simply because he was associated with, and gained nonpublic information from, the bidder, rather than the target.

attach. . . . Similarly, full disclosure forecloses liability under the misappropriation theory: Because the deception essential to the misappropriation theory involves feigning fidelity to the source of information, if the fiduciary discloses to the source that he plans to trade on the nonpublic information, there is no "deceptive device" and thus no §10(b) violation — although the fiduciary-turned-trader may remain liable under state law for breach of a duty of loyalty.[7]

We turn next to the §10(b) requirement that the misappropriator's deceptive use of information be "in connection with the purchase or sale of [a] security." This element is satisfied because the fiduciary's fraud is consummated, not when the fiduciary gains the confidential information, but when, without disclosure to his principal, he uses the information to purchase or sell securities. The securities transaction and the breach of duty thus coincide. This is so even though the person or entity defrauded is not the other party to the trade, but is, instead, the source of the nonpublic information. . . . A misappropriator who trades on the basis of material, nonpublic information, in short, gains his advantageous market position through deception; he deceives the source of the information and simultaneously harms members of the investing public. . . .

The misappropriation theory comports with §10(b)'s language, which requires deception "in connection with the purchase or sale of any security," not deception of an identifiable purchaser or seller. . . . Although informational disparity is inevitable in the securities markets, investors likely would hesitate to venture their capital in a market where trading based on misappropriated nonpublic information is unchecked by law. An investor's informational disadvantage vis-à-vis a misappropriator with material, nonpublic information stems from contrivance, not luck; it is a disadvantage that cannot be overcome with research or skill. See Brudney, *Insiders, Outsiders, and Informational Advantages Under the Federal Securities Laws*, 93 Harv. L. Rev. 322, 356 (1979). . . .

In sum, . . . it makes scant sense to hold a lawyer like O'Hagan a §10(b) violator if he works for a law firm representing the target of a tender offer, but not if he works for a law firm representing the bidder. The text of the statute requires no such result. The misappropriation at issue here was properly made the subject of a §10(b) charge because it meets the statutory requirement that there be "deceptive" conduct "in connection with" securities transactions. . . .

The Eighth Circuit erred in holding that the misappropriation theory is inconsistent with §10(b). . . .

We need not resolve in this case whether the Commission's authority under §14(e) to "define . . . such acts and practices as are fraudulent" is broader than the Commission's fraud-defining authority under §10(b), for . . . Rule 14e-3(a), as applied to cases of this genre, qualifies under §14(e) as a "means

7. Where, however, a person trading on the basis of material, nonpublic information owes a duty of loyalty and confidentiality to two entities or persons — for example, a law firm and its client — but makes disclosure to only one, the trader may still be liable under the misappropriation theory.

reasonably designed to prevent" fraudulent trading on material, nonpublic information in the tender offer context. A prophylactic measure, because its mission is to prevent, typically encompasses more than the core activity prohibited. As we noted in *Schreiber*, §14(e)'s rulemaking authorization gives the Commission "latitude," even in the context of a term of art like "manipulative," "to regulate nondeceptive activities as a 'reasonably designed' means of preventing manipulative acts, without suggesting any change in the meaning of the term 'manipulative' itself." 472 U.S., at 11, n.11. . . . We hold, accordingly, that under §14(e), the Commission may prohibit acts, not themselves fraudulent under the common law or §10(b), if the prohibition is "reasonably designed to prevent . . . acts and practices [that] are fraudulent." 15 U.S.C. §78n(e).

Because Congress has authorized the Commission, in §14(e), to prescribe legislative rules, . . . in determining whether Rule 14e-3(a)'s "disclose or abstain from trading" requirement is reasonably designed to prevent fraudulent acts, we must accord the Commission's assessment "controlling weight unless [it is] arbitrary, capricious, or manifestly contrary to the statute." *Chevron U.S.A. Inc. v. Natural Resources Defense Council, Inc.* . . . In this case, we conclude, the Commission's assessment is none of these.

QUESTION ON UNITED STATES v. O'HAGAN

You work for a broker-dealer in Omaha, Nebraska. One day you happen to glance at your neighbor's desk in the open office and notice buy orders from the legendary billionaire investor Warren Buffett for small stakes in five large public companies. Knowing that the market accords considerable deference to Mr. Buffett's views, you buy six-month calls on shares in all five companies. The stock price for one of these companies declines, the stock prices for the remaining four companies rise, and on net, you make $500,000. Have you violated Rule 10b-5 if Mr. Buffett's purchases were never made public? What if they were announced, as you knew they would be, and their announcement triggered the increases in share prices, just as you expected?

14.4.9   Hacking and Insider Trading—A New Front in the Ongoing War?

There are increasing concerns that hacking into a firm's computer systems could be a way for the technically savvy to gain information that may be used in making trading profits (as well as for other purposes). Hacking presents problems for insider trading jurisprudence because hackers are usually not in a relationship of trust and confidence with the counter-parties to their trades or with the source of information—thereby eliminating liability under *Chiarella* and *O'Hagan*—and they are not usually receiving tips—thereby eliminating liability under *Dirks*.

So how does one address hackers trading on inside information? The Second Circuit confronted this issue head on in *SEC v. Dorozkho*, 574 F.3d 42 (2009). In that case, a hacker (Dorozkho) stole undisclosed negative earnings reports for IMS Health Inc., and shortly thereafter made sizeable profits by purchasing put options on the company's shares. The District Court refused the SEC's request to freeze Dorozkho's assets on the grounds that he had no duty to disclose under §10(b). The SEC appealed, arguing that §10(b) and Rule 10b-5 turned on deception rather than solely on a duty to disclose. While typically insider trading liability involves silent trading (i.e., omitting to say something), it also extends to all misrepresentations or deceptive conduct, including a hacker's scheme to acquire confidential information by misrepresenting his identity. The Second Circuit, per Judge Cabranes, agreed and reversed the District Court's ruling. The case was remanded to the District Court, but Dorozkho absconded and nothing has been heard from him since.

Nonetheless, concerns about hackers and insider trading have only grown over the years as technology and the Internet have become ever more interwoven in our lives. This concern, along with others, led to the Insider Trading Prohibition Act, H.R. 2534, 116th Cong. (2019). The Bill was designed, among other things, to provide a statutory definition of insider trading that would rationalize and expand the scope of what is prohibited. The Bill outlawed trading based on "wrongfully obtained information," including by "theft, bribery, misrepresentation, espionage, . . . a violation of any Federal law protecting computer data or the intellectual property or privacy of computer users, . . . conversion, misappropriation, or other unauthorized and deceptive taking of such information, or . . . a breach of any fiduciary duty, a breach of a confidentiality agreement, a breach of contract, a breach of any code of conduct or ethics policy, or a breach of any other personal or other relationship of trust and confidence." This would surely have covered the fact pattern in *Dorozkho* and much more. The Bill passed the U.S. House of Representatives with some amendments in December 2019 and has been parked in the U.S. Senate for much of 2020 with little hope of action on it in the foreseeable future. As with many things related to insider trading, perhaps the best one can say is stay tuned.

QUESTION ON HACKING AND INSIDER TRADING

If relying on misrepresentations can lead to liability for insider trading, then what about cases where a person gathers information deceptively but not by hacking? For instance, someone in a restaurant holds a mobile phone to his ear (acting like he is engrossed in conversation) to convince the person sitting at the next table that he can't hear what that person is saying. The other person then continues a conversation at the table where he reveals material nonpublic information thinking that the person on the mobile phone isn't listening (when in fact he is). If the person faking the conversation on the mobile phone engaged in securities trading relying on this information, then could that amount to insider trading under *Dorozkho*?

14.4.10   Civil Liability, Civil Fines, and Criminal Penalties for Securities Fraud Violations

As you may already have surmised, the potential criminal sanctions for violating Rules 10b-5 and 14e-3 can be quite severe. But what is the measure of damages available to private plaintiffs in civil actions alleging insider trading? And who has standing to sue? It makes sense that a party to whom an insider had a duty of trust and confidence would have standing. But what about parties who merely traded opposite insiders and were not in a relationship of trust or confidence, as in the case of the target shareholders in *Chiarella*? Logically they should not have standing, even if doing so would make economic sense. But Congress broadened the standing of private parties to sue in 1988.

NOTE ON THE INSIDER TRADING AND SECURITIES FRAUD ENFORCEMENT ACT OF 1988

In 1988, Congress passed the Insider Trading and Securities Fraud Enforcement Act (ITSFEA), H.R. Rep. No. 100-910 (1988), in response to "serious episodes of abusive and illegal practices on Wall Street." In doing so, Congress intended to increase deterrence of insider trading, in part by adding §20A to the Securities Exchange Act (U.S.C. §78t-1 (in your statutory supplement). Section 20A does not define insider trading, but it creates standing for counter-parties to sue insiders who trade on confidential information even if these insiders do not stand in a relationship of trust and confidence to their counter-parties (as in *Chiarella*, where the printer's counter-parties were shareholders in takeover targets, while Chiarella owed a fiduciary duty to his printing company or, at most, to the would-be bidders in tender offers). Fiduciary duty and injury fell by the wayside in §20A. In the interest of deterrence, private parties could sue insiders as trading counter-parties, regardless of whether they suffered an injury as this was conceptualized under Rule 10b-5. But what sort of damages could plaintiffs hope to obtain in a §20A action? The most they could recover was what a genuine victim of insider trading could recover in private actions under Rule 10b-5. And what was this? Consider the following excerpt from *Elkind v. Liggett & Myers, Inc.*

ELKIND v. LIGGETT & MYERS, INC.
635 F.2d 156 (2d Cir. 1980)

MANSFIELD, J.:

[Shareholders brought a class action against Liggett & Myers, Inc. (Liggett), for wrongful tipping of inside information about an earnings decline to certain persons who then sold Liggett's shares on the open market.]

This case presents a question of measurement of damages [in a private Rule 10b-5 insider trading class action]. . . .

The district court looked to the measure of damages used in cases where a buyer was induced to purchase a company's stock by materially misleading statements or omissions. In such cases of fraud by a fiduciary intended to induce others to buy or sell stock the accepted measure of damages is the "out-of-pocket" measure. This consists of the difference between the price paid and the "value" of the stock when brought (or when the buyer committed himself to buy, if earlier). Except in rare face-to-face transactions, however, uninformed traders on an open, impersonal market are not induced by representations on the part of the tipper or tippee to buy or sell. Usually they are wholly unacquainted with and uninfluenced by the tippee's misconduct. They trade independently and voluntarily but without the benefit of information known to the trading tippee.

[Moreover,] it must be remembered that investors who trade in a stock on the open market have no absolute right to know inside information. They are, however, entitled to an honest market in which those with whom they trade have no confidential corporate information. . . .

Recognizing the foregoing, we [suggested in an earlier case] that the district court must be accorded flexibility in assessing damages. . . . [S]everal measures are possible. First, there is the traditional out-of-pocket measure used by the district court in this case. For several reasons this measure appears to be inappropriate. In the first place, . . . it is directed toward compensating a person for losses directly traceable to the defendant's fraud upon him. No such fraud or inducement may be attributed to a tipper or tippee trading on an impersonal market. Aside from this the measure poses serious proof problems that may often be insurmountable in a tippee-trading case. The "value" of the stock traded during the period of nondisclosure of the tipped information (i.e., the price at which the market would have valued the stock if there had been a disclosure) is hypothetical. . . .

[Here the court rejects an out-of-pocket measure of damages on several grounds. One is that trading on inside information on an anonymous market may generate gains for the trader, but it does not impose losses on particular and identifiable victims. A second basis for rejecting out-of-pocket damages in a tipper-tippee scenario is that they would seem to depend on the harm inflicted when the information is tipped, while the information only enters the market when the tippee trades. A third reason is that despite opinion to the contrary, there is no necessary relationship between whether and how insider trading on private information affected share prices when it occurred on one hand, and whether or how public disclosure of this same information affected share prices at the time of disclosure. The court's final and apparently decisive argument against imposing out-of-pocket damages against defendants found to have engaged in insider trading does not rest on concerns about proof or measurement. Rather it is that out-of-pocket damages, no matter how they are fixed, are likely to be "Draconian" and "out of all proportion to the wrong committed."

After rejecting out-of-pocket damages, the court also rejects a second damages measure based on how much insider trading actually affects noisy share prices, which it suspects may often be very little, which the court argues might effectively eliminate damages from private insider trading actions.

At this point, the court finds its Goldilocks spot: the most sensible damages measure is the plaintiffs' out-of-pocket damages as capped — and this is key — by defendant's ill-gotten trading gains. The court addresses the application of this measure in the excerpt from its opinion below. — Eds.]

A [sensible] alternative is (1) to allow any uninformed investor, where a reasonable investor would either have delayed his purchase or not purchased at all if he had had the benefit of the tipped information, to recover any post-purchase decline in market value of his shares up to a reasonable time after he learns of the tipped information or after there is a public disclosure of it but (2) limit his recovery to the amount gained by the tippee as a result of his selling at the earlier date rather than delaying his sale until the parties could trade on an equal informational basis. Under this measure, if the tippee sold 5,000 shares at $50 per share on the basis of inside information and the stock thereafter declined to $40 per share within a reasonable time after public disclosure, an uninformed purchaser, buying shares during the interim (e.g., at $45 per share) would recover the difference between his purchase price and the amount at which he could have sold the shares on an equal informational basis (i.e., the market price within a reasonable time after public disclosure of the tip), subject to a limit of $50,000, which is the amount gained by the tippee as a result of his trading on the inside information rather than on an equal basis. Should the intervening buyers, because of the volume and price of their purchases, claim more than the tippee's gain, their recovery (limited to that gain) would be shared pro rata. . . .

[A]s between the various alternatives we are persuaded . . . that [this] measure . . . offers the most equitable resolution of the difficult problems created by conflicting interests.

QUESTIONS ON ELKIND v. LIGGETT & MYERS, INC.

The *Elkind* disgorgement measure is now the accepted measure of damages in private Rule 10b-5 insider trading cases. How often are plaintiff law firms likely to bring class actions for damages under Rule 10b-5 (or §20A, for that matter)? When might bringing such a class action for insider trading damages make economic sense on the plaintiffs' side? When would it not make sense? Would plaintiffs have brought a class action against *Chiarella*'s printer, even if they had standing to do so under §20A?

A NOTE AND QUESTION ON PUBLIC SANCTIONS FOR INSIDER TRADING

1. Whatever the measure of private civil damages under Rule 10b-5, since 1988, the SEC has had the power to seek a wide range of civil penalties against traders on inside information. It may petition federal district courts

to impose injunctions and severe monetary penalties for securities law violations or it may also seek disgorgement of profits, as well as accountings or audits and court orders that bar violators of the securities laws from acting as corporate officers or directors. Of course, the SEC can also recommend that the Department of Justice prosecute violators of the securities laws under the U. S. Criminal Code. Parties who are convicted after criminal prosecution face particularly severe penalties. For example, §1348 of the U.S. Criminal Code sets the maximum imprisonment sentence at 25 years for anyone convicted of fraud involving the securities of issuers registered under the 1934 Act, while the maximum sentence for criminal violations of the Securities Acts is 20 years. Individuals can also face criminal fines of up to $5 million, while corporate criminal fines range up to $25 million.

2. As between private civil liability for damages and the range of civil and criminal sanctions available to the government, which sanctions bear the burden of deterring insider trading under current law? Could it be otherwise?

14.5   THE OTHER SIDE OF RULE 10b-5: FRAUD-ON-THE-MARKET CLASS ACTIONS

Although Rule 10b-5 establishes the foundations of insider trading law, it also transposes the law of fraud to anonymous securities markets. As we have previously suggested, insider trading is only one variety of securities fraud that can trigger liability under Rule 10b-5. In fact, it may not be the most significant. Many litigators might argue that this honor belongs to another branch of Rule 10b-5 case law that enables (and constrains) shareholder class actions alleging overt securities fraud, and in particular shareholder class actions to recoup damages from what are now termed fraud-on-the-market (FOM) class actions. FOM occurs when false or misleading information — usually originating in the corporation — distorts share prices in otherwise relatively healthy public markets for actively traded stocks. When credible and material misinformation enters the market, shareholders trade at distorted prices and may suffer significant harm as a result. Most often (but not always) misleading corporate information is intended to inflate (or support) share prices, in which case public shareholders may suffer serious losses if they purchase stock at "artificially" high prices and resell it after additional information reveals prior representations to have been false. Less frequently, sellers of stock lose the gains they might otherwise have reaped had they not sold at prices intentionally kept artificially low by the dissemination of false, but credible, information in the market.

Both examples of FOM turn on actors who are able to manipulate stock prices by releasing material information that they knew or should have known was false or misleading. In some cases, these actors may be corporate executives who introduce one large lie in the market by certifying false financial statements or denying important bad news on a conference call with securities analysts. More frequently, one supposes, investors are misled about facts by some combination of exaggerations, omissions, and obfuscations that fall short of bald-faced lies but appear to be — and may well be — a campaign of intentional deception when viewed as a whole. We suppose that even before the 1934 Act an individual investor could press a fraud claim if she could prove that she relied on the public representations of a corporate officer or director and was also (somehow) able to show that he was a counter-party in an anonymous trading market (as the plaintiff did in the *Goodwin* case).

An individual could press a fraud claim on some combinations of these facts. Once the courts transpose the duties that support a traditional securities fraud claim, however, it seems logical to allow FOM class actions. By the 1970s, the principal obstacle to such actions was the requirement that plaintiffs demonstrate their reliance on the defendants' fraudulent statements. By 1980, if not before, some circuits had greatly relaxed the reliance requirement in class actions alleging securities fraud. But it was not until 1988 that the Supreme Court endorsed a rebuttable presumption of reliance on market prices undistorted by fraud, at least in well-functioning public markets. Our editing of the *Basic* case below focuses on the Court's holding that plaintiffs are entitled to a rebuttable presumption of relying on fraud-free securities prices in markets for publicly traded shares. The majority opinion in *Basic* also includes a discussion of the materiality element of securities fraud, which we summarize in the interests of brevity.

14.5.1   Materiality and Reliance in FOM Class Actions

BASIC INC. v. LEVINSON
485 U.S. 224 (1988)

BLACKMUN J.:

This case requires us to apply the materiality requirement [o]f §10(b) of the [1934 Act] and Rule 10b-5 . . . in the context of preliminary corporate merger discussions. We must also determine whether a person who traded a corporation's shares on a securities exchange after the issuance of a materially misleading statement by the corporation may invoke a rebuttable presumption that, in trading, he relied on the integrity of the price set by the market.

[For two years prior to the merger of Combustion Engineering, Inc. and Basic Inc. in December 1978, the companies discreetly negotiated terms for a possible merger between them. Over this same period, Basic made three public statements denying that it was engaged in merger negotiations or knew of any corporate developments that would account for the large volume of market trading in its stock. The plaintiffs in this FOM class action were investors who sold Basic shares at various points between the company's first untrue denial that it was engaged in merger negotiations and a date well after a year later that immediately preceded its announcement of a completed agreement to merge with Combustion Engineering. The plaintiffs alleged, of course, that Basic's three false denials of negotiations that were admitted constituted actionable fraudulent statements under Rule 10b-5. The district court granted summary judgment for the defendants on the theory that a public denial of preliminary merger negotiations was immaterial as a matter of law. The court of appeals reversed, holding that whatever the original status of information about merger agreements, such information became material if the company falsely denied the existence of negotiations that were already underway.

Per Justice Blackmun's majority opinion, what was required to show materiality in a Rule 10b-5 fraud case was a novel question for the Court that was best answered by recalling the balancing test that the Court had used to determine the materiality necessary to force disclosure in proxy contests governed by Rule 14a-9. As formulated in *TSC Industries, Inc. v. Northway, Inc.*, 426 U.S. 438 (1976), a fact is material if there is a substantial likelihood that a reasonable shareholder would consider it important in deciding how to vote in a proxy contest. Disclosing additional facts risks burying shareholders in trivia that degrade their ability to make rational decisions. To strike the right balance between too little and too much disclosure, the *Basic* Court adopted a test originally formulated by Judge Henry Friendly. This test conceptualizes the materiality of information about merger negotiations as a case-specific product of the probability that negotiations will culminate in a merger and the magnitude of the effect that a consummated merger would have on shareholder plaintiffs. Without a doubt, information about Basic's merger negotiations became material well before Basic flatly denied their existence. However, the Court adds a key qualification in a footnote by observing that materiality alone does not create a duty to disclose. Basic might have avoided liability under Rule 10b-5 by refusing to comment on queries about merger negotiations rather than falsely denying that negotiations were underway.

Finally, the Court's decision to adopt a unitary test of materiality rather than a test tailored to policy concerns peculiar to merger negotiations is also notable. Some commentators sided with the district court's conclusion in *Basic* that information about merger negotiations should be immaterial as a matter of law before the parties had reached an agreement in principle about the terms of the proposed merger. Crudely summarized, the pragmatic argument in favor of such a narrow definition of materiality had been that it had protected the confidentiality of its merger negotiations by all necessary means (including its press releases) for the benefit of its shareholders. Disclosure of these negotiations might have put off its competition-shy suitor and so cost its shareholders the opportunity of realizing a large premium in a fully negotiated deal. To its credit, the *Basic* Court refused to engage with the strong conjecture that shareholders would benefit if loyal managers had discretion to lie in limited circumstances.

We now turn to *Basic*'s more controversial holding that plaintiffs in a FOM class action case enjoy a rebuttable presumption of relying on the informational integrity of market price in lieu of the traditional requirement that they demonstrate direct reliance on what defendants had caused to be said or written — such as financial statements, press releases, or oral expressions — that plaintiffs' had individually credited and relied upon.

Justice Blackmun's majority opinion begins its analysis of the reliance presumption by quoting from a prior Third Circuit decision that ruled in favor of the presumption several years before. Thus, the initial quote below reflects the views of the Third Circuit, not necessarily the views of the Court's majority opinion. — EDs.]

> "The fraud on the market theory is based on the hypothesis that, in an open and developed securities market, the price of a company's stock is determined by the available material information regarding the company and its business. Misleading statements will therefore defraud purchasers of stock even if the purchasers do not directly rely on the misstatements. The causal connection between the defendants' fraud and the plaintiffs' purchase of stock in such a case is no less significant than in a case of direct reliance on misrepresentations." *Peil v. Speiser*, 806 F.2d 1154, 1160-1161 (CA3 1986).

Our task, of course, is not to assess the general validity of [this economic] theory, but to consider whether it was proper for the courts below to apply a rebuttable presumption of reliance, supported in part by the fraud-on-the-market theory.

This case required resolution of several common questions of law and fact. . . .

We agree that reliance is an element of a Rule 10b-5 cause of action. . . . Reliance provides the requisite causal connection between a defendant's misrepresentation and a plaintiff's injury. . . . There is, however, more than one way to demonstrate the causal connection. Indeed, we previously have dispensed with a requirement of positive proof of reliance, where a duty to disclose material information had been breached, concluding that the necessary nexus between the plaintiffs' injury and the defendant's wrongful conduct had been established. See *Affiliated Ute Citizens v. United States*, 406 U.S. 128 at 153-154. Similarly, we did not require proof that material omissions or misstatements in a proxy statement decisively affected voting, because the proxy solicitation itself, rather than the defect in the solicitation materials, served as an essential link in the transaction. See *Mills v. Electric Auto-Lite Co.*, 396 U.S. 375, 385-386 (1970).

The modern securities markets, literally involving millions of shares changing hands daily, differ from the face-to-face transactions contemplated by early fraud cases, and our understanding of Rule 10b-5's reliance requirement must encompass these differences. . . .

Presumptions typically serve to assist courts in managing circumstances in which direct proof, for one reason or another, is rendered difficult. . . . The courts below accepted a presumption, created by the fraud-on-the-market theory and subject to rebuttal by petitioners, that persons who had traded Basic shares had done so in reliance on the integrity of the price set by the market, but because of petitioners' material misrepresentations that price had been fraudulently depressed. Requiring a plaintiff to show a speculative state of facts, i.e., how he would have acted if omitted material information had been disclosed, . . . or if the misrepresentation had not been made, . . . would place an unnecessarily unrealistic evidentiary burden on the Rule 10b-5 plaintiff who has traded on an impersonal market. . . .

Arising out of considerations of fairness, public policy, and probability, as well as judicial economy, presumptions are also useful devices for allocating the burdens of proof between parties. . . . [A] presumption of reliance . . . in this case is consistent with, and, by facilitating Rule 10b-5 litigation, supports, the congressional policy embodied in the 1934 Act. . . .

The presumption [of reliance] is also supported by common sense and probability. Recent empirical studies have tended to confirm Congress' premise that the market price of shares traded on well-developed markets reflects all publicly available information, and, hence, any material misrepresentations. It has been noted that "it is hard to imagine that there ever is a buyer or seller who does not rely on market integrity. Who would knowingly roll the dice in a crooked crap game?" *Schlanger v. Four-Phase Systems Inc.*, 555 F. Supp. 535, 538 (S.D.N.Y. 1982). Indeed, nearly every court that has considered the proposition has concluded that where materially misleading statements have been disseminated into an impersonal, well-developed market for securities, the reliance of individual plaintiffs on the integrity of the market price may be presumed. Commentators generally have applauded the adoption of one variation or another of the fraud-on-the-market theory. An investor who buys or sells stock at the price set by the market does so in reliance on the integrity of that price. Because most publicly available information is reflected in market price, an investor's reliance on any public material misrepresentations, therefore, may be presumed for purposes of a Rule 10b-5 action.

The Court of Appeals found that petitioners "made public material misrepresentations and [respondents] sold Basic stock in an impersonal, efficient market. Thus the class, as defined by the district court, has established the threshold facts for proving their loss." 786 F.2d, at 751. The court acknowledged that petitioners may rebut proof of the elements giving rise to the presumption, or show that the misrepresentation in fact did not lead to a distortion of price or that an individual plaintiff traded or would have traded despite his knowing the statement was false. . . .

Any showing that severs the link between the alleged misrepresentation and either the price received (or paid) by the plaintiff, or his decision to trade at a fair market price, will be sufficient to rebut the presumption of reliance. For example, if petitioners could show that the "market makers" were privy to the truth about the merger discussions here with Combustion, and thus that the market price would not have been affected by their misrepresentations, the causal connection could be broken: the basis for finding that the fraud had been transmitted through market price would be gone. Similarly, if, despite petitioners' allegedly fraudulent attempt to manipulate market price, news of the merger discussions credibly entered the market and dissipated the effects of the misstatements, those who traded Basic shares after the corrective statements would have no direct or indirect connection with the fraud. Petitioners also could rebut the presumption of reliance as to plaintiffs who would have divested themselves of their Basic shares without relying on the integrity of the market. For example, a plaintiff who believed that Basic's statements were false and that Basic was indeed engaged in merger discussions, and who consequently believed that Basic stock was artificially underpriced, but sold his shares nevertheless because of other unrelated concerns, e.g., potential antitrust problems, or political pressures to divest from shares of certain businesses, could not be said to have relied on the integrity of a price he knew had been manipulated. . . .

Justice WHITE, with whom Justice O'CONNOR joins, concurring in part and dissenting in part. . . .

At the outset, I note that there are portions of the Court's fraud-on-the-market holding with which I am in agreement. Most importantly, the Court rejects the version of that theory, heretofore adopted by some courts, which equates "causation" with "reliance," and permits recovery by a plaintiff who claims merely to have been *harmed* by a material misrepresentation which altered a market price, notwithstanding proof that the plaintiff did not in any way *rely* on that price. . . . I agree with the Court that if Rule 10b-5's reliance requirement is to be left with any content at all, the fraud-on-the-market presumption must be capable of being rebutted by a showing that a plaintiff did not "rely" on the market price. . . .

But even as the Court attempts to limit the fraud-on-the-market theory it endorses today, the pitfalls in its approach are revealed by previous uses by the lower courts of the broader versions of the theory. . . .

In general, the case law developed in this Court with respect to §10(b) and Rule 10b-5 has been based on doctrines with which we, as judges, are familiar: common-law doctrines of fraud and deceit. . . . But with no staff economists, no experts schooled in the "efficient-capital-market hypothesis," no ability to test the validity of empirical market studies, we are not well equipped to embrace novel constructions of a statute based on contemporary microeconomic theory.[4] . . .

Finally, the particular facts of this case make it an exceedingly poor candidate for the Court's fraud-on-the-market theory, and illustrate the illogic achieved by that theory's application in many cases.

Respondents here are a class of sellers who sold Basic stock between October, 1977 and December 1978, a fourteen-month period. At the time the class period began, Basic's stock was trading at $20 a share (at the time, an all-time high); the last members of the class to sell their Basic stock got a price of just over $30 a share. App. 363, 423. It is indisputable that virtually every member of the class made money from his or her sale of Basic stock.

The oddities of applying the fraud-on-the-market theory in this case are manifest. First, there are the facts that the plaintiffs are sellers and the class period is so lengthy — both are virtually without precedent in prior fraud-on-the-market cases. . . .

[T]here is no evidence that petitioner's officials made the troublesome misstatements for the purpose of manipulating stock prices. . . . Indeed, during the class period, petitioners do not appear to have purchased or sold *any* Basic stock whatsoever. . . .

Third, there are the peculiarities of what kinds of investors will be able to recover in this case. . . . Thus, it is possible that a person who heard the

---

4. This view was put well by two commentators who wrote a few years ago:

"Of all recent developments in financial economics, the efficient capital market hypothesis ("ECMH") has achieved the widest acceptance by the legal culture. . . . Yet the legal culture's remarkably rapid and broad acceptance of an economic concept that did not exist twenty years ago is not matched by an equivalent degree of understanding."

Gilson & Kraakman, *The Mechanisms of Market Efficiency*, 70 Va. L. Rev. 549, 549-550 (1984) (footnotes omitted; emphasis added).

first corporate misstatement and *disbelieved* it — i.e., someone who pur-chased Basic stock thinking that petitioners' statement was false — may still be included in the plaintiff-class on remand. How a person who undertook such a speculative stock-investing strategy — and made $10 a share doing so (if he bought on October 22, 1977, and sold on December 15, 1978) — can say that he was "defrauded" by virtue of his reliance on the "integrity" of the market price is beyond me. And such speculators may not be uncommon, at least in this case. . . .

While the fraud-on-the-market theory has gained even broader accep-tance since 1984, I doubt that it has achieved any greater understanding.

Indeed, the facts of this case lead a casual observer to the almost inescap-able conclusion that many of those who bought or sold Basic stock during the period in question flatly disbelieved the statements which are alleged to have been "materially misleading." Despite three statements denying that merger negotiations were underway, Basic stock hit record-high after record-high during the 14 month class period. It seems quite possible that, like Casca's knowing disbelief of Caesar's "thrice refusal" of the Crown,[11] clever investors were skeptical of petitioners' three denials that merger talks were going on. Yet such investors, the savviest of the savvy, will be able to recover under the Court's opinion, as long as they now claim that they believed in the "integrity of the market price" when they sold their stock (between September and December, 1978). Thus, persons who bought after hearing and relying on the falsity of petitioner's statements may be able to prevail and recover money damages on demand.

And who will pay the judgments won in such actions? I suspect that all too often the majority's rule will "lead to large judgments, payable in the last analysis by the innocent investors, for the benefit of speculators and their lawyers." Cf. *SEC v. Texas Gulf Sulphur Co.*, 401 F.2d 833, 867 (CA2 1968) (en banc) (Friendly, J., concurring). . . .

NOTES AND QUESTIONS ON BASIC INC. V. LEVINSON

1. A couple of years after *Basic* was decided, different commentators argued both sides of the question whether "innocuous" but false denials of merger negotiations ought to enjoy limited protection from Rule 10b-5 liability for the benefit of all shareholders. Compare Jonathan R. Macey & Geoffrey P. Miller, *Good Finance, Bad Economics: An Analysis of Fraud-on-the-Market Theory*, 42 Stan. L. Rev. 1059 (1990) with Ian Ayres, *Back to Basics: Regulating How Corporations Speak to the Market*, 77 Va. L. Rev. 945 (1991).

2. Must the Court accept some form of the Efficient Capital Market Hypothesis (ECMH) to make a rebuttable presumption of reliance on mar-ket prices plausible? Alternatively, is the Court disingenuous when it denies allegiance to any particular theory about the efficiency of share prices but

11. See W. Shakespeare, Julius Caesar, Act I, Scene II.

nonetheless proposes an "inefficient market" defense to the presumption of reliance on market prices? Or put still differently, what is the most minimal empirical assumption that the Court must have made in order to accept the logic of a rebuttable presumption of reliance on share prices?

3. Only a plurality of the *Basic* Court (4–2) joined the majority opinion that created the rebuttable presumption doctrine. As a technical legal matter, *Basic* was therefore not binding precedent in either Supreme Court or lower court litigation. Nevertheless, the federal courts have treated *Basic* as if it were binding precedent despite many suits arguing the contrary. Is this odd or to be expected?

4. The so-called semi-strong form of the ECMH holds that share prices in public stock markets respond rapidly to the public announcement of unanticipated information. Formally stated, this is the claim that share prices reflect novel public information so rapidly that even professional traders cannot profit by trading on it. Markets in which share prices meet this criterion are sometimes said to be "informationally efficient." A much stronger claim is that prices in these markets are also "fundamentally efficient" in the sense that they are best estimates of the value that the market expects investors to receive by holding these shares given available public information. By and large (and most of the time), the prices of exchange-traded stocks appear to be informationally efficient. How might one test whether they are also fundamentally efficient, i.e., whether their current market price is "right" given available public information? Does the *Basic* Court use the term "efficient market" in either of these two senses?

5. How can defendants rebut *Basic*'s presumption of reliance by demonstrating that a stock does not trade in an "efficient market"? What sort of evidence should a trial court credit? See *Cammer v. Bloom*, 711 F. Supp. 1264 (D.N.J. 1989).

6. Justice White's dissent addresses the issue of damages in 10b-5 class actions. As we have previously suggested, this is one of the elephants in the room. A sibling elephant is the question of who ultimately pays for FOM damages or settlement funds? Before reading further, do you expect the same damages measure to apply in insider trading and FOM civil actions? Why — or why not?

7. Can the ECMH be used as a defense? Shouldn't share prices that rapidly reflect all "public" information also enjoy immunity from misinformation that is known to be false by some critical number or percentage of professional traders? See, e.g., *In re Apple Securities Litigation*, 886 F.2d 1109, 1116 (9th Cir. 1989).

14.5.2   Loss Causation in Rule 10b-5 Class Actions

The common law of deceit requires not only reasonable reliance on a misrepresentation but also that their reliance was the proximate cause of their losses. After *Basic* endorsed the rebuttable presumption of reliance that gave legs to shareholder class actions seeking damages for securities fraud, the Supreme Court waited 17 years before addressing FOM class actions again in

Dura Pharmaceuticals Inc. v. Broudo, 544 U.S. 336 (2005). *Dura* provided a brief and rather cautious analysis of loss causation and damages in FOM actions. It stressed the complexity of proving loss causation in FOM actions, which inevitably led to a modest increase in plaintiffs' burden of proof as well as a modest increase in plaintiffs' risk of early dismissal.

Dura stressed that plaintiffs' claim that purchasing shares in reliance on prices distorted by false or misleading information and subsequently selling these shares at a loss was insufficient to establish loss causation. To demonstrate loss causation, plaintiffs must show that defendants' misrepresentation to the market caused their losses by showing that the losses resulting from purchasing shares at inflated prices and reselling them at lower prices were due, in whole or in part, to intervening disclosures that corrected the alleged misrepresentation. This may not be easy to do — or even to allege with the requisite specificity. As *Dura* noted, many factors unrelated to the alleged misrepresentation may have eroded market prices during the period in which plaintiffs held their shares. Put differently, even if plaintiffs had purchased their shares at a price inflated by defendants' misrepresentation, intervening events or market-wide changes might have caused the lower price at which plaintiffs sold — most conspicuously, for example, if these events were correlated with falling share prices before the alleged misrepresentation had been "corrected" by new information entering the market. Indeed, even a precise correlation between a fall in share prices and the moment at which new information corrected defendants' misrepresentation may not demonstrate loss causation if other bad news arising from unrelated "confounding events" became public at virtually the same time that corrective disclosure was made.

The facts in *Dura* featured a pharmaceutical company of the same name that was alleged to have made numerous public misrepresentations between April 15, 1997 and February 24, 1998. Plaintiffs' most plausible claim was that Dura had frequently assured investors that its innovative asthma spray would gain FDA approval and become an important new source of income for the company. Plaintiffs also alleged that Dura had often exaggerated the value of new drugs in its pipeline and issued misleadingly optimistic forecasts about its future revenues and income. Dura's share price rose steadily over the months in which it made these rosy statements. Sadly, however, it was forced to change its tune on February 24, 1998, when it acknowledged a sharp expected drop in the next quarterly earnings report. The following day, Dura's shares lost almost half of their previous market value. A few weeks later, Dura announced that the FDA would not approve the asthma device, contrary to its repeated statements in prior months. After this announcement, Dura's share price suffered a second, more modest fall, from which it fully recovered within a week.

The steep fall in Dura's share prices attracted a FOM shareholder class action on behalf of all investors who purchased Dura shares during its ten-month period of public optimism. The plaintiffs alleged damages equaling the difference between the artificially inflated price they had paid for their shares, and the hypothetical price they would have paid in the absence of Dura's misrepresentations. By the time the case reached the Supreme Court, the courts below had dismissed plaintiffs' complaint for inadequate allegations of scienter in connection with Dura's optimistic forecasts and assessments of its drug pipeline. The surviving portion of the original complaint concerned Dura's allegedly fraudulent statements about the FDA's likely approval of its asthma spray device. On this basis, the Ninth Circuit upheld the complaint, but the Supreme Court reversed.

In the Court's words per Justice Breyer:

> [The Ninth Circuit reasons] at the end of the day plaintiffs need only "establish," *i.e.,* prove, that "the price *on the date of purchase* was inflated because of the misrepresentation." . . . [T]he logical link between the inflated share purchase price and any later economic loss is not invariably strong. Shares are normally purchased with an eye toward a later sale. But if, say, the purchaser sells the shares quickly before the relevant truth begins to leak out, the misrepresentation will not have led to any loss. If the purchaser sells later after the truth makes its way into the marketplace, an initially inflated purchase price *might* mean a later loss. But that is far from inevitably so. . . .

> When the purchaser subsequently resells such shares, even at a lower price, that lower price may reflect, not the earlier misrepresentation, but changed economic circumstances, changed investor expectations, new industry-specific or firm-specific facts, conditions, or other events, which taken separately or together account for some or all of that lower price. . . .

> Given the tangle of factors affecting price, the most logic alone permits us to say is that the higher purchase price will *sometimes* play a role in bringing about a future loss. . . . It may prove to be a necessary condition of any such loss. . . .

> Judicially implied private securities fraud actions resemble in many (but not all) respects common-law deceit and misrepresentation actions. . . . And the common law has long insisted that a plaintiff in such a case show not only that had he known the truth he would not have acted but also that he suffered actual economic loss. (Citations omitted). . . . We cannot reconcile the Ninth Circuit's "inflated purchase price" approach with [the] views of other courts. And the uniqueness of its perspective argues against [its] validity . . . where we consider the contours of a judicially implied cause of action with roots in the common law.

* * *

> Our holding about plaintiffs' need to *prove* proximate causation and economic loss leads us also to conclude that the plaintiffs' complaint here failed adequately to *allege* these requirements. . . . [T]he plaintiffs' lengthy complaint contains only one statement that we can fairly read as describing the loss caused by the defendants . . . [that is, the claim that] plaintiffs "paid artificially inflated prices for Dura['s] securities" and suffered "damage[s]." App. 139a. The statement implies . . . that the plaintiffs considered the allegation of purchase price inflation alone sufficient. The complaint contains nothing that suggests otherwise. . . .

> [I]t should not prove burdensome for a plaintiff who has suffered an economic loss to provide a defendant with some indication of the loss and the causal connection that the plaintiff has in mind. At the same time, allowing a plaintiff to forgo giving any indication of the economic loss and proximate

cause that the plaintiff has in mind would bring about harm of the very sort the statutes seek to avoid [by tightening pleading requirements in the 1995 Private Securities Litigation Reform Act.] . . .

QUESTIONS ON LOSS CAUSATION

1. What should *Dura*'s plaintiffs have alleged about the measure and cause of their damages resulting from the company's misleading reassurances about FDA approval? How attractive would such an allegation have been on these facts?

2. Does *Dura* suggest that stock sold at an inflated price might be associated with diminishing losses over time, as new information and market conditions are reflected in market prices? In other words, are provable shareholder losses likely to decline as more time passes between a misrepresentation and subsequent corrective disclosure? Can plaintiffs ever establish loss causation if they had sold their shares after a sharp drop in share prices but prior to an explicit corrective disclosure?

3. Could it be argued in support of the Ninth Circuit below that the Court misconceives the nature of the loss at stake: that the real loss of buying stock at an inflated price is the loss of subsequent returns on investing the premium that, but for artificial price inflation, the purchaser would not have paid in the market and therefore might have invested elsewhere? On this view, an investor would have incurred a loss at the moment she overpaid for her shares at the inflated price.

4. Can plaintiffs prove loss causation if share prices remain unchanged after a CEO publicly and falsely denies rumors that her company has suffered major losses? Suppose that share prices drop sharply when the rumors prove to be true?

14.5.3   The Role of Class Certification in Recent Challenges to FOM Actions

Rule 10b-5 today is more controversial as support for FOM class actions than it is authority for the severe criminal penalties that courts sometimes impose for insider trading. Corporations and their managers risk enormous civil liability if they were to lose a FOM class action after a genuine trial. This prospect, in turn, is usually enough to guarantee that plaintiffs will enjoy a very large settlement fund if a case might otherwise go to trial. And this prospect, in turn, ensures that defendants fight hard from the beginning to dismiss complaints, obtain summary judgments, and defeat class certifications. In particular, defendants' last and best hope to escape a costly settlement is to defeat plaintiffs' motion for class certification. As a result, class certification hearings often become surrogates for real trials that all know will never occur. Defendants attempt to discredit the merits of plaintiffs' cases, and plaintiffs counter that evidence bearing on the merits of their cases is relevant only after their motions for class certification are granted. The legal point at issue is how one reads F.R.C.P. 23(b)(3), under which class certification hinges on plaintiffs' showing that "questions of law or fact common to class members predominate over any questions affecting only individual members."

In short order the Supreme Court issued three opinions addressing the issue of evidence and class certification. In *Erica P. John Fund, Inc. v. Halliburton Co.*, 131 S. Ct. 2179 (2011) ("*Halliburton I*"), the Court vacated a Fifth Circuit decision that would have required plaintiffs to prove loss causation prior to receiving class certification. In *Amgen Inc. v. Connecticut Retirement Plans & Trust Funds*, 568 U.S. 455 (2013), the Court held that plaintiffs were not required to prove that their alleged misrepresentations were material at the class certification hearing. Finally, the Court's most recent decision, *Halliburton Co. v. Erica P. John Fund, Inc.*, 134 S. Ct. 2398 (2014) ("*Halliburton II*"), addressed a range of legal attacks on *Basic*'s presumption of reliance, including two in support of overruling the reliance presumption entirely and several others urging that it should be limited or otherwise qualified. The arguments for overruling *Basic* were, first, that it had implicitly endorsed the hypothesis that share prices in public equity markets were "efficient" although the academia now rejected this conclusion; and, second, that close analysis of the 1934 Act revealed that *Basic*'s presumption of reliance on market prices had lacked adequate statutory foundation even at the time that *Basic* was decided.

Halliburton II rejected both arguments for overruling *Basic* out of hand. As to the first, the Court observed that academic opinion on the price "efficiency" of share prices was irrelevant since *Basic*'s only real assumption was that credible misinformation would influence share prices in a predictable direction. Chief Justice Roberts, writing for Court, rejected the argument that the *Basic* Court had lacked statutory authority to establish a rebuttable presumption of reliance in FOM cases by invoking the principle of *stare decisis* and, more persuasively, by noting Congress' conspicuous failure to overturn *Basic* even when it legislated other measures to contain abusive shareholder litigation. Chief Justice Roberts authored the *Halliburton II* majority opinion. The excerpt that follows addresses admissible evidence and the burden of proof in FOM class certification hearings.

> Halliburton proposes two alternatives to overruling *Basic* that would alleviate what it regards as the decision's most serious flaws. The first alternative would require plaintiffs to prove that a defendant's misrepresentation actually affected the stock price—so-called "price impact"—in order to invoke the *Basic* presumption. It should not be enough, Halliburton contends, for plaintiffs to demonstrate the general efficiency of the market in which the stock traded. Halliburton's second proposed alternative would allow defendants to rebut the presumption of reliance with evidence of a lack of price impact, not only at the merits stage—which all agree defendants may already do—but also before class certification. . . .
>
> In the absence of price impact, *Basic*'s fraud-on-the-market theory and presumption of reliance collapse. . . . Halliburton argues that since the *Basic* presumption hinges on price impact, plaintiffs should be required to prove it directly in order to invoke the presumption. Proving the presumption's

prerequisites, which are at best an imperfect proxy for price impact, should not suffice. Far from a modest refinement of the *Basic* presumption, this proposal would radically alter the required showing for the reliance element of the Rule 10b-5 cause of action. What is called the *Basic* presumption actually incorporates two constituent presumptions: First, if a plaintiff shows that the defendant's misrepresentation was public and material and that the stock traded in a generally efficient market, he is entitled to a presumption that the misrepresentation affected the stock price. Second, if the plaintiff also shows that he purchased the stock at the market price during the relevant period, he is entitled to a further presumption that he purchased the stock in reliance on the defendant's misrepresentation. By requiring plaintiffs to prove price impact directly, Halliburton's proposal would take away the first constituent presumption. Halliburton's argument for doing so is the same as its primary argument for overruling the *Basic* presumption altogether: Because market efficiency is not a yes-or-no proposition, a public, material misrepresentation might not affect a stock's price even in a generally efficient market. But as explained, *Basic* never suggested otherwise; that is why it affords defendants an opportunity to rebut the presumption by showing, among other things, that the particular misrepresentation at issue did not affect the stock's market price. For the same reasons we declined to completely jettison the *Basic* presumption, we decline to effectively jettison half of it by revising the prerequisites for invoking it.

Even if plaintiffs need not directly prove price impact to invoke the *Basic* presumption, Halliburton contends that defendants should at least be allowed to defeat the presumption at the class certification stage through evidence that the misrepresentation did not in fact affect the stock price. We agree. . . .

There is no dispute that defendants may introduce such evidence at the merits stage to rebut the *Basic* presumption. . . . Nor is there any dispute that defendants may introduce price impact evidence at the class certification stage, so long as it is for the purpose of countering a plaintiff's showing of market efficiency, rather than directly rebutting the presumption. . . . After all, plaintiffs themselves can and do introduce evidence of the existence of price impact in connection with "event studies" — regression analyses that seek to show that the market price of the defendant's stock tends to respond to pertinent publicly reported events. See Brief for Law Professors as Amici Curiae 25-28. In this case, for example, EPJ Fund submitted an event study of various episodes that might have been expected to affect the price of Halliburton's stock, in order to demonstrate that the market for that stock takes account of material, public information about the company. . . .

Defendants — like plaintiffs — may accordingly submit price impact evidence prior to class certification. [In this case defendants may] . . . rely on that same evidence prior to class certification for the particular purpose of rebutting the presumption altogether. . . . Suppose a defendant at the certification stage submits an event study looking at the impact on the price of its stock from six discrete events, in an effort to refute the plaintiffs' claim of general market efficiency. All agree the defendant may do this. Suppose one of the six events is the specific misrepresentation asserted by the plaintiffs. All agree that this too is perfectly acceptable. Now suppose the district court determines that, despite the defendant's study, the plaintiff has carried its burden to prove market efficiency, but that the evidence shows no price impact with respect to the specific misrepresentation challenged in the suit. The evidence at the certification stage thus shows an efficient market, on which the alleged misrepresentation had no price impact. . . . [In this case the plaintiffs' action should not be] certified and proceed as a class action . . . [because] the fraud-on-the-market theory does not apply and common reliance thus cannot be presumed. . . . Under *Basic*'s fraud-on-the-market theory, market efficiency . . . constitute[s] an indirect way of showing price impact. As explained, it is appropriate to allow plaintiffs to rely on this indirect proxy for price impact, rather than requiring them to prove price impact directly, given *Basic*'s rationales for recognizing a presumption of reliance in the first place. . . . But an indirect proxy should not preclude direct evidence when such evidence is available. As we explained in *Basic*, "[a]ny showing that severs the link between the alleged misrepresentation and . . . the price received (or paid) by the plaintiff . . . will be sufficient to rebut the presumption of reliance" because "the basis for finding that the fraud had been transmitted through market price would be gone." 485 U. S., at 248. And without the presumption of reliance, a Rule 10b–5 suit cannot proceed as a class action: Each plaintiff would have to prove reliance individually, so common issues would not "predominate" over individual ones, as required by Rule 23(b)(3). . . .

Our choice . . . is between limiting the price impact inquiry before class certification to indirect evidence, or allowing consideration of direct evidence as well. As explained, we see no reason to artificially limit the inquiry at the certification stage to indirect evidence of price impact. Defendants may seek to defeat the *Basic* presumption at that stage through direct as well as indirect price impact evidence.

QUESTIONS AND NOTES ON HALLIBURTON II

1. To the frustration of many business groups, *Halliburton II* did not overrule *Basic*. But did it affect FOM litigation in more subtle ways? Defendants bear the burden of demonstrating that the misrepresentations alleged by plaintiffs failed to have sufficient "price impact" to qualify plaintiffs for class certification. Does this mean that district courts should deny class certification whenever alleged misrepresentations fail to correlate with changes in share prices?

2. After *Halliburton II*, can plaintiffs argue that but for the misrepresentations of defendants' managers, the market price of a corporation's shares would have fallen dramatically and they would have escaped injury as a result? Explain why or why not.

14.6   INSIDER TRADING AND FOM CLASS ACTIONS: THE ACADEMIC POLICY DEBATES

Most jurisdictions address insider trading and civil suits alleging securities fraud under separate legal regimes. By contrast, U.S. law has generated galaxies of precedents, sub-rules, and authoritative pronouncements, all of which rotate around Rule 10b-5. It is not surprising, then, that one rule has sparked at least two important debates over legal policy in the regulation of securities markets. The first debate centered on insider trading and continued for three decades, from the early 1960s to the early 1990s; the second debate, which addresses the merits of FOM class actions, began in the 1970s and continues to this day. Both debates posed basic normative and conceptual questions although they differed in one key respect. The debate over insider trading policy rarely strayed far from academia while the debate over civil liability for securities fraud has attracted a much wider audience. One reason may be that insider trading has always lacked a vocal constituency outside of academia (almost by definition), while the FOM debate attracts powerful political constituencies as a matter of course. We turn first to the policy behind the law's response to insider trading.

14.6.1   The Insider Trading Debate

The insider trading debate began (and largely remained) a contrarian reaction by market-friendly academics to the SEC's efforts to suppress insider trading under the standard of Rule 10b-5. These scholars not only opposed the SEC's insider trading policy but also developed the affirmative case for deregulating insider trading entirely. One of their principal arguments was that administrators and courts commonly misconceived "fairness" in securities markets and misunderstood the useful role that insider trading actually played.[23] Insider trading was perceived as unfair, they argued, merely because insiders trading on private information earned higher returns than uninformed traders. But this reasoning was faulty because insider trading did not redistribute wealth from outsiders to insiders. Diversified outside investors receive on average exactly what they pay for. Share prices in actively traded markets reflect all public information, including knowledge that insider trading exists and consensus expectations about its likely dimensions. It follows that market prices discount for anticipated levels of insider trading. In competitive capital markets, diversified investors should earn on average the same risk-adjusted returns on their stock portfolios that they could expect to earn by putting their money in other kinds of investment opportunities.[24]

Of course, even "fair" insider trading might not be socially desirable. The proponents of insider trading offered several arguments to make the affirmative case on its behalf (or on behalf of deregulation, if one prefers). The most common of these arguments sketched the ways in which insider trading rights could serve as incentive compensation for key corporate managers and employees.

---

23. No one deserves more credit for originating and disseminating arguments for deregulating than the late Henry Manne, who devoted many pages to refining the case for insider trading over his long and productive academic career. E.g., Henry G. Manne, Insider Trading and the Stock Market (1966). For a lively if polemical summary of Manne's early views, see *In Defense of Insider Trading*, Harv. Bus. Rev. (Nov.-Dec. 1966) at p. 113. Manne's early work either formulates or lays the foundation for virtually all of the substantive arguments authored by deregulatory and "property rights" scholars in later years. Later scholarship in this tradition (including that by Manne himself) has been more rigorous, persuasive, and often more circumspect — but none is (or could be) more original; Manne claimed the field from the deregulatory perspective in 1966. (Of course, Manne also made original and influential contributions in other areas too, most notably his pioneering analysis of the market for corporate control).

24. Kenneth E. Scott, *Insider Trading, Rule 10b-5, Disclosure and Corporate Privacy*, 9 J. Legal Stud. 801 (1980) (arguing that if the existence of insider trading is known, diversification and efficient prices protect uninformed outside traders and ensure that no redistribution occurs).

Henry Manne's early work illustrates one such approach.[25] Unlike most of its later champions, Manne acknowledged from the start that insider trading harms one class of market participants, namely, the class of professional traders and "speculators," whom Manne seemed to regard as a species of market opportunists quite unlike "real" investors who invested for the long term in deserving businesses.[26] Market professionals might prosper despite their short-term trading practices, but it was because they were the first parties after insiders to learn (presumably through legal means) about new information emanating from corporations. The consequence of legally disabling insiders from trading on undisclosed information was to give away value to socially unproductive market professionals. By contrast, enabling trading by corporate insiders would allow firms to reclaim the value of their own information. Implicitly, at least, the argument was that companies should be free to substitute exclusive trading opportunities for other forms of compensation rather than allow free-riding market professionals to claim these opportunities instead. (Indeed, other commentators have suggested the market professionals acting as an interest group may have precipitated the SEC's enthusiasm for suppressing insider trading.[27])

Manne also took the compensation analysis one step further by arguing that insider trading rights would not only be highly efficient but also inexpensive for corporations because they would powerfully motivate insiders to create corporate value in order to trade on it. Later commentators have further elaborated on the potential virtues of insider trading as an incentive device. Among its most widely discussed virtues are: first, that it is very cheap to administer in comparison to explicit contractual incentives because it imposes no negotiation or monitoring costs on corporate employers; second, it efficiently rewards the right corporate agents because they are the first to learn the results of their value-creating activities and can therefore claim trading profits first; and finally, insider trading efficiently ties rewards to the magnitude of agent contributions to corporate value.[28] One might also add that insider trading rights give assurance to managers that their employers will not renege on their promises.

---

25. As usual, Manne makes the point first in the legal and business literatures, see id. A later classic article that further develops this and other Manne arguments with considerable sophistication is, Dennis W. Carlton & Daniel R. Fischel, *The Regulation of Insider Trading*, 35 Stan. L. Rev. 857 (1983).

26. Manne embraced the derogatory label of "speculators." *In Defense of Insider Trading, supra,* note 24, at 114.

27. See, e.g., David D. Haddock & Jonathan R. Macey, *Regulation on Demand: A Private Interest Model, With an Application to Insider Trading Regulation,* 30 J. L. & Econ. 311 (1987).

28. See Carlton & Fischel, *supra* note 26, at 873-874. Several obvious problems with this account include the fact that share prices are noisy and individual contributions to corporate value would have to be very large indeed to generate trading profits. Of course, insiders can leverage trading gains by keeping share prices volatile and trading on derivatives. If they buy calls, they leverage their ability to profit on good news; if they buy puts, they leverage their ability to profit on bad news. Advocates of deregulation such as Carlton and Fischel recognize the possibility that insider trading might induce creation of bad news. They dismiss this concern as unimportant, however, after addressing a variety of other incentives and mechanisms, including self-monitoring among managers, that would constrain insiders to trade only on good news.

Do these incentive arguments make sense to you or are they too good to be true? While you can no doubt guess our answer, a more leisurely way to address the question is to reflect on the hypothetical incentive of insider trading rights when corporations have confidential but highly material information of the sort that is illustrated by many of this chapter's cases. The kinds of information featured in our cases include foreknowledge about M&A transactions (*O'Hagan, Basic,* and *Chiarella*), rich mineral strikes (*Goodwin* and *TGS*), and innovative medical devices (*Dura*). A disproportionate fraction of insider trading cases fall into one of these categories. To make real money from insider trading it helps to have the kind of company that might generate bombshell good news and very volatile share prices.

In the case of companies where mining strikes or medical devices are found, managers typically choose a few investments from a larger set of possible projects on the basis of very imperfect information, and only learn much later whether their investments succeed or fail and by how much. It makes sense for managers to trade only after they learn the outcomes of their investments (but before they publicly disclose these outcomes). This trading interval may be inflexible and a matter of days or it may be flexible and extend over a much longer period. Our interest is in how insider trading rights might affect managerial decisions at two points. The first is when the CEO — assume only the CEO matters — selects her initial investments. Here it is possible (and even likely) that the prospect of future trading on inside information will decouple the CEO's interests from shareholder interests. For example, a CEO might prefer a high-risk/high-return project over a low-risk project with a high probably of yielding modest returns that, still worse, are close to what the market expects. The modest-return project may create more expected value but to select it would be to throw away the CEO's insider trading rights. These rights have an option-like feature: If they affect the CEO's incentives at all in this scenario, they are likely to bias her toward high-risk/high-reward projects that maximize the future value of her insider trading rights. And things are not much better at the second point at which trading rights might influence a CEO's decisions, the point at which she first learns whether a major project has succeeded or failed. Here news of a spectacular success would tempt her to delay disclosure until she had quietly optimized her trading position.

In the event that a CEO could trade on information about an acquisition offer instead of a mining strike, insider trading rights would create similarly perverse incentives. If, as seems likely, the CEOs of target companies have considerable discretion over whether to accept or reject an acquisition offer, the prospect of gaining significant trading profits would presumably incline a target CEO to think more favorably about selling her firm than she might otherwise do. But the consequences for shareholders are not so predictable. A CEO who expected large future benefits from remaining on the job might still reject a very generous bid that shareholders would welcome if they were asked. Indeed, she might even regard her insider trading rights as a kind of one-time future bonus that could be triggered at her discretion by soliciting possible acquirers. Conversely, a retiring or poorly performing CEO might accept or solicit lowball acquisition offers out of fear that he might otherwise lose his job before his firm was sold, and thus he might lose the value of his insider-trading rights forever.

As these hypotheticals illustrate, awarding insider trading rights would be more likely to backfire on shareholders than to motivate value creation. In addition, other factors make insider trading seem even more dysfunctional. One of these is how trading rights might distort information flow within a corporation: They might induce key managers to hoard information and paralyze corporate decision making as a result or, alternatively, they might make it impossible to keep information confidential, in which case all insiders and their tippees would profit indiscriminately at the expense of uninformed traders. A second consideration is that it is still unclear why contractual incentives can't mimic whatever desirable incentive features that insider trading is purported to have. One wonders in this context whether insider trading would have held the same attraction for its champion in the 1960s and 1970s if high-powered negotiated incentive compensation had been as pervasive then as it is today. As for the argument that a corporation owns its confidential information and should therefore be entitled to use it as compensation currency if it wishes, the appropriate response is to ask how many companies today would — if they could — choose to opt out of insider trading prior to making an initial public offering of their stock? The question answers itself. The academic debate over insider trading faded away during the 1990s. But even at its most heated, it never strayed far from the academia. Public sentiment doomed the deregulatory position from the start.

14.6.2   The Academic Policy Debate over FOM Class Actions

Unlike the debate over insider trading, the debate over FOM class actions is very much alive. Since everyone agrees that lying to the market is harmful, the issues in this debate are not as abstract as those that were raised in the insider trading debate. They concern *how* the law should respond to fraudulent misrepresentation rather than whether it should respond at all. Should the law expose corporations as well as their senior managers and directors to the risk of massive liability to disappointed traders for alleged misrepresentations, knowing that corporations and their insurers divide the costs, sometimes after courts refuse to dismiss complaints but always after they certify class actions? Precisely because the damages alleged in class actions are enormous, directors and managers sometimes feel that they are coerced to accept costly settlements regardless of the facts and merely because the alternative might be worse.

The academic critics of FOM class actions, however, are likely to make two other arguments.[29] The first is that these actions are rarely able to deter

29. This discussion relies in part on the concise summary of arguments against the FOM remedy that is provided in James C. Spindler, *Vicarious Liability for Bad Corporate Governance: Are We Wrong About Rule 10b-5?*, 13 Amer. L. and Econ. Rev. 359 (2011). Spindler himself offers an unusual defense of FOM actions that takes managerial loyalty to the interests of current shareholders as the principal explanation for management making misleading statements to the market.

senior managers who mislead the market to advance their own interests rather than those of their corporations and their shareholders. Put differently, managerial fraud is a difficult agency problem that corporate boards can seldom prevent. It follows that sanctions should target the culpable managers — the primary wrongdoers — rather than their corporations. Culpable managers are undeterred partly because they are rarely forced to contribute to FOM settlement funds.[30] It also follows that legal reforms should cap corporate liability while imposing punitive criminal and administrative sanctions on the culpable managers.[31] There is precedent for relying on public enforcement. We largely depend on criminal or administrative sanctions to deter insider trading. Rule 10b-5 authorizes the government to deploy most of the same sanctions against managers who intentionally mislead the market. If deterrence is the problem, public enforcement and sanctions against flesh-and-blood wrongdoers are the solutions.

How one intuits whether FOM class actions actually deter securities fraud depends importantly on certain background assumptions. Most commentators assume that managers who lie do so to advance their own interests while shareholders would prefer them to be truthful. In this case whether FOM class actions can "deter" securities fraud depends on the nitty-gritty power of boards to interdict managerial misconduct and on the power of potential FOM liability to motivate boards to become more vigilant.[32] Although no one can answer these questions with confidence, the many commentators who fear a mismatch between managerial power and shareholder interests in other areas of corporate governance could be forgiven for doubting that corporate civil liability can make a significant difference here.

Different assumptions about shareholder interests and the power of boards can lead to much more favorable expectations about the deterrence effects of FOM civil liability. A challenging article by James Spindler[33] is an example. Spindler posits that current corporate shareholders have a collective interest in maximizing the current share prices even when — or perhaps especially when — their shares are overvalued and can be sold on the market at inflated prices. In addition, he assumes that current shareholders, acting in part through corporate boards, exert very strong pressure on their top managers to maximize current share prices. Besides managing well, managers are expected to support share prices by showing a positive face to the market. In difficult circumstances some managers go much further — to the point of misleading the market.

---

30. See, e.g., Jennifer Arlen & William Carney, *Vicarious Liability for Fraud on the Securities Markets: Theory and Evidence*, 1992 U. Ill. L. Rev. 691 (1992); John Coffee, *Reforming the Securities Class Action: An Essay on Deterrence and Its Implementation*, 106 Colum. L. Rev. 1534 (2006).

31. See, e.g., Donald Langevoort, *On Leaving Corporate Executives Naked, Homeless and without Wheels: Corporate Fraud, Equitable Remedies, and the Debate over Entity versus Individual Liability*, 42 Wake Forrest L. Rev. 627 (2007).

32. See Spindler, *supra* note 30, at 364.

33. Id.

Since no one orders these managers to lie, it might seem obvious that they act for selfish reasons and have no regard for the interests of their shareholders. But Spindler's assumptions suggest a different interpretation. Consider the example of a CEO who will be fired unless he lies about his firm's recent performance, but who believes that his lie — say, a misleading financial report — will never be detected if his firm's performance picks up next year, an improvement which he thinks is likely to happen. By lying, the CEO acts in his own interest but this interest in turn arises under a particular regime of rewards and sanctions that the board has implemented to advance the interests of current shareholders, who always prefer high current share prices. Given their interests, the incentive regime that induces the CEO to lie perfectly aligns his interests with those of his shareholders. After the lie, share prices will remain high indefinitely if firm performance improves or the lie will be discovered as some point and share prices will collapse. Current shareholders prefer either of these outcomes to an immediate collapse of share prices that truthful disclosure might have triggered. As a last step in the argument, consider shareholder interests if the corporation might have to pay enormous civil damages in a FOM class action if the CEO's lie is discovered and share prices collapse as a result. If the damages are large enough and the fraction of current shareholders that will remain shareholders after FOM suits is high enough, it will no longer be in the interest of current shareholders to sponsor an incentive regime that induces lying. If shareholders have the power to promote honesty by changing a CEO's incentives, the conclusion is obvious: FOM class actions strongly deter frauds on the market. The logic is impeccable given the initial assumptions. Which set of assumptions — the "weak" shareholder or "strong" shareholder assumptions — seem more plausible to you?

A second objective of FOM class actions is no less important than deterrence: namely, the compensation of traders who are injured by fraudulent misrepresentations. The critics of FOM actions argue, however, that they compensate no better than they deter, in large part because they start from the misconceived notion that damages paid by corporate defendants can fairly compensate for the harm caused by managerial misrepresentations. The theory of FOM civil liability identifies the injured parties as those who traded after misinformation distorted — usually inflated — price but before the effects of misinformation on price dissipated. Viewing these traders as tort victims who deserve compensation seems entirely right, the conceptual problem arises only when it seems that the corporation will almost always foot the bill. The critics of FOM actions point out that if a corporation must compensate shareholders who bought shares at inflated prices and later sold them at a loss, the result is that one class of innocent shareholders is compensated — those who purchased shares after management lies — at the expense of another class of innocent shareholders — namely, those who purchased shares prior to management's lies and continued to hold them afterwards. FOM actions compensate former shareholders who badly timed their purchases and sales by taxing continuing, long-term shareholders. In addition, another class of former shareholders — those who bought before misinformation entered prices and sold before corrective disclosure was made — are permitted to keep windfall profits that derive in part from having sold shares at inflated prices to many of the very same former shareholders who now seek compensation as members of the plaintiff class. If one assumes, as most commentators do, that the real wrongdoers are opportunistic managers acting for themselves, then there is a strong argument to be made that shifting losses among innocent shareholders is neither compensatory nor fair. Even worse, academic critics of FOM actions argue that these suits reduce the total value available to all innocent shareholders because the corporate defendant usually bears all of the litigation costs that accompany FOM actions. Thus, in the end many critics conclude that these actions are both unfair and wasteful, while other critics reach a slightly cheerier result after considering the mitigating effects of diversification. For diversified investors, at least, shifts in value among classes of shareholders might well be a wash, in which case FOM actions are less unfair on average but no less wasteful. Do you agree with the critics of FOM class actions, and if so, which critics?

Finally, two additional points about the effects of FOM class actions deserve mention. One of these is that this discussion barely touches the surface. FOM actions have many other possible vices and virtues. One possible vice, for example, is that they may systematically favor short-term frequent traders at the expense of long-term investors, and thereby discourage patient capital. On the other hand, perhaps advantaging frequent traders is precisely what corporations should wish to do. Frequent traders support liquid markets and informed share prices, which in the end benefit all shareholders. But frequent traders are also particularly vulnerable to dishonest managers and distorted prices, and therefore deserve additional protection for their trading activity. (Recall a similar argument might be made for a ban on insider trading, which implicitly favors market professionals or "speculators" depending on one's perspective.)

The second notable feature of the critics' arguments is one that we have already flagged. They turn partly on the assumption that managers are solely responsible for feeding misinformation to the market while the high-powered incentives that reward managers for increasing share prices are irrelevant. But in considering fairness, as in considering the deterrence function of liability, a different conclusion follows if one believes that managers merely serve the interests of current shareholders. On the latter assumption, the reason why long-term shareholders should compensate investors who bought shares at inflated prices is clear: The corporation's present owners, its continuing shareholders, were among the potential beneficiaries of managerial lies. It makes sense that they should compensate the only true innocents, i.e., the class of plaintiffs who unknowingly purchased overpriced shares. The conclusion seems right given the assumption. But is the assumption compatible with your intuitions about corporate governance? Could the managerial incentives be that finely tuned and that powerful? Do current shareholders benefit from artificially inflated share prices that are likely to be exposed at some point with serious consequences for the corporation's future credibility?

As the FOM policy debate is still in full throat, we leave these questions for you to consider.

TWO FINAL QUESTIONS

1. Examining 6,000 stock trades by U.S. senators between 1993 and 1998, Professor Alan Ziobrowski and colleagues find that senators beat the market, on average, by an astounding 12 percent annually.[34] Does this evidence indicate that U.S. senators are using inside information to trade? What other explanations are possible?

2. Suppose that the *Basic* Court had rejected a rebuttable presumption of shareholder reliance on market prices, with the consequence that FOM class actions were never brought. In addition, suppose that state courts subscribed to a theory that managerial misstatements harmed corporate reputations, and that the appropriate measure of damages was the decline in the aggregate value of a corporation's shares (called its "market capitalization") that followed after corrective disclosures revealed that its prior share prices had been artificially inflated by managerial misrepresentations. Consider the following questions:

a. Would derivative suits in this alternate universe play the same role that FOM class actions play in our universe? Whom might these suits target? (Note that the corporation, rather than a class of shareholders, is the injured party in this new universe.)

b. Does it make sense to measure the corporation's damages by the drop in its share price caused by correcting its managers' lies? If not, is there a better measure of damages?

c. Regardless of your answers above, might a derivative suit on behalf of the corporation be a better remedy for the harm caused by managers' lies than a FOM class action if all shareholders are equally innocent? Does a derivative action for corporate damages avoid shifting value between equally innocent former shareholders and continuing shareholders? Is it more likely to punish the real wrongdoers than the FOM class action is today? Is it more likely to go to trial rather than settle?

34. Alan J. Ziobrowski, Ping Cheng, James W. Boyd & Brigitte J. Ziobrowski, *Abnormal Returns from the Common Stock Investments of the United States Senate*, 39 J. Fin. & Quant. Anal. 661 (2004).

TABLE OF CASES

INDEX

757